S0-ABC-556

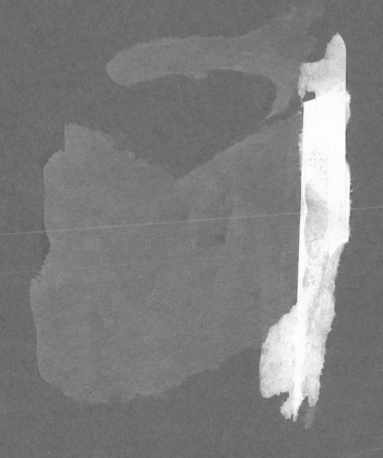

American Government

ROOTS AND REFORM

Karen O'Connor
Professor of Political Science
Emory University

Larry J. Sabato
Robert Kent Gooch Professor of
Government and Foreign Affairs
University of Virginia

Macmillan Publishing Company
New York

Maxwell Macmillan Canada
Toronto

Editor:
Bruce Nichols and
Robert Miller

Development Editors:
Jane Tufts and
David Chodoff

Production Supervisor:
Sharon Lee

Production Manager:
Nicholas Sklitsis

Art Director:
Pat Smythe

Text Designer:
A Good Thing Inc.

Cover Illustration:
Jerry McDaniel

Cover Photo:
Gary Black/Masterfile

Photo Researchers:
Barbara Scott and
Julie Tesser

Illustrations:
A Good Thing Inc.

This book was set in Caxton
by York Graphic Services and
was printed and bound by
Von Hoffman Press.

The cover was printed by
Lehigh Press.

Macmillan Publishing Company
866 Third Avenue, New York, New York 10022

Macmillan Publishing Company is part of
the Maxwell Communication Group of Companies.

Maxwell Macmillan Canada, Inc.
1200 Eglinton Avenue East
Suite 200
Don Mills, Ontario M3C 3N1

Library of Congress Cataloging-in-Publication Data

O'Connor, Karen, 1952–
    American government: roots and reform/Karen O'Connor, Larry J.
Sabato.—Pre-election ed.
        p.   cm.
    Includes bibliographical references and index.
    ISBN 0-02-388887-3
        1. United States—Politics and government.   I. Sabato, Larry J.
II. Title.
JK274.O26   1993
320.973—dc20   92-17330
                            CIP

ISBN 0-02-388895-4   (Pre-election Edition)

Photo credits appear on pages 721–723, which
constitutes a continuation of the copyright page.

Printing: 2   3   4   5   6   7   Year: 3   4   5   6   7   8   9

To Meghan, always the trouper.
Karen O'Connor

To my students over the years,
who all know that
"politics is a good thing."
Larry Sabato

Preface

Teaching introductory American government presents special challenges and rewards. It is a challenge to introduce a new discipline to beginning students. It is a challenge to jump from topic to topic each week. Above all, it is a challenge to motivate large and disparate groups of students to master new material. The rewards offered by success, however, can accumulate in students who pay more attention to their government, who participate in its workings as more informed citizens, and who better understand the workings of democracy as practiced in the United States.

We have witnessed some of these rewards from the lecture podium. With this book, we hope to offer our experiences in written form. Students need perspective and motivation; they also need to be exposed to information that will withstand the test of time. Our goal with this text is to transmit just this sort of information.

Approach

We believe that one cannot fully understand the actions, issues, and policy decisions facing the U.S. government, its constituent states, or "the people" unless these issues are examined from the perspective of how they have evolved over time. Consequently, the title of this book is *American Government: Roots and Reform.* In its pages we try to examine how America is governed today by looking not just at present behavior but also at the Framers' intentions and how they have been implemented over the years. For example, we believe that it is critical to an understanding of the role of political parties in America to understand the Framers' fears of factionalism, how parties evolved, and when and why realignments in party identification occurred. In turn, a comprehension of these processes will help us to understand the kinds of officials who have been elected.

In addition to perennial questions raised by the Framers, we explore issues that the Framers could never have envisioned and how the basic institutions of government have responded to these new demands. Clearly, for example, the Framers could never have envisioned election campaigns in an age of widespread television. It is highly unlikely that an affable former actor, Ronald Reagan, could have been elected president in an earlier century. New demands have periodically forced governmental reform, and understanding the dynamics of change is essential for introductory students.

Our overriding concern is that students understand their government as it exists *today.* In order to do so, they must understand how it was designed in the Constitution. They must appreciate a little of how it reached its current state. Finally, they must understand current political behavior and its effects. Each chapter, therefore, approaches its topic with a combination of perspectives that we feel will best facilitate this approach.

Features

Philosophical Perspective. Every chapter begins with a few sentences from *The Federalist Papers* (with the exception of Chapter 4, which begins with an Anti-Federalist quotation). These passages are explained in captions and then used as references at relevant points in the chapter. From them, students learn that government was born amidst burning issues of representation and power, issues that continue to smolder today.

Historical Perspective. Every chapter uses history to serve two purposes: first, to show how institutions and processes have evolved to their present state, and second, to provide some of the color that makes information memorable. A richer historical texture helps to explain the present; it also helps to free the course from the time-bound nature of newspaper headlines.

Comparative Perspective. Change in Eastern Europe, Latin America, and Asia reminds us of the preeminence of democracy, in theory if not always in fact. As new democratic experiments spring up across the globe, it becomes increasingly important for students to understand the rudiments of presidential versus parliamentary government, of multiparty versus two-party systems, and so on. In order to put American government in perspective, therefore, while avoiding the enormous complexities of huge transnational comparisons, we have used the model of Great Britain as a point of comparison. Throughout our chapter discussions, comparisons are drawn to Great Britain wherever appropriate points arise. By comparing the two governments, students learn the basic differences between presidential and parliamentary democracies.

The following pages demonstrate how these features appear in the text.

SAMPLE TEXT FEATURES

*E*very view we may take of the subject, as candid inquirers after truth, will serve to convince us, that it is both unwise and dangerous to deny the federal government an unconfined authority.

James Madison

FEDERALIST NO. 23

According to the Federalists, the major triumph of the Constitution is the authority it granted the national government over the states ("unconfined" by the states).

Each chapter begins with a quote from *The Federalist Papers* with a caption explaining its context and meaning (this example is from Chapter 2, "The Constitution").

SAMPLE TEXT FEATURES

limited to the states in which the numbers are close. With a direct popular election, where only the national vote total matters, a close count would mean the daunting task of recounting every ballot in the nation.

Overall, although individual elections may sometimes be predictable, the electoral system in the United States is anything but static. New generations—and party-changers in older generations—constantly remake the political landscape. At least every other presidential election brings a change of administration and a focus on new issues. Every other year at least a few fresh personalities and perspectives infuse the Congress, as newly elected U.S. senators and representatives claim mandates and seek to shake up the established order. Each election year the very same tumult and transformation can be observed in the fifty states and in thousands of localities.

The welter of elections may seem like chaos, but from this chaos comes the order and often explosive productivity of a democratic society. For the source of all change in the United States, just as Hamilton and Madison predicted, is the individual citizen who goes to the polls and casts a ballot.

In most societies, there is an insatiable itch for change and a desire to better the conditions of life. In authoritarian countries, repression and violent revolution are the only avenues open to check or provide for change. In democratic nations such as the United States, the voters have the opportunity to orchestrate a peaceful revolution every time they visit their polling places.

Elections take the pulse of average people and gauge their hopes and fears; the study of elections permits us to trace the course of the American revolution over 200 years of voting. Much good and some harm has been accomplished by this explosion of balloting— but all of it has been done, as Hamilton insisted, "on the solid basis of THE CONSENT OF THE PEOPLE."

Summary

Regular elections guarantee mass political action and governmental accountability. They also confer legitimacy on regimes better than any other method of change. There are various types of primary elections in America, as well as general elections, initiatives, referenda, and recall elections. In presidential elections, primaries are sometimes replaced by caucuses in which party members choose a candidate in a closed meeting, but recent years have seen fewer caucuses. After the primary and caucus season finishes, parties hold their national conventions to choose candidates—who generally have been determined in advance by the nominating elections—for the general election. In the general election that follows, statewide popular votes are used to determine the composition of the Electoral College, which ultimately makes the formal choice of a president.

Voters tend to vote retrospectively—that is, they judge candidates based on their past performance, or on the past performance of the party in power. Approximately every thirty-two or thirty-six years, voters have realigned into coalitions that redefine the parties and their candidates. These major realignments are precipitated by one or more critical elections, which polarize voters around new issues and personalities in reaction to crucial developments, such as wars or depressions. Voter participation tends to follow certain patterns: the more educated, affluent, and older the citizens are, the more often they vote; also, whites tend to vote more often than non-whites; Southerners vote less often than non-Southerners.

Chapters refer back to *The Federalist Papers* and the Founders wherever appropriate (this example is from Chapter 12, "Voting and Elections").

SAMPLE TEXT FEATURES

order to best implement their policies, they had to be able to appoint those who subscribed to their political views.

By the time that James A. Garfield, a former distinguished officer in the Civil War, was
elected president in 1880, many reformers were calling publicly for changes in the **civil
service system,** that is, the system by which appointments to the federal bureaucracy
are made. Upon his election to office, Garfield was besieged with office seekers. Washington, D.C., had not seen such a demand for political jobs since the election of Abraham
Lincoln as the first president of the Republican Party. Garfield's immediate predecessor,
Rutherford B. Hayes, had favored the idea of the replacement of the spoils system with a
merit system based on test scores and ability. Congress, however, failed to pass the
legislation he proposed. So, possibly because potential job seekers wanted to secure positions before Congress had the opportunity to act on an overhauled civil service system,
thousands pressed Garfield for positions. This siege prompted Garfield to record in his
diary:

> My day is frittered away with the personal seeking of people when it ought to
> be given to the great problems which concern the whole country.[4]

Although he resolved to reform the civil service, Garfield's life was cut short by the bullets
of an assassin who, ironically, was a frustrated job seeker.

[4] Quoted in Robert G. Caldwell, *James A. Garfield* (Hamden, Conn.: Archon Books, 1965).

People of the Past

William Henry Harrison and Office Seekers

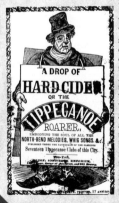

Nominated by the Whig Party in 1839, William Henry Harrison was the "log cabin, hard cider" candidate in the presidential campaign of 1840. Although Harrison was the son of a wealthy Virginia planter, the Whig Party developed an image of Harrison as one who had risen to distinction through his own efforts while retaining the tastes of the ordinary citizen. Harrison went to college and then enlisted in the army where he was promoted to major general. Harrison was a hero in the Battle of Tippecanoe, thus earning the nickname "Tippecanoe" which became the catchy campaign slogan "Tippecanoe and Tyler too" when Harrison selected his running mate, John Tyler.

Harrison ran his campaign without a platform. The advice given to him by Whig leaders was to say nothing about principles or creed. Lots of silly campaign songs were composed and noisy conventions and rallies were held everywhere, but no campaign promises were made.

At his inaugural address on March 4, Harrison droned on for close to two hours. It was a cold and wintry day and Harrison did not wear gloves or an overcoat. Not surprisingly, he developed pneumonia later that month and died on April 4.

Repeatedly dunned by supporters seeking patronage jobs, Harrison's last words were: "I can't stand it . . . Don't trouble me . . . These applications, will they never cease . . . ?" Even on Harrison's deathbed, the problems of a growing bureaucracy continued to hound him.

Every chapter includes a boxed biographical passage highlighting an interesting
personality from America's political past.

SAMPLE TEXT FEATURES

As chair of the Committee of Detail, Wilson had considerable input into the fashioning of the office of chief executive. Rejecting the suggestions of some of the delegates, who initially suggested multiple executives to diffuse the power of the executive branch, the Framers settled on a single chief executive. Borrowing from the constitutions of Pennsylvania, Delaware, New Jersey, and New Hampshire, the Framers called the new chief executive the president. Although the Framers had little difficulty in agreeing that executive authority was to be vested in one person or in agreeing on a title for the new office, the manner of the president's election continued to haunt them, so they turned to a discussion of easier issues.

Qualifications for Office

The Framers mandated that the president (and the vice president, whose major function was to succeed the president in the event of his death or disability) be a natural-born citizen of the United States and at least thirty-five years old. The Framers also insisted that any prospective president had resided in the United States for at least fourteen years. As it was not uncommon for those engaged in international diplomacy to be out of the country for substantial periods of time, the Framers wanted to make sure that prospective presidents spent some time on this country's shores before running for its highest elective office.

How Long Can a President Serve?

Initially, the length of the executive's term of office and his eligibility to seek reelection were the subjects of considerable controversy. Four-, seven-, and eleven-year terms with no eligibility for reelection were suggested by various delegates to the Constitutional Convention. When Elbridge Gerry of Massachusetts arrogantly suggested a fifteen-year term, a better-humored colleague suggested twenty. After all, he noted, it was "the median life of princes."[5] Alexander Hamilton suggested that a president serve during "good behavior." Not surprisingly, the issue of length of term quickly became associated with eligibility to seek reelection. From the beginning, it was clear that if the delegates agreed to allow the state legislatures to choose the president, then shorter terms with the possibility of reelection would be favored. Thus, after the Framers of the Constitution reached agreement on the composition of the electoral college (see Chapter 12), the delegates in favor of a reelection option prevailed, and a four-year term with eligibility for reelection was added to the proposed Article II of the Constitution.

The first president, George Washington (1789–1797), sought reelection only once, and a two-term limit for presidents became traditional. Although Ulysses S. Grant unsuccessfully sought a third term, the two terms established by Washington remained the standard for 150 years, avoiding the Framers' much-feared "constitutional monarch," a perpetually reelected tyrant. In the 1930s and 1940s, however, Franklin Delano Roosevelt ran successfully in four elections as Americans fought first the Great Depression and then World War II. Despite Roosevelt's popularity, negative reaction to his long tenure in office ultimately led to passage (and ratification in 1951) of the Twenty-second Amendment, which limited presidents to two terms or a total of ten years in office, should a vice president assume a portion of a president's unfulfilled term.

Term limitations are rare in parliamentary systems, where the chief executive can remain in office indefinitely, or rather, as long as she or he can command the support of a majority of representatives in the lower house. Margaret Thatcher, prime minister of Britain from 1979 to 1990, was quoted in the run-up to the 1987 general election (which her party, the Conservatives, won) that she intended "to go on and on" as prime minister. In practice, she did not. In theory, she certainly could have.

[5]Quoted in Selma R. Williams, *Fifty-Five Fathers* (New York: Dodd Mead, 1970), p. 77.

References to Great Britain are made when appropriate as a point of comparison (this example is from Chapter 7, "The Presidency").

SAMPLE TEXT FEATURES

Then and Now
Life on the Floor of Congress

Throughout Congress's first several decades, partisan, sectional, and state tensions of the day often found their way onto the floors of the U.S. House and Senate. Many members were armed, and during one House debate thirty members showed their weapons. In 1826, for example, John Randolph of Virginia insulted Henry Clay from the floor of the Senate, referring to Clay as "this being, so brilliant yet so corrupt, which, like a rotten mackerel by moonlight, shined and stunk." Clay immediately challenged Randolph to a duel, of which the only victim was Randolph's coat. In 1856, Representative Preston Brooks of South Carolina, defending the honor of his region and family, assaulted Senator Charles Sumner of Massachusetts on the floor of the Senate. Sumner was disabled and unable to resume his seat in Congress for several years. Guns and knives were abundantly evident on the floor of both House and Senate, along with a wide variety of alcoholic beverages.

Today the House and the Senate are usually much more quiet. In 1984, however, a group of newly elected Republican representatives began taking over the House floor every day after the end of normal hours to berate their Democratic colleagues. The chamber was usually empty but, like all other action on the floor, these speeches were broadcast live on C-SPAN and often used by the members for distribution to local television stations back home. During a particularly strong attack on several Democrats' views on Central America, Representative Newt Gingrich (R.-Ga.) paused suggestively mid-speech, as though waiting for an objection or daring the Democrats to respond. No other House member was on the floor at the time, but since C-SPAN cameras only focus on the speaker, viewers were unaware of that fact.

Speaker Thomas P. O'Neill angrily reacted by ordering C-SPAN cameras to span the empty chamber to expose Gingrich's and other Republicans' tactics, but he failed to inform the Republicans of the change. O'Neill later apologized to the House Minority Leader, Robert Michel, but what Republicans labeled "CAMSCAM" ignited a firestorm on the floor. Incensed by remarks made by Gingrich, O'Neill dropped his gavel, left his spot on the dais, and took to the floor, roaring at Gingrich, "You challenged their [House Democrats'] patriotism, and it is the lowest thing that I have ever seen in my thirty-two years in Congress!" Trent Lott (R.-Ala.) then demanded that the Speaker be "taken down," the House term to call someone to order for violating House rules prohibiting personal attacks. The House Parliamentarian looked in the dictionary to see if the word "lowest" was a slur. As a hush fell on the House, the presiding officer told O'Neill that he had violated House rules. Bristled O'Neill, "I was expressing my views very mildly because I think much worse than I said."

O'Neill's penalty? The rarely invoked enforced silence for the remainder of the day's debate. So uncomfortable with that action was the House Minority Leader that he asked Lott to make a motion exempting O'Neill from the penalty, to which Lott agreed. No other House Speaker has ever been so reprimanded.*

*Alexander Stanley, "Tip Topped: O'Neill Tangles with Some Republican Turks over Camera Angles," *Nation,* May 28, 1984, p. 36.

could allow members to bring lucrative defense contracts back to their districts, encourage the building of bases, or discourage their closing within their districts or states, thus pleasing constituents.

The ability to bring defense contracts, public works contracts, or similar benefits to the district or state improves a member's chances for reelection or for election to higher office.

The Ancillary Package

The ancillary package reflects the pedagogical goals of the text: to provide information in a useful context and with colorful examples. We have tried especially hard to provide materials that are useful for instructors and interesting and helpful to students.

Special Feature

We are particularly pleased to present a unique blend of text, video, and supplementary reading on the perennial subject of how a bill becomes a law. In Chapter 6, we use the Clean Air Act Amendments of 1990 as an example of the complexity of modern legislation, and we refer to it again in Chapter 17, "Domestic Policy," as we illustrate how to analyze public policy. Instructors can supplement this coverage with a video showing highlights of C-SPAN's coverage of the bill, available from Macmillan. After reading about executive lobbying, committees, and floor voting, students will greatly enjoy the chance to see the twists and turns of the Clean Air Act Amendments on video. Furthermore, students can buy at a special reduced price a package from Macmillan combining this text with a copy of *National Journal* reporter Richard Cohen's *Washington at Work: Back Rooms and Clean Air,* covering the amendments in detail. By this means instructors can combine text, video, and a colorful case study in the tradition of *The Dance of Legislation.*

Also Available

Further Readings. To offer more in-depth historical perspective, the text is accompanied by a free book of essays by such political historians as Richard McCormack and Donald Robinson, each covering the evolution of a major institution or process.

Video Library. A full set of videos on every major course topic, including Congress, the presidency, the courts, and elections, is available through Macmillan.

Instructor's Manual. This manual includes lecture ideas, discussion questions, and classroom activities, as well as lecture suggestions for using the free readings, the Clean Air Act book by Richard Cohen, and the video library.

Test Bank. This item contains questions not just on the text, but also on the free readings, the Clean Air Act book, and the video library, allowing instructors to integrate all student materials easily. The *Test Bank* contains more than 1,500 multiple-choice, true/false, and essay questions, as well as midterm and final exams. It is available in a computerized version from the publisher.

Transparencies. A full set of color transparencies is available to complement classroom lectures.

Study Guide. A thorough *Study Guide,* including multiple-choice, matching, and true/false questions, as well as study outlines, is available for students who need help with review work.

Acknowledgments

Karen O'Connor thanks the hundreds of students in her National Government courses who, over the years, have pushed her to learn more about American government and to have fun in the process. She especially thanks Sue Davis, Kaenan Hertz, and Jeff Read for their research assistance and her Emory colleagues Alan Abramowitz, Courtney Brown, Randy Strahan, and Cornell Hooten, who were always willing to share books, ideas, suggestions, and newspaper clippings. She also thanks Dean Howard Hunter of the Emory Law School for providing access to LEXIS and NEXIS, which allowed this book to be as current as possible. Thanks also to Amy Weinhaus at Washington University School of Law, who helped with this project in its early stages, and Gregg Ivers at American University who, like Amy, was always there to offer suggestions, help, and encouragement.

Three students at Emory were especially helpful. Jenny Jacob worked during the summer of 1991 to help organize the edits and updates of several chapters. Laura McColley provided the assistance and fresh perspective that only a graduate student studying for her Ph.D. comprehensive exam in American Government could offer. Laura worked tirelessly on the book and even brought homemade cookies as a reward for completed chapters. During the final stages of this project, John Hermann never complained when asked to read and reread page proofs for any errors on a tight schedule. These students' valuable input, support, and effort helped produce a much better book.

Larry Sabato wishes to thank his University of Virginia colleagues and staff, including Clifton McCleskey, Chairman of the Department of Government and Foreign Affairs; graduate students Bruce Larson and Dan Kritenbrink; and technical assistant Nancy Rae.

Particular thanks from both of us go to Gary Mucciaroni of The College of William and Mary and David Ziegler of Western Washington University for their lengthy and substantive contributions to Chapter 16, "Economic Policy," and Chapter 18, "Foreign Policy," respectively. We also thank Jeff Anderson of Brown University, who helped provide comparisons between the American and British systems of government.

No project such as this can ever be completed on time without tremendous support from the publisher. In Bruce Nichols we have had the rare fortune to work with the best editor in all of political science. He guided this project every step of the way and acted as a cheerleader, friend, stern taskmaster, and even a pushy editor. Though we may have come to verbal (and FAX) blows on a couple of occasions, we all emerged the better for it. One of the nicest aspects of this project was the opportunity to become good friends with Bruce and with Jane Tufts, our development editor. Jane's years of experience and decision to freelance benefitted the book tremendously. Without Jane and Bruce, this book would be nothing like it is today. Although at times we cringed to see the arrival of a Federal Express package from Jane or a FAX from Bruce, they made us write a better book, even if, at times, it must have seemed to them that it was in spite of ourselves.

Other individuals at Macmillan deserve special thanks. David Chodoff assisted with text development and oversaw the development of the line art program. Sharon Lee, our production supervisor, worked prodigiously to coordinate a complicated manuscript and keep it flowing smoothly on a very tight schedule. Nick Sklitsis and John Sollami likewise spent many long hours keeping us on schedule. Barbara Scott, Julie Tesser, and Chris Migdol worked hard to find many excellent photographs. Pat Smythe helped produce a stunning design. Finally, Fred Hamden and Scott Rubin combined to create one of the most impressive marketing campaigns we could ever have imagined.

Many peers reviewed various stages of the manuscript and earned our gratitude in the process: Martin Wiseman, Mississippi State University; Mark Silverstein, Boston University; Steve Mazurana, University of Northern Colorado; Shirley Anne Warshaw, Gettysburg College; Jon Bond, Texas A&M University; Doris Graber, University of Illinois at Chicago; Bruce Oppenheimer, University of Houston; Cary Covington, University of Iowa; Marjorie Hershey, Indiana University; Ruth Bamberger, Drury College; Greg Caldeira, Ohio State University; David Cingranelli, SUNY at Binghamton; Mark Landis, Hofstra University; Charles Hadley, University of New Orleans; Danny Adkison, Oklahoma State University; Kenneth Kennedy, College of San Mateo; Evelyn Fink, Michigan State University.

Finally, we want to thank the many professors and instructors who participated in the class testing of the Pre-Election Preview Edition of *American Government*. Their responses and those of their students were helpful and gratifying.

Peter J. Baxter	Niagara University
Steve Borelli	University of Alabama
Lynn Brink	North Lake College
Alan R. Carter	Schenectady County Community College
Jules Cohn	Borough of Manhattan Community College and John Jay College
Willis Diller	Mid Michigan Community College
William Dowd	Manchester Community College
William Doyle	Johnson State College
Lois Lovelace Duke	Clemson University
Herbert E. Gooch	California Lutheran University
Martin Gruberg	University of Wisconsin-Oshkosh
Stacia L. Haynie	Louisiana State University
David Head	South Georgia College
Marshall R. King	Maryville College
Jean Kingston	California State University, Fresno
Bettie Lu Lancaster	John Brown University
Burdett A. Loomis	University of Kansas
David Maas	University of Alaska
Thomas Mandeville	Clinton Community College
Cecilia G. Manrique	University of Wisconsin-La Crosse
Valerie Martinez	University of North Texas
James L. McDowell	Indiana State University
Nancy E. McGlen	Niagara University
Mary Alice Nye	University of North Texas
Doug Parrott	Sheridan College
Barbara A. Perry	Sweet Briar College
Claude Pomerleau	University of Portland
Hillard Pouncy	Swarthmore College
Linda Simmons	Northern Virginia Community College
Elen C. Singh	Mississippi Valley State University
Priscilla Southwell	University of Oregon
Dennis Sullivan	Dartmouth College
Brenda Teals	Big Bend Community College
Clyde Wilcox	Georgetown University
Karen H. Woodward	Burlington County College

Brief Contents

Contents

PART TWO

Institutions of Government

Post-election Photo Credits

Page	Photographer/Source

Ch. 2 The Constitution

30	Library of Congress

Ch. 7 The Presidency

233	Copyright 1991, USA TODAY. Reprinted with permission.
237 (top right)	Brooks Kraft/Sygma
237 (top middle)	Wally McNamee/Folio, Inc.
237 (top left)	UPI/The Bettmann Archive
237 (bottom left)	AP/Wide World Photos
237 (bottom middle)	UPI/The Bettmann Archive
237 (bottom right)	UPI/The Bettmann Archive

Part Opener 3: Political Behavior

342–343	Peter Turnley/Black Star
388	Peter Turnley/Black Star

Ch. 12 Voting and Elections

425 (left)	AP/Wide World Photos
425 (right)	Allan Tannenbaum/Sygma
426	AP/Wide World
438	AP/Wide World

Ch. 13 The Campaign Process

474	Wally McNamee/Sygma
485	Courtesy of CNN

PART ONE

Foundations of Government

An understanding of American government requires an understanding of its philosophical roots, historical evolution, and present structure and behavior. In this book you will encounter all of these elements, along with some spice to make them interesting: stories, biographies, and behind-the-scenes analysis. Part One begins with basic principles that apply to all parts of our government. In Chapter 1, we define concepts such as *government* and *politics* and explain in more detail how to study government. It is important to place democratic systems in a broad historical and economic context in order to understand their achievements and limitations; therefore Chapter 1 incorporates these perspectives and sets the stage for what follows.

After the introductory chapter, we turn in Chapter 2 to an explanation of the critical founding period of America's governing system, with special emphasis on the creation of the Constitution. Understanding the decisions behind the creation of the Constitution is an essential starting point for studying the government that operates by its rules. We look not only at the original document, but also at the ways it has been interpreted and amended since its inception.

In Chapter 3 we present the main features of America's system of interlocking federal, state, and local governments. These layers, which form complicated, ever-shifting combinations of power and responsibility, differentiate in key ways America's government from other democracies. Since the relationships among the different levels circumscribe nearly every aspect of government, it is important to study their basic principles before examining particular institutions or processes.

Finally, in Chapters 4 and 5, we examine questions of individual rights and liberties. All countries must make basic decisions about how much power should be allocated to the government and how much should be retained by the people. The consequences of such decisions—for example, who votes and who occupies positions of power—can be enormous.

*T*he accumulation of all powers, legislative, executive, and judiciary, in the same hands . . . may justly be pronounced the very definition of tyranny.

James Madison

FEDERALIST NO. 47

The creation of the American system of government, as this quotation from The Federalist Papers indicates, was motivated above all by the need to break away from the English system.

CHAPTER 1

American Government: Roots and Reform

Americans are not the only ones who have wrestled with the need to create a government to meet their own needs. In 1789, spurred by the American Revolution, cries of "Liberté, Egalité and Fraternité" rang out in France as members of the working class rose up against King Louis XVI. The king, members of his family, and many in the French aristocracy were executed by guillotine. Civil unrest continued and mobs controlled the city of Paris until order was restored through the creation of a provisional government.

In the early 1900s in Russia, the radical Bolshevik Party mobilized citizens who were demoralized by war and without jobs or food to overthrow and ultimately execute Czar Nicholas II. The Bolshevik Revolution was followed by a period of civil war, and the Union of Soviet Socialist Republics—which has itself recently succumbed to new unrest—was ultimately created from the ruins of the Russian Empire.

In each of these situations, men and women attempted to create a new system that resolved the classical, age-old question of politics: Who gets what, when, and how?

From the time you get up in the morning to the short time later when you leave for classes or work, this central question of politics pervades your life. The government, for example, sets the standards for whether you wake up on Eastern, Central, or Western Standard Time. It regulates the airwaves and licenses the radio or television broadcasts you might listen to or glance at as you eat and get dressed. Whether or not the water you use as you brush your teeth contains fluoride is a state or local governmental issue. The federal Food and Drug Administration inspects your breakfast meat and sets standards for the advertising on your cereal box, orange juice carton, and other food packaging. Are they really "lite," "high in fiber," or "fresh squeezed"? Only the government can say.

How governments get their powers, and what rights their citizens or subjects retain, is a major focus of this book. All governments—be they that of the United States, those of other democracies such as Great Britain and France, or authoritarian regimes such as that of the former Soviet Union under Stalin—exercise some kind of authority over the daily lives of their citizenry.

Who exercises this power, and how and why they got it, is important to understanding a political system. In short, who governs is a key question. And as we will see, there is no simple answer to that question. For example, do elected representatives actually represent the people who elect them, or do they respond to other interests? High school civics classes teach that elected representatives, working through legitimate channels, produce policies and govern. Yet such simple explanations concerning who governs do not hold together. How, for example, can the Iran-*Contra* affair, which involved charges that the Reagan administration sold arms to Iran to get money to support the *contras* in Nicaragua, be explained in those terms? In this situation, where financial support was given to the *contras* in violation of a congressional directive, laws were undoubtedly broken, yet through 1992 no one who broke them had spent time in prison for doing so.

Political parties, interest groups, and congressional committee assignments all are just part of the answer to the puzzle of who has power and why and how it is used. Consider, for example, the tobacco industry in America. The U.S. Surgeon General requires strong warnings on tobacco products because cigarettes have been linked to cancer. A 1991 draft report from the Environmental Protection Agency concluded that *secondhand* cigarette smoke kills 53,000 nonsmokers annually. Nevertheless, the sale of tobacco has not been banned in the United States. Not only does the government permit smoking, but it also provides *billions* of dollars a year in subsidies to tobacco farmers to increase their profits. Taxes on cigarettes also are lower in the United States than in virtually any other industrialized nation. Because the addictive properties of nicotine undoubtedly would lead to an underground black market for cigarettes like that created for liquor during Prohibition, one can understand the national government's reluctance to ban tobacco products entirely. But addiction alone doesn't explain subsidies or low tax rates.

As we will see in Chapter 15, the powerful tobacco lobby, in conjunction with equally powerful senators and representatives from states in which tobacco is a major cash crop,

Spring Forward, Fall Back

Daylight Savings Time was introduced during World War I as a measure to save coal, which was used to produce electricity for lighting. In order to provide more natural light at the end of the working day clocks are advanced one hour. In the United States, Daylight Savings Time begins on the first Sunday in April (clocks are moved ahead one hour) and ends on the last Sunday in October (clocks are moved back one hour). Any state may decide to remain on Standard Time during this period, as do Arizona and Hawaii; Indiana even allows *counties* to decide whether or not to switch.

Source: USA Today, April 2–4, 1991, p. 1-A.

Lieutenant Colonel Oliver North is sworn in on the occasion of his first appearance before the Senate Iran-*Contra* Committee. An aide to Robert MacFarlane, the head of the National Security Council, North was a key player in the government's secret operation to supply arms to the Nicaraguan *contra* revolutionaries.

Tax rates on cigarettes as a percent of retail price for industrialized nations with the lowest cigarette taxes.	
Canada	69%
Norway	67%
Luxembourg	67%
Finland	67%
Spain	59%
Australia	53%
Switzerland	50%
United States	27%

Source: American Cancer Society, Dr. Gregory Connolly, 1991. Adapted from *Atlanta Constitution*, June 4, 1991, B4.

has been instrumental in seeing that the tobacco industry is allowed to flourish. In contrast, red dye number 2, used to add color to certain food products, was banned in the mid-1970s when it was found to contain cancer-causing agents. Unlike tobacco, it had no supporters (lobbyists) to argue for its continued use in the food industry.

Although, as the examples just given suggest, all governments have problems, it is important to stress the good they can do in their attempts to decide who gets what, when, and how. In the aftermath of the Great Depression in the United States, for example, the government created the Social Security program, which dramatically decreased poverty among the elderly. Our contract laws and judicial system provide an efficient framework for business, assuring people that they have a recourse in the courts should someone fail to deliver as promised. And even something as seemingly mundane as our uniform bankruptcy laws help protect both a business enterprise and its creditors when the enterprise collapses.

Just as it is important to recognize that governments serve many important purposes, it is also important to recognize that government and **politics,** the process by which policy decisions are made, are not static. They are part of a never-ending dynamic process of action and interaction. Governmental actions do not occur in isolation or in a vacuum. The United States and its people, for example, are actors in a world order that from this nation's beginning has affected and continues to affect our laws, policies, and actions. Undoubtedly, the Framers at the Constitutional Convention in Philadelphia were reacting to what they viewed as the tyrannical rule of King George when they drafted Article II of the Constitution, creating a president of the United States. Similarly, the actions of President George Bush and the U.S. Congress in the Persian Gulf War of 1991 were the product of a series of events and reactions to them. The unpopular and unsuccessful Vietnam War, the United States' need for oil, reelection concerns, and probably even President Bush's desire to be viewed as a strong leader—all contributed to some extent to the final decision to deploy troops and then to commence Operation Desert Storm.

Women in combat: Operation Desert Storm. In August, 1990, Iraq invaded the oil-rich country of Kuwait. In response, President Bush sent tens of thousands of troops to contain Iraq's army. With the cooperation of the UN, a multinational force was quickly assembled. Iraq's army was expelled from Kuwait in a brief war in January and February, 1991.

Where Did Our Ideas of Government Come From?

The current American political system did not spring into being overnight. It is the result of an intellectual tradition, as well as the old-fashioned process of trial and error and even luck. To understand how we came to have the form of government we have today, we first need to understand the theories of government that influenced the Founders.

From Aquinas to the Enlightenment

As early as the thirteenth century, classical and medieval theorists such as St. Thomas Aquinas (1225–1274) argued that people naturally fell into groups and that governments were ordained by **natural law**—basic and God-given rules that do not have to be written down so much as discovered. Individual rights to life and liberty were a part of this natural law created by God. In a time when kings ruled as absolute monarchs by divine right, God-given law was accepted as the basic foundation of any government. From this point of view, citizens had to be bound by any government regardless of whether they had a say in its workings. If government reflects God's will, who can argue with it?

In the seventeenth and eighteenth centuries, however, an intellectual revolution swept the European continent, altering the nature of government. Philosophers and scientists such as Isaac Newton (1642–1727) began to argue that the world could be improved through the use of human reason. These theorists directly challenged medieval notions that fate alone controlled an individual's destiny and that kings ruled by divine right. Equally important was the growth of the Protestant faith in this period. Protestantism promoted the belief that people could talk directly to God without the intermediary of a priest. Together these intellectual and religious developments of the Enlightenment period encouraged people to seek alternatives to absolute monarchy and to ponder new methods of governing.

In England, when separatists split from the Anglican church, they did so believing that the ability to speak directly to God gave them the power to participate directly in the governance of their own local congregations. In carrying out their beliefs and establishing self-governing congregations, the separatists were responsible for the first widespread appearance of self-government. The separatists who moved to the English colonies in America brought their beliefs about self-governance with them. The Mayflower Compact reflects this tradition. Although it addresses itself to secular government, its form is akin to the "covenants" (note the use of the word in the compact) that separatist congregations wrote and agreed to when they formed themselves.

A Growing Idea: Popular Consent

Two English theorists in the seventeenth century, Thomas Hobbes (1588–1679) and John Locke (1632–1704), and the eighteenth-century French theorist Jean-Jacques Rousseau (1712–1778) proposed **social contract theories** of government. In contrast to Aquinas and the ideas of God-ordained government, they argued that even before the creation of governments, all individuals were free and equal by natural right. This freedom, in turn, required that all men give their consent to be governed.[1]

Locke and Hobbes. In his classic political treatise *Leviathan* (1651), Hobbes argued pessimistically that man's natural state was war. In his attempt to make sense of King

---

[1] The term *men* is used here because only males were considered fit to vote.

What Do Governments Do?

From the earliest days of recorded civilization, whenever groups of individuals came together, the need for some form of **government** arose. A mechanism was needed for individuals to resolve their differences peacefully and to ward off aggression from outsiders. As societies became more complex, so did the functions of government, such as the coining of money, creation of a public infrastructure of roads, buildings, and so on. Still, the heart of all governments rests on the notion that they are basically "keepers of the peace."

In y name of god Amen· we whose names are vnderwriten, the loyall subiects of our dread soueraigne Lord King Iames by y grace of god, of great Britaine, franc, & yreland king: defendor of y faith, &T

Haueing vndertaken, for y glorie of god, and aduancemente of y christian faith, and honour of our king & countrie, a voyage to plant y first Colonie in y Northerne parts of Virginia· doe by these presents solemnly & mutualy in y presence of god, and one of another, Couenant, & combine our selues togeather into a Ciuill body politick; for our better ordering, & preseruation & furtheranco of y ends aforsaid; and by vertue hereof to enacte, constitute, and frame shuch just & equall lawes, ordinances, Acts, constitutions, & offices, from time to time, as shall be thought most meete & conuenient for y generall good of y Colonie: vnto which we promise all due submission and obedience· In witnes wherof we haue hereunder subscribed our names at Cap= Codd y ·11· of Nouember, in y year of y raigne of our soueraigne Lord king yames of England, franc, & yreland y eighteenth and of scotland y fiftie fourth. An: Dom·1620·]

While on the Mayflower, English colonists drew up a compact declaring their intention to form a "Civil Body Politick," or government, to preserve order and peace.

Charles's restoration to the throne, he mused that life without government was a "state of nature," where, without written, enforceable rules, people would live like animals— foraging for food, stealing, and killing when necessary. To escape the horrors of the natural state, Hobbes argued, men must, in order to protect their lives, give up to government certain rights. Without government, Hobbes warned, life would basically be "solitary, poor, nasty, brutish, and short"—a constant struggle to survive against the evil of others. For this reason, governments had to intrude on people's rights and liberties in order to better control society and provide the proper safeguards for property.

Hobbes argued strongly for a single ruler, no matter how evil, to guarantee the rights of the weak against the strong. Leviathan, a biblical sea monster, was his characterization of an all-powerful government. Moreover, strict adherence to Leviathan's laws, however encompassing or intrusive on liberty, were but a small price to pay for living in a civilized society or, more important, for life itself.

In contrast, John Locke—like many other political philosophers of the era—took the basic survival of man for granted and argued that the major responsibility of government was the preservation of private property. Locke was responding to King James II's abuses of power directed at the Anglican church and Parliament in two of his works, *Essay Concerning Human Understanding* (1690) and *Second Treatise on Civil Government* (1689). Locke denied the divine right of kings to govern. More important, he argued that men were born equal and with equal rights in nature that no king had the power to void. Under what Locke termed "social contract theory," the consent of the people is the only true basis of any sovereign's right to rule. According to Locke, men form governments largely to preserve life, liberty, and property and to assure justice. If governments act improperly, they break their "contract" with the people and therefore no longer enjoy the consent of the governed. Because he believed that true justice comes from laws, Locke argued that the branch of government that

The title page from Thomas Hobbes's *Leviathan,* 1651.

makes laws—as opposed to that which enforces or interprets laws—should be the most powerful.

Locke believed that a chief executive who would administer laws was important, but that he should necessarily be limited by law or by the "social contract" with the governed. Locke's writings influenced many of the American colonists, especially Thomas Jefferson, whose original draft of the Declaration of Independence noted the rights to "life, liberty and property"[2] as key reasons to split from England.

___

[2] Jefferson ultimately and inexplicably changed these words to "Life, Liberty, and the pursuit of Happiness," although most of the signers were far more concerned with property.

People of the Past

Hobbes

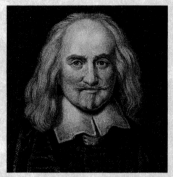

Thomas Hobbes was born in Gloucestershire (Glouster), England in 1588 and began his formal education at the age of four. By the age of six he was learning Latin and Greek, and by the age of nineteen he had obtained his bachelor's degree from Oxford University. In 1608, Hobbes accepted a position as a family tutor with the earl of Devonshire, a post he retained for the rest of his life.

Hobbes was greatly influenced by the chaos of the English Civil War during the mid-seventeenth century. Its impact is evident in his most famous work, *Leviathan* (1651), a treatise on governmental theory that states his views on Man and Citizen. *Leviathan* is commonly described as a book about politics, but it also deals with religion and moral philosophy. Hobbes characterized humans as selfishly individualistic and constantly at war with one another. Without an effective government, argued Hobbes, life would be "solitary, poor, nasty, brutish, and short." People surrendered themselves to rulers in exchange for protection from their neighbors.

Hobbes was quite an energetic man, and at the age of eighty-four he wrote his own autobiography in Latin verse. He died at the age of ninety-one.

Locke

John Locke, born in England in 1632, was admitted to an outstanding public school at the age of fifteen. It was there that he began to question his upbringing in the Puritan faith. At twenty he went on to study at Oxford, where he later became a lecturer in Aristotelian philosophy. Soon, however, he found a new interest in medicine and experimental science.

In 1666, Locke met Anthony Ashley Cooper, the first earl of Shaftesbury, and a strong left-wing politician. It was through Cooper that Locke discovered his own talent for philosophy. In 1689, Locke published his most famous work, *Second Treatise on Civil Government,* in which he set forth a theory of natural rights. He used natural rights to support his "social contract [theory]— the view that the consent of the people is the only true basis of any sovereign's right to rule." Governments exist, he argued, because individuals agree through a contract to form one to protect their rights under natural law. They agree to abide by decisions made by majority vote in the resolution of disputes. Locke died on October 28, 1704 at the age of seventy-two.

Devising a National Government

Although social contract theorists agreed on the need for government, they did not necessarily agree on the form that any government should take. Thomas Hobbes argued for a single leader; John Locke and Jean-Jacques Rousseau saw the need for less centralized locations of power.

A system with a strong ruler, like the British monarchy, was immediately rejected by the colonists after they declared their independence. Most European monarchical systems gave hereditary monarchs absolute power over all forms of activity. Many of the colonists fled from Great Britain to avoid religious persecution and other harsh manifestations of power wielded by George II, whom they viewed as a malevolent despot.

Then and Now
Direct Democracy

The town meeting, which is still the form of government for some places in New England, is an example of direct democracy. Starting in colonial times, the men of the town would congregate at the local meeting hall to discuss issues from public drunkenness to education.

Today some people suggest that electronic voting—by computer or interactive television—may provide a means for returning to direct democracy. Electronic voting could allow all Americans to voice their opinions and possibly even solve the problems inherent with low voter turnouts, especially for local government offices.

Colonists also did not want to create an **oligarchy,** a form of government in which the right to participate is conditioned on the possession of wealth or property. The Greek philosopher Aristotle (384–322 B.C.) defined this form of government as a perversion of an **aristocracy,** often known as the rule of the few. Again, the colonists were fearful of replicating the landed and titled system of the British aristocracy and viewed the formation of a representative form of government as far more in keeping with the ideas of social contract theorists.

The Theory of Democratic Government

As evidenced by the early creation of the Virginia House of Burgesses in 1619, the colonists were quick to create participatory forms of government in which most men (subject to some land-owning requirements) were allowed to participate. The New England town meeting, where all citizens gather to discuss and decide upon issues facing the town, today stands as a surviving example of these forms of **direct democracy.**

Direct democracies, however, soon proved unworkable in the colonies. As more and more settlers came to the New World, town meetings like those in New England were replaced by a system called *indirect* or **representative democracy.** Ironically, this system of government, in which representatives of the people are chosen by ballot, was considered undemocratic by ancient Greeks, who believed that all citizens must have a direct say in their governance.

Representative or indirect democracies, which call for the election of representatives to a governmental decision-making body, were formed first in the colonies and then in the new Union. This type of indirect democracy was later heralded by important political theorists such as the English philosopher John Stuart Mill (1806–1876).[3] Representative democracies are more commonly called *republics,* from the Latin for "public thing." A **republic** is generally intended to serve the interests of the public, not the private interests of rulers or of a privileged class, hence the name.

[3] In his essay *On Liberty* (1859) Mill argues that men could grow only if they experienced minimal governmental restrictions on their liberties, including freedom of thought and discussion.

Types of Government

TYPES	HOW MANY ARE INVOLVED IN THE GOVERNING PROCESS?
Monarchy Example: Eighteenth-century Great Britain	One
Oligarchy Example: El Salvador, 1960s Brazil, 1970s	Small number
Aristocracy Example: Seventeenth-century Poland Haiti, 1980s	Small number
Indirect Democracy Example: United States today	Many
Direct Democracy Example: Ancient Athens	Nearly all

What Are the Characteristics of American Democracy?

The United States is an indirect democracy that places tremendous value on the individual. The American emphasis on **political equality,** the definition of which has varied considerably over time (as discussed in Chapter 5), is a reflection of American stress on the importance of the individual. Although some individuals clearly wield more political clout than others, in theory the adage "one man, one vote" implies a sense of political equality for all.

Majority rule and *preservation of minority rights* are two additional facets of American democracy. Majority rule implies that only policies which collectively garner the support of a majority of individuals will be made into law. This right of the majority to govern themselves is summed up by the term **popular sovereignty.** This term, however, did not come into vogue until pre–Civil War debates over slavery. Supporters of popular sovereignty argued that Western states seeking admission to the Union should be able to decide whether or not they would be added as "free" or "slave" states.

Although preservation of minority rights was not at the forefront of the popular sovereignty debates, American emphasis on majority rule usually has stressed concern with minority rights. As we will see throughout this book, these two concepts are constantly in tension. Debates over slavery, treatment of Japanese-Americans during World War II, persecution of religious minorities, and even more recent debates on civil rights legislation illustrate the conflicts that occur in our democratic system in spite of its emphasis on personal liberty. This emphasis on personal liberty and popular sovereignty is common to many, but not all, democracies. For example, in Britain, sovereign authority is vested not in the people, but in Parliament. Reflecting the centuries of struggle between Parliament and the Crown, the concept of parliamentary sovereignty lends a distinct cast to the struggles and conflicts that unfold in that democracy.

Who Makes Decisions?

How these conflicts are resolved and how much emphasis is placed on individual rights and political freedoms often are determined by how and by whom the government is operated. Over the years several theorists have posited widely different points of view in their attempts to answer this important question. If we subscribe to Harold D. Lasswell's

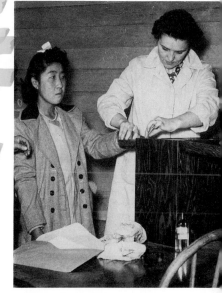

In times of crisis, minority rights are often disregarded. During World War II, Japanese-Americans were interned in large inland camps for fear that their wartime allegiances would lead to espionage. Some forty years later, Congress voted to compensate all those who had been interned.

view of politics as the study of "who gets what, when, and how,"[4] it is critical to understand who makes the decisions in a democratic system.

Elite Theory. One of the most commonly offered explanations of who governs is **elite theory,** posited by the American sociologist C. Wright Mills (1916–1961). In *The Power Elite* (1956), Mills argued that important policies were set by a loose coalition of three groups with some overlap among each. These three major influencers of policy—corporate leaders, military leaders, and a small group of key governmental leaders—are, according to Mills, the true "power elite" in America. Other elite theorists have argued that the news media should be included as a fourth source of political power in the United States. These elite theorists believe that government increasingly has become alienated from the people and is rarely responsive to their wishes.

Bureaucratic Theory. Max Weber (1864–1920), the founder of modern sociology, argued that *all* institutions, governmental and nongovernmental, have fallen under the control of a large and ever-growing bureaucracy. This view is called **bureaucratic theory.** Because all institutions have grown more complex, Weber concluded that the expertise and competence of bureaucrats allows them to wrest power from others, especially elected officials. As we will see in Chapter 8, there is no doubt that in certain policy areas bureaucrats carry increasing amounts of power. Politicians come and go, yet most bureaucrats stay on in their positions for a good part of their working lives.

Pluralist Theory. Another, more widely accepted theory about the nature of power is held by those in the *pluralist* school of thought. According to political scientists like Robert Dahl, the structure of our democratic government allows only for a **pluralist model** of democracy. Dahl argues that resources are scattered so widely in our diverse democracy that no single elite group can ever have a monopoly over any substantial area of policy. In *Who Governs?* (1961), for example, Dahl found that political competition and elections coupled with the growing ethnic and socioeconomic diversity of New Haven, Connecticut, led to a situation in which a single elite could never take and hold power legally. As James Madison argued in Federalist No. 10, a large number of interests and "factions" clashing in the public arena serve to enhance compromise. Dahl found that this need for compromise greatly influenced who governed New Haven in the areas of public education, urban renewal, and political nomination.[5]

Interest Group Theory. Political scientist David Truman concurs with pluralists about the importance of the role of interest groups in a democracy. He postulated what is termed an **interest group theory** of democracy, which is actually not all that different from the pluralist model. According to Truman, interest groups—not elites, sets of elites, or bureaucrats—control the governmental process.[6] Truman believes there are so many potential pressure points in the executive, legislative, and judicial branches of the federal government—as well as at the state level—that groups can step in on any number of competing sides and that government becomes the equilibrium point in the system.

All of these theories provide interesting ways to begin to view how policy decisions are made, whether we are looking at local, state, or national policies. It could be, as Dahl has argued, that no single group or interest can ever have a monopoly over any issue, let alone over larger policy programs. It also stands to reason that the patterns we discover in the United States may apply to a certain extent in other parts of the world.

---

[4] Harold D. Lasswell, *Politics: Who Gets What, When, and How* (New York: McGraw-Hill, 1938).

[5] See also Robert Dahl, *Dilemmas of Pluralist Democracy: Autonomy vs. Control* (New Haven, Conn.: Yale University Press, 1982).

[6] David B. Truman, *The Governmental Process* (New York: Knopf, 1951).

Why a Capitalist System?

When the Framers drafted the Constitution, their tremendous concern with personal property and the need to create a government able to protect it were always at the forefront of their actions and decisions. They were well aware of the need for a well-functioning economy and saw that government had a key role in maintaining one. What a malfunction in the economy is, however, and what steps the government should take to remedy it, were questions that dogged the Framers and continue to puzzle politicians and theorists today.

The private ownership of property and a **free market economy** are key tenets of the American system called **capitalism.** In contrast to socialism, in which the working class owns and controls all means of production and distribution, capitalism favors private control of business and minimal governmental regulation of private industry.

Capitalism. Capitalism is a mode of economic production that can be characterized by the private ownership by individuals or groups of land, factories, raw materials, or other instruments of production. It is the economic system found in the United States, Great Britain, and most parts of Western Europe. In capitalist systems, the laws of supply and demand in the marketplace and free trade set prices of goods and drive production. Unlike in other economic systems, governments play little or no role.

In 1776, at the same time as the signing of the Declaration of Independence, Adam Smith (1723–1790) published *An Inquiry into the Nature and Causes of the Wealth of Nations* (generally known as *The Wealth of Nations*). Smith's book marked the beginning of the modern capitalist era. He argued that free trade would result in full production and economic health. These ideas were greeted with great enthusiasm in the colonies as independence was proclaimed. Colonists no longer wanted to participate in the mercantile system of Great Britain and other Western European nations. These systems bound trade and its administration to national governments. Smith and his supporters saw free trade as "the invisible hand" that produced the wealth of nations. This wealth, in turn, became the inspiration and justification for capitalism.

Under capitalism, sales occur for the profit of the individual. Capitalists believe that both national and individual production is greatest when individuals are free to do with their property or goods as they wish. The conservative political economist Milton Friedman (b. 1912) argues that this kind of free enterprise system is essential to the existence of a free political system like our democracy.[7]

During the late eighteenth century and through the mid-1930s in the United States and in much of the Western world, the idea of ***laissez-faire*** economics (from the French, *to leave alone*) enjoyed exceptional popularity. Governments routinely followed a "hands off" economic policy. By the late 1800s, however, as discussed in Chapters 8 and 16, national governments felt increasing pressure to regulate some aspects of their economies, and true capitalism ceased to exist.[8] The extent of this trend, however, varied by country and over time. In post–World War II Britain, for example, the extent of government economic regulation in industrial policy and social welfare was much greater than that attempted by American policy makers in the same period.

Socialism. Reaction to the overwhelming wealth of millionaire industrialists and a corresponding exploitation of workers in France, England, and ultimately the United

---

[7] Milton Friedman, *Capitalism and Freedom* (Chicago: University of Chicago Press, 1962).

[8] Modern disciples of *laissez-faire* are called libertarians. Libertarians adamantly oppose all forms of government regulation and action unless it is critical to the protection of life, liberty, or property. They argue that while governments are at best an evil necessity, governments are best that govern least.

Communism: A Dying Idea?

The German socialist Karl Marx (1818–1883) grew up in Germany as the socialist movement developed there and in many parts of Western Europe. Its influence on him was profound. He came to argue that government was simply a manifestation of underlying economic forces and could be understood according to types of economic production. All societies went through five stages: (1) primitive communal societies, (2) slavery, (3) feudalism, (4) capitalism, and (5) socialism. According to Marx, history brought with it an evolving economic and political system in which a class struggle between workers and property owners was inevitable. The clash of the interests of these two classes led to the development of the state or government. In turn, governments were used by rich capitalists, called the *bourgeoisie,* to protect their property in much the same way that Charles Beard argued that the Framers of the U.S. Constitution were motivated by their personal economic concerns when they drafted the Constitution (see Chapter 2). In *Das Kapital* (1867), Marx argued that capitalism would always be replaced by socialist states in which the working class would own the means of production and distribution and be able to redistribute the wealth to meet its needs.

Karl Marx

These beliefs ultimately led Marx to suggest, "From each according to his ability, to each according to his needs!" as part of a radical scheme that went further than socialism by advocating an absence of classes and common ownership of the means of sustenance and production. In essence, then, Marx viewed communism as a higher, sixth stage of societies, beyond even socialism. Marx was the first to propound the belief that capitalism was evil and must be overthrown, no matter how violent the means. But the communism espoused by Marx continues to be an "ideal" yet to be implemented and for which there is growing disfavor. The breakup of the Soviet Union is a prime example of this trend.

States led to the development of **socialism,** a philosophy that advocates collective ownership and control of the means of economic production. In direct opposition to the ideas that drove the Founders, socialists called for governmental—rather than private—ownership of all land, property, and industry and, in turn, an equitable distribution of the income from those holdings.

Over the years socialists have been united in their view of a common concern for all men and women, but have been far less in agreement about the means by which to reach a socialist ideal. Some, especially in Western Europe, have argued that socialism can evolve through democratic processes. Thus, in nations like Great Britain, certain critical industries or services such as health care or the coal industry have been *nationalized* or taken over by the state to provide for more efficient supervision and to avoid the major concentrations of wealth that occur when individuals privately own key industries.

In the United States today, many people support the nationalization of health care. But as proposals are being made more frequently to implement some sort of national health insurance or "socialized medicine" of the kind practiced in Canada or Great Britain, charges of "socialism" often have been leveled against those making the proposals. In general, socialism, like many of the other "-isms," has a very negative connotation in the United States, even though many U.S. programs are publicly operated. Medicare and Medicaid, programs of government support for the costs of health care, the nationalization of the country's passenger railroads and their consolidation as Amtrak, and the Social Security retirement system all could be considered examples of democratic socialism.

Totalitarianism. Whereas socialist systems spread the wealth and control of publicly owned industries and other means of production to all members of society, in a **totalitarian** system governments retain unlimited powers for elite rulers. In contrast to governments based on democratic or libertarian beliefs, totalitarian governments have total authority over their people and their economic systems. George Orwell's novel *1984* is perhaps the best depiction of what a pure totalitarian regime would be like. The reign of the Ayatollah Ruhollah Khomeini in Iran from 1979 until his death and that of President Saddam Hussein in Iraq come close to the "total" control of forms of production, the airwaves, education, the arts, and even sports implied by totalitarianism.

Because total control by a single ruler or elite requires technological innovations and weapons of mass destruction that only modern science can provide, totalitarianism, even in partial form, did not present itself to the world until well into the 1900s.[9] Even Adolf Hitler's Germany, perhaps the most totalitarian government that has appeared so far, probably lacked the resources to assert complete control of every aspect of life for all citizens.

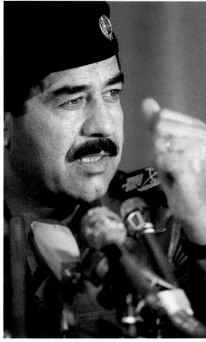
Saddam Hussein

Understanding Our Democratic System

One key to understanding our democratic system is a recognition of the role that history and its lessons have played in the development of the American state. The lessons of history provide a context in which to understand not only policies of the past but also policies today. Crises lead to reform and changing public expectations, all of which contribute to our self-understanding.

The Role of Crises and Reform. As government at all levels continues to grow, we cannot ignore the role that crises have played. The development of the power of the national government as well as realignments in the powers of the various institutions have also been affected by crises, as will be discussed in succeeding chapters. Crises do not only affect the American state; democracies like Britain have witnessed the shaping of their politics, institutions, and conflicts by unforeseen domestic and international crises. The two world wars, for example, greatly strengthened the working-class movement and placed many new issues on the national agenda—for example, nationalization of industry, social welfare, and economic planning.

The Civil War—like other crises, such as the Great Depression and even the Watergate scandal that resulted in Richard Nixon's resignation from the presidency—created major turmoil yet demonstrated that our system can survive in the face of enormous political, societal, and even institutional changes. Most often, these crises have produced considerable reforms. The Civil War led to the dismantling of the slavery system and to the

[9] Hannah Arendt, *The Origins of Totalitarianism* (Cambridge, Mass.: Harvard University Press, 1958).

passage of the Thirteenth, Fourteenth, and Fifteenth Amendments, which led to the seeds of recognition of blacks as American citizens. The Depression led to the New Deal and the creation of a government more actively involved in economic and social regulation. And, more recently, the Watergate scandal resulted in stricter ethics laws that have led to the resignatioi. or removal of many elected officials. The Vietnam War and Watergate also led to a general disillusionment with politics. Only in the aftermath of the success of the United States in the Persian Gulf in 1991 did this disillusionment with government give way to a temporarily renewed sense of national pride.

The Lessons of History. As historians are fond of noting, history often repeats itself. Clear cycles can be seen in the evolution of our democratic system. For example, in the mid-1800s many women's rights activists sought the right to vote on a state-by-state basis and eschewed suggestions to seek a constitutional amendment. This approach later was used in the suffrage movement (1890–1920) by a new generation of women who sought the right to vote, but again it soon proved unworkable as efforts in individual states were costly and often unsuccessful. Women finally decided that an amendment to the U.S. Constitution would be the most expeditious way to secure voting rights.

Today, in the aftermath of a series of decisions indicating an increased willingness on the part of the U.S. Supreme Court to restrict abortion rights, pro-choice forces initially sought to fight for the right to an abortion on a state-by-state basis. But, by mid-1991, the National Abortion Rights Action League (NARAL) had admitted that it had lost far more than it had won with this strategy as state after state passed increasingly restrictive laws. In an effort reminiscent of that adopted by women in the 1920s to obtain the right to vote, NARAL decided to throw all of its efforts behind passage of the national *Freedom of Choice Act,* which would guarantee a woman's right to an abortion free from any state restrictions. Thus, an understanding of the difficulty women have encountered historically helps us to understand the effectiveness of some political strategies today.

Public Expectations. Americans' expectations of their government have grown tremendously in the twentieth century. Although some debate the role of government, public opinion polls reveal most Americans have come to expect "big government" and want the government—especially the national government—to tackle economic and social problems. Whereas libertarians stress that government should not involve itself in the plight of the people or attempt to remedy any social ills, most people today look to it for support for many things, including education, health research, and relief from poverty.

In the 1980s, for example, more than 175,000 people became infected with the AIDS virus, and 109,000 of them died. Although AIDS was first viewed as a rare disease afflicting homosexual men in California and New York, it now is the most common cause of non-accidental death among women in certain age groups. As more people from all groups and of all ages fall victim to AIDS, pressure on the national government increases. Victims or those in high-risk groups are fighting for federal budget increases for AIDS research in addition to anti-discrimination legislation. Others argue for better screening of the blood supply and for compulsory testing of those in the medical profession. Governmental response was urged by C. Everett Koop, U.S. Surgeon General during Ronald Reagan's presidency, who played a major role in the decision to increase the federal governmental effort for AIDS education over the protest of some conservative groups. Thus, as new problems occur, the public increasingly has looked to the government for help and solutions.

In this text we present you with the tools to understand the political system in which you live. We hope that you will approach the study of American politics with an open mind. When you read a daily newspaper or watch a television news program, you are actually engaged in the study of politics. Your study of the processes of government should help you become a better citizen as you become more informed about your government and its operations. We hope that you learn to ask questions. Why was a particular law enacted? How was it implemented? Does your vote count?

Summary

To understand how our current system of government works, it is important to understand choices that were made many years ago. Those who came to the New World often did so to escape many European traditions, including monarchy and aristocracy. Moreover, early settlers were often individualists who found themselves attracted to the ideas of social contract theorists, especially John Locke. Thus, they devised a government system called a representative democracy.

In studying this representative democracy throughout the pages of this book we will be concerned with how decisions that determine who gets what, when, and how are made. Several different theories have been offered about this decision-making process:

1. Elite theory
2. Bureaucratic theory
3. Pluralist theory
4. Interest group theory

No matter which theory you think provides the best lens for viewing the governmental process, it is important to consider the roles of crises and reforms, public expectations, and the lessons of history.

Key Terms

politics	representative democracy	pluralist model
government	republic	interest group theory
natural law	political equality	free market economy
social contract theories	majority rule	capitalism
oligarchy	popular sovereignty	*laissez-faire*
aristocracy	elite theory	socialism
direct democracy	bureaucratic theory	totalitarian

Suggested Readings

Bentley, Arthur. *The Process of Government*. Chicago: University of Chicago Press, 1908.

Dahl, Robert. *Polyarchy: Participation and Opposition*. New Haven, Conn.: Yale University Press, 1971.

_____. *Who Governs?* New Haven, Conn.: Yale University Press, 1961.

Hobbes, Thomas. *Leviathan*.

Locke, John. *Two Treatises of Government,* ed. Peter Lasleti. New York: Mentor, 1960.

Marx, Karl. *Das Kapital*. Chicago: Regnery, 1970.

Mills, C. Wright. *The Power Elite*. New York: Oxford University Press, 1956.

Schumpeter, Joseph A. *Capitalism, Socialism, and Democracy*. New York: Harper, 1942.

Schlesinger, Arthur M. *The Age of Jackson*. Boston: Little, Brown, 1945.

Truman, David. B. *The Governmental Process*. New York: Knopf, 1951.

Weber, Max. *From Max Weber: Essays in Sociology,* trans. and ed. H. H. Gerth and C. Wright Mills. London: Routledge & Kegan Paul, 1948.

$\mathcal{E}$very view we may take of the subject, as candid inquirers after truth, will serve to convince us, that it is both unwise and dangerous to deny the federal government an unconfined authority.

James Madison

FEDERALIST NO. 23

According to the Federalists, the major triumph of the Constitution is the authority it granted the national government over the states ("unconfined" by the states).

CHAPTER 2

The Constitution

The Constitution of the United States

Americans today take their Constitution for granted. It is continually reinterpreted, but it is never seriously questioned as the supreme law of the land. We might amend it every now and then, and we might change our minds over what it allows or does not allow, but we always rely on it.

Yet the Constitution was not automatically adopted without question after it was written. Great Britain did not then have a written constitution, nor does it have one today. Instead, Great Britain had a king, who was guided by a House of Lords to represent the nobility and a House of Commons to represent all others. Moreover, England and English courts were guided by principles of **common law,** the body of law in England that arose from judge-made decisions. Since these ''laws'' were not written, common law underwent many historical changes as it was broadened by local custom and further judicial interpretation. In addition to common law, the British unwritten constitution was and is today comprised of statutory law and conventions, which are rules of behavior that have been adhered to for so long that they are regarded as binding, even though they lack the force of law. This ''unwritten law'' was quite different from the Constitution suggested by the Founders,[1] which carefully created three branches of government and *expressly* gave certain powers to each branch.

In *The Federalist Papers,* its authors—Alexander Hamilton, James Madison, and John Jay—not only had to convince the electorate that the particular wording of the Constitution proposed in 1789 was the best; they also had to convince the public that America needed any sort of written document at all. Moreover, they had to explain why they made the choices they did and how and why the new system would be better than the existing government. Their task was made all the more difficult by the fact that their proposed Constitution took away from the state governments many rights that the colonists had created and had become comfortable with after breaking with Great Britain in 1776. Fortunately, because all thirteen states had drafted written constitutions after independence was declared, most colonists agreed on the need for a written plan of government. Looking outside the continent, however, they saw few models to imitate.

The idea of a written code of laws can be traced to ancient times. But, by the seventeenth and eighteenth centuries, most European legal and governmental systems remained rooted in the notion of the common law and in systems in which a monarch ruled through the **divine right of kings** (see Chapter 1). Since 1215, the British monarch's power had been limited somewhat by the **Magna Carta,** a charter signed by King John guaranteeing the people certain liberties, including landowners' and tenants' rights, the right to trial by jury, the right to reasonable punishments, and some measure of religious freedom. In contrast, other European countries were monarchies with no written guarantees of rights.

In the New World, however, the Massachusetts Bay colonists successfully lived by a few rules set forth in the Mayflower Compact of 1620. And later, in 1781, as discussed in this chapter, the thirteen colonies came together to form a union under the *written* **Articles of Confederation.**

---

[1] Sir William Blackstone attempted to codify or write down the common laws' most widely accepted principles. His several-volume *Commentaries on the Law of England* remains the single best source of English law.

James Madison and Alexander Hamilton, two important early Federalist leaders. Together they were responsible for authoring all but five of *The Federalist Papers.*

For the most part, the Founders charted new territory when they wrote the Constitution in 1789. Their achievement has survived for more than 200 years, and constitutional democracy has spread to many other countries. How did they do it? What issues did they face? What logic did they use? How can we understand their results? This chapter answers these questions by first examining the historical environment from which the Constitution emerged and then by analyzing the document itself.

The Origins of a New Nation

Colonists came to the New World in the early seventeenth century for a variety of reasons. Often it was to escape religious persecution. Others came seeking a new start in an area where land was plentiful. The independence and diversity of the settlers in the New World made the question of how best to rule the new colonies a tricky one. Although the king ruled by decree at home, the Crown's new and distant American possessions were hard to understand, hard to reach, and hard to communicate with. More than merely an ocean separated the two. The colonists were of an independent sort, and it soon became clear that the Crown could not govern the colonies with the same close rein used at home. King James I thus allowed for some local participation through arrangements such as the first elected colonial assembly, the Virginia House of Burgesses, and the elected General Court that governed the Massachusetts Bay Company and its colony after 1629. Almost all of the colonists agreed that the king ruled by divine right; but English monarchs allowed the colonists significant liberties in terms of self-government, religious practices, and economic organization.

For 140 years, this system worked fairly well.[2] By the early 1760s, however, a century and a half of physical separation, colonial development, and the relative self-governance of the colonies had led to weakening ties with—and loyalties to—the Crown. By this time, each of the thirteen colonies had drafted its own written constitution, which provided the fundamental rules or laws for each colony. Moreover, many of the most oppressive British traditions—feudalism, a rigid class system, and the absolute authority of church and king—were nonexistent in the New World. Land was abundant. The restrictive guild and craft systems that severely limited entry into many skilled professions in England did not exist in the colonies. Although the role of religion was central to the lives of most colonists, there was no single state church, and the compulsory British practice of tithing (giving a fixed percentage of one's earnings to the state-sanctioned and -supported church) was nonexistent.

Trade and Taxation

Mercantilism, the theory that the states should predominate over private and colonial interests to the benefit of the Crown, guided many actions of Great Britain toward the colonies. After 1650, for example, Parliament passed a series of navigation acts to prevent its chief rival, Holland, from trading with the English colonies. From 1650 through well into the 1700s, England tried to regulate colonial imports and exports. These policies, however, were difficult to enforce and widely ignored by the colonists, who saw themselves benefiting little from the mercantile system. Thus for years an unwritten agreement existed: The colonists relinquished to the Crown and the British Parliament the authority to regulate trade and conduct international affairs, but they retained the right to levy their own taxes.

[2] For an account of the early development of the colonies, see D. W. Meining, *The Shaping of America,* Vol. 1: *Atlantic America, 1492–1800* (New Haven, Conn.: Yale University Press, 1986).

North America Before and After the Seven Years' War

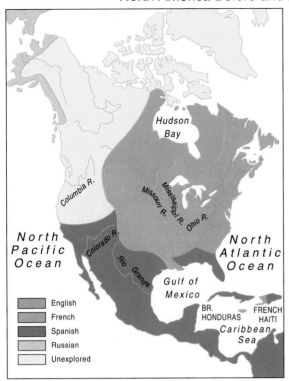

In 1754, before the Seven Years' War

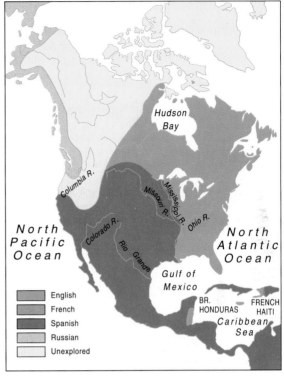

After the Treaty of Paris in 1763

This fragile agreement was soon put to a test. The French and Indian War, fought from 1755 to 1760 on the "Western frontier" of the colonies and Canada, was part of a global war initiated by the British to expand its influence worldwide. The American phase of what internationally was called the Seven Years' War was fought between England and France and its Indian allies. In North America its immediate cause was the rivalry between those two nations, which both claimed the lands between the Allegheny Mountains and the Mississippi River. The surrender of Montréal in 1760 and the Treaty of Paris (signed in 1763) signaled the end of that war. The colonists expected that with the "Indian problem" on the Western frontier now under supposed control, westward migration and settlement could begin in earnest. They were shocked when the Crown decreed in 1763 that there was to be no further westward movement. Parliament believed that expansion into Native American territory would lead to new expenditures for the defense of the settlers, expenditures that were already draining the British treasury, which had yet to recover from the high cost of waging the war.

To raise money to pay for the cost of the war as well as the annual cost of administering the colonies, Parliament enacted the Sugar Act of 1764, which placed taxes on sugar, wine, coffee, and other products commonly exported to the colonies. A postwar colonial depression heightened resentment of the tax. Around the colonies the political cry "No taxation without representation" was heard. Major protest, however, failed to materialize until the imposition of the **Stamp Act** of 1765, which required the purchase of stamps by the payment of a tax on all documents, including newspapers, magazines, and commercial papers. To add insult to injury, Parliament then passed in 1765 the Mutiny or Quartering Act, which required the colonists to furnish barracks or to provide within their own homes living quarters for British troops.

Most colonists, especially those in New England, where these acts hit hardest, were outraged. Again crying, "No taxation without representation," men throughout the colonies organized the Sons of Liberty, under the leadership of Samuel Adams and Patrick Henry. Whereas the sugar tax was a tax on trade—still viewed within the authority of the Crown—the Stamp Act was a direct tax, and protests against it were violent and loud. Riots, often led by the Sons of Liberty, broke out. They were especially violent in Boston, where, for example, the colonial governor's home was burned by an angry mob and British stamp agents were threatened. A boycott of the stamps as well as other British goods was also organized.

First Steps Toward Independence

The colonists called for a meeting of what has been termed the "Stamp Act Congress," the first real meeting of the colonies and the first start toward a unified nation. Nine of the thirteen colonies sent representatives to New York City, where they listed in great detail how they believed their fundamental rights had been violated. Attendees defined what they thought to be the proper relationship between the various colonial governments and the British Parliament; they ardently believed that Parliament had no authority to tax them without colonial representation in the British Parliament. In contrast, the British believed that direct representation of the colonists was impractical and that members of Parliament represented the best interests of all the English, including the colonists.

The Stamp Act Congress and its petitions to the Crown did little to stop the onslaught of taxing measures. Parliament did, however, repeal the Stamp Act and revise the Sugar Act in 1766, largely because of the uproar made by British merchants who were losing large sums of money as a result of the boycotts. Rather than appeasing the colonists, however, these actions emboldened them to increase their resistance. In 1767, when Parliament enacted the Townshend Acts, imposing duties on all kinds of colonial imports, including tea, response from the Sons of Liberty was immediate. Another boycott was announced, and almost all colonists gave up their favorite drink in a united show of resistance to the tax and British authority.

Tensions continued to run high, especially after the British sent 4,000 troops to Boston. These soldiers took over many of the colonists' jobs, such as working on the docks. On March 5, 1770, English troops opened fire on a mob of dock workers, Sons of Liberty, and their "liberty boys" who were taunting them in front of the Boston customs house. Five colonists were killed in what was termed the "Boston Massacre." Following this confrontation, all duties except those on tea were lifted. The tea tax, however, continued to be a symbolic irritant. In 1772, at the suggestion of Samuel Adams, Boston and other towns around Massachusetts set up **Committees of Correspondence** to articulate ideas and to keep communications open around the colony. By 1774, twelve colonies had such committees to maintain a flow of information among like-minded colonists.

Meanwhile, despite dissent in England over treatment of the colonies, Parliament passed another tea tax, designed to shore up the sagging sales of the East India Company: The colonists' boycott had left the British trading house with more than 18 million pounds of unsold tea in its warehouses. To rescue British merchants from literally sinking in tea, Parliament passed in 1773 the Tea Act, which granted a legal monopoly to the financially strapped East India Company. The company was allowed to funnel business to loyalist merchants for the purpose of undercutting colonial merchants, who sold tea imported from other nations. The effect was to drive down the price of tea and hurt colonial merchants who were forced to buy tea at the higher prices from other sources.

When the next shipment of tea arrived in Boston from Great Britain, the colonists responded by throwing the Boston Tea Party. In the dark of night on December 18, 1773, after a militant town meeting presided over by Samuel Adams, about 150 colonists dressed as Indians and made up as blacks, stole their way onto 3 British ships in the Boston Harbor. As a large crowd watched from the docks, they proceeded to open and

THE BLOODY MASSACRE perpetrated in King—t—Street BOSTON on March 5th 1770 by a party of the 29th REGt

UnhappyBoston! fee thy Sons deplore,
Thy hallow'd Walks befmear'd with guiltlefs Gore.
While faithlefs P—n and his favageBands.
With murd'rousRancourftretch their bloodyHands;
Like fierceBarbarians grinning o'er theirPrey,
Approve the Carnage,and enjoy the Day.

If fcalding drops fromRage fromAnguifhWrung
If fpeechlefs Sorrows lab'ring for a Tongue,
Orif a weeping World can ought appeafe
The plaintive Ghofts of Victims fuch as thefe;
ThePatriot's copiousTears for each are fhed,
A gloriousTribute which embalms the Dead.

But know,Fate fummons to that awful Goal,
WhereJUSTICE ftrips theMurd'rer of his Soul:
Should venalC—ts the fcandal of theLand,
Snatch the relentlefsVillain from her Hand.
Keen Execrations on this Plate infcrib'd,
Shall reach aJUDGE who never canbe brib'd.

The unhappy Sufferers were Mefs.s SAML GRAY,SAML MAVERICK,JAMs CALDWELL,CRISPUS ATTUCKS & PATk CARR
Killed. Six wounded; two of them (CHRISTr MONK & JOHN CLARK) Mortally

Paul Revere's engraving of the Boston Massacre was a potent piece of Whig propaganda. Five men were killed, not seven, as the legend states, and the rioters in front of the State House (left) were scarcely as docile as Revere shows them.

then dump nearly 350 chests of tea into the waters below. Similar "tea parties" were held in other colonies. When the news of these actions reached King George, he flew into a rage against the actions of his disloyal subjects. "The die is now cast," the king told his prime minister. "The colonies must either submit or triumph."

His first act was to persuade Parliament to pass the Coercive Acts in 1774. Known in the colonies as the Intolerable Acts, they contained a key provision calling for a total blockade of Boston Harbor until restitution was made for the tea. Another provision reinforced the Quartering Act, again giving royal governors the authority to quarter in the homes of private citizens the additional 4,000 British soldiers sent to patrol Boston.

The First Continental Congress

The British could never have guessed how these actions would unite the colonists. Samuel Adams's Committees of Correspondence spread the word, and food and money were sent to the people of Boston from all over the thirteen colonies. The tax itself was no longer the key issue; now, the extent of British authority over the colonies was the far

People of the Past

Samuel Adams

Although Samuel Adams (1722–1803) today is perhaps best known for the beer that bears his name, Adams's original claim to fame was as a leader against British and Loyalist oppressors (although he did bankrupt his family's brewery business).

Adams was heavily influenced by the writings of John Locke and Locke's belief that it was the "natural right" of man to be self-governing and free from taxation without representation. As a member of the Massachusetts legislature, he advocated defiance of the Stamp Act. With the passage of the Townshend Acts of 1767, he organized a letter-writing campaign urging other colonies to join in resistance. Later, in 1772, he founded the Committees of Correspondence to unite the colonies.

A second cousin of President John Adams, Samuel Adams was a signer of the Declaration of Independence and a member of Massachusetts's constitutional convention that ratified the U.S. Constitution.

more important question. At the request of the colonial assemblies of Massachusetts and Virginia, an intercolonial meeting was agreed upon, with each colonial assembly selecting a group of delegates to attend a continental congress and to speak to the king on behalf of the newly united colonies.

The First Continental Congress met in Philadelphia from September 5 to October 26, 1774. It was made up of fifty-six delegates from every colony except Georgia. The colonists had yet to think of freedom from Great Britain; they simply wanted to iron out their differences with the king. By October they had agreed upon a series of resolutions to oppose the Coercive Acts and establish a formal organization to boycott British goods. The Congress also drafted a Declaration of Rights and Resolves, portions of which later found their way into the Declaration of Independence and the U.S. Constitution.

The Declaration of Rights and Resolves called for colonial rights of petition and assembly, trial by peers, freedom from a standing army, and the selection of representative councils to levy taxes. Finally, the attendees agreed to meet again in Philadelphia in May 1775 unless the king capitulated to their demands.

The Second Continental Congress

King George refused to yield, tensions continued to rise, and a Second Continental Congress was called. Before it could even meet, fighting broke out early in the morning of April 19, 1775, at Lexington and Concord with what is called the "shot heard 'round the world." Eight colonial Minutemen were killed, and 16,000 British troops besieged Boston.

When the Second Continental Congress later convened in Philadelphia on May 10, 1775, delegates were united by their increased hostility. The bloodshed at Lexington left no other course but war. To solidify colonial support for war, a Southerner was selected by representatives from all thirteen colonies in attendance as the commander of the new Continental Army. On June 15, 1775, George Washington of Virginia, who had strongly hinted at his desire to head the army by being the only delegate to appear in a military uniform (he had fought in the French and Indian Wars), was named commander-in-chief. He was given authority to enlist soldiers, and the Congress sent envoys to France to ask for assistance. In a final attempt to avert conflict, the Congress adopted the Olive Branch Petition on July 5, 1775, asking the king to end hostilities. King George rejected the petition and sent an additional 20,000 troops to quell the rebellion. The stage was set for war.

Although the colonists had not gone into the Second Continental Congress expecting to be a free and independent nation, the king's actions seemed to leave them no other choice than to declare their independence. In 1774, Thomas Paine (1737–1809), whose radical political views had gotten him into considerable trouble in Great Britain, came to the colonies with the help of Benjamin Franklin, who saw Paine's potential use to the budding independence movement. Franklin, sensing the need for sentiment to unite the colonies, urged Paine to pen such a document. In January 1776, Paine issued (at first anonymously) *Common Sense,* a pamphlet forcefully arguing for independence from Great Britain. In frank, easy-to-understand language, Paine denounced the corrupt British monarchy and offered reasons for independence. Concerning the English monarchy, Paine wrote, "Ye that dare oppose not only tyranny but the tyrant, Stand forth!"

Events Preceding the Declaration of Independence

1776	Declaration of Independence
1775	Fighting breaks out at Lexington and Concord; Second Continental Congress convened
1774	Coercive or Intolerable Acts; First Continental Congress convened
1773	Tea Act; Boston Tea Party
1772	Committees of Correspondence set up
1767	Townshend Acts; colonists boycott tea
1766	Stamp Act repealed; Sugar Act revised
1765	Stamp Act; Sons of Liberty organized; Stamp Act Congress convened
1764	Revenue Act; Sugar Act
1763	Crown decrees no more westward movement
1760 1754	French and Indian War
1620	Colonies settled and developed Mayflower Compact; settlement in Massachusetts

After the success of *Common Sense,* Thomas Paine wrote a series of essays collectively entitled *The Crisis* to arouse colonists' support for the Revolutionary War. The first *Crisis* papers contain the famous words "These are the times that try men's souls."

Moreover, "Everything that is right," Paine argued, ". . . pleads for separation. The blood of the slain, the weeping voice of nature cries *'Tis Time to Part.'"*

Common Sense, widely read throughout the colonies, was instrumental in changing minds in a very short time. In its first three months of publication, the 47-page *Common Sense* sold 120,000 copies at two shillings a copy, the equivalent of selling 18.75 million books today (given the U.S. population in 1991). There was one copy of *Common Sense* in distribution for every thirteen people in the colonies, a truly astonishing number given the low literacy rate.

The Declaration of Independence

The impact of *Common Sense* on the mood of the nation cannot be underscored adequately. It galvanized the American public and ridiculed all arguments for reconciliation with England. As the mood in the colonies changed, so did that of the Second Continental Congress. On May 15, 1776, Virginia became the first colony to call for independence, instructing one of its delegates to the Second Continental Congress to introduce a resolution to that effect. On June 7, 1776, Richard Henry Lee of Virginia rose to move "(T)hat these United Colonies are, and of right ought to be, free and independent States, and that all connection between them and the State of Great Britain is, and ought to be, dissolved." His three-part resolution—which called for independence, the formation of foreign alliances, and preparation of a plan of confederation—triggered hot debate. A proclamation of independence from Great Britain was tantamount to treason, a crime punishable by death. Although six of the thirteen colonies already had instructed their delegates to vote for independence, the Second Continental Congress was suspended to allow its delegates to return home to their colonial legislatures for final instructions. Independence was not a move to be taken lightly.

At the same time, committees were set up to consider each point of Lee's proposal. A committee of five was selected to begin work on a Declaration of Independence. The Congress selected Benjamin Franklin, John Adams, Robert Livingston, and Roger Sherman as members. Adams lobbied hard for a Southerner to add balance. Thus, owing to his "peculiar felicity of expression" and Southern origins, Thomas Jefferson was selected as chair.

On July 2, twelve of the thirteen colonies (with New York abstaining) voted for independence. Two days later, the Second Continental Congress voted to adopt the Declaration of Independence penned by Thomas Jefferson. On July 9, the Declaration, now with the approval of New York, was read aloud in Philadelphia.[3]

Social Contract Theory

In simple but eloquent language, Jefferson set out the reasons for the colonies' separation from Great Britain. Most of his stirring rhetoric drew heavily on the works of seventeenth- and eighteenth-century political philosophers, particularly the great English political philosopher John Locke, who actually wrote South Carolina's first constitution as a charter when it was formed by the king and mercantile houses in England.

John Locke had long argued that people have certain natural, or God-given, inalienable rights[4] that cannot be taken away by any government. The colonists agreed with

---

[3] See Garry Wills, *Inventing America: Jefferson's Declaration of Independence* (New York: Random House, 1978). Wills argues that the Declaration was signed solely to secure foreign aid in the ongoing war effort.

[4] On John Locke's influence on the Declaration of Independence, see Carl L. Becker, *The Declaration of Independence: A Study in the History of Political Ideas* (New York: Random House, 1942).

him. They had come to cherish, among other things, the right to property. In colonial times "property" did not mean just land; Locke's notion of property rights included life, liberty, and material possessions.

For Locke and his adherents, government existed by the consent of the governed. Under this kind of social contract theory, a group of individuals agree to set up a government for certain defined purposes, and the individuals have the right to resist or remove rulers who deviate from those purposes and goals. Essentially, under social contract theory, government exists for the good of its subjects and not for the benefit of those who govern. Locke argued, furthermore, that rebellion was the ultimate sanction against a government that abused its power.

It is easy to see the colonists' debt to John Locke. In ringing language the Declaration of Independence proclaims:

> *We hold these truths to be self-evident, that all men are created equal, they are endowed by their Creator with certain unalienable Rights, that among these are Life, Liberty and the pursuit of Happiness.*

In 1774 the First Continental Congress had sent a strikingly similar statement to King George. In that declaration it had proclaimed that the colonists were entitled to "life, liberty, and property." In the Declaration of Independence, at the last minute Jefferson had opted to substitute "pursuit of happiness" for "property," but the ideas behind the words were similar. He, and others in attendance at the Second Continental Congress, wanted to have a document that would stand for all time, justifying their break with the Crown and clarifying their notions of the proper form of government. So, Jefferson continued:

> *That to secure these rights, Governments are instituted among Men, deriving their just powers from the consent of the governed. That whenever any Form of Government becomes destructive of these ends, it is the Right of the People to alter or abolish it, and to institute new Government, laying its foundation on such Principles and organizing its Powers in such form, as to them shall seem most likely to effect their Safety and Happiness.*

After this stirring preamble, the Declaration went on to enumerate the wrongs that the colonists had suffered under British rule. All were addressed to the denial of personal rights and liberties, many of which would later be guaranteed by the U.S. Constitution via the Bill of Rights.

After the Declaration was signed and transmitted to the king, the Revolutionary War was fought with a greater vengeance. At a September 1776 peace conference on Staten Island (New York), British General William Howe demanded revocation of the Declaration of Independence. The Americans refused, and the war raged on while the Congress attempted to fashion a new united government.

The First Attempt at Government: The Articles of Confederation

As noted earlier, the British had no written constitution. The body of British common law, conventions, and statutory law had evolved over the ages. Now the colonists in the Second Continental Congress were attempting to codify arrangements that had never before been put into legalistic terminology. To make things more complicated, the delegates had to arrive at these decisions in the wartime atmosphere that prevailed from 1776 to 1780. The document that resulted, known as the Articles of Confederation, created a loose "league of friendship" between the sovereign or independent states.

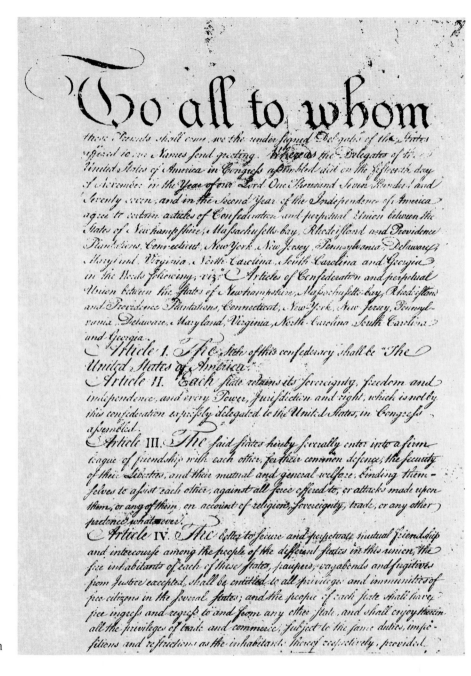

The Articles of Confederation

The Articles created a type of government called a **confederacy,** in which the national government derives its powers from the states that compose it. Although the authority of the states rested on the powers derived directly from the people, the national government held only the powers that the states were willing to give it. Key provisions in the Articles included:

- A national government with a Congress empowered to make peace, coin money, appoint officers for an army, control the post office, and negotiate with Indian tribes

- The retention by each state of its sovereignty or ultimate authority to govern within its territories, and its independence
- One vote in the Continental Congress for each state regardless of size
- The vote of nine states to pass any measure (a unanimous vote for any amendment)
- The selection and payment of delegates to the Congress by their respective state legislatures

Thus, the Articles—passed by the Congress on November 15, 1777, and finally ratified by all thirteen states in 1781—fashioned a government well reflective of the political philosophy of the times.[5] Fearful of a chief executive who would rule tyrannically, however, the Congress made no provision for an executive branch of government. Instead, it provided for a weak president. John Hanson, a member of the Maryland House of Delegates and a member of the first Continental Congress, was the first president under the Articles and therefore is often referred to as the first President of the United States.

Also missing was a strong central government. States operating independently during earlier times did not want to give up their rights to an untested national government, especially in light of their hatred of the Crown and its strong interest in national rule. Despite its flaws, the government under the Articles of Confederation saw the new nation through the Revolutionary War. However, once the British surrendered in 1781 and the new nation found itself no longer united by the war effort, the government quickly fell into chaos.

Problems Under the Articles of Confederation

By 1784, just one year after the Revolutionary army was disbanded, governing the new nation under the Articles of Confederation proved unworkable.[6] Congress could rarely assemble the required quorum of nine states to conduct business. Even when it could, there was little agreement on anything. In order to raise revenue to pay off war debts and run the government, all sorts of land, poll, and liquor taxes were proposed, although Congress had no specific power to tax. Not surprisingly, then, all proposals were rejected. At one point, Congress was even driven out of Philadelphia (then the capital) by its own unpaid army! And, although the national government could coin money, it had no resources to back up the value of its currency. Continental dollars were worth nothing, and trade between states became chaotic as some states began to coin their own money.

In addition, the Articles of Confederation had no provision for a judicial system to handle the growing number of economic conflicts and boundary disputes among the individual states. Several states claimed the same lands to the west; Pennsylvania and Virginia went to war; Vermont threatened to annex itself to Canada.

Another weakness of the Articles was their failure to allow Congress to regulate commerce among the states and with foreign nations. As a result, individual states attempted to enter into agreements with other countries, and foreign nations were suspicious of trade agreements made with the United States. In 1785, for example, Massachusetts banned the export of goods in British ships and doubled duties, and Pennsylvania levied heavy duties on ships of nations that did not have a treaty with the U.S. government.

But its lack of a strong central government was the Articles' greatest weakness. While the war was ongoing, the states acceded the national government's authority to wage armed conflict. Once the war was over, however, each state resumed its sovereign status

---

[5] See Gordon Wood, *The Creation of the American Republic, 1776–1787* (Chapel Hill: University of North Carolina Press, 1969).

[6] For more about the Articles of Confederation, see Merrill Jensen, *The Articles of Confederation* (Madison: University of Wisconsin Press, 1940).

Four Major Failures of the Articles

1. No executive to administer the government
2. No power to tax
3. No authority to regulate commerce
4. No strong central government

and the national government was unable to force the states to abide by the provisions of the Treaty of Peace that had ended the war.

The crumbling economy and a series of bad harvests that made it hard for farmers to get out of debt quickly took their toll on the new nation. George Washington and Alexander Hamilton, both interested in the questions of trade and frontier expansion, soon saw the need for a stronger national government. They were not alone. In 1785 and 1786 the governments of Massachusetts, Virginia, and Maryland encouraged discussion of a strengthened system. Finally, several states joined together to call for a convention in Philadelphia in 1787.

Shays's Rebellion

Before that meeting could take place, however, new unrest broke out in the colonies. In 1780, Massachusetts adopted a state constitution that appeared to favor the interests of the wealthy. The poor and middle class were barred from voting and office holding because of property-owning requirements. And, as the economy of the states worsened, banks foreclosed on farms to pay off debts to Continental Army veterans who were waiting for promised bonuses. Protests were held throughout the summer, and in September 1786, a band of 500 insurgents disrupted judicial proceedings in Springfield, Massachusetts, forcing the courthouse to close. Three months later, frustrations and outrage at a new state law requiring the payment of all debts in cash caused Daniel Shays, a former Revolutionary War army captain, and 1,500 disgruntled and angry farmers to march toward Springfield.

Shays's Rebellion in western Massachusetts

To put down this armed insurrection, the Congress immediately authorized the Secretary of War to call for a new militia. A $530,000 appropriation was made for this purpose, but every state except Virginia refused the Congress's request for money. The governor of Massachusetts then tried to raise a state militia, but because of the poor economy, funds were unavailable in the state treasury to protect the peace. Frantic attempts at private support were made, and a militia was finally assembled. By February 4, 1787, this privately paid force put a stop to Shays and his followers' continued onslaughts, ultimately arresting 150 men and scattering the rest of the rebels throughout Western Massachusetts.

The Miracle at Philadelphia

In the throes of economic turmoil and with domestic tranquility gone haywire, on February 21, 1787, the Congress passed an official resolution that called for a Constitutional Convention in Philadelphia for "the sole and express purpose of revising the Articles of Confederation." All states but Rhode Island sent delegates. Rhode Island was a strong supporter of the government under the Articles and had adopted as its state motto Thomas Paine's famous words "Government is best which governs least." Its absence from the meeting led some present to suggest that its name be changed to "Rogue Island" or that it be dropped from the Union altogether.

New York, too, was almost a holdout, but its governor, George Clinton, was irritated at the Union's refusal to honor his state's claim to the Vermont territory, which, while not a colony, considered itself a separate entity. So, he appointed three delegates, including Alexander Hamilton, whose views on the need for a strong national government had made him a well-known national political figure.

When twenty-nine individuals met in hot, sweltering Philadelphia on May 14, they had much on their minds. While many of them at that initial meeting were intellectuals, others were shrewd farmers or businessmen, and others were astute politicians. All recognized that what they were doing could be considered treasonous. Revising the Articles of Confederation was one thing; to call for an entirely new government, as suggested by the Virginia delegation, was another. So they took their work quite seriously, even to the point of adopting a pledge of secrecy. George Washington, who was unanimously elected the convention's presiding officer, warned:

> Nothing spoken or written can be revealed to anyone—not even your family—until we have adjourned permanently. Gossip or misunderstanding can easily ruin all the hard work we shall have to do this summer.[7]

So concerned about leaks were those in attendance that the delegates agreed to accompany Benjamin Franklin to all of his meals, fearing that the normally gregarious gentleman might get carried away with the mood or by liquor and inadvertently let news of the proceedings slip from his tongue.

The Founders

Fifty-five men out of the seventy-four delegates ultimately chosen by their state legislatures to attend the Constitutional Convention labored long and hard that hot summer behind closed doors in Philadelphia. They are often referred to as the "Founding Fathers," although most, like James Madison, were quite young. Many were in their

[7] Quoted in Selma R. Williams, *Fifty-Five Fathers: The Story of the Constitutional Convention* (New York: Dodd, Mead, 1970), p. 10.

twenties and thirties, and only one—Benjamin Franklin, at eighty-one—was very old. They brought with them a vast amount of political, educational, legal, and business experience. Eight had signed the Declaration of Independence, thirty-nine had attended at least one of the Continental Congresses, and seven were former governors. One-third were college graduates, and thirty-four were lawyers. Notably absent were individuals like Patrick Henry, who once had proclaimed in the Virginia House of Burgess, "Give me liberty or give me death!" Now he stayed away because he "smelt a rat." Also missing were Thomas Jefferson, author of the Declaration of Independence, and John Adams. Both were on ambassadorial stays in Europe. Although some scholarly debate continues concerning the motives of the Founders, it is clear that they were an exceptional lot who ultimately produced a brilliant document reflecting the best efforts of all present.

The Virginia Plan

Soon after George Washington called the meeting to order, Edmund Randolph of Virginia arose to present a framework of government that James Madison had prepared prior to the meeting. The preamble of what is commonly referred to as the Virginia Plan proposed that "a *national* government ought to be established, consisting of a *supreme* Legislative, Executive and Judiciary" (emphasis added). Those in attendance unanimously agreed to debate that idea, and the remainder of Madison's plan was introduced for discussion.

Once the Framers voted to consider Madison's proposals, the die was cast. The purpose of the convention was changed from revision of the Articles to the creation of an entirely new form of government.[8]

The Virginia Plan contained several key elements that shaped the new government and its final structure. It called for:

1. The creation of a national legislature or lawmaking body with two parts, or houses as they were called. One house was to be elected directly by the people; the other house was to be chosen from among persons nominated by the state legislatures. Total representation in the legislature would be in proportion to taxes paid to the federal or national government, corresponding to free population within each state.
2. A single "national Executive" to be chosen by the national legislature for a single term.
3. A Council of Revision, consisting of the national executive and several federal judges, that would have the authority to approve or veto acts of the legislature. Vetoes could be overridden by a vote of both houses of the legislature.
4. A federal judiciary headed by a Supreme Court appointed for life by the legislature.
5. The national government to have the power to override state laws. Since the government was to derive its powers from the people and the states, the Plan argued that the national government should have the ability to operate on both.

During the first few weeks of the convention, discussion of these items dominated the proceedings. After only six days, Virginia's proposal for creation of a new national government was voted upon by the convention. Six states (Massachusetts, Pennsylvania, Delaware, Virginia, North Carolina, and South Carolina) voted in favor of a new, strong national government. Connecticut voted against the proposal. The New York delegation was deadlocked. The New Jersey delegation, unable to reach an agreement, did not vote.

[8] See Samuel Beer, "Federalism, Nationalism and Democracy in America," *American Political Science Review,* Vol. 72 (March 1978), pp. 9–21.

By the narrowest of margins, the Virginia Plan won its first crucial test and gave momentum to those forces favoring a strong central government.

The delegates then debated other sections of the Virginia Plan. The first structural aspect of the new government that the Framers agreed upon was a **bicameral legislature,** that is, a legislature with two distinct bodies. When Thomas Jefferson returned from Paris, he asked Washington why the delegates had agreed to a two-house legislature. "Why do you pour coffee into your saucer?" asked Washington. "To cool it," responded Jefferson. "So," responded Washington, "we pour legislation into the senatorial saucer to cool it."[9]

Delegates initially appeared far from agreement over how members of each house of Congress were to be selected. Many of them appeared to be set against the direct election of members of one house by the people. Many who held to that view feared the idea of democracy. Their elitist views led them to believe that not "all the people" were fit to make decisions concerning the government. They feared the kinds of uprisings that Daniel Shays's actions had typified.

While still fearful of a "mobocracy," or any government rule by a mob, Madison and other supporters of a strong central government continued to insist on direct election of some representatives. They rationalized that without the confidence of the people, government could not long exist.

The Virginia Plan called for a national system with a powerful central government. It was based heavily on the European nation–state model, wherein the national government derives its powers from the people and not from the member states. In contrast, proponents of what was then termed a **federal system** favored a looser confederation of states in which powers could be shared between the national and state governments. Basically comfortable with the arrangements under the Articles of Confederation, they offered another model of government, the New Jersey Plan.

The New Jersey Plan

As supporters of a strong national government continued to debate various aspects of the Virginia Plan, representatives from the smaller states took advantage of a rule of the convention that allowed for reconsideration of any proposal adopted by the convention. Under the direction of William Paterson of New Jersey, the smaller states offered their own plan after about two weeks of deliberation on the Virginia Plan. The New Jersey Plan suggested only that the Articles be strengthened. Its key features included:

1. A one-house legislature with one vote for each state. Representatives to the Congress were to be chosen by state legislatures. The Congress would have the power to raise revenue from duties, stamps, and a post office. All other funds had to be requested from the states.
2. A multi-person "executive" to be chosen by Congress with powers similar to those in the Virginia Plan, except that the executive would not have the authority to veto acts of Congress.
3. The establishment of the acts of Congress as the "supreme law" of the land and authorization of the federal executive to use force to compel obedience.
4. Although there was no provision for a system of national courts, a supreme judiciary with very limited authority would be created.

Not surprisingly, the New Jersey Plan was defeated, but the small states showed that they had sufficient concerns and political clout to force some changes in the Virginia Plan.

[9]Quoted in Doris Faber and Harold Faber, *We the People* (New York: Charles Scribner's Sons, 1987), p. 25.

The Great Compromise

The biggest disagreement raised by the New Jersey Plan concerned representation in the two chambers of Congress. When a deadlock loomed, Connecticut offered the Connecticut Compromise. Each state would have an equal vote in the Senate. Again, deadlock. As Benjamin Franklin put it, "The diversity of opinions turns on two points. If a proportional representation takes place, the small states contend that their liberties will be in danger. If an equality of votes is to be put in its place, large states say that their money will be in danger." He then continued on to comment:

> When a broad table is to be made and the edges of a plank do not fit, the artist takes a little from both sides and makes a good joint. In like manner, both sides must part with some of their demands, in order that they both join in some accommodating position.[10]

A committee was appointed to see if some sort of a compromise could be worked out over the Fourth of July weekend. That committee reported back what became known as the **Great Compromise.** Taking ideas from both the Virginia and New Jersey Plans, it recommended:

1. In one house of the legislature (later called the House of Representatives), there should be 56 representatives—one representative for every 40,000 inhabitants.
2. That house shall have the power to originate all bills for raising and spending money.
3. In the second house of the legislature (later called the Senate), each state should have an equal vote, and representatives would be selected by the state legislatures.[11]

[10] Ibid., p. 31.

[11] For more on the political nature of compromise at the Convention, see Calvin C. Jillson, *Constitution Making: Conflict and Consensus in the Federal Constitution of 1787* (New York: Agathon, 1988).

DOONESBURY   Garry Trudeau

The Constitution denied blacks the right to vote and did not even count them equally with whites for calculating voting districts. It was not until after the Civil War that blacks were first allowed to go to the polls, as depicted in this famous painting.

An additional compromise, however, was necessary before population could be determined. After considerable dissension, representation in the House of Representatives was to be determined on the basis of population, which in turn was to be calculated by adding the *"whole Number of Free Persons"* and *"three fifths of all other Persons."* *"All other Persons"* was the delegates' "tactful" way of referring to slaves. Known as the **Three-Fifths Compromise,** this formula was based on prevailing assumptions that slaves were only three-fifths as productive as white free men.[12]

Although the Southern states sought to count slaves for the purpose of representation, they never even considered that these same slaves should be able to cast ballots for representatives. In fact, throughout most of the colonies, **suffrage,** or the right to vote, was not universal. Instead, it was generally limited to white male property owners.

The Great Compromise ultimately met with the approval of all states in attendance. The smaller states were in good humor because they got equal representation in the Senate; the larger states got proportional representation in the House of Representatives. The small states then could dominate the Senate while the large states, such as Virginia and New York, could control the House. But because both houses had to pass legislation, neither body would be able to dominate the other.

In 1787, Virginia's population was twice that of New York, four times that of New Jersey, and ten times that of Delaware.

---

[12] These kinds of assumptions about slaves were never specifically spelled out in the Constitution. In fact, slavery is nowhere mentioned in the Constitution. Although many of the Framers were morally opposed to slavery, they recognized that if the convention attempted to abolish or seriously restrict it, the Southern states would walk away from the new Union as they eventually did, resulting in the Civil War.

With passage of the Great Compromise and after ten weeks of hard work, agreement existed on most basic principles. On August 6, 1787, a draft of a constitution—seven pages long and with broad margins for notations—was submitted to the delegates. It contained twenty-three articles divided into forty-one separate sections. Still to be included, however, were provisions for an executive branch and a president.

Compromise on the Presidency

By August the Framers had agreed on the idea of a one-person executive, but they disagreed on the length of term of office and how the chief executive should be selected. With Shays's Rebellion still fresh in their minds, the delegates feared putting too much power into the hands of the lower classes. At the same time, representatives from the smaller states feared that the selection of the chief executive by the legislature would put additional power into the hands of the large states.

It was amid these fears that the Committee on Unfinished Portions, whose sole responsibility was to iron out problems and disagreements concerning the new office of chief executive, conducted its work. It recommended that the presidential term of office be fixed at four years instead of the previous seven that had been proposed. By choosing not to mention when the chief executive would be eligible for reelection, they made it possible for a president to serve more than one term. Election of the president was to be by **electors** chosen by the people. And, for the first time at the convention, the new post of vice president was mentioned.

Selecting a President: The Electoral College

In setting up a system for electing the president, the Framers put in place an **electoral college** (see Chapter 7). The electoral college system gave states a key role because each state would select electors equal to the number of representatives it had in the House *and* Senate. Each elector would then vote for two individuals from among those seeking the presidency. The candidate with the most votes, providing it was a majority of all votes cast, would become president; the runner-up would become vice president. In the event of a tie, the House of Representatives would choose one candidate from among those having the five highest vote totals.

The Framers made it nearly impossible for the same state to provide both the president and vice president by adding, *"The Electors shall meet in their respective States and vote by Ballot for two Persons, of whom one at least shall not be an Inhabitant of the same State with themselves."* The delegates were quite happy with this compromise and believed that it was a solution acceptable to all sides. The smaller states believed that they would have an equal voice should the election be forced into the House of Representatives, and the larger states believed they had a good opportunity to elect a president before an election was forced into the House of Representatives.

The Impeachment Process

One more matter remained, however, concerning the president. Still fearful of a leader who might turn out to be more like a British monarch, the Framers were careful to include a provision for removal of the chief executive. They proposed that both the legislative and the judicial branches be involved in the impeachment process. The House of Representatives was given the sole responsibility to investigate and charge a president or vice president with *"Treason, Bribery, or other high Crimes and Misdemeanors."* A majority vote would then result in Articles of Impeachment being issued against the president. In turn, the Senate was given sole responsibility to try the chief executive on the charges issued by the House. A two-thirds vote of the Senate was required to convict and remove the

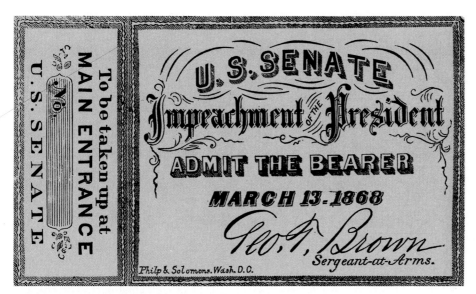

A ticket for entry to the Senate's impeachment trial of Andrew Johnson

president from office. The Chief Justice of the United States was to preside over the Senate proceedings in place of the vice president to prevent the vice president from any appearance of impropriety.

The U.S. Constitution

After the compromise on the presidency, work proceeded quite quickly on the remaining resolutions of the Constitution. A committee of five was chosen to formalize all that had been accomplished in Philadelphia. The final document was largely written by Gouverneur Morris of Pennsylvania, a friend of Washington's who had been the treasurer of the Continental Congress. The committee submitted its work, which included some new proposals as well as changes in accepted ones, to the delegates on August 6, 1787.

The Preamble to the Constitution, the last section to be drafted, contained exceptionally powerful language that formed the bedrock of American political tradition. The Preamble is directly attributable to Morris, who had a true gift for simplifying complex language. Its opening line, *"We the People of the United States,"* boldly proclaimed that a loose confederation of states no longer existed; instead, there was but one American people. As originally proposed the Preamble opened with: "We the people of the States of New Hampshire, Massachusetts, Rhode Island and the Providence Plantations, Connecticut, New Jersey, New York, Pennsylvania, Delaware, Maryland, Virginia, North Carolina, South Carolina and Georgia, do ordain, declare and establish the following Constitution for the government of ourselves and our Posterity." Note how different the remaining phrases ended up under the forceful pen of Morris. The use of the simple phrase *"We the people"* forever ended the question of whence the government derived its power—it came directly from the people and not from the states.

The next phrase of the Constitution explained the need for the new outline of government. *"[I]n Order to form a more perfect Union"* was an indirect way of acknowledging the weaknesses of the Articles of Confederation to govern a growing nation. The goals of the Framers for the new nation were optimistically set out next: to *"establish Justice, insure domestic Tranquility, provide for the common defense, promote the general Welfare, and secure the Blessings of Liberty to ourselves and our Posterity"*; followed by the formal creation of a new government: *"do ordain and establish this Constitution for the United States of America."*

In *The Miracle at Philadelphia* (1966) Catherine Drinker Bowen wrote, "The seven verbs flowed out—to form, establish, insure, provide, promote, secure, ordain. . . . One might challenge the centuries to better these verbs."[13] These powerful words fanned the flames of a new nation. On September 17, the Constitution was finally approved by the delegates from all twelve states in attendance. (Rhode Island had not sent any representatives.) While the completed document did not satisfy all of the delegates, of the forty-one in attendance, thirty-nine ultimately signed the document. The sentiments uttered by Benjamin Franklin probably well reflected those of many others: "Thus, I consent, Sir, to this Constitution because I expect no better, and because I am not sure that it is not the best."[14]

The Basic Principles of the Constitution

The ideas of political philosophers, especially John Locke and the French political philosopher Baron de la Brède et de Montesquieu (1689–1755), heavily influenced the shape and nature of the government proposed by the Founders. Locke's concern with "life, liberty, and property" and his emphasis on individual rights and limited government guided not only the writing of the Declaration of Independence but also that of the Constitution.

The basic structure of the proposed new national government, especially the notion of **checks and balances,** owed much to the writings of Montesquieu. Moreover, the ever-present tension concerning distribution of power reveals the heavy influence of these philosophers as well as the colonists' experience under the Articles of Confederation.[15]

Federalism. Under the Articles of Confederation, only a loose "league of friendship" existed among the states. The Framers believed that a strong national government was necessary for the survival of the new nation. However, they were loath to create a powerful unitary government on the model of Britain, the country from which they had just won their independence. Thus, they fashioned a system now known as federalism wherein there is a division of power between the national government and the states. Whereas opponents argued that a strong national government would infringe on their liberty, James Madison argued that a strong national government with distinct state governments could, if properly directed by constitutional arrangements, be a source of expanded liberties and national unity. The Framers viewed the dividing of governmental authority, between the national government and the states, as a means of checking power with power, and providing "double security" to the people. Throughout the Constitution, such divisions are clearly in evidence. States traditionally set qualifications for citizens to vote in national elections. States were equally represented in the Senate, but always states were to be bound by the Constitution—the supreme law of the land. Later, with passage of the Tenth Amendment (see Chapter 3), the federal structure was clarified further by reserving to the states and to the people all powers not expressly delegated to the national government.

Separation of Powers. Strongly influenced by the writings of John Locke, Madison and many of the Framers clearly feared putting too much power in the hands of any one

---

[13] Quoted in Faber and Faber, p. 43.

[14] Quoted in Richard N. Current, T. Harry Williams, Frank Freidel, and Alan Brinkley, *American History: A Survey,* 6th ed. (New York: McGraw-Hill, 1983), p. 168.

[15] Bernard Bailyn, *The Ideological Origins of the American Revolution* (Cambridge, Mass.: Harvard University Press, 1967).

individual or branch of government. **Separation of powers** is simply a way of parceling out power among the three branches of government. It is also an important aspect of the relationship between the states and the national government. Madison believed that the scheme devised by the Framers would divide the offices of the new government among many individuals and provide each office holder with the "necessary means and personal motives to resist encroachment of the others." In Madison's famous words, "Ambition must be made to counteract ambition." Through a system of separation of powers, law-making, law-enforcing, and law-interpreting functions are assigned to independent branches of government. On the national level (and in most states), the legislature alone has the authority to make laws; the chief executive enforces them, and the judiciary interprets them.

As the Framers envisioned the workings of government, it is unlikely that they foresaw the intermingling of governmental functions that has since evolved. In Article I of the Constitution, the legislative power is vested in the Congress—but the president is also given legislative powers via his ability to veto legislation, although his veto can be overridden by a two-thirds vote in Congress. Implementation of legislation enacted through this process is then made complete by judicial interpretation.

So instead of a pure system of separation of powers, a symbiotic relationship among the three branches of government has existed from the beginning. While today Congress still is entrusted with law making, most legislation originates with the president. And, although the Supreme Court's major function is to interpret the law, its forays into criminal procedure, abortion, and other areas has led many to charge that it has surpassed its constitutional authority and become a law maker.

In this regard, the blurring of the separation of powers has moved the American system a little closer to parliamentary democracies like Britain or Germany. Scholars speak of a "fusion of powers" or "a symbiotic relationship" between the legislature and executive in a parliamentary system, since the executive—typically a prime minister and his or her cabinet—is formed out of the lower house of the legislature. Members of the executive in a parliamentary system usually retain their seats in the legislature, and thus wear two hats: one as a representative of the people and the other as an executive officer.

Check and Balances. A very important principle guiding the Framers as they designed the new government was the principle of checks and balances.[16] Power is checked and balanced because the legislative, executive, and judicial branches of government share some powers and no branch has exclusive domain over any activity. The creation of this system of checks and balances allowed the Framers to minimize the threat of tyranny from any one branch. Thus, for almost every power granted to one branch, an equal power of control was established in the other two branches. The Congress could "check" the power of the president, the Supreme Court, and so on, carefully creating "balance" among the three branches. Following are some examples.

Powers of Congress

- Passes all federal laws
- Establishes lower federal courts and the number of judges
- Can impeach the president
- Can override the president's veto by a two-thirds vote
- Passes the federal budget, which finances the executive branch
- Approves treaties and presidential appointments, including those to the federal courts

---

[16]See. E. P. Panagopoulos, *Essays on the History and Meaning of Checks and Balances* (Landham, Md.: University Press of America, 1985).

Checks on Congressional Powers

- President can veto legislation
- Supreme Court can rule laws unconstitutional
- Both houses of Congress must vote to enact a law, thereby checking power within the legislature

Powers of the President

- Can approve or veto acts of Congress
- Is responsible for carrying out the laws passed by Congress
- Can call Congress into special session
- Can submit legislation to Congress
- Makes foreign treaties
- Nominates Supreme Court justices and federal judges
- Can pardon people convicted in federal court
- Is responsible for execution of court orders
- Is commander-in-chief of armed forces

Checks on Executive Powers

- Congress can override vetoes of legislation by a two-thirds vote
- Senate can refuse to confirm nominees or ratify treaties
- Congress can impeach and remove president
- Congress can declare war
- Supreme Court can declare presidential acts unconstitutional

Powers of the Judiciary

- Can invalidate, on grounds of unconstitutionality, laws passed by Congress
- Can invalidate executive branch orders or actions on grounds of unconstitutionality or absence of authorizing legislation

Checks on Judicial Powers

- Congress can change jurisdiction (authority to hear cases) of the Supreme Court
- Congress can impeach and remove federal judges
- President appoints federal judges (who must be confirmed by the Senate)

The American system of checks and balances contrasts sharply with the British system, which provides for an extreme centralization of power. The "doctrine of parliamentary sovereignty" states that there is no higher legislative authority than Parliament, that no court can declare an act of Parliament to be unconstitutional, that there is no formal limit to what Parliament can legislate upon, and that no Parliament may bind a future Parliament or be bound by previous Parliaments.

The Articles of the Constitution

The final document as signed by the Framers condensed numerous resolutions into the Preamble and seven separate articles. The first three articles established the three branches of government, defined their internal operations, and clarified their relationships with one another. Although all branches were technically to be considered coequal, it is likely that the order of the creation of each branch of government and the relative detail contained in each article reflect the Framers' concern over each branch and its potential for abuse of authority. The four remaining articles define the relationships among the states, declare the national law to be supreme, and set out alternative methods of amending the Constitution.

Article I: The Legislative Branch. Article I vests all legislative powers in the Congress and establishes a bicameral legislature, including the Senate and the House of Representatives. It also sets out the qualifications for holding office in each house, the term of office for each house, methods of selection, and how membership in the House of Representatives is to be apportioned among the states. Operating procedures and the officers for each house are also briefly outlined and described.

Perhaps the most important section of Article I is Section 8. It carefully lists the powers the Framers wished the new Congress to possess. These **enumerated powers**—or specified powers—contain many key provisions that were denied to the Continental Congress under the Articles of Confederation. For example, the new Constitution authorized the Congress to *"regulate Commerce with foreign Nations, and among the several States."* One of the major weaknesses under the Articles was Congress's lack of authority to deal with the trade wars that plagued the member states and affected their business with foreign nations.

After careful enumeration of seventeen powers of Congress, a key clause, often referred to as the **elastic clause,** was added to Article I. It authorized Congress to *"make all Laws which shall be necessary and proper for carrying into Execution the foregoing Powers."* This necessary and proper clause has been the source of tremendous congressional activity never anticipated by the Framers. For example, the Supreme Court has interpreted Congress's authority to regulate commerce coupled with the necessary and proper clause to allow it to ban prostitution (where travel across the state line is involved), regulate trains and planes, establish uniform federal minimum wage and maximum hour laws, and mandate drug testing for certain workers. (See Chapter 6 for more detail on Article I.)

Article II: The Executive Branch. Article II vests the **executive power,** that is, the authority to execute or carry out the laws of the nation, in a president of the United States. Section 1 sets the president's term of office at four years and explains the electoral college. It also states qualifications for office and describes a mechanism for removal from office.

The powers and duties of the president are set out in Section 3. Among the most important are his role as commander-in-chief of the armed forces, the authority to make treaties with the consent of the Senate, and the authority to *"appoint Ambassadors, other public Ministers and Consuls, the "Judges of the supreme Court, and all other Officers of the United States."* Other sections of Article II instruct the president to report directly to Congress *"from time to time,"* in what has come to be known as the "State of the Union" address, and to *"take Care that the Laws be faithfully executed."* Section 4 provides the mechanism for removal of the president, vice president, and other officers of the United States for *"Treason, Bribery, or other high Crimes and Misdemeanors."* (Refer to Chapters 7 and 8 for more information on Article II.)

Article III: The Judicial Branch. Article III establishes a Supreme Court and defines its jurisdiction. During the Philadelphia meeting, the small and large states differed significantly on the desirability of an independent judiciary and on the role of state courts in the national court system. The smaller states feared that a strong unelected judiciary would trample on their liberties. Compromise resulted in Congress's being permitted, but not required, to establish lower national courts. Thus, state courts and the national court

President Bush giving his State of the Union address on January 28, 1992. While the Constitution requires only that the president report to Congress from time to time on the state of the union, over the years the State of the Union message has become a regular event with much pomp and circumstance.

system would exist side by side with distinct areas of authority. Federal courts were given authority to decide cases arising under the federal laws. The Supreme Court also was given the power to settle disputes between states, or between a state and the national government.

Although some delegates to the convention had urged that the president be allowed to remove federal judges, ultimately judges were given appointments for life, presuming "good behavior." And, like the president's, their salaries cannot be lowered while they hold office. This provision was adopted to ensure that the legislature did not attempt to punish the Supreme Court or any other judges for unpopular decisions.

Perhaps the most important power of the Supreme Court is that of **judicial review** (the authority of a court to review acts of the legislature to determine their constitutional validity), although it is not mentioned in the Constitution. That power would later be assumed by the Court after Chief Justice John Marshall, writing for a unanimous Supreme Court in *Marbury* v. *Madison* (1803), concluded that the power could be "implied" from the Constitution. Judicial review is not a feature of all democracies: In Britain, for example, the courts may determine whether a law has been properly applied in a specific instance, but they may not, under the terms of the unwritten constitution, declare an act of Parliament to be unconstitutional. (See Chapter 9 for more information on Article III.)

Articles IV Through VII. Article IV deals with relations between the state and national government and includes the mechanisms for admitting new states to the Union. Article V specifies how amendments can be added to the Constitution. Article VI emphatically announces that the Constitution *"shall be the supreme Law of the Land"* and specifies that all state and national members of the legislature, chief executives, and all judicial officers shall swear an oath to support the Constitution. Mindful of the potential problems of unnecessary religious entanglement that occurred in some colonies, the Constitution specifies that no religious test shall be required for holding any office. The seventh and final article of the Constitution concerns the procedures for ratification of the new Constitution. Before it could become the law of the land, nine of the thirteen states would have to agree to, or ratify, its new provisions.

The Drive for Ratification

While delegates to the Constitutional Convention labored in Philadelphia, the Second Continental Congress continued to govern the former colonies under the Articles. The day after the Constitution was signed, William Jackson, the secretary of the Constitutional Convention, left for New York City, the nation's capital, to hand deliver the official copy of the document. He also took with him a resolution of the delegates calling upon each of the states to submit the new Constitution to a vote. The Framers, however, anticipated resistance from the representatives in the state legislatures and so required the states to call conventions to consider the proposed Constitution.

The Motives of the Framers

Debate about the motives of the Framers filled the air during the ratification struggle and has provided grist for the mill of historians and political scientists over the years. Anti-Federalists, who opposed the new Constitution, charged that Federalist supporters of the Constitution were a self-serving, landed, and propertied elite who had a vested interest in the capitalistic system that had evolved in the colonies. Federalists countered that they simply were trying to preserve a nation.

In 1913, the highly respected political scientist and historian Charles A. Beard published *An Economic Interpretation of the Constitution*. Beard argued that the 1780s were a "critical period" (as the time under governance by the Articles of Confederation had come to be known) not for the nation as a whole, but rather for businessmen who feared that a weak, decentralized government could do further harm to their economic interests. Beard argued that these men wanted a strong national government to promote industry and trade, protect private property, and most importantly, ensure payment of the public debt—much of which was owed to them. Therefore, according to Beard, the Constitution represents "an economic document drawn with superb skill by men whose property interests were immediately at stake."

By the 1950s this view had fallen into disfavor as other historians were unable to find direct links between wealth and the Framers' motives. In the 1960s, however, another group of historians began to argue that social and economic factors were important motives for supporting the Constitution. In *The Anti-Federalists* (1961) Jackson Turner Main posited that while supporters might not have been the united group of creditors suggested by Beard, they were wealthier, came from high social strata, and had greater concern for maintaining the prevailing social order.

In 1969, Gordon Wood's *The Creation of the American Republic* resurrected this debate. Wood deemphasized economics to argue that major social divisions explained support for (or opposition to) the new Constitution. He concluded that the Framers were representatives of a class who favored order and stability over some of the more radical ideas that had inspired the Revolution.

Jackson carried with the Constitution a letter from General George Washington. In a few eloquent words, Washington tried to sum up the sentiments of the Framers and the spirit of compromise that had permeated the long weeks in Philadelphia:

> That it will meet the full and entire approbation of every state is not perhaps to be expected, but each will doubtless consider, that had her interest alone been consulted, the consequences might have been particularly disagreeable or injurious to others; that it is liable to as few exceptions as could reasonably have been expected, we hope and believe; that it may promote lasting welfare of that country so dear to us all, and secure her freedom and happiness is our ardent wish.[17]

The Second Continental Congress immediately accepted the work of the convention and forwarded the proposed Constitution to the states for their vote. It was by no means certain, however, that the new Constitution would be adopted.

During the fall of 1787 and summer of 1788, the new Constitution was debated hotly around the nation. State politicians understandably feared a strong central government. Farmers and many in the lower classes were fearful of a distant national government. And those who had accrued substantial debts during the economic chaos that followed the Revolutionary War feared that a new money policy would plunge them into greater debt. The public in general was very leery of taxes—these were the same people who had revolted against the king's unpopular taxes. At the heart of many of their concerns was the underlying fear of the massive changes that would be brought about by a new system.

Favoring the Constitution were the wealthy merchants, lawyers, creditors, and those who believed that the new nation could not continue to exist under the Articles of Confederation. For them, it all boiled down to one simple question offered by Madison: "Whether or not the Union shall or shall not be continued."

Federalists versus Anti-Federalists. Almost as soon as the ink was dry on the last signature to the Constitution, those who favored the new strong national government chose to call themselves "Federalists." They were well aware that sentiments in the new nation still generally opposed the notion of a strong national government, and proponents did not want to risk being labeled "nationalists." Thus, they tried to get the upper hand in the debate by nicknaming their opponents "Anti-Federalists;" those put in this category insisted instead that they were "Federal Republicans"[18] who believed in a federal system but wanted to protect the state governments from the tyranny of a powerful national government. Ultimately the word *federal* came to mean the form of government embodied in the new Constitution, just as *confederation* meant the "league of states" under the Articles (and later the "Confederacy" of 1861–1865).

Federalists and Anti-Federalists participated in the mass meetings that were held in state legislatures to discuss the pros and cons of the new plan. Public meetings were held and debates were published in newspapers. Indeed, the news media played a powerful role in the adoption debates. The entire Constitution, in fact, was printed in the *Pennsylvania Packet* just two days after the convention's end. Other major papers quickly followed suit. Soon, articles on both sides of the adoption issue began to appear around the nation under various pseudonyms, such as "Caesar" or "Constant Reader," as was the custom of the day.

---

[17] Quoted in Faber and Faber, pp. 51–52.

[18] Federal Republicans were those who favored a republican or representative form of government, not supporters of the modern Republican Party, which did not come into being until 1854 (see Chapter 11).

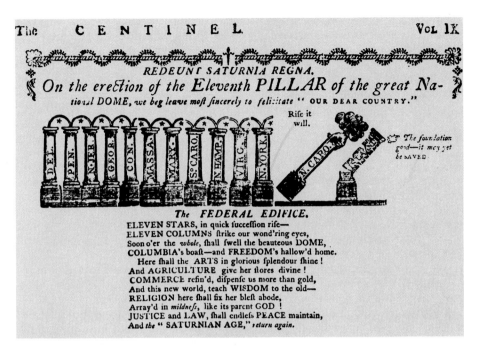

With the Constitution ratified in eleven states and only North Carolina and Rhode Island still uncommitted, cartoonists celebrated certain victory.

One name stood out from all the rest: "Publius" (Latin for "the people"). Between October 1787 and May 1788, eighty-five articles written under that pen name routinely appeared in newspapers in New York, a state where ratification was in doubt. Most were actually written by Alexander Hamilton and James Madison. Hamilton, the young, fiery New Yorker who had been born in the British West Indies, wrote fifty-one, Madison wrote

Federalist and Anti-Federalists Compared

	FEDERALISTS	ANTI-FEDERALISTS
Who Were They?	Property owners, landed rich, merchants of Northeast and Middle Atlantic states	Small farmers, shopkeepers, laborers
Political Philosophy	Elitist: saw themselves and those of their class as best fit to govern (others were to *be* governed)	Believed in decency of common man and in participatory democracy; viewed elites as corrupt; sought greater protection of individual rights
Type of Government Favored	Powerful central government; two-house legislature; upper house (six-year term) further removed from the people, whom they did not trust	Wanted stronger state governments (which were closer to the people) at the expense of the powers of the national government. Sought smaller electoral districts, frequent elections, referendum and recall, large unicameral legislature to provide for greater class and occupational representation
Alliances	Pro-British Anti-French	Anti-British Pro-French

twenty-six, and jointly they penned another three. John Jay, also of New York, who was later to become the first Chief Justice of the United States, wrote five of the pieces. These eighty-five essays became known as *The Federalist Papers.*[19]

Today, *The Federalist Papers* are considered masterful explanations of the Framers' intentions as they drafted the new Constitution. At the time, although they were reprinted widely, they were far too intellectual to have much impact on those who would ultimately vote on the proposed Constitution. Dry and scholarly, they lacked the fervor of much of the political rhetoric that was being espoused elsewhere. *The Federalist Papers* did, however, highlight the reasons for the structure of the new government as well as the benefits that would be provided to all Americans. According to Federalist No. 10, the new Constitution was "a republican remedy for the disease incident to republican government." Moreover, these musings of Madison, Hamilton, and Jay continue to be the best single source of the political theories and philosophies at the heart of our Constitution.

Forced on the defensive, the Anti-Federalists responded with their own series of "letters" written by a variety of Anti-Federalists under the pen names of "Brutus" and "Cato." These letters or essays undertook a line-by-line critique of the Constitution and were designed to counteract *The Federalist Papers.*

The Anti-Federalists argued that a strong central government would render the states powerless.[20] They stressed the strengths of the government under the Articles and argued that the Articles, not the proposed Constitution, created a true federal system. Moreover, they argued that the strong national government would tax heavily, that the Supreme Court would be used to quash the states by invalidating state laws, and that the president eventually would be commander-in-chief of a large and powerful army.

In particular, the Anti-Federalists feared the power of the national government to run roughshod over the liberties of the people. They proposed that the taxing power of Congress be limited, that the executive be curbed by a council, that the military be placed back into the hands of the state militias, and that the jurisdiction of the Supreme Court be limited so as to prohibit the Court from reviewing the decisions of state courts. But their most effective argument concerned the absence of a bill of rights.

James Madison answered these criticisms in Federalists Nos. 10 and 51. In Federalist No. 10, Madison argued that the voters would not always succeed in electing "enlightened statesmen" as their representatives. The greatest threat to individual liberties would therefore come from factions within the government, placing narrow interests above broader national interests and the rights of citizens. Recognizing that no form of government could protect government from unscrupulous politicians, Madison argued that the government was organized in a way that would minimize the effects of political factions. The great advantage of a federal system, Madison maintained, was that it created the "happy combination" of a national government that would be too large to be controlled by any single faction and several state governments that would be smaller and more responsive to local needs.

As an additional level of protection for individuals' rights, Madison argued in Federalist No. 51 for the proposed federal government's separation of powers. Dividing the government's power among three interdependent branches (legislative, executive, and judicial) would prohibit any one branch from either dominating the national government or violating the rights of citizens.

By creating a context for institutional conflict and compromise within the government, Madison hoped that the government would be strong enough to rule the nation effectively, but not strong enough to rule unjustly. "In framing a government which is to be administered by men over men," he wrote in Federalist No. 51, "the great difficulty is

---

[19] Numerous editions of *The Federalist Papers* exist. The most commonly used is one compiled by Clinton Rossiter, ed., *The Federalist* (New York: New American Library, 1961).

[20] See Ralph Ketcham, ed., *The Anti-Federalist Papers and the Constitutional Debates* (New York: New American Library, 1986).

this: you must first enable the government to control the governed; and in the next place oblige it to control itself.''

Debate continued in the thirteen states as votes were taken from December 1787 to June 1788, in accordance with the ratifying process laid out in Article VII of the proposed Constitution. Three states acted quickly to ratify the new Constitution. Two small states, Delaware and New Jersey, voted to ratify before the large states could rethink the notion of equal representation in the Senate. Pennsylvania, where Federalists were well organized, became the third state to ratify. Massachusetts assented to the new government but tempered its support by calling for an immediate addition of amendments including the protection of personal rights. New Hampshire became the crucial ninth state to ratify on June 21, 1788. This action thus completed the ratification process outlined in Article VII of the Constitution and marked the beginning of a new nation. But, because New York and Virginia (which between them accounted for more than 40 percent of the new nation's population) had not yet ratified the Constitution, the practical future of the new nation remained in doubt.

Hamilton in New York and Madison in Virginia worked feverishly to convince delegates to their state conventions to vote for the new government. In New York state, sentiment against the new government was high. In Albany, New York, fighting over the proposed Constitution broke out and resulted in injuries and death. While *The Federalist Papers* undoubtedly had some impact on the delegates, the support of prestigious backers such as Benjamin Franklin and George Washington also helped the ratification effort. Washington, in fact, was widely reported to say, ''There is more wickedness than ignorance in anti-Federalism.'' When news of Virginia's acceptance of the Constitution reached the New York convention, Hamilton was finally able to convince a slim majority

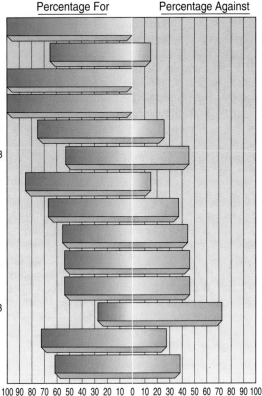

State	Date of Ratification	Vote	Percentage For	Percentage Against
Delaware	Dec. 7, 1787	30–0		
Pennsylvania	Dec. 12, 1787	43–23		
New Jersey	Dec. 18, 1787	38–0		
Georgia	Jan. 2, 1788	26–0		
Connecticut	Jan. 9, 1788	128–40		
Massachusetts	Feb. 16, 1788	187–168		
Maryland	April 26, 1788	63–11		
South Carolina	May 23, 1788	149–73		
New Hampshire	June 21, 1788	57–46		
Virginia	June 25, 1788	89–79		
New York	June 26, 1788	30–27		
North Carolina	Aug. 4, 1788	75–193		
North Carolina	Nov. 21, 1789	194–77		
Rhode Island	May 29, 1790	34–22		

100 90 80 70 60 50 40 30 20 10 0 10 20 30 40 50 60 70 80 90 100

State ratification of the Constitution

Then and Now
Fears of the Anti-Federalists

Many of the fears articulated by the Anti-Federalists have since come true. For one, they feared that the federal government would be able to expand slowly its taxation powers to the point where the states and local governments would find themselves losing their best sources of taxation. This has, in fact, happened; modern tax policy diverts a tremendous majority of individuals' payments to the federal government, which, for all practical purposes, restricts the amount that states and localities can request.

Another fear of the Anti-Federalists was that the creation of a capital city would cause the national government to lose touch with its constituents. The Anti-Federalists proposed that the states superintend any federal capital to guard against this possibility. Today, critics routinely charge that members of Congress have forgotten their roots by living in Washington.

(thirty to twenty-seven) of those present to follow suit. Both states also recommended the addition of a series of structural amendments, and a bill of rights.

Two of the original states—North Carolina and Rhode Island—continued to hold out, largely because they had printed large sums of money and feared what would happen to its value if a national government was instituted. On August 2, 1788, North Carolina became the first state to reject the Constitution on the grounds that no Anti-Federalist amendments were included. Once Congress submitted a bill of rights to the states for their ratification in September 1789, North Carolina ratified the Constitution in late 1789 by a vote of 194 to 77. Rhode Island, the only state that had not sent representatives to Philadelphia, remained out of the Union until 1790. Finally, under threats from its largest cities to secede from the state, the legislature called a convention that ratified the Constitution by a very narrow vote (34 to 32) one year after George Washington became the first president of the United States.

Amending the Constitution

Once the Constitution was ratified, the newly elected Congress immediately proposed a bill of rights. On September 25, 1789, twelve amendments were sent to the states for their ratification. An amendment authorizing the enlargement of the House of Representatives and another to prevent members of the House from raising their own salaries were rejected. The remaining ten amendments, known as the Bill of Rights, were quickly ratified by 1791 in accordance with the procedures set out in Article V. Sought by Anti-Federalists as a protection for individual liberties, they offered numerous specific limitations on the national government's ability to interfere with a wide variety of personal liberties, rights that already were guaranteed by many state constitutions.

The Bill of Rights includes numerous specific protections of personal rights. Freedom of expression, speech, press, religion, and assembly are all guaranteed by the First Amendment. The Bill of Rights also includes numerous guarantees for those accused of crimes—protection against unreasonable searches and seizures (Fourth Amendment), protection against forced self-incrimination, a guarantee of due process of law (Fifth

Amendment), the right to a trial by jury and the right to counsel (Sixth Amendment), and further protections against excessive bail and fines and cruel and unusual punishments (Eighth Amendment). Most, if not all, of these personal rights are protected in Britain, but they are lodged in the common law, not a formal bill of rights. In this regard the United States holds a stronger guarantee of personal liberty.

In addition to guaranteeing these important rights, the Bill of Rights incorporates two amendments that were reactions to British rule—the right to bear arms (Second Amendment) and the right not to have soldiers quartered in their homes (Third Amendment). More general rights are also included in the Bill of Rights. The Ninth Amendment notes that these enumerated rights are *not* inclusive, meaning they are not the only ones to be enjoyed by the people, and the Tenth Amendment states that powers not given to the national government are retained by the states.

Article V: The Constitutional Amendment Process

Article V creates a two-stage amendment process: proposal and ratification.[21] The Constitution specifies two ways to accomplish each stage. Amendments to the Constitution can be proposed by:

1. A two-thirds vote in both houses of Congress, or
2. A two-thirds vote of the state legislatures specifically requesting Congress to call a national convention to propose amendments

The second method has never been used. Historically, it has served as a fairly effective threat, forcing Congress to consider amendments that might otherwise never have been debated. In the 1980s, for example, several states began to call on Congress to enact a balanced-budget amendment. To forestall the need for a special constitutional convention, Congress began to debate the merits of just such an amendment and ultimately enacted the Gramm-Rudman-Hollings Act, which calls for a balanced budget.

Of the thousands of amendments that have been introduced on one or both floors of the Congress, only thirty-three have mustered the requisite two-thirds vote to be sent to the states for their debate and ratification. Only seven proposed amendments sent to the states have failed to achieve ratification.

The ratification process is fairly straightforward. Amendments can be ratified in one of two ways:

1. A favorable vote of three-fourths of the state legislatures
2. A favorable vote of specially called ratifying conventions in three-fourths of the states

The second method was used by the Framers as the means of ratifying the Constitution. The Framers rightly feared that the special interests of the state legislators would preclude a favorable vote by them on the new Constitution. Since ratification of the Constitution, however, the second method has been used to ratify only one amendment. The Eighteenth Amendment, which began the ''Prohibition Era'' by outlawing the sale of alcoholic beverages, was ratified by the more typical first method—using state legislatures. Millions broke the law, others died from drinking homemade liquor, and others made their fortunes selling bootleg or illegal liquor. After a decade of these problems, Congress decided to act. An additional amendment, the Twenty-first, was proposed to repeal the Eighteenth Amendment. The new proposed amendment was sent to the states

---

[21] See Alan P. Grimes, *Democracy and the Amendments to the Constitution* (Lexington, Mass.: Lexington Books, 1978).

FOUR METHODS OF AMENDING THE CONSTITUTION

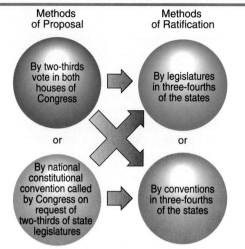

Source: Alex Wellek, ed., *Encyclopedia Dictionary of American Government* (Guilford, Ct: Duskin, 1991), p. 9.

for their ratification,[22] but with a call for ratifying conventions and *not* a vote in the state legislatures. Members of Congress correctly predicted that the move to repeal would encounter opposition in the statehouses, which were largely controlled by conservative rural interests. Via the unusual conventions method, the Twenty-first Amendment repealing the Eighteenth Amendment was ratified within ten months.

The intensity of efforts to amend the Constitution have varied considerably depending on the nature of the change proposed. Whereas the Twenty-first Amendment took only ten months to ratify, an equal rights amendment was introduced in every session of Congress from 1923 until 1972, when Congress finally voted favorably on the proposed amendment. Even then, years of lobbying by women's groups was insufficient to garner necessary support. By 1982, the congressionally mandated date for ratification, only thirty-five states—three short of the number required—had voted favorably on the amendment.[23]

As illustrated in Table 2-1, amendments passed since the Bill of Rights can be organized into four categories: (1) those designed to remedy a structural change in government, (2) those designed to expand rights, (3) those affecting public policy, and (4) those designed to overrule a decision of the U.S. Supreme Court.

Most amendments that change the structure or mechanics of government have been ratified quite easily in response to some sort of "emergency." In the wake of President John F. Kennedy's assassination in 1963, which left the nation without a vice president after Lyndon B. Johnson succeeded to the presidency, the Twenty-fifth Amendment was added to the Constitution to allow the president to fill, subject to the approval of Congress, any vacancy that occurred in that office. For the most part, the public has accepted the structural changes as a natural working out of the kinks in the Constitution.

Amendments expanding rights, especially those concerned with expanding the electorate, make up the next significant group of amendments. Generally, once these amendments are finally able to secure congressional favor, state ratification follows quickly. For example, although women tried for decades to secure a constitutional amendment guar-

[22] David E. Kyvig, *Repealing National Prohibition* (Chicago: University of Chicago Press, 1978).

[23] See Jane J. Mansbridge, *Why We Lost the ERA* (Chicago: University of Chicago Press, 1986).

anteeing their right to vote, once Congress voted favorably on the Nineteenth Amendment, ratification by the states took less than two years.[24]

Amendments designed to alter existing public policies form a third category of constitutional amendments. These amendments always have been regarded as troublesome by constitutional scholars. Many argue that the Constitution should be a basic outline of principles and not a list of desired outcomes. Critics today, for example, fear that efforts to amend the Constitution to prohibit flag burning, allow prayer in schools, or ban abortions would be foolhardy and unnecessary interference with the basic nature of the Constitution. The first two are regarded as particularly risky because they would alter the First Amendment, which to this day has never been amended.

A final category of amendments consists of those that were enacted to overrule specific Supreme Court decisions. As discussed in greater detail in Chapter 9, the Supreme Court is the final authority on what the Constitution means. Once the Court construes a provision of the Constitution, the only way that interpretation can be changed is by the Court itself or by constitutional amendment. Thus, the Supreme Court has become an important mechanism for constitutional change; only two of its decisions have been specifically overruled by constitutional amendments.

In Britain, there is no formal, ''extraordinary'' amendment process. Indeed, a garden-variety act of Parliament, such as the law in 1911 that restricted the legislative competence of the upper house—the House of Lords—can have far-ranging constitutional implications. Britain's unwritten constitution evolves with alterations to the common law,

---

[24] Eleanor Flexner, *Century of Struggle: The Woman's Rights Movement in the United States* (New York: Atheneum, 1974).

Table 2-1   Types of Constitutional Amendments

AFFECTING STRUCTURAL CHANGE		EXPANDING RIGHTS	
12th	Electors required to vote separately for president and vice president (1804)	13th	Bans slavery (1865)
17th	Direct vote of U.S. senators (1913)	14th	Guarantees equal protection and due process (1868)
20th	Date of presidential inauguration changed (1933)	15th	Extends suffrage to black males (1870)
22nd	Presidents limited to two terms (1951)	19th	Extends suffrage to women (1920)
25th	Presidential and vice-presidential succession (1967)	23rd	Residents of District of Columbia given right to vote in presidential elections (1961)
27th	Congressional salaries (1992)	24th	Poll taxes abolished (1964)
AFFECTING PUBLIC POLICY		26th	Extends suffrage to 18-year-olds (1971)
18th	Prohibits liquor sales (1919)	**OVERRULING SUPREME COURT DECISIONS**[a]	
21st	Repeals 18th Amendment (1933)	11th	Prohibits an individual from suing a state without its permission (1798)
		16th	Gives Congress power to tax personal income (1913)

[a] The Fourteenth and Twenty-sixth Amendments also effectively overruled Supreme Court decisions.

The Bill of Rights

FIRST AMENDMENT

Congress shall make no law respecting an establishment of religion, or prohibiting the free exercise thereof; or abridging the freedom of speech, or of the press; or the right of the people peaceably to assemble, and to petition the Government for a redress of grievances.

SECOND AMENDMENT

A well regulated Militia, being necessary to the security of a free State, the right of the people to keep and bear Arms, shall not be infringed.

THIRD AMENDMENT

No Soldier shall, in time of peace be quartered in any house, without the consent of the Owner, nor in time of war, but in a manner to be prescribed by law.

FOURTH AMENDMENT

The right of the people to be secure in their persons, houses, papers, and effects, against unreasonable searches and seizures, shall not be violated, and no Warrants shall issue, but upon probable cause, supported by Oath or affirmation, and particularly describing the place to be searched, and the persons or things to be seized.

FIFTH AMENDMENT

No person shall be held to answer for a capital, or otherwise infamous crime, unless on a presentment or indictment of a Grand Jury, except in cases arising in the land or naval forces, or in the Militia, when in actual service in time of War or public danger; nor shall any person be subject for the same offence to be twice put in jeopardy of life or limb, nor shall be compelled in any criminal case to be a witness against himself, nor be deprived of life, liberty, or property, without due process of law; nor shall private property be taken for public use, without just compensation.

SIXTH AMENDMENT

In all criminal prosecutions, the accused shall enjoy the right to a speedy and public trial, by an impartial jury of the State and district wherein the crime shall have been committed, which district shall have been previously ascertained by law, and to be informed of the nature and cause of the accusation; to be confronted with the witnesses against him; to have compulsory process for obtaining witnesses in his favor; and to have the Assistance of Counsel for his defence.

SEVENTH AMENDMENT

In Suits at common law, where the value in controversy shall exceed twenty dollars, the right of trial by jury shall be preserved, and no fact tried by a jury shall be otherwise re-examined in any Court of the United States, than according to the rules of the common law.

EIGHTH AMENDMENT

Excessive bail shall not be required nor excessive fines imposed, nor cruel and unusual punishments inflicted.

NINTH AMENDMENT

The enumeration in the Constitution, of certain rights, shall not be construed to deny or disparage others retained by the people.

TENTH AMENDMENT

The powers not delegated to the United States by the Constitution, nor prohibited by it to the States, are reserved to the States respectively or to the people.

After the U.S. Supreme Court ruled that flag burning was a constitutionally protected form of expression, several members of Congress proposed that the Constitution be amended to ban flag burning or desecration.

new acts of Parliament, and incremental changes to the host of conventions that regulate political life. Thus, the British constitution is much more flexible and perhaps even more adaptable than its American counterpart; it is also theoretically more open to the abuse of power, particularly with respect to individual liberties.

Informal Methods of Amending the Constitution

The formal amending process is not the only way that the Constitution has been changed over time. Judicial interpretation, popular practice, and technological change also have had a major impact on the way the Constitution has evolved.

Judicial Interpretation. As early as 1803, under the brilliant leadership of Chief Justice John Marshall, the Supreme Court declared that the federal courts had the power to

Amendments That Have Failed State Ratification

1. A provision that would have allowed Congress to regulate the representation of members of the House once the proportions went beyond 100,000 persons per Representative. Proposed: 1789.

2. A provision stripping U.S. citizenship from any individual who "shall accept, claim, receive or retain any title of nobility or honour, or shall without consent of Congress, accept and retain any present pension, office or emolument of any kind whatever, from any emperor, king, prince or foreign power . . ." Proposed: 1811.

3. A provision barring the federal government from interfering with or abolishing slavery. Proposed: 1861.

4. A provision banning child labor. Proposed: 1924.

5. A provision stating that "equality of rights shall not be denied or abridged by the United States or by any State on account of sex." Proposed: 1972.

6. A proposal to give the District of Columbia representation in Congress. Proposed: 1978.

nullify acts of the nation's government when they were in conflict with the U.S. Constitution. Over the years this check on the other branches of government and on the states has increased the authority of the Court and has significantly altered the meaning of various provisions of the Constitution, a fact that prompted Woodrow Wilson to call the Supreme Court "a constitutional convention in continuous session."

For example, when the Framers authorized Congress in Article I, Section 8, to regulate commerce among the states, they could not have imagined the controversial course that interpretation of that clause would take. In *Gibbons* v. *Ogden* (1824), Chief Justice Marshall proclaimed that commerce was "any intercourse between states," including navigation, which allowed Congress to increase its involvement in regulatory activity. Later, in the 1930s, a pro-business Court interpreted the clause very narrowly and repeatedly struck down efforts of Congress and President Franklin Roosevelt to bring the country out of the economic chaos of the Depression. It was not until 1937—in the face of strong public pressure and the threat of congressional attacks—that the Court reread the commerce clause and found constitutional justification for wide congressional power. Since that time, most congressional efforts to regulate any form of business or employment practice have been held to be within the scope of Congress's power.

Some today argue that the original intent of the Framers, as evidenced in Madison's notes from the Constitutional Convention and *The Federalist Papers,* should govern judicial interpretation of the Constitution.[25] Others argue that the Framers knew that a

[25] Speech by Attorney General Edwin Meese III before the American Bar Association, July 9, 1985, Washington, D.C.

changing society needed an elastic, flexible document that could conform to the ages.[26] In all likelihood, the vagueness of the document was purposeful. Those in attendance in Philadelphia recognized that they could not agree on everything and that it was wiser to leave interpretation to those who would follow them.

Cultural Change. Even the most far-sighted authors of the Constitution could not have anticipated the vast changes that have occurred in America. For example, although many hoped for the abolition of slavery, none could have imagined the modern status of blacks or that a black person could be a viable candidate for president. Likewise, few could have anticipated the diverse roles that women would play in society. The Constitution has often been bent to accommodate these changes. Although there is no specific amendment guaranteeing women equal protection of the laws, the courts have interpreted the Constitution to prohibit many forms of discrimination as violations of the Fourteenth Amendment's equal protection clause, despite the fact that the Fourteenth Amendment was not intended to protect women from discrimination.

Technological Change. Technological change has also contributed to a changing Constitution. The Framers could not have envisioned the need for an air traffic control system or for regulation of the airwaves. As computers and other technological advances have allowed the government and, in particular, the bureaucracy (see Chapter 8) to grow, our expectations of the role of government also have changed. It is unlikely that the Founders could have envisioned a Social Security system that has the capacity to mail more than 35 million checks per month to retirees.

Advances in technology have required new interpretations of the Bill of Rights. Wiretapping and other forms of electronic surveillance, for example, are now regulated by the First and Fourth Amendments. Similarly, AIDS testing and drug screening, which involve scientifically advanced tests, must be juxtaposed against constitutional protections.

Toward Reform

When asked in a May 1987 CBS News/New York Times Poll, "Do you think it is too easy or too hard to amend the Constitution, or is the process about right?" 11 percent responded, "Too easy"; 20 percent responded, "Too hard"; and 60 percent responded, "About right." This survey was conducted during the height of the debate over ratification of the Equal Rights Amendment, which, although it failed, was supported by a majority of Americans.

When the Founders met in Philadelphia in 1787, they sought to fashion a constitution that would provide the basic framework for running the nation not only in 1787 but also well into the future. Since ratification of the Bill of Rights in 1791, only sixteen amendments have been added, and only fourteen continue to be functional. (The Twentieth Amendment repealed the Eighteenth Amendment.) The basic framework of government, although modified considerably over time through informal means, remains vital today. Emotionally charged calls for change often have occurred in the wake of highly unpopular Supreme Court decisions such as *Texas* v. *Johnson* (1989), in which the justices ruled that flag burning was a form of political speech protected by the First Amendment. Politicians, veterans' groups, and members of the general public all immediately clamored for passage of a constitutional amendment to limit the reach of the First Amendment and to

[26]Speech by William J. Brennan, Jr., at Georgetown University, Text and Teaching Symposium, October 10, 1985, Washington, D.C.

expressly prohibit flag burning. But, as time passed, cooler heads prevailed, and the move to amend the Constitution faltered.

It would not be surprising to see in the 1990s new efforts to add an equal rights amendment to the Constitution. But because the Framers purposely made it difficult to change the Constitution, ratification of such an amendment is likely to face another uphill battle. The Constitution today remains quite similar to the document ratified in 1789. Reform or change is possible, but the prospect of either remains unlikely.

Summary

Settlers came to the New World for a variety of reasons. While many came to escape British practices such as its inheritance laws, restrictive guild system, or religious persecution, most remained loyal to Great Britain and considered themselves subjects of the king. But over the years, those ties lessened as new generations of Americans were born on colonial soil. A series of taxes levied by the Crown did little to solidify those feelings.

The colonists soon believed that they had no other course than to declare their independence. After waging a successful war of independence, amid economic chaos, steps were soon taken to draft a new constitution.

The miracle at Philadelphia was the result of a series of compromises that combined the principles of popular consent of the government, separation of powers, and federalism. Popular consent was embodied by the direct election of members to the House of Representatives but tempered by the methods of selection for senators and the president. Authority was dispersed among the three branches of government to check tyranny. The federal system gave the national government powers it had lacked under the Articles of Confederation.

Over more than 200 years, our Constitution has endured with few formal changes. It has proved to be a sufficiently elastic document able to meet the needs of the government and the people despite many changes in circumstances.

Key Terms

common law	confederacy	electoral college
divine right of kings	bicameral legislature	checks and balances
	federal system	separation of powers
Magna Carta	Great Compromise	enumerated powers
Articles of Confederation	Three-Fifths Compromise	elastic clause
Stamp Act	suffrage	executive power
Committees of Correspondence	electors	judicial review

Suggested Readings

Bailyn, Bernard. *The Ideological Origins of the American Revolution.* Cambridge, Mass.: Harvard University Press, 1967.

Beard, Charles. *An Economic Interpretation of the Constitution of the United States.* New York: Macmillan, 1913.

Bowen, Catherine Drinker. *Miracle at Philadelphia.* Boston: Little-Brown, 1966.

Hamilton, Alexander, James Madison, and John Jay. *The Federalist Papers,* ed. Isaac Kramnick. New York: Penguin, 1987 (first published in 1788).

Ketchman, Ralph. *The Anti-Federalist Papers and the Constitutional Convention Debated.* New York: New American Library, 1986.

Levy, Leonard W., ed. *Essays on the Making of the Constitution.* New York: Oxford University Press, 1969.

McDonald, Forest. *The Formation of the American Republic.* New York: Penguin, 1967.

Main, Jackson Turner. *The Social Structure of Revolutionary America.* Princeton, N.J.: Princeton University Press, 1965.

Rossiter, Clinton. *1787: Grand Convention.* New York: Macmillan, 1966.

Wood, Gordon S. *The Creation of the American Republic.* Chapel Hill: University of North Carolina Press, 1969.

The power surrendered by the people is first divided between two distinct governments, and then . . . subdivided among distinct and separate departments.

James Madison

FEDERALIST NO. 51

The Founders, fearing tyranny, divided powers among state and national governments. At each level, moreover, powers were divided among executive, legislative, and judicial branches.

CHAPTER 3

Federalism

In *The Federalist Papers,* James Madison, Alexander Hamilton, and John Jay attempted to convince the public that a strong national government drawing its power directly from the people was better than the form of government created by the Articles of Confederation. Under the confederate form of government fashioned by the Articles in 1781, a weak national government depended on the states exclusively for its authority (see Chapter 2). National strength became important—but since the Framers still were inclined to reject anything British, the unitary structure of Britain's government was out of the question.

In this chapter we address the nature of the government created by the Framers and how the Framers attempted to allocate power and the functions of government between one national and several state governments. From the very beginning of the United States of America, the challenge was preserving the traditional independence and rights of the states while establishing an effective national government. Once it became clear that the government under the Articles was ineffective, the Framers recognized the need for a new system. Their solution was to create the world's first **federal system,** although the word *federal* does not itself appear in the Constitution. In the proposed new government, the thirteen sovereign or independent states were bound together under one national government. The result was a system of government that was "neither wholly *national* nor wholly *federal,*" as Madison explained in *The Federalist Papers.*

The relationship between, and the intertwined powers of, the national and state governments are the heart of **federalism,** which draws its origins from the Latin *foedus,* or covenant. Thus, federalism can be envisioned as the written agreement that defines the allocation of power between the national government and the states. Ironically, as discussed in Chapter 2, those who supported the government under the Articles of Confederation argued for what *they* called a federal system. But the fear of being labeled "nationalists" prompted supporters of the new Constitution to call themselves "Federalists," thus co-opting this popular term of the day.

In this chapter we explore the reasons why a federal system was adopted. We also analyze how the relationship and allocation of powers between the national and state governments have changed over time. Political ideology and the Supreme Court have played especially important roles in the development of what political scientists today mean by federalism. As you read this chapter, keep in mind the arguments made by the Framers in support of the system they created. How close to or far from the original intentions of the Founders is the federalism of the twentieth century?

Federalism affects Americans daily. As students, your eligibility for financial aid in terms of federal grants and state-guaranteed loans is just one example of how national and state policies directly affect you. The quality of the highways you travel and the quality of public education in any particular state are also highly dependent on the relationship between the national government and the states. In order to receive federal funds for the building and maintenance of highways, for example, states must follow federal rules about the kinds of roads that can be built. Whereas the national highway system is highly dependent on federal dollars, education traditionally has been regarded as a state matter. Therefore, tremendous differences exist in the amount of money spent per pupil in elementary and secondary schools—from a high of $8,680 a year in New York to a low of $2,767 in Utah in 1990–1991, as shown in Table 3-1. These differences highlight the division of governmental authority inherent in a federal system. As you read on, consider the advantages and disadvantages of this revolutionary system created by the Framers.

The Origins of Federalism

When the Framers met in Philadelphia, they agreed that a new form of government would have to be fashioned to replace the government that existed under the Articles of Confederation. According to noted federalism scholar Daniel J. Elazar, the Framers were

Four Uses of the Term "Federal"

"Federalist Party": New political party that emerged under the leadership of Alexander Hamilton; generally elitist; controlled First Congress

The Federalist Papers: Written by leading Federalists to garner support for the proposed constitution

"Federalist": Name taken by supporters of new proposed government to avoid being called "nationalists"

"Federal system": Term describing distribution of power, originally coined by supporters of government under Articles of Confederation

Table 3-1   Estimated 1990–91 Total Expenditure per Pupil by State

STATES	EXPENDITURE PER PUPIL	STATES	EXPENDITURE PER PUPIL
National average (including Washington, D.C.)	$5,208		
Alabama	3,648	Montana	4,794
Alaska	6,952	Nebraska	4,080
Arizona	4,196	Nevada	4,677
Arkansas	3,419	New Hampshire	5,474
California	4,826	New Jersey	8,451
Colorado	4,702	New Mexico	4,446
Connecticut	8,455	New York	8,680
Delaware	6,016	North Carolina	4,635
District of Columbia	8,221	North Dakota	3,685
Florida	5,003	Ohio	5,629
Georgia	4,852	Oklahoma	3,835
Hawaii	5,008	Oregon	5,291
Idaho	3,211	Pennsylvania	6,534
Illinois	5,062	Rhode Island	6,989
Indiana	4,398	South Carolina	3,843
Iowa	4,877	South Dakota	3,780
Kansas	5,044	Tennessee	3,707
Kentucky	4,390	Texas	4,326
Louisiana	4,041	Utah	2,767
Maine	5,894	Vermont	5,740
Maryland	6,104	Virginia	5,355
Massachusetts	6,351	Washington	5,042
Michigan	5,257	West Virginia	4,695
Minnesota	5,360	Wisconsin	5,946
Mississippi	3,322	Wyoming	5,255
Missouri	4,479		

Source: National Education Association, Washington, D.C., 1990–91.

heavily influenced not only by political considerations, as discussed in Chapter 2, but also by religious, social, and economic factors in their search for a new form of government.

Federalism and the Constitution

The Framers worked to create a system of government that would be familiar to Americans but that could remedy many of the problems experienced under the Articles of Confederation. Alexander Hamilton, one of the strongest proponents of a strong national government, believed that for the nation to survive, it was critical for the national government to be *the* leading force in all political affairs. Like other supporters of the new Constitution, Hamilton articulated three arguments for federalism: the prevention of tyranny, the provision for increased participation in politics, and the creation of laboratories for experiments (by which the states could serve as testing grounds for new policies and programs). Federalists also believed that any concentration of power would work to the disadvantage of the people. They feared that even popularly elected representatives would eventually try to concentrate their control, and tyranny would reign.

To alleviate these fears, the federal government created by the Framers draws its powers directly from the people. As the Framers envisioned, both levels of government—state and national—derive their powers from the people and ultimately are answerable to them. In Federalist No. 51, Alexander Hamilton explained what he perceived to be the beauty of this system: The shifting support of the electorate between the two levels of government would serve to keep each in balance.

Ironically, although they were dissatisfied with the confederacy, the Framers lacked any real idea of what shape the federal system should take. Nevertheless, given their experiences under the Articles, James Madison and his allies believed that the only way to contain factions (special interests) while preserving liberty would be to expand the territory in which factions competed. That is, the Founders believed that they needed to create multiple levels of government—national, state, and local—in order to minimize the influence of special interests.

In fashioning the new federal system of government, the Framers recognized that they would be unable to define precisely how all the relations between the national government and the individual states would work. But the text of the Constitution makes it clear that the balancing and intermingling of powers is at the very core of the federal system. Article II, for example, outlines the president's powers and duties and provides that the machinery of state government be used for election of the president. Furthermore, the president can make treaties only with the concurrence of a two-thirds vote of the Senate, whose members were directly chosen by their respective state legislatures before enactment of the Seventeenth Amendment.

Concurrent Powers. The distribution of powers in the federal system is often described as two overlapping circles. The area where the circles overlap represents **concurrent**, or shared, **powers**—possessed by both the national and state governments. As set out in Article I, Section 8, the Congress has both **enumerated** and **implied powers.** The states possess "police powers" to protect the "health, safety and morals" of their citizens. Because both sets of powers require money to implement, both the national and state governments were given the authority to levy taxes. Other important concurrent

Distribution of Power under Federalism

Federal Powers	Concurrent Powers	State Powers
Coin money	Tax	Establish local governments
Conduct foreign relations	Borrow money	Regulate commerce within a state
Regulate commerce with foreign nations and among states	Establish courts	Conduct elections
Provide an army and a navy	Make and enforce laws	Ratify amendments to the federal Constitution
Declare war	Charter banks and corporations	Take measures for public health, safety, and morals
Establish courts inferior to the Supreme Court	Spend money for the general welfare	Exert powers the Constitution does not delegate to the national government or prohibit the states from using
Make laws necessary and proper to carry out the foregoing powers	Take private property for public purposes, with just compensation	

powers include the right to borrow money, establish courts, charter banks and other corporations, and enact and enforce laws necessary to carry out these powers.

Denied and Reserved Powers. Both the national and state governments are denied the authority to take arbitrary actions affecting constitutional rights and liberties. Neither level of government may pass a **bill of attainder,** a law declaring an act illegal without a judicial trial. Nor can the national or a state government (today) sentence a criminal without due process of law.

National Supremacy. Even during the Constitutional Convention, it was evident that the concept of concurrent powers would lead to conflict and friction between the national government and the states. In fact, the second section of Article VI was added to avoid such conflicts. It provided that:

> *This Constitution, and the Laws of the United States which shall be made in Pursuance thereof, and all Treaties made, or which shall be made, under the Authority of the United States, shall be the supreme Law of the Land; and the Judges in every State shall be bound thereby . . .*

In spite of this language, what *"the supreme Law of the Land"* means has been subject to continuous judicial interpretation and reinterpretation.

Guarantees to and Restrictions on the States. In return for the Anti-Federalists' agreement to the supremacy clause, several guarantees were made to the states in the Constitution. For example, Article IV empowers the national government to ensure that each state has a *"Republican Form of Government,"* meaning one that represents the citizens of the state. Each state is also guaranteed two members in the Senate. The Constitution also guarantees that the national government will provide protection to the states against foreign attacks and domestic rebellion.

Moreover, specific restrictions were imposed on the states in Article I, Section 10. The states were limited in their ability to deal with foreign nations, and they could no longer coin money or tax imports or exports.

Nowhere in the original document are the powers of the states spelled out. Nevertheless, the enumeration of many specific powers to the national government and none to the states is a clear indication of the Federalist leanings of the Framers. It was not until the addition of the Bill of Rights and the Tenth Amendment that the states' powers were better described: *"The powers not delegated to the United States by the Constitution, nor prohibited by it to the States, are reserved to the States respectively, or to the people."*

A completely asymmetric distribution of powers exists in the British unitary state, where local authorities are the only elected public bodies below the national government. British local governments have little power to act for the benefit of the citizens within their jurisdictions. Due to the absence of a specific grant of power from the national legislature, local authorities are not allowed to undertake any action that requires the expenditure of public funds. While British local authorities do in fact collect taxes, employ people, and perform many vital services for their communities, they owe their responsibilities to legislative decisions made in London, the national capital. Not only can the national government add to or subtract from these responsibilities, it can do away with entire categories of local government. In 1986, for example, the Thatcher government abolished the metropolitan county councils over the vociferous objections of the opposition party and targeted local authorities.

Relations Among the States. The Constitution provides that *"Full Faith and Credit shall be given in each State to the public Acts, Records and judicial Proceeding of every other State."* This clause ensures that judicial decrees and contracts made in one state will be binding and enforceable in another. In a similar vein, the Constitution requires states to extradite criminals. Thus, "fugitives" caught in one state are to be returned to the state in which they are wanted on suspicion of having committed a crime or crimes. For example, a free black man originally from Kentucky (a slave state) was accused of helping a female slave from Kentucky escape to Ohio, a free state. In *Kentucky* v. *Dennison* (1861),[1] the Supreme Court ruled that although the governor of Ohio had a *legal* obligation to return the man to Kentucky, the federal government lacked the power to force the governor to do so. In 1987, however, the Supreme Court ruled that *Dennison* must be interpreted in light of the fact that during the Civil War, the federal government's power over the states was at its lowest ebb. In *Puerto Rico* v. *Branstad* (1987), which arose when the governor of Iowa refused to honor Puerto Rico's request for extradition of a man charged with first degree murder, the Court ruled that the extradition clause is binding on the states and is *not* discretionary. The governor believed that the charges against the accused were unreasonable and, on account of the man's race, he would probably not receive a fair trial in Puerto Rico. Nevertheless, because the federal government today has the authority to enforce its provisions, the Court found that Iowa was bound by the Constitution.

The Framers did allow the states to enter into "compacts" with other state to deal with issues like the supervision or governance of rivers, harbors, or other transportation matters. Finally, the Constitution provides that disputes between states are to be settled directly by the Supreme Court under its original jurisdiction (see Chapter 7).

The Evolution and Development of Federalism

The victory of the Federalists—those who supported a strong national government—had long-lasting consequences on the future of the nation. It was clear at the time that the Framers were uncertain as to what the future would hold; over the course of our nation's history the nature of federalism and its allocation of power between the national government and the states have changed dramatically.

Dual Federalism

The kind of federalism that first emerged from 1789 to 1861 in the United States was what we call **dual federalism,** that is, the belief that having separate and equally powerful levels of government is the best arrangement. Dual federalism holds that the national government should not exceed its enumerated powers expressly set out in the Constitution. During this period those in power generally assumed that the national government could promote only a few specific policies dealing with matters like trade and international relations and that the state and national governments existed within separate, distinct, and equal spheres.

The role of state governments in everyday life was far more pervasive than it is today. States controlled labor conditions, race relations, and slavery. Pursuant to various constitutional strictures, states also exercised tremendous powers over the electoral process (including who voted and how congressional districts were drawn), education, property rights, and criminal and family law.

Political Parties. Powerful state political parties reinforced local economic mores and also acted to limit federal authority. Political parties defined election law and electoral districts to help or hinder specific House candidates and in most states controlled the nomination process for House races. They also controlled, through state legislatures, the nomination and election of U.S. senators. (At first, in some states the U.S. House of Representatives was seen as a place where you could "park" one or two of your most

[1] 65 U.S. 66 (1861).

The Evolving Nature of Federalism

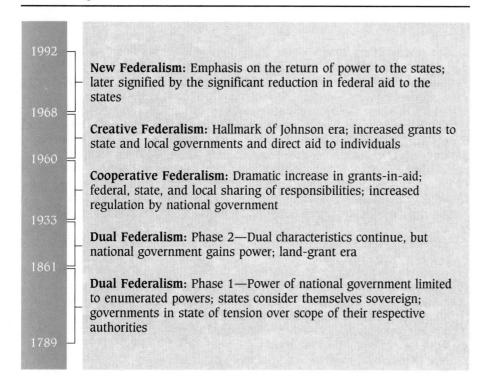

1992

New Federalism: Emphasis on the return of power to the states; later signified by the significant reduction in federal aid to the states

1968

Creative Federalism: Hallmark of Johnson era; increased grants to state and local governments and direct aid to individuals

1960

Cooperative Federalism: Dramatic increase in grants-in-aid; federal, state, and local sharing of responsibilities; increased regulation by national government

1933

Dual Federalism: Phase 2—Dual characteristics continue, but national government gains power; land-grant era

1861

Dual Federalism: Phase 1—Power of national government limited to enumerated powers; states consider themselves sovereign; governments in state of tension over scope of their respective authorities

1789

vociferous and effective opponents to get them out of the state.) As a result, much of what was done in Congress was a function of the bargaining that occurred among those who owed their seats in Congress to their state parties.

Although political parties could gear up to support national issues, voters usually viewed these kinds of measures in terms of their local, rather than national, effects. Therefore, a local party's ability to deliver **patronage**—jobs, public works projects, and so on—was far more important to the local citizenry than who controlled the White House.

Republicanism. As the new government began to work, both the political parties and individual citizens became swept up in notions of **republicanism,** the idea that citizens elect representatives to manage government. Republicanism had two different aspects: First, liberty was defined in terms of the ability of the citizen to participate directly in government through voting; second, liberty was equated with an individual's personal rights. These two ideas were reconciled under the notion of dual federalism. Dual federalism allowed the states to expand voting opportunities to larger segments of the populace yet continue to deny personal liberty to slaves who were deemed private property and thereby not the proper focus of governmental regulation.

The Courts

These competing notions of republicanism often ended up at the core of disputes brought into federal courts. From the beginning, the courts were involved in developing the structure and mechanics of the federal system. At the head of the federal judiciary sat John Marshall, an ardent Federalist who served from 1801 to 1835. In a series of important decisions, Chief Justice Marshall and the Supreme Court reaffirmed the Federalists' beliefs in a strong national government. Federalist sentiments could be seen especially clearly in the Court's broad interpretations of the Constitution's **supremacy clause** and the **commerce clause.**

McCulloch* v. *Maryland. The first major decision of the Marshall Court that defined the relationship between the national and state governments was the case of *McCulloch* v. *Maryland.* In 1816 Congress chartered the Second Bank of the United States. (The charter of the First Bank had been allowed to expire.) The Second Bank was never popular and had detractors on several fronts. As was true since Daniel Shays had marched on the courthouse in Massachusetts, farmers and the poor had a strong suspicion and hatred of banks. In addition, many Jeffersonian Democratic-Republicans—members of the political party that emerged to oppose the Federalist Party—believed that the national government lacked the authority to establish a bank. They believed that because the power to issue corporate charters was not granted to Congress by the Constitution, the Bank of the United States was unconstitutional. States also disliked the national bank; it was the largest corporation in the United States, and it provided stiff competition for state-chartered banks.

In 1818, the Democratic-Republican–controlled Maryland assembly passed a law requiring the Second Bank of the United States to (1) buy stamped paper from the state on which notes issued by the Bank were to be issued, (2) pay the states $15,000 a year, or (3) go out of business. Maryland was not the only state to attempt to tax the U.S. bank out of business. Tennessee, Georgia, Ohio, and North Carolina, for example, enacted laws requiring each branch of the national bank to pay $50,000 to their respective states to stay in business. Illinois and Indiana, which had no branches of the national bank, passed laws prohibiting their establishment.

When James McCulloch, the head cashier of the Baltimore branch of the Bank of the United States, refused to pay the state tax or buy the stamped paper, Maryland brought suit against him and the Bank in state court. Not surprisingly, he was convicted. In 1819, McCulloch appealed his conviction to the U.S. Supreme Court. Arguing on behalf of the federal government and for the constitutionality of the Bank as a proper exercise of congressional power was Daniel Webster, a former Federalist member of Congress and one of the best lawyers in the nation. Among those representing Maryland was Luther Martin, who had been an active opponent of the new Constitution in Philadelphia. There he had railed against the chains being forged for "his country"—meaning Maryland—and its subjugation to new national power. Thirty years later, he saw himself as defending Maryland against the usurpation of its power he had earlier foreseen.[2]

Although Chief Justice John Marshall still presided over the Court, only he and one other Federalist justice remained. The other five justices were Democratic-Republicans appointed by Presidents Jefferson or Madison. In a unanimous opinion, the Court answered the two central questions that had been put to it on appeal: First, did Congress have the authority to charter a bank, and, second, if it did, could a state tax the national bank?

As to the first question—whether Congress had the right to establish a bank or another type of corporation, given that the Constitution does not explicitly mention such a power—Chief Justice Marshall's answer continues to stand as the classic exposition of the doctrine of implied powers and as a reaffirmation of the propriety of a strong national government. He skillfully picked up on arguments that had first been put forth by Alexander Hamilton in support of the First Bank. Marshall explained that although the federal government was limited by the powers set out in the Constitution, the extent of those enumerated powers required judicial interpretation. Therefore, although the word *bank* cannot be found in the Constitution, it does contain enumerated or **express powers**

---

[2]John A. Garraty, ed., *Quarrels That Have Shaped the Constitution* (New York: Harper & Row, 1987), Chapter 3.

specifically giving Congress the authority to levy and collect taxes, issue a currency, and to borrow funds. In its attempts to carry out those enumerated powers, Marshall found, it was reasonable for Congress to consider the chartering of a bank to be "necessary and proper" to the carrying out of its specific powers.

In some of the most famous language from the case, Marshall carefully set out an expansive interpretation of the **necessary and proper clause** of Article I, Section 8, by proclaiming:

> Let the end be legitimate, let it be within the scope of the Constitution, and all means which are appropriate, which are plainly adapted to that end, which are not prohibited, but consistent with the letter and spirit of the Constitution, are constitutional.

With these words, Marshall first enunciated the doctrine of implied powers. The necessary and proper clause gives to Congress the power "*To make all Laws which shall be necessary and proper for carrying into Execution the foregoing Powers, and all other Powers vested by this Constitution in the Government of the United States, or in any Department or Officer thereof.*" Marshall viewed this as a very **elastic clause** that could be stretched to imply other powers from those specifically enumerated in the Constitution. Thus, the powers to levy and collect taxes, issue currency, and borrow funds—expressly noted in the Constitution—could be stretched to imply an authority to charter a bank.

Marshall next addressed the question of whether a federal bank could be taxed by any state government. To Marshall, this was not a difficult question. Once he explained how the chartering of a bank was within the range of powers implied under the necessary and proper clause, he went on to discuss the basic framework of the government set out in the Constitution. According to Marshall, the national government was dependent on the people, not the states, for its powers. Moreover, the Constitution specifically calls for national law to be supreme. Thus, the "instrumentalities," or creations, of the national government—such as the Bank—had to be immune from state challenge or destruction. "The power to tax involves the power to destroy," wrote Marshall in what has become famous language. Such a power, then, was beyond the scope of state authority, because the ability to destroy any federal entity would ultimately make the states supreme over the national government and thereby breach a fundamental constitutional principle.

Gibbons v. *Ogden.*

Gibbons v. *Ogden* (1824) involved a dispute that arose over an action of the New York state legislature granting an exclusive right to operate steamboats on the Hudson River. At the same time, Congress had licensed a ship to sail on the same waters. By the time the case reached the Supreme Court, it was complicated both factually and procedurally. But it addressed one simple, very important question: What was the scope of Congress's authority under the commerce clause? In *Gibbons,* Chief Justice Marshall ruled that Congress's power to regulate interstate commerce included the power to regulate some commercial activities, and that the commerce power had no limits except those specifically found in the Constitution.

Although the Marshall Court boldly supported a strong national government, its Federalist views were tempered by its belief in state sovereignty, or the authority of the states to be supreme in their separate spheres of activity. It was under the leadership of Chief Justice Roger B. Taney, who succeeded Marshall in 1835, that the Supreme Court most fully elaborated the doctrine of dual federalism, which envisions separate functions for the state and national governments.

Taney became Chief Justice in an era of tremendous economic growth and a renewed belief in states' rights. As new business interests and enterprises emerged, they often sought assistance from state governments in the forms of subsidies or tax breaks. In contrast, if businesses needed protection from cheap foreign goods, they sought the assistance of the national government. This assistance generally came in the form of tariffs, which are duties or customs fees charged on merchandise entering into competition with

U.S. goods. The nation was growing at such a rapid pace that the political clout of big business was declining. Changes in many state constitutions extended the right to vote from those who owned property to others, including the poor, farmers, and workers. This expansion of the electorate brought with it a decline in influence for pro-business voters, who tended to view the economy through nationalistic lenses. Chief Justice Taney (1777–1864) saw the Court as above these pressures and as an arbiter of those competing state and nationalistic views. According to Taney:

> This judicial power was justly regarded as indispensable, not merely to maintain the supremacy of the laws of the United States, but also to guard the States from any encroachment upon their reserved rights by the general government.[3]

In a series of cases involving the scope of Congress's power under the commerce clause, the Taney Court further developed doctrines first enunciated by Marshall. The Taney Court emphasized the authority of the states to make laws "necessary to their well being and prosperity."

Slavery-issue Cases. In the 1840s and 1850s, the Supreme Court helped define the respective roles of the state and national governments in the federal system. The comfortable role of the Court as the arbiter of competing national and state interests became troublesome when the Court found itself called upon to deal with the highly political issue of slavery. In cases like *Dred Scott* v. *Sanford* and others, the Court tried to manage the slavery issue by resolving questions of ownership, the status of fugitive slaves, and slavery in the new territories. These cases generally were settled in favor of slavery and states' rights within the framework of dual federalism. Eventually, however, no form of federalism could accommodate the existence of slavery.

Nullification

While the courts were carving out the appropriate roles of each level of government in the federal system, the political debate over states' rights continued to swirl in large part over what is called the doctrine of **nullification,** the purported right of a state to nullify a federal law. As early as 1798, Congress approved the very unpopular Alien and Sedition Acts, which were passed by the Federalist Party–controlled Congress to prevent criticism of the national government (see Chapter 4). Men like Thomas Jefferson and James Madison who opposed the acts suggested that the states had the right to nullify any federal law that *in the opinion of the states* violated the Constitution. The issue, however, was never decided by the Supreme Court because the Alien and Sedition Acts expired before the Court could hear a challenge to them.

The question of nullification came up again in 1828 when the national government enacted a tariff act, most commonly referred to as the "Tariff of Abominations," that raised duties on raw materials, iron, hemp, and flax and reduced protections against imported woolen goods. John C. Calhoun, who served as vice-president from 1825 to 1832 under President Andrew Jackson, broke with Jackson over the tariff bill because it badly affected his home state of South Carolina. Not only did South Carolinians have to pay more for raw materials because of the tariff bill; it was also becoming more and more difficult for them to sell their dwindling crops abroad for a profit. Calhoun thus formulated a theory to justify South Carolina's refusal to abide by the federal tariff law. Later, he used the same nullification theory to justify the Southern states' resistance to national actions to limit slavery.

[3] *Abelman* v. *Booth*, 21 How. 506 (1859).

People of the Past

Dred Scott

Dred Scott was born into slavery in Virginia around 1795. In 1833 he was sold by his original owners, the Blow family, to an army surgeon living in St. Louis. In 1834 he was taken by the doctor to Illinois and later to the Wisconsin Territory, returning to St. Louis in 1838.

Dr. Emerson, the surgeon, died in 1843, and Scott tried to buy his freedom. Before he could, however, he was transferred to Emerson's widow, who moved to New York state, leaving Scott in the custody of his first owners, the Blows. Some of the Blows (Henry Blow later founded the anti-slavery Free Soil Party) and other abolitionists gave money to support a test case seeking Scott's freedom on the ground that his residence in Illinois and later in the Wisconsin Territory, both of which prohibited slavery, in essence made him a free man.

After many delays, in 1857 the U.S. Supreme Court ruled seven to two that Scott was not a citizen and that slaves "were never thought of or spoken of except as property."

At the urging of President James Buchanan, Justice Roger Taney tried to fashion a broad ruling that would settle the slavery question. He ruled that the Congress of the United States lacked the constitutional authority to bar slavery in the territories, thus narrowing the scope of national power while enhancing that of the states. Moreover, for the first time since *Marbury* v. *Madison* (1803) the Court found an act of Congress—the Missouri Compromise—unconstitutional.

Source: Don E. Ferenbacher, "The Dred Scott Case," in *Quarrels That Have Shaped the Constitution,* ed. John A. Garraty (New York: Harper & Row, 1964), Chapter 6.

Calhoun theorized that the federal government was but the agent of the states (the people and the individual state governments) and that the Constitution was simply a compact that provided instructions about how the agent was to act. Thus, according to Calhoun, the U.S. Supreme Court was not competent to pass on the constitutional validity of acts of Congress. Like Congress, the Court was only a branch of a government created by and answerable to the states. Calhoun posited that if the people of any individual state did not like an act of Congress, they could hold a convention to declare that act of Congress null and void. In the state contesting the act, the law would have no force until three-fourths of all of the states ratified an amendment expressly giving Congress that power. Then, if the nullifying state still did not wish to be bound by the new provision, it could secede, or withdraw from the Union. In their fight to keep slavery, which began in the 1850s, the Southern states relied heavily on Calhoun's theories to justify their secession from the Union, which ultimately led to the Civil War.

The Transformation of Dual Federalism

The Civil War forever changed the nature of federalism, as the concept of dual federalism and its emphasis on the role of the states was destroyed along with the Confederacy. In the aftermath of the Civil War and the addition of the Thirteenth, Fourteenth, and Fifteenth Amendments to the Constitution, a profound change occurred in the reunited nation's concept of federalism. After 1861 there was a slow but erratic increase in the role of the national government. According to Daniel J. Elazar, the states and the national government worked together on a variety of projects, including railroad construction, banking, canal building, and ports.[4]

The Supreme Court assisted in this gradual transition to increased federal power, recognizing the need for *national* control over new technological developments such as the telegraph.[5] And, beginning in the 1880s, the Court allowed Congress to regulate many aspects of economic relationships such as the outlawing of monopolies, a type of regulation or power formerly thought to be in the exclusive realm of the states. By the 1890s, passage of laws such as the Interstate Commerce Act and the Sherman Anti-Trust Act allowed Congress to establish itself as the supreme player in a growing national economy.

But the Supreme Court did not consistently enlarge the scope of national power in the pre–New Deal period. In 1895, for example, the United States filed suit against four sugar refiners, alleging that the sale of those four companies would give their buyer control of 98 percent of the U.S. sugar-refining business. The Supreme Court ruled that congressional efforts to control monopolies (through passage of the Sherman Anti-Trust Act) did not give Congress the authority to prevent the sale of these sugar-refining businesses, because manufacturing was not commerce. Therefore, the companies and their actions were beyond the scope of Congress's authority to regulate.

The Great Depression

On October 29, 1929, after steady rises since 1921, the U.S. stock market crashed. The Great Depression of 1929 had actually begun several years before. In 1921 the nation experienced a severe slump in agricultural prices. The construction industry went into decline in 1926, and inventories of consumer goods and automobiles were at an all-time high by the summer of 1929. Bank failures had become common throughout the decade. Thus, when stock prices, which had risen dramatically as a result of widespread speculation, crashed, they took with them the entire national economy.

Rampant unemployment was the hallmark of the Great Depression. To alleviate it and a host of other problems facing the nation, newly elected President Franklin Delano Roosevelt (FDR) proposed in 1933 a variety of innovative programs under the rubric "the New Deal." Just as historical circumstances propelled the writings of Hobbes and Locke discussed in Chapter 1, the economic chaos of the period inspired the New Deal and ushered in a new era in American politics. FDR used the full power of the office of president as well as his highly effective communication skills to sell the American public and Congress on a whole new ideology of government. Not only were the scope and role of national government remarkably altered; so was the relationship between each state, the national government, and the market economy.

The New Deal and a Rapidly Changing Balance of Power

The New Deal period, from 1933 to 1939, was characterized by intense government activity on the national level. It was clear to most politicians that tremendous authority would have to be exercised by the national government to find national solutions to the Depression, which was affecting the citizens of every state in the Union.

In the first few weeks of the legislative session after FDR's inauguration, Congress and the president acted quickly to bolster confidence in the national government. Soon after, Congress enacted an entire series of programs proposed by the president calling for creation of an "alphabetocracy" (agencies known by their initials), including the Federal Emergency Relief Act (FERA), which provided federal emergency relief grants to the

[4] Daniel J. Elazar, *The American Partnership* (Chicago: University of Chicago Press, 1962).
[5] *Pensacola Telegraph* v. *Western Union,* 96 U.S. 1 (1877).

In 1930 during the Depression, an advertisement for free meals for the unemployed at the Willow Tree Restaurant in New York attracted long lines, which were closely watched over by police.

states for unemployment compensation; the Civilian Conservation Corps (CCC), a work relief program for farmers and homeowners; and the Agricultural Adjustment Act (AAA) and the National Industrial Recovery Act (NIRA), which imposed restrictions on production in agriculture and many industries.

As the box on the next page reveals, more than twenty-five separate national programs were enacted as part of the New Deal. These programs tremendously enlarged the scope of the national government. Those who feared this unprecedented use of national power quickly challenged the constitutionality of New Deal programs in court.[6] And at least initially, the Supreme Court often agreed. Through the mid-1930s, the Supreme Court continued to rule that certain aspects of the New Deal went beyond the authority of Congress. In fact, many believe that the Court considered the Depression to be no more than the sum of the economic woes of the individual states and most appropriately handled by the states. The Court's *laissez-faire* or "hands off" attitude toward the economy was reflected in a series of decisions ruling that various aspects of New Deal programs were unconstitutional.

FDR and the Congress were outraged. FDR's frustration with the *laissez-faire* attitude of the Court prompted him to suggest what was ultimately nicknamed his "Court-packing plan." Knowing that there was little he could do to change the minds of those already on the Court, FDR suggested enlarging its size to thirteen justices, which would have given him the opportunity to "pack" the Court with a majority predisposed to the constitutional validity of the New Deal.

Even though Roosevelt was popular, the Court-packing plan was not. Congress and the public were outraged that he even suggested tampering with an institution of government. Nevertheless, the Court appeared to respond to this threat. In 1937, it reversed its series of anti–New Deal decisions, concluding that Congress (and therefore the national government) had the authority to legislate in areas that only *affected* commerce. Congress then used this newly recognized power to legislate in a wide array of areas, including maximum hour and minimum wage laws and child labor. Moreover, the Court soon upheld the constitutionality of the bulk of the massive New Deal relief programs, such as the National Labor Relations Act of 1935, which authorized collective bargaining

[6] Lee Epstein, *Conservatives in Court* (Knoxville: University of Tennessee Press, 1985).

New Deal Legislation

Agricultural Adjustment Act (1938), attempted to stabilize farm prices; succeeded Soil Conservation and Domestic Allotment Act (1936).

Agricultural Adjustment Administration (AAA) (1933), created by Agricultural Adjustment Act and designed to reduce crop surpluses and to restore farmers' purchasing power.

Civilian Conservation Corps (CCC) (1933), agency to give employment on soil, road, and reforestation projects to males between eighteen and twenty-five.

Commodity Credit Corporation (1933), created under AAA to give loans on crops to farmers.

Emergency Banking Relief Act (1933), gave Treasury control of bank openings and gave Roosevelt wide fiscal powers.

Emergency Relief Appropriation Act (1935), created apparatus for federally funded national works programs such as WPA, RA, and REA for unemployed.

Export-Import Bank, established in 1934 to help finance foreign trade.

Farm Credit Administration (FCA), under Farm Credit Act (1933) took over all federal agricultural credit programs.

Federal Communications Commission (FCC), established by Communications Act (1934) to regulate interstate and international telegraph, radio, and cable communications.

Federal Emergency Relief Act (FERA) (1933), authorized grants to states in proportion to amounts spent on relief by the states.

Federal Farm Mortgage Corporation (FFMC), set up in 1934 under FCA to refinance farm debts.

Federal Housing Administration (FHA), established by National Housing Act (1934) to provide home financing and to revive construction of homes.

Home Owners Loan Corporation (HOLC), created under Home Owners Refinancing Act (1933) to refinance non-farm mortgages.

National Industrial Recovery Act (NIRA) (1933), established NRA, PWA, and apparatus for fair trade regulation to revive business and reduce unemployment.

National Labor Relations Board

between unions and employees; the Fair Labor Standards Act of 1938, which prohibited the shipment in interstate commerce of goods made by employees who earned less than the federally mandated minimum wage; and the Agriculture Adjustment Act of 1938, which provided crop subsidies to farmers.

After 1937 the Supreme Court also took a renewed interest in individual liberties, making principles inherent in the Bill of Rights applicable to the states via the Fourteenth Amendment. As we will discuss in Chapter 4, this new interpretation of the Fourteenth Amendment meant that states could no longer abridge most of the rights previously protected from national restraint only by the Bill of Rights.

The Great Depression made necessary new governmental solutions for the problems that were wreaking havoc with the national economy, the economies of the individual states, and the lives of their citizens. In order to improve these economic conditions, all levels of government were forced to work cooperatively with one another. Indeed, most of the New Deal programs relied on states for some sort of participation. The New Deal and its resultant reshaping of federalism also turned away from the locus-of-power questions that were present in early days to a greater emphasis on the role of economics. It

(NLRB), created by National Labor Relations Act (1935) to supervise labor–management relations.

National Recovery Administration (NRA) (1933), administered key programs regulating industry that were authorized by NIRA.

National Youth Administration (NYA) (1935), division of WPA; designed to give employment to people between sixteen and twenty-five.

Public Works Administration (PWA) (1933), established under NIRA to increase employment through projects such as construction of roads and public buildings.

Reconstruction Finance Corporation (1932), Hoover's attempt to revive economy through government loans to financial institutions and railroads.

Resettlement Administration (RA) (1935), designed to reach poor farm families not helped by AAA, through resettlement, loans, and land improvements.

Rural Electrification Administration (REA) (1935), created to bring electricity to isolated areas without private utility service.

Securities and Exchange Commission (SEC), established by Securities Exchange Act (1934) to regulate securities transactions.

Social Security Act (1935), established programs for retirement pensions, unemployment insurance, and other social welfare services.

Soil Conservation and Domestic Allotment Act (1936), unsuccessful substitute for AAA, declared unconstitutional in 1936.

Tennessee Valley Authority (TVA) (1933), corporation created to harness potential of Tennessee Valley and to aid its economic and social welfare.

Works Progress Administration (WPA) (1935), national relief program to use unemployed on public projects; called Works Projects Administration from 1939.

Source: Alex Wellek, ed., *Encyclopedic Dictionary of American Government* (Guilford, Conn.: Dushkin, 1991).

was also a way for members of Congress to bring back "rewards" to their districts, enhancing their prospects for reelection. Thus, as explained in the following section, with the greater concentration of national power that occurred during the New Deal came the expectation that the national government would provide monies to the states.

Models of Federalism

Many view the nature of federalism prior to the Depression and New Deal as well characterized by Morton Grodzins's analogy to a layer cake:

> The federal system is not accurately symbolized by a neat layer cake of three distinct and separate planes. A far more realistic symbol is that of the marble cake. Wherever you slice through it you reveal an inseparable mixture of differently colored ingredients. . . . Vertical and diagonal lines almost obliterate the

horizontal ones, and in some places there are unexpected whirls and an imperceptible merging of colors, so that it is difficult to tell where one ends and the other begins. So it is with federal, state, and local responsibilities in the chaotic marble cake of American government.[7]

This nature of federalism best characterized as a marble cake is often called **cooperative federalism,** a term frequently used to characterize the relationship between the national and state governments that began with the New Deal.

The Changing Nature of Federalism

In the wake of the New Deal, a stronger national government was created, and federalism again experienced a change. States began to take a secondary, albeit important, "cooperative" role in the scheme of governance. Nowhere is this shift in power more clear than in the redevelopment of grant-in-aid programs that began in earnest during the New Deal. It was the tremendous growth in these programs that changed the nature and discussion of federalism from one of "how much power should the national government have" to one of "how much say in the policies of the states can the national government buy."

Grants-in-Aid

As early as 1790, Congress appropriated funds for the states to assume the debts that they had incurred during the Revolutionary War. But it wasn't until the Civil War that Congress enacted its first true grant-in-aid program, in which federal funds were allocated to the states for the support a specific purpose.

Most view the start of this redistribution of funds as beginning with the Morrill Land Grant Act of 1862, which provided for a grant to each state of 30,000 acres of public land for each representative in Congress. Income from this program was to be earmarked for the support of agricultural and mechanical arts colleges. Sixty-nine land-grant colleges—including Texas A&M University, Purdue, and Michigan State University—were established, making this grant-in-aid program the most important single piece of education legislation passed in the United States to that time.

[7] Morton Grodzins, "Centralization and Decentralization in the American Federal System," in *A Nation of States,* ed. Robert A. Goldwin (Chicago: Rand McNally, 1963), pp. 3–4.

Government Spending Before and After the New Deal

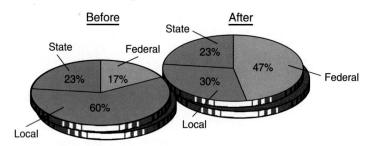

Source: "Significant Features of Fiscal Federalism," in *Advisory Commission on Intergovernmental Relations* (Washington: Government Printing Office, 1979), p. 7.

Purdue University in Indiana is a large land grant school (see text).

Franklin Roosevelt's New Deal program included massive federal dollars for grant-in-aid programs. These grants quickly made the imposition of national goals on the states easier, and once the grant-in-aid idea began to flourish, it often appeared that there could be no stopping it.

By the 1950s and 1960s, grants-in-aid were well entrenched and they often defined federal–state relationships. Moreover, they were frequently viewed by liberal Northern Democrats as a means to bypass the more conservative state legislatures that represented the rural districts of Southern and Midwestern states. ''Bricks and mortar'' education bills, for example, were made to encourage increased state spending on public education. Still, until the 1960s, most grants-in-aid were constructed by or with the cooperation of the states and were designed to assist the states in furthering their traditional responsibilities in the federal system.

In 1964, the Democratic administration of President Lyndon B. Johnson (1963–69) launched its renowned War on Poverty, a broad attempt to combat poverty and discrimination. Federal funds were channeled to states, local governments, and even directly to citizen action groups in an effort to alleviate social ills that the states had been unable to

Then and Now
The Sheppard–Towner Maternity Act of 1923

The Sheppard–Towner Maternity Act (STMA) was enacted by Congress at the urging of women's rights groups who were still flush with the success of their efforts to win the right to vote. The Act called for Congress to make money available to the states for pre- and postnatal care for mothers and their infants. The program was passed largely due to findings that the United States had the highest infant mortality rate in the Western world. Those who had opposed suffrage challenged this first grant-in-aid program in court, arguing that Congress had surpassed its authority under the commerce clause. In *Frothingham* v. *Mellon* (1923) the Supreme Court ruled that federal taxpayers lacked standing to challenge the constitutional validity of these kinds of programs because their interest in the program *as taxpayers* was too remote to give them a sufficient stake in the outcome of the case. Thus, to this day, most congressionally enacted aid programs remain out of the reach of taxpayer challenge.

remedy. Again, the move to fund local groups was made by the most liberal members of Congress to bypass not only conservative state legislatures but also conservative city mayors and councils in cities like Chicago. It was hoped that these new kinds of grants-in-aid would foster a market for national liberally endorsed programs by allowing a variety of participants to come forward to claim federal dollars.

These new grants altered the fragile balance of power that had been at the core of most older grant-in-aid programs. During the Johnson administration, the national government began to use grants-in-aid as a way to further what federal (and not state) officials perceived to be national needs. Thus, grants based on what states wanted or believed they needed began to decline, while those fostering national goals increased dramatically. Moreover, by 1970 federal aid amounted to 19 percent of all state and local government spending; this further enhanced state dependency on the national government.

As Congress increased the number of programs for which cities could be eligible, many critics argued that the system was out of hand. By 1971, there were more than 500 different types of grants-in-aid available, in contrast to only 51 in 1964.[8]

Federal aid to cities and states tripled from 1965 to 1980. One political scientist went as far as to say that in the world of bake-shop metaphors, a "new special" was in the offing to describe this federalism—"fruitcake federalism." Not only was it formless, but it also offered (political) plums to all.

Negative reactions to this far-reaching federalism was not long in coming. States simply wanted more control. Many believed that the situation had produced ridiculous consequences as states and local governments found themselves applying for federal money they didn't even particularly need. These "federal-aid junkies," as one commentator called them, could not resist the lure of federal funds, no matter what the nature of the grant.[9]

Revenue Sharing

In 1971, Richard Nixon proposed the State and Local Assistance Act, noting that "state and local governments need federal money to spend, but they also need greater freedom in spending it." Thus, a program of **revenue sharing,** which was intended to be a new method of redistributing money back to the states was announced. Instead of money going to the states with "strings attached" for specific programs, the intent of revenue

---

[8] Advisory Commission on Intergovernmental Relations, "The Federal Role in the Federal System: The Dynamics of Growth" (Washington: 1980), pp. 120–121.

[9] Samuel H. Beer, "The Modernization of American Federalism," *Publius* 3 (Fall 1973), pp. 74–79.

Governor Lowell Weicker (Ind.-Conn.) in 1991. As federal money to the states diminished in the late 1980s and early 1990s, Weicker proposed Connecticut's first-ever income tax to raise needed funds. The measure was extremely unpopular, but Weicker successfully vetoed several legislative counterproposals, and as of this writing the tax remains in place.

Figure 3-1   The Changing Face of Federal Aid

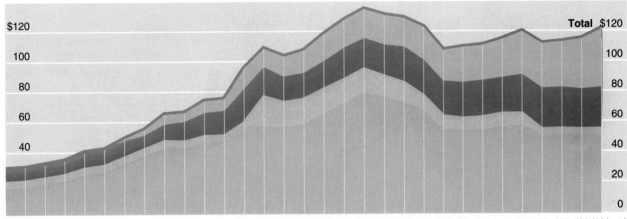

Payments to Individuals   Medicaid   Other Welfare

All Other Aid   Revenue Sharing   Grants to Governments
Includes funds for highways,
the environment, housing,
job training, public health, etc.

Source: Rockefeller Institute of Government, "Legacy of the 80's for States and Cities: Big Bills and Few Options" (*The New York Times,* December 30, 1990, National Edition, p. 10). Reprinted by permission.

sharing was to give money to the states and local governments to spend where they believed the money was most needed.

Revenue sharing was popular with states, which in 1972 were in fiscal crisis, but eventually Congress became disenchanted with the program, over which it had little control. By 1987 it had been phased out completely, as illustrated in Figure 3-1.

The growth of government spending revealed in Figure 3-1 was one reason that Jimmy Carter, a former governor of Georgia, was able to successfully run for president in 1976 as an "outsider" opposed to big government and federal grants mandating state policies. Grants to the states did drop (in terms of real dollars) during the Carter presidency. Still, the impact of his reduction of federal spending on social programs was insufficient to override the rest of his political woes. Ronald Reagan was elected in 1980 pledging a "New Federalism."

Reagan's New Federalism

President Reagan's New Federalism had many facets. The "Reagan Revolution" and its return to conservative principles was typified by the administration's deregulation of many industries (see Chapter 8). President Reagan and his supporters fervently believed that the government should not be in the business of regulating most businesses. "Hack, chop, crunch!" were the sounds of the early 1980s as Reagan's regulatory appointees tried to strip away years of federal regulations.[10]

One area in which deregulation caused problems was the savings and loan industry.

---

[10] Quoted in Kevin Phillips, *The Politics of the Rich and the Poor: Wealth and the American Electorate in the Reagan Aftermath* (New York: HarperCollins, 1991), p. 93.

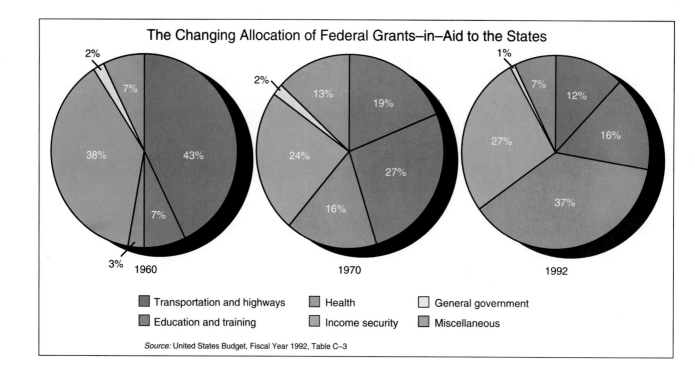

The Changing Allocation of Federal Grants–in–Aid to the States

1960
- 2%
- 7%
- 38%
- 43%
- 7%
- 3%

1970
- 2%
- 13%
- 19%
- 24%
- 27%
- 16%

1992
- 1%
- 7%
- 12%
- 16%
- 27%
- 37%

■ Transportation and highways   ■ Health   □ General government

■ Education and training   ■ Income security   ■ Miscellaneous

Source: United States Budget, Fiscal Year 1992, Table C–3

During the Reagan administration, federal regulators ceased to keep as watchful an eye on lending practices as they had in the past. Prior to 1982, federally chartered savings and loan associations (S&Ls) were required to place almost all of their loans in home mortgages, traditionally a safe investment. But in 1982, when high interest rates made low-interest home mortgages fairly undesirable for banks, new federal laws allowed savings and loans to invest their funds more freely in riskier ventures. As banks had in the 1920s, many S&Ls proceeded to gamble on questionable commercial ventures—and many lost, saddling the American people with a $300 billion price tag for federal nonsupervision of the S&L industry.[11] In the wake of massive deregulation, however,

[11] Ernest F. Hollings, "Bush's Real Problem—the Ruins of Reaganism," *The Washington Post,* April 30, 1989, p. C-1.

April 20, 1989: The sign for the defunct Silverado Banking Company is taken down. As a troubled savings and loan (S&L) institution, Silverado was purchased, merged into another bank, and renamed.

Two Types of Grants-in-Aid

Block Grants   U.S. government gives money to the states for a general purpose, such as education. No strings attached. Preferred by states.

Categorical Grants   U.S. government gives money for more specific purposes and has more control.

Formula Grants   Generally are designated to apply to certain geographical areas within states; local governments must compete for dollars.

Project Grants   Government units and agencies apply for projects that federal agencies have announced. Generally reflect agency agendas; very competitive.

several states did step in to fill the void, but their actions often made it difficult for large corporations that had offices in several states to comply with the morass of differing state regulations that resulted.

President Reagan, picking up on Richard Nixon's special revenue-sharing plan, persuaded Congress to consolidate many categorical grants-in-aid into far fewer, less restrictive block grants. Seventy-seven categorical grants covering a range of programs—including health care, child welfare, and crime—were subsumed by nine block grants. Initially, the states were happy with this action—until they learned that the administration also proposed to cut back on the financing of these programs by 25 percent. In 1980, federal funds made up 26 percent of state expenditures and 17.7 percent of city and county budgets. By 1990, however, federal dollars were 18 percent of state and 6.4 percent of city and county budgets, respectively.

Many programs cut by the Reagan administration involved those that aided the "have nots" of society and disproportionately affected blacks. Throughout the 1960s and even into the 1970s, the poor and less fortunate were often helped by various grants-in-aid programs. Aid to Families with Dependent Children (AFDC); unemployment compensation; the Women, Infants, and Children (WIC) program, which provides food and other assistance to pregnant women and mothers with young children—all were intended to provide minimal levels of subsistence for the poor or those who were temporarily out of work. During the Reagan years, subsidies for these programs decreased as eligibility requirements were increasingly tightened in an effort to balance the national budget.

AFDC, for example, is a program funded largely by the national government. States must meet several conditions to participate, but there is no requirement that states must pay each recipient equally. Although it would be unrealistic to expect a family in rural Alabama to need as much money to live as one that lived in New York City or San Francisco, in 1991 a family of four in Alabama received $155 a month from AFDC while the same family in Alaska received $990, as illustrated in Table 3-2.

AFDC programs were cut by 26 percent between 1977 and 1989. In 1988 in thirty-one states, the maximum amount for a family of three was less than one-half of the amount fixed as the federally defined poverty level. In 1973, AFDC, the largest federal aid program, covered eighty-four out of every one hundred poor children living in poverty; by 1987, it covered only sixty of every one hundred. Although pledges were made that no American would be hurt by budget cuts because they included a "safety net" for the "truly poor," many soon came to realize that the net had more than a few holes.

In 1988, when presidential candidate George Bush called for "a kinder, gentler America," many believed that he would seek to alter the trend of Reagan's "New Federalism"

Table 3-2   Aid to Families with Dependent Children

STATES	MAXIMUM BENEFIT PER MONTH	STATES	MAXIMUM BENEFIT PER MONTH
Alabama	$155	Montana	445
Alaska	990	Nebraska	435
Arizona	353	Nevada	390
Arkansas	247	New Hampshire	575
California	824	New Jersey	488
Colorado	432	New Mexico	373
Connecticut	792	New York	687
Delaware	407	North Carolina	297
District of Columbia	522	North Dakota	491
Florida	346	Ohio	413
Georgia	330	Oregon	541
Hawaii	760	Oklahoma	423
Idaho	357	Pennsylvania	514
Illinois	414	Rhode Island	632
Indiana	346	South Carolina	252
Iowa	495	South Dakota	429
Kansas	470	Tennessee	238
Kentucky	285	Texas	221
Louisiana	234	Utah	470
Maine	569	Vermont	762
Maryland	489	Virginia	410
Massachusetts	628	Washington	624
Michigan	665	West Virginia	312
Minnesota	621	Wisconsin	617
Mississippi	144	Wyoming	390
Missouri	342		

Source: Compiled by Representative Ben Jones's (D-Ga.) Office, January 1991.

policies. But severe budget constraints have made it nearly impossible to restore spending to pre-Reagan levels.

In 1991 Bush did, however, propose what he termed a "New Paradigm." In his fiscal 1992 budget he urged Congress to create a mega-block grant program replacing many categorical grants and consolidating $15 billion in funds allocated to the states. Under this program states would lose an estimated $27.3 billion in federal funds over the next five years. Financially troubled New York would lose $3 billion over the five-year period; other large states, like California and Texas, at least $1 billion. But governors generally hailed the proposed continuation of New Federalism as a means of returning power to the states.

Although grants-in-aid continued during the Reagan and into the Bush years, the discussion of these grants and the philosophies behind their inception forced the states to rethink their position in the federal system. Today, many Republicans, who generally

New Federalism and Budget Cuts Hurt Blacks More Than Whites

It was not quite an accident, nor was it planned, but the budget cuts that President Reagan steamed through Congress in his first two years in office have apparently had a far greater impact on black than on white Americans.

The reason lies in one of the fundamental facts of modern American life: blacks are much more reliant on the federal government than is generally realized.

One out of every four blacks in America is now enrolled in Medicaid, the largest federal welfare program. One in four gets food stamps, the second-largest program. One out of five receives aid to families with dependent children (AFDC), the largest welfare program that pays cash. One of every seven lives in federally subsidized housing.

And in 1981, when Reagan moved to rein in the federal budget, it was precisely these means-tested programs for the poor that came in for some of the sharpest cuts.

. . . [I]n fiscal year 1983, spending was cut 5 percent, food stamps 10 percent and AFDC 13 percent, while the major subsidized housing program was brought to a halt.

Other smaller programs of disproportionate interest to blacks also were hit hard. Job spending was cut 58 percent, child nutrition 29 percent, educational aid to the poor 19 percent, and college student aid 11 percent.

The social "safety net" Reagan promised to keep in place in his early months in office to protect the truly needy did not include most of these programs.

Source: Excerpted from Milton Coleman, "The Politics of Fairness, Part 1: The Budget" (*The Washington Post,* December 4, 1983, Sunday Final Edition, Sec. 1, A–1).

favor a more limited role for the national government, attack grants-in-aid as a way for the national government to annex powers reserved to the states under the Tenth Amendment.

Some would argue that the original reason for these grants—perceived overrepresentation of rural interests in state legislatures, for example—has been removed as the Supreme Court ordered redistricting to ensure better representation of urban and suburban interests. Moreover, state legislatures have become more professional, state and local bureaucracies more responsive, and the delivery of services better. In fact, the greatest growth in government hiring has been in the state and local sectors.

While many argue that these grants are an effective way to raise the level of services provided to the poor, others attack the grants as imposing national priorities on the states. Policy decisions are largely made at the national level, and the states, always in search of funds, are forced to follow the priorities of the national government. States find it very hard to resist the lure of grants, even though many require some sort of state investment of matching or proportional funds.

In response to these criticisms, Republican administrators have supported alternative types of grants, such as block grants, which fall between revenue sharing and grants-in-aid in terms of "strings" that are attached. These alternatives have returned some power to the states, but the massive dollar amounts devoted to federal aid to the states have significantly altered the balance of power in the federal system. It also has created a keen competition among the states for federal funds.

Forcing a National Policy: The Twenty-one-Year-Old Drinking Age

In 1984, only sixteen U.S. senators voted "Nay" on an amendment to the Surface Transportation Act of 1982, a provision designed to withhold 5 percent of federal highway funds from states that did not prohibit those under the age of twenty-one from drinking alcoholic beverages. Because the national government did not have the power to regulate the drinking age, it resorted to the "carrot and stick" nature of federalism. Unless a state raised its drinking age to twenty-one by 1988, Congress would withhold 10 percent of all federal highway grants to the recalcitrant states. In other words, no raised drinking age, no federal dollars. Even most conservative Republican senators—those most attached to the notion of states' rights—supported the provision in spite of the fact that it imposed a national ideal on the states. And, after congressional action, the bill was signed into law by another conservative long concerned with the expansion of national power to the detriment of the states—Ronald Reagan. Ironically, however, states still retain the power to decide who is legally drunk. And, the blood alcohol content required for determining legal intoxication varies dramatically from state to state.

This "carrot and stick" approach was also used to force the states to lower their maximum speed laws to fifty-five miles per hour during the energy crisis of the 1970s. It is by laws such as these that the national government exercises the full force of its power over the states.

The Intergovernmental Lobby

Competition for federal funds has caused state and local governments to hire lobbyists to advance their interests in Washington. School districts, schools systems, cities, states, police chiefs, hospital administrators, and many more all form part of the intergovernmental lobby. Many of these groups have either banded with others or set up offices in Washington to lobby for funds. Many individual cities have offices in the District of Columbia to represent their interests. Others hire full-time or part-time lobbyists to work solely on their behalf to keep abreast of funding opportunities or to lobby for programs that could be useful back home. In the 1990s, searches for federal dollars can be nearly as futile as Ponce de León's search for the Fountain of Youth.

Literally thousands of governments exist in the United States and most have a Washington, D.C. presence. Lobbying puts states in competition with one another as well as with local governments within their boundaries.

Competition is especially keen now that the cumulative impact of "New Federalism" is being felt. At the same time that aid to the state and local governments was declining, states were reluctant to raise taxes.

This "New Federalism" also has changed the nature of politics in the states. Caught by revenue shortfalls caused by the recession of the early 1990s, legal requirements mandating balanced budgets, and growing demands for new social services and the replacement of ones formerly provided by the federal government, governors around the nation are in trouble as they slash services and ask for tax increases. "A governor with

Number of Governments in the U.S. in 1987

U.S. government	1
State governments	50
Local governments	
County	3,042
Municipal (city)	19,200
Township and town	16,691
School district	14,721
Special district	29,532
Total	83,237

Source: U.S. Bureau of the Census, *Statistical Abstract of the U.S.: 1990*, 110th ed. (Washington: 1990).

How Well Did Your State Do in the Scramble for Federal Dollars?

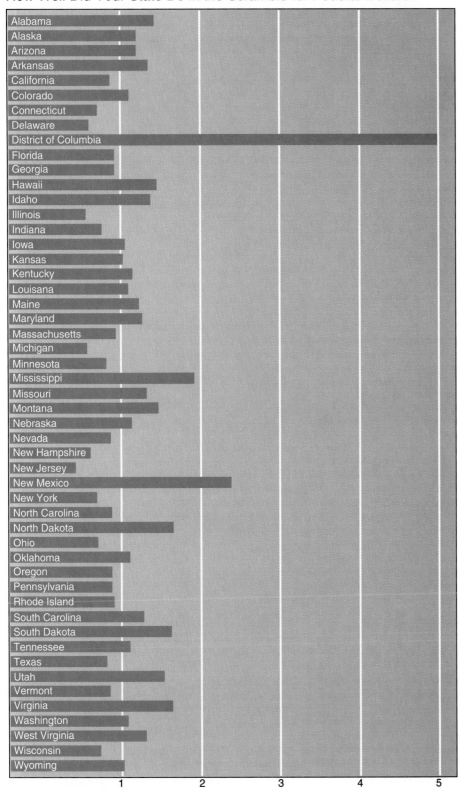

Percent of Federal Taxes from State Residents Returned to State Governments

Source: Harold W. Stanley and Richard G. Niemi, Vital Statistics on American Politics, 3rd ed. (Washington: Congressional Quarterly Press, 1991) Table 10-5, pp. 320–321.

President Bush met with the National Governors' Association in January 1991 and encountered heated debate over the levels of federal funding for state programs.

over a 50 percent approval is more the exception than the rule now, and that just wasn't true three or four years ago," noted one pollster in 1991.[12]

Blaming governors for the effects of New Federalism first became evident in the fall of 1990 when an unprecedented ten incumbent governors chose not to seek reelection and an additional six were defeated. In contrast, only one incumbent senator was ousted. In Virginia, where first-term Democratic Governor L. Douglas Wilder pursued brutal spending cuts to avoid a tax hike, one poll found that 61 percent of state residents disapproved of his performance. In Connecticut, where first-term independent Governor Lowell P. Weicker, Jr., proposed major spending cuts and the imposition of an income tax, 63 percent of those polled in 1991 viewed him unfavorably.

Thus, the anti-regulation and fiscal policies of New Federalism have essentially altered the economic relationship between the national government and the states. Ironically, its plan to return power to the states has actually left the states in a weaker position, at least for the time being. In 1991, legislators in forty-six of the fifty states narrowly avoided missing deadlines for new budget authorizations. Most states are turning to tax increases rather than massive cuts in services. This may eventually allow them to reassert their authority over areas originally left to them in the Constitution and Bill of Rights.

There are parallels to the New Federalism in other countries, some of which are anything but federal. For example, governments in unitary Britain and federal Germany, discouraged by decades of mediocre policy results and tight budgets, drastically overhauled many social and economic programs in the 1980s by combining deep expenditure cuts with a devolution of tasks to subnational governments. National politicians relieved themselves of the political burdens of responsibility with rhetorical flourishes about the values of local democracy, initiative, and autonomy.

Federalism and the Supreme Court

The wealth of the national government has not been the only factor that has altered the nature of the federal system. Historically, the Supreme Court also has played an important role in the configuration of power between the national government and the states,

---

[12] Quoted in David E. Anderson, "Conservative Think Tanks Go Local," *UPI,* June 10, 1991, BC Cycle.

from the days of Marshall's Federalist opinions to *laissez-faire* and then the New Deal. The Supreme Court has periodically interjected itself into numerous areas that the Framers intended to be left within the authority of the states, most notably education and the electoral process.

Education. Although early Congresses tried to encourage the states to develop their university and educational systems through grants-in-aid programs like the Morrill Land Grant Act of 1862, through the 1950s, education was usually considered a function of the states under their police powers, which allow them to provide for public health and welfare. In 1954, in *Brown* v. *Topeka Board of Education,* however, that tradition was shattered when the Supreme Court ruled that state-mandated segregation has no place in the public schools. (See Chapter 5 for greater detail.) *Brown* forced the states to begin to dismantle their school systems and ultimately led the federal courts to play an important role in monitoring the efforts of state and local governments to dismantle the vestiges of segregation.

The Electoral Process. A decade after *Brown,* the Supreme Court also involved itself with one of the most sacred areas of state regulation in the federal system—the conduct of elections. Convention attendees had, as a trade-off for giving the national government more powers, allowed the states control over the qualifications for voting in national elections as well as control over how elections were to be conducted. But in *Wesberry* v. *Sanders* (1964), the Court began to limit the states' ability to control the process of congressional redistricting. In 1966, the Supreme Court invalidated the poll tax, a state-imposed tax of one to five dollars imposed on those who wished to vote. The poll tax was widely used in the Southern states as an effective barrier to the poor, who often were black.[13] Most Southern legislators assailed the Court's decision, viewing it as an illegal interference with their powers to regulate elections under the Constitution and as a violation of state sovereignty. More recently, in 1991 even the increasingly conservative U.S. Supreme Court ruled in two cases that at-large elections of state Supreme Court and trial judges impermissibly diluted the voting strengths of blacks and Hispanics in violation of the Voting Right Act of 1965,[14] thus further limiting the authority of the states.

The Performance of State Functions. In 1974, Congress extended the provisions of the Fair Labor Standards Act (FLSA), which regulated minimum wages and maximum hours for most workers, to cover state and local employees. The National League of Cities, a clearinghouse association of the National Governors' Conference, and several individual states and cities challenged the new measures, arguing that Congress had no authority to regulate the wages of state employees. In *National League of Cities* v. *Usury* (1976) a closely divided Court (five to four), in an opinion written by Associate Justice (later Chief Justice) William Rehnquist, decided that Congress had overstepped its authority. Rehnquist noted that although the Supreme Court had in 1941 upheld the constitutionality of the FLSA and Congress's authority to set minimum wages for employees in the private sector, the 1974 amendment, including state and local employees, had gone too far. For the majority, he wrote:

> This congressionally imposed displacement of state decisions may substantially restructure traditional ways in which the local governments have arranged their affairs. *[Thus] Congress has sought to wield its power in a fashion that would impair the States' "ability to function effectively in a federal system."* (emphasis added)[15]

---

[13]*Harper* v. *Virginia Board of Elections,* 383 U.S. 663 (1966).

[14]*Chisolm* v. *Roemer,* 1991 LEXIS 3627 and *Houston Lawyers' Association* v. *Texas,* 1991 LEXIS 3628.

[15]426 U.S. 833 (1976).

Justice Rehnquist was particularly troubled that the legislation would impair the states' ability to deliver services to their citizens, and thus would affect their ability to function as states. The case was viewed as especially important because it was the first major instance of the Court's establishing any limits on national authority over the states since before the New Deal era. States' rights advocates believed that it was the kind of brake that needed to be applied to the federalism train gone wild. Conservatives hailed the decision as the dawn of a "New Federalism."

Ironically, *National League of Cities* was reversed by an equally divided Court (five to four) just nine years later in *Garcia* v. *San Antonio Metropolitan Authority* (1985).[16] This case also involved the constitutionality of federally imposed minimum wage and maximum hour provisions as they applied to state governments. In *Garcia,* the Court ruled that Congress has broad power to impose its will on state and local governments, even in areas that traditionally have been left to their discretion. The Court ruled that the "political process ensures that laws that unduly burden the states will not be promulgated" and that it should not be up to an "unelected" judiciary to preserve state powers. Furthermore, the majority of the Court concluded that the Tenth Amendment, which had been added to the Constitution as part of the Bill of Rights to ensure that any powers not given to the national government were reserved for the states, was, at least for the time being, essentially meaningless!

Federalism and the New Supreme Court

When Ronald Reagan left Washington to return to California at the end of his second term of office in January 1989, he left a lasting legacy. While president he had had the opportunity to appoint not only the Chief Justice, William Rehnquist, but also Associate Justices Sandra Day O'Connor, Antonin Scalia, and Anthony Kennedy. All were staunch conservatives, but O'Connor in particular, as a former state legislator and then state court judge, held a strong belief that the national government had intruded far too many times on the powers of the states. The Bush appointments of David Souter, a former state attorney general and state court judge, and Clarence Thomas, a leading black conservative, solidify that new, conservative, states' rights–oriented majority.

[16]469 U.S. 528 (1985).

In the wake of the Supreme Court's decision in *Webster* v. *Reproductive Health Services* (1989), individual state governments have taken a more active role in setting guidelines (which may be restrictions) for abortion access. Here, Wichita residents rally for greater restrictions.

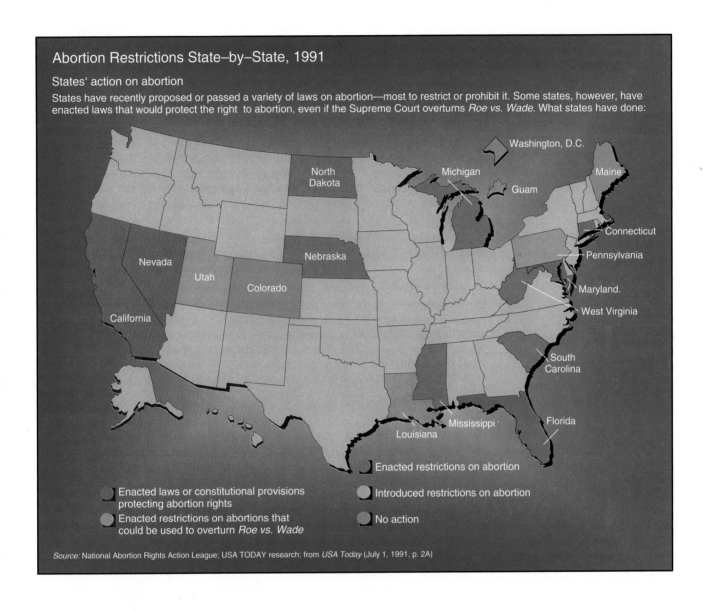

Abortion Restrictions State–by–State, 1991

States' action on abortion

States have recently proposed or passed a variety of laws on abortion—most to restrict or prohibit it. Some states, however, have enacted laws that would protect the right to abortion, even if the Supreme Court overturns *Roe vs. Wade*. What states have done:

Washington, D.C.

North Dakota

Michigan

Guam

Maine

Connecticut

Pennsylvania

Nevada

Utah

Nebraska

Maryland.

Colorado

West Virginia

California

South Carolina

Mississippi

Florida

Louisiana

Enacted restrictions on abortion

Enacted laws or constitutional provisions protecting abortion rights

Introduced restrictions on abortion

Enacted restrictions on abortions that could be used to overturn *Roe vs. Wade*

No action

Source: National Abortion Rights Action League; USA TODAY research; from *USA Today* (July 1, 1991, p. 2A)

Mario M. Cuomo, the liberal Democratic New York governor, has referred to the decisions of this new Court as creating "a kind of new judicial federalism." According to Cuomo, this new federalism can be characterized by the Court's withdrawal of "rights and emphases previously thought to be national."[17] Perhaps most illustrative of this trend was the Supreme Court's decision in *Webster* v. *Reproductive Health Services* (1989)[18] in which the Court gave new latitude—and even encouragement—to the states to fashion more restrictive abortion laws. Since *Webster,* numerous states have enacted new restrictive laws. Moreover, the Court has consistently upheld the authority of the individual states to limit a minor's access to an abortion through imposition of parental consent or notification laws. Other Democrats, including Cuomo, charged that the Bush administration had increasingly handed back to the individual states the financial

[17] Marianne Arneberg, "Cuomo Assails Judicial Hodgepodge," *Newsday,* August 15, 1990, p. 15.
[18] 492 U.S. 490 (1989).

responsibility for what they view as national problems—crime, drugs, teen pregnancy, housing, and education—without funds.

For the most part, recent decisions of the U.S. Supreme Court support Cuomo's characterization of the role of the national government in the newest federalism. But, in spite of its conservative, pro–states' rights leanings, the Court has surprised many with some of its recent decisions. Even before Justice Souter was added to the Court, for example, it upheld the ruling of a lower court judge who had imposed a local tax increase to finance a school desegregation order.[19] National authority also received a boost when the Court ruled that a federal law that limits the authority of state governors to withhold consent for state National Guards' active duty does not violate the militia clauses of the U.S. Constitution. Several governors had argued that the Constitution reserved the power to train militia to the states.[20]

Toward Reform

Inconsistent Court decisions—on the one hand returning costly programs and problems to the states while on the other hand continuing to order costly educational and penal programs—have prompted fifteen state legislatures to approve resolutions calling for amending the Constitution to give the states more authority in relation to the federal government. With the strong support of the Bush administration, these states have proposed two avenues of change, largely in response to recent Court decisions. One seeks to allow the states to initiate amendments without calling a constitutional convention. The other would change the Tenth Amendment to direct the state courts to determine whether the Court had overstepped its boundaries with respect to the states. In the wake of political actions such as these, and many of the justices' pro–states' rights views, it is likely that the newly constituted Rehnquist Court will continue to be a prime mover in efforts to readjust the balance of power and allocation of responsibilities between the national, state, and local governments.

The state and local governments are likely to continue to seek more funds from the national government, but with fewer strings attached. If indeed problems like teen pregnancy, low literacy rates, and crime are local problems with national implications, it will be in the interest of the national government to shore up and even try to equalize aid to the states. The whole can be only as strong as the sum of its parts. Whether politicians with vested interests and definable constituencies can see that and agree on reform in an era of shrinking revenues remains to be seen.

Summary

The inadequacies of the confederate form of government created by the Articles of Confederation led the Framers to create an entirely new, federal system of government. From that summer in Philadelphia until today, the tension between the national and state governments has always been at the core of our federal system.

The Framers originally believed that by dividing governmental powers, no one government, especially the national or federal one, would ever get too powerful. But over the years as the nation grew and faced internal crises—such as the Civil War and the Great Depression—as well as external threats in the form of major wars, the power of the national government increased to meet those emergencies.

[19] *Missouri* v. *Jenkins,* 495 U.S. 33 (1990).
[20] *Perpich* v. *Department of Defense,* 110 S. Ct. 2418 (1990).

In the 1960s, new federal social programs were begun, further binding the states to the national government as it became a major source of revenue for the states. Presidents Nixon, Carter, Reagan, and Bush all have tried to stop the runaway train of national influence and power over functions many argue are best left to the states. To cater to the needs of the states, there is a tendency today to allow states a greater say in federal programs. There is also, however, increasing competition among states for the scarcer federal dollars available.

The increasingly conservative Supreme Court of the 1980s began to take some moves to alter the relationship between the states and the national government. While the federal courts generally require that state mandates and conditions on aid be uniform, they are increasingly allowing states more leeway in the kinds of programs—even laws—they may implement.

Key Terms

federal system	dual federalism	necessary and proper clause
federalism	patronage	elastic clause
concurrent powers	republicanism	nullification
enumerated powers	supremacy clause	cooperative federalism
implied powers	commerce clause	revenue sharing
bill of attainder	express powers	

Suggested Readings

Bowman, Ann O'M, and Richard Kearney. *The Resurgence of the States.* Englewood Cliffs, N.J.: Prentice Hall, 1986.

Derthick, Martha. *The Influence of Federal Grants.* Cambridge, Mass.: Harvard University Press, 1970.

Elazar, Daniel. *American Federalism: A View from the States.* New York: Harper & Row, 1984.

Grodzins, Morton. *The American System.* Chicago: Rand McNally, 1966.

Hamilton, Christopher, and Donald T. Wells. *Federalism, Power, and Political Economy: A New Theory of Federalism's Impact on American Life.* Englewood Cliffs, N.J.: Prentice Hall, 1990.

Peterson, Paul, Barry Rabe, and Kenneth K. Wong. *When Federalism Works.* Washington: Brookings Institution, 1986.

Phillips, Kevin. *The Politics of Rich and Poor: Wealth and the American Electorate in the Reagan Aftermath.* New York: HarperCollins, 1990.

Riker, William H. *Federalism: Origin, Operation, Significance.* Boston: Little, Brown, 1964.

*T*he constitution of this commonwealth . . . provides *that people have a right to* FREEDOM OF SPEECH . . . How long those rights will apertain to you, you yourselves are called upon to say. . . .

Samuel Bryan

"CENTINEL" NO. 1:

Bryan, an Anti-Federalist, argued against the U.S. Constitution because it did not include guarantees of free speech. Because the Pennsylvania Constitution did include such guarantees, Bryan warned Philadelphians that they risked losing hard-won freedoms.

CHAPTER 4

Civil Liberties

When Bryan penned the words opening this chapter on October 5, 1787, he voiced the fears not only of other Anti-Federalists but also of some supporters of the proposed Constitution. Although the Framers—and Alexander Hamilton and James Madison in particular—argued that the checks and balances proposed in the Constitution prevented the national government from usurping the civil liberties of Americans, many others were not so certain. In 1787, most state constitutions explicitly protected a variety of personal liberties—speech, religion, freedom from unreasonable searches and seizures, and trial by jury, among others. It was clear that the national government proposed by the Constitution would redistribute power between the national government and the states in the new federal system. Without specific prohibitions, could the national government be trusted to uphold the rights already enjoyed by its citizens?

Recognition of the increased power that would be held by the new national government led Anti-Federalists to stress the need for a bill of rights to apply to the national government. Note that the Bill of Rights—as drafted by the Framers—applies literally only to the national government. In 1790, it was the power of the national government, not that of the states, that the people feared. Most people believed that they could control the actions of their own state legislators, and most state constitutions included bills of rights.

In this chapter we trace the ratification of the Bill of Rights and the way the **civil liberties** it specifies have evolved since its ratification. Civil liberties are the personal rights and freedoms guaranteed to be immune from government restriction by law, constitution, or judicial interpretation. When we discuss civil liberties like those in the Bill of Rights we are concerned with limits on what governments can and cannot do. In contrast, when we discuss **civil rights,** the subject of Chapter 5, we are concerned with rights—to be free from governmental discrimination based on race or sex, for example—that governments must provide their citizens.

Although the Bill of Rights applies only to the national government, since its ratification many individuals and groups have pressed the Supreme Court to apply its restraints to the states. Over the years the Supreme Court has made some, but not all, of the rights guaranteed by the Bill of Rights binding on the states.

Throughout this chapter we explore the impact of the courts, police, public opinion, political settings, and legislatures on our concept of civil liberties. Changes in Supreme Court personnel, in particular, have made and will continue to make a major difference in this regard.

Although the Bill of Rights and its ratification may seem far removed from or even irrelevant to your life, the liberties contained in it are central to many of today's most controversial issues. Can prayer be a part of a public high school graduation? Can a student be expelled from college for shouting racial slurs on the quad? Can a state prohibit

Racism on campus: At Dartmouth College in 1987, college officials disciplined several students for tearing down shanties erected by anti-apartheid demonstrators. College administrators are increasingly finding themselves between diverse factions of students claiming their First Amendment rights.

physicians from performing an abortion unless it is necessary to save the life of the mother? Can the federal government ban physicians working in federally funded clinics from informing pregnant patients about abortion? Even though the authors of the Bill of Rights probably never envisioned that it would be applied to such situations, each of these issues has found its way into the courts and presents important civil liberties questions.

Complicating our discussion of civil liberties is the notion of rights in conflict. Long ago, political observers learned that whereas many Americans are strong proponents of the Bill of Rights in principle, they are sharply divided when it comes to actual cases involving civil liberties.[1] Although we believe in free speech, we may not want Ku Klux Klan (KKK) members or Nazis parading down our streets or a porn shop opening on our corner. Similarly, we may believe that Americans should be free from unreasonable searches and seizures, but many complain when criminals are released because the results of an illegal search cannot be used in their trials. The courts are repeatedly called upon to address what can be perceived as conflicting liberties. Does one group's right not to be harassed by the KKK outweigh the rights of KKK members to parade or speak their minds? Are the personal freedoms of victims of violent crime outweighed by the constitutional protections guaranteed to their attackers? Issues like these come continually before the courts and legislatures. The way these two branches of government resolve these issues—how the Bill of Rights is interpreted—reflects a delicate balance of many forces, including historical events, technological changes, and personnel changes on the U.S. Supreme Court.

In contrast to the United States, not all democracies have provided a range of civil liberties in a bill of rights that stands beyond the reach of government. Britain's unwritten constitution, for example, makes no such provisions. In that country, freedoms of speech, press, religion, and association reside in the rulings of the common law courts and are very susceptible to curtailment or expansion by Parliament. In the late 1980s, Parliament passed two pieces of legislation at the request of the government of Prime Minister Margaret Thatcher that, viewed from an American vantage point, infringed on civil liberties. First, the media were prohibited from broadcasting live interviews with or quoting directly from members of Sinn Fein, the political wing of the provisional Irish Republican Army (IRA). Although British media have developed techniques for circumventing these restrictions, they have had to accept them as the law of the land. Such an infringement on the free press would be highly unlikely in the United States, where the courts would strike down an act of this kind. Second, in another action directed against the IRA, Parliament passed a law that for all intents and purposes allowed the courts to interpret the silence of an accused defendant as an implicit admission of guilt. Such a law would be inconceivable in the United States because it would contravene the Fifth Amendment.

The Origins of the Bill of Rights

As we saw in Chapter 2, most of the Framers of the Constitution originally opposed the idea of a bill of rights. Late in the Philadelphia Convention, for example, George Mason of Virginia proposed that a bill of rights be added to the preface of the proposed constitution, but his resolution was defeated unanimously.[2] Later, during the Philadelphia

---

[1] James M. Prothro and Charles M. Grigg, "Fundamental Principles of Democracy: Bases of Agreement and Disagreement," *Journal of Politics* 22 (1960), pp. 276–94.

[2] The absence of a bill of rights led George Mason to refuse to sign the proposed Constitution, noting that without it he "would sooner chop off his right hand than put it to the constitution as it now stands." (Quoted in Eric Black, *Our Constitution: The Myth That Binds Us* (Boulder, Colo.: Westview Press, 1988), p. 75.)

Convention and in the subsequent ratification debates, the Federalists advanced three main arguments in opposition to the Bill of Rights:

1. A bill of rights was unnecessary in a constitutional republic founded on the idea of popular sovereignty and inalienable natural, or God-given, rights. Moreover, most state constitutions contained bills of rights, so federal guarantees were unnecessary.
2. A bill of rights would be dangerous. According to Alexander Hamilton in Federalist No. 84, since the national government was a government of enumerated powers (that is, it had only the powers listed in the Constitution), "Why declare that things shall not be done which there is no power to do?"
3. A national bill of rights would be impractical to enforce. Its validity would largely depend on public opinion and the spirit of the people and government.

These arguments, however, failed to carry the day. The insistence of Anti-Federalists on a bill of rights, the conditional ratification of some states pending the addition of these guarantees, and the disagreement among Federalists themselves about the undesirability of a bill of rights led the First Congress to consider a series of amendments to the Constitution. Prompt congressional action put an end to further controversy at a time when national stability and support for the new government were needed.

James Madison and the Bill of Rights

Initially James Madison was convinced that the greatest danger to the personal liberties of citizens lay in the power of popular majorities within the states. Consequently, he saw no great need for a national bill of rights, although he gave considerable thought to the scope of individual rights that needed protection. In 1785, for example, he received a letter from a college friend asking him his views about the kind of constitution the Kentucky Territory should draft after its separation from Virginia. State legislatures, responded Madison, must be constrained by explicitly enumerating exceptions to their authority:

> The [state] Constitution may expressly restrain them [the legislators] from meddling with religion—from abolishing Juries, from taking away the Habeas corpus—from forcing a citizen to give evidence against himself, from controlling the press, from enacting retrospective laws at least in criminal cases, from abridging the right of suffrage, from seizing public property for public use without paying its full value, from licensing the importation of slaves, ...[3]

In his letters to his friend, Madison included many of the important elements that were to find their way into the Bill of Rights. But, most of all, his thoughtful response revealed his concern over the potentially unbridled power of the national legislature.

After the Philadelphia Convention, Madison and Thomas Jefferson, the author of the Declaration of Independence, conducted a lively correspondence about the need for a national bill of rights. Jefferson was far quicker to support such guarantees than was Madison, who continued to voice doubt about their utility. Politics soon intervened, however, when Madison found himself in a close race against James Monroe for a seat in the House of Representatives in the First Congress. The district was largely Anti-Federalist, so to garner support, Madison, in an act of political expediency, issued a series of public letters describing his support for a bill of rights.

Once elected, he kept good on that promise. He became the prime mover and author of the Bill of Rights, although he considered the Congress to have far more important mat-

---

[3] Quoted in Jack N. Rakove, "Madison Won Passage of the Bill of Rights But Remained a Skeptic," *Public Affairs Report* (March 1991), p. 6.

Civil Liberties Specified in the Bill of Rights

Amendment 1: Freedom of religion, speech, press, and assembly. The right to petition the government.

Amendment 2: Right to keep and bear arms.

Amendment 3: Troops may not be quartered in homes in peacetime.

Amendment 4: No unreasonable searches or seizures.

Amendment 5: Grand jury indictment required to prosecute a person for a serious crime. No "double jeopardy" (being tried twice for the same offense). Forcing a person to testify against himself or herself prohibited. No loss of life, liberty, or property without due process.

Amendment 6: Right to a speedy, public, impartial trial with defense counsel and right to cross-examine witnesses.

Amendment 7: Jury trials in civil lawsuits involving amounts in excess of $20.

Amendment 8: No excessive bail or fines, no cruel and unusual punishments.

Amendment 9: Unlisted rights are not necessarily denied.

Amendment 10: Powers not delegated to the United States or denied to states are reserved to the states.

ters to handle and his labors on the Bill of Rights "a nauseous project."[4] The document ultimately adopted by the states in 1791 bore a striking similarity to the ideas expressed in Madison's Kentucky Territory letter, especially his concern with the freedoms of religion and speech.

First Amendment Freedoms

The First Amendment contains some of the most basic and fundamental rights guaranteed to all Americans. A democracy depends on a free exchange of ideas, and the First Amendment shows that the Framers were well aware of this.

The Amendment opens with the words "*Congress shall make no law . . . ,*" and a question that has over the years troubled the Supreme Court and commentators is whether those words should be interpreted *absolutely*. Supreme Court Justice Hugo Black, who served from 1937 to 1971, was the most ardent supporter of the absolutist

Amendment 1

Congress shall make no law respecting an establishment of religion, or prohibiting the free exercise thereof; or abridging the freedom of speech, or of the press; or the right of the people peaceably to assemble, and to petition the Government for a redress of grievances.

[4] Ibid.

approach. To him "no law" meant no law whatsoever. Most other justices, however, have taken less drastic approaches, especially when First Amendment rights appear to be in conflict.

Freedom of Speech and Press

Historically, one of the most volatile areas of the law has been in the interpretation of the First Amendment's mandate that "*Congress shall make no law . . . abridging the freedom of speech, or of the press. . . .*" And, like most other areas protected by the First Amendment, freedoms of speech and press have not been interpreted in an absolutist fashion. Over the years, a hierarchy of protections has emerged, with thoughts at the top, words in between, and actions at the bottom. It may be useful for you to keep this hierarchy in mind as you consider the following situations.

At the top of the protected list is thoughts. In America, with few exceptions, thoughts are considered to be inviolable. Although people may experience a negative reaction for revealing their thoughts—as did presidential candidate Jimmy Carter upon his admission in a *Playboy* magazine article that he had "lusted in his heart" for women other than his wife, for example—the government has no legal right to punish or sanction Americans for what they think. Speech, which stands between thoughts and deeds, can be subject to certain kinds of restraints. Speech that is obscene, **libelous** (false or calling someone into disrepute), **seditious** (advocating the violent overthrow of the government), or that constitutes **fighting words** (inciting or causing injury to those to whom they are addressed) has been interpreted not to be protected by the First Amendment. Often, however, what constitutes any of these exceptions to constitutional protection has troubled the Court. What is considered obscene in rural Mississippi may be commonplace in other sections of the nation.

Freedom of Speech and the Common-Law Tradition

In Great Britain, government censorship of the press and speech had its origins in a 1275 pronouncement from the Crown. Later, in the sixteenth and seventeenth centuries, the King's Council, which sat in what was fearfully called the "Star Chamber" by British subjects, harshly meted out cruel sentences for seditious libel, that is, language tending to incite rebellion against the state. In one of the Star Chamber's most infamous cases, the Trial of William Prynn (1632), Prynn was sentenced to life imprisonment, branded on the forehead, had his nose split, his ears cut off, and was fined £10,000 for publishing a book that criticized actors and actresses. The book was viewed as seditious libel against the queen, because she herself had recently appeared in a play!

The Star Chamber was abolished in 1641, but its precedents were often relied upon by common-law courts. Criminal liability for slander (unlawful, untrue speech) remained a question of law, not one of fact, to be decided by juries. Moreover, partisan publications were discouraged by law. In sum, the British experience concerning speech laws focused largely on issues of prior restraint and not on the protection of speech per se.

Source: David M. O'Brien, *Constitutional Law and Politics, Vol. 2: Civil Rights and Liberties* (New York: Norton, 1991), pp. 337–38.

At the bottom of our First Amendment hierarchy are actions, which are afforded the least protection and thus subject to the most governmental restrictions. You may have a right to shoot a pistol in your back yard, but you can't do it on a city street. As many have commented over the years, "The right to swing your arm ends where the other person's nose begins."

At the time the First Amendment was ratified in 1791, it was considered to protect only against **prior restraint;** that is, the government could not prohibit speech or publication before the fact. The amendment, however, was not considered to provide absolute immunity from governmental sanction for what speakers or publishers might say or print. Over the years, the meaning of this amendment's mandate has been subject to thousands of judicial decisions.

The Alien and Sedition Acts

Less than a decade after ratification of the First Amendment, a constitutional crisis arose over passage by the Federalist Congress of the Alien and Sedition Acts in 1798. These Acts included a series of laws that imposed criminal sanctions for sedition, which the Acts defined as "any false, scandalous writing against the government of the United States." The Sedition Act was passed by Congress to ban any political criticism by the growing numbers of Jeffersonian Democrat-Republicans and to cut down on criticisms of the undeclared war the United States was fighting with France. Federalist judges, who did not even pretend to be objective, imposed fines and even jail terms on at least ten Democrat-Republican newspaper editors for allegedly violating the Acts. Moreover, the Acts were a major issue in the 1800 presidential election campaign, which ultimately saw the close election of their leading opponent, Thomas Jefferson. He quickly pardoned all who had been convicted under the Alien and Sedition Acts, and the Democrat-Republican Congress allowed the Acts to expire before the Supreme Court had an opportunity to hear a challenge to these serious curtailments of the First Amendment.

Slavery, the Civil War, and Rights Curtailments

As a result of the public outcry over the Alien and Sedition Acts, the national government largely got out of the business of regulating sedition, but in its place the states began to prosecute those who published articles critical of governmental policies. In the 1830s, at the urgings of abolitionists, the publication or dissemination of any information about slavery became a punishable offense in the North. In the South, supporters of that "peculiar institution" of slavery enacted laws that prohibited the publication of anti-slavery sentiments, which were viewed as "incendiary," "inflammatory," and "provoking servile insurrection." These laws were reinforced by state practices that included censorship of the mails, whereby Southern postmasters refused to deliver Northern abolitionist papers throughout the South.

During the Civil War, President Abraham Lincoln effectively suspended the free press provision of the First Amendment (as well as many other sections of the Constitution) and even went so far as to order the arrest of the editors of two New York papers that were critical of him. Far from protesting these blatant violations of the First Amendment, the Congress of the United States acceded to them. Right after the war, for example, the Congress actually prevented the Supreme Court from issuing a judgment on a case because members feared it would be critical of the powers Lincoln had taken on during the war. The case of *Ex parte McCardle* (1869)[5] involved a Mississippi newspaper editor who had sought to arouse sentiment against Lincoln and the Union occupation. Even though he was a civilian, McCardle was jailed by a military court without having any charges brought against him. He appealed to the U.S. Supreme Court, arguing that he

[5] 7 Wall. 506 (1869).

was being held unlawfully. Congress, fearing that a victory for McCardle would prompt other Confederate newspaper editors to follow his lead, enacted a law barring the Supreme Court from hearing appeals of cases involving convictions for publishing statements critical of the Union. Because Article III of the Constitution states that Congress has the power to determine the jurisdiction of the Court, the Court complied and said that it had no authority to rule in the matter.

After the war, states also began to prosecute individuals for sedition when they uttered or printed statements critical of the government. Between 1890 and 1900, for example, there were more than 100 state prosecutions for sedition in state courts.[6] Moreover, by the dawn of the twentieth century, public opinion in the United States had become exceedingly hostile to the preachings of such groups as socialists and communists who attempted to appeal to the thousands of new and disheartened immigrants. Socialism and communism became the targets of state laws curtailing speech and the written word. By the end of World War I, at least 32 states had passed laws (often known as criminal syndicalism statutes) to punish seditious libel, and more than 1,900 individuals and over 100 newspapers were prosecuted for violations.[7]

New Restrictions/New Tests

The first major federal law restricting freedom of speech and the press in the twentieth century was the Espionage Act of 1917. Nearly 2,000 Americans were convicted for violating various provisions of the Espionage Act, especially those that made it illegal to urge resistance to the draft or that prohibited the distribution of antiwar leaflets. In 1919, in *Schenck* v. *United States*,[8] the U.S. Supreme Court upheld the conviction of Schenck, a secretary of the Socialist Party, who had been tried and convicted for printing, distributing, and mailing antiwar leaflets to men eligible for the draft, urging them to resist induction. In an opinion written by Justice Oliver Wendell Holmes, the Court concluded that Congress could restrict speech that was "of such a nature as to create a clear and present danger that will bring about the substantive evils that Congress has a right to prevent." Speaking for the unanimous Court, Holmes concluded that the leaflets constituted such a danger, explaining that even the U.S. Constitution does not protect an individual from "falsely shouting fire in a theater and causing a panic." Under the clear and present danger test, situations count, according to the Court. Therefore, whereas the leaflets might have been permissible in peacetime, they posed too much of a danger in wartime. The **clear and present danger test** as applied by the Court also suggested that if no danger existed, or if the speech did not have a "bad tendency"—that is, a tendency to produce the forbidden consequences—the speech would be protected by the First Amendment.

Just a short time later, however, division on the Court concerning the clear and present danger test became apparent. In *Abrams* v. *United States* (1919),[9] Holmes rejected the majority's reliance on the **bad tendency test.** In dissent he wrote that the activities of six anarchists who had been convicted for writing a "silly leaflet" protesting the U.S. government's attempts to overthrow the newly formed Bolshevik government in Russia posed no imminent danger to the United States and therefore should be protected by the First Amendment. The majority, however, remained unconvinced by Holmes's arguments, and from 1919 to 1927, the convictions of defendants in five other cases brought under the Espionage Act were upheld by the Court. The effect of these rulings was that

---

[6] David M. O'Brien, *Constitutional Law and Politics: Civil Rights and Civil Liberties* (New York: Norton, 1991), p. 345.

[7] See Frederick Siebert, *The Rights and Privileges of the Press* (New York: D. Appleton-Century, 1934), pp. 886 and 931–940.

[8] 249 U.S. 47 (1919).

[9] 250 U.S. 616 (1919).

People of the Past

Eugene V. Debs

Eugene Victor Debs was a prominent American socialist and a central figure in challenging the free speech restrictions of the Espionage Act of 1917. He was born in Terre Haute, Indiana in 1855. Debs went to work on the railroads in 1870, and in 1875 he helped form a lodge of the Brotherhood of Locomotive Firemen, an early union, and later served as its national secretary and treasurer and editor of its magazine. In 1893 he helped form the American Railway Union and was made its president.

As part of the Cleveland administration's attempts to crush the Pullman strike of 1894 in Chicago, Debs was held in contempt of court for violating a federal injunction against striking and was sentenced to six months in jail. While in jail, he read widely on the issue of socialism, and in 1897 he transformed the remains of the American Railway Union into the Social Democratic Party of America, which was later called the Socialist Party of America.

Debs ran for president of the United States on the Socialist ticket in 1900, 1904, 1908, and 1912. In 1918, as one of the most visible critics of Woodrow Wilson's decision to enter World War I, he again found himself in court, this time charged with violating the Espionage Act of 1917.

Debs was tried and sentenced to ten years in prison for a speech he delivered in Canton, Ohio at a socialist antiwar rally. In his speech, Debs praised other imprisoned leaders of his party who had been jailed for aiding draft resistors. He accused the U.S. government of using false testimony to convict another antiwar activist and labeled the war a plot by "the predator capitalists in the United States" against the working class "who furnish the corpses. . . . You need to know," he told his listeners, that "you are fit for something better than slavery and cannon fodder."

By the time the appeal of his conviction reached the Supreme Court, a post-war "red scare" had spread through the country. Without even a reference to the "clear and present danger" test enunciated just a week earlier in *Schenck* v. *United States*, his conviction was affirmed by a unanimous Court. Although in *Debs* v. *United States* (1919) Justice Oliver Wendell Holmes conceded that "the main theme" of Debs's speech was the growth and eventual triumph of socialism, he argued that "if a part of the manifest intent of the more general utterance was to encourage those present to obstruct recruiting . . . the immunity of the general theme may not be enough to protect the speech."

Although he was in prison, Debs again ran for president in 1920 and received more than 900,000 votes. President Wilson, still bitter about opposition to the war, refused to pardon Debs before leaving the White House. Wilson's successor, Warren G. Harding, showed more compassion and pardoned Debs in 1921. Debs devoted much of his remaining life to campaigning for improved prison conditions. He died in 1926.

---

speech, especially if it could be construed as adversely affecting national security, would not be protected from governmental infringement by the First Amendment.

The First Amendment Applied to the States: The Incorporation Doctrine

It was during this same period that the Supreme Court began to deal with the power or authority of the states to curb free speech. As discussed in Chapter 2, the Bill of Rights as first adopted was intended to limit the powers of the *national* government to infringe

Until *Gitlow* v. *New York* (1925) involving Benjamin Gitlow (pictured above), it was generally thought that the Fourteenth Amendment did not apply the protections of the Bill of Rights to the states.

upon the rights and liberties of the citizenry. In 1868, however, the Fourteenth Amendment was added to the U.S. Constitution. It contained language suggesting the possibility that some or even all of the protections guaranteed in the Bill of Rights might be interpreted to prevent *state* infringement of those rights. In what is called the **due process clause,** Section 1 of the Fourteenth Amendment reads: "*No State shall . . . deprive any person of life, liberty, or property, without due process of law. . . .*"

Until 1925, the Supreme Court steadfastly rejected numerous arguments that were put forth urging the Court to interpret the due process clause to make various provisions contained in the Bill of Rights applicable to the states. As a consequence, states were free throughout this period to pass sedition laws, knowing that the Supreme Court would uphold their constitutional validity. Then, in 1925, all of this changed dramatically. Benjamin Gitlow, a member of the Left Wing Section of the Socialist Party, was convicted of violating a New York law that, in language very similar to that of the federal Espionage Act, prohibited the advocacy of the violent overthrow of the government. Gitlow had printed 16,000 copies of a manifesto in which he urged the violent overthrow of the U.S. government. The Supreme Court, although it upheld Gitlow's conviction, noted that the states were not completely free to limit forms of expression:

> For present purposes we may and do assume that freedom of speech and of the press—which are protected by the First Amendment from abridgement by Congress—are among the *fundamental personal rights and "liberties"* protected by the due process clause of the Fourteenth Amendment from impairment by the states. (emphasis added)[10]

The development of this **incorporation doctrine**, which makes specific guarantees in the Bill of Rights applicable to the states by incorporating them through the due process clause of the Fourteenth Amendment, led the Supreme Court in the next decade to strike down numerous state laws that restricted First Amendment freedoms.

Perhaps the most famous of these cases was *Near* v. *Minnesota* (1931),[11] the first in which the Supreme Court found that a state law violated freedom of the press as protected by the First Amendment. Jay Near, the publisher of a weekly Minneapolis newspaper, regularly made scurrilous attacks on a variety of groups—blacks, Catholics, Jews, and labor union leaders. Few escaped his hatred. Near's paper was closed under the authority of a state criminal libel law that banned "malicious, scandalous, or defamatory" publications. Near appealed the closing of his paper, and the Supreme Court ruled that "The fact that the liberty of the press may be abused by miscreant purveyors of scandal does not make any the less necessary the immunity of the press from previous restraint."[12] With these words the Court began the process of what is termed **selective incorporation.** As revealed in Table 4-1, not all of the guarantees in the Bill of Rights have yet been made applicable to the states by the due process clause. Instead, the Court has selectively chosen to protect the rights it considers most fundamental.

Selective Incorporation and Fundamental Freedoms. In *Palko* v. *Connecticut* (1937),[13] Frank Palko was charged with first-degree murder for killing two police officers, found guilty of a lesser charge of second-degree murder, and sentenced to life imprisonment. Connecticut appealed, Palko was retried, was found guilty of first-degree murder, and was resentenced to death. Palko then appealed his second conviction on the ground that it violated the Fifth Amendment's prohibition against double jeopardy

---

[10] *Gitlow* v. *New York,* 268 U.S. 652 (1925).

[11] See Fred W. Friendly, *Minnesota Rag* (New York: Random House, 1981).

[12] 283 U.S. 697 (1931).

[13] 302 U.S. 319 (1937).

Table 4-1   Incorporation and the Bill of Rights

AMENDMENT	RIGHT	DATE	CASE
I.	Speech	1925	*Gitlow* v. *New York*
	Press	1931	*Near* v. *Minnesota*
	Assembly	1937	*DeJonge* v. *Oregon*
	Religion	1940	*Cantwell* v. *Connecticut*
II.	Right to bear arms		*Not Incorporated* (Generally, the Supreme Court has upheld reasonable regulations of the right of private citizens to bear arms. Should a tough gun-control law be adopted by a state or local government and a challenge to it be made, a test of incorporation might be presented to the Court in the future.)
III.	No quartering of soldiers		*Not Incorporated* (The quartering problem has not recurred since colonial times.)
IV.	Unreasonable searches and seizures	1949	*Wolf* v. *Colorado*
	The exclusionary rule	1961	*Mapp* v. *Ohio*
V.	Just compensation	1897	*Chicago, B&Q RR. Co.* v. *Chicago*
	Self-incrimination	1964	*Malloy* v. *Hogan*
	Double jeopardy	1969	*Benton* v. *Maryland*
	Grand jury indictment		*Not Incorporated* (The trend in state criminal cases is away from grand juries and toward reliance upon the sworn written accusation of the prosecuting attorney.)
VI.	Public trial	1948	*In re Oliver*
	Right to counsel	1963	*Gideon* v. *Wainwright*
	Confrontation of witnesses	1965	*Pointer* v. *Texas*
	Impartial trial	1966	*Parker* v. *Gladden*
	Speedy trial	1967	*Klopfer* v. *North Carolina*
	Compulsory process	1967	*Washington* v. *Texas*
	Jury trial	1968	*Duncan* v. *Louisiana*
VII.	Right to jury trial in civil cases		*Not Incorporated* (While Warren Burger was Chief Justice he conducted a campaign to abolish jury trials in civil cases to save time and money, and for other reasons.)
VIII.	Cruel or unusual punishment	1962	*Robinson* v. *California*
	Excessive fines or bail		*Not Incorporated*

Source: William C. Louthan, *The United States Supreme Court.* (Englewood Cliffs, N.J.: Prentice Hall, 1991), pp. 205–206.

because the Fifth Amendment had been made applicable to the states by the due process clause of the Fourteenth Amendment.

The Supreme Court upheld Palko's second conviction and the death sentence, thereby choosing not to bind states to the Fifth Amendment's double jeopardy clause. Writing for the majority, Justice Benjamin Cardozo set forth principles that were to guide the Court's interpretation of the incorporation doctrine for the next several decades. Some guarantees found in the Bill of Rights are so *fundamental,* he wrote, that they are made applicable to the states through the due process clause. These rights are fundamental, argued Cardozo, because "neither liberty nor justice would exist if they are sacrificed." Because the Court concluded that the protection against double jeopardy was not a fundamental right, Palko died in Connecticut's gas chamber one year later. Cardozo's argument that those rights were necessary to a "fair and enlightened system of justice" was nonetheless gradually expanded by the Court in later years to include most guarantees contained in the Bill of Rights.

Prior Restraint

In *Near* v. *Minnesota* (1931) the Court set forth a standard to be used to evaluate restrictions on free speech. The Court made it clear that although someone could be punished for libelous statements after the fact, with only a few exceptions, the Court would not tolerate any prior restraint of speech or expression. In 1971, for example, in *New York Times Co.* v. *United States*[14] (also called the "Pentagon Papers" case), the Supreme Court ruled that the U.S. government could not block the publication of secret Defense Department documents illegally furnished to the *Times* by antiwar activists. In 1976, in *Nebraska Press Association* v. *Stuart,*[15] the Supreme Court when even further, noting that any attempt by the government to prevent expression carried "a 'heavy presump-

[14]403 U.S. 713 (1971).
[15]427 U.S. 539 (1976).

Then and Now

Incorporation

James Madison originally proposed seventeen initial amendments to the Constitution, but five were never even sent to the states for their approval. One of those five is particularly significant: "No State shall infringe the equal rights of conscience, nor the freedom of speech, or of the press, nor of the right of trial by jury in criminal cases." This amendment clearly would have prevented the states from infringing these particular liberties. Yet, the many advocates of states' rights in the First Congress easily defeated this proposal.

By the mid-twentieth century, the idea of selective incorporation was firmly ingrained. Nevertheless, it is a *judicially created* doctrine. Today, some speculate that

with a highly conservative Court on record as favoring following the original intentions of the Founders rights selectively incorporated may soon be *deincorporated,* or removed from the list of liberties protected from state infringement by the Constitution. For example, the right of states to give greater aid to religious schools could become constitutionally permissible if the Court were to deincorporate the First Amendment and make it no longer applicable to the states. Similarly, the right to an abortion, which is grounded in several amendments, could be ended if the Court chose not to make certain segments of the Bill of Rights binding on the states.

In this debut installment of a controversial cartoon strip that runs in the Brown University school paper, the PC movement is targetted for sometimes taking to excess its insistence on language free of sexism.

tion' against its constitutionality.''[16] In the *Nebraska* case, a trial court had issued a ''gag order'' barring the press from reporting the lurid details of a crime. In balancing the defendant's constitutional right to a fair trial with the press's right to cover a story, the trial judge concluded that the defendant's right carried a greater weight. The Supreme Court disagreed, holding that the press's right to cover the trial was paramount.

"Politically Correct" Speech

A particularly thorny area emerging as a First Amendment issue is the ability of universities to ban what they view as offensive speech. Since 1989, more than 130 colleges and universities have banned racial slurs directed at minority groups. The University of Connecticut went so far as to ban ''inappropriately directed laughter'' and ''conspicuous exclusion of students from conversations.'' The ''politically correct speech'' movement even has its own cartoon character, ''Politically Correct Man.'' (Actually, ''That's politically correct *person,*'' he proclaimed in his debut as a Brown University comic strip.)

While easy to poke fun at, the PC movement, as it is known, has a serious side. At Dartmouth, a student was expelled for shouting anti-Semitic, anti-black, and anti-homosexual obscenities at students in their dorm rooms at 2:00 A.M. And, at the University of Michigan in 1990 a student was accused of violating the university's regulation that bans speech that victimizes individuals for their sexual orientation when he said during a classroom discussion that he considered homosexuality to be a disease treatable with therapy. The university's code was challenged by the American Civil Liberties Union

[16] Ibid.

The American Civil Liberties Union

The American Civil Liberties Union (ACLU) was created in 1920 by a group that had tried to defend the civil liberties of conscientious objectors to World War I. As the nation's oldest, largest, and premier nonpartisan civil liberties organization, the ACLU works in three major areas of the law: freedom of speech and religion, due process, and equality before the law. The ACLU lobbies for legislation affecting these areas and conducts extensive public education campaigns to familiarize Americans with the guarantees in the Bill of Rights. Its main energies historically have been devoted to litigating to maintain these rights and liberties. The ACLU has been involved in most speech and religion cases heard by the U.S. Supreme Court. It also has specialized projects. The National Prison Project, for example, monitors prison conditions to ensure that prisoner rights are not being violated. Similarly, the Reproductive Freedom Project is one of the most active litigators on behalf of pro-abortion activists. It regularly sponsors challenges to restrictive state abortion laws and files "friend of the court" briefs in cases in which it is not lead counsel. Among the major cases it has participated in since the 1960s are:

- *Mapp* v. *Ohio* (1961): established that illegally obtained evidence can't be used at trial
- *Gideon* v. *Wainwright* (1963): granted indigents the right to counsel
- *Miranda* v. *Arizona* (1966): guaranteed all suspects a right to counsel
- *Tinker* v. *Des Moines Independent School Board* (1969): upheld the right of students to wear black armbands in protest of the Vietnam War

- *Planned Parenthood* v. *Casey* (1992): a challenge to Pennsylvania's restrictive abortion regulations
- *Bowen* v. *Kendrick* (1988): in a defeat for the ACLU, upheld the Adolescent Family Life Act, which bars federal funding of organizations involved in abortions while permitting funding of religious groups advocating self-discipline as a form of birth control.

Although the positions taken by the ACLU on these cases generally have been extremely popular with its members, an outcry arose in 1977 when it decided to represent members of the National Socialist Party who had been denied a parade permit to march in Nazi uniforms through Skokie, Illinois, home to many Jewish concentration camp survivors. The ACLU lost more than 60,000 members who protested its involvement in the case, but it stayed true to its purpose—upholding the First Amendment, no matter how offensive the speech or actions in question.

Recognition of the growing conservative nature of the Supreme Court has caused the ACLU to rethink its litigation strategies. In fact, since 1987 the ACLU's policy has been to stay as far away from the Supreme Court as possible, a major shift in strategy. Formerly the ACLU had appeared before the Court more than any organization except the Justice Department. "We're going to be looking for appropriate ways to bring cases in state courts and to insulate them from Supreme Court review,"* said one ACLU official. Recognizing also that "Civil liberties are not something people intuitively grasp,"† the ACLU is undertaking a campaign to gain more attention for its cause.

*Quoted in Tony Mauro, "Supreme Court v. Civil Liberties; the ACLU's New Strategy of Avoidance," *Legal Times* (June 1, 1987), p. 13.
† Ibid.

and found unconstitutional by a federal district court. In 1991, another federal district court voided a University of Wisconsin rule against hate speech intended to "create a hostile learning environment." The rule had been passed after several racially tinged incidents, including a fraternity slave auction conducted in blackface. Lawyers on both sides of the University of Wisconsin case have pledged to appeal all the way to the Supreme Court.

Libel and Slander

Unlike some forms of speech, the courts will not restrain libelous statements, yet the Supreme Court has consistently ruled that individuals or the press can be sued after the fact for untrue or libelous statements. **Libel** is a written statement that defames the character of a person. If the statement is spoken, it is considered **slander.** In many nations—such as Great Britain, for example—it is relatively easy to sue someone for libel. In the United States, however, the standards of proof are much more difficult. A person who believes that he or she has been a victim of libel, for example, must show that the statements made were untrue. Truth is an absolute defense to libel no matter now painful or embarrassing the revelations are.

It is often more difficult for individuals the Supreme Court considers to be "public persons or public officials" to sue for libel or slander. In the first major case on libel, *New York Times Co.* v. *Sullivan* (1964),[17] the Court overruled an Alabama state court that had found the *Times* guilty of libel for printing a full-page advertisement paid for by civil rights activists (including former First Lady Eleanor Roosevelt) that accused Alabama officials of physically abusing blacks during various civil rights protests. The Supreme Court ruled that a finding of libel against a *public official* could stand only if there were a showing of "actual malice," which would require something to have been written in the "knowledge that it was false or with reckless disregard of whether it was false or not."[18] It is very difficult to prove actual malice, as illustrated by the Supreme Court's decision in *Hustler Magazine* v. *Falwell* (1988).[19] The television evangelist Jerry Falwell, former head of the Moral Majority, sued the publishers of *Hustler* magazine for emotional distress he said he suffered when the magazine published an unflattering cartoon depicting Falwell and his mother engaging in incestuous behavior. The Court deemed the cartoon a parody, which it held was an age-old form of expression that deserved protection, even when it was in bad taste. Thus, as a public figure, Falwell could not recover any money for the distress caused by the suggested untruths.

Obscenity

Since the time of the Founders, obscenity has always been considered to be beyond the protection of the First Amendment. Although some absolutist members of the U.S. Supreme Court, like Justice Black, and the American Civil Liberties Union have argued that the First Amendment protects absolutely *all* speech, this view has never come close to garnering the support of a majority of the justices. Consequently, the dilemma that has continued to face the Court is how to define obscenity and thereby void any First Amendment protection to the works or speech in question.

In 1873, the U.S. Congress prohibited the use of the U.S. mails to disseminate any "obscene" materials. Included in the list of materials considered obscene was any

---

[17] 376 U.S. 254 (1964).
[18] See Anthony Lewis, *Make No Law: The Sullivan Case and the First Amendment* (New York: Random House, 1991).
[19] 485 U.S. 46 (1988).

information on birth control.[20] State courts, following the lead of Congress, also began to enact new anti-obscenity laws and to prosecute writers whose works had any sexual overtones, including James Joyce, D. H. Lawrence, and Theodore Dreiser for his classic *The Great American Tragedy.*

The courts also based their findings of obscenity on a restrictive English common-law test that had been set out in Britain in *Regina* v. *Hicklin* (1868): "whether the tendency of the matter charged as obscenity is to deprive and corrupt those whose minds are open to such immoral influences and into whose hands a publication of this sort might fall."[21] Under a test this broad, many things—especially if they could possibly fall into the hands of children—could be considered obscene. Use of this test prompted Justice Felix Frankfurter to note, "The incidence of this standard is to reduce the adult population of [the United States] to reading what is fit for children."[22]

The Court did not abandon the use of the *Hicklin* test until a majority of the Court agreed with Justice William Brennan in *Roth* v. *United States* (1957).[23] In *Roth,* the Court announced a new test for obscenity: "whether to the average person, applying contemporary community standards, the dominant theme of the material taken as a whole appeals to the prurient interests." In many ways, the *Roth* test brought with it as many problems as it attempted to solve. Throughout the 1950s and 1960s the Court struggled to find a standard by which to judge actions or words obscene and therefore not protected by the First Amendment. In general, only "hardcore" pornography was found obscene by the liberal Warren Court, prompting some to argue that the Court fostered the increase in the number of sexually oriented publications designed to appeal to those living amidst what many called the "sexual revolution."

Richard Nixon made the growth in pornography a major issue when he ran for president in 1968 and pledged to appoint to federal judgeships only those who would uphold "law and order." Nixon's Burger Court began to respond to increased anti-obscenity (also called anti-pornography) legislation and public concern by placing some limits on pornographic materials.

In *Ginzburg* v. *United States* (1968),[24] the Court upheld the conviction of Ralph Ginzburg for "pandering" by selectively mailing his magazine *Eros* from cities including Middlesex, New Jersey; Blue Balls, Montana; and Intercourse, Pennsylvania. Ginzburg's sense of humor was clearly lost on the Court, which decided that he had chosen to exploit the sexual nature of his publication by selective use of provocative postmarks. And, in 1973, the newly constituted Burger Court, with the addition of two Nixon appointees, William H. Rehnquist and Lewis F. Powell, Jr., set out to clarify a new test for obscenity. In *Miller* v. *California* (1973),[25] Burger enunciated concrete rules to be used in obscenity prosecutions that were designed to return to communities a greater role in determining what is obscene, based on local standards.

The *Miller* test redefined obscenity by concluding that a court must ask "whether the work depicts or describes, in a patently offensive way, sexual conduct specifically defined by state law." Moreover, courts were to determine "whether the work, taken as a whole, lacks serious literary, artistic, political or scientific value." And, in place of the contemporary community standards gauge used in earlier cases, the Court defined community standards to mean local, and not national, standards under the rationale that what is acceptable in Times Square in New York City might not be in Peoria, Illinois.

---

[20] Much later, in 1914, Margaret Sanger, who ultimately founded Planned Parenthood, was forced to flee the U.S. to avoid jail after she was found guilty of violating the Comstock Act for using the mails to spread information about contraceptives.

[21] L.R. 2 Q.B. 360 (1868).

[22] *Butler* v. *Michigan,* 352 U.S. 380 (1957).

[23] 354 U.S. 476 (1957).

[24] 383 U.S. 463 (1968).

[25] 413 U.S. 15 (1973).

A Shrinking First Amendment?

In a series of cases in its 1990 term, the U.S. Supreme Court had several opportunities to reinterpret the First Amendment. Nearly every time it did, according to Court watchers, small bites were taken out of the clauses guaranteeing freedom of speech and of the press. Some examples:

1. *On freedom of expression:* The federal government can now prohibit some physicians at federally funded clinics from offering abortion advice even if, in the doctor's judgment, an abortion is medically advisable. In *Rust* v. *Sullivan* the Court ruled five to four that although abortion was a "protected right," the government was not consti-

tutionally required to "subsidize" speech about it.
2. *On libel and public figures:* The Court ruled seven to two that fabricated quotations attributed to a public figure may be libelous only if the changes materially alter the gist or meaning of what the public figure actually said.
3. *On obscenity:* The Court ruled five to four that although erotic nude dancing is a form of expression entitled to some First Amendment protection, a state's interest in protecting the morals of its citizens outweighs any First Amendment rights, thus allowing states to ban nude dancing.

Until recently, however, community standards could not be the sole criterion of obscenity. In *Jenkins* v. *Georgia* (1974),[26] for example, the Court overturned a decision of a Georgia state court that found *Carnal Knowledge* (a movie starring Jack Nicholson, Ann-Margret, and Art Garfunkel that included scenes of a partially nude woman) to be obscene. The Court concluded that the scenes were neither "patently offensive" nor designed to appeal to the "prurient interest." As Justice Potter Stewart had once announced, he couldn't define obscenity, but "I know it when I see it." He didn't see it in *Carnal Knowledge.*

Times and contexts clearly have altered the Court's and indeed, much of America's perceptions of what is obscene. *Carnal Knowledge* now is often shown on television on Saturday afternoons with only minor editing. But today's increasingly conservative Court is showing signs that it will allow communities greater leeway in drafting statutes to deal with obscenity or even, more important, forms of non-obscene expression. In 1991, for example, in *Barnes* v. *Glen Theater,*[27] the Supreme Court voted five to four to allow Indiana to ban totally nude erotic dancing, concluding that its statute didn't violate the First Amendment's guarantee of freedom of expression. Justice Antonin Scalia, concurring in the opinion, went so far as to conclude that the law should be upheld on the ground that moral opposition to nudity is a sufficient reason for the state to ban it altogether.

In a celebrated obscenity case in 1989, a Cincinnati jury found that homoerotic photographs by Robert Mapplethorpe were permissible as expressions of free speech.

[26] 418 U.S. 153 (1974).
[27] 111 S. Ct. 2456 (1991).

Symbolic Speech

In addition to the general protection accorded pure speech, the Supreme Court has extended the reach of the First Amendment to other categories of speech often referred to as **symbolic speech**—symbols, signs, and other methods of expression—as well as to activities like picketing, sit-ins, and demonstrations. In the words of Justice John Marshall Harlan, these kinds of "speech" are part of the "free trade in ideas."

In 1931 the Supreme Court first acknowledged that symbolic speech was entitled to First Amendment protection. In *Stromberg* v. *California*[28] Chief Justice Charles Evans Hughes overturned the conviction of a director of a communist youth camp who raised a red flag every morning as part of the camp's morning exercises. A state law had labeled the display of a red flag as a symbol of opposition to the U.S. government and therefore illegal. Later, in 1943, the Supreme Court struck down a state law requiring students to salute the American flag, thus reaffirming the notion that nonverbal expressions also are entitled to First Amendment protection.[29] In a similar vein, the right of high school students to wear black armbands to protest the Vietnam War was upheld in *Tinker* v. *Des Moines Independent Community School District* (1969).[30]

The burning of the American flag also has been held to be a form of protected symbolic speech. In 1989 a sharply divided Supreme Court (five to four) reversed the conviction of Gregory Johnson, who had been found guilty of setting fire to an American flag during the 1984 Republican national convention in Dallas.[31] A major public outcry against the Court went up, and President George Bush and numerous members of Congress called for a constitutional amendment to ban flag burning. Others, including Justice William J. Brennan, Jr., noted that if not for acts like that of Johnson, the United States would never have been created, nor would a First Amendment guaranteeing a right to political protest exist.

Instead of a constitutional amendment, Congress passed the Federal Flag Protection Act of 1989, which authorized federal prosecution of anyone who intentionally desecrated a national flag. Those who originally had been arrested burned another flag and were convicted; their conviction was again overturned by the Supreme Court. As it had in *Johnson,* the justices divided five to four in holding that the federal law "suffered from the same fundamental flaw" as the earlier state law that was declared in violation of the First Amendment.[32] After that decision by the Court, additional efforts were made to pass a constitutional amendment so that congressional attempts to ban flag burning would not be subject to "interpretation." That effort, however, fell thirty-four votes short in the House of Representatives and nine votes short in the Senate.

Freedom of Religion

Despite the fact that many colonists had fled Europe primarily to escape religious persecution, most colonies actively persecuted other religious groups. The Congregationalist Church of Massachusetts, for example, taxed and harassed those who held other religious beliefs. And, even though several of the colonies had official churches, the colonists were uniformly outraged in 1774 when the British Parliament passed a law establishing Anglicanism and Roman Catholicism as official religions in the colonies. The First Continental Congress immediately sent a letter of protest announcing its "astonishment that a British

---

[28] 283 U.S. 359 (1931).
[29] *West Virginia State Board of Education* v. *Barnette,* 319 U.S. 503 (1943).
[30] 393 U.S. 503 (1969).
[31] *Texas* v. *Johnson,* 491 U.S. 397 (1989).
[32] 110 S. Ct. 2404 (1990).

Parliament should ever consent to establish . . . a religion [meaning Catholicism] that has deluged [England] in blood and dispersed bigotry, persecution, murder and rebellion through every part of the world."[33]

The desire to have the national government free from religious influences is seen in Article VI of the Constitution, which provides that "*no religious Test shall ever be required as a Qualification to any Office or Public Trust under the United States.*" This simple sentiment, however, did not reassure those who feared the new Constitution would curtail individual liberty. Thus, the First Amendment to the Constitution was ultimately ratified to lay those fears to rest.

The Religion Clauses

The First Amendment to the Constitution begins, "*Congress shall make no law respecting an establishment of religion, or prohibiting the free exercise thereof.*" This statement creates the parameters of governmental action. First, the establishment clause directs the national government not to involve itself in religion by creating, in Thomas Jefferson's immortal words, a "wall of separation" between church and state. Second, the establishment clause guarantees that the national government will not interfere with the practice of religion. Like the guarantees concerning speech and freedom of expression, however, these religious clauses are not absolutes. In 1940 in *Cantwell* v. *Connecticut,*[34] the Supreme Court observed that the First Amendment "embraces two concepts— freedom to believe and freedom to act. The first is absolute, but in the nature of things, the second cannot be. Conduct remains subject to regulation of society." For example, in the mid-1800s Mormons traditionally preached the appropriateness of having more than one wife. In 1879, its first encounter with the free exercise clause, the Court upheld the conviction of a Mormon under a federal statute barring that practice. Chief Justice Morrison Waite's opinion made it clear that to do otherwise would provide constitutional protections to a full range of religious beliefs, including those as extreme as human sacrifice. "Laws are made for the government of actions," he wrote, "and while they cannot interfere with mere religious belief and opinions, they may with practices."[35] More recently, in *Department of Human Resources of Oregon* v. *Smith* (1991), the Supreme Court ruled that the free exercise clause allowed Oregon to ban the use of sacramental peyote (an illegal hallucinogenic drug) in some Native American tribes' traditional religious services. The Court upheld the state's right to deny unemployment compensation to two workers who had been fired by a private drug rehabilitation clinic because they ingested an illegal substance.[36] Similarly, the Supreme Court also ruled that it was permissible for Minnesota to compel the Amish to comply with highway safety laws.[37]

The Establishment Clause

Over the years, the Court has been divided over how to apply the establishment clause. Does this clause erect a total wall between church and state, or will some governmental accommodation of religion be allowed?

In 1947, for example, the Court split five to four in upholding the constitutionality of a New Jersey town practice that reimbursed the parents of parochial school students for

The separation of church and state advocated by Thomas Jefferson has not always been clearly defined. In *Lynch* v. *Donnelly* (1984) the Supreme Court upheld the constitutionality of a city-sponsored nativity scene as part of a larger Christmas display in a park. In response to this decision, many municipalities began to erect nativity scenes that were not part of a larger seasonal display. For example, in 1987 the city of Chicago erected, removed, and then re-erected a creche when faced with lawsuits from various groups protesting what they viewed as a unconstitutional intermingling of church and state. At first the city asked local churches to raise a $100,000 bond for protection against litigation. The money was not forthcoming, and the city dismantled the scene. A federal judge then ruled that the city had not violated the First Amendment, and the scene returned.

[33] Continental Congress to the People of Great Britain, October 21, 1774, in *The Founders' Constitution,* Vol. 5, eds. Philip Kurland and Ralph Lerner, (Chicago: University of Chicago Press, 1987), p. 61.

[34] 310 U.S. 296 (1940).

[35] *Reynolds* v. *U.S.,* 98 U.S. 145 (1879).

[36] 494 U.S. 872 (1990).

[37] *Minnesota* v. *Hershberger,* 110 S. Ct. 1918 (1990).

the costs of transporting the children to Roman Catholic schools. In *Everson* v. *Board of Education of Ewing Township*[38] the majority made it clear that the monies spent by the state were not spent in furtherance of a religion; they were instead considered a subsidy to parents, not churches. Writing for the narrow majority, Justice Hugo L. Black suggested, moreover, that a strict separation of church and state did not necessarily prevent a state's "benevolent neutrality" toward religion or religious groups. Over the years, state subsidies that could be considered to aid children or other directly identifiable recipients have been held not to violate the Constitution. This analysis has allowed the Court to permit "released time" for religious instruction outside of the schools (whereby parochial school children are allowed to attend classes in religious instruction off public school grounds),[39] federal aid for the construction of buildings on religiously affiliated college campuses,[40] state-loaned textbooks for parochial school children,[41] and state laws giving parents tax deductions for parochial school tuitions.[42] A similar rationale was used by the Rehnquist Court in 1987 in *Corporation of Presiding Bishops* v. *Amos*[43] to uphold the constitutionality of allowing nonprofit Mormon industries to refuse to hire individuals who were not Mormons.

Prayer in School

While it was upholding these kinds of practices, the Court has held fast to the rule of strict separation between church and state when issues of prayer in school are involved. In *Engel* v. *Vitale* (1962),[44] the Court ruled that the recitation in classrooms of a twenty-two-word nondenominational prayer drafted by the New Hyde Park, New York, school board was not permissible. In 1968, an Arkansas "monkey law" forbidding the teaching of evolution in public schools was ruled unconstitutional under the establishment clause.[45] In 1980, a Kentucky law requiring the posting of the Ten Commandments in public school classrooms was also ruled unconstitutional.[46] Later, in 1985 in *Wallace* v. *Jaffree*,[47] an Alabama law requiring one minute of silence for meditation or voluntary prayer was deemed impermissible.

Even the more conservative Rehnquist Court has been for the most part unwilling to lower the wall of separation when it comes to religious influences in the public schools. In 1987 in *Edwards* v. *Aguillard*,[48] for example, the Court found that a Louisiana statute requiring that creationism be taught as a balance to the teaching of evolution also violated the establishment clause.

Clearly, the Court has gone back and forth in its effort to come up with a workable way to deal with church–state questions. In *Lemon* v. *Kurtzman* (1971)[49] the Court heard a case that challenged direct aid to parochial schools, including the use of state funds to pay teachers' salaries. In its decision, the Court tried—as it often does—to carve out a new "test" by which to measure the constitutionality of these types of laws. To be constitutional, a challenged law or practice must:

---

[38] 330 U.S. 1 (1947).
[39] *McCollum* v. *Board of Education,* 333 U.S. 203 (1948).
[40] *Tilton* v. *Richardson,* 403 U.S. 672 (1971).
[41] *Board of Education* v. *Allen,* 392 U.S. 236 (1968).
[42] *Mueller* v. *Allen,* 463 U.S. 388 (1983).
[43] 483 U.S. 327 (1987).
[44] 370 U.S. 421 (1962).
[45] *Epperson* v. *Arkansas,* 393 U.S. 97 (1968).
[46] *Stone* v. *Graham,* 449 U.S. 39 (1980).
[47] 472 U.S. 38 (1985).
[48] 482 U.S. 578 (1987).
[49] 411 U.S. 192 (1971).

1. Have a secular purpose;
2. Have a primary effect that neither advances nor inhibits religion; and
3. Not foster an excessive government entanglement with religion.

Funding teachers' salaries was found to fail the test and was therefore prohibited by the Constitution.

Since the 1980s, however, the Court has appeared more willing to ignore the *Lemon* test and lower the wall between church and state as long as school prayer is not involved. In 1981, for example, the Court struck down a Missouri law that prohibited the use of state university buildings and grounds for "purposes of religious worship" and that had been used by the university to ban religious groups from using school facilities. With only one dissent, the Court ruled that "University students are . . . less impressionable than younger students and should be able to appreciate that the university's policy is one of neutrality towards religion."[50] This decision was taken as a sign by many members of Congress that this principle could be extended to secondary and even primary schools. In 1984 Congress passed the Equal Access Act, which bars public schools from discriminating against groups of students on the basis of "religious, political, philosophical or other content of the speech at such meetings." The constitutionality of this law was upheld in 1990 in *Board of Education of the Westside Community Schools* v. *Mergens,*[51] when the Court ruled that a school board's refusal to allow a Christian Bible club to meet on school grounds was in violation of the Act. According to Justice Sandra Day O'Connor, writing for the majority, the Act had neither the primary effect of advancing religion nor of excessively entangling government and religion—in spite of the fact that religious meetings would be held on school grounds with a faculty sponsor.

The Free Exercise Clause

As noted earlier, the free exercise clause of the First Amendment proclaims that *"Congress shall make no law . . . prohibiting the free exercise [of religion]."* As in the case of the establishment clause, the Supreme Court has been forced continually to interpret this clause, often trying to balance the sometimes conflicting implications of both. Is it, for example, permissible for a state to bar the use of snakes during religious services although some fundamentalist Christians view snake handling as an important part of their religious services? Is it reasonable to force some men into combat if their religious beliefs bar them from participating? In the latter example, if exemptions (called "conscientious objector deferments") are given to some and not to others, is the government thus favoring one religion over another?

Although the First Amendment guarantees to individuals the right to be free from governmental interference in the exercise of their religion, this guarantee, like other First Amendment freedoms, is not absolute. When secular law comes into conflict with religious law, the right to exercise one's religious beliefs is often denied—especially if the religious beliefs in question are held by a minority or by an unpopular or "suspicious" religious group. Convictions for using illegal drugs, snake handling, and having more than one wife—all tenets of particular religious groups—have been upheld as constitutional. Similarly, states can have Sunday and not Saturday closing laws, even though such laws clearly conflict with the observances of some major religious groups. Nonetheless, the Court has made it clear that the free exercise clause requires that a state or the national government remain neutral toward religion.

Many critics of rigid enforcement of such neutrality argue that the government should do what it can to accommodate the religious diversity in our nation. In the early 1960s,

Members of the Church of God, a faith-healing sect, revived snake handling ceremonies in the 1950s despite a 1940 Kentucky statute that expressly prohibited using poisonous snakes in religious rites. Although banned by law, snake handling practices as part of religious services continue today in many parts of the South.

[50] *Widmar* v. *Vincent,* 454 U.S. 263 (1981).
[51] 110 S. Ct. 2356 (1990).

for example, a South Carolina textile mill shifted to a six-day work week, requiring that all employees work on Saturday. When an employee, a Seventh-Day Adventist whose Sabbath was Saturday, said she could not work on Saturdays, she was fired. When she sought to receive unemployment compensation, her claim was denied, and she thereupon sued to obtain her benefits. Adopting an accommodationist approach, the Supreme Court ordered South Carolina to make an exemption to its law that *required* an employee to be available for work on all but Sundays. The Court ruled that the state law was an unconstitutional violation of the free exercise clause.[52]

This accommodationist approach was further advanced by Chief Justice Warren Burger's majority opinion in *Wisconsin* v. *Yoder,*[53] a challenge to the constitutionality of a Wisconsin law that required all students to stay in school through the age of sixteen. Yoder and several other members of the Old Order Amish religion were convicted of violating the Wisconsin law when they refused to send their children to public or private school after they graduated from the eighth grade. The Amish believed that high school attendance would expose their children to secular influences and "worldly views," thus endangering their way of life. Citing the long, peaceful history of the Amish and their traditional ways, Burger concluded that the statute violated the free exercise clause and interfered with the Amish's practice of their religion.

At times, however, the Court has determined that governmental interests outweigh free exercise rights: In 1986, for example, it ruled that it was reasonable for the military to ban the wearing of yarmulkes by Orthodox Jewish officers,[54] and in 1988 the Court upheld the Forest Service's right to permit road construction and tree harvesting in areas of the national forest traditionally used for religious purposes by Native American tribes.[55]

Although conflicts between religious beliefs and the government are often difficult to settle, the Court has attempted to walk the fine line between the free exercise and establishment clauses. Moreover, in the area of free exercise, the Court often has had to confront questions of "Who is a god?" and "What is a religious faith?"—questions that theologians have grappled with for years. In *U.S.* v. *Seeger* (1965),[56] for example, which involved an appeal of three men who had been denied conscientious objector deferments during the Vietnam War because they did not subscribe to "traditional" organized religions, the Court ruled unanimously that the men were entitled to the deferments because their belief in a "Supreme Being" placed their views parallel to those who practiced traditional religions. In contrast, despite the Court's having ruled that Catholic, Protestant, Jewish, and Buddhist prison inmates must be allowed to hold religious services,[57] in 1987 it held that Islamic prisoners could be denied the same right for security reasons.[58]

The Rights of Criminal Defendants

The Fourth, Fifth, Sixth, and Eighth Amendments provide **due process rights** for those accused of crimes. Procedures for obtaining evidence for the purpose of arresting, trying, and sentencing an individual must be fair. As Table 4-2 indicates, particular amendments, as well as other portions of the Constitution, specifically protect individuals at all stages of the criminal justice process.

[52]*Sherbert* v. *Verner,* 374 U.S. 398 (1963).
[53]406 U.S. 208 (1972).
[54]*Goldman* v. *Weinberger,* 475 U.S. 503 (1986).
[55]*Lyng* v. *Northwest Indian Cemetery Protective Association,* 485 U.S. 439 (1988).
[56]380 U.S. 163 (1965).
[57]*Cruz* v. *Beto,* 405 U.S. 319 (1972).
[58]*O'Lone* v. *Shabazz,* 482 U.S. 342 (1987).

Table 4-2   The Bill of Rights and the Stages of the Criminal Justice System

STAGE	PROTECTIONS
Before a Trial	
1. Evidence gathered	The Fourth Amendment prohibits "unreasonable searches and seizures."
2. Arrest made	The Fifth Amendment bans self-incrimination. The Sixth Amendment guarantees the right to the "Assistance of Counsel."
3. Interrogation held	The Eighth Amendment forbids "excessive bail."
At the Trial	Article III requires a trial by jury.
	The Fifth Amendment bars "double jeopardy" (being tried twice for the same crime).
	The Sixth Amendment requires a "speedy and public trial by an impartial jury."
	The Sixth Amendment guarantees defendants the right to confront witnesses and to call defense witnesses.
Punishment	The Eighth Amendment bans "cruel and unusual punishments."

When we previously examined First Amendment protections, the question was how the specifics contained in that amendment were to be interpreted. In interpreting the amendments dealing with what are frequently termed criminal rights, the courts have to grapple not only with what the amendments mean but also with how their protections are to be carried out. The Eighth Amendment, for example, prohibits *"cruel and unusual punishments,"* but the question of what is cruel and unusual has vexed the Supreme Court for years. In 1972, for example, the Supreme Court found the death penalty to be cruel and unusual punishment. But as crime has increased and public opinion toward the death penalty has changed, so too has the Court's attitude. Today the Court routinely allows executions to be carried out. Perhaps even more than in the area of First Amendment freedoms, prevailing thoughts about the rights of criminal defendants are changing quickly and dramatically as the Rehnquist Court moves away from what some view as the "excesses" of the Warren Court.

When any government prosecutes one of its citizens, the Constitution requires that the processes or procedures it uses be fair. Definitions of fairness, however, have changed substantially over time. Whereas at one time due process required simply a trial by jury, over the years the Supreme Court has ruled, for example, that blacks and women must be given equal opportunities to serve on juries. So, a state system that today excluded blacks or women from jury service would deny a criminal defendant due process rights, and his or her trial could be considered unfair.

The question of how to protect the rights of criminal defendants has been resolved by different societies in different ways. Most democratic nations, including Great Britain, proceed by allowing police to bring to court any information they have collected that is relevant to the guilt or innocence of the party on trial. In these kinds of systems, it makes absolutely *no* difference how the information was obtained. Confessions, evidence seized in "unreasonable" (by American standards) searches or through "bugged" telephones—all are admissible because they are thought to have a strong bearing on the guilt or innocence of the defendant. In the British system, although this "tainted" information is admissible at trial, the police may subsequently be punished for illegal actions they took to secure the evidence. In contrast, in the United States the tradition has been to exclude illegally obtained evidence in order to deter police from abusing the due process rights of all citizens. Under this system, police won't simply stop people on the street or burst into their homes for no reason because, even if they found something illegal, the prohibition in the Fourth Amendment that protects all citizens from *"unreasonable searches and seizures"* would prevent such evidence from being used in court.

Over the years, many individuals have criticized this approach, arguing that it gives criminals more "rights" than their victims. It is important, therefore, to remember that most of these procedural rights apply to individuals charged with crimes *before* they have actually been found guilty. These rights, therefore, were designed to protect the innocent, although, of course, they often have helped the guilty. But as Justice William O. Douglas once noted, "respecting the dignity even of the least worthy citizen . . . raises the stature of all of us."[59] Many continue to argue, however, that only the guilty are helped by the American system and that they should not go unpunished because of a simple police "error." Regardless of your view on this matter, there is no denying that the Court's interpretation of these constitutional provisions has reshaped the course of criminal justice in the United States.

Searches and Seizures

The Fourth Amendment to the Constitution declares: *"The right of the people to be secure in their persons, houses, papers, and effects, against unreasonable searches and seizures, shall not be violated, and no Warrants shall issue, but upon probable cause, supported by Oath or affirmation, and particularly describing the place to be searched, and the persons or things to be seized."* The major purpose of the Amendment was to deny the government the authority to make general searches. The English Parliament often had issued general "writs of assistance" that allowed for such searches. These general warrants were also used against religious and political dissenters, a practice the Framers wanted banned in the new nation. But still, the language that they chose left numerous questions to be answered, such as what is "probable cause" for issuing a warrant, and what are "unreasonable" searches?

In general, once an arrest has been made, the police can search:

1. The person arrested
2. Things in plain view
3. Places or things that the suspect may touch or reach or are otherwise in his or her "immediate control"

In other situations, search warrants must first be obtained from a "neutral and detached magistrate"[60] prior to conducting more extensive searches of houses, cars, offices, or any other place where an individual would reasonably have some expectation of privacy. Consequently, the police cannot require you to undergo surgery to remove a bullet that might be used to incriminate you since your expectation of bodily privacy outweighs the need for evidence.[61] But the police can require you to take a Breathalyzer test to determine if you have been drinking in excess of legal limits.[62]

Homes, too, are presumed to be private. So although firefighters can enter your home to fight a fire without a warrant, if they decide to investigate the cause of the fire, they

---

[59]*Stein* v. *N.Y.,* 346 U.S. 156 (1953).
[60]*Johnson* v. *U.S.,* 333 U.S. 10 (1948).
[61]*Winston* v. *Lee,* 470 U.S. 753 (1985).
[62]*South Dakota* v. *Neville,* 459 U.S. 553 (1983).

Police administering a Breathalyzer test. The courts have upheld the constitutionality of these "seizures" as a valid means of gathering evidence of drunk driving.

must first get a warrant before their reentry.[63] In contrast, under the "open fields doctrine" first articulated by the Supreme Court in 1924,[64] if you own a field and even post "No Trespassing" signs all around, the police can, without a warrant, search your field to see if you are illegally growing marijuana because you cannot have a reasonable expectation to privacy in an open field.[65] In a series of five-to-four decisions, the Rehnquist Court has expanded the open fields doctrine to allow aerial observations of a fenced-in back yard by police looking for marijuana,[66] aerial photography of a Dow Chemical site to inspect for pollution violations,[67] and a nighttime search of a barn in a field by police armed with flashlights but not a warrant.[68]

A common type of warrantless search often occurs "incident to an arrest," meaning simultaneously with an arrest. As already noted, generally in such cases the police may seize only potential evidence on the suspect, in "plain view" or in his or her "immediate control." They may also search if they are in "hot pursuit" of a suspect or if they believe evidence will be destroyed.

Because of their mobile nature, cars have proven problematic for police and the courts. As noted by Chief Justice William Howard Taft as early as 1925, "the vehicle can quickly be moved out of the locality or jurisdiction in which the warrant must be sought."[69] Over the years the Court has become increasingly lenient about the scope of automobile searches. In 1991, for example, the Court upheld a warrantless search of a container found in a car although the police lacked probable cause to search the car itself.[70]

If police suspect that someone is committing or is about to commit a crime, they may "stop and frisk" the suspicious individual. Whereas the liberal Warren Court limited those

[63] *Michigan* v. *Tyler*, 436 U.S. 499 (1978).
[64] *Hester* v. *U.S.*, 265 U.S. 57 (1924).
[65] *Oliver* v. *U.S.*, 466 U.S. 170 (1984).
[66] *California* v. *Ciraolo*, 476 U.S. 207 (1986).
[67] *Dow Chemical Company* v. *U.S.*, 476 U.S. 227 (1986).
[68] *U.S.* v. *Dunn*, 480 U.S. 294 (1987).
[69] *Carroll* v. *U.S.*, 267 U.S. 132 (1925).
[70] *California* v. *Acevedo*, 111 S. Ct. 1982 (1991).

searches to "outer clothing . . . in an attempt to discover weapons which might be used to assault [a police officer],"[71] the Burger and Rehnquist Courts have expanded that rationale. In 1989, the Court upheld a drug-enforcement officer's search of a suspected drug courier at an airport. Chief Justice Rehnquist ruled that there need be only a "reasonable suspicion" for stopping a suspect—a much lower standard than "probable cause."[72]

Searches can also be made without a warrant if consent is obtained, and the Court has ruled that consent can be given by a variety of persons. For example, it has ruled that police can search a bedroom occupied by two persons as long as they have the consent of one.[73]

Testing for Drugs and AIDS

Testing for drugs and AIDS has become an especially thorny search-and-seizure issue. If the government can require you to take a Breathalyzer test, can it require you to be tested for drugs? For AIDS? In the wake of growing public concern over drug use, in 1986 President Ronald Reagan signed an executive order requiring many federal employees to undergo drug tests. While many private employees and professional athletic organizations routinely require drug tests upon application or as a condition of employment, *governmental* requirements present constitutional questions of the scope of permissible searches and seizures. Initially, the federal courts adopted the view that mandatory testing of those in certain occupations such as police and firefighters was unconstitutional *unless* there was some suspicion that the employee had been using drugs. In 1989, however, the Supreme Court ruled that mandatory drug and alcohol testing of employees involved in accidents was constitutional.[74] And in the same year the Court upheld the constitutionality of a compulsory drug-testing program for U.S. Customs Service employees.[75]

Testing for the AIDS virus has also produced questions of unreasonable searches and seizures, especially since those with the virus generally experience discrimination in all walks of life. In July 1991, the Center for Disease Control (CDC) recommended that all health care professionals who perform surgery voluntarily undergo testing to determine if they are infected with the human immunodeficiency virus (HIV), which causes AIDS. If they are, the CDC suggested that they disclose the condition to patients and refrain from practicing unless they are cleared to do so by a local medical review panel. In the absence of federal legislation, however, many medical organizations have refused to comply with the CDC's recommendations. In late October 1991, Congress passed legislation that requires states to adopt the CDC recommendations within one year or risk losing federal funds for numerous health programs, including childhood immunization, drug abuse, and family planning.

The Exclusionary Rule

In 1914 in *Weeks* v. *United States*[76] the U.S. Supreme Court adopted what is called the **exclusionary rule**, which bars the use of illegally seized evidence at trial. The rationale for this was that allowing police and prosecutors to use the "fruits of a poison tree" (a tainted search) would only encourage prohibited activity. Later, in *Mapp* v. *Ohio*

---

[71] *Terry* v. *Ohio*, 392 U.S. 1 (1968).
[72] *U.S.* v. *Sokolov*, 490 U.S. 1 (1989).
[73] *U.S.* v. *Matlock*, 415 U.S. 164 (1974).
[74] *Skinner* v. *Railway Labor Executives' Association*, 489 U.S. 602 (1989).
[75] *National Treasury Employees Union* v. *Von Raab*, 489 U.S. 656 (1989).
[76] 232 U.S. 383 (1914).

(1961),[77] the Court ruled that the exclusionary rule applied to the states via the Fourteenth Amendment. Thus, although the Fourth Amendment itself does not bar the use of evidence obtained in violation of its provisions, the exclusionary rule is a judicially created remedy to deter any violation of the Fourth Amendment.

Although the Warren Court resolved the dilemma of balancing the goal of deterring police misconduct and the likelihood that a guilty individual would go free in favor of deterrence, the Burger and Rehnquist Courts have gradually been chipping away at the exclusionary rule. In *Stone* v. *Powell* (1976)[78] the Burger Court dramatically reduced the opportunities for defendants to seek review of their convictions based on tainted evidence in violation of the Fourth Amendment. If they already had raised the objection in state court, the Supreme Court ruled, convicted defendants could not seek a rehearing on the issue in federal court. Concern that the societal costs of overturning convictions (of guilty individuals) based on illegally obtained evidence outweighed any benefits that the exclusionary rule had in deterring police misconduct prompted Justice Lewis F. Powell, Jr., to note that the exclusionary rule "deflects the truth-finding process and often frees the guilty." Since then, the Court has carved out a variety of "good faith exceptions" to the exclusionary rule that allow the use of "tainted" evidence in a variety of situations, especially when police appeared to be acting or thought that they were acting within the Fourth Amendment's mandates. Thus, it is likely that the rule could be completely abandoned in the next few years.

Self-Incrimination

The Fifth Amendment provides that "*No person shall be . . . compelled in any criminal case to be a witness against himself.*" The Supreme Court has interpreted this guarantee to be "as broad as the mischief against which it seeks to guard,"[79] finding that criminal defendants do not have to take the stand at trial to answer questions, nor can a judge make mention of their failure to do so. Lawyers can't hint that a defendant who refuses to take the stand must be guilty or have something to hide. Moreover, the right not to testify extends to grand jury proceedings, legislative investigations, and even to witnesses in judicial proceedings if the information they may give could result in their own prosecution. "Taking the Fifth" is a shorthand bit of slang that refers to instances when individuals exercise their constitutional right not to incriminate themselves.

The right also means that prosecutors cannot use as evidence in a trial any statements or confessions made by defendants that were not "voluntary." As is the case in many areas of the law, however, the definition of the term *voluntary* has changed over time. For many years, it was not at all unusual for local police to beat a defendant in order to get a confession. Once the Supreme Court ruled in 1936 that confessions given after physical beatings were inadmissible, police began to resort to other measures to force confessions. Defendants, for example, were "given the third degree"—questioned for hours on end with no sleep or food or threatened with physical violence until they were mentally "beaten" into a confession. In other situations family members were threatened. In one case a young mother was told that her welfare benefits would be terminated and her children taken away from her if she failed to talk.[80]

In response to these creative efforts to obtain confessions that were truly not voluntary, in 1966 the Supreme Court delivered its decision in the landmark case of *Miranda* v. *Arizona.*[81] On March 3, 1963, an eighteen-year-old girl was kidnapped and raped on the

[77] 367 U.S. 643 (1961).

[78] 428 U.S. 465 (1976).

[79] *Counselman* v. *Hitchcock,* 142 U.S. 547 (1892).

[80] *Lynumn* v. *Illinois,* 372 U.S. 528 (1963).

[81] 384 U.S. 1602 (1966).

Even though Ernesto Miranda's confession was not admitted as evidence at his retrial, his ex-girlfriend's testimony and that of the victim were enough to convince the jury of his guilt. He served nine years in prison before he was released on parole. After his release, he routinely sold autographed cards inscribed with the Miranda rights now read to all suspects. In 1976, four years after his release, Miranda was stabbed to death in Phoenix in a bar fight during a card game. Two Miranda cards were found on his body, and the person who killed him was read his Miranda rights upon his arrest.

outskirts of Phoenix, Arizona. Ten days later, police arrested Ernesto Miranda, a poor, mentally disturbed man with a ninth-grade education. At the police station, the victim identified Miranda in a lineup as her attacker. Police then took Miranda to a separate room and questioned him for two hours. Although he first denied any guilt, he eventually confessed to the crime and wrote and signed a brief statement describing the crime and admitting his guilt. At no time was he told that he didn't have to answer any questions or that he could be represented by an attorney.

After his conviction, his attorneys appealed his case, arguing that Miranda's Fifth Amendment rights had been violated because his confession had been coerced. In *Miranda* v. *Arizona* the Court found that his confession had not been truly voluntary. Chief Justice Earl Warren, himself a former district attorney and California State Attorney General, noted that because police have a tremendous advantage in any interrogation situation, criminal suspects must be given greater protection. To provide guidelines for police, the Court mandated that "Prior to any questioning, the person must be warned that he has a right to remain silent, that any statements he does make may be used as evidence against him, and that he has a right to the presence of an attorney, either retained or appointed." In response, police all over the nation routinely began to read suspects their **Miranda rights**, a practice you undoubtedly have seen repeated over and over in movies or on TV police dramas.

Although the Burger Court did not enforce the reading of Miranda rights as vehemently as the Warren Court, Chief Justice Burger, Chief Justice Warren's successor, acknowledged that they had become part of established police procedures.[82]

The Rehnquist Court, however, has been more tolerant of the use of coerced confessions and has employed a much more flexible standard. In 1991, for example, it ruled that the use of a coerced confession in a criminal trial does not automatically invalidate a conviction. While Oreste Fulminante was serving time in a federal penitentiary for another crime, he was befriended by an inmate, Anthony Sarivola, who was a paid FBI informer masquerading as an organized-crime figure. Sarivola told Fulminante that he knew Fulminante was getting harsh treatment from other inmates because of rumors that he had murdered a child. He offered him protection in exchange for the truth, and Fulminante admitted that he had killed his eleven-year-old stepdaughter in Arizona and provided details of the crime. When he was released from prison, Fulminante also admitted the facts of the crime to Sarivola's wife, whom he had never met until his release. Subsequently, he was indicted, tried, and convicted in Arizona for murder and sentenced to death. The trial court denied his motion to exclude the confession, which his lawyers argued had been coerced in violation of the Fifth and Fourteenth Amendments. When his appeal ultimately reached the U.S. Supreme Court, a slim five-member majority ruled that the government's use of the defendant's confession could be treated as "harmless error" if other evidence introduced at trial was sufficient to sustain a guilty verdict, thus upholding Fulminante's death sentence.[83] The addition of Justice Clarence Thomas to the Supreme Court in 1991 is unlikely to derail this trend away from a strict reading of *Miranda*.

Right to Counsel

The Sixth Amendment guarantees to an accused person "*the Assistance of Counsel in his defense.*" Historically all that this provision meant was that an individual could hire an attorney to represent him or her in court. Since most criminal defendants are poor, this provision was of little assistance to many of those who found themselves on trial. Recognizing this, Congress required federal courts to provide an attorney for defendants too poor to afford one first in capital cases (those where the death penalty is a possibility) and

[82] *Rhode Island* v. *Innis,* 446 U.S. 291 (1980).
[83] *Arizona* v. *Fulminante,* 111 S. Ct. 2067 (1991).

When Clarence Gideon wrote out his petition for a writ of *certiorari* to the Supreme Court (asking the Court, in its discretion, to hear his case) he had no way of knowing that his case would lead to the landmark ruling on the right to counsel, *Gideon* v. *Wainwright*. Nor did he know that Chief Justice Earl Warren had actually instructed his law clerks to be on the lookout for a *habeas corpus* petition (literally "you have the body," which argues that the person in jail is there in violation of some statutory or constitutional right) that could be used to guarantee the assistance of counsel for defendants in criminal cases.

then eventually in all criminal cases.[84] Congress's decision affected all cases tried in federal courts, but it had no power over state courts, where most criminal cases arise. In 1932 the Supreme Court ordered states to furnish lawyers to defendants in capital cases, but it began to expand the right to counsel to other state offenses only on a piecemeal fashion that afforded the states little direction. Given the cost of providing counsel, this ambiguity often made it cost effective for the states not to provide counsel at all.

In 1963, these ambiguities came to an end when the Court decided to hear the case of *Gideon* v. *Wainwright*.[85] As so poignantly portrayed in Anthony Lewis's book *Gideon's Trumpet* and in the made-for-television movie of the same name starring Henry Fonda, Clarence Earl Gideon, a fifty-one-year-old drifter, was charged with breaking into a Panama City, Florida, pool hall and stealing beer, wine, and some change from a vending machine. At his trial he asked the judge to appoint a lawyer for him because he was too poor to hire one himself. The judge refused, and Gideon was subsequently convicted and

[84] *Johnson* v. *Zerbst*, 304 U.S. 458 (1938).
[85] 372 U.S. 335 (1963).

given a five-year prison term for petty larceny. The case against Gideon had not been strong, but he was unable to point out its weaknesses.

The apparent inequities in the system that had resulted in Gideon's conviction continued to bother him. Eventually he borrowed some lined paper from a prison guard and, after consulting the prison library, drafted and mailed to the U.S. Supreme Court a petition asking it to overrule the state Supreme Court decision.

In a unanimous decision, the U.S. Supreme Court agreed with Gideon and his court-appointed lawyer, Abe Fortas, a former associate justice of the Supreme Court. Writing for the Court, Justice Hugo Black explained that "lawyers in criminal courts are necessities, not luxuries." Therefore, the Court concluded, the state *must* provide an attorney to poor defendants in felony cases. Underscoring the Court's point, Gideon was acquitted when he was retried with a lawyer by his side to argue his case.

In 1972 the Burger Court expanded the *Gideon* rule, mandating that states must provide counsel to any poor defendant in even a misdemeanor criminal case if conviction could result in a jail term.[86] The Court also extended the right-to-counsel provision to every stage in a criminal case, from strong suspicion and/or arrest through preliminary hearings to sentencing and even beyond. States and the national government must even provide counsel for one appeal of a conviction, but not more. (Some states extend this to more than one appeal.)

Jury Trial

The Sixth Amendment (and to a lesser extent, Article III of the Constitution) provides that a person accused of a crime shall enjoy the right to a speedy and public trial by an impartial jury—that is, a trial in which a group of the accused's peers act as a fact-finding, deliberative body to determine his or her guilt or innocence. The Supreme Court has held that jury trials must be made available if a prison sentence of six or more months is possible.

"Impartiality" is a requirement of jury trials that has undergone significant change, with the method of selecting jurors being the most frequently challenged part of the process. For example, whereas potential individual jurors who have prejudged a case are not eligible to serve, no groups can be systematically excluded from serving. In 1880, for example, the Supreme Court ruled that blacks could not be excluded from state jury pools (lists of those eligible to serve).[87] And, in 1975, the Court ruled that to bar women from jury service violated the mandate that juries be a "fair cross section" of the community.[88]

In the 1980s the Court expanded the requirement that juries reflect the community by invalidating various indirect means of excluding blacks. For example, when James Batson, a black man, was tried for second-degree burglary, the state prosecutor used all of his peremptory challenges[89] to the jury to eliminate all four potential black jurors, leaving an all-white jury. The state court judge overruled Batson's lawyer's contention that the exclusion of blacks violated Batson's constitutional rights, and Batson was found guilty. The Supreme Court, however, overturned his conviction. While noting that lawyers historically used peremptory challenges to select juries they believed most favorable to the outcome they desired, the Court held that the use of peremptory challenges specifically to exclude black jurors violated the equal protection clause of the Fourteenth Amendment.

---

[86] *Argersinger* v. *Hamlin,* 407 U.S. 25 (1972).

[87] *Strauder* v. *West Virginia,* 100 U.S. 303 (1880).

[88] *Taylor* v. *Louisiana,* 419 U.S. 522 (1975).

[89] Peremptory challenges are discretionary challenges. A lawyer representing an abortion clinic protestor would use peremptory challenges to rid the jury of abortion advocates. "For cause" challenges are those based on some legal reasoning and not a personal hunch about the best persons to serve on the jury. In a capital case, persons who are morally opposed to the death penalty could be removed "for cause." *Batson* v. *Kentucky,* 476 U.S. 79 (1986).

Cruel and Unusual Punishment

The Eighth Amendment prohibits "cruel and unusual punishments," a concept rooted in the English common-law tradition. In the 1500s, religious heretics and those critical of the Crown were subjected to torture to extract confessions and then equally hideous death by the rack, disembowelment, or other forms of barbarity. The English Bill of Rights and its safeguard against "cruel and unusual punishments" was a result of public outrage against those practices. The same language found its way into the U.S. Declaration of Independence and into the Bill of Rights. Prior to the 1960s, however, little judicial attention was paid to the meaning of that phrase, especially in the context of the death penalty.

The death penalty was in use in all of the colonies at the time the Constitution was adopted, and so its constitutionality went unquestioned. In fact, in two separate cases in the late 1800s the Supreme Court ruled that deaths by public shooting and, soon after, electrocution were not "cruel and unusual" forms of punishment in the same category as "punishments which inflict torture, such as the rack, the thumbscrew, the iron boot, the stretching of limbs and the like. . . . "[90]

In the 1960s the National Association for the Advancement of Colored People (NAACP) Legal Defense Fund orchestrated a carefully designed legal attack on the constitutionality of the death penalty in the belief that it was applied more frequently to blacks convicted of crimes than to members of other groups.[91] Public opinion polls also revealed that in 1971, on the eve of the NAACP's first major death sentence case to reach the Supreme Court, support for the death penalty had fallen below 50 percent (see Figure 4-1).

With the "timing" just right, in 1972 in *Furman* v. *Georgia,* the Supreme Court upheld the NAACP's position and effectively put an end to capital punishment by declaring that as imposed (in an often arbitrary manner) it constituted cruel and unusual punishment in violation of the Eighth and Fourteenth Amendments. Following this decision, various state legislatures enacted new laws designed to meet the Court's objections. In 1976, after reviewing a number of these state laws, the Supreme Court reinstated the constitutionality of the death penalty in a seven-to-two decision.[92] Troy Gregg had murdered two hitchhikers and was awaiting execution on Georgia's death row. Although his lawyers argued that to put him to death would constitute cruel and unusual punishment, the Court concluded that the death penalty "is an expression of society's outrage at particularly offensive conduct . . . . [I]t is an extreme action, suitable to the most extreme of crimes." Before he could be executed, Troy Gregg escaped from Georgia's death row in July 1980 using a hand-crafted hacksaw and a homemade prison guard uniform. He and three other inmates escaped to North Carolina, where Gregg was beaten to death before he could be caught by authorities.

It is fairly clear that unless minors are involved, the Supreme Court now is unwilling to intervene to overrule state courts' imposition of the death penalty. In 1987 in *McCleskey* v. *Kemp,*[93] yet another Georgia case, a five-to-four Court ruled that the death penalty did not violate the equal protection clause because it discriminated against blacks. Despite the testimony of social scientists and clear evidence that the state was eleven times more likely to seek the death penalty against a black defendant, the Court upheld Warren McCleskey's sentence. It noted that even if statistics clearly show overall discrimination, "racial bias is an inevitable part of our criminal justice system" and therefore not enough to invalidate Georgia's death penalty law. Within hours of that loss, McCleskey's lawyers

---

[90] *O'Neil* v. *Vermont,* 144 U.S. 323 (1892).

[91] See Michael Meltsner, *Cruel and Unusual: The Supreme Court and Capital Punishment* (New York: Random House, 1973).

[92] *Gregg* v. *Georgia,* 428 U.S. 153 (1976).

[93] 481 U.S. 279 (1987).

Figure 4-1 **Public Opinion on the Death Penalty**

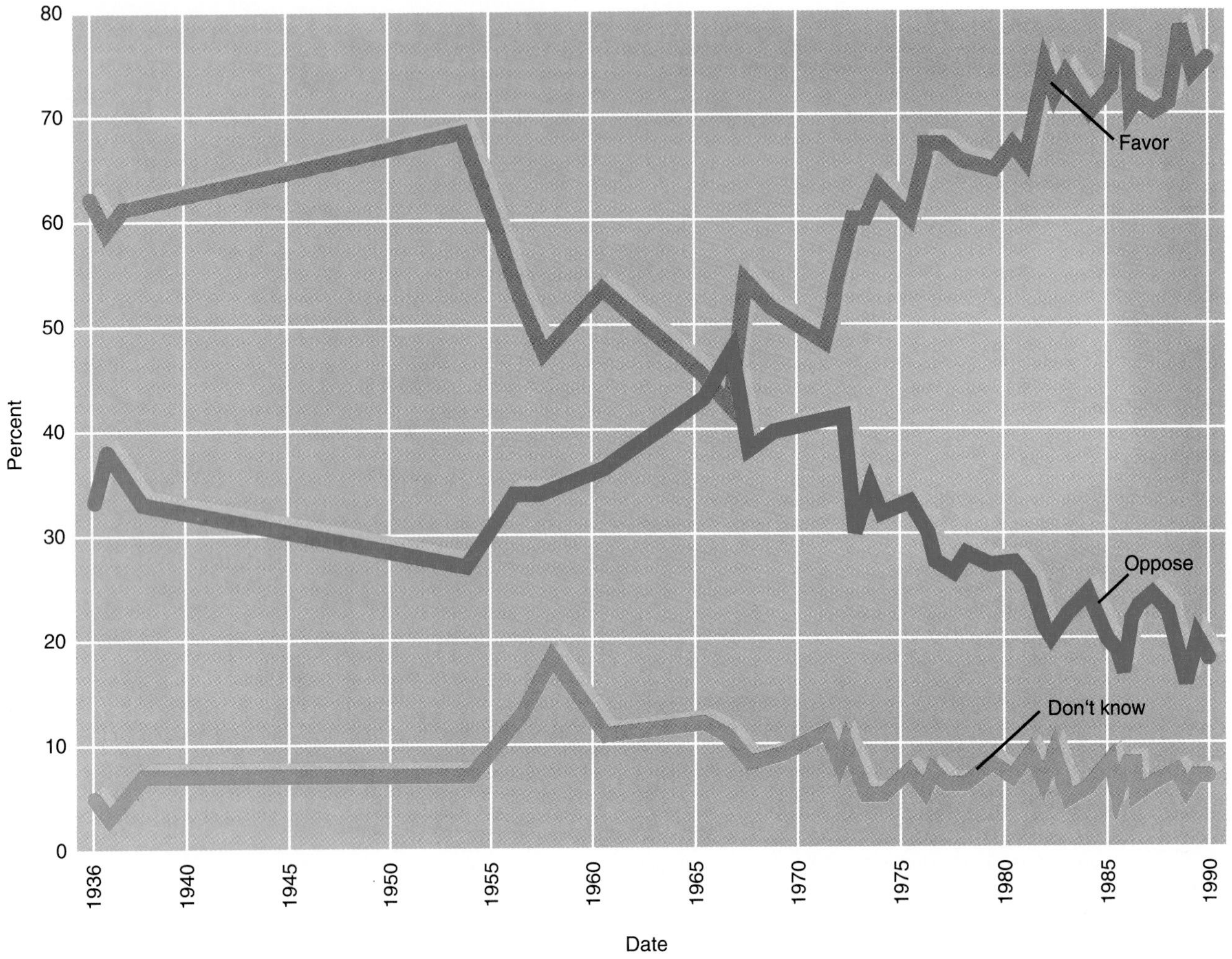

Note: Questions: 1936–1937 – "Are you in favor of the death penalty for murder?" 1953- February 1972, November 1972, April 1976, January 1985, November 1985–
"Are you in favor of the death penalty for persons convicted of murder?" All others–"Do you favor or oppose the death penalty for persons convicted of murder?"

* Includes qualified yes or qualified no.

Sources: 1936 through February 1972, November 1972, April 1976, January 1981, January 1985, November 1985, and September 1988: Gallup surveys; others from
General Social Survey.

filed a new appeal, arguing that the informant who gave the only testimony against McCleskey had been placed in his (McCleskey's) cell illegally. By the time his lawyers stood before the Supreme Court again three years later, the Court was more conservative. And, again, their appearance produced an equally if not more important ruling on the death penalty and criminal procedure from the Supreme Court. In the second *McCleskey* case, *McCleskey* v. *Zant,*[94] the Court found that McCleskey's lawyers should have raised the issue of the informant during the first appeal, in spite of the fact that the lawyers were originally told by the state that the witness was not an informer. The decision served to set new standards, making it much more difficult for death-row inmates to file repeated

[94] 111 S. Ct. 2841 (1991).

Warren McCleskey and the Death Penalty

When forty-six-year-old Warren McCles-key, a former aerospace company worker, was put to death in Georgia's electric chair on September 26, 1991, his death marked a new era in criminal law. McCleskey's path to immortality began on a dark night in 1978 when an off-duty Atlanta police officer was shot and killed as he investigated a break-in at a downtown Atlanta furniture store. There was never any question that McCleskey was there; the question was whether he killed the officer. McCleskey maintained his innocence to the end.

In McCleskey's first appeal, decided in 1987, the Supreme Court rejected his claim that death penalty laws are un-constitutional *even* if statistics indicate that racial discrimination affected the way the death sentence was imposed. In his second appeal, decided in 1991 in a six-to-three ruling, the Court rebuffed McCleskey's appeal in a decision that severely restricts the ability of state prisoners to seek more than one habeas corpus review. A "writ of habeas cor-pus" allows prisoners who have ex-hausted their state-level appeals to bring constitutional challenges—in sep-arate appeals with no time limit—to the federal courts. Experts anticipate that the decision will shorten the average time between commission of a crime and execution—currently nine years— to six or seven years.

Writing for the majority of the Court, Justice Anthony Kennedy said that death row inmates can bring additional appeals only when they can show that some external factor, such as improper suppression of evidence, prevented them from raising the claim in the first appeal. In addition, a prisoner must show that the new evidence would have had a substantial effect on the conviction or sentence.

In his second appeal, McCleskey had argued that his Sixth Amendment right to counsel was violated by the state when a cellmate—who the police had placed with McCleskey to gather incrim-inating evidence on the promise of re-ducing the charges against him— coerced McCleskey to confess to the murder and then testified against him at trial. Even though another court ruled that this government action was illegal because the jury was not told that the witness was an informant, the Supreme Court said McCleskey's lawyers should have raised the issue earlier. Even a last-minute attempt by his attorneys, who filed affidavits from two of McCles-key's original jurors saying they would *not* have voted for the death sentence had they been told an informant had been planted in the cell, was not enough to convince the Court to stop his execution.

appeals, a practice frequently decried by many of the justices. Ironically, McCleskey's accuser was freed the night before McCleskey was electrocuted.

The Right to Privacy

The Framers failed to mention a right to privacy in the original Constitution, and when the First Congress met to draft the Bill of Rights, no mention was made of it then. Never-theless, as Justice William O. Douglas noted in 1965, the notion of privacy is "older than the Bill of Rights." It is questionable, however, whether the Framers would ever have considered birth control, surrogate motherhood, or in vitro fertilization the proper subjects of constitutional protection.

What Is the Right to Privacy?

Although the Constitution is silent about the right to privacy, the Bill of Rights contains many indications that the Framers expected that some areas of life were "off limits" to governmental regulation. The freedom of religion found in the First Amendment implies a right to exercise private, personal beliefs. The guarantee against unreasonable searches and seizures contained in the Fourth Amendment similarly implies that persons are to be secure in their homes and should not fear that police will show up at their doorsteps without cause. As early as 1928 Justice Louis Brandeis hailed privacy as "the right to be left alone—the most comprehensive of the rights and the most valued by civilized men." It was not until 1965, however, that the Court attempted to explain the origins of the right.

Birth Control

In 1965 in *Griswold* v. *Connecticut*[95] the Supreme Court heard arguments concerning the constitutionality of an 1879 Connecticut law that prohibited the dissemination of information about and the sale of contraceptives. In 1943 and again in 1961, groups seeking legislative repeal of the law had challenged its constitutionality; however, the Supreme Court refused to address the merits of the case, finding that a doctor who had not been charged with violating the statute had no standing (legal right) to bring the case. In the 1961 decision, however, four justices dissented, and soon two in the majority retired. But because Justice Felix Frankfurter's majority opinion had stressed the fact that the law had long gone unenforced, officials of the Planned Parenthood organization decided that they would need to have parties actually charged with violating the law in order to challenge its constitutionality. So, Estelle Griswold, the executive director of Planned Parenthood League of Connecticut, and Dr. C. Lee Buxton opened up a birth-control clinic and were arrested ten days later. After they were convicted in the state courts, they appealed to the U.S. Supreme Court. Seven justices decided that various portions of the Bill of Rights cast "penumbras"—unstated liberties on the fringes or in the shadow of more explicitly stated rights—thereby creating zones of privacy, including a married couple's right to plan a family. Later, the Court expanded the right of privacy to include the right of unmarried individuals to have access to contraceptives. "If the right of privacy means anything," wrote Justice William J. Brennan, "it is the right of the individual, married or single, to be free from unwarranted governmental intrusion into matters so fundamentally affecting a person as the decision to bear or beget a child."[96]

Abortion

In the early 1960s, the combined effects of a worldwide panic that arose after pregnant women who had been given the drug thalidomide to control morning sickness bore severely deformed babies, a nationwide measles epidemic that resulted in the birth of hundreds of severely deformed babies, the increasing medical safety of abortions, and the growing women's rights movement put pressure on the legal and medical establishments for changes in laws that would guarantee a woman's access to safe and legal abortion. By the late 1960s, fourteen states had voted to liberalize their abortion policies, and four states allowed abortion in the early stages of pregnancy without any criminal penalty. But many women's rights activists wanted more. They argued that deciding whether to

[95] 381 U.S. 481 (1965).
[96] *Eisenstadt* v. *Baird,* 410 U.S. 113 (1972).

carry a pregnancy to term was a woman's fundamental constitutional right. In 1973, in one of the most controversial decisions ever handed down, seven members of the Court agreed with this position.

The woman whose case became the catalyst for pro-choice and anti-abortion groups was an itinerant circus worker who found herself pregnant. Already the mother of a toddler she had to leave in her mother's care, she decided to terminate the pregnancy. Unable to secure a legal abortion and frightened by the conditions she found when she sought an illegal, back-alley abortion, Norma McCovey then turned to two young Texas lawyers who were looking for a plaintiff who would allow them to challenge Texas's restrictive statute, which allowed abortions only when they were necessary to save the life of the mother. Although McCovey was unable to obtain a legal abortion and later gave birth and put the baby up for adoption, she allowed her lawyers to proceed to use her, under the pseudonym Jane Roe, as their plaintiff to challenge the Texas law as enforced by Henry Wade, the district attorney of Dallas County, Texas. When the case finally came before the Supreme Court, Justice Harry A. Blackmun, a former lawyer at the Mayo Clinic, relied heavily on medical evidence to invalidate the Texas law. Blackmun divided pregnancy into three parts. In the first trimester, the Court concluded, a woman's right to privacy gave her an absolute right, free from state interference, to terminate a pregnancy. In the second trimester, the state's interest in the health of the mother gave it the right to regulate abortions—but only to protect the woman's health. Only in the third trimester—after the potential viability of the fetus—did the Court find that the state's interest in potential life outweighed the woman's privacy interests. Even in the third trimester, however, abortions to save the life or health of the mother were to be legal.

Roe v. *Wade* unleashed a torrent of political controversy. Anti-abortion groups, caught off guard, scrambled to recoup their losses in Congress. Representative Henry Hyde (R.-Ill.) persuaded Congress to ban the use of Medicaid funds for abortions for poor women, and the constitutionality of the Hyde Amendment was upheld by the Supreme Court in 1977 and again in 1980.[97]

Throughout the 1970s until today, the right to an abortion and its constitutional underpinnings in the right to privacy have been under attack by well-organized anti-abortion groups. The Reagan and Bush administrations also have been strong advocates of the anti-abortion position, regularly urging the Court to overrule *Roe.* They came close to victory in *Webster* v. *Reproductive Health Services* (1989).[98] In *Webster* the Court upheld state-required fetal viability tests in the second trimester that would increase the cost of an abortion considerably. The Court also upheld Missouri's refusal to allow abortions to be performed in state-supported hospitals or by state-funded doctors or nurses. Perhaps most noteworthy, however, were the facts that four justices seemed willing to overrule *Roe* v. *Wade* and that Justice Antonin Scalia publicly rebuked his colleague Sandra Day O'Connor, the only woman on the Court, for failing to provide the critical fifth vote to overrule *Roe.*

At this writing, the outlook for the continued vitality of *Roe* v. *Wade* is unclear. As we saw in *Rust* v. *Sullivan* (1991), discussed earlier, the Court ruled five to four that although the right to an abortion was a "protected right," the government didn't have to subsidize it. (Justice David Souter, the Court's newest member at that time, joined the conservative, anti-abortion faction led by Chief Justice William H. Rehnquist.) Spurred on by these positive signals from the Court and heartened by the appointment of Justice Clarence Thomas, a former Roman Catholic seminarian, to the Court, anti-abortion activists are helping states such as Utah and Pennsylvania defend the constitutionality of newly enacted abortion laws. Also, the political fallout over the issue has caused candidates at all levels to reevaluate their position as more and more voters show an interest in an office seeker's position on abortion. In 1989, for example, L. Douglas Wilder and James J. Florio, both pro-choice candidates, were chosen governor of Virginia and New

Civil disobedience: In 1991 in Wichita, Kansas, Operation Rescue anti-abortion activists felt so strongly about their cause that they staged massive civil disobedience demonstrations outside of an abortion clinic. Operation Rescue first adopted this tactic in 1988 during the Democratic National Convention in Atlanta, Georgia. Since then, clinics in a variety of U.S. cities have been the target of these sit-ins, which often have led to arrest of the protesters.

[97] *Beal* v. *Doe,* 432 U.S. 438 (1977) and *Harris* v. *McRae,* 448 U.S. 297 (1980).
[98] 492 U.S. 490 (1989).

Jersey, respectively, in elections that placed abortion at the center of debate. Although pro-choice candidates may profit from their position on this highly emotional issue, it is unlikely that the Court's upcoming decisions will give them much to rejoice about.

Homosexuality

Although the Supreme Court has ruled that the right to privacy includes the right "whether or not to beget children," it has declined to interpret the right of privacy to include the right to engage in homosexual acts. In 1985 the Court, in a four-to-four decision (in Justice Lewis Powell's absence for illness), upheld a lower court decision that overturned an Oklahoma law allowing the dismissal of teachers who advocate homosexual relations. When Professor Lawrence Tribe of the Harvard Law School took to the lectern to argue against the constitutionality of a Georgia statute that prohibited consensual heterosexual and homosexual oral or anal sex, he pitched his arguments toward Justice Powell, who he knew would be the crucial swing vote in this controversial area. But his efforts were ultimately to no avail.

On a Saturday morning in 1986 in Atlanta, Michael Hardwick was arrested in his bedroom by a police officer who was there to serve an arrest warrant on Hardwick for his failure to appear in court on another charge. (One of his roommates let the police officer in and directed him to Hardwick's room.) After Hardwick's arrest on a sodomy charge, the local prosecutor decided not to pursue charges under the sodomy law. Nonetheless, Hardwick, a local gay activist, joined forces with the American Civil Liberties Union to challenge the constitutionality of the law. In a five-to-four decision the Supreme Court upheld the law. At conference, Justice Powell reportedly seemed torn by the case. He believed that the twenty-year sentence that came with conviction was excessive but was troubled by the fact that Hardwick hadn't actually been tried and convicted. Although he originally voted with the majority to overturn the law, he was bothered by the broadness of Justice Blackmun's original draft of the majority opinion and therefore changed his mind, making the minority view upholding the law the new majority.[99]

In light of the current composition of the Court and the AIDS crisis, it is highly unlikely that the right to privacy will at any time soon be extended to gays. In fact, during the 1991 confirmation hearings of Justice Clarence Thomas, the question often seemed more one of whether a majority of the court will continue to find a right to privacy at all within the "penumbras" of the Bill of Rights.

Toward Reform

The addition of the Bill of Rights to the Constitution was one of the first acts of the First Congress. Since that time, no amendments have been added to the Constitution to alter the basic liberties guaranteed by the Bill of Rights. In the 1980s, in the aftermath of the flag burning controversy, many called for the enactment of an amendment to ban flag burning. But reluctance to in any way alter the First Amendment's far-reaching protections ultimately led to the defeat of such proposals. Opponents argued fervently that this nation was built upon political protest and that free expression should be constitutionally protected at all costs, no matter how repugnant to the majority.

While little has been done in the way of making changes to the Constitution, over the years the Supreme Court has been a major player in "reforming" the Constitution. Many have viewed the Court as a continuing Constitutional Convention whose decisions have refined and even created new rights through judicial interpretation. Today, a considerable

---

[99] Reported in David M. O'Brien, *Constitutional Law and Politics*, Vol. 1 (New York: Norton, 1991), p. 1223. See *Hardwick* v. *Bowers*, 478 U.S. 186 (1986).

controversy exists over the appropriateness of policy making by a non-elected judiciary. Since the 1950s, the Court at times has found itself the target of congressional threats to limit its ability to hear cases. Generally, these proposals have occurred when the Court has appeared to be lenient toward those advocating unpopular ideas such as communism or flag burning. At times the Court has backed down, at times it has not.

Summary

The Bill of Rights is a fundamental part of the American tradition. Within its provisions are the heart of Americans' protections from the excesses of government the Framers sought to avoid. Disputes over the scope of its provisions are common, and over the years all three branches of government—especially the legislative and the judicial—have played key roles in defining them.

Key freedoms guaranteed by the First Amendment deal with religion, speech, and press. Procedural rights guaranteed to those accused of a crime are found in the Fourth, Fifth, Sixth, and Eighth Amendments. And other rights, such as that of privacy, although not found in the printed words of the Constitution, have been found in the shadow or "penumbras" of specific provisions.

All of these rights—whether protected by specific amendments or not—are subject to frequent judicial scrutiny and have evolved and been expanded or contracted over time. Each new Supreme Court has contributed to these developments, and it is likely that these liberties will continue to take different shapes and contours as they are interpreted anew.

Key Terms

civil liberties	clear and present danger test	libel
civil rights	bad tendency test	slander
libelous	due process clause	symbolic speech
seditious	incorporation doctrine	due process rights
fighting words	selective incorporation	exclusionary rule
prior restraint		Miranda rights

Suggested Readings

Chafe, Zachariah, Jr. *Free Speech in the United States.* Cambridge, Mass.: Harvard University Press, 1948.

Clor, Harry M. *Obscenity and Public Morality.* Chicago: University of Chicago Press, 1967.

Friendly, Fred. *Minnesota Rag: The Dramatic Story of the Landmark Case That Gave New Meaning to Freedom of the Press.* New York: Random House, 1981.

Leonard, Levy, et al. *The First Amendment.* New York: Macmillan, 1986.

Lewis, Anthony. *Make No Law: The Sullivan Case and the First Amendment.* New York: Random House, 1991.

Manwaring, David R. *Render unto Caesar: The Flag Salute Controversy.* Chicago: University of Chicago Press, 1962.

O'Brien, David M. *Constitutional Law and Politics, Vol. 2: Civil Rights and Civil Liberties.* New York: Norton, 1991.

Pfeffer, Leo. *Religion, State and the Burger Court.* Buffalo, New York: Prometheus Books, 1984.

Rubin, Eva. *Abortion, Politics, and the Court.* Westport, Conn.: Greenwood Press, 1982.

The true state of the case is that [slaves] partake of both these qualities: being considered by our laws, in some respects, as persons, and in other respects as property.

James Madison

FEDERALIST NO. 54

The institution of slavery represents America's most profound betrayal of civil rights in its entire history. It would take some of the country's most tumultuous times—including the Civil War and the civil rights movement of the 1960s—to begin to rectify the evils of slavery and its legacy.

CHAPTER 5

Civil Rights

While the Declaration of Independence boldly proclaimed, "We hold these truths to be self-evident, that all men are created equal, that they are endowed by their Creator with certain inalienable rights . . . ," the Constitution is silent on the concept of equality. The Founders were guided in their drafting of the Constitution and later of the Bill of Rights by the high premium they placed on the notion of liberty. They firmly believed that all men, at least all white men, were equally entitled to life, liberty, property, and the pursuit of happiness.

The well-to-do members of the Constitutional Convention—in spite of pleas like those of Abigail Adams to her husband, John, cautioning him not to "forget the ladies" in the new code of laws—generally never gave even a thought to what today we call **civil rights,** the powers or privileges guaranteed to individuals and protected by law from arbitrary infringement by the government or any individual. Although the right to a trial by jury, found in the Sixth Amendment, can be considered a civil right, more commonly we think of civil rights as those policies that explicitly and specifically extend basic rights to blacks, women, and other minorities who historically have faced discrimination and differential treatment. One could go so far as to say that civil liberties concern rights that the government may not infringe; civil rights concern rights that the government must provide.

What we think of today as issues of major importance—the treatment of blacks and voting—were issues addressed by the Framers, but, as James Madison's reflections in Federalist No. 54 on the "Three-Fifths Compromise" indicate, black slaves were treated in the new Constitution more like property than persons. Whereas earlier the Declaration of Independence had so eloquently proclaimed that "all men are created equal," the delegates to the Constitutional Convention put political expediency before the immorality of slavery. In fact, the Constitution specifically provided that the importation of slaves could not be prohibited for twenty years!

Once slavery was sanctioned, the question then became: "How were slaves to be considered for purposes of determining state population?" Delegates from the slave states—who insisted that slaves were property, not persons—fought to include those same slaves as persons for the purpose of calculating state populations upon which representation in the House of Representatives was to be based. In contrast, representatives from states in which slavery was on the wane argued that slaves be included only for purposes of calculating direct taxes, which the Framers had already agreed would be apportioned among the states according to population. This controversy led to the "Three-Fifths Compromise" in which each slave would be counted as "three-fifths" of a free man for purposes of representation *and* taxation. Why three-fifths? A committee of twelve members representing each state at the Constitutional Convention concluded that a slave was, on the average, "three-fifths" as productive as a free man.

Slaves at work in South Carolina.

There was never any question that white women would be considered full citizens for purposes of determining state population. And there was no question about whether women could vote. They could not. Voting qualifications were left to the states and, given that most states had numerous requirements that had to be met before a man could vote, the Framers appeared unfazed by limits on suffrage, the legal right to vote. In fact, a proposal for universal suffrage for males was quickly rejected by the Framers. In general the idea of voting rights or any other kind of rights was not something that particularly troubled the Framers. They were more concerned with fashioning a workable government. Once the Constitution was ratified, however, one of the first orders of business for the First Congress was passage of the Bill of Rights, which was immediately added to the Constitution to ensure that a number of personal liberties would be free from curtailment by the national government. These are what we call civil liberties, freedoms expressly guaranteed to the individual upon which the government cannot infringe.

In the early years after the Revolutionary War, women had voted in some parts of Virginia and New Jersey, but those rights were terminated by the adoption of state constitutions limiting suffrage to white property-owning males.

The Framers had a narrow view of equal rights. Generally the notion was limited to mean the right of *some* citizens to equal treatment by the *national* government. Since that time, however, the concept of civil rights has changed dramatically. The addition of the Fourteenth Amendment, one of three amendments passed after the Civil War, introduced the notion of equality into the Constitution for the first time by specifying that states could not deny their citizens *"equal protection of the laws."*

Since its addition to the Constitution, the Fourteenth Amendment has generated more litigation to determine and specify its meaning than any other provision of the Constitution. Within a few years of its ratification, women—and, later, blacks and other minorities and disadvantaged groups—took to the courts to seek expanded civil rights in all walks of life. But the struggle to expand rights was not limited to the courts. Public protest, civil disobedience, legislative lobbying, and appeals to public opinion all have been part of the arsenal of those seeking full equality.

As we will see, the Constitution now has been interpreted to protect blacks and women from discrimination or any other unequal treatment that violates their civil rights. The Supreme Court, however, has chosen not to interpret the **equal protection clause** of the Fourteenth Amendment as prohibiting discrimination against a variety of others, including, for example, the poor, the handicapped, the elderly, and those afflicted with AIDS. Congress, however, *has* acted to extend rights to many of those groups by passage of various laws. Recently, after the Supreme Court retreated from many of its earlier civil rights decisions, Congress found itself deadlocked with the president over an attempt to reinstate earlier Court doctrine. A compromise civil rights bill was finally passed in late 1991.

In many ways, this is a strange period to be studying civil rights. Over time, since passage of the Civil War Amendments, there has been a fairly consistent pattern of the expansion of civil rights to more and more groups. Full equality still has not been reached by everyone, but major improvements and progress have been made. But as we saw in the case of civil liberties, the Rehnquist Court is increasingly reversing earlier civil rights victories, especially those affecting blacks. How far the tide will turn is yet to be seen.

Civil rights and equality are burning issues in Britain, although the form and content differ substantially. During the nineteenth century in Britain, a major issue was the right to vote. By the end of the century, all adult males could vote, while women were accorded the right to vote in two successive stages: the first in 1918, when women over the age of thirty were granted suffrage, and the second in 1928, when women twenty-one and older were allowed to vote. In the twentieth century in Britain, equality and civil rights for women and racial and ethnic minorities have taken center stage. With the United States as a reference point, the British political system has generated both advantages and disadvantages for these groups. The unitary form of government and the strong political left provide—at least technically—ready vehicles for rapid, sweeping legislative change. Women and minorities, for example, have not had to contend with an obstructionist tier of state governments in obtaining greater rights. Still, getting the attention of highly organized political parties and a centralized government has not always been easy.

Moreover, the absence of a codified bill of rights has made it more difficult than it is in the United States to seek judicial reform.

To better understand how notions of equality and civil rights have changed in this country, we examine the evolution of black rights and women's rights in tandem from a historical perspective. Until recently the struggles for black rights and women's rights have been closely intertwined. To appreciate how each group as drawn ideas, support, and success from the other, we discuss their parallel developments. Additionally, as blacks and women have gained fuller equality, their actions have become the model for other groups that considered themselves disadvantaged in the political system—Hispanics, gays, the elderly, and the poor, for example. This chapter includes an examination of these recent developments.

Landmark Events in the Quest for Civil Rights: The Nineteenth Century

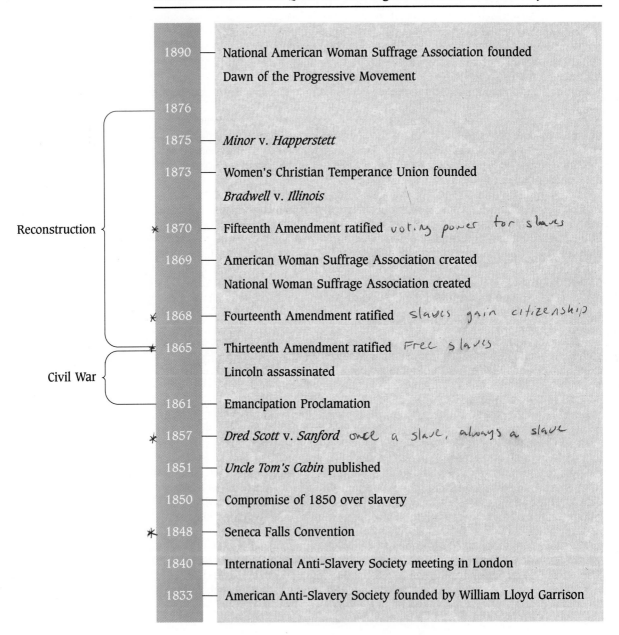

	1890	National American Woman Suffrage Association founded
		Dawn of the Progressive Movement
	1876	
	1875	*Minor* v. *Happerstett*
	1873	Women's Christian Temperance Union founded
		Bradwell v. *Illinois*
Reconstruction	✳ 1870	Fifteenth Amendment ratified *voting power for slaves*
	1869	American Woman Suffrage Association created
		National Woman Suffrage Association created
	✳ 1868	Fourteenth Amendment ratified *slaves gain citizenship*
	✳ 1865	Thirteenth Amendment ratified *Free slaves*
		Lincoln assassinated
Civil War	1861	Emancipation Proclamation
	✳ 1857	*Dred Scott* v. *Sanford* *once a slave, always a slave*
	1851	*Uncle Tom's Cabin* published
	1850	Compromise of 1850 over slavery
	✳ 1848	Seneca Falls Convention
	1840	International Anti-Slavery Society meeting in London
	1833	American Anti-Slavery Society founded by William Lloyd Garrison

To facilitate our discussion, we look at the evolution of civil rights in four distinct eras:

1. The abolition of slavery and winning the right to vote, 1840–90
2. The Progressive Movement and the push for equality, 1890–1954
3. The civil rights movement and beyond, 1955–80
4. The Reagan Revolution and beyond, 1981–

In each period major advances were made, although full equality still remains a dream for many Americans.

Slavery, Abolition, and Winning the Right to Vote, 1840–90

The period from 1840 to 1890 was one of tremendous change and upheaval in America. The Civil War was fought and slaves were freed, yet the promise of equality guaranteed to blacks by the Civil War Amendments failed to become a reality. And, while women's rights activists also began to make claims for equality, often using the arguments enunciated for the abolition of slavery, they too fell far short of their goals.

The Development of Slavery

After 1793, with the invention of the cotton gin, a machine that allowed seeds to be separated from cotton very quickly, the agricultural South grew increasingly reliant on slaves to plant and harvest fields. More and more acres of farmland were converted to cotton production, an increasingly profitable venture. When Congress decided to ban slave trade in 1808 (after the expiration of the twenty-year period guaranteed by the Constitution), the number of blacks in the United States began to decline just as the "need" for slaves grew. In 1820, blacks made up 25 percent of the population. By 1840 that figure had fallen to 20 percent. As the South was becoming even more agricultural because of the cotton gin, technological advances were helping turn the Northern states into an increasingly industrialized region. Factories were springing up all over the Northeast. The increased industrialization of the North exacerbated the cultural and political differences between the regions.

Slavery presented the national government with a divisive political issue. Conflicts between Northern and Southern states over the admission of new states to the Union with "free" or "slave" status emerged as the nation grew westward. The first major sectional crisis occurred in 1820, when the territory of Missouri applied for admission to the Union as a "slave state"—that is, one in which slavery would be legal. Missouri's admission would have weighted the Senate in favor of slavery and was therefore opposed by Northern senators. Henry Clay of Kentucky suggested the Missouri Compromise of 1820, which allowed the admission of Missouri as a slave state along with the admission of the state of Maine (formed out of the territory of Massachusetts with the permission of Congress and Massachusetts) as a free state. The compromise additionally set forth the principle that all territory north of the line 36 degrees 30 minutes would be admitted as free; all below, as slave states.

Other compromises concerning slavery were eventually necessitated as the nation continued to grow. In the Compromise of 1850, for example, (1) California was admitted as a free state, (2) the territories of Utah and New Mexico were created out of land acquired from Mexico, (3) slave trade was abolished in the District of Columbia, and (4) a more stringent fugitive slave law was passed to appease the South. The resultant Fugitive Slave Law, whose purpose was to achieve the return of escaped slaves, denied runaway slaves the right to a trial by jury as well as the right to testify in a court of law upon their capture.

The Abolitionist Movement: The First Civil Rights Movement

The political controversies that occurred over the compromises, while solidifying the South, fueled the fervor of those who opposed slavery. In the early 1800s, opponents of slavery encouraged private charities to purchase slaves and transport them to the west coast of Africa, where the independent nation of Liberia was founded in the 1820s by eighty-eight black settlers.[1] Although some slaves obtained freedom this way, this solution to the problem was not all that practical. Few owners were willing to free their slaves, and the trip and conditions in Africa were dangerous. The anti-slavery movement might have fizzled had it not been for the infusion of leadership in the person of William Lloyd Garrison, a white New Englander who became active in the movement in the early 1830s. Garrison and his growing band of followers believed that slavery was morally wrong and called for its total abolition, not colonization of Africa, as a solution. He was the first person in the United States to call for "immediate and complete emancipation" of all slaves. Garrison founded and edited *The Liberator,* an abolitionist newspaper that commenced publication in 1831 and quickly became a forceful and outspoken forum for opponents of slavery. Arguing the need to extend civil rights, or what he termed "citizenship rights," to blacks, Garrison quickly amassed a sizable group of disciples. With the support of British anti-slavery leaders he founded the American Anti-Slavery Society in 1833; by 1838 it had more than 250,000 members. To put this number in perspective, that would be like the National Association for the Advancement of Colored People [NAACP] having 3.8 million members in the United States today! (In contrast, the NAACP's 1990 membership was only 400,000 members.)

The nearly 250,000 freed blacks in the North found solace in the efforts of the Anti-Slavery Society. Frederick Douglass, the most prominent black American of the pre–Civil War period, joined the call for an end to slavery and greater equality for blacks. He also edited a widely read and powerful voice against slavery, *The North Star.*

The Women's Rights Tie-in. Slavery was not the only inequality that people began to question in the decades that followed adoption of the Constitution. In 1840, for example, Garrison and even Douglass parted from the Anti-Slavery Society when it refused to accept their demand that women be allowed to participate equally in all of its activities. At that time, societal rules demanded that women not speak out in public and most laws acted to make women second-class citizens. In most states, for example, women could not divorce their husbands or keep their own wages and inheritances. And, of course, they could not vote.

It is not surprising to find that in 1840, the same year that Garrison broke with the Anti-Slavery Society and formed the American Equal Rights Association, two women who later were to be the founders of the women's movement first came to question their gender's status. Attending the 1840 meeting of the International Anti-Slavery Society in London with their husbands, Elizabeth Cady Stanton and Lucretia Mott were denied seats on the floor of the conference solely because they were women. As they sat in the balcony apart from the male delegates, they paused to compare their status to that of the slaves they sought to free. Believing that women were not all that much better off than slaves, they resolved to call a meeting to address these issues. It was not until 1848, however, that they sent out a "call" or notice for the first women's rights convention. Three hundred women and men, including Frederick Douglass, traveled to the sleepy little town of Seneca Falls, New York in order to attend the first meeting for women's rights.

[1] By 1831, only 1,420 slaves had returned to Liberia.

Then and Now

The Liberator and *Modern Maturity*

Over the years, newspapers have played an important role in rousing public sentiment against the denial of basic civil rights to blacks, women, and other minorities. William Lloyd Garrison used the pages of *The Liberator* to give voice to Northern sentiments against slavery. Later, W.E.B. DuBois edited *The Crisis,* which served to spread the word about the NAACP and its activities. *The Revolution,* edited by Susan B. Anthony, served a similar purpose for informing women about women's rights conventions, activities, and so on.

Disadvantaged groups today also make good use of the print media to "spread the word." The widest-circulated magazine in the United States is *Modern Maturity,* the in-house publication of the American Association of Retired Persons (AARP). A slick, bi-monthly publication, *Modern Maturity* has a paid circulation of 22 million. The AARP uses *Modern Maturity* to publicize its programs, such as AARP/Vote, which mobilizes the elderly to vote and urges its readers to lobby Congress for various AARP-sponsored programs.

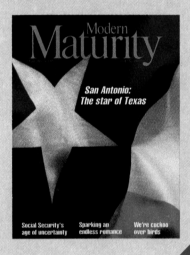

The Seneca Falls Convention (1848).

The Seneca Falls Convention attracted women and men from all over New York State. Many of them had strong ties to the abolitionist movement and believed that all men and women should be able to enjoy all rights of citizenship. Not surprisingly, then, the convention issued a Declaration of Sentiments (modeled after the U.S. Declaration of Independence), which described the "absolute tyranny" of men over women. Later, at the same meeting, resolutions calling for the abolition of legal, economic, and social discrimination against women were passed. All the documents reflected the attendees' dissatisfaction with contemporary moral codes, divorce and criminal laws, and the limited opportunities for women in education, the church, and careers in medicine, law, and politics. Only the call for an expanded franchise—the legal right of women to vote—failed to win unanimous approval. Those who attended the Seneca Falls meeting continued to press for women's rights along with the abolition of slavery. The two movements had many of the same supporters, and the messages of each were carried in both abolitionist and women's rights newspapers.

The 1850s: The Calm Before the Storm.

By 1850, much was changing in America—the Gold Rush had spurred westward migration, cities grew as people were

People of the Past

Frederick Douglass

Frederick Douglass (1817–1895), a leading advocate of civil rights for both blacks and women, was the son of a slave and an unknown white man. Although born into slavery, Douglass learned how to read and write. Once he escaped to the North, he became a well-known orator and journalist. He spoke to abolitionist groups about his experiences as a slave and included these experiences in his autobiography, *Narrative of the Life of Frederick Douglass.* His life was also romanticized by others in song.

In 1847 he started his own newspaper, *The North Star,* in Rochester, New York. Douglass was a strong abolitionist, who urged President Abraham Lincoln to emancipate the slaves and who helped to recruit black soldiers for the Union forces in the Civil War. His home in Rochester, New York, was a station along the Underground Railroad. Douglass was also a firm believer in women's suffrage and he attended the Seneca Falls Convention in 1848. Douglass was appointed to several minor federal posts, including that of minister to Haiti from 1889 to 1891. He was considered the greatest black leader of his time. When he died in 1895, five states adopted resolutions of regret, and two U.S. senators and one Supreme Court justice were among his honorary pallbearers.

Uncle Tom's Cabin, by Harriet Beecher Stowe.

lured from their farms, railroads and the telegraph increased communication and mobility, and immigrants flooded into the United States. Reformers called for change, the women's movement gained momentum, and slavery continued to tear the nation apart. The Compromise of 1850 did little to quell those fires, and its Fugitive Slave Act, in fact, prompted Harriet Beecher Stowe, the sister of well-known abolitionist preachers, to pen *Uncle Tom's Cabin,* a story that depicted the evils of slavery as a slave family was torn apart. *Uncle Tom's Cabin* was published from 1851 to 1852 in a series of forty installments in an anti-slavery newspaper. The nation hung on Stowe's every word as persons all around the United States read about the horrors visited on a slave family by its evil overseer, Simon Legree. All forty installments were published the next year as a book. It sold more than 300,000 copies in a single year and unleashed the potent power of the pen.

The tremendous national reaction to Stowe's work, which later prompted Abraham Lincoln to remark that Stowe was "the little woman who started the big war," had not yet faded when the 1820 Missouri Compromise became the lightning rod of the first major civil rights case to be addressed by the U.S. Supreme Court. As discussed in Chapter 3, in *Dred Scott* v. *Sanford* (1857),[2] the Supreme Court bluntly ruled that the first Missouri Compromise, which prohibited slavery north of the 36 30′ line, was unconstitutional. Furthermore, the Court found that slaves were not U.S. citizens and therefore could not bring lawsuits to federal court.

Writing for the majority, Chief Justice Roger Taney concluded that even free blacks "had no rights which the white man was bound to respect; and the Negro might justly and lawfully be reduced to slavery for his benefit." Although the cause of equal rights

[2] 60 U.S. (19. How.) 393 (1857).

clearly lost, the outrageous statements of the justices gave fuel to the increasingly powerful anti-slavery movement in the United States. Ironically, after the case was decided, Scott's owner decided to free him anyway.

The Civil War (1861–65) and Its Aftermath: Civil Rights Laws and Constitutional Amendments

There were many causes of the Civil War, including: (1) the political conflict between the North and South over the doctrines of nullification and secession, (2) the increasing political strength of the Northern states in Congress, (3) Southern agrarianism versus Northern industrialization, and (4) the clash of conservative Southern culture with more progressive Northern ideas. Slavery, however, was clearly the key issue.

During the war, abolitionists kept their activities alive and were rewarded in 1862 when President Lincoln issued the **Emancipation Proclamation,** which provided that all slaves in states still in active rebellion against the United States would automatically be freed on January 1, 1863. Designed as a measure to gain favor for the war in the North, the Emancipation Proclamation did not free all slaves. That did not occur until congressional passage and the ultimate ratification of the Thirteenth Amendment.

The Civil War Amendments. Enacted in 1865, the **Thirteenth Amendment** was the first of the three so-called Civil War Amendments. It stated that:

> *neither slavery nor involuntary servitude . . . shall exist within the United States, or any place subject to their jurisdiction.*

Although Southern states were required to ratify the Thirteenth Amendment as a condition of their readmission to the Union after the war, most quickly passed laws that were designed to dramatically restrict opportunities for newly freed slaves. Called the **Black Codes,** these laws prohibited blacks from voting, sitting on juries, or even appearing in public places. Although Black Codes differed from state to state, most were modeled after pre–Civil War provisions and were designed to reinstate the old status quo. All the codes, for example, empowered local law-enforcement officials to arrest unemployed blacks, fine them for vagrancy, and hire them out to employers to satisfy their fines. Some state codes went so far as to require blacks to work on plantations or to be domestics. (The Black Codes laid the groundwork for Jim Crow laws, which would institute segregation in all walks of life.)

To invalidate some of the Black Codes, the outraged Reconstructionist Congress, controlled by Radical Republicans, enacted the Civil Rights Act of 1866. President Andrew Johnson vetoed the legislation, but for the first time in history Congress overrode a presidential veto and passed the legislation anyway. This act made blacks citizens of the United States and gave the national government the power to intervene when states attempted to restrict their citizenship rights in matters such as voting. Congress reasoned that blacks were unlikely to fare well if they could file discrimination complaints only in state courts, where judges were elected; passage of a federal law allowed them to seek redress in the federal courts.

Because controversy remained over the constitutionality of the act (since the constitution gives states the right to determine qualifications of voters), the **Fourteenth Amendment** was simultaneously proposed by Congress. One of its key provisions guaranteed citizenship to all freed slaves:

> *All persons born or naturalized in the United States, and subject to the jurisdiction thereof, are citizens of the United States and of the State wherein they reside.*

Reconstruction

In the aftermath of the Civil War, the national government was faced with the problem of bringing the Southern states back into the Union. Its efforts to do so are generally referred to as *Reconstruction.* Aside from measures of political integration, Reconstruction encompassed physical and financial rehabilitation as well. In 1863, for example, President Abraham Lincoln established the "ten percent plan," which allowed a state to reformulate its own government once 10 percent of its voting population had pledged an oath of loyalty to the Union. Following Lincoln's assassination, President Andrew Johnson similarly granted amnesty to all Southerners who pledged loyalty to the Union and began reconstructing state governments. However, the Radical Republicans, who had found Lincoln and Johnson too conciliatory toward the South, declared the Southern state governments illegal and divided the region into five military districts, each governed by a major general. New state governments were formed, run by coalitions of scalawags (white Southerners who agreed with the Radical Republicans), carpetbaggers (immigrants from the North who took their name from the cloth baggage they used), and Negroes. Because these governments were imposed on Southerners from the outside, they were weak and could be maintained only through the use of military force. The "carpetbag regimes" were corrupt, and conditions in the South worsened under the Reconstruction pol-

Source: Bettmann Archive.

Thomas Nast, the most famous political cartooner of the day, drew this rendition of a "carpetbagger" headed South with a bag on his back. The bag contains the faults of his own he never sees, while he so easily sees the faults of Southerners.

icies of the Radical Republicans. The Fifteenth Amendment, which allowed Negroes to vote, was passed in part to dilute the strength of the Radical Republicans in Congress. Finally, the closeness of the 1876 presidential campaign between Republican Rutherford B. Hayes and Democrat Samuel J. Tilden brought promises from Hayes to improve conditions in the South. Hayes won the election, and Reconstruction ended. Republicans, however, did not receive any future support from Southerners, who blamed the Civil War and Reconstruction on the Republican Party.

Other key provisions of the Fourteenth Amendment barred states from abridging

- *the privileges and immunities of citizenship*

or depriving

- *any person of life, liberty, or property without due process of law.*

Unlike the Thirteenth Amendment, which had near-unanimous support in the North, the Fourteenth Amendment was opposed by many women. During the Civil War, women's rights activists, including Elizabeth Cady Stanton and Susan B. Anthony, put aside their claims for expanded rights for women, most notably the ballot, and threw their energies into the war effort. They were convinced that once slaves were freed and blacks were given the right to vote, women similarly would be rewarded with the franchise. They were wrong.

After ratification of the Fourteenth Amendment, women's rights activists met in Washington, D.C. in early 1869 for the first National Woman's Suffrage convention. There, activists argued against passage of any new amendment that would extend suffrage to black males and not to women. The convention resolved that "a *man's* government is worse than a *white* man's government, because, in proportion as you increase the tyrants, you make the condition of the disenfranchised class more hopeless and degraded."

In spite of these arguments, the **Fifteenth Amendment** was passed by Congress in February, 1869. It stated:

The right of citizens of the United States to vote shall not be denied or abridged by the United States or any State on account of race, color or previous condition of servitude.

Congress shall have the power to enforce this article by appropriate legislation.

Women's rights activists were shocked when Congress failed to include a provision enfranchising females. Abolitionists' and the American Equal Rights Association's continued support of the Fifteenth Amendment prompted many women's rights supporters to leave that movement to work solely for the cause of women's rights. Twice burned, Anthony and Stanton decided to form their own National Woman Suffrage Association (NWSA) to achieve that goal.[3] In spite of NWSA's opposition, however, the Fifteenth Amendment was ratified in 1870.

Civil Rights and the Supreme Court

While the Congress was clear in its wishes that the rights of blacks be expanded and that Black Codes be rendered illegal, the Supreme Court was not nearly so protective of those rights under the Civil War Amendments. In the first two tests of the scope of the Fourteenth Amendment, the Supreme Court ruled that the citizenship rights guaranteed by the Fourteenth Amendment applied only to rights of national citizenship and not state citizenship. Ironically, neither case involved blacks. In *The Slaughterhouse Cases* (1873),[4] the Court upheld the right of Louisiana to create a monopoly in the operation of slaughterhouses despite the Butcher's Benevolent Association's claim that this action deprived its members of their livelihood and thus the privileges and immunities of citizenship guaranteed by the amendment. Similarly, in *Bradwell* v. *Illinois* (1873),[5] when Myra Bradwell petitioned the Supreme Court, asking it to find that Illinois's refusal to allow her to practice law (although she passed the bar exam) violated her citizenship rights guaranteed by the privileges and immunities clause, her arguments fell on deaf ears. In *Bradwell,* the Court went even further than it had in *The Slaughterhouse Cases* by ruling that it was reasonable for the state to bar women from the practice of law because "the natural and proper timidity and delicacy which belongs to the female sex evidently unfits it for

[3] Ellen Carol DuBois, *Feminism and Suffrage* (Ithaca, New York: Cornell University Press, 1980).
[4] 83 U.S. (16 Wall.) 36 (1873).
[5] 83 U.S. (16 Wall.) 130 (1873).

Women in the Law

In 1869, Arabella (Belle) Mansfield (1846–1911) was the first woman admitted to the bar in the United States. Mansfield's high honors on her examination had led her two examiners to comment that this was "the very best rebuke possible to the imputation that ladies cannot qualify for the practice of law." A few editorials ridiculed the idea of a female lawyer, but otherwise there was little interest in the event.

Whereas there were only a handful of female lawyers in the United States in 1873 when the Supreme Court ruled that states could bar women from the practice of law, by 1990 women made up 45 percent of all law students and 20 percent of the legal profession.

many of the occupations of civil life." The combined message of these two cases was that state and national citizenship were separate and distinct. In essence, the Supreme Court ruled that neither blacks nor any others could be protected from discriminatory state action because the Fourteenth Amendment did not enlarge the limited rights guaranteed by U.S. citizenship.

Claims for expanded rights and requests for a clear definition of U.S. citizenship rights continued to fall on deaf ears in the halls of the Supreme Court. In 1875, for example, the Court heard *Minor* v. *Happersett*,[6] the culmination of a series of test cases launched by women's rights activists.[7] Virginia Minor, a close friend of Susan B. Anthony's, decided after planning with Anthony and other NWSA members, to attempt to register to vote in her hometown of St. Louis, Missouri. When the registrar refused to record her name on the list of eligible voters, Minor sued, arguing that the state's refusal to let her vote violated the privileges and immunities clause of the Fourteenth Amendment. Rejecting her claim, the justices ruled unanimously that voting was not a privilege of citizenship.

Failures in the Court and mounting Southern resistance to black equality led Congress to pass the Civil Rights Act of 1875, designed to grant blacks equal access to public accommodations such as theaters, restaurants, and transportation. It also prohibited the exclusion of blacks from jury service. After 1877, however, as Radical Republicans lost their hold on Congress and Reconstruction was dismantled, national interest in the legal condition of blacks waned. Most white Southerners had never believed in equality for the new **freedmen,** as former slaves were called. Any rights freedmen received had been contingent upon federal enforcement. Once federal troops were no longer available to guard polls and prevent whites from excluding black voters, Southern states moved to limit black access to the ballot. Other aspects of life also were soon limited by judicial decisions upholding **Jim Crow** laws, anti-black statutes that discriminated against blacks with respect to attendance in public schools and the use of such public facilities as railroads, restaurants, and theaters. Many also barred interracial marriage. All of these laws, at first blush, appeared to conflict with the Civil Rights Act of 1875. In 1883, however, a series of cases decided by the Supreme Court severely damaged the vitality of the 1875 Act. In the **Civil Rights Cases**[8] (actually five separate cases involving the convictions of private individuals who were found to have violated the Civil Rights Act when they refused to extend accommodations to blacks in theaters, a hotel, and a railroad), the Supreme Court ruled that Congress could prohibit only state or governmental action and *not* private acts of discrimination. The Court thus seriously limited the scope of the Thirteenth and Fourteenth Amendments by concluding that Congress had no authority to prohibit private discrimination in public accommodations.

The Court's opinion in the *Civil Rights Cases* provided a rationale for the enactment of wide-ranging racially discriminatory state laws and moral reinforcement for the Jim Crow system. Southern states viewed the Court's ruling as an invitation to restrict the reach of the Thirteenth, Fourteenth, and Fifteenth Amendments, virtually eviscerating those provisions.

In devising ways to make certain that blacks did not vote, Southerners had to avoid the *intent* of the Fifteenth Amendment. It did not *guarantee* suffrage; it simply said that states could not deny anyone the right to vote on account of color. So, to exclude blacks in a seemingly racially neutral way, Southern states used two devices before the 1890s: (1) poll taxes (small taxes on the right to vote that often came due when poor black sharecroppers had the least amount of money on hand) or some form of property-owning qualifications and (2) "literacy" or "understanding" tests, which allowed local registrars to administer difficult reading-comprehension tests to those they did not know (and therefore could not personally attest to their fitness to vote).

[6] 88 U.S. (21 Wall.) 162 (1875).
[7] Karen O'Connor, *Women's Organizations' Use of the Courts* (Lexington, Mass.: Lexington Books, 1980).
[8] 109 U.S. 3 (1883).

Jim Crow laws led to segregated hotels, restaurants, and other public facilities permeating and defining the Southern way of life.

Who Was Jim Crow?

The term "Jim Crow" symbolizes the continued discrimination of blacks in the South through state-enacted "separate but equal" laws following *Plessy* v. *Ferguson* (1896). Blacks could be denied the use of public facilities if separate-but-equal facilities existed for them. The name Jim Crow came from a song-and-dance routine first performed in the 1830s, by Thomas Dartmouth Rice in which, having blackened his face with a burnt cork, he sang:

> Weel a-bout and turn a-bout
> And do just so
> Every time I weel about
> I jump Jim Crow

Thus was born what was to become the popular minstrel show wherein whites made fun of black songs and speech. Jim Crow was "a comic, jumping, stupid rag doll of a man." The term "Jim Crow" quickly became a synonym for "Negro."* The actual identity of Jim Crow, however, is unknown. Historians suggest that he may have been a soldier whom Rice saw in Kentucky or Ohio, a slave in one of several states, or "old man Crow" himself, a legendary slaveholder.

The Jim Crow laws created separate facilities for blacks in such places as railroad cars, restaurants, and schools. The last was perhaps the most damaging to blacks, because the schools for black children were not given the same funding or quality of teachers as the schools for white children. It was not until 1954, in *Brown* v. *Board of Education of Topeka* that racial segregation was ruled unconstitutional.

*Source: Davis, Kenneth C. *Don't Know Much About History* (New York: Crown, 1990), p. 215.

These voting restrictions had an immediate impact. By the late 1890s, black voting had fallen by 62 percent while white voting had fallen by only 26 percent from the Reconstruction period. To make certain that these devices did not further hurt poor or uneducated white voters, many Southern states passed what were called **grandfather clauses,** statutes that allowed anyone to vote if his grandfathers had done so *before* Reconstruction began. This effectively denied the ancestors of any slaves the right to bypass wealth or literacy requirements.

While blacks continued to face wide-ranging discrimination on all fronts, women, too, continued to confront discrimination. During this period, married women, by law, could not be recognized as legal entities. Women often were treated in the same category as juveniles and imbeciles and in many states were not entitled to their wages, inheritances, or custody of their children.

The Push for Equality, 1890–1954

The year 1890 saw the dawn of the **Progressive Movement,** characterized by a concerted effort to reform political, economic, and social affairs. Evils like child labor, the concentration of economic power in the hands of a few industrialists, limited suffrage, political corruption, business monopolies, and prejudice against blacks were all targets of reform efforts. Distress over the legal inferiority of blacks was aggravated in 1896 by the U.S. Supreme Court's decision in *Plessy* v. *Ferguson,* a case that some commentators point to as the darkest hour of the Court.

***Plessy* v. *Ferguson:* "Separate But Equal."** In 1892, a group of blacks in Louisiana decided to test the constitutionality of a Louisiana law—a key provision of its Black Code—that mandated racial segregation on all public trains. They found an "ideal" individual to test the law. Homer Adolph Plessy was seven-eighths Caucasian with blond hair and blue eyes. But, although he was "white" in appearance, he was widely known in the community to have had a black great-grandmother. His coloring made him an excellent subject for a potential test case of the Louisiana code. Plessy boarded a train in

Although *Plessy* concerned segregated railroad cars, the principle of "separate but equal" applied to many areas of American life. One of the most detrimental arenas of segregation was the school system, where separate most certainly did not imply equal.

New Orleans and proceeded to the "whites only" car. He was arrested when he refused to leave his seat and take one in the car reserved for blacks. Plessy sued the railroad company, arguing that segregation was illegal under the provisions of the Fourteenth Amendment.

The Supreme Court disagreed. After analyzing the history of blacks in the United States, the majority concluded that the Louisiana law was constitutional. The justices based the decision on their belief that separate facilities for blacks and whites provided equal protection of the laws. After all, they reasoned, blacks were not prevented from riding on the train; the Louisiana statute required only that the races travel separately. *Plessy* v. *Ferguson*[9] is famous because of the Court's enunciation of what is called the "separate but equal doctrine," which, like the *Civil Rights Cases,* opened up new avenues for states to discriminate against blacks with the law on their side.

Justice John Marshall Harlan (1877–1911), the lone dissenter on the Court, criticized the majority and argued that it was senseless to hold constitutional a law "which, practically, puts the badge of servitude and degradation upon a large class of our fellow citizens."

Not surprisingly, the separate-but-equal doctrine soon came to mean only "separate" as the Jim Crow system became a way of life in the American South. In 1898, the Court upheld the constitutionality of literacy tests (*Williams* v. *Mississippi*[10]) and indicated its apparent willingness to allow the Southern states to define their own suffrage standards—whether or not they disproportionately affected blacks. One year later, in 1899, the Supreme Court chose to ignore the fact that educational opportunities for black children were far inferior to those of whites. In *Cumming* v. *County Board of Education,*[11] black parents who were also taxpayers challenged their tax assessments because the money was used to support a "whites only" high school. The Board of Education originally had supported a black public high school, but when funds got tight, the school was closed in order to use funds for a black elementary school. The Court rejected the parents' challenge, unanimously upholding the constitutionality of this disparate treatment. The justices appeared to be very concerned that the relief requested could have impaired the functioning of the white high school or required that it be closed altogether.

Thus, by 1900 equality for blacks was far from the promise first offered by the heady passage of the Civil War Amendments. Again and again the Supreme Court nullified the intent of the amendments and sanctioned racial segregation while the states avidly followed its lead. While discrimination was widely practiced in many parts of the North, Southern states passed laws legally imposing segregation in education, housing, public accommodations, employment, and most other spheres of life. **Miscegenation laws,** for example, prohibited blacks and whites from marrying. Laws alone were not the only practices designed to keep blacks in a secondary position. Jim Crow established a way of life with strong social as well as legal codes. Juan Williams notes in *Eyes on the Prize:*

There were Jim Crow schools, Jim Crow restaurants, Jim Crow water fountains, and Jim Crow customs—blacks were expected to tip their hats when they walked past whites, but whites did not have to remove their hats even when they entered a black family's home. Whites were to be called "sir" and "ma'am" by blacks, who in turn were called by their first names by whites. People with white skin were to be given a wide berth on the sidewalk; blacks were expected to step aside meekly.[12]

[9]163 U.S. 537 (1896).
[10]170 U.S. 213 (1898).
[11]175 U.S. 528 (1899).
[12]Juan Williams, *Eyes on the Prize: America's Civil Rights Years, 1954–1965* (New York: Penguin, 1987), p. 10.

Landmark Events in the Quest for Civil Rights: From *Plessy* v. *Ferguson* to
Brown v. *Board of Education*

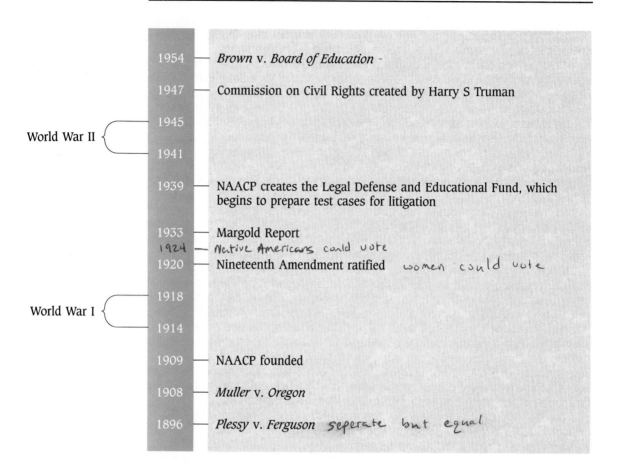

1954	*Brown* v. *Board of Education*
1947	Commission on Civil Rights created by Harry S Truman
1945	World War II
1941	
1939	NAACP creates the Legal Defense and Educational Fund, which begins to prepare test cases for litigation
1933	Margold Report
1924	Native Americans could vote
1920	Nineteenth Amendment ratified women could vote
1918	World War I
1914	
1909	NAACP founded
1908	*Muller* v. *Oregon*
1896	*Plessy* v. *Ferguson* seperate but equal

Notwithstanding these degrading practices, by the early 1900s a small cadre of blacks (largely from the North) had been able to attain some education and were ready to push for additional rights. They found some progressive citizens and politicians amenable to their cause.

The Founding of the National Association for the Advancement of Colored People

In 1909, a handful of individuals active in a variety of progressive causes—including women's suffrage and better working conditions for women and children—met to discuss the idea of a group devoted to the problems of "the Negro." Major race riots had recently occurred in several American cities, and progressive reformers who sought change in political, economic, and social relations were concerned about these outbreaks of violence and the possibility of others. Oswald Garrison Villard, the influential publisher of the New York *Evening Post*—and grandson of William Lloyd Garrison—called a conference to discuss the problem. At that meeting, a Committee of Forty was established, and this group soon evolved into the National Association for the Advancement of Colored People (NAACP). This committee included Garrison; Jane Addams of Hull House, who was vice president of the National American Woman Suffrage Association; Moorfield Storey, a past

The Niagara Movement

The earliest attempt at organizing a black protest toward securing civil rights was the Niagara Movement, organized in 1905 by W.E.B. DuBois, a young black Harvard graduate. A group of young black intellectuals met at Niagara Falls to discuss the need for political action to secure civil rights. Meeting at Harper's Ferry, New York, the following year, members of the movement pledged:

William E. DuBois (second from the right in the second row) is pictured with the original leaders of the Niagara Movement in this 1905 photo taken on the Canadian side of Niagara Falls.

> We will not be satisfied to take one jot or title less than our full manhood rights. We claim for ourselves every single right that belongs to a free-born American, political, civil and social; and until we get these rights we will never cease to protest and assail the ears of America.

The movement never gained much strength, however, and it existed for less than five years and attracted fewer than one hundred followers. Other blacks criticized the movement as not being representative of those living in the South, where the influence of Booker T. Washington prevailed. Washington, a former slave who worked as a janitor to pay his way through Hampton Normal and Agricultural School, became a schoolteacher and built Alabama's Tuskegee Institute into the major vocational training school for blacks in the country. Washington's philosophy was one of accommodation and acceptance, emphasizing the need for blacks to become educated and believing that with time they would gradually come to be recognized and awarded their political rights. In contrast, those involved in the Niagara Movement were the first to make immediate demands for civil rights, a strategy the black population as a whole apparently was not yet ready to embrace.

president of the American Bar Association; and W.E.B. DuBois, a founder of the Niagara Movement, a group of educated blacks who took their name from their first meeting place, Niagara Falls, in Ontario, Canada. (They met there because no hotel on the American side of the Falls would accommodate them.)

Key Women's Groups

The NAACP was not the only group getting off the ground. The struggle for women's rights was revitalized by the formation of the National American Woman Suffrage Association (NAWSA) in 1890 when two women's groups, the National Woman Suffrage Association and its more conservative rival (composed largely of American Equal Rights Association members) merged, with Susan B. Anthony as president. Unlike the National Woman Suffrage Association, which had sought a wide variety of expanded rights for women, this new association was devoted largely to securing women's suffrage. Its task

The *Muller* Opinion

According to the Court in *Muller*:

That woman's physical structure and the performance of maternal functions place her at a disadvantage in the struggle for subsistence is obvious. . . . As healthy mothers are essential to vigorous offspring, the physical well-being of women becomes an object of public interest and care in order to preserve the strength and vigor of the race. . . . As minors [children], though not to the same extent, she has been looked upon in the courts as needing especial care that her rights may be preserved.

was greatly facilitated by the proliferation of women's groups that emerged during the Progressive era (1890 to World War I). In addition to the rapidly growing temperance movement, which sought to ban the sale of alcohol, groups were created to seek protective legislation in the form of maximum hour or minimum wage laws for women and to work for improved sanitation, public morals, education, and the like. Other organizations that were part of what was called the "club movement" were created to provide increased cultural and literary experiences for middle-class women, who with the increased industrialization of the United States found themselves for the first time with some time on their hands to pursue activities other than those centered on the home.

One of the most active groups lobbying on behalf of women during this period was the National Consumers' League (NCL), which insisted that hard-fought-for Oregon legislation limiting women to ten hours of work a day be properly defended before the U.S. Supreme Court. Curt Muller had been convicted of employing women in his small laundry more than ten hours a day, a violation of the Oregon statute, which had been passed after extensive NCL lobbying. When the U.S. Supreme Court agreed to hear his appeal, the NCL sought permission from the state to conduct the defense of the statute.

At the urging of NCL attorney and future Supreme Court Justice Louis Brandeis, NCL members amassed an impressive array of sociological and medical data that were incorporated into what was to become known as "The Brandeis Brief." The Brandeis Brief and *Muller* v. *Oregon* (1908) are widely regarded as the first time that sociological and other "nonlegal" data were used to convince the Court to take a position not indicated by other legal precedents. The brief submitted by Brandeis contained only three pages of legal argument while more than one hundred were devoted to nonlegal data. The Brandeis Brief was a tactic that was soon to be used widely by civil rights groups. The NAACP, in fact, eventually hired a statistician to help its lawyers amass data to help present evidence of discrimination to the courts.

Women who sought the vote did so using reasoning reflective of the Court's position in *Muller.* Discarding the earlier notion of full equality, NAWSA based its claim on the right to vote largely on the fact that women, as mothers, should be enfranchised. Furthermore, although many members of the suffrage movement were NAACP members, the new women's movement—called the **suffrage movement** because of its focus—took on racist overtones as women argued that if undereducated blacks could vote, why couldn't women? Some NAWSA members even argued that "the enfranchisement of women would ensure immediate and durable white supremacy."[13]

Diverse attitudes clearly were present in the growing suffrage movement, which often tried to be all things to all people. Its roots in the Progressive Movement gave it an exceptionally broad base that transformed NAWSA from a small organization of just over 10,000 members in the early 1890s to a true social movement of more than 2 million members in 1917. By 1920, this coalition was able to secure ratification of the Nineteenth, or the Susan B. Anthony, Amendment to the Constitution. This amendment guaranteed women the right to vote fifty-five years after blacks were enfranchised by the Fifteenth Amendment.[14]

After passage of the suffrage amendment in 1920, the fragile alliance of diverse women's groups that had come together to fight for the vote quickly disintegrated. Women returned to their "home" groups, such as the NCL, the Women's Christian Temperance Union, or a book club, to pursue their narrower goals of protective legislation, prohibition, or self-improvement. In fact, after the tumult of the suffrage movement, organized activity on behalf of women's rights did not reemerge until the 1960s. In the meantime, however, the NAACP continued to fight racism. In fact, its activities and those of others in the civil rights movement would give impetus to a new women's movement.

[13] Judith Papachristou, *Women Together* (New York: Knopf, 1976), p. 144.
[14] Eleanor Flexner, *Century of Struggle* (New York: Atheneum, 1971).

Litigating for Equality

During the 1930s, leaders of the NAACP began to sense that the time was right to launch a full-scale challenge to the constitutionality of *Plessy*'s "separate but equal" doctrine. In 1933, Nathan Ross Margold, a white, Harvard-educated NAACP attorney, wrote what has come to be known as the *Margold Report.* In it, he set out a legal theory and strategic plan designed to overrule *Plessy.* Using the Margold plan as its foundation, the NAACP mapped out a long-range strategy that would first target segregation in professional and graduate education. Clearly, the separate-but-equal doctrine and the proliferation of Jim Crow laws stood as a bar to any hope of full equality for blacks. Traditional legislative channels were unlikely to work given the limited or nonexistent political power of blacks in the 1930s. Thus, the federal courts and a long-range litigation strategy were the NAACP's only hope.

Test Cases. The NAACP opted first to challenge the constitutionality of Jim Crow law schools. In 1935, all Southern states maintained fully segregated elementary and secondary schools. Colleges and universities were also segregated, but most states did not provide for postgraduate education for blacks. NAACP lawyers chose to target law schools because they were institutions that judges could well understand.

Lloyd Gaines, a graduate of Missouri's all-black Lincoln University, sought admission to the all-white University of Missouri Law School in 1936. He was immediately rejected, but the state offered to build a law school at Lincoln (although no funds were allocated for the project) or, if he didn't want to wait, to pay his tuition at an out-of-state law school. Gaines lost his appeal of this rejection in the lower court, and the case was appealed to the U.S. Supreme Court[15].

Gaines's case was filed at an auspicious time. As you may recall from Chapter 3, a "constitutional revolution" occurred in 1937. Prior to 1937, the Court was most receptive to and most interested in the protection of economic liberties. In 1937, however, the Court reversed itself in a series of cases and began to place individual freedoms and personal liberty on a more protected plain. Thus, in 1938, it was to a far more sympathetic Supreme Court that Gaines's lawyers finally pleaded his claims. NAACP attorneys argued that the creation of a separate law school of any less caliber than that of the University of Missouri would not and could not afford Gaines an *equal* education. In *Missouri* ex rel. *Gaines* v. *Canada* (1938), the justices agreed with the NAACP's contention and ruled that Missouri had failed to meet the separate-but-equal requirements of *Plessy.* The state's offer to send Gaines to an out-of-state law school was simply insufficient, and the Court ordered Missouri to admit Gaines to the school.

Recognizing the importance of the Court's ruling, in 1939 the NAACP created a separate, tax-exempt, legal defense fund to devise a strategy to build on *Gaines* in order to bring about equal education opportunities for all black children. The first head of the NAACP Legal Defense and Educational Fund (LDF), as it was called, was Thurgood Marshall, who later became the first black to serve on the U.S. Supreme Court (1967–91). Sensing that the Court would be more amenable to the NAACP's broader goals if it was first forced to address a variety of less threatening claims to educational opportunity, Marshall and the LDF brought a series of carefully crafted test cases to the Court after *Gaines.*

The first case involved a forty-six-year-old black mail carrier, Herman Sweatt, who in 1946 applied for admission to the all-white University of Texas Law School and was rejected on racial grounds. Sweatt sued, and the judge gave the state six months to establish a law school or to admit him to the University of Texas. The university then rented a few rooms in downtown Houston and hired two local black attorneys to be

Lloyd Gaines was the subject of the major test case, *Missouri* ex rel. *Gaines* v. *Canada,* which contested the principle of segregated schools. Gaines chose to attend the University of Michigan, from which he strangely disappeared.

[15]*Missouri ex rel. Gaines* v. *Canada,* 305 U.S. 337 (1938).

part-time faculty members. (At that time there was only one full-time black law school professor in the United States.) Although this was acceptable to the lower court judge, the state legislature, seeing the handwriting on the wall, authorized $3 million for the creation of the Texas State University for Negroes. One hundred thousand dollars of that money was to be for a law school. A law school ''better'' than the one in Houston was created in Austin across the street from the state capitol. It consisted of three small basement rooms, a library of more than 10,000 books and access to the state law library, and three part-time first-year instructors as the ''faculty.'' Sweatt declined the opportunity to secure a legal education there and instead chose to pursue his case.

While working on *Sweatt,* the NAACP LDF and Marshall also decided to pursue another case. Thurgood Marshall chose to use the case of George W. McLaurin, a retired university professor who had been denied admission to the doctoral education program at the University of Oklahoma. Marshall reasoned that McLaurin, at sixty-eight years of age, would be immune from the charges that blacks wanted integration in order to intermarry. After a lower court ruling, the university modified its procedures and allowed him to attend the school on a quasi-segregated basis. The university reserved a dingy alcove in the cafeteria for him to eat in during off hours. McLaurin was given a table to himself in the library behind a shelf of newspapers. And, in what surely ''was Oklahoma's most inventive contribution to legalized bigotry since the adoption of the 'grandfather clause,'[16] McLaurin was forced to sit alone just outside the classrooms while lectures were given and seminars were held inside.

The Supreme Court handled these two cases—*Sweatt* and *McLaurin*—as companion cases. The eleven Southern states filed an *amicus curiae,* or friend of the court, brief in which they argued that *Plessy* should govern both cases. The NAACP received assistance, however, from an unexpected source—the U.S. government. In a dramatic departure from the past, the administration of Harry S Truman filed a friend of the court brief urging the Court to overrule *Plessy.* Since the late 1870s, the U.S. government had never sided against the Southern states in a civil rights matter and had never submitted an *amicus* brief supporting the rights of black citizens. President Truman believed that because many blacks had fought and died for their country in World War II, this kind of executive action was proper. The Court traditionally gives great weight to briefs from the U.S. government. The Court again failed to overrule *Plessy,* but the justices found that the measures taken by the states in each case failed to live up to the strictures of the separate-but-equal doctrine. The Court unanimously ruled that what had been done in each situation was inadequate to afford a sound education. In the *Sweatt* case, for example, the Court declared:

> The University of Texas Law School possesses to a far greater degree those qualities which are incapable of objective measurement but which make for greatness in a law school. Such qualities, to name but a few, include the reputation of the faculty, experience of the administration, position and influence of the alumni, standing in the community, traditions and prestige.[17]

These sentiments were echoed in the *McLaurin* decision. Although the petitioner could not claim that the facilities were unequal, the Court held, his isolation was unconstitutional because the restrictions ''[impaired] and [inhibited] his ability to study, engage in discussion and exchange views with other students, and in general, to learn his profession.''[18]

After these decisions were handed down in 1950, the NAACP LDF concluded that the time had come to launch a full-scale attack on the separate-but-equal doctrine. The deci-

[16]Richard Kluger, *Simple Justice* (New York: Vintage, 1975), p. 268.
[17]339 U.S. 629 (1950).
[18]339 U.S. 637 (1950).

sions of the Court were encouraging, and the position of the U.S. government and the population in general appeared to be more receptive to an outright overruling of *Plessy.*

Brown v. *Board of Education of Topeka, Kansas* (1954).

Brown v. *Board of Education of Topeka (Brown I)*[19] was actually four cases brought from different areas of the South and the border states. According to U.S. Supreme Court Justice Tom Clark of Texas, the Court "consolidated them and made *Brown* the first so that the whole question would not smack of being purely a Southern one."[20] All four cases involved public elementary or high school systems that mandated separate schools for blacks and whites.

In *Brown,* NAACP lawyers, again headed by Thurgood Marshall, decided to argue that *Plessy*'s separate-but-equal doctrine was unconstitutional under the Fourteenth Amendment and that if the Court was still reluctant to overrule *Plessy,* the only way to equalize the schools was to integrate them. A major component of the NAACP's legal strategy was to prove that the intellectual, psychological, and financial damage that befell blacks as a result of segregation precluded any court from ever finding equality.

In *Brown* and *Bolling* v. *Sharpe,*[21] a challenge to discrimination in the District of Columbia schools, the NAACP LDF presented the Supreme Court with evidence of the harmful consequences of state-imposed racial discrimination. To buttress its claims the NAACP introduced the soon-to-be-famous "doll study," conducted by Kenneth Clark, a prominent black sociologist who long had studied the effects of segregation on black children. He conducted his research by showing black children black dolls and white dolls, then asking them which doll they liked better. Most liked the white doll better, and many added that the black doll looked "bad." Nearly half of the black children saw themselves as a white doll. This information was then used to illustrate the negative impact of racial segregation and bias on a black child's self-image.

The legal briefs of the NAACP were supported by important *amicus curiae* briefs submitted by the U.S. government and other major civil rights groups, labor unions, and religious groups decrying racial segregation. On May 17, 1954, Chief Justice Earl Warren delivered the fourth opinion of the day, *Brown* v. *Board of Education of Topeka.* Writing for the Court, Warren stated:

> To separate [school children] from others . . . solely because of their race generates a feeling of inferiority as to their status in the community that may affect their hearts and minds in a way very unlikely ever to be undone.

> We conclude, unanimously, that in the field of public education the doctrine of "separate but equal" has no place.[22]

There can be no doubt that *Brown* was the most important civil rights case decided in the twentieth century. It immediately evoked an uproar that shook the nation. Some called the day the decision was handed down "Black Monday." The governor of South Carolina decried the decision, saying, "Ending segregation would mark the beginning of the end of civilization in the South as we know it." The governor of Georgia predicted that segregation would result in intermarriage and "mongrelization of the races." The NAACP lawyers who had argued these cases and those leading to *Brown,* however, were jubilant.

Since 1890, remarkable changes had occurred in the civil rights of Americans. Women had won the right to vote, and after a long and arduous trail of litigation in the federal courts, the Supreme Court had finally overturned the worst case of the era, *Plessy* v. *Ferguson.* The Court boldly proclaimed that separate but equal (at least in education)

[19] 347 U.S. 483 (1954).
[20] Williams, p. 31.
[21] 347 U.S. 497 (1954).
[22] 347 U.S. 483 (1954).

Why It's Called *Brown* v. *Board of Education of Topeka*

Seven-year-old Linda Brown of Topeka, Kansas, lived close to a good public school, but it was reserved for whites. So every day she had to cross railroad tracks in a nearby switching yard on her way to catch a run-down school bus that would take her across town to a school reserved for black students. Her father, Oliver Brown, concerned for her safety and the quality of her education, became increasingly frustrated with his youngster's having to travel far from home to get an education.

"The issue came up, and it was decided that Reverend Brown's daughter would be the goat, so to speak," recalled a member of the Topeka NAACP. "He put forth his daughter to test the validity of the [law], and we had to raise the money."*

The NAACP continued to gather plaintiffs and test cases from around the nation. The Supreme Court first agreed to hear *Brown* and *Briggs* v. *Elliott* (South Carolina) in 1952. Two days before they were to be heard, the Court issued a postponement and added *Davis* v. *Prince Edward County* (Virginia) to its docket. Just a few weeks later, the Court added *Bolling* v. *Sharpe*

Source: AP/Wide World.

Ten years after the Court's decision in *Brown* v. *Board of Education,* Linda Brown Smith stood in front of the school whose refusal to admit her ultimately led to the Court's 1954 ruling named after her. The decision came too late for her, but her two younger sisters were able to attend integrated schools.

from the District of Columbia and *Gebhart* v. *Belton* (Delaware). The Court clearly wanted to hear cases from a cross section of the nation. But the justices chose to hear them all under the name *Brown* v. *Board of Education of Topeka* to stress that segregation was not just a Southern problem.

*Quoted in Juan Williams, *Eyes on the Prize: America's Civil Rights Years, 1954–1965* (New York: Penguin, 1987), p. 21.

would no longer pass constitutional muster. The question then became how *Brown* would be interpreted and implemented. Could it be used to invalidate other Jim Crow laws and practices? Would blacks be truly equal under law?

The Civil Rights Movement, 1954–68

Since 1954, profound changes have occurred in our notion of civil rights. First blacks and then women have built upon existing organizations to forge successful movements for increased rights. *Brown* served as a catalyst for change, sparking the development of the modern civil rights movement. Women's work in that movement and the student protest movement that arose to voice disagreement with the U.S. government's involvement in Vietnam would lead women to form their own organizations to press for full equality. As blacks and women became more and more successful, they served as the model for others who sought equality—Hispanics, Native Americans, the poor, the elderly, and gays.

Landmark Events in the Quest for Civil Rights: From 1955 to 1982

1982	Equal Rights Amendment fails to be ratified
1972	Equal Rights Amendment sent to states for ratification
1971	*Reed* v. *Reed*
1968	Martin Luther King assassinated
1966	National Organization for Women formed
	Black ghetto riots
1965	Voting Rights Act
1964	Martin Luther King wins Nobel Peace Prize
	Summer riots in Northern ghettos
	Civil Rights Act of 1964
	Twenty-fourth Amendment banning poll taxes ratified
1963	John F. Kennedy assassinated
	March on Washington, D.C.
	Martin Luther King leads March on Birmingham
	Betty Friedan's *The Feminine Mystique* published
1961	Freedom Rides begin
1960	First sit-ins
1956	Montgomery Bus Boycott
1955	Rosa Parks arrested

School Desegregation After *Brown*

In its landmark decision of 1954, the Court did not address the question of how equal educational opportunity and racial segregation were to be achieved. The Supreme Court technically has no army to enforce its decisions, and the Southern states saw their very way of life threatened by *Brown.* One year later, however, in what is referred to as *Brown II,*[23] the Court ruled that racially segregated systems must be dismantled "with all deliberate speed." To facilitate implementation, the Court placed enforcement of *Brown* in the hands of non-elected federal district court judges, who were considered more immune from local political pressures than were regularly elected state court judges.

The NAACP continued to resort to the courts to see that *Brown* was implemented while the South entered into a near-conspiracy to avoid the mandates of *Brown II.* In Arkansas, for example, Governor Orval Faubus, facing a reelection bid, announced that he would not "be a party to any attempt to force acceptance of change to which people are overwhelmingly opposed." So, although Arkansas announced a limited Phase (integration) Plan designed to begin integration slowly on a grade-by-grade basis beginning in the high schools, the day before school was to begin Governor Faubus went on television to announce that he planned to surround Little Rock's Central High School with National Guardsmen to prevent black students from entering. While the federal courts in Arkansas continued to order the admission of black children, the governor remained adamant. Finally, President Dwight Eisenhower was compelled to send federal troops to Little Rock to protect the rights of the nine students who had attempted to attend Central High.

In reaction to the governor's outrageous conduct, the Court took an unprecedented action. In ruling that the governor and state legislature had violated the supremacy clause of Article IV of the Constitution, each justice signed the unanimous opinion individually to underscore his personal support. (Unanimous opinions are usually written and signed by a single justice.) *Cooper* v. *Aaron* (1958)[24] boldly proclaimed, "No state legislator or executive or judicial officer can war against the Constitution without violating his undertaking to support it." Their actions were ruled constitutionally repugnant and these kinds of "evasive schemes" illegal.

The saga of Little Rock is telling and illustrative of the massive resistance to *Brown* and the NAACP throughout the South. It is hard to imagine these kinds of confrontations occurring today—a governor calling a press conference to announce that he would defy a federal order, a president sending in federal troops to protect the rights of black citizens against the state militia, legislation requiring the NAACP to identify its members, and massive violence in a public high school. All of this was duly recorded in the press and on television in vivid detail. And all of this added fuel to the fire of others around the South.

A New Move for Black Rights

In early 1955, soon after *Brown II,* a Montgomery, Alabama, teenager was forcibly removed from a bus when she refused to leave her seat in the middle of the vehicle to move to the back of the bus, where the "blacks only" seats were. The local NAACP immediately went to her aid. Its Youth Council adviser, Rosa Parks, in particular, wanted the girl to challenge the constitutionality of the segregated bus system in court. Parks was especially sympathetic to the young girl because Parks herself had been ejected from a bus years before for refusing to enter through the back door. So, Parks and other NAACP officials began to raise money for litigation and made speeches around town to garner public support. There were problems, however, with the potential plaintiff, and the NAACP decided it was better not to go forward with that particular individual.

[23] 349 U.S. 294 (1955).
[24] 358 U.S. 1 (1958).

Rosa Parks then apparently took it upon herself to be the next potential plaintiff. Amidst the hustle and bustle of the Montgomery, Alabama Christmas rush on December 1, 1955, Rosa Parks made history when she refused to leave her seat on a bus to move to the back and make room for a white male passenger. Parks was arrested for violating an Alabama Jim Crow law banning integration of public facilities, including buses. After being freed on bond, Parks and the NAACP decided to enlist city clergy to help her cause. At the same time, other activists (primarily women) mimeographed and distributed 35,000 handbills calling for blacks to boycott the Montgomery bus system on the day of Parks's trial. Black ministers throughout the city used Sunday services to urge their members to support the boycott. That Monday, blacks walked, carpooled, or used black-owned taxicabs. That evening, local ministers came together and decided that the boycott should be continued. A twenty-six-year-old minister, Martin Luther King, Jr., was selected to lead the newly formed "Montgomery Improvement Association." King was new to town, and church leaders had been looking for a way to get him more involved in civil rights work.

As the boycott dragged on, Montgomery officials and local business owners began to harass the city's black citizens. But King urged Montgomery's black citizens to continue their protest. The residents held out despite suffering personal hardship for their actions, ranging from harassment to bankruptcy to job loss. By the end of 1956, a federal court applied the principles of *Brown* to the boycott issue and ruled that the segregated bus system violated the equal protection clause of the Fourteenth Amendment. After a year of walking, blacks ended their protest as the buses were ordered to integrate. The first effort at nonviolent protest had been won.

After a ruling from the U.S. Supreme Court that banned segregation on public buses operated by the city of Montgomery, Alabama, Rosa Parks, whose refusal to give up her seat on the bus sparked the Montgomery Bus Boycott, takes a seat on an integrated bus.

New Groups Formed. The recognition and respect that King earned within the black community helped him to launch the Southern Christian Leadership Conference (SCLC) in 1957 soon after the Montgomery bus boycott's end. Unlike the NAACP, which had Northern origins and had come to rely largely on litigation as a means of achieving expanded equality, the SCLC had a Southern base and was rooted more closely in black religious culture. The SCLC's philosophy was reflective of King's growing belief in the importance of nonviolent protest.

On February 1, 1960, students at North Carolina Agricultural and Technical College participated in the first "sit-in." Angered and frustrated by their inability to be served at local lunch counters but heartened by the success of the Montgomery bus boycott, students marched to the local Woolworth's and ordered a cup of coffee. They were refused service. So the students sat until police came and carted them off to jail. Soon thereafter, black college students around the South joined together to challenge the Jim Crow laws in the region. These mass actions immediately brought extensive attention from the national news media.

With the assistance of an $800 grant from the SCLC, over spring break 1960, 200 student delegates—black *and* white—met at Shaw University in North Carolina to consider recent sit-in actions and to plan for the future. Later that year two more meetings were held in Atlanta, Georgia, and the Student Nonviolent Coordinating Committee (SNCC) was formed.

Among the SNCC's first leaders were Marion Barry, who went on to serve as mayor of Washington, D.C. (1978–90); John Lewis, who at this writing is a member of Congress who serves as the Deputy House Majority Whip; and Marian Wright (Edelman), who first became an NAACP lawyer and later the founder and head of the Children's Defense Fund. While the SCLC generally worked with church leaders in a community, SNCC was much more of a grassroots organization. Always perceived as more radical than the SCLC, SNCC tended to focus its organizing activities on the young, black or white.

In addition to taking up the sit-in bandwagon, SNCC also came to lead what were called **freedom rides,** which were designed to focus attention on segregated public accommodations. Bands of college students and other civil rights activists traveled throughout the South by bus in an effort to force bus stations to desegregate. These protesters

A prime objective of the protesters in Birmingham was to focus national attention on their cause. For the first time in American history, a majority of the public owned television sets and could see the horrors of police brutality. But the print media continued to be a powerful tool. This picture was reprinted over and over again and even frequently mentioned on the floor of Congress over debates on the Civil Rights Act of 1964.

frequently were met with brutal violence as local police chose not to defend protesters' basic constitutional rights to free speech and peaceful assembly against angry mobs of segregationists who assembled in wait. It was not only blacks who participated in these freedom rides; increasingly, white college students from the North began to play an important role in SNCC.

While SNCC continued to sponsor sit-ins and freedom rides, in 1963 Martin Luther King, Jr., launched a series of massive nonviolent demonstrations in Birmingham, Alabama, long considered a major stronghold of segregation. Thousands of blacks and whites marched to Birmingham in a show of solidarity. Peaceful marchers were met there by Birmingham Police Commissioner Eugene "Bull" Conner, who ordered his officers to use dogs, clubs, the spray from fire hoses, and other tactics on the marchers, whose ranks included small children. All of the marchers, including the children, suffered badly at the hands of local police. Americans across the nation watched in horror as they witnessed the brutality and abuse that was heaped on the protestors. As the marchers hoped, these shocking scenes helped convince President John F. Kennedy to propose important civil rights legislation.

The Civil Rights Act of 1964

The older faction of the civil rights movement, as represented by SCLC, and the younger branch, represented by SNCC, both sought a similar goal: implementation of Supreme Court decisions and an end to racial segregation and discrimination. The cumulative effect of collective actions such as sit-ins, boycotts, marches, and freedom rides—as well as the tragic bombings and deaths inflicted in retaliation—led to congressional passage of the first major piece of civil rights legislation since the post–Civil War era.

In 1963, President Kennedy requested that Congress pass a law banning discrimination in public accommodations. Seizing the moment and recognizing the potency of a show of massive support, Reverend King called for a monumental march on Washington, D.C., to demonstrate widespread support for legislation to ban discrimination in *all* walks of life, not just public accommodations. Held only four months after the Birmingham demonstrations, the "March on Washington for Jobs and Freedom" was attended by more than 250,000 people who heard King's now-immortal "I Have a Dream" speech, delivered from the Lincoln Memorial. Before Congress had the opportunity to vote on any legislation, however, Kennedy was assassinated in Dallas, Texas.

It was clear that national laws outlawing discrimination were the only answer, as Southern legislators would never vote to repeal Jim Crow laws. But through the 1960s, blacks lacked sufficient political power or the force of public opinion to sway enough congressional leaders. Their task was further stymied by loud and strong opposition from Southern members of Congress, many of whom, because of the Democratic Party's total control of the South, had been in office far longer than most and therefore held powerful committee chairmanships that were awarded on seniority. The Senate Judiciary Committee was controlled by a coalition of Southern Democrats and conservative Republicans, and the House Rules Committee was chaired by a Virginian who was opposed to any civil rights legislation and who, by virtue of his position, could block such legislation in committee.

When Vice President Lyndon B. Johnson, a Southern-born former Senate majority leader, succeeded John F. Kennedy and became president, he put civil rights reform at the top of his legislative priority list, and civil rights activists gained a critical ally. Thus, through the 1960s, the movement subtly changed in focus from peaceful protest and litigation to legislative lobbying. Now its focus had broadened from integration of school and public facilities and voting rights to issues of housing, jobs, and equal opportunity.

The push for civil rights legislation in the halls of Congress was also helped by changes in public opinion. As illustrated in Figure 5-1, between 1959 and 1965 Southern attitudes toward integrated schools had changed enormously as the proportion of Southerners who responded that they would not mind if their child attended a school that was half black increased dramatically.

In spite of strong presidential support and the sway of public opinion, however, the Civil Rights Act of 1964 did not sail through Congress easily. Southern senators, led by

Martin Luther King, Jr., addressing the march on Washington in March, 1963.

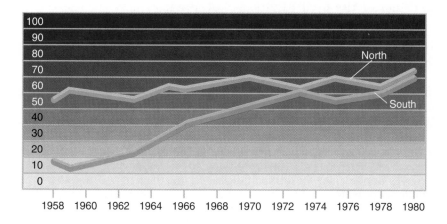

**Figure 5-1
Attitudes of Whites to Integrated Education, North and South.**
Percentage of whites who would not object to their children attending a school with half black, half white enrollment.

Source: Howard Schman, Charlotte Steeh, and Lawrence Bobo, *Racial Attitudes in America* (Cambridge, Mass.: Harvard University Press, 1985), p. 69.

South Carolina's Strom Thurmond, a Democrat who later switched to the Republican Party, conducted the longest filibuster in the history of the Senate. For eight weeks they held up voting on the bill until cloture (see Chapter 6) was invoked and the filibuster brought to an end. Once passed, the **Civil Rights Act of 1964:**

- Barred discrimination in the "full and equal enjoyment" of goods and services in any public accommodation based on race, color, religion, or national origin
- Authorized the Attorney General to initiate lawsuits to force desegregation of public schools on behalf of private individuals
- Made illegal the use of literacy tests or other administrative devices or tests designed to impede black voting
- Barred discrimination in any program or activity receiving federal assistance
- Prohibited discrimination in employment on grounds of race, color, religion, national origin, or sex
- Created the Equal Employment Opportunity Commission to monitor and enforce the bans on employment discrimination.

While these changes were occurring in the law of the land, other changes were sweeping the nation. Violence began to rock the nation as ghetto riots broke out in the Northeast. Although Northern blacks were not subject to Jim Crow laws, many lived in poverty and faced pervasive daily discrimination and its resultant frustration. From 1964 to 1968, many Northern blacks took to the streets, burning and looting.

Violence also marred the continued activities of civil rights workers in the South. During the summer of 1964 three civil rights workers—one black, two white—were killed in Neshoba County, Mississippi. In 1965, King again led his supporters on a massive march, this time from Selma to the Alabama state capital in Montgomery in support of additional voting rights protections. Again, Southern officials unleashed a reign of terror in Selma as they used whips, dogs, cattle prods, clubs, and tear gas to deter the protestors. One marcher was killed. Again, Americans watched in horror as they witnessed this brutality on their television screens. This march and the public's reaction to it led to quick passage of the Voting Rights Act of 1965, which suspended the use of literacy tests and authorized the federal government to monitor all elections in areas where discrimination was found to be practiced or where less than 50 percent of the voting-age public was registered to vote in the 1964 election.

The Effect of the Civil Rights Act of 1964

Many Southerners were adamant in their belief that the 1964 and 1965 Acts were unconstitutional because they went beyond the scope of Congress's authority to legislate under the Constitution.

Public Accommodations. The Supreme Court heard the first challenge to the 1964 Act on an expedited review, which bypassed the intermediate courts. In 1964 in *Heart of Atlanta Motel* v. *United States,*[25] the operator of a hotel that refused black guests asked the Court to rule that Section 2 of the Act barring discrimination in public accommodations be declared unconstitutional. Hotel attorneys argued that the Act exceeded congressional authority granted by the commerce clause to "regulate interstate commerce." Justice Tom C. Clark, writing for the Court, disagreed and found that Congress was acting within the scope of its authority when it acted to prohibit discrimination in any commercial enterprises engaged in interstate commerce.

[25] 379 U.S. 241 (1964).

Education. One of the key provisions of the Civil Rights Act of 1964, Title VI, authorized the Justice Department to bring actions against school districts that had yet to comply with *Brown* v. *Board of Education.* In 1964, a full decade after *Brown,* fewer than 1 percent of all black children in the South attended integrated schools.[26]

In 1968, the Supreme Court ruled that a "freedom of choice plan" under which pupils could choose which school they attended was unconstitutional when it resulted in overwhelmingly majority black and white schools.[27] In 1969, the Supreme Court ruled unanimously that state-sanctioned dual school systems must cease immediately.[28]

Just two years later, in *Swann* v. *Charlotte-Mecklenburg School District* (1971),[29] the Supreme Court ruled that lower federal courts could order busing as an appropriate remedy to end dual school systems. The school board had assigned students to the schools closest to their homes without regard to race. Under this new plan, only about half of all black children attended formerly white schools. In interpreting Title VI's provisions, the Court ruled:

- Plaintiffs must show that the school district engaged in intentional discrimination.
- A history of **de jure** (or by statutory law) **discrimination** coupled with the presence of all black or white schools creates a legal presumption that the school board intended to discriminate.
- The remedy for segregation is not freedom of choice alone. Other permissible remedies to end the vestiges of discrimination include busing, racial quotas in the assignment of students and teachers, and the redrawing of district lines.
- There is no constitutional requirement that all schools in every school district reflect the racial composition of the entire school district.

Busing, however, was considered appropriate only when the discrimination was a result of what is termed *de jure* discrimination. The distinction that the Court drew in *Swann* between *de jure* and *de facto* discrimination is extremely important. The Court was careful to note its approval of busing as a remedy for intentional, governmental-imposed or -sanctioned discrimination, which is called *de jure* or by-law discrimination. In contrast, *de facto* discrimination, which most frequently occurs as a result of housing patterns and private acts of discrimination, is considered to have happened without governmental involvement and is therefore unintentional. This is true even where, as was the case in *Swann,* the Court found that although various government agencies typically contribute to segregated housing patterns, that fact was not enough to prove a discriminatory intent if *de facto* discrimination is present. Busing was found not to be an appropriate remedy for *de facto* discrimination.

This distinction was critical as the Justice Department and the NAACP LDF turned their attention to segregated school systems in both the North and South. Busing has been a highly emotional issue since *Swann.* Few parents want to see their child bused, and most Americans argue that it is better for their children to attend schools close to their homes. In fact, the relative quality of local school districts are often the reason why many families move to particular neighborhoods or localities. When busing was ordered in urban school districts, many whites fled to the suburbs.

Truly integrated schools are becoming more and more difficult to achieve. Take the city of Atlanta, Georgia, for example. In the early 1980s, the public elementary school

---

[26] Paul Brest and Sanford Levinson, *Processes of Constitutional Decision-making,* 2nd ed. (Boston: Little, Brown, 1983), pp. 471–480.

[27] *Green* v. *County School Board,* 391 U.S. 430 (1968).

[28] *Alexander* v. *Holmes County Board of Education,* 396 U.S. 19 (1969).

[29] 402 U.S. 1 (1971).

School busing in the wake of the *Swann* decision was particularly contentious in Boston in the 1970s. Over the years, the use of forced busing has found itself in increasing disfavor with the Supreme Court. In *Board of Education of Oklahoma City Public Schools* v. *Dowell* (1991), the Court concluded that school districts that were previously required by law to end racial discrimination could end the use of forced busing in favor of a return to neighborhood schools, even if that resulted in schools that were overwhelmingly white or black.

population was approximately 90 percent black, whereas the student population in school districts in the areas that ringed the city ranged from 5 to 30 percent black. Clearly, it would be useless to order busing within Atlanta alone. So, the NAACP and the American Civil Liberties Union asked the federal courts to require busing between the surrounding areas and the city. The Supreme Court rejected this plea because there was no showing of intentional discrimination on the part of the outlying school districts.[30]

Employment. The Civil Rights Act of 1964 prohibits employers from discriminating against employees for a variety of reasons, including race and sex. (In 1978 the Act was amended to prohibit discrimination based on pregnancy.)

In one of the first major cases decided under the Act, brought by the NAACP LDF, the Supreme Court found that employers could be found liable under the Act if the *effect* of their employment practices was to exclude blacks from certain positions. So in 1971 in *Griggs* v. *Duke Power Company,*[31] black employees were allowed to show with statistical evidence that black workers had been permitted to work in but one department of Duke Power Company. Those jobs involved heavy manual labor and were considered to be the least desirable in the company. Blacks were effectively kept out of better positions because the company had instituted high school education requirements and/or the passing of a special test. Many of the black applicants, of course, had been deeply affected by the inferior education provided by North Carolina segregated school systems.

[30]*Armour* v. *Nix,* 448 U.S. 908 (1980).
[31]401 U.S. 424 (1971).

The Supreme Court ruled that although the tests did not appear on their face to discriminate against blacks, their effects—that there were no black employees in any other departments—were sufficient to shift to the employer the burden of proving that there was no discrimination. Thus, the Duke Power Company would have to prove that the tests were "a business necessity" that had a "demonstrable relationship to successful performance. . . ."

The notion of "business necessity" as articulated by the courts and the Civil Rights Act was especially important for women. For years, women had been kept out of many occupations as employers argued that their customers preferred to deal with male personnel. Conversely, males were barred from flight-attendant positions because the airlines believed that passengers preferred to be served by women. The airlines justified their "females only" employment policy by noting that flyers often became nervous and male passengers would feel uneasy if they had to seek comfort from another male. Similarly, many large factories, manufacturing establishments, and police and fire departments outrightly refused to hire women by using arbitrary height and weight requirements. Like the tests in *Griggs,* these requirements often could not be shown to be related to job performance and were eventually ruled illegal by the federal courts.

As noted earlier, one of the key provisions of the Civil Rights Act allowed the Justice Department and/or the **Equal Employment Opportunity Commission** (EEOC) to enforce key provisions of the Act. Employment discrimination litigation is very expensive and beyond the means of most salaried workers. Thus, if the EEOC chooses to enforce the

Voting Rights

Both the Civil Rights Act of 1964 and the Voting Rights Act of 1965 were intended to guarantee voting rights to blacks nearly a century after passage of the Fifteenth Amendment. Black voters have used their strength at the ballot box to elect black officials. Only seventy blacks held public office in the eleven Southern states covered by the Act in 1965; by the early 1980s more than 2,500 blacks held elected office in those states.

Today most Voting Rights Act cases deal not with bars to black voting but with the drawing of election lines. As amended in 1982, the Voting Rights Act not only prohibits state legislatures from diluting black voting strength by distributing black voters among white districts or packing them into one black district, it also *requires* states to create as many black districts as possible. The redrawing of election-district lines comes under careful scrutiny after each national census. Most Southern states must have all revisions in their districts "pre-cleared" by the U.S. Justice Department, which is charged with enforcing the Voting Rights Act. Recently, the Republican Justice Department has insisted that the maximum number of black districts be drawn, recognizing that the more black districts there are, the more likely it will be to gain Republican districts elsewhere in a state (since 90 percent of blacks are Democrats).

The results of the 1990 census will undoubtedly give rise to numerous lawsuits. Blacks, however, are no longer at the forefront of this movement. Throughout the Southwest, instead, Hispanic voters are increasingly going to court to protect their voting rights, which they frequently see as diluted by unfavorable drawing of legislative district lines by state legislatures.

law vigorously and bring cases on behalf of individuals, an employee's chances of proving discrimination are increased tremendously, especially since the courts generally look with favor on claims brought by the U.S. government. In fact, the failure of the EEOC to investigate claims of sex discrimination contributed to the rise of the current women's rights movement.

The Women's Rights Movement. Just as women had been involved in the abolitionist movement in the 1800s, women from all walks of life also participated in all phases of the civil rights movement. Women were important members of both SNCC and more traditional groups like the NAACP and the SCLC.[32] Yet they often found themselves treated as second-class citizens. At one point, Stokely Carmichael, chair of SNCC, openly proclaimed that ''the only place for women [in the civil rights movement] is prone [on their backs].[33] Statements and attitudes like these led some women to found early women's liberation groups that were generally quite radical and small in membership.

As discussed earlier, initial efforts to convince the Supreme Court to declare that women were enfranchised under the Fourteenth Amendment were uniformly unsuccessful. The paternalistic attitude of the Supreme Court, and perhaps society as well, continued well into the 1970s. As late as 1961, Florida required women who wished to serve on juries to travel to the county courthouse and register for that duty. In contrast, all men who were registered voters were eligible to serve. When Gwendolyn Hoyt was convicted of bludgeoning her adulterous husband to death with a baseball bat, she appealed her conviction, claiming that the exclusion of women from juries prejudiced her case. She believed that female jurors—her peers—would have been more sympathetic to her and the emotional turmoil that led to her attack on her husband and her claim of ''temporary insanity.'' She therefore argued that her trial by an all-male jury violated her rights guaranteed by the Fourteenth Amendment. In rejecting her contention, in *Hoyt* v. *Florida*[34] Justice John Harlan (the grandson of the lone dissenting justice in *Plessy*) wrote:

> Despite the enlightened emancipation of women from the restrictions and protections of bygone years, and their entry into many parts of community life formerly considered to be reserved to men, a woman is still regarded as the center of home and family life.

These kinds of attitudes and decisions were not sufficient to forge a new move for women's rights. Shortly after *Hoyt,* however, three incidents or events occurred to move women to action. In 1961, soon after his election, President John Kennedy had created a President's Commission on the Status of Women. The Commission's report, *American Women,* released in 1963, documented pervasive discrimination against women in all walks of life. In addition, the civil rights movement and publication of Betty Friedan's *The Feminine Mystique* (1963), which led women to question their lives and status in society, added to their dawning recognition that something was wrong. Soon after, the Civil Rights Act of 1964 prohibited discrimination based not only on race, but also on sex. Ironically, that provision had been added to Title VII of the Civil Rights Act by Southern Democrats. Title VII's aim was to prevent discrimination in employment. The Southern senators saw a prohibition against sex discrimination in employment as a joke and viewed its addition as a means to discredit the entire Act and ensure its defeat. Thus it was added at the last minute, and female members of Congress seized the opportunity to garner support for the measure.

---

[32] Mary King, *Freedom Song* (New York: Morrow, 1987).
[33] Quoted in Jo Freeman, *The Politics of Women's Liberation* (New York: Longman, 1975), p. 57.
[34] 368 U.S. 57 (1960).

In 1966, women activists formed the National Organization for Women (NOW). From its inception, NOW was closely modeled after the NAACP. Women in NOW were quite similar to those who created the NAACP; they wanted to work within the system to prevent discrimination. Initially most of this activity was geared toward two goals: achievement of equality through passage of an equal rights amendment to the Constitution, or by judicial decision. But because the Supreme Court failed to extend constitutional protections to women, the only recourse that remained was an amendment.

The Equal Rights Amendment. Not all women agreed with notions of full equality for women. Members of the National Consumers' League, for example, feared that an ERA would invalidate protective legislation of the kind specifically ruled constitutional in *Muller* v. *Oregon* (1908). Nevertheless, from 1923 to 1972, a proposal for an equal rights amendment was made in every session of every Congress.

Finally, in 1972, in response to NOW, the National Women's Political Caucus, and a wide variety of other women's groups, Congress passed the proposed Equal Rights Amendment by overwhelming majorities (84–8 in the Senate; 354–24 in the House). Every president since Harry Truman backed it, and public opinion favored its ratification.

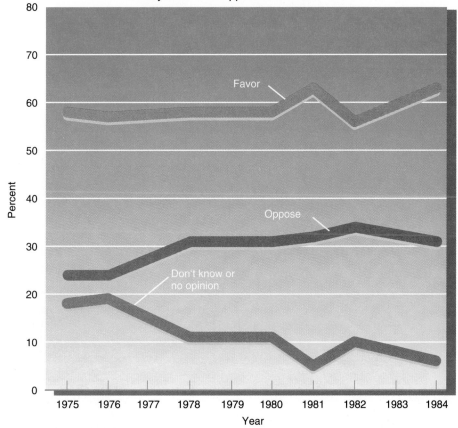

Public Opinion on the ERA

Have you heard or read about the Equal Rights Amendment to the U.S. Constitution which would prohibit discrimination on the basis of sex? Do you favor or oppose this amendment?

Source: The Gallup Poll (1982), 1440, (1984) 242.

The amendment provided that

- Equality of rights under the law shall not be denied or abridged by the United States or by any state on account of sex.
- The Congress shall have the power to enforce, by appropriate legislation, the provisions of this article.

Within a year, twenty-two states had ratified the amendment, most by overwhelming margins. In early 1973, however, the Supreme Court decided in *Roe* v. *Wade*[35] that women had a constitutionally protected right to privacy that included the right to terminate a pregnancy.

Almost overnight *Roe* gave those who opposed the ERA political fuel. Although privacy rights and the ERA have nothing to do with each other, opponents effectively persuaded many in unratified states that the two were linked. If abortion was legal, why not marriages between and adoptions by homosexuals? They also claimed that the ERA would force women out of their homes and into the workforce as husbands would no longer be responsible for their wives' support.[36]

These arguments and the amendment's potential to make women eligible for the draft brought the ratification effort to a near standstill. In 1974–75, the amendment only squeaked through the Montana and North Dakota legislatures, and two states—Nebraska and Tennessee—voted to rescind their earlier ratifications.

By 1978, one year before the deadline for ratification was to expire, thirty-five states—three short of the three-fourths necessary for ratification—had voted for the amendment.

[35] 410 U.S. 113 (1973).
[36] Ree L. Lee, *A Lawyer Looks at the ERA* (Provo, Utah: Brigham Young University Press, 1980).

Eleanor Smeal, President of the National Organization for Women, led NOW's effort to have Congress extend the deadline for ratification of the Equal Rights Amendment. In spite of the ratification extension, NOW and a coalition of other women's groups were unable to convince a sufficient number of state legislators of the need for an equal rights amendment.

Efforts in key states such as Illinois and Florida failed as opposition to the amendment intensified.

Faced with the prospect of defeat, amendment supporters heavily lobbied Congress to extend the deadline. Congress extended the time period for ratification by three years, but to no avail. Additional states ratified the amendment, but three more rescinded their votes.

Thus, what began as a simple correction to the Constitution turned into a highly controversial change. Opponents needed only to stall ratification in twelve states while supporters had to convince legislators in thirty-eight. Hurting the effort was the success that women's rights activists had had in the courts. When women first sought the ERA in the late 1960s, the Supreme Court had yet to rule that women were protected by the Fourteenth Amendment from any kind of discrimination, thus necessitating the need for an amendment. But, as the Court widened its interpretation of the Constitution to protect women from some sorts of discrimination, in the eyes of many the need for a new amendment became less urgent.

Litigation for Equal Rights. While several women's groups worked toward passage of the ERA, NOW and several other groups, including the Women's Rights Project of the American Civil Liberties Union (ACLU), acted to form litigating arms to pressure the courts. An immediate roadblock that women faced was the Supreme Court's interpretation of the equal protection clause of the Fourteenth Amendment.

The Equal Protection Clause and Constitutional Standards of Review

As noted earlier, the Fourteenth Amendment protects all U.S. citizens from state action that violates equal protection of the laws. But early on, the Supreme Court decided that certain rights were entitled to a heightened standard of review. As early as 1937,[37] the Supreme Court recognized that certain rights were so fundamental that a very heavy burden would be placed on any government that sought to restrict those rights. When fundamental rights such as First Amendment freedoms or **suspect classifications** such as race are involved, the Court uses a heightened standard of review called **strict scrutiny** to determine the constitutional validity of the challenged practices. Beginning with *Brown* v. *Board of Education,* the Supreme Court viewed race-based distinctions with the same strict scrutiny. In legal terms, this means that if a statute or governmental practice makes a classification based on race, the statute is presumed to be unconstitutional unless the state can provide ''compelling affirmative justifications''—that is, unless the state can prove the law is necessary to accomplish a permissible goal. During the 1960s and into the 1970s, the Court routinely stuck down as unconstitutional practices and statutes that discriminated on the basis of race. ''White only'' public parks and recreational facilities, tax-exempt status for private schools that discriminated, and statutes that prohibited racial intermarriage were declared unconstitutional. In contrast, the Court refused even to consider the fact that the equal protection clause might apply to discrimination against women. Finally, in 1971, in a case brought by the Women's Rights Project of the American Civil Liberties Union, the Supreme Court ruled that an Idaho law which granted male parents an automatic preference over female parents as the administrator of their deceased children's estates violated the equal protection clause.

Reed v. *Reed,*[38] the Idaho case, turned the tide in terms of constitutional litigation. While the Court did not rule that sex was a suspect classification, it concluded that the equal protection clause of the Fourteenth Amendment prohibited unreasonable

[37]*Palko* v. *Connecticut,* 302 U.S. 319 (1937).
[38]404 U.S. 71 (1971).

The Equal Protection Clause and Standards of Review Used by the Supreme Court to Determine If It Has Been Violated

TYPES OF CLASSIFICATION	STANDARD OF REVIEW	TEST	EXAMPLE
What Kind of Statutory Classification Is in Issue?	What Standard of Review Will Be Used?	What Does the Court Ask?	How Does the Court Apply the Test?
Fundamental freedoms: Religion, assembly, press, privacy, "suspect" classifications (including race)	Strict scrutiny or heightened standard	Is classification *necessary* to the accomplishment of a permissible state goal?	*Brown* v. *Board of Education* (1954) Racial segregation not necessary to accomplish the state goal of educating its students.
Gender	Intermediate standard	Does it serve an important governmental objective, and is it substantially related to those ends?	*Craig* v. *Boren* (1976) Keeping drunk drivers off the roads may be an important governmental objective, but allowing eighteen- to twenty-one-year-old women to drink alcoholic beverages while prohibiting men of the same age from drinking is not substantially related to that goal.
Others (including age, wealth, and sexual preference)	Minimum rationality standard	Is there any rational foundation for the discrimination?	*Hardwick* v. *Bowers* (1986) It is rational for Georgia to prohibit consensual sodomy because of traditional taboos against homosexual behavior.

classifications based on sex. And, by 1976, the Court ruled that sex-discrimination complaints would be judged by a new, judicially created intermediate standard of review a step below strict scrutiny. In *Craig* v. *Boren* (1976),[39] the owner of the Honk 'n' Holler Restaurant in Stillwater, Oklahoma, and Craig, a male under twenty-one, challenged the constitutionality of the state law that prohibited the sale of 3.2 percent beer to males under the age of twenty-one and to females under the age of eighteen. The state introduced a considerable amount of evidence in support of the statute, including:

- Eighteen- to twenty-year-old males were more likely to be arrested for driving under the influence than were females of the same age
- Youths aged seventeen to twenty-one are more likely to be injured or to die in alcohol-related traffic accidents, with males exceeding females
- Young men were more inclined to drink and drive than females

The Supreme Court found that this information was "too tenuous" to support the legislation. In coming to this conclusion, the Court carved out a new "test" to be used in examining claims of sex discrimination. According to the Court, "[T]o withstand constitutional challenge, . . . classifications by gender must serve important governmental objectives and must be substantially related to achievement to those objectives." As *Craig* demonstrates, men, too, can use the Fourteenth Amendment to fight gender-based discrimination. Since 1976, the Court has applied that intermediate standard to most claims involving gender that it has heard. Thus, the following kinds of practices have been found to violate the Fourteenth Amendment:

[39] 429 U.S. 190 (1976).

- Single-sex public nursing schools
- Laws that consider males adults at twenty-one years but females at eighteen years
- Laws that allow women and not men to receive alimony

In contrast, the Court has upheld the following governmental practices and laws:

- Draft-registration provisions for males only
- Statutory rape laws that apply only to female victims

The level of review used by the Court is crucial. Clearly, a statute that excluded blacks from a draft registration would be unconstitutional. But, because gender is not subject to the same higher standard of review that is used in racial-discrimination cases, the exclusion of women from the requirements of the Military Selective Service Act was ruled permissible because the government policy was considered to serve "important governmental objectives."

The reader can perhaps better understand, then, why women's rights activists continue to argue that until the passage of an equal rights amendment, women will never come close to enjoying the same rights as men. An amendment would automatically raise the level of scrutiny that the Court applies.

Statutory Remedies for Discrimination. In part because of the limits of the intermediate standard of review, women's rights activists began to bombard the courts with sex-discrimination cases filed under Title VII of the Civil Rights Act, which prohibits discrimination in employment, or Title IX of the Education Amendments of 1972, which bars educational institutions receiving federal funds from discriminating against female students. Key victories under Title VII include:

- Consideration of sexual harassment as discrimination
- Inclusion of law firms in the coverage of the Act
- Allowance of voluntary affirmative action programs to redress historical discrimination against women

Title IX, which parallels Title VII, has also greatly expanded the opportunities for women in elementary, secondary, and post secondary institutions. It was lobbied for heavily by women's groups, which, like the NAACP before them, saw the eradication of educational discrimination as a key way to improve other facets of women's lives. Most of today's college students, especially those in their late teens or early twenties, did not go through school being excluded from home economics or shop classes on account of their sex. Nor, probably, did many attend schools that simply had no team sports for females. Yet, this was commonly the case in the United States prior to passage of Title IX.

The effectiveness of Title IX was sorely hampered in 1984 by a Supreme Court decision, *Grove City College* v. *Bell*.[40] Grove City College was a small religious college in Pennsylvania that accepted no federal funds. It refused any public funds in large part to assure its independence from federal rules and regulations. Many students in attendance there were the recipients of federal student loans. When the university refused to sign a letter stating that it was in full compliance with Title IX, the Carter adminstration's Justice Department moved to terminate funds to the students at Grove City College. Students at the college sued. By the time the case reached the Supreme Court, Ronald Reagan had been elected president.

[40] 465 U.S. 555 (1984).

Building on the Successes of Blacks and Women

In the wake of the successes of blacks and women in achieving greater rights, other traditionally disenfranchised groups have organized to gain fuller equality. Recognizing that litigation and the use of test-case strategies were key to many of the gains made by blacks and women, other groups saw the wisdom of litigation as a civil rights tool. With the assistance of the Ford Foundation, for example, Mexican-Americans founded the Mexican American Legal Defense and Education Fund (MALDEF) in 1968. Modeled after the NAACP LDF, MALDEF has played a major role in bringing test cases trying to force school districts to allocate more funds to schools that have predominantly low-income minority populations, implement bilingual education programs, force employers to hire Chicanos, and challenge election rules and apportionment plans that undercount or dilute Hispanic voting power.

Native Americans, historically ill treated by American law, also were helped by Ford money, which facilitated the creation of the Native American Rights Fund in 1970. It has sponsored hundreds of cases involving tribal fishing rights key to their economic survival, tribal land claims, and taxation of tribal profits.

The elderly, the fastest-growing group in America, also have resorted to litigation to gain civil rights. The American Association of Retired Persons (AARP) was founded in 1958 and today counts more than 22 million members over the age of 55. In conjunction with the National Senior Citizens' Law Center, founded in 1972, AARP often participates in litigation involving the concerns of senior citizens, including pension and retirement issues, Medicaid benefits, Social Security disability benefits, and mandatory retirement.

One of the latest groups to use litigation to achieve civil rights is gays. In the late 1970s, the Lambda Legal Defense and Education Fund, the Lesbian Rights Project, and Gay and Lesbian Advocates and Defenders were founded by gay activists dedicated to ending legal restrictions on the civil rights of homosexuals. Although these groups have won important victories in the courts concerning AIDS discrimination, insurance policy survivor benefits, and even some employment issues, they generally have not been as successful as other disadvantaged groups.

In 1986 in *Hardwick* v. *Bowers,* for example, the Supreme Court ruled that a Georgia law which made illegal private acts of consensual sodomy (whether practiced by homosexuals or by heterosexual married adults) was constitutional. Gay-rights groups had argued that a constitutional right to privacy included the right to engage in consensual sex within one's home, but the Court disagreed. Although privacy rights may attach to relations of "family, marriage, or procreation," those rights did not extend to gays, wrote Justice Byron White for the Court. In a concurring opinion—his last written on the Court—Chief Justice Warren Burger called sodomy "the infamous crime against nature." Although four dissenters practically accused the majority of homophobia, it was clear that the Court spoke for many Americans, some of who had gone so far as to argue that AIDS was God's curse on gays. Gays have yet to win the public's sympathy or that of the Supreme Court.

The Reagan Administration and Civil Rights and Beyond, 1980–

The Reagan administration abandoned the position taken by the Carter Justice Department and urged the Court to find that institutions receiving federal funds were *not* required to comply with the ever-widening net of anti-discrimination statutes that covered race, sex, age, handicaps, and national origin. Instead, the Court was asked to find that only those programs directly affected by the federal funding were bound by federal anti-discrimination provisions.

In a decision that was widely hailed by conservatives and bemoaned by civil rights activists, the Court agreed with the Reagan administration and limited the coverage of anti-discrimination statutes to the university programs directly receiving federal funds and not to the entire institution. In essence, in one fell swoop, the Court eviscerated one of the most potent weapons in the civil rights movement's arsenal—the potential withdrawal of thousands and even millions of dollars as penalties for noncompliance.

The Reagan administration's victory in *Grove City College,* however, was short-lived. An angry Democratic House of Representatives quickly acted to pass the Civil Rights Restoration Act to overrule the case. But, at the urging of the Reagan administration, the Republican-controlled Senate of the 98th and 99th Congresses failed to pass the Act. After the Democrats regained control of the Senate in the 1986 elections, the Democratic 100th Congress in 1988 passed the Civil Rights Restoration Act over the veto of President Reagan.

Affirmative Action

The civil rights debate has often centered on the argument between equality of opportunity versus equality of results. Most civil rights and women's rights organizations argue that the lingering and pervasive burdens of racism and sexism can be overcome only by taking race or gender into account in fashioning remedies. They argue that the Constitution is not and should not be color or sex blind. Therefore, busing should be used to integrate schools if necessary, and women should be given child-care assistance to allow them to compete equally in the marketplace.

The counter-argument holds that if it was once wrong to use labels to discriminate against a group, it should be wrong to use those same labels to help a group. Laws should be neutral or color blind. According to this view, quotas or other forms of **affirmative action,** policies designed to give special attention or compensatory treatment to members of a previously disadvantaged group, should be illegal. As early as 1871, Frederick Douglass ridiculed the idea of racial quotas, arguing that they would promote "an image of blacks as privileged wards of the state." They were "absurd as a matter of practice" because they could be inferred to argue that blacks "should constitute one-eighth of the poets, statesmen, scholars, authors and philosophers."

The debate over affirmative action and equality of opportunity became particularly intense during the Reagan years in the wake of public opinion and two court cases that were generally decided in favor of affirmative action.

In 1978, the Supreme Court for the first time fully addressed the issue of affirmative action. Allen Bakke, a thirty-one-year-old paramedic, originally sought admission to several medical schools and was rejected because of his age. The next year, he applied to the University of California at Davis and was placed on the waiting list. The Davis Medical School maintained two separate admissions committees—one for white students and another for minority students. Bakke was not admitted to the school, although his grades and standardized test scores were better than those of all of the black students admitted to the school. In *Regents of the University of California* v. *Bakke,*[41] a badly divided Court concluded that Bakke's rejection had been illegal because the use of strict quotas was inappropriate. The medical school, however, was free to "take race into account."

Bakke was quickly followed in 1979 by another case in which the Court ruled that a factory and a union could voluntarily adopt a quota system in selecting black workers over more senior white workers for a training program.[42]

For a while the Court continued to uphold more affirmative action plans, especially when there was clear-cut evidence of prior discrimination, although it was by five-to-four votes. And, in 1987, in *Johnson* v. *Santa Clara Transportation Agency,*[43] the Court for the first time ruled that a public employer could use a voluntary plan to promote women even if there was no judicial finding of prior discrimination.

In all of these cases the Reagan administration powerfully urged the Court to invalidate the plans in question, to no avail. But with changes in personnel on the Court, including the appointment in 1986 of Chief Justice William Rehnquist, a strong opponent of affirmative action, the continued efforts of the Reagan administration finally began to pay off as the Court heard a new series of cases that began to signal an end to the advances of civil rights law. In a three-month period in 1989, the Supreme Court handed down five civil rights decisions limiting affirmative action programs and making it harder to prove employment discrimination.

In February 1990 congressional and civil rights leaders unveiled legislation designed to make it easier for minorities and women to fight job bias in the courts. In introducing the Civil Rights Act of 1990, Senator Edward M. Kennedy (D.-Mass.) noted that the act was necessary to overrule the Court's rulings, which "were an abrupt and unfortunate departure from its historic vigilance in protecting" the rights of minorities. The bill sought to blunt the effort of recent Court rulings by:

- Barring harassment or firing of employees based on racial bias. (The Court had ruled that the 1866 Civil Rights Act, used by a North Carolina credit union worker to press her racial-bias claim, barred only hiring discrimination, not on-the-job harassment.)

- Forcing employers to show that any practice with proven discriminatory impact was prompted by business necessity. (The Court had ruled in a case from Alaska involving cannery workers that the burden of proof belongs with workers who allege they are the victims of discrimination.)

- Making it clear that it is always illegal to use race, ethnicity, gender, or religion as a criterion for employment decisions. (The Court had ruled that the burden of proof belongs to employers if accused of discriminating illegally in personnel decisions; however, the ruling was vague enough to confuse lower courts.)

- Making court-approved affirmative action plans designed to remedy discrimination permanent. (The Court had made it easier for white men to challenge such plans years after they were put into effect.)

- Easing the deadlines for workers who sue over allegedly biased seniority systems. (The Court had ruled that the time frame for filing such lawsuits is determined by when a seniority plan is adopted, not when an individual worker is affected.)

- Assuring victims of intentional discrimination the right to sue for monetary damages.

[41] 438 U.S. 265 (1978).
[42] *United Steelworkers of America* v. *Weber,* 443 U.S. 197 (1979).
[43] 480 U.S. 616 (1987).

The bill passed both houses of Congress but was vetoed by President Reagan's successor, George Bush, and Congress failed to override the veto. In late 1991 Congress and the White House reached a compromise on a weaker version of the civil rights bill, which was passed by overwhelming majorities in both the House (381 to 31) and Senate (93 to 5). Quotas were prohibited by the new act. Moreover, in the wake of the Clarence Thomas hearings and their focus on sexual harassment, victims of sexual harassment were given the explicit right to sue for intentional discrimination. The act also overruled the Supreme Court rulings noted above.

Toward Reform

In March 1990, civil rights activists met in Selma, Alabama, to recreate the famous march from Selma to Birmingham on the twenty-fifth anniversary of that occasion. Clearly, tremendous inroads had been made in the years since so much blood was shed in Alabama. All around the nation, individuals who played major roles in the civil rights movement are in important positions of power. A new generation of black and female leaders is emerging as additional barriers continue to fall. The civil rights movement had international effects as well. In the late 1960s and 1970s, the leaders of racial minority communities in Britain consciously patterned their organizations on American models. Moreover, the urban riots that rocked Liverpool, Birmingham, and London during the 1980s evoked the image of those in the United States during the hot summers of the 1960s. The emergence of the British feminist movement also looked to the United States for both positive and negative lessons.

In this country, the political environment for blacks and women is changing. The Bush administration is not particularly receptive to the expansion of civil rights. As vacancies occur on the Supreme Court, Bush, like Reagan, has appointed conservatives as replacements. Bush's replacement for Thurgood Marshall, Clarence Thomas, the black former head of the EEOC who himself was the beneficiary of an affirmative action program at Yale Law School, is against quotas. The conservative shift on the Court makes it unlikely that decisions in the near future will be as aggressively pro-rights as in the recent past. Additionally, blacks and women are hampered by their very successes. Leaders have found it increasingly more difficult to mobilize followers since the most blatant discriminatory practices have been put to an end and disagreement exists on how to achieve remaining goals. For example, although all blacks still agree on the need for improved educational opportunities, they disagree on how best to achieve that goal. At a time when 40 percent of the black men in the United States are functionally illiterate and many cities are overwhelmingly black, busing is no longer the issue. For some, the trend in the 1990s should be toward reinstating all-black schools with a focus on black pride. In 1990 and 1991 several big cities, including Detroit and Milwaukee, set up all-male black elementary and high schools designed to provide black youngsters from female-headed households with positive black male role models and a better education. The constitutionality of these schools, however, is being challenged in court by women's rights groups who believe that gender-segregated schools—black, white, or racially mixed—are unconstitutional.

To some extent, the civil rights movement has come full circle. Opportunities for blacks and women have improved, lessening (in the eyes of some) the need for further reform. Equality of opportunity enjoys more support than equality of results. The American public no longer believes that blacks and women need additional help from the government. Most believe that the quality of life for blacks has gotten better. But as the Supreme Court continues to chip away at civil rights long enjoyed by many, there may be a pro-rights backlash helped by a Democratic administration.

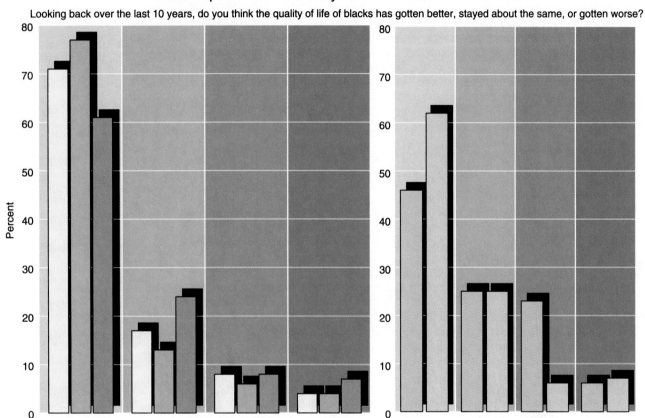

Public Opinion on the Quality of Life for African Americans

Looking back over the last 10 years, do you think the quality of life of blacks has gotten better, stayed about the same, or gotten worse?

Source: The Gallup Poll Monthly (June 1990).

Summary

While the Framers and other Americans basked in the glory of the newly adopted Constitution and Bill of Rights, their protections did not extend to all Americans. Black slaves could not vote or enjoy any other rights of citizenship. Five blacks were counted as three citizens when determining state population for representation in the House. Women, while counted for purposes of representation, were also not allowed to vote.

The "Compromise" reached by the Framers to settle the slavery question later erupted: first into a political war and soon after into a real war that culminated with the passage of the Civil War Amendments, which gave newly freed slaves full citizenship rates and the right to vote.

In spite of these constitutional changes, Southern states continued to discriminate against blacks—their actions facilitated by decisions of the U.S. Supreme Court, such as *Plessy* v. *Ferguson*. The Court was also not receptive to claims of sexual discrimination.

Groups such as the NAACP launched a test case strategy to bring about a reversal of *Plessy* v. *Ferguson*. Boycotts, sit-ins, and non-violent marches were used to draw attention to the plight of black Americans, particularly in the South.

Drawing on lessons from the civil rights struggle, women also united to achieve equal rights. Although they had gained the right to vote in 1920, their progress in the educational and employment spheres had been severely limited.

While efforts to add an equal rights amendment to the Constitution were unsuccessful, significant progress toward equality was made in the courts and elsewhere. But today, governmental policy is in a state of flux. Beginning in 1989, the Supreme Court has shifted to the right and appears less amenable to previous decisions on affirmative action and discrimination.

Key Terms

civil rights

equal protection clause

Emancipation Proclamation

Thirteenth Amendment

Black Codes

Fourteenth Amendment

Fifteenth Amendment

freedmen

Jim Crow

Civil Rights Cases

grandfather clauses

Progressive Movement

miscegenation laws

suffrage movement

Brown v. *Board of Education of Topeka*

freedom rides

Civil Rights Act of 1964

de jure discrimination

Equal Employment Opportunity Commission

suspect classifications

strict scrutiny

affirmative action

Suggested Readings

Browning, Rufus P., Dale Rogers Marshall, and David H. Tabb. *Protest Is Not Enough.* Berkeley: University of California Press, 1984.

Bullock, Charles III, and Charles Lamb, eds. *Implementation of Civil Rights Policy.* Monterey, Calif.: Brooks/Cole, 1984.

Flexner, Eleanor. *Century of Struggle.* New York: Atheneum, 1971.

Freeman, Jo. *The Politics of Women's Liberation.* New York: Longman, 1975.

King, Mary. *Freedom Song.* New York: Morrow, 1987.

Kluger, Richard. *Simple Justice.* New York: Vintage, 1975.

Mansbridge, Jane J. *Why We Lost the ERA.* Chicago: University of Chicago Press, 1986.

Sindler, Allan P. *Bakke, DeFunis, and Minority Admissions.* New York: Longman, 1978.

Verba, Sidney, and Gary R. Orren. *Equality in America: The View from the Top.* Cambridge, Mass.: Harvard University Press, 1985.

Vose, Clement E. *Constitutional Change: Amendment Politics and Supreme Court Litigation Since 1900.* Lexington, Mass.: Heath, 1972.

Williams, Juan. *Eyes on the Prize: America's Civil Rights Years, 1954–1965.* New York: Penguin, 1987.

Woodward, C. Vann. *The Strange Career of Jim Crow.* New York: Oxford University Press, 1957.

PART TWO

Institutions of Government

Political institutions such as Congress and the presidency form the core of a government's decision-making apparatus. We need to understand how these institutions are designed, how they have changed over time, and how they function today. The United States has been governed by more than one hundred Congresses, over forty presidents, and thousands of federal judges; but while the individuals have changed, all three respective governmental branches have remained intact. Studying these branches allows us to address the question central to any investigation of a political system—that of how such institutions shape behavior.

In Chapter 6, we turn to Congress. Since law making defines much of governance, the legislature is a natural starting point for institutional analysis. Congress is a complex body comprising 535 representatives and senators. We will study it both from the point of view of the individual member and from that of committees, caucuses, and parties.

In Chapter 7, we examine the presidency in a historical context and in its modern form. The nation's chief executive has wielded a varying amount of power over the years, and it is important to understand why and how that power has evolved. In Chapter 8, we examine the bureaucratic structure of the executive branch. The administration of America's government has grown dizzyingly complex and therefore requires a complete chapter for proper explanation.

Finally, we look at the judiciary in Chapter 9, with special emphasis on the Supreme Court. It is the judicial branch that most carefully considers the principles of the Constitution and the changing interpretations of the rights and liberties discussed in Part One. The judiciary must consider fundamental questions of fairness and power, and their decisions deeply affect the fabric of American life.

In republican government, the legislative authority naturally predominates. The remedy for this inconvenience is to divide the legislature into different branches . . . .

Alexander Hamilton

FEDERALIST NO. 51

By dividing Congress into two houses—the Senate and the House of Representatives—the Framers believed that they could diffuse its power and keep it from dominating the federal system.

CHAPTER 6

Congress

In all democratic nations, the primary institution for representing the interests of the citizenry is an elected legislature. When the Framers met in Philadelphia, there was no question about whether the new government would have a legislature. Instead, the delegates considered how it was to be structured (unicameral or bicameral, that is, consisting of one house or two), the nature of the powers to be given to it, and whom the body should represent.

In the centuries since the writing of the Constitution and the creation of the Congress, it has evolved in size, shape, and power. Consider the following:

- In a republican government, the legislative authority naturally predominates[1]
- "Congress is the dominant, nay, the irresistible power of the federal system"[2]
- In 1991, in the aftermath of the Clarence Thomas hearings to the U.S. Supreme Court, Congress enjoyed the confidence of only 11 percent of the people, and criticisms of the Senate, its members, and its rules and procedures abounded.[3]

In the sections that follow, we will come to terms with these various pronouncements about Congress by examining its members, its structure, and the procedures used to exercise and facilitate its lawmaking and oversight functions. As these have changed throughout history, so has Congress itself.

The Roots and Evolving Powers of Congress

Congress's powers evolved from Americans' experiments in the colonies and under the Articles of Confederation. When the colonists came to the New World, their general approval of Britain's parliamentary system led them to adopt similar two-house legislative bodies in the individual colonies. One house was directly elected by the people; the other was a Crown-appointed council that worked under the authority of the colonial government.

While originally established as advisory bodies to the royal governors appointed by the king, the colonial assemblies gradually assumed more power and authority in each colony, particularly over taxation and expenditures. The assemblies also legislated on religious issues and established quality standards for such colonial goods as flour, rice, tobacco, and rum. Prior to the American Revolution, colonists turned to these legislatures, the only bodies directly elected by the people, to represent and defend their interests against British infringement.

Colonists often drew parallels between their assemblies and the British Parliament, but they broke with British tradition in one significant way. The British Parliament was based on the concept of **virtual representation**—that is, although members of Parliament were elected from specific districts, they were considered to represent the *entire* country. Because members were the "virtual" or actual representatives of all English people, they could legislate for British subjects in America as well. Colonists argued for a system of **actual representation,** in which members represented only those voters who elected them.

---

[1] *Federalist Papers,* No. 51.

[2] Woodrow Wilson, *Congressional Government: A Study in American Politics* (New York: Meridan Books, 1956). (Originally published in 1885.)

[3] Ronald Brownstein, "Times Poll Finds Prosperity Issue Hampers Democrats," *Los Angeles Times,* November 27, 1991, p. A-1.

Theories of Representation in Congress

Over the years, members of Congress and political theorists have held different ideas about how best to represent constituents. Edmund Burke, who served as a member of the British House of Commons (1765–97), argued that once elected, a representative need not vote the way constituents would expect him to. According to Burke, a representative is a "trustee" expected to listen to the opinions of his constituents but trusted by them to use his or her own best judgment in making final decisions. A second theory of representation holds that representatives are "delegates" who should vote or represent the opinions of their constituents regardless of whether those opinions are their own.

Members of Congress do not clearly fall into the categories of trustee or delegate. It is often unclear how constituents feel about a particular issue, or there may be conflicting opinions within a single constituency. With these difficulties in mind, a third theory of representation holds that "politicos" alternately don the hats of trustee or delegate, depending on the issue. On an issue of great concern to their constituents representatives will most likely vote as delegates; on other issues, perhaps those that are less visible, representatives will act as trustees and use their best judgment.

The Continental Congress

The Continental Congress was formally established by the Articles of Confederation in 1771. The Congress was established to govern the union of the states and was given power over national affairs, particularly those relating to the Revolutionary War. But, as described in Chapter 2, the Congress had no independent sources of income and had to depend on the states for money and supplies. After the war was over, the states reverted to considering themselves as sovereign nations, and many believed that the national government under the Articles of Confederation was inadequate to serve the needs of the new nation. Discontent grew, eventually leading to the new Constitution in Philadelphia.

The Constitution and the Structures and Duties of the New Congress

Article I of the Constitution created the legislative branch of government we know today. The kind of two-house legislature created by the Framers is called a bicameral legislature. All states except Nebraska follow this model. As discussed in Chapter 2, the Great Compromise resulted in each state being represented by two senators, regardless of the state's population, whereas the number of representatives in the "lower" house, the House of Representatives, is determined by state population. (After the 1990 Census, California, the most populous state, will have fifty-four representatives; Alaska, Delaware, North Dakota, South Dakota, Vermont, and Wyoming, the least populous states, will have but one representative each.) Members of the Senate were to be elected to six-year terms by state legislatures with one-third of that body up for reelection every two years; the Seventeenth Amendment, added in 1913, provides for the direct election of senators.

The Capitol building, Washington, D.C.

In contrast to senators' six-year terms, members of the House of Representatives were to be elected to two-year terms by a direct vote of the eligible voters in each congressional district. Because each state's representation is based on population, the Constitution called for a national census every ten years. Until the first census could be taken, the Constitution fixed the number of representatives at sixty-five. In 1790, then, one member represented 37,000 people. As the population of the new nation grew and states were added to the Union, the House became larger and larger. In 1910 the House expanded to 435 members and in 1929, the House decided to fix its size at 435 by statute. Population shifts were to be handled every ten years after the census by the reapportionment of representatives among the states, a process discussed in greater detail later in this chapter.

The new Congress bore the marks of its colonial and revolutionary heritage. The directly elected House of Representatives assured local interests a voice in national affairs. The House was also considered to be the most "democratic" section of the new government because it was (at the time) the *only* directly elected part of the national government. Moreover, the bicameral nature of the new legislature created another check on national power: No bill can be passed into law without the approval of both houses of Congress. Each body can veto the policy desires of the other.

The modern British legislature is also bicameral. The House of Commons is comprised of 650 representatives hailing from electoral districts around the country; in this regard, it is the functional equivalent of the U.S. House of Representatives. The House of Lords, or upper house, has no American counterpart. Comprised of "peers" who represent only themselves as individuals, the Lords is a functioning vestige of Britain's centuries-long trek from absolute monarchy to parliamentary democracy. More than 1,000 peers sit in the Lords by virtue of hereditary lineage, appointment by the Crown on the recommendation of the Prime Minister, or the position they hold in government. However, owing to a series of twentieth-century parliamentary acts that sharply reduced its powers, the House of Lords plays only a marginal role in legislative affairs. The real center of legislative authority is in the House of Commons.

As we discuss the Congress in this chapter and elsewhere, the distinctions between the House and the Senate will often seem to blur. Yet there are important differences in

The Old Senate Chamber

Table 6-1   Some Differences Between the House and Senate

The House	The Senate
CONSTITUTIONAL DIFFERENCES	**CONSTITUTIONAL DIFFERENCES**
Initiates all revenue bills	Offers "advice and consent" to many major presidential appointments
Initiates impeachment procedures and passes impeachment bills	Tries impeached officials
Elected every two years	Elected every six years
Comprises 435 members (apportioned by population)	Comprises 100 members (two from each state)
	Approves treaties
DIFFERENCES IN OPERATION	**DIFFERENCES IN OPERATION**
More centralized, more formal:	Less centralized, less formal:
Stronger leadership	Weaker leadership
Rules Committee fairly powerful in controlling time and rules of debate (in conjunction with the majority leader)	No Rules Committee; limits on debate come through unanimous consent or cloture of filibuster
More impersonal	More personal
Power less evenly distributed	Power more evenly distributed
Members are highly specialized	Members are generalists
Emphasizes tax and revenue policy	Emphasizes foreign policy
Seniority important in determining power	Seniority less important in determining power
CHANGES IN THE INSTITUTION	**CHANGES IN THE INSTITUTION**
Power is becoming centralized in the hands of key committees and the leadership	Senate workload increasing and informality breaking down
House procedures are becoming more efficient with less debate and fewer amendments	Members are becoming more specialized; debate and deliberations less frequent
Turnover is low	Turnover is moderate

each body, as revealed in Table 6-1. Both houses share Congress's most important power—that of law making. Both houses also participate in another major function of Congress: oversight of the executive branch. But their working styles are quite different.

The Constitution specifically delegates to Congress **legislative powers,** which are shared by the two houses. No bill can become law, for example, without the consent of both houses. Examples of other shared powers include the power to declare war, raise an army and navy, coin money, regulate commerce, establish the federal courts and their jurisdiction, establish rules of immigration and naturalization, and to *"make all Laws which shall be necessary and proper for carrying into Execution the foregoing Powers."*

The Framers' intentions and the difference in size and constituencies of the two deliberative bodies have led to other differences. The Constitution specifies that certain powers vest in only one house. The House of Representatives was charged with originating all revenue bills. Over the years, however, this mandate has been blurred, and it is not unusual to see budget bills being considered simultaneously in both houses, especially

The Powers of Congress

The powers of Congress, found in Article I, Section 8 of the Constitution, are to:

- Lay and collect taxes and duties
- Borrow money
- Regulate commerce with foreign nations and among the states
- Establish rules for naturalization (that is, the process of becoming a citizen) and bankruptcy
- Coin money, set its value, and fix the standard of weights and measures
- Punish counterfeiting
- Establish a post office and post roads
- Issue patents and copyrights
- Define and punish piracies, felonies on the high seas, and crimes against the law of nations
- Create courts inferior to (that is, below) the Supreme Court
- Declare war
- Raise and support an army and navy and make rules for their governance
- Provide for a militia (reserving to the states the right to appoint militia officers and to train the militia under congressional rules)
- Exercise legislative powers over the seat of government (the District of Columbia) and over places purchased to be federal facilities (forts, arsenals, dockyards, and "other needful buildings")
- "Make all laws which shall be necessary and proper for carrying into execution the foregoing powers, and all other powers vested by this Constitution in the government of the United States" (Note: This "necessary and proper," or "elastic," clause has been expansively interpreted by the Supreme Court, as explained in Chapter 2.)

since each must approve all bills in the end, whether or not they involve revenues. The House also has the power of **impeachment**, the authority to charge the president, vice president, or other "civil officers," including federal judges, with *"Treason, Bribery or other high Crimes and Misdemeanors."* Only the Senate is authorized to conduct trials of impeachment, with a two-thirds vote being necessary before a federal official can be removed from office.

Only one president, Andrew Johnson, has been impeached by the House, but he was acquitted by the full Senate by a one-vote margin. More recently, as we will discuss in greater detail in Chapter 7, President Richard M. Nixon resigned from office in 1974 after the House Judiciary Committee voted to impeach him for his role in the Watergate scandal. In 1986, for the first time in fifty years, the House voted to impeach federal judge Harry R. Claiborne after he was convicted in federal court of income-tax evasion but refused to resign from the bench. After a trial in the Senate, he was removed from the bench after being convicted on three of the four articles of impeachment that the House had brought against him. In 1988 the process was repeated when Florida's first black federal judge, Alcee Hastings, was impeached even though he was acquitted of bribery charges in a U.S. federal district court.

The Senate not only has the sole authority to convict and remove federal officials from their positions, but it also has the power to approve major presidential appointments, including federal judges, ambassadors, and Cabinet and sub-Cabinet positions. The Senate, too, must approve by a two-thirds vote all treaties entered into by the president. Failure by the president to court the Senate can be costly. For example at the end of World War I, President Woodrow Wilson worked long and hard to get other nations to accept the Treaty of Versailles, which contained the charter of the proposed League of Nations. He overestimated his support in the Senate, however, and that body refused to ratify the treaty, thereby dealing Wilson and his international stature a severe setback.

The Members: Who Are They, and What Do They Do?

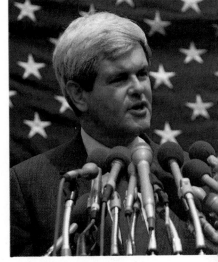

Being a member of Congress is a glamorous and exciting job. Newt Gingrich (R.-Ga.) once gleefully remarked, "There are very few games as fun as being a congressman."[4] It is also a hard job that requires one to continually seek reelection, expend enormous sums of money, and work very long hours, often for far less pay than could be earned in the private sector.

Although the U.S. Constitution sets out the formal, or legal, requirements for membership in the House and Senate (see Table 6-2), in reality these formal requirements are only part of the picture. There also seem to be informal requirements for a successful election campaign. Membership in one of the two major parties is virtually essential. Election laws in various states often discriminate against independents (those without party affiliation) and minor-party candidates (see Chapter 12). Money is another must. Most members of Congress are well-off if not wealthy. The Senate, moreover, has often been called the "Millionaires' Club" because so many very rich individuals serve in that chamber: ten of the thirteen richest members of Congress serve in the Senate. In the 103rd Congress (1993–95) nearly half are millionaires and more than 20 percent have a net worth of more than $2 million. In contrast, only 7 percent of present House members have that kind of wealth.

While everyone in the 103rd Congress may not be millionaires, the Congress has the "look" of a private club, just as the Congresses before it. In the 103rd Congress, the average age of all members is 53.1 years, 45 percent are lawyers, and 32 percent describe their profession as finance or banking. Moreover, Protestants collectively constitute the largest religious group—58 percent—and most members have a college education. But some changes are occurring. Over the years, more and more women and minorities have been running for office and winning (see Figure 6-1). In the 103rd Congress, for example, a record fifty-four women serve: six in the Senate and forty-eight in the House. Thirty-eight blacks also hold office in the House, the largest number ever to be elected, and one black woman, Carol Moseley Braun, was elected to the senate.

Representative Newt Gingrich, the second most powerful Republican in the House, has been a thorn in the side of House leaders, and he isn't too popular back at home—at least with the Democratic majority that controls the Georgia legislature. As a result of the 1990 census, Georgia was given an additional congressional district. An outraged Gingrich complained that Democratic legislators had carved his congressional district into four pieces "in an effort to destroy me." Gingrich only narrowly won reelection in 1990 against a poorly funded, relatively unknown challenger. His home was then thrown into the overwhelmingly Democratic district of John Lewis, the Deputy House Whip, which forced Gingrich to run in a new district in 1992.

[4] Hedrick Smith, *The Power Game* (New York: Ballantine Books, 1989), p. 97.

Table 6-2   Constitutional Qualifications

	HOUSE OF REPRESENTATIVES	SENATE
Age	25 years[a]	30 years[b]
Citizenship	U.S. for at least 7 years	U.S. for at least 9 years
Residency	In state from which elected	In state from which elected

[a] The youngest House member of the 102nd Congress was 30.
[b] The youngest Senate member of the 102nd Congress was 42.

Figure 6-1   Increase in Women and Minorities in Congress

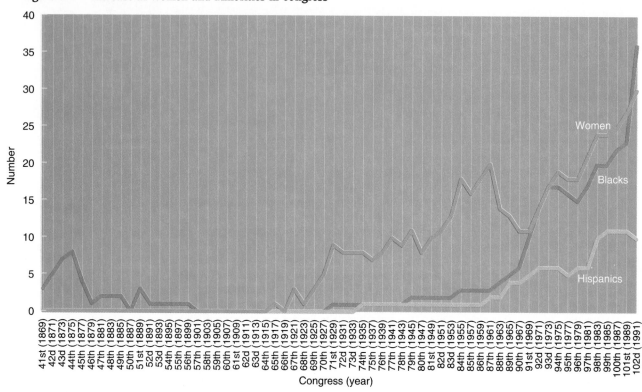

Source: Norman J. Ornstein *et. al., Vital Statistics on Congress* (Washington: CQ Press, 1992), pp. 38–39; Harold W. Stanley and Richard G. Niemi, *Vital Statistics on American Politics*, 3rd ed. (Washington: CQ Press, 1992), p. 201.

Does it make a difference if members of Congress actually come from or are members of a particular group? Some would argue a resounding no. Senator Edward Kennedy (D.-Mass.), for example, is one of the wealthiest members of the Senate, yet he has been an effective champion of the poor, women, and other minorities throughout his six terms in the Senate. But recent studies reveal that female legislators are more likely than their male counterparts to sponsor legislation of concern to women.[5] In the 101st Congress, for example, two bills supported by most women in Congress were passed: an extension of Medicare to cover mammograms for women over sixty-five and the establishment of a $30 million screening program for breast and cervical cancer for poor women, who die of these diseases at higher rates than the rest of the population. Representative Mary Rose Oakar (D.-Ohio), who cosponsored these bills, noted that she made progress by seeking help from male representatives whose wives had had breast cancer. "There are at least ten of them, and when it hits you in the family, boy, do attitudes change."[6] Without a push from women, however, it is unlikely that even those male representatives would have acted.

The fact that there were only two women in the one-hundred-member Senate was highlighted when the Senate Judiciary Committee initially failed to act on a sexual harassment complaint filed with the committee against Judge Clarence Thomas during the

[5] Beth Reingold, "Representing Women: A Comparison of Female and Male Legislators in Arizona and California" (Ph.D. dissertation, University of California, Berkeley, 1992).

[6] Quoted in Stacey Edwards, "Health Act to End Discrimination in Health Issues, Mikulski Says," *States News Service,* February 27, 1991.

hearings for his confirmation to the U.S. Supreme Court in 1991. When a female reporter from National Public Radio was leaked a copy of an FBI statement alleging improper conduct by Thomas, a national outcry went up. In arguing for a delay in the vote on the nomination of Thomas, Senator Paul Simon, (D.-Ill.), a member of the Senate Judiciary Committee, noted: "I think there is, in a body that is ninety-eight males to two women, a lack of sensitivity toward women's concerns and black and Hispanic concerns. If there were twenty women who were members of the Senate, we could delay the vote right now."[7] Seven female House members were so upset that the Senate would not hold a

[7] Quoted in Maureen Dowd, "The Thomas Nomination: The Senate and Sexism; Panel's Handling of Harassment Allegation Renews Questions About an All-Male Club," *The New York Times,* October 8, 1991, p. A-1.

Women in Congress

Congress clearly does not represent the American public demographically. Although women make up more than 50 percent of the nation's population, only 6 percent of the members of the 102nd Congress were female.

At current election rates it will take centuries for them to reach parity with their percentage of the population, a goal of many feminists. Eleanor Smeal of the Fund for Feminist Majority estimates that at the rate women are winning seats in Congress, they won't hold half the seats until 2334.

Success in getting women elected to Congress has been slow for several reasons. First, because most incumbents are men, women are provided few opportunities to compete in open races in which they would have a better chance of winning. Also, until recently there simply has not been a large number of female candidates running for Congress.

The women who have been elected, however, have made their mark as outspoken activists for various causes. In 1916, Representative Jeannette Rankin (R.-Mont.) became the first woman elected to Congress. In her two terms (1917–19; 1941–43) she actively supported child labor laws, women's suffrage, eight-hour work days, and birth control. She is, however, best known for her opposition to World

Wars I and II: She cast the lone ballot against U.S. entry into each war. Likewise, former Representative Elizabeth Holtzman (D.-N.Y.) was an outspoken critic of the Vietnam War. As junior members of the House of Representatives, both Holtzman and Barbara Jordan (D.-Tex.) served on the House Judiciary Committee and took active roles in the effort to bring articles of impeachment against President Richard Nixon.

Historically, the women who have served in Congress have not been afraid to speak out. Senator Margaret Chase Smith (R.-Me.), for example, was the first senator to speak out against Senator Joseph McCarthy's campaign against suspected communists in the 1950s. Her "Declaration of Conscience," a forceful speech delivered against Senator McCarthy in an era when personal attacks were unheard of on the floor, was the first speech she delivered as a senator.

Female representatives also have played prominent roles in efforts to expand women's rights. It was Martha Griffiths (D.-Mich.) who successfully added "sex" to the list of discriminatory qualifications prohibited by the Civil Rights Act of 1964 and Bella Abzug (D.-N.Y.) who led the fight for congressional passage of the Equal Rights Amendment.

Seven female House members attempted to gain entrance to a meeting of Senate Democrats in 1991 to demand that allegations of sexual harassment receive a full hearing before the Senate vote to confirm Clarence Thomas to the Supreme Court.

new round of hearings on the issue that they tried to gain entrance to a meeting of Senate Democrats discussing the matter, but were denied entrance. Once refused entry, they immediately set about lobbying senators for new hearings, collaring them as they came off the floor. "It's a perfect example," said Karen Johnson of the National Federation of Republican Women, "of why we need more women in the U.S. Senate."[8]

What Do Members of Congress Do?

According to the only study ever done on this subject, an average member of the House of Representatives spends 11.18 hours a day working on congressional-related activities. According to Hedrick Smith, a Pulitzer Prize–winning reporter for the *New York Times:*

> [D]ays are a kaleidoscopic jumble: breakfast with reporters, morning staff meetings, simultaneous committee hearings to juggle, back-to-back sessions with lobbyists and constituents, phone calls, briefings, constant buzzers interrupting

[8] Quoted in Dennis Cauchon and Andrea Stone, "Rising Tide of Anger," *USA TODAY,* October 6, 1991, p. 3-A.

A Perk Scandal

From 1838 to 1992, members of Congress used the private House bank to deposit their paychecks and to pay their personal bills. The bank paid no interest on deposits, nor did it charge for overdrafts. In 1992, in the aftermath of revelations that a majority of members of the 102nd Congress had bounced checks drawn to their accounts in the House bank, it was closed. (The bank had permitted House members to bounce 8,331 checks without penalty in one year.) Some representatives were found to have written rubber checks that totaled over $100,000, proving to much of the public that perks given to members of Congress as well as their recent salary increases had put the members out of touch with their constituents. Not only did "Rubbergate" lead to defeats of some of the more notorious "bouncers" in the 1992 elections, but the U.S. Attorney's office also began investigating a broad range of possible illegal activities, from check kiting to fraud.

House and Senate challengers in the 1992 elections tried to make the most of the perk scandal and the public's anti-incumbency mood. For example, in Massachusetts, Republican Peter Blute mounted a successful campaign against Democrat Joseph Early—who had 140 overdrafts—by running ads accusing Early of a "terrible addiction: perkomania." Blute also derided Early's frequent trips abroad, giving him the nickname "Tahiti Joe."

Nonetheless, although a handful of the worst abusers were defeated, most incumbents survived "Rubbergate" and the outcry over perks. House Republican Whip Newt Gingrich of Georgia, for example, who had criticized Democrats for their bounced checks yet had twenty-two himself, was targeted for defeat by numerous national liberal groups. His opponent labeled him a "perk monster" and widely ridiculed him for using a government limousine to ride the 150 yards from his apartment to his office, but Gingrich won reelection handily. Most Americans may like to complain about Congress, but they continue to send their representatives back to Washington.

office work to make quorum calls and votes on the run, afternoon speeches, evening meetings, receptions, fund-raisers, all crammed into four days so they can race home for a weekend gauntlet of campaigning. It's a rat race . . . [9]

Senator David Durenburger (R.-Minn.) once recalled the advice he received from one senior senator: "If you want really to keep on a fast track, always have more than two things to do for any space on your schedule. Go into politics because there's always too much to do."[10] One of the toughest and most time-consuming things that members do is to seek reelection.

Although the hours are long and the pace is hectic, many individuals simply love the game of politics. Moreover, being a member of Congress is viewed by many as a highly prestigious and influential job. The salary and perquisites or bonuses that go with the job (often called "perks") aren't bad either.

Members of Congress receive the following:

- An annual salary of $129,500 (the Speaker earns $160,000, the same as the vice president and Chief Justice)
- Free life insurance and a generous retirement plan
- Free office space in Washington and in their congressional districts back home
- A staff allowance of $515,760 for each House member and $814,000–$1,764,000 for each senator (depending on the population of his or her state), plus $280,000 for committee aides
- An expense account for telephone, stationery, and so on
- Thirty-two fully reimbursed round trips home a year
- Travel allowances and free travel to foreign lands on congressional inquiries (often called junkets by critics)
- Nearly unlimited franking (free mailing) privileges.
- Access to free congressionally owned and operated video and film studios to record messages for their constituents
- Discounts in Capitol Hill tax-free shops and restaurants (The bean soup at $1.40 a cup in the Senate Dining Room is famous.)
- $10.00 haircuts at the congressional barbershop
- Free reserved parking at Washington National Airport
- Use of the House gym for $100 a year or of the Senate "baths." (Women members were not allowed to use the House gym until 1985.) Soap is provided free by Representative Dan Rostenkowski [D.-Ill.], whose district is home to the Helene Curtis Company.

Changes in Representation: Reapportionment and Redistricting

The U.S. Constitution requires that a census, which entails the counting of all Americans, be taken every ten years. Congressional districts then must be redrawn by state legislatures to reflect population shifts so that each member in Congress will represent approximately the same number of residents. Reapportionment, which allots or reapportions the number of representatives each state gets, is often a very contentious process because of the high political stakes involved. When state population shifts occur, states gain or lose

[9] Smith, p. 108.
[10] Ibid.

The Original "Gerrymander" Cartoon, 1812

A Modern Day Georgia Gerrymander, 1991

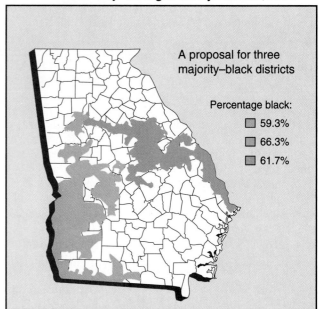

A proposal for three
majority–black districts

Percentage black:

☐ 59.3%

☐ 66.3%

☐ 61.7%

congressional seats. For example, in the 1990 census (as in most censuses since 1960), many Northeastern states lost congressional seats as they lost population, while the South, Southwest, and West gained seats because of the population explosion that has occurred in those areas, which collectively are known as the "sunbelt." For example, New York lost five congressional seats after the 1980 census and an additional three in 1990. Conversely, after the 1980 census, Florida picked up four seats and an additional four after the 1990 census.

Through the process of **redistricting,** or the redrawing of congressional districts to reflect population shifts, the majority party in each statehouse tries to assure that the maximum number of representatives from its political party can be elected to Congress. This redistricting process, which has gone on since the first census in 1790, is often called **gerrymandering.** The term was coined in 1812 when the powerful Republican governor of Massachusetts, Elbridge Gerry, persuaded the state legislature to create an oddly shaped district in order to favor the election of a fellow Republican. The story goes that upon seeing how the district was drawn, one critic observed, "Why, that looks like a salamander!" to which another retorted, "That's not a salamander, that's a gerrymander." The two most common forms of gerrymandering are "packing" and "cracking." Packing involves drawing a district so that it has a large number of supporters from a particular political party, thus making it a "safe" district. Cracking means dividing up supporters of the opposition party so that they become minorities in a number of districts, thus weakening their influence. No matter whether cracking or packing is used, districts often take unusual shapes.

Creative redistricting and the actions of state legislators have often created problems that have ended up in litigation. The Supreme Court faced the question of apportionment in *Baker* v. *Carr* (1962).[11] The Court found that a Tennessee legislative apportionment plan that failed to alter district lines despite large shifts in population was unconstitutional because it violated the constitutional principle of equal protection of the law. Furthermore, the Court ruled that the equitable apportionment of voters among districts was a legal question of constitutional rights and *not a political question,* thereby allowing the courts to direct relief in cases of malapportionment. Two years later, in *Reynolds* v. *Sims*

[11] 369 U.S. 186 (1962).

(1964),[12] based on the principle of "one man, one vote," the Supreme Court ruled that congressional as well as state legislative districts must have "substantially equal" populations.

More recently, in 1986 the Court ruled that any gerrymandering of a congressional district that purposely dilutes minority strength—a common reason for gerrymandering in the past—was illegal under the 1982 Voting Rights Act.[13] Consequently, whereas the drawing of districts to enhance party strength is permissible, redistricting plans that dilute black or Hispanic political clout are not.

New Members, New Styles

The 1970s witnessed a change in the types of candidates elected to the U.S. Congress. Many of these newcomers were the products of media-driven campaigns and the skillfull use of television. Once in Washington, they were more effective than older colleagues at getting national attention. This new group rose to public prominence not necessarily through their expertise or long service, but because television could make an individual a "star."

While new methods of gaining power were becoming more important, a procedural development also was taking on increased significance. The informal Senate tradition of allowing holds to be placed on bills began to be used with increasing frequency for political leverage and delay. A hold is a tactic by which a senator asks to be informed before a particular bill is brought to the floor. This request signals the Senate leadership and the sponsors of the bill that a colleague may have objections to the bill and should be consulted. Holds, which Senate Historian Larry DeNardis calls "silent filibusters," come in various forms. (As discussed later in this chapter, a filibuster is a way of halting action on a bill by means of long speeches or unlimited debate in the Senate.)

- A "consult," "informational," or "Mae West" hold (nicknamed after an early Hollywood movie star whose trademark phrase was "come up and see me sometime"): generally the senator has an amendment to offer or wants a leader to "come up and see me sometime" about the bill
- A "regular" or "real" hold: can mean that the member does not want the bill put to a vote and is trying to exercise a form of **senatorial courtesy,** a practice by which senators can have near-veto power over laws or appointments that affect their state in a specific way
- A "trading stock" hold: used as a bargaining chip to gain support on some future bill

The hold system has recently come under attack by some Senate members. "It's gotten out of control," says Senator Bennett Johnston (D.-La).[14] In the first session of the 102nd Congress, for example, holds were placed on more than two-thirds of the 250 bills reported out of committee in the Senate.

How Congress Works

Every two years, a new Congress is seated. After determining qualifications of new members, the Congress organizes its business for the coming session; it elects leaders, chooses committee assignments for the two-year period, and sets its agenda. Each year members

---

[12] 377 U.S. 533 (1964).

[13] *Thornburg* v. *Gingles,* 478 U.S. 30 (1986).

[14] Quoted in "Senate 'Holds' System Developing as Sophisticated Tactic for Leverage, Delay," *1991 Daily Report for Executives,* August 26, 1991, No. 165, p. C-1.

of Congress introduce up to 10,000 bills and eventually pass between 700 and 2,000; therefore, having rules and organization is critical. The primary organizing principles that drive Congress are political parties and the committee system.

The Role of Political Parties

When the first Congress met in 1789 in the nation's temporary capital in New York City, it consisted of only twenty-six senators and sixty-five representatives. Those men faced the enormous task of creating much of the machinery of government as well as that of drafting a bill of rights, for which the Anti-Federalists had argued so vehemently. During their debates, the political differences that divided Americans during the early years of the union were renewed. When Alexander Hamilton, the first Secretary of the Treasury and a staunch Federalist, proposed to fund the national debt and create a national bank, for example, he aroused the ire of those who feared vesting the national government with too much power. This conflict led Hamilton's opponents to create the Democratic-Republican Party to counter the Federalists, creating a two-party system in Congress. Control of the political parties quickly gave Congress far more powers. The Democratic-Republican **party caucus** (a formal gathering of all party members) nominated Thomas Jefferson (1804), James Madison (1808 and 1812), and James Monroe (1816) for president, all of whom were elected.

At the beginning of each new Congress—the 103rd Congress meets in 1993–94—the members of each party gather in caucus or conference. Historically these caucuses have enjoyed varied powers, but today the party caucuses—called "caucus" by House Democrats and "conference" by House and Senate Republicans and Senate Democrats—are used by party members to select leaders and make decisions on pending issues.

The **majority party** in each House is the one with the greatest number of members. Being in the majority party allows members of that party to choose the major officers of Congress and thereby control debate on the floor, hold all committee chairmanships, and have a majority on all committees. For almost thirty years the Democrats controlled both houses of Congress with few interruptions. In 1980, the Republican Party won control of the Senate for the first time in twenty-eight years, but the Democrats regained their majority in the 1986 elections. In parliamentary systems like Britain's, the majority party in the House of Commons is entitled to form the government.

The House of Representatives

Today, the House of Representatives is more than four times larger than the Senate (see Figure 6-2). Even in the First Congress in 1789, it was almost three times larger than the Senate. It is not surprising, then, that from the beginning, the House has been more tightly organized, more elaborately structured, and governed by stricter rules. Traditionally, loyalty to the party leadership and voting along party lines have been more common in the House than in the Senate. House leaders also play a key role in moving along the business of the House.

Partisan considerations especially affected the internal structure of the House of Representatives in the pre–Civil War years. As it increased in size, more permanent **standing committees** were created to divide up the House's work load (see Table 6-3 on page 192). Appointments to those committees were made by the **Speaker of the House,** and that position became correspondingly powerful.

The Speaker of the House is the only officer of the House of Representatives specifically mentioned in the Constitution. The Speaker is elected by the entire House and is traditionally a member of the majority party, as are all committee chairs. While typically not the member with the longest service, the Speaker generally has served in the House for a long time and in other House leadership positions as sort of an apprenticeship. The Speaker is elected at the beginning of each new Congress and generally is reelected until

The First Standing Committee

The First Standing Committee, the Ways and Means Committee, was established in 1795. Given the House of Representatives' important function of originating all money bills, the creation of this committee was consistent with the House's perceived need to keep a close watch on the Treasury Department, since Alexander Hamilton, the Secretary of the Treasury, had considerable disdain for the chamber directly elected by the people.

Figure 6-2   Congress Grows

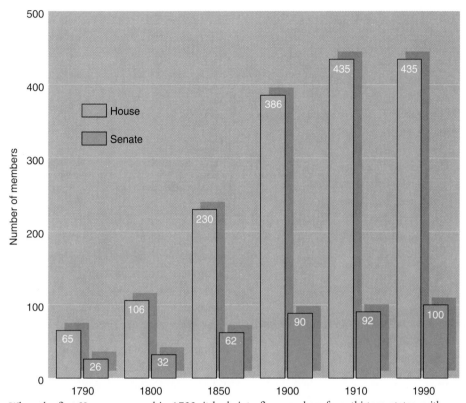

When the first House convened in 1789, it had sixty-five members from thirteen states, with each member representing 30,000 people. In the 1890s, each member represented 173,901 people, and in 1910 the number of representatives in the House was increased to 435, with each member representing 210,583 constituents. In 1929, the size of the House was fixed by statute at 435 members. In 1990, there was one representative for every 573,394 people. In 1991, in the wake of the 1990 census, the state of Montana filed a lawsuit after it appeared that its two congressional districts would be combined into one statewide district of more than 800,000 people, which would be the nation's largest. State officials argued that Montana residents would be underrepresented in the House, but a federal district court disagreed.

he chooses to retire. The Speaker presides over the House, oversees House business, is the official spokesperson for the House of Representatives and second in the line of presidential succession. Moreover, he is the House liaison with the president and generally has great political influence within the chamber. Through his parliamentary and political skills he is expected to smooth the passage of party-backed legislation through the House.

The first "powerful" Speaker was Henry Clay, elected to the position in 1810. Clay dominated the Democratic-Republican Party caucus and kept party members in line by the use of his power to appoint committee members and committee chairs. Not only did Clay use the party caucus, which he controlled, to decide which issues were to be addressed on the House floor, but he also used his power as Speaker to appoint his "hawk" allies to key positions on the Military and Foreign Affairs Committees in anticipation of the War of 1812.

Table 6-3   Standing Committees of the Senate and House

SENATE COMMITTEES	HOUSE COMMITTEES[a]
Major Committees *(Senators limited to service on two)* Agriculture, Nutrition, and Forestry Appropriations Armed Services Banking, Housing, and Urban Affairs Budget Commerce, Science, and Transportation Energy and Natural Resources Environment and Public Works Finance Foreign Relations Governmental Affairs Judiciary Labor and Human Resources **Minor Committees** *(Senators limited to service on just one)* Rules and Administration Small Business Veterans Affairs	**Exclusive Committees** *(Representatives on one of these committees cannot serve on any other committee except Budget)* Appropriations Rules Ways and Means **Major Committees** *(Representatives can serve on only one major committee)* Agriculture Armed Services Banking, Finance, and Urban Affairs Education and Labor Energy and Commerce Foreign Affairs Judiciary Public Works and Transportation **Nonmajor (Minor) Committees** District of Columbia Government Operations House Administration Interior and Insular Affairs Merchant Marine and Fisheries Post Office and Civil Service Science, Space, and Technology Small Business Standards of Official Conduct (Ethics Committee) Veterans Affairs

[a]As classified by House Democratic Caucus rules. The Republican Party is not bound by these rules but generally follows them, especially those regarding exclusive committees.

Modern Speakers do not enjoy the formal powers of their predecessors who served before 1910. Nevertheless, they have substantial powers based largely on their personal ability to persuade. Thomas Foley presides over the 103rd Congress, composed of 259 Democrats and 176 Republicans. Foley was a prominent lawyer in his native state of Washington prior to his election to the 89th Congress in the Democratic landslide of 1964. Foley moved through the ranks of the House leadership, serving first as the Democratic whip and then the majority leader. He became the forty-ninth Speaker in June 1989.

After the Speaker, the next most powerful people in the House are the majority and minority leaders, who are elected in their individual party caucuses. The majority leader

People of the Past

Henry Clay

Henry Clay (1777–1852) was a congressional giant of his time. As leader of the Whig Party, five times an unsuccessful presidential candidate, secretary of state under John Quincy Adams, and Speaker of the House of Representatives for six terms—longer than anyone else in the nineteenth century—Clay played an active role in national politics for over forty years.

Clay's personality and skill in oratory won him authority in Washington. As Speaker of the House of Representatives, in 1812, Clay became the leader of the "War Hawks," urging President James Madison to declare war on Great Britain to prevent British control of the seas, which Madison did on June 1, 1812.

As a presidential candidate, Clay developed his "American System," calling for national defense, construction of roads and canals with federal aid, protection of home industry through duties on foreign imports, and establishment of a second Bank of the United States. Clay wanted federal land in the West to be sold rather than given away to homesteaders so that the proceeds could be used to build schools and roads. The American System became the major plank in the platform of Clay's Whig party.

Clay is remembered as the Great Compromiser. As a Southerner and a slaveholder on the one hand, and a friend to Northern industry on the other, Clay mediated between North and South over the question of slavery. Clay played a major role in three landmark compromises: the Missouri Compromise of 1820, the Tariff Compromise of 1850, and the Compromise of 1850. Clay hoped that the last of these compromises would prevent the Civil War.

Although Clay did not prevent the Civil War and his Whig party disappeared shortly after his death, many features of his American System were later put into operation by the Republican Party.

---

at this writing, Richard Gephardt (D.-Mo.), is the second most important person in the House; his counterpart on the other side of the aisle (the House is organized so that Democrats sit on the left side and Republicans on the right side of the center aisle) is the present minority leader, Robert Michel (R.-Ill). Gephardt and Michel work closely with Foley, and the majority leader helps the Speaker schedule proposed legislation for debate on the House floor.

The Speaker and majority and minority leaders are assisted in their leadership efforts by the majority and minority whips. The concept of whips originated in the British House of Commons, where they were named after the "whipper in," the rider who keeps the hounds together in a fox hunt. Party whips, who were first designated in the House in 1899 and in the Senate in 1913, do, as their name suggests, try to "whip" fellow Democrats or Republicans into line on partisan issues. They try to maintain close contact with all members on important votes, prepare summaries of content and implications of bills, get "nose counts" during debates and votes, and in general get members to toe the party line. They are elected by party members in caucuses. The current House Whip, David Bonior (D.-Mich.), was elected in 1991.

Other important components of the partisan apparatus in the House include a Steering and Policy Committee that assigns Democratic representatives to House committees. The Republicans have a Committee on Committees that performs this function. Each party also has a Congressional Campaign Committee to assist members in their reelection bids.

Formal and Informal Powers of the Speaker of the House

FORMAL	INFORMAL
Presides over House when in session	Acts as national party leader when president is from different party
Plays a major role in committee assignments. Appoints 12 of 33 members of the Democratic Steering Committee, which functions as the "Committee on Committees" to select committee members	Sets the public agenda through ability to attract media attention
Appoints or plays a major role in the selection of other party leaders	Helps other members with fund raising by making appearances at events in their districts
Exercises considerable control over assignment of bills to particular committees	

The Senate

The Constitution specifies that the presiding officer of the Senate is the president of the Senate. The vice president of the United States fills this job. Because he is not a member of the Senate, he votes only in the case of a tie. The official chair of the Senate is the *president pro tempore*—at this writing, Robert C. Byrd (D.-W.Va)—who is selected by the majority party and presides over the Senate in the absence of the vice president. The position of president pro tempore is today primarily an honorary office that generally goes to the most senior senator of the majority party. Once elected, the *pro tem,* as he is called, stays in that office until there is a change in the majority party in the Senate. Since presiding over the Senate is a rather dull duty, neither the vice president nor the president pro tempore performs the task often. Instead, the duty of presiding over the Senate rotates among junior members of the chamber.

The true leader of the Senate is the majority leader. Although not as powerful as the Speaker of the House, he sets the Senate agenda, refers legislation to committees, and assigns members to committees. George Mitchell (D.-Me.), a quiet, studious man, was elected to this position by the fifty-six Democrats in the Senate. In contrast, leading the forty-four Senate Republicans is the acerbic and witty minority leader, Robert Dole (R.-Kans.). (Dole served as the majority leader during the Republicans' control of the Senate from 1984 to 1987.) The majority and minority whips round out the leadership positions in the Senate and perform functions similar to their House counterparts. Because of the Senate's smaller size, organization and formal rules have never played the same role in the Senate as they do in the House. Until recently, it was a "Gentlemen's Club" whose folkways—unwritten rules of behavior—governed its operation. One such folkway stipulated that political disagreements not become personal criticisms. A senator who disliked another referred to him as "the able, learned and distinguished senator." A member who really couldn't stand another called him "my very able, learned and distinguished colleague." Referring to members of their body by title and not by name, senators would sometimes go out of their way not to offend one another on the floor. For example, the following took place on the Senate floor while Lyndon B. Johnson served in the Senate and was printed in the *Congressional Record.*

> *Mr. [Lyndon] Johnson of Texas:* The Senator from Texas does not have any objection, and the Senator from Texas wishes the Senator from California to know that the Senator from Texas knew the Senator from California did not criticize him. . . . [15]

[15] Quoted in Donald R. Matthews, *U.S. Senators and Their World* (Chapel Hill, N.C.: The University of North Carolina Press, 1960), pp. 97–98.

Speaker of the House Thomas Foley (D.-Wash.) with Senate Minority Leader Robert Dole (R.-Kans.).

The Committee System: Legislation and Oversight

Committees are not mentioned in the Constitution. Originally, they were created on an ad hoc (as necessary) basis, but they had historical precedents in the British Parliament and in the colonial legislatures. These ad hoc committees were dissolved as soon as their specific tasks were accomplished. By the Second Congress, 350 such committees had been formed, and soon the increasing scope of congressional activities made the establishment, dissolution, and reestablishment of ad hoc committees increasingly time-consuming and inconvenient.

Over the years, as issues became more complex, specialization became an absolute necessity. Thus, a more institutionalized committee system was created in 1816, and committees have been added over time. Committees allow members of Congress to specialize and become experts in a small number of areas instead of attempting to be "jacks of all trades, masters of none." The establishment of subcommittees further subdivides issues and allows for even greater specialization. In addition, some committee assignments allow members to act on behalf of the specific interests of their constituents. Western representatives, for example, favor an assignment to the Interior and Insular Affairs Committee because of that committee's jurisdiction over all Western lands.

"Congress in session is Congress on exhibition, whilst Congress in its committee rooms is Congress at work" is even more true today than when Woodrow Wilson wrote it in 1883.[16] A quick look at the floor of the House or the Senate would lead most to conclude that not much goes on up on "the Hill" (as the Capitol is often called). Unless a vote is in progress, few members are on the floor. Instead, they are attending committee or subcommittee meetings, where most of the real work of Congress goes on. These "little legislatures" and their subcommittees are where all bills (proposed laws) are first considered.

Types of Committees

There are four types of congressional committees: standing, ad hoc or select, joint, and conference. The House and Senate standing committees listed earlier in Table 6-3 were created by statute. The House has twenty-two standing committees, and each has an

[16]Wilson, p. 79.

average of about thirty-five members. Together, they have a total of 157 subcommittees that collectively act as the eyes, ears, and hands of the House. They consider issues roughly parallel to those of the departments represented in the president's cabinet. For example, there are committees on agriculture, the judiciary, veterans affairs, transportation, and labor.

Standing committees have tremendous power. They can defeat bills, delay them, amend them so that they are radically changed, or hurry them through the process. In Wilson's words, once a bill is referred to a committee, it "crosses a parliamentary bridge of sighs to dim dungeons of silence from whence it never will return." Thus, a committee reports out to the full House or Senate only a small fraction of the bills first assigned to it. Bills can be "forced" out of a House committee by a **discharge petition** signed by a majority (218) of the membership, but legislators are reluctant to take this drastic measure. Since World War II, fewer than five bills have been enacted into law through this procedure. In 1971, for example, a discharge petition was used to force the proposed Equal Rights Amendment out of the Judiciary Committee, where it had been stalled by the committee's powerful chair, Emanuel Celler (D.-N.Y.). It later went on to be passed by the full House on a vote of 350 to 15. Generally, however, few members are willing to sign any discharge petition.

The Senate has sixteen standing committees that range in size from sixteen to twenty-nine members. It also has more than eighty-five subcommittees, allowing nearly all senators the opportunity to chair one. In contrast to the House, whose members hold few committee assignments (an average of two standing and four subcommittees), senators are spread more thinly, with each serving on an average of three committees and seven subcommittees. Whereas the committee system allows House members to become policy or issue specialists, Senate members are often generalists. Senator Max Baucus (D.-Mont.) is typical; he sits on the Agriculture, Nutrition and Forestry, Finance, Small Business, and Environment and Public Works committees. Daniel Patrick Moynihan (D.-N.Y.) sits on six committees and chairs two subcommittees. Senate committees enjoy the same power over framing legislation as do House committees, but the Senate is more likely to force bills out of committee by the use of discharge petitions. During the 1960s, in particular, the Senate was regularly forced to use discharge petitions to bypass the Judiciary Committee to get full consideration of civil rights laws. The Judiciary Committee as chaired by Senator James Eastland (D.-Miss.) became known as the "graveyard of civil rights legislation." (From 1953 to 1963 only 1 of 121 civil rights bills emerged from Eastland's fiefdom.)

Committee Membership

To gain a seat on a committee, one must be associated with either of the two main political parties. This becomes important on the rare occasions when an independent or third-party candidate is elected to one of the chambers. In 1990, for example, when independent socialist Bernard Sanders of Vermont was elected to the House of Representatives, he had to choose a party affiliation for the purposes of committee placement. (He chose the Democratic Party.)

New members and those seeking changes in their assignments inform their party's selection committee of their preferences. Generally preferences can be filled because junior members do not request more influential or prestigious committees like Ways and Means in the House or Armed Services in the Senate. Instead, they request assignments based on their own interests or expertise or on a particular committee's ability to help their prospects for reelection.

For example, in his first term in the Senate, Robert Kerrey (D.-Neb.) was assigned to the Agriculture Committee, where he could advance his state's farm industry. Representatives also seek committee assignments that have access to what is known as the **pork barrel**, or "bringing home the bacon." Until the recent end of the Cold War a seat on the "bread and butter" Armed Services Committee, for example, was particularly attractive. It

Then and Now
Life on the Floor of Congress

Throughout Congress's first several decades, partisan, sectional, and state tensions of the day often found their way onto the floors of the U.S. House and Senate. Many members were armed, and during one House debate thirty members showed their weapons. In 1826, for example, John Randolph of Virginia insulted Henry Clay from the floor of the Senate, referring to Clay as "this being, so brilliant yet so corrupt, which, like a rotten mackerel by moonlight, shined and stunk." Clay immediately challenged Randolph to a duel, of which the only victim was Randolph's coat. In 1856, Representative Preston Brooks of South Carolina, defending the honor of his region and family, assaulted Senator Charles Sumner of Massachusetts on the floor of the Senate. Sumner was disabled and unable to resume his seat in Congress for several years. Guns and knives were abundantly evident on the floor of both House and Senate, along with a wide variety of alcoholic beverages.

Today the House and the Senate are usually much more quiet. In 1984, however, a group of newly elected Republican representatives began taking over the House floor every day after the end of normal hours to berate their Democratic colleagues. The chamber was usually empty but, like all other action on the floor, these speeches were broadcast live on C-SPAN and often used by the members for distribution to local television stations back home. During a particularly strong attack on several Democrats' views on Central America, Representative Newt Gingrich (R.-Ga.) paused suggestively mid-speech, as though waiting for an objection or daring the Democrats to respond. No other House member was on the floor at the time, but since C-SPAN cameras only focus on the speaker, viewers were unaware of that fact.

Speaker Thomas P. O'Neill angrily reacted by ordering C-SPAN cameras to span the empty chamber to expose Gingrich's and other Republicans' tactics, but he failed to inform the Republicans of the change. O'Neill later apologized to the House Minority Leader, Robert Michel, but what Republicans labeled "CAMSCAM" ignited a firestorm on the floor. Incensed by remarks made by Gingrich, O'Neill dropped his gavel, left his spot on the dais, and took to the floor, roaring at Gingrich, "You challenged their [House Democrats'] patriotism, and it is the lowest thing that I have ever seen in my thirty-two years in Congress!" Trent Lott (R.-Miss.) then demanded that the Speaker be "taken down," the House term to call someone to order for violating House rules prohibiting personal attacks. The House Parliamentarian looked in the dictionary to see if the word "lowest" was a slur. As a hush fell on the House, the presiding officer told O'Neill that he had violated House rules. Bristled O'Neill, "I was expressing my views very mildly because I think much worse than I said."

O'Neill's penalty? The rarely invoked enforced silence for the remainder of the day's debate. So uncomfortable with that action was the House Minority Leader that he asked Lott to make a motion exempting O'Neill from the penalty, to which Lott agreed. No other House Speaker has ever been so reprimanded.[*]

[*]Alexander Stanley, "Tip Topped: O'Neill Tangles with Some Republican Turks over Camera Angles," *Nation*, May 28, 1984, p. 36.

could allow members to bring lucrative defense contracts back to their districts, encourage the building of bases, or discourage their closing within their districts or states, thus pleasing constituents.

The ability to bring defense contracts, public works contracts, or similar benefits to the district or state improves a member's chances for reelection or for election to higher office.

Floor Plan of the Capitol Building

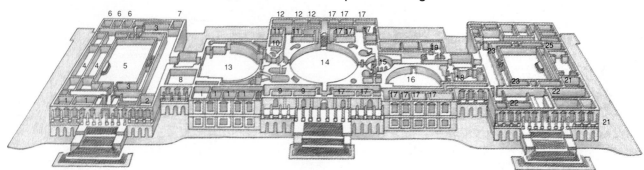

House of Representatives
1 Speaker's Office
2 Committee on Ways and Means
3 Cloakrooms
4 Members' Retiring Room and Lobby
5 House Chamber
6 Committee on Appropriations
7 Minority Whip
8 House Reception Room
9 House Conference Room
10 Committee Meeting Room
11 Representatives' Offices
12 Minority Leader

Central Area
13 Statuary Hall
14 Rotunda
15 Senate Rotunda
16 Old Senate Chamber

Senate
17 Senators' Offices
18 Senate Conference Room
19 Minority Leader
20 Majority Leader
21 Office of the Vice President
22 Senators' Reception Room
23 Cloakrooms
24 Senate Chamber
25 President's Room

In 1984, Jesse Helms (R.-N.C.), for example, turned down the chairmanship of the Senate Committee on Foreign Relations to stay on the less prestigious Committee on Agriculture, Nutrition, and Forestry, where he could better ensure continued support for the tobacco industry so vital to his home state's economy.

There always are members, however, who end up with "bad" committee assignments. After her 1968 election, Representative Shirley Chisholm (D.-N.Y.), the first black woman elected to Congress, was assigned to the House Agriculture Committee. "Apparently all they know here in Washington about Brooklyn is that a tree grows there," complained Chisholm. "I think it would be hard to imagine an assignment that is less relevant to my background or to the needs of the predominantly black and Puerto Rican people who elected me," she protested. In spite of the fact that some urban Democrats welcome serving on the committee that oversees the food stamp program, Chisholm fought for a different assignment and ultimately landed one on the Veterans Affairs Committee. "There are a lot more veterans in my district than there are trees," she later explained.[17]

In both the House and the Senate, committee membership generally reflects the party distribution within that chamber. For example, if the Democrats are the majority party and hold two-thirds of the seats, they control the chairmanship of and usually hold two-thirds of the seats on a committee, with the Republicans making up the other one-third. This distribution is based on tradition, not rules. Moreover, some committees have traditions of either partisanship or bipartisanship. For instance, the House Armed Services Committee has a tradition of strong bipartisanship and therefore has a large number of minority members. In contrast, the House Rules Committee has tended to be more

[17] Reported in Roger H. Davidson and Walter J. Oleszek, *Congress and Its Members,* 3rd ed. (Washington: CQ Press, 1990), p. 206 and *Woman's Almanac* (New York: Newspaper Enterprise Association, 1977), p. 200.

partisan and has a higher number of majority members. Since 1980, over the objections of House Republicans, Democrats have made several key committees disproportionately Democratic in order to assure control, since conservative Democrats increasingly were voting with the Republican minority. In fact, several Republican representatives even filed suit in federal court against Democratic leaders to gain more equitable distribution on committees, but the case was dismissed.

Although most committees in one house parallel one in the other, one committee unique to the House of Representatives plays a key role in the lawmaking process: the House Rules Committee. This committee reviews most bills after they come from a committee before they go to the full chamber for consideration. Performing a "traffic cop" function, this committee gives each bill what is called a rule, which contains the date the bill will come up for debate, the time that will be allotted for discussion, and often even specifications concerning what kinds of amendments can be offered. Members of this committee are directly appointed by the Speaker.

Types of Committees

- *Standing committees* are the committees to which proposed bills are referred for consideration. Fewer than 10 percent of the more than 10,000 measures sent to committees are ever reported out of these committees. They are called "standing" because they continue from one Congress to the next; therefore, they are generally viewed as the permanent workshops of congressional lawmaking.

- *Ad hoc* or *select committees* are temporary committees appointed for specific purposes with fairly limited mandates, generally to conduct special investigations or studies and to report back to the chamber that established them. Unlike standing committees, select committees do not ordinarily draft and report legislation.

- *Joint committees* are formed with members from both houses of Congress, generally to coordinate investigations or special studies. In practice, they are set up to expedite business between the houses and to help focus public attention on major matters such as the economy, taxation, or scandals. A joint committee, for example, was formed to investigate the Iran-*Contra* scandal.

- *Conference committees* are a special kind of joint committee with the explicit function of reconciling differences in bills passed by the House and Senate. The conference committee is made up of members from the House and Senate committees that originally considered the bill. Because the Constitution mandates that all bills pass both houses in the same form, compromises are often needed between the versions that pass each house of Congress. Once the committee comes up with a satisfactory compromise bill, it is presented to both houses of Congress for their approval. At this point, they can only accept or decline the compromise legislation; they cannot change or amend it in any way.

House–Senate Committee Comparison

CATEGORY	HOUSE	SENATE
Number of standing committees	22	16
Total committee assignments per member	About 7	About 11
Power or prestige committees	Appropriations, Budget, Rules, Ways and Means	Appropriations, Armed Services, Finance, Foreign Relations; almost every Senator assigned to one of these four
Treaties and nominations submitted by the president	No authority	Committees review
Floor debate	Representatives' activity is somewhat confined to the bills reported from the panels on which they serve	Senators can choose to influence any policy area regardless of their committee assignments
Subcommittee government	The norm on many committees	Notable on some but not most committees
Committee consideration of legislation	More difficult to bypass	Easier to bypass (for example, by allowing "riders"—unrelated policy proposals—to measures pending on the floor)
Committee chairmen	Subject to party and House rules that limit their discretionary authority over committee operations	Freer reign to manage and organize their committees
Committee staff	Less assertive in advocating ideas and proposals	More aggressive in shaping the legislative agenda
Eligibility for subcommittee chairmanships	Representatives of the majority party usually must wait at least one term	Majority senators, regardless of their seniority, usually chair subcommittees

Source: Roger H. Davidson and Walter J. Oleszek, *Congress and Its Members,* 3rd ed. (Washington: CQ Press, 1990), p. 205.

The Power of Committee Chairs

The position of committee chair is one of tremendous power and prestige. When House Speakers were strong, as was the case with Joseph Cannon, they personally selected all committee chairs on the basis of friendships and loyalty. After the revolution of 1910, committee chairs were chosen by seniority—the person of the majority party with the most continuous service on the committee was automatically made chair.

In 1971 and again in 1973, moderate and liberal Democrats pushed through a series of changes in the House designed to break the hold that conservative committee chairs from the South had long enjoyed because of the seniority system. In 1971, however,

House Democrats voted to elect committee chairs by secret ballot in the party caucus at the beginning of the session, and seniority was no longer the sole criterion for becoming a House chair. (In the Senate there was little change, because seniority is not nearly so important there; however, if one-fifth of the party caucus requests it, a secret ballot may be used to elect committee chairs.)

In the wake of these reforms—and the election in 1974 of a bumper crop of "Young Turks," seventy-five new liberal House Democrats—in 1975, three long-entrenched House chairs who were considered dictatorial, on the conservative fringes of the party, or both, were removed from their positions. Later, in 1985, eighty-year-old Melvin Price was voted out as chair of the Armed Services Committee, in spite of his promise to resign at the end of the term and passionate pleas from Speaker Thomas P. O'Neill.

Although their power was reduced by these reforms, committee chairs still establish the agenda for the committee in conjunction with the ranking minority member and may sit as a nonvoting member on all subcommittees. Moreover, committee chairs call meetings, strategize, recommend majority members to sit on conference committees, and are in charge of the committee staff. The chair may choose not to schedule a hearing on a bill so that the bill can die, may convene meetings when opponents are absent, and may adjourn meetings when things are going badly. Personal skill, influence, and expertise are a chair's best allies.

The Rise of Subcommittees

Another reform that occurred in the early 1970s was the adoption of "the subcommittee bill of rights," which decentralized committee power enormously. It took power away from the committee chairs of the 22 House standing committees and divided it among 157 subcommittees whose chairs now control their own budgets and staffs. Previously, subcommittee chairs were appointed by the committee chair. House Democrats now require that committee Democrats bid for subcommittee chairs and that their choices be accepted by a vote of party members on that committee. Seniority is generally used, but this new method does give majority party members the right to reject a subcommittee chair.[18]

Before the rule changes, committee chairs often chose to head important subcommittees themselves or appointed their close friends to those positions. As the power and number of subcommittees have increased, House Democrats abolished the practice of multiple subcommittee chairships, allowing each member to chair only one. This allowed so many House members to become subcommittee chairs and have their own base of power that former Representative Morris K. Udall (D.-Ariz.) once joked that if he passed a young colleague in the hall and didn't remember his name, he'd simply greet him with "good morning, Mr. Chairman," knowing he'd be right about half the time.[19]

As the work load of Congress has increased, so has the importance of subcommittees, leading to the rise of what some term "subcommittee government." On some committees it has become the norm that committee members simply defer to the judgment of the subcommittee and its specialists to speed up the legislative process.

Party and Special-Interest Caucuses

While understanding the roles of parties and the committee system is key to understanding Congress, special-interest caucuses also play central roles. The first special-interest caucus, which dates back to the early Congresses, were organized around political

---

[18] Steven S. Smith and Christopher J. Deering, *Committees in Congress,* 2nd ed. (Washington: CQ Press, 1990), p. 126.

[19] Ibid.

Representative Bella Abzug
(D.-N.Y.)

parties. The Democratic-Republican Caucus, for example, nominated candidates successfully for several presidential contests from 1800 to 1824.

Today, special-interest groups or caucuses exist within each party. Liberal Democrats belong to the Democratic Study Group, conservative Republicans to the Arms Control Caucus. Moreover, conservative Southern Democrats—called "boll weevils" because, like their namesake, they bore from within the boll—created the Conservative Democratic Forum in the early 1980s. Its nearly sixty members meet for breakfast every Thursday at 9:00 A.M. in the Speaker's dining room for off-the-record discussions.

Other **special-interest caucuses,** including those involving farmers, footwear, and freshmen members of Congress allow members from either party to cross party lines to band together with others who have a common interest. In the 102nd Congress, there were over seventy such caucuses, including the black caucus, the women's caucus, and caucuses formed to promote certain industries, such as textiles, tourism, wine, coal, steel, mushrooms, and cranberries. Many of these caucuses lie low unless their interests are threatened. In the 1970s, when an influx of mushrooms from China and Taiwan threatened the sale of U.S. mushrooms, the sixty-member Mushroom Caucus sprang into action to defend its product.

Black legislators formed their own caucus in 1971, and lobbyists from major women's rights groups urged the women in Congress to do likewise. But senior female House members were opposed to the idea, and others feared being associated with the abrasive style and progressive agenda of Bella Abzug (D.-N.Y.), who was known to millions by the hats she wore at all times. Thus, the Congresswoman's Caucus was not formed until 1977, with fifteen of the eighteen women in the House joining. The caucus soon changed its name to the Congressional Women's Caucus but was hurt by the refusal of several Republican women to join after their election in 1980. The caucus reorganized in 1981, changed its name to the Congressional Caucus for Women's Issues, and opened its doors to men. In 1991 it had 154 members, 128 of them men, making it one of the largest caucuses in the House. It has been instrumental in garnering support for increased research support for women's health issues and the Family and Medical Leave Act, among other issues. In 1991, it outlined the Women's Health Equity Act, a package of twenty-two bills designed to improve women's health through new initiatives in research, services, and prevention. The caucus also has requested that government agencies include women in their drug trials and other health studies.

Members also strongly identify by their class—that is, the year in which they were elected. For example, the largest "new" class in years was the class of 1974, when the Watergate scandal and the resignation of President Richard M. Nixon resulted in a Democratic landslide that produced seventy-five new House Democrats. In 1978, thirty-six new Republicans arrived in the House, followed by fifty-two more in 1980. Members of the same classes share information with one another and form networks that often solidify as the members' tenure in the House increases.

State and regional caucuses are another important source of information exchange among members and across party lines. Large state delegations, such as those of California, New York, and Texas, often work together, regardless of party lines, to bring the bacon home to their states. Some state caucuses hold weekly meetings to assure that their interests are adequately represented on important committees and to keep abreast of pending legislation that might affect their states.

Regional caucuses cut across not only state lines but both houses of Congress as well. In the early years of the nation, members of Congress even roomed in boarding houses organized around regions. These "boarding house networks"[20] enforced discipline through the threat of social ostracism. While these kinds of strictures no longer exist today, informal frostbelt and sunbelt caucuses exist to advance sectional interests. The

[20]James Sterling Young, *The Washington Community, 1800–1820* (New York: Columbia University Press, 1966), pp. 98–105.

frostbelt or Northeast-Midwest Coalition, for example, was formed in the 1970s when the energy crisis prompted many firms and factories to move to lower-cost locations in the South. In 1990 its members called for California and Texas to pay larger shares of the bailout costs of the savings and loan industry. "The leading culprit in this Texas-sized problem is none other than the Lone Star State itself—a veritable bailout blackhole," charged Representative Olympia v. Snowe (R.-Me.) a frostbelt spokesperson. Reaction from the sunbelt caucus was quick. Representative Steve Bartlett (R.-Tx.) retorted: "This is merely Texas-bashing for home consumption."[21]

Staff

When we think of "Congress," we generally think of the Capitol itself or the 535 members who work there. But Congress is much more. Critical to its ability to function is its large staff, which now consists of more than 30,000 employees (19,000 on Capitol Hill). In the recent past, so many aides have been hired that Congress has been forced to build new office buildings for itself as well as to convert nearby hotels, apartments, and federal buildings into offices just to house its aides.

Congress is the only legislature in the world with such a vast staff. The British Parliament, for example, has a negligible number of staffers to assist its members, and individual members are rarely in a financial position to keep more than one or two full-time staffers to assist them both in London and in their home constituency. In fact, the British parliamentary internship programs, so popular at American universities, not only provide participants with an experience they will never forget, but help in a small way to fill a chronic institutional gap in staffing requirements.

Since the 1950s, and especially since the 1970s, the size of congressional staffs has risen dramatically, as have the kinds of problems staffers are called upon to address. Problems with a constituent's mail delivery, lost Social Security checks, information for students doing school term papers, and constituents' tickets for Washington tourist attractions are only some of the congressional duties that come under the label of **constituency service.** While members routinely service their constituents through pork barrel, that is, bringing federal grants and projects to cities, businesses, colleges, and other groups in their districts, they also help through casework, another form of constituency service performed by staffers that helps constituents cut through the maze of bureaucratic red tape to get government assistance to which they believe they are entitled.

More and more frequently, a member of Congress uses his or her staff allowance to maintain offices back home in the district in order to help with constituent problems. In fact, about one-third of House staffers and one-quarter of Senate staffers do not work in Washington. Congress also has added to the size of its staff in an effort to reassert itself in the lawmaking process. It has hired additional staff to help members with their committee duties and work for the committees themselves. In essence, Congress has created a mini-bureaucracy that has many parallels to the executive bureaucracy discussed in Chapter 8.

Staff members generally work for one of the following: (1) for members of Congress directly as personal aides, (2) for committees directly, or (3) for one of the congressional support agencies (see later).

In 1991, there were about 12,500 staff members for the House and 7,200 for the Senate. The average size of a House member's personal staff in Washington is eighteen; the average senator has two times that figure. Senators from more populous states get proportionately more staff. House staff sizes are generally similar, given that House district sizes are comparable. In 1991, each House member received $475,000 to be allotted to hire his or her staff members. By way of comparison, House members each received $366,648 in 1983, while British members of Parliament were given $17,046.

The Library of Congress was established by Congress in 1800 with a grant of $5,000 and Thomas Jefferson's donation of his entire library. It was burned by the British during the War of 1812. It administers the Congressional Research Service, which answers all kinds of inquiries for information by members of Congress, and in this way functions as a private research tool. The Library also registers the copyrights on all books published in the United States.

---

[21] William J. Eaton "Battling Caucuses—Congressional Cheer-Leaders Rally Round Their Caucuses," *Los Angeles Times,* July 31, 1990, p. A-5.

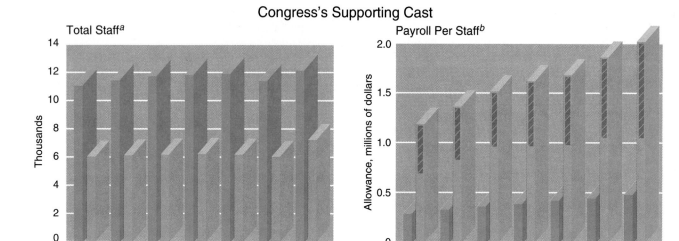

Congress's Supporting Cast

Total Staff[a]

Payroll Per Staff[b]

House of Representatives   Senate   Range

[a] Personal staff of senators and representatives and staff of officers, leaders and committees of the House and Senate, excluding joint committees and support agencies like the Library of Congress.

[b] Payroll allowance for personal staff of senators and representatives other than committee chairmen and ranking minority members of committees. Senator's allowances vary based on their states' populations.

Source: Martin Tolcin, "19,000 Congressional Aides Discover Power but Little Glory on Capitol Hill," *The New York Times,* November 12, 1991, p. A-22. Reprinted by permission. Data from American Enterprise Institute, *Vital Statistics on Congress* 1991–92.

Congress has developed four support agencies—the Congressional Research Service, the General Accounting Office, the Office of Technology Assessment, and the Congressional Budget Office—in order to provide the specialized knowledge necessary for members of Congress to make informed decisions on complex issues.

Congressional Research Service (CRS). Created in 1914 as the Legislative Research Service (LRS), the CRS is administered by the Library of Congress and responds to more than a quarter of a million congressional requests for information each year. The CRS is staffed with almost 900 employees, many of whom have advanced academic training. The service provides nonpartisan studies of public issues, compiling facts on both sides of issues, and it conducts major research projects for committees at the request of members. The CRS also prepares summaries of all bills introduced and tracks the progress of major bills. All of this information is available via computer terminals in the Senate and House Offices.

General Accounting Office (GAO). The GAO was established in 1921 as an independent regulatory agency for the purpose of auditing the financial expenditures of the executive branch and federal agencies. Today, staffed with more than 5,000 employees, the GAO has expanded to perform four additional functions: It sets government standards for accounting, it provides a variety of legal opinions, it settles claims against the government, and it conducts studies upon congressional request. Through its investigation of the efficiency and effectiveness of agencies, the GAO has acted as a watchdog of military funds in particular, often making headlines by reporting when products are bought far above market value price.

Office of Technology Assessment (OTA). The OTA, an agency of about one hundred employees, was created in 1972 to study and evaluate the long-range effects of

Staff Salaries

In 1991 congressional pay raises and scales for aides went up. Officers of the House, such as the parliamentarian and senior leadership aides, now earn $115,092. This top salary can also be earned by three aides on each committee. Each committee can also pay up to $108,837 for a maximum of nine staffers. Individual member aides can be paid as much as $101,331.

new and existing technology. The OTA has dealt with such issues as the impact of computers on privacy rights and the effect of the chemical Agent Orange on Vietnam veterans and their children.

Congressional Budget Office (CBO). The CBO was created in 1974 in order to evaluate the economic effect of different spending programs and to provide information on the cost of proposed policies. The CBO employs more than 200 people on its staff and is responsible for analyzing the president's budget and economic projections, thereby providing Congress with a valuable second opinion for use in budget debates.

How Members Make Decisions

As a bill wends its way through the labyrinth of the lawmaking process, members are confronted with the question: How should I vote? Although most legislation pertains to fairly mundane matters, members nonetheless fear that they will "miss" something in a bill and vote the "wrong" way, alienating voters at home. Unless a bill is controversial, this could be easy to do. In the 101st Congress, 6,683 bills were introduced in the House and 968 were passed. In the Senate, 3,669 bills were introduced and 980 passed. Only 650 bills were passed by both Houses, but they amounted to over 5,700 pages of new laws, as revealed in Figure 6-3.

In an effort to avoid making any voting mistakes, members look to a variety of sources for "cues." Major cue givers include political parties, colleagues, interest groups, staff members, the president, and, of course, constituents. And, frequently, how a

Figure 6-3 Number and Length of Bills Passed by Congress, 1947–1990

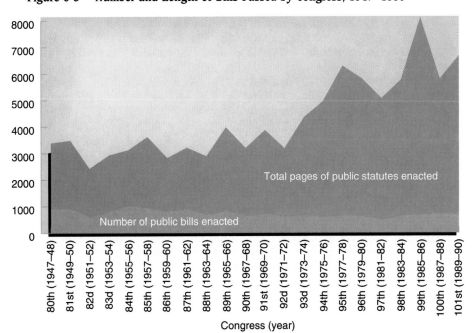

Source: Norman J. Ornstein *et. al., Vital Statistics on Congress 1991–1992* (Washington: CQ Press, 1992), Table 6-4, p. 156.

member ultimately decides or votes on any particular measure will vary according to the issues involved and in the context in which they are presented.[22]

Political Parties

Not all issues voted on in Congress divide members along party lines. In fact, only one-third to one-half of the votes in Congress are considered to be party votes (that is, when a majority in one party opposes a majority in the other). However, on these party votes members vote with their party between 70 and 80 percent of the time. Political parties have an interest in increasing their representation in Congress and maintaining party unity on votes in Congress. Toward that end, party officials have several resources of influence.

Members of Congress elected on a partisan ticket will feel a degree of obligation to their party. Although the national political parties have little say in who gets a party's nomination for the U.S. Senate or the House, once a candidate has emerged successfully from a primary contest (see Chapter 12), both houses have committees that provide campaign assistance since it is to each party's advantage to win as many seats as possible in each house. Once a member is elected, especially if he or she was the recipient of financial support or campaign visits from popular members, party leaders expect some degree of loyalty in return.

Each party in Congress also has a whip system used to disseminate information, keep track of who is voting with the party and who is not, and influence and pressure the undecided. Generally this pressure is subtle; however, in some instances, party leaders turn on the heat. For example, when in 1987 Senate Democratic leaders wanted to override a veto by President Ronald Reagan, they adopted a "babysitting" strategy in which wavering Democrats were accompanied at all times by two other Democrats with the "right" views. Obviously the party cue can be strong at times, and going along on legislation of importance to the party leadership can have its rewards.

Although it is rare to see a vote along straight party lines, in recent years there has been a general trend toward party unity on floor votes, especially in the House. On some votes, members always stick together. The vote for the Speaker, for example, is made strictly along party lines, with Democrats, the usual majority party, seeing their candidate win. Voting for a Speaker can be considered an "easy" vote, but Democrats have not always been so united. During the 1960s, Southern Democrats stood united against party leaders in both Houses who supported sweeping civil rights legislation. Since passage of the Voting Rights Act of 1965, more and more blacks have voted in the South, pushing conservative Democrats to take more moderate positions on race to attract voters, creating a greater trend toward party unity in Congress.

In Britain, virtually all votes (called *divisions*) taken in the House of Commons divide Members of Parliament along party lines; indeed, in this sense we speak of British parliamentary parties as "disciplined," as they are able to marshal the support of their members on questions before the legislature.

Colleagues

Because members, especially those in the House, tend to specialize, they tend to look to certain of their colleagues for what Donald Matthews and James A. Stimson call cues.[23] Each member has a different set of cue givers, depending on the issue involved. A cue

---

[22] Aage R. Clausen, *How Congressmen Decide: A Policy Focus* (New York: St. Martin's Press, 1973).

[23] Donald R. Matthews and James Stimson, *Yeas and Neas* (Chapel Hill: University of North Carolina Press, 1975).

giver may be a respected member of the state delegation or a committee chair or subcommittee chair whom a member particularly admires or who has a reputation for exceptional expertise. In the Senate, for example, the highly respected Senator Sam Nunn (D.-Ga.) presently heads the Armed Services Committee, and many members often take from him cues as to how to vote on arms appropriations bills. Others can be friends who tend to think the same way as the representative does. Members also trade votes with friends or even foes. For example, vote trading often takes place on specialized bills designed to bring home the bacon to certain areas. A yea vote by an unaffected member often is given in exchange for the promise of a future yea vote on a similar piece of legislation affecting his or her district.

Staff

Given the amount of work members have, they tend to rely heavily on members of their staff for information on pending legislation. Generally staff members prepare summaries of bills and brief the representative or senator based on their research. If the bill is non-ideological or one that the member has no real position on, staff members can be very influential. Staff members also do research on and even draft bills that a member wishes to introduce.

Staff aides are especially crucial in the Senate. Because senators have so many committee assignments and are often spread so thin, they frequently rely heavily on aides. The next time you see a televised Senate hearing, notice how each senator has at least one aide sitting behind him or her, ready with information and often even with questions for the senator to ask. Some believe that staff members have become too important, too powerful, and that their bosses are too dependent on them. Says Senator Lloyd Bentson (D.-Tx.), "I get so damned tired of members who can't go any place without staff. They don't know the issues themselves."[24] Still, while others argue that aides are helpful, it is unlikely that any would keep their positions for long if they regularly disagreed with their boss.

Interest Groups

The primary function of most interest-group lobbyists is to provide information to supportive or potentially supportive legislators and their staffs. It's likely, for example, that a representative knows that the National Organization for Women (NOW) favors a parental leave act. What the legislator needs to get from NOW is information and substantial research on the cost and impact of such legislation. Who would be covered? What impact would the act have on employers' profitability, and on American children? It is in presenting this kind of information that an interest group can solidify a member's support or influence a member leaning in its direction. Pressure groups often urge their members in a particular state or district to call or write their senator or representative. Lobbyists can't vote, but voters back home can, thus drawing attention to the issue and buttressing the group's appeal for support.

Constituents

Constituents—the people who live and vote in a member's district or state—are always in mind when a member casts a vote. It is rare for a legislator to vote against the wishes of his or her constituency regularly, particularly on issues of welfare rights, domestic policy,

---

[24] Martin Tolchin, "19,000 Congressional Aides Discover Power But Little Glory on Capitol Hill," *The New York Times,* November 12, 1991, p. A-22.

Figure 6-4 **How Members View Their Districts**

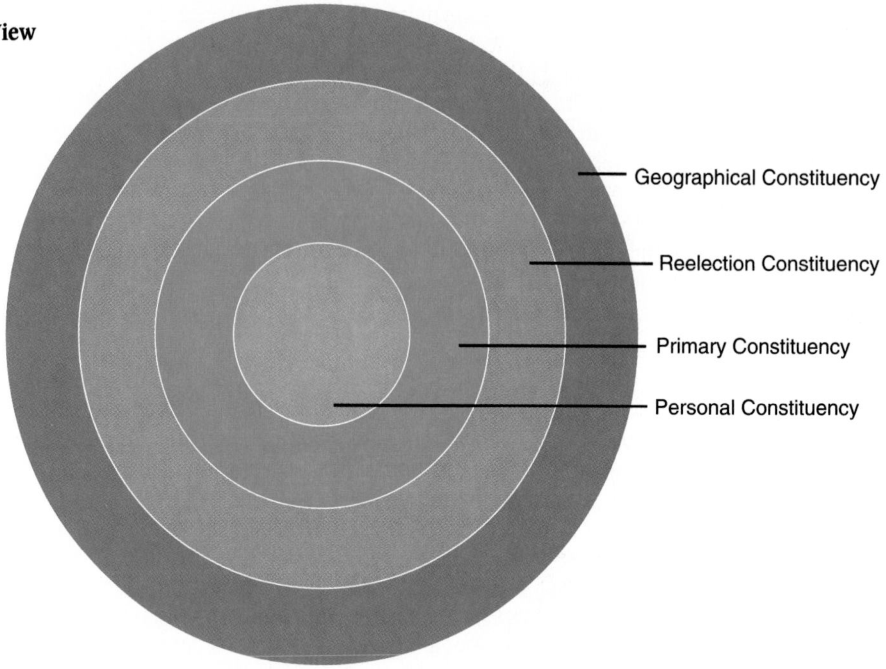

- Geographical Constituency
- Reelection Constituency
- Primary Constituency
- Personal Constituency

Source: Richard Fenno, *Homestyle: House Members in Their Districts* (Glenview III: Scott, Foresman, 1978).

or other highly salient issues such as affirmative action, abortion, or war. Most constituents often have strong convictions on one or more of these issues. For example, during the 1960s, representatives from Southern states could not hope to keep their seats for long if they voted in favor of proposed civil rights legislation. But gauging how voters feel about any particular issue is often not easy. Because it is virtually impossible to know how the folks back home feel on all issues, a representative's perception of their preferences is important.

Political scientist Richard Fenno concludes that members perceive their constituencies to consist of four groups, as illustrated in Figure 6-4. Members initially describe their "geographical constituency"—the location and size of the district—and its internal makeup, or socioeconomic and political characteristics, and the proportion of people who are "blue collar," Jewish, Democratic, or elderly, for example. Within the geographical constituency, members define a "reelection constituency," consisting of the people who the member thinks vote for him or her. This is the member's perceived political base; to disagree with the reelection constituency could cost the member his or her seat. Within the reelection constituency is a smaller group consisting of the member's strongest supporters, the "primary constituency." These loyalists vote for the member and provide campaign assistance and financial support. The fourth and final constituency is made up of the people closest to the member—his or her "personal constituency"—including friends and advisers. Thus, a member of Congress may perceive his district in a variety of ways, and sometimes the four constituencies may be in conflict. The typical voter in the district may have quite different views from those of the member's strongest supporters. Although most of the member's constituency will usually be unaware of the member's voting decisions, it would be foolish for a representative or senator to ignore an overwhelming majority of his or her constituents' views on an issue of salience.

The President

Over the years, especially since the presidency of Franklin Delano Roosevelt, Congress has allowed the president to play an ever-growing role in the legislative process. Today, for example, Congress often finds itself responding to executive branch proposals, as it did in the case of the Clean Air Act Amendments of 1990 discussed later in this chapter. Critics of Congress point to its slow, unwieldy process and the complexity of national problems as reasons why Congress often doesn't seem to act on its own.

Individual members, especially if the president is popular with voters, often find themselves voting in support of legislation supported by the White House. Legislators "on the fence" often find themselves targeted by the White House or inundated with dinner invitations to state dinners. Lyndon Johnson was a master of this strategy, as is George Bush.

Although the president, especially a popular one, undoubtedly can have an impact on how a member votes, political scientist John Kingdon found that overall, colleagues and constituents have the greatest impact of the many factors discussed here. But, voting is a complex process, and it is unlikely that one faction ever prevails for any single member over a set of issues.[25]

[25] John Kingdon, *Congressmen's Voting Decision,* 2nd ed. (New York: Harper and Row, 1981).

Support for the President in Congressional Votes

The graph shows the percentage of votes each year in which the outcome was the one favored by the president. Appropriations bills are not included.

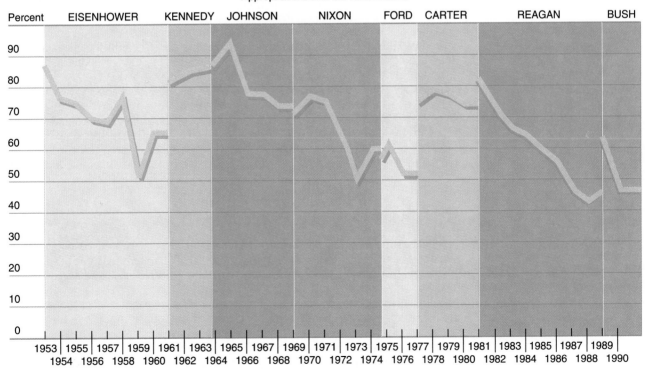

Source: Scores compiled by Congressional Quarterly, Inc. Reprinted with the permission of Congressional Quarterly, Inc.

The Lawmaking Function of Congress

Chief among the responsibilities of Congress is its lawmaking function. Proposals for legislation can come from the president, executive agencies, committee staffs, interest groups, or even private individuals, but only members of the House or Senate actually can formally submit a bill for congressional consideration. Once a bill is proposed, it usually reaches a dead end. Of the more than 6,000 bills introduced each year in Congress fewer than 25 percent are enacted or made into law, as revealed in Figure 6-3. It is probably useful to think of Congress as a system of multiple vetoes, which was what the Framers desired. They wanted to disperse power, and as Congress has evolved it has come closer and closer to the Framers' intentions. As a bill goes through Congress, a dispersion of power occurs as roadblocks to passage must be surmounted at numerous steps in the process. In addition to realistic roadblocks, caution signs and other opportunities for delay abound. A member who sponsors a bill must get through *every* obstacle; in contrast, successful opposition means "winning" at only one of many stages, including: (1) the subcommittee, (2) the House full committee, (3) the House Rules Committee, (4) the House, (5) the Senate subcommittee, (6) the full Senate committee, (7) the Senate, (8) floor leaders in both Houses, (9) the House–Senate Conference Committee, and (10) the president.

In Britain, the daily rhythm of parliamentary activity contrasts sharply with that in the U.S. Congress. The emphasis is overwhelmingly on formal debate, in which government and opposition teams clash regularly and in animated fashion. For an individual Member of Parliament (MP), the fastest route to prestige and influence is to shine in debate and thus come to the attention of the party leadership. Consequently, there are few incentives for members to spend a lot of time in committee, since committee work takes the MP off the debate floor and encourages cross-party cooperation. The combination of strong parliamentary parties and a neglected committee system leads to a situation where Parliament, though a spirited forum, is a relatively weak institution in the overall governmental scheme. Virtually all bills emanate from the executive, and the scope for an individual MP's influence on the legislative process is slim. The British parliament is, to employ the conventional distinction, a debating parliament, not a working parliament (like the U.S. Congress or the German Bundestag).

The story of how a bill becomes a law in the United States can be told in two different ways. The first is the "textbook" method—you may have seen a flowchart on a television show that tracks the course of a bill from inception through subcommittee and committee action and finally to presidential approval or veto. The textbook method provides a greatly simplified road map of the process to make it easier to understand. A second method looks at an actual example of how a particular bill became a law and shows the true complexities of the process.

How a Bill Becomes a Law: The Textbook Way

A bill must survive three stages before it becomes a law. A bill may be killed during any of these stages; therefore, it is much easier to defeat a bill than it is to get one passed. The House and Senate have parallel processes, and often the same bill is introduced in each chamber at the same time.

Although a bill must be introduced by a member of Congress, it is often sponsored by a whole list of other members in an early effort to show support for the bill. Once introduced, the bill is sent to the clerk of the chamber, who gives it a number (for example, HR 1, or S 1—indicating House or Senate bill number one for the session). The bill is then printed, distributed, and sent to the appropriate committee for consideration.

The first stage of action takes place within the committee. The committee usually refers the bill to one of its subcommittees, which researches the bill and decides whether to hold hearings on it. The subcommittee hearings provide the opportunity for those on

How a Bill Becomes a Law: The Textbook Way

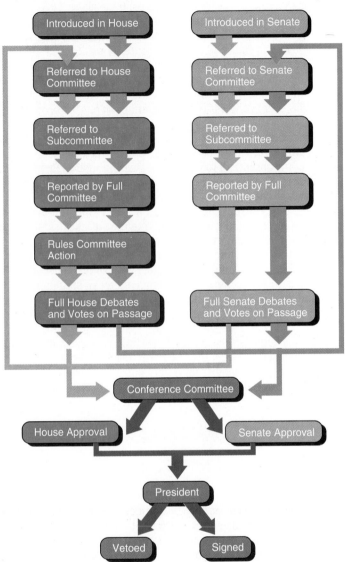

both sides of the issue to voice their opinions. Most of these hearings are now open to the public because of 1970s sunshine laws, which require open sessions. After the hearings, the bill is revised, and the subcommittee votes to approve or defeat the bill. If the subcommittee votes in favor of the bill, it is returned to the full committee, which then either rejects the bill or sends it to the House or Senate floor.

The second stage of action takes place on the House or Senate floor. Before the bill may be debated on the floor, it must be sent to the Rules Committee to be given a rule and a place on the calendar, or schedule. The rule given to the bill determines the limits on the floor debate and specifies what types of amendments, if any, may be attached. The calendar categorizes the bills. The House has five different calendars: The Union calendar is for all revenue or money bills. The House calendar deals with all major, nonmoney bills, such as civil rights or family leave legislation. The Private calendar is for bills that affect only one member, such as immigration issues or other private matters. The Consent calendar is for noncontroversial issues such as declaring National Garden Week or Mothers' Day. The Discharge calendar is for discharge petitions alone, which allow the entire House to vote to "discharge" or remove a bill from a committee.

When the day arrives for floor debate, the House may choose to form a "Committee of the Whole" that allows the House to deliberate with the presence of only one hundred members to expedite consideration of the bill. This practice was borrowed from the British and used in the colonial legislatures as well. On the House floor the bill is debated, amendments are offered, and a vote is taken by the full House. If the bill survives, it is sent to the other chamber of Congress for consideration if it has not been considered there simultaneously.

Unlike the House, where debate is necessarily limited given the size of the body, bills may be held up by **filibusters** in the Senate. Filibusters, which allow for unlimited debate on a bill, grew out of the absence of rules to limit speech in the Senate and are often used to "talk a bill to death." The filibuster became an increasingly common feature of Senate life during the slavery debates. In 1917, after eleven senators waged a filibuster against an important foreign policy matter supported by President Woodrow Wilson, the Senate adopted a rule to avoid the potential disaster of tying the president's hands during World War I. To end a filibuster, cloture must be invoked. To cut off debate, sixteen senators must first sign a motion for cloture. Then, a roll-call vote is taken. Two-thirds of the senators present—subsequent changes now require only sixty—must vote in the affirmative to end a filibuster. Each member of the Senate then can speak for one hour before debate is closed and the legislation on the floor is brought to a vote. If the other chamber approves a different version of the same bill, a conference committee is established to iron out the differences.

The third stage of action takes place within the conference committee. The conference committee, whose members are from the original House and Senate committees, revises the bill and returns it to each chamber for a final vote. No changes or amendments are allowed at this stage. If the bill is passed it is sent to the president, who either signs it or vetoes it.

Filibusters

The term "filibuster" is derived from the Dutch word *vrijbuiter,* meaning "freebooter," and translated into English it means "continuous talking." The filibuster is today commonly known as a tactic senators may use in an effort to talk a bill to death. In 1854, for example, senators attempted to talk to death the Kansas–Nebraska Act in an effort to forestall deciding the issue of slavery.

There are no rules on the content of a filibuster as long as the senator keeps on talking. Often a senator will read from a phone book, recite poetry, or read cookbooks in order to delay a vote. Often, a team of senators will take turns speaking to keep the filibuster going in hopes that a bill will be tabled or killed. In 1964, for example, a group of Northern liberal senators continued a filibuster for eighty-two days in an effort to prevent amendments that would weaken a civil rights bill. It has been the Southern senators, however, who have made the most use of the filibuster in their efforts to circumvent or at least delay civil rights legislation. Senator Strom Thurmond (D.-S.C.)* holds the record for the longest one-man filibuster; in 1957 he opposed civil rights legislation in a personal filibuster that lasted more than twenty-four hours.

*Thurmond changed his party affiliation from Democrat to Republican on September 16, 1964, shortly after passage of the Civil Rights Act of 1964.

The president has ten days to consider the bill and has four options. (1) He can sign the bill, at which point it becomes law. (2) He can veto the bill. Congress may override the president's veto with a two-thirds vote in each chamber, a very difficult task. (3) He can wait the full ten days, at the end of which time the bill becomes law without his signature if Congress is still in session. (4) If the Congress adjourns before the ten days are up the president can choose not to sign the bill, and it is thus "pocket vetoed." **Pocket vetoes** figuratively allow bills stashed in the president's pocket to die. The only way for the bill to become law is for it to be reintroduced in the next session and go through the process all over again. Because Congress sets its own date of adjournment, technically the session could be continued the few extra days necessary to prevent a pocket veto. Extensions are unlikely, however, as sessions are scheduled to adjourn close to the November elections or the Christmas holidays.

How a Bill Really Becomes a Law: The Clean Air Act Amendments of 1990

Passage of the Clean Air Act Amendments of 1990, while following the general steps outlined above, was far more complex and interesting. Like most major modern legislation, this act officially began with the White House. After campaigning for president in 1988 as an environmentalist, George Bush promised in his inaugural address to send Congress a major clean air legislative package. Over the next several months, an executive team was assembled: Robert Grady of the Office of Management and Budget (OMB); William Reilly, the head of the Environmental Protection Agency (EPA), and several aides; Roger Porter, the president's domestic policy adviser; and, in an unusual move, C. Boyden Gray, the White House chief counsel. Gray was a close adviser to the president and considered by many to be the "real clean air nut" in the administration. Notably excluded were members of the Department of Energy.

After considerable discussion, study, and interviewing of academics and others, this team hammered together a vast proposal in Bush's name. Fully 140 representatives and 25 senators, led by Representative John Dingell (D.-Mich.) and Senator John Chafee (R.-R.I.), introduced it as a bill in each house.

In the Senate, the bill was assigned to the Environment and Public Works Committee, which is so pro-environmentalist that it is out of sync with the rest of the Senate. When its version of the bill was reported back to the floor, the committee had stretched the bill's provisions so much that the package was unacceptable to the full Senate. Automobile tail pipe emission standards, for example, were far too strict. Instead of igniting a flurry of amendments and arguments, individual senators ignored the extreme bill entirely because they didn't want to touch it. Supporters knew that calling a vote would bring defeat, but they couldn't figure out how to amend the act to make it acceptable to the majority.

George Mitchell, the Senate majority leader, then took over in a typical modern party leadership maneuver. He called a series of closed-door negotiations that included representatives of the administration, Robert Dole (the minority leader), and other key senators who were called in on those points in which they had a vested interest. After six long weeks of hard negotiating, this process produced an agreement among Democrats, Republicans, and the administration on every single point in the package, including tail pipe emissions and air-quality standards. As a group, the participants agreed to fight off every amendment that might be proposed from the floor, with the stipulation that any amendment successfully passed would free up any party to walk away from the deal.

This process, though extraordinary by historical standards, has become quite common on major bills as political parties have strengthened and the committees have proven unsuccessful at managing a more unruly Senate or House floor. When the act was brought to the floor, the powerful team led by Mitchell, Dole, and the White House succeeded in fending off all major amendments—only a few minor adjustments were

How a Bill Really Becomes a Law: The Clean Air Act Amendments of 1990

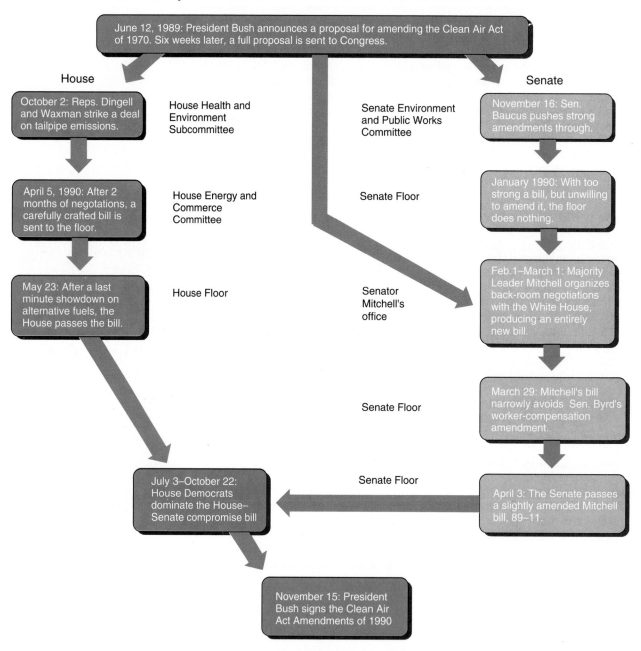

June 12, 1989: President Bush announces a proposal for amending the Clean Air Act of 1970. Six weeks later, a full proposal is sent to Congress.

House

October 2: Reps. Dingell and Waxman strike a deal on tailpipe emissions.

House Health and Environment Subcommittee

April 5, 1990: After 2 months of negotiations, a carefully crafted bill is sent to the floor.

House Energy and Commerce Committee

May 23: After a last minute showdown on alternative fuels, the House passes the bill.

House Floor

July 3–October 22: House Democrats dominate the House–Senate compromise bill

Senate Environment and Public Works Committee

Senate Floor

Senator Mitchell's office

Senate

November 16: Sen. Baucus pushes strong amendments through.

January 1990: With too strong a bill, but unwilling to amend it, the floor does nothing.

Feb.1–March 1: Majority Leader Mitchell organizes back-room negotiations with the White House, producing an entirely new bill.

Senate Floor

March 29: Mitchell's bill narrowly avoids Sen. Byrd's worker-compensation amendment.

Senate Floor

April 3: The Senate passes a slightly amended Mitchell bill, 89–11.

November 15: President Bush signs the Clean Air Act Amendments of 1990

allowed to pass—and the Senate proceeded to pass the resultant package by an overwhelming margin.

In the House, meanwhile, the Energy and Commerce Committee had much more say, partly because of the typically greater expertise in technical issues that members of the more populous House can afford to obtain. First a rule was assigned to the bill so that no amendment could be offered without the approval of key committee members. The powerful chair of the committee, John Dingell, had been trying to scuttle clean air legislation for years in order to protect his constituents, Detroit auto workers. The Environment and

Health subcommittee of his panel, however, was chaired by Henry Waxman (D.-Cal.), who for just as many years had championed clean air for his smog-ridden constituents in Los Angeles. Now that Bush had broken the legislative deadlock with a proposal, Dingell knew he would have to deal with Waxman and have the committee report out some kind of bill.

Taking a cue from the Senate, these two pulled back behind closed doors in informal negotiations that only indirectly involved other members of the committee. When they reached a deal on tailpipe emissions, their biggest sticking point, the official committee proceedings got back on track. Unlike what had transpired in the Senate, however, none of these behind-the-scenes or committee negotiations involved the White House. This was because House Republicans had become so ineffectual after so many years of Democratic control that the Democrats, in effect, could ignore them and their party leader in the White House. Dingell, Waxman, Speaker Thomas Foley, and their colleagues were much more willing to slam the door on those on the other side of the aisle than their counterparts in the Senate had been.

Once both houses passed versions of the bill, the conference committee phase commenced. Because of House members' greater knowledge and expertise, they controlled the course of deliberations, making the bill stronger than the one originally proposed by the White House. President Bush was in no position to veto the stronger bill, however, because he had taken part (through his teammates) in the Senate's side of the deal making and had campaigned so loudly on the environment. In the end, therefore, the House crafters like Waxman who wanted a strong bill were able to carry the day.

Congress and the President

Culminating the months of wheeling and dealing that took place over passage of the Clean Air Amendments of 1990, George Bush signed the bill into law on November 15, 1990. Looking on were Environmental Protection Agency Administrator William Reilly and Bush's Energy Secretary James Watkins.

Over the years the balance of power between Congress and the executive branch has seesawed. The post–Civil War Congress attempted to regain control of the vast executive powers that President Abraham Lincoln, recently slain, had taken from them. Angered at the refusal of Lincoln's successor, Andrew Johnson, to go along with its radical "reforms" of the South, Congress passed the Tenure of Office Act, which prevented the president, under the threat of civil penalty, from removing any Cabinet-level appointments of the previous administration. Johnson accepted the challenge and fired Lincoln's Secretary of War, who many believed was guilty of heinous war crimes. The House voted to impeach Johnson, but only the desertion of a handful of Republican senators prevented him from being removed from office. (The effort fell short by one vote.) Nonetheless, the president's power had been greatly weakened, and the Congress again became the center of power and authority in the federal government.

Beginning in the early 1900s, however, a series of strong presidents acted at the expense of congressional power. Theodore Roosevelt, Franklin Roosevelt, and Lyndon Johnson, especially, all viewed the presidency as carrying with it enormous powers. Although these presidents facilitated an expansion of the role of the federal government, over time the perception grew that presidents were abusing their power, particularly after the events of the Vietnam War and Watergate. By the 1970s, then, scholars were discussing the "imperial presidency,"[26] and Congress made efforts to reassert itself through exercising its oversight function zealously.

Oversight of the Executive Branch

According to political scientists Roger Davidson and Walter Oleszek, oversight is exercised in a variety of ways, the most common being hearings and investigations. The purpose of most hearings is to make sure that laws passed by Congress are routinely and

[26]Arthur Schlesinger, *The Imperial Presidency* (New York: Houghton Mifflin, 1973).

properly administered by the executive branch. Authorizations and frequent reviews of agency performance and appropriations are probably the most effective types of oversight. Since money is the life blood of any agency, threatening its funding can often assure compliance with congressional wishes. Two other devices that help Congress with oversight are (1) sunset laws and (2) the legislative veto.

Sunset laws specify end dates for new programs at the time they are authorized by Congress and can be continued only after Congress reauthorizes the program. The purpose of these sunset laws is to make certain that Congress does not continue to fund programs that have outlived their usefulness or that are inefficient.

Legislative vetoes, a procedure by which one or both houses of Congress could disallow an act of an executive agency by a simple majority vote, also help Congress perform its oversight function. Provisions for so-called legislative vetoes were first added to statutes in 1932 but were not used frequently until the 1970s. They were usually included in laws that delegated congressional powers to the executive branch while retaining the power of Congress to restrict their use. By 1981, more than 200 statutes contained legislative veto provisions.

In *Immigration and Naturalization Service* v. *Chadha* (1983) the U.S. Supreme Court ruled that the legislative veto as it was used in many circumstances was unconstitutional. The Court concluded that although the Constitution gave Congress the power to make laws, the Framers were clear in their intent that Congress should separate itself from executing or enforcing the laws. In spite of *Chadha,* however, the legislative veto continues to play an important role in executive–legislative relations.

Special Oversight Functions of the Senate

The Constitution grants the Senate the important power of advice and consent with respect to presidential appointments and treaties. The presidential appointment of all ambassadors, Cabinet secretaries and many undersecretaries, Federal Reserve positions and the federal judiciary are subject to senatorial consent. In general, the confirmation process begins in the appropriate committee. The committee holds hearings and makes a recommendation to the full body. A simple majority vote of the full Senate is necessary for

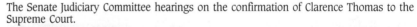

The Senate Judiciary Committee hearings on the confirmation of Clarence Thomas to the Supreme Court.

confirmation. Quite often, these hearings are perfunctory and routine, as discussed in Chapter 7. However, periodically a battle ensues over a presidential nominee.

The Senate ratifies treaties by a two-thirds majority. A major arms control treaty, SALT II, was withdrawn from Senate consideration in the fall of 1979 when it became certain that it had little chance for ratification. This was a major political defeat for President Jimmy Carter. President Ronald Reagan fared better when he won Senate approval of the Intermediate Nuclear Forces (INF) Treaty in 1988.

Congressional Efforts to Reassert Its Oversight Function

The Constitution divides foreign policy powers between the executive and the legislative branches. The president has the power to wage war and negotiate treaties, whereas the Congress has the power to declare war and the Senate has the power to ratify treaties. Throughout the twentieth century, the executive branch has become preeminent in foreign affairs despite the constitutional division of powers. This is partly due to the series of crises and the development of nuclear weapons in this century; both have necessitated quick decision making and secrecy, which is far easier to manage in the executive branch. Congress, with its 535 members, has a more difficult time reaching a consensus and keeping secrets. After years of playing second fiddle to a series of presidents from Theodore Roosevelt to Richard Nixon, a "snoozing Congress" was "aroused"[27] and seized for itself the authority and expertise necessary to go head-to-head with the chief executive. In a delayed response to Lyndon B. Johnson's conduct of the Vietnam War, in 1973 Congress passed the **War Powers Act** over President Nixon's veto, requiring any president to obtain congressional approval before committing U.S. forces to a combat zone. It also requires that the president notify Congress within forty-eight hours of committing troops to foreign soil. In addition, the president must withdraw troops within sixty days unless Congress votes to declare war. The president is also required to consult with Congress prior to committing troops if at all possible.

Until recently, the War Powers Act has been of limited effectiveness in claiming a larger congressional role in international crisis situations. Presidents Gerald R. Ford, Carter, and Reagan never consulted Congress in advance of committing troops, citing the need for secrecy and swift movement, although they did notify Congress shortly after the incidents. They contended that the War Powers Act was probably unconstitutional—although it has been upheld by the Supreme Court—because it limits presidential prerogatives as commander-in-chief. President Bush, however, after months of refusing to acknowledge that Congress had a role, consulted with Congress before and after committing troops in the Persian Gulf in 1990–91 and even requested a congressional resolution for the conduct of the war. On January 12, 1991, a solemn and sharply divided Congress voted to authorize the president to go to war against Iraq if it didn't end its occupation of Kuwait. Along Republican Party lines, with the support of a few Democrats, the Senate voted 52 to 47 for the Authorization for Use of Military Force Against Iraq Resolution. Minutes later the House voted 250 to 183. With these votes, Congress had acted after months of indecision about its role in the conflict that had begun when Iraq invaded Kuwait on August 2, 1990. Much of the debate over the resolution underscored the fact that the Democratic-controlled Congress had acted too late to do anything but support the president. Even Democratic House Majority Leader Richard Gephardt (D.-Mo.) underscored the need for a united national front before the vote, noting "Whatever our decision, we will leave this room one again and whole again."[28]

[27] *The Wall Street Journal,* April 13, 1973, p. 10.
[28] Quoted in "Bush Is Given Authorization to Use Force Against Iraq," *Congressional Quarterly Weekly Report,* January 12, 1991, p. 65.

Unlike his predecessors, then, President Bush had followed the intent as well as the letter of the act. The future effectiveness of the War Powers Act in carving out a larger role for Congress in foreign affairs remains in the hands of the president.

Congress has made similar efforts to regain control over economic policy. In 1974, Congress passed the Budget and Impoundment Control Act in response to President Nixon's refusal to spend money on certain programs authorized by Congress. The act also created budget committees in the House and in the Senate and the Congressional Budget Office (CBO) to analyze budget proposals and their potential impact on the economy. Prior to 1974, the Office of Management and Budget (OMB) in the executive branch controlled the budget process and Congress had no way of systematically evaluating budgets or their impact. "The creation of the CBO began to redress the balance of power," said Stuart Eisenstadt, the Carter White House domestic policy chief.[29] It ended the president's monopoly on information and gave Congress a powerful weapon. In 1977, for example, Joseph A. Califano, then the Secretary of Health, Education, and Welfare, proposed some changes in welfare programs, estimating their cost at $5 billion in 1978. The newspaper headline the day after read "CBO to Carter: Welfare Reform $17 Billion." The Carter White House knew immediately that the reform would be killed. Eisenstadt said, "Our program's over. There's no way Congress is going to pass what they think is a $17 billion welfare reform proposal."[30]

Knowing it could not trust the executive branch to provide it with accurate information, Congress also expanded the staffs of members and the committee staffs in both houses. It also added to the research service of the Library of Congress, and other support services were expanded.

Toward Reform

Although the Congress today is very different from that which first sat in New York City in 1789, much of what it has become has its roots in the reforms that took place in 1910. The process of decentralization that was started then was continued by additional reforms in 1946 and in the 1960s and 1970s.

Term Limits

A reform controversy that has been sweeping the United States in the 1990s is the debate over term limitations—the proposal that would set an exact, maximum number of elective terms that any legislator could serve. Already some form of term limitation has been adopted for state legislators in Oklahoma, Colorado, and California by means of a popular vote. The Colorado referendum also applied term limits to the state's congressional representatives, though some constitutional experts doubt its validity. (Constitutional requirements for House and Senate elections, they contend, cannot be imposed by referendum or initiative.) Voters in Washington state, however, defeated term limits in 1991.

Generally, the term-limit proposals call for a maximum term of service of from six to twelve years for state legislators, with a separate limit for each house of the legislature. For Congress, U.S. House members could serve from six to twelve years, and U.S. senators from twelve to eighteen years in total—the number of years depending on the proposal.

The idea of term limitation is an old one. Many of the Founders believed in the regular rotation of offices among worthy citizens, and for the most part this was the practice in the early years of the republic. There is also a precedent for term limitation in the office of

[29] Quoted in Smith, p. 23.
[30] Ibid.

governor. From the very first, Americans were suspicious of executive power and have preferred to restrict their governors to a fixed number of terms in the statehouse, and even today, the two-term limit (with each term four years in length) is the gubernatorial norm. And, of course, the president of the United States has been limited to two full four-year terms since the Twenty-second Amendment was ratified after the death of four-term President Franklin D. Roosevelt.

The modern advocates of term limits for members of Congress argue that incumbents have too many advantages in running for office and that limits are the only sure way to build in more competition and ensure turnover. They believe that many good people now hesitant to start a lengthy second career in politics would be willing to serve for a short period of time, just as some of the Founders had envisioned. Many Republicans are especially strong supporters of term limits, seeing this reform as an opportunity to eliminate entrenched Democratic incumbents who constitute a majority of both houses of Congress and most state legislatures. Republicans believe they will gain under a term limits scheme because many Democrats will be forced out of office and the resulting "open seats" with no incumbent will be more vulnerable to Republican takeover. Also, the business-based, private enterprise-centered Republican Party has more difficulty than the government service-oriented Democrats in recruiting candidates for full-time, semi-permanent political careers. With limited tenure requiring less long-term commitment to government service, Republicans think they can convince more of their qualified activists to run.

Term-limit opponents have a very different view of this reform. They note that the people already have the power to limit terms—and to do so more severely than the reformers' proposals advocate. If the electorate so desires, for example, it could replace the entire U.S. House of Representatives every two years. This does not happen because many voters are pleased with the representation provided by their legislators. Yet term limits deny these constituents their right to retain a good member of Congress in office if they so desire; under term limitation, good and bad legislators are ousted equally and without distinction. Term-limit opponents also note that the loss of senior, experienced legislators means the diminishing of an important check on other actors in the legislative process who would *not* be limited by term, such as lobbyists, legislative staff, and executive department bureaucrats. Few Americans are any more fond of these groups than they are of legislators. This last problem with term limits is an example of the *unintended consequences* of reform. The American system of government is so complex that each new action can produce somewhat unpredictable reactions, and wise reformers must be alert to the "ripple effects" of their proposals.

Term limits are undeniably popular with a large majority of the American people, as public opinion polls have consistently shown. Most (but not all) academics, newspaper columnists, and opinion leaders remain opposed to term limits, however. The debate about term limitations will undoubtedly continue to rage for years to come. Where do *you* stand?

Summary

When the Framers met in Philadelphia they knew that a new form of stronger, more centralized government was needed to govern a growing nation. After considerable debate, Article I, creating a bicameral legislature, was written. Fear of the masses, however, led the Framers to make only the larger, less prestigious House of Representatives directly elected by the people. Senators, to be the elder statesmen, were to be elected by the state legislatures, a compromise and a reflection of the Federalists' general distrust of the populace.

Over the years as the size of the nation increased and new problems, particularly slavery, presented themselves, the power of each house has changed, as has its size and way of doing business. The quick development of political parties led to fuller articulation of both sides of issues, but Congress often found itself then, and continues to find itself today, locked in partisan battles in addressing critical national problems. Because the House of Representatives, in particular, became quite unwieldy, a rigid committee system and elaborate process for law making was established to allow Congress to fulfill its major functions of law making and oversight.

Just as the size and nature of Congress has changed over the years, so has the nature of its members. Members of Congress have become more "professional," as most now view it as a full-time, long-term job instead of as a stepping stone to another office. For a variety of reasons, while most of the American public voices displeasure at Congress as a body, individual members, especially in the House, enjoy what is termed an incumbency effect whereby few who seek reelection are ever defeated.

In exercising their most important function—law making—members of Congress are affected by a variety of factors, including their political party, colleagues, staff, interest groups, constituents, and the president. Dissatisfaction with congressional decision making has led some to call for term limits.

Key Terms

virtual representation	senatorial courtesy	pork barrel
actual representation	party caucus	special-interest caucuses
legislative powers	majority party	constituency service
impeachment	standing committees	filibuster
redistricting	Speaker of the House	pocket veto
gerrymandering	discharge petition	War Powers Act

Suggested Readings

Aberbach, Joel D. *Keeping a Watchful Eye.* Washington: Brookings Institution, 1990.

Cain, Bruce, John Ferejohn, and Morris Fiorina. *The Personal Vote.* Cambridge, Mass.: Harvard University Press, 1987.

Dodd, Lawrence C., and Bruce I. Oppenheimer. *Congress Reconsidered,* 4th ed. Washington: CQ Press, 1985.

Fenno, Richard F., Jr. *Congressmen in Committees.* Boston: Little, Brown, 1973.

———. *Home Style.* Boston: Little, Brown, 1978.

Hinckley, Barbara. *Coalitions and Politics.* San Diego: Harcourt Brace Jovanovich, 1981.

Jones, Rochelle, and Peter Woll. *The Private of Congress.* New York: Free Press, 1979.

Loomis, Burdett. *The American Politician.* New York: Basic Books, 1988.

Mayhew, David R. *Congress: The Electoral Connection.* New Haven, Conn.: Yale University Press, 1974.

Sabato, Larry J. *PAC Power.* New York: Norton, 1984.

Smith, Hedrick. *The Power Game.* New York: Ballantine, 1988.

Strahan, Randall. *New Ways and Means: Reform and Change in a Congressional Committee.* Chapel Hill, N.C.: University of North Carolina, 1990.

Energy in the Executive is a leading character in the definition of good government."

Alexander Hamilton

FEDERALIST NO. 70

Hamilton, James Madison, and the other Federalists argued against those who wanted to curb presidential power.

CHAPTER 7

The Presidency

In 1787, when Alexander Hamilton penned the words opening this chapter, he was expressing the views of the majority of the Framers. Most saw a need for a chief executive, but they feared putting significant powers in the hands of any one individual. Under the Articles of Confederation there had been no executive branch of government, and the eighteen different men who served as the "president" of the Continental Congress of the United States of America were "president" in name only—they had no actual authority or power in the new nation. Yet, because the Framers were so sure that George Washington, whom they had trusted with their lives during the Revolutionary War, would become the first president of the new nation, many of their deepest fears were calmed. They agreed upon the necessity of having one individual speak on behalf of the new nation, and they all agreed that that one individual should be George Washington.

Distrust of a powerful chief executive led to the deliberate vagueness of the Constitution's prescriptions for the presidency. In contrast to the laundry list of provisions concerning the authority of the legislative branch found in Article I, in Article II the Constitution lists far fewer powers of the president. Though the Framers nearly unanimously agreed about the need for a strong central government and a greatly empowered Congress, they did not agree about the proper role of the president or the sweep of his authority.

It is highly unlikely that the Framers—even Alexander Hamilton, who was probably the greatest proponent of a strong chief executive—ever envisioned the growth in executive power that has occurred over the years. Just think of the differences in governance faced by two Georges—Washington and Bush. George Washington supervised the nation from a temporary headquarters with a staff of but one aide—his nephew, paid out of Washington's own funds—and only four Cabinet members. In contrast, in 1991 George Bush presided over a White House staff of nearly 400, a Cabinet of 14 members, and an executive branch of government that employed more than 3 million people. Both presidents faced staggering national budget deficits, but what was considered staggering in Washington's day pales in comparison to the national deficit of nearly $3 trillion George Bush confronts.

In this chapter we look at how the presidency has evolved from its humble origins in Article II of the Constitution to its current stature as the most powerful branch of government. We then discuss the "modern presidency" (from the election of Franklin Delano Roosevelt in 1932 to the present) as a single office and as the basis of a presidential establishment of staff, Cabinet positions, and an executive bureaucracy.

The five most recent presidents: George Bush, Ronald Reagan, Jimmy Carter, Gerald Ford, and Richard Nixon.

The Roots of the Office of President of the United States

The earliest example of executive power in the colonies was the royal governor, appointed by the king of England and normally entrusted with the "powers of appointment, military command, expenditure, and—within limitations—pardon, as well as with large powers in connection with the powers of law making."[1] The royal governors often found themselves at odds with the colonists and especially with the elected colonial legislatures. As representatives of the Crown, the governors were distrusted and disdained by the people, many of whom had fled from Great Britain to escape royal domination. "'The executive magistrate' was the natural enemy, the legislative assembly the natural friend of liberty, a sentiment strengthened by the contemporary spectacle of George III's domination of Parliament."[2]

Once the colonists broke from England in 1776, their distrust of a chief executive continued. Most state constitutions reduced the office of governor to a symbolic head—elected annually by the legislature and stripped of most rights we today assume an executive must possess, such as the right to call the legislature into session or to veto its acts. The constitution adopted by Virginia in 1776 illustrates this sentiment. It cautioned that "the executive powers of government" were to be exercised "according to the laws" of the state, and that no powers could be claimed by the governor on the basis of "any law, statute, or custom of England."[3]

Although most of the states opted for a "symbolic" office of governor, some states did entrust wider powers to their chief executives. The New York governor, for example, was elected directly by the people, possessed the power to pardon, was designated "commander-in-chief" of the state militia, and was charged with the duty that "laws [be] faithfully executed to the best of his ability."

When the Framers met in Philadelphia to consider a new type of government, they were able to draw on the experiences of the states as well as the ideas of the political theorists John Locke and Baron de La Brède et de Montesquieu, who had written extensively on the role of a chief executive.

The Framers and the Creation of the Presidency

As we saw in Chapter 2, the delegates to the Philadelphia Convention quickly decided to dispense with the Articles of Confederation and fashion a new government composed of three branches—the legislative (to make the laws), the executive (to execute, or implement, the laws), and the judicial (to interpret the laws). Early on at the meeting the Virginia delegation proposed its "Virginia Plan" as a format for the new government. Among its provisions was a proposal for a single national executive elected by the legislature and ineligible for a second term. Echoing the Virginia experience, and wary of a strong executive, its delegates wanted an executive strictly accountable to the legislature.

In contrast, James Wilson of Philadelphia suggested a single, more powerful president who would be elected by the people and "independent of the legislature." Wilson also suggested giving the executive an absolute veto over the acts of Congress. "Without such a defense," he wrote, "the legislature can at any moment sink it [the executive] into non-existence."[4]

---

[1] Edward S. Corwin, *The President: Office and Powers, 1787–1957,* 4th ed. (New York: New York University Press, 1957), p. 5.

[2] Ibid., p. 6.

[3] F. N. Thorpe, ed., *American Charters, Constitutions, Etc.* (Washington, 1909), VIII, pp. 3816–17.

[4] Quoted in Corwin, p. 11.

As chair of the Committee of Detail, Wilson had considerable input into the fashioning of the office of chief executive. Rejecting the suggestions of some of the delegates, who initially suggested multiple executives to diffuse the power of the executive branch, the Framers settled on a single chief executive. Borrowing from the constitutions of Pennsylvania, Delaware, New Jersey, and New Hampshire, the Framers called the new chief executive the president. Although the Framers had little difficulty in agreeing that executive authority was to be vested in one person or in agreeing on a title for the new office, the manner of the president's election continued to haunt them, so they turned to a discussion of easier issues.

Qualifications for Office

The Framers mandated that the president (and the vice president, whose major function was to succeed the president in the event of his death or disability) be a natural-born citizen of the United States and at least thirty-five years old. The Framers also insisted that any prospective president had resided in the United States for at least fourteen years. As it was not uncommon for those engaged in international diplomacy to be out of the country for substantial periods of time, the Framers wanted to make sure that prospective presidents spent some time on this country's shores before running for its highest elective office.

How Long Can a President Serve?

Initially, the length of the executive's term of office and his eligibility to seek reelection were the subjects of considerable controversy. Four-, seven-, and eleven-year terms with no eligibility for reelection were suggested by various delegates to the Constitutional Convention. When Elbridge Gerry of Massachusetts arrogantly suggested a fifteen-year term, a better-humored colleague suggested twenty. After all, he noted, it was "the median life of princes."[5] Alexander Hamilton suggested that a president serve during "good behavior." Not surprisingly, the issue of length of term quickly became associated with eligibility to seek reelection. From the beginning, it was clear that if the delegates agreed to allow the state legislatures to choose the president, then shorter terms with the possibility of reelection would be favored. Thus, after the Framers of the Constitution reached agreement on the composition of the electoral college (see Chapter 12), the delegates in favor of a reelection option prevailed, and a four-year term with eligibility for reelection was added to the proposed Article II of the Constitution.

The first president, George Washington (1789–1797), sought reelection only once, and a two-term limit for presidents became traditional. Although Ulysses S. Grant unsuccessfully sought a third term, the two terms established by Washington remained the standard for 150 years, avoiding the Framers' much-feared "constitutional monarch," a perpetually reelected tyrant. In the 1930s and 1940s, however, Franklin Delano Roosevelt ran successfully in four elections as Americans fought first the Great Depression and then World War II. Despite Roosevelt's popularity, negative reaction to his long tenure in office ultimately led to passage (and ratification in 1951) of the Twenty-second Amendment, which limited presidents to two terms or a total of ten years in office, should a vice president assume a portion of a president's unfulfilled term.

Term limitations are rare in parliamentary systems, where the chief executive can remain in office indefinitely, or rather, as long as she or he can command the support of a majority of representatives in the lower house. Margaret Thatcher, prime minister of Britain from 1979 to 1990, was quoted in the run-up to the 1987 general election (which her party, the Conservatives, won) that she intended "to go on and on" as prime minister. In practice, she did not. In theory, she certainly could have.

---

[5] Quoted in Selma R. Williams, *Fifty-Five Fathers* (New York: Dodd Mead, 1970), p. 77.

Succession

Originally, the Constitution was not precise about what would happen were a president to die in office or be unable to fulfill his duties. Eight presidents have died in office from illness or assassination. William Henry Harrison was the first president to expire in office— he caught a cold at his inauguration in 1841 and died one month later. (When John Tyler succeeded to Harrison's presidency, there was even some question about the extent of his presidential authority because at that time the Constitution stated only that presidential powers and duties "shall devolve on the Vice President.") The first president to be assassinated was Abraham Lincoln in 1865. Richard Nixon, facing impeachment and likely conviction in 1974, became the first president to resign from office.

Whether as a result of death or resignation, the vice president has always taken over the reins of office. The Constitution directs Congress to select a successor if there is no vice president. To clarify this, Congress passed the Presidential Succession Act of 1947, which lists—in order—those in line (after the vice president) to succeed the president:

1. Speaker of the House of Representatives
2. President pro tempore of the Senate
3. Secretaries of State, Treasury, and Defense, and other Cabinet heads in order of their departments' creation (see page 255)

The Succession Act has never been used, as there have been no vacancies in the office of vice president when something happened to the president. The Twenty-fifth Amendment was added to the Constitution in 1967 to assure that this will continue to be the case. In the case of a vacancy in the vice presidency, the Twenty-fifth Amendment directs the president to appoint a new vice president, subject to the approval (by a simple majority) of both houses of Congress.

The Twenty-fifth Amendment has been used twice in its relatively short history. In 1973 President Richard M. Nixon selected the House minority leader, Gerald R. Ford, to replace Vice President Spiro T. Agnew when Agnew resigned in the wake of charges that he had accepted bribes while a local public official in Maryland and while vice president. Less than a year later, when Vice President Ford became the thirty-eighth president after Nixon's resignation, he appointed former four-term New York State Governor Nelson A. Rockefeller to the vice presidency. This set up for the first time in U.S. history a situation in which neither the president nor the vice president had been elected to those positions.

How Can a President Be Removed?

Another point of dissention among the delegates in Philadelphia concerned the appropriateness of including a process for removing the chief executive from office, called the impeachment process. Benjamin Franklin, a staunch supporter of impeachment, noted that "historically, the lack of power to impeach had necessitated recourse to assassination,"[6] and he urged the rest of the delegates to formulate a legal mechanism to remove the president and vice president.

Just as the veto power was a check on Congress, the impeachment provision ultimately contained in Article II was adopted as a check on the power of the president (as well as the judiciary). Each house of Congress was given a role to play to assure that the chief executive could be removed only for *"Treason, Bribery, or other high Crimes and Misdemeanors."* If, after a thorough investigation, the House of Representatives was persuaded that the president had engaged in any of these offenses, it could vote to impeach the president. If **articles of impeachment** were returned against the president

---

[6] Winston Solberg, *The Federal Convention and the Formation of the Union of the American States* (Indianapolis: Bobbs-Merrill, 1958), p. 235.

What Happens If a President Can't Do His Job?

When the twentieth president, James A. Garfield, was wounded by an assassin's bullet in July 1881, he lingered until mid-September. In 1919, President Woodrow Wilson had what many believed to be a nervous collapse in the summer and a debilitating stroke in the fall that incapacitated him for several months. His wife refused to admit his advisers to his sickroom, and rumors flew about "the First Lady President" as many suspected it was his wife and not Wilson who was issuing written orders.

A section of the Twenty-fifth Amendment allows the vice president and a majority of the Cabinet (or some other body determined by Congress) to deem a president unable to fulfill his duties. It sets up a procedure to allow the vice president to become "acting president" if the president is incapacitated. The president can also voluntarily relinquish his power. Following the

Woodrow Wilson, with his wife Edith.

spirit of the amendment, before he underwent surgery for cancer of the colon in 1985, President Ronald Reagan sent his vice president, George Bush, a letter that made Bush the acting president for eight hours.

by a simple majority vote, a trial of the president was to be held in the Senate, with the Chief Justice of the United States presiding over the Senate hearing and the vote on the articles. A two-thirds majority vote in the Senate to remove the president on any count of impeachment would lead to his automatic removal from office. As noted in Chapter 6, only one president, Andrew Johnson in 1868, has ever been impeached by the House of Representatives.

Formal procedures for succession, removal, and impeachment have no parallels in the British parliamentary system. When the prime minister resigns, dies in office, or loses the confidence of the majority party in Parliament, one of two things can happen: (1) either a new prime minister is named out of the sitting Parliament, again from the majority party, or (2) Parliament is "dissolved" and new elections are held, with a new prime minister emerging from the new Parliament.

The Vice President

The office of vice president was given only short shrift by the Framers. They sensed the need to have an immediate official "stand in" for the president but gave little thought to the office beyond that point. Initially, for example, the vice president's one and only function was to assume the office of president in the case of the death of the president or some other emergency. Further debate, however, led the delegates to make the vice president the presiding officer of the Senate (except in cases of presidential impeachment) with the authority to vote only in the event of a tie because they feared that if the Senate's presiding officer were chosen from the Senate itself, one state would be short a representative.

With so little authority, until recently the office of vice president has been considered unimportant and a sure place for a public official to disappear into obscurity. John Adams wrote to his wife, Abigail, about his position as America's first vice president, saying that it was "the most insignificant office that was the invention of man . . . or his imagination conceived."[7] A similar sentiment is evident in a story told by Thomas R. Marshall, Woodrow Wilson's little-remembered vice president: "Once there were two brothers. One ran away to sea. The other was elected vice president, and nothing was heard of either of them again."[8] Franklin Delano Roosevelt's first vice president, John Nance Garner, more bluntly observed that his job was not worth "a pitcher of warm spit."

Power and fame generally come to only those vice presidents who become president. Only "one heartbeat away" from the presidency, the vice president serves as a constant reminder of the president's mortality. In part, this has added to a trend of uneasy relationships between presidents and vice presidents that began as early as Adams and Jefferson. As the historian Arthur M. Schlesinger, Jr., once noted, "The Vice President has only one serious thing to do: that is, to wait around for the President to die. This is hardly the basis for a cordial and enduring friendship."[9]

In the past, presidents chose their vice presidents largely to "balance"—politically, geographically, or otherwise—the presidential ticket, with little thought given to the possibility of the vice president becoming president. Franklin Roosevelt, for example, a liberal New Yorker, selected Garner, a conservative Texan, to be his running mate in 1932. After serving two terms, Garner—who openly disagreed with Roosevelt over many policies, including the former's Court-packing plan (see Chapter 9) and his belief that Roosevelt should not seek a third term—sought the 1940 presidential nomination himself.

In general, as presidential candidates have begun to select running mates who might eventually take over the reins of the nation's highest office, once elected, they have given them more and more responsibility as well as access to information vital to the country's national security. The office of vice president has begun to come into its own after years of deserved ridicule and insignificance.

How much power a vice president has, however, depends upon how much the president is willing to give him. Although Jimmy Carter, a Southerner, chose Walter F. Mondale, a Northerner, as his running mate in 1976 to balance the ticket, he was also the first president to give his vice president more than ceremonial duties. Mondale—a former senator from Minnesota with Washington connections—became an important adviser to President Carter, who had run for office as a Washington "outsider." Whereas previous vice presidents had tried to make numerous trivial tasks appear significant, Mondale's opinion was that if a job was important, it had already been assigned to someone else. Therefore, he did his best to carve out a new role as an adviser to the president, an activity encouraged by Carter.

The "Mondale model" of an active vice president set the expectations for what the influence, powers, and limitations of modern vice presidents should be. Although

Former President Jimmy Carter conferring with Walter Mondale, his vice president.

[7] Alfred Steinberg, *The First Ten: The Founding Presidents and Their Administrations* (New York: Doubleday, 1967), p. 59.

[8] As a presiding officer in the Senate, Marshall helped break the monotony of a lengthy speech on "What This Country Needs" by quipping his well repeated words: "What this country needs is a really good five-cent cigar." Carol Haas, *In the World of Politics* (Hauppauge, New York: Barron's Educational Services, 1991), p. 223.

[9] "Is the Vice Presidency Necessary?" *Atlantic* 233 (May 1974), p. 37.

Watergate and Its Effect on the Presidency

Richard Nixon, in a recorded conversation from the Oval Office:

> I don't give a shit what happens, I want you to stonewall it, let them plead the Fifth Amendment, cover up or anything else, if it'll save the plan.

Nixon's plan was to get reelected to the presidency by any means necessary. What Nixon did not anticipate was getting caught. On June 17, 1972, five men were arrested during a break-in at the Democratic National Committee's (DNC) headquarters in the Watergate office complex in Washington, D.C. The men were caught with burglary tools, bugging devices, and a stack of $100 bills; their mission was to install listening devices in the phones of the DNC in order to learn of campaign strategies and information that could be used against the Democratic presidential nominee, who was to be selected the next month at the 1972 Democratic National Convention. Among the burglars was James W. McCord Jr., the security director of the Committee to Re-Elect the President (CREEP). Later, two former White House aides working for CREEP, G. Gordon Liddy and E. Howard Hunt, were also arrested for their role in the planning of the break-in. Immediately after the arrests, the White House and CREEP shredded all documents in their possession that might link the burglars to the White House. Meanwhile, Nixon assured the press that there was no connection between him or his staffers and the burglary.

On September 15, 1972, Liddy, Hunt, and the Watergate burglars were indicted for burglary by a federal grand jury. On November 7, 1972, Nixon was reelected for a second term with virtually no one paying much attention to the break-in. On December 8, Hunt's wife was killed in a plane crash.Perhaps significantly, she was carrying $10,000 in $100 bills.

The highly publicized **Watergate** trials, began on January 8, 1973, and all five defendants pleaded guilty; Liddy and Hunt were later convicted in a separate trial. On March 19, 1973, McCord came forward with more information, which he detailed in a letter to Judge John J. Sirica, who had accepted his plea of guilty. In it he explained that he and the other Watergate defendants had been pressured to remain silent and that other highly placed public officials were involved, including John N. Mitchell, a close friend of Richard Nixon's who had resigned from his position as U.S. Attorney General to head CREEP.

On April 20, L. Patrick Gray, the director of the FBI, resigned after admitting he had destroyed evidence connected to the Watergate case. Ten days later Attorney General Richard Kleindienst and top presidential aides John D. Ehrlichman and H. R. Haldeman resigned; and Nixon fired the presidential counselor, John Dean.

In June, Dean testified before the specially impaneled Senate Watergate Committee that Nixon had participated in an attempt to cover up the Watergate affair, that the break-in was part of a larger program of political espionage, and that the president was a party in an attempt to cover that up too. In July, Alexander P. Butterfield, a former White House aide, disclosed that the president had secretly tape recorded all conversations that took place in the Oval Office. The committee immediately demanded the tapes, but the president refused to turn them over, citing "executive privilege" and continuing to maintain his innocence. The committee then obtained subpoenas for several of the taped conversations. The White House special prosecutor, Archibald Cox, who had been appointed by Nixon "to investigate" the break-in, also requested the tapes and refused to accept a White House compromise that would have provided him with a "synopsis" of their content. When Cox refused to back down, the president ordered him to be

Rosemary Woods, Richard Nixon's secretary, in her office.

fired. Both the Attorney General Elliot L. Richardson and his deputy William D. Ruchelshaus refused to carry out the president's order. Cox was finally fired by Solicitor General Robert H. Bork.

Three days later, the House Judiciary Committee announced that it would begin hearing impeachment charges against Nixon. Finally, on October 30, Nixon reluctantly turned over the requested tapes, but two were "missing." Moreover, one contained a "mysterious" 18½-minute gap that the White House claimed was erased accidentally by Nixon's secretary, Rose Mary Woods. (Later analysis of the tape revealed that the erasure had been deliberate.) By January 1974, Nixon was still refusing to surrender the additional 500 tapes and documents subpoenaed by the Senate Watergate Committee. As Nixon steadfastly refused to turn over the tapes, the Court, acknowledging the gravity of the matter, agreed to hear the case immediately. Nixon implied that, absent a unanimous Supreme Court ruling, he might not comply with the Court's decision.

On July 24, 1974, a unanimous Court ruled in *United States* v. *Nixon* that there was no absolute "executive privilege" that could justify Nixon's refusal to comply with a court order to produce information. The president was ordered to turn over the tapes, and within hours the White House agreed to comply. One of the three tapes released revealed that the president had ordered not only a halt to the FBI's investigation of the Watergate break-in but also a subsequent coverup to prevent the discovery that his campaign was involved. This was the "smoking gun" congressional investigators had been looking for. On July 27, 1974, the House Judiciary Committee approved the first of three articles of impeachment against Nixon. On August 9, Nixon resigned.

One month later President Gerald R. Ford pardoned Nixon, arguing that it was necessary to prevent the spectacle of having a former president on trial and that it was time for the nation to turn its attentions elsewhere.

Watergate made a lasting impression on the presidency. It proved that the system created by the Framers worked: Under threat of certain impeachment and conviction, a president was succeeded in an orderly, nonviolent fashion. Watergate also facilitated the 1976 election of Jimmy Carter, who ran as an "outsider" in opposition to the corrupting influences of Washington. It also spurred many reforms in existing ethics laws.

Vice President Dan Quayle

President Ronald Reagan, Carter's successor, announced that his vice president, George Bush, would be given responsibilities in foreign affairs, national security, and dealings with Congress, Reagan did not appear as willing to utilize the vice president as did Carter. However, Bush, a former director of the Central Intelligence Agency (CIA), was given the unprecedented responsibility of heading the National Security Crisis Management team. Following the assassination attempt on President Reagan in March 1981, Vice President Bush worked closely with the recuperating president to keep the government in order.

The increased responsibilities of the vice president have made the office an unofficial training ground for future presidents. Since 1952, the only elected vice president who has not received his party's nod to run for president was Alben W. Barkley, who served under President Truman. Of the six vice presidents who have run for president since 1960, four have been elected. (Nixon's first vice president, Spiro Agnew, was indicted, and Gerald Ford's vice president, Nelson Rockefeller, chose not to seek the nomination in 1976. Hubert Humphrey, who served under Lyndon B. Johnson, and Walter Mondale, who was Carter's vice president, ran but were not elected.) In light of this trend, many political observers were surprised when George Bush selected a relatively obscure U.S. senator from Indiana, J. Danforth Quayle, to be his running mate in 1988.

The Constitutional Powers of the President

Despite the Framers' shared faith in George Washington as their intended first president, it took considerable compromise to overcome their continued fear of a king. The specific powers of the executive branch that the Framers agreed upon are enumerated in Article II of the Constitution. Over the years, the expected limits of these specific constitutional powers have changed as individual presidents asserted themselves in the political process. Some presidents are powerful and effective; others just limp along in office. Much of the president's authority stems from his position as the symbolic leader of the nation and his ability to wield power. When the president speaks—especially in the area of foreign affairs—he speaks for the nation in one voice. But at the base of all presidential authority is Article II.

Executive Power

Perhaps the most important section of Article II is its first sentence. It provides that *"The executive Power shall be vested in a President of the United States of America."* Just what "executive power" was to mean was left quite vague by the Framers. As administrative head of the executive branch, the president was charged with taking *"Care that the Laws be faithfully executed."* He was also given the authority to appoint (with the consent of the Senate) heads of departments to assist him in that task. In Federalist No. 77, Alexander Hamilton commented that "no objection could be made to this class of authorities . . . " It was only much after 1789 that the scope of these provisions became the subject of substantial controversy.

Veto Power

Proponents of a strong executive argued that the president should have an absolute **veto** over acts of Congress—that is, that he should be able to reject any congressional proposal and have his word be final. Opponents of this idea, including Benjamin Franklin, countered that in their home states the executive veto "was constantly made use of to extort money" from the legislature. James Madison, however, made the most compelling argument for some sort of a compromise on the issue:

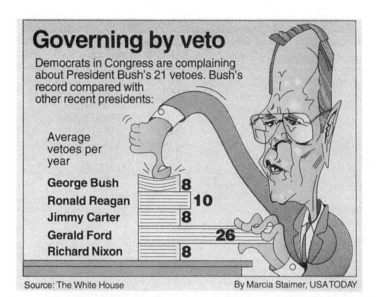

Governing by veto

Democrats in Congress are complaining about President Bush's 21 vetoes. Bush's record compared with other recent presidents:

Average vetoes per year

George Bush	8
Ronald Reagan	10
Jimmy Carter	8
Gerald Ford	26
Richard Nixon	8

Source: The White House   By Marcia Staimer, USA TODAY

Until October 7, 1992, George Bush enjoyed an unprecedented string of congressional failures to override his vetoes. In fact, until October 1992, when the Senate (74–24) and House (308–114) voted overwhelmingly to override his veto of a bill to reregulate the cable television industry, congressional leaders had been unable to muster sufficient support to override *any* Bush veto.

Experience has proven a tendency in our governments to throw all power into the legislative vortex. The Executives of the States are in general little more than Ciphers, the legislatures omnipotent. If no effectual check be devised for restraining the instability and encroachments of the latter, a revolution of some kind or other would be inevitable.[10]

In keeping with the system of checks and balances, then, the veto power prevailed, but as a "qualified negative." Although the president was given the authority to veto, or disapprove of, any act of Congress (with the exception of joint resolutions that propose constitutional amendments), Congress was given the authority to override executive vetoes by a two-thirds vote of both Houses. The power of the veto derives from Congress's usual inability to muster enough votes to override one; there have been approximately 2,500 presidential vetoes, and only 100-odd have been overridden.

George Bush has not been reluctant to use his veto power and, until October 1992 enjoyed the honor of never having had one of his vetoes overridden. He has vetoed bills that were considered to enjoy wide support, including bills authorizing parental leave and several versions of a civil rights bill. In 1991, for example, although a $6.5 billion bill providing twenty additional weeks of unemployment compensation was passed by margins of 300 to 118 in the House and 65 to 35 in the Senate, the Congress was not able to override Bush's veto. Congress later passed a similar version of the bill, which President Bush signed when Senate Democrats used his veto to argue that he was insensitive to the plight of the jobless.

The Appointment Power

The Constitution authorizes the president to appoint, with the advice and consent of the Senate, *"Ambassadors, other public Ministers and Consuls, judges of the supreme Court, and all other Officers of the United States, whose Appointments are not herein otherwise provided for, and which shall be established by Law. . . ."* Today, with the growth of the Executive Office of the President—as well as of the Cabinet, executive agencies, and commissions discussed in Chapter 8—the president has accumulated the authority to make more than 3,000 appointments to his administration (and technically more than 100,000 if military officers are included). Although only about half of these

[10] Quoted in Solberg, p. 91.

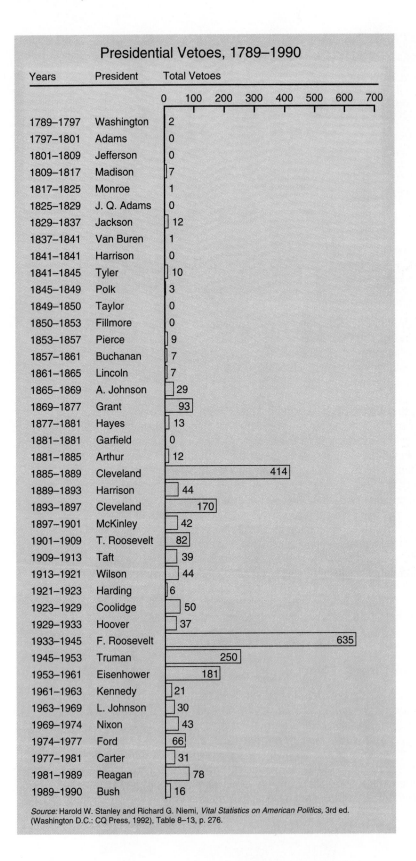

Presidential Vetoes, 1789–1990

Years	President	Total Vetoes
1789–1797	Washington	2
1797–1801	Adams	0
1801–1809	Jefferson	0
1809–1817	Madison	7
1817–1825	Monroe	1
1825–1829	J. Q. Adams	0
1829–1837	Jackson	12
1837–1841	Van Buren	1
1841–1841	Harrison	0
1841–1845	Tyler	10
1845–1849	Polk	3
1849–1850	Taylor	0
1850–1853	Fillmore	0
1853–1857	Pierce	9
1857–1861	Buchanan	7
1861–1865	Lincoln	7
1865–1869	A. Johnson	29
1869–1877	Grant	93
1877–1881	Hayes	13
1881–1881	Garfield	0
1881–1885	Arthur	12
1885–1889	Cleveland	414
1889–1893	Harrison	44
1893–1897	Cleveland	170
1897–1901	McKinley	42
1901–1909	T. Roosevelt	82
1909–1913	Taft	39
1913–1921	Wilson	44
1921–1923	Harding	6
1923–1929	Coolidge	50
1929–1933	Hoover	37
1933–1945	F. Roosevelt	635
1945–1953	Truman	250
1953–1961	Eisenhower	181
1961–1963	Kennedy	21
1963–1969	L. Johnson	30
1969–1974	Nixon	43
1974–1977	Ford	66
1977–1981	Carter	31
1981–1989	Reagan	78
1989–1990	Bush	16

Source: Harold W. Stanley and Richard G. Niemi, *Vital Statistics on American Politics,* 3rd ed. (Washington D.C.: CQ Press, 1992), Table 8–13, p. 276.

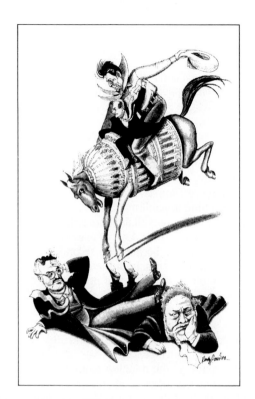

Cartoon depicting President Reagan riding Congress with Supreme Court nominee Anthony Kennedy, over Senate-rejected nominees Douglas Ginsburg (left) and Robert Bork (right).

are in policy-making positions, this power gives a president considerable influence over policy making. In the context of his ability to make appointments to the federal courts, especially, his influence can be felt far past his term of office. As noted previously, appointments to the federal bench, Cabinet-level positions, and other key spots are subject to Senate confirmation. The British prime minister enjoys a similarly broad power of appointment; however, the prime minister does not have to seek the approval of either chamber of the legislature for executive and bureaucratic appointments. This ability to select an executive team without the formal participation of Parliament is one of the many sources of the prime minister's power.

Once a president sends appointments to the Senate, they are traditionally given great respect—especially those for the Cabinet. Although Senator Nancy Kassebaum (R.-Kan.) has commented, ''I firmly believe that our founding fathers did not intend for the United States Senate to be a rubber stamp,''[11] it is rare for the Senate to reject a presidential appointment. President Dwight D. Eisenhower's nomination of Lewis L. Strauss to be Secretary of Commerce was rejected by a forty-nine to forty-six vote because of a combination of policy differences and lingering questions about Stauss's integrity. After Eisenhower, it was thirty years before the next Cabinet nominee was rejected. In fact, the Senate's rejection of President Bush's nominee for Secretary of Defense, former Senator John G. Tower (R.-Tex.), marked only the eighth time in history that a president's choice for a Cabinet post has been rejected. Tower's nomination was rejected on a vote of fifty-three to forty-seven because of charges of a potential conflict of interest with defense contractors (whom he had worked for since retiring from the Senate), excessive drinking, and womanizing.

Certain kinds of nominees receive more congressional scrutiny than others. Regulatory commission members, discussed in detail in Chapter 8, are located in the world of politics somewhere between the legislative and executive branches, yet appointed by the president. Supreme Court appointees also lie outside the executive branch of government and are increasingly subject to greater senatorial review and public, televised grilling. During the Nixon administration two Supreme Court nominees were rejected after

---

[11] ''Senate Votes to Reject Tower; Bush Nominates Rep. Cheney,'' *The National Bureau of National Affairs, Inc. Federal Contracts Report,* March 13, 1989, Vol. 51, No. 11, p. 465.

questions were raised about their competence and commitment to civil rights. President Reagan experienced opposition to some of his federal district court appointments on the same grounds. Reagan's second nominee to the Supreme Court, Judge Robert Bork, was rejected by the Senate on a vote of fifty-eight to forty-two because of his perceived hostility to the rights of blacks and women and to abortion. Reagan then nominated Judge Douglas Ginsburg whose nomination was withdrawn when allegations of Ginsburg's drug use with students while he was a Harvard law professor were made public. Anthony Kennedy, Reagan's third choice, was finally confirmed in 1988.

In 1991 Clarence Thomas, President Bush's nominee to the Supreme Court, faced the closest vote resulting in confirmation for a justice—fifty-two to forty-eight—in the past century. In spite of charges that Thomas had sexually harassed a former employee—charges that resulted in three days of televised Senate hearings that at one point lasted until after 2:00 A.M.—he became the second black to serve on the Court.

In general, few nominees are turned down. When a nominee appears to be "in trouble," presidents often withdraw the nomination or hint that it would be wise for the nominee to do so. For example, after Robert Gates was nominated by President Reagan in 1987 to succeed CIA Director William J. Casey, Gates withdrew his name amid questions of the agency's involvement in the Iran-*Contra* affair. Later, however, he was renominated to the position by President Bush and after 138 days of questioning by the Senate Select Committee on Intelligence, he was ultimately confirmed.

Senatorial courtesy, the tradition requiring that members of the Senate defer to the judgments of their colleagues concerning nominees from their home states, often grants senators of the president's party a virtual veto over appointments to jobs in their states. Although this limits the president's discretion in filling state-specific jobs, especially federal district court vacancies, "national" positions provide the opportunity for the president to shape the direction and image of his administration. There are, of course, some traditions—such as the nomination of a Westerner to be Secretary of the Interior—but these are not requirements. The quality of presidential appointments directly reflects upon the president. Presidents Ulysses S. Grant, Warren G. Harding, and Richard Nixon, for example, were hurt by the low quality of some of their appointments. Likewise, President Ronald Reagan's reputation suffered when the behavior of several of his appointees led to numerous resignations, the prosecution of ex–White House aides Michael Deaver and Lyn Nofziger, the investigation of Attorney General Edwin Meese III, and the conviction for perjury of Rita Lavelle of the Environmental Protection Agency, among others.

The Pardoning Power

Presidents also can exercise a check on judicial power through their constitutional authority to grant reprieves or pardons. **Pardons,** which restore all rights and privileges of citizenship, usually go to specific individuals for crimes for which they have been convicted. In the case of the most famous presidential pardon ever granted, in 1974 President Gerald Ford pardoned former President Richard M. Nixon, who had not been formally charged with any illegalities, "for any offenses against the United States, which he, Richard Nixon, has committed or may have committed while in office." This unilateral pardon unleashed a torrent of public criticism that many blame for Ford's ultimate defeat in his 1976 bid for the presidency.

Even though pardons are generally directed toward a specific individual, presidents historically have used their pardoning power to offer general amnesties. Presidents Washington, John Adams, Madison, Lincoln, Andrew Johnson, Theodore Roosevelt, and Jimmy Carter all used general pardons to grant amnesty to large classes of individuals for illegal acts. Carter, for example, incurred the wrath of many veterans' groups when he made an offer of unconditional amnesty to approximately 10,000 men who had fled the United States or gone into hiding to avoid being drafted to serve in the Vietnam War.

Chief law enforcer: National Guard troops sent by President Eisenhower enforce federal court decisions ordering the integration of public schools in Little Rock, Arkansas.

Commander-in-chief: President Bush and his wife Barbara with troops in the Persian Gulf.

Leader of the party: Presidential candidate Bill Clinton accepts the Democratic Party's nomination for president at the party's 1992 convention.

The President's Many Hats

Key player in the legislative process: President Reagan and legislative leaders of both parties after budget negotiations in 1988.

Shaper of domestic policy: President Lyndon B. Johnson conferring with the Reverend Martin Luther King, Jr. and other black leaders about Johnson's War on Poverty.

Chief of state: President Nixon and his wife Pat at a state dinner in China celebrating renewed relations between that country and the United States.

238 ■ Chapter 7 The Presidency

The Power to Convene Congress and Make Treaties

The veto and appointment powers are not the only ones that impose a relationship between the president and Congress. Not only does the Constitution require the president to inform the Congress periodically of *"the State of the Union,"* but it also authorizes the president to convene either or both houses of Congress on *"extraordinary Occasions."* In Federalist No. 77 Hamilton justified this secondary power by noting that because the Senate and the chief executive enjoy concurrent powers to make treaties, "it might often be necessary to call it together with a view to this object, when it would be unnecessary and improper to convene the House of Representatives."

The British prime minister possesses vis-à-vis the legislature one power that the President does not: the power to dissolve Parliament and call new elections. While a Parliament has a maximum life of five years, technically speaking, the prime minister can call an election at any time, which gives the party in power a significant advantage in terms of picking the optimal time—politically and economically—to go to the people. This power contributes to an executive that is ascendant over its legislature.

The president's power to make treaties with foreign nations is checked by the Constitution's stipulation that all treaties be approved by at least two-thirds of the members of the Senate. The chief executive can also *"receive ambassadors,"* wording that has been interpreted to allow the president to recognize the very existence of other nations.

Historically, the Senate ratifies about 70 percent of the treaties submitted to it by the president.[12] Only sixteen that have been put to a vote have been rejected, often under highly partisan circumstances. Perhaps the most notable example of the Senate's disinclination to ratify a treaty was its defeat of the Treaty of Versailles submitted by President Woodrow Wilson. The Treaty was an agreement among the major nations to end World War I and called for, at Wilson's insistence, the creation of the League of Nations—a precursor of the United Nations—to foster continued peace and international disarmament. In struggling to gain international acceptance for the League, Wilson had taken American support for granted. This was a dramatic miscalculation. Isolationists, led by Senator William Jennings Bryan (D.-Neb.), opposed U.S. participation in the League on the grounds that the League would place the United States in the center of every major international conflict. Proponents countered that, League or no League, the United States had emerged from World War I as a world power and that membership in the League would enhance its new role. The vote in the Senate for ratification was very close, but the isolationists prevailed—the United States stayed out of the League, and Wilson was devastated.

The Senate also may require substantial amendment of a treaty prior to its consent. When President Carter, for example, proposed the controversial Panama Canal Treaties in 1977, the Senate required several conditions to be ironed out between the Carter and Torrijos administrations before its approval was forthcoming.

Presidents often try to get around the *"advise and consent"* requirement of treaties by entering into **executive agreements**, which allow the president to enter into secret and highly sensitive arrangements with foreign nations without congressional approval. Since the days of George Washington, presidents have used these agreements, and their use has been upheld by the courts. Although executive agreements are not binding on subsequent administrations, since 1900 they have been used far more frequently than treaties, thus further cementing the role of the president in foreign affairs.

Commander-in-Chief of the Military

One of the most important executive powers is the president's authority over the military. Article II states that the President is *"Commander-in-Chief of the Army and Navy of the United States."* The Framers saw this grant of authority as consistent with state practices.

[12]Benjamin I. Page and Mark P. Petracca, *The American Presidency* (New York: McGraw-Hill, 1983), p. 268.

According to Hamilton, it amounted to "nothing more than the supreme command and direction of the military and naval forces." Since the eighteenth century, this power has proved to be wide-ranging.

The Constitution quite specifically grants Congress the authority to declare war. Nevertheless, presidents since Abraham Lincoln have used the commander-in-chief clause in conjunction with the chief executive's duty to *"take Care that the Laws be faithfully executed"* as authority to broaden other powers.

They also have used it to wage war. Modern presidents continually clash with Congress over the ability to commence hostilities. The Vietnam War, in which 58,000 American soldiers were killed and 300,000 were wounded, at a cost of $150 billion, was conducted without a congressional declaration of war. In fact, acknowledging President Johnson's claim to war-making authority, Congress passed the Gulf of Tonkin Resolution in 1964 with only two dissenting votes.

During that highly controversial war, Presidents Johnson and then Nixon routinely assured members of Congress that victory was near. In 1971, however, publication of the Pentagon Papers revealed what many had suspected all along—Lyndon Johnson had systematically altered casualty figures and distorted key facts to place the conduct of the war in a more positive light. In 1973, Congress passed the War Powers Act to limit the authority of the president to introduce American troops into foreign nations without congressional approval (as noted in Chapter 6). President Nixon's veto of the act was overridden by a two-thirds majority in both houses of Congress.

The Development of Presidential Power

Each man who has assumed the presidency has brought with him some expectation of presidential authority. After John F. Kennedy had been in office two years, however, he noted publicly that the nation's problems "are more difficult than I had imagined" and that "there are greater limitations upon our ability to bring about a favorable result than I had imagined."[13] Moreover, political scientist Richard Neustadt argues, presidents historically have been limited in their ability to turn the formal powers of the presidency into effective policy making. The tension that limitation produces puts them in a position that Neustadt likens to that of "a cat on a hot tin roof."

A president's personal expectation of authority often has been tempered by the Supreme Court's interpretation of constitutional provisions concerning the scope of presidential power, by the president's personality, and by the times in which the president serves. The postwar era of good feelings and economic prosperity presided over in the 1950s by the grandfatherly former war hero Dwight Eisenhower, for instance, called for a very different kind of leader from the Civil War–torn nation governed by Abraham Lincoln.

The presidency that we see today is quite different from the office assumed by George Washington in 1789. According to Benjamin Page and Mark Petracca, two main trends are responsible for the office's evolution: (1) a phenomenal growth in presidential tasks, responsibilities, and delegated authority and (2) democratization of the office, which has brought the president closer to the people.

The First Three Presidents

Each of the first three presidents—George Washington, John Adams, and Thomas Jefferson—contributed significantly to the development of the office of the chief executive, although in different ways. When George Washington was sworn in as the first president

[13] *Public Papers of the Presidents* (1963), p. 889.

of the United States on a cold, blustery day in New York City in April 1789, he took over an office and government that were really yet to be created. Eventually a few hundred postal workers were hired, and Washington appointed a small group of Cabinet advisers and clerks. During Washington's two terms the entire federal budget was only about $40 million, or approximately $10 for every citizen in America. In contrast, in 1990 the federal budget was $1.17 trillion, or $4,680 for every man, woman, and child.

As the first president, Washington set several important precedents for future presidents:

- He took every opportunity to establish the primacy of the national government. When John Hancock, the governor of Massachusetts, came to New York City, for example, Washington insisted that Hancock call upon *him* (to show his respect) rather than the other way around. For two days, Washington played an uncomfortable waiting game, but his patience and insistence paid off when the governor finally came to pay his respects. In 1794, Washington's use of the militia of four states to put down the Whiskey Rebellion, an uprising of 3,000 Western Pennsylvania farmers opposed to the payment of federal excise tax on liquor, also helped establish the idea of federal supremacy and the authority of the executive branch to collect the taxes levied by Congress. (Leading these 1,500 troops was Alexander Hamilton, Secretary of the Treasury.)
- Washington began the practice of regular meetings with his advisers (called the Cabinet), thus establishing the Cabinet system, the popular name for the meeting of the executive departments.
- He asserted the prominence of the role of the chief executive in the conduct of foreign affairs. He sent envoys to negotiate the Jay Treaty with Great Britain and then, over senatorial objection, continued to assert his authority to negotiate treaties first and then, second, simply submit them to the Senate for its approval. He made it clear that the Senate's function was limited to approval and *not* negotiation.

During the terms of the next two presidents, Adams and Jefferson, both of whom had participated in the early founding of the nation, several other notable precedents occurred that were to affect the development of the office of the chief executive.

- Adams's poor leadership skills heightened the divisions between Federalists and Anti-Federalists and probably quickened the development of political parties (see Chapter 11).
- Jefferson used the developing party system to establish strong ties with the Congress and thus expand the role of the chief executive in the legislative process.
- Although ostensibly against a strong federal government, Jefferson used the **inherent powers** of the presidency first advocated by the Federalist Alexander Hamilton to double the size of the country through the Louisiana Purchase, which gave the United States ownership of substantial lands west of the Mississippi River.

Congressional Triumph: 1804–1933

Although the first three presidents made enormous contributions to the office of the chief executive and established important precedents that would guide the conduct of those who came after them, the very nature of the way government had to function in its formative years caused the balance of power to be heavily weighted in favor of a strong Congress. Americans routinely had far more intimate contacts with their representatives in Congress, whereas to most, the president seemed a remote figure.

By the end of Jefferson's first term, it was clear that the Framers' initial fear of an all-powerful, monarchical president was unfounded. Congress played a key role in the fashioning of the new government and organized itself in the process. The strength of Congress and the relatively weak presidents who came after Jefferson allowed Congress to be the most powerful branch of government. In fact, with but two exceptions—Andrew Jackson and Abraham Lincoln—most presidents from Jefferson to Franklin Roosevelt failed to exercise the powers of the presidency in any powerful way.

Exception to the Rule, No. 1: Jackson. The first president truly to act as a strong *national* leader was Andrew Jackson. By 1828, eleven new states had been added to the Union, and the number of white males eligible to vote had expanded enormously as property requirements for voting were removed by nearly all states. When Jackson of Tennessee was elected the seventh president in 1828, he was the first one who was not a Virginian or an Adams. His election launched a new era and the beginning of "Jacksonian democracy," which embodied a Western, frontier, egalitarian spirit. The masses loved him, and legends were built on his common-man image. When Jackson was asked to give a postmastership to a soldier who had lost his leg on the battlefield and needed the job to support his family, he was told that the man hadn't voted for him. "If he lost his leg fighting for his country," said Jackson, "that is vote enough for me."[14]

Jackson effectively used his image and power to buttress the party system by relying heavily on **patronage,** whereby he filled presidential appointments with loyal followers of his Democratic Party. Frequently finding himself at odds with Congress, Jackson also made extensive use of the veto power. His veto of twelve bills surpassed that of the combined total of nine vetoes used by his six predecessors. He also reasserted the supremacy of the national government (and the presidency) by facing down South Carolina's nullification of a federal tariff law.

Exception to the Rule, No. 2: Lincoln. Echoing the views of Jackson was the presidential leadership style of Abraham Lincoln. The unprecedented emergency of the Civil War caused Lincoln to assume powers that no president before him had claimed as his own. Lincoln believed that he needed to act quickly, and he frequently did so without first obtaining the approval of Congress. Among the many "questionable" acts of Lincoln were:

- Suspension of the writ of *habeas corpus* (allowing those in prison to petition to be released), citing the need to jail persons even suspected of disloyal practices (see Chapter 4)
- Expansion of the size of the U.S. army above congressionally mandated ceilings
- Institution of a blockade of Southern ports, thus initiating a war without the approval of Congress
- Closing of the mails to treasonable correspondence

According to Lincoln, his circumvention of the Constitution was necessary to save the nation and was legal because of the inherent powers of his office. He argued that the Constitution conferred upon the president an inherent power to make sure that the laws of the United States are faithfully executed. He simply refused to allow the nation to crumble because of what he viewed as technical requirements of the Constitution. Noting the secession of the Southern states and their threat to the sanctity of the Union, Lincoln queried, "Are all of the laws *but one* to go unexecuted, and the Government itself go to pieces lest that one be violated?"[15]

KING ANDREW THE FIRST.

Andrew Jackson's presidential leadership was so heavy-handed that cartoonists depicted him as "King Andrew the First." Here he is shown treading the Constitution underfoot while wielding veto power and a royal scepter.

[14] Quoted in Paul F. Boller, Jr., *Presidential Anecdotes* (New York: Penguin Books, 1981), p. 78.

[15] Abraham Lincoln, "Special Session Message," July 4, 1861, in *Borzoi Reader in American Politics,* Edward Keynes and David Adamany, eds. (New York: Knopf, 1973), p. 539.

People of the Past

Presidential Candidate Victoria Woodhull

Victoria Woodhull (1838–1927), a notorious spiritualist, was the first woman to open a brokerage firm on Wall Street. Bankrolled by leading industrialist Cornelius C. Vanderbilt, the "Bewitching Broker" began to dabble in politics in 1868. She and her sister, Tennessee Clafin, published *Woodhull and Clafin's Weekly,* a paper that publicized their controversial views. Believing marriage to be a form of sexual bondage, Woodhull publicly advocated free love—a woman's right to love whom she pleased outside of the bonds of matrimony. In addition, Woodhull regularly used her newspaper to campaign for legalized prostitution, dress reform, and many other controversial causes.

Woodhull was regularly vilified in the press not only for her public pronouncements but also for her personal living arrangements. Although she was divorced from her first husband, Woodhull continued to live not only with him, but also with another man. The "Terrible Siren," as she was nicknamed by the press, claimed to be married to her lover, but no record of their marriage was ever found, although they did obtain a license to wed.

Thus, when she chose to address Congress on the opening day of National Woman Suffrage Association's convention (NWSA), it was not surprising that Woodhull's actions attracted public attention. Many NWSA members, however, chose to ignore her infamous reputation and went to the Capitol to hear her before their meeting commenced. NWSA leaders Susan B. Anthony and Elizabeth Cady Stanton befriended Woodhull. When Woodhull tried to take control of the NWSA meeting and urged NWSA to form a new political party to allow Woodhull to enter the presidential race of 1872, however, Anthony and Stanton quickly disassociated themselves and NWSA from her. Undaunted, Woodhull held her own convention on May 10, 1872, at which she was nominated as the presidential candidate of the "Equal Rights" party. But by election day, Woodhull was in jail, accused of harboring two husbands.

In 1877 Woodhull moved to London, England where she later married John Biddulph Martin of Martin's Bank, London. She died at the age of eighty-eight after spending the last years of her life trying to disown her past.

Few presidents other than Jackson and Lincoln subscribed to a broad and expansive interpretation of executive power prior to the administration of Franklin Delano Roosevelt (1933–45). Neither Jackson nor Lincoln was succeeded by strong presidents; the nation was possibly just not yet ready to submit to a series of strong presidents.

The Growth of the Modern Presidency

Before the days of instantaneous communication, the nation could afford to allow the relatively slow deliberative processes of Congress to make most decisions. As the times have changed, and national leaders from around the world all look to electronic media such as the Cable News Network (CNN) for coverage of events, the need for one individual to act quickly on behalf of the nation seems clear.

The Role of Crises. That need appears especially true in times of crises, which long have played a key role in the development of presidential authority. Lincoln, for example, one of the most powerful presidents, governed during the peculiar circumstances of a national civil war. Times of danger to the union required that a strong leader take up the reins of government. In the twentieth century, especially, presidential—as opposed to congressional—decision making has become more and more important. Much of this growth can be traced to the four-term presidency of Franklin Delano Roosevelt (FDR), which included several crises.

FDR and the Modern Presidency. Taking office in 1933 in the midst of a major crisis, the Great Depression, FDR noted the disarray in the national economy and concluded in his inaugural address, "This nation asks for action and action now." To jump-start the American economy he asked Congress for "broad executive powers to wage a war against the emergency, as great as the power that would be given to me if we were in fact invaded by a foreign foe."[16]

Just as Lincoln had taken bold steps upon his inauguration, Roosevelt also acted quickly. He immediately fashioned his "New Deal" plan, which he had promised Americans when he accepted the Democratic nomination for president. The New Deal was a package of bold and controversial programs designed to invigorate the failing American economy. As part of that plan, Roosevelt

- Declared a bank holiday to end public runs of the depleted resources of many banks
- Persuaded Congress to pass broad pieces of legislation providing for emergency relief, public works jobs, regulation of farm production, and improved terms and conditions of work for thousands of workers in a variety of industries
- Regularized the practice of sending legislative programs from the executive branch to Congress for its approval instead of only reacting to congressional proposals
- Increased the size of the federal bureaucracy from fewer than 600,000 to more than 1 million workers

Throughout Roosevelt's unprecedented twelve years in office (he was elected to four terms but died shortly after beginning the last one), which saw the nation go from the economic "war" of the Great Depression to the real conflict of World War II, the institution of the presidency changed profoundly and permanently. All kinds of agencies were created to implement New Deal programs, and the executive branch became more and more involved in a wide variety of programs. To his successors FDR left the "modern presidency," including a burgeoning (many would say bloated) federal bureaucracy (see Chapter 8), an active and usually leading role in foreign policy, and a nationalized executive office as methods of technology—first radio and then television—brought the president closer to the public than ever before.

Roosevelt established a new relationship between the presidency and the people. In his radio addresses—or "fireside chats," as he liked to call them—he spoke to the public in a relaxed and informal manner, yet he discussed serious issues. He opened his radio addresses with "My friends . . . ," which made it seem as though he were speaking directly to each listener. As a result of these chats, Roosevelt began to receive about 4,000 letters per day, in contrast to the 40 letters per day received by his predecessor, Herbert Hoover. The head of the White House correspondence section remembered that "the mail started coming in by the truckload. They couldn't even get the envelopes open."[17] One letter that found its way to the White House was simply addressed "My Friend, Washington, D.C." Roosevelt "personalized" the presidency—his style was successful, and his innovations became the routine and the expected.

The rhetorical and personalized styles of post-FDR presidents are very different from those of nineteenth-century presidents. George Washington believed that the purpose of public appearances was to "see and be seen," and not to discuss policy issues. Today presidents use every opportunity to sell their programs. Whereas the rhetoric of early presidents was written, formal, and addressed principally to Congress, today oral speeches addressed to the public at large are the norm. Abraham Lincoln was applauded

---

[16] Quoted in Page and Petracca, p. 57.
[17] Merlin Gustafson, "The President's Mail," *Presidential Studies Quarterly* 8 (1978), p. 36.

Out of the Mouths of Presidents

Warren G. Harding was the first president to employ a formal speech writer—Judson Welliver, who is said to have coined the phrase "the Founding Fathers." According to former Ronald Reagan speech writer Peggy Noonan, author of *What I Saw at the Revolution,* "Speeches are important because they are one of the great constants of our political history. For 200 years, from "Give me liberty or give me death" (Patrick Henry) to "Ask not what your country can do for you . . . ," (John Kennedy), they have been not only the way we measure public men, they have been how we tell each other who we are." Some famous lines:

- "A kinder, gentler nation," spoken by George Bush, written by Peggy Noonan
- "The New Federalism," spoken by Richard Nixon, written by Patrick Buchanan
- "Nattering nabobs of negativism," spoken by Vice President Spiro T. Agnew, written by William Safire (founder of the Judson Welliver Society, the organization of former presidential speech writers, which includes Clark Clifford, Bill Moyers, Jack Valenti, and Pierre Salinger)

for refusing to speak about the impending Civil War. In contrast, Ronald Reagan was hailed as "the Great Communicator."

Presidential Involvement in the Legislative Process. When FDR first sent a legislative package to Congress, he broke with the traditional model of law making. Political scientists described this new process as one in which "the president proposes and the Congress disposes." Increased public expectations have allowed most presidents since FDR to take an active role in all stages of the legislative process.

Although the public looks to the president to set the agenda, "merely placing a program before Congress is not enough," once declared President Lyndon Johnson. "Without constant attention from the administration, most legislation moves through the congressional process at the speed of a glacier."[18] The president's most important power is his ability to construct coalitions to work for passage of his legislation. Frequently, presidents must "deal" with legislators and have "goodies" to trade for votes. Ronald Reagan's first budget director, David Stockman, once estimated that "the last 10 or 20 percent of the votes needed for a majority of both houses [on the 1981 tax cut bill] had to be bought, period." Concessions took the form of real estate tax shelters, special breaks for oil lease holders, and loopholes in the corporate income tax. "The hogs were really feeding," said Stockman. "The greed level, the level of opportunism, just got out of control."[19] When asked by the administration if his vote could be bought, one represent-

[18]Lyndon B. Johnson, *The Vantage Point* (New York: Holt, Rinehart and Winston, 1971), p. 448.
[19]David Stockman, *The Triumph of Politics* (New York: Harper and Row, 1986), p. 251.

ative from Louisiana retorted, "No, but it can be rented." With votes bought and rented, the president ultimately was able to get what he wanted from Congress.

FDR and Lyndon B. Johnson (LBJ) were among the best presidents at "working" Congress. On the whole, presidents have a hard time getting Congress to pass their programs. In Nixon's first term only 35 percent of his publicly requested programs were enacted. Kennedy had fared little better. Even LBJ who was able to get about 57 percent of his programs through Congress, noted: "You've got to give it all you can, that first year . . . before they start worrying about themselves. . . . You can't put anything through when half the Congress is thinking how to beat you."[20]

Presidential Involvement in the Budgetary Process. Although the Framers gave Congress the power of the purse, the economic disaster set off by the stock market crash of 1929 allowed FDR to assert himself in the congressional budgetary process. In 1939 the Bureau of the Budget, which had been created in 1921 to help the president tell Congress how much money it would take to run the executive branch of government, was made part of the newly created Executive Office of the President. In 1970, President Nixon changed its name to the Office of Management and Budget (OMB) to underline its function in the executive branch.

OMB works exclusively for the president and employs hundreds of budget and policy experts. As a powerful resource of the president, OMB reports allow the president to attach price tags to his legislative proposals and to defend the presidential budget. The OMB budget is a huge document, and even those who prepare it have a hard time deciphering all of its provisions.

While even OMB directors may not know all the details and intricacies of the federal budget, their reputed expertise often gives them an advantage over members of Congress. And, political observers believe that the importance of the executive branch will increase in the wake of the Balanced Budget and Emergency Deficit Reduction Act of 1985 (often called "Gramm-Rudman," for two of the three senators who sponsored it). This act outlined debt ceilings and targeted a balanced budget for 1993.

Critics argue that Gramm-Rudman is an unconscionable shift of power to the chief executive. "With this additional power," according to Senator Bill Bradley (D.-N.J.), a president, "if he plays hard ball, could dismantle the nondefense portion of the budget and wreak havoc with America's poor."[21] Other critics note that the president's power also has been increased by the Act's requirement that the president bring the budget in line by reducing or even eliminating cost-of-living and similar automatic spending programs found in programs such as Social Security. This requirement gives a president enormous power, but it depends heavily on his ability to garner public support for such cost-cutting measures.

Winning Support. According to scholar Thomas Cronin, a president has three ways to improve his role as a legislative lobbyist. He can use patronage to win supporters. Invitations to the White House and campaign visits to members of Congress running for office are two such ways to curry favor with legislators. Inattention to key members can prove deadly to a president's legislative program. House Speaker Thomas P. ("Tip") O'Neill reportedly was quite irritated when the Carter team refused O'Neill's request for extra tickets to Carter's inaugural, and this did not exactly get the president off to a good start with the powerful Speaker. In contrast, President Reagan was famous for giving out gift cufflinks and theater tickets along with plugs for legislation he favored.

A second way a president can bolster support for his legislative package is to use party

[20] Quoted in Thomas E. Cronin, *The State of the Presidency,* 2nd ed. (Boston: Little Brown, 1980), p. 169.

[21] Bill Bradley, "Congress at Its Worst," *The Washington Post National Weekly Edition,* October 28, 1985, p. 29.

support. As the informal leader of his political party, he should be able to use that position to his advantage in Congress, where party loyalty is very important. This strategy works best when the president has carried members of his party into office on his coattails, as was the case in the Johnson and Reagan landslides of 1964 and 1984, respectively.

Party support for the executive's proposals in the legislature is much less problematic in parliamentary systems. For example, since the British prime minister holds office precisely because he or she enjoys the support of the majority party in Parliament, many of the roadblocks that plague legislative–executive relations in the United States do not exist.

The third way a president can influence Congress is through close contact with the American people. By "going public" on a position, the president can bring constituent pressures on key members of Congress. The quality and effectiveness of all three strategies are often dependent on what is often termed "**presidential style**."

Presidential Style

A president's ability to get things done depends on many factors, including his character and approach to office, the perception of others of his ability to lead, and his ability to mobilize public opinion to support his actions. As he was leaving office, Harry S Truman mused about what surprises awaited his successor, Dwight Eisenhower, a former general: "He'll sit here and he'll say, 'Do this! Do that!' *And nothing will happen.* Poor Ike—it won't be a bit like the army. He'll find it very frustrating."[22]

Presidential Character

The forty men who have held the nation's highest office are a diverse lot. (George Bush is considered the forty-first president because Grover Cleveland served as the twenty-second and twenty-fourth presidents, having been elected to nonconsecutive terms in 1884 and 1892.) Some have been quite unassuming in their approach to the office. James Madison, for example, wore out-of-date knee britches, silk stockings, and a sword. He met visitors in ink-spotted clothing and worn-down shoes, often looking more like an unkempt clerk than president of the United States.[23] More recently, Jimmy Carter also adopted an unassuming approach to the presidency. During the energy crunch of the 1970s he ordered White House thermostats set to a chill 65 degrees and suggested that his advisers wear sweaters to work. Carter often appeared before the nation in cardigan sweaters instead of suits. He tried to build his "common man" image by carrying his own luggage and prohibiting the Marine band from playing the traditional fanfare "Hail to the Chief" to signify his arrival on official occasions.

In contrast, other presidents have been much more attuned to the trappings of office. Many believe that the Kennedys did it best. During the thousand days they lived in the White House it became a royal palace—"Camelot." John F. Kennedy (JFK) and his family had looks, youth, and wealth, and JFK was a gifted orator. When Jacqueline Kennedy filled the White House with expensive antiques she was praised; when Nancy Reagan bought new china for the White House she was widely attacked and lampooned as "Queen Nancy."

How one approaches the job of president often reflects long-held behaviors. Political scientist James David Barber has suggested that patterns of behavior, many that may be

---

[22] Quoted in Richard E. Neustadt, *Presidential Power: The Politics of Power from FDR to Carter* (New York: Wiley, 1980), p. 9.
[23] Boller, p. 50.

ingrained during childhood, exist and can help explain presidential behavior.[24] Barber believes that there are four **presidential character** types, based on (1) energy level (whether the president is active or passive) and (2) the degree of enjoyment a president finds in his job (whether the president has a positive or negative attitude about his job). Barber believes that active and positive presidents are more successful than passive and negative presidents. Active-positive presidents generally enjoyed warm and supportive childhood environments and are basically happy individuals open to new life experiences. They approach the presidency with a characteristic zest for life and have a drive to lead and succeed. In contrast, passive presidents find themselves reacting to circumstances, are likely to take direction from others, and fail to make full use of the enormous resources of the executive office. Table 7-1 classifies presidents since Taft according to Barber's categories.

A classic example of an active-positive president is Franklin Delano Roosevelt. Reared in tremendous wealth, Roosevelt enjoyed a considerable amount of self-confidence in spite of his severe health problems (he was paralyzed from the waist down by polio). Roosevelt simply loved the game of politics. When he suffered setbacks—such as the Supreme Court's rulings that portions of his New Deal legislative program were unconstitutional—he repeatedly sought new ways to achieve his policy objectives. Other active-positives such as John F. Kennedy and George Bush enjoyed similar stable family relationships and relished the idea of being president. Even during the dark days of the Iraqi occupation of Kuwait in 1990, President Bush kept to his vacation schedule of water sports, running, and golf while handling the crisis from Kennebunkport, his Maine vacation home. Although his anguish and concern about the situation were clear, he did not appear to experience the dark bouts of gloom that pervaded the presidencies of Lyndon Johnson, Richard Nixon, and even Abraham Lincoln, who Barber considers active-negative presidents.

Although an active-positive president, George Bush was often criticized for sharing one active-negative feature with LBJ: a tendency to surround himself with "yes men." "Bush wants twins around him, and that can be dangerous," concludes Barber.[25] Even the conservative political columnist William Safire has noted an "absence of creative tension [which] has generated little excitement or innovation . . . as a result of the Bush

[24] James David Barber, *The Presidential Character: Predicting Performance in the White House,* 3rd ed. (Englewood Cliffs, N.J.: Prentice Hall, 1985).

[25] Quoted in Larry Berman and Bruce W. Jentleson, "Bush and the Post-Cold-War World: New Challenges for American Leadership" from Colin Campbell and Bert A. Rockman, *The Bush Presidency: First Appraisals* (Chatham, N.J.: Chatham House, 1991), p. 103.

Table 7-1   Barber's Presidential Personalities

	ACTIVE	PASSIVE
POSITIVE	F. D. Roosevelt Truman Kennedy Ford Carter[a] Bush	Taft Harding Reagan
NEGATIVE	Wilson Hoover L. B. Johnson Nixon	Coolidge Eisenhower

[a] Some scholars think that Carter better fits the active-negative typology.

emphasis on the appearance of unanimity. We miss the Rooseveltian turbulence that often leads to original thinking."[26]

Although Barber's typology can be a fun way to begin to discuss the stages and characters of the men who have served as president, some disagree with his approach and its ability to predict presidential success. Garry Wills, for example, describes Barber's work as an example of the "games academics play."[27]

The Power to Persuade. A president is many things to many people. The demands of his office require that he be a symbol of the nation, a political organizer, and a moral teacher. But to do this job, according to George Reedy, he must be able to do two things: First, he must be able to resolve policy questions that will not yield to quantitative, empirical analyses, and, second, he must be able to persuade enough of the country that his actions are the right ones so that he can carry them out without national strife.[28] Exercising the constitutional powers of the chief executive are not enough; a president's personality and ability to persuade others are key to amassing greater power and authority.

Frequently, the difference between great and mediocre presidents centers on their ability to grasp this fact of political life. Truly "great" presidents, such as Lincoln and Franklin Roosevelt, understood that the White House was a locus of power from which decisions could flow to shape the national destiny. They recognized that their day-to-day activities were designed to bolster support for their policies and to secure backing that could translate their intuitive judgment into meaningful action. On the other hand, mediocre presidents have tended to regard the White House as "a stage for the presentation of performances to the public" or a fitting honor to cap a career.[29]

Presidential character and political skills often determine how effectively a president can exercise the broad powers of the modern president. Political scientist Richard Neustadt has developed a model of how presidents win, lose, or maintain their personal power and influence. According to Neustadt, "Presidential power is the *power to persuade,*" and the power to persuade comes largely from an individual's ability to bargain.

When Neustadt's *Presidential Power* was first published in 1960, it was widely hailed as a guidebook for those interested in wielding power. Both Presidents Kennedy and Johnson studied it intensely, and Kennedy even hired Neustadt as a staff consultant.

Neustadt argued that there were nine steps to achieving a successful presidency. (Notice how closely related many of his points are to key elements of Barber's typology of successful presidents.)

1. To be a successful leader, a president must have a will for power.
2. The ability of a president to win over others is key to getting other institutions of government to act. He must be the agenda setter for the national government.
3. Introverts cannot be successful presidents. Instead, a president must be receptive and sensitive to the thoughts and ideas of others in order to come to effective compromises and solutions to national problems.
4. Because members of Congress are motivated by the prospect of reelection, the president must get members of Congress to see that his way is also in their best interest.
5. A president must be able to ride out events and crises.
6. A strong, effective president must be his own intelligence officer and not rely on others to assess the political and power stakes involved in particular actions. A successful president cannot delegate the job of chief politician.

[26] William Safire, "Bush's Cabinet: Who's Up," *New York Times Magazine,* March 25, 1990, p. 32.
[27] Gary Wills, *The Kennedy Imprisonment* (Boston: Little Brown, 1982), p. 186.
[28] George Reedy, *The Twilight of the Presidency* (New York: New American Library), p. 38.
[29] Ibid, pp. 38–39.

The Best and the Worst Presidents

Who was the best president and who was the worst? Many surveys of scholars have been taken over the years to answer this question, and virtually all have ranked Abraham Lincoln the best and Warren G. Harding the worst. A 1982 *Chicago Tribune* poll,* for example, came up with these results:

TEN BEST PRESIDENTS

1. Lincoln (best)
2. Washington
3. F. Roosevelt
4. T. Roosevelt
5. Jefferson
6. Wilson
7. Jackson
8. Truman
9. Eisenhower
10. Polk (10th best)

TEN WORST PRESIDENTS

1. Harding (worst)
2. Nixon
3. Buchanan
4. Pierce
5. Grant
6. Fillmore
7. A. Johnson
8. Coolidge
9. Tyler
10. Carter (10th worst)

Lincoln broke all kinds of laws and violated the Constitution to keep the nation together in its darkest hour—the Civil War. Had he not succeeded he would undoubtedly be ranked with Harding at the bottom of the heap.

And just who was Harding? In 1923 he said "This is a hell of a job! I have no trouble with my enemies. I can take care of my enemies all right. But my damn friends, my God-damned friends . . . they're the ones who keep me walking the floor nights." Indeed, it *was* Harding's friends who got him into trouble. He was elected in a landslide victory in 1920 not so much because of his popularity, but because of public backlash against World War I and Woodrow Wilson's League of Nations fiasco. When he came to Washington, he brought with him "friends" more bent on enriching themselves than on public service. They found abundant opportunities for corruption, including the sale of alien properties in the aftermath of World War I, the sale of U.S. ships, the enforcement of Prohibition after 1921, outlays for the care of veterans, and the management of oil-rich lands. Eventually numerous scandals surfaced during Harding's administration. The head of the Veteran's Bureau was forced to resign and was ultimately jailed for corruption. Other scandals were emerging when Harding suddenly died in 1923.

*Arthur Murphy, "Evaluating the Presidents of the United States," *Presidential Studies Quarterly* 14 (1984), pp. 117–126.

7. A president must always act as an expert even if he is not. The public looks to their president to know a lot about all important issues.

8. Popularity and prestige are pluses for any president. Conversely, public disapproval encourages the resistance of the Washington community to his programs.

9. Because presidential power is so difficult to attain, a president must always remain mindful of the need for multiple channels of information, the importance of persuasion in bargaining situations, and the art of the deal. Confrontational demands should be avoided at all costs.

President Ronald Reagan was often praised for controlling the media's representation of the White House.

Truly effective presidents have the ability and power to persuade not only what Neustadt calls Washingtonians[30]—a group that includes members of Congress, interest-group leaders, and media moguls—but also the general public.

FDR and LBJ both had excellent reputations among law makers for being able to get their legislative packages through Congress. Presidents Kennedy and Carter had more mixed successes, whereas Richard Nixon believed (wrongly) that the power of his office was enough to get recalcitrant legislators to support his programs. He failed to grasp the importance of the need to persuade members of Congress personally of the soundness of legislation he sought.

The recognition of and ability to persuade the public are also key elements of a successful presidency. Even before the days of FDR's personal presidency, others reached out to gain public support for their programs. Theodore Roosevelt (1901–09) referred to the presidency as a "bully pulpit" that he used to try to garner support for progressive programs. Woodrow Wilson took a whistle-stop train tour around the country to try (in vain) to build support for the League of Nations. It wasn't until the development of commercial air travel and television that presidents were able to communicate directly with the people.

Harry S Truman was the first president to address the nation on television, although neither he nor Eisenhower, his successor, used that medium to any degree. By the 1960s, television and jet transportation were no longer novel. John F. Kennedy, the first real "media darling," made even his press conferences media events as he used his good looks and quick sense of humor to his advantage to drum up public support for his programs.

Political scientist Sam Kernell refers to these kinds of direct, presidential appeals to the electorate as "going public."[31] Going public, in essence, often means that a president will go over the heads of members of Congress to gain support from the people, who, in turn, can place pressure on other elected officials in Washington.

Presidents Carter and Reagan—both Washington outsiders—used direct appeals to the public with widely different degrees of success. Jimmy Carter often went on TV to gain support for his policies, but his low-key, "toned down," and "de-pomped styles" failed to stir television audiences.[32] None of his efforts was nearly so successful as those of Ronald Reagan, who earned the nickname that says it all: "the Great Communicator." Reagan, a former actor, understood the use of television as a medium from the beginning. In a 1981 television address explaining and drumming up support for his proposed tax cuts, he exhorted the public "to put aside any feeling of frustration . . . about our political institutions . . . [and] contact your senators and congressmen."[33] According to Kernell, the public's reaction was "swift and overwhelming."[34] Democrats, especially those from the South, joined with Republicans to enact the tax cuts.

Public Opinion and Presidential Popularity

Most presidents do all that they can to woo public opinion, and certain "cycles" of popularity have occurred since 1938, when pollsters first began to track presidential popularity. As revealed in Figure 7-1, until the presidency of George Bush, the general trend has been increasingly lower rates of support for presidents, even Ronald Reagan. Many credit this trend to events such as Vietnam, Watergate, the Iran hostage crisis, and the Iran-*Contra* scandal, which have made the public increasingly skeptical of presiden-

[30] Neustadt, p. 44.

[31] Sam Kernell, *Going Public: New Strategies of Presidential Leadership* (Washington: CQ Press, 1986).

[32] Neustadt, p. 235.

[33] Quoted in Kernell, p. 120.

[34] Ibid.

Figure 7-1   Presidential Approval Since 1938

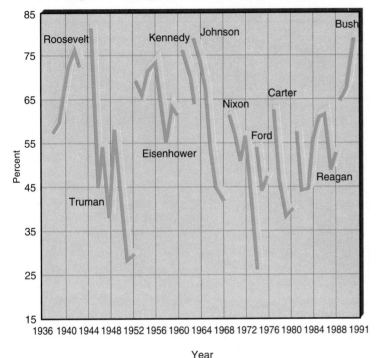

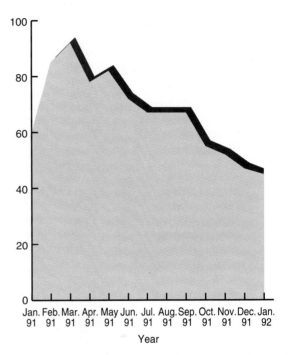

Source: Harold W. Stanley and Richard G. Niemi, *Vital Statistics on American Politics*, 3rd ed. (Washington D.C.: CQ Press, 1992), Figure 8–1, p. 279, from Gallup Poll data, 1938–1991.

Source: Gallup Poll data.

These graphs show the percent of people responding ''Approve'' to the question, ''Do you approve or disapprove of the way [incumbent president] is handling his job as president?''

tial performance. The sole exception to this pattern is George Bush, who was the first president in a long time to reclaim a ''pride in America'' sentiment, which occurred in the aftermath of the major and, perhaps more important, quick victory in the 1991 Persian Gulf war. Even Bush's popularity, however, plummeted as the good feelings from the Gulf war faded and Americans began to feel the pinch of recession.

Presidential popularity follows a cyclical pattern. Typically, presidents enjoy their highest level of popularity at the beginning of their terms. Presidents try to take advantage of this ''honeymoon'' period and work hard to get their programs passed by Congress as soon as possible. Each action a president takes, however, is divisive—some people will approve, and others will disapprove. And disapproval tends to have a cumulative effect. Inevitably the honeymoon ends about mid-way through the term.

Although surges caused by major international events do occur, they generally don't last long. As revealed in Table 7-2, each of the last ten presidents experienced at least one ''rallying'' point based on a foreign event. Rallies lasted an average of ten weeks, with the longest being seven months.[35]

[35] Michael R. Kagay, ''History Suggest Bush's Popularity Will Ebb,'' *The New York Times,* May 22, 1991, p. A-10.

Table 7-2   Temporary Rises in Popularity

Gallup poll measurements of the size and duration of the largest increase in each president's approval rating before and after dramatic international events.

	PERCENTAGE POINT INCREASE IN PUBLIC APPROVAL	DURATION OF THE INCREASE, IN WEEKS
Franklin D. Roosevelt Pearl Harbor	12	30
Harry S Truman Truman Doctrine	12	N.A.[a]
South Korea invaded	9	10
Dwight D. Eisenhower Bermuda conference/ Atoms for peace speech	10	20
John F. Kennedy Cuban missile crisis	13	31
Lyndon B. Johnson Speech halting bombing of North Vietnam and withdrawing from 1968 campaign	14	19
Richard M. Nixon Vietnam peace agreement	16	15
Gerald R. Ford Mayaguez incident	11	25
Jimmy Carter Hostages seized in Iran	19	30
Ronald Reagan Beirut bombing/Grenada invasion	8	N.A.[b]
First summit with Gorbachev	7	4
George Bush Iraqi invasion of Kuwait	14	9
Gulf war begins	18	30

[a]No polls conducted
[b]Overlapping events

Source: The New York Times, May 22, 1991, p. A-10. Information from the Gallup Organization.

A president's overall approval rating may allow him to make some unpopular policy decisions. George Bush's unprecedented sustained popularity until mid-1991 occurred in spite of the fact that voters had given him low marks for his handling of the economy, education, and health care, as indicated in Table 7-3. No other presidents, however, were so lucky. Even Ronald Reagan, whom many called the "Teflon president" because criticisms seemed to roll off him, suffered a beating in public opinion polls as unemployment rates rose in his first term and the Iran-*Contra* hearings proceeded in his second.

Two Presidencies

Even when George Bush enjoyed phenomenally high popularity ratings, most Americans were unhappy with his domestic policies. So was the Democratically controlled Congress. Presidents generally enjoy far more congressional support for their conduct of foreign affairs than their handling of domestic and economic matters. Political scientist Aaron

Table 7-3   Public Approval of George Bush's Handling of Specific Issues, November 1989

Although Bush's overall approval rating in November, 1989 was 70 percent, he received low marks for his handling of domestic issues.

"[Do] you approve or disapprove of the way President Bush is handling _____?"

	APPROVE	DISAPPROVE
Federal budget deficit	32%	53%
Poverty and homelessness	30	59
Economic conditions	40	51
The drug problem	53	41
Environmental issues	46	40
Abortion issue	38	45
Education policy	53	35
Foreign policy	65	21
The situation in Eastern Europe	63	16
Relations with the Soviet Union	81	11
The situation in Central America	40	39

Source: George C. Edwards, "George Bush and the Public Presidency: The Politics of Inclusion," in Colin Campbell, S. J., and Bert A. Rockman, eds., *The Bush Presidency: First Appraisals* (Chatham, N.J.: Chatham House, 1991), p. 136. Information from Gallup poll, 9–12 November 1989.

Wildavsky concludes that America really has **two presidencies**—a strong leader in foreign affairs, and a weak one on the domestic side.[36] For example, even though the congressional vote to authorize the president to use force in the Persian Gulf was close and along partisan lines, once the president was given authorization, the often partisan Congress was united in its support of the president. In contrast, there appears to be little agreement concerning the measures to be taken to improve the economy.

The Presidential Establishment

As the responsibilities and scope of presidential authority have grown over the years, so has the executive branch of government. No longer is the executive branch the small group of men who gathered around George Washington's dining room on Cherry Street in Philadelphia before they went to New York City. Today a president is surrounded by advisers of all types—from the Attorney General to advise him on legal issues to the Surgeon General to advise him on health matters. His personal staff, the vice president, and the Cabinet all help him fulfill his duties as chief executive.

The Cabinet

Although the Founders had discussed the idea of some form of national executive council, they did not include a provision for one in the Constitution. They did, however, recognize the need for departments of government and departmental heads.

[36] Aaron B. Wildavsky, "The Two Presidencies," *Transaction,* December, 1966, pp. 7–14.

D.C.—Still a Man's Town

Washington, D.C. is still considered a man's town, and the White House is no different. During his first two years in office, George Bush named 185 women to full-time presidential appointments—19.4 percent of all of his appointments—compared with 101 for Jimmy Carter and 105 for Ronald Reagan.

Still, Bush's inner circle had what one staffer calls "a male prep school, locker room atmosphere." Of the fifteen officials on the White House senior staff with the top rank of assistant to the president, only one was a woman—Secretary of the Cabinet Edith E. Holiday. Of the twenty deputy assistants, seven were women who worked in intergovernmental affairs, public liaison, personnel, and scheduling—traditionally female positions.

Then and Now

A Tale of Two Georges

On April 30, 1789, thirteen guns sounded in New York City to signal the beginning of the inaugural day of the first president of the United States, George Washington. Around noon, a delegation from Congress arrived to escort Washington, who greeted them in powdered hair, a brown suit, and silk stockings. They went in a carriage drawn by four horses amidst a cheering crowd to the steps of Federal Hall in New York City. After his swearing in, Washington went to church to offer up a prayer and then went home for dinner.

During Washington's administration, a string of measures were pushed through Congress to make the new nation stronger. A national currency was instituted, the Bank of the United States was established, manufacturing and trade were fostered by tariffs and bounties, and inventions were protected by patent and copyright laws. While the United States reorganized the armed forces and built new fortifications in the East and West, national security was preserved by a neutrality proclamation in regard to an ever-widening European war between France and Great Britain.

Unlike some presidents to follow him, Washington reveled in the dignity of the office. He rode in a carriage drawn by six cream-colored horses or alone on a white steed with a saddle trimmed in gold. His house had fourteen white servants and seven slaves to help with elaborate dinners. And, as it had been celebrated since the Revolutionary War, his birthday was a day of celebration in many towns across the new nation. "Even Cincinnatus received no adulations of this kind," the *National Gazette* observed. "Surely the office [the President] enjoys is a sufficient testimony of the people's favor, without worshipping him likewise."

Washington's appreciation of regality was also evident in his tours through the new nation. From October to November 1789, he traveled through New England in a hired coach accompanied by his aide, his private secretary, six servants, nine horses, and a luggage wagon.

During Washington's tenure, the entire U.S. national budget for 8 years was about $40 million, or approximately $10 for each U.S. citizen. Most people were farmers; only 3 percent lived in cities.

The nation of Geoge Bush in January 1989 was quite different, as was the man. George Bush delivered his inaugural address amidst exceptionally tight security. He went back to the White House with its large professional staff, which includes even an expert chef. The house where the president resides today is not only surrounded by a tall iron fence, it is fortified with brick barriers on Pennsylvania Avenue.

George Bush was a more informal man than the first George who served as president. Like Washington, however, he enjoyed traveling and spent a considerable amount of time away from Washington. Both Georges were wealthy and enjoyed large inherited homes—for Washington, Mt. Vernon; for Bush, a large estate in Kennebunkport, Maine. Unlike Washington, however, Bush served only one term.

Consequently, although there is no provision for a cabinet in the Constitution per se, Article II, Section 2, states that the president *"may require the Opinion, in writing, of the Principal Officer in each of the executive Departments, upon any Subject relating to the Duties of their respective Offices. . . ."*

Just prior to and immediately after Washington's inauguration in New York City on April 30, 1789, he consulted with Hamilton, Madison, and others concerning their views of the powers and duties of the president. Collectively they adopted the position that department heads should be assistants to the president, rather than to Congress. These sentiments led Washington to ask Congress to create three executive departments—one for foreign affairs (State), one for military affairs (War, which was incorporated into the Defense Department in 1947), and one for fiscal matters (Treasury). He viewed these advisers as a council of sorts and frequently called them together. He also established the tradition that Cabinet members were to be loyal to the president. After his Secretary of State disagreed with Washington's support of the Jay Treaty, he fired him.

Over the years the Cabinet has grown as departments have been added, in large part because of social changes in the nation. As interest groups pressured Congress and the president to recognize their demands, they often were rewarded by the creation of an executive department headed by a secretary. As a member of the president's Cabinet, the secretary was assumed to have regular access to him.

Today the Cabinet is composed of thirteen secretaries and the Attorney General:

- The Department of State (1789): responsible for the making of foreign policy, including treaty negotiation
- The Department of the Treasury (1789): responsible for government funds
- The Department of Defense (1789; 1947): created by consolidating the former Departments of War, the Army, the Navy, and the Air Force
- The Department of Justice (1870; head is the Attorney General): the government's attorney
- The Department of the Interior (1849): manages the nation's natural resources, including wildlife and public lands
- The Department of Agriculture (1862): administers farm and food stamp programs and aids farmers
- The Department of Commerce (1903): aids businesses and conducts the U.S. census (originally the Department of Commerce and Labor)
- The Department of Labor (1913): runs manpower programs and aids labor in various ways
- The Department of Health and Human Services (1953): runs health, welfare, and Social Security programs; created as the Department of Health, Education, and Welfare (lost its education function in 1979)
- The Department of Housing and Urban Development (1965): responsible for urban and housing programs
- The Department of Transportation (1966): responsible for mass transportation and highway programs
- The Department of Energy (1977): responsible for energy policy and research, including atomic energy
- The Department of Education (1979): responsible for the federal government's education programs
- The Department of Veterans Affairs (1989): responsible for programs aiding veterans
- (The vice president, the U.S. Trade Representative, and the Director of the Office of Management and Budget also were considered part of the Bush Cabinet.)

Secretary of State James A. Baker III, right, is greeted by Israel's then–Foreign Minister David Levy, center, upon arriving in Tel Aviv in March, 1991, to pursue the possibility of Middle East peace talks.

From the beginning, Cabinet secretaries have found themselves in the curious position of having two masters. They serve the president and must report to Congress on the activities of their respective departments. The inevitable clash between these two roles first surfaced in 1833. Disliking the National Bank, Andrew Jackson ordered his Secretary of the Treasury to transfer federal funds to another bank. The secretary believed the National Bank to be sound, and Congress had recently voiced its support of the bank by way of a resolution to that effect. Accordingly, the secretary refused to comply with Jackson's direct order, whereupon he was promptly removed.

Instances like this are not uncommon. Although individual members of the Cabinet may be very close to the president—John Kennedy's Attorney General was his brother Robert, and George Bush's Secretary of State, James Baker, was a longtime friend—more often than not Cabinets today as a body have little influence on the president. Kennedy, for example, was almost openly scornful of the institution. During the Cuban Missile Crisis, he not only ignored the Cabinet (rarely holding meetings) but also enlarged the

National Security Council (see Chapter 18) and directed policy through an ad hoc "executive" committee made up of officials in whom he had special confidence.[37] Distrust of his Cabinet and of the agendas of several of its members led President Carter to fire four of his Cabinet secretaries on the advice of his White House staffers. Several staffers had scores to settle with all four, and the staffers' ability to "roll" them—Washington talk for "overturning them, toppling them, bringing them down, as a wrestler or street mugger might"—reflects the power of those in the Executive Office of the President.

Although it bears the same name, the British Cabinet is quite distinct from its American counterpart. There are some similarities: for example, Cabinet officials in both countries are appointed by their respective chief executives and provide political guidance to the bureaucracy. However, British Cabinet ministers hail exclusively from the legislature (indeed, they retain their seats in Parliament while they serve as executive officers), and they participate in a collective executive decision-making body—the Cabinet—for which there is no counterpart in the United States. As a result, although the prime minister is clearly "first among equals" in the Cabinet, the decisions of the British government are issued formally in the name of the Cabinet, not the prime minister.

The Executive Office of the President

The **Executive Office of the President** (EOP) is actually several offices, a "mini-bureaucracy" located in the ornate Executive Office Building located next to the White House on Pennsylvania Avenue. FDR established the EOP in 1939 because his New Deal programs needed oversight. The EOP has expanded over time to include eight advisory and policy-making agencies responsible to the executive branch. Three of the most important include the National Security Council, the Council of Economic Advisors, and the Office of Management and Budget.

The National Security Council (NSC) was established in 1947 in order to advise the president on American military and foreign policies. The NSC is composed of the president, the vice president, and the Secretaries of State and Defense. The president's special assistant for security affairs runs the staff of the NSC, coordinates information and options, and advises the president.

The Council of Economic Advisors (CEA) consists of three economic experts appointed by the president. The CEA prepares the *Annual Report of the Council of Economic Advisors* and advises the president on economic policy. Through constant analysis of the economy and economic trends, the CEA attempts to anticipate rather than react to economic events.

The Office of Management and Budget (OMB) was created in 1970 as a replacement for the Bureau of the Budget (created in 1921). The OMB has the responsibility for preparing the president's budget proposal, designing the president's program, and reviewing the progress, budget, and program proposals of the executive department agencies.

Although the president appoints the members of each of these bodies, they, too, still must perform their tasks in accordance with congressional legislation. Thus, like the Cabinet, depending on who serves in key positions, these mini-agencies may not be truly responsible to the president.

White House Staff

George Washington's closest confidants were Alexander Hamilton and Thomas Jefferson—both Cabinet secretaries—but that has rarely been the case with modern presidents. As the size and complexity of the government grew, Cabinet secretaries presided over their own ever-burgeoning staffs, and presidents increasingly looked to a different inner circle

[37] Reedy, p. 77.

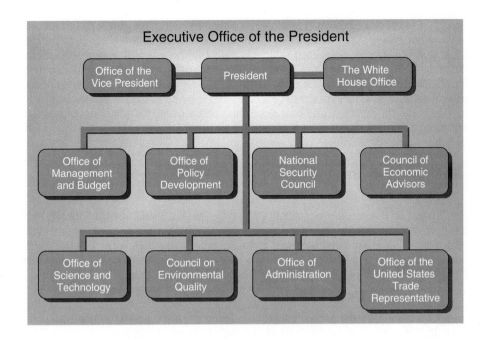

Executive Office of the President

- Office of the Vice President
- President
- The White House Office

- Office of Management and Budget
- Office of Policy Development
- National Security Council
- Council of Economic Advisors

- Office of Science and Technology
- Council on Environmental Quality
- Office of Administration
- Office of the United States Trade Representative

of informal advisers. By the 1830s Andrew Jackson had chosen to rely on his own inner circle, nicknamed his "Kitchen Cabinet," instead of his department heads to advise him. So too, FDR surrounded himself with New York political operatives and his more intellectual "brain trust"; Jimmy Carter brought several Georgians to the White House with him; and Ronald Reagan initially surrounded himself with fellow Californians—Edwin Meese III, William French Smith (the Attorney General), and Michael Deaver.

These aides are as diverse as their duties, and loyalty is often their strong suit. Richard Nixon's first chief of staff, H. R. Haldeman, for example, believed it was his role to "take the heat" for any presidential gaffes. According to him, "Every president needs a son of a bitch and I'm Nixon's. I get what he wants done and I take the heat instead of him."[38] This loyalty led President Nixon to consider Haldeman his alter ego.

Although each president organizes his staff in different ways, presidents typically have a chief of staff. John Sununu, the former governor of New Hampshire whom George Bush credited with his key primary victory there in 1988, was his first chief of staff. Although close aide James Baker urged Bush to adopt a triumvirate style, Bush made Sununu a strong chief of staff who organized the rest of his staff on hierarchical lines. In late 1991, John Sununu was forced to resign in the wake of a series of public relations disasters. Bush quickly replaced him with Transportation Secretary Samuel K. Skinner. "You want a chief of staff who will be a bit of a lightning rod who will deflect attention from the president" on sensitive and negative issues, reflected Stuart E. Eizenstadt, Jimmy Carter's assistant for domestic policy. "The tough call is when so much lightning gets stored up in the rod that it creates an energy field around which people are uncomfortable."[39]

In addition to a chief of staff, presidents typically have a national security adviser to provide them with daily briefings on international affairs. During the Persian Gulf war, National Security Adviser Brent Scowcroft played an important role in advising President Bush. Other key staffers include those who help plan domestic policy, maintain relations with Congress and interest groups, deal with the media, provide economic expertise, and

[38] Quoted in Page and Petracca, p. 169.
[39] Quoted in James Gertzenzang and Jack Nelson, "Sununu's Future as Bush's Top Aide Being Questioned," *Los Angeles Times,* November 13, 1990, p. A-1.

George Bush with new Chief of Staff Samuel Skinner, winter 1991.

execute political strategies. As the demands on the president have grown so has the size of the White House staff—from 51 in 1943, to 247 in 1953, to a high of 583 in 1972. Since that time, staffs have been trimmed, generally running in the near 400-person range. In 1991 the Bush White House had 397 employees. White House office space is limited, so many staffers are relegated to the old Executive Office Building next door. In spite of small offices, most prefer to be located in the White House. In Washington, who has the ear of the president and how close one's office is to his is a measure of power—not the size of the office itself.

Toward Reform

The presidency is a peculiar institution. Only forty men have held the position, and each has been different in style and temperament. Some have been smart, some not too intelligent. Others have appeared to thrive in office; others have labored under the strain. Several have broken laws for different reasons and to very different fates. Lincoln earned a place in history as one of the greats; Richard Nixon resigned to avoid impeachment.

Over the years various reforms have been proposed to "improve" the presidency, but the consensus appears to be that as an institution it works fairly well. Most serious calls for reform have not been concerned with the Framers' chief fear—a too-powerful president. Instead they have centered on giving the president greater power.

The Two-Term Limitation

Ever since passage of the Twenty-second Amendment, some have argued against the two-term limit, believing it, too, to be "undemocratic." After all, if a president is enjoying the support of the people and doing a good job, why shouldn't he be allowed to seek a third or fourth term? Early in the second terms of Richard Nixon and Ronald Reagan, some of their supporters launched trial balloons concerning third terms, but to little avail.

Although it is likely that calls for change in the office, election procedures, and term of office will continue, change is highly unlikely as long as the system continues to work with some degree of effectiveness.

The Line-Item Veto

George Bush, like several other presidents, often used the veto power, as well as threat of its use, an exceptionally powerful tool in convincing Congress to adopt programs more to his liking. Although none of his twenty-two vetoes through March 1992 were overridden, he continued to call for a line-item veto. Line-item vetoes, a power enjoyed by many governors, allows a chief executive to disprove of particular items in a legislative-passed budget instead of vetoing the entire legislative proposal. Picking up on calls made earlier by President Ronald Reagan, Bush supporters in the Senate introduced legislation that would give the president the authority to kill spending measures he dislikes. Senator Robert C. Byrd (D.-W. Va.), in fact, made an eight-hour impassioned speech likening the Republican's line-item veto proposal to "quack medicine better regarded as snake oil."[40] Republican sponsors, who were not surprised by the fifty-four to forty-four vote against the measure, said they had introduced the measure not only to give the president what he wants, but also to prod the president into an election-year confrontation with Democrats over pork barrel spending often used to enrich the districts of particular Democratic legislators. A line-item veto would allow a president to do away with more outrageous examples of "pork," or what a president might see as needless fat in the budget.

[40] "Senate Rejects Giving Bush Line-Item Veto," *The New York Times,* February 28, 1992, p. A-6.

While Bill Clinton also supports the line-item veto, the Senate vote, and the more likely need for a constitutional amendment authorizing this change, makes its adoption unlikely. Like the abolition of the two-term limitation, most Americans seem leery of making any major changes to the power of the presidency.

Summary

The Founders feared a tyrannical monarch. Therefore, after a considerable amount of deliberation and discussion, they created the office of chief executive. They wanted to fashion an office that could balance the need to have one individual speak on behalf of the nation, but they didn't want to give him tyrannical powers. Over the years the power of the president has expanded tremendously. Individual presidents have used their personal skills to bolster specific authorities found in the Constitution to make the presidency an office of every-growing power—especially in times of crises and in foreign affairs.

Most presidents begin their terms with the confidence and approval of most Americans. With the sole exception of George Bush, however, their honeymoons don't last long. Scandals, the economy, and conflicts with Congress all quickly take their toll on presidential popularity and with it the ability to get legislative programs enacted.

To get his programs enacted, the president often draws on the help and expertise of Cabinet secretaries, members of the Executive Office of the President, and White House staffers. Each has different roles to play, with White House staffers often exercising enormous influence. The existence of all of these aides has increased the tendency of the president to initiate legislation, although his successes on "the Hill," especially in domestic affairs, still remains marginal.

Key Terms

articles of impeachment	executive agreement	presidential character
Watergate	inherent powers	two presidencies
veto	patronage	Executive Office of the President
pardon	presidential style	

Selected Readings

Campbell, Colin, S. J., and Bert Rockman. *The Bush Presidency: First Appraisals.* Chatham, N.J.: Chatham House, 1991.

Corwin, Edwin S. *The Presidential Office and Powers,* 4th ed. New York: New York University Press, 1957.

Cronin, Thomas. *The State of the Presidency.* Boston: Little, Brown, 1975.

Edwards, George C., III. *At the Margins.* New Haven, Conn.: Yale University Press, 1989.

George, Alexander L. *Presidential Decisionmaking in Foreign Policy.* Boulder, Colo.: Westview Press, 1980.

Kellerman, Barbara. *The Political Presidency.* New York: Oxford University Press, 1984.

Neustadt, Richard. *Presidential Power,* revised ed. New York: Wiley, 1980.

Page, Benjamin I., and Mark P. Petracca, *The American Presidency.* New York: McGraw-Hill, 1983.

Reedy, George E. *The Twilight of the Presidency.* New York: New American Library, 1970.

Tulis, Jeffrey K. *The Rhetorical Presidency.* Princeton, N.J.: Princeton University Press, 1987.

Watson, Richard A., and Norman C. Thomas. *The Politics of the Presidency,* 2nd ed. Washington: CQ Press, 1988.

The true test of a good government is its aptitude and tendency to produce a good administration.

Alexander Hamilton

FEDERALIST NO. 86

Hamilton believed that the separation of powers to appoint and confirm key members of the bureaucracy (appointment by the president, confirmation by the Senate) would ensure against poor selections.

CHAPTER 8

The Bureaucracy

Alexander Hamilton could not have envisioned that the power of the president to appoint "a good administration" would ultimately result in an executive branch that numbered over 3 million workers in 1991. This enormous arm of the executive branch, which makes up a large part of the **bureaucracy,** assists the president in carrying out his constitutionally mandated charge to enforce the laws of the nation. As the bureaucracy has grown, some have come to refer to it as the "fourth branch" of government. Without the bureaucracy, government as we know it would come to a grinding halt. The military could not function, social service programs would cease, and all air traffic would be grounded. These examples are but a small fraction of the workings of the bureaucracy. Harold D. Lasswell once defined political science as the "study of who gets what, when, where and how."[1] It is in the study of the bureaucracy that those questions can perhaps best be answered.

Even though the bureaucracy performs many tasks that we have come to take for granted, attacking the bureaucracy often appears to be a national pastime. Candidates for public office constantly criticize the bureaucracy and speak about it as though it were a foreign power to be conquered. Said President Jimmy Carter, "Our government . . . is a horrible bureaucratic mess. It is disorganized, wasteful, has no purpose and its policies are incomprehensible or devised by special interest groups with little regard for the welfare of the average citizen." Members of Congress even joke that there is a game called "Bureaucracy" in which "There is only one rule. The first one to move loses." Even *Roget's Thesaurus* equates the term "bureaucracy" with officialism and red tape.

The bureaucracy is harshly criticized elsewhere, too. The British civil service has been accused at various times of being distant and imperious, inefficient, inexpert, and even responsible for the country's poor economic performance in the postwar period.

This chapter traces the growth of the bureaucracy and examines how it is organized, how it interacts with the three branches of government, how it implements policy, and what role it plays in our national system of government.

As you read the pages that follow, you will see why many people, including presidents, have criticized the bureaucracy. We hope, however, that you will also see that the bureaucracy has in many respects grown to meet the needs of a growing nation and the rising expectations and demands of the American public.

What Is the Bureaucracy?

Bureaucracy is actually a term used to refer to any large, complex organization in which employees have specified responsibilities and work within a hierarchy of authority. The word *bureau* initially referred to the cloth covering of desks or writing tables used by seventeenth-century French government officials. Later, in the eighteenth century, the term "bureau" was coupled with the suffix *-cracy,* which long had been used to signify rule of government (as in *aristocracy, democracy,* or *theocracy*). In Britain, the bureaucracy is commonly referred to as the civil service or *Whitehall,* the name of the building in London that houses many government ministries. In looking at our government, when we refer to the bureaucracy and **bureaucrats**—employees of particular governmental agencies or units who possess expertise in certain issue areas—we mean the various departments, agencies, bureaus, offices, and other government units that administer our nation's laws and policies. In effect, the bureaucracy converts the intentions of elected officials and appointed judges into policies.

In many ways, the American bureaucracy is distinctive because political authority over the bureaucracy is not in a single set of hands but is instead shared by many

[1] Harold D. Lasswell, *Politics: Who Gets What, When, and How* (New York: McGraw-Hill, 1938).

institutions. Although it was the president who could remove officials from their positions in the new executive branch, it has always been questionable how much authority the chief executive actually exercises over that branch. Because of the system of checks and balances created by the Framers, Congress authorizes the creation of departments, funds them, and passes the laws that the agencies are to implement. Therefore, it is unclear with whom bureaucratic loyalty lies.

In Great Britain today, bureaucrats take orders from the ministers in charge of their departments but are not directly accountable to the Parliament. In the United States, the bureaucracy can be thought of as the arm of the government that links the three branches of the national government and the federal system together. The Congress makes the laws, but it must rely on the executive branch of government and the bureaucracy to enforce them. So, for example, when Congress enacted the Civil Rights Act of 1964 to eliminate discrimination in employment, it created the Equal Employment Opportunity Commission (EEOC) to enforce its provisions. The head of EEOC is appointed by the president with the advice and consent of the Senate. The EEOC often reflects the political views of the chief executive. During the Lyndon B. Johnson presidency, for example, the EEOC was generally given high marks for its handling of claims of racial discrimination[2]; in contrast, the Reagan and Bush administrations have been accused of lax enforcement and being reluctant to issue forceful rules to prevent or discourage discrimination.

Commissions like the EEOC have the power not only to make rules but also to settle disputes between parties concerning the enforcement and implementation of those rules. More often than not, however, those agency determinations end up being challenged in the courts. Almost every type of agency decision has the likelihood of ending up in court. Yet because most administrative agencies that make up part of the bureaucracy enjoy reputations for special expertise in clearly defined policy areas, the judiciary routinely defers to administrative decision makers.

The bureaucracy facilitates interactions within the federal system. While many bureaucratic agencies act directly on the people—the Internal Revenue Service collects taxes directly from individuals, and the Postal Service delivers mail to your door—other bureaucratic agencies interact routinely with state and local governments and act as key players in the continuing definition and redefinition of federalism. For example, federal "grants-in-aid" for programs to deal with poverty and disability are supervised by the Social Security Administration, a division of the Department of Health and Human Services, which sets up guidelines for eligibility, distributes money to the states, and oversees the implementation of the various state programs.

Is Bureaucracy a Dirty Word?

The bureaucracy's reach, its hierarchical structure, and the fact that it is monitored by all three branches of government often make it difficult for the executive branch to exert control over the bureaucracy. Although Harry S Truman as president once displayed on his desk a placard proclaiming, "The buck stops here," these days the president may not even know where the buck *is,* much less where it has stopped! The development of the bureaucracy has made it hard for the president to know exactly what is going on or if his direct orders are being followed.

Americans dislike the bureaucracy for a variety of reasons. Conservatives charge that the bureaucracy is too liberal and that its functions constitute unnecessary government meddling in our lives. They argue that the bureaucracy is too large, too powerful, and too unaccountable to the people or to elected officials. In contrast, liberals view the

---

[2] Women's groups, however, founded the National Organization for Women out of their frustration with the EEOC's failure to consider complaints of sexual discrimination. See Jo Freeman, *The Politics of Women's Liberation* (New York: Longman, 1975).

Government has been accused of red tape problems for many years. In this 1897 cartoon, President McKinley is shown having difficulty driving Congress toward prosperity because of the red tape of congressional conflict.

UNPLEASANT PLIGHT OF THE "ADVANCE AGENT OF PROSPERITY."

bureaucracy as too slow, too unimaginative to solve America's problems, and too zealous a guardian of the status quo. Whether conservative, liberal, or moderate, most Americans think that the bureaucracy works poorly and is too wasteful. Tales of governmental payments for $640 toilet seats and $7,622 coffee makers don't help the public's image of the bureaucracy.

Roots of the Bureaucratic System

Over the years, the bureaucracy has grown because Congress and the president have agreed on the need for new agencies to assist them in lawmaking and law-enforcing. Wars, national emergencies, and changes in demographics, technology, and public expectations are just some of the reasons for that growth. Of the bureaucracy President Gerald Ford once wrote, "One of the enduring truths of the nation's capital is that bureaucrats survive. Agencies don't fold their tents and quietly fade away after their work is done. They find Something New to Do. Invariably, that Something New involves more people with more power and more paperwork—all involving more expenditures."[3] Thus, as over the years new demands for governmental services have been created and new agencies established, the total size of the bureaucracy has grown enormously.

[3] Gerald R. Ford, *A Time to Heal: The Autobiography of Gerald R. Ford* (New York: Harper and Row, 1979), p. 272.

The Early Years

Just as the legislative, executive, and judicial branches started out modestly, so did the bureaucracy (or federal service, as some preferred to refer to it). The presidency of George Washington was quite uncomplicated, and so too was the administration that was hired to support him.

At the core of the origins of the bureaucracy was the first Cabinet. While the Constitution does not mention the Cabinet, Article II does note that the President *"may require the Opinion, in writing, of the principal Officer in each of the executive Departments, upon any Subject relating to the Duties of their respective Offices."* George Washington's executive branch consisted of three departments that were holdovers from those already established under the Articles of Confederation: State (called Foreign Affairs under the Articles), War, and Treasury. The head of each department was to be called the *secretary.* Since the president often would need legal advice, the Congress created an office of Attorney General. The Attorney General was considered a Cabinet member from the start, although he did not become head of a department—the Justice Department—until after the Civil War. Individuals appointed to positions within each department were to be subject to approval by the U.S. Senate but were "removable by the president" alone. Even the first Congress realized how important it was for a president to be surrounded by those in whom he had complete confidence and trust.

Differing views of the role of the national government, and of the executive branch in particular, were apparent right away in the differing styles of the first Cabinet secretaries. The State Department, headed by Thomas Jefferson, had but nine employees. Jefferson, always the opponent of big national government, saw no need for additional staff members. In contrast, Secretary of the Treasury Alexander Hamilton perceived himself to head the most critical new department. He was charged with collecting taxes, issuing money, and printing postage stamps, all key governmental responsibilities crucial to the survival of the new nation. Therefore, he sought a large staff whose views of the importance of the department and its role in forging an economically stable nation were consistent with his. Hamilton's belief in the need for a strong national government and a strong national economy set the stage for later national government intervention in the economy.

From 1816 to 1861, the size of the federal bureaucracy grew dramatically, increasing eight times over. Much of this growth was directly attributable to increased demands on existing departments such as the Post Office (as the Postal Service was then called), which was forced to expand to meet the needs of a growing and westward-expanding population. The Post Office, in fact, was removed from the jurisdiction of the Treasury Department in 1829 by Andrew Jackson. Recognizing the tremendous potential increases in the demands on the Post Office, Jackson promoted the Postmaster General to Cabinet-level rank, thereby giving him greater control over the office and its immense number of positions.

The Post Office Department was not the only new department created during this period. On his last day in office, President James K. Polk (1845–49) signed into law a bill creating the Department of the Interior. He recognized the need not only for a department to be in charge of the millions of new acres the United States had acquired but also for a governmental agency to deal with the Native Americans who lived on the land. The new department was given responsibility for supervising the use of natural resources on those lands, issuing patents on new inventions, and conducting the census every ten years (a task initially performed by the Treasury Department and later the Department of Commerce).

The Civil War and Its Aftermath

The Civil War (1861–65) inalterably changed the nature of the federal bureaucracy. As the nation geared up for war, thousands of additional employees were added to existing departments. The Civil War also spawned the need for new governmental agencies. A

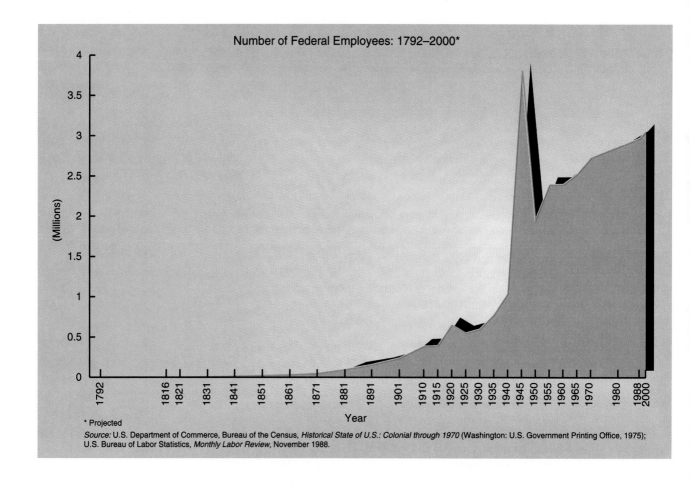

Number of Federal Employees: 1792–2000*

* Projected

Source: U.S. Department of Commerce, Bureau of the Census, *Historical State of U.S.: Colonial through 1970* (Washington: U.S. Government Printing Office, 1975); U.S. Bureau of Labor Statistics, *Monthly Labor Review*, November 1988.

series of poor harvests and marketing problems led President Abraham Lincoln, who understood that one needs food in order to conduct a war, to create the Department of Agriculture in 1862, although it was not given full Cabinet-level status until 1889.

After the Civil War, the need for big government continued unabated. In 1866 the Pension Office was established to pay benefits to the thousands of Northern veterans who had fought in the war (more than 127,000 men were initially eligible for benefits).

Other new departments were added through 1900. Agriculture became a full-fledged department and began to play an important role in informing farmers about the latest developments in soil conservation, livestock breeding, and planting techniques. The increase in the types and nature of government services provided resulted in a parallel rise in the number of federal jobs. And many of those jobs were used by the president or leaders of the president's political party for patronage, that is, jobs, grants, or other special favors given as rewards to friends and political allies for their support.

How to Become a Bureaucrat: From Spoils to Merit

The phrase spoils system was coined by a New York state senator in 1832 to legitimize the firing of public-office holders of the defeated political party and their replacement with loyalists of the newly elected party. "To the victor belongs the spoils" was a phrase frequently used to justify the practice of filling public job vacancies with friends. President Andrew Jackson, in particular, faced severe criticism for populating the federal government with his political cronies. But many presidents, including Jackson, argued that in order to best implement their policies, they had to be able to appoint those who subscribed to their political views.

By the time that James A. Garfield, a former distinguished officer in the Civil War, was elected president in 1880, many reformers were calling publicly for changes in the **civil service system,** that is, the system by which appointments to the federal bureaucracy are made. Upon his election to office, Garfield was besieged with office seekers. Washington, D.C., had not seen such a demand for political jobs since the election of Abraham Lincoln as the first president of the Republican Party. Garfield's immediate predecessor, Rutherford B. Hayes, had favored the idea of the replacement of the spoils system with a merit system based on test scores and ability. Congress, however, failed to pass the legislation he proposed. So, possibly because potential job seekers wanted to secure positions before Congress had the opportunity to act on an overhauled civil service system, thousands pressed Garfield for positions. This siege prompted Garfield to record in his diary:

> My day is frittered away with the personal seeking of people when it ought to be given to the great problems which concern the whole country.[4]

Although he resolved to reform the civil service, Garfield's life was cut short by the bullets of an assassin who, ironically, was a frustrated job seeker.

[4] Quoted in Robert G. Caldwell, *James A. Garfield* (Hamden, Conn.: Archon Books, 1965).

People of the Past

William Henry Harrison and Office Seekers

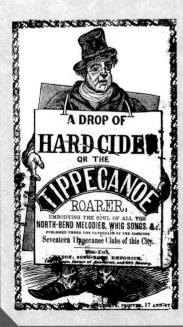

A DROP OF
HARD CIDER
OR THE
TIPPECANOE
ROARER,
EMBODYING THE SOUL OF ALL THE
NORTH-BEND MELODIES, WHIG SONGS, &c.
PUBLISHED UNDER THE PATRONAGE OF THE GLORIOUS
Seventeen Tippecanoe Clubs of this City.

Nominated by the Whig Party in 1839, William Henry Harrison was the "log cabin, hard cider" candidate in the presidential campaign of 1840. Although Harrison was the son of a wealthy Virginia planter, the Whig Party developed an image of Harrison as one who had risen to distinction through his own efforts while retaining the tastes of the ordinary citizen. Harrison went to college and then enlisted in the army where he was promoted to major general. Harrison was a hero in the Battle of Tippecanoe, thus earning the nickname "Tippecanoe" which became the catchy campaign slogan "Tippecanoe and Tyler too" when Harrison selected his running mate, John Tyler.

Harrison ran his campaign without a platform. The advice given to him by Whig leaders was to say nothing about principles or creed. Lots of silly campaign songs were composed and noisy conventions and rallies were held everywhere, but no campaign promises were made.

At his inaugural address on March 4, Harrison droned on for close to two hours. It was a cold and wintry day and Harrison did not wear gloves or an overcoat. Not surprisingly, he developed pneumonia later that month and died on April 4.

Repeatedly dunned by supporters seeking patronage jobs, Harrison's last words were: "I can't stand it . . . Don't trouble me . . . These applications, will they never cease . . . ?" Even on Harrison's deathbed, the problems of a growing bureaucracy continued to hound him.

An artist's representation of President Garfield's assassination. He was killed by an unhappy office seeker.

Public reaction to Garfield's death was a turning point in the evolution of the federal bureaucracy. In 1883 Congress passed the **Civil Service Reform Act of 1883,** more commonly known as the **Pendleton Act,** to reduce patronage. It created a bipartisan three-member Civil Service Commission, which operated until 1978. Under its provisions, about 15 percent of the positions in the federal civil service were classified into grades or levels to which appointments would be made on the basis of performance on competitive examinations. This was called the **merit system.** (In 1952, President Truman mandated that 93 percent of all jobs in the federal service be appointed under a merit system.) The Pendleton Act also made it illegal to fire a civil servant for failure to contribute to a political party or campaign.

The Growth of Regulation

As Congress attempted to reform the bureaucracy by appointing more career civil servants, concern with good government was at least in part responsible for the creation by Congress in 1887 of the first independent **regulatory commission.** The Interstate Commerce Commission (ICC) was created to control price fixing and other unfair practices of the nation's railroads and began the tradition of establishing regulatory commissions or agencies to eliminate or restrict actions or behaviors considered harmful. It also marked a shift in the focus of the bureaucracy from service to regulation. In the case of the ICC, Congress was reacting to public outcries over the exorbitant rates charged by railroad companies for hauling freight. Independent regulatory agencies such as the ICC are created by Congress to be independent of direct presidential authority. Members of these commissions, although appointed by the president, hold their jobs for fixed terms and are not removable by the president.

The 1900 election of Theodore Roosevelt, a progressive Republican, to the presidency strengthened the movement toward regulation and increased the size of the bureaucracy. Intolerable labor practices—including low wages, long hours, substandard working conditions, the refusal of employers to recognize the rights of workers to join a union, and the fact that so many businesses had grown so large and powerful that they could force workers to accept substandard conditions or not work at all—led Roosevelt to ask Congress to establish a joint Department of Commerce and Labor in 1903 to oversee employer–employee relations.

In 1913, President Woodrow Wilson created a separate Department of Labor because it was clear that one agency could not well represent the interests of two factions that had such decidedly different perspectives. The creation of this new department reflected the economic and societal changes that were occurring in the United States as immigration increased and the economy became increasingly industrialized. One year later, in 1914, Congress created the Federal Trade Commission (FTC) to protect small businesses and the public from unfair competition and the monopoly powers of big business.

Also affecting the size of government and the possibilities for growth was the ratification in 1913 of the Sixteenth Amendment to the Constitution. It gave Congress the authority to implement a federal income tax to supplement the national treasury, thus providing an infusion of funds to support new agencies, services, and governmental programs.

Laissez-faire **Attitudes.** During the early 1900s, while Progressives raised the public cry for regulation of business, many Americans, especially businessmen, continued to resist such moves. They believed that the role of the federal government was not to regulate but instead to facilitate the national economy through a commitment to *laissez-faire,* a French term literally meaning "to let do." In America in the early 1900s the term was used to describe a governmental hands-off policy concerning the economy. The courts, especially the U.S. Supreme Court, were at the forefront of the philosophical debate over how much power the national government had to regulate the private sector. In a series of key decisions made through 1937, the Supreme Court repeatedly invalidated key provisions in congressional legislation designed to regulate various aspects of the economy. The Court and others who subscribed to *laissez-faire* principles of a free enterprise system argued that natural economic laws at work in the marketplace control the buying and selling of goods. Thus, it was believed that the government had no right to step in to try to regulate business in any way.

The New Deal and the U.S. Supreme Court

In the wake of the high unemployment and weak financial markets of the Great Depression, Franklin Roosevelt's solution for economic revitalization included the creation of innumerable new government agencies to regulate business practices and various aspects of the economy. Although the Supreme Court stood adamantly opposed to increased regulation and bureaucratization, Roosevelt and the Congress advanced far-ranging economic legislation. The desperate mood of the nation supported these moves as most Americans began to change their idea of the proper role of government and governmental services. Formerly Americans believed in a hands-off approach; they now

Poor working conditions in the early 1900s: a sweatshop in New York.

believed that it was the government's job to get the economy going and get Americans back to work.

Within the first one hundred days of Roosevelt's administration, Congress approved every new regulatory measure proposed by the president. The first, the National Industrial Recovery Act (NIRA), was an unprecedented attempt to regulate industry. Congress next enacted the Agricultural Adjustment Act (AAA), which provided government support for farm prices and regulated production to ensure market-competitive prices. Soon thereafter Congress approved legislation reforming the Federal Reserve System, requiring the separation of investment and commercial banking in an effort to forestall further bank collapses. Congress also set up the Federal Deposit Insurance Corporation (FDIC) to insure bank deposits, and the Federal Securities Act gave the Federal Trade Commission the authority to supervise and regulate the issuance, buying, and selling of stocks and bonds. The NIRA and the AAA especially were unique governmental ventures into the private economy because they allowed tremendous bureaucratic discretion.

Until 1937, however, the Supreme Court refused to allow Congress or the president to delegate such far-ranging authority to regulate the economy to the bureaucracy, and at the same time it challenged Congress's authority to legislate in these areas. *Laissez-faire* was alive and well at the Court, and attempts to end the economic slump through greater governmental involvement were repeatedly stymied by the justices. In 1937, however, the Court became more in sync with public and elite opinion. In a series of cases discussed in Chapter 9, the Supreme Court reversed a number of its earlier decisions and upheld what some have termed the "alphabetocracy." For example, the Court in 1937 upheld the constitutionality of the National Labor Relations Act of 1935 (NLRA), which allowed recognition of unions and established formal arbitration procedures for employers and employees. Subsequent decisions upheld the validity of the Fair Labor Standards Act (FLSA) and the Agricultural Adjustment Act (AAA).

Once these new programs were declared constitutional, there was a need for an everexpanding bureaucracy to monitor the numerous programs created by the new laws. With the growth in the bureaucracy came more abuses in the employment of governmental bureaucrats and, in turn, more calls for reform.

The Hatch Act. As an increasing proportion of the American workforce came to work for the U.S. government as a result of the New Deal recovery programs, many began to fear that the members of the civil service would have major roles to play not only in implementing public policy but also in the election of members of Congress and even the president. Consequently, in 1939 Congress enacted what is commonly known as the **Hatch Act,** which was designed to prohibit the use of federal authority to affect elections and the pressuring of federal employees to make political contributions, work for a particular party, or campaign for a particular candidate. In effect, the Hatch Act was designed to neutralize the civil service politically by prohibiting civil servants from taking activist roles in partisan campaigns; under its provisions, federal employees may not run for public office, campaign for or against candidates, make speeches, raise funds for candidates, organize political rallies, circulate petitions, or participate in registration drives that seek voters for one party only. Civil servants may still vote, discuss political issues and candidates, participate in get-out-the-vote drives, contribute money to campaigns and attend fund-raising functions, join political clubs or parties, wear political buttons or display stickers, and sign nominating petitions—they just can't run the show or attempt to influence others.

Although presidents as far back as Thomas Jefferson have advocated efforts to limit the opportunities for federal civil servants to influence the votes of others, many have criticized the Hatch Act. Critics argue that it denies millions of federal employees the First Amendment guarantees of freedom of speech and association and discourages political participation among a group of people who would otherwise be strong political activists. Critics also argue that civil servants *should* become more involved in campaigns, particularly at the state and local level, in order to better understand the needs of the citizens they serve. Despite its controversial nature, the Hatch Act has survived to protect the neutrality of civil servants from partisan influences.

World War II and Its Aftermath

During World War II, tax rates were increased tremendously to support the war, and they never again fell to prewar levels. This huge infusion of new monies and veterans' demands for services led to a variety of programs and a much bigger government. The G.I. Bill, for example, provided college loans for returning veterans and reduced mortgage rates to allow them to buy homes. Again, Americans became accustomed to the increasingly important role that the national government was playing, often at the expense of the states, in entirely new areas such as middle-class housing.

Not only was the national government involved in more service programs that affected more people, but it was involved in more regulation as well. Homes bought with Veterans' Housing Authority loans, for example, had to meet certain specifications.

After World War II, the civil rights movement and President Lyndon B. Johnson's War on Poverty (see Chapter 5) also produced additional growth in the bureaucracy. As discussed earlier, the Equal Employment Opportunity Commission (EEOC) was created in 1964; the Department of Housing and Urban Development and the Department of Transportation were created in 1966. Also created was the Organization for Economic Opportunity (OEO) to coordinate welfare programs. These expansions of the bureaucracy corresponded to increases in presidential power. Remember that most major expansions in the power of the presidency have occurred during times of war or economic emergency. Most of the important changes that occurred in the size of the bureaucracy through the 1960s also occurred in response to war or economic chaos.

This pattern is not unique to the United States. In Britain, the two world wars left the country with a vastly expanded bureaucracy capable, among other things, of economic planning, and delivering a wide variety of social services.

The Modern Bureaucracy

One of the most difficult tasks facing those who study the bureaucracy is that of determining whether bureaucracies are responsive to citizens as well as to elected and appointed officials. We often think of bureaucrats as "them." But they are actually quite like "us." To understand the modern bureaucracy, it is essential to understand who bureaucrats are, how the bureaucracy is organized, and how it works.

Who Are Bureaucrats?

Federal bureaucrats are career government employees who work in the executive branch, in the 14 Cabinet-level departments and the more than 60 independent agencies that comprise more than 2,000 bureaus, divisions, branches, offices, services, and other subunits. There are approximately 3 million federal bureaucrats (in contrast to only 800,000 in Great Britain) coming from all walks of life—they vary in race, religion, ethnicity, level of education, and income. Although the representation of women and minorities is still low, Congress has ordered federal agencies to make special efforts in their recruitment of minority and other disadvantaged groups. And overall, women and other minorities are better represented in the bureaucracy as a proportion of the workforce than in the nation as a whole.

More than 90 percent of bureaucrats are selected by merit standards, which include tests (such as civil service or foreign service exams) and educational criteria. Merit

Characteristics of Federal Civilian Employees, 1988

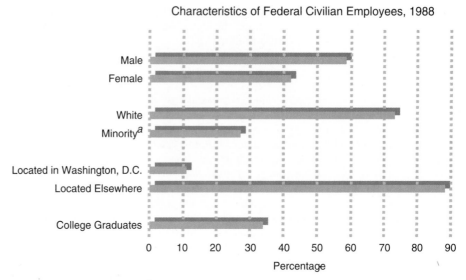

Percentage

a Black, Asian, Native American, and Hispanic

Sources: Statistical Abstract of the United States, 1990 (Washington: U.S. Government Printing Office, 1990), pp. 323–326. Office of Personnel Management, *Federal Civilian Workforce Statistics, Employment and Trends as of November 1988* (Washington: U.S. Government Printing Office, 1989), pp. 70.

systems protect federal employees from being fired for political reasons. Positions in the politically neutral civil service in Britain are also filled on the basis of competitive examinations; nevertheless, most entrants continue to come from either Oxford University or Cambridge University, and this has given the bureaucracy an elitist image.

At one time federal employees were underpaid in comparison with their civilian counterparts, but now salaries are largely competitive except at the senior ranks. Most federal employees have a GS (Graded Service) job rank; these range from GS-1 to GS-18. Rankings are determined by position and employee qualifications.

A Senior Executive Service (SES) was created in 1978 at the urging of President Jimmy Carter.[5] It represents a compromise between two traditions—a president-led

[5] See Mark W. Huddleston, "The Carter Civil Service Reforms," *Political Science Quarterly* (Winter 1981–82), pp. 607–622.

The Civil Service exam.

bureaucracy and one composed of experts. The SES contains approximately 8,000 top-level career employees (spread throughout the various agencies) who receive higher salaries than GS employees but can be moved or transferred by the order of the president. Unlike regular presidential appointees, they cannot be fired by the president at will.

While the stereotypical image of a bureaucrat is that of the "paper pusher," more than 15,000 job skills are represented in the federal government, and its workers are perhaps the best trained and most skilled and efficient in the world. Working for the government are forest rangers, FBI agents, foreign service officers, computer programmers, security guards, librarians, administrators, engineers, plumbers, lawyers, doctors, postal carriers, and zoologists, among others. The diversity of government jobs mirrors the diversity of jobs in the private sector. Thirty-seven percent of the federal workforce are employees of the army, navy, air force, or another defense agency. Although people tend to perceive the welfare bureaucracy in monstrous proportions, only 15 percent of the bureaucracy works for welfare agencies.

Another myth is the perception that most bureaucrats work in Washington. In reality, only about 12 percent of the 3 million federal bureaucrats work in the nation's capital; the rest are located in regional, state, and local offices scattered throughout the country. The decentralization of the bureaucracy facilitates accessibility. The Social Security Administration, for example, has numerous offices so that its clients have a place to take their paperwork, questions, and problems. Decentralization also helps distribute jobs and incomes across the country. Although the Centers for Disease Control might easily have been located in Washington, it is instead located in Atlanta, Georgia. Likewise, the headquarters for the National Aviation and Space Administration (NASA) is located in Houston, Texas.

Many Americans also believe that the federal bureaucracy is growing bigger each year. While it *is* true that the number of *government* employees has been increasing, the growth has taken place primarily at the state and local levels, while the federal workforce has remained fairly stable (as revealed in Figure 8-1).

The stability of an agency and the expansion or reduction of its employees are up to Congress; legislators have the power to abolish existing agencies or to create new ones as they see fit. But as one study conducted several years ago reveals, old government agencies not only never die, they hardly ever fade away either. Of 175 agencies in selected areas operating in 1923, all but 27 were alive and well fifty years later.[6]

Moreover, as each president has entered office, most have pledged to eliminate an agency or two or, at the very least, combine some. But, as President Ronald Reagan, who campaigned in part on a pledge to eliminate the Department of Education, soon learned, abolishing an agency is easier said than done. (Reagan, in fact, ended up elevating the Veterans Administration to the Department of Veterans Affairs by an act of Congress in 1988.) More common are the actions of President Carter. In 1978, he proposed reforms in the civil service system. The Civil Service Commission was split into two agencies, the Office of Personnel Management (OPM) and the Merit Systems Protection Board. OPM, in charge of hiring most civil service workers, has elaborate rules for hiring, promotion, and firing. Until the 1978 reforms, it was virtually impossible to fire a federal worker. Reforms urged by President Carter gave OPM more latitude, but because of the strength of federal employee unions and the regulations that protect federal workers, it is still difficult to remove an employee whose performance is unsatisfactory.

Even the U.S. Supreme Court has gotten involved with the government's right to terminate protected workers. In *Arnett* v. *Kennedy* (1974), the Court ruled that federal jobs were private property, in the same manner that one's house or car is. According to the Supreme Court, the due process clause of the Fifth Amendment protects federal

---

[6] Herbert Kaufman, *Are Government Organizations Immortal?* (Washington: Brookings Institution, 1976).

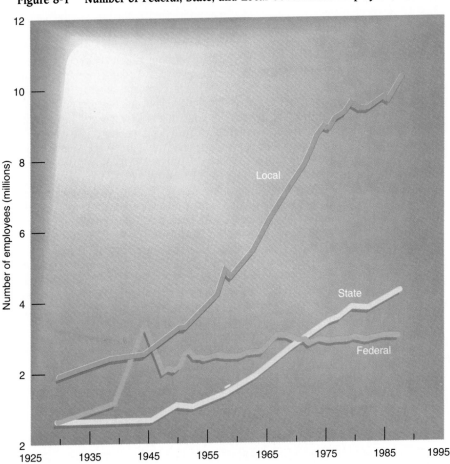

Figure 8-1   Number of Federal, State, and Local Government Employees, 1929–1988

Source: Harold W. Stanley and Richard G. Niemi, *Vital Statistics on American Politics*, 3rd ed. (Washington: CQ Press, 1991), p. 315. 1929–1944, 1949, 1954, 1959, 1964, 1969–1988: U.S. Advisory Commission on Intergovernmental Relations, *Significant Features of Fiscal Federalism, 1990*, vol. 2 (Washington: U.S. Advisory Commission on Intergovernmental Relations, 1990), p. 177; other years: Bureau of the Census, *Historical Statistics of the United States*, Series Y189–198 (Washington: U.S. Government Printing Office, 1975), p. 1100.

employees who have been fired and requires the government to provide an appeals procedure before termination.

The courts and Congress also have attempted to uphold the rights of **whistle blowers,** federal employees who publicly disclose waste or mismanagement in their agencies. In the past, whistle blowers were sometimes punished or transferred to undesirable positions. During the Nixon administration, for example, when a top Pentagon employee testified before Congress about huge cost overruns on the C-5A troop transport plane, President Nixon was so angered that he ordered Defense Department officials to "get rid of that ----." Recently, however, whistle blowers have been honored and awarded for serving the public interest. And in 1989, with the support of President George Bush, Congress passed legislation to ensure protection for whistle blowers. The legislation grants relief to federal employees who can link a demotion or firing to whistle blowing. It also allows whistle blowers to appeal their cases in the federal courts. Federal law even provides financial rewards for whistle blowers in some instances.

Formal Organization

While even experts can't agree on the exact number of separate agencies that make up the bureaucracy,[7] there are probably more than 400. A distinctive feature of the bureaucracy is its division into areas of specialization: One agency handles occupational safety, for example, another specializes in education, another in foreign affairs, another in employment discrimination, and another deals with the environment. Because each concentrates on a particular issue area, no two agencies are identical, but they do fall into four general groups (each is a mini-bureaucracy in its own right): (1) departments, (2) government corporations, (3) independent agencies, and (4) regulatory commissions.

Departments. The largest units of the federal bureaucracy are the fourteen executive branch departments headed by Cabinet members called secretaries (except the Justice Department, which is headed by the Attorney General), who are responsible for establishing the department's general policy and overseeing its operations. As discussed in Chapter 7, Cabinet secretaries are directly responsible to the president, although they are often viewed as having two masters—the president and those affected by their department. Cabinet secretaries are also tied to Congress, from which they get their appropriations and discretion to implement legislation and make rules.

Although departments vary considerably by size, prestige, and power, they share certain features. Each department covers a broad area of responsibility generally reflected by the name of the department. Each secretary is assisted by a deputy or undersecretary

[7] On the difficulty of counting the exact number of government agencies see David Nachmias and David H. Rosenbloom, *Bureaucratic Government: U.S.A.* (New York: St. Martin's Press, 1980).

How to Fire a Federal Bureaucrat

Firing a bureaucrat can be very difficult. To fire a member of the competitive civil service, explicit procedures must be followed:

1. At least thirty days written notice must be given to an employee in advance of their firing or demotion for incompetence or misconduct.

2. The written notification must contain a statement of reasons for the action and specific examples of unacceptable performance.

3. The employee has the right to reply both orally or in written form to the charges and has the right to an attorney.

4. Appeals from any adverse action against the employee can be made to the three-person Merit Systems Protection Board (MSPB), a bipartisan body appointed by the president and confirmed by the Senate.

5. All employees have a right to a hearing and the right to an attorney in front of the MSPB.

6. All decisions of the MSPB are appealable by the employee to the U.S. Court of Appeals.

Departments of the Executive Branch

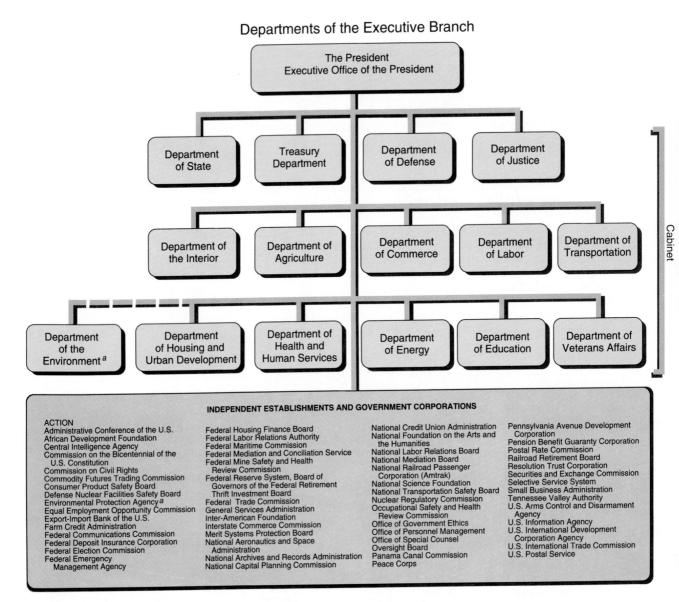

[a] Congress is currently considering a proposal to raise the Environmental Protection Agency to Cabinet rank as the Department of the Environment.

Source: United States Government Manual 1990–91 (Washington: Government Printing Office).

to take part of the administrative burden off of his or her shoulders, as well as by several assistant secretaries who direct major programs within the department. In addition, each secretary, like the president, has numerous assistants who help with planning, budgeting, personnel, legal services, public relations, and other key staff functions. All departments are subdivided into smaller agencies, bureaus, offices, and services, and it is at this level that the real work of each agency is done. Most departments are subdivided along function lines, but the basis for division may be geography, work processes (for example, the Economic Research Service in the Department of Agriculture), or clientele (such as the Bureau of Indian Affairs in the Department of Interior).

In addition to national offices in Washington, D.C., or its immediate suburbs, each executive department has regional offices to serve all parts of the United States. The Department of Health and Human Services (HHS) follows a typical departmental organization (see Figure 8-2). The Secretary of HHS presides over a variety of smaller agencies, centers, and programs. The Centers for Disease Control, a division of the Public Health Service that has played such an important role in conducting research on the AIDS virus, is under his jurisdiction. So, too, are programs that provide assistance to poor pregnant women, and the Social Security Administration, a major bureaucracy in its own right. In mid-1991 HHS was reorganized to consolidate its many programs and divisions that deal with families and children. The new Administration for Children and Families combines in one agency Head Start (which provides preschool education to the poor); job opportunities and basic skills programs; Aid to Families with Dependent Children; child-support enforcement; Adoption Assistance; foster care; child abuse programs; and two block grant programs. This new division alone has an annual budget of more than $25 billion and a staff of more than 2,000.

Some departments are directed by law to foster and promote the interests of a given clientele—that is, a specific segment or group in the U.S. population. Such departments are called **clientele agencies.** Some of the most well known are listed below.

- Department of Agriculture
- Department of Commerce and Labor
- Department of Education
- Department of Energy
- Department of Health and Human Services

- Department of Housing and Urban Development
- Department of the Interior
- Department of Labor
- Department of Transportation
- Department of Veterans Affairs

Figure 8-2   Organization of the Department of Health and Human Services

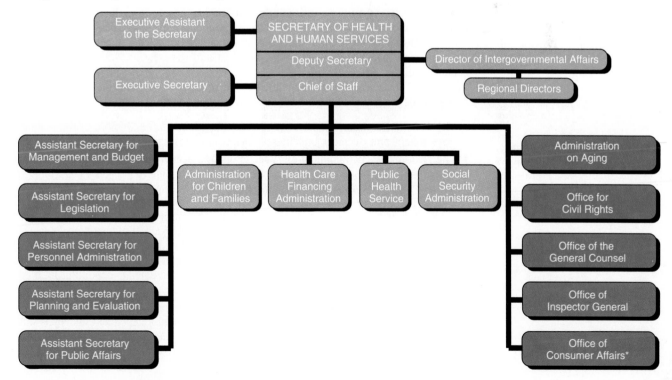

*Located administratively in HHS, but reports to the president

Because these agencies were created to assist certain segments of society and their particular interests, it is not surprising that clientele groups have become powerful lobbies with their respective agencies in Washington. The clientele agencies and groups are also active at the regional level, where clientele agencies devote a substantial part of their resources. One of the most obvious examples of the regional type of "outreach" performed by these agencies is the Extension Service of the Department of Agriculture. Agricultural extension agents are scattered throughout the farm belt and routinely work with farmers on farm productivity and other problems. Career bureaucrats in the Agriculture Department know that farm interests will be dependable allies year in and year out. Congress and/or the president are not nearly so reliable, as they must balance the interests of farmers with those of other segments of society.

Government Corporations. **Government corporations** are businesses set up and created by Congress that theoretically perform functions that could be provided by private businesses. Unlike other governmental agencies, government corporations charge for their services. For example, the largest government corporation, the U.S. Postal Service—whose functions could be handled by a private corporation, such as Federal Express or the United Parcel Service (UPS)—exists to ensure delivery of mail throughout the United States at supposedly cheaper rates than a private business might charge. Similarly, the Tennessee Valley Authority (TVA) provides electricity at reduced rates to millions of Americans in the Appalachian region of the Southeast, a generally low-income area that failed to attract construction by private utility companies.

In cases like that of the TVA where the financial incentives for private industry are minimal, the Congress often believes that it must act. In other cases it steps in to salvage valuable public assets. For example, when passenger rail service in the United States no longer remained profitable, Congress stepped in to create Amtrak and thus nationalized the passenger-train industry to keep passenger trains running.

Independent Agencies. **Independent agencies** closely resemble Cabinet departments but have narrower areas of responsibility. Generally speaking, all agencies that are not corporations or do not fall under the departments are called independent agencies. Many of these agencies are tied to the president and Congress as closely as executive departments.

Heads of these agencies are appointed by the president and serve, like Cabinet secretaries, at his pleasure. Among the largest independent agencies are:

- The General Services Administration, which functions as the landlord of the federal government and oversees buildings, supplies, purchasing, and rents
- The National Science Foundation, which supports academic and scientific research
- The Central Intelligence Agency, which coordinates intelligence activities at different levels of government as a means of strengthening national security

Independent agencies most frequently exist apart from executive departments for practical or symbolic reasons. The National Aviation and Space Administration (NASA), for example, could have been placed within the Department of Defense. Symbolically, however, that kind of placement could have conjured up thoughts of a space program dedicated solely to military purposes rather than for civilian satellite communication or scientific exploration.

Regulatory Boards or Commissions. Another type of independent agency is the independent regulatory board or commission, such as the National Labor Relations Board, the Federal Reserve Board, and the Securities and Exchange Commission (SEC).[8]

---

[8] The classic work on regulatory commissions is Marver Bernstein, *Regulating Business by Independent Commission* (Princeton, N.J.: Princeton University Press, 1955).

Corporations, Independent Agencies, and Regulatory Agencies

SOME GOVERNMENT CORPORATIONS

Amtrak
Export-Import Bank
Federal Deposit Insurance Corporation
Government National Mortgage Association
Resolution Trust Corporation
Pennsylvania Avenue Development Corporation
Pension Benefit Guaranty Corporation
U.S. Postal Service
Tennesee Valley Authority

SOME INDEPENDENT AGENCIES

ACTION
Central Intelligence Agency
Federal Emergency Management Agency
General Services Administration
National Aeronautics and Space Administration
National Archives and Records Administration
Peace Corps
Selective Service System
Small Business Administration
U.S. Information Agency

SOME REGULATORY AGENCIES OR COMMISSIONS

Consumer Product Safety Commission
Commodity Futures Trading Commission
Equal Employment Opportunity Commission
Federal Communications Commission
Federal Election Commission
Federal Housing Finance Board
Federal Trade Commission
Interstate Commerce Commission
National Labor Relations Board
Nuclear Regulatory Commission
Securities and Exchange Commission

Congress began to set up regulating commissions as early as 1887, recognizing the need for close and continuous guardianship of particular economic activities. Once the Supreme Court decided to allow Congress to begin to regulate aspects of the economy, the number of independent regulatory agencies—now over sixty—grew. Older boards and commissions, such as the Interstate Commerce Commission (ICC), SEC, and Federal Reserve Board, are generally charged with overseeing a certain industry. Regulatory agencies created since the 1960s are more concerned with how the business sector relates to public health and safety. The Occupational Safety and Health Administration (OSHA), for

A Food and Drug Administration testing lab, at which scientists look for decomposition in fish and crabs.

example, promotes job safety, and the Environmental Protection Agency (EPA) regulates industrial pollution. (In 1990, President Bush supported elevating the EPA to Cabinet-level status.)

Most of the older agencies are "independent" by virtue of their relative freedom from immediate political pressure. They are headed by a board composed of several members (always an odd number to avoid ties) who are selected by the president and confirmed by Congress. (Commissioners are appointed for fixed, staggered terms to increase the chances of a bipartisan board.) Unlike executive department heads, they cannot be easily removed by the president. In 1935, the U.S. Supreme Court ruled that in creating independent commissions, the Congress had intended that they be independent panels of experts removed as much as possible from immediate political pressures.[9]

Newer regulatory boards lack this kind of autonomy and freedom from political pressures; they are generally headed by a single administrator who can be removed by the president. These boards and commissions, such as the EEOC, are therefore far more susceptible to political pressure and political wishes.

The mark that presidential appointments can have on these commissions cannot be questioned. When Jimmy Carter was president, he appointed Michael Pertschuk, a public-interest law activist, to head the Federal Trade Commission (FTC), which became a staunchly proconsumer commission. President Reagan's choice to replace Pertschuk was economist James Miller III, who was known for his anti-regulationist, free market beliefs. Miller's appointment gave Reagan supporters a majority on the five-member commission. Under Miller's leadership the FTC abandoned its practice of policing the industry for false advertising and instead adopted a policy of making investigations only in response to specific complaints filed with the commission. American business generally hailed Miller's actions, but consumer activists were outraged because the change in policy meant that the FTC would be less aggressive. In this case, a change in presidents clearly led to a change in policy.

[9]295 U.S. 602 (1935).

Policy Making

It is hard enough to design public policies and programs that look good on paper. It is harder still to formulate them in words and slogans that resonate pleasingly in the ears of political leaders and the constituencies to which they are responsive. And it is excruciatingly hard to implement them in a way that pleases anyone at all, including the supposed beneficiaries or clients.[10]

The awesome task of implementing public policy is delegated to the federal bureaucracy. When Congress creates any kind of department, agency, or commission, it is actually delegating some of the congressional powers listed in Article I, Section 8, of the U.S. Constitution. Therefore, the laws creating agencies carefully describe their purpose and give them the authority to make numerous policy decisions, which have the effect of law. Congress recognizes that it does not have the time, expertise, or ability to involve itself in every detail of every program; therefore, it sets general guidelines for agency action and leaves it to the agency to work out the details. And, more often than not, when Congress is unable to agree upon clear-cut guidelines, it passes that political hot potato to an agency for it to resolve.

A good example of how Congress often passes the buck is the Occupational Safety and Health Act of 1970. It provided only a rough expression of the desired end results of ensuring a safe and healthy workplace for every man and woman in the nation. The legislation, however, was silent on how two competing interests were to be balanced: the rights of workers injured, killed, or exposed to hazards on the job and the interests of employers who, in order to minimize risks, would have to expend large sums of money in order to comply with OSHA mandates. Congress left it to the Occupational Safety and Health Administration (OSHA) to determine how to implement the act.

The same thing apparently occurred with passage of the Clean Air Act Amendments of 1990. After much political wrangling, they were sent to the EPA to draft regulations for a law that, according to one representative of the utility industry, contained all sorts of "discontinuities and contradictions."[11]

Implementation is the process by which a law or policy is put into operation. Essentially, bureaucrats are implementors. They take the laws and policies made by Congress, the president, and the courts and develop rules and procedures for making sure they are carried out. Most implementation involves what is called **administrative discretion,** the ability to make choices concerning the best way to implement congressional intentions. If Congress does not like an agency's actions, it can pass laws that invalidate specific rules or procedures.

Rule Making

The administrative discretion conferred upon bureaucratic agencies is exercised through two formal administrative procedures: rule making and adjudication. Rule making is the administrative process that results in regulations. **Regulations** are the rules that govern the operation of all government programs. Mountains of rules and regulations, published in the *Federal Register* and the *Code of Federal Regulations,* have been developed by administrative agencies.

In the case of the Occupational Safety and Health Act, for example, although all parties that pressed for the law were in agreement that industrial hazards (such as breathing asbestos-filled air) were more potentially harmful to a worker's health than

---

[10] Eugene Bardach, *The Implementation Game* (Cambridge, Mass.: MIT Press, 1977), p. 3.

[11] Stacey Evers, "Politics Pollute Clean Air Act," States News Service, December 22, 1991.

Every year, thousands upon thousands of pages of regulations are created, modified, replaced by still more of the same, and published in the *Federal Register.*

Contents

Federal Register

Vol. 57, No. 37

Tuesday, February 25, 1992

Agency for Health Care Policy and Research
NOTICES
Meetings:
  Health Care Policy, Research, and Evaluation National
    Advisory Council, 6504

Agriculture Department
See also Forest Service
PROPOSED RULES
Federal regulatory review, 6483

Air Force Department
NOTICES
Meetings:
  Scientific Advisory Board, 6496, 6497

Army Department
NOTICES
Meetings:
  Science Board, 6497
Military traffic management:
  International and domestic carrier evaluation reporting
    systems; standardization, 6497

Centers for Disease Control
NOTICES
Grants and cooperative agreements; availability, etc.:
  Infant immunization coalitions, 6504

Energy Department
See also Federal Energy Regulatory Commission; Hearings
  and Appeals Office, Energy Department
NOTICES
National energy strategy report; availability, 6498
Natural gas exportation and importation:
  Kimball Energy Corp., 6499
  Teco Gas Marketing Co., 6500

Environmental Protection Agency
PROPOSED RULES
Hazardous waste:
  Land disposal restrictions—
    Newly identified and listed wastes and contaminated
      debris; potential treatment standards, 6487

Equal Employment Opportunity Commission
NOTICES
Meetings; Sunshine Act, 6550

Federal Aviation Administration
RULES
Standard instrument approach procedures, 6468, 6473
PROPOSED RULES
Airworthiness directives:
  Boeing; correction, 6551
NOTICES
Airport noise compatibility program:
  Minneapolis-St. Paul International Airport, MN, 6541

were safety hazards (such as dangerous heavy machinery), OSHA chose first to address safety rather than health concerns. Not surprisingly, regulation writers found it easier to address safety concerns—they are easier to describe, assess, and control. If a worker falls from a platform, for example, the cause is clear—no railing or restraint system. Moreover, the results—a broken arm, leg, or neck (or all three) are easier to quantify than the lingering effects of some chemicals and their possible relationship to cancer.

But regulation writers got carried away in an effort to bring about quick compliance with the act. The first set of regulations took up nearly 250 pages in the *Federal Register,* a daily publication of the federal government that contains all proposed and final regulations of all federal agencies. Some regulations were intricately detailed, such as ones requiring toilets to have hinged, open front seats.[12]

Because regulations often involve political conflict, the Administrative Procedure Act (first passed in 1946) established rule-making procedures in order to give everyone the chance to participate in the process. The act requires that (1) public notice of the time, place, and nature of the rule-making proceedings be provided in the *Federal Register,* (2) interested parties be given the opportunity to submit written arguments and facts relevant to the rule, and (3) the statutory purpose and basis of the rule be stated. Once rules have been written, thirty days must elapse before they take effect.

Sometimes agencies are required by law to conduct a formal hearing before issuing rules. Evidence is gathered and witnesses testify and are cross-examined by opposing interests. The process can take weeks or even months, at the end of which agency administrators must review the entire record and then justify the rules they issue. Although cumbersome, the process has reduced criticism of the rules and bolstered the agency's standing with the courts.

Even when groups have had the opportunity to testify, they may be unhappy about the outcome of regulations. Critics of OSHA complained that its regulations were ridiculous and not cost effective. After only a year of operation, members of Congress were besieged with complaints prompting efforts to amend and even repeal the act. Even

[12]Dennis J. Palumbo, *Public Policy in America* (New York: Harcourt Brace Jovanovich, 1988), p. 196.

President Gerald Ford spoke out against the "overzealous" and "nitpicking" regulations being issued by OSHA.[13] By 1977, OSHA finally revoked 1,100 of its safety regulations.

Similar problems have occurred more recently in the case of the EPA and the Clean Air Act Amendments. The process has been complicated by the White House's industry-oriented Council on Competitiveness, headed by the vice president, which has forcibly weakened more than one hundred EPA rules. The president, as head of the executive branch, has made the Council responsible for reviewing all new federal regulations that could place undue burdens on industry. Thus, the Council directed the EPA in ways that Congress specifically had rejected, a move that drew the ire of members of the House Health and Environment Subcommittee. According to its chair, Representative Henry Waxman (D.-Cal.), by November 15, 1991 (one year after passage of the act), the EPA had failed to take any of the sixteen important actions required by statute. The subcommittee has been particularly chagrined by Vice President Quayle's refusal to answer questions about the Council and its role in the rule-making process.[14] Environmental interest groups charge that the Bush administration is trying to "gain through regulation what it lost in legislation."[15]

Administrative Adjudication

Rule making is what is called a quasi-legislative process because an agency ultimately writes a regulation that has the force of a law made by Congress. Administrative adjudication is a quasi-judicial process in which a bureaucratic agency settles disputes between two parties in a manner similar to the way courts resolve disputes. Both of these functions are referred to as "quasi" (meaning "almost") because law making by any body other than Congress or adjudication by any body other than the judiciary would be a violation of the constitutional principle of separation of powers.

On occasion a person or business is accused of not complying with the law or an agency's regulations. Some agencies are routinely involved in administrative adjudication, which is generally less formal than a trial.

Various agencies and boards employ administrative law judges to conduct the hearings. Although these judges are employed by the agency, they are strictly independent and cannot be removed except for gross misconduct. OSHA, for example, is charged with trying to settle disputes between employers and employees who allege violations of the act. It also fines employers for infractions of its safety regulations; in 1991 it levied $180 million in fines and through closer oversight hopes to raise that amount to $1.5 billion by 1995. In virtually every case adjudicated by an agency, appeals to the federal courts are guaranteed.

Despite thousands and thousands of pages of rules and regulations and the resolution of specific conflicts through adjudications, many real-life situations are still left ambiguous. Usually "street level" bureaucrats implement policy, using their on-the-spot bureaucratic discretion. In the case of OSHA, however, local inspectors initially were not given the opportunity to exercise discretion. Instead, they were ordered to issue citations for any violation, however small. In its early years, 95 percent of OSHA's citations were for small, nonserious infractions, such as failure to replace towels in restrooms, failure to post OSHA notices, and failure to keep accurate records of employee injuries or illnesses.[16]

A worker from the Environmental Protection Agency disposing of toxic waste.

[13] James Q. Wilson, *Bureaucracy: What Government Agencies Do and Why They Do It* (New York: Basic Books, 1989), p. 198.

[14] Federal News Service, Hearing of the Health and Environment Subcommittee, November 14, 1991, NEXIS.

[15] Ibid.

[16] Frank J. Thompson. *Health Policy and the Bureaucracy: Politics and Implementation* (Cambridge, Mass.: MIT Press, 1981), p. 9.

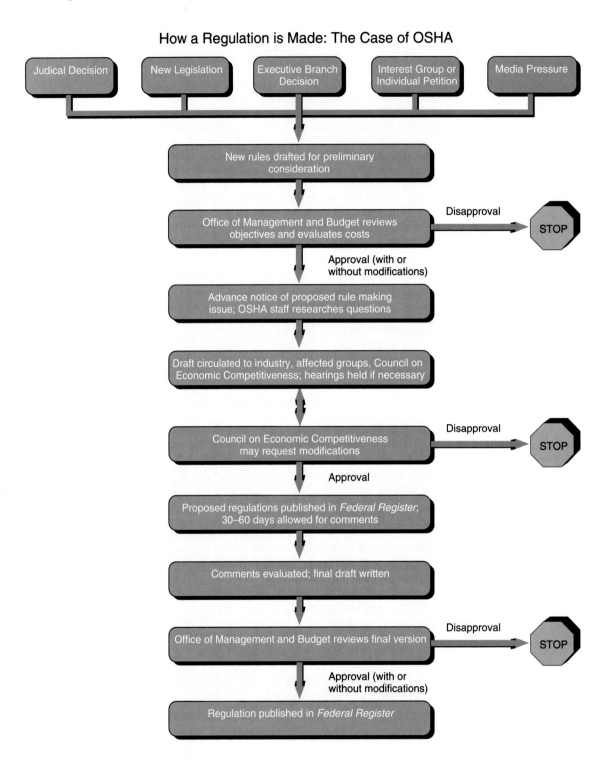

How a Regulation is Made: The Case of OSHA

OSHA also is empowered to refer cases to the Department of Justice for possible criminal prosecution if employers willfully violate OSHA standards and an employee death results. Recently OSHA has been far more vigilant in enforcing *all* of its rules. Under a new administrator, OSHA referred more cases to the Justice Department in the first half of 1991 than any other period in its history. Inspections and fines have also increased.

Making Agencies Accountable

The question of to whom bureaucrats should be responsible is one that continually comes up in any debate. Should the bureaucracy be held accountable to itself, to organized interest groups, to the president, or to the Congress? While many would argue that bureaucrats should be responsive to the public interest, the public interest is difficult to define. As it turns out, several factors do work to control the power of the bureaucracy and, to some degree, the same kinds of checks and balances that operate between the three constitutional branches of government exist to check the bureaucracy.

Many argue that the president should be in charge of the bureaucracy. It is up to him to see that popular ideas and expectations are translated into administrative action. So, upon the election of conservative Republican presidents—such as Ronald Reagan and George Bush—who favor cutbacks in federal programs and limited governmental regulation of the economy, the bureaucracy should respond accordingly. But under our constitutional system, the president is not the only actor in the policy process. Congress creates the agencies, funds them, and establishes the broad rules of their operation. Moreover, Congress continually reviews the various agencies through oversight committee investigations, appropriations hearings, and informal hearings.

The problem of accountability in the bureaucracy is even more acute in Britain. The oversight function provided by Parliament, though improved over the course of the 1980s, has generally been inadequate. Moreover, since political appointees constitute no more than the top two or three layers of the bureaucracy, the vast majority of civil servants are shielded from national election results and therefore, some would argue, executive control. The perception is of a small set of relatively inexperienced ministers against a large, permanent, expert civil service. It is no wonder, critics argue, that elections produce so little change in government policies. Although often exaggerated, these concerns have sparked numerous attempts at reform of the civil service.

Executive Control

As crises have caused the expansion of the size and scope of the American national government in general and of the executive branch and the bureaucracy in particular, presidents have delegated more and more power to bureaucrats. Recognizing this, each chief executive tries to appoint the best possible persons to carry out his wishes and policy preferences. Presidents may make thousands of appointments to the executive branch; in doing so, they have the opportunity to appoint individuals who share similar goals. And although that actually amounts to less than 1 percent of all federal jobs, they are usually the top policy-making positions.

While some spots go to party loyalists, campaign workers, or close friends, others go to "experts," although generally carefully screened ones who share the president's basic approach to government and political beliefs. President Reagan, in particular, looked for agency heads who shared his political philosophies. He appointed James Watt, the former head of a conservative public-interest law firm (the Mountain States Legal Foundation), to head the Department of the Interior. While at the Mountain States Legal Foundation, Watt had headed a successful litigation program that had challenged many key public-lands regulatory programs run by the Department of the Interior.[17] Reagan also picked James Miller III, an economist well known for his extensive writings in opposition to all trade regulation, to head the Federal Trade Commission (FTC). In just one year, 1981, Miller terminated 25 percent of all of the FTC's pending cases against business firms. But this scheme of things is not without its problems. In late 1990, for example, George

[17]Karen O'Connor and Lee Epstein, "Rebalancing the Scales of Justice," *Harvard Journal of Law and Public Policy* (Fall 1984), pp. 483–506.

RU 486 and the Bureaucracy

It was classic congressional melodrama, replete with passionate witnesses and hostile questions. But in the end, no one knew who the villain was.

"We're talking at cross purposes," complained Solomon Sobel, director of the Food and Drug Administration's Division of Metabolism and Endocrine Drug Products.

They did so for 3½ hours yesterday in an often-contentious hearing at which the chairman of a House subcommittee charged that the FDA's ban on importation of RU 486, the French "abortion pill," is "arbitrary, political and unscientific." Rep. Ron Wyden (D.-Ore.) also accused the FDA of trucking to antiabortion prejudice in the Bush administration and thereby causing "needless suffering" for Americans denied access to the drug.

FDA officials countered that their policy is mandated by U.S. law, which prohibits the import of unapproved drugs. The agency, said FDA counsel Sandra Barnes, "has no other choice but to enforce the statute—which Congress has not seen fit to change." Ronald Chesemore, FDA associate commissioner for regulatory affairs, stressed that agency officials "place no restrictions on research."

At issue was a year-old import ban on personal use of RU 486, a drug available in France to induce abortion, but which is also thought to have exceptional promise in treating breast cancer, endometriosis, meningioma (a form of brain cancer), and [a] gland disorder called Cushing's syndrome, and many other maladies involving hormonal effects on the body.

William Regelson of the Medical College of Virginia told the hearing that more study of the effects of RU 486 could lead to "major medical breakthroughs" in treating diseases as diverse as hypertension and AIDS. But, he said, "we're stymied by this emotionalism related to fertilization. I get the feeling that the FDA got carried away by the pressures of Right-to-Lifers."

Regelson dismissed arguments about the personal hazards of unsupervised use of RU 486: "We don't deny patients morphine because people on the street are abusing narcotics."

FDA officials responded that, in fact, the compound can be imported legally

Bush's Secretary of Education, Lauro Cavazos, the first Hispanic to serve in the Cabinet, was forced to resign. Bush had run for president stressing his commitment to education, yet the administration was continually under attack for its failure to take the lead on educational issues. Education groups charged that Cavazos was ineffective. The White House, especially then–Chief of Staff John Sununu, believed that Cavazos was unassertive and ineffective, thus undermining Bush's wish to be known as the "education president."[18] In fact, only two hours after Cavazos's "resignation" was announced, Bush made a speech urging new educational reforms, in effect acknowledging that his appointed secretary had failed to make much progress in this area.

Many presidents have expressed dismay over their inability to oversee the day-to-day workings of the bureaucracy. John F. Kennedy was known to complain, for example, that the State Department was a "bowl of jelly" and giving anyone at State an instruction was

---

[18]Richard Benedetto, "Scholarship Decision Causes White House Anxiety," *USA Today,* December 15, 1990.

for FDA-approved clinical trials, several of which are under way. Chesemore kept reiterating that the agency's ban extends only to individual use of the drug for abortion. The personal-use ban, Chesemore said, was implemented after the agency became concerned that "publicity about the use of these drugs overseas would lead to unsupervised use or clandestine distribution" in this country.

But Wyden, chairman of the House subcommittee on regulation, business opportunities, and energy (and the only committee member present at the hearing), blamed the FDA for ignoring evidence of the drug's safety and creating a climate of regulatory "resistance" to RU 486 through the import ban instead of performing as an "active advocate" for medical research.

As a result, he said, the drug's manufacturer, Roussel Uclaf, has made it difficult, and often impossible, for U.S.

researchers to get reliable supplies of RU 486.

Kathryn Horwitz of the University of Colorado, who studies the actions of sex hormones on cancer, testified that she can no longer obtain the drug for basic research because her test-tube studies of its effects on cancer cells don't fit the requirements of clinical trials.

Several other witnesses criticized the FDA policy while emphasizing the drug's therapeutic promise. Myron Allukian, Jr., past president of the American Public Health Association, testified that the FDA's "bureaucratic barrier" demonstrates "profound ignorance of the potential of RU 486" and "sends the wrong message to researchers, academics, health professionals and the public." He urged the FDA to disregard RU 486's ability to cause abortions "and treat it like any other drug that has demonstrated potential to improve the quality of life. . . ."

Source: Curt Suplee, "Hill Holds Heated Hearing on RU 486: FDA Denies Antiabortion Bias in Banning Drug with Several Uses," *The Washington Post,* November 20, 1990, p. A-21. Reprinted with permission.

comparable to putting it in a dead letter box.[19] George Bush faced similar problems. In December 1990, for example, the Assistant Secretary for Civil Rights in the Department of Education announced that it was illegal for colleges and universities supported by federal monies to give scholarships designated solely for minority students. Although the White House strongly opposed quotas, the ruling deeply embarrassed Bush, who learned of it only after it was reported in the press. Still smarting from the wide criticisms he received over his vetoing of a civil rights bill, Bush ordered his aides to come up with a way to reverse the policy.[20]

To give direction to bureaucrats, presidents can issue **executive orders.** Executive orders are presidential directives to an agency that provide the basis for carrying out laws or for establishing new policies. Even before Congress acted to protect women from discrimination by the federal government, for example, the National Organization for

[19] Arthur Schlesinger, Jr., *A Thousand Days* (Greenwich, Conn.: Fawcett Books, 1967), p. 377.
[20] Andrew Rosenthal, "White House Retreats on Ruling That Curbs Minority Scholarships," *The New York Times,* December 18, 1990, p. A-1.

Making Agencies Accountable

The president has the authority to:

- Appoint and remove agency heads and a few additional top bureaucrats
- Reorganize the bureaucracy (with congressional approval)
- Make changes in the annual budget proposals of agencies
- Ignore legislative initiatives originating within the bureaucracy
- Initiate or adjust policies that would, if enacted by Congress, alter the bureaucracy's activities

Congress has the authority to:

- Reduce the annual budget of an agency
- Pass legislation that alters the bureaucracy's activities
- Abolish existing programs
- Investigate bureaucratic activities, forcing bureaucrats to testify about them
- Influence presidential appointments of agency heads and other top bureaucratic officials
- Write legislation in such a way as to limit the bureaucracy's discretion (e.g., sunset laws)

The courts have the authority to:

- Rule on whether bureaucrats have acted within the law and require policy changes to comply with the law
- Force the bureaucracy to respect the rights of individuals through hearings and other proceedings

Women convinced President Lyndon Johnson to sign Executive Order 11375 in 1967. It amended an earlier order that prohibited the federal government from discriminating on the basis of race, color, religion, or national origin in the awarding of federal contracts. Nevertheless, although the president signed the order, the Office of Federal Contract Compliance, the executive agency charged with implementing the order, failed to draft appropriate guidelines for implementation of the order until several years later.[21] A president can direct an agency to act, but it may take some time for his orders to be carried out. Given the many "jobs" of any president, few can ensure that all of their orders will be carried out, or, as was the case with minority scholarships, that they will like all rules that are made.

Presidents also try to control the bureaucracy by reorganizing it, but in general these efforts are not particularly successful.[22] All recent presidents have tried to streamline the bureaucracy, a persistent theme of government reform, to make it more accountable. President Nixon's plan to combine fifty domestic agencies and seven different departments into four large "super departments" was the most ambitious. This proposal would have given Nixon tighter control of domestic programs, but it was fought tooth and nail by the agencies to be consolidated and their clientele groups. It was also opposed by certain members of Congress, who feared that centralization would reduce their power and cause further congressional reorganization as the committee structure would have to be changed to better monitor the proposed new agencies. In the end, with the exception of the creation of the Office of Management and Budget to replace the old Bureau of the

---

[21] Irene Murphy, *Public Policy on the Status of Women* (Lexington, Mass.: Lexington Books, 1974).

[22] Peter Woll, *American Bureaucracy,* 2nd ed. (New York: Norton, 1977), p. 244.

Budget and the establishment of the Domestic Council within the Executive Office of the President, none of Nixon's plan got through Congress.

Because sweeping changes are seldom adopted, most presidents try only to tinker with the bureaucracy. Minor changes, however, don't appear to be of much real consequence, and the same problems of control generally reemerge elsewhere.[23] According to political scientists Benjamin I. Page and Mark P. Petracca, "In any case, reorganization is only an ultimate weapon—of last resort—in a continuing widespread struggle between presidents and the bureaucracy.[24]

[23] James G. March and Johan P. Olson, "Organizing Political Life: What Administrative Reorganization Tells Us About Government," *American Political Science Review* 77 (June 1983), pp. 281–296.

[24] Benjamin I. Page and Mark P. Petracca, *The American Presidency* (New York: McGraw-Hill, 1983), p. 224.

Presidents and Cabinet Changes

PRESIDENT	TERM OF OFFICE	CABINET CHANGE	PRESIDENT	TERM OF OFFICE	CABINET CHANGE
1. George Washington	1789–97	Created Secretaries of State, Treasury, and War and Attorney General	27. William H. Taft	1909–13	
			28. Woodrow Wilson	1913–21	Divided Department of Commerce and Labor into Department of Commerce, Department of Labor
2. John Adams	1797–1801	Added Secretary of Navy			
3. Thomas Jefferson	1801–09		29. Warren Harding	1921–23	
4. James Madison	1809–17		30. Calvin Coolidge	1923–29	
5. James Monroe	1817–25		31. Herbert Hoover	1929–33	
6. John Quincy Adams	1825–29		32. Franklin D. Roosevelt	1933–45	
7. Andrew Jackson	1829–37	Added Postmaster General	33. Harry S. Truman	1945–53	Combined War Department and Department of Navy into Department of Defense
8. Martin Van Buren	1837–41				
9. William Henry Harrison	1841		34. Dwight D. Eisenhower	1953–61	Added Department of Health, Education and Welfare (HEW)
10. John Tyler	1841–45				
11. James K. Polk	1845–49	Added Secretary of Interior	35. John F. Kennedy	1961–63	
12. Zachary Taylor	1849–50		36. Lyndon B. Johnson	1963–69	Added Departments of Housing and Urban Development (HUD) and Transportation (DOT)
13. Millard Fillmore	1850–53				
14. Franklin Pierce	1853–57				
15. James Buchanan	1857–61		37. Richard M. Nixon	1969–74	Deleted Postmaster General
16. Abraham Lincoln	1861–65				
17. Andrew Johnson	1865–69		38. Gerald R. Ford	1974–77	
18. Ulysses S. Grant	1869–77		39. Jimmy Carter	1977–81	Divided HEW into Departments of Education and Health and Human Services (HHS); added Department of Energy
19. Rutherford B. Hayes	1877–81				
20. James A. Garfield	1881				
21. Chester A. Arthur	1881–85				
22. Grover Cleveland	1885–89	Added Department of Agriculture to Cabinet	40. Ronald Reagan	1981–89	Added Department of Veterans Affairs
23. Benjamin Harrison	1889–93				
24. Grover Cleveland	1893–97		41. George Bush	1989–	Proposed making Environmental Protection Agency a Cabinet-level department; passed by Senate late 1991
25. William McKinley	1897–1901				
26. Theodore Roosevelt	1901–09	Created Department of Commerce and Labor			

President Bush swearing in Secretary of Labor Lynn Martin.

Presidents have been much more successful in creating new agencies, generally under the guise of making the bureaucracy more efficient and accountable. In 1965 Lyndon B. Johnson convinced Congress that the nation's decaying cities needed federal help. The result was the creation of the Department of Housing and Urban Development to implement Johnson's ideas for urban development and renewal. Similarly, Jimmy Carter, reacting to the energy crisis, asked Congress to establish a Department of Energy to plan conservation policies for industry and private citizens. This tendency to create new agencies has increased the president's ability to control and coordinate bureaucratic functions.

Congressional Control

Congress, too, plays an important role in checking the power of the bureaucracy. As indicated throughout this chapter, Congress exercises considerable oversight over the bureaucracy through its extensive use of its investigatory powers. It is not at all unusual for a congressional committee or subcommittee to hold hearings on a particular problem and then to direct the relevant agency to study the problem or find ways to remedy it. Representatives for the agencies also appear before these committees on a regular basis to inform members about agency activities, ongoing investigations, and so on.

Not only does Congress have a statutory responsibility to oversee the bureaucracy; it also has the power of appropriations, which it wields like the sword of Damocles over the heads of various agency officials.[25] The House Appropriations Committee routinely holds hearings that agency heads are forced to come before in order to justify their budget requests. Authorization legislation originates in the various legislative committees that oversee particular agencies (such as Agriculture, Veterans Affairs, Education, and Labor) and sets the maximum amounts that agencies can spend on particular programs. While some authorizations, such as Social Security, are permanent, others, including the State Department and Defense Department procurements, are watched closely and are subject to annual authorizations.

Once funds are authorized, they must then be appropriated before they can be spent. Appropriations originate with the House Appropriations Committee, not the specialized legislative committees. Often, the Appropriations Committee appropriates sums smaller than those authorized by the legislative committee. Thus, the Appropriations Committee, a budget cutter, has an additional oversight function.

Congress can also pass new legislation that clarifies policies or that even overturns regulations or rules. Still, in all, the congressional oversight function is not a particularly glamorous one. Little political capital is likely to be earned through oversight unless the problems addressed are of interest to a member's district or otherwise worthy of publicity. Consequently, whereas the head of the subcommittee overseeing the Food and Drug Administration's failure to regulate diet centers may get a considerable amount of favorable publicity, those exercising the tedious yet exceptionally critical oversight of the Federal Deposit Insurance Corporation are unlikely to get any constituent rewards. It was this problem that contributed to the savings and loan crisis.

Because the oversight function is difficult and has few rewards, Congress has turned much of this function over to the General Accounting Office (GAO; see page 204), whose major function was once to track how money is spent in the bureaucracy. Today, the GAO also monitors how policies are implemented. The Congressional Budget Office also conducts oversight studies. If it or the GAO uncovers problems with an agency's work, Congress is immediately notified.

---

[25] In Greek and Roman legends, Damocles was a courtier and constant flatterer of Dionysus, King of Syracuse. He coveted the happiness and glory of kings until Dionysus gave a banquet in his honor. Damocles enjoyed the banquet immensely until he looked up and saw a sword over his head, hung by a single thread. The sword was meant to teach him of the constant danger faced by the kings he so envied.

Then and Now

Child Labor and the Bureaucracy

Through the mid 1900s, children worked for low wages and often in extremely hazardous conditions. Children of the poor often didn't attend school or dropped out at an early age. Children who did not earn money by running errands or peddling newspapers often were employed in the textile industry. By 1900, 13 percent of all textile trade workers were children under the age of sixteen. In the South, children under fifteen made up 25 percent of the workforce in the cotton mills, and half of them were under twelve! Most manufacturers preferred to hire children for unskilled jobs because they could be paid less than adults.

In the Progressive era, reformers advocated a variety of measures to alleviate these conditions, which they saw as a major societal problem. They urged age limits on employment, compulsory school attendance laws, and legislation to require students to stay in school until a certain age. The National Child Labor Committee was formed in 1904 to urge states and the national government to adopt child labor laws to regulate the hours worked by children. In 1918, however, the U.S. Supreme Court ruled that a national child labor law was unconstitutional because Congress lacked the authority to regulate it under its commerce powers.

Opponents of child labor next sought a constitutional amendment to ban child labor. Congress passed the amendment in 1924, but the conservative political climate of the 1920s combined with strong opposition from church groups, farmers, and Southerners who feared the government's involvement in family matters prevented its ratification by the states.

When the Depression hit the United States, attitudes about labor and governmental regulation changed dramatically. Codes developed under the National Industrial Recovery Act reduced child labor, and the Fair Labor Standards Act of 1938 (which was upheld by the Supreme Court) set both maximum hours and minimum wages for all workers and, in effect, prohibited the employment of children in manufacturing and mining under the age of sixteen.

Child labor continues to be a problem today in spite of federal law that bars children under twelve from working. Many states also have stringent laws. Nevertheless, the American Friends Service Committee found that children comprised about 25 percent of all farm laborers—many of them the children of migrant workers. Labor Department statistics indicate that the problem has gotten worse. From 1985 to 1989, the number of illegally employed minors jumped 128 percent—from 9,000 to 22,500, with many of them in fast-food restaurants. Information for 1988 from 26 states reveals that children suffered over 31,500 injuries at work. "Our feeling is strong that child labor is an extremely serious problem now, and it is approaching a crisis stage," said Jeffrey F. Newman of the National Child Labor Committee (NCLC). "It is not as serious yet as it was in 1900 or 1919, but it certainly has been moving in that direction . . . and if it is not checked, I think we could easily find ourselves in a situation where we could turn the clock back 100 years."[*]

In response to pressure from the NCLC and other concerned groups, then–Secretary of Labor Elizabeth Dole targeted repeat offenders and ordered her assistant secretary for employment standards to develop a comprehensive plan to combat child labor.

In March 1990 the department staged "Operation Child Watch" as 500 federal investigators inspected over 4,000 businesses and found more than 15,500 minors working in conditions banned by the Fair Labor Standards Act. Penalties exceeded $2.9 million.

[*]Quoted in Kirk Victor, "Kids on the Job," *National Journal,* July 14, 1990, p. 1712.

Judicial Control

The oversight function of the judiciary is less direct than that of the other two branches of government. Although injured parties can bring suit against agencies for their failure to enforce the law or can even challenge agency interpretations of the law, in general the courts give great weight to the opinions of bureaucrats and usually defer to their expertise.

The courts have, however, ruled that agencies must give all affected individuals their due process rights guaranteed by the U.S. Constitution. A Social Security recipient's checks cannot be stopped, for example, unless that individual is provided with reasonable notice and an opportunity for a hearing.

Iron Triangles and Issue Networks

While Congress and the president continually criticize the bureaucracy and, indeed, often take steps to control it, the strong ties that agencies enjoy with interest groups on the one hand and congressional committees and subcommittees on the other help to explain the uphill battle to "control" the bureaucracy.

As discussed in Chapter 15 and as shown in Figure 8-3, the relatively stable relationships and patterns of interaction that occur among an agency, interest groups, and congressional committees or subcommittees are known as **iron triangles** or subgovernments.

Policy-making subgovernments are called iron because they are virtually impenetrable to outsiders and largely autonomous. Even presidents have difficulty piercing the workings of these subgovernments, which have endured over time. Examples of iron triangles abound. Senior citizens' groups (especially the American Association of Retired Persons), the Social Security Administration, and the House Subcommittee on Aging all are likely to agree on the need for increased Social Security benefits. Similarly, the Department of Veterans Affairs, the House Committee on Veterans Affairs, and the American Legion and Veterans of Foreign Wars—the two largest organizations representing veterans—are usually in agreement on the need for expanded programs for veterans.

The policy decisions made within these iron triangles often foster the interests of a clientele group but have little to do with the advancement of national policy goals. Often these decisions conflict with other governmental policies and tend to tie the hands of larger institutions, such as Congress and the president. The White House is often too busy dealing with international affairs or crises to deal with smaller issues like veterans' benefits. Likewise, Congress defers to its committees. Thus, these subgovernments decentral-

The recently created Cabinet position of Secretary of Veterans Affairs, overseeing the Department of the same name, is an office that helps veteran groups such as the Veterans of Foreign Wars work with the House and Senate Veterans Affairs Committees, often resulting in government expenditures for benefits such as VA hospitals.

Figure 8-3   How the Iron Triangle Works at One Agency: The Occupational Safety and Health Administration

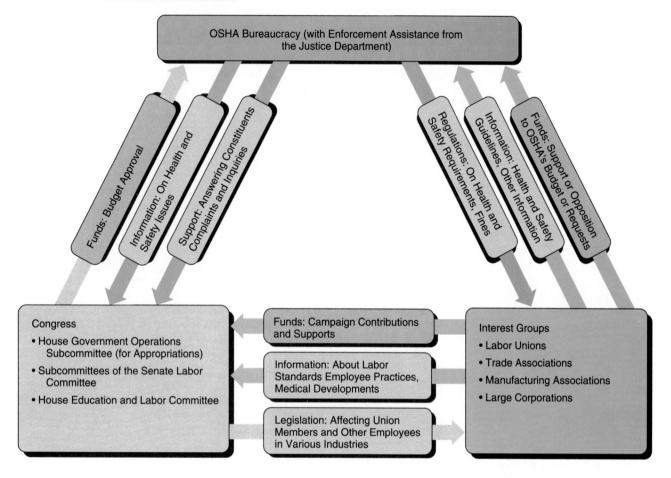

ize policy making and make it more difficult to control.[26] Of course, one precondition for an iron triangle is a strong legislature. In Britain, where Parliament is quite weak, iron triangles are a rarity. Instead, close relationships between interest groups and the bureaucracy have evolved in numerous policy areas; perhaps the term "iron bars" would be more appropriate.

Although iron triangles are quite stable and have a relatively small set of actors, what Hugh Heclo describes as **issue networks** are quite different.[27] He argues that this system of separate subgovernments is overlaid with an amorphous system of issue networks that are made up of "a large number of participants with quite variable degrees of mutual commitment or dependence on others in their environment."[28] Unlike iron triangles, issue networks are constantly changing as members with technical expertise become involved in various issues. Environmentalists interested in the chemical Agent Orange

[26] For more on iron triangles, see Randall Ripley and Grace Franklin, *Congress, Bureaucracy and Public Policy,* 4th ed. (Homewood, Ill.: Dorsey Press, 1984).

[27] "Issue Networks and the Executive Establishment," in Anthony King, ed., *The New American Political System* (Washington: American Enterprise Institute, 1978), pp. 87–124.

[28] Ibid., p. 102.

Iron Triangles at Work

Iron triangles and issue networks explain how much of the business of regulation is conducted. For example, in the aftermath of the gigantic Perrier recall—in which the Perrier Bottling Company of France recalled millions of bottles of its expensive mineral water—the Food and Drug Administration began to test the quality of bottled waters sold in the United States. After the FDA provided Congress with information on fifty-two kinds of domestic and imported bottled waters, the Energy and Commerce Committee held public hearings on the safety of these waters, many of which proved to be no safer than New Jersey tap water. Three staffers of that committee and its Investigative Subcommittee along with two lawyers for the International Bottled Water Association traveled not to various sites in the United States to examine how waters were bottled but instead to Paris to visit the Perrier and Evian plants and to meet with French health officials. Later they drove to Milan and Florence to visit plants there. From there they went to Brussels to visit another bottler and then flew to London for more meetings. Staffers from the General Accounting Office, meanwhile, were sent to visit U.S. bottlers in Douglas County, Georgia. When the committee got around to holding its hearings, only information on two plants—both of those visited by GAO staffers—was singled out for criticism. Data on all other fifty plants were kept confidential. Did the fact that lawyers for the association accompanied key staffers on fact-finding missions to desirable foreign locations have anything to do with FDA actions or the conduct of the congressional oversight hearings? You decide.

Source: Jeff Nesmith, "Bottled Water Probe Full of Leaks," *Atlanta Journal & Constitution,* April 14, 1991, p. H-1.

and its health consequences, for example, might attempt to pierce the Veterans Affairs iron triangle but only while Agent Orange needed to be dealt with in that arena.

Problems with the Modern Bureaucracy

As the modern bureaucracy has grown, so has its problems. Not only do the executive branch and Congress have difficulty in overseeing the actions of the numerous bureaus, agencies, and commissions, but often the right hand of any agency itself doesn't know what its left hand is doing. This confusion is complicated by the presence of interagency committees, which have been established to coordinate the implementation of various public policies that require interdepartmental cooperation.

Other factors that contribute to problems with the bureaucracy include red tape, waste, conflict, and duplication.

Size Problems

The size of the bureaucracy has led to a system that allows some bureaucrats to begin to believe that they, and not elected officials, actually make laws and policy. And, as rules and regulations have become increasingly complex, the red tape (complex rules and procedures that must be followed before anything can get done) and waste in the system have grown. Often the paperwork and maze of regulations that one must get through before a license can be obtained or before a veteran can receive his or her first benefits, for example, are so overwhelming that many people are discouraged from ever applying for what is rightfully theirs. Moreover, as the bureaucracy has grown and the involvement of the federal government in all walks of life has increased, waste and duplication frequently occur. Stories in the news media abound about the use of research money to purchase expensive carpets for department heads instead of to discover a cure for the common cold.

Duplication of services and faulty coordination are also problems in an ever-mushrooming bureaucracy. As discussed earlier, in 1991 the Department of Health and Human Services underwent a massive reorganization to streamline programs because so many of them existed to deal with the problems faced by unmarried women with small children. Streamlining is the exception rather than the rule most times, however. It is far more likely to see a situation where programs abound not in just a single agency but in a variety of agencies, making duplication and even turf wars between agencies inevitable. For example, both the Customs Service and the Drug Enforcement Administration are charged with intercepting drugs brought into this country illegally. Lack of coordination and bickering have thus hurt the overall fight against illegal drugs as these two agencies compete.

System Problems

The lack of evaluation programs, increasing decentralization within agencies, and the vagueness of rules governing the bureaucracy and its programs also present major obstacles in reforming the bureaucracy.

Often, the success of a program may be difficult to gauge because there are no precise standards of evaluation. Moreover, if information concerning success is not available or cannot be measured with any precision, it becomes difficult for policy makers to know what to do with the program. Should it be continued, changed, or eliminated?

One of the most interesting examples of the difficulty of measuring success can be seen in the Head Start program. One of the Great Society programs initiated by Congress and Lyndon Johnson in the 1960s, it was designed to help low-income and minority students to do better in school. Head Start programs provided preschool enrichment classes for these youngsters on the theory that this "head start" would allow poorer children to compete in school on a more equal footing with those from more privileged

The Head Start program identifies deserving preschool children and provides much-needed education, nutrition, and socializing.

Women's basketball at the University of Texas.

backgrounds. Initially, the results were disappointing when it appeared that children enrolled in Head Start did no better in school than those who did not participate in the program. In spite of these discouraging results, the program was continued, although critics were quick to point to early lack of results. Later, however, long-term studies of the effectiveness of the program revealed that the Head Start program did have a positive effect on school performance.[29]

Decentralized authority also presents a problem constantly faced by the bureaucracy. Not only do most agencies have several regional offices making coordination difficult, but the structure of the federal system creates problems. While an agency in Washington, D.C., may have clear ideas concerning how a particular program should work, state and local officials may have very different ideas.

Vague directives are yet another problem that haunts bureaucrats. Congress often states only broad policy goals and leaves implementation of the specifics up to bureaucrats. This way Congress cannot be blamed for any particularly unpopular interpretations.

One particularly controversial policy was at the heart of Title IX of the Education Amendments of 1972, which, emulating aspects of the Civil Rights Act of 1964, mandated that

> No person in the United States shall, on the basis of sex, be excluded from participation in, be denied the benefits of, or be subjected to discrimination under any education program or activity receiving federal financial assistance.

The law further instructed the Secretary of Health, Education, and Welfare (it now applies to the Secretary of Education) to ''prepare and publish proposed regulations . . . which shall include with respect to intercollegiate athletic activities reasonable provisions considering the nature of particular sports'' to implement the amendments. Supporters of women's athletics and college and universities went around and around with HEW officials over the intent of Congress. Supporters of women's sports argued that discrimination against women in all sports was prohibited. Others said that ''revenue producing'' sports such as basketball and football were exempt.

Finally, in December 1978—six years after passage of the amendments—the Office for Civil Rights in HEW released a ''policy interpretation'' of the law dealing largely with the section that concerned intercollegiate athletics.[30] More than thirty pages of text were devoted to dealing with one hundred or so words from the statute. Football was recognized as unique, so it could be implied that male-dominated football programs could continue to outspend women's athletic programs. The more than sixty women's groups that had lobbied for equality of spending were outraged and turned their efforts toward seeking more favorable rulings on the construction of the statute from the courts.

We can probably expect similar litigation over the Clean Air Act. Vague directives from Congress often result in more confusion and make policy implementation extremely difficult.

Toward Reform

Politicians and the public regularly criticize the bureaucracy and call for its reform. It's too big, too inefficient, too decentralized, too unresponsive, and too out of control. Over the years, a wide variety of proposals for reform have been made, including reorganization, deregulation, and sunset laws.

[29] Fred M. Hechinger, ''Blacks Found to Benefit from Preschooling,'' *The New York Times,* September 11, 1984, p. C-4.

[30] See Joyce Gelb and Marian Lief Palley, *Women and Public Policies* (Princeton, N.J.: Princeton University Press, 1982), Chapter 5.

Reorganization

As discussed earlier, many presidents have called for total reorganization of the bureaucracy. Richard Nixon's proposal to consolidate several existing agencies into four super departments was the most dramatic, but it went nowhere. It makes sense, as with the situation in the Department of Health and Human Services, to consolidate all programs dealing with teenage mothers into one more easily manageable unit. Yet efforts like these to consolidate and combine programs often meet with resistance from bureaucrats and interest groups that fear a loss of power or, in times of recession, jobs.

Deregulation

Many argue that the government is too deeply involved in regulating various aspects of the economy. Therefore, since the 1970s major efforts have been made to deregulate, thereby freeing businesses from governmental rules and regulations. **Deregulation** allows market forces to drive the economy and govern prices.

Shortly after taking office, President Jimmy Carter announced that one of his major goals was to free the American people from "the burden of overregulation." One of the hallmarks of the Carter years, then, was the deregulating of numerous industries.

The airlines were the first to be deregulated. In 1978, at Carter's urgings, Congress passed legislation allowing airlines to select the routes they wanted to fly and to establish fares as they saw fit. Prior to this deregulation, the Civil Aeronautics Board (CAB) had allocated routes and set fares. Although many agree that the CAB had overregulated the airlines, the results of deregulation have been mixed. Some smaller cities no longer have air service as airlines dropped less lucrative lines. Similarly, deregulation led to increased competition that ultimately drove several major carriers from the skies and into bankruptcy.

The Reagan administration took up the deregulation campaign where Carter left off. Reagan's efforts to deregulate industries involved in health and safety were particularly controversial. A major scandal arose in his administration over efforts to lessen regulation of the environment, and more than twenty officials of the Environmental Protection Agency were forced to resign.

Air traffic is heavily regulated by the Federal Transportation Commission, although a period of deregulation in the 1980s and 90s led to tremendous shakeouts and instability.

Author Karen Berger holds a silicone gel breast implant at a press conference in November, 1991. Berger testified at a Food and Drug Administration hearing considering banning the implants due to health fears.

The question "How much government?" relates directly to the larger question of the role of government in a democracy. Many people, especially conservatives, believe that government regulation of the economy is ill advised. In contrast, many liberals believe that government regulations concerning the public health and welfare are very much needed. According to this group, individuals without the financial and investigatory abilities of the national government are unlikely to learn enough about certain potentially harmful products until it is too late.

The Food and Drug Administration within the Department of Health and Human Services is responsible for approving new products, product labeling, and the content of food and drugs to ensure public safety. In 1992, after public outcries, congressional hearings, and interest-group and media pressure on the FDA, it announced that it would limit the use of silicon breast implants. This was only after years of testimony and increasing medical evidence—including that from FDA scientists—showed that implants leaked and might be associated with other health hazards. Although more than 3 million women in the United States have had cosmetic breast implants, without the force and resources of the FDA, there would have been little that private citizens could have done to reveal the problem.

Sunset Laws

Another reform gaining momentum is passage of **sunset laws,** which provide that an agency is automatically abolished after a fixed period of years unless Congress extends its life. The theory behind this reform is that new agencies will not have the opportunity to be "captured" by special interests and will perform their duties freer of outside influences and more in accord with the public interest.

Summary

The bureaucracy plays a major role in America as a shaper of public policy, earning it the nickname the "fourth branch" of the government. In this chapter, we have traced the evolution of the bureaucracy from a handful of Cabinet assistants to the largest single employer in the United States. Most of these employees are a part of the civil service system and hold a variety of positions. Others, largely those in key policy positions, are appointed by the president.

The bureaucracy can be divided into four general categories: Cabinet departments, government corporations, independent agencies, and regulatory boards or commissions. Each of these entities plays a key role in policy making.

Bureaucrats use considerable administrative discretion in turning laws and executive directives into policy. Yet, to keep the bureaucracy accountable, all three branches try to exercise some control over its workings. The president and Congress, in particular, have a variety of mechanisms at their disposal to check the bureaucracy. Bureaucrats' strong ties to interest groups and the presence of iron triangles, however, often make the bureaucracy hard to control.

Key Terms

bureaucracy	Hatch Act	regulations
bureaucrats	whistle blowers	executive orders
civil service system	clientele agencies	iron triangles
Pendleton Act (Civil Service Reform Act of 1883)	government corporations	issue networks
	independent agencies	deregulation
merit system	implementation	sunset laws
regulatory commission	administrative discretion	

Suggested Readings

Derthick, Martha and Paul J. Quirk. *The Politics of Deregulation.* Washington: Brookings Institution, 1985.

Dodd, Lawrence and Richard Schott. *Congress and the Administrative State.* New York: Wiley, 1979.

Gormley, William T. Jr. *Taming the Bureaucracy: Muscles, Prayers and Other Strategies.* Princeton, N.J.: Princeton University Press, 1989.

Knott, Jack H. and Gary J. Miller. *Reforming Bureaucracy: The Politics of Institutional Choice.* Englewood Cliffs, N.J.: Prentice Hall, 1987.

Rourke, Francis E. *Bureaucracy, Politics and Public Policy.* Boston: Little, Brown, 1984.

Seidman, Harold and Robert Gilmour. *Politics, Position, and Power,* 4th ed. New York: Oxford University Press, 1986.

Stillman, Richard J. *The American Bureaucracy.* New York: Nelson Hall, 1987.

Weiss, Carol H. and Allen H. Barton., ed. *Making Bureaucracies Work.* Beverly Hills: Sage Publications, 1980.

Wilson, James Q. *Bureaucracy: What Government Agencies Do and Why They Do It.* New York: Basic Books, 1989.

> . . . the judiciary, from the nature of its functions, will always be the least dangerous to the political rights of the Constitution; because it will be least in a capacity to annoy or injure them.
>
> *Alexander Hamilton*

FEDERALIST NO. 78

The Framers worried most about the tyranny of taxation and military despotism. Because the judiciary cannot normally make policy in these areas, Hamilton feared the courts far less than he feared Congress or the president.

The Judiciary

When Alexander Hamilton wrote under the pen name Publius to urge support of the U.S. Constitution in 1787, he firmly believed that the judiciary would be "the least dangerous" branch of government. And in its formative years it *was* the least dangerous branch. So seemingly inconsequential was the judicial branch that when the national government made its move to the District of Columbia, Congress forgot to include any space to house the justices of the Supreme Court! Last-minute conferences with the Capitol architects led to the allocation of a small area in the basement of the Senate wing of the Capitol Building for a courtroom. There was no other space allowed for the justices, however.

Today, the role of the courts, particularly the U.S. Supreme Court, is significantly different from what it was in 1788, the year the national government came into being. The "least dangerous branch" is now perceived by many as having too much power. During different periods of its history the role and power of the federal courts have varied tremendously. They have often played a key role in creating a strong national government and have boldly led the nation in social reform. Yet at other times, they have stubbornly stood as a major obstacle to important social and economic change.

In this chapter we explore the development of the national judiciary. The Framers could never have envisioned that the authority of the Supreme Court and other federal courts would grow to include issues as diverse as the right of married couples to use birth control, the right of parents to withdraw life-support systems from their children, or the authority of the government to limit construction of a dam to save a small endangered fish called a snail darter. As recent battles over nominations to the Supreme Court reveal, a growing segment of the public views the Court as the final word on many important, controversial issues.

A note on terminology before we start: When we refer to the Supreme Court, the Court, or high court here, we mean the U.S. Supreme Court, which sits at the pinnacle of the federal and state court systems. The Supreme Court is also referred to by the name of the Chief Justice who presided over it during a particular period (e.g., the Marshall Court is the Court presided over by John Marshall from 1801 to 1835). When we use the term "courts," we refer to all federal or state courts unless otherwise noted.

The old chambers of the Supreme Court located in the basement of the U.S. Senate.

In this chapter we pay special attention to the political nature of the courts and examine how the power of the courts, especially that of the Supreme Court, has expanded over time. We look at how—and, more important, why—judges are appointed to the federal bench. We also examine the role of the courts in the legal process and how the Supreme Court arrives at its decisions. And finally, we speculate as to the future of the Court as an institution and as a policy maker.

The Creation of the Judicial Branch

James Madison's records of the Philadelphia Convention make it clear that the Framers devoted little time to the writing or the content of Article III, which created the judicial branch of government, largely because they believed that it posed little of the potential threat of tyranny that they feared from the other two branches. One scholar has even suggested that for at least some delegates to the Constitutional Convention, "provision for a national judiciary was a matter of theoretical necessity . . . more in deference to the maxim of separation [of powers] than in response to clearly formulated ideas about the role of a national judicial system and its indispensability."[1] There was debate among the Framers, however, concerning the need for any federal courts below the level of the Supreme Court, and some argued in favor of deciding all cases in state courts, with only appeals going before the Supreme Court. Others argued for a system of federal courts; a compromise left the final choice to Congress. Moreover, one of the Court's most important powers, that of judicial review, the authority to review acts of the other branches of government and the states, is not even contained in Article III of the Constitution, which vests *"The judicial Power of the United States . . . in one supreme Court, and in such inferior Courts as the Congress may from time to time ordain and establish."* Although there was some debate over whether the Court should have the power of judicial review, the question was left unsettled in the final document [and not finally resolved until *Marbury* v. *Madison* (1803) discussed on pages 306–307]. This vagueness was not all that unusual given the numerous compromises that took place in Philadelphia. Anti-Federalists, however, were not so nearly in agreement about the need for a supreme court, in particular, or a federal judiciary, more generally, especially one whose members had life tenure and the ability to interpret what was to be *"the supreme law of the land,"* a phrase that Anti-Federalists feared would give the Court too much power.

Had it been viewed as the potential policy maker the Court is today, it is highly unlikely that the Founders would have agreed on Article III's provision of life tenure with "good behavior" for federal judges. This feature was agreed upon because as Alexander Hamilton wrote in Federalist No. 78, the ability to "withstand legislative encroachment afford[s] a strong argument for permanent tenure of judicial offices." That is, the Framers didn't want the justices (or any federal judges) subject to the whims of politics, the public, or politicians. Moreover, Hamilton argued that the "independence of judges" was needed "to guard the Constitution and the rights of individuals." Therefore, because the Court was envisioned by the Framers as quite powerless, Alexander Hamilton stressed the need to place federal judges above the fray of politics. Although there is no denying that judges are political animals and carry the same prejudices and preferences to the bench that others do to the statehouse, Congress, or the White House, the provision of life tenure for *"good behavior"* has functioned well.

Some checks on the power of the judiciary were nonetheless included in the Constitution. Congress can alter the Court's jurisdiction (its ability to hear certain kinds of cases).

---

[1] Julius Goebal Jr., *History of the Supreme Court of the United States,* Vol. 1: *Antecedents and Beginnings to 1801* (New York: Macmillan, 1971), p. 206.

Congress can also propose constitutional amendments that, if ratified, will effectively reverse judicial decisions, and it can impeach and remove federal judges. In one further check, it is the president who—with the *"advice and consent"* of the Senate—appoints all federal judges.

The Judiciary Act of 1789

In spite of the Framers' intentions, the pervasive role of politics in the judicial branch became quickly evident with the passage of the Judiciary Act of 1789. Congress spent nearly the entire last half of its first session deliberating the various provisions of the act that were needed to give form and substance to the federal judiciary. As one early observer noted, "The convention has only crayoned in the outlines. It left it to Congress to fill up and colour the canvas."[2]

The Judiciary Act was drafted largely by U.S. Senator Oliver Ellsworth, a former member of the Constitutional Convention from Connecticut who later served on the Supreme Court as its second Chief Justice from 1796 to 1800. The act established the basic three-tiered structure of the federal court system. At the bottom were thirteen district courts—one in each state—each staffed by a federal judge. Appeals from the district courts were to be made to one of the three circuit courts. Each circuit court was composed of one district court judge and two Supreme Court justices. Although the Constitution mentions *"the supreme Court,"* it was silent on its size. Therefore, Congress set the size of the Court at six—establishing the position of Chief Justice and five associate justices.

From the beginning, the circuit court duties of the Supreme Court justices presented problems for the prestige of the Court. Few good lawyers were willing to accept nominations to the high court because its circuit court duties entailed a substantial amount of travel—most of it on horseback over poorly maintained roads in frequently inclement weather. Southern justices often tallied up as much as 10,000 miles a year on horseback. George Washington tried to prevail upon several friends and supporters to fill vacancies on the Court as they appeared, but most declined the "honor." John Adams, the second president of the United States, ran into similar problems. When he asked John Jay, the first Chief Justice, to resume the position after he resigned to become governor of New York, Jay declined the offer. Given Jay's view of the Court and its performance statistics, his refusal wasn't surprising. Jay had once remarked of the Court that it had neither "energy, weight and dignity" nor "public confidence and respect." In fact, the Court heard no cases in its first two years of existence and had heard fewer than seventy by 1801. Moreover, in an indication of its status, one associate justice had left the Court to become Chief Justice of the South Carolina Supreme Court. (Although such a move would be considered a step down today, keep in mind that in the early years of the United States many viewed the states as more important than the new national government.)

Hampered by frequent changes in personnel, limited space for its operations, no clerical support, and no system of reporting its decisions, the Court and its meager activities did not impress many people.

The Jay Court (1790–95)

In spite of all its problems, in its first decade the Court took several actions to help mold the new nation. First, by declining to render advisory opinions, the justices attempted to establish the Supreme Court as an independent, nonpolitical branch of government. Although John Jay frequently rendered advice to the president in private, the Court refused to answer questions posed to it by Washington concerning the construction of international laws and treaties. The justices wanted to avoid the appearance of prejudging an issue that could later arise before them.

The early Court also tried to advance principles of nationalism and to maintain the

Burdens of the Early Court

We really, sir, find the burdens laid upon us so excessive that we cannot forbear representing them in strong and explicit terms. That the task of holding twenty-seven Circuit Courts a year, in the different States, from New Hampshire to Georgia, besides two sessions of the Supreme Court at Philadelphia, in the two most severe seasons of the year, is a task which, considering the extent of the United States and the small number of Judges, is too burdensome. That to require of the Judges to pass the greater part of their days on the road, and at inns, at a distance from their families, is a requisition which in their opinion, should not be made unless in cases of necessity.

Source: Letter to the president of the United States, August 19, 1792, signed by all the justices. Quoted in Charles Warren, *The Supreme Court in United States History,* Vol. I (Boston: Little, Brown, 1926), pp. 88–89.

[2] Quoted in Ibid., p. 280.

supremacy of the national government over the states. As circuit court jurists, the justices rendered numerous decisions on such matters as national suppression of the Whiskey Rebellion (see Chapter 2), which strengthened Congress, and the constitutionality of the Alien and Sedition Acts (see Chapter 4), which made it a crime to criticize the executive branch of government or its actions.

During the ratification debates Anti-Federalists had warned that Article III extended federal judicial power to controversies *"between a State and Citizens of another State,"* meaning that a citizen of one state could sue any other state in federal court, a prospect unthinkable to defenders of state sovereignty. Although Federalists, including Hamilton and Madison, had scoffed at the idea, the nationalist Supreme Court proved them wrong in *Chisholm* v. *Georgia* (1793).[3] In *Chisholm,* the Court interpreted its jurisdiction under Article III, Section 2, to include the right to hear suits brought by a citizen of one state against another state. Writing in *Chisholm,* Justice James Wilson, for example, denounced the "haughty notions of state independence, state sovereignty, and state independence." The states' reaction to this perceived attack on their authority led to passage and ratification (in 1798) of the Eleventh Amendment, which specifically limited judicial power by specifying that the federal courts' authority did not "extend to any suit . . . commenced or prosecuted against one of the United States by citizens of another State. . . ."

Finally, in a series of circuit and Supreme Court decisions, the Jay Court paved the way for announcement of the doctrine of judicial review by the third Chief Justice, John Marshall. (Oliver Ellsworth served from 1796 to 1800.) Justices "riding cicircuit" frequently held state laws unconstitutional because they violated the U.S. Constitution. And, in *Hylton* v. *United States* (1796),[4] the Court evaluated for the first time the constitutionality of an act of Congress. In *Hylton,* the Court ruled that an excise tax on carriages that had been enacted by Congress was not a direct tax and was therefore valid even though it was not apportioned evenly among the states (as called for in the Constitution).

John Jay (1745–1829), one of the authors of *The Federalist Papers,* was the first Chief Justice of the U.S. Supreme Court, a position he held from 1789 to 1795. While serving as Chief Justice, he left the country for a year to lead a diplomatic mission to Great Britain which resulted in an agreement that bears his name—the Jay Treaty. Jay was one of the architects of New York's first state constitution, and while still Chief Justice, he ran unsuccessfully for governor of that state. He was elected as governor in 1794 while in England. Jay resigned as Chief Justice in 1795 to assume the New York governorship.

The Marshall Court (1801–35)

John Marshall was appointed Chief Justice by President John Adams in 1801, three years after he declined to accept a nomination as associate justice. An ardent Federalist who had declined Washington's offer to become Attorney General, Marshall later came to be considered the most important justice ever to serve on the high court. Part of his reputation is the result of the duration of his service and the historical significance of this period in our nation's history. Marshall also, however, brought much needed respect and prestige to the Court through his decisions in a progression of cases and a series of innovations.

One of Marshall's first innovations on the Court was to discontinue the practice of *seriatim* opinions, which was the custom of the King's Bench in Great Britain. Prior to the Marshall Court, each justice delivered his own opinion in order. (*Seriatim* is Latin for "in a series.") There was no single "opinion of the Court" as we are accustomed to today. For the Court to take its place as a coequal branch of government, Marshall strongly believed, the justices needed to speak as a *Court* and not as six individuals. In fact, during Marshall's first four years in office, the Court routinely spoke as one, and the Chief Justice wrote twenty-four of its twenty-six opinions.

Judicial Review

Alexander Hamilton first publicly mentioned the idea of judicial review in Federalist No. 78: "whenever a particular statute contravenes the Constitution, it will be the duty of the judicial tribunals to adhere to the latter and disregard the former." There is no counterpart

[3] 2 Dall. 419 (1793).
[4] 3 Dall. 171 (1796).

People of the Past

John Marshall

John Marshall (1755–1835) was born in a log cabin in Germantown, Virginia, the first of fifteen children of Welsh immigrants. Although tutored at home by two clergymen, it was his father who inspired Marshall, introducing him to English literature and Sir William Blackstone's influential book, *Commentaries on the Laws of England.* After serving in the Continental Army and acquiring the rank of captain, Marshall taught himself law. He attended only one formal course at the College of William and Mary before being admitted to the bar. Marshall practiced law in Virginia where he and his wife lived and raised a family. Of their ten children, only six survived childhood.

Marshall served as a delegate to the Virginia legislature from 1782 to 1785, 1787 to 1790, and 1795 to 1796 and played an instrumental role in Virginia's ratification of the U.S. Constitution in 1787. As the leading Federalist in Virginia, Marshall was offered several positions in the Federalist administrations of George Washington and John Adams—including Attorney General and associate justice to the Supreme Court—but he refused them all. Finally, Washington persuaded him to run for the House of Representatives in 1799. Marshall was elected, but his career in the House was brief, for he became Secretary of State in 1800 under John Adams. When Oliver Ellsworth resigned as Chief Justice of the Supreme Court in 1800, Adams nominated Marshall.

Marshall was well-suited to the leisurely pace of the Supreme Court in its early days. He enjoyed the outdoors, socializing in the clubs and saloons around Richmond, and he excelled at quoits (similar to horseshoes).

Marshall dominated the Court during his thirty-four years as Chief Justice and increased public respect for the Court by establishing the following tenets:

- The practice by which the view of the Court is expressed in a single opinion instead of a series of opinions, as had been the case. Marshall insisted on unanimity and discouraged dissenting and concurring opinions, thereby winning for the Court the prestige it needed to resolve many of the conflicts and controversies that came before it.
- The Court as the final arbiter of constitutional questions, with the right to declare congressional acts void [*Marbury* v. *Madison* (1803)].
- The authority of the Supreme Court over the judiciaries of the various states, including the Court's power to declare state laws invalid [*Fletcher* v. *Peck* (1810); *Martin* v. *Hunter's Lessee* (1816); *Cohens* v. *Virginia* (1821)].
- The supremacy of the federal government and Congress over state governments through a broad interpretation of the "necessary and proper" clause [*McCulloch* v. *Maryland* (1819)].

During the Marshall era the Court operated like a family firm. The justices came to Washington for only a few months, so they lived together in a boarding house where they often discussed cases at dinner over wine.

Personalities and individual characteristics had a tremendous influence on the Court. Although Marshall had little experience in the practice of law and none as a judge prior to his appointment to Chief Justice, his personality and leadership capabilities allowed him to shape the Court and the federal judiciary into a branch of the government with authority and respect.

to judicial review in the British political system. Under the terms of Britain's unwritten constitution and the doctrine of parliamentary sovereignty, courts cannot declare acts of Parliament to be unconstitutional. Nonetheless, because this function is not mentioned in the U.S. Constitution, the actual authority of the Supreme Court to review acts of Congress to determine their constitutionality was initially in question. Although the Supreme

Court had often reviewed acts of Congress, in the early years it had not found any to be unconstitutional. ***Marbury* v. *Madison*** (1803) today is viewed as providing the cornerstone of judicial review, the authority of the U.S. Supreme Court to review acts of Congress and the state legislatures to determine their constitutionality.

In the final hours of the Adams administration, William Marbury was appointed a justice of the peace for the District of Columbia. But in the confusion of winding up matters, John Marshall, Adams's Secretary of State, failed to deliver Marbury's commission. Marbury then asked James Madison, Thomas Jefferson's Secretary of State, for the commission. Under direct orders from Jefferson, who was irate over the Adams administration's last minute appointment of several federal judges (whose appointments were quickly ratified by the Federalist Congress), Madison refused to turn over the commission. Marbury and three other Adams appointees who were in the same situation then filed a writ of *mandamus* (a legal motion) asking the Supreme Court to order Madison to deliver their commissions.

Political tensions ran high as the Court met to hear the case. Jefferson threatened to ignore any order of the Court. Marshall realized that he and the prestige of the Court could be devastated by any refusal of the executive branch to comply with the decision. Responding to this challenge, in a brilliant opinion that in many sections reads more like a lecture to Jefferson than a discussion of the merits of Marbury's claim, Marshall concluded that although Marbury and the others were entitled to their commissions, the Court lacked the power to issue the writs sought by Marbury. Marshall further ruled that the parts of the Judiciary Act of 1789 that had extended the jurisdiction of the Court to allow it to issue writs was inconsistent with the Constitution and therefore unconstitutional.

Although the immediate effect of the decision was to deny power to the Court, its long-term effect was to establish the rule that "it is emphatically the province and duty of the judicial department to say what the law is." Since *Marbury,* the Court has routinely exercised this power of judicial review to determine the constitutionality of acts of Congress, the executive branch, and the states.

The Judicial System

The judicial system in the United States can best be characterized as a dual system consisting of the federal court system and the judicial systems of the fifty states. Both are basically three-tiered. As depicted in Figure 9-1, at the bottom are district trial courts, where litigation begins. In the middle are appellate courts in the state systems and the Courts of Appeals in the federal system. And a supreme court sits at the top of the pyramid as the final word in each system. The Courts of Appeal and supreme courts are **appellate courts** that with few exceptions review cases on appeal that already have been decided in lower courts. To appeal means to take a case to a higher court. All three court types hear cases that deal with two types of law: criminal and civil.

Criminal and Civil Law

Criminal law refers to the branch of law dealing with crimes and their punishments. A crime is an action considered to be an offense against authority or a violation of a duty owed to the public. Crimes are graded according to their severity as felonies, misdemeanors, or offenses. Some acts—for example, murder, rape, and robbery—are considered crimes in all states. Others—such as sodomy and some forms of gambling such as lotteries or bingo—are illegal only in some states. Moreover, although all states outlaw murder, their penal, or criminal codes treat the crime quite differently; as discussed in Chapter 4, the penalty for murder differs considerably from state to state.

Figure 9-1   The American Court System

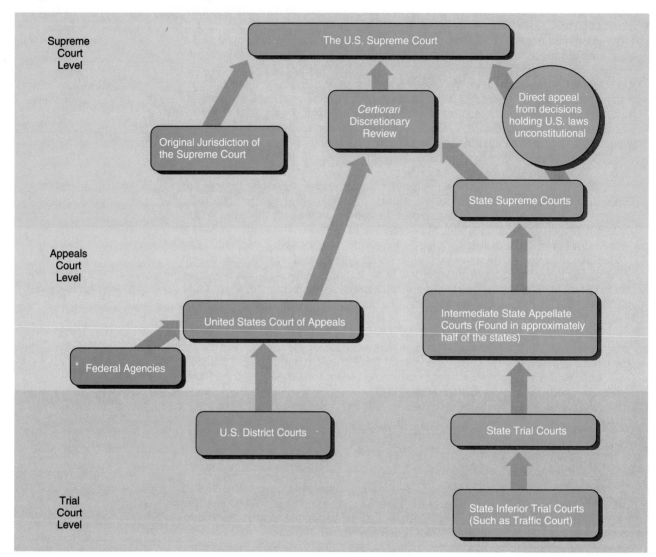

The body of law grading, describing, and setting punishments for crimes is known as criminal law. In contrast to civil law, criminal law assumes that society itself is the victim of the illegal act; therefore, the government prosecutes or brings an action on behalf of an injured party (acting as a plaintiff) in criminal but not civil cases. Criminal trials are often depicted on television programs like "Perry Mason" and "L.A. Law."

In criminal cases, a defendant is charged with violating a specific law. A state prosecutor or district attorney then generally takes the case before a **grand jury** to see if there are sufficient reasons to issue an **indictment**—a formal accusation—and proceed to trial. If an indictment is issued, the defendant can often negotiate or plea-bargain with the prosecutor for reduced charges in exchange for a guilty plea.

Civil law, on the other hand, is used to regulate relationships between private individuals or companies. Because the actions at issue don't constitute a threat to society, persons who believe they have been injured by another party must take action on their own to seek judicial relief. Civil cases, then, involve lawsuits filed to recover something of value, whether it is the right to vote, fair treatment, or monetary compensation for an item or service that cannot be recovered. Most cases seen on the television program "The People's Court" are civil cases. Divorce and child-custody proceedings, employment discrimination claims, and disputes arising from contracts or accidents are all examples of civil law. Divorce and child-custody cases generally involve only issues of state law and so are not heard, except in rare cases, in the federal court system. Allegations of employment discrimination based on gender or race, however, are generally filed in federal court because such discrimination violates the Civil Rights Act of 1964, a federal statute.

Before a criminal or civil case gets to court, much has to happen. In fact, very few of the legal disputes that arise in the United States ever get to court. Most individuals and companies involved in civil disputes routinely settle their disagreements out of court. Often these settlements are not reached until minutes before the case is to be tried. And many civil cases that go to trial are settled during the course of the trial—before the case can be handed over to the jury or submitted to a judge for a decision or determination of guilt.

Each civil and criminal case has a plaintiff who brings charges against a defendant. Sometimes the government is the plaintiff. The government may bring criminal or civil charges against a person or corporation for violating the law on behalf of the citizens of the state or national government. Cases are known by the name of the plaintiff first, and of the defendant, second. So in *Marbury* v. *Madison,* William Marbury was suing the U.S. government and James Madison as its Secretary of State for not delivering his judicial commission. During trials, judges must often interpret the intent of laws enacted by Congress and state legislatures as they bear on the issues at hand. To do so, they read reports, testimony, and debates on the relevant legislation and study the results of other similar legal cases.

Jurisdiction

In addition to two types of law, there are two kinds of jurisdiction, that is, the authority of the court to decide a certain question: original and appellate. *Original jurisdiction* refers to a court's ability to hear disputes as a trial court. (The William Kennedy Smith rape trial, for example, was heard before a state trial court.) Trial courts determine the facts of the case. More than 90 percent of all cases end at this stage.

Appellate jurisdiction refers to a court's ability to review cases already decided by a trial court. Appellate courts do not review the factual record; instead, they review legal issues to make certain that the law was applied properly.

The Federal Court System

The federal district courts, circuit courts of appeal, and the Supreme Court are called **constitutional** (or Article III) **courts** because they are established (or Congress is authorized to establish them) in Article III of the Constitution. Judges who preside over these courts are selected by the president (with the advice and consent of the Senate), and they serve lifetime terms as long as they engage in "good behavior."

In addition to constitutional courts, there are **legislative courts**, courts that are set up by Congress, generally for special purposes. The U.S. Court of Military Affairs (which hears appeals of cases involving the military), the Court of Customs and Appeals (which hears appeals from decisions of customs courts and the Patent Office), and bankruptcy courts (which hear cases involving bankruptcy proceedings) are examples of legislative courts. The judges who preside over these courts are appointed by the president (subject to Senate confirmation) and serve fixed, limited terms.

District Courts

As we saw earlier, Congress recognized the need for federal trial courts soon after ratification of the Constitution. Thirteen district courts were created by the Judiciary Act of 1789, and by 1992 there were ninety-four federal district courts. Because of one of the compromises of the Judiciary Act of 1789, no district court cuts across state lines. Every state has at least one district court, and the largest states—California, New York, and Texas—each have four.[5]

Federal district courts have the authority to hear only specific types of cases. (Cases involving all other kinds of issues generally must be heard in state court.) Although the rules governing district court jurisdiction can be complex, the cases heard there generally fall into three categories:

1. They present a federal question based on a claim under the U.S. Constitution, a treaty with another nation, or a federal statute. Federal question jurisdiction can involve criminal or civil law.
2. They involve the federal government as a party.[6]
3. They involve cases in which citizens are from different states, and the amount of money at issue is more than $50,000.[7]

The losing party in a case heard and decided in a federal district court may appeal the decision to the appropriate Circuit Court of Appeals.

Each federal judicial district has a U.S. Attorney, who is nominated by the president and confirmed by the Senate. The size of the staff and the number of Assistant U.S. Attorneys who work in each district depend on the amount of litigation in each district. U.S. Attorneys, like district attorneys within the states, have a considerable amount of discretion as to whether they pursue criminal or civil investigations or file charges against individuals or corporations.

The Courts of Appeals

The Circuit Courts of Appeals, the intermediate appellate courts in the federal system, were established in 1789 to hear appeals from federal district courts. Originally called circuit courts, each is now officially known as the United States Court of Appeals for the [circuit number] Circuit. There are eleven numbered circuit courts. A twelfth, the D.C. Circuit, handles most appeals involving federal regulatory commissions and agencies, including, for example, the National Labor Relations Board and the Securities and Exchange Commission.

The Courts of Appeals are staffed by 156 judges who are appointed by the president, subject to Senate confirmation. The number of judges within each circuit varies—depending upon the workload and the complexity of the cases—and ranges from six to twenty-eight. Each circuit is supervised by a chief judge, the most senior judge in terms of service below the age of seventy. In deciding cases, judges are divided into rotating three-judge panels, made up of both the active judges within the circuit, visiting judges (primarily district judges from the same circuit), and retired judges. In rare cases, by majority vote all the judges in a circuit may choose to sit together ("en banc") to decide a case.

---

[5] David W. Neubauer, *Judicial Process: Law, Courts and Politics* (Pacific Grove, Calif.: Brooks/Cole, 1991), p. 57.

[6] The most commonly filed cases in the federal district courts involve challenges to determinations made by the Social Security Administration concerning disability payments. In fact, more than 50 percent of the civil cases heard by federal district courts involve these kinds of cases.

[7] Cases involving citizens from different states generally can be filed in either state or federal court.

The Courts of Appeals have no original jurisdiction. Rather, Congress has granted these courts appellate jurisdiction over two general categories of cases: appeals from criminal and civil cases from the district courts and appeals from administrative agencies. Criminal and civil case appeals constitute about 90 percent of the workload of the Courts of Appeals. In contrast, appeals from administrative agencies make up only about 10 percent of the workload. And because so many agencies are located in Washington, D.C., the D.C. Circuit Court of Appeals hears an inordinate number of such cases. The D.C. Circuit Court of Appeals, then, is considered the second most important court in the nation because its decisions regulate the regulatory agencies.

Once a decision is made by a federal Court of Appeals, a litigant no longer has an automatic right to an appeal. The losing party may submit a petition to the Supreme Court to hear the case, but the Court grants few of these requests. The Courts of Appeals, then, are the courts of last resort for almost all federal litigation.

In general, Courts of Appeals try to correct errors of law and procedure that have occurred in the lower court or administrative agency. Courts of Appeals hear no new testimony; instead, lawyers submit written arguments, called **briefs** (also submitted in trial courts), and then appear to argue the case and orally present their arguments to the court. In deciding these cases, the judges rely on the briefs, oral argument, and **precedents** (past decisions) in making their decisions.

Although decisions of any Court of Appeals are binding on only the district courts that are within the geographic confines of the circuit, decisions of the U.S. Supreme Court are binding throughout the nation and establish precedents. This reliance on past decisions or precedents to formulate decisions in new cases is called ***stare decisis*** (a Latin phrase meaning "let the decision stand"). The principle of *stare decisis* allows for continuity and predictability in our judicial system. If a party goes to court, it is incumbent on his or her lawyer to know how a court has acted in similar cases. Although *stare decisis* can be helpful in predicting decisions, at times judges carve out new ground and ignore, decline to follow, or even overrule precedents in order to reach a different conclusion in a case involving similar circumstances. In one sense, that is why there is so much litigation in America today. Parties know that one cannot always predict the outcome of a case; if such prediction were possible, there would be little reason to go to court.

The Supreme Court

At the top of the judicial ladder is the U.S. Supreme Court. In reviewing cases from the U.S. Courts of Appeals and state supreme courts, it acts as the final interpreter of the U.S. Constitution. Not only does it decide many major cases with tremendous policy significance each year, it also ensures uniformity in the interpretation of national laws and the Constitution, resolves conflicts among the states, and maintains the supremacy of national law in the federal system.

Since 1869, the U.S. Supreme Court has consisted of eight associate justices and one Chief Justice, who is nominated by the president specifically for that position. There is no special significance about the number nine, and the Constitution is silent about the size of the Court. Between 1801 and 1869 Congress altered the size of the Court several times. The least number on the Court was six; the most, ten. In 1866 Congress reduced the size of the Court from ten to eight so that President Andrew Johnson, who was very unpopular with Congress (and who escaped being removed from office by the Senate by just one vote), could not fill two vacancies that existed. When the more popular former war hero Ulysses S. Grant took office, the number was increased to nine, where it has remained. There have been only 106 justices of the Court since 1790.

The Chief Justice presides over public sessions of the Court, conducts the Court's conferences, assigns the writing of opinions (if he is in the majority, otherwise the most senior justice in the majority makes the assignment), and administers the oath of office to the president and the vice president on Inauguration Day. Any federal judge may administer the oath, as has happened when a president dies in office. By law, the Chief Justice, like the rest of the justices, is authorized to hire four clerks. Chief Justice William Rehnquist, however, has a tradition of hiring only three. He also has several secretaries and a messenger to help him with his duties. In 1972 Congress authorized the position of administrative assistant to serve at the pleasure of the Chief Justice. Chief Justice Warren E. Burger (1969–86) used his assistant to help him in his nonlegal judicial duties by conducting research, monitoring judicial administration, supervising Court operations, and educating the public about the role of the Supreme Court.

In addition to their law clerks, justices are assisted in their duties by personal secretaries and other members of the Court's support staff, including

- The Clerk of the Court: the Court's official business manager, who accepts all filings, administers the Court's docket, and prepares the Court's formal judgments
- The Marshal of the Court: the Court's general manager, paymaster, and chief security officer
- The Reporter of Decisions: edits opinions and supervises their printing in the Court's official reporter, *The United States Reports*
- The Public Information Officer: answers questions from the press and public about the Court and the justices
- The Legal Office: serves as in-house counsel on questions regarding the Court or the building and also assists with screening petitions when necessary.

It is not uncommon to hear a disgruntled party emerge from a local courthouse and angrily vow to take his or her appeal "all the way to the Supreme Court." In reality, this seldom happens. Although the Court received a record 6,316 petitions for review in 1990, it accepted only 125 cases for plenary (full) review—down from 146 in 1989 and 170 in 1988. Furthermore, the appellate process (the process of appealing decisions of one court to a higher court) is costly and lengthy. A case could take at least five years to

Chief Justices of the Supreme Court

CHIEF JUSTICE	NOMINATING PRESIDENT	YEARS OF SERVICE
John Jay	Washington	1789–1795
John Rutledge[a]	Washington	1795
Oliver Ellsworth	Washington	1796–1800
John Marshall	Adams	1801–1835
Roger B. Taney	Jackson	1836–1864
Salmon P. Chase	Lincoln	1864–1873
Morrison R. Waite	Grant	1874–1888
Melville W. Fuller	Cleveland	1888–1910
Edward D. White	Taft	1910–1921
William Howard Taft	Harding	1921–1930
Charles Evans Hughes	Hoover	1930–1941
Harlan Fiske Stone	F. Roosevelt	1941–1946
Fred M. Vinson	Truman	1946–1953
Earl Warren	Eisenhower	1953–1969
Warren E. Burger	Nixon	1969–1986
William H. Rehnquist	Reagan	1986–present

[a]Not confirmed by the Senate.

Then and Now

Law Clerks

As early as 1850, the justices of the Supreme Court beseeched Congress to approve the hiring of an "investigating clerk" to assist each justice, particularly in copying opinions. Congress denied the request, so when the first law clerk was hired by Justice Horace Gray in 1882, the clerk was paid by the justice himself. A top graduate from Harvard Law School, Justice Gray's clerk served as an assistant and a barber. Finally, in 1886 Congress appropriated $1,600 a year to provide for a "stenographer clerk" for each justice. Although today clerks generally serve for periods of one to two years, Chief Justices Charles Evans Hughes and William Howard Taft and Justice Frank Murphy employed their clerks for five years or longer.

Over time, the number of clerks employed by the justices has increased. In 1989, for example, there were thirty-three clerks serving the nine justices, whereas twenty years ago there were half as many. Generally each justice hires four clerks, who each earn approximately $40,000 a year.

The justices have complete discretion over whom they hire and the nature and amount of the work they assign. Clerks are typically selected from candidates at the top of their graduating class from prestigious law schools. They perform a variety of tasks, ranging from searching every page of *United States Reports* for some particular information to playing tennis or taking walks with the justices. Clerks spend most of their time researching material relevant to particular cases, reading and summarizing cases, and helping justices write opinions. Just how much help they provide in the writing of opinions is not known. Although it is occasionally alleged that a particular clerk wrote a particular opinion delivered by a justice, no such allegation has ever been proved. The relationship between clerks and the justices for whom they work is close and confidential, and many aspects of the relationship are kept secret. Clerks may sometimes talk among themselves about the views and personalities of their justices, but rarely has a clerk leaked such information to the press.

Supplementing the assistance provided by clerks is the Court's Legal Office, established in 1973. The office is staffed by two attorneys, each serving four years. They provide advice to the justices and the clerks of the Court on matters of procedure and any questions directly concerning the Court.

The growing workload of the Court makes the services of the Court's Legal Office and an increasing number of law clerks a necessity.

---

get to the Supreme Court, and litigation of more than twenty years duration is not out of the question as cases get bounced back and forth on different issues between courts of different levels. For example, many inmates have been on death row for ten or more years as they await the appeals of their cases on various grounds. Criminal cases, including death penalty cases, come before the Court through its appellate jurisdiction. A much less common way for a case to reach the Court is through its original jurisdiction.

Original Jurisdiction. The Constitution specifically sets out the scope of the Court's original jurisdiction, that is, cases for which the Court functions as a trial court having the first, or original, hearing in the case. The Court has original jurisdiction ". . . *over all Cases affecting Ambassadors, other public Ministers and Consuls, and those in which a State shall be a party. . . .*" Most cases arising under the Court's original jurisdiction involve disputes between two states, usually over issues such as ownership of offshore oil deposits, territorial disputes caused by shifting river boundaries, or controversies caused by conflicting claims over water rights such as when a river flows through two or more states.[8] In earlier days, the Court would actually sit as a trial court and hear evidence and

[8] Neubauer, p. 370.

argument. Today, the Court usually appoints a Special Master—often a retired judge or an expert on the matter at hand—to hear the case in a district court on behalf of the Supreme Court and then report his or her findings and recommendations back to the Court. It is rare for more than one or two of these cases to come to the Court in a year.

Appellate Jurisdiction. Most cases arrive at the Court under its appellate jurisdiction, that is, its authority to hear appeals from other courts in the state or federal systems. The appellate jurisdiction of the Court can be changed by the Congress at any time, a power that has been a potent threat to the authority of the Court. The Judiciary Act of 1925 gave the Court discretion over its own jurisdiction, meaning that it does not have to accept all appeals that come to it. This so-called "Judge's Bill" was largely written by the Court itself under the direction of Chief Justice William Howard Taft, incidentally the only member of the Court who had been president of the United States. The idea behind the bill was that the intermediate Courts of Appeal should be the final word for almost all federal litigants, thus freeing the Supreme Court to concentrate on constitutional issues unless the Court decided that it wanted to address other issues. The Court, then, is not expected to exercise its appellate jurisdiction simply to correct errors of other courts. Instead, appeal to the Supreme Court should be taken only if the case presents important issues of law, or what is termed "a substantial federal question." Since 1988, all appellate cases that come to the Court arrive there on a petition for a **writ of *certiorari*** (from the Latin "to be informed"), which literally are requests for the Supreme Court—at its discretion—to order up the records of the lower courts for purposes of review.

All petitions for *certiorari* must meet two criteria:

1. They must come from the U.S. Court of Appeals or from a state court of last resort. Generally, this means that the case has been decided by the state supreme court.
2. The case must involve a federal question. This means that the case must present questions of interpretation of federal constitutional law or involve a federal statute or treaty. The reasons why the Court should accept the case for review and legal argument supporting that position are set out in the petition (also called a brief).

How Lower Court Judges Are Selected

The selection of all federal judges is a very political process: They are nominated by the president and must be confirmed by the U.S. Senate. Most presidents generally have indicated their intention to make judicial appointments in a nonpartisan manner. But, because judges are appointed for life and enjoy significant prestige, federal judgeships often are considered to be "political plums" used to reward the party faithful. Typically, federal judges have held other offices, such as those of state court judge or prosecutor. Most have been involved in politics, which is what brings them into consideration for a position on the federal bench. Griffin Bell, Attorney General in the Carter administration and former federal circuit court judge, once remarked, "For me, becoming a federal judge wasn't very difficult. I managed John F. Kennedy's presidential campaign in Georgia. And I was campaign manager and special counsel for the governor [Carter]."[9]

Of the judgeships for the three constitutional courts, those for federal district courts are most frequently seen as "rewards." And it is often senators and not the president who view these seats on the bench as theirs to bestow on their political allies.

Although there are specific, detailed provisions in Articles I and II concerning the

[9] Quoted in Nina Totenberg, "Will Judges Be Chosen Rationally?" *Judicature* (August/September 1976), p. 93.

Characteristics of Appointees to Federal District Courts from Johnson to Bush

	JOHNSON APPOINTEES	NIXON APPOINTEES	FORD APPOINTEES	CARTER APPOINTEES	REAGAN APPOINTEES	BUSH APPOINTEES[a]
Occupation (percent)						
Politics/government	21.3	10.6	21.2	4.4	12.8	10.4
Judiciary	31.1	28.5	34.6	44.6	37.2	47.9
Lawyer	44.3	58.1	44.2	57.7	47.3	39.5
Other	3.3	2.8	0.0	3.5	2.8	2.1
Experience (percent)						
Judicial	34.4	35.2	42.3	54.5	46.6	50.0
Prosecutorial	45.9	41.9	50.0	38.6	44.1	38.0
Neither	33.6	36.3	30.8	28.2	28.3	27.1
Political affiliation (percent)						
Democrat	94.3	7.3	21.2	92.6	4.8	4.2
Republican	5.7	92.7	78.8	4.4	93.1	93.8
Independent	0.0	0.0	0.0	2.9	2.1	2.1
Religion (percent)						
Protestant	58.2	73.2	73.1	60.4	60.3	64.6
Catholic	31.1	18.4	17.3	27.7	30.0	22.9
Jewish	10.7	8.4	9.6	11.9	9.3	12.5
Race/ethnicity (percent)						
White	93.4	95.5	88.5	78.7	92.4	95.8
Black	4.1	3.4	5.8	13.9	2.1	2.1
Asian-American	0.0	0.0	3.9	0.5	0.7	0.0
Hispanic	2.5	1.1	1.9	6.9	4.8	2.1
Sex						
Percent female	1.6	0.6	1.9	14.4	8.3	10.4
Net worth (percent)						
Under $200,000	NA	NA	NA	35.8[b]	17.6	6.2
200–499,999	NA	NA	NA	41.2[b]	37.6	29.2
500–999,999	NA	NA	NA	18.9[b]	21.7	31.2
1,000,000+	NA	NA	NA	4.0[b]	23.1	33.3
Total number of appointees	122	179	52	202	290	48
Average age at nomination (years)	51.4	49.1	49.2	49.7	48.7	49.6

[a] Appointees through December 1990.
[b] These figures are for appointees confirmed by the 96th Congress. Professor Elliot Slotnick of Ohio State University provided the net worth figures for all but six Carter district court appointees for whom no data were available.

Source: Sheldon Goldman, "The Bush Imprint on the Judiciary: Carrying on a Tradition," *Judicature 74* (April–May 1991).

qualifications for president, senator, and member of the House of Representatives, the Constitution is curiously silent on the topic of qualifications for federal judge. This may have been because of an assumption that all federal judges would be lawyers, but to make such a requirement explicit might have marked the judicial branch as too elite for the tastes of common men and women. Also, it would have been impractical to require formal legal training, given that there were so few law schools in the nation and the fact that most lawyers became licensed after clerking or apprenticing with another lawyer.[10]

Nominations to District Courts

Each year a large number of federal district court judgeships become available through death and retirement. Other openings occur as Congress continually adds new positions in an effort to meet the increasing demands on the federal court system. Because there are so many vacancies at any one time, the president generally does not become personally involved in the selection of lower court judges. Presidents Jimmy Carter and Ronald Reagan, for example, each appointed more than 200 judges to the federal district courts, and many of their nominees were unknown to them.

Until the election of Ronald Reagan, presidents generally deferred selection of district court judges to the choice of senators of their own party who represented the state in which a vacancy occurred on the federal bench. In turn, members of the Senate generally deferred to the wishes of their colleagues who were doing the sponsoring, a practice called senatorial courtesy. At one point, by tradition, the Senate would refuse to confirm presidential nominees unless the nominee had been approved by the senator(s) of the nominee's home state.

Senatorial courtesy has been an important source of political patronage for senators, but it also helps the system run more smoothly. In fact, it has the practical effect of what Attorney General Robert F. Kennedy characterized as ". . . senatorial appointment with the advice and consent of the President."[11]

The process was disrupted by the actions of President Reagan, particularly during his second term, when his new Attorney General, Edwin Meese III, became very involved in the process of judicial selection. Meese appointed a special assistant to handle judicial selection and used personal interviews of prospective nominees to an unprecedented degree in order to ascertain the candidate's overall "judicial philosophy," that is, what the prospective jurist thinks about legal issues (see pages 331–333). Moreover, Meese was willing to go head to head with senators to make sure that only judges sharing the administration's political philosophy were appointed to the bench.

President George Bush continued the policy of minimizing the home-state senators' role in the confirmation process, but his first Attorney General, Richard Thornburgh, tried to minimize some of the overt politicization of the Reagan administration. Bush requested that senators forward three choices to him for any district court vacancy. These names were reviewed by the president's Committee on Federal Judicial Selection after the prospective nominees had been interviewed by various Justice Department officials including the Deputy Attorney General and the Solicitor General (see pages 326–327), to ascertain their judicial philosophy and position on controversial issues such as civil rights and abortion. One name was then selected for nomination. This practice incensed Republican senators, in particular, who view district court judgeships as an important way to reward friends and campaign workers. Moreover, the Bush administration's insistence on nominees who were "philosophically conservative"[12] resulted in a considerable number of vacancies on the federal bench. In December 1991, 103 vacancies existed on the

[10] John R. Vile and Mario Perez-Reilly, "The U.S. Constitution and Judicial Qualifications: A Curious Omission," *Judicature* (December/January 1991), pp. 198–202.

[11] Quoted in David M. O'Brien, *Storm Center: The Supreme Court in American Politics,* 2nd ed. (New York: Norton, 1990), p. 70.

[12] Sheldon Goldman, "The Bush Imprint on the Federal Judiciary: Carrying on a Tradition," *Judicature* (April/May 1991), p. 297.

649-member federal district court bench, and President Bush had nominated only 37 individuals to those posts.

Nominations to Courts of Appeals

Senatorial courtesy does not operate to the same degree in the selection of the more prestigious Courts of Appeals judgeships largely because the jurisdiction of each circuit includes at least three states. When vacancies on the Courts of Appeals occur, presidents frequently consult senators of the various states in the circuit, but ultimately the Justice Department plays the key role in selection.

To ensure diverse representation of blacks, women, and other minorities traditionally underrepresented on the federal bench, President Jimmy Carter established a Judicial Nominating Commission. In turn, commissions (consisting of lawyers and laypersons selected by the president) were established within each circuit. The members were charged with submitting three to five names to the president for his consideration. According to political scientist Elliot E. Slotnick, in spite of President Carter's efforts to depoliticize the process, the judges selected in this manner were no different from those chosen more traditionally. Like those chosen in the past, they were overwhelmingly from the president's party and were likely to have been involved in party politics.[13]

The commissions were abandoned by President Reagan and since then the Justice Department (and, increasingly the White House counsel) has played a key role in the selection of Courts of Appeals judges. Unlike Carter, Reagan became very involved in some Senate battles on behalf of his conservative nominees. In particular, Attorney General Meese actively defended several conservative nominations, including that of Daniel Manion to an appeals court position in 1986 that resulted in a close and bitter Senate vote that the Reagan administration ultimately lost, although the president lobbied several senators personally.

As of December 1, 1991, twenty-one vacancies existed on the already overburdened circuit courts, but only seven nominations were pending before the Senate Judiciary Committee.

Court of Appeals Judge Edith Jones from Houston, Texas. Judge Jones, generally considered to be a conservative, was often mentioned as a possible Republican appointee to the Supreme Court during the Bush administration.

How a Justice Gets to the U.S. Supreme Court

As noted, the Constitution is silent on the qualifications for appointment to the Supreme Court (as well as to other constitutional courts). In Great Britain, where the Lord Chancellor is the highest court official (and formally appointed by the Crown but actually chosen by the prime minister), ideology is generally not a concern in any court appointments; experience as a trial judge is. In the United States, Supreme Court justices generally have had little previous judicial experience on any level. Of the 106 justices who have served or are serving on the Court, only 22 had ten or more years of experience on any bench, and 42 had no judicial experience at all. Justice Oliver Wendell Holmes once remarked that a judge should be a "combination of Justinian, Jesus Christ and John Marshall."[14]

According to insurance company statistics, only conductors of symphony orchestras enjoy longer life spans than Supreme Court justices.

Like other federal court judges, the justices of the Supreme Court are nominated by the president and must be confirmed by the Senate. Historically, however, because of the special place the Supreme Court enjoys in our constitutional system, its nominees have encountered more opposition than district or Court of Appeals judges. As the role of the Court has increased over time, so too has the amount of attention given to nominees. And

[13] Elliot E. Slotnick, "Federal Appellate Judge Selection During the Carter Administration: Recruitment Changes and Unanswered Questions," *Justice System Journal* 6 (Fall 1981), pp. 293–304.

[14] Quoted in Judge Irving R. Kaufman, "Charting a Judicial Pedigree," *The New York Times,* January 24, 1981, p. 23.

with the increased attention has come increased opposition, especially to nominees with controversial views.

Nomination Criteria

Justice Sandra Day O'Connor once remarked that "You have to be lucky" to be appointed to the Court.[15] Although luck is certainly important, over the years nominations to the bench have been made for a variety of reasons. Depending on the timing of a vacancy, a president may or may not have a list of possible candidates or even a specific individual in mind. Until recently, presidents often have looked within their circle of friends or their administration to fill a vacancy. Nevertheless, whether the nominee is a friend or someone known to the president only by reputation, at least six criteria are especially important.

1. *Competence and ethical standards.* Most prospective nominees are expected to have had at least some judicial or governmental experience. John Jay, the first Chief Justice, was one of the authors of *The Federalist Papers* and was active in New York politics. John Marshall was a former Secretary of State. Many recent appointees to the Court have had prior judicial experience. Moreover, Justices John Paul Stevens, Anthony Kennedy, Antonin Scalia, David Souter, and Clarence Thomas all served on the U.S. Court of Appeals. Unlike most recent justices, however, Thomas had served on the Court of Appeals for only eighteen months, and he had never argued a case in federal court, leading the American Bar Association's Standing Committee on the Federal Judiciary (see page 321) to rate him only Qualified, the lowest acceptable rating.

   It is rare for the ethical standards or personal lives of prospective members of the Court to be challenged. In 1968, upon Lyndon Johnson's nomination of Associate Justice Abe Fortas to the position of Chief Justice, enough questions were raised about the propriety of Fortas's business dealings that his nomination was withdrawn. More recently, in 1991 the nation sat riveted to their television sets as they watched Clarence Thomas being questioned about charges of sexual harassment levied against him by a former employee, Anita Hill. Although these charges were not enough to stand in the way of his confirmation, they did result in one of the closest confirmation votes ever for a Supreme Court justice—fifty-two to forty-eight.

2. *Ideological or policy preferences.* Most presidents seek to appoint to the Court individuals who share their policy preferences, and almost all have political goals in mind when they appoint a justice. Upon the death of staunch Federalist Justice William Cushing, for example, Thomas Jefferson wrote to one of his allies, "I observe old Cushing is dead. At length, then, we have a chance of getting a Republican majority in the Supreme Judiciary. For ten years has that branch braved the spirit and will of the nation. . . . The event is a fortunate one, and so timed as to be a godsend to me."[16]

   More recently, Presidents Richard Nixon and Ronald Reagan were very successful in molding the Court to their own political beliefs. Both publicly proclaimed that they were nominating individuals who favored a **strict constructionist** approach to constitutional decision making—that is, an approach that emphasizes the initial intentions of the Framers (see pages 331–333). Justices William Rehnquist and Antonin Scalia, in particular, have been very vocal in

---

[15] Quoted in Lawrence Baum, *The Supreme Court,* 3rd. ed. (Washington: CQ Press, 1989), p. 108.

[16] Quoted in William H. Rehnquist, *The Supreme Court: How It Was, How It Is* (New York: Morrow, 1987), p. 237.

The current Supreme Court. From left to right (front row): John Paul Stevens, Byron R. White, William H. Rehnquist, Harry A. Blackmun, Sandra Day O'Connor; (back row): David H. Souter, Antonin Scalia, Anthony M. Kennedy, Clarence Thomas.

The Supreme Court, 1992

NAME	YEAR OF BIRTH	YEAR OF APPOINTMENT	LAW SCHOOL	APPOINTING PRESIDENT	PRIOR JUDICIAL EXPERIENCE	PRIOR GOVERNMENT EXPERIENCE
Byron R. White	1917	1962	Yale	Kennedy	—	Deputy U.S. Attorney General
Harry A. Blackmun	1908	1970	Harvard	Nixon	U.S. Court of Appeals	—
William H. Rehnquist[a]	1924	1972	Stanford	Nixon	—	Assistant U.S. Attorney General
John Paul Stevens	1920	1975	Chicago	Ford	U.S. Court of Appeals	—
Sandra Day O'Connor	1930	1981	Stanford	Reagan	Arizona Court of Appeals	State Legislator
Antonin Scalia	1936	1986	Harvard	Reagan	U.S. Court of Appeals	—
Anthony M. Kennedy	1936	1988	Harvard	Reagan	U.S. Court of Appeals	—
David H. Souter	1940	1990	Harvard	Bush	U.S. Court of Appeals	New Hampshire Attorney General
Clarence Thomas	1949	1991	Yale	Bush	U.S. Court of Appeals	Chair, Equal Employment Opportunity Commission

[a]Promoted to Chief Justice by Reagan in 1986.

support of this view, believing that it is inappropriate for the judiciary to make policy through broad or expansive interpretations of the Constitution.[17] Instead, they argue, the Court should construe the Constitution narrowly.

Whereas his predecessors forwarded some fairly controversial nominees to the Senate Judiciary Committee for its approval, in contrast, President Bush looked to a nominee with virtually no public record when his first vacancy occurred. Many believe that it was the absence of any controversial pronouncements in David Souter's background that prompted his nomination. Upon Souter's nomination, Bush said that Supreme Court justices should be beyond the "flames of political passion" and urged the Senate to avoid allowing abortion or any other issue to become a "litmus test."[18] Some viewed Bush's self-stated goal of de-politicizing the selection of Supreme Court justices with skepticism that appeared warranted when Bush nominated Clarence Thomas to the high court in 1991. Thomas was well regarded in conservative circles and known for his writings and strong opinions on affirmative action and the role of the states in the federal system.

3. *Rewards.* Historically, many of those appointed to the Supreme Court have been personal friends of presidents. Abraham Lincoln, for example, appointed one of his key political advisers to the Court. More recently, Lyndon Johnson appointed two longtime friends, Abe Fortas and Tom Clark. In addition, most presidents select justices of their own party affiliation. Chief Justice Rehnquist was long active in Arizona Republican Party politics, as was Justice O'Connor before her appointment to the bench; both were appointed by Republican presidents. Party activism can also be used by presidents as an indication of a nominee's commitment to certain ideological principles.

4. *Pursuit of political support.* During Ronald Reagan's successful campaign for the presidency in 1980, some of his advisers feared that the "gender gap" would hurt him. Polls repeatedly showed that he was far less popular with female voters than with men. Particularly troublesome was his vocal opposition to the pending Equal Rights Amendment. To gain support from women, Reagan announced during his campaign that should he win, he would appoint a woman to fill the first vacancy on the Court. When Justice Potter Stewart, a moderate, announced his early retirement from the bench, President Reagan nominated Sandra Day O'Connor of the Arizona State Court of Appeals to fill the vacancy.

5. *Religion.* Ironically, religion, which has historically been an important issue, was hardly mentioned during the most recent Supreme Court vacancies, even though Clarence Thomas made much of the importance of his religious upbringing. When his nomination was announced he went so far as to thank the Catholic nuns who had taught him when he was a boy. Through 1992, of the 106 justices who have served on the Court, almost all have been members of traditional Protestant faiths. Only nine have been Catholic and only five have been Jewish.[19] At two times during the Rehnquist Court, more Catholics—Brennan, Scalia, and Kennedy and then Scalia, Kennedy, and Thomas—have served on the Court at one time than at any other period in history. Today, however, it is clear that religion cannot be taken as a sign of a justice's conservative or liberal ideology: When William Brennan was on the Court, he and Antonin Scalia were at ideological extremes.

[17]But see Sue Davis, *Justice Rehnquist and the Conservative Judicial Philosophy* (Princeton, N.J.: Princeton University Press, 1989).

[18]Laurene McQuillan, "Bush Urges Senate to Avoid Abortion Litmus Test on Souter," *Reuters,* July 24, 1990, NEXIS.

[19]Clarence Thomas is considered Catholic here, although he currently attends an Episcopalian church, having been barred from Catholic sacraments because of his remarriage.

6. *Race.* Only two black justices have ever served on the Court. Race was undoubtedly a critical issue in the appointment of Clarence Thomas to replace Thurgood Marshall, the first black justice. But instead of acknowledging his wish to retain a "black seat" on the Court, President Bush announced that he was "picking the best man for the job on the merits," a claim that was met with considerable skepticism by many observers.

The Supreme Court Confirmation Process

Before 1900, about one-fourth of all presidential nominees to the Supreme Court were rejected by the Senate. In 1844, for example, President John Tyler sent six nominations to the Senate, and all but one were defeated. In 1866 Andrew Johnson nominated his brilliant Attorney General, Henry Stanberry, but the Senate's hostility to Johnson led it to *abolish* the vacancy instead of letting him fill it.

As noted earlier, the Constitution gives the Senate the authority to approve all nominees to the federal bench, and it takes this duty most seriously when considering nominees to the Supreme Court. Ordinarily, all nominations are referred to the Senate Committee on the Judiciary, which is composed of fourteen members. In the 102nd Congress, all but one are lawyers. As detailed later, this committee then investigates the nominees, holds hearings, and votes on its recommendation for Senate action. The full Senate then deliberates on the nominee before voting. A simple majority vote is required for confirmation.

Investigation. Once a president settles on a nominee to the Supreme Court, the nominee's name is sent to the Federal Bureau of Investigation. While the FBI conducts an extensive background check, the Senate Judiciary Committee also begins to investigate the background of the nominee. (The same process is used for nominees of the lower federal courts, although such investigations generally are not nearly as extensive as for Supreme Court nominees.)

To begin its task, the Senate committee asks each nominee to complete a lengthy questionnaire detailing previous work (dating as far back as high school summer jobs), judicial opinions written, judicial philosophy, speeches, and even all interviews ever given to members of the press. Committee staffers also get in touch with potential witnesses who might offer testimony concerning the nominee's fitness for office.

At the same time, the president also forwards the name of his nominee to the American Bar Association (ABA), the politically powerful organization that represents the interests of the legal profession. After its own investigation, the ABA rates the nominee, based on his or her qualifications, as Highly Qualified, Qualified, or Not Qualified. (The same system is used for lower federal court nominees.)

David Souter, Bush's first nominee to the Court, received a unanimous rating of Highly Qualified from the ABA. In contrast, Clarence Thomas (well before the charges of sexual harassment became public), was given only a Qualified rating, with two members voting Not Qualified. Of the twenty-two previous nominees rated by the ABA, he was the first to receive less than at least a unanimous Qualified rating.

Lobbying by Interest Groups. Whereas the ABA is an organization that is asked formally to rate nominees, other groups also are keenly interested in the nomination process. Until recently interest groups have played a minor and backstage role in most appointments to the U.S. Supreme Court. Although interest groups generally have not lobbied on behalf of any one individual, in 1981 women's rights groups successfully urged President Reagan to honor his campaign commitment to appoint a woman to the high court.

It is more common for interest groups to lobby against a prospective nominee. Even this, however, is a relatively recent phenomenon. In 1937, the National Association for the Advancement of Colored People (NAACP) lobbied unsuccessfully against the appointment of Hugo Black to the Supreme Court. Although the Alabama native was a former member of the Ku Klux Klan, the NAACP was unable to mobilize sufficient opposition to block his confirmation. More successful was the American Federation of Labor (AFL), which in 1930 was able to block the nomination of Judge John J. Parker, chief judge of the U.S. Fourth Circuit Court of Appeals. The AFL opposed Parker's nomination because he supported agreements that allowed employers to prohibit their employees from joining or assisting a labor union. Moreover, Parker's hostile racial sentiments caused the NAACP to join the chorus against his nomination. Most observers credit this alliance of interests as being key to the success of the effort to block the Parker nomination. After a sixteen-week fight, he became the first nominee rejected in the twentieth century on a narrow vote of forty-one to thirty-nine.

In 1987, the nomination of Robert H. Bork to the Supreme Court produced an unprecedented amount of interest-group lobbying on both sides of the nomination. The Democratic-controlled Judiciary Committee delayed the hearings, thus allowing liberal interest groups time to mobilize the most extensive radio, television, and print media campaign ever launched against a nominee to the U.S. Supreme Court in spite of the fact that he sat with distinction on the D.C. Court of Appeals, was a former U.S. Solicitor General, a top-ranked law school graduate, and a Yale Law School professor. (His actions as Solicitor General, especially his firing of the Watergate Special Prosecutor—see page 231—however, made him a special target for traditional liberals.)

In the national elections of 1986, Democrats had recaptured the majority in the U.S. Senate after six years as the minority party. Many new Democratic senators were elected from the South, and all could attribute their victories to the power of the black vote. When President Reagan nominated Judge Bork, long an outspoken opponent of affirmative action and any kind of judicial activism, civil rights groups contacted key Democratic senators to remind them of their narrow victories and who was responsible for them. Interest groups also banded together and carefully planned the testimony they would give before the Judiciary Committee in opposition to Bork.

These interest groups and the media also used the time between the nomination and the confirmation hearings to garner unprecedented amounts of information on the nominee—even Judge Bork's personal video-rental preferences were brought to public attention. In the end, Bork's nomination was defeated by a vote of fifty-eight to forty-two.

The Senate Committee Hearings. The Committee chair often can play a particularly crucial role in the confirmation hearings because he can set the tone of the proceedings and either encourage or discourage aggressive questioning of nominees. Until 1929, all but one Senate Judiciary Committee hearing on a Supreme Court nominee had been conducted in executive session—that is, closed to the public. The 1916 hearings on Louis Brandeis, the first Jewish justice, were conducted in public and lasted nineteen days, although Brandeis himself was never called to testify. Felix Frankfurter, who was nominated in 1939 to replace Brandeis, was the first nominee to testify in any detail before the committee. Although subsequent revelations about Brandeis's payment of Frankfurter to participate in cases (while Brandeis was on the Court) raise questions about the fitness of both Frankfurter and Brandeis for the bench, no information about Frankfurter's legal arrangements with Brandeis were unearthed during the committee's investigations or Frankfurter's testimony.

Until recently, modern nomination hearings were no more thorough in terms of the attention given to nominees' backgrounds. Chief Justice Warren E. Burger, for example, was confirmed in 1969 by the Senate on a vote of ninety-four to three just nineteen days after he was nominated.

In recent hearings it has become standard for nominees to dodge tough questions when they are asked them. In 1981, when Sandra Day O'Connor became the first nominee to appear before television cameras in the committee room, she generally declined to comment on cases or issues that might ultimately arise before the Court. So did nominees Anthony Kennedy, Antonin Scalia, and David Souter. The Clarence Thomas hearings originally proceeded true to this form. Democratic senators tried not only to pin Judge Thomas down on his views on a variety of controversial issues but also question him about the numerous speeches he had delivered and conservative articles he had written. Like most nominees before him, Thomas steadfastly refused to answer these questions. At one point he even responded to a series of questions on abortion by saying that he had never even discussed it, a response that many found difficult to believe.

After Thomas's initial hearings and a seven-to-seven committee vote, Nina Totenberg, a reporter for National Public Radio, reported on the eve of the vote of the full Senate that a complaint of sexual misconduct had been made to Senate staffers and was contained in the FBI report but had not been mentioned during the hearings. Reacting to public pressure and to Thomas's own request to clear his name, the Senate committee then held an unprecedented additional several days of hearings. As the nation sat transfixed before its television sets, Anita Hill, a law professor, recounted in graphic detail her allegations of Clarence Thomas's on-the-job sexual harassment of her while he headed the Equal Employment Opportunity Commission (ironically, the federal agency charged with investigating such complaints). Thomas angrily denounced her charges, characterizing the whole Senate hearing process as a "high-tech lynching."

The Vote in the Senate. After hearings are concluded, the Senate Judiciary Committee usually makes a recommendation to the full Senate. Any rejections of presidential nominees to the Supreme Court generally occur only after the Senate Judiciary Committee has recommended against a nominee's appointment. Few recent confirmations have been close; prior to Clarence Thomas's fifty-two to forty-eight vote, Rehnquist's nominations as associate justice (sixty-eight to twenty-six) and as Chief Justice (sixty-nine to thirty-three) were the closest in recent history.

Anita Hill testifies before the members of the Senate Judiciary Committee as they consider the appointment of Clarence Thomas to the Supreme Court.

The Supreme Court Today

Given the judicial system's vast size and substantial power (at least indirectly) over so many aspects of our lives, it is surprising that so many Americans know next to nothing about the judicial system in general and the Supreme Court in particular. Until very recently, Senate Judiciary Committee hearings concerning nominees were conducted with little or no publicity, and little attention has been paid to the personnel of the Court. Even today, at a time when the Court is enjoying unprecedented media attention, few Americans can correctly name the Chief Justice, let alone the other eight justices. One news poll indicated that more Americans knew of Judge Joseph Wapner of the TV show "The People's Court" than knew of Chief Justice Rehnquist. Another poll conducted in 1989 for the Court's 200th anniversary revealed that fewer than one-fourth of Americans queried knew how many justices sit on the Court, and nearly two-thirds could not name a single member of the Court.

Although much of this ignorance can be blamed on the American public's lack of interest, part of the problem stems from the Court itself. Its rites and rituals contribute to the Court's mystique and encourage a "cult of the robe." Consider, for example, the way in which judicial proceedings are conducted. Oral arguments are not televised, and deliberations concerning the outcome of cases are conducted in utmost secrecy. In contrast, C-SPAN brings us daily coverage of various congressional hearings and floor debate on bills and important national issues.

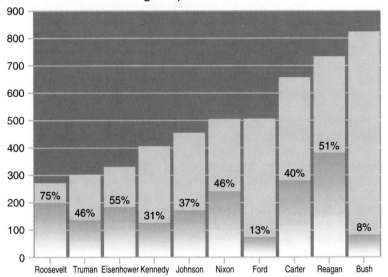

Number of Judges Appointed Compared to Total Authorized Judgeships from Roosevelt to Bush

President	Supreme Court	Court of Appeals[a]	District Courts[b]	Total	Total Judgeships[c]
Roosevelt (1933–45)	9	52	136	197	262
Truman (1945–53)	4	27	102	133	292
Eisenhower (1953–61)	5	45	127	177	322
Kennedy (1961–63)	2	20	102	124	395
Johnson (1963–69)	2	41	125	168	449
Nixon (1969–74)	4	45	182	231	504
Ford (1974–77)	1	12	52	65	504
Carter (1977–81)	0	56	206	262	657
Reagan (1981–89)	3	83	292	378	740
Bush (1989–90)	1	18	48	67	825

[a] Does not include the appeals court for the Federal Circuit
[b] Includes district courts in the territories
[c] Total judgeships authorized in president's last year in office

Source: "Imprints on the Bench," *CQ Weekly Report*, January 19, 1991, p. 173. Reprinted by permission.

Deciding to Hear a Case

Although more than 6,000 cases a year are now filed at the Supreme Court, this was not always the case. From 1790 to 1801, the Court heard only eighty-seven cases under its appellate jurisdiction.[20] In its early years, the bulk of the justices' workload involved their circuit-riding duties. From 1862 to 1866, only 240 cases were decided. Creation of the Courts of Appeals in 1891 resulted in an immediate reduction in Supreme Court filings—from 600 in 1890 to 275 in 1892.[21] As recently as the 1940s, fewer than 1,000 cases were filed annually. Since that time, filings have increased at a fairly steady rate.

About half of the petitions to the Court are filed *in forma pauperis* (literally from the Latin, "in the form of a pauper"). About 80 percent of these are filed by indigent prison inmates seeking review of their sentences. Permission to proceed *in forma pauperis* (IFP) allows the petitioner to avoid filing and printing costs. Any criminal

[20] Stephen L. Wasby, *The Supreme Court in the Federal Judicial System,* 3rd ed. (Chicago: Nelson-Hall, 1988), p. 192.
[21] Ibid.

defendant who has had a court-appointed lawyer in a lower court proceeding is automatically entitled to proceed in this fashion.

In recent years the Court has tended more and more to deny requests to file *in forma pauperis.* In *In re Sindram* (1991), for example, the Rehnquist Court chastised Michael Sindram for filing his petition *in forma pauperis* to require the Maryland courts to expedite his request to expunge a $35 speeding ticket from his record. Sindram was no stranger to the Supreme Court. During the previous three years he had filed forty-two separate motions on various legal matters, twenty-four of them in the 1990 term. In denying Sindram's request to file as an indigent, the majority noted that "[t]he goal of fairly dispensing justice . . . is compromised when the Court is forced to devote its limited resources to the processing of repetitious and frivolous requests." Along with the order denying the petition, the Court issued new rules to provide for denial of "frivolous" or "malicious" IFP motions.[22]

Unlike other courts, the Supreme Court controls its own docket through the *certiorari* process and decides which cases it wants to hear, rejecting most cases that come to it. The Clerk of the Court's office transmits petitions for writs of *certiorari* to the Chief Justice's office, where his clerks first review the petitions, and then to the individual justices' offices. All the justices on the Rehnquist Court except Justice John Paul Stevens participate in what is called the "cert pool." As part of the pool, they review their assigned fraction of petitions and share their notes with each other. Those cases that the justices deem noteworthy are then placed on what is called the discuss list—a list of cases to be discussed—prepared by the Chief Justice's clerks and circulated to the chambers of the justices. Only about 30 percent of submitted petitions make it to this list. During one of the justices' weekly conference meetings, the cases on the list are reviewed. The Chief Justice speaks first, then the rest of the justices speak in turn according to seniority.

The decision process ends when the justices vote, and by custom, *certiorari* is granted according to the **Rule of Four**—when at least four justices vote to hear a case. Justice Stevens has suggested that this be changed to a "rule of five" to reduce the Court's caseload. According to Stevens, between 23 and 30 percent of the cases in the 1979, 1980, and 1981 terms had the support of only four justices.[23]

If *certiorari* is granted, the case is slated for oral argument and decision. As Figure 9-2 illustrates, even under the Rule of Four, very few cases make it this far. Although the number of cases filed has increased, the number the Court accepts for oral argument and decision has actually been declining.

The content of the Court's docket is every bit as significant as its size. Prior to the 1930s, the Court generally heard cases of interest only to the immediate parties. In the 1930s, cases requiring the interpretation of constitutional law began to take a growing portion of its workload, leading the Court to take a more important role in the policy-making process. In the 1930s, only 5 percent of the Court's cases involved questions concerning the Bill of Rights. By the late 1950s, one-third of filed cases involved such questions, and by the 1960s, half did.[24] In 1990, only 30 percent of the Court's caseload dealt with constitutional questions.

Characteristics of a Supreme Court Case. The reasons the Court decides to hear cases are many and diverse. The Court doesn't offer reasons, and "the standards by which the justices decide to grant or deny review are highly personalized and necessarily discretionary" noted former Chief Justice Earl Warren. Moreover, he continued, "those standards cannot be captured in rules or guidelines that would be meaningful."[25] Political

---

[22] 111 S. Ct. 596 (1991).

[23] Wasby, p. 206.

[24] See Wasby, p. 198. Much of this change occurred as the result of an increase in state criminal cases, of which nearly 100 percent concerned constitutional questions.

[25] "Retired Chief Justice Warren Attacks . . . Freund Study Group's Composition and Proposal," *American Bar Association Journal* 59 (July 1973), p. 728.

Figure 9-2   Supreme Court Caseload, 1950–1991

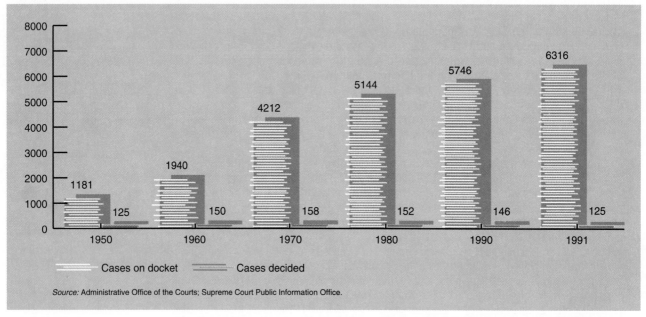

Cases on docket ≡≡≡   Cases decided ≡≡≡

Source: Administrative Office of the Courts; Supreme Court Public Information Office.

This figure shows the upward trend of case filings at the U.S. Supreme Court since 1950. Also shown is the fairly constant number of cases that the justices have actually accepted for full review and for which they have issued opinion. The Court decides only one or two cases a term under its original jurisdiction. Almost all the rest of its workload consists of appeals from lower federal or state courts.

scientists have nonetheless attempted to determine the characteristics of the cases the Court accepts. Among the cues they have identified are the following:

- The case involves conflict among the circuit courts.
- The federal government is the party asking for review.
- The case presents a civil rights or civil liberties question.
- There are signs of group interest in the case as indicated by *amicus curiae* briefs.

One of the most important cues for predicting whether the Court will hear a case is the position the U.S. **Solicitor General** takes on it. The Solicitor General, appointed by the president, is the third-ranking member of the Justice Department and is responsible for handling all appeals on behalf of the U.S. government to the Supreme Court. The Solicitor's staff is like a small, specialized law firm within the Justice Department. But because it has such a special relationship with the Supreme Court it is often referred to as the Court's "ninth and a half member."[26] It even has a suite of offices within the Supreme Court itself. Moreover, the Solicitor General appears as a party or as an ***amicus curiae,*** or friend of the Court in more than 50 percent of the cases heard by the Court each term.

This special relationship with the Court helps explain the overwhelming success the

[26]Kathleen Werdegar, "The Solicitor General and Administrative Due Process," *George Washington Law Review 482* (1967–1968).

Solicitor General's office enjoys before the Supreme Court. But, because of this special relationship, the Solicitor General often finds himself playing two conflicting roles: representing the president's policy interests before the Court and representing the broader interests of the United States in Court. At times, solicitors find these two roles difficult to reconcile. Former Solicitor General Rex E. Lee (1981–85), for example, noted that on more than one occasion he had refused to make in Court arguments advanced by the Reagan administration (a stand that ultimately forced him to resign his position). Said Lee, "I'm not the pamphleteer general; I'm the solicitor general. My audience is not 100 million people; my audience is nine people. . . . Credibility is the most important asset that any solicitor general has."[27]

The credibility of the Solicitor General became an even bigger issue during the tenure of Lee's replacement, Charles Fried, who was appointed by Reagan in 1985. On behalf of the administration, Fried regularly urged the Court (unsuccessfully) to reverse its prior decisions on abortion and affirmative action, causing him to lose credibility with the Court. In contrast, President Bush's Solicitor General, Kenneth Starr, was highly regarded in legal circles and was a close friend of several members of the Court.

Starting the Case

Once the Court decides to hear a case, a flurry of activity begins. If a criminal defendant is proceeding *in forma pauperis,* an expert lawyer is appointed by the Court to prepare and argue the case. Unlike the situation in many state courts, where appointed lawyers are often novice attorneys, it is considered an honor to be asked to represent an indigent before the Supreme Court in spite of the fact that such representation is on a *pro bono,* or for no fee, basis.

Whether or not they are being paid, lawyers on both sides of the case begin to prepare their written arguments for submission to the Court. In these briefs, lawyers cite prior case law and make arguments as to why the Court should find in favor of their client.

More often than not, these arguments are echoed or expanded upon in *amicus curiae* briefs filed by interested parties, especially interest groups. Often, lawyers will seek the support of sympathetic interest groups to buttress their claims before the Court, although most *amicus* briefs are filed independently without requests from one of the two major parties.

Since the 1970s, interest groups have increasingly used the *amicus* brief as a way to lobby the Court. Because litigation is so expensive, few people have the money (or time or interest) to pursue a perceived wrong all the way to the U.S. Supreme Court. All sorts of interest groups, then, find that joining ongoing cases through *amicus* briefs is a useful way of advancing their policy preferences. "Cases do not arrive on the doorsteps of the Supreme Court like orphans in the night," correctly observed the political scientist Richard C. Cortner.[28] Major cases such as *Brown* v. *Board of Education* (1954), *Roe* v. *Wade* (1973), and *Hardwick* v. *Bowers* (1986) all attracted large numbers of *amicus* briefs as part of interest groups' efforts to lobby the judiciary and bring about desired political objectives.

Interest groups also provide the Court with information not necessarily contained in the major-party briefs. Interest groups not only often help with writing briefs, they also frequently assist in practice moot-court sessions. In these sessions, the lawyer who will argue the case before the nine justices goes through a complete rehearsal, with prominent lawyers and law professors playing the roles of the various justices.

---

[27] Quoted in Elder Witt, *A Different Justice: Reagan and the Supreme Court* (Washington: CQ Press, 1986), p. 133.

[28] Richard C. Cortner, *The Supreme Court and Civil Liberties* (Palo Alto, CA: Mayfield, 1975), p. vi.

Oral Arguments by Attorneys

After briefs and *amicus* briefs are submitted on each side, oral argument takes place. The Supreme Court's annual term begins the first Monday in October, as it has since the late 1800s, and runs through early July. In the early nineteenth century, sessions of the Court lasted only a few weeks twice a year. Today justices hear oral argument from the beginning of the term until early April. Special cases, such as *U.S.* v. *Nixon* (1974), have been heard later. During the term, "sittings," periods of about two weeks in which cases are heard, alternate with "recesses," also about two weeks long. Oral arguments are usually heard Monday through Wednesday during sittings.

Oral argument is generally limited to the immediate parties to the case, although it is not uncommon for the U.S. Solicitor General to appear to argue orally as an *amicus curiae.* Oral argument at the Court is fraught with time-honored tradition and ceremony. At precisely 10:00 every morning when the Court is in session, the Court Marshal (dressed in a cutaway) emerges to intone "Oyez! Oyez! Oyez!" as the nine justices emerge from behind a reddish-purple velvet curtain to take their places on the raised and slightly angled bench. (From 1790 to 1972, the justices sat on a straight bench. Chief Justice Burger modified it so that justices at each end could see and hear better.) There, the Chief Justice sits in the middle with the justices to his right and left alternating in seniority.

Almost all attorneys are allotted one-half hour to present their cases, and this allotment includes the time taken by questions from the bench. Justice John Marshall Harlan once noted that there was "no substitute" for this method in getting at the heart of an issue and in finding out where the truth lies."[29] As the lawyer for the appellee approaches the mahogany lectern, a green light goes on, indicating that the attorney's time has begun. A white light flashes when five minutes remain. When another light, a red one, goes on, Court practice mandates that counsel stop immediately. One famous piece of Court lore told to all attorneys concerns one counsel who continued talking and reading from his prepared argument after the light went out. When he looked up, he found an empty bench—the justices had quietly risen and departed while he continued to talk. On

---

[29] Quoted in Wasby, pp. 224–25.

Oral Arguments

Oral arguments are a holdover from the nineteenth century, when the Court relied much more heavily on oral arguments than on written briefs. In those days, oral arguments could last for days. In *McCulloch* v. *Maryland,* for example, the Court permitted the lawyers to argue for nine days because the issues at stake were considered to be so significant. Daniel Webster, the finest oral advocate of his time, argued the case for McCulloch.

The strain of oral argument can take its toll on even the most seasoned lawyers. Solicitor General Stanley Reid once fainted. On another occasion, one lawyer got so caught up in his argument that his teeth popped right out of his mouth. Undaunted, he caught them in mid-air and flipped them back into place, hardly missing a beat of his argument. Not a single justice even smiled until after leaving the bench for the day.

another occasion, Chief Justice Charles Evans Hughes stopped a leader of the New York bar in the middle of the word *if.*

Questions asked at oral argument can be very important. Lawyers are routinely interrupted as justices pepper them with inquiries. Lawyers are prohibited by formal rules from reading from prepared texts, but they may use notes. Other kinds of aids are usually barred, but the Court allowed the deaf lawyer in *Rowley Board of Education* v. *U.S.* (1982),[30] a case involving the amount of assistance a public school district had to provide a deaf student, to use a video display screen from which he could read questions from the justices that were typed into it by a stenotypist.

Questioning from the bench can become quite active, especially if the case is controversial. Justice Scalia, the most active jurist currently on the bench, frequently interrupts counsel with questions or comments. Several other justices have, in fact, privately expressed irritation over his "bull doggedness" from the bench. In one series of eight cases, Justice William J. Brennan did not ask a single question whereas Justice Scalia asked 126. The Court also will often ask one side more questions than another. In the companion case to *Brown* v. *Board of Education,* for example, the lawyer defending segregation was interrupted only 11 times, whereas Thurgood Marshall, as counsel for the NAACP, was interrupted 127 times.[31] Continual interruptions can fluster even the most experienced of lawyers. During the 1960 term, Justice Felix Frankfurter repeatedly questioned an obviously nervous lawyer, only to hear Justice William O. Douglas answer the questions. "I thought you were arguing the case," Frankfurter yelled to the lawyer, who answered, "I am, but I can use all the help I can get."[32]

Although many Court watchers have tried to figure out how a particular justice will vote based on the questioning at oral argument, most find that the questions do not help much in predicting the outcome of a case. Nevertheless, many believe that oral argument has several important functions. Oral argument is the only opportunity for even a small portion of the public (who may attend the hearings) and the press to observe the workings of the Court. It assures lawyers that the justices have heard their case, and it forces lawyers to focus on arguments believed important by the justices.

Oral argument also legitimizes the judicial function and allows the justices to communicate with their colleagues. It also provides the Court with additional information, especially concerning the Court's broader political role, an issue not usually addressed in written briefs. For example, the justices can ask how many people might be affected by its decision or where the Court (and country) would be heading if a case were decided in a particular way.

The Conference and Vote

The justices meet in closed conference on Wednesday afternoons and Fridays when the Court is hearing oral argument. The Wednesday conferences deal with cases heard on Mondays; the Friday conferences with cases heard on Tuesdays and Wednesdays and with *certiorari* petitions and appeals. These conferences highlight the importance and power of the Chief Justice, who presides over them and makes the initial presentation of each case. Each individual justice then discusses the case in order of seniority on the Court, the most senior justice first and the most junior justice last.

Most accounts of the decision-making process reveal that at this point some justices try to change the minds of others but that most enter the conference room with a clear

[30] 458 U.S. 176 (1982).

[31] Milton Dickens and Ruth E. Schwartz, "Oral Argument Before the Supreme Court: Marshall v. Davis in the School Segregation Cases," *Quarterly Journal of Speech* 57 (February 1971), p. 39.

[32] Reported in Anthony Lewis, "The Justices' Supreme Job," *The New York Times Magazine,* June 11, 1961.

idea of how they feel. Although other Courts have followed different procedures, on the Rehnquist Court the justices generally vote at the same time they discuss the case. Initial conference votes are not final, and this allows justices to change their minds before final votes are taken later.

Writing the Opinions of the Court

After the initial vote, the Court must provide legal reasons for its positions. The reasoning behind any decision is often as important as the outcome because, under our system of *stare decisis,* both are likely to be relied on later by lower courts confronted with cases that involve similar issues. The Chief Justice, if he is in the majority, has the job of assigning the writing of the opinion, in which the reasons behind a decision are set forth. This privilege enables him to wield tremendous power. (If he is in the minority, the assignment falls to the most senior justice in the majority.) During the Burger Court years (1969–86), the Chief Justice was heavily criticized for his tendency to wait to announce his vote at conference so that he could be in the majority (even when his initial comments indicated a different opinion) and thus assign the opinion (often to himself) and possibly weaken its overall impact. Today, however, the Chief Justice is regularly in the majority, so tactics like Burger's are no longer considered necessary.

The justice assigned to write the majority opinion circulates drafts of the opinion to all members of the Court. Informal caucusing and negotiation then often take place as justices may "hold out" for word changes or other modifications as a condition of their continued support of the majority opinion. At the same time, **dissenting opinions** written by those who disagree with the outcome or **concurring opinions** written by those who agree with the outcome but not the legal rationale for the opinion (or who may wish to clarify their support further) also circulate through the various chambers. The justices are often assisted in their writing of opinions by their clerks, who also can serve as intermediaries to other justices by talking among themselves.

This kind of communal work can result in poorly written opinions, as was the case with *U.S.* v. *Nixon* (1974). Although the court order for Nixon to turn over tape recordings of his conversations (see Chapter 7) was issued under Chief Justice Burger's name, many believe that it was a combination of several justices' contributions and additions. Sensing the need for the Court to speak unanimously on such an important decision— one that pitted two branches of government against each other—Justice Burger apparently made concessions to get support.[33] This process led to sometimes confused prose.

Recently, tensions have grown on the Court concerning some issues, and dissents or concurring opinions have become quite pointed. The protocol of the Court has always been characterized by politeness—since the ascendancy of Chief Justice Roger Taney to the Court in 1836, the justices have begun each session with a round of handshaking— but this has not stopped some justices from openly ridiculing their brethren from the bench. Justice Scalia, for example, publicly criticized Justice O'Connor's opinion in *Webster* v. *Reproductive Health Services* (1989), saying that her "'assertion that a fundamental rule of judicial restraint' requires [the Court] to avoid reconsidering *Roe* [v. *Wade*] cannot be taken seriously."

How the Justices Vote

A number of scholars have formulated numerous theories concerning how Supreme Court justices vote. Some have tried to predict voting patterns by examining individual justices' social background characteristics (such as their education or party identifica-

---

[33] Bob Woodward and Scott Armstrong, *The Brethren* (New York: Simon and Schuster, 1979), pp. 65, 288–347.

tion). Others have attempted to predict voting based on the factual patterns in a case,[34] and others have relied on their perceptions of the justices' roles.[35] All of this research indicates to one degree or another that justices do not make decisions in a vacuum. Each is influenced by a variety of factors, and many in fact were appointed to the Court with the expectation that they would further a particular ideology or approach.

The Effects of Ideology

Since the 1940s, the two most prevailing ideologies in the United States have been conservative and liberal. On the Supreme Court, justices with "conservative" views generally vote against affirmative action, abortion rights, expanded rights for criminal defendants, and increased power for the national government. In contrast, "liberals" tend to support the parties advancing these positions.

Over time, however, scholars have generally agreed that identifiable voting blocs have occurred on the Court. During the New Deal period, for example, five justices, a critical conservative bloc, routinely voted to strike down the constitutionality of New Deal legislation. Traditionally, such voting blocks or coalitions have centered on liberal/ conservative splits on issues like states' rights (conservatives supporting and liberals opposing), economic issues (conservatives being pro-business; liberals, pro-labor), and civil liberties and civil rights (conservatives being less supportive than liberals). On death-penalty cases, for example, Justices William Brennan and Thurgood Marshall (sometimes joined by John Paul Stevens) consistently voted against the imposition of the death penalty. The current Rehnquist Court, however, has fewer of these blocs because its members are for the most part ideologically homogeneous. All but Harry Blackmun and Stevens take conservative positions on most issues.

Judicial Philosophy

Closely tied to liberal and conservative views are notions of judicial philosophy. One of the primary issues of judicial power focuses on the activism/restraint debate. Advocates of judicial restraint argue that courts should allow the decisions of other branches to stand, even when they offend judges' own sense of principles.[36] Restraintists defend their position by asserting that the federal courts are composed of unelected judges, which makes the judicial branch the least democratic branch of government. Consequently, the courts should defer policy making to other branches of government as much as possible.

Restraintists refer to *Roe* v. *Wade* (1973), the case that liberalized abortion laws, as a classic example of judicial activism run amok. They maintain that the Court should have deferred policy making on this sensitive issue to the states or to the other branches of the federal government—the legislature and executive—because they are elected and therefore are more receptive to the majority's will.

Advocates of judicial activism contend that judges should use their power broadly to further justice, especially in the areas of equality and personal liberty. Activists argue that it is the courts' appropriate role to correct injustices committed by the other branches of

---

[34] See, for example, Jeffrey A. Segal, "Predicting Supreme Court Cases Probabilistically: The Search and Seizure Cases, 1962–1981," *American Political Science Review* 78 (September 1978), pp. 891–900, where he argues that the facts of the case are a critical determinant in Supreme Court voting.

[35] According to James L. Gibson, role theory, which posits that individual justices act differently in different cases primarily due to differing expectations about what is proper, helps explain how the justices vote. James L. Gibson, "Discriminant Functions, Role Orientations and Judicial Behavior: Theoretical and Methodological Linkages," *Journal of Politics* 39 (November 1977), pp. 984–1007.

[36] Stanley C. Brubaker, "Reconsidering Dworkin's Case for Judicial Activism," *The Journal of Politics* 46 (1984), p. 504.

Comparison of Dissent Rates: Great Dissenters of the Past versus Recent Justices

JUSTICE	NUMBER OF DISSENTING OPINIONS	AVERAGE PER TERM
The Great Dissenters		
W. Johnson (1804–34)	30	1.0
J. Catron (1837–65)	26	0.9
N. Clifford (1858–81)	60	2.6
J. Harlan (1877–1911)	119	3.5
O. Holmes (1902–32)	72	2.1
L. Brandeis (1915–39)	65	2.9
H. Stone (1925–46)	93	4.6
H. Black (1937–71)	310	9.1
F. Frankfurter (1939–62)	251	10.9
J. Harlan (1955–71)	242	15.1
The Burger and Rehnquist Courts (through 1990)		
W. Douglas (1969–74)	231	38.5
J. Stevens (1975–90)	318	21.2
W. Brennan Jr. (1969–90)	379	18.0
T. Marshall (1969–90)	322	15.3
W. Rehnquist (1971–90)	250	13.1
P. Stewart (1969–81)	130	10.8
B. White (1969–90)	217	10.6
H. Blackmun (1971–90)	203	10.5
A. Scalia (1986–90)	32	8.3
L. Powell Jr. (1971–87)	159	9.9
S. O'Connor (1981–90)	64	7.0
W. Burger (1969–86)	111	6.3
A. Kennedy (1987–90)	17	5.6

Source: David O'Brien, *Constitutional Law and Politics: Struggles for Power and Governmental Accountability,* Vol. 1 (New York: Norton, 1991), p. 164.

government. Explicit in this argument is the notion that courts need to protect oppressed minorities.[37]

Activists point to *Brown* v. *Board of Education* (1954) as an excellent example of the importance of judicial activism. In *Brown,* the Supreme Court ruled that racial segregation in public schools was in violation of the equal protection clause of the Fourteenth Amendment. Segregation was nonetheless practiced after passage of the Fourteenth Amendment, and an activist would point out that if the Court had not reinterpreted its provisions,

[37] Donald L. Horowitz, *The Courts and Social Policy* (Washington: Brookings Institution, 1977), p. 538.

many states probably would still have laws or policies mandating segregation in public schools.

The debate over activism versus restraint often focuses on how the Court should translate the meaning of the Constitution. Advocates of judicial restraint generally agree that judges should be strict constructionists, that is, they should interpret the Constitution as it was written and intended by the Framers. They argue that in determining the constitutionality of a statute or policy, the Court should rely on the explicit meanings of the clauses in the document, which can be found by looking at the intent of the Framers.

Edwin Meese III, the U.S. Attorney General in the Reagan administration, is a leading interpretivist. Meese asserts that "judges [are] expected to resist any political effort to depart from the literal provisions of the Constitution.[38] Meese also argues that "the text of the document and the original intention of those who framed it would be the judicial standard in giving effect to the Constitution.[39]

In contrast, non-interpretivists argue that the Framers intended the Constitution to be a flexible document whose provisions must be interpreted in light of changing historical circumstances and needs. They believe that judges must move beyond the text of the Constitution and impart to it values that are not explicitly in the document, all the while explaining what the Constitution means for a developing and dynamic system.

Former Supreme Court Justice William Brennan subscribes to the non-interpretivist school. Brennan's point of view is that "Our Constitution was not intended to preserve a preexisting society but to make a new one, to put in place new principles that the prior political community had not sufficiently recognized."[40]

Of late, most activist, non-interpretivist judges, such as Justice Brennan, have tended to be liberal. There is, however, no necessary connection between activism and liberalism. Some believe, for example, that the conservative Rehnquist Court could adopt an activist approach as it puts its conservative stamp on its construction or interpretation of statutes or the Constitution.

[38] Edwin Meese III, *The Great Debate: Interpreting Our Written Constitution* (Washington: The Federalist Society, 1986), p. 2.

[39] Ibid., p. 1.

[40] William Brennan Jr., *The Great Debate: Interpreting Our Written Constitution* (Washington: The Federalist Society, 1986), p. 18.

President Ronald Reagan with Attorney General Edwin Meese, who strongly supported the doctrine of judicial restraint.

Effects of Public Opinion and Interest-Group Lobbying

According to Chief Justice Rehnquist,

> Judges, so long as they are relatively normal human beings, can no more escape being influenced by public opinion in the long run than can people working at other jobs. And if a judge on coming to the bench were to decide to hermetically seal himself off from all manifestations of public opinion, he would accomplish very little; he would not be influenced by current public opinion, but instead would be influenced by the state of public opinion at the time he came to the bench.[41]

Public opinion can act as a check on the power of the courts as well as an energizing factor. Activist periods on the Supreme Court have generally corresponded to periods of social or economic crisis. For example, the Marshall Court supported a strong national government, much to the chagrin of a series of pro-states' rights Democratic-Republican presidents in the early crisis-ridden years of the republic. Similarly, the Court capitulated to political pressures and public opinion when after 1936, it reversed many of its decisions blocking President Roosevelt's New Deal legislation.

The courts also can be the direct target of public opinion. During the spring of 1989 the Supreme Court was subjected to unprecedented lobbying as groups and individuals on both sides of the abortion issue marched and sent appeals to the Court. Earlier, in the fall of 1988, Justice Harry Blackmun, author of *Roe* v. *Wade,* had warned a law school audience in a public address that he feared that the decision was in jeopardy. This in itself was a highly unusual move; until recently, it was the practice of the justices never to comment on cases or the Court.

Speeches like Blackmun's put pro-choice advocates on guard, and many took advantage of the momentum that had built around their successful campaign against the nomination of Robert Bork. In 1989, their forces mounted the largest demonstration on Washington in the history of the United States when more than 300,000 people marched from the White House to the Supreme Court. In addition, full-page advertisements appeared in prominent newspapers, and supporters of *Roe* v. *Wade* were urged to contact members of the Court to voice their support. Justice Sandra Day O'Connor, the Court's lone woman, was targeted by many who viewed her as the crucial swing justice on the issue. Mail at the Court, which usually averages about 1,000 pieces a day, rose to an astronomical 46,000 pieces when *Roe* reached the Court, virtually paralyzing normal lines of communication. Several justices spoke out against this kind of "extra-judicial" communication and voiced their belief in its ineffectiveness. In *Webster* v. *Reproductive Health Services* (1989) Justice Scalia even bemoaned:

> We can now look forward to at least another Term with carts full of mail from the public, and streets full of demonstrators, urging us—their unelected and life tenured judges who have been awarded those extraordinary, undemocratic characteristics precisely in order that we might follow the law despite the popular will—to follow the popular will.

But the fact remains that the Court is very dependent on the public for its prestige as well as for compliance with its decisions. In times of war and other emergencies, for example, the Court frequently has decided cases in ways that commentators have attributed to the sway of public opinion and political exigencies. In *Koramatsu* v. *The United States* (1944), for example, the high court upheld the obviously unconstitutional intern-

[41] William H. Rehnquist, "Constitutional Law and Public Opinion," paper presented at Suffolk University School of Law, Boston, April 10, 1986, pp. 40–41.

The 1989 pro-choice rally in Washington, D.C. was part of an intense lobbying effort to influence the Court's decision in the *Webster* case. Justice Sandra Day O'Connor, viewed as a swing vote on the case, was a particular target of the lobbying.

ment of Japanese-American citizens during World War II. Moreover, Chief Justice Rehnquist himself has suggested that the Court's restriction on presidential authority in *Youngstown Sheet & Tube* (1952), which invalidated President Harry Truman's seizure of the nation's steel mills, was largely attributable to Truman's unpopularity and that of the Korean War.[42]

[42] In *Youngstown Sheet and Tube Co.* v. *Sawyer,* 343 U.S. 579 (1952), the Supreme Court ruled that President Truman's seizure and operation of U.S. steel mills in the face of a strike threat were unconstitutional because the Constitution implied no such broad executive power. See Alan Westin, *Anatomy of a Constitutional Law Case* (New York: Macmillan, 1958).

The Court Versus the American Public

In recent years, the Court has both agreed and disagreed with the public on various issues, such as:

Should TV and other recording devices be permitted in the Supreme Court?

Court: No   Public: Yes (59%)

Should a parent be forced to reveal the whereabouts of a child even though it could violate Fifth Amendment rights?

Court: Yes   Public: Yes (50%)
                        No (39%)
                        Don't Know (11%)

Should a family be allowed to decide to end life-support systems?

Court: Yes   Public: Yes (88%)

Before getting an abortion, whose consent should a teenager be required to gain?

Court: Public:
One parent   Both parents (38%)
                    One parent (37%)
                    Neither parent (22%)

A 1990 study of the American public's knowledge and perceptions of the Court indicated that only 44 percent believed that the Court decides cases primarily on the basis of facts and law. Nearly 50 percent believe that the Court decides based on other factors, including political pressures (28 percent), political/personal beliefs (18 percent), or religious beliefs (1 percent). Although theoretically the Court was envisioned to be above these pressures—witness the selection process, for example—the American public does not appear to be particularly upset about the role of politics and personal beliefs in the decision-making process. In fact, those polled want the Court to take a more active role in the areas of discrimination against women and minorities.

Making Policy

When the Court decides to hear (or not to hear) a case, it takes its first step in policy making. Thus, it is through interpreting statutes or the Constitution that federal courts, and the Supreme Court in particular, make policy in several ways. Judges can interpret a provision of a law to cover matters not previously understood to be covered by the law or can "discover" new rights, such as that of privacy, from their reading of the Constitution.

This power of the courts to make policy presents difficult questions for democratic theory, as noted by Justice Scalia in *Webster,* because democratic theorists believe that the power to make law resides only in the people or their elected representatives. Yet court rulings, especially Supreme Court decisions, routinely affect policy far beyond the interests of the immediate parties.

One measure of how powerful courts are is that more than 100 federal laws have been declared unconstitutional, as shown in Table 9-1. Although many of these laws have not been particularly significant, others have been. For example, in *Immigration and Naturalization Service* v. *Chadha* (1983)—discussed in Chapter 6—the Court found that legislative vetoes were unconstitutional.

Another measure of the power of the Supreme Court is its ability to overrule itself. Although the Court generally abides by the informal rule of *stare decisis,* by one count, since 1810 it has overruled itself in more than 140 cases. *Brown* v. *Board of Education* (1954), for example, overruled *Plessy* v. *Ferguson* (1896), thereby reversing years of constitutional interpretation that had concluded that racial segregation was not a violation of the Constitution. Moreover, in the past few years, the Court has repeatedly reversed earlier decisions in the areas of criminal defendants' rights, affirmative action, and the establishment of religion, thus revealing its powerful role in determining national policy.

A measure of the growing power of the federal courts is the degree to which they now handle questions or issues that, after *Marbury* v. *Madison,* had been considered to be political questions more appropriately left to the other branches of government to decide. Prior to 1962, for example, the Court refused to hear cases questioning the size (and populations) of congressional districts, no matter how unequal they were.[43] The boundary of a congressional district was considered to be a political question. Then, in 1962, writing for the Court, Justice William Brennan concluded that simply because a case involved a political issue did not mean that it involved a political question, thus opening up the floodgates to cases involving a variety of issues that the Court formerly had declined to address.[44]

Not all acts of Congress are easily challenged, and not everyone can challenge a law. Litigants (those who bring a case) must have what is called standing to sue. Over the years this has come to mean that a person bringing a lawsuit must have a strong interest and personal stake in the outcome of the case. Generally these individuals must show the

[43] See *Colegrove* v. *Green,* 328 U.S. 549 (1946), for example.
[44] *Baker* v. *Carr,* 369 U.S. 186 (1962).

Table 9-1   Federal, State, and Local Laws Declared Unconstitutional by the Supreme Court, by Decade, 1789–1990

YEARS	FEDERAL	STATE AND LOCAL
1789–1799	0	0
1800–1809	1	1
1810–1819	0	7
1820–1829	0	8
1830–1839	0	3
1840–1849	0	9
1850–1859	1	7
1860–1869	4	23
1870–1879	7	36
1880–1889	4	46
1890–1899	5	36
1900–1909	9	40
1910–1919	6	118
1920–1929	15	139
1930–1939	13	93
1940–1949	2	58
1950–1959	5	60
1960–1969	16	149
1970–1979	20	193
1980–1990	18[a]	125
Total	126	1,151

[a] In *Immigration and Naturalization Service* v. *Chadha* (1983), the Burger Court struck down the legislative veto, which effectively invalidated 212 other statutes.

Source: Lawrence Baum, *The Supreme Court,* 4th ed. (Washington: CQ Press, 1992).

court that they have sustained or are in immediate danger of sustaining a direct and substantial injury from another party or some action of the government.

Recently the courts have been more willing to allow people to sue under a tactic called a class-action lawsuit, which allows a small number of individuals to sue on behalf of themselves *and* the class of all other citizens who are similarly situated. Class-action lawsuits are frequently used in the areas of civil rights and prisoners' rights when a large group of people may be affected by a practice but do not have the resources to bring individual lawsuits. Opinions in these cases can have particularly far-ranging results.

Implementing Court Decisions

President Andrew Jackson, annoyed about a particular decision handed down by the Marshall Court, is alleged to have said "John Marshall has made his decision; now let him enforce it." Jackson's statement raises a question: How do Supreme Court rulings translate into public policy? In fact, although judicial decisions carry legal and even moral authority, all courts must rely on other units of government to carry out their directives. Judicial implementation is the term that refers to how and whether judicial decisions are translated into actual public policies affecting more than the immediate parties to the lawsuit.

How well a decision is implemented often depends on how well crafted or popular it is. Hostile reaction in the South to *Brown* v. *Board of Education* (1954) and the absence of precise guidelines to implement the decision meant that the ruling went largely unenforced for years. The *Brown* experience also highlights how much the Supreme Court needs the support of both federal and state courts as well as other governmental agencies to carry out its judgments.

Charles Johnson and Bradley C. Canon suggest that the implementation of judicial decisions involves what they call an *implementing population* and a *consumer population*.[45] The implementing population consists of those people responsible for carrying out a decision. It varies depending on the policy and issues in question, but can include lawyers, judges, public officials, police officers and police departments, hospital administrators, government agencies, and corporations. The consumer population consists of those people who might be directly affected by a decision.

For effective implementation of a judicial decision, the first requirement is that the members of the implementing population must act to show that they understand the original decision. For example, in 1964 the Supreme Court ruled in *Reynolds* v. *Sims*[46] that every person should have an equally weighted vote in electing governmental representatives. This "one person, one vote" decision might seem simple enough at first glance, but in practice it can be very difficult to understand. The implementing population in this case consists chiefly of state legislatures and local governments, who determine voting districts for federal, state, and local offices (see Chapter 6). If a state legislature draws districts such that black voters are spread thinly across a number of separate constituencies, the chances are slim that any particular district will elect a representative who is especially sensitive to blacks' concerns. Does that violate "equal representation"? (In practice, the courts and the Justice Department have intervened in many cases to ensure that elected officials will include minority representation.)

The second requirement is that the implementing population must actually follow Court policy. Thus, when the Court ruled that men could not be denied admission to a state-sponsored nursing school, the implementing population—in this case the university administrators and Board of Regents of the nursing school—had to enroll qualified male students.

Judicial decisions are most likely to be smoothly implemented if responsibility for implementation is concentrated in the hands of a few highly visible public officials, such as the president or a governor. By the same token, these officials can also thwart or impede judicial intentions. Recall from Chapter 5, for example, the effect of Governor Orval Faubus's initial refusal to allow black children to attend all-white public schools in Little Rock, Arkansas.

The third requirement for implementation is that the consumer population must be aware of the rights that a decision grants or denies them. Teenagers seeking an abortion, for example, are consumers of the Supreme Court's decisions on abortion. They need to know that most states require them to inform their parents of their intention to have an abortion or get parental permission to do so. Similarly, criminal defendants and their lawyers are consumers of Court decisions on, say, the exclusionary rule. They need to know the implications of recent Supreme Court decisions for evidence presented at trial.

[45] Charles Johnson and Bradley C. Canon, *Judicial Policies' Implementation and Impact* (Washington: CQ Press, 1984), Chapter 1.
[46] 377 U.S. 533 (1964).

Toward Reform

Clearly the American public regards the Supreme Court as a powerful policy maker. In a 1990 poll, most respondents said they believed that the Court was more powerful than the president (31 versus 21 percent) and that the Court was close to being as powerful as Congress (38 percent).

Considering how poorly informed the American public is about the Court, interest in its activities is fairly high. It is likely to grow as more Americans come to understand the importance of the Court in shaping our social and economic agenda and as Court appointments continue to get extensive media coverage.

In the wake of the Clarence Thomas hearings, much was said about the need to reform the judicial selection process. Criticism was directed in particular at Senate confirmation hearings, special interest groups, and ideological politics. As time has passed, however, little has been done in response to these concerns. Historically, in fact, there has been little inclination to tinker with the judicial system—even though the courts have grown in power—except when the Supreme Court has stepped on too many toes. Congress and the president have, from time to time, limited, or attempted to limit, the jurisdiction of the Court. When Democratic-Republicans were unable to get rid of Federalist judges by impeachment, they abolished the federal circuit courts. Following the Civil War, radical Republicans cut the size of the Court and changed its appellate jurisdiction to prevent it from hearing a case involving the constitutionality of some Reconstruction legislation.[47] And in 1936, President Franklin Roosevelt tried unsuccessfully to change the size of the Court so that he could pack it with supporters of his New Deal.

More recently, proposals have been made to alter the Court's jurisdiction on matters such as abortion, but not much has come of them. If the current Court continues its

[47] *Ex parte McCardle,* 74 U.S. 506 (1869).

July 6, 1991: Protesters rallied in Washington, D.C. against the Supreme Court's ruling in *Rust* v. *Sullivan* barring federally funded clinics from discussing abortion. Marchers wore gags or tape across their mouths to dramatize feelings about the high court's "gag order."

conservative pattern, it may someday find itself in conflict with a more liberal Democratic president and Congress. The result might be new calls to change the Court's jurisdiction. The history of such conflicts however, suggests, that the Court would be likely to adapt in a way that would avoid any major alterations to the judiciary by the other branches of government.

Summary

The courts and the judiciary occupy a peculiar place in our democratic system. Unelected by the people, federal judges serve for life with no direct responsibility or accountability to those who can be affected so profoundly by their decisions.

Many of the Framers viewed the judicial branch of government as little more than a minor check on the other two branches, ignoring Anti-Federalist concerns about an unelected judiciary and its potential for tyranny. Although *tyrannical* is not usually a term used to describe the Supreme Court or any other court, the judiciary certainly has taken a place in the American political system unintended by the Framers.

The structure of the courts in the United States is complicated by the existence of both a national and state judicial systems. At the federal level, although the Constitution only mentions the Supreme Court, it allows Congress to establish additional lower courts, which it did in the Judiciary Act of 1789 and again in 1891, establishing the three-tiered structure we have today.

Most litigation begins in the district courts where trials are held and juries are empaneled. There are ninety-four district courts. Their areas of jurisdiction are based on population, but there is at least one district court in every state. The decisions of district courts may be reviewed by the Courts of Appeals, whose purpose is not to retry cases, but to review them for errors in procedure. The Supreme Court is the ultimate appellate court.

The judiciary structure is similar at the state level. Many states, however, have two tiers of trial courts: one for minor criminal offenses, and one for major criminal offenses. Many of the states have intermediate courts of appeals, and all states have a supreme court.

Federal judges are nominated by the president and confirmed by the Senate. Over the years, the Senate's role in the confirmation process and the process itself have changed. Calls for reform of the process can be attributed in part to the public's perception that the Supreme Court has grown in importance as a policy maker and to public debate over what the Court's role should be. The activism/restraint debate has been with us since the Founding period, but the recent conservative shift of the Court has led to a renewed debate on the proper role of the courts in the federal system.

Because the Supreme Court deals with issues involving deeply felt social values or political beliefs, its decisions have an impact reaching beyond the immediate parties in dispute. The Court is not authorized to implement its decisions and must rely on other units of government to do so.

In interpreting the law and deciding conflicts among interest, the Court unquestionably makes policy. An opinion may be broad or narrow, have far-reaching implications for future cases, or have little impact beyond the case at hand. The impact of a decision is determined by the type of decision, how the Court presents it, and how the decision is implemented.

Key Terms

Marbury v. *Madison*	constitutional courts	strict constructionist
appellate courts	legislative courts	*in forma pauperis*
criminal law	briefs	Rule of Four
grand jury	precedents	Solicitor General
indictment	*stare decisis*	*amicus curiae*
civil law	writ of *certiorari*	dissenting opinions
		concurring opinions

Suggested Readings

Abraham, Henry. *The Judicial Process,* 5th ed. New York: Oxford University Press, 1986.

Baum, Lawrence. *American Courts: Process and Policy.* Boston: Houghton Mifflin, 1989.

———. *The Supreme Court,* 4th ed. Washington: CQ Press, 1992.

Garraty, John, ed. *Quarrels That Have Shaped the Constitution.* New York: Harper & Row, 1987.

Levy, Leonard W., et al., eds. *American Constitutional History.* New York: Macmillan, 1989.

Marshall, Thomas. *Public Opinion and the Supreme Court.* Boston: Unwin and Hyman, 1989.

Neubauer, David W. *Judicial Process: Law, Courts and Politics.* Pacific Grove, Calif.: Brooks/Cole, 1991.

O'Brien, David M. *Storm Center: The Supreme Court in American Politics,* 2nd ed. New York: Norton, 1990.

O'Connor, Karen. *Women's Organizations' Use of the Courts.* Lexington, Mass.: Lexington Books, 1980.

Wasby, Stephen. *The Supreme Court in the Federal Judicial System,* 3rd ed. Chicago: Nelson-Hall, 1988.

Woodward, Bob, and Scott Armstrong. *The Brethren: Inside the Supreme Court.* New York: Simon and Schuster, 1979.

PART THREE

Political Behavior

This section examines the mechanisms for citizen involvement in America's democracy. Political participation by citizens is a hallmark of all democratic systems, and the specific process by which the public wields influence over its governing institutions are essential subjects of study.

We begin in Chapter 10 with an analysis of public opinion. How does the public come to form and express its views on government? What exactly is "the public"? Over the years, how have politicians heard the many voices that make up the public?

In Chapter 11 we look at political parties. How do groups of citizens come together into parties? How do politicians use parties to help organize institutions such as Congress and the presidency? These are the key questions addressed in this chapter.

In Chapters 12 and 13 we examine elections, both from the perspective of the voter (Chapter 12) and from that of the campaigning politician (Chapter 13). We look at the role of elections in America's governance and the changing behavior of politicians over the years in response to elections. We conclude with an analysis of the 1992 elections and bring together questions of individual voters, parties, and politicians in the most current national presidential contest.

In Chapter 14 we look at the impact of the media on politics. How do citizens understand their government through the prism of the media? How do governmental officials use the media to help them govern more effectively?

Finally, in Chapter 15, we examine interest groups—private groups of voters who organize to further particular political goals. No interest group comprises all citizens, but many citizens have either direct or indirect affiliation with one or more groups. Understanding how groups have changed over the years, how they work today, and what influence they wield is an important dimension in understanding political behavior.

I have often taken notice

that Providence has been pleased to

give this one connected country to

one united people—a people

descended from the same ancestors,

speaking the same language,

professing the same religion, attached

to the same principles of government,

very similar in manners and

customs. . . .

John Jay

FEDERALIST NO. 2

The Framers may well have wished for all Americans to share a common culture. At no time, however, has the American public resembled Jay's description.

CHAPTER 10

Public Opinion

When John Jay wrote so glowingly of the sameness of the American people in 1787, he and other writers of *The Federalist Papers* believed that Americans had more in common than not. Jay spoke of shared public opinion and the need for a national government. But Jay overstated the universality of the public's support for a strong national government. Moreover, while Americans at the time generally shared one language, religion, and a common ancestry, existing class differences were already producing the kind of factions that the Federalists feared.

The Federalist Papers were themselves one of the first major attempts to change public opinion—in this case, to gain public support for the newly drafted U.S. Constitution. Even prior to publication of *The Federalist Papers,* Thomas Paine's *Common Sense* and later his *Crisis* papers were widely distributed around the colonies to stimulate patriotic feelings and increase public support for the Revolutionary War. From the very early days of the republic political leaders recognized the importance of public opinion and used all the means at their disposal to manipulate it for their purposes.

The proper role of public opinion in the making of policy is just one question we explore in this chapter. Others concern how political attitudes and public opinion have been manipulated and measured over time, how these attitudes are formed, and what enduring issues have been important to politicians and the public.

What Is Public Opinion?

At first blush, **public opinion** seems to be a very straightforward term: It is what the public thinks about a particular issue or set of issues. Historically, and as it is used here, public opinion generally has meant the opinions held by ordinary citizens that governmental officials take into account when making policy. Since the 1930s, governmental decision makers have relied heavily on **polls**—interviews with a sample of citizens that are used to estimate public opinion of the entire population—to determine what the public is thinking. According to the prominent pollster George Gallup, polls have played a key role in defining issues of concern to the public, shaping administrative decisions, and helping "speed up the process of democracy" in the United States.[1] But as we discuss

[1] Allan M. Winkler, "Public Opinion," in Jack Greene, ed., *The Encyclopedia of American Political History* (New York: Charles Scribner's Sons, 1988), p. 1038.

Popular opinion: After the allied forces successfully pushed Iraq out of Kuwait, American public support for the war reached very high levels, as evidenced by this victory parade in New York City.

later in this chapter, what the public thinks about various issues is difficult to know simply because public opinion can change so quickly. For example, two weeks before the United States bombed Iraq in January 1991, public opinion polls revealed that 61 percent of the American public believed that the U.S. should engage in combat in Iraq. One week after the invasion, 86 percent reported that they approved of President Bush's handling of the situation.

These kinds of changes illustrate the difference between what one analyst calls "popular opinion," as opposed to "public opinion." Robert Nisbet defines **popular opinion** as the widely fluctuating changes in public support for governmental policies based on "transitory thoughts that citizens have about topical events."[2] Public opinion, on the other hand, reflects long-lasting, deeply felt political beliefs.

Throughout our nation's history, political thinkers have argued that a just government rests on the wishes of the people. In Federalist No. 10, for example, James Madison articulated this classical liberal precept by identifying the necessity of governmental response to the will of the people as opposed to responding to momentary mood swings influenced by dramatic events (what Nisbet would call popular opinion). According to Madison, governments need respond only to those enduring beliefs shared by the public.

Not all commentators agree with Madison. According to George Gallup, the founder of modern-day polling, leaders must constantly take public opinion—no matter how short-lived—into account. Like the Jacksonians of a much earlier era, Gallup was distrustful of leaders who were not in tune with the common man. According to Gallup,

> In a democracy we demand the views of the people be taken into account. This does not mean that leaders must follow the public's view slavishly; it does mean that they should have an available appraisal of public opinion and take some account of it in reaching their decision.[3]

While Gallup undoubtedly had a vested interest in fostering reliance on polls, his sentiments accurately reflect the feelings of many political thinkers concerning the role of public opinion and governance. Majoritarians like Gallup believe that the government should do what a majority of the public wants done. In contrast, pluralists argue that the public as a whole doesn't have consistent opinions on day-to-day issues but that subgroups within the public often hold strong views on some issues. Pluralists believe that the government must allow for the expression of these minority opinions and that democracy works best when these different voices are allowed to fight it out in the public arena.

Early Efforts to Influence Public Opinion

One can hardly read a newspaper or a news magazine or watch television without hearing the results of the latest public opinion poll on abortion, crime, AIDS, or some other social problem, or a report on the most recent presidential popularity rating. But even before polling, by the early 1800s, the term "public opinion" was frequently being used by the educated middle class. As more Americans became educated, they became more vocal about their opinions and were more likely to vote. A more educated, reading public led to increased demand for newspapers, which in turn provided more information about the process of government. And as America grew, there were more elections and more opportunities for citizens to express their political opinions through the ballot box. As a result of these trends, political leaders were more frequently forced to try to gauge public opinion in order to remain responsive to the wishes and desires of their constituents.

[2] Robert Nisbet, "Popular Opinion versus Public Opinion," *Public Interest,* 1975, p. 167.
[3] *Public Opinion Quarterly* 29 (Winter 1965–66), p. 547.

Northern support for the abolitionist movement increased tremendously with the 1851–52 serial publication of Harriet Beecher Stowe's *Uncle Tom's Cabin.* This 1851 Boston advertisement warns fugitive slaves to avoid contact with the police.

CAUTION!!
COLORED PEOPLE
OF BOSTON, ONE & ALL,

You are hereby respectfully CAUTIONED and advised, to avoid conversing with the
Watchmen and Police Officers of Boston,

For since the recent ORDER OF THE MAYOR & ALDERMEN, they are empowered to act as

KIDNAPPERS
AND
Slave Catchers,

And they have already been actually employed in KIDNAPPING, CATCHING, AND KEEPING SLAVES. Therefore, if you value your LIBERTY, and the *Welfare of the Fugitives* among you, *Shun* them in every possible manner, as so many *HOUNDS* on the track of the most unfortunate of your race.

Keep a Sharp Look Out for KIDNAPPERS, and have TOP EYE open.
APRIL 24, 1851.

Election Reform

Initiative: A method by which state and local voters can propose laws or constitutional amendments. Generally, special-interest groups draft the initiatives and then circulate them on petitions. Usually the initiative must attract the signatures of at least 5 to 10 percent of the registered voters in the state or community in order to get on the ballot.

Referendum: The practice of putting pieces of legislation proposed by the state legislature before the voters for their approval or disapproval.

Recall: A procedure for demanding the ouster of elected public officials prior to the end of their term.

An example of the power of public opinion is found in the public's response to the serialization of Harriet Beecher Stowe's *Uncle Tom's Cabin* in 1851 through 1852. *Uncle Tom's Cabin* was one of the most powerful propaganda statements ever issued about slavery, and by the time the first shots of the Civil War were fired at Fort Sumter in 1861 more than 1 million copies of the book were in print. While Stowe's words alone could not have caused the public outrage over slavery that contributed to Northern support for the war, her book convinced the majority of the American people of the justness of the abolitionist cause and strengthened public opinion against slavery.

Decades later, one of the hallmarks of the Progressive era of the late nineteenth and early twentieth centuries was the restructuring of government to be more responsive to the views of the people. Many governmental reforms were enacted to make legislative assemblies more responsive to public opinion. During this period measures such as the **initiative, referendum,** and **recall** and the restructuring of primary elections were undertaken to give more citizens an opportunity to voice their views in the electoral process.

During the Progressive era there was also a growing belief that the pressure of public opinion would act as a safeguard in the conduct of both domestic and international affairs. In 1909, speaking out on behalf of compulsory arbitration of international disagreements to avoid war, President William Howard Taft (1909–13) noted that once a court hearing was held and the dispute decided, "few nations will care to face the condemnation of international public opinion and disobey the judgment [of the international court]."[4] He obviously hadn't envisioned leaders like Adolf Hitler or Saddam Hussein.

During World War I, while some argued that public opinion didn't matter at all, President Woodrow Wilson argued that public opinion would temper the actions of international leaders. Therefore, only eight days after the start of the war, Wilson created a Committee on Public Information. Run by a prominent journalist, the committee immediately undertook to unite American public opinion behind the war effort. It used all of the tools available—pamphlets, posters, and speakers who exhorted the patrons of local movie houses during every intermission—to garner support and favorable opinion for the war. In the words of the committee's head, it was "the world's greatest adventure in advertising."[5]

In the wake of World War I, Walter Lippmann, a well-known journalist and author who was extensively involved in propaganda activities during the war, publicly voiced his concerns about how easily public opinion could be manipulated and his reservations about the weight it should be given. In his seminal work, *Public Opinion* (1922),

[4] Quoted in Winkler, p. 1031.
[5] Quoted in Winkler, p. 1035.

"The world's greatest adventure in advertising:" During World War I, the Committee on Public Information created a vast gallery of posters designed to shore up public support for the war effort.

Lippmann wrote, "Since Public Opinion is supposed to be the prime mover in democracies, one might reasonably expect to find a vast literature. One does not find it."[6] In the 1920s, polling as we know it today had not been developed.

Early Efforts to Gauge Public Opinion

Modern-day public opinion polling as we know it today did not begin to develop until the 1930s. Researchers in a variety of disciplines, including political science, heeded Lippmann's call to learn more about public opinion and set about trying to use scientific methods to measure political thought through the use of surveys or polls. As methods for gathering and interpreting data improved, survey data began to play an increasingly important role in all walks of life, from politics to retailing.

Even before the 1930s, many had tried to predict the results of political elections. As early as 1824, for example, one Pennsylvania newspaper tried to predict the winner of that year's presidential contest. Later, in 1883, the *Boston Globe* sent reporters to selected election precincts to poll voters as they exited voting booths in an effort to predict the results of key contests. And in 1916, *Literary Digest,* a popular magazine, began mailing survey postcards to potential voters in an effort to predict election outcomes. *Literary Digest* drew its survey sample from "every telephone book in the United States, from the rosters of clubs and associations, from city directories, lists of registered voters [and] classified mail order and occupational data."[7] Using the data it received back from the millions of postcard ballots it sent out throughout the United States, it correctly predicted every presidential election from 1920 to 1932.

Literary Digest correctly predicted the popular vote in four presidential elections by using **straw polls** with such accuracy that its polling methods were widely hailed as

[6] Ibid.
[7] *Literary Digest* 122, 22 August 1936, p. 3.

A typical polling instrument.

```
                                          NATIONAL STUDY

   INTERVIEWER_____              STUDY #__5483____
   TARRANCE & ASSOCIATES                    CODING_____
   GREENBERG-LAKE                           COMPUTER_____
   PERSONAL/CONFIDENTIAL                    FINANCE_____
                                            INTERVIEWING_____


   Hello, I'm _____ of Tarrance & Associates, a national
   research firm.  We're calling from our national telephone center.
   We're talking to people in the nation today about public leaders
   and issues facing us all.

   A.   Are you registered to vote
        in your state and will you be
        able to vote in the election
        for President that will be
        held in 1992?


        _____
        IF "NO", ASK:  Is there someone
        else at home who is registered
        to vote?  (IF "YES", THEN ASK:
        MAY I SPEAK WITH HIM/HER?)
                                        Yes (CONTINUE)

                                        No  (THANK AND TERMINATE)
```

Then and Now
Straw Polls

In the early 1900s, polls like those conducted by *Literary Digest* reached out to as many potential respondents as possible, with no regard for modern sampling techniques which require that respondents be selected or sampled according to strict rules of cross-sectional representation. Respondents, in essence, were like "straws in the wind," hence the term straw polls.

Literary Digest's sample had three fatal errors. First, the sample was drawn in a biased fashion that used telephone directories and lists of automobile owners. This technique oversampled the upper middle class and rich, groups heavily Republican in political orientation. Moreover, in 1936, voting polarized along class lines. Thus, the oversampling of wealthy Republicans was particularly problematic because it severely underestimated the Democratic vote. *Literary Digest*'s second problem was timing: It sent out questionnaires in early September. Thus, the changes in public sentiment that occurred as the election drew closer went uncovered. Its third error occurred because of a problem we now call self-selection:

Only highly motivated individuals sent back the cards—only 22 percent of those surveyed responded. Those who respond to mail surveys are quite different from the general electorate; they often are wealthier and better educated and care more fervently about issues. *Literary Digest,* then, failed to observe one of the now well-known cardinal rules of survey sampling, that "one cannot allow the respondents to select themselves into the sample."*

Although these crude techniques are now looked upon with disfavor by serious students of public opinion, straw polls are still common today. Interest groups, for example, frequently poll their members on relevant issues. Perhaps the most common form of straw poll used today are those conducted by local television news programs. Many have nightly features asking viewers to call in their sentiments (with one phone number for pro and another for con). The results of these unscientific polls vary widely because those who feel very strongly about the issue often repeatedly call in their votes.

Source: Robert S. Erikson, Norman Luttbeg, and Kent Tedin, *American Public Opinion: Its Origin, Content and Impact* (New York: Wiley, 1980), p. 28.

"amazingly right" and "uncannily accurate."[8] In 1936, however, its luck ran out. *Literary Digest* predicted that Alfred M. Landon (whose daughter is current U.S. Senator Nancy Kassebaum, who like her father, is a Kansas Republican) would beat President Franklin Roosevelt by a margin of 57 percent to 43 percent. Roosevelt, however, won in a landslide election, receiving 62.5 percent of the popular vote and carrying every state except Vermont and Maine.

The Gallup Poll

At least one pollster, however, correctly predicted the results of the 1936 election: George Gallup, who had written his dissertation on measuring the readership of newspapers. Gallup attracted considerable national attention when he correctly predicted the outcome of the 1936 presidential election. Although he underpredicted Roosevelt's victory by nearly 7 percent, the fact that he got the winner right was what everyone remembered.

Through the late 1940s, the number of polling groups and increasingly sophisticated polling techniques grew by leaps and bounds as new businesses and politicians relied on their information. In 1948, however, the polling industry suffered a severe, although

[8]*Literary Digest* 125, 14 November 1936, p. 1.

People of the Past

George Gallup

George Gallup earned a Ph.D. in journalism from the University of Iowa; his dissertation examined methods of measuring the readership of newspapers. He first became interested in polling when his mother-in-law ran for public office in 1932. She was running against a popular incumbent, and most observers considered her candidacy a lost cause. Nevertheless, because of the Democratic landslide of 1932, she was swept into office on the coattails of Franklin Roosevelt.

Gallup's interest in politics, fostered by his experience in his mother-in-law's campaign and his academic background in journalism and advertising, led him to take a job at a New York advertising agency. In 1935 he founded the American Institute of Public Opinion, head-quartered at Princeton University in New Jersey. At the institute, Gallup refined a number of survey and sampling techniques to measure the public's attitudes on social, political, and economic issues. Weekly reports called the Gallup Polls were sent to more than forty subscribing newspapers.

Gallup attracted considerable national attention when he correctly predicted the outcome of the 1936 presidential election. Recognizing many of the flaws of *Literary Digest*'s poll, he relied on a sample of a few thousand people who represented the voting population in terms of important demographic variables, such as age, gender, political affiliation, and region.

fleeting, setback. George Gallup and many other pollsters incorrectly predicted that Thomas E. Dewey would defeat President Harry S Truman.

In spite of errors like these, pollsters have been quick to defend their craft. Gallup readily admitted the mistakes that affected his 1948 poll, including the early cutoff date of his sample, noting, "we are continually experimenting and we are continually learning."[9] He consistently argued that the judgment of the masses was basically good and often far better than that of their leaders.

[9] Benjamin Ginsburg, *The Captive Public* (New York: Basic Books, 1986).

Not only did advance polls in 1948 predict that Republican nominee Thomas E. Dewey would defeat Democratic incumbent Harry S Truman, but based on early and incomplete vote tallies, some newspapers' early editions even on the day *after* the election declared Dewey to have won. Here a triumphant Truman holds aloft the *Chicago Tribune*.

Political Socialization: The First Step Toward Forming Opinions

Political scientists believe that many of our attitudes about issues are grounded in political values, which are acquired through a process called **political socialization.** Political socialization "is the process through which an individual acquires his [or her] particular political orientations—his [or her] knowledge, feelings and evaluations regarding his [or her] political world."[10] Through the process of political socialization we become aware of political facts and events and form political values. Family, schools, houses of worship, peers, friends, and the media are often important influences or agents of political socialization. Try to remember your earliest memory of the president of the United States. For many of you it was probably Jimmy Carter or Ronald Reagan (older students hopefully remember more distant presidents). What did you think of him? Of the Republican or Democratic parties? It is likely that your earliest feelings or attitudes were shaped by what your parents thought about that particular president and his party. Similar processes also apply to your early attitudes about political parties, the flag, and the United States.

Those who study political socialization argue that children who grew up during the Vietnam era (1964–73) or during the Watergate scandal had far more negative feelings about the president than children who grew up in households that approved of President Reagan.

The Family

The family's influence can be traced to two factors, communication and receptivity. Children, especially during their preschool years, spend tremendous amounts of time with their parents and early on learn their parents' political values, even though these concepts may be vague. One study, for example, found that the most important visible public figures for children under the age of ten were police officers and, to a much lesser extent, the president. Children almost uniformly view both as "helpful." But by the age of ten or eleven, children become more selective in their perceptions of the president. By this age, children raised in Democratic households are much more likely to be critical of a Republican president than those raised in Republican households.

In 1958, 72 percent of the children in Republican households adopted their parents' party identification. By 1988, 58 percent of children in Republican households identified themselves as Republicans. This figure could rise again, because the popular presidency of Ronald Reagan may leave a long-lasting affection for the Republican Party among many young people only now coming of age, in spite of the fact that his image has been somewhat tarnished since he left office.

School

Researchers report mixed findings concerning the role of the schools in the political socialization process. There is no question that in elementary school children are taught respect for their nation and its symbols. Most school days begin with the Pledge of Allegiance, and patriotism and respect for country are important, although subtle, components of most school curricula. In 1991, for example, few school children were taught to question U.S. involvement in the Persian Gulf. Instead, at almost every school in the nation, children were encouraged or even required to write servicemen and servicewomen in the Gulf, involving these children with the war effort and implying school support for the war.

[10]Richard Dawson, et al. *Political Socialization,* 2nd ed. (Boston: Little-Brown, 1977), p. 33.

High schools are also important agents of political socialization. They continue the elementary school tradition of building good citizens and often reinforce textbook learning with trips to the state or national capital. They also offer courses on current American affairs. Better-informed citizens vote more often as adults. Presentation of civic information is especially critical at the secondary school stage because the formal education of many Americans ends with high school.

Learning at the college level is often different from that encountered in grade school or high school. Many college courses and texts like this one are designed in part to provide you with the information necessary to think critically about issues of major political consequence. It is common in college for students to be called upon to question the appropriateness of certain political actions or to discuss underlying reasons for certain political or policy decisions. Therefore, most researchers believe that college has a liberalizing effect on students. Since the 1920s, studies have shown, students get more liberal each year they are in college.

Peers

Although the influence of the schools on political socialization is often called into doubt, peers—that is, children about the same age as a young person—do seem to have an important effect on the socialization process. Whereas parental influences are greatest during the tender years from birth to five, a child's peer group becomes increasingly more important as the child gets older.

The Impact of Events

While there is no doubt that parents—and, to a lesser degree, school and peers—play a role in a person's political socialization, the role of key political events is also very important. You probably do not have a single professor who cannot remember what she or he was doing on the day that President John F. Kennedy was killed, November 22, 1963. This tragic and dramatic event is indelibly etched in the minds of virtually all citizens who can remember it. Later, President Richard M. Nixon's fall from grace and forced resignation in 1973 also had a profound impact on the socialization process of all Americans, possibly to the greatest extent on young people, who were forced to face the fact that their government was not always right or honest. In fact, one of the problems in discussing political socialization is that many of the major studies on this topic were conducted in the aftermath of these and other crucial events, including the civil rights movement and the Vietnam War, all of which produced a marked increase in Americans' distrust of government. The findings reported in Figure 10-1 on this subject might not have been so negative if a different generation of adolescents had been surveyed. In a study of Boston children conducted in the aftermath of the Watergate scandal, for example, one political scientist found that children's perception of the president went from that of a benevolent to a "malevolent" leader.[11]

Social Groups

Also affecting the development and continuity of political beliefs and opinions are group effects, that is, certain characteristics that allow a person to be lumped into categories. Among the most important of these groups are religion, educational attainment, income, region, and race. More recently, researchers have learned that gender and age are becoming increasingly important determinants of public opinion, especially on certain issues.

---

[11] F. Christopher Arterton, "The Impact of Watergate on Children's Attitudes Toward Political Authority," *Political Science Quarterly* 89 (June 1974), p. 273.

Figure 10-1 **Attitudes of American Adolescents to the United States and Its Symbols, Government, and Institutions**

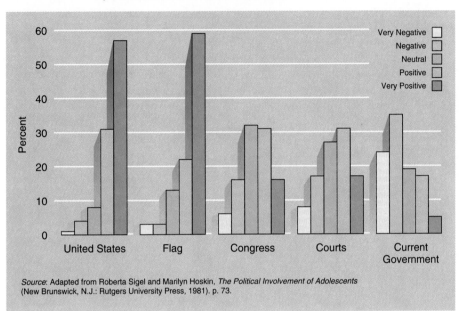

Source: Adapted from Roberta Sigel and Marilyn Hoskin, *The Political Involvement of Adolescents* (New Brunswick, N.J.: Rutgers University Press, 1981). p. 73.

Religion. Religion plays a very important role in the life of Americans. As shown in Figure 10-2, far more Americans attend church regularly than do citizens of Europe. In 1988, 56 percent of Americans identified themselves as Protestant, 28 percent as Catholic, 2 percent as Jewish, and 2 percent other. Only 9 percent claim to have no religious affiliation. Over the years analysts have found continuing opinion differences among these groups, with Protestants being the most conservative on many issues and Jews the most liberal, as shown in Figure 10-3.

Shared religious attitudes tend to affect voting and stances toward particular issues. Catholics tend to vote Democratic more than do Protestants. For example, Catholics overwhelmingly cast their ballots for John Kennedy, who became the first Catholic president, in 1960. Catholics as a group also favor aid to parochial schools, most Jews support aid to Israel, and many fundamentalist Protestants support organized prayer in public schools.

Region. Regional differences have been important to the development and maintenance of public opinion since colonial times. As America grew and developed into a major industrial nation, waves of immigrants with new religious traditions and customs entered the United States and often settled in areas they viewed as hospitable to their way of life. For example, thousands of Scandinavians settled in cold, snowy, rural Minnesota, and many Irish settled in the urban centers of the Northeast, as did many Poles, Italians, and Jews. All brought with them unique views about many issues as well as about the role of government. Many of these regional differences continue to affect public opinion today, sometimes resulting in conflict at the national level.

Recall, for example, that during the Constitutional Convention most Southerners staunchly advocated a weak national government. The Civil War was fought in part because of basic differences in philosophy toward government (states' rights in the South versus national rights in the North) and the question of the moral and political validity of the institution of slavery.

Figure 10-2   Weekly Church Attendance

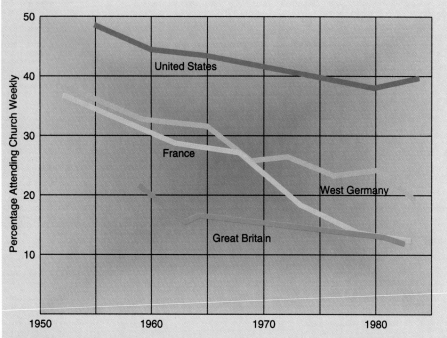

Source: Russell Dalton, *Citizen Politics in Western Democracies* (Chatham, N.J.: Chatham House, 1988), p. 162. Reprinted by permission. Data derived from: *United States*, Gallup (1980); *Britain*, Civic Culture Study, British Election Studies; *West Germany*, Civic Culture Study, West German Election Studies; *France*, IFOP Polls, Inglehart 1968 Election Study, European Community Studies.

Figure 10-3   Liberal/Conservative Self-Identification of Protestants, Catholics, and Jews

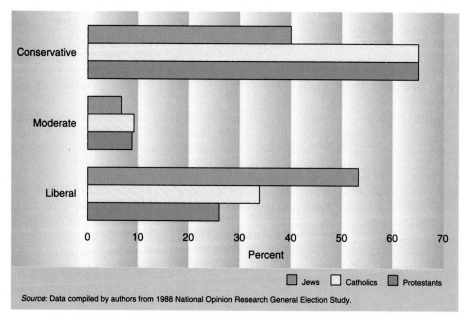

Source: Data compiled by authors from 1988 National Opinion Research General Election Study.

TABLE 10-1   Does the South Differ?

Percentage giving "liberal" response among white Protestants living in different regions, 1988.

ISSUE	EAST	MIDWEST	SOUTH	WEST
Economic and welfare issues:				
More government health care	48%	35%	37%	39%
Government job guarantees	19	19	22	21
Increase Social Security	56	50	59	53
Cut military spending	32	35	21	30
Civil rights and civil liberties issues:				
Aid to minorities	16	14	14	23
Homosexual rights	56	56	47	52
Women's equality	63	65	62	69
Right to abortion	65	49	45	60
Average percentage liberal, all issues	41%	37%	34%	41%

Source: Compiled by Daron Shaw. Reprinted with permission of the Center for Political Studies, University of Michigan.

As we know from the advent of modern political polling, the South has continued to lag behind the rest of the nation on support for civil rights, while continuing to favor return of power to the states at the expense of the national government, as revealed in Table 10-1.

During the drive to ratify the Equal Rights Amendment (1972–81), much was made by Southern legislators about whether the national government should mandate how the states treat "their women." And, not surprisingly, it was the Southern states that effectively blocked passage of the ERA.

Southerners also are much more supportive of a strong national defense and they accounted for 41 percent of the troops in the Persian Gulf in the early days of the war, even though they make up only 28 percent of the general population.

At one time, the South was so overwhelmingly Democratic that it was referred to as "the Solid South." Although they were conservative, Southerners' Democratic leanings stemmed from their reaction to the policies of Abraham Lincoln, a Republican. This Democratic bias has eroded recently because of massive migration to the South from the Northeast and Midwest (both hard hit by the economic recession of the 1970s), an escalating number of the elderly retiring to warmer climates, and an increased perception that the Democratic Party is too liberal. Since 1972, for example—with the exception of "native son" Jimmy Carter in 1976—every Republican presidential candidate has carried the South. Today it is not unusual for Southern states to send Republican representatives to Congress, and often the Democrats elected in the South are more conservative than their Northern Republican colleagues.

Race. Race is an exceptionally important factor in elections and in the study of public opinion. The direction and intensity of black political opinion is often quite different from that of whites. As revealed in Figure 10-4, blacks support affirmative action plans at significantly higher levels than whites.

Figure 10-4   Black versus White Attitudes

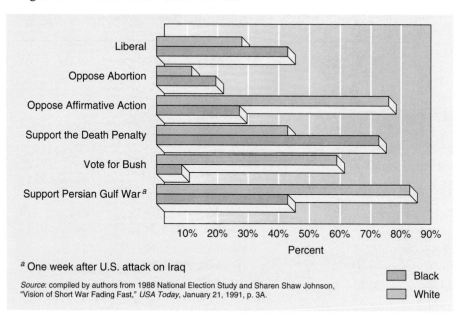

a One week after U.S. attack on Iraq

Source: compiled by authors from 1988 National Election Study and Sharen Shaw Johnson, "Vision of Short War Fading Fast," *USA Today*, January 21, 1991, p. 3A.

Blacks, however, are not the only racial or ethnic minority group in America. Native Americans, Hispanics, and Asian or Pacific Islanders, who made up 0.8, 9, and 2.9 percent of the population, respectively, in 1990, are identifiable minorities who often respond differently to issues than do whites. Generally, Hispanics and Native Americans hold similar opinions on many issues largely because significant proportions of these minority-group members belong to low-income groups and find themselves to be targets of discrimination.

Gender. From the time that the earliest public opinion polls were taken, women have been known to hold more negative views about war and military intervention and more strongly positive attitudes about issues touching on social welfare concerns, such as education, juvenile justice, capital punishment, and the environment. The reasons for this "gender gap" have been sought by many researchers. Some suggest that women's more "nurturing" nature and their prominent role as mothers lead women to have more liberal attitudes on issues affecting the family or the safety of their children. As revealed in polls taken in the late 1980s, women continue to hold very different opinions from men on a variety of issues, as shown in Table 10-2.

Ironically, during the debate over the Equal Rights Amendment, men preferred the amendment more than did women voters. Men also appear today to support a woman's right to an abortion to a greater extent than women.

Age. As Americans live longer, senior citizens are becoming a potent political force. In states like Florida, to which many Northern retirees have flocked to seek relief from cold winters and high taxes, the elderly have voted as a bloc to defeat school tax increases and to pass tax breaks for themselves. As a group, senior citizens are much more likely to favor an increased governmental role in the area of medical insurance while opposing any cuts in Social Security benefits.

In the future, the "graying of America" will have major social and political consequences. As discussed in Chapter 12, the elderly vote in far larger numbers than their

Table 10-2 Gender Differences on Issues of War, Peace, and Social Spending

ISSUES FAVORED	MALES	FEMALES
Increase defense spending	34	24
Aid to *contras*	42	21
"Star Wars" spending	24	10
No return to a peacetime draft	48	61
Initial sending troops to gulf	72	53
Increase spending on food stamps	18	24

Source: Data supplied by Center for the Study of Women and Politics.

younger counterparts. Moreover, the fastest-growing age group in the United States is that of citizens over the age of sixty-five. So, not only are there more persons in this category, but they are also the most active at the ballot box and will undoubtedly continue to have their wishes heard and heeded.

Political Ideology

An individual's coherent set of values and beliefs about the purpose and scope of government is called his or her **political ideology.** In sharp contrast to spur-of-the-moment responses, these sets of values, often greatly affected by political socialization, prompt citizens to favor a certain set of policy programs. Conservatives are likely to support smaller, less activist governments. In contrast, liberals favor big governments that play active roles.

Democratic primary candidate Bill Clinton campaigned hard in Florida to attract the elderly vote.

Conservative Versus Liberal

We often hear the terms "conservative" and "liberal" applied to politicians, but what do these ideological labels mean? As it happens, both terms have evolved over the years, and William Safire described these changes in his Political Dictionary.

CONSERVATIVE: A defender of the status quo who, when change becomes necessary in tested institutions or practices, prefers that it come slowly, and in moderation.

In modern U.S. politics, as in the past, "conservative" is a term of opprobrium to some, and of veneration to others. Edmund Burke, the early defender of the conservative philosophy, argued that the only way to preserve political stability was by carefully controlling change and seeking a slow, careful integration of new forces into venerable institutions.

The philosophy has had some famous detractors as well. Benjamin Disraeli, who was to become a Conservative prime minister of Great Britain, wrote in his sprightly novel *Coningsby:* "Conservatism discards Prescription, shrinks from Principle, disavows Progress; having rejected all respect for antiquity, it offers no redress for the present, and makes no preparation for the future. . . ."

The political origin of the word can be traced to the *Senat Conservateur* in the 1795 French Constitution, and it was used in its present English sense by British statesman, later Prime Minister, George Canning in 1820. . . . It was soon applied in America to the Whigs.

Today the more rigid conservative generally opposes virtually all governmental regulation of the economy. He or she favors local and state action over federal action and emphasizes fiscal responsibility, most notably in the form of balanced budgets.

But there exists a less doctrinaire conservative who admits the need for government action in some fields and for steady change in many areas. Instead of fighting a rear-guard action, he seeks to achieve such change within the framework of existing institutions, occasionally changing the institutions when they show need of it.

LIBERAL: Currently one who believes in more government action to meet

The terms "liberal" and "conservative" are tricky. Liberal and conservative ideologies focus on the function of liberty and equality in our society and on the proper role of government. The terms reflect opposing attitudes on a wide range of economic, social, and political issues. Although many Americans continue to identify themselves as liberals or conservatives, over the years these terms have had very different meanings. During the nineteenth century, for example, a liberal was one who supported freedom from undue governmental control; in contrast, conservatives supported governmental power and favored a role for religion in public life. Today, these terms have very different meanings to the general public. **Liberals** now are considered to favor extensive governmental involvement in the economy and the provision of social services and to take an activist role in protecting the rights of women, the elderly, minorities, and the environment. In contrast, **conservatives** are thought to believe that a government is best that governs least and that big government can only infringe on individual personal and economic rights. Conservatives also believe that domestic problems like homelessness, poverty, and discrimination are better dealt with by the private sector than by the government.

While political scientists and politicians often talk in terms of liberal and conservative individual needs; originally one who resisted government encroachment on individual liberties. In the original sense the word described those of the emerging middle classes in France and Great Britain who wanted to overthrow the dominant aristocracy.

In U.S. politics the word was used by George Washington to indicate a person of generosity or broad-mindedness, as he expressed distaste for those who would deprive Catholics and Jews of their rights.

The word became part of the American vocabulary in its earlier meaning during a rump convention of Republicans dissatisfied with the presidency of Ulysses S. Grant, held in Cincinnati in 1872. German-born Carl Schurz, who chaired the convention, used the word often. So did the leading journalist-thinker of the rebellion, Edwin L. Godkin of *The Nation.* The short-lived party born of the convention was called "The Liberal Republican" party.

In its present usage, the word ac-quired significance during the presidency of Franklin D. Roosevelt, who defined it this way during the 1932 campaign for his first term: ". . . say that civilization is a tree which, as it grows, continually produces rot and dead wood. The radical says: 'Cut it down.' The conservative says: 'Don't touch it.' The liberal compromises: 'Let's prune, so that we lose neither the old trunk nor the new branches.'"

Liberalism takes criticism from both right and left. President Herbert Hoover in a magazine article referred to ". . . fuzzy minded totalitarian liberals who believe that their creeping collectivism can be adopted without destroying personal liberty and representative government." Sometimes even liberals cannot avoid the temptation to assault the term. Adlai Stevenson, the Democrats' presidential candidate in 1952 and 1956, once described a liberal as "one who has both feet firmly planted in the air."

Source: William Safire, *Safire's Political Dictionary: The New Language of Politics* (New York: Random House, 1978).

ideologies, the general public does not appear to be as enamored of this kind of labeling. When asked, most Americans respond that their political beliefs are "middle of the road" or moderate, although a substantial number call themselves conservatives. Less than 25 percent of the American public labels itself "liberal." While America has become more conservative in recent years, the term "liberal" has even come to be a label to be avoided. In the 1988 presidential election, George Bush was able to stick the label "liberal" on his opponent, Michael S. Dukakis. In the minds of the public "liberal" was associated with big government, big spending, and support for affirmative action programs. The more the "liberal" label came to be associated with Dukakis, the more his support eroded.

The labels "liberal" and "conservative" can be quite misleading. Studies reveal, for example, that many who call themselves conservative actually take fairly liberal positions on many policy issues.[12] Those who take conservative stances against "big

[12] Lloyd Free and Hadley Cantril, *The Political Belief of Americans* (New York: Simon and Schuster, 1968).

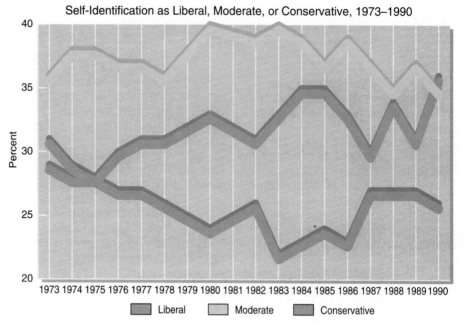

Self-Identification as Liberal, Moderate, or Conservative, 1973–1990

Note: "Liberal" equals the combined percentages of those identifying themselves as extremely liberal, liberal, or slightly liberal; "conservative" equals the combined percentages of those identifying themselves as extremely conservative, conservative, or slightly conservative.

Source: General Society Survey, National Opinion Research Center, University of Chicago.

government" often support increased government spending for the elderly, education, or health care. Thus, conservative or liberal ideology does not necessarily allow us to predict political opinions. In a "perfect" world, liberals would be liberal and conservatives would be conservative. Instead, Americans are inconsistent. Studies reveal that anywhere from 20 to 68 percent will take a traditionally "conservative" position on one issue and a traditionally "liberal" position on another.[13]

Americans do have political ideologies. The political culture in the United States places a high premium on individual liberty, equality, and the right of self-government, but these values lead many to hold a set of political beliefs that no longer allow for their placement on a single liberal-conservative continuum. Instead, many today put differing emphases on the role of government in economic, social, and political spheres. It is not at all unusual to see a person who could be considered liberal on social issues such as abortion and civil rights hold conservative views on economic or "pocketbook" issues.

How We Form Political Opinions

Many of us hold opinions on a wide range of political issues. In general, many of those values can be traced to the wide variety of social groups and different experiences each of us has had. Some individuals (called ideologues) think about politics and vote strictly on

[13] Philip E. Converse, "The Nature of Belief Systems in Mass Publics," in *Ideology and Discontent,* David E. Apter, ed. (New York: Free Press, 1964), pp. 206–221.

The American Voter and Ideology

In 1960, Angus Campbell and three colleagues tried to determine the ideological sophistication of the American electorate by assessing their responses to questions about numerous issues and the 1956 presidential election. Only 12 percent of the electorate responded in ideological terms. Forty-two percent assessed the candidates based on their "benefits of groups" (blacks, laborers, businesspersons, etc.), whereas others tended to evaluate candidates based on what was termed "the nature of the times." Moreover, 22 percent—nearly one-quarter of the sample—did not appear to be motivated by any issue or ideological underpinnings. These voters judged candidates on their personalities alone.

Other studies have concluded that the electorate of the 1950s was relatively apathetic and not representative of other eras. For example, in *The Changing American Voter* (1976), the authors argued that voters from 1956 to 1972 were much more interested in politics and more ideologically sophisticated than those of the 1950s. Other studies have found that the more ideological the candidates are—for example, as in the 1964 Goldwater/Johnson race—the more likely are voters to respond in ideological terms.

*Norman H. Nie, Sidney Verba, and John R. Petrocik, *The Changing American Voter* (Cambridge, Mass.: Harvard University Press, 1976).

the basis of liberal or conservative ideology. Most don't. In this section we explore how most people—those who are not ideologues—make up their minds on political issues. Chief among the factors that lead citizens to form political opinions are personal benefits, political knowledge, and cues from various leaders or opinion makers.

Personal Benefits

Most people will choose policies that benefit them personally. You've probably heard the adage "People vote with their pocketbooks." Taxpayers generally favor lower taxes, hence the popularity of candidates pledging "No new taxes." Similarly, the elderly usually support Social Security increases, and blacks support strong civil rights laws and affirmative action programs.

Some government policies, however, don't really affect us *individually*. Abortion, legalized prostitution, and the death penalty are often perceived as moral issues, and individuals often form attitudes toward them based on underlying values acquired through their socialization process.

When individuals are faced with policies that don't affect them personally and don't involve moral issues, they have difficulty forming an opinion. Foreign policy is an area where this phenomenon is especially true. Americans often know little of the world around them. Unless moral issues such as apartheid in South Africa or human-rights violations in China are involved, American public opinion is likely to be quite volatile in the wake of any new information. For example, George Bush's popularity fell as soon as Americans viewed the results of Saddam Hussein's ravaging of the Kurds (see Figure 10-5).

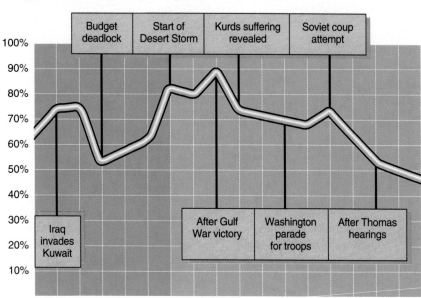

Figure 10-5   Bush's Popularity, July 1990 to December 1991

Source: For July 1990 through October 1991, *Atlanta Journal and Constitution*, November 1, 1991, p. A-3. Reprinted by permission. Data supplied by Gallup Organization.

Political Knowledge

Americans enjoy a relatively high literacy rate, and most Americans graduate from high school. And, unlike Great Britain, most Americans enjoy access to a range of higher education opportunities. In spite of that access to education, however, Americans' level of actual political knowledge is low. After the 1986 elections, for example, only 22 percent of people surveyed could correctly identify their representative in Congress. One Gallup study done in 1988, moreover, found that 75 percent of all Americans were unable to locate the Persian Gulf on a map. Two-thirds couldn't find Vietnam. Americans aged eighteen to twenty-four scored the lowest, with two-thirds not being able to point to France on an outline map.[14]

E. D. Hirsch Jr. criticizes the schools for their failure to teach "cultural literacy."[15] Americans, he concludes, frequently lack basic contextual knowledge—where Africa is, when the Civil War was fought and why, for example—necessary to sort out the rest of the information they receive. So, although millions of Americans read a daily newspaper and watch television news, they still have low levels of knowledge. In fact, one study of citizens' ability to recall the facts of recent major news stories revealed that less than 15 percent of those surveyed could get the facts right, prompting its authors to conclude that "ignorance is widespread, if not rampant."[16] Political scientist Doris Graber echoes that

[14] "Geography: A Lost Generation," *Nation,* August 8, 1988, p. 19.

[15] E. D. Hirsch, Jr., *Cultural Literacy* (Boston: Houghton Mifflin, 1986).

[16] Lee Sigelman and Ernest Yanarella, "Public Information on Public Issues," *Social Science Quarterly* 67 (June 1986), p. 404.

American Political Ignorance

	PERCENT UNABLE TO IDENTIFY
Name of vice president (1986)	23%
Name of the Speaker of the House (1986)	44
Party with most members in Senate before election (1984)	70
Chief Justice of United States (1986)	86

Source: National Opinion Research Center, General Social Surveys and Center for Political Studies, American National Election Studies.

sentiment: "By and large . . . people do not seem to gain much specific information from the media.[17]

In spite of their low levels of knowledge, Americans are still generally willing to offer opinions on a wide range of issues, from abortion to the budget to the Stealth bomber. These low levels of knowlege, however, can lead to the rapid opinion shifts on issues that we called popular opinion earlier in this chapter. The ebb and flow of popular opinion can be affected dramatically by political leaders.

Cues from Leaders

Given the visibility of political leaders and their access to the media, it is easy to see the important role they play in influencing public opinion. Political leaders, members of the news media, and a host of other experts have regular opportunities to influence public opinion, given the weakness with which most Americans hold many of their political beliefs. The president—particularly a popular one—can heavily sway public opinion. Political scientist John E. Mueller concludes, in fact, that there is a group of citizens— called followers—who are inclined to rally to the support of the president no matter what he does.[18] According to Mueller, the president's strength, especially in the area of foreign affairs (where public information is lowest), derives from the "majesty" of his office and his singular position as head of state.[19] Recognizing this, presidents often take to television to drum up support for their programs.[20]

How We Measure Public Opinion

To guide their policy decisions, public officials use a variety of measures—election results, the number of telephone calls pro and con on any particular issue, letters to the editor in hometown papers, the size of demonstrations or marches—as indicators of public opinion. The most commonly relied upon measure of public sentiment continues to be the public opinion survey, more popularly called a poll.

[17]Doris Graber, *Mass Media and American Politics,* 2nd ed. (Washington: CQ Press, 1984), p. 157.
[18]John Mueller, *War, Presidents and Public Opinion,* (New York: Wiley, 1973), p. 69.
[19]Ibid.
[20]Roderick P. Hart, *The Sound of Leadership: Presidential Communication in the Modern Age* (Chicago: University of Chicago Press, 1987).

Poll Wording

Polls, supported by each side in the abortion debate, differ depending on how the question is worded:

One poll, partly paid for by the National Right to Life Committee, asked: "The U.S. Supreme Court recently ruled that the federal government is not required to use taxpayer funds for family planning programs to perform, counsel, or refer for abortion as a method of family planning. Do you favor or oppose this ruling?"

Favor	48%
Oppose	48%
Don't know/refuse	4%

Source: Wirthlin Group poll of 1,000 adults taken on June 17–19; margin of error is 3 percentage points

Another poll, commissioned by Planned Parenthood, asked: "Do you favor or oppose that Supreme Court decision preventing clinic doctors and medical personnel from discussing abortion in family planning clinics that receive federal funds?"

Oppose	65%
Favor	33%
Not sure	2%

Source: Lou Harris and Associates poll of 1,254 adults, May 31–June 5; margin of error: 3 percentage points

Source: "Words Affect Poll Numbers," *USA Today,* June 25, 1991, p. 7-A

The polling process most often begins when someone says, "Let's find out about X and Y." Xs or Ys can be many things. People may want to know how to shape a candidate's campaign strategy, how to market a new product, how to determine the popularity of certain television shows, or how to form public policy on issues of health care or housing. Potential candidates for local office may want to know how many people have heard of them (the device used to find out is called a name recognition survey). Better-known candidates contemplating higher office might want to know how they might fare against an incumbent. News organizations routinely poll potential voters over the course of a campaign (or duration of a war, presidential term, and so on) to measure changes in public opinion and to measure the fluctuations in a candidate's popularity as Election Day nears.

Determining the Content and Phrasing the Questions

Once a candidate, politician, or news organization decides that it wants to find out about the public's attitudes via a poll, special care has to be taken in constructing the questions to be asked. For example, if your professor asked you "Do you think my grading procedures are fair?" rather than "In general, how fair do you think the grading is in your American Politics course?" you might give a slightly different answer. The wording of the first question tends to put you on the spot and personalize the grading style; the second question is more neutral. Even more obvious differences appear in the real world of polling, especially when interested groups want a poll to have particular results. Responses to highly emotional issues such as abortion, busing, and affirmative action are often skewed depending upon the wording of the question. As discussed in the box entitled "Poll Wording," respondents' answers to questions about abortion appear to differ considerably depending upon how the questions are worded. Support for abortion can range from around 40 to 90 percent, depending on the question asked. Moreover, respondents often react to emotional cues, and this also tends to skew the survey results.

Selecting the Sample

Once the decision is made to take a poll, pollsters must determine the universe, or entire group whose attitudes they wish to measure. This universe could be all Americans, all voters, all city residents, all women, or all Democrats. Although in a perfect world each individual would be asked to give an opinion, this kind of polling is simply not practical. Consequently, pollsters take a sample of the universe in which they are interested. One way to do this is by **random sampling**, which simply means using a method of selection that gives each potential voter or adult the same chance of being selected. In theory, this sounds good, but it is actually impossible to achieve because no one has lists of every person in any group. Most national surveys and commercial polls use samples of 1,000 to 1,500 individuals and use a variation of the random sampling method called **stratified** or **multistage** area **sampling**. Simple random samples aren't very useful at predicting voting because they may undersample (or oversample) key populations that are not likely to vote. Although the *Literary Digest* sample discussed earlier was a straw poll (see page 351) and not a random sample, it suffered from an oversampling of voters drawn from telephone directories and car registrations, hardly representative of the general electorate in the midst of the Depression.

To avoid these problems, stratified sampling makes use of census data, which provide the number of residences in an area and their location. Researchers divide the country into four sampling regions, and then a set of counties and standard metropolitan statistical areas are randomly selected in proportion to the total national population. Generally, about eighty primary sampling units are chosen. Once certain primary sampling units are selected, often they are used for many years because it is cheaper for polling companies to train interviewers to work in a fixed area.

Public Opinion on Abortion, 1962–1990 (percent)

| | | | | | | AS FORM | |
| | MOTHER'S | | BIRTH | LOW | SINGLE | OF BIRTH | ANY |
YEAR	HEALTH	RAPE	DEFECT	INCOME	MOTHER	CONTROL	REASON
1962	77	—	55	15	—	—	—
1965	70	56	55	21	17	15	—
1969	80	—	63	23	—	—	—
1972	83	75	75	46	41	38	—
1973	91	81	82	52	47	46	—
1974	90	83	83	52	48	45	—
1975	88	80	80	51	46	44	—
1976	89	81	82	51	48	45	—
1977	89	81	83	52	48	45	37
1978	88	81	80	46	40	39	32
1980	88	80	80	50	46	45	39
1982	90	83	81	50	47	46	39
1983	87	80	76	42	38	38	33
1984	88	77	78	45	43	41	37
1985	87	78	76	42	40	39	36
1987	86	78	77	44	40	40	38
1988	86	77	76	40	38	39	35
1989	88	80	78	46	43	43	39
1990	89	81	78	46	43	43	42

Note: "—" indicates not available. Question: "Please tell me whether or not you think it should be possible for a pregnant woman to obtain a legal abortion [in the order asked in the survey] if there is a strong chance of serious defect in the baby? If she is married and does not want any more children? If the woman's own health is seriously endangered by the pregnancy? If the family has a very low income and cannot afford any more children? If she became pregnant as a result of rape? If she is not married and does not want to marry the man? The woman wants it for any reason?"

Sources: 1962 and 1969: Gallup surveys; 1965: National Opinion Research Center surveys; 1972–1988: General Social Survey. Compiled in Harold W. Stanley and Richard G. Niemi, *Vital Statistics on American Politics* (Washington: CQ Press, 1991), p. 35.

About twenty respondents from each primary sampling unit are selected to be interviewed. Generally four or five city blocks or areas are selected and then four or five target families from each district are used. Large, sophisticated surveys like the National Election Study and General Social Survey attempt to sample from lists of persons living in each household. The key to the success of this method is not to let people volunteer to be interviewed—volunteers often have different opinions from those who don't volunteer.

Stratified sampling (the most rigorous sampling technique) is generally not used by most survey organizations. Instead, they randomly survey every 10th, 100th, or 1,000th person or household. If those individuals are not at home, they go to the home or apartment next door.

Not all polls are based on probability sampling. A less reliable but frequently used method is known as **nonprobability sampling**. The *Literary Digest* poll is one good example, as are the polls taken by local television stations. Such "straw polls" are not

A Common Poll Description

Most major poll reports now include a section containing information on how the poll was conducted. The following was from a poll on women's issues reported in the New York Times *on August 20, 1989.*

HOW THE POLL WAS TAKEN

The New York Times Poll on women's issues is based on telephone interviews conducted June 20 through June 25 with 1,497 adults around the United States, excluding Alaska and Hawaii.

The sample of telephone exchanges called was selected by a computer from a complete list of exchanges in the country. The exchanges were chosen so as to assure that each region of the country was represented in proportion to its population. For each exchange, the telephone numbers were formed by random digits, thus permitting access to both listed and unlisted numbers. The numbers were then screened to limit calls to residences.

Women were sampled at a higher rate than men so that there would be enough women interviewed to provide statistically reliable comparisons among various subgroups of women. The results of the interviews with 1,025 women and 472 men were then weighted to their correct proportions in the population.

Results were also weighted to take account of household size and number of residential telephone lines and to adjust for variations in the sample relating to region, race, age, and education.

A group of 978 of these respondents were interviewed a second time from July 25 through 30, after the Supreme Court's decision allowing states more freedom to restrict abortion. Respondents in the second survey amounted to 79 percent of the 1,236 randomly selected people who were asked to participate, but 258 declined or were not reached despite several attempts.

In theory, in nineteen cases out of the twenty the results based on either such samples will differ not by more than three percentage points in either direction from what would have been obtained by seeking out all American adults.

The percentages reported are the particular results most likely to match what would be obtained by seeking out all adult Americans. Other possible percentages are progressively less likely the more they differ from the reported results.

The potential sampling error for smaller subgroups is larger. For example, for men it is plus or minus five percentage points in both the first and second surveys. For women it is plus or minus three percentage points in the first survey and plus or minus four percentage points in the second survey. For women aged eighteen to twenty-nine in the first survey, it is plus or minus six percentage points.

In addition to sampling error, the practical difficulties of conducting any survey of public opinion may introduce other errors into the poll.

representative samples, because only those aware of the poll and highly motivated about it are included in the sample.

Another kind of nonprobability sample involves "surveys" taken by organized interests. Generally, these groups send "questionnaires" to their members, and the tallies of these very biased polls are then sent to the press, members of Congress, and members of the executive branch.

A more reliable nonprobability sample is a **quota sample** in which pollsters draw their sample based on known statistics. Thus, assuming a citywide survey has been commissioned, if that city is 30 percent black, 15 percent Hispanic, and 55 percent white, interviewers will use those figures to determine the proportion of particular groups that they will sample in that city. These kinds of surveys are often conducted at local malls and shopping centers. Perhaps you've wondered why the man or woman with the clipboard has clearly passed you up to ask questions of other shoppers. Now you know it is likely that you failed to fit into one of the categories of individuals that particular pollster was charged with locating. Although this kind of sampling technique can yield fairly impressive findings, the degree of accuracy falls short of that of surveys based on probability samples. Moreover, these polls generally oversample visible populations such as shoppers. The views of stay-at-homes, who may be glued to CNN, C-SPAN, or soap operas are therefore underrepresented.

Kinds of Polls

The most common form of polls are random-digit dialing surveys, in which a computer randomly selects telephone numbers to be dialed. Because it is estimated that as many as 95 percent of the American public have phones in their homes, samples selected in this manner are likely to be fairly representative. George Gallup observed in 1967 that the quickest and cheapest way to poll people is by telephone.

> but you run into a problem. . . . You're more likely to reach conservatives and more Republicans than Democrats. If you could reach people in theaters or bars or massage parlors, you'd find the Democrats.[21]

In spite of Gallup's obvious biases and stereotyping, he came to the proper conclusion that some telephone polls can be less than accurate. Other possible problems with telephone surveys include:

- They are not particularly useful for detailed and/or lengthy surveys.
- Nationally more than 20 percent of all phone numbers are unlisted; in San Francisco that proportion is 48 percent. (This does not present a problem when random dialing is used.)
- They underrepresent women, who generally are more likely not to list their phone numbers. (Again, this is not a problem with random dialing.)
- Because of the large number of telephone sales calls and solicitations and other "unwanted" calls, the refusal rate for phone survey participation is around 30 percent.
- They undersample the poor. The Public Interest Research Group estimates that 27 percent of those with incomes under $15,000 do not have telephones in their homes.

In spite of these problems, most polls done for newspapers and news magazines are conducted this way.

---

[21] Quoted in Eric Pace, "George H. Gallup Is Dead at 82," *The New York Times,* July 28, 1984, p. A-1.

Individual, in-person interviews are conducted by some groups such as the University of Michigan for its National Election Studies. Some analysts favor such in-person surveys, but others argue that the unintended influence of the questioner or pollster is very important and can lead to errors. How the pollster dresses, relates to the person being interviewed, and even asks the questions can affect responses. (Some of these problems can also affect the results of telephone surveys.)

Probably the most criticized kind of polls are **exit polls**, conducted at selected polling places on Election Day. Generally, large news organizations send pollsters to selected precincts to sample every tenth voter as they emerge from their polling place. These results then are used to help the network predict the outcome of key races, often just a few minutes after the polls close in a particular state and generally before voters in other areas—sometimes in a later time zone—have cast their ballots. In 1980, his own polling and the results of network exit polls led President Jimmy Carter to concede defeat three hours before the polls closed on the West coast, leading many to criticize Carter and network predictions for harming other Democrats' chances. (Many Democrats argued that if the presidential election had already been "called," voters were unlikely to go to the polls.) In the aftermath of that controversy, all networks agreed not to predict the results of presidential contests until all polling places were closed.

Exit polls have also been faulted because it appears that not all voters are willing to reply truthfully to pollsters' questions. In 1989, for example, when L. Douglas Wilder ran for the Virginia governorship, exit polls were way off. Surveys done before the race showed the black lieutenant governor winning by margins of 4 to 15 percent. A television exit poll showed him winning by 10 percent. Wilder won, but with a razor-thin margin of only 6,582 votes out of a record 1.78 million cast. Clearly, pollsters had been lied to or misled by "some Democratic-leaning white Virginians who could not bring themselves to vote for a black candidate . . . and few voters are secure enough in their bigotry to confess such blatant bias."[22] It seems that many white voters were unwilling

---

[22] Walter Shapiro, "Breakthrough in Virginia," *Time,* November 20, 1989, p. 54.

Governor L. Douglas Wilder of Virginia, whose election in 1989 demonstrated some of the difficulties of polling. Despite advance surveys and exit polls that indicated a comfortable lead, Wilder's actual margin of victory was razor-thin. Apparently, voters, for fear of admitting racism, were unwilling to admit that they had voted against him.

to say that they had not voted for Wilder; therefore, they told pollsters that they *had* voted for Wilder, the black candidate, when they had not. A similar phenomenon occurred during the Louisiana gubernatorial primary in 1991. Many whites who voted for David Duke, the former Ku Klux Klansman, apparently lied to pollsters, who underpredicted his support. Duke received a majority of the white vote, although he ultimately was soundly defeated in the general election.

Shortcomings of Polling

The accuracy of any poll depends on the quality of the sample that was drawn. Small samples, if properly drawn, can be very accurate if each unit in the universe has an equal opportunity to be sampled. If a pollster, for example, fails to sample certain populations, his or her results may reflect that shortcoming. Often, the opinions of the poor and/or homeless are underrepresented because insufficient attention is given to making certain that these groups are representatively sampled.

There comes a point in sampling, however, where increases in the size of the sample have little effect on a reduction of the **sampling error**, the difference between the actual universe and the sample.

All polls contain errors. Standard samples of approximately 1,500 individuals provide fairly good estimates of actual behavior (in the case of voting, for example). Typically, the **margin of error**, or sampling error, in a sample of 1,500 will be about 3 percent. If you ask "Do you like ice cream?" of 1,500 people and 52 percent say "yes" and 48 percent say "no," the results are too close to tell whether more people like ice cream than not. Why? Because the margin of error implies that somewhere between 55 percent (52 + 3) and 49 percent (52 − 3) of the people like ice cream while between 51 percent (48 + 3) and 45 percent (48 − 3) do not. The margin of error in a close election makes predictions very difficult.

Public opinion polls may also be "off" when they attempt to gauge attitudes about issues that some or even many individuals don't care about or about which the public has little information. For example, few Americans probably care about the elimination of the electoral college. If a representative sample were polled, many would answer pro or con without having given much consideration to the question.

Low levels of knowledge or the inability to understand complex issues also confound pollsters. The Gramm–Rudman Act, for example, was passed in late 1986 amidst considerable publicity because it would force limits on federal spending in an effort to balance the budget and forestall the need for the much-feared (at least by many members of Congress) balanced budget constitutional amendment. After President Reagan signed the Gramm–Rudman bill into law, a Washington Post/ABC poll asked respondents if they had "read or heard anything about Congress passing the Gramm–Rudman bill, which requires the government to balance the federal budget by 1991." Only sixty out of every one hundred respondents had. Among those 60 percent, only three-fifths reported having an opinion about its provisions.

The poll would have received far more responses if the "have you heard" question had not been used as a filter to exclude those who knew nothing about the bill. If the poll had asked only, "Do you favor or oppose the Gramm–Rudman Act?" many of the 40 percent who hadn't heard of the bill might nevertheless have responded pro or con. Most academic public opinion research organizations, such as the National Election Study, for example, use some kind of filter question that first asks respondents whether or not they have thought about the question. These screening procedures generally allow surveyors to exclude as many as 20 percent of their respondents, especially on complex issues like the federal budget. Questions on more personal issues such as moral values, drugs, crime, race, and women's role in society get far fewer "no opinion" or "don't know" responses.

Public Opinion on a Variety of Issues, 1990

"Do you think it would be best for the future of this country if we take an active part in world affairs, or if we stay out of world affairs?"

Active part: 68%   Stay out: 27%   No opinion: 4%

"Would you favor or oppose a law which would require a person to obtain a police permit before he or she could buy a gun?"

Favor: 79%   Oppose: 20%   Don't know: 2%

"There has been discussion lately about a constitutional amendment which would make it illegal to burn or desecrate the United States flag. Some people favor a flag-burning amendment because they say the flag is America's unique symbol and deserves constitutional protection from desecration. Others oppose a flag-burning amendment because they say burning the flag is a form of freedom of speech, no matter how offensive, which is protected by the Bill of Rights. Which of these two opinions comes closest to your own?"

Favor: 66%   Oppose: 29%   No opinion: 5%

"The U.S. Supreme Court has ruled that no state or local government may require the reading of the Lord's Prayer or Bible verses in public schools. What are your views on this—do you approve or disapprove of the court ruling?"

Favor: 40%   Oppose: 56%   No opinion: 4%

Source: Harold W. Stanley and Richard G. Niemi, *Vital Statistics on American Politics* (Washington: CQ Press, 1991).

Another shortcoming of polls concerns their inability to measure intensity of feeling about particular issues. Whereas a respondent might answer affirmatively to any question, it is likely that his or her feelings about issues such as abortion, the death penalty, or support for American troops in the Gulf are far more intense than his or her feelings about the electoral college.

Exit polls can be undertaken by news networks, newspapers, polling organizations, or, as in this case, directly by candidates' campaigns.

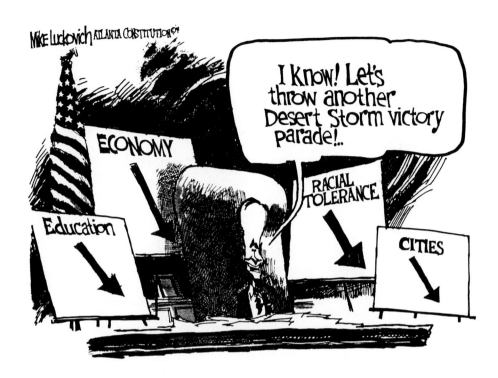

How Public Opinion Affects Politicians, Politics, and Policy

George Gallup once remarked, "It is not incumbent upon a leader, even in a democracy, to follow the wishes of the people slavishly. But the very nature of democracy makes it imperative that public opinion be taken into account in reaching decisions about legislative goals."[23] Politicians and government officials spend millions of dollars each year taking the "pulse" of the public. Even the federal government spends millions annually on polls and surveys designed to evaluate programs and to provide information for shaping policies.

We know that politicians rely on polls, but it's difficult to say just how much. Several political scientists have attempted to study whether public policy is responsive to public opinion, with mixed results.[24] As we have seen, public opinion can fluctuate, making it difficult for a politician or policy maker to assess. Some critics of polls and their use by politicians argue that they hurt democracy and make leaders weaker. Some say that politicians are simply driven by the results of polls that do not reflect serious debate of issues. In response to this argument, George Gallup retorted, "One might as well insist that a thermometer makes the weather."[25]

Polls can clearly distort the election process by creating what are called "bandwagon" and "underdog" effects. In a presidential campaign, an early victory in the Iowa caucuses or the New Hampshire primary, for example, can boost a candidate's standings in the polls as the rest of the nation begins to think of him or her in a more positive light. New

[23] Quoted in Pace, p. A-1.
[24] See for example, Benjamin Page and Robert Shapiro, "Effects of Public Opinion on Policy," *American Political Science Review* 57 (March 1983), pp. 175–190.
[25] Quoted in Pace, op. cit.

supporters jump on the bandwagon. A strong showing in the polls, in turn, leads to more and larger donations, the lifeblood of any campaign. Herbert Asher has noted that "bad poll results, as well as poor primary and caucus standings, may deter potential donors from supporting a failing campaign."[26]

Political scientist Benjamin Ginsburg argues that public opinion polls weaken democracy,[27] claiming that they allow governments and politicians to say they have considered public opinion in spite of the fact that polls don't always measure the intensity of feeling on an issue or might overreflect the views of those who lack sufficient information to make educated choices. He further argues that democracy is better served by politicians' reliance on calls and letters—active signs of interest—than the passive voice of public opinion.

Summary

Public opinion is what the public thinks about an issue or a particular set of issues. As Americans with a belief in democracy, most of us would argue that the government needs to be responsive to public opinion. But, in reality, public opinion is very complex and difficult to measure or gauge with any precision.

Almost since the first elections in the United States, various attempts have been made to predict elections and to measure how voters feel about particular candidates. Over the years, polling to measure public opinion has become more and more sophisticated and more accurate because pollsters are better able to sample the public to determine their attitudes and positions on issues. Pollsters recognize that their sample must be reflective of the population whose ideas and beliefs they wish to measure.

The first step in forming opinions occurs through a process called political socialization. The family, school, your peers, and the social group to which you belong—including your religion, region, race, gender, and age—all affect how you view political events and issues, as do the major events themselves. Our political ideology—whether we are liberal, conservative, or moderate—also provides a lens by which we filter our political views.

Political interest, information on issues and events, and even the views of others affect our ultimate views of a variety of issues, including race relations, the death penalty, abortion, and federal taxes. Knowledge of the public's views on these issues is often used by politicians to tailor campaigns or to drive policy decisions.

Key Terms

public opinion	political socialization	multistage sampling
polls	political ideology	nonprobability sampling
popular opinion	liberals	quota sample
initiative	conservatives	exit polls
referendum	random sampling	sampling error
recall	stratified sampling	margin of error
straw polls		

[26] Herbert Asher, *Polling and the Public: What Every Citizen Should Know* (Washington: CQ Press, 1988), p. 109.
[27] Ginsburg, Chapter 4.

Suggested Readings

Asher, Herbert. *Polling and the Public: What Every Citizen Should Know.* Washington: CQ Press, 1988.

Campbell, Angus, et al. *The American Voter.* New York: Wiley, 1960.

Crespi, Irving. *Public Opinion, Polls, and Democracy.* Boulder, Colo.: Westview Press, 1989.

Ginsburg, Benjamin. *The Captive Public.* New York: Basic Books, 1986.

Graber, Doris. *Processing the News: How People Tame the Information Tide.* New York: Longman, 1984.

Jennings, M. Kent and Richard Niemi. *Generations and Politics: A Panel Study of Young Adults and Their Parents.* Princeton, N.J.: Princeton University Press, 1981.

Key, V. O., Jr. *Public Opinion and American Democracy.* New York: Alfred E. Knopf, 1961.

Niemi, Richard G., John Mueller, and Tom Smith. *Trends in Public Opinion: A Compendium of Survey Data.* New York: Greenwood Press, 1989.

Yeric, Jerry L. and John R. Todd. *Public Opinion: The Visible Politics,* 2nd ed. Itasca, Ill.: Peacock, 1989.

There are two methods of curing the mischiefs of faction: The one, by removing its causes; the other, by controlling its effects.

James Madison

FEDERALIST NO. 10

Of all the phenomena feared by the Framers, political parties have proved to be the most pervasive and lasting. In this famous passage, Madison expresses distrust of factions.

CHAPTER 11

POLITICAL PARTIES

Many of the Founders harbored a deep distrust of political parties and other "factions," fearing the divisiveness they might engender at a time when the success of the infant federal Constitution was still far from certain. In this regard we need only remember President George Washington's 1796 farewell address in which he warned the new nation "in the most solemn manner against the baneful effects of the spirit of party generally." Judging by his arguments in Federalist No. 10, James Madison held the same views as far back as the 1780s. Yet Madison was wise enough to understand that the "cure" for factionalism—the absence of liberty—is far worse than the disease. And Madison recognized the inevitability that factions of various sorts, whether narrow special-interest groups or broad-based parties, would form in any republic.

Madison also correctly foresaw that the mechanisms of the federal system would temper the "mischiefs of faction." The division of governmental powers among several branches; the layers of federal, state, and local governments; the numerous checks and balances in the Constitution; and the vigorous competition among and between the factions themselves all help to counteract or limit the ill effects of faction. In fact, for a variety of reasons that this chapter will explain, the United States is the only industrial democracy with just two parties of consequence.

In the centuries since Madison and Washington's criticisms of faction, we have come to see political parties in a new light. Far from an evil to be tempered, they have provided our system of government with the stability and choice that preserve it. As this chapter explains, the political scientist E. E. Schattschneider was not exaggerating when he wrote, ". . . modern democracy is unthinkable save in terms of the parties."[1]

What Is a Political Party?

Any definition of "political party" must be kept general, because there are so many kinds of parties in the United States. In some states and localities, party organizations are strong and well entrenched, whereas in other places the parties exist more on paper than in reality. This diversity would probably please James Madison, validating as it does his vision of a varied federalism. But it also complicates our task of explaining and understanding the political parties.[2]

At the most basic level a **political party** is a group of office holders, candidates, activists, and voters who identify with a group label and seek to elect to public office individuals who run under that label. Notice how pragmatic this concept of party is. The goal is to *win* office, not just compete for it. This objective is in keeping with the practical nature of Americans and the country's historical aversion to most ideologically driven, "purist" politics (as we will see later in this chapter). Nevertheless, the group label—also called **party identification**—can carry with it clear messages about ideology and issue positions. Although this is especially true of minor, less broad-based parties that have little chance of electoral success, it also applies to the national, dominant political parties—the Democrats and the Republicans.

The definition of "party" also identifies the three groups of individuals who make up any political party: (1) the office holders and candidates who run under the party's banner (the **governmental party**), (2) the workers and activists who staff the party's formal organization (the **organizational party**), and (3) the voters who consider themselves to be allied or associated with the party (the **party-in-the-electorate**). We exam-

---

[1] E. E. Schattschneider, *Party Government* (New York: Holt, Rinehart and Winston, 1942), p. 1. This book stands as one of the most eloquent arguments for a strong political party system ever penned.

[2] For more information on this topic, see Larry Sabato, *The Party's Just Begun: Shaping Political Parties for America's Future* (Glenview, Ill.: Scott, Foresman/Little, Brown, 1988).

ine each of these groups later in the chapter after first reviewing the history and development of political parties in the United States.

The Evolution of American Party Democracy

It is one of the great ironies of the early republic that George Washington's public farewell, which warned the nation against parties, marked the effective end of the brief era of partyless politics in the United States. Washington's unifying influence ebbed as he stepped off the national stage, and his vice president and successor, President John Adams, occupied a far less exalted position. Adams was allied with Alexander Hamilton, and to win the presidency in 1796 he narrowly defeated Thomas Jefferson, Hamilton's erstwhile rival in Washington's Cabinet. Hamilton and Jefferson, before ratification of the Constitution, had been leaders of the Federalists and Anti-Federalists, respectively (see Chapter 2). Over the course of Adams's single term, two competing congressional party groupings (or caucuses) gradually organized around these clashing men and their principles. Hamilton's Federalists supported a strong central government, whereas the Democratic-Republicans of Thomas Jefferson and his ally, James Madison, inherited the mantle of the Anti-Federalists, and preferred a federal system in which the states were relatively more powerful. (Jefferson actually preferred the simpler name "Republicans"—a very different group from today's party of the same name—but Hamilton insisted on calling them "Democratic-Republicans" to link them to the radical democrats of the French Revolution.) In the presidential election of 1800, the Federalists supported Adams's bid for a second term, but this time the Democratic-Republicans prevailed with their nominee, Jefferson, who became the first American president elected as the nominee of a political party.

Jefferson was deeply committed to the ideas of his party, but not nearly as devoted to the idea of a party system. He regarded his party as a temporary measure necessary to defeat Adams and Hamilton. Neither Jefferson's party nor Hamilton's enjoyed widespread "party identification" among the citizenry akin to that of today's Democrats and Republicans. Although Southerners were overwhelmingly partial to the Democratic-Republicans and New Englanders to the Federalists, no broad-based party organizations existed on either side to mobilize popular support. Just as the nation was in its infancy, so too was the party system, and attachments to both parties were weak at first.

The Early Parties Fade

After the spirited confrontations of the republic's early years, political parties faded somewhat in importance for a quarter of a century. The Federalists ceased nominating presidential candidates by 1816, having failed to elect one of their own since Adams's victory in 1796, and by 1820 the party had dissolved. James Monroe's presidency from 1817 to 1825 produced the so-called Era of Good Feelings, when party politics was nearly suspended at the national level. Even during Monroe's tenure, though, party organizations continued to develop at the state level, fueled in part by the enormous increase in the electorate that took place between 1820 and 1840, when most states abolished property requirements as a condition of suffrage. In this twenty-year period, the number of votes cast in presidential contests rose from 300,000 to more than 2 million.

At the same time, American politics was being democratized in other ways. By the 1820s all the states except South Carolina had switched from state legislative selection of presidential electors to popular election of electoral college slates. This change helped to transform presidential politics. No longer just the concern of society's upper crust, the election of the president became a matter for all qualified voters to decide.

The party base broadened along with the electorate. Small caucuses of congressional party leaders had previously nominated candidates, but after much criticism of the system as elitist and undemocratic, it gave way to nominations at large party conventions. The country's first major national presidential nominating convention was held in 1832 by the Democratic Party,[3] the successor to the old Jeffersonian Democratic-Republicans. (The shortened name had gradually come into use in the 1820s.) Formed around the charismatic populist President Andrew Jackson, the Democratic party attracted most of the newly enfranchised voters, who were drawn to Jackson's style. Jackson's strong personality helped to polarize politics, and opposition to the president coalesced into the Whig Party, which was descended from the Federalists and whose early leaders included Henry Clay, the Speaker of the House from 1811 to 1820. The incumbent Jackson defeated Clay in the 1832 presidential contest and became the first chief executive who won the White House as the nominee of a truly national, popularly based political party.

The Whigs and the Democrats continued to strengthen after 1832, establishing state and local organizations almost everywhere. Their competition was usually fierce and closely matched, and they brought the United States the first broadly supported two-party system in the Western world.[4] Unfortunately for the Whigs, the issue of slavery sharpened many already present and divisive internal party tensions that led to its gradual dissolution and replacement by the new Republican Party. Formed in 1854 by anti-slavery activists, the Republican Party set its sights on the abolition (or at least the containment) of slavery. After a losing presidential effort for John C. Frémont in 1856, it was able to assemble enough support from the Whigs, anti-slavery Northern Democrats, and others to win the presidency for Abraham Lincoln in a fragmented 1860 vote. In that year, the South voted solidly Democratic, beginning a habit so strong that not a single Southern state voted Republican for president again until 1920.

The British political system, which has also been characterized by competition between two political parties with significant third-party activity, provides an interesting contrast to the American case. It took the massive extension of suffrage in 1867 to prompt the emergence of two modern, mass political parties (the Liberals and the Conservatives), which were needed to organize and mobilize the now unwieldy electorate. In

---

[3] The National Republican (one forerunner of the Whig Party) and the Anti-Masonic Parties each had held more limited conventions in 1831.

[4] By contrast, Great Britain did not develop truly national, broad-based parties until the 1870s.

The Six American Party Systems

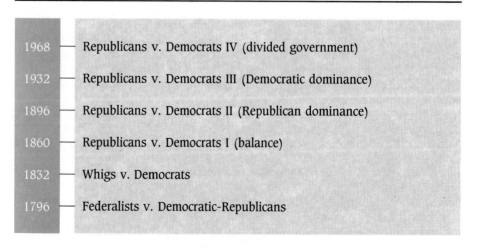

1968	Republicans v. Democrats IV (divided government)
1932	Republicans v. Democrats III (Democratic dominance)
1896	Republicans v. Democrats II (Republican dominance)
1860	Republicans v. Democrats I (balance)
1832	Whigs v. Democrats
1796	Federalists v. Democratic-Republicans

the aftermath of World War I, the Liberals gave way to the Labour Party as the Conservatives' principal contender for power.

Democrats and Republicans: The Golden Age

From that election in 1860 to this day, the same two great parties—the Republicans and the Democrats—have dominated American elections, and control of an electoral majority has seesawed back and forth between them. The dominance of the Republicans (now often called the Grand Old Party, or GOP—see the sidebar explanation) in the post–Civil War Reconstruction era eventually gave way to a closely competitive system from 1876 to 1896, in part because the Democrats were more successful at integrating new immigrants to port cities like New York. In the latter years of the nineteenth century, however, the Republicans skillfully capitalized on fears of a growing anti-establishment, anti–big business sentiment in the Democratic Party and fashioned a dominant and enduring majority of voters that essentially lasted until the early 1930s, when the Great Depression created the conditions for a Democratic resurgence.

Franklin Roosevelt's New Deal coalition of 1932 (consisting of the South, ethnics, organized labor, farmers, liberals, and big-city "machines"—as well-oiled party organizations are sometimes called) basically characterized both the Democratic Party and the prevailing national majority until at least the late 1960s. Since 1970, neither party has been clearly dominant, as more and more voters have seemed to view their partisan attachments as less important. Simultaneously, the Republicans have dominated presidential elections, and Democrats have won most congressional contests. (This development will be discussed later in this chapter.)

The Modern Era versus the Golden Age

The modern era seems very distant from the "golden age" of parties from the 1870s to the 1920s. Immigration from Europe (particularly Ireland, Italy, and Germany) fueled the development of big-city party organizations that ruled with an iron hand in their domains. Party and government were virtually interchangeable, and the parties were the providers of needed services, entertainment, and employment. These party organizations

The Grand Old Party

Ever since the 1880s, the term "Grand Old Party" has been used to refer to the Republican Party. The phrase seems to have taken its inspiration from Great Britain, where Prime Minister William Gladstone was dubbed "the Grand Old Man" or "GOM" in 1882. Soon after that, "GOP" made its bow in headlines appearing in the *New York Tribune* and the *Boston Post.*

This Thomas Nast cartoon, from November 7, 1874, was one of the earliest uses of the Republican elephant as a symbol of the party. Nast was a die-hard Republican. Here he labeled the *New York Herald's* stance against Republican candidate Ulysses S. Grant as "Caesarism"—that is, corrupt and autocratic. The *Herald* is depicted as a Democratic donkey in lion's clothing; Republican planks such as reforming the corrupt Democratic New York Tammany machine are threatened by the media's revolt. Should the elephant fall, it would descend into Nast's "chaos" of the Democratic South's post–Civil War claims.

were a central element of life for millions, sponsoring community events (parades and picnics), providing social services such as helping new immigrants to settle in and giving food and temporary housing to those in immediate need—all in exchange for votes. The parties offered immigrants not just services but also the opportunity for upward social mobility as they rose in the organization. As the hope for social advancement, the parties engendered among their supporters and office holders intense devotion that helped to produce startlingly high voter turnouts—75 percent or better in all presidential elections from 1876 to 1900, compared with only about 50 percent today[5]—as well as the greatest party-line voting ever achieved among party contingents in Congress and many state legislatures.[6]

Is the Party Over?

The heyday of the party—at least this certain kind of party—has passed. In the twentieth century many social, political, technological, and governmental changes have contributed to party decline. Historically, the government's gradual assumption of important functions previously performed by the parties—such as printing ballots, conducting elections, and providing social welfare services—had a major impact. Social services began to be seen as a right of citizenship rather than a privilege extended in exchange for a person's support of a party, and as the flow of immigrants slowed dramatically in the 1920s, party organizations gradually withered in most places. Although party organizations have always been more formidable in Western European countries, there too a tangible decline has taken place over the past few decades.

At the same time, the **direct primary,** whereby party nominees were determined by the ballots of qualified voters rather than at party conventions, was widely adopted by the states in the first two decades of the twentieth century. The primary removed the power of nomination from party leaders and workers, giving it instead to a much broader and more independent electorate and thus loosening the tie between the party nominee and the party organization. **Civil service laws** also removed much of the patronage used by the parties to reward their followers. (Civil service laws require appointment on the basis of merit and competitive examinations, whereas patronage—also called the **spoils system**—awards jobs on the basis of party loyalty.) These changes were encouraged by the Progressive Movement (consisting of politically liberal reformers), which flourished in the first two decades of the twentieth century.

In the post–World War II era, extensive social changes fed the movement away from strong parties. Broad-based education gave rise to **issue-oriented politics,** or politics that focuses on specific issues, such as civil rights, tax cutting, environmentalism, and abortion, rather than on party labels. Issue politics tends to cut across party lines and encourages voters to **ticket-split**—the act of voting for candidates of different parties for various offices in the same election. Another post–World War II social change that has affected the parties is the shift in the population. Millions of people have moved out of the cities, which are easily organizable because of population density, and into the sprawling suburbs, where a sense of privacy and detachment can often deter the most energetic of organizers.

Politically, many other trends have also contributed to the parties' decline. Television has come to dominate American politics, and the medium naturally emphasizes candidate personality rather than abstract concepts such as party labels. The modern parties

---

[5] Voter turnout in presidential elections from 1876 to 1900 ranged from 75 to 82 percent of the potential (male) electorate, compared with 50 to 55 percent in contemporary elections. See *Historical Statistics of the United States: Colonial Times to 1970,* Part 2, Series Y-27-28 (Washington: Government Printing Office, 1975), based on unpublished data prepared by Walter Dean Burnham.

[6] Frank Sorauf, *Party Politics in America,* 5th ed. (Boston: Little, Brown, 1984), p. 22.

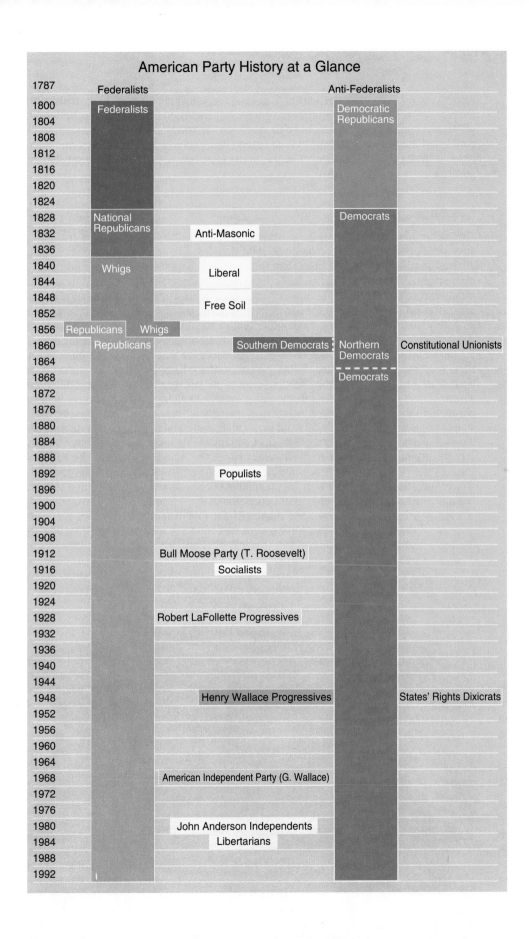

American Party History at a Glance

1787	Federalists			Anti-Federalists	
1800	Federalists			Democratic Republicans	
1804					
1808					
1812					
1816					
1820					
1824					
1828	National Republicans			Democrats	
1832		Anti-Masonic			
1836					
1840	Whigs				
1844		Liberal			
1848		Free Soil			
1852					
1856	Republicans Whigs				
1860	Republicans	Southern Democrats		Northern Democrats	Constitutional Unionists
1864					
1868				Democrats	
1872					
1876					
1880					
1884					
1888					
1892		Populists			
1896					
1900					
1904					
1908					
1912		Bull Moose Party (T. Roosevelt)			
1916		Socialists			
1920					
1924					
1928		Robert LaFollette Progressives			
1932					
1936					
1940					
1944					
1948		Henry Wallace Progressives			States' Rights Dixicrats
1952					
1956					
1960					
1964					
1968		American Independent Party (G. Wallace)			
1972					
1976					
1980		John Anderson Independents			
1984		Libertarians			
1988					
1992					

have many rivals for the affections of their candidates, including **political consultants,** the hired guns who manage campaigns and design television advertisements. Both television and consultants have replaced the party as the "middleman" between the candidate and the voter. It is little wonder that many candidates and office holders who have reached their posts without much help from their parties remain as free as possible of party ties.

Lessons

The parties' decline can easily be exaggerated, however. Viewing parties in the broad sweep of American history, it becomes clear that first, although political parties have evolved considerably and changed form from time to time, they usually have been reliable vehicles for mass participation in a representative democracy. In fact, the gradual but steady expansion of suffrage itself was orchestrated by the parties. As one political scientist concluded, "In the search for new segments of the populace that might be exploited profitably, the parties have kept the movement to liberalize the franchise well ahead of the demand. . . . The enlargement of the practicing electorate has been one of the principal labors of the parties, a truly notable achievement for which the parties have never been properly credited."[7] Second, the parties' journey through American history has been characterized by the same ability to adapt to prevailing conditions that is often cited as the genius of the Constitution. Flexibility and pragmatism mark both and help to ensure both their survival and the success of the society they serve. Third, despite massive changes in political conditions and frequent dramatic shifts in the electorate's mood, the two major parties have not only achieved remarkable longevity, they have almost consistently provided strong competition for each other and the voters at the national level. Of the twenty-seven presidential elections in the century-plus from 1884 to 1988, for instance, the Republicans won fifteen and the Democrats twelve. Even when calamities have struck the parties—the Great Depression in the 1930s or the Watergate scandal of 1973–74 for the Republicans (see Chapter 7), the Civil War or left-wing McGovernism in 1972 for the Democrats—they have proved tremendously resilient, sometimes bouncing back from landslide defeats to win the next election.

[7] Schattschneider, p. 48.

Franklin D. Roosevelt, right, then–governor of New York, with vice-presidential nominee John N. Garner (left), on the rear platform of the governor's train in Topeka, Kansas, where Roosevelt made the first major speech of his presidential campaign. The severity of the Depression, blamed on the incumbent Republican administration, gave Roosevelt and the Democrats a strong and long-lasting boost.

Perhaps most of all, history teaches us that the development of parties in the United States has been inevitable, as James Madison feared. Human nature alone guarantees conflict in any society; in a free state, the question is simply how to contain and channel conflict productively without infringing on individual liberties. The Founders' utopian hopes for the avoidance of partisan faction have given way to an appreciation of the parties' constructive contribution to conflict definition and resolution during the years of the American republic.

The Roles of the American Parties

Conflict definition and resolution is one vital purpose served by the party system in America. But the parties play many other roles, too, and they accomplish much more for politics and society, as the following sampler suggests.

Mobilizing Support and Gathering Power

The effect of party affiliation is enormously helpful to elected leaders. They can count on disproportionate support among their partisans in times of trouble, and in close judgment calls they have a home-court advantage. Therefore the parties aid office holders by giving them maneuvering room and by mobilizing support for their policies. For example, when the president addresses the nation and requests support for his policies, his party's activists are usually the first to respond to the call, perhaps flooding Congress with telegrams urging action of the president's agenda. Because there are only two major parties, pragmatic citizens who are interested in politics or public policy are mainly attracted to one or the other standard, creating natural majorities or near-majorities for party office holders to command. The party creates a community of interest that bonds disparate groups over time into what is called a **coalition**—and this eliminates the necessity of creating a new coalition for every campaign or every issue. Imagine the chaos and mad scrambles for public support that would constantly ensue without the continuity provided by the parties.

A Force for Stability

As mechanisms for organizing and containing political change, the parties are a potent force for stability. They represent continuity in the wake of changing issues and personalities, anchoring the electorate in the midst of the storm of new political people and policies. Because of its unyielding, pragmatic desire to *win* elections (not just contest them), each party in a sense acts to moderate public opinion. The party tames its own extreme elements by pulling them toward an ideological center in order to attract a majority of votes on Election Day.

Another aspect of the stability the parties provide can be found in the nature of the coalitions they forge. There are inherent contradictions in these coalitions that, oddly enough, strengthen the nation even as they strain party unity. Franklin Roosevelt's Democratic New Deal coalition, for example, included many blacks and most Southern whites—opposing elements nonetheless joined in common political purpose. This party union of the two groups, as limited a context as it may have been, surely provided a framework for acceptance of change and contributed to reconciliation of the races in the civil rights era. Nowhere can this reconciliation be more clearly seen than in the South, where most state Democratic parties remained predominant after the mid-1960s by building on the ingrained Democratic voting habits of both whites and blacks to create new, moderate, generally integrated societies.

People of the Past

Plunkitt of Tammany Hall

Tammany Hall was a powerful New York City political organization during the mid-nineteenth and early twentieth centuries. Originally formed as a social club in 1797, it had been transformed into an influential political machine by 1850, with membership including most of the city's prominent Democrats.

Of all the organization's politicians, one of the most renowned at the turn of the twentieth century was ward boss George Washington Plunkitt. The son of Irish immigrants, Plunkitt worked his way up through the ranks of the organization—starting as a teenager—to become the leader of the city's Fifteenth Assembly District. (An assembly district is made up of many smaller units, called election districts.) Remembered as one of the shrewdest politicians of his time, Plunkitt was born poor but died a millionaire, acquiring most of his wealth through what he called "honest graft," a term best described in his own candid words:

> My party's in power in the city, and its goin' to take a lot of public improvements. Well, I'm tipped off, say, that they're going to lay out a new park at a certain place.
>
> I see my opportunity and I take it. I go to that place and I buy up all the land I can in the neighborhood. Then the board of this or that makes it public, and there is a rush to get my land, which nobody cared particular for before.
>
> Ain't it perfectly honest to charge a good price and make a profit on my investment and foresight? Of course, it is. Well, that's honest graft.

Source: William L. Riordon, ed., *Plunkitt of Tammany Hall* (New York: Dutton, 1963).

For Plunkitt, then, there was a difference between honest and dishonest graft, "between political looters and politicians who make a fortune out of politics by keepin' their eyes wide open":

> The looter goes in for himself alone without considerin' his organization or his city. The politician looks after his own interests, the organization's interests, and the city's interests all at the same time.

No less illustrative of Plunkitt's brand of politics was the way he looked after constituents' interests. During Tammany's reign, the population of New York City was made up predominantly of poor immigrants, mostly Irish, for whom Plunkitt and his fellow district leaders served as a bridge between the Old and New Worlds and a way out of the slums. Besides assimilating these newcomers to life in the United States and acquainting them with the processes of self-government, the ward bosses used the patronage* at their disposal to provide tangible benefits as well. Be it a job, liquor, a pushcart license, even cash, the ward boss was always happy to help out a needy constituent—in exchange, of course, for loyalty at the ballot box during election time. Again, in Plunkitt's own words:

> Every good man looks after his friends, and any man who doesn't isn't likely to be popular. If I have a good thing to hand out in private life, I give it to a friend. Why shouldn't I do it in public life?

Unity, Linkage, Accountability

Parties provide the glue to hold together the disparate elements of the fragmented American governmental and political apparatus. The Founders designed a system that divides and subdivides power, making it possible to preserve individual liberty but difficult to coordinate and produce action in a timely fashion. Parties help to compensate for this drawback by linking all the institutions of power one to another. Although rivalry between the executive and legislative branches of American government is inevitable, the partisan affiliations of the leaders of each branch constitute a common basis for cooperation, as any president and his fellow party members in Congress usually demonstrate daily. Each time President George Bush has nominated a new Supreme Court justice, for instance, Republican members of the Senate have been the first to speak up on the nominee's behalf and have orchestrated confirmation efforts.

Another thing, I can always get a job for a deservin' man. I make it a point to keep on the track of jobs, and it seldom happens that I don't have a few up my sleeve ready for use. I know every employer in the district and in the whole city, for that matter. And they ain't in the habit of sayin' no to me when I ask them for a job.

In contrast to the issue-oriented or image-appeal politics we know today, Plunkitt's politics can be viewed as *personal.* As he put it, the Tammany leader "learned how to reach the hearts of the great mass of voters. He does not bother about reaching their heads." Plunkitt understood the value of this personalized, community-oriented politics to both voters and leaders, and his advice to aspiring politicians was simply to "study human nature and act accordin'." Such a study, however, was not to be conducted through books—"books is a hindrance more than anything else"—but through the community itself:

To learn real human nature you have to go among the people, see them and be seen. I know every man, woman, and child in the Fifteenth District, except them that's been born this summer—and I know some of them, too. I know what they like and what they don't like, what they are strong at and what they are weak in, and I reach them by approachin' at the right side.

For a number of reasons, Plunkitt's brand of politics

had all but disappeared by the mid-twentieth century. First, a drastic decline of immigration during the 1920s strangled the fuel line that fed the fires of city machines. Second, many of these services gradually came to be viewed as a right of citizenship rather than as a reward for supporting a particular party; therefore, government replaced party organizations as the dispensers of benefits. Most important, however, and much to the chagrin of Plunkitt himself, were the new civil service laws passed by reformers in the 1920s to combat the alleged corruption of machine politics. These laws struck at the heart and soul of machine politics—the spoils system—inducing Plunkitt to deem them "the biggest fraud of the age," tantamount to the ruin of the nation:

There can't be no real patriotism while it lasts. How are you goin' to interest our young men in their country if you have no offices to give them when they work for their party? . . . I know more than one man in the past years who worked for the ticket and was just overflowin' with patriotism, but when he was knocked out by the civil service humbug he got to hate his country and became an anarchist.

For better or worse, however, the reformers prevailed, and by the mid-twentieth century civil service had come to dominate government at every level, consigning Plunkitt's brand of politics to America's past.

Patronage (also called the "spoils system"): The resources available to a politician to reward constituents for their support. Such resources usually take the form of appointive offices, grants, or licenses.

Even within each branch there is intended fragmentation, and party once again helps to narrow the differences between the House of Representatives and the Senate, or between the president and his chiefs in the executive bureaucracy. Similarly, the division of national, state, and local governments, while always an invitation to conflict, is made more workable and easily coordinated by the intersecting party relationships that exist among office holders at all levels. Party affiliation, in other words, is a sanctioned and universally recognized basis for mediation and negotiation laterally among the branches and vertically among the layers.

The party's linkage function does not end there. Party identification and organization are natural connectors and vehicles for communication between the voter and the candidate as well as between the voter and the office holder. The party connection is one means of increasing accountability in election campaigns and in government. Candidates on the campaign trail and elected party leaders in office are required from time to time to

Women working for Democrat Ann Richards, who won election to the governorship of Texas in 1990. Campaign fund raising is often performed by loyal party followers.

account for their performance at party-sponsored forums, nominating primaries, and conventions.

Political parties, too, can take some credit for unifying the nation by dampening sectionalism. Since parties must form national majorities to win the presidency, any single, isolated region is guaranteed minority status unless it establishes ties with other areas. The party label and philosophy are the bridge that enables regions to join forces, and in the process a national interest, rather than a merely sectional one, is created and served.

The Electioneering Function

The election, proclaimed H. G. Wells, is "democracy's ceremonial, its feast, its great function," and the political parties assist this ceremony in essential ways. First, the parties funnel talented (and, granted, some not-so-talented) individuals into politics and government. Thousands of candidates are recruited each year by the two parties, as are many of candidates' staff members—the ones who manage the campaigns and go on to serve in key governmental positions once the election has been won.

This function is even more crucial in the British parliamentary system. In the postwar period, the *only* avenue to national power—i.e., the prime minister's office or a choice seat on the Cabinet—has been through either the Conservative Party or the Labour Party. That is, ambitious politicians must work their way up through the party hierarchy, building a support coalition along the way.

Elections can have meaning in a democracy only if they are competitive, and in America they probably could not be without the parties. Even in the South, traditionally the least politically competitive American region, the parties today regularly produce reasonably vigorous contests at the state (and, increasingly, the local) level.

Party as a Voting and Issue Cue

A voter's party identification acts as an invaluable filter for information, a perceptual screen that affects how he or she digests political news. Therefore, party affiliation provides a useful cue for voters—particularly for the least informed and least interested, who can use the party as a shortcut or substitute for interpreting issues and events they may not fully comprehend. But even better-educated and more involved voters find party identification helpful. After all, no one has the time to study every issue carefully or to become fully knowledgeable about every candidate seeking public office.

Policy Formulation and Promotion

U.S. Senator Huey Long (D.-La.), one of the premier spokesmen for "the people" of this century, was usually able to capture the flavor of the average man's views about politics. Considering an independent bid for president before his assassination in 1935, Long liked to compare the Republican and Democratic parties to the two patent medicines offered by a traveling salesman. Asked the difference between them, the salesman explained that the "High Populorum" tonic was made from the bark of the tree taken from the top down, while "Low Populorum" tonic was made from bark stripped from the root up. The analogous moral, according to Long, was this: "The only difference I've found in Congress between the Republican and Democratic leadership is that one of 'em is skinning us from the ankle up and the other from the ear down!"[8]

Long would certainly have insisted that his fable applied to the **national party platforms,** the most visible instrument by which parties formulate, convey, and promote public policy. Every four years, each party writes for the presidential nominating conventions a lengthy platform containing its positions on key issues. Most citizens in our own era undoubtedly still believe that party platforms are relatively undifferentiated, a mixture of pabulum and pussyfooting. Yet the political scientist Gerald Pomper's study of party platforms from 1944 through 1976 demonstrated that each party's pledges were consistently and significantly different, a function in part of the varied groups in their

[8] As quoted in Ken Bode, "Hero or Demagogue?" *The New Republic* 195, March 3, 1986, p. 28.

U.S. Senator Huey Long (D.-La.)

coalitions.[9] Interestingly, some 69 percent of the specific platform positions were taken by one party but not the other. On abortion, for example, the Democrats are strongly for it while the Republicans are firmly against it in their most recent platforms.

Granted, then, party platforms are quite distinctive. Does this elaborate party exercise in policy formulation mean anything? One could argue that the platform is valuable, if only as a clear presentation of a party's basic philosophy and a forum for activist opinion and public education. But platforms have much more impact than that. Cynics will be amazed to discover that about two-thirds of the promises in the victorious party's presidential platform have been completely or mostly implemented; even more astounding, one-half or more of the pledges of the *losing* party find their way into public policy (with the success rate depending on whether the party controls one, both, or neither house of Congress).[10] The party platform also has great influence on a new presidential administration's legislative program and the president's State of the Union address. And while party affiliation is normally the single most important determinant of voting in Congress and in state legislatures,[11] the party-vote relationship is even stronger when party platform issues come up on the floor of Congress. Gerald Pomper concludes: "We should therefore take platforms seriously—because politicians appear to take them seriously."

Besides mobilizing Americans on a permanent basis, then, the parties convert the cacophony of hundreds of identifiable social and economic groups into a two-part (semi)harmony that is much more comprehensible, if not always on key and pleasing to the ears. The simplicity of two-party politics may be deceptive given the enormous variety in public policy choices, but a sensible system of representation in the American context might well be impossible without it. And those who would suffer most from its absence would not be the few who are individually or organizationally powerful—their voices would be heard under almost any system. As the political scientist Walter Dean Burnham has pointed out, the losers would be the many individually powerless for whom the parties are the only effective devices yet created that can generate collective power on their behalf.[12]

One-Partyism and Third-Partyism

The two-party system has not gone unchallenged. At the state level two-party competition was severely limited or non-existent in much of the country for most of this century.[13] Especially in the one-party Democratic states of the Deep South and the rock-ribbed Republican states of Maine, New Hampshire, and Vermont, the dominant party's primary nomination was often equivalent to election, and the only real contest was an unsatisfying intraparty one in which colorful personalities often dominated and a half-dozen major candidacies in each primary proved confusing to voters.[14] Even in most two-party states there existed dozens of cities and counties that had a massive majority of voters aligned with one or the other party and therefore were effectively one-party in local elections. In Britain, one-partyism at the subnational level is a relatively common

[9] Gerald M. Pomper with Susan Lederman, *Elections in America,* 2nd ed. (New York: Longman, 1980), pp. 145–50, 167–73.
[10] See David E. Price, *Bringing Back the Parties* (Washington: CQ Press, 1984), pp. 284–88.
[11] See, for example, Sarah McCally Morehouse, "Legislatures and Political Parties," *State Government* 59:1, (1976), p. 23.
[12] Walter Dean Burnham, *Critical Elections and the Mainsprings of American Politics* (New York: Norton, 1970), pp. 132–33.
[13] See V. O. Key Jr., *American State Politics: An Introduction* (New York: Knopf, 1956).
[14] See V. O. Key Jr., *Southern Politics in State and Nation* (New York: Knopf, 1949).

phenomenon; for example, certain regions like the Northeast have voted overwhelmingly for the Labour Party in general election after general election.

Historical, cultural, and sectional forces primarily accounted for the concentration of one party's supporters in certain areas. The Civil War's divisions, for instance, were mirrored for the better part of a century in the Democratic predisposition of the South and the Republican proclivities of the Yankee Northern states. Whatever the combination of factors producing **one-partyism**—a political system in which one party dominates and wins virtually all contests—the condition has certainly declined precipitously in the last quarter century.[15]

The spread of two-party competition, while still uneven in some respects, is one of the most significant political trends of recent times, and virtually no one-party states are left. There are no purely Republican states anymore, and the heavily Democratic contingent has been reduced to, at most, Alabama, Georgia, Louisiana, Mississippi, Arkansas, and Maryland. (Note, though, that in each of these states one or more Republicans have been elected to the governorship or U.S. Senate since 1970, and the Deep South states usually vote Republican in presidential contests as well.)

Ironically, the growth of two-party competition has been spurred less by the developing strength of the main parties than by party weakness, illustrated by the decline in partisan loyalty among the voters. In other words, citizens now are somewhat more inclined to cross party lines to support an appealing candidate regardless of party affiliation, thus making a victory for the minority party possible whether or not it has earned the victory through the party's own organizational hard work. It should also be noted that the elimination of pockets of one-party strength adds an element of instability to the system, since at one point even in lean times of national electoral disaster, each party was assured of a regional base from which a comeback could be staged. Nonetheless, the increase in party competitiveness can be viewed positively, since it eliminates the odious effects of one-partyism and guarantees a comprehensible and credible partisan choice to a larger segment of the electorate than ever before.

Minor Parties

Third-partyism has proved more durable than one-partyism, though its nature is sporadic and intermittent, and its effects on the political system are on the whole less weighty. Given all the controversy third parties generate, one could be excused for thinking that they were extraordinarily important on the American scene. But as Frank Sorauf has concluded, third parties in fact "have not assumed the importance that all the [academic] attention lavished on them suggests."[16] Not a single minor party has ever come close to winning the presidency, and only eight minor parties have won so much as a single state's electoral college votes. Just four third parties (the farmer-backed Populists in 1892, Theodore Roosevelt's Bull Moose Party in 1912, the reform-minded Progressives in 1924, and former Alabama Governor George Wallace's racially-based American Independent Party in 1968) have garnered more than 10 percent of the popular vote for president.[17] (Roosevelt, incidentally, abandoned the Republican Party—under whose banner he had won the presidency in 1904—in order to form the Bull Moose Party—composed mainly of reformist Republicans.)

---

[15] See John F. Bibby, Cornelius P. Cotter, James L. Gibson, and Robert J. Huckshorn, "Parties in State Politics," in Virginia Gray, Herbert Jacob, and Kenneth Vines, eds., *Politics in the American States,* 4th ed. (Boston: Little, Brown, 1983), Table 3.3, p. 66; also Larry Sabato, *Goodbye to Good-Time Charlie: The American Governorship Transformed,* 2nd ed. (Washington: CQ Press, 1983), pp. 116–38.

[16] Sorauf, p. 51.

[17] Roosevelt's 1912 effort was the most successful; the Bull Moose Party won 30 percent of the popular vote for president (though only 17 percent of the electoral college votes). Roosevelt's is also the only third party to run ahead of one of the two major parties (the Republicans).

The "Bull Moose" Party

Theodore Roosevelt was so impressed during his hunting expeditions in the Western United States with the great strength and stamina of the bull moose that "as strong as a bull moose" became one of his favorite expressions.

In 1912, when he refused to support Republican President William Howard Taft (1909–13) for reelection, the "Bull Moose" became the nickname and symbol of the independent movement he led.

A 1912 cartoon from the Utica, New York *Saturday Globe* shows the scare thrown to the Republicans and Democrats by Theodore Roosevelt's Bull Moose Party.

THE APPEARANCE OF THE NEW PARTY IN THE POLITICAL FIELD

Third parties find their roots in sectionalism (as did the South's states' rights Dixiecrats, who broke away from the Democrats in 1948); in economic protest (such as the agrarian revolt that fueled the Populists, an 1892 prairie-states party); in specific issues (such as the Prohibition Party's proposed ban on the sale of alcoholic beverages); in ideology (the Socialist, Communist, and Libertarian Parties are examples); and in appealing, charismatic personalities (Theodore Roosevelt is perhaps the best case). Many of the minor parties have drawn strength from a combination of these sources. The American Independent Party enjoyed a measure of success because of a dynamic leader (George Wallace), a firm geographic base (the South), and an emotional issue (civil rights). Above all, third parties make electoral progress in direct proportion to the failure of the two major parties to incorporate new ideas or alienated groups or to nominate attractive candidates as their standard-bearers. Certainly in the media age, this latter qualification has grown in importance. The 1980 independent presidential bid of U.S. Representative John Anderson (R.-Ill.) was spurred not by geography or specific issues or Anderson's persona but by intense dissatisfaction among some voters with the major-party nominees (Jimmy Carter and Ronald Reagan).[18]

Explanations

Third parties in the United States are akin to shooting stars that appear briefly and brilliantly but do not long remain visible in the political constellation. In fact, the United States is the only major Western nation that does not have at least one significant, enduring national third party, and there are a number of explanations for this. Unlike many European countries that use **proportional representation** (awarding legislative seats in proportion to the number of votes received) and guarantee parliamentary seats to any

[18] Anderson received only 7 percent of the vote in the end, though at points in the contest polls had shown him with well above 20 percent.

faction securing as little as 5 percent of the vote, the United States has a "single member, plurality" electoral system that requires a party to get one more vote than any other party in a legislative district or in a state's presidential election in order to win. To paraphrase the legendary coach Vince Lombardi, finishing first is not everything, it is the only thing in American politics; placing second, even by a smidgen, doesn't count. This condition encourages the grouping of interests into as few parties as possible (the democratic minimum being two).

Other institutional factors undergird the two-party system as well:

- The laws in most states make it difficult for third parties to secure a place on the ballot by requiring large numbers of signatures, whereas the Democratic and Republican parties are often granted automatic access.

- Democrats and Republicans in the state legislatures may have little in common, but one shared objective is to make sure that the political pie is cut into only two sizable pieces, not three or more smaller slices.

- The public funding of campaigns (financing from taxpayer dollars), where it exists, is far more generous for the two major parties. At the national level, for instance, third-party presidential candidates receive money only *after* the general election, *if* they have garnered more than 5 percent of the vote, and *only* in proportion to their total vote; the major-party candidates, by contrast, get large, full general election grants immediately upon their summer nominations.

- The news media are biased—legitimately so—against minor parties, which are usually given relatively little coverage compared with that given to major-party nominees. The media are only reflecting political reality, of course, and it would be absurd to expect them to offer equal time to all comers. Still, it is a vicious cycle for minor-party candidates: A lack of broad-based support produces slight coverage, which minimizes their chances of attracting more adherents.

Beyond the institutional explanations are historical, cultural, and social theories of two-partyism in America. The **dualist theory,** frequently criticized as overly simplistic,

A New Third Party

In the fall of 1991, a panel formed by the National Organization for Women (NOW) recommended the creation of a new political party that would attract more women and minority members than do the Republicans and the Democrats. The party would be organized and led by NOW, once approved by the full membership of that organization at a national convention.

The new party will face several challenges. For one, as NOW's president Molly Yard argued, its sponsor has many other issues on its agenda, and the formation of a serious national political party requires tremendous efforts and resources. For another, any meaningfully large party that attracts women and minority members risks diluting the strength of the Democrats without creating enough momentum to place its own candidates in major positions. There are potentially offsetting advantages, however. In the past, serious third-party challenges have influenced the agenda set by the major parties. It is also possible to field a targeted group of candidates that can accomplish a lot without being the major party in power.

suggests that there has always been an underlying binary nature to U.S. politics. Whether it was the early conflict between Eastern financial interests and Western frontiersmen, the sectional division of North and South, the more current urban-versus-rural or urban-versus-suburban clashes, or even the natural tensions of democratic institutions (the government against the opposition, for instance), dualists believe that the processes and interests of politics inevitably reduce the players into two great camps.

Other political scientists emphasize the basic social consensus existing in American life. Despite great diversity in our heritage, the vast majority of Americans accept without serious question the fundamental structures of our system: The Constitution, the governmental set-up, a lightly controlled free enterprise economy, and so on. This consensus, when allied with certain American cultural characteristics developed over time (pragmatism, acceptance of the need for compromise, a lack of extreme and divisive social-class consciousness), produces the conditions necessary for relatively non-ideological, centrist politics that can naturally support two moderate alternative parties but has little need for more.

The passion for power and victory that drives both Democrats and Republicans overrides ideology and prevents rigidity. Unless a kind of rigor mortis takes hold in the future in one or both major parties—with say, the capture of the party organization by unyielding extremists of right or left—it is difficult to imagine any third party becoming a major, permanent force in American politics. The corollary of this axiom, though, is that the

George C. Wallace

Few third-party candidates for president have even thrown a scare into the major-party nominees the way George Corley Wallace did in 1968. A strong supporter of racial segregation, Wallace was elected Democratic governor of Alabama in 1962. Barred by the state constitution from seeking a second consecutive term, Wallace had his wife, Lurleen, run for governor in 1966. She won, but died of cancer in 1968 while still in office.

Wallace then formed the American Independent Party and ran for president in 1968, charging that "there isn't a dime's worth of difference between Democrats and Republicans." His opposition to school busing to achieve racial balance as well as his pro–Vietnam War stance won Wallace much white support in the Deep South. In the end, Wallace won 46 electoral college votes (all in the South) and 13.5 percent of the popular votes cast. Republican Richard Nixon won the election with 43.4 percent of the popular vote; Democrat Hubert Humphrey garnered 42.7 percent. The conservative Wallace nearly drained enough votes from Nixon to elect the far more liberal Humphrey.

Wallace was reelected Alabama's governor in 1970 and 1974. While campaigning for president again in 1972, this time as a Democrat, Wallace was shot and paralyzed from the waist down by a gunman in Laurel, Maryland. Though he recovered enough to continue his political career in Alabama, Wallace never fully regained his health or his political fire. Wallace's racial views moderated with time after he renounced segregation, and he won the support of many black voters in his last election as governor in 1974. He retired from public life in January 1979.

Third Party and Independent Presidential Candidates Receiving 5 Percent or More of Popular Vote

CANDIDATE (PARTY)	YEAR	PERCENT OF POPULAR VOTE	ELECTORAL VOTES
John B. Anderson (Independent)	1980	6.6	0
George C. Wallace (American Independent)	1968	13.5	46
Robert M. LaFollette (Progressive)	1924	16.6	13
Theodore Roosevelt (Bull Moose)	1912	27.4	88
Eugene V. Debs (Socialist)	1912	6.0	0
James B. Weaver (Populist)	1892	8.5	22
John C. Breckinridge (Southern Democrat)	1860	18.1	72
John Bell (Constitutional Union)	1860	12.6	39
Millard Fillmore (Whig-American)	1856	21.5	8
Martin Van Buren (Free Soil)	1848	10.1	0
William Wirt (Anti-Masonic)	1832	7.8	7

Source: Congressional Quarterly Weekly Report, October 18, 1980, p. 3147 (as adapted).

major parties must be eternally vigilant to avoid ideologically inspired takeovers, perhaps by expanding participation in party activities to as broad-based a group of voters as possible.

For the foreseeable future, though, third parties likely will continue to play useful supporting roles similar to their historically sanctioned ones: They can popularize ideas that might not receive a hearing otherwise. They can serve as vehicles of popular discontent with the major parties and thereby induce change in major-party behavior and platforms. They may well presage and assist future party realignments as they have sometimes done in the past. In a few states third parties will also continue to take a unique part in political life, as the Conservative and Liberal Parties of New York State do.[19] But in a two-party system that is supplemented by generous means of expressing dissent and registering political opposition in other ways (court challenges, interest-group organizing, and so on), third parties will continue to have a limited future in the United States.

[19] New York election law makes the Conservatives and Liberals (and, more recently, the Right to Life [anti-abortion] Party) potential power brokers since as an alternative to placing their own adherents on the ballot they can instead, nominate the candidates of a major party to run under their labels, thus encouraging the major parties and their nominees to court them assiduously.

The Basic Structure of American Political Parties

The structure of the two major parties is not elaborate. Figure 11-1 summarizes the levels of each party, from grassroots base to pinnacle.

National Committees

The first national party committees were skeletal and formed some years after the creation of the presidential nominating conventions in the 1830s. Every four years, each party holds a national convention to nominate its presidential and vice-presidential candidates. First the Democrats in 1848 and then the Republicans in 1856 established national governing bodies (the Democratic National Committee, or DNC, and the Republican National Committee, or RNC) to make arrangements for the conventions and to coordi-

**Figure 11-1
Political Party Organization in America: From Base to Pinnacle**

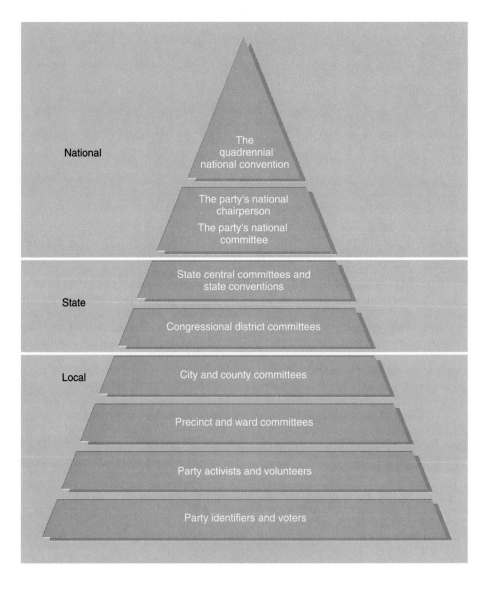

National — The quadrennial national convention

The party's national chairperson

The party's national committee

State — State central committees and state conventions

Congressional district committees

Local — City and county committees

Precinct and ward committees

Party activists and volunteers

Party identifiers and voters

nate the subsequent presidential campaigns. The DNC and RNC were each composed of one representative from each state—expanded to two in the 1920s after the post of state committeewoman was established—and the states had complete control over the selection of their representatives to the national committees. In addition, to serve their interests the congressional party caucuses in both houses organized their own national committees, loosely allied with the DNC and RNC. The National Republican Congressional Committee (NRCC) was started in 1866 when the Radical Republican congressional delegation was feuding with Abraham Lincoln's moderate successor, President Andrew Johnson, and wanted a counterweight to his control of the RNC. At the same time House and Senate Democrats set up a similar committee. After the popular election of U.S. senators was initiated in 1913 with the ratification of the Seventeenth Amendment to the Constitution, both parties organized separate Senate campaign committees. This three-part arrangement of national party committee, House party committee, and Senate party committee has persisted in both parties until the present day, and each party's three committees are located together in Washington.

The memberships of both the RNC and DNC have grown considerably in size over the decades, but the DNC's expansion has been much greater, and it is now more than twice the size of the RNC—390 DNC members to just 165 for the RNC. Since 1972 the Democrats have also abandoned the principle of equal DNC representation for all states and have assigned the number of committeepersons on the basis of each state's population and its past voter support for the party's candidates. Although the national conventions formally ratify all national committee members, the real choices are made in the states, with selection methods varying from election at state party conventions (the most common means) to primary election to selection by state central committees or designation by the party delegation to the national presidential convention.

Leadership

The key national party official is the chairperson of the DNC or RNC. Although the chair is formally elected by the national committee, he or she is usually selected by the sitting president or newly nominated presidential candidate, who is accorded the right to name the individual for at least the duration of his or her campaign. Only the postcampaign out-of-power party committee actually has the authority to appoint a chairperson independently. The committee-crowned chairpersons generally have the greatest impact on the party because they come to their posts at times of crisis when a leadership vacuum exists. (A defeated presidential candidate is technically the head of the national party until the next nominating convention, but the reality is naturally otherwise as a party attempts to shake off a losing image.) The chair often becomes the prime spokesperson and arbitrator for the party during the four years between elections, and he or she is called upon to damp down factionalism, negotiate candidate disputes, raise money, and prepare the machinery for the next presidential election. Balancing the interests of all potential White House contenders is a particularly difficult job, and strict neutrality is normally expected from the chair.

Ron Brown, former chairman of the Democratic National Committee

In recent times both parties have benefited from adept leadership while out of power. RNC Chairman William Brock during the Carter presidency and DNC Chairman Paul Kirk during the second Reagan term both skillfully used their positions to strengthen their parties organizationally and to polish the party images. Brock and Kirk frequently appeared on news shows to give the out-of-power party's viewpoint. By contrast, party chairpersons selected by incumbent presidents and presidential candidates tend to be close allies of the presidents or candidates and often subordinate the good of the party to the needs of the campaign or White House. During the Carter presidency, for example, DNC Chairman Kenneth Curtis and his successor John White were creatures of the White House who acted as cheerleaders for their chief executive but did little to keep the Democratic Party competitive with the then-strengthening GOP organization.

Because of their command of presidential patronage and influence, a few national-party chairpersons selected by presidents have become powerful and well known, such as Republican Mark Hanna during the McKinley presidency (1897–1901) and Democrat James Farley under President Franklin Roosevelt. Most presidentially appointed chairs, however, have been relatively obscure; the chance for a chairperson to make a difference and cut a memorable figure generally comes when there is no competition from a White House nominee or occupant. Until December 1992, the DNC chair was Ronald Brown, an attorney and the first black to hold a party chairmanship; his Republican counterpart was Richard Bond, a long-time Republican political operative and former protegé of Lee Atwater. Atwater, a master strategist who died in 1991 of a brain tumor at the age of forty-one, had been President Bush's 1988 campaign manager before assuming the RNC chairmanship in 1989.

National Conventions

Much of any party chairperson's effort is directed at planning the presidential nominating convention, or **national convention,** the most publicized and vital event on the party's calendar. Until 1984, gavel-to-gavel coverage had been standard practice on all national television networks, and even after the recent cutbacks by some news organizations, a substantial block of time is still devoted to the conventions. (In 1992, for example, all the networks gave at least a couple of prime-time hours per night to convention coverage.) Although the nomination of the presidential ticket naturally receives the lion's share of attention, the convention also fulfills its role as the ultimate governing body for the party itself. The rules adopted and the platform passed at the quadrennial conclave are durable guideposts that steer the party for years after the final gavel has been brought down. Most of the recent party chairpersons, in cooperation with the incumbent president or likely nominee, have tried to orchestrate carefully every minute of the conventions in order to project just the right image to voters at home. By and large, they have succeeded, though at the price of draining some spontaneity and excitement from the process.

From 1974 to 1982 the Democratic Party also held a **midterm convention** (also called a mini-convention). Designed to provide party activists a chance to express themselves on policy and presidential performance (whether the chief executive was a Democrat or a Republican), the midterm convention instead mainly generated worry among the party leadership and elected officials about the factional infighting and ideological posturing that might be on display before a national audience. While none of the midterm gatherings was a disaster (and none a roaring success, either), by 1986 the Democrats had decided to avoid potential divisiveness and save the $2 million necessary to hold the convention, and it was canceled.

States and Localities

Although national committee activities of all kinds attract most of the media attention, the party is structurally based not in Washington but in the states and localities. Except for the campaign finance arena, virtually all governmental regulation of political parties is left to the states, for example, and most elected officials give their allegiance to the local party divisions they know best. Most important, the vast majority of party leadership positions are filled at subnational levels.

The pyramidal arrangement of party committees provides for a broad base of support. The smallest voting unit, the precinct, usually takes in a few adjacent neighborhoods and is the fundamental building block of the party, and each of the more than 100,000 precincts in the United States potentially has a committeeman or committeewoman to represent it in each party's councils. The precinct committeepersons are the key foot soldiers of any party, and their efforts are supplemented by party committees above them in the wards, cities, counties, towns, villages, and congressional districts.

The state governing body supervising this collection of local party organizations is usually called the state central (or executive) committee, and it comprises representatives from all major geographic units, as determined by and selected under state law. Generally, state parties are free to act within the limits set by their state legislatures without interference from the national party, except in the selection and seating of presidential convention delegates. National Democrats have been particularly inclined to regulate this aspect of party life.

Informal Groups

The formal structure of party organization is supplemented by numerous official, semi-official, and unaffiliated groups that combine and clash with the parties in countless ways. Both the DNC and RNC have affiliated organizations of state and local party women (The National Federation of Democratic Women and the National Federation of Republican Women), and there are youth divisions as well (the Young Democrats of America and the Young Republicans' National Federation), which have a generous definition of "young"—up to and including age thirty-five. The state governors in each party have their own party associations, too.

Just outside the party orbit are the supportive interest groups and associations that often provide money, labor, or other forms of assistance to the parties. Labor unions, progressive political action committees (PACs), teachers, black and liberal women's groups, and the Americans for Democratic Action are some of the Democratic Party's organizational groups, while business PACs, the Chamber of Commerce of the United States, fundamentalist Christian organizations, and some anti-abortion agencies work closely with the Republicans. Similar party-interest group pairings occur in Britain. Trade unions have aligned themselves with the Labour Party, providing the bulk of the party's contributions, while business has been closely allied with the Conservatives.

Each U.S. party also has several institutionalized sources of policy ideas. Though unconnected to the parties in any official sense, these so-called think tanks (institutional collections of policy-oriented researchers and academics) are quite influential. During the Reagan administration, for instance, the right-wing Heritage Foundation placed many dozens of its conservatives in important governmental positions, and its issue studies on subjects from tax reform to South Africa carried considerable weight with policy makers. The more moderate and bipartisan American Enterprise Institute also supplied the Reagan team with people and ideas. On the Democratic side, liberal think tanks have proliferated during the party's Reagan and Bush–induced exile. More than a half-dozen policy institutes formed after 1980 (the beginning of the current Republican presidential ascendancy) in an attempt to nurse the Democrats back to political health. The Center for National Policy and the Progressive Policy Institute, to cite two, have sponsored several conferences and published a number of papers on Democratic policy alternatives.

Finally, there are extraparty organizations that form for a wide variety of purposes, including "reforming" a party or moving it ideologically to the right or left. In New York City, for example, Democratic reform clubs were established in the late 1800s to fight the Tammany Hall machine (the city's dominant Democratic organization at the time), and about seventy clubs still prosper by attracting well-educated activists committed to various liberal causes. More recently, both national parties have been favored (or bedeviled) by the formation of new extraparty outfits. The Democrats are being pushed by both halves of the ideological continuum. The Democratic Leadership Council (DLC) was launched in 1985 by moderate-conservative Democrats concerned about what they perceived as the leftward drift of their party and its image as the captive of liberal special-interest groups. It is composed of more than one hundred current and former Democratic office holders (such as Senator Sam Nunn of Georgia and House Majority Leader Richard Gephardt of Missouri). The DLC is not always popular with the national party leadership, which sometimes views it as a potential rival. Party leaders have been equally concerned

Then and Now
The Political Machines

When Americans think of local political parties, legendary Chicago Mayor Richard J. Daley's machine most quickly comes to mind. In the 1950s and 1960s his machine dominated Chicago politics, controlling judges, politicians, municipal agencies, and the police and fire departments. The force behind the Daley machine was its control of municipal and county elections, in which supporters were rewarded with patronage and other tangible benefits, and opponents were disciplined accordingly. But after more than two decades of command, the Daley machine gradually faded with the mayor's death in 1977, decimated by in-fighting, reformers, and court rulings that struck at the heart of the patronage system.

That all party organizations have gone the way of Chicago's is a commonly held belief, even among political observers. But recent studies of the 7,300 county-level party organizations in the United States have revealed that many local parties—Democratic as well as Republican—are surprisingly active and have not really become less so over the decades. While the weakening of the party organization is unmistakable in many cities and counties, and most county parties have no paid staff, central party headquarters, or even a telephone listing, some local parties appear to have a life of their own aided by substantial help from the state and (on the

Republican side) national committees. These local organizations seem to endure and sometimes prosper despite party reversals at state or national levels. In the most successful cases, this is due to one of two sources of strength: either a well-nourished grassroots organization fed by patronage or a technologically advanced party with a solid base of ideologically attuned contributors and supporters.

A present-day example of the former, more traditional local organization is the Republican Party of Nassau County, New York. No doubt Mayor Daley would have found much to like about this rigid and hierarchial machine that controls more than 20,000 jobs and features an elaborate superstructure of ward chairpersons, precinct committee members, and block captains who turn out the vote on Election Day. Originally built on New York City's out-migration of blue-collar Irish and Italian ethnics who wanted to dissociate themselves from the city's liberal politics, the machine now takes great care to recruit young people, in part by distributing plum summer jobs. Many of these youths go on to base their whole careers on service to the party. In the best tradition of machine politics, aspiring office holders are expected to work their way up the ladder slowly, toiling for years in the back rooms and the neighborhoods, de-

Thomas Nast, a famous cartoonist for *Harper's* in the late nineteenth century, drew dozens of cartoons attacking the New York Democratic machine run out of Tammany Hall (see the "Then and Now" box above).

livering votes for the party candidates and dollars for the party war chest.

But the Nassau County machine is not without its problems. Corruption charges against some of its leaders have been proven, and its command of so many patronage positions is under attack. Yet electoral success keeps the organization humming, and it regularly wins a large majority of the area's county, state legislative, and congressional posts. The machine has even produced one of New York's U.S. senators, Alfonse D'Amato. First elected in 1980, D'Amato was a supervisor of Nassau's Hempstead township and a top leader of the party organization prior to his Senate bid. Learning constituency-service politics well in the county machine, he attended assiduously to his state's interests just as he had done for his township, earning a landslide reelection in a 1986 campaign that even included an endorsement from the liberal *New York Times*.

If Chicago and Nassau Country represent the old-style political machine, then the Waxman–Berman machine in California may suggest the future directions of strong local parties. Named after its founder, liberal Democratic Congressman Henry A. Waxman and Howard L. Berman, this Los Angeles–based machine has built its success on direct mail and new campaign technologies rather than on patronage and ward committee members. In many ways, Waxman–Berman is the polar opposite of the Nassau Country organization: informal, candidate (not party) centered, and a creation of California's anti-party environment. Also unlike their Nassau brethren, who virtually ignore national politics and concentrate on local offices, Waxman, Berman, and their allies care little about local politics; most of their energies are devoted to electing congressional candidates and influencing national and international policy.

While the differences between the traditional and modern political machines are substantial, there is one fundamental link between them: They both accumulate power by helping friends win elective and appointive office. The new technologically advanced model of strong local parties probably has more of a future than the older, ethnically based or patronage-fed machine. Yet the latter should not be dismissed so easily, not only because it has proven hardier in some places than many expected but also because there is a great deal to be said for such personalized, neighborhood-oriented parties. Indeed, the ideal self-sustaining part might be a carefully crafted combination of modern technology and community service–centered organization.

about a left-leaning force organizing from within the partisan ranks, Jesse Jackson's National Rainbow Coalition. The Coalition is partly a vehicle for Jackson's presidential ambitions, but beyond that, its goals of mass membership, hundreds of state and local charter affiliates, and endorsements of independent candidates when Democratic nominees are found to be "unacceptable" present a challenge to the Democratic Party in the eyes of at least some party officials. Republicans have their extraparty agents too, the most prominent of which is North Carolina Senator Jesse Helms's Congressional Club, one of the largest political action committees in the United States. Mirroring the philosophy of its founder, the Club is fiercely conservative. And much like Jesse Jackson and the Rainbow Coalition at the opposite end of the political spectrum, Helms and the Club will maneuver within or without the party as circumstances dictate.

The Party in Government

The structure of political parties reviewed so far has been organizational, self-contained, and apart from governing institutions. Another dimension of party exists—and thrives—*within* government, as a critical, essential mechanism of all its branches and layers.

The Congressional Party

In no segment of American government is the party more visible or vital than in the Congress. In this century the political parties have dramatically increased the sophistication and impact of their internal congressional organizations. Prior to the beginning of every session, each party in both houses of Congress gathers (or "caucuses") separately to select party leaders (House Speaker or minority leader, Senate majority and minority leaders, party whips, and so on) and to arrange for the appointment of members of each chamber's committees. In effect, then, the parties organize and operate the Congress. Their management systems have grown quite elaborate; the web of deputy and assistant whips for House Democrats now extends to about one-fourth of the party's entire membership. Although not invulnerable to pressure from the minority, the majority party in each house generally holds sway, even fixing the size of its majority on all committees— a proportion frequently in excess of the percentage of seats it holds in the house as a whole.

Discipline. Congressional party leaders have some substantial tools at their disposal to enforce a degree of discipline in their troops. While seniority usually determines most committee assignments, an occasional choice plum may be given to the loyal and withheld from the rebellious. A member's bill can be lovingly caressed through the legislative process, or it can be summarily dismissed without so much as a hearing. Pork barrel— government projects yielding rich patronage benefits that sustain many a legislator's electoral survival—may be included or deleted in the appropriations process. Small favors and perquisites (such as the allocation of desirable office space or the scheduling of floor votes for the convenience of a member) can also be useful levers. Then, too, there are the campaign aids at the command of the leadership: money from party sources, endorsements, appearances in the district or at fund-raising events, and so on. On rare occasions, the leaders and their allies in the party caucus may even impose sanctions of various sorts (such as the stripping of seniority rights or prized committee berths) to punish recalcitrant law makers.[20]

In spite of all these weapons in the leadership's arsenal, the congressional parties lack the cohesion that characterizes parliamentary legislatures. This is not surprising, since the costs of bolting the party are far less in the United States than in, say, Great Britain. A disloyal English member of Parliament might very well be replaced as a party candidate at the next election; in America, it is more likely that the independent-minded member of Congress would be electorally rewarded—hailed as a free spirit, an individual of the people who stood up to the party bosses. Moreover, defections from the ruling party in a parliamentary system bring a threat of the government's collapse and with it early elections under possibly unfavorable conditions; fixed election dates in the United States mean that the consequences of defection are much less dire. Also, a centralized, unicameral parliament (in which executive and legislative branches are effectively fused) permits relatively easy hierarchial, programmatic control by party leaders.

The separate executive branch, the bicameral power-sharing, and the extraordinary decentralization of Congress's work are all institutional obstacles that limit the effectiveness of coordinated party action. Finally, party discipline is hurt by the individualistic

---

[20] Such cases are few, but a deterrent nonetheless. Several U.S. senators were expelled from the Republican caucus in 1925 for having supported the Progressive candidate for president the previous year. In 1965 two Southern House Democrats lost all their committee seniority because of their 1964 endorsement of GOP presidential nominee Barry Goldwater, as did another Southerner in 1968 for his backing of George Wallace's third-party candidacy. In early 1983 the House Democratic caucus removed Texas Representative Phil Gramm from his Budget Committee seat because of his "disloyalty" in working more closely with Republican committee members than with his own party leaders. (Gramm resigned his seat in Congress, changed parties, was reelected as a Republican, and used the controversy to propel himself into the U.S. Senate in 1984.)

nature of American politics: campaigns that are candidate centered rather than party oriented; diverse electoral constituencies to which members of Congress must understandably be responsive; the largely private system of election financing that indebts legislators to wealthy individuals and nonparty interest groups more than to their parties; and the importance to law makers of attracting the news media's attention—often more easily done by showmanship than by quiet, effective labor within the party system.

Results. These are formidable barriers to the operation of responsible, potent legislative parties. Therefore, it is impressive to discover that party labels have consistently been the most powerful predictor of congressional roll-call voting, and in the last few years even more votes have been closely following the partisan divide. While not invariably predictive, as in strong parliamentary systems, a member's party affiliation has proven to be the indicator of his or her votes more than 70 percent of the time in recent years; that is, the average representative or senator sides with his or her party on about 70 percent of the votes that divide a majority of Democrats from a majority of Republicans. In most recent years more than half of the roll-call votes in the House and Senate also found majorities of Democrats and Republicans on opposite sides.

High levels of party cohesion are especially likely to be seen when votes are taken in several areas. The votes that organize the legislative chambers (such as the election of a Speaker), set up the election machinery and campaign laws, and seat-challenged members command nearly unanimous support on behalf of the party's basic interests. Those votes involving key parts of the president's program also frequently divide the parties. Finally, certain policy issues (such as Social Security, welfare programs, and union–management relations) as well as party platform issues that directly and manifestly affect the party's image or its key constituencies produce substantial party voting.[21]

Until the decade of the 1980s there had been a substantial decline in party voting in Congress. At the turn of the century almost three-quarters of all the recorded votes saw a majority of one party voting against a majority of the other party, and astoundingly a third or more of a session's roll calls would pit at least 90 percent of one party against 90

---

[21] See Julius Turner with Edward V. Schneier Jr., *Party and Constituency: Pressures on Congress* (Baltimore: John Hopkins University Press, 1970), pp. 33–39.

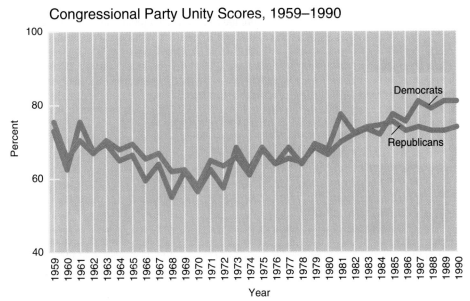

Congressional Party Unity Scores, 1959–1990

A party unity vote is one in which a member of Congress votes with his or her party on issues that divide a majority of Democrats from a majority of Republicans. This graph traces the average percentage of party unity votes for all members of Congress from 1959 to 1990.

Source: Congressional Quarterly Almanacs (Washington: Congressional Quarterly, Inc).

A party vote is one in which a majority of Democrats and Republicans vote on opposite sides. This graph traces party votes as a percentage of total votes from 1954 to 1990 for each house of Congress.

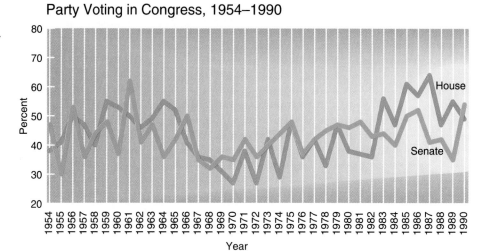

Party Voting in Congress, 1954–1990

Source: *Congressional Quarterly Almanacs* (Washington: Congressional Quarterly, Inc).

percent or more of the other party. This was at a time when two Speakers of the House (Republicans Thomas B. Reed and Joseph G. Cannon, who in succession controlled the Speakership most of the years between 1889 and 1911) possessed almost dictatorial authority and therefore could enforce strict voting discipline. But a rebellious House drastically curtailed the Speaker's powers between 1909 and 1911, a development that combined with internal GOP strains and splits to reduce party harmony and unity in congressional voting.

Two decades later, when the Democrats of the New Deal coalition held sway, they also had their own fractures and contradictions (blacks versus whites, Northern liberals versus Southern conservatives, urban versus rural areas, and so forth). The effect of these tensions and the other anti-party trends discussed earlier was to leave party majorities opposing each other on only about 40 percent of recorded votes through the latter 1960s and the 1970s. In the past several years, however, party voting has increased noticeably. In 1990, for instance, the average Democratic member voted with his or her party (on votes dividing party majorities) about 81 percent of the time, while the average Republican did so in more than 74 percent of the cases.

There are many reasons for the recent growth of congressional party unity and cohesion. Some are the result of long-term political factors. Both congressional parties, for instance, have gradually become more ideologically homogeneous and internally consistent. Southern Democrats today are more moderate and far closer philosophically to their Northern counterparts than the South's legislative barons of old ever were; similarly, there are few liberal Republicans left in either chamber of Congress, and GOP House members from all regions of the country are—with a few exceptions—moderately to solidly conservative. At the same time, strong two-party competition has come to almost all areas of the nation, and the electoral insecurity produced by vigorous competition seems to encourage party unity and cooperation in a legislature (perhaps as a kind of "circling the wagons" effect).[22]

The circumstances of contemporary politics are also producing greater legislative cohesion. There is growing dissatisfaction on the Republican side of the House aisle with that party's seemingly permanent minority status, and the increased militancy of some GOP members of Congress (such as Minority Whip Newt Gingrich of Georgia) has raised

[22] Joseph A. Schlesinger, "The New American Political Party," *American Political Science Review* 79, (1985), p. 1168.

the partisan hackles of many Democrats, polarizing the House a bit more along party lines. On the other side of the Capitol, the continuing, close partisan struggle over control of the Senate since 1980 has appeared to increase the party consciousness of both groups of senators.

One of the least recognized but most enduring effects of the Watergate scandal was to stimulate the strengthening of the congressional parties long after Richard Nixon had departed the White House. The Watergate-spawned election of seventy-five reform-minded freshman Democrats in 1974 led to a revolt against the seniority system in early 1975. Three unresponsive senior chairmen were deposed, the power of the committee system was diminished, and a crucial barrier to the influence of party thus fell. When a rigid seniority system protected independent-minded members, not surprisingly, committee chairs often voted against their party's wishes. After the 1975 display of caucus muscle, though, chairpersons dramatically increased their solidarity with the party majority, scoring even higher than backbenchers (junior members) on party unity scales.[23]

The political party campaign committees have also played a role in the renewed cohesiveness observed within Congress. Each national party committee has been recruiting and training House and Senate candidates as never before and devising common themes for all nominees in election seasons—work that may help to produce a consensual legislative agenda for each party. The carrot and stick of party money and campaign services, such as media advertising production and polling, is also being used to convert candidates into party team players. Clearly, the more important the party organization can be to a legislator's election and reelection, the more attention a legislator is likely to pay to his or her party.

The Presidential Party

Political parties may well be more central to the operation of the legislative branch than the executive branch, but it is the presidential party that captures the public imagination and shapes the electorate's opinion of the two parties. In our very personalized politics, voters' perceptions of the incumbent president and the presidential candidates determine to a great degree how citizens perceive the parties.

A chief executive's successes are his party's successes; the president's failures are borne by the party as much as the individual. The image projected by a losing presidential candidate is incorporated into the party's contemporary portrait, whether wanted or not. As the highest elected candidate of the national party, the president naturally assumes the role of party leader, as does the White House nominee of the other party (at least during the campaign).

The juggling of contradictory roles is not always easy for a president. Expected not only to bring the country together as ceremonial chief of state and to forge a ruling consensus as head of government, the president must also be an effective commander of a sometimes divided party. Along with the inevitable headaches party leadership brings, though, there are clear and compelling advantages that accompany it. Foremost among them is a party's ability to mobilize support among voters for a president's program. Also, the executive's legislative agenda might be derailed more quickly without the common tie of party label between the chief executive and many members of Congress; all presidents appeal for some congressional support on the basis of shared party affiliation, and they generally receive it. In recent decades, the average legislator of the president's party has backed the chief executive two-thirds to three-quarters of the time, whereas the average member of the opposition has done so only one-third to one-half the time. There is considerable variance among presidents, of course, since circumstances and executive skill differ. Ronald Reagan's support among GOP senators was exceptionally high, for

---

[23] Sara Brandes Crook and John R. Hibbing, "Congressional Reform and Party Discipline: The Effects of Change in the Seniority System on Party Loyalty in the U.S. House of Representatives," *British Journal of Political Science* 15 (April 1985), pp. 207–26.

instance, whereas Jimmy Carter and Dwight Eisenhower (in his second term) had more than the usual degree of trouble with their House partisans.

These party gifts to the president are reciprocated in other ways. In addition to compiling a record for the party and giving substance to its image, presidents appoint many activists to office, recruit candidates, raise money for the party treasury, campaign extensively for party nominees during election seasons, and occasionally provide some "coattail" help to fellow office seekers who are on the ballot in presidential election years.

Pro-Party Presidents. Some presidents take their party responsibilities more seriously than others. In this century Democrats Woodrow Wilson and Franklin Roosevelt were exceptionally party oriented and dedicated to building their party electorally and governmentally. In his first term Wilson worked closely with Democratic congressional leaders to fashion a progressive and successful party program, and Roosevelt was responsible for constructing the enduring New Deal coalition for his party and breathing life into a previously moribund Democratic National Committee. Republican Gerald Ford, during his brief tenure from 1974 to 1977, also achieved a reputation as a party builder, and he was willing to undertake campaign and organizational chores for the GOP (especially in fund raising and in barnstorming for nominees) that most other presidents minimized or shunned. Perhaps Ford's previous role as House minority leader made him more sensitive to the needs of his fellow party office holders.

Managing relations with the legislature is much less problematic in the British parliamentary system. The party in government consists of individuals from the majority in Parliament, who continue to hold their seats in Parliament. Moreover, the life of the Parliament is tied intimately to the life of the government; should the latter fall, the former almost certainly will. This provides the party in power with a compelling argument to use with recalcitrant partisans in the legislature.

The scores represent the percentage of recorded votes on which members were in agreement with the president's announced position.

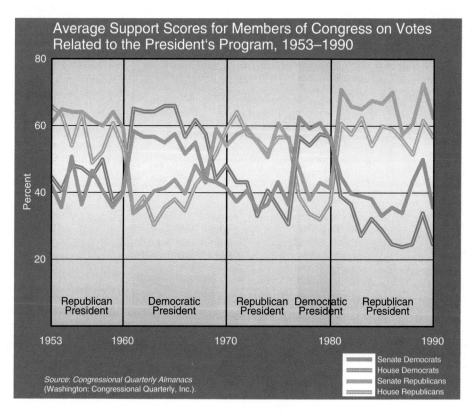

Average Support Scores for Members of Congress on Votes Related to the President's Program, 1953–1990

Source: Congressional Quarterly Almanacs (Washington: Congressional Quarterly, Inc.).

Nonpartisan Presidents. Most modern chief executives have been in an entirely different mold. Dwight Eisenhower elevated "nonpartisanship" to a virtual art form, and while it may have preserved his personal popularity, it proved a disaster for his party. Despite a full two-term occupancy of the White House, the Republican Party remained mired in minority status among the electorate, and Eisenhower never really attempted to transfer his high ratings to the party. Lyndon Johnson kept the DNC busy with such trivial tasks as answering wedding invitations sent to the First Family, and when many of the Democratic senators and representatives elected on his presidential coattails were endangered in the 1966 midterm election, LBJ canceled a major campaign trip on their behalf lest his policies get tied too closely to their possible defeats. Democrats lost forty-seven House seats, three Senate seats, and eight governorships in a 1966 debacle Johnson did little to prevent.

In 1972 Richard Nixon discouraged the GOP from nominating candidates against conservative Southern Democrats in order to improve his own electoral and congressional position, since the grateful unopposed legislators would presumably be less likely to cause Nixon trouble on the campaign trail or in Congress. Nixon also subordinated the party's agenda almost wholly to his own reelection. Shunting aside the Republican National Committee, Nixon formed the Committee to Re-Elect the President, which, unfortunately for him, became known by what Nixon critics called the most appropriate acronym of our time: CREEP. So removed were party leaders from CREEP's abuses (see the box on Watergate in Chapter 7) that the Republican Party organization itself escaped blame during the Watergate investigations.

Jimmy Carter also showed little interest in his national party. Elected as an outsider in 1976, Carter and his top aides at first viewed the party as another extension of the Washington establishment they had pledged to ignore. Carter and his DNC chairmen failed to develop the Democratic Party organizationally and financially to keep it competitive during a critical period, while the Republicans were undergoing a dramatic revitalization stimulated by their desire to recover from the Watergate scandal. Later, during his fateful 1980 reelection campaign, Carter was properly criticized for diverting DNC personnel and resources to his presidential needs rather than permitting them to pursue essential partywide electoral tasks.

Reagan and Bush. Carter's two Republican successors have taken a very different approach. Ronald Reagan was one of the most party-oriented presidents of recent times.[24] In 1983 and in 1984, during his own reelection effort, Reagan made more than two dozen campaign and fund-raising appearances for all branches of the party organization and candidates at every level. More than 300 television endorsements were taped as well, including one for an obscure Honolulu city council contest. Reagan also showed a willingness to get involved in the nitty-gritty of candidate recruitment, frequently calling in strong potential candidates to urge them to run. During the intense and ultimately unsuccessful battle to retain control of the U.S. Senate for the Republicans in 1986, Reagan played the good soldier, visiting twenty-two key states repeatedly and raising $33 million for the party and its candidates. Unlike Eisenhower, Reagan was willing to attempt a popularity transfer to his party and to campaign for Republicans whether they were strongly loyal to him personally or not; unlike Johnson, Reagan was willing to put his prestige and policies to the test on the campaign trail; unlike Nixon, Reagan spent time and effort helping underdogs and longshot candidates, not just likely winners; unlike Carter, Reagan signed more than seventy fund-raising appeals for party committees and took a personal interest in the further strengthening of the GOP's organizational capacity. George Bush, a former RNC chairman, emulated the Reagan model in his own presidency.

[24] Rhodes Cook, "Reagan Nurtures His Adopted Party to Strength," *Congressional Quarterly Weekly* 43 (September 28, 1985), pp. 1927–30.

In the midterm elections of 1990, President George Bush appeared at a rally in Rochester, Minnesota to try and boost the reelection chances of Senator Rudy Boschwitz (R.-Minn.). As in most midterm contests, however, the 1990 races witnessed losses in both houses of Congress by the president's party. Boschwitz was unseated by political science professor Paul Wellstone, a Democrat.

However, neither Reagan nor Bush were very successful in providing much coattail help to their party's nominees lower down on the ballot. Reagan's initial victory in 1980 was one factor in the election of a Republican Senate, but his landslide reelection in 1984 had, like Nixon's in 1972, almost no impact on his party's congressional representation. And Bush provided no coattails at all to the GOP in 1988. There is little question that the coattail effect—whereby party nominees lower on the ballot can receive additional votes generated by a popular presidential candidate—has diminished sharply compared with a generation ago.[25] Partly, the decreased competitiveness of congressional elections has been produced by artful redistricting and the growing value of incumbency.[26] But voters are also less willing to think and cast ballots in purely partisan terms—a development that limits presidential leadership and hurts party development. (We return to this subject in the next chapter.)

The Parties and the Judiciary

Americans view the judiciary as "above politics" and certainly nonpartisan, and many judges are quick to agree. Yet not only do members of the judiciary sometimes follow the election returns and allow themselves to be influenced by popular opinion, they are also products of their party identification and possess the very same partisan perceptual screens as all other politically aware citizens.

Legislators are far more partisan than judges, but it is wrong to assume that judges reach decisions wholly independent of partisan values. First of all, judges are creatures of the political process, and their posts are considered patronage plums. Those who are not elected are appointed by presidents or governors for their abilities but also as members of the executive's party and increasingly as representatives of a certain philosophy of or approach to government. In this century every president has appointed judges overwhelmingly from his own party; Jimmy Carter and Ronald Reagan, for instance, drew 95 percent or more of their judicial choices from their respective parties. Furthermore, Democratic executives are naturally inclined to choose for the bench liberal individuals who may be friendly to the welfare state or critical of some business practices. Republican executives generally lean toward conservatives for judicial posts, hoping they will be tough on criminal defendants, anti-abortion, and restrained in the use of court power. Research has long indicated that party affiliation is in fact a moderately good predictor of judicial decisions, at least in some areas.[27] In other words, party matters in the judiciary just as it does in the other two branches of government, although it certainly matters less on the bench than in the legislature and in the executive.

Many judges appointed to office have had long careers in politics as loyal party workers or legislators. Supreme Court Justice Sandra Day O'Connor, for example, was an active member of the National Republican Women's Club and is a former Republican state legislator. Some jurists are even more overtly political, since they are elected to office. In a

[25] George C. Edwards III, *Presidential Influence in Congress* (New York: Freeman, 1980); and Herbert M. Kritzer and Robert B. Eubank, "Presidential Coattails Revisited: Partisanship and Incumbency Effects," *American Journal of Political Science* 23 (1979), pp. 615–26.

[26] Lyn Ragsdale, "The Fiction of Congressional Elections as Presidential Events," *American Politics Quarterly* 8 (1980), pp. 375–98; and Thomas E. Mann and Raymond E. Wolfinger, "Candidates and Parties in Congressional Elections," *American Political Science Review* 74 (1980), pp. 617–32.

[27] See Sidney Ulmer, "The Political Party Variable on the Michigan Supreme Court," *Journal of Public Law* 11 (1962), pp. 352–62; Stuart Nagel, "Political Party Affiliation and Judges' Decisions," *American Political Science Review* 55 (1961), pp. 843–50; David W. Adamany, "The Party Variable in Judges' Voting: Conceptual Notes and a Case Study," *American Political Science Review* 63 (1969), pp. 57–73; Sheldon Goldman, "Voting Behavior on the United States Courts of Appeals, 1961–1964," *American Political Science Review* 60 (1966), pp. 374–83; and Robert A. Carp and C. K. Rowland, *Policymaking and Politics in the Federal District Courts* (Knoxville: University of Tennessee Press, 1983).

majority of states at least some judicial positions are filled by election, and seventeen states hold outright partisan elections, with both parties nominating opposing candidates and running hard-hitting campaigns. In some rural counties across America, local judges are not merely partisanly elected figures; they are the key public officials, controlling many patronage jobs and the party machinery itself. Obviously, therefore, in many places in the United States, judges by necessity and by tradition are not above politics but in the thick of it. Although election of the judiciary is a questionable practice in light of its specially sanctioned role as impartial arbiter, partisan influence exerted both by jurists' party loyalties and by the appointment (or election) process is useful in retaining some degree of accountability in a branch often accused of being arrogant and aloof.

The Parties and State Governments

Most of the conclusions just reached about the party's relationship to the legislature, the executive, and the judiciary apply to those branches on the state level as well. The national parties, after all, are organized around state units, and the basic structural arrangement of party and government is much the same in Washington and the state capitals. Remarkably, too, the major national parties are the dominant political forces in all fifty states. This has been true consistently; unlike Great Britain or Canada, the United States has no regional or state parties that displace one or both of the national parties in local contests. Occasionally in American history a third party has proven locally potent, as did Minnesota's Farmer-Labor Party and Wisconsin's Progressives, both of which elected governors and state legislative majorities earlier in this century. But over time, no such party has survived,[28] and every state's two-party system mirrors national party dualism, at least as far as labels are concerned.

Parties and Governors.

There are some party-oriented differences at the state level, though. Governors in many states tend to possess even greater influence over their parties' organizations and legislators than do presidents. Many governors have far more patronage positions at their command than does a president, and these material rewards and incentives give governors added clout with activists and office holders. In addition, tradition in some states permits the governor to take a role in selecting the legislature's committee chairs and party floor leaders, and some state executives even attend and help direct the party legislative caucuses—activities no president would ever undertake. Moreover, forty-three governors possess a power denied the national executive—the item veto, which permits the governor to veto single items (such as individual pork barrel projects) in appropriations bills. Whereas a president must often accept objectionable measures as part of a bill too urgent or important to be vetoed, a governor gains enormous leverage with legislators by means of the item veto.

Parties and State Legislatures.

Just as the party relationship between the executive and the legislature tends to be stronger at the state level than in Washington, so also is the party role in the legislature itself more high-profile and effective. Most state legislatures surpass the U.S. Congress in partisan unity and cohesion. While fewer than half of congressional roll calls in the post–World War II era have produced majorities of the two parties on opposite sides, a number of state legislatures (including Massachusetts, New York, Ohio, and Pennsylvania) have achieved party voting levels of 70 percent or better

[28] The Farmer-Labor Party did survive in a sense; having endured a series of defeats, it merged in 1944 with the Democrats, and Democratic candidates still officially bear the standard of the Democratic-Farmer-Labor (DFL) Party. At about the same time, also having suffered severe electoral reversals, the Progressives stopped nominating candidates in Wisconsin. The party's members either returned to the Republican Party, from which it had split early in the century, or became Democrats.

Republicans and States' Rights

The party names "Democrat" and "Republican" have remained constant since 1860, but the philosophies the names represent have not. The Republican Party first gained power in 1860, determined to preserve the federal Union and to battle those who believed that states had the right to secede. By the New Deal era, though, the GOP had become the advocate of states' rights, and the party's officials often sounded the alarm against federal encroachment on state prerogatives—a policy that continues today. Conversely, the Democratic Party has been transformed from the more conservative and states' rights–oriented party in the 1800s to the more liberal and pro-government party of today.

in some years. Not all states display party cohesion of this magnitude, of course. Nebraska has a nonpartisan legislature, elected without party labels on the ballot; and the lack of two-party competition in the South has left essentially one-party legislatures split into factions, regional groupings, or personal cliques. As real interparty competition reaches the legislative level in Southern states, however, party cohesion in the legislatures is likely to increase.

One other party distinction is notable in many state legislatures. Compared with the Congress, state legislative leaders have much more authority and power, and this is one reason why party unity is higher in the state capitols.[29] The strict seniority system that usually controls committee assignments in Congress is less absolute in most states, and legislative leaders often have considerable discretion in appointing the committee chairs and members. The party caucuses, too, are usually more active and influential in state legislatures than in their Washington counterparts. In some legislatures, the caucuses meet weekly or even daily to work out strategy and count votes, and nearly one-fourth of the caucuses bind all the party members to support the group's decisions on key issues (such as appropriations measures, tax issues, and procedural questions). Not just the leaders and caucuses but the party organizations as well have more influence over legislators at the state level. State legislators are far more dependent than their congressional counterparts on their state and local parties for election assistance. Whereas members of Congress have large government-provided staffs and lavish perquisites to assist (directly or indirectly) their reelection efforts, state legislative candidates need party workers and, increasingly, the party's financial support and technological resources at election time.

The Modern Transformation of Party Organization

The parties are not just convenient labels for office holders; they are functioning organizations with bureaucracies in virtually every hamlet in America. However, the vitality of the organizations varies widely from place to place and from era to era.

The modern Republican Party has thoroughly outclassed its Democratic rival in almost every category of campaign service and fund raising. There are a number of explanations for the disparity between the two major parties. Until 1980 the Republicans were almost perennially disappointed underdogs, especially in congressional contests, and they therefore felt the need to give extra effort. The GOP had the willingness, and enough electoral frustrations, to experiment with new campaign technologies that might hold the key to elusive victories. Also, since Democrats held most of the congressional offices and thus had most of the benefits of incumbency and staff, Republican nominees were forced to rely more on their party to offset built-in Democratic advantages. The party staff, in other words, compensated for the Democratic congressional staff, and perhaps also for organized labor's divisions of election troops, which were usually at the beck and call of Democratic candidates. Then, too, one could argue that the business and middle-class base of the modern GOP has a natural managerial and entrepreneurial flair possessed and demonstrated by the party officers drawn from that talented pool of people.

Whatever the causes, the contemporary Republican Party has organizational prowess unparalleled in American history and unrivaled by the Democrats. The Republicans have outraised the Democrats by large margins in all recent election cycles, never by less than two to one and usually by a considerably higher ratio. Democrats must struggle to secure enough money to meet the basic needs of most of their candidates, while in the words of a past chairman of the Democratic Senatorial Campaign Committee, "The single biggest problem the Republicans have is how to legally spend the money they have."[30]

[29]Sarah McCally Morehouse, "Legislatures and Political Parties," *State Government* 59:1 (1976), pp. 19–24.
[30]Senator George J. Mitchell (D.-Me.) as quoted in the *Washington Post,* February 9, 1986, p. A-14.

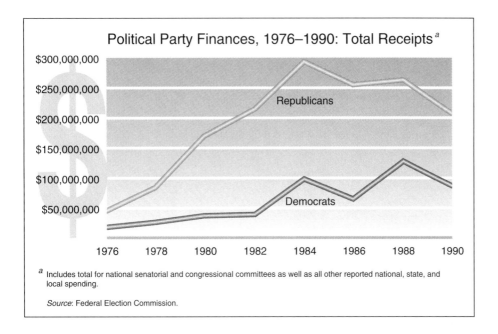

Political Party Finances, 1976–1990: Total Receipts[a]

[a] Includes total for national senatorial and congressional committees as well as all other reported national, state, and local spending.

Source: Federal Election Commission.

Most of the Republican money is raised through highly successful mail solicitation, which was begun in the early 1960s and accelerated in the mid-1970s when postage and production costs were relatively low. From a base of just 24,000 names in 1975, for example, the national Republican Party has expanded its mailing list of proven donors to several million by the 1990s. Mailings produce about three-quarters of total revenue, and they do so with an average contribution of under $35. In this fashion the GOP may have broadened its committed base, because contributing money usually strengthens the tie between a voter and any organization. Most of the rest of the GOP's funds come from larger donors who secure membership in various Republican contributor groups. For

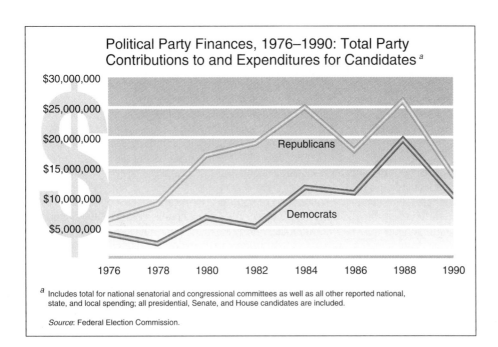

Political Party Finances, 1976–1990: Total Party Contributions to and Expenditures for Candidates[a]

[a] Includes total for national senatorial and congressional committees as well as all other reported national, state, and local spending; all presidential, Senate, and House candidates are included.

Source: Federal Election Commission.

instance, the Republican National Committee designates any $10,000 annual giver an "Eagle."

The Republican cash is used to support a dazzling variety of party activities and campaign services, including the following.

Party Staff

Several hundred operatives are employed by the national GOP in election years, and even in the off years, well over one hundred hold full-time positions. There is great emphasis on field staff—that is, staff members sent to and stationed in key districts and states who maintain close communication between local and national party offices.

Voter Contact

The Republicans frequently conduct massive telephone canvassing operations to identify likely Republican voters and to get them to the polls on Election Day. In 1986, for instance, the GOP used paid callers in seventeen phone centers across the country to reach 10.5 million prospective voters in twenty-five states during the general election campaign. Nearly 5.5 million previously identified Republicans were re-called just before Election Day, many of them hearing an automated message from the president: "This is Ronald Reagan and I want to remind you to go out and vote on Tuesday. . . ." In addition, 12 million pieces of "persuasive" (non–fund-raising) mail were sent to households in the last two weeks of the campaign.

Polling

The national Republican committees have spent millions of dollars for national, state, and local public opinion surveys, and they have accumulated an enormous storehouse of data on American attitudes generally and on marginal districts in particular. Many of the surveys are provided to GOP nominees at a cut-rate cost. In important contests the party will frequently commission **tracking polls**—continuous surveys that enable a campaign to chart its daily rise or fall. The information provided in such polls is invaluable in the tense concluding days of an election.

Media Advertising

The national Republican Party operates a sophisticated in-house media division that specializes in the design and production of television advertisements for party nominees at all levels. About seventy to one hundred candidates are helped in an election cycle. Not only do they obtain expert and technically superior media commercials, but the party also offers its wares for a minimal fee, often including the actual buying of time—that is, the purchase of specific time slots on television shows for broadcasting the spots. The candidates thus save the substantial commissions and fees usually charged by independent political consultants for the same services.

Perhaps of greater significance than the production of candidates' commercials is the GOP's advertising for the party itself. Since 1978 the Republicans have aired spots designed to support not specific candidates but the generic party label. Beginning with the 1980 election, the GOP has used institutional advertising to establish basic election themes. "Vote Republican—for a Change" spots attacked the Democratic Congress in 1980. Then–House Speaker Thomas P. "Tip" O'Neill was lampooned by an actor who ignored all warning signs and drove a car until it ran out of fuel. ("The Democrats are out of gas," announced the narrator as "Tip" futilely kicked the automobile's tire.) Another ad starred an unemployed factory worker from Baltimore, a lifelong Democrat who plain-

I AM A REPUBLICAN BECAUSE . . .

I believe that the proper function of government is to do for the people those things that have to be done but cannot be done, or cannot be done as well, by individuals, and that the most effective government is government closest to the people.

I believe that good government is based on the individual and that each person's ability, dignity, freedom and responsibility must be honored and recognized.

I believe that free enterprise and the encouragement of individual initiative and incentive have given this nation an economic system second to none.

I believe that sound money management should be our goal.

Party advertising: The parties spend money on their own individual candidates as well as on slates of candidates ("vote Republican"); sometimes they even create general advertisements to encourage voters to identify with a party.

tively asked, "If the Democrats are so good for working people, then how come so many people aren't working?"

In the 1982 midterm congressional elections the defensive focus of a $15 million institutional campaign was "give the guy [Reagan] a chance" and "stay the course" with the president in the midst of a deep recession and high unemployment. For instance, a white-haired mailman was seen delivering Social Security checks fattened with a cost-of-living increase, reminding elderly voters that Reagan had kept his promise, and urging, "for gosh sake, let's give the guy a chance." The spot, like the earlier 1980 ads, was highly rated by viewers, and although some moderate Republican candidates resisted being tied to Reagan during one of the most unpopular periods of his presidency, pre- and post-election surveys suggested that the GOP-sponsored media campaign had been, on the whole, helpful to the party and to individual candidates.

Campaign Staff Training and Research

The party trains many of the political volunteers and paid operatives who manage the candidates' campaigns. Since 1976 the Republicans have held annually about a half-dozen week-long "Campaign Management Colleges" for staffers, and in 1986 the party launched an ambitious million-dollar "Congressional Campaign Academy" that offers two-week, all-expenses-paid training courses for prospective campaign managers, finance directors, and press relations staff. Early in each election cycle the national party staff also prepares voluminous research reports on Democratic opponents, analyzing their public statements, votes, and attendance records. The reports are made available to GOP candidates and their aides.

Results

Despite its financial edge and service sophistication, all is not well in the Republican organizational paradise. Success has bred self-satisfaction and complacency, encouraged waste, and caused the party to place too much reliance on money and technology and not enough on the foundation of any party movement—people. As former U.S. Senator Paul Laxalt (R.-Nev.), outgoing general chairman of the national Republican Party, was forced to admit in 1987:

> We've got way too much money, we've got way too many political operatives, we've got far too few volunteers. . . . We are substituting contributions and high technology for volunteers in the field. I've gone the sophisticate route, I've gone the television route, and there is no substitute for the volunteer route.[31]

As Laxalt implied, technology and money can probably only add 2 or 3 percentage points to a candidate's margin. The rest is determined by the nominee's quality and positions, the general electoral tide prevailing in any given year, and the energy of party troops in field.

Parties, like people, change their habits slowly. The Democrats were reluctant to alter a formula that had been a winning combination for decades of New Deal dominance. The prevailing philosophy was, "Let a thousand flowers bloom"; candidates were encouraged to go their own way, to rely on organized labor and other interest groups allied with the Democrats, and to raise their own money, while the national party was kept subservient and weak.

The massive Democratic defeats suffered in 1980 forced a fundamental reevaluation of the party's structure and activities. Democrats, diverse and quarrelsome by nature, came to an unaccustomed consensus that the party must change to survive, that it must dampen internal ideological disputes and begin to revitalize its organization. Thus was born the committment to technological and fund-raising modernization, using the Republican Party's accomplishments as a model, that drives the Democratic Party today.

Comprehension of the task is but the first step to realization of the goal, so even after more than a decade, Democrats still trail their competitors by virtually every significant measure of party activity. Yet the financial figures of party finances (receipts), graphed earlier on page 411, can be read a different way. While the GOP has consistently maintained an enormous edge, the Democrats have considerably increased their total receipts, now raising many times more than just a few years ago. The Democrats lose the money competition with the Republicans by a country mile, but viewed in another context, the new Democratic Party greatly outdistances the old. That is no small achievement.

The decision in 1981 to begin a direct-mail program for the national party was a turning point. From a list of only 25,000 donors before the program began, the DNC's support base has grown to 500,000. The Democrats have imitated the Republicans not just in fund raising but also in the uses to which the money is put. For instance, in 1986 the party opened a $3 million media center that produces television and radio spots at rates greatly reduced from those charged by independent political consultants. The Democratic Party is attempting to do more for its candidates and their campaign staffs, too, creating the Democratic National Training Institute in 1985. The Institute coordinates campaign schools for party workers from around the country.

Thus, both party organizations have grown mightier in recent years—at the very time when political parties have seemed to be in decline in some other ways. Most important, many voters appear to have less of a sense of partisan identification and loyalty today than in generations past. Why is this so?

The Party-in-the-Electorate

A political party is far more than its organizational shell, however dazzling the technologies at its command, and its reach extends well beyond the relative handful of men and women who are the party-in-government. In any democracy, where power is derived directly from the people, the party's real importance and strength must come from the

---

[31] As quoted in a speech to the RNC by the Associated Press, January 24, 1987, and in the *Washington Post,* same date, p. A-3.

citizenry it attempts to mobilize. The party-in-the-electorate—the mass of potential voters who identify with the Democratic or Republican labels—is the third and most significant element in the party triad, providing the foundation for the organizational and governmental parties. But in some crucial respects it is the most troubled of the three special components of the American political parties. In recent decades fewer citizens have been willing to pledge their fealty to the major parties, and many of those who have declared their loyalties have done so with less intensity. Also, voters of each partisan stripe are increasingly casting ballots for some candidates of the opposing party, and partisan identification is a less reliable indicator of likely voting choices today than it once was.

Party Identification

Most American voters *identify* with a party but do not *belong* to it. There is no universal enrolled party membership; there are no prescribed dues; no formal rules concerning an individual's activities; no enforceable obligations to the party assumed by the voter. The party has no real control over or even an accurate accounting of its adherents, and the party's voters subscribe to few or none of the commonly accepted tenets of organizational membership, such as regular participation and some measure of responsibility for the group's welfare. Rather, party identification or affiliation is an informal and impressionistic exercise whereby a citizen acquires a party label and accepts its standard as a shorthand summary of his or her political views and preferences. However, just because the acquisition is informal does not mean that it is unimportant. The party label becomes a voter's central political reference symbol and perceptual screen, a prism or filter through which the world of politics and government flows and is interpreted. For many Americans, party identification is a significant aspect of one's political personality and a way of defining and explaining oneself to others. The loyalty generated by the label can be as intense as any enjoyed by sports teams and alma maters; in a few areas of the country, ''Democrat'' and ''Republican'' are still fighting words.

On the whole, though, Americans regard their partisan affiliation with lesser degrees of enthusiasm, viewing it as a convenience rather than a necessity. The individual identifications are reinforced by the legal institutionalization of the major parties. Because of restrictive ballot laws, campaign finance rules, the powerful inertia of political tradition, and many other factors, voters for all practical purposes are limited to a choice between a Democrat and a Republican in virtually all elections—a situation that naturally encourages the pragmatic choosing up of sides. The party registration process that exists in about half of the states, requiring a voter to state a party preference (or independent status) when registering to vote and restricting participation in primaries to party registrants, also is an incentive for voters to affiliate themselves with a party.[32]

Whatever the societal and governmental forces undergirding party identification, the explanations of partisan loyalty at the individual's level are understandably more personal. Not surprisingly, parents are the single greatest influence in establishing a person's first party identification. Politically active parents with the same party loyalty raise children who will be strong party identifiers, while parents without party affiliations or with mixed affiliations produce offspring more likely to be independents. Early socialization is hardly the last step in the acquisition and maintenance of a party identity; marriage and other facts of adult life can change one's loyalty. So can charismatic political personalities, particularly at the national level (such as Franklin Roosevelt and Ronald Reagan), cataclysmic events (the Civil War and the Great Depression are the best examples), and maybe intense social issues (for instance, abortion). Interestingly, social class is not an especially strong indicator of likely partisan choice in the United States, at least in comparison with Western European democracies. Not only are Americans less inclined than

---

[32] See Steven E. Finkel and Howard A. Scarrow, ''Party Identification and Party Enrollment: The Difference and the Consequence,'' *Journal of Politics* 47 (May 1985), pp. 620–42.

Europeans to perceive class distinctions—preferring instead to see themselves and most others as members of an exceedingly broad middle class—but other factors, including sectionalism and candidate-oriented politics, tend to blur class lines in voting.

Declining Loyalty

Over the past two decades many political scientists as well as other observers, journalists, and party activists have become increasingly anxious about a perceived decline in partisan identification and loyalty. Many public opinion surveys have shown a significant growth in independents at the expense of the two major parties. The Center for Political Studies/Survey Research Center (CPS/SRC) of the University of Michigan, for instance, has charted the rise of self-described independents from a low of 19 percent in 1958 to a peak of 38 percent twenty years later. Before the 1950s, although the evidence is more circumstantial because of the scarcity of reliable survey research data, there are indications that independents were many fewer in number, and party loyalties considerably firmer.

Yet the recent decline of party identification can be exaggerated, and in some ways there has been remarkable stability in the voters' party choices. Over more than thirty years, during vast political, economic, and social upheavals that have changed the face of the nation, the Democratic Party has nearly consistently drawn the support of a small majority and the Republican Party has attracted a share of the electorate in the low-to-mid-30-percent range. Granted, there have been peaks and valleys for both parties. The Johnson landslide of 1964 helped Democrats top the 60 percent mark, while the Reagan landslide of 1984 and the post–Persian Gulf war glow of 1991 sent Democratic stock below the majority midpoint. The Goldwater debacle of 1964 and the Watergate disaster of 1974 left the Republicans with under a third of the populace; Reagan's reelection brought the GOP to the threshold of 40 percent. Some slight average erosion over time in Democratic Party strength is certainly apparent, as is a small Republican gain during the Reagan and Bush eras. Yet these sorts of gradations are more akin to rolling foothills than towering mountain ranges. The steady nature of modern partisanship goes beyond the fortunes of each party. Identification with the two parties in modern times has never dipped below 83 percent of the American electorate (recorded during the disillusionment spawned by Watergate in 1974) and can usually be found in the mid-to-upper-80-percent range.

When pollsters ask for party identification information, they generally proceed in two stages. First, they inquire whether a respondent considers himself or herself a Democrat, Republican, or independent. Then the party identifiers are asked to categorize themselves as "strong" or "not very strong" supporters, while the independents are pushed to reveal their leanings with a question such as, "Which party do you normally support in elections—the Democrats or the Republicans?" It may be true that some independent respondents are thereby prodded to pick a party under the pressure of the interview situation, regardless of their true feelings. But research has demonstrated that independent "leaners" in fact vote very much like real partisans, in some elections more so than the "not very strong" party identifiers. There is reason to count the independent leaners as closet partisans, though voting behavior is *not* the equivalent of real partisan identification.

In fact, the reluctance of "leaners" to admit their real party identities is in itself worrisome because it reveals a change in attitudes about political parties and their proper role in our society. Being a socially acceptable, integrated, and contributing member of one's community once almost demanded partisan affiliation; it was a badge of good citizenship, signifying that one was a patriot. Today the labels are avoided as an offense to a thinking person's individualism, and a vast majority of Americans insist they vote for "the person, not the party." The reasons for these anti-party attitudes are not hard to find. The growth of an issue-oriented politics that cuts across party lines for those voters who feel intensely

Party Identification, 1952–1991 [a]
Percent, by Year

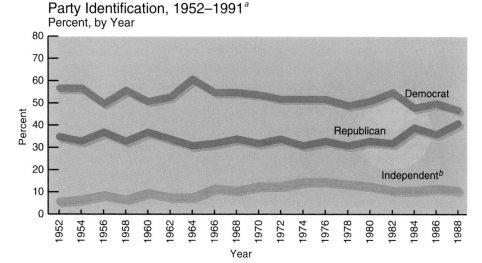

[a]Partisan totals do not add to 100% since "apolitical" and "other" responses were deleted. Sample size from poll to poll varied, from a low of 1,130 to a high of 2,850.

[b]Pure independents only. Independent "leaners" have been added to Democratic and Republican totals.

Source: Center for Political Studies/Survey Research Center of the University of Michigan, made available through the Inter-University Consortium for Political and Social Research. Also, Leon D. Epstein, *Political Parties in the American Mold* (Madison: University of Wisconsin Press, 1986), Table 8.1, p. 257.

about certain policy matters is partly to blame. So too is the emphasis on personality politics by the mass media (especially television) and political consultants. Underlying these causes, though, is a far more disturbing and destructive long-term phenomenon: the perceived loss of party credibility and the decline of the party's tangible connections to the lives of everyday citizens. Although the underlying partisanship of the American people has not declined significantly since 1952, voter-admitted partisanship has dropped considerably. About three-quarters or more of the electorate volunteered a party choice without prodding from 1952 to 1964, but since 1970 an average of under two-thirds has been willing to do so. Professed independents (including leaners) have increased from around a fifth of the electorate in the 1950s to a third or more in the 1970s and 1980s. Also cause for concern is the marginal decline in strong Democrats and strong Republicans. Strong partisans are a party's backbone, the source of its volunteer force, candidates, and dependable voters. Even a slight shrinkage in these ranks can be troublesome.

Group Affiliations

Just as individuals vary in the *strength* of their partisan choice, so too do groups vary in the degree to which they identify with the Democratic party or the Republican Party. There are enormous variations in party identification from one region or demographic group to another. Consider the following examples.

● Geographic region: While all other geographic regions are relatively closely contested between the parties, the South still exhibits the Democratic Party affinity cultivated in the last century and stoked in the fires of the Civil War. In all regions, party strengths vary by locality, with central cities almost everywhere heavily Democratic, the swelling suburbs serving as the main source of GOP partisans, and the small town and rural areas split evenly between the two major parties.

● Gender: Women and men differ sharply in their partisan choice, a phenomenon called the **gender gap**, which has yawned at least since 1980. Women generally favor the Democratic Party by 5 to 10 percent, and men give the GOP a similar edge. Besides women's rights issues, female concerns for peace and social compassion may provide much of the gap's foundation. For instance, women are usually much less likely than men to favor American military action, and they are less inclined to support cuts in government funding of social welfare programs.

- Race and ethnicity: Blacks are the most dramatically different population subgroup in party terms. The 80 percent-plus advantage they offer the Democrats dwarfs the edge given to either party by any other segment of the electorate, and their proportion of strong Democrats (about 40 percent) is 3 times that of whites. Blacks account almost entirely for the slight lead in party affiliation that Democrats normally enjoy over Republicans, since the GOP has recently been able to attract a narrow plurality of whites to its standard. Perhaps as a reflection of the massive party chasm separating blacks and whites, the two races differ greatly on many policy issues, with blacks overwhelmingly on the liberal side and whites closer to the conservative pole. An exception, incidentally, is abortion, where religious beliefs may lead blacks to the more conservative stance. The much smaller population group of Hispanics supplements blacks as a Democratic stalwart; by more than three to one, Hispanics prefer the Democratic label. An exception is the Cuban-American population, whose anti–Fidel Castro tilt leads to Republicanism.

- Age: Young people are becoming more Republican. While polls in 1972 indicated that the group of eighteen- to twenty-four-year-olds, and particularly students, were the only age group to support Democratic presidential nominee George McGovern,[33] by the 1990s the eighteen- to thirty-four-year-old age group was the most Republican of all. Much of this margin was derived from strong student affiliation with the Republicans. The most Democratic age group, by contrast, is that of

---

[33] Even the eighteen- to twenty-four-year-olds were very closely split between McGovern and Nixon in most polls, but McGovern ran more than a dozen percentage points better among the very young than among the electorate as a whole.

Professor Stephen Carter of Yale Law School, author of *Reflections of an Affirmative Action Baby,* in which he expresses ambivalence about the effects of affirmative action on black Americans. Traditionally, Democrats have supported affirmative action while Republicans have opposed it.

the thirty-five- to forty-nine-year-olds, whose political views were shaped in part by the era of civil rights, Vietnam, and Watergate.

- Social and economic factors: Some traditional strengths and weaknesses persist for each party by occupation, income, and education. The GOP remains predominant among executives, professionals, and white-collar workers, whereas the Democrats lead substantially among blue-collar workers and the unemployed. Labor union members are also Democratic by two-and-a-half to one. The more conservative retired population leans Republican. Women who do not work outside the home are less liberal and Democratic than those who do. Occupation, income, and education are closely related, of course, so many of the same partisan patterns can be detected in all three classifications. Democratic support usually drops steadily as one climbs the income scale. Similarly, as years of education increase, identification with the Republican Party climbs—until graduate school, when the Democrats rally a bit and only narrowly trail GOP partisans.

- Religion: The party preferences by religion are also traditional, but with modern twists. Protestants—especially Methodists, Presbyterians, and Episcopalians—favor the Republicans by a few percentage points, whereas Catholics and, even more so, Jews are predominantly Democratic in affiliation. Less polarization is apparent all around, though.[34] Democrats have made inroads among many Protestant denominations over the past three decades, and Republicans can now claim more than a quarter of the Jewish population and nearly 40 percent of the Catholics. The "born again" Christians, who have received much attention in recent years, are somewhat less Republican than commonly believed. The GOP usually has just about a 10 percent edge among them, primarily because so many blacks classify themselves as members of this group.

- Marital status: Even marital status reveals something about partisan affiliation. Those who are married, a traditionally more conservative group, and those who have never married, a segment weighted toward the premarriage young who currently lean toward the Republicans, are closely divided in party loyalty. But the widowed are Democratic in nature, probably because there are far more widows than widowers, the gender gap once again expressing itself. The divorced and the separated, who may well be experiencing economic hardship and appear to be more liberal than the married population, are a substantially Democratic group.

- Ideology: Ideologically, there are few surprises. Lending credence to the belief that both parties are now relatively distinct philosophically, liberals are overwhelmingly Democratic and conservatives are staunchly Republican in most surveys and opinion studies.

As party identification has weakened, so too has the likelihood that voters will cast ballots predictably and regularly for their party's nominees. (The next chapter will discuss this in some detail.) In the present day—as at the founding of the republic—Americans are simply not wedded to the idea or the reality of political parties.

The strong party system that prevails in Great Britain provides an illuminating contrast. A large majority of Britons strongly identifies with either the Conservatives (Tories) or the Labour Party, and voters rarely switch allegiances on Election Day. Of course the British parliamentary system is party based while American politics is far more personality oriented. In Britain a voter essentially casts a ballot for a party rather than a person who will serve as prime minister; in the United States, many voters pick presidents more

[34] The presidential election of 1960 may be an extreme case, but John Kennedy's massive support among Catholics and Nixon's less substantial but still impressive backing by Protestants demonstrates the polarization that religion could once produce. See Philip E. Converse, "Religion and Politics: The 1960 Election," in Angus Campbell et al., *Elections and the Political Order* (New York: Wiley, 1966), pp. 96–124.

The "Gender Gap"

Some political scientists argue that the difference in the way men and women vote first emerged in 1920, when newly enfranchised women registered overwhelmingly as Republicans. It was not until the 1980 presidential election, however, that a noticeable and possibly significant *gender gap* emerged. This time, the Democratic Party was the apparent beneficiary. While Ronald Reagan trounced incumbent Democratic President Jimmy Carter, he did so with the votes of only 46 percent of the women, compared to 54 percent of the men.

This gender gap continues to persist at all levels of elections. In 1990, exit polls conducted after seventy races revealed a gender gap in 61 percent of the races analyzed. In 1992, as in previous elections, more voters were women (54 percent) than men (46 percent). Again, more women—47 percent—voted for the Democrat (Clinton) than men—41 percent. Among working women the gap was even more pronounced—51 percent voted for Clinton, only 31 percent for Bush.

by their characters and personalities than on the basis of their party labels. The British parties also polarize the electorate because of the strong ideological cast of the Tories (free enterprise) and the Labour Party (socialist). While there are clear differences between a liberal Democratic Party and a conservative Republican Party, the American contrast is far less sharp than that of the United Kingdom. Nevertheless, observers of British politics point to recent developments that resonate with the American experience. Within the past two decades, a general "dealignment" of the electorate has taken place, with stable party allegiances on the decline. Hardest hit has been the Labour Party, which has apparently lost its grip on traditional sources of support among the working class.

Toward Reform

The following is a list of attributes that healthy parties should possess and some suggested means for helping them secure and maintain these attributes.

Attributes	Possible Means
Fairness and legitimacy	Promote an open structure within the parties, which invites participation by *all* interested citizens.
Broad electoral appeal	Prevent party takeover by ideological extremists.
Participation	Get local parties more involved in meeting the needs of the community and neighborhoods.
Accountability	Keep parties in closer touch with their constituents.
Conflict control	Grant more power to party leaders so that they can control factional conflict within the party.
Resources	Broaden the financial base of the parties.
Autonomy	"Deregulate" the parties; allow them to set their own rules as much as possible instead of having government do it for them.
Policy capacity	Establish an active policy council in each party to work on position papers year round.
Incentives	Increase patronage positions so more party workers can be rewarded.
Candidate assistance	Provide services such as television advertisement production and placement to the party's candidates.

The effect of all of these measures would be to strengthen the parties. Stronger parties would help bring apathetic voters back into the fold of electoral participation and would also provide a strong unifying force to overcome regional disputes in Congress.

Summary

Political parties encompass three separate components: (1) the governmental party comprises the office holders and candidates who run under the party's banner; (2) the electoral party comprises the workers and activists who staff the party's formal organization; (3) the party-in-the-electorate refers to the voters who consider themselves to be allied or associated with the party. Over the years, there have been six major party systems, marked by voter alignments into distinct coalitions.

Parties perform several functions. They create a community of interest that over time bonds disparate groups. They moderate extreme views into more pragmatic, stable, centrist positions. They offer voters a cue for judgment, allowing them to hold politicians responsible for large policy questions. And they serve as a forge for new policy positions by creating national platforms every four years.

The American party system is uniquely a two-party system. While brief periods of one-partyism can prevail, especially below the national level, the greatest proportion of all federal, state, and local elections are contests between the Republican and Democratic parties only.

In recent years, the party-in-the-electorate seems to be declining, insofar as more and more voters prefer to call themselves independent. Moreover, voters have frequently chosen to elect Democratic Congresses and Republican presidents, suggesting that the voters' loyalty to neither party is strong.

Key Terms

political party	spoils system	third-partyism
party identification	issue-oriented politics	proportional representation
governmental party	ticket-split	dualist theory
organizational party	political consultants	national convention
party-in-the-electorate	coalition	midterm convention
direct primary	national party platforms	tracking polls
civil service laws	one-partyism	gender gap

Suggested Readings

Broder, David S. *The Party's Over.* New York: Harper & Row, 1971.

Epstein, Leon. *Political Parties in the American Mold.* Madison: University of Wisconsin Press, 1986.

Kayden, Xandra, and Eddie Mahe. *The Party Goes On.* New York: Basic Books, 1985.

Key, V. O. Jr. *Politics, Parties, and Pressure Groups,* 5th ed. New York: Thomas Y. Crowell, 1964.

Maisel, L. Sandy, ed. *The Parties Respond.* Boulder, Colo.: Westview Press, 1990.

Polsby, Nelson W. *Consequences of Party Reform.* New York: Oxford University Press, 1983.

Pomper, Gerald M., ed. *Party Organizations in American Politics.* New York: Praeger, 1984.

Price, David E. *Bringing Back the Parties.* Washington: CQ Press, 1984.

Riordan, William L., ed. *Plunkitt of Tammany Hall.* New York: Dutton, 1963. (First published in 1905.)

Sabato, Larry J. *The Party's Just Begun: Shaping Political Parties for America's Future.* Glenview, Ill.: Scott, Foresman/Little, Brown, 1988.

Schattschneider, E. E. *Party Government.* New York: Holt, Rinehart and Winston, 1942.

Sorauf, Frank J., and Paul Allen Beck. *Party Politics in America,* 6th ed. Glenview, Ill.: Scott, Foresman/Little, Brown, 1988.

Sundquist, James L. *Dynamics of the Party System,* revised ed. Washington: The Brookings Institution, 1983.

Wattenberg, Martin P. *The Decline of American Political Parties, 1952–1988.* Cambridge, Mass.: Harvard University Press, 1988.

The fabric of the American empire ought to rest on the solid basis of THE CONSENT OF THE PEOPLE. The stream of national power ought to flow immediately from that pure, original fountain of legitimate authority.

Alexander Hamilton

FEDERALIST NO. 22

Both of the chief authors of The Federalist Papers included passages designed to win over the hearts of the colonists. Here Hamilton argues eloquently that elections are the linchpin of democracy, allowing the public to vote into office any candidate they please.

CHAPTER 12

Voting and Elections

Despite the noble sentiments expressed in the quotation that opens this chapter, both Hamilton and Madison did not desire a pure democracy, believing as they did that "mob rule" was an excess to be avoided at all costs. Nonetheless, they would surely have agreed with the novelist H. G. Wells, who, as noted earlier, declared an election to be "democracy's ceremonial, its feast, its great function." For it is through free and competitive elections that the consent of the people is obtained and the government gains its democratic legitimacy.

The United States of America is a democrat's paradise in many respects because it probably conducts more elections for more offices more frequently than any nation on earth. Moreover, in recent times the American **electorate**—those citizens eligible to vote—has been the most universal in the country's history; no longer can one's race or sex or creed prevent participation at the ballot box.

But Hamilton's eloquent words in Federalist No. 22 have been realized only after two centuries of struggle. In Hamilton's time, and long thereafter, women could not vote; slaves could not vote; members of certain religions could not vote in some jurisdictions; those without property were barred from the ballot box in many places, and so on. The history of American elections is in part a study of the contrast between Hamilton's high ideals and the harsh reality of a limited suffrage (the right to vote). Although the denial of a basic right to millions of Americans throughout the country's history is a tragic and depressing fact, the gradual but steady broadening of the voting franchise is an inspiring triumph for those whose courage won them a full measure of freedom—and also for the American system, which has repeatedly proven its ability to redeem itself by fulfilling Hamilton's vision.

The Purposes Served by Elections

Both the ballot and the bullet are methods of governmental change around the world, and surely the former is preferable to the latter. Although the United States has been unable to escape the bullet's awful effects, most change has come to us through the election process. Regular elections guarantee mass political action and enable citizens to influence the actions of their government. Election campaigns may often seem unruly, unending, harsh, and even vicious, but imagine the stark alternative: violence and disruption. Societies that cannot vote their leaders out of office are left with little choice other than to force them out by means of strikes, riots, or coups d'etat.

Popular election confers on a government legitimacy that it can achieve no other way. Even many authoritarian and communist systems around the globe recognize this and, from time to time, hold "referenda" to endorse their regimes or one-party elections even though these plebiscites offer no real choice that would ratify their rule. The *symbolism* of elections as mechanisms to legitimize change, then, is important, but so is their practical value. After all, elections are the means to fill public offices and staff the government. The voters' choice of candidates and parties helps to organize government as well. Because candidates advocate certain policies, elections also involve a choice of platforms and point the society in certain directions on a wide range of fronts, from abortion to civil rights to national defense to the environment.

Regular elections also ensure that government is accountable to the people it serves. At fixed intervals the electorate is called upon to judge those in power. If the judgment is favorable, and the incumbents are reelected, the office holders may continue their policies with renewed resolve. Should the incumbents be defeated and their challengers elected, however, a change in policies will likely result. Either way, the winners will claim a **mandate** (literally, a command) from the people to carry out their platform.

Sometimes the claim of a mandate is suspect because voters are not so much endorsing one candidate and his or her beliefs as rejecting his or her opponent. Frequently this is because the electorate is exercising **retrospective judgment**, that is, voters are render-

Democrat Bill Clinton with his running mate Al Gore (left) and Republican President Bush with Vice President Dan Quayle (right) accept their parties' nominations during the presidential election campaign of 1992.

ing judgment on the performance of the party in power. This judgment makes perfect sense since voters can evaluate the record of office holders far better than they can predict the future actions of the out-of-power challengers. Consider for a moment how voters retrospectively judged recent presidential administrations in reaching their ballot decisions:

- *1968:* No one could know what Richard Nixon's promised "secret plan to end the Vietnam War" really was, but the electorate knew that President Lyndon Johnson had failed to resolve the conflict. Result: Republican Nixon elected over Johnson's Democratic vice president, Hubert Humphrey.

- *1972:* The American people were satisfied with Nixon's stewardship of foreign affairs, especially his good relationship with the Soviet Union, the diplomatic opening to China, and the "Vietnamization" of the war. The Watergate scandal (involving Nixon's coverup of his campaign's bugging of the Democrats' national headquarters) was only in its infancy, and the president was rewarded with a forty-nine-state sweep over Democrat George McGovern.

- *1976:* Despite confusion about Jimmy Carter's real philosophy and intentions, the relatively unknown Georgia Democrat was elected president as voters held President Gerald Ford responsible for an economic recession and his pardon of Richard Nixon for Watergate crimes.

- *1980:* Burdened by hard economic times and the Iranian hostage crisis (one year before Election Day, Iranian militants had seized fifty-three Americans whom they held until January 20, 1981), Carter became a one-term president as the electorate rejected the Democrat's perceived weak leadership. At age sixty-nine, Ronald Reagan was not viewed as the ideal replacement by many voters, and neither did a majority agree with some of his conservative principles. But the retrospective judgment on Carter was so harsh that an imperfect alternative was considered preferable to another term of the Democrat.

- *1984:* A strong economic recovery from a midterm recession and an image of strength derived from a defense buildup and a successful military venture in Grenada combined to produce a satisfied electorate and a forty-nine-state landslide reelection for Reagan over Carter's vice president, Walter Mondale.

- *1988:* Continued satisfaction with Reagan—a product of strong economic expansion and superpower summitry—produced an electoral endorsement of Reagan's vice president, George Bush. Bush was seen as Reagan's understudy and natural successor; the Democratic nominee, Michael Dukakis, offered too few convincing reasons to alter the voters' considered retrospective judgment.

Whether one agrees or disagrees with these election results, there is a rough justice at work here. When parties and presidents please the electorate, they are rewarded; when they preside over hard times, they are punished. A president is usually not responsible for all the good or bad developments that occur on his watch, but the voters nonetheless hold him accountable—not an unreasonable way for citizens to behave in a democracy.

Different Kinds of Elections

So far we have referred mainly to presidential elections, but in the American system, elections—like Heinz products—come in fifty-seven varieties (almost).

Primary Elections

First, **primary elections** are those in which voters decide which of the candidates *within* a party will represent the party's ticket in the general elections. And the primaries themselves vary in kind. For example, **closed primaries** allow only a party's registered members to vote, and **open primaries** allow independents and sometimes members of the other party to participate. (Closed primaries are considered healthier for the party system because they prevent members of one party from influencing the primaries of the opposition party.) There is also the **blanket primary**, in which voters are permitted to vote in either party's primary (but not both) on an office-by-office basis. Happily, the **white primary**, in which all nonwhite voters were systematically excluded from voting, is no longer in existence. White primaries ended when the Supreme Court ruled in *Smith* v.

By the end of the 1992 primary season Bill Clinton had secured the nomination of the Democratic Party for president, but polls suggested that he was poorly regarded by the electorate-at-large. In June, he appeared on "The Arsenio Hall Show" in what turned out to be the beginning of a campaign to improve his image.

Open and Closed Primaries

STATES WITH CLOSED PRIMARIES	STATES WITH OPEN PRIMARIES
Arizona	Alabama
California	Alaska[a]
Colorado	Arkansas
Connecticut	Georgia
Delaware	Hawaii
Florida	Idaho
Iowa	Illinois
Kansas	Indiana
Kentucky	Louisiana[b]
Maine	Michigan
Maryland	Minnesota
Massachusetts	Mississippi
Nebraska	Missouri
Nevada	Montana
New Hampshire	North Dakota
New Jersey	Rhode Island
New Mexico	South Carolina
New York	Tennessee
North Carolina	Texas
Ohio	Utah
Oklahoma	Vermont
Oregon	Virginia
Pennsylvania	Washington[a]
South Dakota	Wisconsin
West Virginia	
Wyoming	

[a] These open-primary states also employ the "blanket primary."

[b] Nonpartisan primary system (that is, all candidates from both parties run for office in an October primary, and if no candidate secures a majority in that election, the two top finishers run against each other in a second primary held in November).

Allwright (1944) that they violated the Fifteenth Amendment to the Constitution. Finally, when none of the candidates in the initial primary secures a majority of the votes, there is a **runoff primary**, a contest between the two candidates with the greatest number of votes.

General Elections

Once the party candidates for various offices are chosen, **general elections** are held, in which voters decide which candidates will actually fill the nation's elective public offices. These come at many levels, including municipal, county, state, and national. While primaries are contests between the candidates *within* each party, general elections are contests between the candidates of *opposing* parties.

General elections come in many varieties because Americans perceive the various offices as substantially different from one another. In sizing up presidential candidates, voters look for leadership and character, and they base their judgments partly on foreign policy and defense issues that do not arise in state and local elections. Leadership qualities are vital for gubernatorial and mayoral candidates, as are the nuts and bolts issues (taxes, schools, roads, etc.) that dominate the concerns of state and local governments. Citizens often choose their congressional representatives very differently than they select presidents. Knowing much less about the candidates, people will sometimes base a vote on simple name identification and visibility. This way of deciding one's vote obviously helps incumbents and therefore to some degree explains the high reelection rates of incumbent U.S. representatives: Since World War II, 92 percent of all U.S. House members seeking another term have won, and in several recent election years the proportion has been above 95 percent.

Finally, members of Congress have a luxury available to no president: the ability to duck responsibility. Whereas presidents are held accountable for everything that happens, legislators can always blame the other 534 people in Congress for inaction, mistakes, and problems.

Initiative, Referendum, and Recall

Two other types of elections are referenda and initiatives. Used in about twenty states, initiatives and referenda involve voting on *issues* (as opposed to voting for candidates). An initiative is a process that allows citizens to propose legislation and submit it to the state electorate for popular vote, as long as they have a certain number of signatures on petitions supporting the proposal. A referendum is a procedure whereby the state legislature submits proposed legislation to the state's voters for approval. Although both of these electoral devices provide for more direct democracy, they are not problem-free. In the 1990 elections, for instance, California had so many referenda and initiatives on its ballot that the state printed a lengthy two-volume guide in an attempt to explain them all to voters. Despite this, many Californians complained that it was virtually impossible for even a reasonably informed citizen to vote intelligently on so many issues.

One other kind of election (or "de-election") is the recall, a procedure found in many states whereby an incumbent can be removed from office by popular vote. Recall elections are very rare, and sometimes they are thwarted by the official's resignation or impeachment prior to the vote. For example, Arizona Governor Evan Mecham was impeached and ousted in 1988 by the state legislature for mishandling campaign finances (among other offenses) just a few weeks before a recall election had been scheduled.

British election varieties pale in comparison. There, one encounters national elections to the House of Commons, which must be called sometime during the five-year life of a Parliament; local elections, which are held every three years; elections to the European Parliament, which occur at five-year intervals; and three instances of national referenda.

Presidential Elections

Variety aside, no American election can compare to the presidential contest. This spectacle, held every four years, brings together all the elements of politics and attracts the most ambitious and energetic politicians on the national stage. The election itself is a marathon—not a single election but a collection of fifty separate state elections in each party, held over a six-month period, to pick convention delegates. The election of delegates is followed in midsummer by the parties' grand national conventions and then by yet another set of fifty separate state elections all held on the Tuesday after the first Monday in November. This lengthy process exhausts candidates and voters alike, but it also allows the diversity of America to be displayed in ways a shorter, more homogeneous presidential election process could not. Every state has its moment in the sun, every local and regional problem a chance to be aired, every candidate an opportunity to break away from the pack.

The state party organizations employ a number of methods to elect national convention delegates. There are six basic systems of delegate selection.

1. *Winner-take-all:* Under this system, the candidate who wins the most votes in a state secures all of that state's delegates. The Democrats moved away from this mode of delegate selection in 1976, and they no longer permit its use because of the arguable unfairness to all candidates except the primary winner. Republicans do *not* prohibit winner-take-all contests, thus enabling a GOP candidate to amass a majority of delegates more quickly. This can give the GOP candidate a head start in planning for the general election.

2. *Proportional representation:* Under this system, candidates who secure a threshold percentage of votes (usually around 15 percent) are awarded delegates in proportion to the number of popular votes won. This system is now strongly favored by the Democrats and is used in many states' primaries. Although proportional representation is probably the most fair way of allocating delegates to candidates, its downfall is that it renders majorities of delegates more difficult to accumulate—and, thus, it can lengthen the contest for the nomination.

3. *Proportional representation with bonus delegates:* This system also awards delegates to candidates in proportion to the popular vote won, but in addition it gives one bonus delegate to the winner of each district. The appeal of this system is that it is a compromise between pure proportional representation and the winner-take-all rule.

4. *Beauty contest with separate delegate selection:* The results of this type of primary have no bearing on actual delegate selection, which usually takes place in later conventions. The "beauty contest" serves as an indication of popular sentiment for the conventions to consider as they choose the actual delegates.

5. *Delegate selection with no beauty contest:* Under this system the primary election chooses delegates to the national conventions who are not linked on the ballot to specific presidential contenders. Well-known names and party-endorsed delegates are often favored under this system.

6. *The caucus:* The caucus is the oldest, most party-oriented method of choosing delegates to the national conventions. Traditionally, the caucus was a closed meeting of party members in each state that selected the party's choice for presidential candidate. In the late nineteenth and early twentieth centuries, however, these caucuses came to be viewed by many as elitist and anti-democratic, and reformers succeeded in replacing them with direct primaries in most places. While there are still presidential nominating caucuses today, such as in Iowa, they are now more open and attract a wider range of the party's membership.

Primaries versus Caucuses

The mix of preconvention contests has changed over the years, with the most pronounced trend being the shift to primaries: Just seventeen states held presidential primaries in 1968, compared with thirty-eight in 1992. The growth in primaries is supported by some who claim that they are more democratic. The primaries are open not only to party activists, but also to anyone, wealthy or poor, urban or rural, Northern or Southern, who wants to vote. Theoretically, then, representatives of all these groups have a chance at winning the presidency. Related to this, advocates argue that presidential primaries are the most representative means by which to nominate presidential candidates. They are a true barometer of a candidate's popularity with the party rank and file. Finally, the proponents of presidential primaries claim that they constitute a rigorous test for the candidates, a chance to display under pressure some of the very skills needed to be a successful president.

Critics of presidential primaries, however, see the situation somewhat differently. First, they argue, although it may be true that primaries attract more participants than do caucuses, this quantity is more than matched by the quality of caucus participation. Compared with the unenlightening minutes spent at the primary polls, caucus attendees spend several hours or more learning about politics and the party, listening to speeches by candidates or their representatives, and taking cues from party leaders and elected officials. Moreover, voters may not know very much about any of the field of candidates in a primary, or they may be excessively swayed by the media, popularity polls, and television ads.

Critics also argue that the scheduling of primaries unfairly affects their outcomes. For example, the earliest primary is in the small, atypical state of New Hampshire, and it receives far more media coverage than warranted simply because it is first. Such excessive coverage undoubtedly skews the picture for larger states that hold their primaries later. Last, the critics argue, the qualities tested by the primary system are by no means a complete list of those a president needs to be successful. For instance, skill at playing the media game is by itself no guarantee of an effective presidency. Similarly, the exhausting schedule of the primaries may be a better test of a candidate's brawn than his or her brain.

The primary proponents have obviously had the better of the arguments so far, though the debate continues, as do efforts to experiment with the schedule of primaries. From time to time, proposals are made for **regional primaries**. Under this system, the nation would be divided into five or six geographic regions (such as the South or the

Senator Robert Kerry (D.-Neb.) campaigning in New Hampshire in February, 1992. New Hampshire's position as the first primary has historically given it unusual influence on presidential elections; candidates spend more time there (often six weeks or more) than anywhere else.

Midwest), and all the states in each region would hold their primary elections on the same day, with perhaps one regional election day per month from February through June of presidential election years. This change would certainly cut down on candidate wear and tear. Moreover, candidates would be inspired to focus more on regional issues. On the other hand, regional primaries would probably cost candidates at least as much as the state-by-state system, and the system might needlessly amplify the differences and create divisive rifts among the nation's regions.

Occasionally a regional plan is adopted. In 1988, for instance, fourteen Southern and border South states joined together to hold simultaneous primaries on "Super Tuesday" (March 8) in order to maximize the South's impact on presidential politics. This was an attempt by conservative Democrats to influence the choice of the party nominee. Their effort failed, however, since the two biggest winners of Super Tuesday were liberals Jesse Jackson (who won six Southern states) and Michael Dukakis, who carried the mega-states of Texas and Florida. This outcome occurred because, in general, the kinds of citizens who vote in Democratic primaries in the South are not greatly different from those who cast ballots in Northern Democratic primaries—most tend toward the liberal side of the ideological spectrum.

The primary schedule has also been altered by a process called frontloading, the tendency of states to choose an early date on the primary calendar. Fully half or more of all the delegates to both party conventions are now chosen before the end of April (see Table 12-1). This trend is hardly surprising given the added press emphasis on the first contests and the voters' desire to cast their ballots before the competition is decided. Ever since 1976, when the then-unknown Jimmy Carter scored an upset win in the Iowa

Table 12-1   1992 Presidential Nominating Season at a Glance

	DELEGATE D	COUNT R	FORM OF DELEGATE SELECTION	DATE OF MAIN EVENT
Alabama	62	38	Open Primary	June 2
Alaska	18	19	Closed Caucus (D)/Open Caucus (R)[a]	April 2
Arizona	47	37	Closed Caucus	March 7
Arkansas	43	27	Open Primary	May 26
California	382	201	Closed Primary	June 2
Colorado	54	37	Open Primary[a]	March 3
Connecticut	61	35	Closed Primary	March 24
Delaware	19	19	Closed Caucus (D)/Open Caucus (R)	March 3
District of Columbia	29	14	Closed Primary	May 5
Florida	160	97	Closed Primary	March 10
Georgia	88	52	Open Primary	March 10
Hawaii	26	14	Closed Caucus	March 10
Idaho	24	22	Open Caucus (D)/Open Primary (R)	March 3
Illinois	183	85	Open Primary	March 17
Indiana	86	51	Open Primary	May 5
Iowa	57	23	Open Caucus[a]	February 10
Kansas	42	30	Open Primary[a]	April 7

(continued)

Table 12-1   1992 Presidential Nominating Season at a Glance (continued)

	DELEGATE COUNT		FORM OF DELEGATE SELECTION	DATE OF MAIN EVENT
	D	R		
Kentucky	62	35	Closed Primary	May 26
Louisiana	69	38	Closed Primary	March 10
Maine	30	22	Open Caucus[a]	February 23
Maryland	80	42	Closed Primary	March 3
Massachusetts	107	38	Open Primary[a]	March 10
Michigan	148	72	Closed Primary	March 17
Minnesota	87	32	Open Caucus	March 3
Mississippi	45	32	Open Primary	March 10
Missouri	86	47	Open Caucus	March 10
Montana	22	20	Open Primary	June 2
Nebraska	31	24	Closed Primary	May 12
Nevada	23	21	Closed Caucus	March 7
New Hampshire	24	23	Open Primary[a]	February 18
New Jersey	117	60	Closed Primary	June 2
New Mexico	33	25	Closed Primary	June 2
New York	268	100	Closed Primary	April 7
North Carolina	93	57	Closed Primary	May 5
North Dakota	20	17	Open Caucus (D)/Open Primary (R)	June 9
Ohio	167	83	Open Primary	June 2
Oklahoma	52	34	Closed Primary	March 10
Oregon	53	23	Closed Primary	May 19
Pennsylvania	188	90	Closed Primary	April 28
Rhode Island	28	15	Open Primary[a]	March 10
South Carolina	50	36	Open Primary	March 7
South Dakota	20	19	Closed Primary	February 25
Tennessee	77	45	Open Primary	March 10
Texas	214	121	Open Primary	March 10
Utah	28	27	Open Caucus	April 20
Vermont	19	19	Open Caucus	March 31
Virginia	92	54	Open Caucus	April 11
Washington	80	35	Open Primary	May 19
West Virginia	38	18	Closed Primary (D)/Open Primary (R)[a]	May 12
Wisconsin	91	35	Open Primary	April 7
Wyoming	19	20	Closed Caucus	March 7
Puerto Rico	57	14	Open Primary	March 15
U.S. Territories	12	12		
Democrats Abroad	9			
Unassigned	262			
Total	**4,282**	**2,206**		

[a]Independents may participate; voters registered by party may participate only in their party's primary or caucus.
Source: Congressional Quarterly Weekly.

caucuses, Iowa's first-in-the-nation delegate selection in February has drawn enormous attention. So has the first primary state, New Hampshire, which holds its election shortly after the Iowa caucuses (see Tables 12-2 and 12-3). In fact, the New Hampshire primary has the distinction of having voted for the eventual winner of the presidency in every election since 1952. Despite this record, the focus on early contests, coupled with frontloading, can result in a party's being saddled with a nominee too quickly, before press scrutiny and voter reflection are given enough time to separate the wheat from the chaff.

Table 12-2   Recent New Hampshire Primary Results

YEAR	TURNOUT	TOP CANDIDATES	PERCENT
Democrats			
1988	123,512	Michael Dukakis	36
		Richard Gephardt	20
		Paul Simon	17
		Jesse Jackson	8
		Albert Gore	7
1984	101,131	Gary Hart	37
		Walter Mondale	28
		John Glenn	12
		Jesse Jackson	5
		George McGovern	5
1980	111,930	Jimmy Carter	47
		Edward Kennedy	37
		Jerry Brown	10
1976	82,381	Jimmy Carter	28
		Morris Udall	23
		Birch Bayh	15
		Fred Harris	11
		Sargent Shriver	8
1972	88,854	Edmund Muskie	46
		George McGovern	37
Republicans			
1988	157,644	George Bush	38
		Robert Dole	28
		Jack Kemp	13
		Pete du Pont	10
		Pat Robertson	9
1984	75,570	Ronald Reagan	86
1980	147,157	Ronald Reagan	50
		George Bush	23
		Howard Baker	13
		John Anderson	10
1976	111,674	Gerald Ford	49
		Ronald Reagan	48
1972	117,208	Richard Nixon	68
		Paul McCloskey	20
		John Ashbrook	10

Source: Congressional Quarterly Weekly.

Table 12-3   Recent Iowa Caucus Results

YEAR	TURNOUT	TOP CANDIDATE	PERCENT
Democrats			
1992	30,000		
		Tom Harkin	76.5
		Uncommitted	11.9
		Paul Tsongas	4.1
		Bill Clinton	2.8
		Bob Kerrey	2.5
		Jerry Brown	1.6
		Others	0.6
1988	126,000	Richard Gephardt	31
		Paul Simon	27
		Michael Dukakis	22
		Jesse Jackson	9
1984	75,000	Walter Mondale	49
		Gary Hart	16
		George McGovern	10
1980	100,000	Jimmy Carter	59
		Ted Kennedy	31
Republicans			
1992[b]	—	—	—
1988	108,838	Robert Dole	37
		Pat Robertson	25
		George Bush	19
		Jack Kemp	11
1984[a]	—	—	—
1980	106,051	George Bush	32
		Ronald Reagan	30
		Howard Baker	15

[a]In 1984, incumbent president Reagan faced no opposition.
[b]Republicans did not hold an Iowa caucus in 1992.
Source: Congressional Quarterly Weekly.

The Party Conventions

The seemingly endless nomination battle does have an end point: the national party convention held in the summer of presidential election years. The out-of-power party traditionally goes first, in late July, followed by the party holding the White House in mid-August. Preempting some of prime-time television for four nights, these remarkable conclaves are hard for the public to ignore; indeed, they are pivotal events in shaping the voters' perceptions of the candidates.

Yet the conventions once were much more than this: They were deliberative bodies that made actual decisions, where party leaders held sway and deals were sometimes cut in "smoke-filled rooms" to deliver nominations to little-known contenders (called "dark horses"—see the "Then and Now" feature on page 436). But this era pre-dated the modern emphasis on reform, primaries, and proportional representation, all of which have combined to make conventions mere ratifying agencies for pre-selected nominees.

It was in the 1830s that the national nominating convention replaced the congressional caucus (an organization of all the party's members of Congress) as the means for selecting the presidential ticket. The national convention consists of a delegation from each state. The delegation, whose size is determined by the national party, includes leaders from the state's various localities. Consequently, the nominee of the convention is, in effect, the choice of a congregation of state and local parties.

The first national convention was held in 1831 by the Anti-Masonic Party. In 1832 Andrew Jackson's nomination for reelection was ratified by the first Democratic National Convention. Just four years later, in 1836 Martin Van Buren became the first non-incumbent candidate nominated by a major party convention (the Democrats) to win the presidency. Unlike the congressional caucus system, the convention is compatible with the federal separation of powers and provides for the broad participation of party members. In addition to selecting the party's presidential ticket, the convention also drafts the party's platform (see Chapter 11) and establishes party rules and procedures.

From the 1830s to the mid-twentieth century, the national conventions remained primarily under the control of the important state and local party leaders—the so-called bosses or kingmakers—who would bargain within a splintered, decentralized party. During these years state delegations in the convention consisted mostly of **uncommitted delegates** (that is, those who had not pledged to support any particular candidate). These delegates were selected by party leaders, and this enabled the latter to broker agreements with prominent national candidates. Under this structure a state party leader could exchange delegation support for valuable political plums—for instance, a Cabinet position or even the vice presidency—for an important state political figure.

The convention today, however, is fundamentally different. First, its importance as a party conclave, at which compromises on party leadership and policies can be worked

In 1836 Martin Van Buren became the first non-incumbent candidate nominated by a major party convention to win the presidency. Previously a loyal vice president to Andrew Jackson (and the last sitting vice president to win the presidency before George Bush in 1988), Van Buren proceeded to solidify the Democrats' party politics through patronage and active leadership.

Then and Now
Dark Horses versus Well-worn Horses

The national party convention of the present day is a different animal from that of the past. No longer is it a deliberative forum for choosing the party presidential nominee; rather, the convention now merely ratifies the choices of the preconvention state caucuses and primaries. A look at the Republican and Democratic Party conventions sixty years apart—in 1920 and 1980—will illuminate one key contrast between the old-style and new-style conventions: the absence of dark horses—relatively unknown candidates who emerge at the convention and occasionally win a nomination as a compromise choice to break a deadlock.

The 1920 Republican convention featured a rift in the party. On one side was the party's old presidential faction, moderate and internationalist, with Abraham Lincoln and Theodore Roosevelt serving as its models. On the other side stood the more conservative wing of the party, with Senator Henry Cabot Lodge of Massachusetts at the helm and including most if not all of Capitol Hill's GOP leadership.

The "presidential" party during those days usually exerted more influence in presidential nominations than did the congressional party. But this changed in 1920 because Lodge's congressional party had garnered more power and influence during the latter part of Democratic President Woodrow Wilson's White House tenure (1913–21), when Wilson was seriously ill and his policies were under attack. Could the two wings of the party compromise on a presidential candidate for 1920? Any such compromise would undoubtedly be difficult to come by because most potential candidates were aligned firmly with one wing of the party or the other.

Senator Warren G. Harding of Ohio was one possible compromise candidate. A small-town politician and one-time editor of a staunchly Republican Ohio newspaper, Harding had a reputation in the Senate based primarily on his capacity to win allies in all factions of the Republican Party. But Harding's chances appeared bleak at the outset of the convention, and after the first ballot, he was considerably behind a number of other Republican hopefuls. Yet, several frontrunners continued to deadlock in ballot after ballot, testing the patience of the delegates who were baking in the hot Chicago summer.

The weather, combined with the seemingly unresolvable convention impasse, spurred a group of influential Senate leaders to meet at a nearby hotel room to attempt to hammer out a compromise—the classic gathering of party leaders behind the closed doors of a smoke-filled room. At the meeting, Harding's name continued to be floated. Although most of the party leaders questioned the Ohioan's convictions and leadership abilities, he did have some attractive qualities: He was handsome (it was said that Harding "looked like a president"), he hailed from a politically important state, and he could be expected to work with leaders of both party factions. As such, the GOP kingmakers decided to test the waters with Harding but agreed to reconvene later in the more likely event that the delegates rejected him. Harding soon went to work to ensure that no new meeting would be needed, however, and he campaigned vigorously for his candidacy throughout the evening, roaming the halls and trying to convince any delegate he could find of his credibility as a candidate.

The deadlock at the convention continued for a few more ballots, but the frazzled delegates gradually realized that Harding perhaps was the only candidate with the potential to secure a majority. This sent frontrunners scurrying around the convention to build a coalition to

out, has diminished. Second, although it still formally selects the presidential ticket, most nominations are settled well in advance. The conventions really serve to ratify the results of primary elections and caucuses. There are three areas in which new preconvention political processes have lessened the role of the convention.

1. *Delegate selection.* The selection of delegates to the conventions is no longer the function of party leaders but of primary elections and grassroots caucuses. Moreover, recent reforms, especially by the Democratic Party, have generally weakened any remaining control by local party leaders over delegates. A prime exam-

stop Harding. They failed, however, and dark-horse candidate Harding—on the tenth ballot—secured enough votes to win the nomination.

The Democrats also needed a candidate to unite the party in 1920, one who could emphasize Wilson's successes yet downplay his failures. After thirty-eight ballots at the Democratic National Convention, no majority candidate had yet emerged, instilling in Wilson a hope that the party might again turn to him as the nominee, despite his deteriorated physical condition. It was one thing for the Democrats to remain loyal to Wilson—which they did by endorsing his policies and paying him homage in the party platform—and another for the party to nominate him for a third term. A turn to Wilson was ultimately unnecessary, as Ohio Governor James M. Cox finally secured the nomination on the forty-fourth ballot.

Conditions are very different today. Nominations are no longer decided in smoke-filled back rooms at the conventions; instead, the critical moments occur well beforehand in the highly visible primary-and-caucus obstacle course that creates not dark horses but well-worn horses by convention time. In 1980, for example, many Democrats were dissatisfied with the Carter presidency. The situation was so dismal for the incumbent president that a strong nomination challenge came from a prominent fellow Democrat, Senator Edward M. Kennedy of Massachusetts. At first, the polls were encouraging for Kennedy—he enjoyed a two-to-one margin over Carter in the summer of 1979. But the Iran hostage crisis—the seizing by Iranian militants of more than fifty Americans from the U.S. embassy in Tehran—led to a sharp rise in public support for Carter, ultimately giving him a decisive margin over Kennedy in the vital early contests. Despite the initial strong challenge from Kennedy and the party's dissatisfaction with Carter's presidency, the latter's nomination was secured by April 1980, before the primaries had ended and four months before the Democratic convention opened. Even with a deep fissure in the Democratic Party, no dark-horse candidate emerged because most delegates arrived at the convention already bound by the rules of the party to Carter or Kennedy.

No dark-horse candidate emerged in the Republican field in 1980 either. The most well-known of the Republicans was a former movie actor and California governor, Ronald Reagan, sixty-nine years old and a conservative who appealed to the right wing of the party. Moderate U.S. Senate Minority Leader Howard Baker of Tennessee and Senator Robert Dole of Kansas were both in the running, as were former Texas Governor John Connally, Representative John Anderson of Illinois (who would later declare himself an independent candidate for president), and George Bush, a former member of Congress from Texas and U.S. ambassador to China. Though Bush won the Iowa precinct caucuses (the first major contest in 1980), Reagan won handily in the next big challenge, New Hampshire, securing almost twice Bush's vote. Like the Democratic nomination, the Republican contest was settled four months before the party convention, and only the brokering over Reagan's choice of a vice-presidential running mate was left to generate excitement at the convention.

The 1980 conventions are typical of those in the modern era, where presidential candidates secure victory by appealing directly to the people, not the party leaders. For better or worse, the deliberative conventions at which dark-horse candidates flourished, such as those of 1920, are probably consigned to the American political past.

ple of this is the Democrats' abolition of the **unit rule**, a traditional party practice under which the majority of a state delegation (say, twenty-six of fifty delegates) could force the minority to vote for its candidate. Another new Democratic Party rule decrees that a state's delegates be chosen in proportion to the votes cast in its primary or caucus (so that, for example, a candidate who receives 30 percent of the vote gains about 30 percent of the convention delegates). This change has had the effect of requiring delegates to indicate their presidential preference at each stage of the selection process. Consequently, the majority of state delegates now come to the convention already committed to a

The Texas delegation to the 1992 Republican convention announces the votes that clinched the nomination of President Bush for a second term.

candidate. Again, this diminishes the discretionary role of the convention and the party leaders' capacity to bargain. In sum, the many complex changes in the rules of delegate selection have contributed to the loss of decision making by the convention. And although many of these changes were initiated by the Democratic Party, the Republicans were carried along as many Democrat-controlled state legislatures enacted the reforms as state laws. There have been new rules to counteract some of these changes, however. For instance, since 1984 the number of delegate slots reserved for elected Democratic Party officials—called **superdelegates**—has been increased, so that all Democratic governors and 80 percent of the congressional Democrats are now included as voting delegates at the convention.

2. *National candidates and issues.* The political perceptions and loyalties of voters are now influenced largely by national candidates and issues, a factor that has undoubtedly served to diminish the power of state and local party leaders in the convention. The national candidates have usurped the autonomy of state party leaders with their preconvention capacity to garner delegate support. And issues, increasingly national in scope, are significantly more important to the new, issue-oriented party activists than to the party professionals, who, prior to the late 1960s, had a monopoly on the management of party affairs.

3. *The news media.* The mass media have helped to transform the national conventions into political extravaganzas for the television audience's consumption. They have also helped to preempt the convention, by keeping count of the delegates committed to the candidates; as a result, the delegates and even the candidates now have much more information about nomination politics well before the convention. From the strategies of candidates to the commitments of individual delegates, the media cover it all. Even the bargaining within key party committees—formerly done in secret—is now subject to some public scrutiny, thanks to open meetings. The business of the convention has been irrevocably shaped to accommodate television: Important roles are now assigned to attractive speakers, and most crucial party affairs are saved for prime-time viewing hours.

Extensive media coverage of the convention has its pros and cons. On the one hand, such exposure helps the party launch its presidential campaign with fanfare. On the other hand, it can expose rifts within a party, as happened at the Vietnam War–torn 1968 Democratic convention in Chicago, when "hawks" supporting the war and President Lyndon Johnson clashed with the antiwar "doves" both on the convention floor and in street demonstrations around the convention hall. Whatever the case, it is ironic that saturation media coverage of pre-election events has helped to cause the convention's loss of anticipation and exhilaration.

Some reformers have spoken of replacing the conventions with national direct primaries, but it is unlikely that the parties would agree to this. Although its role in nominating the presidential ticket has often been reduced to formality, the convention is still a valuable political institution. After all, it is the only real arena where the national political parties can command a nearly universal audience while they celebrate past achievements and project their hopes for the future.

Who Are the Delegates? In one sense, party conventions are microcosms of America: every state, most localities, and all races and creeds find some representation there. Yet delegates are an unusual and unrepresentative collection of people in many other ways. It is not just their exceptionally keen interest in politics that distinguishes delegates. These activists are ideologically more pure and financially better off than most Americans.

In 1988, for example, both parties drew their delegates from an elite group that had income and educational levels far above the average American's (see Table 12-4). Yet the distinctiveness of each party was also apparent. Democratic delegates tended to be younger and more likely to be black, female, divorced or single, and a member of a labor union. Republicans drew their delegates more heavily from those over forty-five years old, whites, married men, and Protestants. GOP conventioneers were also more likely to be elected or appointed officials and to have been at previous party conventions.

Table 12-4   A Comparison of Delegates to the 1988 Presidential Nominating Conventions

	DEMOCRATIC DELEGATES	REPUBLICAN DELEGATES
Level of Education		
High school or less	12%	13%
Some college	19	23
College graduate	22	32
Graduate school	46	34
Household Income		
Under $12,000	2%	1%
$12,000 to $19,999	4	2
$20,000 to $29,999	10	6
$30,000 to $49,999	29	22
$50,000 or more	55	69
Ideology		
Very liberal	8%	0%
Liberal	33	2
Moderate	41	34
Conservative	4	51
Very conservative	1	8

(continued)

Women as Delegates

Since 1980 Democratic Party rules have required that women comprise 50 percent of the delegates to its national convention. The Republican Party has no similar quotas. Nevertheless, both parties have tried to increase the role of women at the convention. Some "firsts" for women at conventions include:

1876—First women to address a national convention

1890—First women delegates to both party's convention

1940—First woman to nominate a presidential candidate

1951—First woman asked to chair a national party

1972—First women keynote speaker

Source: Center for the Study of American Women in Politics.

Table 12-4   A Comparison of Delegates to the 1988 Presidential Nominating Conventions (continued)

	DEMOCRATIC DELEGATES	REPUBLICAN DELEGATES
Age		
18–30	5%	3%
31–44	43	23
45–64	45	59
65 and older	7	14
Race		
White	73%	94%
Black	21	2
Hispanic	4	3
Other	2	1
Marital Status		
Married	68%	84%
Divorced	14	6
Widowed	4	5
Single	15	5
Labor Union		
Member	27%	4%
Not a member	73	96
Sex		
Male	51%	64%
Female	49	36
Past Convention Attendance		
Was a delegate or alternate before	30%	44%
Not a delegate or alternate before	70	56
Public or Party Position		
Elected public/party official	49%	52%
Appointed public/party official	10	20
Both elected and appointed	11	5
Not an official	31	23
Religion		
Protestant	42%	66%
Catholic	30	22
Other/None	28	12

Source: Figures are from a *Washington Post* telephone poll of 501 Republican delegates from July 26 to August 6, 1988, and 504 Democratic delegates from June 21 to July 10. Margin of sampling error is plus or minus 5 percentage points. Figures do not include those who declined to answer the question. Other totals may not add up to 100 percent because of rounding.

The contrast in the two parties' delegations is no accident; it reflects not only the differences in the party constituencies but also conscious decisions made by party leaders. After the tumultuous 1968 Democratic National Convention (which, as noted previously, was torn by dissent over the Vietnam War), Democrats formed the McGovern–Fraser Commission (named for Senator George McGovern and Representative Donald Fraser) to examine the condition of the party and to propose changes in its structure. As a direct consequence of the commission's work, the 1972 convention was the most broadly representative ever of women, blacks, and young people, because the party required these groups to be included in state delegations in rough proportion to their numbers in the population of each state. (Delegations failing this test were not seated.) This new mandate was very controversial, and it has since been watered down considerably. Nonetheless, women and blacks are still more fully represented at Democratic conventions (as Table 12-4 shows) than at Republican conventions. GOP leaders have placed far less emphasis on proportional representation, and instead of procedural reforms, Republicans have concentrated on strengthening their state organizations and fund-raising efforts, a strategy that has clearly paid off at the polls.

The delegates in each party also exemplify the philosophical gulf separating the two parties (see Table 12-5). Democratic delegates are well to the left of their own party's voters on most issues, and even further away from the opinions held by the nation's electorate as a whole. Republican delegates are a mirror image of their opponents—considerably to the right of GOP voters and even more so of the entire electorate. Although it is sometimes said that the two major parties do not present American citizens with a "clear choice" of candidates, it is possible to argue the contrary. Our politics are perhaps too polarized, with the great majority of Americans—moderates and pragmatists overwhelmingly—left underrepresented by parties too fond of ideological purity.

The philosophical divergence is usually reflected in the party platforms, even in years like 1988 when one party attempts to water down its rhetoric and avoid specifics. (The Democrats did so in 1988; the Republicans have done so in some earlier years, such as 1968.)

Selected Contrasts in the 1988 Party Platforms

	Domestic Policy	
	REPUBLICANS	DEMOCRATS
Abortion	"Support human life amendment to the Constitution . . . oppose the use of public revenues for abortion"	"The fundamental right of reproductive choice should be guaranteed regardless of ability to pay"
AIDS	"Emphasize . . . abstinence from drug abuse and sexual activity outside of marriage"	"Protection of the civil rights of those suffering from AIDS"
Taxes/ Budget	"Oppose any attempts to increase taxes . . . call for a balanced-budget amendment and a line-item veto"	"Time for America to reinvest in its people . . . significantly increas[e] federal funding for education . . . homelessness should be ended"
Foreign and Defense Policy		
Strategic Defense Initiative ("Star Wars")	"Committed to rapid and certain deployment"	"Ban space weapons in their entirety"
South Africa	"Deplore the apartheid system"	"Declare South Africa a terrorist state and impose comprehensive sanctions"
Central America	"Assist [*contras*] with both humanitarian and military aid"	"Deliver the promise of peace . . . by the Arias Peace Plan"

Sources: 1988 Democratic and Republican Party Platforms.

Table 12-5 Comparison of the Views of the Public with Those of Delegates to the 1988 Presidential Nominating Conventions

This table displays the views held by delegates to the 1988 Democratic and Republican National Conventions, and it contrasts those views with the positions taken by average citizens who identify with the Democratic Party or the Republican Party, as well as by all the voters taken as a whole. Notice how liberal the Democratic delegates are and how conservative the Republican delegates are, compared with the other groups of less politically active citizens.

Question: "I am going to read a few statements. After each, please tell me if you agree with the statement or disagree with it, or if, perhaps, you have no opinion about the statement." (Figures show percentage who agreed with the statement.)

	REPUBLICAN DELEGATES	DEMOCRATIC DELEGATES	REPUBLICANS	DEMOCRATS	ALL VOTERS
A. The Equal Rights Amendment should be ratified.	29%	90%	56%	74%	64%
B. Black people in the United States are still a long way from having the same chance in life that white people have.	45	83	48	60	53
C. The government should raise taxes now as one means of dealing with the federal budget deficit.	8	44	26	36	31
D. There is nothing wrong with using the CIA to support governments that are friendly to the United States and to undermine hostile foreign governments.	65	21	56	38	46
E. Large corporations have too much power for the good of the country.	14	67	66	79	73
F. We should stop building nuclear power plants because of safety and waste problems.	10	61	48	63	55
G. The military draft should be reinstituted.	26	22	37	37	37
H. There should be a constitutional amendment outlawing abortion.	36	6	36	35	35
I. The government should institute and operate a national health care program.	15	82	61	83	72
J. The United States can meet its national security obligations with a much smaller military.	15	81	43	65	55
K. The United States should take all steps, including the use of force, to prevent the spread of communism.	67	26	65	54	59

Question: "I'm going to read you two statements. I'd like you to tell me if you agree more with the first statement or more with the second statement, or if, perhaps, you can't make up your mind."

The government in Washington should see to it that everyone who wants to work has a job.	12%	70%	30%	57%	44%
It is not the role of government to see to it that everyone has a job.	83	23	66	40	52
No opinion.	5	7	4	3	4

Question: "Would you say you favor smaller government with fewer services or large government with many services?"

	REPUBLICAN DELEGATES	DEMOCRATIC DELEGATES	REPUBLICANS	DEMOCRATS	ALL VOTERS
Smaller government	90%	18%	66%	41%	53%
Large government	4	62	28	54	41
No opinion	6	20	6	5	6

Source: Figures are from a *Washington Post* telephone poll of 501 Republican delegates from July 26 to August 6, 1988, 504 Democratic delegates from June 21 to July 10, and a Washington Post–ABC News telephone poll of 1,147 registered voters from July 6–11, including 560 self-identified Democrats and independents leaning toward the Democratic Party and 501 Republicans and Republican leaners. Margin of sampling error is plus or minus 5 percentage points for figures based on delegates, Republicans and Democrats, and 3 points for figures based on all voters.

The Electoral College: How Presidents Are Elected

Given the enormous output of energy, money, and tears expended just to nominate two major-party presidential contenders, it is difficult to believe that the general election could be more arduous than the nominating contests—but it usually is. The actual campaign for the presidency (and other offices) will be described in the next chapter, but the object of the exercise is clear: winning a majority of the electoral college, a uniquely American institution that consists of duly elected representatives of each state who cast the final ballots that actually elect a president.

The electoral college was the result of a compromise between Founders like Roger Sherman and Elbridge Gerry, who argued for selection of the president by the Congress, and those such as James Madison, James Wilson, and Gouverneur Morris, who favored selection by direct popular election. The electoral college compromise, while not a perfect solution, had practical benefits. Since there were no mass media in those days, it is unlikely that common citizens, even reasonably informed ones, would know much about a candidate from another state. This could have possibly left voters with no choice but to vote for someone from their own state, thus making it improbable that any candidate would secure a national majority. On the other hand, the **electors** (members of the electoral college) would be men of character with a solid knowledge of national politics, able to identify, agree upon, and select prominent national statesmen. Basically, there are three essentials to understanding the Founders' design of the electoral college: (1) It was meant to work *without* political parties, (2) it was designed to cover both the nominating *and* electing phases of presidential selection, and (3) it was constructed to produce a nonpartisan president.

The machinery of the electoral college was somewhat complex. Each state designated electors (through appointment or popular vote) equal in number to its representation in the House and Senate. The electors met in their respective states, each having *two* votes for president, the latter an attempt by the Founders to ensure that at least one candidate would secure a majority of electoral votes needed for victory. The candidate who won the most votes, providing he received a majority of the total number of electors, won the presidency; the candidate securing the second greatest number of votes won the vice presidency. If two candidates received the same number of votes, and both had a majority of electors, the election was decided in the House of Representatives, with each state delegation acting as a unit and having one vote to cast. In the event that no candidate secured a majority, the election would also be decided in the House, with each state delegation having one vote to cast for any of the top five electoral vote winners. In both of these scenarios a majority of the total number of states was necessary to secure victory.

But the Founders' idea of nonpartisan presidential elections lasted barely a decade, ending for the most part after George Washington's two terms. In 1796, their arrange-

People of the Past

How Rutherford B. Hayes Was Elected President in 1876

The story of Rutherford B. Hayes's ascent to the presidency is a fascinating one. It began with the dismal record of Republican President Ulysses S. Grant's administration, the corruption and incompetence of which was so well established by 1876 that the Republican Party's only hope of winning that year's presidential election was probably in running an obscure candidate. It was under these circumstances that Hayes, a little-known former governor of Ohio, received his party's nomination over James G. Blaine of Maine by only five votes on the seventh ballot at the Republican National Convention in Cincinnati. Conversely, Hayes's Democratic opponent, New York Governor Samuel J. Tilden, easily secured his party's nomination on the second ballot.

National prominence aside, both candidates considered themselves reformers. Having played a crucial role in the breakup of the Democrats' New York City machine run by party boss William M. Tweed, Tilden staked his reputation on reform. And Hayes went so far as to vow that, if elected, he would not seek a second term, ensuring that patronage would not be used to secure his re-election.

Again, however, the Grant administration's record combined with the nation's depressed economy made Democrat Tilden the likely victor of the election. Accepting this seemingly inevitable conclusion, Hayes retired to bed early on election evening, and with good reason: Early, unofficial election returns indicated that Tilden had carried New York, New Jersey, Connecticut, Indiana, and most of the South, apparently giving him 203 elec-

toral votes, 18 more than the 185 needed to win. The contest was not yet finished, though. Hayes carried most of the Western United States, and he could still win if he captured the Southern states that had Republican governors. In these states the vote leaned to Tilden but was extremely close. Not ready to concede, Republican Party operative General Daniel E. Sickles telegraphed Republican leaders in Florida, Louisiana, and South Carolina, explaining that "with your state for Hayes, he is elected," and admonishing them to "Hold your state." The Republicans responded with newfound assurance of a Hayes victory, which fueled the ensuing controversy.

In the three Southern states contacted by Sickles, Republican-dominated election boards disputed the legitimacy of many Democratic votes. During the late nineteenth century, voter fraud was rampant, as many states had no registration laws and political parties printed their own ballots. Therefore each state had an election board charged with counting ballots and discounting fraudulent votes. In South Carolina the 5-member board discarded enough allegedly fraudulent votes to give Hayes a narrow 600-vote victory. Florida's election board, too, ultimately pruned enough supposedly fraudulent votes to secure for Hayes a 900-vote victory. Even in Louisiana—where Tilden ostensibly won by 6,300 votes—the election board threw out 15,000 votes, 13,000 of which were Democratic. This allowed Hayes to carry the state by 3,000 votes.

On December 6, 1876, each state's electors formally

ment for presidential selection produced a president and vice president with markedly different political philosophies, which, as we noted earlier, is a circumstance unthinkable in modern times. This happened when a tie vote in the electoral college sent the election into the House of Representatives, which selected Federalist John Adams as president and his political opponent, the Democratic-Republican Thomas Jefferson, as vice president.

The Election of 1800. By the election of 1800, both of the two emerging national parties—the Federalists and the Democratic-Republicans—nominated presidential and vice presidential candidates through their respective congressional caucuses before electors had even been chosen in the states. At the same time, the national parties were also gaining influence in the states, and this resulted in the selection of electors committed to cast their ballots and sent them to Congress for official tallying. In most states the process occurred without incident. But the exceptions—Florida, Louisiana, Oregon, and South Carolina—each forwarded conflicting electoral votes to Washington. Consequently, the result of the initial Washington count included twenty disputed electoral votes—all, of course, claimed by both the candidates—along with 184 electoral votes for Tilden and 165 for Hayes.

How could this crisis be resolved? The Constitution states only that electoral votes be "directed to the President of the Senate," who "shall, in the presence of the Senate and House of Representatives, open all the certificates and the Votes shall then be counted." The document makes no mention of who decides which votes to include when a state's votes are in dispute. Enjoying a majority in the Senate, the Republicans argued that Michigan Republican Thomas W. Ferry, the president of the Senate, should decide. (Henry Wilson, who as vice president of the United States would have been the Senate's presiding officer, had died in office in 1875.) The Democrats, who controlled the House and commanded a comfortable majority in Congress as a whole, contended that the House and the Senate combined should decide. Neither side was able to persuade the other, so in the end a compromise was forged: A bipartisan commission was set up to decide the fate of the disputed electoral votes, the results of which would be final unless *both* houses of Congress vetoed them.

The parties turned next to the issue of the commission's composition, with the result being another moderate compromise. The commission would include four Supreme Court justices—two Democrats and two Republicans—who would in turn select a fifth judge, assumed by most to be Judge David Davis, an independent. Additionally, the commission would include ten members of Congress—five representatives and five senators, of whom half would be Republicans and half Democrats. Unexpectedly, however, Judge Davis refused the invitation to sit on the commission, and Republican Supreme Court Justice Joseph Bradley was chosen instead, giving the Republicans an eight-to-seven majority on the commission.

The commission's partisan colors became obvious as it decided which electoral votes to accept from the four disputed states. In all cases, the Republican majority gave Hayes the disputed electoral votes and, therefore, a 185–184 overall electoral college victory. Thus was the presidency awarded to Rutherford B. Hayes in 1876—despite his receiving far fewer popular votes than Tilden, even after accounting for voter fraud. Despite encouragement from some supporters to march on Washington and seize control of the government, Tilden accepted the results and permitted Hayes to enter the White House. But Hayes was never regarded as a legitimate occupant of 1600 Pennsylvania Avenue by many Tilden backers, and he was frequently referred to as "His Fraudulency" throughout his single term in office from 1877 to 1881.

their presidential and vice-presidential nominees. In other words, the once-deliberative electors lost their independent judgment and assumed the less important role of instructed party agents. This was, of course, a far cry from the nonpartisan system envisioned by the Founders.

The republic's fourth presidential election also revealed a glitch in the Founders' plan. In 1800, Thomas Jefferson and Aaron Burr were, respectively, the Democratic-Republican Party's candidates for president and vice president, and supporters of the Democratic-Republican Party controlled a majority of the electoral college. Accordingly, each Democratic-Republican elector in the states cast one of his two votes for Jefferson and the other one for Burr, a situation that resulted in a tie for the presidency between Jefferson and Burr, since there was no way under the constitutional arrangements for electors to earmark their votes separately for president and vice president. And even though most understood Jefferson to be the actual choice for president, the Constitution mandated that a tie be decided by the House of Representatives. And so it was, of course, and in Jefferson's favor—but only after much energy was expended to persuade lame-duck Federalists not to give Burr the presidency.

The Twelfth Amendment, ratified in 1804 and still the constitutional foundation for presidential elections, was an attempt to remedy the confusion between the selection of vice presidents and presidents that emerged in the election of 1800. To do this, the amendment provided for separate elections for each office, with each elector having only *one* vote to cast for each. In the event of a tie or when no candidate received a majority of the total number of electors, the election still went to the House of Representatives; now, however, each state delegation would have one vote to choose from among the *three* candidates with the greatest number of electoral votes.

The electoral college modified by the Twelfth Amendment fared better than the original design, but it has not been problem-free. For example, in the 1824 election between John Quincy Adams and Andrew Jackson, neither presidential candidate secured a majority of electoral votes, once again throwing the election into the House, which, despite the fact that Jackson had more electoral and popular votes than Adams, selected the latter as president. On two other occasions in the nineteenth century the presidential candidate with fewer popular votes than his opponent won the presidency. In the 1876 contest between Republican Rutherford B. Hayes and Democrat Samuel J. Tilden no candidate received a majority of electoral votes, and the House decided in Hayes's favor even though he had only one more (disputed) electoral vote and 250,000 fewer popular votes than Tilden (see the "People of the Past" box). In the election of 1888, President Grover Cleveland secured about 100,000 more popular votes than did Benjamin Harrison, yet Harrison won a majority of the electoral college vote, and with it the presidency.

Before the election of 1876, Cartoonist Nast was quite confident the Republican Party would easily trample Samuel Tilden and Thomas Hendricks, the Democratic nominees for president and vice president.

After the election: Nast's elephant, battered and bandaged, moan with Pyrrhus, "Another such victory and I am undone." Hayes was elected by a margin of a single electoral vote.

The Electoral College in the Twentieth Century. Although generally more stable, the twentieth century has also witnessed a number of near crises pertaining to the electoral college. For instance, in the already turbulent year of 1968, the potential for the presidential election to be decided in the House was raised considerably with the entrance into the race of third-party candidate George Wallace. And the election of 1976 was almost a repeat of those nineteenth-century contests in which the candidate with fewer popular votes won the presidency: Even though Democrat Jimmy Carter received about 1.7 million more popular votes than Republican Gerald Ford, a switch of some 8,000 popular votes in Ohio and Hawaii would have secured for Ford enough votes to win the electoral college, and hence the presidency.

Patterns of Presidential Elections

The electoral college results reveal more over time than simply who won the presidency. They show which party and which region(s) are coming to dominance, and how voters may be changing party allegiances in response to new issues and generational change.

Party Realignments. Usually such movements are gradual, but occasionally the political equivalent of a major earthquake swiftly and dramatically alters the landscape. During these rare events, called **party realignments**,[1] existing party affiliations are

[1] On the subject of realignment, see Walter Dean Burnham, *Critical Elections and the Mainsprings of American Politics* (New York: Norton, 1970); Kristi Andersen, *The Creation of a Democratic Majority* (Chicago: University of Chicago Press, 1979); and John R. Petrocik, "Realignment: New Party Coalitions and the Nationalization of the South," *Journal of Politics* 49 (May 1987), pp. 347–75.

Superdelegates

Occasionally, a political party finds a new idea in an old one. Such is the case with the Democrats and "superdelegates." Before 1972 most delegates to a Democratic National Convention were not bound by primary results to support a particular candidate for president. This freedom to maneuver meant that conventions could be exciting and somewhat unpredictable gatherings, where last-minute events and deals could sway wavering delegates. Since 1972 all the Democratic conventions have been predetermined by primary elections and the party has been committed to a nominee for weeks or months prior to the convention.

Democrats attempted to add more flexibility to their 1984, 1988, and 1992 conventions and to add the "peer review" of potential nominees that used to take place when party bosses made decisions behind closed doors by allotting several hundred superdelegate slots—positions reserved for the party's high elected and appointed officials. To this point, though, superdelegates have made little practical difference, since they usually support the candidate who has won the primaries. However, if the primary results are ever split and a convention is deadlocked, superdelegates could prove to be critical in the selection of the party's presidential candidate, just as the bosses of old were.

subject to upheaval: Many voters may change parties, and the youngest age group of voters may permanently adopt the label of the newly dominant party.

A major realignment is precipitated by one or more **critical elections**, which may polarize voters around new issues and personalities in reaction to crucial developments, such as a war or an economic depression. In Britain, for example, the first postwar election held in 1945 was critical, since it ushered the Labour Party into power for the first time and introduced to Britain a new interventionist agenda in the fields of economic and social welfare policies. In the entire history of the United States, there have been six party alignments, as indicated by the timeline on page 380; three tumultuous eras in particular have produced significant critical elections. First, during the period leading up to the Civil War, the Whig Party gradually dissolved and the Republican Party developed and won the presidency. Second, the populist radicalization of the Democratic Party in the 1890s enabled the Republicans to greatly strengthen their majority status and make lasting gains in voter attachments. Third, the Great Depression of the 1930s propelled the Democrats to power, causing large numbers of voters to repudiate the GOP and embrace the Democratic Party. In each of these cases, fundamental and enduring alterations in the party equation resulted.

The last confirmed major realignment, then, happened in the 1928–36 period, as Republican Herbert Hoover's presidency was held to one term because of voter anger about the Depression. In 1932 Democrat Franklin D. Roosevelt swept to power as the electorate decisively rejected Hoover and the Republicans. This dramatic vote of "no confidence" was followed by substantial changes in policy by the new president, who demonstrated in fact or at least in appearance that his policies were effective. The people responded to his success, accepted his vision of society, and ratified their choice of the new president's party in subsequent presidential and congressional elections.

Simultaneously, the former majority party (Republican) reluctantly but inevitably adjusted to its new minority role. So strong was the new partisan attachment for most voters that even when short-term issues and personalities that favored the Republican Party dislodged the Democrats from power, the basic distribution of party loyalties did not shift significantly. In 1952, 1956, 1968, and 1972, then, Republicans won the presidency, but the New Deal Democratic coalition was still visible in the voting patterns, and it survived to emerge again in future elections.

These are four examples of alignment-*deviating* presidential elections—elections whose results (the victories of Republicans Dwight Eisenhower and Richard Nixon) were at odds with what would be expected, given the underlying Democratic voting majority in the electorate at the time. (Eisenhower won mainly because of his war record and appealing personality, and Nixon gained the White House thanks to internal splits in the Democratic Party over the Vietnam War and racial issues.) We can contrast these four deviating elections with the alignment-*maintaining* elections of 1940, 1944, 1948, 1960, 1964, and 1976, when the New Deal coalition prevailed in the presidential contests, as Democrats Franklin Roosevelt, Harry Truman, John Kennedy, Lyndon Johnson, and Jimmy Carter won office.

Until recent times, at least, major realignments had been spaced about thirty-six years apart in the American experience. With the aid of timely circumstances, realignments are accomplished in two primary ways.[2] Some voters are simply converted from one party to the other by the issues and candidates of the time. New voters may also be mobilized into action: Immigrants, young voters, and previous nonvoters may become motivated and then absorbed into a new governing majority. However vibrant and potent they may be at first, party coalitions age, tensions increase, and grievances accumulate. The majority's original reason for existing fades, new generations do not remember the traumatic

---

[2]Barbara Farah and Helmut Norpoth, "Trends in Partisan Realignment, 1976–1986: A Decade of Waiting," paper prepared for delivery at the annual meeting of the American Political Science Association, Washington, D.C., August 27–31, 1986.

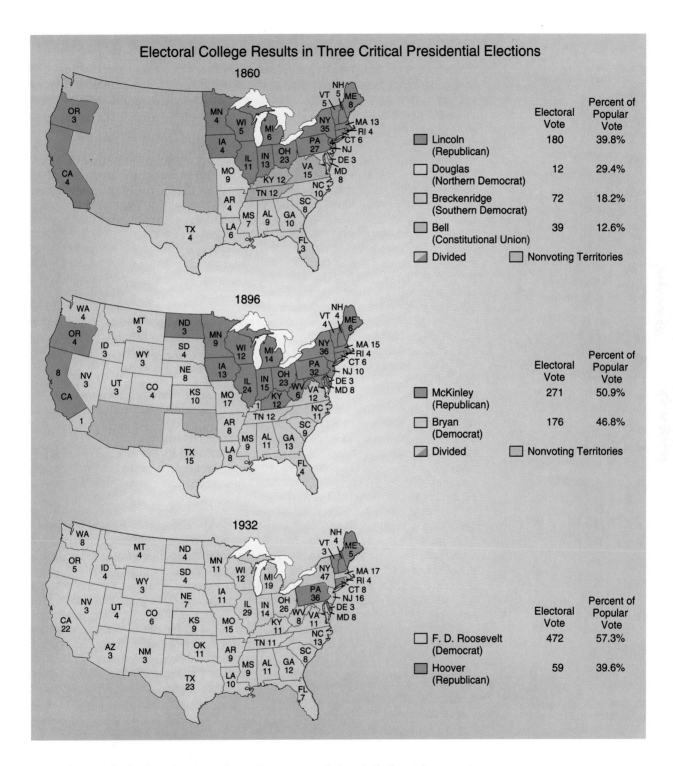

Electoral College Results in Three Critical Presidential Elections

1860

	Electoral Vote	Percent of Popular Vote
Lincoln (Republican)	180	39.8%
Douglas (Northern Democrat)	12	29.4%
Breckenridge (Southern Democrat)	72	18.2%
Bell (Constitutional Union)	39	12.6%
Divided		Nonvoting Territories

1896

	Electoral Vote	Percent of Popular Vote
McKinley (Republican)	271	50.9%
Bryan (Democrat)	176	46.8%
Divided		Nonvoting Territories

1932

	Electoral Vote	Percent of Popular Vote
F. D. Roosevelt (Democrat)	472	57.3%
Hoover (Republican)	59	39.6%

events that originally brought about the realignment, and they lack the stalwart party identifications of their ancestors. New issues arise, producing conflicts that can be resolved only by a breakup of old alignments and a reshuffling of individual and group party loyalties. Viewed in historical perspective, party realignment has been a mechanism that ensures stability by controlling unavoidable change.

By no means is a critical realigning era the only occasion when changes in partisan affiliation are accommodated. In truth, every election produces realignment to some degree, since some individuals are undoubtedly pushed to change parties by events and by their reactions to the candidates. Recent research suggests that partisanship is far more responsive to current issues and personalities than had been believed earlier, and that major realignments are just extreme cases of the kind of changes in party loyalty registered every year.[3]

Secular Realignment. Although the term *realignment* is usually applied only if momentous events such as war or depression produce enduring and substantial alterations in the party coalitions, political scientists have long recognized that a more gradual rearrangement of party coalitions could occur.[4] Called **secular realignment**, this piecemeal process depends not on convulsive shocks to the political system but on slow, almost subterranean demographic shifts—the shrinking of one party's base of support and the enlargement of the other's, for example, or simple generational replacement (that is, the dying off of the older generation and the maturing of the younger generation). A recently minted version of this theory, termed rolling realignment,[5] argues that in an era of weaker party attachments (such as we currently are experiencing), a dramatic full-scale realignment may not be possible. Still, a critical mass of voters may be attracted for years to one party's banner in waves or streams, if that party's leadership and performance are consistently exemplary. Something of this nature began in Britain when Margaret Thatcher led the Conservatives to victory in 1979; thereafter, the Labour Party has lost its hold on traditional sources of support and now faces a difficult road to restored political viability.

Some also contend that the decline of party affiliation has in essence left the electorate *dealigned* and incapable of being realigned as long as party ties remain tenuous for so many. Voters shift with greater ease between the parties during dealignment, but little permanence or intensity exists in identifications made and held so lightly. If nothing else, the obsolescence of realignment theory may be indicated by the calendar; if major realignments occur roughly every thirty-six years, we are long overdue. The last major realignment took place between 1928 and 1936, so the next one might have been expected in the late 1960s and early 1970s.

As the trends toward ticket-splitting, partisan independency, and voter volatility suggest, there is little question that we have been moving through an unstable and somewhat "dealigned" period at least since the 1970s. The foremost political question today is whether dealignment will continue (and in what form) or whether a major realignment is in the offing. Each previous dealignment has been a precursor of realignment,[6] but no law requires that realignment succeed dealignment, especially under modern conditions. It may be that the outlines of the Democratic New Deal coalition will continue to be seen and to prevail in American politics, or that the system may be so dealigned that only short-term and transitory majority coalitions are possible. The other alternative—plausible but without hard evidence to support it as yet—is one more to the liking of Republican activists: a full-scale or rolling realignment of the electorate that builds on the electoral successes of the Reagan and Bush years and producing a stable GOP majority.

[3] Morris Fiorina, *Retrospective Voting in American National Elections* (New Haven, Conn.: Yale University Press, 1981); and Charles H. Franklin and John E. Jackson, "The Dynamics of Party Identification," *American Political Science Review* 77 (1983), pp. 957–73.

[4] See, for example, V. O. Key Jr., "A Theory of Critical Elections," *Journal of Politics* 17 (February 1955), pp. 3–18.

[5] The less dynamic term *creeping realignment* is also sometimes used.

[6] See Paul Allen Beck, "The Dealignment Era in America," in Russell J. Dalton et al., *Electoral Change in Advanced Industrial Democracies: Realignment or Dealignment?* (Princeton, N.J.: Princeton University Press, 1984), p. 264. See also Philip M. Williams, "Party Realignment in the United States and Britain," *British Journal of Political Science* 15 (January 1985), pp. 97–115.

Of course, Republican analysts have been attempting to convince the political world of the reality of major realignment ever since Ronald Reagan's decisive presidential victory in 1980, just as another contingent had tried to do following Richard Nixon's successes in 1968 and 1972. As evidence, GOP boosters point to increased levels of Republican identification, especially by the young, and a string of presidential victories that supposedly imply a Republican ''lock'' on an electoral college majority.

Democrats have insisted that the Republican claims are nothing more than wishful thinking. Resurrecting a popular advertising slogan used as a 1984 campaign retort, Democrats ask, ''Where's the beef?,'' noting their overwhelming edge in local offices, continuous firm control of the House of Representatives, and recapture of the Senate in 1986. Clearly, major changes in the American electorate have been occurring, but these changes may or may not constitute a major critical realignment of party balance. Democrats are not the dominant party they once were, but the GOP has not obtained majority status either. The struggle between the parties for dominance continues, and the outcome is as yet uncertain. For the moment, as for much of the modern era, Americans seem to prefer ''divided government,'' giving the Republicans charge of the presidency and the Democrats the Congress. This may not be a conscious choice, but it is the undeniable result of the electorate's voting habits in recent times. In twenty-six of the forty years since 1952, the presidency has been Republican and one or both houses of Congress Democratic. By contrast, in a parliamentary system like Britain, divided government is an impossibility since the executive is formed out of the legislature.

Congressional Elections

Many elements of the different kinds of elections are similar: Candidates, voters, issues, and television advertisements are constants. But there are distinctive aspects of each as well. Compared with presidential elections, congressional elections are a different animal.

First, most candidates for Congress labor in relative obscurity. While there are some celebrity nominees for Congress—television stars, sports heroes, even local TV news anchors—the vast majority of party nominees are little-known state legislators and local office holders. For them, just getting known, establishing name identification, is the biggest battle. No major-party presidential nominee need worry about this elementary stage because so much media attention is focused on the race for the White House. This is not so for congressional contests, which receive remarkably little coverage in many states and communities.

The Incumbency Advantage

Under these circumstances, the advantages of **incumbency** (that is, already being in office) are enhanced, and a kind of electoral inertia takes hold: Those in office tend to remain in office. Every year the average member of the U.S. House of Representatives expends about $750,000 in taxpayer funds to run the office. Much of this money directly or indirectly promotes the legislator by means of mass mailings and constituency services—the term used to describe a wide array of assistance provided by a member of Congress to voters in need. (Examples: tracking a lost Social Security check, helping a veteran receive disputed benefits, finding a summer internship for a college student, and so on.) In addition to these institutional means of self-promotion, most incumbents are highly visible in their districts. They have easy access to local media, cut ribbons galore, and speak frequently at meetings and community events. Nearly a quarter of the people in an average congressional district claim to have met their representative, and about half recognize their legislator's name without prompting.

This spending and visibility pays off: Reelection rates for sitting House members range well above 90 percent in most election years. Frequently the reelection rate for

Senator Robert Byrd (D.-W.V.) making a speech. Former majority leader of the Senate, Byrd has become a master at promoting himself to his state. His pork barrel tactics have included legislation that relocates federal offices to West Virginia, bringing lots of jobs with them.

What a Difference a Term Makes

In 1990 only one non-incumbent woman, Joan Kelly Horn (D. -Mo.), was elected to the U.S. House of Representatives, and she won by just fifty-four votes. Between 1990 and 1992, however—thanks to redistricting required by the 1990 census and a wave of retirements that followed in the wake of the check-cashing scandal and the Thomas hearings—the greatest number of seats in history came open in the House. In 1992, women won an unprecedented twenty-four new seats in the House (bringing the total to forty-seven) and four new seats in the Senate (bringing the total to six). Ironically, Joan Kelly Horn was one of only fifteen incumbent Democratic House members defeated.

senators is as high, but not always. In a "bad" year for House incumbents, "only" 88 percent will win (as in the Watergate year of 1974), but the senatorial reelection rate can drop much lower on occasion (to 60 percent in the 1980 Reagan landslide, for example). There is a good reason for this. A Senate election is often a high-visibility contest that receives much more publicity than a House race. So while House incumbents remain protected and insulated in part because few voters pay attention to their little-known challengers, a Senate-seat challenger can become well known more easily—and thus be in a better position to defeat an incumbent.

Scandals and Coattails

For the relatively few incumbent members of Congress who *do* lose their reelection bids, two explanations are paramount: scandals and coattails. Scandals come in many varieties in this age of the investigative press. The old standby of financial impropriety (bribery, payoffs, and the like) has been supplemented by other forms of career-ending incidents, such as personal improprieties (sexual escapades, for instance). The power of incumbency is so strong, however, that many legislators survive even serious scandal to win reelection. Congressman Barney Frank (D.-Mass.), for instance, an acknowledged homosexual, hired a male prostitute who then proceeded to run a prostitution service out of Frank's apartment in Washington. This situation became public knowledge in 1989. Though Frank claimed ignorance of the man's activities, he admitted having some of his parking tickets "fixed." Despite the sordid nature of this arrangement, most of Frank's constituents were satisfied with his representation of them and easily reelected him in 1990.

More commonly, the defeat of a congressional incumbent comes as a result of the presidential coattail effect. As Table 12-6 shows, successful presidential candidates usually carry into office a substantial number of congressional candidates of the same party in the year of their election. Notice the overall decline in the strength of the coattail effect in modern times, however, as party identification has weakened and the powers and

Table 12-6   Congressional Election Results, 1948–90

PRESIDENTIAL ELECTION YEARS			OFF-YEAR ELECTIONS		
Gain or loss for president's party			Gain or loss for president's party		
Year/President	House	Senate	Year	House	Senate
1948: Truman (D)	+76	+9	1950	−29	−6
1952: Eisenhower (R)	+24	+2	1954	−18	−1
1956: Eisenhower (R)	−2	0	1958	−48	−13
1960: Kennedy (D)	−20	−2	1962	−4	+3
1964: Johnson (D)	+38	+2	1966	−47	−4
1968: Nixon (R)	+7	+5	1970	−12	+2
1972: Nixon (R)	+13	−2	1974	−48	−5
1976: Carter (D)	+2	0	1978	−15	−3
1980: Reagan (R)	+33	+12	1982	−26	+1
1984: Reagan (R)	+15	−2	1986	−5	−8
1988: Bush (R)	−3	−1	1990	−9	−1

perks of incumbency have grown. Whereas Harry Truman's party gained seventy-six House seats and nine additional Senate seats in 1948, George Bush's party actually *lost* three House seats and one Senate berth in 1988, despite Bush's handsome 54 percent majority. The gains can be minimal even in presidential landslide reelection years such as 1972 (Nixon) and 1984 (Reagan). Occasionally, though, when the issues are emotional and the voters' desire for change is strong enough, as in Reagan's original 1980 victory, the coattail effect can still be substantial.

Off-year Elections

Elections in the middle of presidential terms—**off-year elections**—present a different threat to incumbents. This time it is the incumbents *of the president's party* who are most in jeopardy. Just as the presidential party usually *gains* seats in presidential election years, it usually *loses* seats in off years. The problems and tribulations of governing normally cost a president some popularity, alienate key groups, or cause the public to want to send the president a message of one sort or another. An economic downturn or a scandal can underline and expand this circumstance, as the Watergate scandal of 1974 and the recession of 1982 demonstrated. What is most apparent from the off-year statistics of Table 12-6, however, is the frequent tendency of voters to punish the president's party much more severely in the sixth year of an eight-year presidency (1958, 1966, 1974).[7] After only two years voters are still willing to "give the guy a chance," but after six years voters are often restless for change. Finally, notice in the table that Senate elections are less inclined to follow these rules than House elections. The idiosyncratic nature of Senate contests is due to both their intermittent scheduling (only a third of the seats come up for election every two years) and the existence of well-funded celebrity candidates who can sometimes swim against whatever political tide is rising.

[7] The Kennedy–Johnson years (1961–1969) and the Nixon–Ford years (1969–1977) are each considered an eight-year unit for our purposes here.

Senator Paul Wellstone (D.-Minn.) during his successful campaign to unseat incumbent Rudy Boschwitz in 1990. Boschwitz was the only Senate incumbent who lost in 1990, but Wellstone's victory for the Democrats mirrored several seats that his party gained in the House.

Voting Behavior

Whether they are casting ballots in congressional or presidential elections, voters behave in certain distinct ways and exhibit unmistakable patterns to those political scientists who study them.

The first clear division is between those citizens who vote and those who do not. About 40 percent of the adult population in the United States vote regularly, whereas 25 percent are occasional voters. Thirty-five percent rarely or never vote. There are many differences, socioeconomic and attitudinal, between voters and nonvoters. First, those who vote are usually more highly educated than nonvoters. While a high percentage of registered voters have four or more years of college, many nonvoters tend to have less schooling. This fact certainly suggests that institutions of higher education provide citizens with opportunities to learn about and become interested in politics.

There is also a relationship between income and voting. A considerably higher percentage of citizens with annual incomes over $40,000 vote than do citizens with incomes under $10,000. Income level is, to some degree, connected to education level, as wealthier people tend to have more opportunities for higher education. Wealthy citizens are also more likely than poor ones to think that the "system" works for them and that their votes make a difference. By contrast, lower-income citizens often feel alienated from politics, possibly believing that conditions will remain the same no matter for whom they vote.

There is also a correlation between age and voter participation rates. A much higher percentage of citizens thirty and older vote than do citizens younger than thirty, although voter turnout decreases over the age of seventy because of physical infirmity. Regrettably, less than half of the eighteen- to twenty-four age group is even registered to vote. The most plausible reason for this is that younger people are more mobile and have not yet put down roots in a community, and since registration is not automatic, people who relocate have to go to some effort to register.

Another voter difference is related to race: Whites vote more regularly than blacks. This is due in part to the relative income and educational levels of the two racial groups. Blacks tend to be poorer and have less formal education than whites, and, as mentioned earlier, both of these are factors in voter turnout. Significantly, though, highly educated and wealthier blacks tend to participate in elections to a *greater* degree than their white counterparts.

Although socioeconomic factors undoubtedly weigh heavily in voter participation rates, an interest in politics must also be included as an important factor. Many citizens who vote have grown up in families interested and active in politics, and they in turn stimulate their children to take an interest. Conversely, many nonvoters simply do not care about politics or the outcome of elections, never having been taught their importance at a younger age.

Those who are highly interested in politics constitute only a small minority of the American populace. For example, the most politically active Americans—party and issue-group activists—make up less than 5 percent of the United States' 250 million people. And those who contribute time or money to a party or a candidate during a campaign make up only about 10 percent of the total population. On the other hand, although these percentages appear low, they translate into millions of Americans who contribute more than just votes to the system.

Why Is Voter Turnout So Low?

There is no getting around the fact that the United States has the lowest voter participation rate of any nation in the industrialized world, and it is declining. Only about half of the eligible electorate (that is, those age eighteen and over) voted in the 1988 general presidential election, compared with 62 percent in 1960. In contrast, turnout for British

---

Voter Participation

In addition to income, education, age and race, there are other important variables in voter turnout, including region and sex. Fewer voters show up at the polls in the South than in any other region. By contrast, the highest rate of turnout is usually found in the Midwest, where aggressive voter registration efforts are often held and the culture has long encouraged citizen activism. Voter turnout varies less between the sexes. In the 1950s and 1960s men were slightly more likely than women to cast a presidential ballot, but by 1988 women were a bit more inclined than men to come to the polls. The difference, however, is slight.

A campaign to register voters in Connecticut.

Voter Turnout Around the World

Almost all democracies around the globe have voter turnouts much larger than the United States', as this table shows. Only Switzerland has a voter turnout lower than that of the United States. One reason for America's poor showing is our requirement that citizens *register* to vote before being able to participate in elections. In all other nations listed in this table (except for France) citizens are *automatically* registered by the government or, in the cases of Australia and New Zealand, are compelled by law both to register and to vote.

COUNTRY	AVERAGE TURNOUT IN NATIONAL ELECTIONS[a]
Australia	84%
Austria	88
Belgium	88
Canada	67
Denmark	87
Finland	82
France	77
West Germany	84
Ireland	77
Israel	82
Italy	94
Japan	73
Netherlands	82
New Zealand	84
Norway	81
Sweden	88
Switzerland	43
United Kingdom	75
United States	54

[a] Either all parliamentary elections or, for France and the United States, presidential elections held from 1970 to 1979.

Source: Robert W. Jackman, "Political Institutions and Voter Turnout in the Industrial Democracies," *American Political Science Review* 81 (June 1987), p. 420.

postwar elections has fluctuated between 72 and 84 percent. There are a number of reasons for the low American rates. First, unlike the United States, some nations—such as Australia and Belgium—have *compulsory* voting laws, and not surprisingly they enjoy voter turnout rates in excess of 95 percent. (In some cases, citizens pay a tax if they do *not* vote.) Second, many nations also automatically register all of their citizens to vote. In the United States, citizens must jump the extra hurdle of voter registration. Indeed, it is no coincidence that voter participation rates dropped markedly after reformers pushed through strict voter registration laws in the early part of the twentieth century. Also a factor in the United States' low voter turnout are stringent absentee ballot laws. Many states, for instance, require citizens to apply in person for absentee ballots, a burdensome requirement given that one's inability to be present in his or her own state is often the reason for absentee ballots in the first place. Another explanation for low voter turnout in this country is the sheer number and frequency of elections, which few if any other democracies can match. Yet an election cornucopia is the inevitable result of federalism and the separation of powers, which results in layers of often separate elections on the local, state, and national levels.

Although some of the blame for low voter participation can be laid on the institutional factors we have just reviewed, voter attitudes play an equally important part. As noted previously, alienation afflicts some voters and others are just plain apathetic—possibly

Voter turnouts have varied dramatically in the course of U.S. history, but since the 1830s, presidential elections have always drawn more voters to the polls than midterm congressional elections.

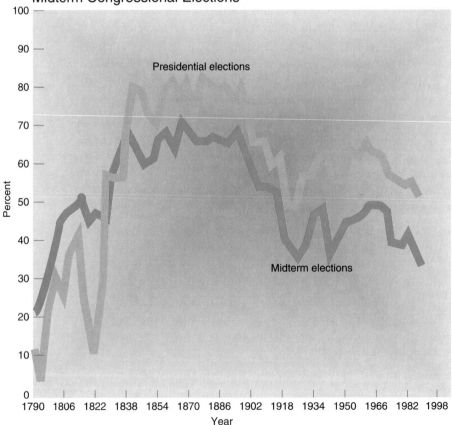

Source: Adapted from Harold W. Stanley and Richard G. Niemi, *Vital Statistics on American Politics*, 3rd ed. (Washington: CQ Press, 1992), Figure 3–1, p. 85.

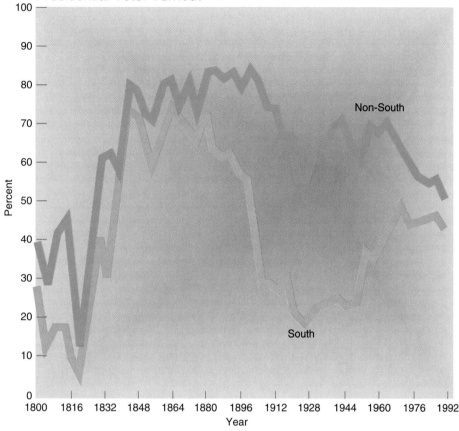

The South Versus the Non-South for Presidential Voter Turnout

Source: Harold W. Stanley and Richard G. Niemi, *Vital Statistics on American Politics*, 3rd ed. (Washington: CQ Press, 1992), Figure 3–2, p. 86.

Mainly because of racially discriminatory registration restrictions, the South had dramatically lower voter turnout than the rest of the nation from the post–Civil War period until the 1960s, when civil rights laws (especially the Voting Rights Act of 1965) eliminated much of the turnout difference. Note that voter participation in the South still remains somewhat below that of the other regions.

because of a lack of pressing issues in a particular year, satisfaction with the status quo, or uncompetitive (even uncontested) elections. Furthermore, many citizens may be turned off by the quality of campaigns in a time when petty issues and personal mudslinging are more prevalent than ever.

Reformers have suggested many ideas to increase voter turnout in the United States. Always on the list is raising the political awareness of young citizens, a reform that inevitably must involve our nation's schools. No less important, and perhaps simpler to achieve, are the institutional reforms. To begin with, many observers propose making it easier for citizens to register to vote. The typical thirty-days-before-an-election registration deadline could be shortened to a week or ten days. After all, most people become more interested in voting as Election Day nears. Mail-in registration could also be instituted so that a citizen need not take time off from work to register. Better yet, all U.S. citizens could be registered automatically at the age of eighteen. Absentee ballots could also be made easier to obtain by eliminating the in-person requirement. A more concise and clear ballot might help, too. A short ballot, where only a few offices are up for election, keeps a sharper election focus for easily distracted citizens; the long ballot, where few offices are appointive and a dozen or more statewide posts are elective, pleases populists but usually results in uninformed voting. Another worthwhile idea is the proposal to make Election Day a holiday. Besides removing an obstacle to voting (the busy workday), this might focus more voter attention on the contests in the critical final hours. Finally, reformers have long argued that strengthening the political parties would increase voter turnout, because parties have historically been the organizations in the United States best suited for and most successful at mobilizing citizens to vote. During the late 1800s and early 1900s, America's "Golden Age" of powerful political parties, one of their primary activities was getting out the vote on Election Day. And even today, the parties' Election Day get-out-the-vote drives increase voter turnout by as many as several million in national contests. Other ideas to increase voter turnout are less practical or feasible. For example, holding fewer elections might sound appealing, but it is difficult to see how this could be accomplished without diluting many of the central tenets of federalism and separation of powers that the Founders believed essential to the protection of liberty.

A New Voting Pattern: Ticket-Splitting

Among citizens who do cast their ballots, an important voting trend cannot be ignored. Citizens have been increasingly deserting their party affiliations in the polling booths, and the practice of ticket-splitting—voting simultaneously for candidates of both parties for different offices—has soared dramatically.

The evidence of this development abounds. As already reviewed, Republican presidential landslides in 1956, 1972, 1980, and 1984 were accompanied by the election of substantial Democratic majorities in the House of Representatives. Divided government, with the presidency held by one party and one or both houses of Congress held by the other party, has never been as frequent in American history as it is today. From 1920 to 1944 about 15 percent of the congressional districts voted for presidential and House candidates of different parties, but from 1960 to 1988, at least 25 percent of the districts cast split tickets in any presidential year, and in 1984 nearly 50 percent of the districts did so. Similarly, at the statewide level only 17 percent of the states electing governors in presidential years between 1880 and 1956 elected state and national executives from different parties. Yet from 1960 to 1988 fully 40 percent of states holding simultaneous presidential and gubernatorial elections recorded split results.

These percentages actually understate the degree of ticket-splitting by individual voters. The Gallup Poll has regularly asked its respondents, "For the various political offices, did you vote for all the candidates of one party, that is, a straight ticket, or did you vote for the candidates of different parties [ticket-splitting]?" Since 1968 the proportion of voters who have ticket-split in presidential years has consistently been around 60 percent of the total.[8] Other polls and researchers have found reduced straight-ticket balloting and significant ticket-splitting at all levels of elections, especially since 1952.

Not surprisingly, the intensity of party affiliation is a major determinant of a voter's propensity to split the ticket. Strong party identifiers are the most likely to cast a straight-party ballot; pure independents are the least likely. Somewhat greater proportions of ticket-splitters are found among high-income and better-educated citizens, but there is little difference in the distribution by gender or age. Blacks exhibit the highest straight-party rate of any population subgroup; about three-quarters of all black voters stay in the Democratic Party column from the top to the bottom of the ballot.

There are a number of explanations for the modern rise of ticket-splitting, many of them similar to the perceived causes of the dip in party identification levels (see Chapter 11). The growth of issue-oriented politics, the mushrooming of single-interest groups, the greater emphasis on candidate-centered personality politics, and broader-based education are all often cited. So too is the marked gain in the value of incumbency. Thanks in part to the enormous fattening of congressional constituency services, incum-

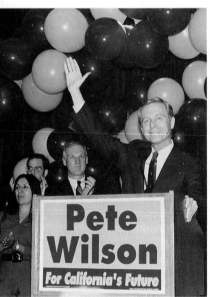

Governor Pete Wilson (R.-Cal.), who presides over a divided state government (the state assembly is controlled by the Democrats). Wilson, a fiscal conservative but social moderate, exemplifies a trend among new politicians that combines elements of both parties' historic positioning. Among the 1992 Democratic candidates for president, Paul Tsongas, Bill Clinton, and Bob Kerrey all shared fiscal conservatism and social tolerance.

---

[8] Cited in Everett Carll Ladd Jr., "On Mandates, Realignments, and the 1984 Presidential Election," *Political Science Quarterly* 100 (Spring 1985), p. 23.

bent U.S. representatives and senators have been able to attract a steadily increasing share of the other party's identifiers.[9]

Toward Reform

Most proposals for electoral reform center on the electoral college, starting with the *faithless elector*—that is, the elector who does not vote for the candidate to whom he or she is committed. In the twentieth century alone, electors have been faithless in seven elections: 1948, 1956, 1960, 1968, 1972, 1976, and 1988. In 1960 Alabama and Mississippi harkened back to the original design of the electoral college by electing a considerable number of "unpledged" electors, rather than supporting either Democrat John Kennedy or Republican Richard Nixon.

Electors in about half the states are required by law to cast a ballot for the presidential and vice-presidential candidates who win the most votes in the state. While some legal scholars have questioned the constitutionality of these laws, the Supreme Court has upheld them, though the laws are obviously difficult to enforce. Any law to remedy the problem of the faithless elector would therefore have to be in the form of a constitutional amendment, either mandating that electors vote for the candidate who wins a state's popular vote or removing altogether the office of elector and automatically awarding a state's electoral votes to the winner of its popular vote.

Other proposals for reforming the electoral college include getting rid of it altogether—that is, holding a direct national election. Such a change would have several major consequences: (1) The popular vote would be the only determinant for winning the presidency. (2) The slight advantage given lightly populated states under the electoral college would be eliminated. Currently, each state (from tiny Rhode Island to gargantuan California) is given the same two additional electoral votes on top of the votes it receives to match the number of representatives it sends to the U.S. House of Representatives. (3) More minor-party candidates would run, since they would no longer be encumbered by the winner-take-all rules of the states and could accumulate votes nationally. In order to preclude a candidate with only a small plurality of the popular vote from winning the election, however, any reasonable plan for a direct national contest would have to stipulate that the winner receive a certain percentage of the popular vote (perhaps 40 percent), with a runoff election necessary between the top two contenders if no one secures that proportion. A constitutional amendment proposing this reform was passed by a wide margin in the House of Representatives in 1969. However, in a vote ten years later, the Senate failed to come up with the two-thirds majority needed to send the proposal on to the states for ratification.

Defenders of the electoral college concede its problems, but argue that they are not serious enough to warrant change. Moreover, many still see value in the electoral college. To begin with, the electoral college helps preserve the contours of federalism by stressing states as the building blocks of presidential victories. Its elimination would hurt small states, which under the current system enjoy slight overrepresentation thanks to the two "senatorial" electoral votes. Finally, opponents of reform argue against an important component of direct popular elections: the *recount* (another count and tally of all votes cast on election day). In extremely close elections, such as the 1960 contest between John Kennedy and Richard Nixon, recounts in a few states with sizable blocs of electoral votes are inevitable, but at least under the electoral college system, recounts can be

---

[9] Thomas E. Mann and Raymond E. Wolfinger, "Candidates and Parties in Congressional Elections," *American Political Science Review* 74 (September 1980), pp. 617–32; Albert D. Cover, "One Good Term Deserves Another: The Advantage of Incumbency in Congressional Elections," *American Journal of Political Science* 21 (August 1977), p. 535; and Gary C. Jacobson, *The Politics of Congressional Elections* (Boston: Little, Brown, 1983), p. 86.

limited to the states in which the numbers are close. With a direct popular election, where only the national vote total matters, a close count would mean the daunting task of recounting every ballot in the nation.

Overall, although individual elections may sometimes be predictable, the electoral system in the United States is anything but static. New generations—and party-changers in older generations—constantly remake the political landscape. At least every other presidential election brings a change of administration and a focus on new issues. Every other year at least a few fresh personalities and perspectives infuse the Congress, as newly elected U.S. senators and representatives claim mandates and seek to shake up the established order. Each election year the very same tumult and transformation can be observed in the fifty states and in thousands of localities.

The welter of elections may seem like chaos, but from this chaos comes the order and often explosive productivity of a democratic society. For the source of all change in the United States, just as Hamilton and Madison predicted, is the individual citizen who goes to the polls and casts a ballot.

In most societies, there is an insatiable itch for change and a desire to better the conditions of life. In authoritarian countries, repression and violent revolution are the only avenues open to check or provide for change. In democratic nations such as the United States, the voters have the opportunity to orchestrate a peaceful revolution every time they visit their polling places.

Elections take the pulse of average people and gauge their hopes and fears; the study of elections permits us to trace the course of the American revolution over 200 years of voting. Much good and some harm has been accomplished by this explosion of balloting— but all of it has been done, as Hamilton insisted, "on the solid basis of THE CONSENT OF THE PEOPLE."

Summary

Regular elections guarantee mass political action and governmental accountability. They also confer legitimacy on regimes better than any other method of change. There are various types of primary elections in America, as well as general elections, initiatives, referenda, and recall elections. In presidential elections, primaries are sometimes replaced by caucuses in which party members choose a candidate in a closed meeting, but recent years have seen fewer caucuses. After the primary and caucus season finishes, parties hold their national conventions to choose candidates—who generally have been determined in advance by the nominating elections—for the general election. In the general election that follows, statewide popular votes are used to determine the composition of the Electoral College, which ultimately makes the formal choice of a president.

Voters tend to vote retrospectively—that is, they judge candidates based on their past performance, or on the past performance of the party in power. Approximately every thirty-two or thirty-six years, voters have realigned into coalitions that redefine the parties and their candidates. These major realignments are precipitated by one or more critical elections, which polarize voters around new issues and personalities in reaction to crucial developments, such as wars or depressions. Voter participation tends to follow certain patterns: the more educated, affluent, and older the citizens are, the more often they vote; also, whites tend to vote more often than non-whites; Southerners vote less often than non-Southerners.

Key Terms

electorate	white primary	electors
mandate	runoff primary	party realignments
retrospective judgment	general elections	critical elections
primary elections	regional primaries	secular realignment
closed primaries	uncommitted delegates	incumbency
open primaries	unit rule	off-year elections
blanket primary	superdelegates	

Suggested Readings

Asher, Herbert B. *Presidential Elections and American Politics,* 4th ed. Chicago: Dorsey Press, 1988.

Bartels, Larry M. *Presidential Primaries and the Dynamics of Public Choice.* Princeton, N.J.: Princeton University Press, 1988.

Berelson, Bernard R., Paul F. Lazarsfeld, and William N. McPhee. *Voting: A Study of Opinion Formation in a Presidential Campaign.* Chicago: University of Chicago Press, 1954.

Burnham, Walter Dean. *Critical Elections and the Mainsprings of American Politics.* New York: Norton, 1970.

Campbell, Angus, Philip E. Converse, Warren E. Miller, and Donald E. Stokes. *The American Voter.* New York: Wiley, 1960.

Ceaser, James W. *Presidential Selection: Theory and Development.* Princeton, N.J.: Princeton University Press, 1979.

Fiorina, Morris P. *Retrospective Voting in American National Elections.* New Haven, Conn.: Yale University Press, 1981.

Jacobson, Gary C. *The Politics of Congressional Elections,* 2nd ed. Boston: Little, Brown, 1987.

———. *The Electoral Origins of Divided Government.* Boulder, Colo.: Westview Press, 1990.

Kelley, Stanley Jr. *Interpreting Elections.* Princeton, N.J.: Princeton University Press, 1983.

Key, V. O. Jr., with the assistance of Milton C. Cummings. *The Responsible Electorate.* Cambridge, Mass.: Harvard University Press, 1966.

Nie, Norman H., Sidney Verba, and John R. Petrocik. *The Changing American Voter.* Cambridge, Mass.: Belknap Press of Harvard University, 1966.

Polsby, Nelson W., and Aaron Wildavsky. *Presidential Elections: Contemporary Strategies of American Electoral Politics,* 7th ed. New York: Free Press, 1988.

Wayne, Stephen J. *The Road to the White House,* 2nd ed. New York: St. Martin's Press, 1984.

*P*eople] will enter into the

public service under circumstances

which cannot fail to produce a

temporary affection at least to their

constituents. There is in every breast

a sensibility to marks of honor, of

favor, of esteem, and of confidence,

which, apart from all considerations

of interest, is some pledge for grateful

and benevolent returns.

James Madison

FEDERALIST NO. 57

In this passage Madison expresses his belief that public servants will be held in high esteem and honor by the constituents who have elected them—at least for a while.

CHAPTER 13

The Campaign Process

James Madison could not have conceived of television, much less negative "attack" commercials used to sully the reputations of all contenders in modern campaigns—so we can forgive him for assuming that every winner is awarded the "temporary affection" of his or her constituents. But in another sense Madison is correct. Each victorious candidate manages to secure the votes of a plurality of those going to the polls on Election Day. The candidate accomplishes this personal triumph by means of the campaign, the process of seeking and winning votes in the run-up to an election.

So far we have focused upon the election decision itself and have said little about the campaign conducted prior to the balloting. Although modern electioneering is advanced, with dazzling technologies and strategies employed to attract voters, its basic purpose is primitive: one person asking another for support, an approach unchanged since the dawn of civilization. The art of campaigning involves the science of polls, the planning of sophisticated mass mailings, and the coordination of electronic telephone "banks" to reach voters. Yet it also involves the diplomatic skill of stitching together disparate individuals and groups to achieve a fragile but election-winning majority. How candidates perform this exquisitely difficult task is the subject of this chapter.

At the Starting Block: Ambition and Strategy

In Federalist No. 57 Madison suggests one of the vital motivations that leads candidates to seek public office: the desire for "marks of honor" and "esteem." Fortunately for our democracy, a fair number of people find the often intangible rewards of public service to be sufficient inducement to enter the public arena. They are willing to put up with abuse from citizens, criticism from the press, invasion of their privacy, and frequently a lessening of income in order to win the honor of office. Despite the common notion that "the office seeks the man or woman," it is personal *ambition* that leads most candidates to the starting gate.[1] The ambition is not always selfish. In addition to a desire for power, a candidate may wish to push an issue or cause dear to his or her heart.

[1] See Alan Ehrenhalt, *The United States of Ambition* (New York: Random House, 1990).

Appealing to various groups: During the first week of March 1992, Governor Bill Clinton campaigned hard in Florida. A densely populated state with a wide range of voters, Florida has been a key early contest for several recent election cycles. On March 4 in Miami, Clinton reiterated a pledge for tax cuts for working people, a position that helped him gain a plurality of both black and white Democratic voters in the statewide contest on March 10.

Whatever their motivations, candidates quickly recognize the realities of running for office. The candidate's campaign must be geared to appeal to both rank-and-file voters and the leaders of various groups and voting blocs (such as business, labor, and key ethnic populations). The candidate must find issues that motivate voters, and he or she must take defensible stands on the controversies of the day. Unavoidably, the candidate must also raise large sums of money in order to compete, as we will discuss later.

The Structure of a Campaign

A campaign for high office (such as the presidency, a governorship, or a U.S. Senate seat) is a highly complex effort akin to running a multimillion-dollar business, while campaigns for local offices are usually simple mom-and-pop operations. But all campaigns, no matter what their size, have certain aspects in common. Indeed, each campaign really consists of several campaigns that are being run simultaneously, including the following.

1. The **nomination campaign.** The target here is the party elite, the leaders and activists who choose nominees in primaries or conventions. Party leaders are concerned with electability while activists are often ideological and issue oriented, so a candidate must appeal to both bases.
2. The **general election campaign.** A far-sighted candidate never forgets the ultimate goal: winning the general election. Therefore, he or she tries to avoid taking stands that, however pleasing to party activists in the primary, will alienate a majority of the larger general election constituency.
3. The **personal campaign.** This is the public part of the campaign. The candidate and his or her family and supporters make appearances, meet voters, hold press conferences, and give speeches.
4. The **organizational campaign.** Behind the scenes, another campaign is humming. Volunteers telephone voters and distribute literature, staffers organize events, and everyone raises money to support the operation.
5. The **media campaign.** On television and radio the candidate's advertisements (termed **paid media**) air frequently in an effort to convince the public that the candidate is the best person for the job. Meanwhile, campaigners attempt to influence the press coverage of the campaign by the print and electronic news reporters—the **free media.**

British election campaigns could not be more distinctive. In the first place, candidate selection is controlled by local party organizations. Second, the national parties control key facets of the campaign, insofar as they provide the financing, which is regulated by national statute, and they execute the campaign strategy. As a result, national party platforms—not candidate personalities—play a dominant role in the campaign. Finally, the power of the prime minister to call elections at his or her discretion—literally at a moment's notice—produces campaigns of a mere four to five weeks in duration.

In order to better comprehend campaigns, let's examine a few aspects of each of them, remembering that they must all mesh together successfully for the candidate to win.

The Nomination Campaign

A new candidate gets "sea legs" early on, as he or she adjusts to the pressures of being in the spotlight day in and day out. This is the time to learn that a single careless phrase could end the campaign or guarantee a defeat. This is also the time to seek the support of party leaders and interest groups and test out themes, slogans, and strategies. The press and public will be far more forgiving of mistakes made at this point, and they will take far less notice of shifts in strategy than they will later in the general election campaign.

At this time, there is a danger not widely recognized by candidates: Surrounded by friendly activists and ideological soulmates in the quest to win the party's nomination, a candidate can move too far to the right or left and become too extreme for the November electorate. Conservative Barry Goldwater, the 1964 Republican nominee for president, and liberal George McGovern, the 1972 Democratic nominee for president, both fell victim to this phenomenon in seeking their party's nomination, and they were handily defeated in the general elections by Presidents Lyndon Johnson and Richard Nixon, respectively.

The General Election Campaign

Once the choice is clear between the two major-party nominees, both candidates can go to work. Most significant interest groups are courted for money and endorsements, although the results are mainly predictable: liberal, labor, and minority groups usually back Democrats, while conservative and business organizations support Republicans. The most active and intense groups are often huddled around emotional issues such as abortion and gun control, and these organizations can produce a bumper crop of money and activists for favored candidates.

Virtually all candidates adopt a brief theme, or slogan, to serve as a rallying cry in their quest for office. Some of the presidential campaign slogans have entered national lore (see Table 13-1), but most are nondescript and can fit many candidates ("She thinks like us," "He's on our side," "She hears you," "You know where he stands"). Candidates try to avoid controversy in their selection of slogans, and some openly eschew ideology. (An ever-popular one of this genre: "Not left, not right—forward!") The clever candidate also attempts to find a slogan that cannot be lampooned easily. In 1964 Barry Goldwater's handlers may have regretted their choice of "In your heart you know he's right" when Lyndon Johnson's supporters quickly converted it into "In your guts you

---

Table 13-1   Famous Presidential Campaign Slogans

PRESIDENTIAL CANDIDATE	SLOGAN
William Henry Harrison (Whig, 1840)	"Tippecanoe and Tyler, Too"[a]
Calvin Coolidge (Republican, 1924)	"Keep Cool with Coolidge"
Herbert Hoover (Republican, 1928)	"A Chicken in Every Pot, a Car in Every Garage."
Dwight Eisenhower (Republican, 1952)	"I Like Ike"
Lyndon Johnson (Democrat, 1964)	"All the Way with LBJ"
Barry Goldwater (Republican, 1964)	"In Your Heart You Know He's Right"
George Wallace (Independent, 1968)	"Send Them a Message"
Richard Nixon (Republican, 1968)	"Nixon's the One!"
Richard Nixon (Republican, 1972)	"Now More Than Ever"
Jimmy Carter (Democrat, 1976)	"Why Not the Best?"
Ronald Reagan (Republican, 1984)	"It's Morning in America"

[a]Tippecanoe was a nickname given Harrison—a reference to his participation in the battle of Tippecanoe—and Tyler was Harrison's vice presidential candidate, John Tyler of Virginia.

Right-wing 1964 Republican candidate Barry Goldwater's famous slogan, "In your heart, you know he's right" was quickly lampooned by incumbent Democratic opponent President Lyndon Johnson's campaign as "In your guts you know he's nuts."

know he's nuts." (Democrats were trying to portray Goldwater as a warmonger after the Republican indicated a willingness to use nuclear weapons in Vietnam and elsewhere under some conditions.)

The Personal Campaign

In the effort to show voters that they are hard-working, thoughtful, and worthy of the office they seek, candidates try to meet personally as many citizens as possible in the course of a campaign. A candidate for high office may deliver up to a dozen speeches a day, and that is only part of the exhausting schedule maintained by most contenders. The day may begin at 5:00 A.M. at the entrance gate to an auto plant with an hour or two of handshaking, followed by similar gladhanding at subway stops until 9:00. Strategy

On February 12, 1992, President Bush formally announced his candidacy in Washington and then quickly flew to New Hampshire to begin campaigning with voters at the Bedford, New Hampshire Mall.

sessions with key advisers and preparation for upcoming presentations and forums may fill the morning. A talk at a luncheon, afternoon fund raisers, and a series of television and print interviews crowd the afternoon agenda. The light fare of cocktail parties is followed by a dinner speech, perhaps some telephone or neighborhood canvassing of voters, and a civic-forum talk or two. More meetings with advisers and planning for the next day's events can easily take a candidate past midnight. With only a few hours of sleep, it starts all over again, and after months of this kind of grueling pace, the candidate may well be on auto pilot and unable to think clearly. Beyond the strains this fast-lane existence adds to a candidate's family life, this hectic schedule leaves little time for reflection and long-range planning. And is it any wonder that many candidates commit gaffes and appear to have foot-in-mouth disease under these conditions?

Of course there are considerable rewards to be had on the campaign trail that balance the personal disadvantages. A candidate can affect the course of his or her government and community and in so doing become a person who is admired and respected by peers. Meeting all manner of people, solving problems, gaining exposure to every facet of life in one's constituency—these help a public person live life fully and compensate for the hardships of the campaign trail.

The Organizational Campaign

If the candidate is the public face of the campaign, the organization behind the candidate is the private face. Depending on the level of the office sought, the organizational staff can consist of a handful of volunteers or hundreds of paid specialists supplementing the work of thousands of volunteers. The most elaborate structure is found in presidential campaigns. Tens of thousands of volunteers distribute literature and visit neighborhoods. They are directed by paid staff that may number 300 or more, including a couple of dozen lawyers and accountants. At the top of the organizational chart are the campaign manager and the key political consultants, the hired handlers who provide technologies, services, and strategies to the campaign. The best-known consultants for any campaign are usually the **media consultant,** who produces the candidate's television and radio advertisements; the **pollster,** who takes the public opinion surveys that guide the cam-

Media consultants arrange everything from paid advertising to daily photo opportunities, such as this Oval Office setting for President Bush.

Figure 13-1   The Organizational Campaign

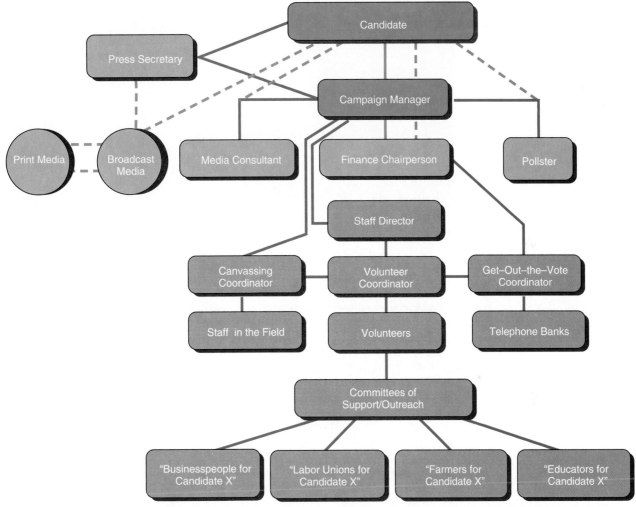

Every campaign is organized a bit differently, but most campaigns for office have the common elements listed here. Note that the key personnel (such as the consultants and the finance chair) have direct access to the candidate, even though they technically report to the campaign manager.

paign; and the **direct mailer,** who supervises direct-mail fund raising. After the candidate, however, the most important person to the campaign is probably the finance chair, who is responsible for bringing in the large contributions that pay most of the salaries of the consultants and staff.

In addition to raising money, the most vital work of the candidate's organization is to get in touch with voters. Some of this is done in person by volunteers who walk the neighborhoods going door-to-door to solicit votes. Some is accomplished by telephone as volunteers use computerized telephone banks to call targeted voters with scripted messages. Both contact methods are termed **voter canvass.** Most canvassing takes place in the month before the election, when voters are paying attention. Close to Election Day, the telephone banks begin the vital **get-out-the-vote** (GOTV) effort, reminding supporters to vote and arranging for their transportation to the polls if necessary. (See Figure 13-1 for a summary graph of a campaign's basic organization.)

Conservative Republican challenger Pat Buchanan, running against his own party's incumbent President Bush, struggled with low funds throughout the campaign. Trying to make the most of his money, he used intentionally inflammatory commercials that would be remembered despite their scarcity. In this commercial he attacked the National Endowment for the Arts' support of what Buchanan termed "shocking and blasphemous" artworks.

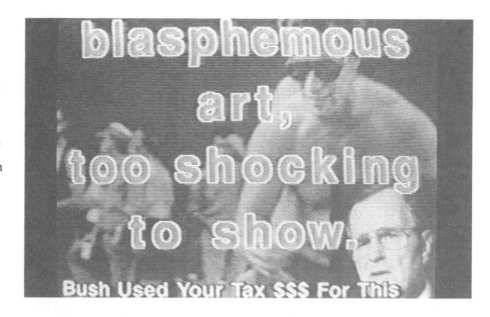

The Media Campaign

What voters actually see and hear of the candidate is mainly determined by the free media (newspaper and television coverage) and the paid media (such as television advertising) accompanying the campaign. The two kinds of media are fundamentally different: Paid advertising is completely under the control of the campaign, whereas the press is totally independent. Great care is taken in the design of the television advertising, which takes many approaches. **Positive ads** stress the candidate's qualifications, family, and issue positions with no direct reference to the opponent. **Negative ads** attack the opponent's character and platform and (save for a brief legal identification at the ad's conclusion) may not even mention the candidate paying for their airing. **Contrast ads** compare the records and proposals of the candidates—obviously with a bias toward the sponsor.

Occasionally, these advertisements are relatively long (from four-and-a-half-minute ads up to thirty-minute documentaries), but usually the messages are short **spot ads** of sixty-, thirty-, or ten-second durations. There is little question that the category of advertisements showing the greatest growth in the past two decades has been negative spots. While voters normally need a reason to vote *for* a candidate, they also frequently vote *against* the other candidate—and negative ads can provide the critical justification for such a vote.

Prior to the 1980s, well-known incumbents usually ignored negative attacks from their challengers, believing that the proper stance was to be "above the fray." But after some well-publicized defeats of incumbents in the early 1980s in which negative television advertising played a prominent role,[2] incumbents began attacking their challengers with relish. The new rule of politics became "An attack unanswered is an attack agreed to." In a further attempt to stave off brickbats from challengers, incumbents even began anticipating the substance of their opponents' attacks and airing inoculation advertising early in the campaign to protect themselves in advance of the other side's spots. For example, a senator who fears a broadside about her voting record on Social Security issues might air advertisements featuring senior citizens praising her support of Social Security.

[2] Five liberal Democratic U.S. senators, including George McGovern of South Dakota, were defeated in this fashion in 1980, for example.

People of the Past

William Henry Harrison and the Media Campaign of 1840

The political historian Keith Melder, among others, has argued that William Henry Harrison's 1840 run for the presidency was the first media campaign, complete with the creation of an image and the means for selling it to the public.

Harrison's campaign began with his pursuit of the Whig Party's nomination, for which Harrison—an accomplished general but a political novice—ran against Henry Clay and Daniel Webster, both experienced politicians. In the very first Whig national convention, party leaders unfriendly to Clay and Webster rigged the rules in Harrison's favor, guaranteeing his nomination. They also added Virginian John Tyler to the ticket as the vice-presidential candidate for geographical balance. (Harrison, although also a native of Virginia, was governor of Indiana.) Moreover, since the party was divided over many issues, the leadership decided early on that waging a colorful and insubstantial campaign would be the best route to victory in a year when the incumbent Democratic president, Martin Van Buren, was already weakened by a severe economic depression.

Ironically, Harrison's key image was provided not by his own party but by a Democratic newspaper out of Baltimore, which caricatured Harrison as a cider-swilling, log cabin–dwelling simpleton. Unfortunately for the Democrats, the Whig Party took hold of this sarcasm and converted it into a powerful campaign theme for the candidate. Harrison, the Whig Party claimed, resided in a log cabin (actually, only the original structure of his home was made from logs) and supposedly possessed all the virtuous qualities of the hard-working frontiersman.

The log cabin issue was pushed vigorously by the Whigs, who used banners, ribbons, songs, and "cabin raisings"—the construction of log cabins in many communities to serve as the local Whig Party headquarters—to get their message to the public. The Whig Party created a campaign newspaper—named, of course, the *Log Cabin*—that featured speeches by eloquent Whigs and, in a true harbinger of things to come, peddled campaign banners and log cabin gadgets considered indispensable to the loyal Harrison supporter. In another first, the candidate himself spoke often (a total of twenty-three speeches) on behalf of his candidacy. Before 1840, it was considered improper for the candidate to participate directly in the electioneering process.

The Harrison campaign of 1840, then, was the first to sell a candidate as a national product, and it became the model for many presidential campaigns to follow. The Democrats complained mightily about Whig "showboating," but when Harrison easily defeated Van Buren, the Whig methods seemed vindicated. As for the voters, they clearly preferred the new style of campaigning. Not only did Harrison win handsomely, but nearly 80 percent of those eligible to vote turned out at the polls—a remarkable proportion at that time, or in ours. (In 1988 only 50 percent of the eligible voters cast a ballot for president.) Tragically for Harrison, his election was the high point of the briefest of all presidencies. After catching cold at his March 1841 inauguration, Harrison died in April, serving for only one month as president.

The Candidate or the Campaign: Which Do We Vote For?

One important point about media and organizational techniques needs to be made. Much is said and written about them during the campaign, and they are often presented as political magic. Yet although campaign methods have clearly become very sophisticated, the technologies still often fail the candidates and their campaigns. The political consultants who develop and master the technologies of polling, media, and so on frequently make serious mistakes in judgment and despite popular lore and journalistic legend, few candidates are the creations of their clever consultants and dazzling campaign techniques. Partly this is because politics always has been (and always will be) far more art than science, not subject to precise manipulation or formulaic computation. *In the end—in most cases—the candidate wins or loses the race according to his or her abilities, qualifications, communication skills, and weaknesses.* Although this simple truth is warmly reassuring, it has been remarkably overlooked by election analysts and reporters seemingly mesmerized by the exorbitant claims of consultants and the flashy computer lights of their technologies.[3]

The voter deserves much of the credit for whatever encouragement we can draw from this candidate-centered view of politics. Granted, citizens are often inattentive to politics and, in effect, force candidates to use empty slogans and "glitz" to attract their attention. But it is also true that most voters want to take the real measure of candidates and retain a healthy skepticism about the techniques of running for office. The political cartoonist Tom Toles suggested as much when he depicted the seven preparatory steps the modern candidate takes: (1) set out to discover what voters want; (2) conduct extensive polling;

[3] See Larry Sabato, ed., *Campaigns and Elections: A Reader in Modern American Politics* (Glenview, Ill.: Scott, Foresman, 1989), pp. 3–4.

Famous "Soundbites" from Recent Presidential Campaigns

1988 "Read my lips; no new taxes."
— George Bush (R)

"This election isn't about ideology; it's about competence."
— Michael Dukakis (D)

"Stop lying about my record!"
— Senator Bob Dole (R), speaking to George Bush during their campaign for the Republican nomination.

"I knew Jack Kennedy, he was a friend of mine. And Senator, you're no Jack Kennedy."
— Democratic vice-presidential nominee Lloyd Bentsen, responding in an October debate to GOP nominee Dan Quayle's comparison of himself to Kennedy.

"Follow me around . . . [you'll] be very bored."
— Gary Hart (D) to a reporter shortly before his May 1987 weekend with model Donna Rice.

1984 "Where's the beef?"
— Walter Mondale to his Democratic rival Gary Hart, who claimed to have "new ideas."

1980 "There you go again . . ."
— Ronald Reagan (R) to President Jimmy Carter (D), in response to some of Carter's charges against Reagan in a debate.

"Are you better off today than you were four years ago?"
— Reagan's oft-repeated question to the voters.

"I'll whip his ass."
— President Carter's pledge to defeat Senator Edward Kennedy's challenge to his renomination.

The accommodations of the Democratic Party contenders vary from a Regency Hotel suite to the basement of a city brownstone. Here, campaign workers of Governor Bill Clinton worked out of offices in Times Square, New York.

(3) study demographic trends; (4) engage in sophisticated interpretation of in-depth voter interviews; (5) analyze results; (6) discover that what the voters want is a candidate who doesn't need to do steps one through five; (7) pretend you didn't. The chastened politician tells his assembled throng, "I follow my conscience."[4]

Modern Campaign Challenges

The modern candidate faces two major challenges: communicating through the media and raising the money needed to stay in the race. We will consider these in turn.

The News Media

The news media present quite a challenge to candidates. Although politicians and their staffs cannot control the press, they nonetheless try to manipulate coverage. Three techniques are employed to accomplish this aim. First, the staff often seeks to isolate the candidate from the press, thus reducing the chances that reporters will bait a candidate into saying something that might damage his or her cause. Naturally, the media are frustrated by such a tactic and insist on as many open press conferences as possible. Second, the campaign stages "media events"—activities designed to include brief, clever quotes called soundbites and staged with appealing backdrops so that they are all but irresistible to television news in particular. In this fashion the candidate's staff can successfully fill the "news hole" reserved for campaign coverage on the evening news programs and in the morning papers. Third, the handlers and consultants have perfected the technique termed "spin"—that is, they put the most favorable possible interpretation for their candidate on any circumstance occurring in the campaign, and they "work" the press to sell their point of view or at least to ensure that it is included in the reporters' stories. **Candidate debates,** especially the televised presidential variety, are showcases for the consultants' spin patrol, and teams of staffers from each side swarm the press rooms to declare victory even before the candidates finish their closing statements.

In Britain, where the House of Commons is structured to provide continuous debate between government and opposition, resort to such media extravaganza is for the most part superfluous. To be sure, television plays an increasingly important role as a forum for

[4] From a 1987 cartoon by Tom Toles, copyrighted by the *Buffalo News.*

party clashes in British politics, but in no way does it achieve the prominence of American television.

Televised Debates. Candidate debates are media extravaganzas that are a hybrid of free and paid media. Like ads, much of the candidate dialogue (jokes included) is canned and pre-packaged. Yet spontaneity cannot be completely eliminated, and gaffes, quips, and slips of the tongue can sometimes be revealing. President Gerald Ford's insistence during an October 1976 debate with Jimmy Carter that Poland was not under Soviet domination may well have cost him a close election. Ronald Reagan's refrain, "Are you better off today than you were four years ago?" neatly summed up his case against Carter in 1980; moreover, Reagan's easygoing performance reassured a skeptical public that wanted Carter out of the White House but was not certain it wanted Reagan in. Senator John Kennedy's visually impressive showing in the first 1960 presidential debate dramatically reduced the utility of two-term Vice President Richard Nixon's "experience" edge. Not only was Nixon ill at the time, he was also poorly dressed and poorly made up for television. Interestingly, most of those who heard the debate on radio—and therefore could not see the contrast between the pale, anxious, sweating Nixon and the relaxed, tanned Kennedy—thought that Nixon had won.

The importance of debates can easily be overrated, however. A weak performance by Reagan in his first debate with Walter Mondale in 1984 had little lasting effect, in part because Reagan did better in the second one. And most of the debates in 1960, 1976, 1980, and 1988 were unmemorable and electorally inconsequential. Debates usually just firm up the voting predispositions of most Americans and cannot change the fundamentals of an election (the state of the economy, scandal, presidential popularity, and so on). Nonetheless, because debates are potentially educational and focus the public mind on the upcoming election, they are useful. Since they have been held in every presidential campaign from 1976 on, debates are now likely to be an expected and standard part of the presidential election process.[5] They are also an established feature of campaigns for governor, U.S. senator, and many other offices.

---

[5] Incumbents or frontrunners refused to participate in suggested presidential debates in 1964, 1968, and 1972, but precedent would now probably make such a decision a costly one for any presidential contender, even an incumbent.

Democratic candidate Bill Clinton makes a point during the second of three presidential debates in the 1992 election campaign. This debate, held in Richmond, Virginia, had an unusually informal format that allowed the candidates to move about the stage as they responded to questions from an audience of uncommitted voters.

The "Outsider" Candidate

Whenever Washington is especially unpopular, most presidential candidates adopt the "outsider" label and become crusaders for change. Democrat Jimmy Carter did this successfully in 1976 against longtime insider Gerald Ford, but he was on the receiving end when he lost to Ronald Reagan in 1980. Reagan, who attacked the federal government even while in office, never lost the outsider glow and used it again in 1984 to defeat former Vice President Walter Mondale, another insider. George Bush, a classic insider, profited from peace, prosperity, and Reagan's successes to win election in 1988, but in 1992 a serious recession again tarnished Washington's image. Democrats jockeyed to portray themselves as outsiders, and Bush joined the eventual Democratic nominee, Bill Clinton, in trying to portray himself as one also. Both were outflanked by Ross Perot, who was untainted by any prior political candidacy. In 1992, then, Americans were treated to the amusing spectacle of an incumbent president, a long-serving governor, and a billionaire all claiming "outsider" innocence.

Can the Press Be "Handled"? Whether in debates or elsewhere, efforts by candidates to manipulate the news media often fail because the press is wise to their tactics and determined to thwart them. Not even the candidates' paid media is sacrosanct anymore. The press, especially major newspapers throughout the country, has taken to analyzing the accuracy of the television advertisements aired during the campaign—a welcome and useful addition to journalists' scrutiny of politicians. Less welcome are some other news media practices in campaigns. Many studies have shown that the media are obsessed with the horse race aspect of politics—who's ahead, who's behind, who's gaining—to the detriment of the substance of the candidates' issues and ideas. Public opinion polls, many of them taken by the news outlets themselves, dominate coverage, especially on television, where only a few minutes a night are devoted to politics.

Related to the proliferation of polls is the media's expectations game in presidential primary contests. With polls as the "objective" backdrop, journalists set the margins by which contenders are expected to win or lose—so much so that even a clear victory of five percentage points can be judged a setback if the candidate had been projected to win by twelve or fifteen points. Finally, the news media often overemphasize trivial parts of the campaign, such as a politician's minor gaffe, and give far too much attention to the private lives of candidates. This superficial coverage and the resources needed to generate it are displacing serious journalism on the issues. These subjects will be taken up again in the next chapter, which deals with the news media.

Raising the Money

To run all aspects of a campaign successfully requires a great deal of money. In 1990 alone, nearly $450 million was raised and spent in U.S. House and Senate races. In close, competitive races for the House,[6] the winning candidate spent about $550,000, and the losing party nominee $350,000. Victorious Senate candidates in medium-size to large

[6] A "close, competitive race" is defined as one in which the winner received 55 percent or less of the vote.

states spent from $1.3 million up to $13.3 million, and the losers sometimes matched or exceeded the winners' total. (As the humorist Will Rogers once remarked early in the twentieth century, "Politics has got so expensive that it takes lots of money even to get beat with.")

All this political money is regulated by the federal government under the terms of the Federal Election Campaign Act, first passed in 1971 but substantially strengthened after Watergate in 1974 and again in 1976. (Still more amendments were passed in 1979.) Table 13-2 summarizes some of the important provisions of this law, which limits what individuals, interest groups, and political parties can give to candidates for president, U.S. senator, and U.S. representative. These limits on contributions are discussed in the passages that follow, but the goal of all limits is the same: to prevent any single group or individual from gaining too much influence over elected officials, who naturally feel indebted to campaign contributors.

Given the cash flow required by a campaign and the legal restrictions on political money, raising the funds necessary to run a modern campaign is a monumental task. Consequently, presidential and congressional campaigns have squads of fund raisers on staff. These professionals rely on several standard sources of campaign money.

Individual Contributions. Individual contributions are donations from individual citizens. The maximum allowable contribution under federal law for congressional and presidential elections is $1,000 per election to each candidate, with primary and general

Table 13-2   Current Contribution Limits (under the Federal Election Campaign Act)

CONTRIBUTIONS FROM	GIVEN TO CANDIDATE (PER ELECTION)[a]	GIVEN TO NATIONAL PARTY (PER CALENDAR YEAR)	TOTAL ALLOWABLE CONTRIBUTIONS (PER CALENDAR YEAR)
Individual	$1,000	$20,000	Limited to $25,000
Political action committee[b]	$5,000	$15,000	No limit
Any political party committee[c]	$5,000	No limit	No limit
All national and state party committees taken together	To House candidates: $30,000 plus "coordinated expenditures"[d] (of $55,240 per candidate in 1992)		
	To Senate candidates: $27,500 plus "coordinated expenditures"[d] (of $110,480 per candidate in smallest states to $2.5 million in California in 1992)		

[a]Each of the following is considered a *separate* election: primary (or convention), run-off, general election.
[b]Multicandidate PACs only. Multicandidate committees have received contributions from at least fifty persons and have given to at least five federal candidates.
[c]Multicandidate party committees only. Multicandidate committees have received contributions from at least fifty persons and have given to at least five federal candidates.
[d]Coordinated expenditures are party-paid general election campaign expenditures made in consultation and coordination with the candidate.

elections considered separate. Individuals are also limited to a total of $25,000 in gifts to all candidates combined each calendar year. Most candidates receive a majority of all funds directly from individuals, and most individual gifts are well below the maximum level.

Political Action Committee (PAC) Contributions. Donations from **political action committees** are those from interest groups (labor unions, corporations, trade associations, and ideological and issue groups). Under federal law these organizations are required to establish officially recognized fund-raising committees, called PACs, in order to participate in federal elections. (Some but not all states have similar requirements for state elections.) Approximately 4,200 PACs are registered with the Federal Election Commission—the governmental agency charged with administering the election laws— and in 1990 all PACs together gave $150 million to Senate and House candidates. (By contrast, individual citizens donated nearly $250 million.) On average, PAC contributions account for 38 percent of the "war chests" (campaign funds) of House candidates and 22 percent of the treasuries of Senate candidates. (Interest groups are treated in more detail in Chapter 15.)

Political Party Contributions. Candidates also receive donations from the national and state committees of the Democratic and Republican Parties. As we saw in Chapter 11, the political parties can give substantial contributions to their congressional nominees. In 1990 the Democrats funneled $10 million to their standard-bearers, and the Republicans sent nearly $14 million to theirs. In competitive races the parties may provide 15 to 17 percent of their candidates' total war chests.

Candidates' Personal Contributions. Candidates and their families may donate to the campaign. The Supreme Court ruled in 1976 in *Buckley* v. *Valeo* that no limit could be placed on the amount of money candidates can spend from their own families' resources, as such spending is considered a First Amendment right of free speech. For wealthy politicians like U.S. Senators John D. Rockefeller IV (D.-W.Va.) or Herb Kohl (D.-Wisc.), this allowance may mean personal spending in the millions. Most candidates, though, commit well under $100,000 in family resources to their election bids; Ross Perot, who publicly committed to spend millions, was not the usual candidate.

Public Funds. Public funds are donations from general tax revenues. Only presidential candidates (and a handful of state and local contenders) receive public funds. Under the terms of the Federal Election Campaign Act of 1971 (which first established public funding of presidential campaigns), a candidate for president can become eligible for public funds during the nominating contest by raising at least $5,000 in contributions of $250 or under in each of twenty states. Once this is certified, the candidate can apply for federal **matching funds,** whereby every dollar raised from individuals in amounts less than $251 is matched by the federal treasury on a dollar-for-dollar basis. This assumes there is enough money in the Presidential Election Campaign Fund to do so. The fund is accumulated by taxpayers who designate $1.00 of their taxes for this purpose each year when they send in their tax returns; only about 20 percent of taxpayers check off the appropriate box, even though participation does not increase their tax burden. For the general election, the two major-party nominees are given a lump-sum payment in the summer before the election ($55 million each in 1992) from which all their general election campaign expenditures must come. A candidate of a third party receives a smaller amount proportionate to his or her November vote total *if* he or she gains a minimum of 5 percent of the vote. Note that in such a case the money comes to third-party campaigns only *after* the election is over. The only third-party candidate to qualify for general election funds so far has been John Anderson, the independent candidate for president in 1980 who garnered 7 percent of the national vote.

Women's PACs Continue to Make a Difference

Women's political action committees made a real difference in the 1990 and 1992 elections. In 1990, women's PACs contributed over $2.6 million to candidates and in 1992 approximately double that.

EMILY's List, which stands for Early Money Is Like Yeast (it makes the dough rise), is the largest contributor to women's campaigns. Founded in 1985, its members contributed nearly $1.5 million to female candidates in 1990. Anne Richards, who ran a hotly contested race for Texas governorship in 1990, credits EMILY's List with providing crucial funding at key times, allowing her to win her race. EMILY's List expects to spend over $3 million in the 1992 elections.

Source: Center for the American Woman and Politics, *CAWP News & Notes* (Winter 1991), pp. 10–11.

Independent Expenditures. There is also spending by individuals, groups, and PACs that is undertaken independent of any campaign or candidate. This spending is *not* under the direction or control of the campaign staff and is unlimited because First Amendment free speech is involved. Sometimes the spending is positive and advocates the election of a candidate, whereas on other occasions it is negative, urging the defeat of a targeted candidate. Liberals, conservatives, environmentalists, supporters of Israel, and trade groups representing realtors, doctors, and auto dealers have all used this supplementary method of campaign spending over the years. In addition, untold millions are spent by labor, corporate, and community groups for grassroots organizing, voter registration, volunteer participation, and internal political communications with their members and employees. Depending on the sponsoring group, all of this activity has a political effect—favoring one candidate or party and hurting others—but that is not always obvious or well publicized. Also, unlike all the other forms of contributions discussed earlier, it is usually not necessary to disclose these indirect gifts to the Federal Election Commission.[7]

Are PACs a Good or Bad Part of the Process?

Of all these forms of spending, probably the most controversial is that involving PAC money. Some observers claim that PACs are the embodiment of corrupt "special interests" that use campaign donations to "buy" the votes of legislators. Most political scientists in the field of campaign finance have quite a different opinion, viewing PACs as a natural and diverse manifestation of interest-group politics in a democracy.

Although a good number of PACs of all persuasions existed prior to the 1970s, it was during this decade—the decade of campaign reform—that the modern PAC era began. Spawned by the Watergate-inspired revisions of the campaign-finance laws, PACs grew in number from 113 in 1972 to nearly 4,200 by the early 1990s, and their contributions to congressional candidates multiplied almost eighteen-fold, from $8.5 million in 1971–72 to $149.9 million in 1989–90 (see Figures 13-2 and 13-3). The rapid rise of PACs has inevitably proved controversial, yet many of the charges made against political action committees are exaggerated and dubious.

Some people argue that PACs are dangerously novel and have flooded the political system with money. Although the widespread use of the PAC structure is new, the fact remains that special-interest money of all types has *always* found its way into politics, and before the 1970s it did so in less traceable and far more disturbing and unsavory ways because, before PACs, little of the money given to candidates was regularly disclosed for public inspection. And although it is true that PACs contribute a massive sum to candidates in absolute terms, it is not clear that there is *proportionately* more interest-group money in the system than before. The proportion of House and Senate campaign funds provided by PACs has certainly increased since the early 1970s, but *individuals,* most of whom are unaffiliated with PACs, together with the political parties still supply more than three-fifths of all the money spent by or on behalf of House candidates and three-quarters of the campaign expenditures for Senate contenders. So while the importance of PAC spending has grown, PACs clearly remain secondary as a source of election funding and therefore pose no overwhelming threat to our system's legitimacy.

It can be argued that contemporary political action committees are another manifestation of what James Madison called factions. Through the flourishing of competing interest groups or factions, said Madison in Federalist No. 10, liberty would be preserved. In any democracy, and particularly in one as pluralistic as that of the United States, it is essential that groups be relatively unrestricted in advocating their interests and positions. Not only is unrestricted political activity by interest groups a mark of a free society, but it also

---

[7] All *direct* contributions over $100 must be disclosed to the Federal Election Commission, and the report is supposed to include the name, address, and occupation of each donor.

Figure 13-2   Growth in Total Number of PACs

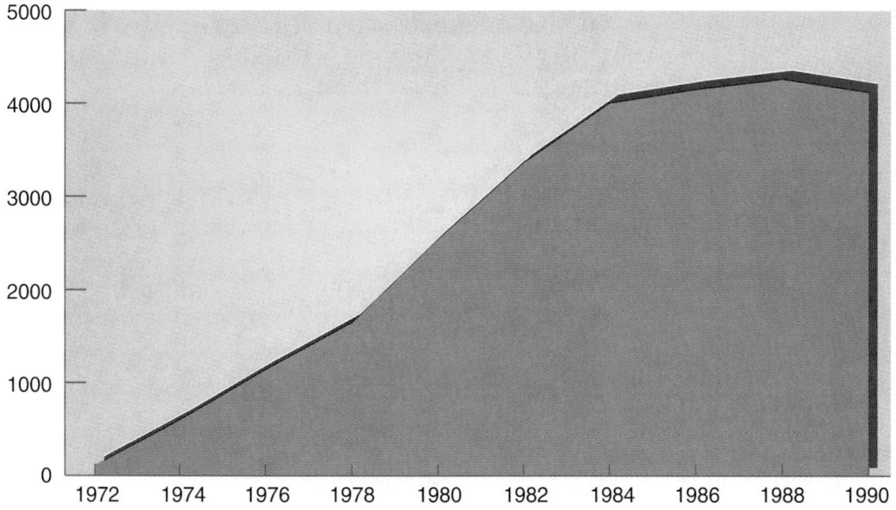

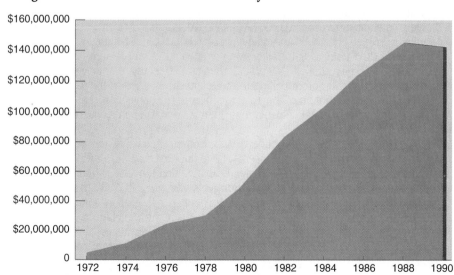

^{a}As of December 31st of every other year, starting in 1972.

Source: Federal Election Commission.

provides a safety valve for the competitive pressures that build on all fronts in a democracy. It also supplies a means of keeping representatives responsive to legitimate needs.

The election outlays of PACs, like the total amount expended in a single election season, seem huge. But the price of elections in the United States is less than or approximately the same as in some other nations, measured on a per voter basis (see Table

Figure 13-3   Growth in Total Contributions by PACs to House and Senate Candidates^a

^{a} For two-year election cycles ending in years shown.

Source: Federal Election Commission.

Table 13-3   The Costs of Elections Around the Globe

COUNTRY	AMOUNT OF MONEY SPENT PER VOTER[a] IN RECENT NATIONAL ELECTIONS (IN DOLLARS)
United States	$ 3.25[b]
Venezuela	26.35[c]
Great Britain	0.50[c]
Ireland	3.93[c]
Canada	1.43[c]
Germany (West only)	3.20[c]
Israel	4.34

[a]"Voters" include all those who were of age to vote, whether or not they were registered.

[b]Includes both presidential and congressional elections.

[c]Figure does not include free television broadcast time or other government subsidies not available to candidates in the United States.

Source: Howard Penniman, "U.S. Elections: Really a Bargain?" *Public Opinion* (June/July 1984), p. 51.

13-3).[8] Moreover, the cost of all American elections taken together is less than the annual advertising budgets of many individual private corporations to sell cereals, dog food, cars, and toothpaste. These days it is expensive to communicate, whether the message is political or commercial. The costs of television time, polling, consultants, and so on have soared over and above the inflation rate.

A Summary of Contributions and Expenses

A glance at Table 13-4 gives an idea of where all the money comes from and goes. A "typical" U.S. Senate candidate in 1992 received most of his or her war chest from relatively small individual donations. PACs supplied about 22 percent, the political party committees 15 percent, and the candidates about 3 percent. The single greatest outlay (40 percent of the total) was for television advertising; the next-largest item, staff and consultant salaries, was half of TV's cost (20 percent). The other 40 percent of the budget was spent on everything from polling to travel expenses. Keep in mind that in a large state with a dozen or more media markets (concentrated population centers with many television and radio stations), expenditures often balloon to $5 million, $10 million, and even more.

Some candidates have more difficulty than others in raising the necessary dollar amounts. Those in power, the incumbents, have the least trouble, although challengers who face incumbents weakened by scandal can also find the task of financing the campaign relatively easy. The size of a **challenger's** war chest is really the key variable. There is a point of diminishing returns for incumbent spending, as most office holders are already well known to the voters. But the challenger's name and platform are likely to be obscure. If the challenger can raise and spend enough to get his or her basic message across, there is a reasonable chance that the election will be at least moderately competi-

---

[8]See Howard Penniman, "U.S. Elections: Really a Bargain?" *Public Opinion* (June/July 1984), p. 51.

Table 13-4 Campaign for the U.S. Senate, 1992: A "Typical" Candidate's Budget of $2 Million

FUNDS FROM	TOTAL $	% OF TOTAL
Political action committees (PACs)	$ 440,000	22%
Contributions from individuals	1,200,000	60
Political party	300,000	15
Candidate's own money (including family loans)	60,000	3
TOTAL	$2,000,000	100%

ARE SPENT ON		
Television (and radio) advertising	$ 800,000	40%
Staff salaries and consultant fees	400,000	20
Polling	75,000	4
Print media (literature, mail, buttons, etc.)	60,000	3
Canvassing/get-out-the-vote efforts	125,000	6
Office rent, equipment, and travel	300,000	15
Fund-raising expenses	190,000	10
Legal and accounting services	50,000	2
TOTAL	$2,000,000	100%

tive. As is more common, though, if the challenger is starved for funds, the contest will probably turn into a romp for the well-heeled incumbent.

Bringing It Together: The 1992 Presidential Campaign and Election

A year before the November 1992 presidential election, it looked likely to be a rather boring, predictable affair, much like the 1984 contest that had resulted in a landslide reelection for President Reagan. Most of the strongest potential Democratic candidates, such as New York Governor Mario Cuomo and New Jersey U.S. Senator Bill Bradley, decided not to run for president, and President Bush was still riding a wave of popularity from the Persian Gulf war. In the end, however, 1992 produced one of the most exciting and competitive contests for the White House in modern times.

The Party Nomination Battle

President Bush's hopes for an uncontested renomination were shattered when he was challenged by conservative television commentator Patrick J. Buchanan. Buchanan attacked Bush on the economy, on his 1990 abandonment of his 1988 "no new taxes" campaign pledge, and on National Endowment of the Arts funding of such controversial projects as a film about black gay males. Buchanan achieved his high watermark on February 19, with 37 percent of the vote in the first primary, New Hampshire. This state had saved Bush's candidacy in 1988 after his third-place finish in the Iowa caucuses. In 1992, however, many of its citizens felt Bush had abandoned them during the recession,

Then and Now

The Television Advertising Campaigns of 1952 and 1992

Forty years—and a world of difference—separate the presidential campaigns of 1952 and 1992 when viewed through the camera lens of television advertising.

The initial, landmark year for political television was 1952. Television had become truly national, not just regional, and portions of the political parties' national conventions were first broadcast. With 45 percent of the nation's households owning televisions, the presidential campaign was forced to take notice. Republican presidential nominee Dwight Eisenhower's advisers were particularly intrigued with the device, seeing it as a way to counter his stumbling press-conference performances and to make him appear more knowledgeable.

Eisenhower's advertising campaign was a glimpse of the future. Two associates of Ted Bates and Company advertising agency of New York designed the spots, targeted them to play in key swing areas of the country, and arranged a television and radio saturation blitz in the last three weeks of the campaign along with the Batten, Barton, Durstine, and Osborn (BBD & O) advertising agency, which actually bought the air time. The three primary themes of the commercials (corruption, high prices, and the Korean War) were chosen after consultation with the pollster George Gallup. There was an extraordinarily large number of spots (forty-nine produced for television, twenty-nine for radio); most of them were twenty seconds in length, the rest sixty seconds. They played repeatedly in forty-nine selected counties in twelve non-Southern states as well as in a few targeted Southern states. In New York City alone, 130 Eisenhower television ads were broadcast at station breaks just on the day before the election. The GOP's media strategy appeared to have been successful, and the Neilsen ratings showed that Eisenhower's telecasts consistently drew higher ratings than those of his Democratic opponent, Adlai Stevenson.

The commercials themselves were simplistic and technically very primitive in comparison with modern fare. Eisenhower had a peculiarly stilted way of speaking while reading cue cards, and his delivery was amateurish if sincere and appealing. If nothing else, the GOP commercials from 1952 reveal that the issues in American politics never seem to change. Eisenhower's slogan "It's Time for a Change" is a perennial production, for exam-

ple. One advertisement was a clever adaptation of the "March of Time" newsreel series that preceded the main features in American movie theaters of the period, and various news clips of Eisenhower accompanied the audio:

NARRATOR: The man from Abilene. Out of the heartland of America, out of this small-frame house in Abilene, Kansas, came a man, Dwight D. Eisenhower. Through the crucial hours of historic D-Day, he brought us to the triumph and peace of VE-Day. Now, another crucial hour in our history. The big question . . .

MAN'S VOICE: General, if war comes, is this country really ready?

EISENHOWER: It is not. The administration has spent many billions of dollars for national defense. Yet today we haven't enough tanks for the fighting men in Korea. It is time for a change.

NARRATOR: The nation, haunted by the stalemate in Korea, looks to Eisenhower. Eisenhower knows how to deal with the Russians. He has met with Europe's leaders, has got them working with us. Elect the number-one man for the number-one job of our time. November fourth, vote for peace, vote for Eisenhower.

Yet this spot had an odd ring to it, perhaps because the approach ignored the intimate nature of television, which reaches its viewers in the home's cozy quarters as opposed to the blare of a newsreel in an auditorium. Some other Eisenhower commercials used an even less effective format whereby a film showed Eisenhower mechanically giving his responses to off-camera questions.

By the best estimates this first media blitz cost the Republicans close to $1.5 million. During that campaign the Democrats spent only about $77,000 on television, and the new spots they produced played on New Deal themes and Republican responsibility for the Great Depression: "Sh-h-h-h. Don't mention it to a soul, don't spread it around . . . but the Republican party was in power back in 1932 . . . 13 million people were unemployed . . . bank doors shut in your face. . . ." The Democrats, who had wanted to run an ad blitz but could not raise the money to pay for it, turned instead to broadsides about the GOP's "soap campaign." George Ball, then a staffer in Stevenson's organization and later a major figure in the Johnson White House, set the tone for all the critical reactions to media politics that would follow when he charged that the Republican ad managers

conceived not an election campaign in the usual sense, but a super colossal, multimillion-dollar production designed to sell an inadequate ticket to the American people in precisely the way they sell soap, ammoniated toothpaste, hair tonic, or bubble gum. They guarantee their candidates to be 99⁴⁴/₁₀₀ percent pure; whether or not they will float remains to be seen.

The poet Marya Mannes was moved to write "Sales Campaign" in reaction to the Eisenhower advertising effort. It read, in part: "Phillip Morris, Lucky Strike, Alka Seltzer, I Like Ike."

For better or worse, the pattern was set for future campaigns. The campaign of 1992 was no exception,

even though all three presidential camps produced television advertising that was far more sophisticated than that of 1952.

Ross Perot, the Independent candidate, aired mainly half-hour and hour-long commercials in the final weeks of campaign '92, whereas Republican George Bush and Democrat Bill Clinton televised mostly brief, highly negative attack ads. One improvement in the process is worth noting, however. The news media undertook to check the accuracy of the assertions in the 1992 advertisements, and many major newspapers and television networks published and aired their findings. For example, Howard Kurtz, *The Washington Post*'s media reporter, wrote "background" analyses of many campaign advertising spots. These critiques—two of which are reproduced on this page—were printed in the *Post* for all to see.

Candidate: President Bush
Producer: The November Co.
Time: 30 seconds

Audio: Bill Clinton says he'll only tax the rich to pay for his campaign promises. But here's what Clinton economics could mean to you. [On screen: John Canes, steamfitter, $1,088 more in taxes. Lori Huntoon, scientist, $2,072 more in taxes.] 100 leading economists say this plan means higher taxes and bigger deficits. [Julie and Gary Schwartz, sales reps, $1,191 more in taxes. Wyman Winston, Housing Lender, $2,072 more in taxes.] You can't trust Clinton economics. It's wrong for you. It's wrong for America.

Background: This ad is misleading because it rests on a series of assumptions about Clinton's economic plan, all of which are in dispute. Viewers are not told the incomes of the people featured in the ad or the budget assumptions the Bush camp uses; the specific tax-hike figures are simply presented as fact. The commercial assumes that 1) Clinton's tax plan will have a revenue shortfall, 2) Clinton's spending cuts won't save as much as he says, and 3) Clinton's middle-class tax cut won't be enacted. Even if all those assumptions are correct, Clinton would still have the option of scaling back his spending plans, raising other taxes or increasing the deficit. The key verb in the ad: what Clinton's plan *could* mean to you.

Candidate: Bill Clinton
Producer: Clinton–Gore Creative Team
Time: 30 seconds

Audio: 1988. [Bush: Read my lips.] Then George Bush signed the second biggest tax increase in American history. [Bush: Read my lips.] George Bush increased taxes on the middle class. Bush doubled the beer tax and increased the gas tax by 56 percent. Now Bush wants to give a $108,000 tax break to millionaires. $108,000. Guess who's going to pay? We can't afford four more years.

Background: This is a response to an earlier Bush ad detailing Clinton's tax increases in Arkansas. It even uses Bush's tag line, "Guess who's going to pay?" The ad is accurate in saying Bush signed the second largest U.S. tax hike in 1990, but fails to mention that the Democratic Congress agreed to the increase. The tax increase on the "middle class" refers to the hike in beer and gas taxes. The "tax break to millionaires" largely refers to Bush's proposed capital-gains tax cut, which would effect anyone with profits on property or securities. The $108,000 savings is subject to dispute since it is based on projections of a typical millionaire's capital gains.

Source: Howard Kurtz, "30-Second Politics," *The Washington Post*, October 2, 1992. Reprinted by permission.

1992 Party Primaries

Democrats

	Number of Primaries Won	Percent of Total Votes
Clinton	32	51.9
Brown	2	19.9
Tsongas	4	18.1
Uncommited/ others	1	10.1

A total of 20,179,973 votes were cast in 39 primaries.

Republicans

	Number of Primaries Won	Percent of Total Votes
Bush	39	73.0
Buchanan	0	22.4
Uncommited/ others	0	3.6
Duke	0	1.0

A total of 13,025,824 votes were cast in 39 primaries.

Source: Congressional Quarterly Weekly Supplements 50, July 4, 1992, p. 71 and August 8, 1992, p. 67.

which was much more severe in their state than in the country as a whole. Buchanan also won 36 percent of the vote in Georgia on March 3, but faded thereafter. Although Bush eventually racked up nearly all of the delegates to the Republican convention, his overall showing in the primaries was anemic compared to most of his Republican predecessors. Bush won just 73 percent of all the votes cast in GOP contests in 1992, far less than Presidents Eisenhower (86 percent), Nixon, (87 percent), and Reagan (99 percent) in their reelection years.

Democrats sponsored one of their standard free-for-alls for the presidential nomination. The leading announced candidate from the beginning was Governor Bill Clinton of Arkansas, although his status as frontrunner was shaky. He was plagued by mini-scandals that threatened to drive him from the race: an alleged affair with an Arkansas woman named Gennifer Flowers, his possible evasion of the draft during the Vietnam War, and youthful experimentation with marijuana (self-admitted, with the silly proviso that he had "never inhaled").

Clinton survived and managed to outflank all his rivals, one by one. The most serious was former Massachusetts U.S. Senator Paul Tsongas, whose tough fiscal message—"no more Santa Claus"—attracted white middle- and upper-class Democrats concerned about the budget deficit and America's deep-seated economic problems. Tsongas won the New Hampshire primary, with Clinton a respectable second. Senator Tom Harkin of Iowa, Senator Bob Kerrey of Nebraska, and former Governor of California Jerry Brown each won other early contests, but starting with Georgia on March 3, Clinton began to generate unstoppable momentum. On "Super Tuesday" (March 10), he swept the Southern contests, but Tsongas did well outside the South. Then on March 17, Clinton won both Illinois and Michigan decisively. Short of money, Tsongas joined Harkin and Kerrey on the inactive list. Brown persisted, winning a few more contests, but Clinton effectively ended his challenge with a decisive win in New York on April 7. From then on, Clinton scored relatively easy victories everywhere, even in Brown's home state of California on June 2. Voter turnouts were low, however—overall just 12 percent of the voting-age population—and Democrats appeared more resigned than enthusiastic as they looked to a Clinton candidacy. Nonetheless, Clinton's 51.9 percent of the total Democratic primary votes was a solid showing.

The Third Force: Ross Perot

On February 20, 1992, Texas billionaire Ross Perot, appearing on CNN's "Larry King Live," announced that if Americans in all fifty states put him on their ballots, he would run for president. Capitalizing on widespread discontent with the two major party nominees, he then launched a most improbable pseudo-candidacy that derived in good part from his intense dislike of fellow Texan Bush.

Although Perot declared a willingness to spend "whatever it takes"—estimates ranged from $100 to $300 million—of his own fortune to be competitive, he actually spent little in the early months of his unannounced candidacy. Instead, he cleverly used the free media, especially the soft-edged talk shows and morning TV ("Larry King Live," "Donahue," "Today"), to advance himself while offering little of detailed substance. With the political press at bay, he could project accessibility with little risk; with party identification on the decline, his independent stand was a magnet for many alienated voters anxious for "change" and an end to politics as usual; and with nearly unlimited resources, he was not forced to waste time in a money chase. His folksy image and "can-do" approach to gridlocked government proved popular and he rocketed to the top of the opinion polls.

Gradually, though, some less flattering facts about Perot began to filter out. The tycoon's autocratic, authoritarian manner unsettled some, as did his penchant for conspiracy theories and alleged investigation of adversaries' private lives. Still, with a seemingly firm hold on millions of Americans, Perot cast a long Texas shadow over both parties—until he abruptly declined to run on July 16, 1992, the last day of the Democratic National

Convention. Unable to work with the feisty Texan, his campaign manager and other key aides had resigned just prior to the withdrawal. Feeling outraged and betrayed, many of Perot's supporters abandoned him, while others urged him to reverse his decision. Stung by the label of "quitter," and claiming disappointment that Bush and Clinton had not adopted his debt reduction platform, Perot abruptly changed course yet again on October 1 and announced his Independent candidacy. But his luster was clearly gone and his appeal sharply diminished.

The Party Conventions

Democrats gathered first in convention, in New York City from July 13–17. The week before, Clinton had named Tennessee Senator Albert Gore, Jr. as his running mate. The privileged son of a senator and an unsuccessful candidate for president in 1988, Gore struck many as similar to Clinton: young (44), Southern, and moderate-liberal. The un-usual pairing of two Southerners on the ticket signaled the Democrats' determination to fight for GOP-leaning Dixie's electoral votes, and the match of two post–World War II "baby boom" generation candidates guaranteed a vigorous campaign and an appeal for change. Gore's strengths in foreign policy and the environment as well as his Vietnam-era military service balanced several of Clinton's prominent weaknesses.

Ross Perot on "Larry King Live." His appearance on this and other television talk shows in the spring and early summer of 1992 helped boost his standing in the polls before he abruptly declined to run in July. He reversed himself again on October 1 and joined the race as an Independent.

Democrats were enormously pleased and encouraged by the course of their convention, which they used to showcase a "new" Democratic Party more to the liking of mainstream America. With the exception of Jerry Brown, all of Clinton's former rivals for the nomination warmly embraced him; New York Governor Mario Cuomo gave a stirring nomination speech; a platform incorporating important centrist positions on economics and government (for example, that government programs were not the solution to every problem) was adopted; and the Clinton–Gore ticket was given a rousing sendoff. Following Perot's stunning announcement that he would not run for president, most Perot voters appeared to switch to Clinton as the other "change" candidate, and as the convention concluded, the nominee skyrocketed to a twenty-four-point lead over President Bush in a CNN–Gallup survey. Buoyed by this large convention "bounce" and armed with the opportunities provided by a weak economy, Democrats looked forward to the coming campaign and tried not to look back to 1988, when Michael Dukakis had squandered a smaller 17-point advantage and lost to George Bush.

Clinton quickly proved that he had learned from Dukakis's mistakes. Setting a pattern he would follow to Election Day, he campaigned vigorously and nearly continuously between the Democratic and Republican conventions, much of the time on a bus tour with his running mate, aggressively countering every attack made by the Bush forces and launching many attacks of his own. Combined with more bad economic news and a listless Bush response, these techniques helped him maintain his lead through the GOP convention and beyond.

Republicans prepared for their party conclave with trepidation. A few conservative activists and columnists called for Bush to step aside and not seek reelection, while other Republicans suggested that Vice President Quayle should step aside. Instead, Bush reaffirmed his ticket, and then delighted his party by moving Secretary of State James Baker—one of the architects of his 1988 victory—out of the State Department and over to the White House to serve as chief of staff and campaign manager.

On that upbeat note, the Republican National Convention opened in Houston, Texas on August 17. That evening Pat Buchanan enthusiastically endorsed President Bush, but his harsh address, reflecting the influence of the right wing on the tone and substance of the convention, alienated many moderate Americans. Framing the November battle from the Republican perspective, the convention organizers emphasized "family values," foreign policy, and Congress bashing. President Bush gave a generally well-regarded closing address on these themes.

In retrospect, many observers concluded that the convention had been poorly organized, and in particular, that giving prominence to the negative messages of Buchanan and others may have been a mistake. Most polls showed Bush achieved some "bounce" from his convention, but much less than Clinton had secured from his. Bush, it became increasingly clear, would be hard pressed to catch up.

The Fall Campaign and General Election Results

As the campaign developed in the months following the Republican convention, each of the more than 275 pre-election polls showed Bill Clinton ahead. Without question, he ran a technically superb campaign; his strategy, television advertising, use of the media, and energetic stumping (frequently on a bus) were on target and exceptionally clever. Fielding the best Democratic campaign team in a generation, he successfully projected a moderate image that appealed to a wide range of voters. Keeping his message focused on the weak economy, he was able to win back many so-called "Reagan" Democrats—registered Democrats who had voted for Republican presidential candidates since 1980. Appearing on MTV and—with saxophone in hand—on "The Arsenio Hall Show," Clinton also appealed directly and effectively to the young. Clinton campaigners were quick to respond to Republican attacks, faxing counterstatements and "truth sheets" almost instantaneously to networks and print reporters.

Bush's campaign, in contrast, was slow to organize and even slower to focus on consistent themes. It hopped, skipped, and jumped among topics as diverse as "family values," experience, trust, Clinton's draft evasion and anti-war demonstrating, and the Arkansas record. Even Republicans admit their party had rarely, if ever, mismanaged a presidential campaign so badly. It reminded most observers of the inept effort made by Michael Dukakis in 1988—the same year that a finely crafted and executed campaign by George Bush won him the presidency.

Although the differences between the two campaigns was certainly a factor in the outcome of the election, it is also true that any election involving an incumbent president is essentially a referendum on his incumbency, and in that sense, George Bush lost the election every bit as much as Bill Clinton won it. Here are some of the reasons—beyond his lackluster campaign—that Bush forfeited his second term:

- *The economy.* The U.S. economy, the most basic of all forces in presidential elections, suffered a serious recession in 1990–91 and recovered only fitfully and painfully in the months leading up to the election. In many ways relating to their pocketbooks, voters simply did not believe they were better off than four years earlier, which predisposed them to change the status quo. Clinton and Perot continually hammered away at Bush about the recession and the rising national debt, making the economy the most important issue in the campaign.

- *Presidential domestic inaction and the end of the Cold War.* Known as a "foreign policy president" because of his love of international relations, Bush often seemed disinterested in domestic affairs. His repeated declarations that the economy was improving—designed to increase consumer confidence—made him appear out of touch. Meanwhile, festering problems across America (decaying inner cities, infrastructure deterioration, a perceived decline in the quality of health care and education) caused many to yearn for a candidate who placed domestic matters at the top of his agenda. The end of the Cold War and the collapse of communism also helped focus the election squarely on domestic policy, leaving foreign affairs on the periphery.

- *Vice-presidential candidates.* Bush's vice president, Dan Quayle, was certainly more competent than the news media and the late-night comics portrayed him, but his public image was so negative that he undoubtedly hurt Bush. By contrast, Clinton's vice-presidential pick, Al Gore, was widely viewed as an asset, and the news media gave him extremely positive reviews.

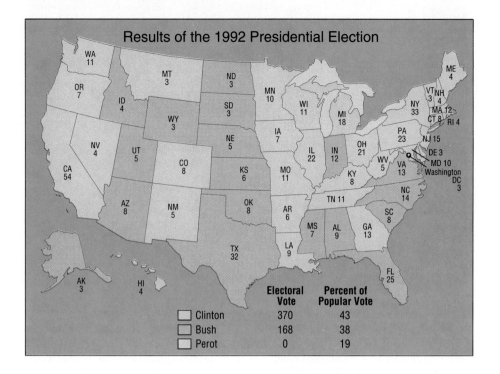

Results of the 1992 Presidential Election

	Electoral Vote	Percent of Popular Vote
Clinton	370	43
Bush	168	38
Perot	0	19

- *The Perot factor*. The billionaire Independent had an intense hatred for his fellow Texan Bush and aimed most of his fire at the president—even charging late in the campaign (with absolutely no evidence) that the GOP planned to disrupt his daughter's wedding. Most of Perot's support was drawn from the white, suburban upper-middle class, a predominantly Republican constituency, and Bush likely suffered disproportionately as a result.

- *Scandals*. Two scandals haunted Bush's reelection effort: Iran-*Contra* and Iraq-gate. The Iran-*Contra* scandal originated in the Reagan administration and involved the illegal sale of U.S. arms to Iran, with some of the profits improperly diverted to fund the anti-communist *contras* fighting a civil war in the Central American country of Nicaragua. Bush, who was vice president at the time, had repeatedly claimed he was "out of the loop" on this policy, but the release of a memorandum written by Reagan Defense Secretary Casper Weinberger just days before the election suggested that he was very much in the loop. The revelation cost Bush the last-minute campaign momentum he had generated. The Iraq-gate scandal took some of the luster off of Bush's leadership in the Persian Gulf war. It referred to the U.S. policy of arming Iraq's leader, Saddam Hussein, in the years leading up to his invasion of Kuwait in 1990 and the possible postwar cover-up of the Bush administration's decisions in this matter. Both scandals hampered efforts by the Bush team to raise questions about Clinton's character (marital infidelity, youthful marijuana usage, and draft evasion).

- *News media bias*. Republicans claimed that the national media, particularly the networks, *The Washington Post*, and *The New York Times*, were tilting heavily to Clinton and putting Bush and the economy in the worst possible light. Although there may be some truth to this criticism, it is questionable how much media bias affected the final election outcome.

Election Results. The Reagan–Bush majority coalition that had governed for twelve years simply buckled under the weight of all these burdens. "Reagan" Democrats returned en masse to the Democratic fold. Young people between the ages of 18 and 30 also moved into Clinton's column after supporting the GOP in 1980, 1984, and 1988. Many

Bill Clinton and Al Gore, with their wives Hillary and Tipper, acknowledge victory in Little Rock, Arkansas on election night.

women also shifted to Clinton, a result of a bad economy, the Democrat's pro-abortion position, and the Anita Hill–Clarence Thomas hearings of the U.S. Senate when Thomas's nomination to the Supreme Court was under consideration in 1991. Some exit poll findings suggested women comprised as much as 54 percent of the voters on November 3, 1992, so Clinton's edge among women was especially important.

Clinton's Electoral College victory (370 for Clinton, 168 for Bush, and 0 for Perot) was much broader than his popular vote plurality (43 percent for Clinton, 38 percent for Bush, and 19 percent for Perot). He was thus to be a "minority president"—elected by less than half the popular vote[9]—but one whose win was nonetheless impressive. After all, since World War II only two other challengers—Jimmy Carter in 1976 and Ronald Reagan in 1980—had ousted incumbents from the White House, and no other president had been as popular as Bush was earlier in his term. Bush became the tenth president to lose a bid for reelection.[10]

The Democrats won states in every region of the country. They swept the economically hard-hit Northeast, winning even reliably Republican New Hampshire. Except for Indiana, home of Dan Quayle, the Midwest was solidly Democratic, as was the Pacific Coast. (The Republicans ceded giant California's fifty-four electoral votes to the Democrats months before the election when polls showed them in a hopeless position there.)

President Bush achieved a respectable showing only in the South. But even in this region, which had long been solidly Republican, Florida and Texas stayed loyal to Bush by only narrow margins, and the Democrats stole Georgia and Louisiana as well as Clinton's Arkansas and Gore's Tennessee. Bush also held onto some Rocky Mountain and Plains states, but significantly, he forfeited four states that had nearly consistently voted Republican in modern times: Colorado, Montana, Nevada, and New Mexico.

By the standards of recent history, Clinton's Electoral College majority was the most impressive and diverse for a Democrat since Lyndon Johnson's landslide election in 1964. And Bush's collapse from his 427 Electoral College votes in 1988 to 168 in 1992 was stunning. Bush fared far worse than Gerald Ford, who won 240 Electoral College votes in his losing 1976 bid. Still, Jimmy Carter, who captured just forty-nine Electoral College votes in his 1980 reelection bid, holds the post–World War II record for decisive defeat of an incumbent.

[9] Fifteen of our forty-two chief executives were elected with less than a majority. The most recent prior to Clinton was Richard Nixon, who (like Clinton) garnered 43 percent of the votes in 1968's three-way race.

[10] The other defeated presidents (and year of defeat) were John Adams (1800), John Quincy Adams (1828), Martin Van Buren (1840), Grover Cleveland (1888), Benjamin Harrison (1892), William Howard Taft (1912), Herbert Hoover (1932), Gerald Ford (1976), and Jimmy Carter (1980).

Like the presidential election, congressional elections also demonstrated the growing clout of women and minorities. Four new women were elected to the U.S. Senate, two from the same state: Barbara Boxer (D.-Ca.), Dianne Feinstein (D.-Ca.), Carol Moseley Braun (D.-Ill.), and Patty Murray (D.-Wash.). They joined two other women (Democrat Barbara Mikulski of Maryland and Republican Nancy Kassebaum of Kansas) in the Senate that convened in January 1993. Braun was also the first black woman ever elected to the U.S. Senate. In the House, the number of women jumped from twenty-eight to forty-eight, the number of blacks from twenty-five to thirty-eight, and the number of Hispanic-Americans from eleven to seventeen. Finally, the first Korean-American was elected to the House (Republican Jay Kim of California) and a Native American, Democrat Ben Nighthorse Campbell, won a Senate seat from Colorado. This growing diversity and representativeness in Congress was perhaps the most notable result of the congressional elections. Party balance changed little. Democrats maintained solid control of both houses, staying even in the Senate (for a total of 57 out of 100) and losing ten seats in the House (for a total of 258 out of 435).

Voter turnout was up in 1992 after a long and worrisome decline. About 55 percent of Americans aged 18 and over turned up at the polling places in 1992 (and about 80 percent of those *registered* to vote did so). These numbers were a significant increase over 1988, when just 50 percent of those 18 and older voted. But it is still well below the 62 percent of 1960 and the even higher turnouts regularly recorded in the last century.

Toward Reform

In response to the growing concern about the amounts of money spent on federal elections, both Republicans and Democrats have sponsored major campaign-finance reform bills in Congress. But changing the rules of the game can alter the results of elections, and not surprisingly the Democratic proposals favor Democratic candidates and the Republican proposals favor Republican candidates. For many years now as a consequence, Congress has been at an impasse on campaign reform—with Republican presidents promising to veto any Democratic-passed bill.

Democrats favor setting a limit on the amount of money any congressional candidate can spend to win office. (For the House a candidate might be limited to $600,000; the Senate limit would depend on each state's population, with a more heavily populated state having a higher limit.) Republicans are adamantly against these spending caps, arguing that the limits mainly hurt challengers who are not as well known as incumbents and need to spend more money to increase their name identification. For example, from 1978 to 1988 only seven of the thirty-two winning Senate challengers remained within the spending limits proposed by the Democrats. Republicans also claim that they must spend more than Democrats because they have access to no volunteer group comparable to organized labor, which aids Democrats overwhelmingly, and hence the GOP candidates must normally pay campaign workers.

Of course, both parties' positions on this issue are rooted in self-interest: The Republicans are more successful than Democrats at raising money, and the Democrats want to limit that advantage. Moreover, the cost to either party of conceding too much on this issue is the possibility of relinquishing control of Congress for a long time to come. This makes it an issue that does not easily lend itself to compromise.

Yet many experts inside and outside of Congress argue that there are many other ideas concerning campaign finance that would create a more wholesome system without resorting to spending limits. One such idea is to limit the influence of political action committees (PACs). Critics charge that PACs reduce political competition by giving overwhelmingly to incumbents, while at the same time they corrupt the system by indebting legislators to the special interests that form PACs. Abolishing PACs altogether, however, is very probably unconstitutional, as doing so would violate the First Amendment's guarantee of free political association; and restricting their contribution limits too much would just divert their money into other forms of political spending that are not easily revealed (such as funneling cash to state and local parties in states that do not require full campaign-finance disclosure). As reformers through the years have discovered, it is nearly impossible to dam the flow of political money in a free and open democratic system in which participation is encouraged.

A better way to control PACs and special-interest groups is to increase the influence and level of spending by parties. This would limit PACs *indirectly* by augmenting the power of a rival source of campaign funds. As we discussed in Chapter 11, parties can be strengthened in many ways, especially by loosening or eliminating current restrictions on what citizens may give to a party or what a party may donate to its candidates. In addition, parties ought to be the recipients of some free advertising time on all television and radio stations. This time could then be allocated to its most needy nominees—incumbents who are in trouble, as well as promising challengers. Since candidates spend a major portion of their campaign funds for media advertising time—up to 60 percent in some Senate races—such a reform could conceivably help to cut the burgeoning costs of campaigns. And it would aid challengers and less wealthy candidates in particular, balancing some of the advantages of incumbency. The United States, incidentally, is the only large democratic country in the world that does not provide some free media time to parties or candidates.

Campaign-finance reform is a favorite Washington topic, but for all the good (and bad) ideas that are proposed, little legislation is ever passed. Many incumbents prefer not to alter the system that, whatever its faults, elected them. Democrats and Republicans are at loggerheads over the partisan effects of various reforms, and therefore a Republican president would likely veto any bill passed by a Democratic Congress. The American people also remain skeptical of political parties, and little popular support can be found for their cause. The last set of campaign-finance reforms passed in the wake of Watergate, and it may take another scandal or two to generate enough momentum to pass a successor package of reforms in the Congress.

Summary

As this analysis of the 1992 election suggests, the campaign process in the United States is far from perfect. Campaigns stretch out seemingly interminably, unlike in Great Britain, where the entire parliamentary election process is confined to four or five weeks. Moreover, candidates in the United States are often judged on trivial issues, voters cast many ballots for the "lesser of evils," and some contenders for lower office never raise enough money to get a fair hearing. But those who follow campaigns also would do well to remember the wise words of one of this century's greatest political scientists, V. O. Key Jr. Key's central observation was simple but powerful: "Voters are not fools."[11] Not every citizen devotes enough time to politics, and many are woefully uninformed at times. But virtually all voters know their basic interests and cast their ballots accordingly. They are not always right in their judgments, yet over time there is a rough justice to election results. Parties and office holders who produce a measure of prosperity and happiness for the electorate are usually rewarded, and those who do not keep the home folks satisfied may be forced to find another line of work.

Campaigns, the process of seeking and winning votes in the run-up to an election, consist of five separate components: the nomination campaign in which party leaders and activists are courted to ensure that the candidate is nominated in primaries or conventions; the general election campaign in which the goal is to appeal to the nation as a whole; the personal campaign in which the candidate and his or her family make appearances, meet voters, hold press conferences, and give speeches; the organizational campaign in which volunteers telephone

---

[11]See V. O. Key Jr., *The Responsible Electorate* (Cambridge, Mass.: Harvard University Press, 1966).

voters, distribute literature, organize events, and raise money; and the media campaign, waged on television and on the radio.

Campaign staffs combine volunteers with a manager at the top and key political consultants—including media consultants, a pollster, and a direct mailer. In recent years, media consultants have assumed greater and greater importance, partly because the cost of broadcasting has skyrocketed, so that campaign media budgets consume the lion's share of available resources.

Campaign finance rises periodically as a reform issue, because candidates who outspend their opponents tend to win, and raising money is easier for some than for others. Incumbents enjoy a fund-raising edge as well as advantages due to name recognition and some of the perks of office, such as mailing privileges. Campaigns receive money from several sources. Individual contributions are currently limited to $1,000 per candidate per election; political action committees, which represent interest groups, are limited to $5,000. In addition, candidates can receive large supplements from their party, and they can spend as much of their own money as they like.

Key Terms

nomination campaign	organizational campaign	free media
general election campaign	media campaign	media consultant
personal campaign	paid media	pollster
direct mailer	negative ads	political action committees
voter canvass	contrast ads	public funds
get-out-the-vote	spot ads	matching funds
positive ads	candidate debates	challenger

Suggested Readings

Abramson, Paul R., John H. Aldrich, and David W. Rohde. *Change and Continuity in the 1988 Elections.* Washington: CQ Press, 1990.

Alexander, Herbert E., and Monica Bauer. *Financing the 1988 Election.* Boulder, Colo.: Westview Press, 1991.

Goldenberg, Edie, and Michael W. Traugott. *Campaigning for Congress.* Washington: CQ Press, 1984.

Jackson, Brooks. *Honest Graft: Big Money and the American Political Process.* Washington: Farragut, 1990.

Kern, Montague. *30-Second Politics: Political Advertising in the Eighties.* New York: Praeger, 1989.

Orren, Gary R., and Nelson W. Polsby, eds. *Media and Momentum: The New Hampshire Primary and Nomination Politics.* Chatham, N.J.: Chatham House, 1987.

Patterson, Thomas E. *The Mass Media Election.* New York: Praeger, 1980.

Sabato, Larry J. *Campaigns and Elections: A Reader in Modern American Politics.* Glenview, Ill.: Scott, Foresman, 1989.

———. *PAC Power: Inside the World of Political Action Committees.* New York: Norton, 1985.

———. *Paying for Elections: The Campaign Finance Thicket.* New York: Priority Press for the Twentieth Century Fund, 1989.

———. *The Rise of Political Consultants: New Ways of Winning Elections.* New York: Basic Books, 1981.

Salmore, Barbara G., and Stephen Salmore. *Candidates, Parties, and Campaigns,* 2nd ed. Washington: CQ Press, 1989.

Sorauf, Frank J. *Money in American Elections.* Glenview, Ill.: Scott, Foresman, 1988.

What is the liberty of the press? Who can give it any definition which would not leave the utmost latitude for evasion?

Alexander Hamilton

FEDERALIST NO. 84

Hamilton asserted that the rights of a free press, like all other democratic rights, ultimately depend on the support of the public.

CHAPTER 14

The News Media

The passage by Hamilton that opens this chapter is a pointed reminder that many of the Founders did not share the belief that guaranteed freedom of the press was fundamental to American democracy. Actually, Federalists such as Hamilton agreed to include freedom of the press and the other amendments in the Bill of Rights only to satisfy states' righters and secure passage of the Constitution. And, in fact, there is not much evidence that even the staunchest advocates of the Bill of Rights favored *absolute* freedom of the press, that is, a free press unbalanced by other legitimate rights such as those of personal privacy, fair trial, copyright protection, and national security.[1] The surprising truth is that the Founders devoted little thought and debate to the free press clause because it was not considered a matter of the highest importance. Even its position as the *First* Amendment is deceptive. Originally the rights of free speech and press were included in the third amendment to the proposed Bill of Rights, but the first two amendments were not ratified by the original states. So, what we now herald as the all-powerful, preeminent First Amendment was a product of political compromise, relative inattention, and historical accident!

Nonetheless, the simple words *"Congress shall make no law . . . abridging the freedom of speech, or of the press"* have shaped the American republic as much as or more than any others in the Constitution and its amendments. With the Constitution's sanction, as interpreted by the Supreme Court over two centuries, a vigorous and highly competitive press has emerged. Composed of **print press** (newspapers, magazines, journals) and **electronic media** (television and radio), the news media in the United States arguably have more freedom and are less controlled today than any other press in the world. How this freedom evolved, the ways in which it is manifested, and whether press freedom is used responsibly are subjects that we examine in this chapter.[2]

The American Press of Yesteryear

Journalism—the process and profession of collecting and disseminating the news (that is, new information about subjects of public interest)—has been with us in some form since the dawn of civilization.[3] Yet its practice has often been remarkably uncivilized, and it was far more so at the beginning of the American republic than it is today.

A hint of future directions appeared in the very first newspaper published in America in 1690, which carried a report that the king of France "used to lie with" his son's wife. George Washington escaped most press scrutiny but detested journalists nonetheless; his battle tactics in the Revolutionary War had been much criticized in print, and an early draft of his "Farewell Address to the Nation" at the end of his presidency (1796) contained a condemnation of the press that has often been described as savage.[4] Thomas Jefferson was treated especially harshly by elements of the early American press. For example, one Richmond newspaper editor, angered by Jefferson's refusal to appoint him a postmaster, concocted a falsehood that survives to this day: that Jefferson kept a slave as his concubine and had several children by her.[5] One can understand why Jefferson, normally a defender of a free press, commented that "even the least informed of the people have learned that nothing in a newspaper is to be believed."

Jefferson probably did not intend that statement literally, since he himself was instru-

[1] See Dom Bonafede, "First Amendment on Trial," *National Journal* 23 (July 20, 1991), p. 1833.
[2] For more on this topic, see Larry Sabato, *Feeding Frenzy* (New York: The Free Press, 1991).
[3] See Mitchell Stephens, *A History of News: From the Drum to the Satellite* (New York: Viking, 1989).
[4] Charles Press and Kenneth VerBurg, *American Politicians and Journalists* (Glenview, Ill.: Scott, Foresman, 1988), pp. 8–10.
[5] See Merrill D. Peterson, *Thomas Jefferson and the New Nation* (New York: Oxford University Press, 1970), pp. 185–87.

The History of American Media

1960	First televised presidential campaign debates
1952	First presidential campaign advertisements aired on television
1948	First televised election
1928	First radio broadcast of an election
1900	Muckraking in fashion
1890	Yellow journalism spreads
1833	First "penny press"
1789	First party newspapers circulated
1690	First newspaper published

mental in establishing the *National Gazette,* the newspaper of his political faction and viewpoint. The *Gazette* was created to compete with a similar paper (called the *Gazette of the United States*) founded earlier by Alexander Hamilton and his anti-Jefferson Federalists. The era of party newspapers extended from Washington's tenure through Andrew Jackson's presidency. The editor of Jackson's party paper, *The Globe,* was included in the president's influential "kitchen cabinet" (a group of informal advisers), and all of Jackson's appointees with annual salaries greater than $1,000 were required to buy a subscription. (Incidentally, from George Washington through James Buchanan, who left office in 1861, all government printing contracts were awarded to the newspaper associated with the incumbent administration.)

A Less Partisan Press

The partisan press eventually gave way to the "penny press." In 1833 Benjamin Day founded the *New York Sun,* which cost a penny at the newsstand. It was politically a more independent publication than the party papers, and it was not tied to one party. The *Sun* was the forerunner of the modern press built on mass circulation and commercial advertising to produce profit. By 1861 the penny press had so supplanted partisan papers that President Abraham Lincoln (who succeeded Buchanan) announced that his administration would have no favored or sponsored newspaper.

The press thus became markedly less partisan but not necessarily more respectable. Mass-circulation dailies sought wide readership, and, then as now, readers were clearly attracted by the sensational and the scandalous. The sordid side of politics became the entertainment of the times. One of the best-known examples occurred in the presidential campaign of 1884, when the *Buffalo Evening Telegraph* headlined "A Terrible Tale" about Grover Cleveland, the Democratic nominee.[6] In 1871, while sheriff of Buffalo, the

---

[6]For a delightful rendition of this episode, see Shelley Ross, *Fall from Grace* (New York: Ballantine, 1988), Chapter 12.

The first issue of *The Sun,* Benjamin Day's nonpartisan paper costing a penny in 1833.

bachelor Cleveland had allegedly fathered a child. Even though the woman in question had been seeing other men too, Cleveland willingly accepted responsibility since all the other men were married, and he had dutifully paid child support for years. Fortunately for Cleveland, another newspaper, the *Democratic Sentinel,* broke a story that helped to offset his own scandal: Republican presidential nominee James G. Blaine and his wife had had their first child just three months after their wedding. There is a lesson for politicians in this double-edged morality tale. Cleveland acknowledged his responsibility forthrightly and took his lumps, whereas Blaine backed and filled and told a fabulously elaborate, completely unbelievable story about having had two marriage ceremonies six months apart. Cleveland won the election (though other factors also played a role in his victory).

The era of the intrusive press was in full flower. First **yellow journalism** and then **muckraking** were in fashion. Pioneered by prominent publishers such as William Randolph Hearst and Joseph Pulitzer, yellow journalism[7] featured pictures, comics, and color designed to capture a share of the burgeoning immigrant population market—and also oversimplified and sensationalized many news developments. The front-page "editorial crusade" became common, the motto for which frequently seemed to be "Damn the truth, full speed ahead." The muckrakers—so named by President Theodore Roosevelt after a special rake designed to collect manure[8]—took charge after the turn of the century in a number of newspapers and nationally circulated magazines. Journalists such as Upton Sinclair and David Graham Phillips searched out and exposed real and apparent misconduct by government, business, and politicians in order to stimulate reform.[9] There was no shortage of corruption to reveal, of course, and much good came from these efforts. But an unfortunate side effect of the emphasis on crusades and investigations was

[7] The name strictly derived from printing the comic strip "Yellow Kid" in color.

[8] Doris A. Graber, *Mass Media and American Politics,* 3rd ed. (Washington: CQ Press, 1989), p. 12.

[9] See Thomas C. Leonard, *The Power of the Press: The Birth of American Political Reporting* (New York: Oxford University Press, 1986), Chapter 7.

the frequent publication of gossip and rumor without sufficient proof. The modern press corps may also be guilty of this offense, but it has achieved great progress on another front. Throughout the nineteenth century, payoffs to the press were not uncommon. Andrew Jackson, for instance, gave one in ten of his early appointments to loyal reporters,[10] and during the 1872 presidential campaign the Republicans slipped cash to about 300 newsmen.[11] Wealthy industrialists also sometimes purchased editorial peace or investigative cease-fire for tens of thousands of dollars. Examples of such press corruption today are exceedingly rare, and not even the most extreme of the modern media's critics believe otherwise.

As the news business grew, its focus gradually shifted from passionate opinion to corporate profit. Newspapers, hoping to maximize profit, were more careful not to alienate the advertisers and readers who produced their revenues, and the result was less harsh, more "objective" reporting. Meanwhile, media barons became pillars of the establishment; for the most part, they were no longer the anti-establishment insurgents of yore.

Technological advances obviously had a major impact on this transformation in journalism. High-speed presses and more cheaply produced paper made mass-circulation dailies possible. The telegraph and, later, the telephone made news gathering easier and much faster. And, of course, nothing else could compare to the inventions of radio and television. Radio became widely available in the 1920s, and for the first time, millions of Americans were hearing national politicians instead of merely reading about them. With television—first introduced in the late 1940s and nearly a universal fixture in American homes by the mid-1950s—citizens could see and hear candidates and presidents. The removal of newspapers and magazines as the foremost conduits between politicians and voters had profound effects on the electoral process, as we discuss shortly.

[10] Richard L. Rubin, *Press, Party, and Presidency* (New York: Norton, 1981), pp. 38–39.
[11] Stephen Bates, *If No News, Send Rumors* (New York: St. Martin's Press, 1989), p. 185.

"Uncle Sam's Next Campaign—the War Against the Yellow Press." In this 1898 cartoon in the wake of the Spanish American War, yellow journalism is attacked for its threats, insults, filth, grime, blood, death, slander, gore, and blackmail, all of which is "lies." The cartoonist is suggesting that after winning the foreign war, the government ought to attack its own yellow journalists at home.

The Contemporary Media Scene

The editors of the first partisan newspapers could scarcely have imagined what their profession would become more than two centuries later. The number and diversity of media outlets existing in the 1990s are stunning: many thousands of daily and weekly newspapers, periodicals (magazines, newsletters, computerized information services), and radio and television stations and networks. In some ways the news business is more competitive than at any time in history, yet paradoxically, the news media have expanded in some ways and contracted in others, dramatically changing the ways in which they cover politics.

The growth of the political press corps is obvious to anyone familiar with government or campaigns. Just since 1983, for example, the number of print (newspaper and magazine) reporters accredited at the U.S. Capitol has jumped from 2,300 to more than 4,100; the gain for broadcast (television and radio) journalists was equally impressive and proportionately larger, from about 1,000 in 1983 to more than 2,400 by 1990.[12] On the campaign trail a similar phenomenon has been occurring. In the 1960s a presidential candidate in the primaries would attract a press entourage of at most a couple of dozen reporters, but in the 1990s a hundred or more print and broadcast journalists can be seen tagging along with a frontrunner. Consequently, a politician's every public utterance is made, reported, and intensively scrutinized and interpreted in a media pressure cooker.

Although there are more journalists, they are not necessarily attracting a larger audience, at least on the print side. Daily newspaper circulation has been stagnant for twenty years at 62 to 63 million papers per day (see Figure 14-1). On a per household basis, circulation has actually fallen 44 percent over these two decades.[13] Barely half of the adult population reads a newspaper every day; and, among young people age eighteen to twenty-nine, only a third are daily readers—a decline of 50 percent in two decades. Along with the relative decline of readership has come a drop in the overall level of competition. In 1880, 61 percent of U.S. cities had at least two competing dailies, but by 1990 a mere 2 percent of cities did so. Not surprisingly, the number of dailies has declined significantly, from a peak of 2,600 in 1909 to 1,611 today.[14] And most of the remaining dailies are owned by large media conglomerates called chains. In 1940, 83 percent of all daily newspapers were independently owned, but by 1990 just 24 percent remained out of the clutches of a chain (such as Gannett, Hearst, Knight-Ridder, and Newhouse).

Part of the cause of the newspapers' declining audience has been the increased popularity of television as a news source. As Table 14-1 on page 500 shows, at the dawn of the 1960s a substantial majority of Americans reported that they got most of their news from newspapers, but by the latter half of the 1980s television was the people's choice by an almost two-to-one margin.[15] Moreover, by a margin of 55 to 21 percent, Americans now say that they are inclined to believe television over newspapers when conflicting reports about the same story arise. Of course, most individuals still rely on *both* print and broadcast sources,[16] but there can be little question that television news is increasingly

---

[12] Barbara Matusow, "Washington's Journalism Establishment," *The Washingtonian* 23 (February 1989), pp. 94–101, 265–70.

[13] See Eleanor Randolph, "Extra! Extra! Who Cares?" *Washington Post,* April 1, 1990, pp. Cl, 4.

[14] Sunday newspapers are exceptions to the trend. More than one hundred new Sunday papers were created in the decade of the 1980s, and Sunday circulation as a whole has increased 25 percent since 1970.

[15] Harold W. Stanley and Richard G. Niemi, eds., *Vital Statistics on American Politics* (Washington: CQ Press, 1988), Table 2-8, p. 58.

[16] See Evans Witt, "Here, There, and Everywhere: Where Americans Get Their News," *Public Opinion* 6 (August/September 1983), pp. 45–48; June O. Yum and Kathleen E. Kendall, "Sources of Political Information in a Presidential Primary Campaign," *Journalism Quarterly* 65 (Spring 1988), pp. 148–51, 177.

Figure 14-1   Circulation of Daily Newspapers, 1850–1990

Year	Number of Daily Newspapers	Circulation (in thousands)	Circulation as a Percentage of Population
1850	254	758	3.3%
1890	1,610	8,387	13.3%
1909	2,600	24,212	26.2%
1919	2,441	33,029	31.0%
1927	2,091	41,368	35.7%
1937	2,065	43,345	34.1%
1947	1,854	53,287	37.0%
1958	1,778	58,713	33.6%
1963	1,766	63,831	33.7%
1970	1,748	62,100	30.3%
1980	1,745	62,200	27.3%
1985	1,676	62,800	26.2%
1990	1,611	62,324	25.0%

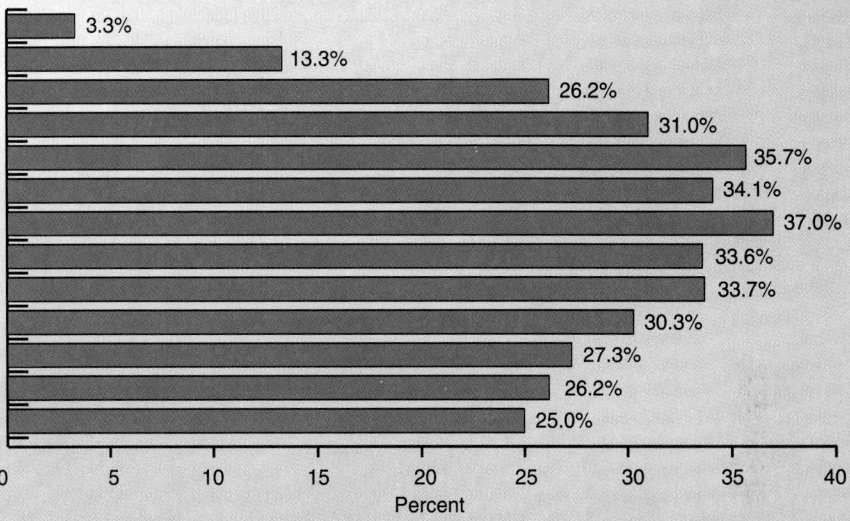

Percent: 0 5 10 15 20 25 30 35 40

Source: Adapted from Harold W. Stanley and Richard G. Niemi, *Vital Statistics on American Politics*, 3rd ed. (Washington: CQ Press, Table 2–3, pp. 56–57.

The number of daily newspapers peaked in 1909, and it has fallen sharply since. The proportion of Americans who subscribe to newspapers has also dropped steadily since 1947, and only a quarter of the American population subscribes to a daily newspaper today.

important. Despite its many drawbacks (such as simplicity, brevity, and entertainment orientation) television news is "news that matters."[17] Although not totally eclipsing newspapers, television frequently overshadows them, even as it often takes its agenda and lead stories from the headlines produced by print reporters (especially those working for the "print elite," such as the *New York Times,* the *Washington Post,* the *Wall Street Journal,* the Associated Press, United Press International, *Time, Newsweek,* and *U.S. News & World Report*). Regrettably, busy people today appear to have less time to review the printed word, and consequently they rely more on television's brief headline summaries to stay in touch.

The television news industry differs from its print cousin in a variety of ways. For one, the number of outlets has been increasing, not declining as with newspapers. The three major networks now receive broadcast competition from Cable Network News (CNN), "Headline News," Cable Satellite Public Affairs Network (C-SPAN), and PBS's "MacNeil/ Lehrer NewsHour." Although the audiences of all the alternate shows are relatively small compared with those of the network shows, they are growing while the networks' audience shares contract. The potential for cable expansion is still large, too; less than half of all American households are currently wired for cable. Adding to television's diversity, the national TV news corps is often outnumbered on the campaign trail by local television reporters. Satellite technology has enabled any of the 1,300 local stations willing to invest in the hardware an opportunity to beam back reports from the field. On a daily basis, local TV news is watched by more people (67 percent of adults) than network news (49 percent), so increased local attention to politics has some real significance.

[17]This was the fundamental conclusion of Shanto Iyengar and Donald R. Kinder, *News That Matters* (Chicago: University of Chicago Press, 1987).

Table 14-1   Use and Trustworthiness of News Media

In the 1950s newspapers provided most of the average American's news, and papers were more "believable" than television. By the 1980s television had triumphed over newspapers in both categories, and TV had also eclipsed the influence of radio and magazines.

	1959	1963	1967	1972	1976	1982	1986
Source of most news[a]							
Television	51%	55%	64%	64%	64%	64%	66%
Newspapers	57	53	55	50	49	44	36
Radio	34	29	28	21	19	18	14
Magazines	8	6	7	6	7	6	4
People	4	4	4	4	5	4	4
Most believable[b]							
Television	29%	36%	41%	48%	51%	53%	55%
Newspapers	32	24	24	21	22	22	21
Radio	12	12	7	8	7	6	6
Magazines	10	10	8	10	9	8	7
Don't know/no answer	17	18	20	13	11	11	12

[a]Question: "First, I'd like to ask you where you usually get most of your news about what's going on in the world today—from the newspapers or radio or television or magazines or talking to people or where?" (more than one answer permitted)

[b]Question: "If you got conflicting or different reports of the same news story from radio, television, the magazines, and the newspapers, which of the versions would you be most inclined to believe—the one on the radio or television or magazines or newspapers?" (only one answer permitted)

Source: Adapted from Harold W. Stanley and Richard G. Niemi, *Vital Statistics on American Politics,* 3rd ed. (Washington: CQ Press, 1992), Table 2-13, p. 75.

The decline of the major networks' audience shares and the local stations' decreasing reliance on the major networks for news—coupled with stringent belt tightening ordered by the networks' corporate managers—resulted in severe news staff cutbacks at NBC, CBS, and ABC during the 1980s. These "economy measures" have affected the quality of broadcast journalism. Many senior correspondents bemoan the loss of desk assistants and junior reporters who did much of the legwork necessary to get less superficial, more in-depth pieces on the air. As a consequence, stories requiring extensive research are often discarded in favor of simplistic, eye-catching, "sexy" items that increasingly seem to dominate campaign and government coverage.

Media That Matter

Every newspaper, radio station, and television station is influential in its own bailiwick, but only a handful of media outlets really matter in a national sense. The United States has no nationwide daily newspapers to match the influence of Great Britain's *The Times,* the *Guardian,* and the *Daily Telegraph,* all of which are avidly read in virtually every corner of the United Kingdom. The national orientation of the British print media can be traced to the smaller size of the country and London's role as both the national capital and the largest cultural metropolis. The vastness of our country and the existence of many large cities such as New York, Los Angeles, and Chicago effectively preclude a nationally united print medium in the United States.

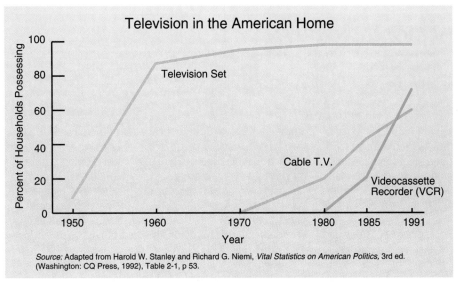

Television in the American Home

Source: Adapted from Harold W. Stanley and Richard G. Niemi, *Vital Statistics on American Politics,* 3rd ed. (Washington: CQ Press, 1992), Table 2-1, p 53.

Television sets have been standard equipment in the average American home since the 1960s. Cable television and VCRs were added only in the 1980s, when both technological innovations joined U.S. households with phenomenal speed.

However, national distribution of the *New York Times,* the *Wall Street Journal, USA Today,* and the *Christian Science Monitor* does exist, and other newspapers such as the *Washington Post* and the *Los Angeles Times* have substantial influence from coast to coast. These six newspapers also have a pronounced effect on what the four national **networks** (ABC, CBS, NBC, and CNN) broadcast on their evening news programs—or, in the case of CNN, around the clock. A major story that breaks in one of these papers is nearly guaranteed to be featured on one or more of the network news shows. These news shows are carried by hundreds of local stations—called **affiliates**—that are associated with the national networks and may choose to carry their programming. Two **wire**

The CNN cable network has emerged as a strong competitor for traditional network news shares. During the 1991 Gulf War, millions of Americans tuned into CNN for constant coverage.

People of the Past

Pioneers of the Broadcasting Industry

One of the first and most prominent broadcast journalists in the United States was the CBS radio anchor Edward R. Murrow. Trained in language and public speaking through childhood Bible readings and endowed with a richly textured voice, Murrow was a superb radio reporter who later adapted his skills to the new medium of television.

Murrow joined CBS in 1935 as director of "talks and education," a position that entailed setting up radio speeches by prominent public officials. In 1937 he became European director of "talks," stationed in London, a move that would prove to be the catalyst for his career as a radio newscaster. When Germany invaded Austria on March 11, 1938, Murrow was on assignment in Poland, but he was soon directed to go to Vienna. Once in Austria, which he reached only with great difficulty, Murrow's dramatic eyewitness accounts of Adolf Hitler's takeover mesmerized both Europe and the United States.

Murrow's finest moment, however, came in the 1940 "Battle of Britain"—the German bombing campaign that flattened much of London. Probably more than any other broadcast journalist, Murrow brought the air battle to the forefront of American public attention. Murrow was so respected by British authorities that only he and two other reporters—NBC's Fred Bates and John MacVane—were permitted to broadcast without first clearing their information with British censors. Murrow, Bates, and MacVane all did rooftop broadcasts during Germany's bombing raids, but CBS's were the most listened to because of Murrow's special talents.

After the war, in 1946, Murrow became vice president of news and public affairs at CBS. His task was to set the course of that network's radio newscasting, and one of his achievements was the development of CBS's first documentary unit. Yet Murrow did not really enjoy administration, and a few years later he returned to the field as a journalist, this time on television. Among his many accomplishments were hard-hitting CBS programs on the right-wing extremism of U.S. Senator Joseph R. McCarthy (R.-Wisc.) and on the poverty and exploitation of migrant workers. In 1961 Murrow was appointed director of the United States Information Agency by President John F. Kennedy; he died of cancer in 1965.

Meanwhile, NBC television was establishing the first broadcast news anchor team for its evening news show. Chet Huntley and David Brinkley hosted "The Huntley–Brinkley Report" each night for fifteen minutes. The two had first been paired to cover the 1956 Democratic and Republican presidential conventions, and it was obvious from the start that they were compatible and appealing. Huntley, a North Carolina native who got his start with United Press International, had a solemn, serious style of reporting. Brinkley, a Montanan who started his media career working for KPCB-AM in Seattle while a senior at the University of Washington—he was at once a disc jockey, a writer, salesman, and a janitor—had a sharp, witty tone that complemented Huntley nicely. Americans quickly became accustomed to their style and their signature signoff at program's end: "Goodnight, David." "Goodnight, Chet." "And goodnight for NBC News."

"The Huntley–Brinkley Report" ran for fourteen years, from 1956 to 1970. In 1963 its time slot was increased to a half hour, mostly in response to competition from CBS, which had initiated the first half-hour news show on network television, anchored by another rising star, Walter Cronkite. In 1970 the team broke up when Chet Huntley decided to retire. While Huntley has since died, David Brinkley still broadcasts a Sunday talk show, though he has changed networks, working now for ABC News.

services, the Associated Press (AP) and United Press International (UPI), also nationalize the news. Most newspapers subscribe to one or both services, which not only produce their own news stories but also put "on the wire" major stories produced by other media outlets. AP is the older of the two, having been founded in 1848, and it is also financially healthier than UPI, which has suffered massive staff cutbacks in recent years.

The national newspapers, wire services, and broadcast networks are supplemented by a number of national news magazines whose subscribers number in the millions. *Time,*

Newsweek, and *U.S. News & World Report* bring the week's news into focus and head-line one event or trend for special treatment. Other news magazines stress commentary from an ideological viewpoint, including *The Nation* (left-wing), *The New Republic* (moderate-liberal), and *The National Review* (conservative). These publications have much smaller circulations, but their readerships are composed of activists and opinion leaders, and therefore they have disproportionate influence.

Circumstances can conspire to make a publication of lesser importance into a relative giant. For example, the *Manchester Union-Leader* in New Hampshire and the *Des Moines Register* in Iowa are closely read by a national political audience in the months leading up to the early presidential contests in these states. (In presidential election years, New Hampshire has the nation's first scheduled primary, and Iowa has the first caucus.)

How the Media Cover Politicians and Government

Covering the Presidency

In the U.S. system of government the three branches are roughly equal in power and authority, but in the world of media coverage, the president is first among equals. All television cables lead to the White House, and a president can address the nation on all networks almost at will. Congress and the courts appear divided and confused institutions on the tube—different segments contradicting others—whereas the commander-in-chief is in clear focus as chief of state and head of government. The situation is scarcely different in other democracies. In Britain, all media eyes are on No. 10 Downing Street, the office and residence of the prime minister.

Since Franklin Roosevelt's time, the presidential press conference has been used by chief executives to shape public opinion and explain their actions. The presence of the press directly in the White House enables a president to appear even on very short notice and to televise live, interrupting regular programming. The White House's press-briefing room is a familiar sight on the evening news, not just because presidents use it so often but also because the presidential press secretary has almost daily question-and-answer

Presidential press conferences: After summit meetings with Soviet President Mikhail Gorbachev in May 1990, President Bush gave an informal press conference outside the White House. Press conferences can be spontaneous, like this one, or prearranged, as they often are in the White House press room.

Presidential News Conferences, 1929–1991

President		Total Number of Press Conferences	Average Number of Press Conferences per Month
Hoover	(1929–33)	268	
Roosevelt	(1933–45)	998	
Truman	(1945–53)	334	
Eisenhower	(1953–61)	193	
Kennedy	(1961–63)	65	
Johnson	(1963–69)	135	
Nixon	(1969–74)	39	
Ford	(1974–77)	39	
Carter	(1977–81)	59	
Reagan	(1981–89)	53	
Bush	(1989–91)[a]	45	

[a] As of June 15, 1991.

Source: Adapted from Harold W. Stanley and Richard G. Niemi, *Vital Statistics on American Politics*, 3rd ed. (Washington: CQ Press, 1992) Table 2–4, p. 59.

sessions there. The press secretary's post has existed only since Herbert Hoover's administration (1929–33), and the individual holding it is the president's main conduit of information to the press. A number of presidents have chosen for this vital position close aides who were very familiar with their thinking. For example, John Kennedy had Pierre

Press Secretary Marlin Fitzwater

President Bush's press secretary was an old hand at his job—he was also President Reagan's press secretary. This unusual continuity was partly the result of the close relationship that existed between Republican presidents Reagan and Bush; the change of administration in 1989 did not necessarily mean a change in personnel. Fitzwater had served from 1985 to 1987 as Bush's press spokesperson while Bush was vice-president. Bush then passed Fitzwater along to Reagan when Rea-

gan needed a replacement for presidential press secretary Larry Speakes when the latter resigned in 1987.

Unlike many other press secretaries who have had a long personal and political relationship with their presidents, most of Fitzwater's career was with the federal government as a speech writer and press relations manager for various executive departments and commissions. Fitzwater earned his undergraduate degree in journalism from Kansas State University in 1965.

The White House Press Corps

Perhaps the most visible part of the national press corps is the group of correspondents who work at the White House. Every network, many large television stations, and virtually all big-city daily newspapers have at least one representative who works in the White House to cover the president and his chief advisers. Other media outlets representing foreign countries are also given access to the White House and are included in the presidential press corps.

White House reporters do not have the run of the place, of course. They are usually restricted to the press room, which is used by the president to make announcements and to hold informal question-and-answer sessions. Small cubicles adjoining the press room are also provided for many news outlets. Although presidential appearances in the press room rarely occur more than once or twice a week, the president's news secretary appears daily to "brief" reporters on the chief executive's current schedule and activities. Frequently the press secretary also makes announcements on behalf of the president

(perhaps the chief executive's comment on just-released economic statistics, for example).

Formal presidential news conferences, often held in the East Room of the White House, are an elaborate production, especially if held during prime-time hours. All the networks carry them live and in full, and correspondents jockey to attract the president's attention. The best-known reporters are nearly guaranteed to be selected, and these are prime opportunities for them—and the news organizations they represent. Over the years, many of the networks' most prominent professionals have served on the White House beat, including CBS's Dan Rather and Lesley Stahl, NBC's Tom Brokaw, and ABC's Sam Donaldson.

It is not always easy for the president to have reporters literally underfoot. But the instantaneous access they give the president to the American people is essential to his work, and the scrutiny of the chief executive they offer the American people is vital to the voters as well.

Salinger (now an ABC News foreign correspondent), Lyndon Johnson had Bill Moyers (who now hosts many PBS documentaries), and Jimmy Carter chose his longtime Georgia associate Jody Powell. Probably the most famous recent presidential press secretary is James Brady, who was wounded and disabled in the March 1981 assassination attempt on President Ronald Reagan.

Covering Congress

Press coverage of Congress is very different. The size of the institution alone (535 members) and its decentralized nature (bicameralism, the committee system, and so on) make it difficult for the media to survey. Most news organizations solve this problem by concentrating coverage on three groups of individuals. First, the leaders of both parties in both houses receive the lion's share of attention because only they can speak for a majority of their party's members. Usually the majority and minority leaders in each house and the Speaker of the House are the preferred spokespersons, but the whips also secure a substantial share of air time and column inches. Second, key committee chairs

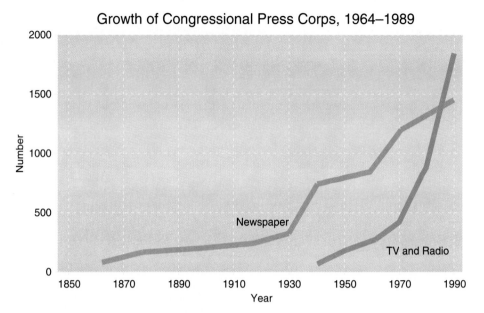

Growth of Congressional Press Corps, 1964–1989

Source: Adapted from Harold W. Stanley and Richard G. Niemi, *Vital Statistics on American Politics*, 3rd ed. (Washington: CQ Press, 1992), Figure 2–1, p. 58.

Steady growth in the number of reporters covering Congress has occurred from the time of the Civil War to the present day. But only in the 1980s did TV and radio newspeople begin to out-number newspaper journalists. Press corps members are those correspondents entitled to admission to the Senate and House press galleries and radio and television galleries.

command center media stage when subjects in their domain are newsworthy. Heads of the most prominent committees (such as Ways and Means or Armed Services) are guaranteed frequent coverage, but even the chairs and members of minor committees or subcommittees can achieve fame when the time and issue are right. For example, normally the U.S. Senate Subcommittee on Surface Transportation is not a hotbed of media interest, but when the subjects before it were drug selling and prostitution at highway truck stops, reporters and cameras packed the hearing room in 1989, showering attention on an obscure Nebraska senator, James Exon (the subcommittee chairman). Third, local newspapers and broadcast stations will normally devote some resources to covering their local senators and representatives, even when these legislators are junior and relatively lacking in influence. Most office holders, in turn, are mainly concerned with the "care and feeding" of their local media contingents, as these reporters are the ones who directly and regularly reach the voters in their home constituencies.

One other kind of congressional news coverage is worth noting: investigative-committee hearings. Occasionally, a sensational scandal leads to televised congressional committee hearings that transfix and electrify the nation. In the early 1950s Senator Joseph R. McCarthy (R.-Wisc.) held a series of hearings to expose and root out what he claimed were communists in the State Department and other U.S. government agencies. The senator's irresponsible style of investigation, involving many wild charges made without proof and the smearing of some innocent opponents with the communist label, gave rise to the term "McCarthyism." The Watergate hearings of 1973 and 1974 made heroes out of two committee chairs, Senator Sam Ervin (D.-N.C.) and U.S. Representative Peter Rodino (D.-N.J.), for uncovering many of the facts behind the Watergate scandal and then pursuing the impeachment of President Richard Nixon. (Nixon resigned in August 1974, before the full House could vote on his impeachment.) In 1987 the Iran-*Contra* hearings—set up to investigate a complicated Reagan administration scheme in which arms were sold to Iran and then the profits were diverted to the Nicaraguan anti-communist *contras*—also created a popular hero. This time, however, he was not the committee chair but a witness, Lieutenant Colonel Oliver North, a White House aide deeply involved in the scandal. North's boyish appeal and patriotic demeanor projected well on television, where all the hearings were carried live (as were the McCarthy and Watergate hearings). More recently, in October 1991, the nation was treated to another televised committee spectacle when Supreme Court nominee Clarence Thomas was accused of sexual harassment (see the box on the Thomas hearings on page 508).

Covering the Courts

The most different branch of government, in press coverage as in so many other respects, is the court system. Cloaked in secrecy—because judicial deliberation and decision making are conducted in private—the courts receive scant coverage under most circumstances. However, a volatile or controversial issue such as abortion can change the rules, especially when the Supreme Court is rendering the decision. Each network and major newspaper has one or more Supreme Court reporters, usually well schooled in the law, and their "instant analysis" of court opinions interprets the decisions for the millions of lay people without legal training. Gradually, the admission of cameras into state and local courtrooms across America is offering citizens a more in-depth look at the operation of the judicial branch. As yet, though, the Supreme Court permits no televised proceedings.

Even more than the Court's decisions, presidential appointments to the high court are the focus of intense media attention. As the judiciary has assumed a more important role in modern times, the men and women considered for the post are being subjected to withering scrutiny of their records and even their private lives. Media disclosure that Douglas Ginsberg had smoked marijuana extensively as an adult forced President Reagan to withdraw his Supreme Court nomination in 1987, for example.

Watergate and the Era of Investigative Journalism

The Watergate scandal of the Nixon administration—which stemmed from White House efforts to eavesdrop on officials of the Democratic National Committee and then cover up presidential involvement in the scheme—had the most profound impact of any modern event on the manner and substance of the press's conduct. In many respects Watergate began a chain reaction that today allows for intense scrutiny of public officials' private lives. Moreover, coupled with the civil rights movement and Vietnam, Watergate shifted the orientation of journalism away from mere description (providing an account of happenings) and toward prescription—helping to set the campaign's (and society's) agenda by focusing attention on the candidates' shortcomings as well as certain social problems.

A new breed and a new generation of reporters were attracted to journalism, and particularly its investigative role. As a group they were idealistic, though aggressively mistrustful of authority, and they shared a contempt for "politics as usual." The Vietnam and Watergate generation today dominates journalism: They and their younger colleagues hold sway over most newsrooms, with two-thirds of all reporters now under the age of thirty-six and an ever-increasing share of editors and executives drawn from the Watergate-era class.[18]

Of course, many of those who found journalism newly attractive in the wake of Watergate were not completely altruistic. Young and ambitious journalists saw the happy fate of the *Washington Post*'s young Watergate sleuths Bob Woodward and Carl

---

[18] American Society of Newspaper Editors, *The Changing Face of the Newsroom* (Washington: ASNE, May 1989), p. 29.

The Clarence Thomas Hearings

Like Watergate and the Iran-*Contra* scandal, Clarence Thomas's nomination to the Supreme Court in 1991 gave rise to a television extravaganza that mesmerized the American people. The U.S. Senate's Judiciary Committee hearings on allegations of sexual harassment lodged against Thomas drew a large audience for three full days in early October 1991.

A few months earlier, President Bush had nominated Thomas, a black conservative, to succeed retiring Justice Thurgood Marshall, a pillar of the civil rights movement. Thomas appeared to be heading to an easy Senate confirmation when National Public Radio's correspondent Nina Totenberg reported the harassment charges just days before Thomas's scheduled confirmation vote. The all-male Senate Judiciary Committee had earlier disregarded the charges, in part because the chief accuser, University of Oklahoma Law School Professor Anita Hill, was reluctant to come forward publicly. But the information was leaked to National Public Radio and other news outlets, and soon the Senate was forced to postpone the confirma-

tion vote and to hold an additional Judiciary Committee hearing to investigate the allegations, which dated back to Thomas's chairmanship of the Equal Employment Opportunity Commission during the Reagan presidency. (Hill had also been an EEOC employee and one of Thomas's subordinates.)

The hearings became a national obsession—a real-life soap opera made for television. Hill's graphic accusations of Thomas's advances and vivid sexual allusions shocked many Americans, who were equally riveted by Thomas's angry denial of the charges and denouncement of the Judiciary Committee inquiry as "a high-tech lynching." Convincing and sincere character witnesses for both sides were produced, leaving most viewers puzzled about the truth. In the absence of hard evidence, a substantial majority of citizens (as measured by public opinion polls) eventually sided with Thomas, and he managed to win confirmation in the full Senate by a vote of fifty-two to forty-eight—the narrowest affirmative vote for a Supreme Court justice in this century.

The most damaging political conse-

Bernstein, who gained fame, fortune, and big-screen portrayals by Robert Redford and Dustin Hoffman in the movie *All the President's Men.* The young were attracted not just to journalism but to a particular *kind* of journalism. Their role models were not respected, established reporters but two unknowns who succeeded by refusing to play by the rules their seniors had accepted. Whatever their motives, though, journalism's new breed has been determined to "get to the bottom" of each new scandal.

In the post-Watergate press there is a volatile mix of guilt and fear at work. The guilt stems from regret that experienced Washington reporters failed to detect the telltale signs of the Watergate scandal early on; that even after the story broke, most journalists underplayed the unfolding disaster until forced to take it more seriously by the two wet-behind-the-ears *Post* cubs; that over the years journalism's leading lights had gotten too close to the politicians they were supposed to check and therefore for too long failed to tell the public about dangerous excesses in the government. The press's ongoing fear is deepseated and complements the guilt. Every journalist is apprehensive about missing the next "big one," of being left on the platform when the next scandal train leaves Union Station.

The intense media attention focused on the Senate Judiciary Committee's confirmation hearings of Judge Clarence Thomas created a three-way spectacle: the senators, the testifiers (pictured above is Thomas), and the media themselves.

quences of the hearings were visited on the senators themselves. Both sides agreed that the Senate had handled the matter poorly—first, by not treating Hill's accusations seriously, then by conducting a public spectacle. The Watergate hearings made heroes of many of the participating legislators (such as U.S. Senator Sam Ervin of North Carolina, the folksy chairman of the Senate Watergate panel). But the Thomas hearings only diminished the reputations of most senators who had the misfortune to be in the spotlight. Democrats such as Senator Edward M. Kennedy of

Massachusetts, not known to have a spotless private life, were derided for hypocrisy, while Republicans such as Arlen Specter of Pennsylvania and Alan Simpson of Wyoming were criticized for their often harsh questioning of Anita Hill.

The contrast between the Watergate and the Thomas hearings demonstrates that intense media coverage is a double-edged sword: When the television lights are trained on elected officials, they can easily emerge as national heroes—or national objects of scorn.

The Post-Watergate Era

In the post-Watergate era, the sizable financial and personnel investments many major news organizations have made in investigative units almost guarantee that greater attention will be given to scandals and that probably more of them—some real and some manufactured—will be uncovered.

The "Character Issue" in Media Coverage of Politicians

Another clear consequence of Watergate has been the increasing emphasis placed by the press on the character of candidates. The issue of character has always been present in American politics—George Washington was not made our first president for his policy positions—but rarely if ever has character been such an issue as it has in elections from 1976 onward. Jimmy Carter's 1976 presidential campaign was characterized by moral posturing in the wake of Watergate. Edward Kennedy's 1980 presidential candidacy was destroyed in part by lingering character questions; and the 1988 race witnessed an explosion of character concerns so forceful that several candidates (such as Gary Hart) were badly scarred by it.

The character issue may in part have been an outgrowth of the "new journalism" popularized by the author Tom Wolfe in the 1970s.[19] Contending that conventional journalism was sterile and stripped of color, Wolfe and others argued for a reporting style that expanded the definition of news and, novel-like, highlighted all the personal details of the newsmaker. Then, too, reporters had witnessed the success of such books as Theodore H. White's "Making of the President" series and Joe McGinniss's *The Selling of the President 1968,* which offered revealing behind-the-scenes vignettes of the previous election's candidates with their hair down.[20] Why not give readers and viewers this information before the election?, the press reasoned. And there was encouragement from academic quarters as well. "Look to character first" when evaluating and choosing among presidential candidates, wrote Duke University political science professor James David Barber in an acclaimed and widely circulated 1972 volume, *The Presidential Character* (see Chapter 7).[21]

Whatever the precise historical origins of the character trend in reporting, it is undergirded by certain assumptions. First, the press sees that it has mainly replaced the political parties as the "screening committee" that winnows the field of candidates and filters out the weaker or more unlucky contenders. (This fact may be yet another reason to support the strengthening of the political parties. Politicians are in a much better position than the press to provide professional "peer review" of their colleagues who are seeking the presidency.) Second, many journalists believe it necessary to tell people about any of

---

[19]See Tom Wolfe, *The New Journalism* (New York: Harper & Row, 1973), especially pp. 9–32.

[20]The first and best in White's series was *The Making of the President 1960* (New York: Atheneum, 1961). See also Joe McGinniss, *The Selling of the President 1968* (New York: Trident, 1969).

[21]See James David Barber, *The Presidential Character* (Englewood Cliffs, N.J.: Prentice Hall, 1972), p. 445.

Bill Clinton and the character issue: Early in the primary season leading up to the elections of 1992, accusations of infidelity emerged against Democratic frontrunner Bill Clinton. In an attempt to turn the tide, Clinton and his wife Hillary addressed the charges on "60 Minutes" immediately after NBC's television broadcast of the Superbowl. Although Clinton lost his lead in New Hampshire polls and finished second to Senator Paul Tsongas there, he went on to reclaim frontrunner status.

Then and Now

The Character Issue from Grover Cleveland to Gary Hart

The "character issue"—which focuses press attention on the private-life activities and personalities of candidates—has been with us throughout American history, as the text's reference to President Grover Cleveland's child born out of wedlock suggests.

Yet the intensity and the reach of the character issue has grown over the centuries, and particularly in recent years, as Democratic presidential candidate Gary Hart discovered to his chagrin in 1987. The press corps had long heard stories about Hart's alleged extramarital affairs, but no useful evidence had come to light. The situation changed dramatically in May 1987, shortly after Hart declared his candidacy for a second run at the White House.

The *Miami Herald* received an anonymous tip that Hart would be meeting an attractive model for a weekend tryst in Washington, D.C. This tip closely followed Hart's public insistence that the "womanizing" rumors about him were false and that his once-rocky marriage was again on firm ground. Hart had said to one reporter, E. J. Dionne of the *New York Times,* "Follow me around. . . . [You'll] be very bored."

Bored the *Miami Herald* was not when it decided to stake out Hart's Washington townhouse. The paper's reporters apparently observed Hart and Donna Rice, the model, inhabiting the townhouse, although the journalists' surveillance was not continuous and both house entrances were not always covered. Despite the flaws, the circumstances were suspicious enough to generate a major scandal that dominated Hart's campaign.

Hart tried to fight back, insisting on his innocence and his right to privacy, but his damage-control operation collapsed in the face of other revelations, such as the disclosure that Hart and Rice had earlier taken an overnight cruise to Bimini on the aptly christened yacht *Monkey Business.* Hart's exit from the campaign came after Paul Taylor, a *Washington Post* reporter, asked the candidate, "Have you ever committed adultery?" Hart declined to answer, but the meaning of the query soon became clear: The *Post* had identified yet another woman with whom Hart had had a long-standing relationship. Faced with that potential disclosure and caught up in an overwhelming media maelstrom, Hart withdrew from the race on May 8, 1987, with a bitter blast at the "intrusive" press that had brought him down. He briefly reentered the presidential contest in December, but by then Hart was a spent force and received only a handful of votes in the early 1988 contests.

Probably no event from the 1988 presidential campaign has proved to be as memorable as the undoing of Gary Hart. The Hart episode also marked a milestone for the news media. They had helped to eliminate the Democratic Party's frontrunner before a single voter's ballot had been cast in the primaries, and they had done it by aggressively investigating the private life of the unlucky candidate.

a candidate's foibles that might affect his or her public performance. The press's third supposition is that it is giving the public what it wants and expects, more or less. Perhaps television has conditioned voters to think about the private "lives of the rich and famous." The rules of television prominence now seem to apply to all celebrities equally, whether they reside in Hollywood or Washington.

Loosening of the Libel Law. Another factor permits the modern press to undertake "character" investigations. In the old days, a reporter would think twice about filing a story critical of a politician's character, and the editors probably would have killed the story had the reporter been foolish enough to do so. The reason? Fear of a libel suit. (Recall from Chapter 4 that libel is published defamation of character that unjustly injures a person's reputation.) The first question editors would ask about even an ambiguous or suggestive phrase about a public official was, "If we're sued, can you prove beyond a doubt what you've written?"

Such inhibitions were ostensibly lifted in 1964, when the Supreme Court ruled in ***New York Times Co.* v. *Sullivan***[22] that simply publishing a defamatory falsehood was not enough to justify a libel judgment. Henceforth a public official would have to prove "actual malice," a requirement extended three years later to all public figures, such as Hollywood stars and prominent athletes.[23] The Supreme Court declared that the First Amendment requires elected officials and candidates to prove that the publisher either believed the challenged statement was false or at least entertained serious doubts about its truth and acted recklessly in publishing it in the face of those doubts. The "actual malice" rule has made it very difficult for public figures to win in libel cases.

Despite *Sullivan,* the threat of libel litigation (and its deterrent effect on the press) persists for at least two reasons. First, the *Sullivan* protections do little to reduce the expense of defending defamation claims. The monetary costs have grown enormously, as have the required commitments of reporters' and editors' time and energy. Small news organizations without the financial resources of a national network or the *New York Times* are sometimes reluctant to publish material that might invite a lawsuit because the litigation costs could threaten their existence. The second reason for the continuing libel threat is a cultural phenomenon of heightened sensitivity to the harm that words can do to an individual's emotional tranquility. As a result, politicians are often more inclined to sue their press adversaries, even when success is unlikely.

But high costs and the politicians' propensity to sue cut both ways. The overall number of libel suits filed in recent years has dropped because plaintiffs also incur hefty legal bills, and—perhaps more important—they have despaired of winning. Some news outlets have added another disincentive by filing countersuits charging their antagonists with bringing frivolous or nuisance actions against them.

In practice, then, the loosening of libel law has provided journalists with a safer harbor from liability in their reporting on elected officials and candidates. Whether it has truly diminished press self-censorship, especially for less financially endowed media outlets, is a more difficult question. However, at least for the wealthy newspapers and networks, the libel laws are no longer as severe a restraint on the press as they once were.

The Question of Bias

Whenever the media break an unfavorable story about a politician, the politician usually counters with a cry of "biased reporting"—a claim that the press has told an untruth, only part of the truth, or reported facts out of the complete context of the event. Who is right? Are the news media biased? The answer is simple and unavoidable: Of course they are. Journalists are fallible human beings who inevitably have values, preferences, and attitudes galore—some conscious, others subconscious, but all reflected at one time or another in the subjects or slants selected for coverage. Given that the press is biased, it is important to know in what ways it is biased and when and how the biases show.

Truth be told, most journalists lean to the left. First of all, those in the relatively small group of professional journalists (not much over 100,000, compared with more than 4 million teachers in the United States) are drawn heavily from the ranks of highly educated social and political liberals, as a number of studies, some conducted by the media themselves, have shown.[24] Journalists are substantially Democratic in party affiliation and voting habits, progressive and anti-establishment in political orientation, and well to

[22] 376 U.S. 254 (1964). See also Steven Pressman, "Libel Law: Finding the Right Balance," *Editorial Research Reports* 2 (August 18, 1989), pp. 462–71.

[23] *Curtis Publishing Co.* v. *Butts,* 388 U.S. 130 (1967); *Associated Press* v. *Walker,* 388 U.S. 130 (1967).

[24] American Society of Newspaper Editors, p. 33; William Schneider and I. A. Lewis, "Views on the News," *Public Opinion* 8 (August/September 1985), pp. 6–11, 58–59; and S. Robert Lichter, Stanley Rothman, and Linda S. Lichter, *The Media Elite* (Bethesda, Md.: Adler & Adler, 1986).

the left of the general public on most economic, foreign policy, and social issues (such as abortion, affirmative action, gay rights, and gun control). Second, many dozens of the most influential reporters and executives entered (or reentered) journalism after stints of partisan involvement in campaigns or government, and a substantial majority worked for Democrats.[25] Third, this liberal press bias does indeed show up frequently on screen and in print. A study of reporting on the abortion issue, for example, revealed a clear slant to the "pro" side on network television news, matching in many ways the reporters' own abortion-rights views.[26] Additionally, the media list to the left on the agenda of topics they choose to cover.[27] In the latter half of the 1980s, for instance, television gave enormous attention to the homelessness issue; in the process, some experts in the field believe, the broadcasters both exaggerated the problem and grossly overstated the role of unemployment in creating the condition of homelessness.[28]

The public, incidentally, senses that most members of the press have somewhat different beliefs from those of the citizenry at large. The Times Mirror Center for the People and the Press, which has commissioned an enlightening series of Gallup surveys on public attitudes toward journalism, found in 1989 that 76 percent of a random sample of the U.S. adult population saw "a great deal" or "a fair amount" of political bias in news coverage.[29] And 68 percent believed that news organizations tended to favor one side rather than deal fairly with all sides on political and social issues. (Just four years earlier, the proportion citing one-sidedness had been only 53 percent.) By decisive margins, respondents who chose to classify press bias saw it as leaning toward the liberal rather than toward the conservative or moderate.

Conservative politicians do not need a Gallup survey to convince them that the press is biased against them. For decades, right-of-center Republican leaders have railed against the "liberal media." When former President Dwight Eisenhower attacked the "sensation-seeking" press at the 1964 GOP convention, which nominated Barry Goldwater for president, delegates raged against the media assemblage, cursing and shaking their fists at them. No one has ever launched a more vigorous assault against the American media than did Vice President Spiro T. Agnew, who in November 1969 derided the "small band of network commentators and self-appointed analysts . . . who not only enjoy a right of instant rebuttal to every presidential address but more importantly wield a free hand in selecting, presenting, and interpreting the great issues in our nation."

The events of many national election years underscore conservative complaints. Richard Nixon's claim of a Democratic tilt during his 1968 presidential race was supported in a much-circulated—and greatly criticized—1971 book by *TV Guide*'s Edith Efron, *The News Twisters,*[30] in which the author claimed that network news shows had

[25] See Dom Bonafede, "Crossing Over," *National Journal* 21 (January 14, 1989), p. 102; Richard Harwood, "Tainted Journalists," *Washington Post,* December 4, 1988, p. L6; Charles Trueheart, "Trading Places: The Insiders Debate," *Washington Post,* January 4, 1989, pp. D1, 19; and Kirk Victor, "Slanted Views," *National Journal* 20 (June 4, 1988), p. 1512.

[26] "*Roe* v. *Webster,*" *Media Monitor* 3 (October 1989), pp. 1–6; also David Shaw, "Abortion and the Media," (four-part series) *Los Angeles Times,* July 1, 1990, pp. A1, 50–51; July 2, 1990, pp. A1, 20; July 3, 1990, pp. A1, 22–23; July 4, 1990, pp. A1, 28–29.

[27] The importance of the agenda-setting function is discussed throughout Shanto Iyengar and Donald R. Kinder, *News That Matters.* See especially pp. 4 and 33.

[28] David Whitman, "Who's Who Among the Homeless," *The New Republic* 199, June 6, 1988, pp. 18–20.

[29] Times-Mirror Center for the People and the Press, "The People and the Press, Part 5: Public Attitudes Toward News Organizations," based on an in-person random sample survey of 1,507 adult Americans, conducted by the Gallup organization between August 9 and 28, 1989 (margin of error: plus or minus 3 percent).

[30] Edith Efron, *The News Twisters* (Los Angeles: Nash, 1971). See the criticisms of Efron's study in Paul Weaver, "Is Television News Biased?" *Public Interest* (Winter 1972), pp. 57–74; and also in Robert L. Stevenson, Richard A. Eisinger, Barry M. Feinberg, and Alan B. Kotok, "Untwisting The News Twisters: A Replication of Efron's Study," *Journalism Quarterly* 50 (Summer 1973), pp. 211–19.

Early media pressure on Dan Quayle: Immediately after George Bush's 1988 surprise choice of Senator Dan Quayle to be his running mate, the media swarmed over Quayle's political track record, National Guard service record, and even his academic record. Here, reporters surround Quayle in his home state of Indiana.

emphasized pro-Democratic and anti-Republican statements throughout the general election campaign. More recently, the 1984 and 1988 campaigns have stoked conservative fires. Regarding the former, the ticket of Walter Mondale and Geraldine Ferraro received far kinder, more positive coverage than did the Reagan–Bush team, according to a study by the political scientists Michael J. Robinson and Maura Clancey.[31] Four years later George Bush still received a highly negative press, though Michael Dukakis fared no better.[32] Most rankling to conservatives, though, was this pair of findings: The most liberal candidate for president in 1988, Jesse Jackson, garnered the best press,[33] and the most conservative of the four national party nominees, Dan Quayle, secured the worst.

The right wing is not alone in its disgruntlement with the news media. For very different reasons, the left wing joins in the condemnation. Liberals, while acknowledging the press's early tough line on Quayle, have taken the media to task for not keeping the pressure on him throughout the 1988 campaign. The failure of the media to analyze and criticize the sometimes exaggerated claims made in George Bush's anti-Dukakis advertisements is also cited. To the left, the perceived press kindness toward Bush was merely a continuation of its genuflection to Ronald Reagan during his presidency. "Because of the government manipulation and voluntary self-censorship the major American news organizations too often abdicated their responsibility . . . during the Reagan years," wrote the left-wing media critic Mark Hertsgaard.[34] Like others of his persuasion over the years, Hertsgaard points to the conservative status-quo interests of the corporate elites who run most media organizations to explain why a Ronald Reagan would be pampered by the press.

There are many conservatives well placed in the American television and print commentary arenas to do the pampering, whether prompted by the media moguls or not. Right-of-center television hosts (John McLaughlin, William F. Buckley Jr., Patrick J. Buchanan—who became a Republican presidential candidate for 1992—and so on) dominate the public broadcasting agenda, and conservative columnists (especially James J. Kilpatrick, George F. Will, William Safire, and Rowland Evans and Robert Novak) have much larger circulations than most of their liberal counterparts (such as Carl Rowan and Ellen Goodman). Conservative Paul Harvey is the premier radio commentator, too. Even the mainstream news shows rely disproportionately on white, male, moderate-to-

[31] Michael J. Robinson and Maura Clancey, "General Election Coverage: Part 1," *Public Opinion* 7 (December/January 1985), pp. 49–54, 59.

[32] See Robert S. Lichter, Daniel Amundson, and Richard E. Noyes, "Election '88 Media Coverage," *Public Opinion* 11 (January/February 1989), pp. 18–19, 52.

[33] See Robert S. Lichter, Daniel Amundson, and Richard E. Noyes, *The Video Campaign: Network Coverage of the 1988 Primaries* (Washington: American Enterprise Institute, 1988).

[34] See Mark Hertsgaard, *On Bended Knee: The Press and the Reagan Presidency* (New York: Farrar, Straus & Giroux, 1988).

conservative voices, as a recent study of guests on "Nightline" and the "MacNeil/Lehrer News-Hour" has shown.[35] This generous measure of conservative commentary is supplemented by the heavily Republican tilt of newspaper editorial pages. In the fifteen presidential elections from 1932 to 1988 inclusive, a majority of the nation's dailies editorially supported the Republican nominee on fourteen of those occasions.[36] (The only exception was 1964.)

The question of media bias surfaces frequently in Britain, too. Many of the national newspapers sport openly acknowledged editorial lines: for example, the *Daily Telegraph* generally supports the position of the Conservative Party, the *Daily Mirror* sides with Labour, while the *Manchester Guardian* tends to adopt a Social Democratic position. It was precisely because of these open political loyalties that the appearance in 1987 of *The Independent* as a self-declared nonpartisan newspaper created such a splash. The broadcast media are by law required to maintain political impartiality, although they have been a frequent target of conservative criticism for their supposedly leftist leanings.

Other Sources of Bias. From left to right, all of these criticisms have some validity in different times and circumstances, in one media forum or another. But these critiques ignore some non-ideological factors probably more essential to an understanding of press bias. Owing to competition and the reward structure of journalism, the deepest bias most political journalists have is the desire to get to the bottom of a good campaign story—which is usually negative news about a candidate. The fear of missing a good story, more than bias, leads all media outlets to the same developing headlines and encourages them to adopt the same slant. One of the newspapers that broke important negative information about Dan Quayle in 1988 was none other than the Quayle family-owned paper, the *Indianapolis News.* (The story concerned Quayle's service in the National Guard rather than the military during the Vietnam War.)

A related non-ideological bias is the effort to create a horse race where none exists. Newspeople, whose lives revolve around the current political scene, naturally want to add spice and drama, minimize their boredom, and increase their audience. Other human, not just partisan, biases are at work. Whether the press likes or dislikes a candidate personally is often vital. Former Governor Bruce Babbitt and U.S. Representative Morris K. Udall, both wisecracking, straight-talking Arizona Democrats, were press favorites in their presidential bids (in 1988 and 1976, respectively), and both enjoyed favorable coverage. Richard Nixon, Jimmy Carter, and Gary Hart—all aloof politicians—were disliked by many reporters who covered them, and they suffered from a harsh and critical press.

Finally, in their quest to avoid bias, reporters frequently seize on non-ideological offenses such as gaffes, ethical violations, and campaign-finance problems. These "objective" items are intrinsically free of partisan taint and can be pursued without guilt.

For all the emphasis here on bias, it is undeniably true that the modern news media are far more fair than their American ancestors ever were. News blackouts of the editors' enemies, under which all positive information about the targeted politicians was banned from print, were once shockingly common but are now exceedingly rare and universally condemned. No longer do organized groups of reporters take out advertisements to support or oppose candidates, or send telegrams to the president and members of Congress advocating certain public policies—events that occurred as late as the 1970s.

---

[35] Fairness and Accuracy in Reporting (FAIR), "All the Usual Suspects: MacNeil-Lehrer and Nightline" (New York: FAIR, May 1990).

[36] See Nick Thimmesch, "The Editorial Endorsement Game," *Public Opinion* 7 (October/November 1984), pp. 10–13. However, there has been an accelerating trend toward neurality on the editorial pages. In 1964, 1968, and 1972 only 23 percent of the pages made no endorsement in the presidential contest; in 1984 the figure was 33 percent and in 1988, 55 percent. See Martin P. Wattenberg, *The Decline of American Political Parties* (Cambridge, Mass.: Harvard University Press, 1990), Chapter 9.

In sum, then, press bias of all kinds—partisan, agenda-setting, and non-ideological—can and does influence the day-to-day coverage of politicians. But bias is not the be-all and end-all that critics on both the right and left often insist it is. Press tilt has a marginal to moderate effect, and it is but one piece in the media's news mosaic.

The Media's Influence on the Public

Some bias in media coverage clearly exists, as we have just discussed. But how does this bias affect the public that reads or views biased reporting?

In most cases the press has surprisingly little effect. To put it bluntly, people tend to see what they want to see; that is, human beings will focus on parts of a report that reinforce their own attitudes and ignore parts that challenge their core beliefs. Most of us also selectively tune out and ignore reports that contradict our preferences in politics and other fields. Therefore, a committed Democrat will remember certain bits of a televised news program about a current campaign—primarily the bits that reinforce his or her own choice—and an equally committed Republican will recall very different sections of the report or remember the material in a way that supports the GOP position. In other words, most voters are not empty vessels into which the media can pour their own beliefs. This fact dramatically limits the ability of news organizations to sway public opinion.

And yet the news media *do* have some influence (called **media effects**) on public opinion. Let's examine how this is so.

- First, reporting can sway those people who are uncommitted and have no strong opinion in the first place. On the other hand, this sort of politically unmotivated individual is probably unlikely to vote in a given election, and therefore the media influence is of no particular consequence.

- Second, the press has a much greater impact on topics far removed from the lives and experiences of its readers and viewers. News reports can probably shape public opinion about events in foreign countries fairly easily. Yet what the media say about rising prices, neighborhood crime, or child rearing may have relatively little effect because most citizens have personal experiences and well-formed ideas about these subjects.

- Third, news organizations can help tell us what to think *about,* even if they cannot determine *what* we think. As mentioned earlier, the press often sets the agenda for government or a campaign by focusing on certain issues or concerns. For example, in the week following the *Exxon Valdez* oil tanker's massive spill off the Alaska coast in 1989, every national network devoted extensive coverage to the accident. And sure enough, concern about the environment quickly began to top the list of national problems considered most pressing by the public, as measured by opinion polls. Without the dramatic pictures and lavish media attention that accompanied the spill, it is doubtful that the environment would have risen so quickly to the forefront of the country's political agenda.

How Politicians Use the Media

Our emphasis so far has mainly been on the ways and means of press coverage of politicians. But the other side of the story is at least as interesting: how politicians use the media to achieve their ends. In the chapter on campaigns, we discussed the "media events" (press conferences at picturesque locations and the like) that are staged to attract coverage. Other manipulations of the press can be more subtle, however. Frequently, elected officials will pass along "tips" to reporters, seeking to curry favor or produce stories favorable to their interests. (Reporters and editors usually decide whether to publish the tip based on its **newsworthiness** and not on the motivations of their sources.)

On other occasions, candidates and their aides will go "on background" to give trusted newspersons juicy morsels of negative information about rivals. **On background**—meaning that none of the news can be attributed to the source—is one of several journalistic devices used to solicit and elicit information that might otherwise never come to light. **Deep background** is another such rule; whereas "background" talks can be attributed to unnamed senior officials, "deep background" news must be completely unsourced, with the reporter giving the reader no hint about the origin of the information. An even more drastic form of obtaining information is the **off-the-record** discussion, in which nothing at all the official says may be printed. (If a reporter can obtain the same information elsewhere, however, he or she is free to publish it.) By contrast, in an **on-the-record** session, such as a formal press conference, every word an official utters can be printed—and used against him or her. It is no wonder that office holders often prefer the nonpublishable alternatives!

Clearly, these rules are necessary for reporters to do their basic job—informing the public—but ironically, the same rules keep the press from fully informing their readers and viewers. Every public official knows that journalists are pledged to protect the confidentiality of their sources, and therefore the rules can sometimes be used to their own benefit—by, say, giving reporters derogatory information to print about one's rivals without having to be identified as the source. However regrettable the manipulation, it is an unavoidable part of the process.

Some politicians do not manipulate the press so much as they use it well when their talents match the needs of their day's dominant form of media. Franklin D. Roosevelt's folksy manner and mellifluous voice, for example, were tailor-made for radio, and his "fireside chats" in the 1930s reassured a nation shaken by the Great Depression. John F. Kennedy was America's first television-wise president; handsome, witty, and vibrant, JFK perfected the art of televised press conferences to win public support for his actions. Twenty years later Ronald Reagan, an actor by training, also made masterful use of television in going around Congress to appeal directly to the citizenry, as he did in winning congressional approval for his tax cuts and economic policies in 1981.

Other presidents of lesser media talents also adapt to the media realities of their time. Bush could not have been more unlike his charismatic predecessor, and his awkward gestures, high-pitched, nasal voice, poor speech delivery, and choppy sentence structure

President Franklin Roosevelt during a fireside chat in 1941. Roosevelt's skillful use of radio boosted his popularity throughout his tenure in the White House.

were often widely lampooned. Nonetheless Bush and his aides recognized that he was at his best in informal, less staged settings where his hands-on experience and detailed knowledge of government were apparent. Consequently, Bush rarely employed the Oval Office speech to the nation or the prime-time news conferences that were Reagan's favorite forms of talking to the nation. Instead, Bush held mid-morning White House press room briefings and many one-on-one press interviews.

Government Regulation of the Electronic Media

Not only do politicians manipulate the media, but the U.S. government *regulates* the electronic component of the media. Unlike radio or TV broadcasters, the print media are exempt from most forms of government regulation, though even print media must not violate community standards for obscenity, for instance. There are two reasons for this unequal treatment: First, the airwaves used by the electronic media are considered public property and are only leased by the federal government to private broadcasters. Second, those airwaves are in limited supply, and without some regulation, the nation's many radio and television stations would interfere with one another's frequency signals. As it happened, it was not the federal government but rather private broadcasters, frustrated by the numerous instances in which signal jamming occurred, who initiated the call for government regulation in the early days of the electronic media. Newspapers, of course, are not subject to these technical complexities.

The first government regulation of the electronic media came in 1927, when Congress enacted the Federal Radio Act, which established the Federal Radio Commission (FRC) and declared the airwaves to be public property. In addition, the act required that all broadcasters be licensed by the FRC. In 1934 the Federal Communications Commission (FCC) replaced the FRC as the electronic media regulatory body. The FCC is composed of five members, of whom not more than three can be from the same political party. These members are selected by the president for five-year terms on an overlapping basis. Because the FCC is shielded from direct, daily control by the president or Congress—though both have influence over the FCC commissioners—it is an independent regulatory agency (see Chapter 8). In addition to regulating public and commercial radio and television, the FCC also oversees telephone, telegraph, satellite, and foreign communications in the United States.

Under the FCC's rules, television stations must apply for license renewal every five years, radio stations every seven years. Until the 1980s, the FCC's criteria for license renewal were how well a station served its community, how judiciously it used the public airwaves, and how much time it devoted to public affairs. In fact, though, few licenses were ever withdrawn, and the tests for license renewal were never truly rigorous. Regulation of the broadcast industry became even looser—nearly non-existent, in fact—during the Reagan administration. For example, license renewal became something of a formality, with most stations able to complete the process simply by dropping a postcard in the mail. The FCC holds a formal hearing only if the license is challenged by a competing group of individuals who want to operate a station at the assigned frequency.

The FCC also regulates private ownership of broadcast stations. For instance, in the 1940s it said that a single person or corporation could own only one radio and one television station in any one community or "media market." In the 1950s it enacted the 7-7-7 rule, limiting to seven each the number of AM, FM, and TV stations a single company could own throughout the nation. In addition, the FCC forbids ownership of a daily newspaper and a television station in the same media market. Yet deregulation has recently prevailed in the area of ownership rules, too. During the Reagan years, the FCC expanded the limits on ownership of AM, FM, and television stations from 7 to 12, thereby making the 7-7-7 rule the 12-12-12 rule. In 1992, the FCC further expanded the limits of ownership of AM and FM stations, such that the 12-12-12 rule became a new 12-30-30 rule.

Content Regulation

The government also subjects the electronic media to substantial **content regulation** that, again, does not apply to the print media. Charged with ensuring that the airwaves "serve the public interest, convenience, and necessity," the FCC has attempted to promote equity in broadcasting. For example, the **equal time rule** requires that broadcast stations sell campaign airtime equally to all candidates *if* they choose to sell it to any, which they are under no obligation to do. An exception to this rule is a political debate: Stations may exclude from this event lesser-known and minor-party candidates.

Another noteworthy FCC regulation is the **right-of-rebuttal rule,** which requires that a person attacked on a radio or television station be offered the opportunity to respond. This rule was judicially sanctioned in the 1969 Supreme Court case *Red Lion Broadcasting Company* v. *FCC,* in which the Court ruled that Fred Cook, the author of a book on U.S. Senator Barry Goldwater of Arizona (the 1964 Republican nominee for president), must be afforded the chance to answer an attack on him aired by a Pennsylvania radio station.

Perhaps the most controversial FCC regulation was the **fairness doctrine.** Implemented in 1949 and in effect until 1985, the fairness doctrine required broadcasters to be "fair" in their coverage of news events—that is, they had to cover the events adequately and present contrasting views on important public issues. Many broadcasters disliked the rule, however, claiming that fairness was simply too difficult to define and that the rule abridged their First Amendment freedoms. They also argued that it ultimately forced broadcasters to lessen coverage of controversial issues because of fear of a deluge of airtime requests from interest groups involved in each matter. In a hotly debated 1985 decision, the FCC, without congressional consent, abolished the fairness doctrine, arguing that the blossoming of the electronic media in the United States during the preceding forty years had created enough diversity among the stations to render unnecessary the ordering of diversity within them. In 1986 a federal circuit court of appeals vindicated the FCC decision, holding that it did not need congressional approval to abolish the rule. Seeking to counter the FCC's decision, Congress attempted to write the fairness doctrine into law, which, if successful, would have forced the FCC to implement it. Yet although both the House and the Senate passed the bill, President Reagan ended the controversy for the moment by vetoing it, citing his First Amendment concerns about government regulation of the news media.

Extreme left- or right-wing candidates like Republican David Duke often battle for equal time on the major networks. In reality, however, air time is so expensive and fringe candidates have such a hard time raising large sums of money, that the networks can offer equal time without the candidates' being able to take advantage of it.

The abolition of the fairness doctrine has by no means ended debate over its merit, however. Proponents, still trying to reinstate it, argue that its elimination results in a reduction of quality programming on public issues. In their view, deregulation means more advertisements, soap operas, and situation comedies wasting airtime, leaving less room for public discourse on important matters. Opponents of the fairness doctrine, on the other hand, continue to call for less regulation, arguing that the electronic media should be as free as the print media—especially because the electronic media are now probably more competitive than the print media.

Confidentiality of Sources

Another vital aspect of news media practice, both print and electronic, has been influenced by legal statutes and court decisions: the confidentiality of sources. How much a reporter can learn from a source often depends on the journalist's guarantees of confidentiality to his or her source, that is, a pledge not to reveal the origin of information he or she may print or air.

Only a small number of states have laws protecting the confidentiality of reporters' sources, and no federal law provides such protection. Therefore, the courts have decided the degree to which confidentiality is protected, largely on a case-by-case basis. For example, in *Branzburg* v. *Hayes* (1972), the Supreme Court ruled that the First Amendment does not protect reporters from having to testify and possibly divulge sources before state or federal grand juries. "The investigation of crime by grand juries," the Court held, "implements a fundamental governmental role of securing the safety of the person and property of the [citizen]." Compared with this overriding governmental interest, the protection of sources is an insufficient reason to treat reporters subpoenaed by grand juries differently from other citizens—or so the high court held.

Journalists have maintained that rulings like that in *Branzburg* hinder the press's efforts at gathering the news—that without a guarantee of confidentiality, sources will be reluctant to provide crucial information. In response, the Court has noted that although confidentiality of sources does not outweigh the government's interest in prosecuting criminals, a journalist's confidentiality pledge is protected in most cases.

Censorship

While not free of government regulation, the media in the United States enjoy considerably more liberty than do their counterparts in Great Britain. One of the world's oldest democracies, Great Britain nonetheless owns that nation's main electronic medium, the British Broadcasting Company (BBC). And the BBC, along with the privately owned media, are subjected to unusually strict regulation on the publication of governmental secrets. For example, the sweeping Official Secrets Acts of 1911 makes it a criminal offense for a Briton to publish any facts, material, or news collected in his or her capacity as a public minister or civil servant. The act was invoked recently when the British government banned the publication of a 1987 novel, *Spy Catcher,* written by Peter Wright, a former British intelligence officer, who undoubtedly collected much of the book's information while on the job. In the United States, only government officials can be prosecuted for divulging classified information; no such law applies to journalists. Nor can the government, except under extremely rare and confined circumstances, impose prior restraints on the press—that is, the government cannot censor the press. This principle was clearly established in *New York Times* v. *United States* (1971), a case in which the Supreme Court ruled that the government could not prevent publication by the *New York Times* of the "Pentagon Papers," classified government documents about the Vietnam War that had been stolen, photocopied, and sent to the *Times* and the *Washington Post* by Daniel Ellsberg, an anti-war activist. "Only a free and unrestrained press can effectively expose deception in the government," Justice Hugo Black wrote in a concurring opinion for the Court. "To find that the President has 'inherent power' to halt the publication of news by resort to the courts would wipe out the First Amendment."

To assist the media in determining what is and is not publishable, Britain provides a system called "D-notice," which allows journalists to submit questionable material to a review committee before its publication. But D-notice has not quelled argument over media freedom in the United Kingdom. Indeed, the debate came prominently to the fore during the 1982 Falkland Islands war between Britain and Argentina, where it centered on questions of how much information the public had a right to know and whether the media should remain neutral in covering a war in which the nation is involved. Once again, however, the British government prevailed in arguing for continued strict control of the media, declaring, "There can be sound military reasons for withholding the whole truth from the public domain, [or] for using the media to put out 'misinformation.'"[37]

Similar questions and arguments arose in the United States during the 1991 Persian Gulf war. Reporters were upset that the military was not forthcoming about events on and off the battlefield, while some Pentagon officials and many in the general public accused the press of telling the enemy too much in their dispatches. Unlike in Great Britain, however, the U.S. government had little recourse but to attempt to isolate offending reporters by keeping them away from the battlefield. Even this maneuver was highly

[37] House of Commons, Defense Committee, *The Handling of the Press and Public Information during the Falklands Conflict* (London: Her Majesty's Stationery Office, 1982), p. x.

In 1971, the Supreme Court ruled in *New York Times* v. *United States* that the government could not prevent publication of the "Pentagon Papers." Here Daniel Ellsberg, who had stolen and copied the classified "Pentagon Papers," is greeted by well-wishers after the Court's decision.

controversial and very unpopular with news correspondents because it directly interfered with their job of reporting the news.

Such arguments are an inevitable part of the landscape in a free society. Whatever their specific quarrels with the press, most Americans would probably prefer that the media tell them too much rather than not enough. Totalitarian societies have a tame journalism, after all; so press excesses may be the price of unbridled freedom. Without question, a free press is of incalculable value to a nation, as the recent revolution in the Soviet Union (now the Commonwealth of Independent States) has shown. The 1991 coup against then-Soviet President Mikhail Gorbachev failed in part because the coup leaders could not smother the public's continued desire for freedom, stoked by the relatively uncensored television and print journalism that existed in the final years of Gorbachev's rule.

In the United States, freedom is secured mainly by the Constitution's basic guarantees and institutions. But freedom is also ensured by the thousands of independently owned and operated newspapers, magazines, and broadcast stations. The cacophony of media voices may often be off-key and harsh, but its very lack of orchestration enables us all to continue to sing the sweet song of freedom.

Toward Reform

The phenomenal growth of cable television during the past two decades has given new competition to the three major commercial television networks (ABC, CBS, and NBC). With almost half of all American households now wired for cable TV, the networks' share of the national television audience has declined steadily. Today fewer than six in every ten viewers are watching the three networks during many prime-time hours, compared with the networks' near-monopoly twenty years ago.

Some aspects of cable television's recent growth have been undesirable, at least in the eyes of critics. A case in point is the trend toward cross ownership—the possession of commercial and cable stations by the same people and corporations. As cable has become more popular and therefore more threatening to the commercial networks, these networks have been buying some cable franchises, and other media giants such as Time

Warner Communications and Times-Mirror have done the same. The concentration of commercial and cable television ownership in relatively few hands can be troubling, not least because this development can reduce the diversity of programming that was originally cable's great promise.

So far, though, any fair observer would conclude that cable television has greatly increased consumer choice and made available many new options for the American public. The large number of cable channels and information services suggests as much. In March 1988, for instance, 77 percent of all houses that subscribed to cable had access to thirty or more channels, and 90 percent had access to twenty or more channels.

One vital difference between cable and commercial television is the emergence of interactive systems—cable systems that allow interaction between the sender and the consumer. These interactive systems permit viewers to respond instantly to televised polls by using hand-held devices, for example, and potentially such an arrangement could lead to televised "town meetings" on issues of general interest. Of course, such developments must be viewed with caution as well as enthusiasm: Instant polls are unscientific and imprecise, as there is not random selection of the participants, and those who respond to such public affairs programming constitute only a minute and usually unrepresentative proportion of the population.

The rise of cable television is also having a significant effect on political campaigns. For example, cable systems are carrying a large number of local candidate debates. Although debates for state and national offices are televised frequently by the commercial stations, campaigns for local offices have often been neglected, largely because they are of interest to only a relatively small audience. Cable channels are so numerous that access for local candidates is much less of a problem. Cable channels also permit candidates to target paid political advertisements at small, select audiences. Such narrowcasting to targeted groups—as opposed to broadcasting to a large, diversified audience—enables candidates to tailor a message to Hispanics watching a Spanish-language channel, or sports fans who watch ESPN, or younger voters who watch MTV.

In general, then, cable means more choice in media and less influence for the commercial networks. This change can prove to be beneficial, as diversity and decentralization often do, or cable could turn out to be just more wasted fluff in programming that is distinct only because it is packaged a bit differently. Consumers of television—all of you who make up the audience—will help to determine which of these roads cable television takes.[38]

Summary

The modern media consist of print press (newspapers, magazines, journals) and electronic media (television and radio). In the United States the media are relatively uncontrolled and free to express many views, although that has not always been the case. Until the mid-to-late 1800s, when independent papers first appeared, newspapers were partisan, that is, they openly supported a particular party. In this century, first radio in the late 1920s and then television in the late 1940s have revolutionized the transmission of political information, leading to more candidate-centered, entrepreneurial politics in the age of television.

The media have shifted focus in recent years, first toward investigative journalism in the Watergate era, and then toward character issues. Studies have shown that by framing issues for debate and discussion, the media have clear and recognizable effects on voters.

The government has gradually loosened its restrictions on the media. Officially, the Federal Communications Commission licenses and regulates broadcasting stations, although in practice it has been quite willing to grant and renew licenses, and recently it has reduced its

---

[38] For further reading, see Jeffrey B. Abramson, F. Christopher Arterton, and Gary R. Orren, *The Electronic Commonwealth: The Impact of Media Technologies on Democratic Politics* (New York: Basic Books, 1988).

regulation of licensees. Additionally, cable transmission was first allowed on a widespread basis in the late 1970s, from whence it has grown to a large supplier of information. Finally, content regulations have loosened, with the courts using a narrow interpretation of libel.

Key Terms

print press

electronic media

yellow journalism

muckraking

networks

affiliates

wire services

New York Times Co. v. Sullivan

media effects

newsworthiness

on background

deep background

off the record

on the record

content regulation

equal time rule

right-of-rebuttal rule

fairness doctrine

Suggested Readings

Arterton, F. Christopher. *Media Politics: The News Strategies of Presidential Campaigns.* Lexington, Mass.: Lexington Books, 1984.

Berkman, Ronald, and Laura W. Kitch. *Politics in the Media Age.* New York: McGraw-Hill, 1986.

Broder, David S. *Behind the Front Page.* New York: Simon and Schuster, 1987.

Cook, Timothy E. *Making Laws and Making News: Media Strategies in the U.S. House of Representatives.* Washington: The Brookings Institution, 1989.

Crouse, Timothy. *The Boys on the Bus.* New York: Ballantine, 1973.

Entman, Robert M. *Democracy Without Citizens: Media and the Decay of American Politics.* New York: Oxford University Press, 1989.

Epstein, Edward Jay. *News from Nowhere: Television and the News.* New York: Random House, 1973.

Graber, Doris A. *Mass Media and American Politics,* 3rd ed. Washington: CQ Press, 1989.

Iyengar, Shanto, and Donald R. Kinder. *News That Matters.* Chicago: University of Chicago Press, 1987.

Lichter, S. Robert; Stanley Rothman; and Linda S. Lichter. *The Media Elite.* Bethesda, Md.: Adler & Adler, 1986.

Press, Charles, and Kenneth VerBurg. *American Politicians and Journalists.* Glenview, Ill.: Scott, Foresman, 1988.

Ranney, Austin. *Channels of Power: The Impact of Television on American Politics.* New York: Basic Books, 1983.

Sabato, Larry. *Feeding Frenzy: How Attack Journalism Has Transformed American Politics.* New York: Macmillan/The Free Press, 1991.

Stephens, Mitchell. *A History of News: From the Drum to the Satellite.* New York: Viking, 1989.

A zeal for different

opinions concerning religion,

concerning government, and many

other points . . . have, in turn,

divided mankind . . . inflamed them

with mutual animosity, and rendered

them more disposed to vex and

oppress each other than to cooperate

for the common good.

James Madison

FEDERALIST NO. 10

Madison believed that one of the principal purposes of government is to control the effects of competing interest groups. As noted in Chapter 11, the Framers hoped to avoid the formation of official political parties; at the private level, however, they surely knew that the formation of interest groups was inevitable.

CHAPTER 15

Interest Groups

An **interest group** can be defined as "any group that, on the basis of one or more shared attitudes, makes certain claims upon other groups in society for the establishment, maintenance, or enhancement of forms of behavior that are implied by the shared attitudes."[1] The Founders feared the counterdemocratic efforts of factions, or what we call interest groups today. When James Madison wrote Federalist No. 10 he undoubtedly had in mind many of the groups of debtors and propertyless persons who had participated in the Shays's Rebellion (see Chapter 2). In his own words, "creditors" and "debtors" are divided, naturally, "into different classes, actuated by different sentiments and views." Madison knew from his days in the Virginia Assembly that factions were inevitable and that the struggle among groups was inevitable in the political process. This knowledge led him and the other Framers to tailor a governmental system of checks and balances that would allow selfish interests to check one another in the natural course of the political process. As discussed in Chapter 2, Madison and many of the other Framers were intent on creating a government of many levels—local, state, and national, as well as a national government consisting of three branches. It was their belief that this division of power would prohibit any one individual or group of individuals from becoming too powerful. Decentralizing power also would neutralize the effect of special interests, which would be unable to spread their efforts throughout so many different levels of government. Thus, the "mischief of faction" could be lessened.

Ironically, *The Federalist Papers* were a key component of one of the most skillful and successful examples of interest-group activity in the history of this nation. As discussed in Chapter 2, "unless the Federalists [themselves an interest group] had been as shrewd in manipulation as they were sound in theory, their arguments could not have prevailed."[2] They were only one of many interest groups that existed in that era.

Over the years, as we explore in the following sections, interest groups have proliferated. In 1831–32, Alexis de Tocqueville, a French aristocrat and philosopher, toured the United States extensively. A keen observer of American politics, he was very much impressed by the tendency of Americans to join groups in order to participate in the policy-making process. "Whenever at the head of some new undertaking you see government in France, or a man of rank in England, in the United States you will be sure to find an association," wrote de Tocqueville. Remember, de Tocqueville was writing about the profusion of groups in America just forty years after Madison warned about factionalism and at the same time that the modern political party as we know it today was taking form. Nevertheless, he was impressed by the ability of groups to influence the formal institutions of government, noting:

> It is true that they [representatives of these associations] have not the right, like the others, of making the laws; but they have the power of attacking those which are in force and of drawing up beforehand those which ought to be enacted.[3]

So, in but a few decades, "associations" had become an integral part of American life. de Tocqueville rattled off the numerous kinds of groupings that appeared to link Americans—a list that could be multiplied many times over today. Just think of the number of interest groups or voluntary associations to which you belong. It's likely that you belong to some kind of organized religion; a political party; a town, college, or university social, civic, athletic, or academic group, or a more general special-interest group such as Greenpeace, the National Rifle Association, the National Right-to-Life Committee, or the National

[1] David B. Truman, *The Governmental Process: Political Interests and Public Opinion* (New York: Knopf, 1951), p. 33.

[2] Samuel Eliot Morrison and Henry Steel Commager, *The Growth of the American Republic* (New York: Oxford University Press, 1930), p. 163.

[3] Alexis de Tocqueville, *Democracy in America,* Vol. 1, trans. Phillips Bradley (New York: Knopf, Vintage Books, 1945; orig. published 1835), p. 191.

A nation of groups: When issues arise affecting particular segments of the electorate, interest groups tend to organize in response. The groups can be narrowly based, even to the point of representing a single company, or they can be very broad, as with the National Organization for Women, pictured above in a 1990 demonstration outside the Saudi embassy protesting that government's treatment of women.

Abortion Rights Action League. Even if you don't belong to one of these groups, you undoubtedly have heard of their activities or know someone who is a member.

Not all groups are political, but they may become politically active when their members feel that a government policy threatens or affects group goals. Most politically active groups make use of a technique called **lobbying** to make their interests heard and understood by those who are in a position to influence or cause change in governmental policies. Depending on the type of group and on the role it is looking to play, lobbying can take many forms. You probably have never thought of the Boy Scouts or Girl Scouts of America as "political." Yet, when Congress began debating legislation dealing with discrimination in private clubs, representatives of both organizations testified in an attempt to persuade Congress to allow them to remain single-sex organizations. Similarly, you probably don't often think of garden clubs as political. Yet, when issues of highway beautification come before a legislature, representatives from numerous garden clubs are likely to be there.

In this chapter, we explore the roles played by various kinds of interest groups and their development since the days of the Founders. After tracing the general development of groups and their involvement in politics in the United States, we look to see why people join groups, why groups flourish, and the kinds of tactics they employ as they attempt to pressure government to achieve their policy objectives.

The Roles Interest Groups Play

Americans have long debated the nature of interest groups and their role in a democratic society. Do interest groups contribute to the betterment of society, or are they an evil best controlled by government? Recognizing the inevitability of interest groups, James Madison came down on the side of creating a structure or system of government that would attempt to control the effects of group advocacy.

Interest groups often fill voids left by the traditional political parties and give Americans another opportunity to take their claims directly to the government. Groups allow un- or underrepresented groups an opportunity to have their voices heard, thereby making the government and its policy-making process more representative of diverse populations and perspectives. There is also a downside to interest groups. Because groups make claims on society, they can increase the cost of public policies. The elderly can push for more costly health care and Social Security programs, women for improved athletic programs, the handicapped for improved access to public buildings, industry for tax loopholes and veterans for improved benefits. Many Americans believe that interest groups exist simply to advance their own selfish interests, with little regard for the rights of other groups or, more importantly, people not represented by any organized group.

Whether good or bad, interest groups play an important role in American politics. In addition to *enhancing* the democratic process by providing increased representation and participation, they increase public awareness about important issues, help frame the public agenda, and often monitor programs to guarantee effective implementation.

Representation

Just as members of Congress are assumed to represent the interests of their constituents in Washington, D.C., interest groups are assumed to represent the interests of their members to policy makers at all levels of government. In the 1950s, for example, the National Association for the Advancement of Colored People (NAACP) was able to articulate and present the interests of black citizens to national decision makers even though blacks had little or no electoral clout, especially in the South. Without the efforts of the civil rights groups discussed in Chapter 5, it is unlikely that either the courts or Congress would have acted as quickly to make discrimination illegal. All sorts of groups, whether they are composed of railroad workers, physical therapists, campers, or homosexuals, have found that banding together and hiring a person to advocate their interests in Washington, D.C., or a state capital increase the likelihood that issues of concern to them will be addressed and, they hope, favorably acted upon. To represent their members, groups testify at hearings, communicate with government officials, and take part in a variety of other activities, as shown in Table 15-1.

Pressuring the government: One of the most famous interest group leaders in recent decades, Ralph Nader (right), who leads various groups on behalf of consumers, gave a news conference in Washington in 1988 with New York State Attorney General Robert Abrams. At this conference, Nader blasted the Food and Drug Administration for trying to kill a rule requiring fruit juice companies to reveal the amount of real juice in their products.

Table 15-1 Percentage of Groups Using Each of Techniques of Exercising Influence

1. Testifying at hearings	99%
2. Contacting government officials directly to present your point of view	98
3. Engaging in informal contacts with officials— at conventions, over lunch, etc.	95
4. Presenting research results or technical information	92
5. Sending letters to members of your organization to inform them about your activities	92
6. Entering into coalitions with other organizations	90
7. Attempting to shape the implementation of policies	89
8. Talking with people from the press and the media	86
9. Consulting with government officials to plan legislative strategy	85
10. Helping to draft legislation	85
11. Inspiring letter-writing or telegram campaigns	84
12. Shaping the government's agenda by raising new issues and calling attention to previously ignored problems	84
13. Mounting grassroots lobbying efforts	80
14. Having influential constituents contact their member of Congress	80
15. Helping to draft regulations, rules, or guidelines	78
16. Serving on advisory commissions and boards	76
17. Alerting members of Congress to the effects of a bill on their districts	75
18. Filing suit or otherwise engaging in litigation	72
19. Making financial contributions to electoral campaigns	58
20. Doing favors for officials who need assistance	56
21. Attempting to influence appointments to public office	53
22. Publicizing candidates' voting records	44
23. Engaging in direct-mail fund raising for your organization	44
24. Running advertisements in the media about your position on issues	31
25. Contributing work or personnel to electoral campaigns	24
26. Making public endorsements of candidates for office	22
27. Engaging in protests or demonstrations	20

Source: Kay Lehman Schlozman and John T. Tierney, "More of the Same: Washington Pressure Group Activity in a Decade of Change," *Journal of Politics* 45 (1988), pp. 351–75.

Political Participation

Interest groups enhance political participation by motivating like-minded individuals to work toward a common goal. Legislators are often far more likely to listen to or be concerned about the interests of a group as opposed to the interests of any one individual. The congressional testimony of Kimberly Bergalis, the first known individual to contract AIDS from a dentist, was given heavy media coverage. Yet the likelihood that Congress will approve mandatory testing of all health care workers without the backing of one or more organized groups to support Bergalis's requests are slim. In contrast, after the Supreme Court ruled in 1976 that pregnancy discrimination was not prohibited by the Civil Rights Act of 1964, hordes of lobbyists from various women's rights groups descended on Congress. In response, Congress quickly enacted the Pregnancy Discrimination Act of 1978 to ban that practice.

Education

As interest groups attempt to gain members and influence policy making, they educate potential members, elected and unelected policy makers, and the public at large in the process. For example, in 1987, when President Ronald Reagan nominated Judge Robert H. Bork of the Washington, D.C. Court of Appeals to the U.S. Supreme Court, an unprecedented coalition of liberal interest groups banded together to stop his nomination. They not only took out a series of full-page advertisements in leading newspapers to inform the public about Judge Bork's likely effect on the Court and on its handling of issues such as abortion and civil rights, they even produced a series of television ads to urge constituents to contact their senators and ask them to vote against his nomination. Similarly, when Congress was debating the "Brady Bill" (to limit the sale of handguns) in 1991, groups on both sides of the debate used mass mailings and print ads to educate the public. Such educational campaigns are, of course, decidedly biased, but they do raise public awareness of issues.

An advertisement created by Handgun Control, Inc., a single-issue group that has spent years encouraging legislation to limit private ownership of handguns.

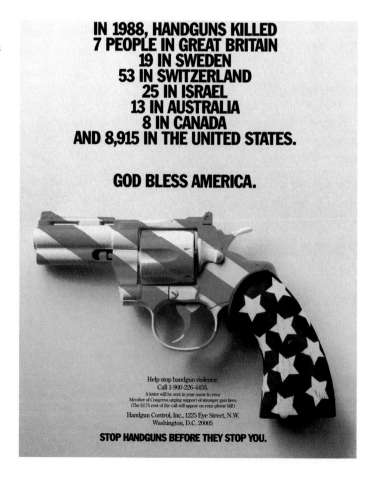

Agenda Building

An interest group's role in educating the public on issues is related to its role in building the government's policy agenda. As groups mobilize to push their policy goals, they often bring into the public forum issues that might not have otherwise surfaced at that time. The Humane Society, for example, has been around since the turn of the century, but it was not until more aggressive groups like PETA—People for the Ethical Treatment of Animals—made the public aware of the wide-scale testing of many products on animals that the pressure of the general public effectively forced many manufacturers to alter their testing programs. Putting issues on the public agenda, then, does not necessarily mean that an interest group pressures a governmental body to act; it can mean that the public is made sufficiently aware of a certain practice or policy to work for changes to be made.

Program Monitoring

In addition to trying to bring about action in the form of laws or regulations, interest groups often find it useful, once a law is passed or a regulation written that affects them, to monitor how that law or regulation is implemented. The National Organization for Women (NOW), for example, created the Project on Educational Equity Review (PEER) to monitor the enforcement of Title IX, the purpose of which is to ban sex discrimination in schools receiving federal funding. Its newsletter, *PEER Perspective,* provides detailed analyses of Title IX legislative and administrative activity. Moreover, PEER staffers are in regular contact with government officials to discuss enforcement and to lobby against regulations that would hinder the enforcement of Title IX.

Types of Interest Groups

A wide variety of interest groups engage in the activities noted here. Although there can be considerable overlap, interest groups can usually be characterized as falling into one of the following categories.

Economic Interests

Most groups have some sort of economic interest, even if it only involves attracting enough donations to pay the telephone bill or send out the next mailing. **Economic-interest groups** are a special case: Their primary purpose is to promote the economic interests of their members. Historically, business (including trade and professional groups), labor, and agricultural interests have been considered the "big three" of economic interest groups.

Groups that mobilize to protect particular economic interests generally are the most fully and effectively organized of all the types of interest groups. They exist to make profits and to obtain economic benefits for their members. In order to achieve their goals, however, they often find that they must resort to political means.

The Public Interest

Political scientist Jeffrey Berry defines a **public-interest group** as "one that seeks a collective good, the achievement of which will not selectively and materially benefit the membership or activists of the organization."[4] Unlike the economic interests noted

[4] Jeffrey Berry, *Lobbying for the People: The Political Behavior of Public Interest Groups* (Princeton, N.J.: Princeton University Press, 1977), p. 7.

previously, public-interest groups do not tend to be particularly motivated by selfish considerations. As Berry shows, the public interest has many faces: environmentalists, good-government groups such as Common Cause, peace groups, church groups, political groups, and groups that speak out for those who cannot (such as children, the mentally ill, or animals). Members of the American Civil Liberties Union (ACLU), for example, a public-interest organization that fights against, among other things, government entanglement with religion, stand to realize no financial gain when the ACLU argues that the government should not allow nativity scenes to be erected on public lands. Similarly, its members get no direct economic benefits when the ACLU challenges the constitutionality of New York State's practice of awarding college scholarships to students based on their SAT scores. (The ACLU successfully argued that the SATs discriminate against women.)

Single-Issue versus Multi-Issue Groups

Most of the economic- and public-interest groups discussed in the preceding section are **multi-issue groups,** that is, they are concerned with more than just a single issue. Whereas, for example, the AFL-CIO, the largest labor union in America, was formed to represent the interests of organized labor, it is also concerned with health care, Social Security, and civil rights as well as with other issues. Similarly, the NAACP is interested primarily in race relations, but it is also involved in other areas, including education, the criminal justice system, housing, and welfare rights—all areas of potential concern to its members.

Of late, we have seen the growth of **single-issue groups,** organized to influence policy in only one area. Single-issue groups differ from multi-issue groups both in the range and intensity of their interests. Concentration on one area generally leads to greater zeal in a group's lobbying efforts. The most visible single-issue groups today are those organized on both sides of the abortion debate. Anti-abortion groups like Operation Rescue and pro-choice groups like the National Abortions Rights Action League (NARAL) are good examples of single-issue groups. Today, virtually all kinds of interests are pursued single-mindedly. Drug- or AIDS-awareness groups, environmental groups, and anti-nuclear power groups, for example, could all be classified as single-issue groups.

The Origins of American Interest Groups

Interest groups tend to arise in response to changes: political changes, changes in the population, technological changes, or changes in society itself. During the 1770s, for example, many groups arose to fight for independence; during the 1830s and 1840s, many religious groups were formed, and the anti-slavery movement grew out of them. After the Civil War, trade unions flourished, and the Grange was founded to help farmers. Business associations proliferated in the 1880s and 1890s. In the early 1900s other groups were created in reaction to big business and other social and economic forces. Finally, the 1960s fostered the growth of public-interest groups. Some social scientists explain this kind of ebb and flow of group activity by referring to **wave theory** (also called disturbance theory), which hypothesizes that groups form in part to counteract the activities of other groups or organized special interests. According to this view, the government's role is to provide a forum in which the competing demands of groups and the majority of the U.S. population can be heard and balanced. Political scientist David B. Truman argues that the government's role in managing competing groups is to balance their conflicting demands. Nevertheless, when examining the evolution and growth of

Wave Theory in Action: Business and Labor

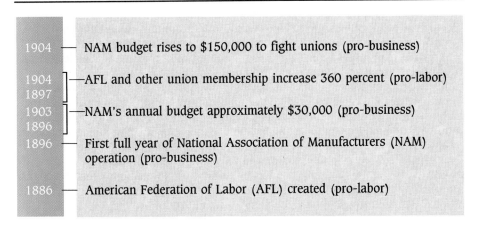

1904 — NAM budget rises to $150,000 to fight unions (pro-business)

1904
1897 — AFL and other union membership increase 360 percent (pro-labor)

1903
1896 — NAM's annual budget approximately $30,000 (pro-business)

1896 — First full year of National Association of Manufacturers (NAM) operation (pro-business)

1886 — American Federation of Labor (AFL) created (pro-labor)

interest groups in the United States, we are not always looking at clashes of one group against another, but of one group against the majority of the American public.

After the early years of our republic, there have been three waves of interest-group formation and activity. As we examine the three waves, we look at what caused them and what effects they have had on our government.

The Early Years: The Colonial Period to 1830

When the colonists first came to America in 1619, many did so to escape religious persecution. They then organized themselves into colonies based on their own religious preference. Catholics founded Maryland, the Puritans founded Massachusetts, and the Quakers founded Pennsylvania, for example. In essence, these colonies became some of the first special-interest groups in the New World: They were governmental units organized along religious lines and designed to further certain religious, moral, and policy preferences.

Soon thereafter, skilled laborers such as bricklayers and blacksmiths who banded together in craft guilds and trade associations became some of the first interest groups in the United States as they formed associations to restrict competition in the wake of an influx of new settlers who wanted their jobs. And, as we saw in Chapter 2, groups of colonists dissatisfied with the actions of the king formed the Sons of Liberty and participated in the Boston Tea Party as a demonstration of political protest. Although social or political protest is not necessarily a tactic employed by all groups, throughout history numerous groups have resorted to protests or even illegal activities when more conventional methods of lobbying have failed.

The highly agricultural nature of the new nation was reflected in some of the earliest regional societies. In 1785 the Philadelphia Society for Promoting Agriculture, the goal of which was to advance "products of the land within the American states," counted Benjamin Franklin as one of its active members and George Washington as an honorary member. The Society for Promoting and Improving Agriculture and Other Rural Concerns was founded around the same time in Charleston, South Carolina. Poor communications networks prevented any of these associations' becoming national in scope. And none was particularly political in nature.

The First Wave of American Interest Groups: National Groups Emerge (1830–80)

Although all kinds of local groups proliferated throughout the colonies and in the new states, it was not until the 1830s, as communications networks improved, that the first groups national in scope began to emerge. It is interesting to note that an identical flowering of associational activity occurred in Britain at this time.

Many of these first national groups were single-issue groups deeply rooted in the Christian religious revivalism that was sweeping the nation. Concern with humanitarian issues such as temperance (total abstinence from alcoholic beverages), peace, capital punishment, education, and, most important, slavery, led to the founding of numerous groups dedicated to solving these problems. Among the first of these groups was the American Anti-Slavery Society, founded in 1833 by William Lloyd Garrison. The only woman allowed to speak at its first meeting, Lucretia Mott, went on to organize the first large gathering of women's rights activists in Seneca Falls, New York in 1848. But no national women's groups were formed until after the Civil War.

In the wake of continued immigration and growing poverty in large, increasingly industrialized cities, concern for the fate of the poor led to the founding of the Young Men's Christian Association (YMCA) in Boston in 1851. Although today many people associate the YMCA with sports and recreation, its founders initially viewed these kinds of activities only as a means of reaching out to the children of immigrants and the poor in urban centers to help integrate them into society and a Christian lifestyle.

The Women's Christian Temperance Union (WCTU) was founded in 1874 with the goal of outlawing the sale of liquor. Its members, many of them quite religious, believed that the consumption of alcohol was an evil injurious to family life because many men drank away their paychecks, leaving no money to feed or clothe their families. Many women who felt that the national suffrage associations (whose aim was to get women the right to vote) were too radical joined the WCTU to do good for others. Churches and Southerners, in particular, supported the WCTU's goal of prohibiting the manufacture and sale of all alcoholic beverages. The WCTU's activities included conventional and noncon-

The First Wave of American Interest Groups

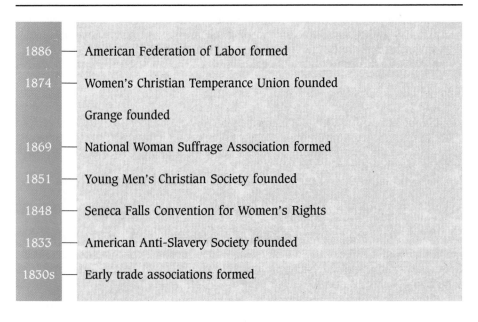

1886	American Federation of Labor formed
1874	Women's Christian Temperance Union founded
	Grange founded
1869	National Woman Suffrage Association formed
1851	Young Men's Christian Society founded
1848	Seneca Falls Convention for Women's Rights
1833	American Anti-Slavery Society founded
1830s	Early trade associations formed

ventional forms of activity: organizing prayer groups, lobbying for prohibition legislation, conducting peaceful marches, and engaging in more violent protests that included destruction of saloons. By the 1890s, the WCTU had more than 200,000 female members at a time when the total U.S. population was 63 million. (In contrast, in 1991, the membership of National Organization for Women was 250,000 when the total population was nearly 249 million.)

Like the WCTU, the Grange was also formed during the period following the Civil War. It was created by six government employees as an educational society for farmers to teach them about the latest agricultural developments. Although its charter formally stated that the Grange was not to become involved in "politics," in 1876 it formulated a detailed plan to pressure Congress to enact legislation favorable to farmers. In response to the growth of large businesses and monopolies that affected the prices of livestock and harvests, the Grange's members banded together to influence the traditional political parties to deal more effectively with big-business interests. The Grange's women's auxiliaries also provided a first and very important mechanism for women to assemble, a situation that was later used effectively by women's suffrage groups looking for other bases of support.

The Civil War also fostered the creation of a national communications network of telegraph lines and railroads. After the war, for the first time in history, railroads, radio, and telegraphs existed to bring people, manufactured goods, agricultural products, and information to the far corners of the nation. At the same time, the federal bureaucracy grew enormously, giving interest groups new targets for their lobbying efforts (see Chapter 8).

Perhaps the most effective interest group of the day was the railroad industry. In a move that couldn't take place today because of its clear impropriety, the Central Pacific Railroad sent its own **lobbyist** to Washington, D.C. in 1861, where he eventually became the clerk (staff administrator) of the committees of both houses of Congress that were charged with overseeing regulation of the railroad industry. Subsequently, the Central Pacific Railroad (later called the Southern Pacific) received from Congress vast grants of lands along its route and large subsidized loans from the national government. The railroad became so important that it later went on to have nearly total political control of the California state legislature.

After the Civil War, business interests began to play even larger roles in both state and national politics. A popular saying of the day noted that the Standard Oil Company did everything to the Pennsylvania legislature except refine it. Increasingly large trusts, monopolies, business combinations, and corporate conglomerations in the oil, steel, and sugar industries became sufficiently powerful to control many representatives in the state and national legislatures.

The Second Wave of National Group Activity (1890–1920)

By the 1890s, a profound change had occurred in the nation's political and social outlook. Rapid industrialization and an influx of immigrants created a host of problems, including crime, poverty, squalid and unsafe working conditions, widespread political corruption, and high prices caused by monopolistic business practices. Many Americans began to believe that new measures would be necessary to impose order on this growing chaos and to curb some of the more glaring problems brought on by industrialization and immigration. The political and social movement that grew out of these concerns was called progressivism.

The Progressive Movement. Not even the progressives themselves could agree on what the term "progressive" actually meant. To some it was a broad societal vision. Others believed that it encompassed a set of moral and humanitarian goals. And to others it was a set of particular good-government reforms. Desire for reform led to an explosion of all types of interest groups: single-issue, trade, labor, and the first public-interest groups. Politically, the movement took the form of the Progressive Party, which sought on many fronts to limit or end the power of the industrialists' near-total control of the steel, oil, railroad, and other key industries.

During its formative stages, the Progressive Movement was epitomized by the rapid growth of settlement houses—welfare centers that provided community services such as child care, reading and English language lessons, and job training for the less fortunate—across the United States. Jane Addams, a young social worker, established one of the first settlement houses, Hull House, in Chicago in 1889. By 1900, there were more than 400 such houses across the nation.

In addition to providing many services to the poor, settlement houses provided room and board for innumerable progressive activists. Here, prominent thinkers met and exchanged ideas; settlement house residents, in essence, were the Progressive Movement. They were active in women's suffrage, in reform of the treatment of juvenile offenders, in education systems (including implementation of a system of kindergartens), and in the reform of corrupt city governments. Many went on to found groups that would later form the core of the civil rights and public-interest movements of the 1960s.

Living at one time or another at Hull House, for example, were Julia Lathrop, the future head of the Federal Children's Bureau and director of the Immigrants' Protective League; members of the future Boards of Directors of the National Association for the Advancement of Colored People (established in 1909) and the American Civil Liberties Union (established in 1919); John Dewey, an educational reformer and inventor of the Dewey Decimal library cataloging system; Eugene V. Debs, president of the American Railway Union; Margaret Dreier Robins, the president of the Women's Trade Union League; and executive directors of the National Child Labor Committee and the National Consumers' League.

Progressive groups relied heavily on the support of the public for various appeals to legislators for reform. For example, the National Consumers' League (NCL) was founded in 1899 by wealthy women to work for improved working conditions for women and children. At that time, women and children worked for long hours at low wages in substandard buildings lacking proper ventilation or safety features. In addition to extensive lobbying (at the state and national levels) for maximum hour and minimum wage laws for women and children, the NCL's local organizations published a list of approved retailers who treated their employees well by providing them fair wages for reasonable hours in a safe environment. It also started the "shop early" movement at Christmastime to encourage consumers to do their holiday shopping before the Christmas rush. The NCL believed that such a campaign would prompt consumers to do everything possible to reduce the burden placed on shop girls.

Many members of the NCL were also members of the National American Woman Suffrage Association, which was the key organization pushing for a constitutional amendment to give women the right to vote. During the Progressive era, women's organizations were second only to trade organizations in number and influence on Capitol Hill.

In response to the pressure applied by progressive groups, the national government began to regulate business. Because businesses had a vested interest in keeping wages low and costs down, more business groups organized to consolidate their strength and to counter progressive moves. Not only did governments have to mediate progressive and business demands, but they also had to accommodate the role of organized labor, which often allied itself with progressive groups against big business.

Organized Labor. Although there were several early unsuccessful attempts to organize local labor groups into national unions, it was not until the creation of the American Federation of Labor (AFL) in 1886 that there was any real national union activity. The AFL for the first time brought skilled workers from several trades together into one stronger national organization. By 1902, its membership exceeded 1 million workers. However, its effectiveness in mobilizing for higher wages for workers triggered more and

Jane Addams, who in 1889 founded Hull House in Chicago and helped launch the Progressive Movement. She is pictured here in 1914.

People of the Past

Florence Kelley

Florence Kelley (1859–1932) was the third of eight children born to William Darrah Kelley, a self-educated lawyer who later enjoyed a long career in Congress. Kelley's five sisters died in infancy, and since she was ill quite often herself, her early schooling took place at home. She read her father's entire library and developed strong interests in social reform at an early age. She was particularly influenced by her aunt Sarah, a Quaker reformer and abolitionist, who refused to use cotton or sugar in personal protest against slave labor. Kelley's father was a strong believer in women's suffrage and he encouraged her to enter Cornell University. There, Kelley earned a bachelor's degree in 1876 and applied to the University of Pennsylvania to study law, but was refused because of her sex.

While traveling in Europe, Kelley met M. Carey Thomas, the first American woman to earn a Ph.D., who urged Kelley to attend her alma mater, the University of Zurich. There Kelley translated several major works by Karl Marx and Friedrich Engels and she met and married a Polish medical student and socialist. They had three children before returning to New York City. Kelley's husband abused her, however, and finally in 1891, she took her children and fled to Chicago, where she obtained a divorce and reverted back to her maiden name.

In Chicago, Kelley joined Jane Addams and other women reformers at Hull House, one of the nation's first social settlements. Concerned with child labor, she published a pamphlet in 1892, *Our Toiling Children.* Three years later she published *Hull House Maps and Papers* based on her investigations of the "sweating" system in garment factories and a survey of the condition of city slums. Described as a "guerilla warrior" in the "wilderness of industrial wrongs," Kelley pushed to get legislation limiting the hours a woman could work, prohibiting child labor, and controlling tenement sweatshops. Frustrated by her inability to get cases prosecuted, Kelley took night classes and earned a law degree from Northwestern University in 1894.

To attack child labor from another angle, Kelley eagerly accepted the position of general secretary of the newly established National Consumers' League, a position she held from 1899 until her death in 1932. The NCL used consumer pressure to ensure that goods were manufactured under acceptable working conditions. Kelley spoke to groups all over the country on behalf of her cause. She established sixty Consumers' Leagues in twenty states and organized two international conferences. She helped set up the New York Child Labor Committee in 1902 and the National Child Labor Committee in 1904.

Kelley pursued a number of other interests as well. She was a founding member of the National Association for the Advancement of Colored People and the Women's International League for Peace and Freedom. She was also active from 1911 onward in the Intercollegiate Socialist Society, serving as its president from 1918 to 1920. In 1912 she joined the Eugene V. Debs Socialist Party of America. She also served as vice president of the National Woman Suffrage Association for several years and lobbied for women's legislation as an active member of the Women's Joint Congressional Committee that was founded in the early 1920s after passage of the Nineteenth Amendment.

Under Kelley's leadership, the NCL launched a successful defense of protective legislation in the courts. Kelley's efforts were also key to congressional passage of the Sheppard–Towner Maternity and Infancy Act in 1921.

better business organization. As business interests pushed states for "open shop" laws (which would outlaw unions in their factories), the AFL became increasingly political. It was also forced to react to the success of big businesses' use of legal injunctions to prohibit union organization. In Britain, labor organized at the national level much earlier: The Trades Union Congress (TUC), a federation of individual unions, formed in 1868.

Conversely, organized business appeared somewhat later in Britain than in the United States: The Federation of British Industry (FBI) opened its doors in 1916, some twenty-one years after its American counterpart, the National Association of Manufacturers, began operations.

In 1914, massive lobbying by the AFL and its members led to passage of the Clayton Act, which the labor leader Samuel Gompers hailed as the "Magna Carta" of the labor movement. This law allowed unions to organize free from prosecution and also guaranteed their right to strike, a powerful weapon against employers.

Business Groups and Trade Associations. The National Association of Manufacturers (NAM) was founded in 1895 by manufacturers who had suffered business reverses in the economic panic of 1893 and who believed that they were being affected adversely by the growth of organized labor. NAM first became politically active in 1913 when a major tariff bill was under congressional consideration. NAM's tactics were "so insistent and abrasive" and its expenditures of monies so lavish that President Woodrow Wilson was forced to denounce its lobbying tactics as an "unbearable situation."[5] Congress immediately called for an investigation of NAM's activities but found no member of Congress willing to testify that he had ever even encountered a member of NAM (probably because many of them had been "bought" with illegal contributions and gifts).

The second major business organization came into being in 1912, when the National Chamber of Commerce was created with the assistance of the Secretary of Commerce and Labor. (This was before that Cabinet post was split into the Department of Commerce and the Department of Labor.) The administration of President William Howard Taft believed that the government should have one body to consult with concerning the interests of business. Also, regional chambers of commerce saw the need to operate on the national level. They had been distressed by the progressive, seemingly anti-business, anti-monopoly policies of President Theodore Roosevelt (who left office in 1909) and were alarmed by the increased political activity of organized labor.

NAM, the Chamber of Commerce, and other **trade associations** representing specific industries were effective spokespersons for their member companies. They were unable to defeat passage of the Clayton Act, but groups such as the Cotton Manufacturers planned elaborate and successful court campaigns to overturn key provisions of the act in the courts.[6] And, the Clayton Act aside, innumerable pieces of pro-business legislation were passed by Congress, whose members continued to insist that they had never been contacted by business groups.

In 1928 the bubble burst for some business interests. At the Senate's request, the Federal Trade Commission (FTC) undertook a massive investigation of the lobbying tactics of the business community. The examination of Congress by the FTC revealed extensive illegal lobbying by yet another group, the National Electric Light Association (NELA). Not only did the NELA lavishly entertain members of Congress, it also went to great expense to educate the public on the virtues of electric lighting. Books and pamphlets were produced and donated to schools and public libraries to sway public opinion. Needy teachers and ministers who were willing to advocate electricity were "helped" with financial grants. These tactics were considered unethical by many, and business was held in public disfavor. It was these kinds of activities that led the public to view lobbyists in a negative light.

The battles among business, labor, and progressive groups well illustrate the wave theory of interest groups. Though issues changed and the Progressive Movement gave way under the weight of the Depression and World War II, the general balance of groups maintained itself until well past the mid-twentieth century.

---

[5] Quoted in Grant McConnell, "Lobbies and Pressure Groups," in Jack Greene, ed. *Encyclopedia of American Political History,* Vol. 2 (New York: Macmillan, 1984), p. 768.
[6] Lee Epstein, *Conservatives in Court* (Knoxville: University of Tennessee Press, 1985).

The Third Wave of Interest-Group Activity (1960–)

After the Depression, the New Deal, and America's entry into World War II, many progressive groups fell into disarray. Others continued, but with less vitality. Many business, labor, and professional groups, however, continued to flourish. According to a study conducted by Kay Lehman Schlozman and John Tierney, nearly 70 percent of today's Washington, D.C.–based political organizations established their offices after 1960. Nearly half opened their offices after 1970. Not surprisingly, given the social and economic thrust of President Lyndon Johnson's "Great Society" programs, most of the new groups were formed to take advantage of the money and opportunities those programs offered.

From 1960 to 1992, the number of interest-group representatives registered (as required by law) in Washington increased from fewer than 500 to 6,083. The federal government had clearly become the primary target of policy change, and it was natural for groups to concentrate their resources in the nation's capital.

Then and Now
Lobbying

The exact origin of the term "lobbying" is disputed. In the mid-seventeenth century there was a room located near the floor of the English House of Commons where members of Parliament would congregate and could be approached by their constituents and others who wanted to plead a particular cause. Similarly, in the United States, people often waited outside the chambers of the House and Senate to speak to members of Congress as they emerged. Because they waited in the lobbies to argue their cases, by the nineteenth century they were commonly referred to as "lobbyists." Another piece of folklore explains that when Ulysses S. Grant was president he would frequently walk from the White House to the Willard Hotel on Pennsylvania Avenue just to relax in its comfortable and attractive lobby. Interest group representatives and those seeking favors from Grant would crowd into that lobby and try to press their claims. Soon they were nicknamed lobbyists.

Lobbying reached an infamous peak in the late 1800s when railroads and other big businesses openly bribed state and federal legislators to obtain favorable legislation. Congress finally got around to regulating some aspects of lobbying in 1946 with the Regulation of Lobbying Act, which required paid lobbyists to register with the House and Senate and to file quarterly financial reports, including an account of all contributions and expenditures as well as the names and addresses of those to whom they gave $500 or more. Organizations also were required to submit financial reports, although

they did not have to register officially. The purpose of the act was to publicize the activities of lobbyists and remove some of the uncertainty surrounding the influence of lobbying on legislation. In 1954, however, a lower court ruled the act unconstitutional. Although the Supreme Court reversed the decision, the Court's narrow interpretation undermined the effectiveness of the act. The Court ruled that the act was applicable only to persons or organizations who solicited, collected, or received money for the principal purpose of influencing legislation by directly lobbying members of Congress. Consequently, many lobbyists do not register at all. The National Association of Manufacturers, for example, was formed in 1895, but did not register as a lobbying group until 1975. Of the organizations that do register, more than 90 percent do not file complete financial reports.

As a result of a series of hearings held in 1991, Congress is expected to consider legislation creating a unified lobbying disclosure law to reduce many of the loopholes in the current regulations. While lobbyists are currently required to disclose all meetings with House and Senate members, time spent with personal or committee staff is not counted. And while the expenses incurred during those meetings with members of Congress must be reported, the total spending of lobbyists remains unknown. Stricter regulations on lobbying will reveal a more accurate picture of who is trying to influence legislation and with how much money.

Public-Interest Groups. During the 1960s and 1970s, the progressive spirit found renewed vigor in the rise of public-interest groups. Generally, these groups devoted themselves to representing the interests of blacks, women, the elderly, the poor, and consumers or working on behalf of the environment. Many of their leaders and members had been active in the civil rights and anti–Vietnam War movement efforts of the 1960s. Other groups, like the ACLU and NAACP, which had survived for nearly a century gained renewed vigor.

Common Cause and the Nader Network. The civil rights and anti-war movements of the 1960s and 1970s left many Americans feeling cynical about a government which they believed failed to respond to the will of the majority. They also believed that if citizens banded together, they could make a difference. Thus, two major new public-interest groups—Common Cause and Ralph Nader's Public Citizen, Inc.—were founded during this period. Common Cause, a "good government" group similar to some of the early progressive good-government groups, has effectively challenged aspects of the congressional seniority system, successfully urged the passage of sweeping campaign-financing reforms, and played a major role in the enactment of legislation authorizing federal financing of presidential campaigns. It continues to lobby for accountability in government and for more efficient and responsive governmental structures and practices.

Perhaps more well known than Common Cause is the collection of groups headed by Ralph Nader under the name Public Citizen, Inc. In 1965 Nader, a young lawyer, was thrust into the public limelight with the publication of his book *Unsafe at Any Speed.* In it he charged that General Motors' (GM) Corvair was unsafe to drive, and he produced voluminous evidence of how the car could flip over at average speeds on curved roads. He later testified about auto safety in front of Congress in 1966 and then learned that General Motors had spied on him in an effort to discredit his work. The subsequent $250,000 that GM paid to Nader in an out-of-court settlement allowed him to establish the Center for the Study of Responsive Law in 1969. It analyzed the activities of regulatory agencies and concluded that few of them enforced anti-trust regulations or cracked down on deceptive advertising practices. Nader then turned again to lobbying Congress,

Common Cause, a good government group, has lobbied for a number of governmental reforms over the last several decades. Recently, the group has advocated campaign finance reform by means of both voluntary candidate choice and statutory change, as shown in the Common Cause flyer below. Although statutory change is the only guarantee of victory, voluntarism can happen: In 1992, for example, Democratic primary candidate Jerry Brown refused to accept contributions of over $100.

Ask Presidential Candidates to "Take the Pledge" by Making a Public Commitment Now to:

★ Prevent the use of huge Watergate-style "soft money" contributions to support their 1992 campaign for president.

★ Support the legislative provisions passed by the United States Senate last year to end the use of huge Watergate-style "soft money" contributions to support presidential campaigns.

which led him to create Public Citizen, Inc., to act as an umbrella organization for what was to be called the "Nader Network" of groups.

These good-government groups have had a significant impact on governmental policy making, as have other public interest groups, including those concerned with the environment and women's issues. As discussed throughout this text, both have enjoyed considerable success in the legislative forum.

Conservative Backlash: Religious and Ideological Groups. The growth and successes that various public-interest groups had in the 1960s and 1970s ultimately created a conservative backlash. Many of these liberal groups' advances were made through litigation, that is, by challenging existing laws and practices through the courts. As discussed in detail in Chapter 9, since the days of the progressive National Consumers' League, liberal groups had targeted the courts, especially the Supreme Court, in an effort to secure their goals. Women and blacks won many rights through expanded readings of the equal protection clause of the Fourteenth Amendment and judicial interpretation of the requirements of the Civil Rights Act of 1964 (such as the end of segregated schools and the right to a job free from discrimination), and the Nader groups and environmentalists secured many governmental regulations that adversely affected business interests. Conservative groups quickly took notice of these successes and began responding to them.

By the mid- to late 1970s, conservatives became very concerned about the successes of liberal groups in shaping and defining the public agenda, and religious and ideological conservatives became a potent force in American politics. The largest new religious conservative group was the Reverend Jerry Falwell's Moral Majority, founded in 1978. At one point, the Moral Majority had an extensive television ministry and in its peak year, 1984, raised $11 million for political lobbying. It was widely credited with assisting Ronald Reagan's 1980 presidential victory as well as the defeats of several liberal Democratic senators that same year; Falwell claimed to have sent 3 to 4 million newly registered voters to the polls.[7] In June 1989, Falwell announced that he was terminating the Moral Majority after the movement suffered from a series of financial and sexual scandals involving television evangelists. To some extent, the end of the Reagan era seemed to trigger an end to the effectiveness of the religious right in national politics. Other conservatives, however, were not so daunted.

In 1973, friends of Ronald Reagan, who was then the governor of California, were dismayed by the repeated successes in the courts of liberal public-interest groups. Liberal groups were continually victorious in challenging the "reforms" of the Reagan administration—particularly those concerning welfare and the environment. Reaganites were incensed that these liberal groups continually went to court claiming to represent the "public interest." Therefore, Reagan supporters in California founded the Pacific Legal Foundation, the chief aim of which was to present the conservative side of the public interest in court. In the late 1970s, the Pacific Legal Foundation was sufficiently successful to justify the creation of regional law centers throughout the United States.[8] The conservative firms' goals were to bring to court cases that would secure the reversal of liberal decisions involving the environment, affirmative action, and other issues of concern to conservatives. As the Supreme Court has taken a more conservative turn, these conservative public-interest firms are renewing their efforts to bring to the Court test cases on issues involving civil rights, affirmative action, the environment, and prayer in schools.

[7] Peter Stienfels, "Moral Majority to Dissolve; Says Mission Accomplished," *The New York Times,* June 12, 1989, p. A-14.

[8] Karen O'Connor and Bryant Scott McFall, "Conservative Interest Group Litigation in the Reagan Era and Beyond," in Mark P. Petracca, ed. *The Politics of Interests* (Boulder, Colo.: Westview Press, 1992), pp. 263–281.

Business Groups. Conservative public-interest groups were not the only ones organized to advance conservative views beginning in the 1970s. Many members of the business community believed that both the Chamber of Commerce and the National Association of Manufacturers were too reactionary and shrill in their condemnation of governmental policies and practices. In addition, some members of the business community believed that both were too slow to act and therefore were ineffective representatives of big business. To fill this perceived void and to counter the effects of the Nader Network, the Business Roundtable was created in 1972. Largely made up of the chief executive officers of major businesses, the Roundtable uses its members for direct lobbying and policy formation. It is "a fraternity of powerful and prestigious business leaders that tells 'business's side of the story' to legislators, bureaucrats, White House personnel, and other interested public officials."[9] One of its first battles led to the defeat of Carter administration–backed legislation that would have created a federal consumer protection agency, a pet project of Ralph Nader's.

Unlike public-interest groups, organizations like the Chamber of Commerce and the Business Roundtable enjoy many of the benefits other businesses do as lobbyists: They already have extensive organization, expertise, large numbers, a strong financial base, and a longstanding relationship with key actors in government. Such natural advantages have led to huge numbers of business groups. One observer describes their proliferation this way:

> If you want to understand government, don't begin by reading the Constitution. It conveys precious little of today's statecraft. Instead, read selected portions of the Washington Telephone Directory, such as pages 354–58, which contain listings for all of the organizations with titles beginning with the word "National." . . . There are, of course, the big ones, like the National Association of Manufacturers, and the National Association of Broadcasters. But the pages teem with others, National Cigar Leaf Tobacco Association, National Association of Mirror Manufacturers, National Association of Miscellaneous Ornamental and Architectural Product Contractors, National Association of Margarine Manufacturers.[10]

These national groups devote tremendous resources to fighting government regulation. And quite often, they find themselves on the opposite side of organized labor on any issue.

Organized Labor. Labor became a stronger force in American politics when the American Federation of Labor and the Congress of Industrial Organizations merged in 1955. The new AFL-CIO immediately turned its energies to pressuring the government to protect concessions won from employers at the bargaining table. Concentrating its efforts largely on the national level, the AFL-CIO and other unions have been active in a wide range of issues, including minimum wage laws, the environment, civil rights, medical insurance, and consumer and education issues. But the once-fabled political clout of organized labor has recently been on the wane. By the late 1970s it was clear that even during a Democratic administration (Carter's), organized labor lacked the impact it had had during earlier decades. During the Reagan administration, organized labor's influence fell to an all-time modern-day low. In spite of the tremendous resources behind the AFL-CIO and other unions, membership has dropped, and continues to do so.

[9] David Mahood, *Interest Groups Participation in America: A New Intensity* (Englewood Cliffs, N.J.: Prentice Hall, 1990), p. 23.

[10] Quoted in Ronald J. Hrebrenar and Ruth K. Scott, *Interest Group Politics in America,* 2nd ed. (Englewood Cliffs, N.J.: Prentice Hall, 1990), p. 263.

Members of the AFL-CIO, the major institution of organized labor in contemporary America, marching in a 1991 rally in Washington.

Professional Associations. In contrast to the labor union situation, the political influence of professional societies continues to expand. The American Medical Association (AMA), for example, is implementing an even stronger, more intensive lobbying effort to try to fend off attempts to establish a system of national guaranteed health care of the kind in Great Britain. In the early 1960s, the AMA spent millions of dollars in an

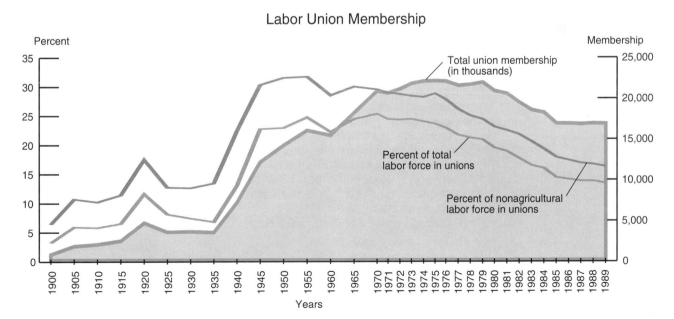

Labor Union Membership

Source: Harold W. Stanley and Richard G. Niemi, *Vital Statistics on American Politics*, 3rd ed. (Washington: CQ Press, 1992) Table 6-11, p. 190.

unsuccessful effort to fight Medicare. Once some sort of medical assistance for the aged was inevitable, the AMA turned its efforts toward the drafting and implementation of legislation and regulations, an effort that produced considerable financial rewards for physicians. According to a report of the Federation of American Scientists:

> The old and the poor constituted an enormous pool of previously unfinanced health care needs. Once their needs began to be financed, demand for health care jumped still farther ahead of supply. For those who provided health services, these programs were a bonanza. The doctors were committed only to "reasonable" charges. . . . Naturally, their charges rose.[11]

The AMA, however, has experienced internal problems since the 1980s. In 1985 and 1986, its political action committee (PAC; see pages 477–479) declined from first to second place in terms of the dollars it contributed to the campaigns of candidates for office. However, the AMA remains a potent force on Capitol Hill.

The National Education Association, which represents the interests of teachers, professors, and administrators, is another influential professional association. It was instrumental in the establishment of the Department of Education during the Carter administration. Also influential is the American Bar Association (ABA), which represents many of the nation's lawyers. As discussed in Chapter 9, the ABA plays a key role in nominations to the federal bench via its rating of the candidates.

What Makes an Interest Group Successful?

Throughout our nation's history, all kinds of interests in society have organized to pressure the government for policy change. Some have been successful, and some have not. E. E. Schattschneider once wrote, "Pressure politics is essentially the politics of small groups. . . . Pressure tactics are not remarkably successful in mobilizing general interests."[12] He was correct; historically, corporate interests often prevail over the concerns of public interest groups such as environmentalists.

To understand this point better, it's important to distinguish between an actual and a potential group. Theoretically, all women could be members of a women's rights group, all campers members of a conservation group, or all gun owners members of the National Rifle Association. These potential groups include *all* people who might be group members because they share a common trait or interest.[13] An actual group consists of only those people who actually join, and it is always smaller than the potential group.

Groups vary tremendously in their ability to enroll potential members, as revealed in Table 15-2. Economist Mancur Olson notes that all groups, whether economic or noneconomic, provide some **collective good**—that is, something of value, such as money, a tax write-off, a good feeling, or a better environment—that can't be withheld from a non-group member.[14] If one union member at a factory gets a raise, for example, all other workers at that factory will too. Therefore, those who don't join or work for the benefit of the group still reap the rewards of the group's activity. This phenomenon is called the

[11] Ibid., p. 275.

[12] E. E. Schattschneider, *The Semi-Sovereign People* (New York: Holt, Rinehart and Winston, 1960), p. 35.

[13] Truman, p. 511.

[14] Mancur Olson, *The Logic of Collective Action: Public Goods and the Theory of Groups* (Cambridge, Mass.: Harvard University Press, 1965).

Table 15-2   Potential versus Actual Interest Groups

The goal of most groups is to mobilize all potential members. Often that task is impossible. As Olson points out, the larger the group, the more difficult it is to mobilize. To illustrate the potential versus actual membership phenomenon, here are several examples of groups and their potential memberships.

POPULATION	GROUP	NUMBER OF POTENTIAL MEMBERS	NUMBER OF ACTUAL MEMBERS
Governors	National Governors' Association	55	55 (includes territories)
Political Science Faculty	American Political Science Association	17,000	8,250
Doctors	American Medical Association	548,000	288,000
Women	National Organization for Women	127,000,000	250,000
Blacks	National Association for the Advancement of Colored People (NAACP)	30,600,000	500,000

free rider problem. Consequently, Olson asserts, potential members are unlikely to join a group because they realize that they will receive many of the benefits the group achieves regardless of their participation. Not only is it irrational for free riders to join any group, but the bigger the group, the greater the free rider problem. Small groups like the AMA or the American Political Science Association have an organizational advantage because in a small group, any individual's share of the collective good may be great enough to make it rational to join.

The Role of Leaders

Interest-group theorists frequently acknowledge the key role that leaders play in the formation and viability of groups. The role of an interest-group leader is similar to that of an entrepreneur in the business world. As in the marketing of a new product, an interest-group leader must have something attractive to offer in order to convince members to join. Potential members of the group must be convinced that the benefits of joining outweigh the costs. Union members, for example, must be persuaded that the cost of their union dues will be offset by the union's winning higher wages for them. The leader of the group must convince potential members that the group can effectively lobby the government and achieve particular goals.

Without the powerful pen of William Lloyd Garrison in the 1830s, who knows whether the abolitionist movement would have been as successful? Similarly, Frances Willard was the prime mover behind the WCTU, as were Marian Wright Edelman of the Children's Defense Fund in 1968, and the Reverend Jerry Falwell of the Moral Majority in the 1980s. Most successful groups, especially public-interest groups, are led by charismatic individuals who devote most of their energies to "the cause."

Leaders often differ from the rank and file of the group in that they are usually more future oriented, better educated, and affluent. Accounts of the early efforts of a former elementary school teacher, Susan B. Anthony, to secure the vote for women indicate that she did not expect that suffrage would be forthcoming quickly. Her belief in the future led her to continue where more faint-hearted individuals might not have bothered. Similarly, without Ralph Nader, a Yale-educated lawyer, there might not be a Public Citizen, Inc.

Suffrage leader Susan B. Anthony in later life. Although she died before passage of the Nineteenth Amendment, her efforts on its behalf were critical.

Group Structure

The success of any group can be affected by its leader's choice of organizational structure, which is often based on the activities and goals of the group. There are two basic group structures: federated and unitary. A federated association is basically one made up of other groups. Key functions (such as lobbying or education), authority, and activities are divided between the national office and the state or local affiliates. The National Organization for Women, for example, is a federated association; it has a national office in New York City, and affiliates in all fifty states. The National Association for the Advancement of Colored People (NAACP) also employs a federated structure and often relies on its 1,700 adult and 450 college affiliates in forty-eight states to alert it to discriminatory practices or policies.

Unitary associations have only one level of decision making and organization. The Business Roundtable, for example, is a unitary association. So too is the American Political Science Association, although numerous independent regional and state political science associations exist.

Funding

Funding is crucial to all interest groups. In a 1983 study, Jack L. Walker found that patrons—those who fund groups—were key to many interest-group successes.[15] Government, foundations, and wealthy individuals all serve as patrons who provide crucial startup funds for groups, especially public-interest groups.

Groups also rely heavily on membership contributions, dues, and other fund-raising activities. During the 1980s, conservative groups, for example, relied heavily on the direct mail skills of the marketing wizard Richard Viguerie to raise monies for a variety of conservative causes. In the 1990s, pro-choice groups have successfully appealed to supporters by requesting funds to campaign for legislation in anticipation of the Supreme Court's reversal of *Roe* v. *Wade.*

Membership

E. E. Schattschneider has noted that our interest-group system has a decidedly "upper class bias," and he concluded that 90 percent of the population does not participate in the interest-group, or what he calls pressure-group, system. Since the 1960s, survey data have revealed that group membership is drawn primarily from those with higher income and education levels. Those who are wealthier can afford to belong to more organizations because they have more money and, often, more leisure time. Money and education are also associated with greater confidence that one's actions will bring results, a further incentive to devote time to organizing or supporting interest groups.

People who do belong to groups often belong to more than one. This overlapping membership can often affect the cohesiveness of a group. Imagine, for example, that you are an officer in the college Young Republicans. If you call a meeting, people may not attend because they have academic, athletic, or social obligations. Divided loyalties such as these often affect the success of a group.

Organizations are usually composed of three kinds of members. At the top are a relatively small number of leaders who devote most of their energies to the single group. The second tier of members are generally involved psychologically as well as organizationally. They are the workhorses of the group—they attend meetings, pay dues, and chair committees to see that things get done. In the bottom tier are the rank and file,

---

[15]Jack Walker, "The Origins and Maintenance of Interest Groups in America," *American Political Science Review 77* (June 1983), pp. 390–406.

members who don't actively participate. They pay their dues and call themselves group members, but they do little more. Most group members fall into this last category.

What Interest Groups Do

In a word, interest groups lobby. The name "lobbyist" refers to any representative of a group who attempts to influence a policy maker by any one or more of the variety of tactics illustrated earlier in Table 15-1. Lobbying is the process by which interest groups attempt to assert their influence on the policy process.

As Table 15-1 indicates, there are at least twenty-seven ways to lobby, and these various methods can be classified either as inside lobbying (lobbying governmental employees directly) or outside lobbying (involving indirect appeals to government employees through candidates for office or through the public itself).

As journalist Hedrick Smith has noted, lobbying carries a very bad image: ". . . lobbying kindles an image of wickedness only barely less disreputable than the skullduggery of the Mafia."[16] A group's ability to take advantage of the political process and to exert influence depends on many factors, including its size, financial strength, and the nature of the demands it makes.[17] Groups don't necessarily have much control over these factors, but they can choose which strategies to adopt. Research indicates that interest groups don't change basic policy making, but they do affect small but significant provisions attached to many bills.

Inside Lobbying

Inside lobbying is carried out to give an interest group the kind of direct access necessary to influence the policy process. Access to important policy makers is key and exceptionally important in congressional and executive branch lobbying and to a lesser extent in lobbying the Supreme Court. Interest groups who inside lobby traditionally try to persuade key governmental decision makers *and* the public of the correctness of their positions. Generally, they do this by testifying at hearings, getting in touch with legislators, and providing information that decision makers might not have the time, opportunity, or interest to gather on their own. Of course, information provided by the groups is designed to present the group's position in a favorable light.

Lobbying Congress. Members of Congress are the targets of a wide variety of lobbying activities: individual letters from interested constituents, campaign contributions, speaking fees, or the outright payment of money for votes. Of course, the last item is illegal, but there are numerous documented instances of money changing hands for votes.

Lobbying is a skill that has developed over the years. In 1869, for example, women meeting in Washington, D.C., for the second annual meeting of the National Woman Suffrage Association marched to Capitol Hill to hear one of their members (unsuccessfully) ask Congress to pass legislation to enfranchise women under the terms of the Fourteenth Amendment.

Practices such as these floor speeches are no longer permitted. Today, lobbyists try to develop close relationships with senators and representatives to enhance their access to the policy-making process. A symbiotic relationship between members and interest-

[16] Hedrick Smith, *The Power Game* (New York: Random House, 1988), p. 231.
[17] Berry, p. 62.

John E. Jacob (behind microphones) of the National Urban League and leaders of other organizations lobbying for a civil rights bill at the Capitol in 1991.

group representatives often develops. Representatives and their staff members, who face an exhausting workload and legislation they know little about, frequently look to lobbyists for information. According to one aide:

> My boss demands a speech and a statement for the *Congressional Record* for every bill we introduce or co-sponsor—and we have a lot of bills. I just can't do it all myself. The better lobbyists, when they have a proposal they are pushing, bring it to me along with a couple of speeches, a *Record* insert, and a fact sheet.[18]

Not surprisingly, lobbyists work most closely with representatives who share their interests. A lobbyist from the National Rifle Association (NRA), for example, would be unlikely to try to influence a liberal representative who was on record as strongly in favor of gun control. Instead, it is far more effective for a group like the NRA to provide useful information for its supporters and to those who are undecided.

A lobbyist's effectiveness depends largely on his or her reputation for fair play and provision of accurate information. No member of Congress wants to look uninformed. As one member noted:

> It doesn't take very long to figure out which lobbyists are straightforward, and which ones are trying to snow you. The good ones will give you the weak points as well as the strong points of their case. If anyone ever gives me false or misleading information, that's it—I'll never see him again.[19]

Because inside lobbying is so important, many especially effective lobbyists often are former members of Congress, former staff aides, former White House officials or Cabinet officers, or Washington insiders. This type of lobbyist frequently drops in to visit members of Congress or their staff members and often takes them to lunch, golf, or parties.

Every year hundreds of White House aides or key executive branch staffers take

[18] Quoted in Kay Lehman Schlozman and John T. Tierney, *Organized Interests and American Society* (New York: Harper & Row, 1986), p. 85.

[19] Quoted in Norman J. Ornstein and Shirley Elder, *Interest Groups, Lobbying and Policy Making* (Washington: CQ Press, 1978), p. 77.

lucrative jobs in the private sector as lobbyists. While much of that activity may be ethically questionable, most is not illegal. There are well-publicized exceptions, however. Michael K. Deaver, once a top aide to President Ronald Reagan, was convicted of perjury in connection with a grand jury investigation of his use of his former government contacts to help clients in his public relations firm. Similarly, Lyn Nofziger, another Reagan aide, was convicted for violating the Ethics in Government Act (his conviction was later overturned) for lobbying the White House on behalf of various labor unions and businesses too soon after he left public service.

Successful lobbyists are also available when a member of Congress might need them. In 1977 when the Senate was being threatened by a filibuster over gas deregulation, during the all-night session

> The Natural Gas Committee, organized with a $600,000 annual budget to work solely for deregulation, set up a post just outside the Senate Chamber by commandeering a corridor bench and stacking it with manila envelopes full of position papers on pending amendments. . . .
>
> "We keep a person sitting at a window seat with the files," said one lobbyist for the committee, which represents more than one hundred companies. "Everybody knows where he is. We also have a group of runners because there isn't even a phone there. . . .
>
> To cope with the staggering pile of 508 inhibiting amendments . . . the gas industry put a computer to work cranking out "instant economic replay" to a terminal in the National Gas Committee's Connecticut Avenue headquarters, with the results quickly taxied to Capitol Hill.[20]

While these kinds of tactics are still used, lobbyists have been dramatically affected by the decentralization of congressional power that has occurred over the years (see Chapter 6). The weakening of the power of committee chairs, the diffusion of power to junior House members, and the proliferation of subcommittees have required interest groups to

---

[20] Ibid., pp. 85–86.

Former presidential aide Michael Deaver, in 1986, was the subject of an FBI investigation into his lobbying activities after he left the Reagan administration to start his own public relations firm. He eventually was convicted of perjury.

Ethics in Government Act

In 1978, in the wake of Watergate, Congress passed the Ethics in Government Act. Its key provisions dealt with financial disclosure and employment after government service:

Financial disclosure: The president, vice president, and top-ranking executive employees must file annual public financial disclosure reports that list:

- The source and amount of all earned income; all income from stocks, bonds, and property; any investments or large debts; and the source of a spouse's income, if any.
- Any position or offices held in any business, labor, or nonprofit organizations.

Employment after government services: Former executive branch employees may not:

- Represent anyone before any agency for two years after leaving government service on matters that came within the former employees' sphere of responsibility (even if they were not personally involved in the matter).
- Represent anyone on *any* matter before their former agency for one year after leaving it, even if the former employees had no connection with the matter while in the government.

Sources: National Journal (November 19, 1977), pp. 1796–1803; and *Congressional Quarterly Weekly Report* (October 28, 1978), pp. 3121–3127.

expand the scope and intensity of their lobbying efforts. Despite the changing climate in Congress, however, interest groups' role in the policy-making process remains important.

Lobbying the Executive Branch and Executive Agencies. As the scope of the federal government has expanded, lobbying the executive branch has increased in importance and frequency. Groups often target one or more levels of the executive branch because there are so many potential access points—the president and White House staff, the numerous levels of the bureaucracy, and the independent regulatory commissions. Groups try to work closely with the administration to influence policy decisions at their formulation and implementation stages. And, like the situation with congressional lobbying, the effectiveness of a group often lies in its ability to provide decision makers with important information.

Historically, group representatives have met with presidents or their staff members to urge policy directions. In 1992, representatives of the auto industry even accompanied President Bush to lobby the Japanese for more favorable trade regulations. Most presidents also specifically set up staff positions "explicitly to serve as brokerages or clearinghouses to provide greater access to presidential attention for professional, demographic or specialized organizations."[21] Political scientist Thomas Cronin has suggested that "presidents have appointed either an aide or an office for every American dilemma."[22] Among these are offices of domestic policy, economic policy, science and technology, consumer

[21.]Thomas Cronin, *The State of the Presidency* (Boston: Little, Brown, 1975), p. 123.
[22]Ibid.

affairs, the environment, and minority affairs. At various times, special liaison offices have been created to deal with women, Jews, blacks, and bankers, among others.

An especially strong link exists between interest groups and the regulatory agencies (see Chapter 8). Because of the highly technical aspects of much regulatory work, many groups employ Washington attorneys to deal directly with the agencies. So great is interest-group influence in the decision-making process of these agencies that many charge that the agencies have been captured by the interest groups. The Interstate Commerce Commission (ICC), for example, was created in 1887 at the urgings of progressive groups to protect the public from the rampant price fixing and other corrupt practices that were commonplace in the railroad industry. Yet the ICC—heavily influenced by the railroads themselves—frequently set trucking and railroad freight shipping fees at high levels. At one point, early in the 1900s, the ICC and the trucking association even shared offices in the same federal building! Even after the extensive deregulation that took place during the Carter and Reagan administrations, some groups still complained that certain agencies were unduly influenced by some groups. The National Coal Association (NCA), for example, has argued that the ICC has granted excessive increases in rail freight rates that adversely affect the coal industry. The head of the NCA once remarked: "I used to say that the I.C.C. is a wholly owned subsidiary of the Association of American Railroads. But now I'm older and wiser and as a consequence of these outrageous decisions I now contend that the I.C.C. is a wholly owned subsidiary of the coal-carrying railroads."[23]

With or without former government officials on their staffs, interest groups strive to form stable and cozy relationships with Congress and the bureaucracy to achieve their goals. The term "iron triangle" is commonly used to describe the informal, yet semi-permanent relationship of these three actors in the policy process.[24] (See Chapter 8.)

Being part of an iron triangle has significant advantages for interest groups. They cement their access to key legislators and bureaucrats by building loyalties, thereby maintaining these triangles. Each corner of the triangle has something to offer the others, and these relationships tend to become ironclad. As described in Chapter 8, interest group ties to congressional subcommittees, staffers, and bureaucrats are an invaluable source of influence.

Similar group behavior can be observed in Britain. Since interest groups tend to concentrate their lobbying efforts where it will do them the most good, this leads to perceptibly different patterns of interaction in the British case, however. Since Parliament lacks institutional clout, interest groups tend to cluster around the bureaucracy and the occasional government minister who is known to be open to influence. As a result, one rarely observes classic iron triangles in the British system.

Lobbying the Courts. Finally, the courts have proved a useful target for interest groups. Although you might think that the courts decide cases that affect only the parties involved or that they should be immune from political pressures, interest groups have for years recognized the value of lobbying the courts, especially the Supreme Court. As shown earlier in Table 15-1, 72 percent of the Washington-based groups surveyed participated in litigation as a lobbying tool. Groups participate in litigation because they recognize that judicial decisions can bring about major policy changes.

Outside Lobbying

Lobbying Congress, the president, or the courts are all conventional methods of inside lobbying. Other conventional and even nonconventional forms of pressure-group activity can be categorized as outside lobbying.

[23] Quoted in Hrebrenar and Scott, p. 216.
[24] Some also speak of iron rectangles, reflecting the growing importance of the courts in the process.

Grassroots Lobbying. As its name implies, grassroots lobbying is a form of pressure-group activity that attempts to involve those at the bottom level. It often involves door-to-door informational or petition drives—a tried and true method of lobbying. As early as the 1840s, for example, women (who could not even vote) used petition campaigns to persuade state legislators to enact Married Women's Property Acts to give women control of their earnings and a greater legal say in the custody of their children. Today, environmentalists frequently go door-to-door to alert their friends and neighbors about pending legislation, the creating or locating of hazardous waste materials, or other threats.

When these forms of pressure-group activity are unsuccessful or appear to be too slow to achieve results, some groups resort to more forceful measures to attract attention to their cause. In April 1992, for example, women's rights activists concerned about reproductive freedom held one of the largest mass marches to date in Washington, D.C. During the civil rights movement, as discussed in Chapter 5, Martin Luther King Jr. and his followers frequently resorted to nonviolent marches to draw attention to the plight of blacks in the South. These forms of organized group activity were legal. Proper parade permits were obtained and government officials notified. The protesters who tried to stop the freedom marchers, however, were engaging in illegal protest activity, another form of activity sometimes resorted to by interest groups.

Protest Activity. Since the Revolutionary War, violent, illegal protest has been one of the tactics of organized interests. The Boston Tea Party, for example, involved the breaking of all sorts of laws although no one was hurt physically. Other forms of protest such as the Shays's Rebellion ended in tragedy for some of their participants.

Groups on both ends of the political spectrum historically have resorted to violence. Abolitionists, anti-nuclear activists, anti-war activists, animal-rights advocates, and others on the "left" have broken laws, damaged property, and even injured or killed innocent bystanders. On the "right," groups like Operation Rescue and the Ku Klux Klan have broken the laws and even hurt or killed people in furtherance of their objectives. From the early 1900s until the 1960s, blacks were routinely lynched by KKK members. Today, Operation Rescue members regularly block the entrances to abortion clinics; other anti-abortion groups have taken credit for clinic bombings.

Most groups, however, have few members so devoted as to put everything on the line for their cause. It is far more likely for a group's members to opt for more conventional forms of lobbying or to influence policy through the electoral process.

Election Activities. Many groups claim to be nonpartisan, that is, nonpolitical. Usually they try to have friends in both political parties to whom they can look for assistance and access. Some organizations, however, routinely endorse candidates for public office, pledging money, group support, and often even campaign volunteers. Endorsements from some groups may be used by a candidate's opponent to attack the candidate. When several labor unions endorsed Walter Mondale in his 1984 campaign against President Ronald Reagan, he was labeled a "tool of the labor unions" by Republicans.

Some ideological groups rate candidates to help their members (and the general public) evaluate the voting records of members of Congress. The American Conservative Union (conservative) and the Americans for Democratic Action (liberal)—two groups at ideological polar extremes—routinely rate candidates and members of Congress based on their votes on key issues of importance to the group, as illustrated in Table 15-3.

Other groups target certain individuals and campaign against them to show their clout and to scare other elected officials into paying more attention to them. Beginning in 1970, for example, Environmental Action (EA) labeled twelve members of the House of Representatives "the dirty dozen" because of their votes against bills that the group believed were necessary to protect the environment. Over the years, the designation of more than thirty members of Congress with a similar label was widely publicized by the media and through direct-mail campaigns to voters interested in the environment. To

Table 15-3   1990 Group Ratings of Select Members of Congress[a]

MEMBER	AMERICAN CONSERVATIVE UNION (ACU)	AMERICANS FOR DEMOCRATIC ACTION (ADA)
Sen. Edward M. Kennedy (D.-Mass.)	0	100
Rep. Theodore S. Weiss (D.-N.Y.)	4	100
Rep. Barbara Boxer (D.-Calif.)	4	94
Rep. Vic Fazio (D.-Calif.)	4	89
Sen. Paul Simon (D.-Ill.)	13	94
Sen. Robert Kerrey (D.-Neb.)	13	83
Sen. Lloyd Bentsen (D.-Tex.)	32	44
Sen. John C. Danforth (D.-Mo.)	43	39
Sen. Nancy Kassebaum (D.-Kan.)	64	44
Rep. Newt Gingrich (R.-Ga.)	86	39
Sen. Jesse A. Helms (R.-N.C.)	100	6
Rep. William E. Dannemeyer (R.-Calif.)	100	4

[a]Members are rated on a scale from 1 to 100, with 1 being the lowest and 100 being the highest.

date, only seven members to earn EA's anti-environmental nickname have stayed in office. Similarly, in 1980, the Moral Majority targeted several liberal Democratic senators who were up for reelection and saw all of them defeated. Its clout, although short-lived, clearly made many vulnerable senators think twice about risking the wrath of what seemed to be a very powerful group able to produce results at the polls.

Another interest-group strategy is to form a political party to publicize a cause and even possibly win a few public offices. In 1848, the Free Soil Party was formed to publicize the crusade against slavery; twenty years later, the Prohibition Party was formed to ban the sale of alcoholic beverages. Similarly, in 1976, the National Right-to-Life Party was formed to publicize the anti-abortion position; and the National Organization for Women has held numerous serious discussions about the advisability of forming a new women's party. (See the box on page 393 in Chapter 11.)

The effectiveness of an interest group in the election arena has often been overrated by members of the news media. In general, it is very difficult to assess the effect of a particular group's impact on any one election because of the number of other factors that are present in any election or campaign. However, the one area in which interest groups do seem able to affect the outcome of elections directly is through a relatively new device called the political action committee.

Interest Groups and Political Action Committees. Throughout most of history, powerful interests and individuals have often used their money to "buy" politicians or their votes. Even if outright bribery was not involved, huge corporate or other interest-group donations certainly made some politicians look as if they were in the "pocket" of certain special interests. Congressional passage of the Federal Election Campaign Act began to change most of that. The 1971 Act required candidates to disclose all campaign contributions and limited the amount of money that they could spend on media advertising. In 1974, in the wake of the Watergate scandal (see Chapter 7), amendments to the act made it more far-reaching. They sharply limited the amount any interest group could give to a candidate for federal office. However, they also made it legal for corporations and labor unions to form political action committees, often referred to as PACs, that could make contributions to candidates for national elections. (See Chapter 13 for more on this subject.) Technically, a PAC is a political arm of a business, labor, trade, professional, or other interest group legally authorized to raise funds on a voluntary basis from employees or members in order to contribute to a political candidate or party.

The 1971 Federal Election Campaign Act as amended in 1974 was challenged in court by an unusual alliance of conservatives and liberals, including the New York Civil Liberties Union and the American Conservative Union. The Supreme Court upheld most of the act's provisions in Buckley v. Valeo *(1976) but found that a limit on spending violated the First Amendment.*

Toward Reform

Since the turn of the century, when good-government groups formed in response to blatant political corruption and the conflicts of interest between big business and government, the public has been uniform in its support of reforming and reducing the influence of "special interests." But, as James Madison pointed out centuries earlier in Federalist No. 10, it may be dangerous for governments to regulate factions too strictly, for such actions could limit liberty itself. Madison optimistically believed that competition between factions could be balanced by governments, but as we have seen in this chapter, all groups are not created equal. Generally, the wealthy and the powerful and the groups that represent them have more political sway than the poor and disenfranchised.

In 1946, in an effort to limit the power of lobbyists, Congress passed the Federal Regulation of Lobbying Act, which required anyone hired to lobby any member of Congress to register and file quarterly financial reports. Few lobbyists actually file these reports, and the Justice Department has not even opted to try to enforce the provisions of the act, believing its vagueness makes it virtually unenforceable. While some good-government groups argue that the laws should be strengthened, civil liberties groups such as the American Civil Liberties Union (see page 106) argue that registration provisions violate the First Amendment's freedom of speech and the right of petition.

In 1992, in the wake of the Savings and Loan scandal and the 1991 recession, Congress passed fairly sweeping reform legislation aimed at limiting interest groups. It called for curtailing special interest group PAC contributions, providing some public financing for congressional campaigns, and for tighter registration provisions for lobbyists. While many who criticize PACs supported the legislation, most Republican legislators voted against the bill, and it was vetoed by President George Bush. In 1992, the Senate voted fifty-two to forty-eight for a PAC reform law, which was vetoed by President Bush. Most observers believe that President Clinton will sign such a bill into law if Congress presents him with one.

Summary

Interest groups play a variety of roles in the American political process. They can increase representation of diverse interests in governmental decision making. They also increase political participation and educate the public and governmental officials about important issues. As they educate, they also help to put issues on the public agenda that might never get there without pressure-group activity. Once interest group-sponsored initiatives are adopted, groups often monitor those programs to make sure they are properly implemented.

America has always been a nation of joiners. National groups first emerged in the United States in the 1830s. Since that time, the type, nature, sophistication, and tactics of groups have changed dramatically.

A variety of different types of interest groups have emerged over the years. Groups exist that claim to represent specialized economic interests or the public interest; they also lobby on behalf of a single issue or a wide array of programs.

Just as groups are diverse, so are the ways in which they measure success. Strong leaders or patrons are critical to the success of most interest groups as are adequate resources, whether in the form of a dedicated membership or a reliable source of funds.

Leaders and funds allow groups to engage in a variety of lobbying activities. Depending on the goals of a particular group, its leaders and members may direct their efforts to one or more branches or levels of government using inside or outside strategies, or both.

Adverse reaction to the potential power of interest groups and the possibility of inappropriate influence has led Congress periodically to draft legislation to regulate lobbying. PACs, in particular, have come under an increasing amount of criticism.

Key Terms

interest group

lobbying

economic-interest groups

public-interest groups

multi-issue groups

single-issue groups

wave theory

lobbyist

trade associations

collective good

free rider problem

Suggested Readings

Berry, Jeffrey M. *The Interest Group Society,* 2nd ed. Glenview, Ill.: Scott, Foresman/Little, Brown, 1989.

———. *Lobbying for the People: The Political Behavior of Public Interest Groups.* Princeton, N.J.: Princeton University Press, 1977.

Cigler, Allan J., and Burdett A. Loomis, eds. *Interest Group Politics,* 3rd ed. Washington: CQ Press, 1991.

Hrebenar, Ronald J., and Ruth K. Scott. *Interest Group Politics in America,* 2nd ed. Englewood Cliffs, N.J.: Prentice Hall, 1990.

O'Connor, Karen, and Nancy E. McGlen. *Women's Rights.* New York: Praeger, 1983.

Olson, Mancur, Jr. *The Logic of Collective Action: Public Goods and the Theory of Groups.* Cambridge, Mass.: Harvard University Press, 1965.

Sabato, Larry. *PAC Power: Inside World of Political Action Committees.* New York: Norton, 1984.

Schlozman, Kay Lehman, and John T. Tierney. *Organized Interests and American Democracy.* New York: Harper & Row, 1986.

PART FOUR

Public Policy

We close the book with an examination of the policies that American government produces. What combination of institutional (Part Two) and behavioral (Part Three) knowledge explains government's policy results? This is the key question of Part Four.

We begin in Chapter 16 with economic policy because it is the nerve center of American politics. Internally, the government's budget sets the parameters for its entire range of activity. Externally, the manner in which the government manages the broader economy largely determines its popular support. Without both a healthy overall economy and an acceptable budget for their own activities, few governments can succeed.

Discussing domestic policy in Chapter 17, we first ask the question, "How should public policy be analyzed?" Examining a specific policy area requires a set of analytic tools, and we provide these at the start of the chapter. We then use them to examine welfare, education, and health, three key areas of modern governmental activity.

We finish in Chapter 18 with an examination of foreign and military policy. One of the government's most basic tasks is to keep the peace and protect the national interest, and the United States has taken many different approaches to that task over the years. We will examine its successes and failures in historical context, offering analysis along the way. We conclude with a section considering America's role in a changing world—an appropriate question to end the book, since its answer requires consideration of all aspects of America's government.

The most common and durable source of factions has been the various and unequal distribution of property. Those who hold and those who are without property have ever formed distinct interests in society. . . .

James Madison

FEDERALIST NO. 10

Even among the Founders, economic interests and policy preferences varied. Alexander Hamilton favored manufacturing; Thomas Jefferson favored agriculture. They often disagreed on policy questions.

CHAPTER 16

Economic Policy

Most of us think of economics and politics as separate spheres. The former is concerned with the production and distribution of goods and services, whereas the latter deals with collective choices made by government. Economic decisions, primarily made through markets, are made by private, self-interested consumers, firms, and workers. Political decisions, on the other hand, are primarily made through elections, legislatures, and public bureaucracies. While politics includes self-interested behavior, it also involves agreement on the broader "public interest."

In reality, economic and political spheres are closely linked, and they have become increasingly so during this century. Indeed, the growth of government involvement in economic affairs is a distinctive feature of modern times. One crude measure of this involvement is the proportion of our nation's economic resources that is directly controlled by government. We measure the value of the total output of goods and services of the economy by calculating the **gross domestic product** (GDP).[1] Figure 16-1 (later in this chapter) shows that total spending by government as a proportion of GDP has more than tripled in the past sixty years. In 1929, on the eve of the Great Depression, total government spending was only 10 percent of GDP; by 1989 it had risen to 32 percent, or about one-third of GDP.

These figures understate the degree of government involvement because they do not take into account other ways, besides spending, in which government affects the economy. For example, through tax policy the government provides incentives to encourage people to invest their money in particular industries, to help finance the costs of health care for employees, and to encourage home ownership and charitable contributions. And through its regulatory activities, the government affects the price of many goods and services, the levels of pollution that industries can introduce into the air and water, the

---

[1] You may be more familiar with gross *national* product (GNP), which is distinguished from GDP because it includes the earnings of American-owned assets located abroad. Because most other countries use GDP rather than GNP, the former will be used throughout most of this chapter for ease of comparison between the United States and other nations.

The Pervasiveness of Government Regulation

In Chapter 1 we described government's involvement in a typical morning routine:

From the time you get up in the morning to the short time later when you leave for classes or work, this central question of politics pervades your life. The government, for example, sets the standards for whether you wake up on Eastern, Central, or Western Standard Time. It regulates the airwaves and licenses the radio or television broadcasts you might listen to or glance at as you eat and get dressed. Whether or not the water you use as you brush your teeth contains fluoride is a state or local governmental issue. The federal Food and Drug Administration inspects your breakfast meat and sets standards for the advertising on your cereal box, orange juice carton, and other food packaging. Are they really "lite," "high in fiber," or "fresh squeezed"? Only the government can say.

All of these examples represent regulatory activities undertaken by legislatures and government bureaucracies, which amount to governmental intervention in the economy.

safety of the products we purchase, and conditions in the workplace. For good or ill, then, government can influence the decisions and behavior of private economic agents in a variety of ways.

Government Intervention in Historical Perspective

Government has never been an insignificant force in the nation's economic affairs. From the very beginning, it played a crucial role in fostering economic development. The policies of Alexander Hamilton, the first Treasury Secretary, included land, tax, tariff, and credit policies intended to bolster American manufacturing. Later on, the government built roads and canals, offered land grants to build the transcontinental railroad, and established tariffs (taxes on imported goods) to shield the new manufacturing from foreign competition. From the start, corporations were chartered by the government. The whole process of industrialization was dependent on the reinterpretation of common law by state courts in order to protect industrialists from tort actions (lawsuits that result from a wrongful act, injury, or damage) and damages to their property.

Laissez-faire and the Rise of Industrial Capitalism

After the Civil War, the United States entered a period of rapid economic growth. With the establishment of a mature industrial economy, Hamiltonian economic development policies were no longer considered necessary, and the nation entered a period in which the doctrine of *laissez-faire* dominated. *Laissez-faire* is a French term for "let (people) do as they please," meaning that government should interfere only minimally in the private market. This idea had existed at least since 1776, when Adam Smith wrote his classic *The Wealth of Nations,* in which he argued that by being free to pursue his or her own self-interest in the market each individual contributed to the welfare of all other individuals in society. The decisions of millions of individuals pursuing their self-interest acted as a "hidden hand" to efficiently allocate resources, requiring little direction from the "visible hand" of the government. The role of government in such an economy is to establish a legal framework for the market to function within—protecting property rights, enforcing contracts, and so on—and to provide such basic public facilities as roads and bridges that cannot be provided through the market. Though *laissez-faire* was always more myth than reality, unsolicited government intervention virtually ended after the Civil War. In striking down state and federal regulatory statutes, the Supreme Court essentially incorporated *laissez-faire* doctrine as the public policy of the United States.

The minimal role for government prescribed by the *laissez-faire* doctrine was ill suited to the kind of economic order that was emerging, however. The rise of industrial capitalism involved a shift from subsistence farming to factory production for mass markets. People began working in factories for wages. Industrialization created a new set of challenges and vulnerabilities that did not exist in an agriculture-based economy: industrial accidents and diseases, pollution of the air and water, the emergence of powerful monopolies that could exploit workers and consumers, unemployment and the loss of income because of **business cycles.** Business cycles are "boom and bust" swings in the economy, in which people are thrown out of work and financial markets become chaotic during "bust" periods.

Along with industrialization came urbanization—the shift of population from the country to cities, where factories were located, and a large influx of immigrants from Europe. The sheer density of people required that government invest in "infrastructure" (bridges, roads, sewer and water facilities, and so on); provide or regulate public utilities (gas, electricity, telephones, and the like); and establish police, fire, and similar public-welfare services.

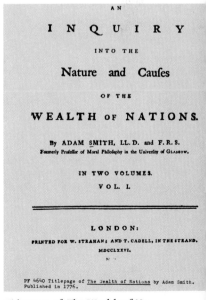

A N

I N Q U I R Y

INTO THE

Nature and Caufes

OF THE

WEALTH OF NATIONS.

By ADAM SMITH, LL. D. and F. R. S.
Formerly Profeffor of Moral Philofophy in the Univerfity of GLASGOW.

IN TWO VOLUMES.
VOL. I.

LONDON:
PRINTED FOR W. STRAHAN; AND T. CADELL, IN THE STRAND.
MDCCLXXVI.

PF 4640 Titlepage of The Wealth of Nations by Adam Smith.
Published in 1776.

Title page of *The Wealth of Nations,* Adam Smith's classic 1776 book arguing that free market mechanisms are the best engine for economic progress.

Market Failures

Economists have developed different criteria for deciding when government intervention in the market is warranted. One of these is called *market failure.* This refers to the presence in the market of imperfections that prevent the allocation of resources in accord with consumers' valuations. Three market failures that are most important are:

- *Public Goods:* These are goods and services that cannot be provided through the market because it is difficult or impractical to restrict their use to paying customers. A meal at the local McDonald's is not a public good because it is possible to exclude people who do not pay for the food from partaking of it. By contrast, it is difficult to restrict the use of streets and parks to paying customers. If government did not provide these goods by forcing people to pay taxes for them, individuals would be tempted to act as "free riders"— enjoying the benefit while not paying for the cost. Even if it were technically possible to exclude such free riders (by having private toll roads or private parks with high fences around them), the costs of controlling access and collecting tolls would be so large that the alternative— having government pay for streets and parks—makes the most sense.

- *Natural Monopolies:* These include goods and services for which it is impractical or inefficient to have a competitive market. For many public utilities— such as electricity, natural gas, cable television, and telephone service—it would be wasteful or impractical to have more than one provider. To make sure that the providers of these services do not charge the public exorbitant rates, they are either provided directly by local governments or are regulated by them.

- *Externalities:* An "externality" exists when some of the benefits (a "positive externality") or the costs (a "negative externality") of an economic transaction are absorbed by individuals who are not parties to the transaction. They are effects on third parties that occur as incidental by-products of another person's or firm's activity. Education is an example of a positive externality. One reason the government supports much of the costs of education is that the benefits of education are spread throughout society. Not only will you and your school benefit from your "purchase" of an education, but so will your future employers, the customers and clients for whom you will produce, and the economy as a whole. Negative externalities involve costs, rather than benefits, but they justify government intervention on the same principle. For instance, part of the cost of producing paper is the water that will be fouled by paper manufacturers who discharge pollutants into streams and lakes. These costs to society, however, are not included in the cost of the paper sold to consumers and do not appear on the manufacturer's profit and loss statement. As a result, government must regulate paper manufacturers by requiring, under penalty of law, that they stop or limit their discharges or find other ways to reduce their pollution.

The Progressive Era

The growth of concentrated economic power and chronic depressions led many to conclude that unbridled capitalism was threatening democracy and social stability. Woodrow Wilson is said to have declared, "we are all caught in a great economic system which is heartless."[2] The early decades of the twentieth century, then, ushered in what we have come to know as modern "progressive liberalism," a blending of Hamiltonian means to achieve Jeffersonian (i.e., democratic, egalitarian) ends. New controls over corporate power and social reforms were enacted under the progressive presidencies of Wilson and Theodore Roosevelt. New regulatory agencies were established, such as the Federal Trade Commission (FTC) and the Federal Reserve System, and existing ones, such as the Interstate Commerce Commission (ICC) and the Anti-trust Division of the Justice Department, were given new powers. The FTC and Anti-trust Division are responsible for preventing businesses from engaging in unfair methods of competition and unfair or deceptive practices affecting commerce, and with forestalling or reversing actions (such as mergers and acquisitions) that might substantially lessen competition. The ICC was charged with regulating the rates charged by railroads and other forms of transportation. The Federal Reserve was given the power to regulate financial institutions.

The New Deal

With the outbreak of World War I the Progressive era came to an end. During the 1920s the nation entered a period of prosperity and conservative politics that halted the expansion of federal intervention. The economic boom came to an abrupt end in 1929 with the cataclysmic downturn known as the **Great Depression.** The economic devastation of the Depression was unparalleled before or since it occurred. It came suddenly and lasted for a prolonged period of about ten years. Contrasted with the prosperity of the 1920s, the downturn seemed even worse. Louise Armstrong, writing about Chicago in 1932, put it this way: "One vivid, gruesome moment of those dark days we shall never forget. We saw a crowd of some fifty men fighting over a barrel of garbage which had been set outside the back door of a restaurant. American citizens fighting for scraps of food like animals."[3]

The stock market crash of October 1929 was the most visible symbol of what was happening. Investors seemed to lose all confidence in the economy. There had been financial panics and depressions before, but none on this scale had ever happened. The Depression was felt worldwide, but it hit the United States especially hard. It devastated virtually every sector of the economy, including business, finance, labor, agriculture, and housing. No social class or income group was spared.

The Depression was perceived by many intellectuals and experts as a massive institutional failure of the capitalist system. No one had doubted capitalism's ability to produce abundance before this time. Even though many people thought that the abundance was distributed inequitably and that some people were exploited, the system's productive capacity had not been called into question. Also, before the Depression few people thought that the government had any legitimate role in reviving a stagnant economy. Now these assumptions came under considerable doubt.

The Depression marked a watershed in American history because it established the federal government as ultimately responsible for maintaining economic stability. This obligation still exists today. Even the most fervent believers in free markets and opponents of government intervention accept this principle. The public now expects the

[2] Woodrow Wilson, *The Great Quotations,* comp. George Seldes (New York: Lyle Stewart, 1966), p. 750.

[3] Quoted in F. L. Allen, *Since Yesterday* (New York: Harper and Bros., 1940), p. 64.

government to guarantee a healthy economy and will punish elected officials at the polls for poor economic performance.

The response to the Depression in the United States was President Franklin D. Roosevelt's New Deal, the label given by Roosevelt to a wide variety of initiatives intended to relieve destitution and revive the economy.[4] Other nations, like Germany, were not so lucky; there, the Depression helped bring undemocratic regimes to power. Still other countries in Europe, like Britain and France, stumbled along until the latter half of the 1930s, when rearmament policies began to revive their stagnant economies.

The first step the New Deal took was to revive the financial system. On the eve of the Depression, investors were involved in a variety of risky investments. They engaged in speculation—betting that stock prices would keep rising. Stock prices did not reflect the worth of the corporations but were inflated because of the speculative bidding. Suddenly the psychology changed, and all confidence that stock prices would continue to rise disappeared. Instead of buying stocks, people began selling them in a frenzy. Much of the speculation was financed with borrowed money—in effect, by using other people's savings to gamble on stock prices. When the stock market crashed and speculators could not repay their loans, people's savings were lost because the banks had lent their money to the speculators. When depositors realized what had happened, they demanded their money. The bank panics exacerbated the crisis because banks could not meet these demands.

Financial Reforms. The New Deal enacted banking reforms and in 1934 created the Securities and Exchange Commission (SEC), which established a system of controls on

[4] See Jonathan R. T. Hughes, *The Governmental Habit: Economic Controls from Colonial Times to the Present* (New York: Basic Books, 1977), Chapter 5.

Then and Now
Regulation of Financial Markets

Throughout the nineteenth century and until after the Great Depression of the 1930s, the U.S. economy was plagued periodically by financial panics. Downturns in the business cycle were accompanied by runs on banks, widespread defaults on loans, bankruptcies of large enterprises, and sharp declines in stock prices. Panics, often preceded by speculative booms in real estate or securities, usually resulted when a spectacular failure caused a sudden, drastic reappraisal of business prospects. From 1790 to 1907 there were twenty-one panics, or about one every five or six years. The stock market crash in October 1929 set off a succession of banking panics, with more than 9,000 bank failures between 1930 and 1933. There were virtually no means available to prevent these disasters, to keep them from spreading, or to ease their effects.

In response, Congress established the Federal Reserve System in 1914 as the nation's "central bank."

The Federal Reserve was empowered to create money to meet the seasonal needs of business and to counteract panics. In addition, the Federal Reserve imposed controls over bank reserves, accounting procedures, and management; produced a uniform currency; cleared checks and collections, and handled government finance. The Federal Reserve injects money into the financial system by purchasing government bonds. So when "the Fed" decides that more money is needed by the economy, it prints new money and promptly spends some (on bonds).

Today the Federal Reserve plays a critical role in stabilizing the financial system. For instance, without the Fed in operation, the 1987 stock market crash could have had a more devastating impact. When the stock market crashed, the Federal Reserve immediately flooded the financial markets with money in order to prevent further panic.

A construction project of the Works Progress Administration (WPA), a New Deal government program created to provide jobs and build roads, bridges, parks, and other public facilities.

investors and banks to prevent rampant borrowing and lending for speculation. The commission sets down "margin requirements" that permit no more than half of the money used for investments in securities to be borrowed. The Federal Reserve Board was given new powers to set banks' reserve requirements and interest rates. For depositors, the Federal Deposit Insurance Corporation (FDIC) was established in 1933 to insure deposits of bank customers, thus bolstering public confidence in the financial system and heading off panics.

Roosevelt also took emergency measures to relieve the destitution of the jobless. At the height of the Depression, one-quarter of all workers were unemployed. The first program was the FERA (Federal Emergency Relief Act), which provided grants to the states to provide welfare payments. Roosevelt, however, preferred "work" relief to "direct" relief because he believed that people should be given the dignity of a job. Therefore he established a succession of programs to create jobs for the unemployed. The New Deal was a veritable "alphabet soup" of such programs. The most famous was the Works Progress Administration (WPA), which provided jobs and helped to build many roads, bridges, parks, and other public facilities that are still in use today.

The National Industrial Recovery Act. The boldest New Deal initiative was the **National Industrial Recovery Act** (NIRA) of 1933. Because the Depression was seen as a catastrophic malfunctioning of the economic system, it was believed that temporary relief measures were insufficient. Many New Dealers believed that the Depression was caused by "overproduction" that had resulted from too much competition. Too many goods had flooded the market, pushing prices and wages too low. Unregulated market competition had driven businesses to slash workers' wages and lengthen the work week. The lost purchasing power contracted the economy further, producing a downward spiral.

The solution was sought in having business, labor, and government cooperate with one another in *planning* the economy. The NIRA, administered by the National Recovery Administration (NRA), was the most comprehensive effort in modern American history to control the market by having government subvert its basic principles.[5] For the New

---

[5] Donald R. Brand, *Corporatism and the Rule of Law: A Study of the National Recovery Administration* (Ithaca, N.Y.: Cornell University Press, 1988); Theda Skocpol and Kenneth Finegold, "State Capacity and Economic Intervention in the Early New Deal," *Political Science Quarterly* 97 (Summer 1982), pp. 255–78.

The WPA

The largest and most famous of the New Deal's job-creation programs was the WPA—the Works Progress Administration. Enacted in the midst of the Great Depression, the program had the purpose of not simply providing jobs for the unemployed—it was also intended to build public works, and this it did on a massive scale. The variety and magnitude of what the WPA accomplished is staggering. From 1935 to 1941 more than 600,000 miles of roads and streets were built or repaired, enough to encircle the world twenty-four times! Bridges were constructed or rebuilt, 116,000 of them; and nearly 600 airplane landing fields were constructed. More than 100,000 public libraries, schools, and other public buildings were erected. If only the *new* buildings were distributed evenly among the 3,000 counties in the United States, each county would have had about ten. WPA projects included draining swamps and repairing library books; teaching illiterate adults and serving school lunches; building stadiums and painting murals; planting trees and harvesting oysters. The projects ranged from modest ones costing a few hundred dollars to the building of major municipal airports and bridges, each of which cost tens of millions of dollars.

The WPA was not free of controversy and criticism. Some people objected in principle to the government's provision of jobs to so many people, and others complained that too much of the money was wasted on "make work" and used by politicians to reward their friends.

Source: Donald S. Howard, *The WPA and Federal Relief Policy* (New York: Russell Sage Foundation, 1943).

Dealers, the NIRA was nothing less than an attempt to alter fundamentally the individualist, competitive ethic of capitalism. According to Roosevelt, "We have always known that heedless self-interest was bad morals; we know now that it is bad economics."[6] Cooperation between government, business, and labor unions was to replace competition as the basic principle of economic organization.

The NIRA governed the U.S. economy from 1933 to 1935. It included provisions to strengthen labor's economic power by developing minimum wage requirements and promoting trade union organization and collective bargaining with employers. Unions would be able to gain higher wages for their members, and this in turn would help maintain purchasing power in the economy. Because business would bear substantially increased costs from these reforms, and because business cooperation was essential to the success of the NIRA, anti-trust laws would be relaxed (that is, restrictions on free enterprise would be lifted) and trade associations would be able to cooperate in drafting "codes of fair trade" that would apply to all members of the relevant industry. The codes were subject to the approval of the NRA.

By 1935 the NRA had approved 874 industry codes that had been drafted by the trade associations. Of these, 560 provided some form of intra-industry price fixing and 422 provided for the direct exchange of price information. Many codes also arranged for

[6] Franklin D. Roosevelt, Inaugural Address, 20 January 1937.

Government Intervention in the Economy During the New Deal

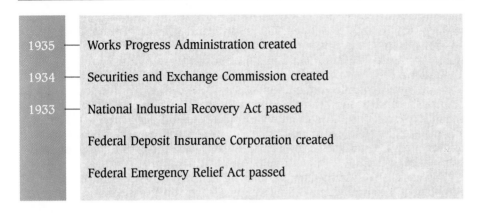

1935	—	Works Progress Administration created
1934	—	Securities and Exchange Commission created
1933	—	National Industrial Recovery Act passed
		Federal Deposit Insurance Corporation created
		Federal Emergency Relief Act passed

dividing markets and restricting output from and entry into markets, all in an effort to force prices up and establish orderly markets. The codes, contrivances to control prices, wages, hours of work, and production, were everything that Adam Smith had deplored.

In the end, the NIRA failed. First, businessmen cooperated with NIRA provisions for a while, but economic self-interest soon reasserted itself. To gain a competitive advantage over rivals who continued to adhere to the codes, some businesses cheated by slashing their wages and prices. Eventually, even those businesses committed to the NRA felt compelled to do the same. The NRA tried to enforce the codes but failed because the task was overwhelming and violations were often difficult to detect. Second, the codes of fair trade competition were becoming a vehicle for uncontrolled business cartelization. (A cartel exists when firms band together to control the level of output or prices; hence, cartelization refers to the banding together of firms.) Prices increased faster than wages, eating into labor's purchasing power. Appeals to self-restraint failed. The NIRA was premised upon voluntary cooperation and public-spiritedness. Without moral enthusiasm to sustain it, the program was doomed to failure. The social consensus necessary for the NIRA to succeed simply did not exist. The long-established traditions of competition, self-interested behavior, and distrust of government were too formidable to overcome.

In spite of the failure of the NIRA, parts of the New Deal became immensely successful and are permanent fixtures of the American political landscape. The Social Security Act of 1935, in particular, set up social insurance programs to guard against destitution during old age and periods of unemployment or disability.[7] The New Deal's most important legacy, however, is in terms of its broader public philosophy, rather than its specific programs. The New Deal made legitimate government intervention in the economy and irrevocably established Washington's responsibility for national economic performance.

The Keynesian Consensus

If anyone can be called the "intellectual founder" of modern government intervention in the economy it is the British economist John Maynard Keynes. Keynes (pronounced *kanes*) revolutionized economic thinking by overturning orthodox (i.e., *laissez-faire*) economic theories that were dominant before the 1930s. What Keynes provided was crucial—an intellectual justification for government intervention.

Until Keynes, most economists believed that the economy was guided by the "hidden

---

[7] Martha Derthick, *Policymaking for Social Security* (Washington: The Brookings Institution, 1979).

hand" of the price mechanism, which would automatically bring the economy to the full use of its human and capital resources. Unemployment was considered a temporary phenomenon that would disappear when workers realized that their wage demands were too high, and that to be hired by employers they would have to accept less. Governmental efforts to end the Depression would either have no effect or would make the crisis worse. The appropriate policy was a balanced budget.

Keynes argued that no automatic mechanism would allow the economy to recover from the Great Depression on its own. What was needed was for the government to deliberately create a large deficit, which would pump resources back into the economy and thus spur recovery. The stimulus would produce income that in turn would be spent creating additional jobs and income, and so on. Such a policy would not only stimulate recovery from a depression but could also be used to *prevent* economic downturns at the first sign of trouble.

Unschooled in **Keynesianism,** the "new economics of Keynes," Franklin Roosevelt was not totally convinced that deficits were good. The New Deal's deficit spending was not so much an economic recovery program as it was a humanitarian effort to relieve suffering. In any event, the deficits created were too limited to bring the country out of the Depression; when the economy improved in 1937 Roosevelt cut expenditures, and the country went back into depression in 1938. It was the government's spending during World War II, not the New Deal, that brought the economy out of the doldrums. The massive deficits of those years validated Keynes's argument that deficit spending could bring an end to most unemployment. Keynes's ideas, widely ignored during the inter-world war years (1920–38), were quickly adopted in Britain and other industrialized European democracies immediately after the end of World War II.

The Full Employment Bill. Despite the conversion of most of the economics profession to Keynesian thinking by the end of World War II, it was not until much later that American policy makers adopted the new strategy of fiscal management. The Keynesian prescription was first attempted in the 1945 full employment proposal advanced by liberals in Congress.[8] The plan, sponsored by Senator James Murray (D.-Mont.), would have established a "right to employment," a guarantee that anyone willing and able to work would have a job (this is what Murray meant by **full employment**). It also stipulated that the president would submit a "National Production and Employment Budget" that would estimate the size of the labor force, the total national production needed to provide jobs for it, and the total investment needed to meet that level of production. If the anticipated level of private investment was insufficient to absorb the entire labor force, the federal government would provide such additional investment and spending needed to reach full employment.

Murray's proposal was killed in Congress by a conservative coalition of Republicans and Southern Democrats, who feared that it would lead to excessive government spending and government control of the economy. What Congress passed instead, the Employment Act of 1946, was a much watered-down version of the original proposal. It excluded any "right" to a job or commitment to achieving full employment, and any mechanism for doing so. The Act was a perfect example of symbolism over substance. Its main contribution to economic management was the creation of the **Council of Economic Advisers** (CEA), an agency lodged in the Executive Office of the President to help advise the chief executive on economic policy. The CEA brought professional economists into the highest levels of the federal government.

The 1950s were characterized by a checkered economic performance that included several recessions. The administration of President Dwight D. Eisenhower held firm to the pre-Keynesian doctrine of balanced budgets, and fears of inflation kept both Congress and the president from using fiscal policy to stimulate the economy.

[8] Stephen K. Bailey, *Congress Makes a Law: The Story of the Employment Act of 1946* (New York: Columbia University Press, 1951).

People of the Past

Walter Heller

Walter Heller with President John F. Kennedy.

Walter Heller was the most influential economist in Washington through much of the 1960s. He is given a great deal of credit for the adoption of modern, Keynesian techniques of economic management in the United States. For Heller, policy makers spent the Eisenhower years foolishly clinging to balanced budgets. As chairman of President John F. Kennedy's Council of Economic Advisers, Heller was a tireless advocate of the aggressive use of fiscal policy to stimulate economic growth. His policy prescription went beyond the notion of using a fiscal stimulus to get out of recessions; he proposed that it be used to eliminate slack in the economy altogether, even when the economy was not in recession. As CEA chairman, Heller kept up a steady flow of information to Kennedy on the state of the economy and the benefits that would accrue from a tax cut. Heller served, in effect, as the president's tutor—educating him in the "new economics" and persuading him to push Congress to adopt a tax cut. His persistence bore fruit with the passage of the Tax Reduction Act of 1965.

Heller received his undergraduate degree from Oberlin College and his Ph.D. from the University of Wisconsin in 1941. His career was split between academia and government service. After working in the Treasury Department, he taught for many years at the University of Minnesota. He then held several posts as an economic adviser in the federal government until he was named chairman of the CEA. Heller was described in *Current Biography* in 1961 as "a practical economist interested in public service," and as one who "brings to 'the dismal science' a light and lucid touch." He died in 1987 at the age of seventy-six.

The Triumph of "Commercial Keynesianism." In 1961, John F. Kennedy, an activist president committed to getting the country "moving again," took office and brought Keynesian economists to Washington. They believed that the new techniques of economic management should be used not only to lift the economy out of recessions but also to stimulate economic growth to its fullest capacity. As Kennedy remarked, "The mere absence of war is not peace. The mere absence of recession is not growth."[9]

There was still the problem of how to make deficits (budget shortfalls when expenses exceed revenues), which most policy makers regarded as irresponsible, politically appealing. Keynesian economists understood that for many conservatives and members of the business community, deficits could be made more palatable if they were created by *cutting taxes* rather than by increasing spending. Business had long complained of high, "confiscatory" taxes as a drag on the economy. Moreover, a tax cut had the advantage of increasing *private* consumption because with lower taxes, consumers had more money to spend, creating a higher demand for what the private sector produced. Higher government spending, on the other hand, meant spending on public goods and services, with fewer resources left over for private consumption, and a shift in decisions over the allocation of resources from the private to the public sector.[10]

The result was the passage of the Tax Reduction Act of 1965. Hence, the proponents

[9] John F. Kennedy, State of the Union message, 14 January 1963.
[10] Robert M. Collins, *The Business Response to Keynes: 1929–1964* (New York: Columbia University Press, 1981), Chapter 6.

of a brand of Keynesianism that was much more congenial to business had triumphed two decades after those of a radically different Keynesian program had been defeated. The tax stimulus helped expand the economy through the rest of the 1960s and drove the unemployment rate down below 4 percent, its lowest rate in peacetime and very close to what most people considered to be full employment. It is interesting to note that at the same time in Britain and France, both left-wing and right-wing governments were experimenting with intervention and planning as a means of spurring the growth of their economies. Policy decisions often echo across the Atlantic Ocean, regardless of political ideology.

Guns and Butter

The cut in tax rates of the 1960s was not the only action by government that helped to stimulate economic growth. Two other factors contributed as well: spending on the military (guns) and spending on domestic needs (butter). First, the United States had emerged from World War II as the world's most powerful military power. With the rise of the Soviet Union as a powerful potential military adversary in its own right, it fell to the United States to assume a leadership role in containing communism and Soviet expansion. This responsibility involved undertaking massive military commitments, and consequently a large defense budget. It is no coincidence that the low unemployment rate in the late 1960s was achieved at the same time that U.S. involvement in the Vietnam War escalated. Defense spending not only adds stimulus to the economy, it also greatly affects the structure of the domestic economy. A substantial number of industries are defense related, and many firms contract directly with the federal government or with giant defense manufacturers.

Also, both a cause and effect of economic expansion was greater spending on domestic programs. Major programs were launched during this period to build the interstate highway system, provide health care for the elderly and poor, and implement food stamp and other social programs for the disadvantaged. Existing programs, particularly Social Security, were expanded. The prosperity of the times produced the tax revenue that made it possible to fund these programs; conversely, spending on the programs added further stimulus to the economy.

The Post-Keynesian Era

Neither economic stability nor the Keynesian consensus lasted long, however. As the 1960s came to a close, spending on the Vietnam War produced inflation, which is a rise in the level of prices generally. The inflation was blamed on President Lyndon Johnson for failing to raise taxes to pay for the war, and on his successor, President Richard Nixon, who stimulated the economy further just prior to his reelection in 1972. Soon afterward, policy makers faced an unprecedented problem—**stagflation,** which is simultaneously high rates of inflation *and* of unemployment. This was primarily the result of a series of "supply shocks" that buffeted the economies of the industrialized world. The most important was the quadrupling of oil prices and embargo launched by the international oil cartel OPEC (the Organization of Petroleum Exporting Countries). The sudden oil-price rises rippled throughout the entire economy, and the transfer of income from the industrial countries to OPEC reversed economic growth, creating high unemployment.

Stagflation rendered the conduct of macroeconomic management much more difficult. Efforts to drive unemployment rates down by stimulating the economy would simply exacerbate the already high inflation; conversely, reducing the fiscal stimulus to the economy would worsen an already high jobless rate. As the "misery index"—the sum of the inflation and unemployment rates—remained in double digits, the tools of modern economic management suddenly appeared obsolete. Policymakers were on the horns of a dilemma, and two of them, Presidents Gerald Ford and Jimmy Carter, suffered defeats at the polls in 1976 and 1980, respectively, largely because of poor economic performance.

Unemployment in modern America: A healthy economy is a major goal of all presidential administrations. Without it, voters lose jobs and presidential approval tends to drop. Presidents Ford and Carter both lost bids for reelection in the midst of high unemployment and inflation.

Competition from Abroad. During this same period, the U.S. economy became more interdependent with those of other countries. This meant not only that many American export industries relied increasingly on markets abroad, but also that, even more so, domestic firms faced stiff competition from foreign producers. Japanese and European competitors, in particular, were especially effective in penetrating U.S. markets for

From "Free Trade" to "Fair Trade"

In the 1930s Congress passed the "Smoot–Hawley" trade bill, which sharply raised tariffs on imported goods. This action set off a "trade war" as other nations retaliated with their own tariffs. The result was a contraction in the volume of world trade, and Smoot–Hawley was blamed as a principal culprit in the Great Depression. In the wake of that bitter experience, after World War II the United States adopted a policy of "free trade." It negotiated a series of agreements with countries around the world to reduce tariff barriers to minimal levels by the 1970s. The policy was a great success. The volume of international trade exploded, and this helped fuel the postwar boom. Starting in the 1970s, however, American industries began facing serious competition, principally from Japan and European nations. Our relatively open economy made it possible for foreign competitors to penetrate markets that formerly had been dominated by domestic firms. At the same time, many American businessmen and workers complained of "unfair trade"—that many foreign governments had erected "non-tariff" trade barriers that kept out American exports, and that their industries received government subsidies that American firms did not receive. Other observers argue that the inability of American industry to compete is due less to the actions of foreign governments than to the inadequacies of American business itself.

textiles, steel, autos, machine tools, and electronic goods. The most visible sign of this change is that the United States has run **trade deficits** (when the value of imports exceeds that of exports) almost every year since 1971. Americans' incomes also grew more slowly than those of our competitors. Citizens generally sensed that America was experiencing a "decline," and particular industries pressured the government for relief in the form of **protectionism**—the erection of barriers against foreign competitors, such as tariffs.

The Conservative Attack on Government Intervention. By the late 1970s, the perception had grown widespread that much of the problem with the American economy was a government that had grown too large and intrusive. At best, it appeared that the government was incapable of dealing with stagflation and international competition; at worst, government itself was to blame for the economic problems besetting the nation. The latter thesis—that, in the words of Ronald Reagan, "government is the problem, not the solution"—had a certain plausibility. After all, had not inflation and other indicators worsened during the same time that taxes, deficits, regulations, and the money supply also rose?[11] The case for an economic policy more attuned to the growing anti-government spirit seemed obvious.

The conservatives who rose to power in the 1980s were anti-Keynesian because they rejected the notion of government practicing "discretionary" fiscal management and because they sought a reduction in the size of the public sector. The new economic policy contained four components: **monetarism,** which stipulated that growth in the money supply should be restrained by close adherence to a fixed "rule" that limited it to the rate of growth in the economy; **supply-side** tax cuts for individuals and corporations; cuts in domestic spending and balanced budgets; and deregulation. A "tight" money policy would end inflation. Tax cuts would spur economic growth and reduce unemployment, not by stimulating demand as in Keynesian theory but by providing incentives for people to work harder, save, and invest. Balancing the budget would lower interest rates and inflation, and deregulation would both lower inflation and reduce the cost of doing business.

Anti-Keynesianism was not confined to the North American continent during this period. At approximately the same time, Margaret Thatcher took over the leadership of the Conservative Party in Britain and inaugurated a supply-side revolution scarcely distinguishable from the Reagan program. In 1981, France's first postwar Socialist government reversed course in the face of massive international economic pressure and implemented a set of economic policies that could just as easily have come from their conservative opponents.

Parts of this strategy were incompatible with other parts. It proved impossible to balance the budget because the combination of large tax cuts, monetary restraint, a defense buildup, and only modest cuts in domestic spending added up to persistently large deficits. Ironically, though the Reagan administration rejected Keynesianism as an economy theory, the massive deficits created by this policy mix were much more consistent with a Keynesian policy than with old-fashioned Republican fiscal orthodoxy. Lower oil prices and monetary restraint reduced inflation, although at the cost of a deep recession in 1982–83, the worst economic downturn since the Great Depression. Coming out of the recession, the combination of large tax cuts and "military Keynesianism" set the stage for a period of recovery that lasted until 1990. The economy, however, did not "grow out of the deficit," as predicted by supply-side theory.

The Growth of Government in Perspective. The forces that we discussed earlier—industrial capitalism, urbanization, international interdependence, and Keynesian ideas—

---

[11] See Herbert Stein, *Presidential Economics: The Making of Economic Policy from Roosevelt to Reagan and Beyond* (Washington: American Enterprise Institute, 1988), Chapters 6 and 7.

Figure 16-1   Total Government Spending in the United States as a Percent of Gross Domestic Product, 1929–1989

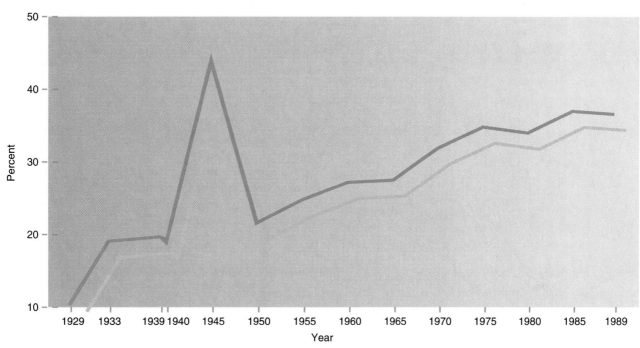

Source: U.S. Department of Commerce, Census Bureau, *Statistical Abstract of the United States*, (Washington: Government Printing Office, various years); Organization for Economic Cooperation and Development, *Economic Outlook*, (Paris: OECD, Various years).

account for the long-term trend of growing government involvement in the economy. They also help to explain the sharper and more short-term rises and falls in the growth pattern. Figure 16-1 reveals that government grew rapidly during the Depression and World War II, and actually shrank in the postwar economic recovery.

Despite all the concern about the size of government in the Reagan years, government spending was no smaller at the end of the 1980s, when Reagan left Washington, than it was when he took office at the beginning of the decade. In 1970 total government spending was about 32 percent of GNP, in 1980 it stood at about 31 percent, and in 1989 it was still 32 percent. There was a slight decrease in the *federal* government's share of total spending. There was also a noticeable change in the *composition* of federal spending, with defense spending accounting for between 24 and 28 percent of GNP annually during the 1980s, compared with between 23 and 24 percent annually during the post–Vietnam War years in the 1970s. Perhaps the most important change is that interest payments on the public debt were almost 15 percent of GNP in 1989 (compared with less than 9 percent in 1980), a result of the large budget deficits created in that decade.

Another way to look at the size of government in the United States is by comparing it with those of other industrialized democracies. When we do this we see that government in the United States is smaller and less involved in the economy than governments elsewhere. Figure 16-2 shows that among fifteen nations, the U.S. government spends less than almost any other. In addition, many European governments own railroads, airlines, public utilities, companies engaged in energy extraction and production, and broadcasting and telecommunications networks. In the United States, most such industries are privately owned and operated. Likewise, most countries provide more generous benefits and broader coverage for old-age pensions, unemployment insurance, medical

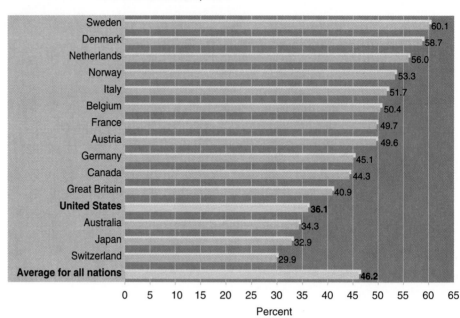

Figure 16-2 Total Government Spending as a Percent of Gross Domestic Product for Selected Nations, 1989[a]

[a] Figures for Japan, Belgium, and Norway are for 1988.

Source: Organization for Economic Cooperation and Development, *Economic Outlook*, (Paris: OECD, June 1990).

care, and other social welfare programs. The U.S. government funds very little public housing and does not provide sickness pay and paid parental leave.[12]

Objectives and Instruments of Economic Policy

Virtually everyone agrees that there are three primary goals of economic policy: high **employment,** low **inflation,** and **economic growth.** We all want jobs, stable prices, and higher incomes to purchase the greatest abundance of goods and services that our economy can produce. Although pursuit of these objectives is universally supported, different political interests often stress one or more of them over the other(s). Labor unions, for instance, stress the need for all workers to have jobs and rising incomes. Businesspeople want higher profits and opportunities for growth. Bankers and other holders of monetary assets place a premium on stable prices.

U.S. Economic Performance: Past and Present

Figures 16-3 and 16-4 show how the United States has performed over the past three decades on two important indicators, the rates of unemployment and inflation. With regard to the first, rates of unemployment in the United States have been consistently higher than in most other industrial democracies. This changed in the mid-1980s,

[12] Anthony King, "Ideas, Institutions, and the Policies of Governments," *British Journal of Political Science* 3 (July and October 1973), pp. 219–313 and 409–23.

Figure 16-3   Rates of Unemployment: The United States and Six Other Nations, 1960–1990

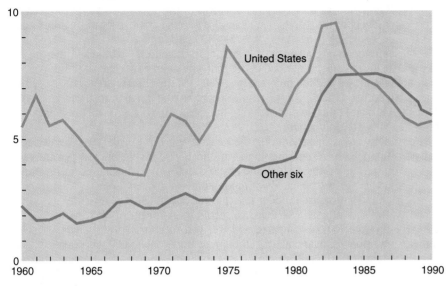

Source: Organization for Cooperation and Development, *Economic Outlook* (Paris: OECD, various years).

Figure 16-4   Rates of Inflation: The United States and Six Other Nations, 1960–1990

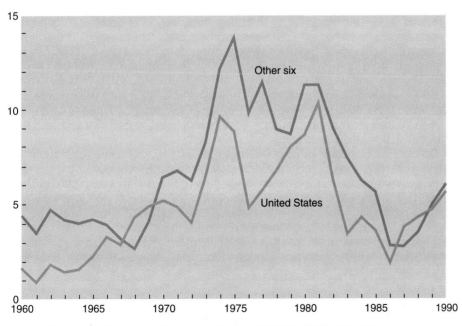

Source: Organization for Cooperation and Development, *Economic Outlook* (Paris: OECD, various years).

however, when the U.S. rate dipped below the average for six of its competitors (France, West Germany, Great Britain, Italy, Japan, and Sweden). Figure 16-3 also shows that the unemployment rate has risen steadily since its low point of 3 to 4 percent in the mid- to late 1960s. Even with the drop in unemployment in the 1980s, it has yet to reach the relatively low levels of the 1960s. One can also see the sharp rises in unemployment during the recessions of 1961, 1971, 1973–74, 1980, and 1982–83.

The rate of inflation (Figure 16-4) reveals a different pattern. In this case, it is the U.S. economy that has usually performed better than the average for the six other nations. Only in the late 1960s and the mid- to late 1980s did the U.S. inflation rate exceed the average of the other nations. Figure 16-4 also shows that inflation rose considerably in the United States and other countries during most of the 1970s, primarily because of the oil-price "shocks" of that period.

The economy's performance during the Reagan and Bush years has been decidedly mixed. The unemployment rate was higher in the 1980s (averaging 7.2 percent, compared with 6.1 percent in the 1970s) and economic growth somewhat lower (averaging 2.7 percent in the 1980s, compared with more than 2.8 percent in the 1970s). In addition, Americans' real disposable (after tax) income stagnated, and productivity growth was modest. Only on inflation was there a discernible improvement, with an average rate of 4.7 percent in the 1980s, compared with 7.1 percent in the 1970s. Under President George Bush we find a similar pattern, although definitely a less bright economic picture. Inflation has remained under control, but in the summer of 1990 the nation entered a recession from which a full recovery was not expected until at least 1992. The rate of economic growth for the Bush administration in its first three years was lower than for any other administration since the Great Depression.

Macro- and Microeconomic Tools

In attempting to achieve and stabilize high employment, growth, and price stability, the government has an array of instruments at its disposal. These may be divided into two broad categories—"macroeconomic" and "microeconomic." Macroeconomic instruments affect the *overall level* of economic activity by regulating aggregate flows of income and expenditure. The two most important of these are fiscal and monetary policies.

Fiscal policy is conducted through the federal budget. What is important here is not the composition of the budget (how the government spends the money), but the *overall, or "aggregate," levels of spending and revenue* and, in turn, the size of the deficit or surplus that is produced. When total revenue (what the government absorbs from taxes, customs duties, and user fees) equals total spending, there is a balanced budget. When revenue exceeds spending, the budget is in surplus; and when spending exceeds revenue, a deficit is created. In the case of a deficit, the government must finance the shortfall through borrowing. The unpaid portion of accumulated deficits over time constitutes the **national debt** of the United States.

Deficits may be created either by cutting taxes, increasing spending, or some combination of the two. Conversely, the budget moves into surplus with either the raising of taxes, spending cuts, or some combination of the two. When deficits are created they can stimulate economic growth, expanding incomes and the number of jobs. When this happens, consumers are able to spend more money, which allows business to expand production further and hire more workers. Conversely, when taxes are raised and/or spending is cut, the budget moves into balance or surplus. In this case, the rate of economic growth may slow down. If it slows too much, incomes will stagnate or shrink, and people may be put out of work.

Monetary policy has to do with regulating the level of credit in the economy, primarily through raising and lowering interest rates and expanding or contracting the size of the money supply. If interest rates are rising, businesses will be discouraged from expanding their production and hiring new workers because borrowing will cost them more.

The Tools of Economic Policy

MACROECONOMIC

Fiscal Policy:

Manipulating total levels of spending and taxation and, consequently, the size of the budget deficit. Affects rates of unemployment, inflation, and income growth.

Example: The rate of economic growth begins to slow, and unemployment begins to rise. Congress enacts a tax cut and/or increases spending, creating more income for people to spend and, in turn, stimulating job growth.

Monetary Policy:

Manipulating interest rates and the money supply. Affects rates of unemployment, inflation, and income growth.

Example: The demand for goods and services rises until the economy reaches its full productive capacity. Prices and wages begin to rise in response, creating inflation. The Federal Reserve Board dampens demand by increasing interest rates and limiting the supply of money, slowing the growth in jobs and income.

MICROECONOMIC

Tax Expenditures:

Providing incentives to individuals and businesses to undertake actions the government deems desir-able by promising them that they will pay less in taxes if they do so.

Examples: Encouraging the purchase of houses by allowing individuals to deduct from their taxable incomes the interest payments on mortgages; encouraging business investment by allowing businesses to deduct part of the cost of new plant and equipment.

Subsidies and Loans:

Providing grants and loans to individuals, businesses, and state and local governments to make it easier for them to undertake specific actions the government deems desirable.

Examples: Providing local governments with grants to repair bridges and highways; providing loans to small businesses in areas with high unemployment; providing loans to college students to finance their educations.

Regulations:

Rules imposed by government on businesses and other organizations to control their behavior in the marketplace.

Examples: Mandating that automobile companies design and produce cars that conserve fuel; restricting misleading or fraudulent advertising practices by businesses; setting rates that utility companies can charge for their services.

In addition, potential home and auto buyers will find it more difficult to take out loans, and this will affect the level of demand in those industries. If interest rates continue to rise, production may actually shrink, and the ranks of the unemployed will grow. The same is true when growth in the money supply slows. When this happens, banks will have less money to lend to borrowers, and this situation will slow the expansion of production and employment. On the other hand, when interest rates fall and the money supply expands, these occurrences will have the opposite effects—making it easier for businesses and consumers to borrow, thus expanding production, consumer demand, and job opportunities.

Hence, macroeconomic tools have powerful impacts on levels of unemployment, prices, and economic growth. When fiscal and monetary policies are too "tight" (i.e., restrictive) they can slow economic growth and increase unemployment; when they are too "loose" (i.e., expansionary) they can "overstimulate" the economy and lead to inflation. In theory, monetary and fiscal policies are supposed to be coordinated so that they are moving the economy in the same direction. For any number of reasons, however, such coordination is often difficult.

When the government uses *micro*economic instruments, it seeks to intervene at the level of specific sectors of the economy and particular industries. These tools come in a variety of forms. For instance, government may provide loans to new small businesses that are unable to borrow capital from private banks, subsidies in the form of grants-in-aid to local governments to help create jobs in areas where unemployment is high, or tax incentives ("tax expenditures") to encourage businesses to invest in new plant and equipment.

One of the most important instruments at the government's disposal is regulation. Regulations are rules written by government agencies that can be enforced by penalizing those who violate them. They prohibit businesses and other private economic actors from engaging in behavior deemed undesirable. There are two main types of regulation—the older "economic regulation" and the newer "social regulation." The former includes regulations intended to ensure "fair trade" practices, to set prices and rates of various goods and services, and to establish requirements for entry into various markets. Social regulations have to do with mandating health and safety conditions in the workplace, prohibiting discrimination and encouraging the hiring of underrepresented groups, stipulating product-quality and safety standards, and setting emission controls to reduce pollution of the environment.

Most of the remainder of this chapter examines further the use and impacts of these instruments.

Monetary Policy

Monetary policy, along with fiscal policy, is the major instrument used to regulate the economy as a whole. Monetary policy is concerned with regulating the supply of money (credit) and interest rates. Almost the entire economy operates through money, the medium through which virtually all income and spending transactions take place. By controlling the printing press, the government has exclusive control over currency and, therefore, seems to control how much money is in the economy. But the "money supply" includes more than currency; it also includes bank deposits and other monetary assets. When people and organizations deposit their money into financial institutions (banks and savings and loans), these deposits are lent to borrowers. The lending of money, in effect, creates new deposits—new money that did not exist previously.

The government limits the ability of banks to create new money through the Federal Reserve System. The "Fed," as it is called, consists of a Board of Governors, which sits in Washington, and twelve regional federal reserve banks. Seven governors, one of whom is the chair, sit on the board; they are appointed by the president and confirmed by the Senate for fourteen-year terms. Because of his leadership position on the Board, and because of the importance of monetary policy to the performance of the economy, the chair of the Federal Reserve has often been characterized as "the second most powerful man in the United States."

The most important policy-making body at the Federal Reserve is the Federal Open Market Committee. On it sit twelve members, including all seven governors plus five representatives from the regional federal reserve banks. The seats for the five regional banks rotate among the twelve regions, except for the New York federal reserve, which, because of its importance, retains a permanent seat.

Former Congressman Wright Patman (D.-Tex.) once declared, "A slight acquaintance with American constitutional theory and practice demonstrates that, constitutionally, the

Organization of the Federal Reserve System

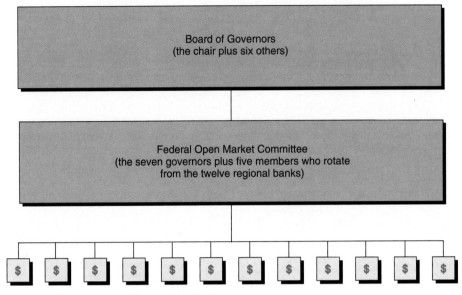

Twelve Regional Federal Reserve Banks

Federal Reserve is a pretty queer duck."[13] Indeed, the Fed is a curious mixture of private interests and public supervision. The Board of Governors shares its power with the twelve regional reserve banks, whose presidents are not appointed by the president of the United States, but are elected by each district's board of directors. A majority of the directors, in turn, are elected by the commercial "member banks" in each region. While the Fed is part of the government, it is also set apart from it. Similar to those of federal judges, the long terms enjoyed by Federal Reserve governors are intended to afford them independence and impartiality so that monetary policy is not influenced by "political" considerations. Critics claim that this arrangement is both unrealistic and undemocratic. After all, how could *any* decision made by the Federal Reserve not be "political," given that it will affect the economic fortunes of the entire nation? And why should such critical public policy decisions be removed from direct control by the people's representatives in Congress and the White House? Defenders of the Fed's independent status, on the other hand, argue that monetary policy is too complex and technical to be entrusted to elected officials. Moreover, independent judgment is necessary because it would be too tempting for politicians to manipulate monetary policy for their own short-term ends (such as reelection), rather than for the long-term needs of the economy.

Within rough limits, the Federal Reserve can determine the total amount of deposits and thus the size of the total money supply. Other things being equal, the greater the money supply, the lower interest rates will fall. As noted earlier, lower interest rates make it more attractive for consumers to borrow to finance major purchases and for corporations to expand their production. Consequently, expanding the money supply expands income and the supply of jobs. Limiting the size of the money supply does just the opposite—it makes it more difficult to borrow, thus slowing consumer borrowing and business expansion. Certain industries are more sensitive to monetary policy than others. Those that are directly affected by interest-rate fluctuations are the most quickly and profoundly affected. Housing construction (mortgages) and consumer durables (e.g.,

---

[13] Quoted in William Greider, *Secrets of the Temple: How the Federal Reserve Runs the Country* (New York: Simon and Schuster, 1987), pp. 49–50.

Money and Mystique at the Fed

For all of its power and importance, the Federal Reserve System is a mysterious entity to most Americans. One observer has likened it to a religious institution, a characterization that seems bizarre at first but that upon closer examination reveals a bit of truth about the Fed. Housed in a dignified marble "temple" on Constitution Avenue in Washington, the high priests of monetary policy direct the economy in ways that are hidden from, and incomprehensible to, the average citizen. Their deliberations take place in secret. Their debates are conducted in the technical language of economics. Their powers to create money and make it disappear inspire awe and fear. Such powers cannot be entrusted to ordinary mortals but must be exercised only by priests undefiled by "political considerations."

The Fed's mystique has not been lost on the Fed itself, which has often portrayed itself as the master of an arcane science. A former officer of the Fed described the induction of economists into the fraternity of the Fed staff as "taking the veil," similar to nuns entering a convent. One member of Congress described the senior economists at the Fed as "the monks." Richard Syron, a vice president of the Boston Fed, compared the institution to the Catholic church:

> The System is just like the Church. That's probably why I feel so comfortable with it. It's got a pope, the chairman; and a college of cardinals, the governors and bank presidents; and a curia, the senior staff. The equivalent of the laity is the commercial banks. . . . We even have different orders of religious thought like Jesuits and Franciscans and Dominicans only we call them pragmatists and monetarists and neo-Keynesians.

Source: Quotation and paraphrasing from William Greider, *Secrets of the Temple: How the Federal Reserve Runs the Country* (New York: Simon and Schuster, 1987), Chapter 2.

---

cars) are financed through installment loans. As a result, these areas of the economy are the first to "go soft" when interest rates rise.

This is a simple model, of course. Business expansion and contraction are also critically dependent on whether investors and businesspeople have "confidence" that investment will be profitable. These decisions, in turn, depend on a host of factors, one of which is government policy (or expectations of what that policy will be in the future). The point to keep in mind is that the Fed's decisions are profoundly important for the economy. If the Fed seeks to limit the money supply and drive up interest rates, it can halt or prevent a recovery, resulting in business bankruptcies and joblessness. On the other hand, if it seeks to expand the money supply and drive down interest rates too low or too quickly, it may "overheat" the economy and create inflation.

Tools of the Federal Reserve. In its conduct of monetary policy, the Federal Reserve relies on three powerful instruments that affect interest rates and the money supply.

- *Reserve Requirements* The Fed specifies what proportion of banks' deposits can be used to make loans. Raising the ratio of reserves against deposits restricts the ability of banks to make new loans; lowering it allows banks to expand their loans.

- *The Discount Rate*   Most major banks are members of the Federal Reserve. The discount rate is the interest rate at which member banks can borrow from their regional federal reserve bank when they need additional reserves. Raising the discount rate restricts the expansion of reserves and consequently the ability to lend out deposits; lowering the discount rate relaxes the restriction, making it easier to lend.

  Both of these instruments are also used to safeguard against the collapse of banks if they overextend their borrowing.

- *Open-Market Transactions*   The Fed can buy or sell U.S. government securities, which are interest-bearing Treasury bonds that are bought and sold by investors. When the Fed *buys* securities from bond traders, it pays for them by creating deposits for the traders' clients in the federal reserve banks. These deposits serve as additions to reserves for commercial banks. The added reserves permit commercial banks to expand their loans by some multiple of the new reserves. Conversely, when the Fed *sells* government securities, the buyers' payments are charged against commercial banks' reserve accounts, reducing them and requiring banks to contract deposits by a multiple of the amount of the purchase. Because of the flexibility and direct impact of open-market transactions, they are considered the Fed's most important policy instrument.

The Federal Budget and the Conduct of Fiscal Policy

Monetary policy is largely decided by the independent Federal Reserve Board, but fiscal policy is an entirely different matter. Here, much like the lawmaking process described in Chapter 6, the president and Congress struggle to come to agreement.[14]

The Budget and Accounting Act of 1921 assigned to the president the task of preparing a budget and submitting it to Congress. Assisting the president in this endeavor is the **Office of Management and Budget** (OMB). The president sends his budget to Congress in January of each year, but the agencies of the executive branch begin their preparations months before. The OMB provides instructions and guidance to the various agencies of the executive branch, and the agencies proceed to submit their budget requests. As one would expect, each federal agency usually believes in the wisdom of its own programs and seeks to expand or at least maintain its budget. The OMB's role, on the other hand, is to develop a budget that reflects the *president's* priorities and control the spending of individual agencies. President Lyndon Johnson once quipped that "my Cabinet consists of nine salesmen and one credit manager."[15] Agency requests are frequently revised downward by the OMB, and this process sometimes sets the stage for agencies to appeal to the president. More often than not, the president will support the OMB in such appeals. During the early years of the Reagan administration, this traditional "bottom-up" procedure for budget preparation was replaced by a "top-down" process in which the OMB made the major budget decisions (except for the Defense Department) and imposed them on the agencies.

Under Article I of the Constitution, Congress alone has the power to "appropriate" money. Many of the budget battles over the years have occurred in Congress. But because the president must sign a budget bill into law, the White House is never too far off stage. Congressional legislative committees may authorize that given sums of money be spent on the programs that fall under their jurisdictions, but the *funding* decisions for those programs are the domain of the House and Senate appropriations committees. The appropriations committees have traditionally defined their role in terms of "protecting the

Alan Greenspan, chairman of the Federal Reserve, testifying before Congress. Because of the enormous power of the "Fed," public statements by its leader are always closely watched. Often, when the chairman testifies to Congress, his statements are examined closely for signals of future changes in monetary policy, and hundreds of private investors react accordingly.

---

[14] This discussion of the budget-making process draws heavily on James E. Anderson, *Public Policymaking: An Introduction* (Boston: Houghton Mifflin, 1990), Chapter 5.

[15] Lyndon B. Johnson, remark during a meeting of the Business Council, December 1963.

purse strings" of the federal treasury. The committees often deny funding that the legislative committees authorize. At times the legislative committees have circumvented the appropriations committees through **backdoor spending**—authorizing agencies to borrow money from the Treasury or to contract for the purchase of goods and services in the future. The appropriations committees have opposed these practices.

For many years the budgetary process was highly fragmented and chaotic. Appropriations and revenue decisions were considered separately by different committees. Spending decisions were divided into a number of appropriations bills that were approved sequentially. This process had two shortcomings. First, it made it difficult to establish clear priorities, such as between defense and domestic programs, or among programs within each category. Second, and just as important, it essentially left to accident the determination of *total* expenditure and revenue levels and hence the size of the deficit or surplus.

This fragmented system contrasts with the centralized framework in place in the United Kingdom. Although complaints about interminable budget wrangles, departmental egoism, and runaway expenditure are not uncommon, the executive retains a much firmer grip on the process than in the United States. Parliament's weakness as an institution, combined with the monopoly of control exercised by Her Majesty's Treasury over all critical facets of the budgetary process, leaves a much more manageable political field for the prime minister to navigate.

The Budget and Impoundment Control Act of 1974. To gain greater control over the budget process, Congress enacted the Budget and Impoundment Control Act of 1974. This act established a formal budget process that involves setting overall levels of revenue and expenditures, as well as establishing priorities among different "functional" areas (e.g., defense, transportation, agriculture, and education). New budget committees were established in each chamber to perform these tasks, as was the **Congressional Budget Office** (CBO), a professional staff of technical experts to help the budget committees in their work.

The budget process consists of a timetable, displayed in the accompanying timeline. The budget committees hold hearings on the president's budget, soliciting advice from the OMB, the executive agencies, and other interested parties. The committees formulate concurrent budget resolutions, which set forth targets for the overall levels of spending and revenue, as well as for each functional area included in the budget. The appropriations committees are expected to work within these targets when making their appropriations decisions. Congress votes on these resolutions and may amend them.

If the appropriations bills exceed the limits set forth in the budget resolution, a "reconciliation" process ensues. The budget committees direct the legislative committees to make changes in the programs under their jurisdictions to bring them into line with the targets set forth in the budget resolution. Unlike the budget resolution, reconciliation requires presidential approval. The reconciliation process was used extensively during the early years of the Reagan administration as a principal means through which the president achieved the cuts in the domestic budget that he sought.

Action on all appropriations bills is supposed to be completed before the start of the new fiscal year on October 1. Commonly, however, some or all of the bills have not been passed or approved by the president. Congress must then pass a continuing resolution that enables agencies to continue operating until their regular appropriations are approved.

The budget process instituted in 1974 was an effort to make budgeting more rational and comprehensive, to overcome the fragmentation and incoherence of the process it replaced. It was the latter features that led many analysts to describe budgeting as incremental—that is, the consideration of only a limited number of policy options that depart only marginally from the status quo. The president and Congress do not start from scratch every year in setting their budget priorities; instead, they usually accept the previous year's priorities as a starting point and then make relatively small changes in the budget. Appropriations committees take an agency's current budget as its "base" and then add

Federal Budget Process

Early January	President submits budget to Congress.
February 15	Congressional Budget Office (CBO) reports to the Budget Committees on fiscal policy and budget priorities.
February 25	Congressional committees submit views and estimates on spending to the Budget Committee.
April 1	Senate Budget Committee reports its budget resolution. (There is no similar requirement for the House Budget Committee.)
April 15	Congress acts on the concurrent budget resolution.
June 10	House Appropriations Committee completes action on regular appropriations bills.
June 15	Congress passes a reconciliation bill.
June 30	House completes action on all appropriations bills.
August 20	CBO reports on estimated deficit and needed reductions in spending.
August 25	Office of Management and Budget (OMB) estimates budget deficit and orders any necessary budget cuts.
October 1	New fiscal year begins.
October 15	"Automatic" budget cuts by OMB become effective if Congress has not adopted an alternative, and the president issues an order.
November 15	General Accounting Office issues compliance report on the order.

an "increment," something more than the base but usually less than the increase requested by the agency.

The Deficit and the Debt. Two aspects of federal budgeting that have drastically exceeded incrementalism in recent times are the deficit and the national debt. The recession of the early 1980s, the 1981 tax cut, and rising expenditures for national defense and domestic programs have all contributed to massive annual deficits and a cumulative national debt that tripled between the mid-1970s and the mid-1980s. Deficits, which rarely exceeded $60 billion before the 1980s, averaged $150 billion during that decade (see Figure 16-5). On the other hand, these figures may not be especially meaningful because the economy has also grown. Although the budget deficit in the 1960s was usually less than 1 percent of GNP—compared with between 3 and 5 percent of GNP during the 1980s—today's deficit is still a modest fraction of the overall economy.

Figure 16-5   Federal Budget Surplus/Deficit, 1960–1989

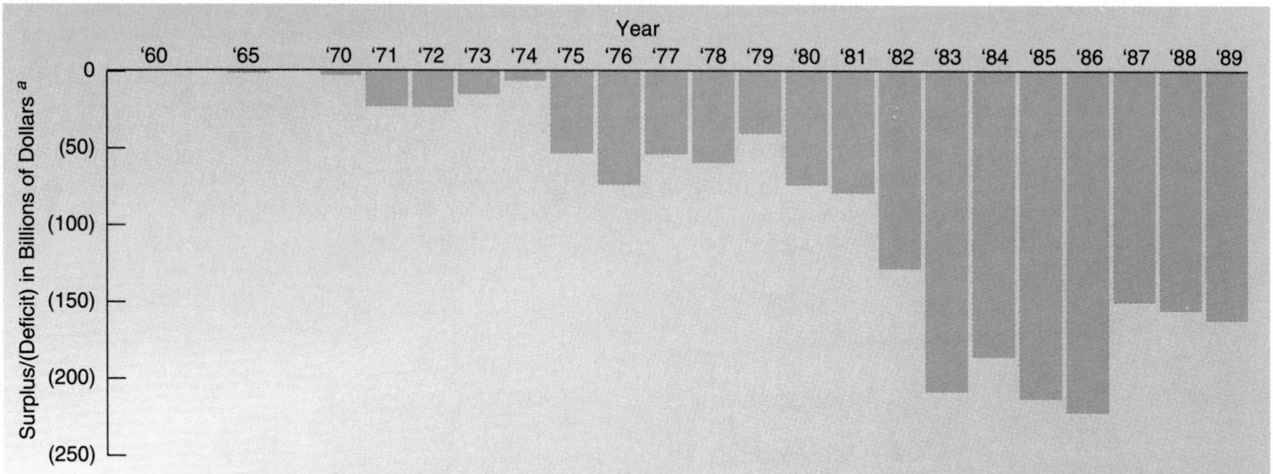

a In current dollars (not adjusted for inflation)

Source: U.S. Department of Commerce, Census Bureau, *Statistical Abstract of the United States* (Washington: Government Printing Office, 1991).

Similarly, although the national debt has grown enormously, it is about the same proportion of GNP that it was in the 1960s.[16] In addition, while the national debt has grown, so too has the value of the government's assets. By one calculation, assets approximately equaled liabilities in 1960, but by 1980 assets exceeded liabilities by $279 billion.[17]

Strong partisan differences between the Democratic-controlled Congress and the Republican president over the size and composition of the budget led to a virtual breakdown in conventional budgetary procedures in the 1980s. The alarming size of the deficits led to the adoption of the Balanced Budget and Emergency Deficit Control Act of 1985, better known for the names of its three sponsors in the Senate—Phil Gramm, Warren Rudman, and Ernest Hollings. As originally enacted, the **Gramm–Rudman–Hollings Act** called for reducing the deficit over six years, reaching zero in 1991. After protracted negotiations, several programs were exempted from the automatic budget cuts, including Social Security, veterans' pensions, Medicaid, food stamps, Aid to Families with Dependent Children, child nutrition, and interest on the national debt. Non-exempt programs would shoulder across-the-board cuts.

In 1987 Gramm–Rudman–Hollings was amended to ease the time schedule for reducing the deficit. Most members of Congress found it unacceptable to make the cuts of $45 billion called for in the law, as did the Reagan administration, which sought to avoid cuts in the military budget. The new legislation revised the annual deficit-reduction targets and amended how the cuts were to be carried out.

Because Congress has failed to meet the deficit targets contained in the original Gramm–Rudman–Hollings, the law has not been a success. It has succeeded only in the sense that deficits may have been higher had it not been in effect. In setting deficit-reduction targets into law, Congress is free to change them (as occurred in 1987). In addition, the law can be regularly skirted through budgetary "gimmickry" and by forecasting rosy

[16] James D. Savage, *Balanced Budgets and American Politics* (Ithaca, N.Y.: Cornell University Press, 1988), Chapter 2.

[17] Robert Eisner and Paul J. Peiper, "A New View of the Federal Debt and Budget Deficits," *American Economic Review* 74 (March 1984), p. 23.

Senators (left to right) Warren B. Rudman (R.-N.H.), Phil Gramm (R.-Tex.), and Ernest F. Hollings (D.-S.C.), who cosponsored a 1985 law that attempted to control spiraling deficits. The budget process has proven very difficult to control, however, and their original statute was revised and superseded by the budget agreement of 1990.

economic conditions (upon which spending and revenue levels are based) that deceptively underestimate the size of the deficit in the future.

Tax Policy

An adage observes that "nothing is more certain in life than death and taxes." Equally certain is the disdain with which Americans greet tax increases, a reaction that dates back to the Boston Tea Party. Until this century, the federal government relied for revenue primarily on excise taxes on goods and tariffs levied on imports. Until the late 1930s the politics of taxation was regionally based. The Northeast favored tariffs to protect its industrial goods from competition; the South and West, which would bear a disproportionate burden of the cost of tariffs, favored taxes on income and wealth.

The Income Tax. The first federal **income tax** was enacted during the Civil War because of the need for revenue,[18] but this tax and another enacted in 1894 were later repealed. The individual income tax became permanent with the passage of the Sixteenth Amendment in 1913. The effort to pass the income-tax amendment and law was led by progressives in Congress and coincided with Democratic control of Congress and the White House. The income tax quickly emerged as a major source of revenue to finance the U.S. role in World War I. Today it is the federal government's most important source of revenue.

Although the Progressives sought to use the income tax to achieve greater income equality, they were in the minority in this objective. The major impetus to the enactment and expansion of the income tax was the government's need for revenue and the influence of Southern and Western regions in Congress. Throughout its history, there is little evidence that majorities in Congress ever intended to use the income tax to redistribute income, and in fact little income has been redistributed. The income tax paid by most Americans has been approximately proportional to their income.

[18]The following discussion of the history of the income tax relies on John F. Witte, *The Politics and Development of the Federal Income Tax* (Madison: University of Wisconsin Press, 1985), Section III.

Similar to budget policy, changes in tax policy tend to be highly incremental. Provisions in the tax law tend to be changed in lots of minor ways from year to year. Tax levels and rates tend to rise and fall in small increments. The use and modification of exemptions, deductions, investment credits, and other provisions have taken place gradually over time. With the exception of the Tax Reform Act of 1986, discussed in the next section, little time is spent considering radical proposals for change.

Tax Expenditures and Tax Reform. One of the most important long-term trends in the income tax has been the growth in "tax expenditure" provisions. Tax expenditures—or "loopholes," as they are commonly known—allow individuals and corporations to pay less money in taxes. They are called "tax expenditures" because the government is spending money, in effect, by forgoing the collection of taxes that it would otherwise collect. These come in a variety of forms: deductions for interest paid on home mortgages, credits to businesses that invest in new plants and equipment, and exclusions from income of employer contributions to health insurance, for example. Many tax expenditures, such as the home mortgage interest deduction, benefit broad segments of the public, whereas others are targeted toward much more narrow interests. In all cases, the government uses the income tax to provide incentives for encouraging a wide array of objectives. Hence, tax expenditures have transformed the income tax into a multipurpose policy tool, far beyond the original objective of simply raising revenue for the government.

As laudable as many of these objectives are, the accumulation of tax expenditures has had several undesirable consequences. One is increased complexity. The tax code began as an eight-page amendment to a tariff bill. By the 1980s, the code and the rules elaborated to enforce it occupied entire bookshelves. This provides many jobs for tax lawyers and accountants, but the incomprehensibility of the tax code overwhelms the average citizen. Tax expenditures also create inequity. Those who can take advantage of these provisions can significantly reduce their tax liability. This diminishes what economists call "vertical equity" (the idea that more affluent people should pay a higher proportion of their income in taxes than people with less income) and "horizontal equity" (the idea that people at the same income levels should pay the same amount in taxes). Another problem with tax expenditures is that they erode the "tax base"—the total income subject to taxation. As such, they represent losses of revenue that the government would otherwise collect, forcing it either to raise tax rates higher on a smaller income base or to borrow and, thus, increase the size of the deficit. Finally, the economic benefits from tax expenditures are dubious. Many experts argue that by influencing investment decisions, tax expenditures distort market efficiency and hence dampen economic growth.

The unfairness and economic irrationality of the tax code had reached absurd proportions by the mid-1980s. Many large and profitable corporations were paying little or no federal income taxes. For instance, a mother of three children in Milwaukee in 1983 who earned $12,000 paid more in taxes than Boeing, General Electric, du Pont, and Texaco *combined.* A package of GE light bulbs cost more than GE's entire contribution to the cost of government. Generous tax breaks for investing in commercial real estate resulted in "see-through" skyscrapers—buildings without tenants—in many cities. Individuals were investing in new buildings because of the tax advantages, not because of a strong demand for office space. In California, a group of dentists' investment in jojoba beans allowed them to take large deductions during the three years it takes to determine whether a plant is female and could therefore produce more beans. One member of Congress complained, "We shouldn't be giving tax breaks to anything that takes three years to figure out its sex."[19]

Despite these problems, the conventional wisdom was that the political appeal of tax

[19] From Jeffrey H. Birnbaum and Alan S. Murray, *Showdown at Gucci Gulch: Lawmakers, Lobbyists, and the Unlikely Triumph of Tax Reform* (New York: Random House, 1987), pp. 10–12.

expenditures was too strong to eliminate or curtail them. Those groups that benefited from the provisions, many with powerful lobbying organizations in Washington, would fiercely resist change. As a very large group, taxpayers were less able and likely to mobilize in favor of reform because each one would benefit only marginally from reform. Each beneficiary of a loophole, on the other hand, felt much more intense about the issue because they stood to lose considerably from reform.

Despite these obstacles, Congress passed the Tax Reform Act of 1986, which represents a dramatic reversal of the growth of tax expenditures.[20] The proponents of tax reform included an unusual alliance of liberal Democrats, who traditionally champion the elimination of tax breaks for the wealthy and big corporations, and conservative Republicans, who saw eliminating tax expenditures as a way to cut tax rates for individuals and corporations as a whole. Reformers attacked tax expenditures for all the reasons discussed previously, but the "fairness" issue was their most potent political argument in favor of change. In the end, it was this issue above all others that compelled a majority of legislators to approve reform, despite the pressure they were under from the lobbyists who fought the measure.

Regulation and Deregulation

The final economic tool of government that we will explore is regulation. Regulation is a crucial aspect of government involvement in the economy, even though it hardly shows up in the federal budget. To a great degree, regulation has been a substitute in the United States for government ownership and control of industries, which exists in many European countries. Business regulation was introduced in the late nineteenth century for a variety of reasons: to restrain monopoly, to nurture infant industries, to stabilize markets and maintain adequate supplies of goods and services at reasonable prices, and to assure that small towns and remote areas would be served by transportation and utility companies.

Nevertheless, beginning in the 1950s and 1960s, economists and political scientists began criticizing regulation. They found that regulation often produced monopoly profits, excessive costs, discriminatory rates, and wasted energy. Their major conclusion was that rather than serve consumers' interests, many federal regulatory agencies had become "captured" by the industries, or that they served the industries all along. Regulatory commissioners had the power to set the rates that industries could charge for their services and to issue operating licenses. These regulations made it extremely difficult for industries to engage in price competition and for new competitors to enter the market. The result was that consumers were forced to pay higher prices and had fewer choices than they would have enjoyed in a more competitive market. The regulated firms, on the other hand, were assured of higher profits and larger shares of the market.

Some of the restrictions imposed by regulatory commissions were truly senseless and bizarre. In the case of trucking, for instance, some truckers could carry empty ginger ale bottles but not empty cola or root beer bottles. Others were exempt from regulation if they carried frozen TV dinners—unless they contained chicken or seafood. Livestock were exempt from regulation, unless they were being taken to a show; then they were not . . . unless it was a 4-H show—then they were. Raisins were exempt if they were coated with honey, cinnamon, or sugar, but not if they were covered with chocolate. To preserve their regulated turf, trucking companies often filed protests with the regulatory commission against rival carriers. In one case, an exasperated competitor announced that it wished to carry yak fat from Omaha to Chicago. Even though yak fat didn't exist, thirteen different companies filed protests challenging the competition![21]

---

[20] Timothy J. Conlan, Margaret T. Wrightson, and David R. Beam, *Taxing Choices: The Politics of Tax Reform* (Washington: CQ Press, 1990), Birnbaum and Murray.

[21] Dorothy Robyn, *Braking the Special Interests: Trucking Deregulation and the Politics of Policy Reform* (Chicago: University of Chicago Press, 1987), pp. 18–19.

The Regulation of Trucking

A vast array of items that we purchase are shipped from manufacturers to stores by truck. For many years the rates that trucking companies could charge for this service were set by the Interstate Commerce Commission (ICC). The rates that the companies could charge were fixed collectively by "rate bureaus" around the country—organizations made up of the trucking firms themselves. In effect, the rate bureaus acted much like cartels. All rates had to be approved by the ICC, but in practice the commission would simply rubber-stamp what the rate bureaus had decided. The task of reviewing thousands of rates per day was overwhelming, and the ICC was extremely sympathetic to the industry and protective of it. In theory, any regulated firm could undercut the fixed rate, but few did because the other carriers would file protests with the commission. The ICC made it virtually impossible for there to be price competition in another way as well—by erecting "barriers to entry" for new firms that sought to join the trucking business. New firms had to prove that existing firms were not already providing a needed service and that they would not be damaged by the additional competition. It was considered irrelevant if the new firm promised to offer its service at a lower cost to consumers. In addition, applications for entry were open to challenge by established firms, and these challenges often cost the new competitors hundreds of thousands of dollars in legal costs.

Source: Dorothy Robyn, *Braking the Special Interests: Trucking Deregulation and the Politics of Policy Reform* (Chicago: University of Chicago Press, 1987), Chapter 2.

Local governments regulate taxicabs by issuing medallions like this one. A car must have a medallion to be officially recognized as a taxi. At airports, for example, there are often curb access areas restricted to taxis only.

Although regulatory agencies were intended to regulate "in the public interest," many critics argued that regulators had been "captured" by interest groups, so that they only helped the firms they were supposed to regulate. As the **capture theory** of regulation gradually became widely accepted in the post–World War II era, "deregulation" became a fashionable policy option.[22] Although several industries were the targets of reformers who advocated deregulation, three in particular became especially vulnerable: telecommunications, trucking, and the airlines. All three cases represented dramatic reversals of a half-century or more of regulation. As in the case of tax reform, the regulated industries were adamantly opposed to deregulation and mobilized to defeat it, while consumers remained unorganized and politically inert.

Deregulation succeeded because it appealed to Democrats and Republicans, conservatives as well as liberals. On both sides of the political spectrum, "policy entrepreneurs" emerged in government—highly committed individuals willing to invest their resources in bringing it about. An alliance in the mid-1970s developed between Senator Edward M. Kennedy (D.-Mass.) and President Gerald Ford, starting off the deregulation movement. Following Ford, President Jimmy Carter also became a strong supporter of deregulation. Liberals no longer saw economic regulation as a tool for safeguarding the public against monopoly profits and chaotic markets. Instead, they saw it as a way in which big busi-

[22] Martha Derthick and Paul J. Quirk, *The Politics of Deregulation* (Washington: The Brookings Institution, 1985).

ness, with the help of a "captured" government agency, was able to charge unreasonably high prices, provide inadequate service, and engage in anti-competitive behavior. It was consumerism that attracted Kennedy to the issue; deregulation attracted Ford's support because he saw regulation as a cause of inflation and because deregulation was consistent with conservative beliefs in less government and freer markets.

Almost all economists also favored deregulation, and many of them were appointed to the regulatory commissions. The first push to deregulate came from within the commissions themselves, thus making it easier for Congress to follow with legislation. The substantial empirical evidence mustered by reformers not only showed the efficiency gains that could accrue from deregulation but also credibly countered predictions by opponents that deregulation would have disruptive effects.[23]

In addition, the reformers found a constituency willing to help them in the fight for deregulation. The sharp rise in fuel prices in the mid-1970s prompted businesses that shipped their goods by truck to organize to fight against motor carrier regulation. Farm groups, the National Federation of Independent Businesses, the National Association of Manufacturers, and others joined to fight for reform in an ad hoc coalition that included liberal-oriented consumer groups, conservative "public interest" organizations, and a variety of others representing more specific organizations.

An even more ambitious program of deregulation was underway in Britain at the same time. Margaret Thatcher was following through on her campaign pledge to privatize many of Britain's nationalized industries, including gas and telecommunications; to sell off public housing to tenants; and to contract out many public services to the private sector. There is scarcely any question that this broad-ranging initiative will constitute her most lasting legacy in Britain.

Today, the pendulum seems to have completed its swing toward deregulation. The broad consensus among liberals and conservatives that made it possible to accomplish "pro-competitive" deregulation does not exist in the area of **social regulation**—regulations imposed on firms to protect the environment, to make the workplace safe and healthful, to protect consumers from unsafe products and fraud, and to end discrimination in hiring. Even in some of those areas where deregulation was accomplished, such as air transport, there have been calls to "re-regulate." The initial wave of competition that followed airline deregulation has given way to an industry in which competitors have been driven out of the market.

Elizabeth Dole, former Secretary of Labor for President Bush. As head of the Environmental Protection Agency in the 1980s she was widely credited with strengthening the integrity of that regulatory agency after earlier accusations of "capture" by anti-regulatory interests.

Toward Reform: Alternative Directions for U.S. Economic Policy

Where is our economy headed in the future? The contemporary U.S. economy faces a series of challenges. Along with perennial concerns about maintaining price stability and low unemployment, the nation has not been able to achieve the rates of economic growth and productivity that it reached in earlier decades. Real disposable income has been virtually stagnant since the early 1970s. There is concern that American industry is unable to compete with powerful competitors, especially the Japanese. What were once secure, thriving domestic industries either no longer exist, are under severe pressure, or survive only because they are shielded from foreign competition.

It is no surprise, therefore, that over the past decade or two there have been a variety of far-reaching proposals advanced to restore American economic preeminence. Many of these proposals, according to Kenneth Dolbeare, can be categorized into three distinct "strategies for economic renewal": cowboy capitalism, yankee capitalism, and full

[23] Robyn, Chapter 4.

employment democracy.[24] The first favors minimal government "interference" in the marketplace and views most public spending, taxation, and regulation as bad for the economy. The other two strategies favor strong government action, seeing it as a necessary instrument for attaining prosperity. Yankee capitalism wants to use government to strengthen American business, especially in international competition. Full employment democracy wants to use government to redistribute economic resources and opportunities, and it views the power of business as problematic in that endeavor.

Each one has antecedents in American history. Cowboy capitalism looks for inspiration to the late nineteenth century, when *laissez-faire* economic doctrine and the myth of rugged individualism reigned supreme. Yankee capitalism finds its roots in Alexander Hamilton's policies, which assigned government a key, active role in guiding and promoting economic development. It also looks to nations like Japan, France, and Germany as models for the kind of public–private sector collaboration that they believe is needed. Full employment democrats look to Franklin Roosevelt and the New Deal, in particular, but also to the democratic-egalitarian political philosophies of Thomas Jefferson and Andrew Jackson.

Cowboy Capitalism

The most influential of the three thus far has been cowboy capitalism, the "free market" solutions advanced by the Reagan and Bush administrations. It calls for restoring economic growth and productivity by reducing tax burdens (especially on the affluent), federal spending (or at least slowing its rate of growth), and regulations on business. Since control over resources by government distorts incentives, reducing taxes and spending will allow the market to work more efficiently. Lower taxes and less regulation will create incentives for people to work, save, and invest and for business to expand production. The major economic proposal put forward by the Bush administration has been to reduce the tax on capital gains income (such as earnings from the sale of stocks). Such a proposal would help not just those mainly affluent taxpayers who would gain directly, but the economy as a whole as this money is invested in productive enterprises. To control inflation, the Federal Reserve is called on to restrain the growth in the money supply.

Supply-side tax cuts, according to this perspective, are the key to achieving non-inflationary economic growth because they increase productivity. Greater productivity means that more goods can be produced at lower per unit costs, thus keeping inflation under wraps. Sluggish productivity is due to government taxes and regulations, which discourage work and investment and raise the costs of production. Supply-siders are unconcerned about deficits because only demand-side (i.e., Keynesian) deficits are inflationary. When the tax cuts are kept out of the hands of consumers and used instead to increase the supply of goods and services, inflation is avoided. In addition, the boost in economic growth will expand the amount of taxes collected by the government, thus closing the deficit in the long run.

If the Fed follows a monetary policy that keeps money-supply growth disciplined and steady, it will not give in to pressures to inflate or deflate the economy. With stable prices, investors will be encouraged to invest for the long term because they will have confidence that their profits will not be eroded by inflation.

Although both supply-siders and "monetarists" agree on the wisdom of freer markets, they disagree on key points. Supply-siders see monetary restraint as a threat to the robust economy that they anticipate tax cuts will produce. Monetarists view the large deficits created by tax cuts as problematic because they place the Federal Reserve in the untenable position of having to choose between "accommodating" the deficit by expand-

---

[24] Kenneth M. Dolbeare, *Democracy at Risk: The Politics of Economic Renewal* (Chatham, N.J.: Chatham House, 1986).

ing the money supply (which might cause inflation) and not accommodating it and thereby allowing government borrowing to raise interest rates and "crowd out" private investment. Supply-siders, on the other hand, are less concerned about deficits. As Ronald Reagan once quipped, "The deficit is big enough to take care of itself."

Yankee Capitalism

Proponents of the second major program for economic renewal, yankee capitalism, come mainly from the academic community but also include "enlightened" segments of big business and high finance. Its political following is among moderates and "neo-liberals" in the Democratic Party, who see the need to recapture middle-class support by stressing economic growth rather than by redistributing income and opportunity.

A wide array of specific proposals have been advanced under the rubric of yankee capitalism, but two elements are essential. The first has to do with institutional arrangements rather than policies: a closer relationship, or "partnership," among government, business, and labor. Greater consultation and cooperation between government and industry, in particular, is needed to overcome the adversarial relationship between the two. In an international economy that has become increasingly competitive, American business cannot simply go it alone. Nations in which foreign firms and governments act in concert are able to develop trade strategies that leave American firms at a disadvantage.

The second element of yankee capitalism is an industrial policy. Although many different industrial policies are advanced, most stress developing new policy tools or refashioning existing tools to assist the process of readjustment from declining "sunset" industries (those in which the United States is no longer competitive or in which markets are shrinking) to new "sunrise" industries that offer the best prospects for economic growth and international competitiveness. Some of these include the creation of public-investment banks that would channel capital toward industries with potential for growth, a government agency to partially finance research and development into new products and production processes, greater public investment in "human capital" (education and training) to upgrade the skills of the workforce, and policies to cushion the shock of readjustment for declining industries.

Full Employment Democracy

The third alternative for the future, full employment democracy, represents the most liberal desires of the electorate. Advocates of full employment democracy draw their support from the liberal wing of the Democratic Party, especially among labor unions, civil rights groups, and advocates who speak and lobby on behalf of disadvantaged members of society. They share with yankee capitalists a belief in the inadequacy of free markets and a faith in activist government, but they stress the needs of working people rather than those of business. Making sure that everyone who is able to work has a job at a decent wage and attaining a more equitable distribution of income must come before profits and business expansion. Full employment policy advocates seek to fulfill the promise of the original full employment proposal of 1945 and the Humphrey–Hawkins full employment legislation passed in 1978.

A right to a job would be firmly established, just as citizens are guaranteed other rights in a democracy. Full employment advocates argue that the achievement of full employment is not inherently incompatible with price stability and market efficiency. Massive investment in public works would provide meaningful work at above-poverty-level wages to those who cannot find it in the private sector, and it would also strengthen an economy that now relies upon an aging system of roads, bridges, and other public facilities. From reductions in the military budget and the use of public and private pension funds, new investments in private projects would be made through a national network of

Reforms for the Future

A BALANCED-BUDGET AMENDMENT

Amending the Constitution to mandate that the federal government balance its budget has been a favorite policy option of conservative politicians such as former President Ronald Reagan. Proponents of such an amendment argue that it would lead to greater prudence and discipline in government spending, help to restrain the growth of government, and improve the performance of the economy. Critics of the idea claim that it would increase conflict among various interests in society, making them fight over limited resources, and that it would hamper the government's management of the economy and its ability to respond to emergencies. In particular, having to balance the budget during recessions would simply aggravate the downturn. In addition, such an amendment would constrain the government's ability to respond to citizens' needs and demands for public spending. Proponents of the idea counter that the amendment could include provisions to make it more flexible to respond to such contingencies. Some conservatives also have criticized the idea on the grounds that instead of restraining government spending, a balanced-budget amendment would merely require raising taxes to bring the budget into balance.

RE-REGULATION

Calls for the re-regulation of certain industries that were deregulated in the 1970s are the result of unintended consequences of deregulation. The airline industry, in particular, has become a target of re-regulation proponents. Immediately after deregulation, competition flourished among airlines, with new entrants into the market and reduced fares for consumers. But in more recent years, fares have risen and the industry has become more concentrated, with bankruptcies and leveraged buyouts of one airline by another reducing the number of competitors. None of the current proposals would return to government control over routes, schedules, and fares. They do, however, contemplate giving the federal Transportation Department new authority to force airlines to sell off highly profitable computerized reservation systems, which help the airlines that own them to increase their share of the market. They also would permit the government to grant competing airlines access to airports at which one or two companies dominate passenger service.

publicly run development banks. Finally, to achieve greater income equality, advocates of full employment democracy call for changes in the income-tax structure that would make it truly progressive.

Summary

The history of government involvement in the economy over the course of the past century is one of increased intervention. The development of a modern, industrial, capitalist economy posed significant challenges from which government could not retreat. During the Progressive era the government's regulatory powers were greatly extended to restrain monopoly, prevent financial panics, assure the purity of food and safeness of drugs, and for other purposes. The next expansion of the government's role came under the New Deal in the 1930s, a response to the emergency of the Great Depression. New regulatory controls were instituted over financial markets, an array of job-creation programs were launched, Social Security retirement benefits and unemployment insurance were established, and the ill-fated National Industrial Recovery Act was enacted.

The challenges of a mature industrial economy were accompanied by the emergence of new economic theories that made government intervention legitimate. After World War II the federal government adopted Keynesian tools of economic management—particularly the use of deficits to stimulate economic growth. This was a rejection of *laissez-faire* doctrine, which had dominated economic thinking until the Depression. Americans reshaped Keynes's prescription in a conservative direction by opting to create deficits by cutting taxes rather than by increasing spending. Although government has always played a critical role in the U.S. economy and that role remains substantial, it nevertheless has been more limited than in most other industrial nations.

The three major goals of economic policy are high employment, price stability, and economic growth. Historically, the United States tends to have higher rates of unemployment but lower rates of inflation than most other industrialized democracies. American rates of economic growth and productivity have been below those of many of our most important competitors, such as Japan, which have also been able to penetrate many of our domestic markets.

Government has a number of policy instruments at its disposal as it attempts to improve economic performance. Fiscal and monetary policies affect the overall level of demand for goods and services, and consequently the price level, unemployment, and income growth. Fiscal policy has to do with manipulating aggregate, or total, spending and taxation, and the resultant surplus or deficit. Deficits, whether created through tax cuts or increased spending, tend to stimulate economic growth, whereas balanced budgets and surpluses tend to depress it. Fiscal policy is made by Congress and the president through the budget process. Despite reforms in the process, it has been very difficult for both branches to develop the kind of consensus necessary to reduce the large budget deficits that currently exist.

Monetary policy is concerned with the level of interest rates and the supply of money. Generally, lower interest rates and an expanded money supply will stimulate economic growth, whereas higher rates and a shrinking money supply will tend to dampen growth, but they will also keep a lid on inflation. How the Federal Reserve Board conducts monetary policy critically affects the ability of banks to lend funds to corporate and individual borrowers, and this, in turn, affects the level of stimulus in the economy. The Fed sets reserve requirements for banks, raises or lowers the discount rate, and purchases and sells government securities ("open-market transactions"). The Fed is an independent agency of the executive branch, expected to make its decisions in an objective and nonpolitical fashion. The board is headed by a powerful chair, who, along with the other governors, is appointed by the president and confirmed by Congress. Their terms last fourteen years.

The government's use of other policy instruments, such as tax expenditures and regulation, is intended to affect particular industries and groups in the economy. Here the United States, which, like Great Britain, has relied for the most part on a *laissez-faire* approach to regulating specific firms, finds itself without many of the capabilities available to Japan or even France. Tax expenditures are incentives that permit corporations and individuals to pay less in taxes in order to promote some desirable outcome. These range from incentives to encourage business investment to those that encourage individuals to donate to charities. Regulations are rules written by government to inhibit undesirable conduct on the part of business and other economic actors. These range from economic regulations setting prices that businesses can charge for their services to those that establish limits on the emissions of factories and other polluters. Many tax expenditures have recently been eliminated or curtailed under tax reform. Similarly, a variety of industries have been deregulated.

Where the American economy is headed is uncertain, as is the direction of economic policy. Three main alternative strategies have been put forward to meet the economic challenges that the nation faces. Cowboy capitalism is the free market solution, which calls for reducing government taxes, spending, and regulation. Yankee capitalism favors close cooperation between business and government and a variety of measures under the rubric of "industrial policy" to boost American competitiveness. Proponents of full employment democracy call for establishing a right to employment for all Americans and for massive public investments to create sufficient employment opportunities at decent wages.

Key Terms

gross domestic product	protectionism	Office of Management and Budget
business cycle	monetarism	backdoor spending
Great Depression	supply-side	Congressional Budget Office
National Industrial Recovery Act	employment	
	inflation	Gramm–Rudman–Hollings Act
Keynesianism	economic growth	income tax
full employment	fiscal policy	
Council of Economic Advisers	national debt	capture theory
stagflation	monetary policy	social regulation
trade deficits		

Suggested Readings

Bailey, Stephen. *Congress Makes a Law: The Story Behind the Employment Act of 1946.* New York: Columbia University Press, 1951.

Brand, Donald R. *Corporatism and the Rule of Law: A Study of the National Recovery Administration.* Ithaca, N.Y.: Cornell University Press, 1988.

Collins, Robert. *The Business Response to Keynes: 1929–1964.* New York: Columbia University Press, 1981.

Conlan, Timothy J.; Margaret T. Wrightson; and David R. Beam. *Taxing Choices: The Politics of Tax Reform.* Washington: CQ Press, 1990.

Derthick, Martha, and Paul J. Quirk. *The Politics of Deregulation.* Washington: The Brookings Institution, 1985.

Destler, I. M. *American Trade Politics,* 2nd ed. Washington: International Institute of Economics, 1992.

Dolbeare, Kenneth M. *Democracy at Risk: The Politics of Economic Renewal.* Chatham, N.J.: Chatham House, 1986.

Edsall, Thomas B. *The New Politics of Inequality.* New York: Norton, 1984.

Eisner, Robert. *How Real Is the Federal Deficit?* New York: Free Press, 1986.

Fraser, Steve, and Gary Gerstle. *The Rise and Fall of the New Deal Order.* Princeton, N.J.: Princeton University Press, 1988.

Hughes, Jonathan R. T. *The Governmental Habit.* New York: Basic Books, 1977.

Mucciaroni, Gary. *The Political Failure of Employment Policy, 1945–1982.* Pittsburgh: University of Pittsburgh Press, 1990.

Olson, Mancur. *The Rise and Decline of Nations: Economic Growth, Stagflation, and Social Rigidities.* New Haven, Conn.: Yale University Press, 1982.

Peretz, Paul, ed. *The Politics of American Economic Policy Making.* Armonk, N.Y.: Sharpe, 1987.

Pfiffner, James P., ed. *The President and Economic Policy.* Philadelphia: Institute for the Study of Human Issues, 1986.

Reich, Robert B. *The Next American Frontier.* New York: Times Books, 1983.

Robyn, Dorothy. *Braking the Special Interests.* Chicago: University of Chicago Press, 1987.

Savage, James D. *Balanced Budgets & American Politics.* Ithaca, N.Y.: Cornell University Press, 1988.

Schwarz, John. *America's Hidden Success: A Reassessment of Twenty Years of Public Policy.* New York: Norton, 1983.

Schick, Allen, ed. *Making Economic Policy in Congress.* Washington: American Enterprise Institute, 1983.

Stein, Herbert. *Presidential Economics: The Making of Economic Policy from Roosevelt to Reagan and Beyond.* Washington: American Enterprise Institute, 1988.

Sundquist, James L. *Politics and Policy: The Eisenhower, Kennedy and Johnson Years.* Washington: The Brookings Institution, 1968.

Tufte, Edward R. *Political Control of the Economy.* Princeton, N.J.: Princeton University Press, 1978.

Vogel, David. *Fluctuating Fortunes: The Political Power of Business in America.* New York: Basic Books, 1989.

Weatherford, M. Stephen. "Political Business Cycles and the Process of Economic Policy-making," *American Politics Quarterly* 16 (January 1988), pp. 99–136.

Weir, Margaret, and Theda Skocpol. "State Structures and the Possibilities for 'Keynesian' Responses to the Great Depression," in Peter B. Evans, Dietrich Rueschemeyer, and Theda Skocpol, eds., *Bringing the State Back In.* New York: Cambridge University Press, 1985.

Wildavsky, Aaron. *The New Politics of the Budgetary Process.* Glenview, Ill.: Scott, Foresman, 1988.

Wilson, James Q., ed. *The Politics of Regulation.* New York: Basic Books, 1980.

Witte, John. *The Politics and Development of the Federal Income Tax.* Madison: University of Wisconsin Press, 1985.

Woolley, John T. *Monetary Politics: The Federal Reserve and the Politics of Monetary Policy.* London: Cambridge University Press, 1984.

[Congress shall have the]

"power to make all laws which shall

be necessary and proper for carrying

into execution the foregoing powers,

and all other powers vested by this

Constitution . . ."

Few parts of the Constitution

have been assailed with more

intemperance than this. . . .

James Madison

FEDERALIST NO. 44

Without the "elastic clause" quoted in this passage, Congress would have virtually no authority to undertake what is now called domestic policy.

CHAPTER 17

Domestic Policy

As James Madison indicated in Federalist No. 44, the Framers heatedly debated how strictly to limit the federal government. The elastic clause, discussed in Chapter 6, was viewed with particular distrust by many because it allowed Congress broad and undefined authority to pass "necessary" laws. Fortunately for the federal government, Madison and the Federalists won their argument for the elastic clause, thereby setting the stage for a wealth of federal domestic policy making.

By means of the elastic clause, Congress could expand its sphere of activity greatly as long as it remained focused on "all other powers vested by this Constitution in the government of the United States." Over the years, Congress has steadily widened its interpretation of what is possible under these terms, and the scope of domestic policy has correspondingly expanded.

The Growth of Government

In earlier chapters, we have seen how modern American government involves itself in many different areas. Cleaning the air, regulating the food we eat, and setting Daylight Savings Time are just three examples. For much of our history, however, government has been much less active than it is today.

In the early days of the republic, American government essentially concerned itself with only two functions: defense and watching over the economy. Domestic policy amounted to what is called the **economic watchdog model** of government: The economy, including all daily activities of the people, was allowed to run on its own with the government standing by to help solve problems and crises. This was truly an era of

The growth of our public agenda is not necessarily inexorable. Education, entirely a private affair in the colonial era, began to be government-controlled and public on a statewide basis only when public responsibility was authorized by state constitutions. That private-to-public transfer was not automatic or entirely accepted. In this cartoon, Thomas Nast complains that the Catholic church (a sponsor of its own school system) was undermining public education in the period after the Civil War. The value of public education is still subject to hot debate.

THE AMERICAN RIVER GANGES.

THE PRIESTS AND THE CHILDREN.

**Table 17-1   Growth and Distribution of U.S. Public-
Sector Employment, Selected Years, 1944–87**

YEAR	Number Employed (thousands)			
	TOTAL PUBLIC SECTOR	FEDERAL	STATE	LOCAL
1944	6,537	3,365	700	2,472
1949	6,203	2,047	1,037	3,119
1954	7,232	2,373	1,149	3,710
1959	8,487	2,399	1,454	4,634
1964	10,064	2,528	1,873	5,663
1969	12,685	2,969	2,614	7,102
1975	14,986	2,890	3,268	8,828
1977	15,459	2,848	3,481	9,130
1981	15,968	2,865	3,726	9,377
1982	15,918	2,848	3,747	9,324
1984	16,436	2,942	3,898	9,595
1987[a]	17,481	3,030	(14,451)	

[a]Office of Management and Budget estimates, 1988.

Source: Compiled in D. B. Robertson and D. R. Judd, *The Development of American Public Policy* (New York: Scott Foresman, 1989), p. 156.

limited government. Disputes had to be brought to the government's attention by means of lawsuits; there were very few taxes; schools, road systems, and virtually all other common needs were met either privately or at the local or state level.

Over our 200-year history, however, the government has expanded in size and activity. Growth has not been perfectly steady; sometimes the government has grown explosively, sometimes it has held even or, extremely rarely, declined slightly. But as a rule, the future has always meant more, not less, government.

This growth has occurred in all parts of the government. Congress has grown to match a growing population and an increase in the number of states. As there have been more and more members of Congress, there have been more legislators able to specialize their interests and champion particular areas of governmental activity. In Chapter 8, we noted that the federal bureaucracy has grown as well—to more than 3 million workers. Table 17-1 shows the incredible growth of the bureaucracy at all levels just since World War II. These employees have been added either by presidential or congressional orders, as new areas of activity have required more managers, overseers, and regulators. But new employees do not just manage existing policies; they inevitably create momentum to modify and/or extend those policies, thereby creating new areas of government involvement.

In Chapter 15, we noted that the number of interest groups has also grown. Although interest groups are private, they add more pressure on the government to expand its activities. In 1964, for example, interest groups like Martin Luther King Jr.'s Southern Christian Leadership Conference helped bring America's racial prejudice into public focus, eventually leading to the Civil Rights Act, which in turn led to a larger bureaucracy, including the Equal Employment Opportunities Commission, formed by the act to help enforce its provisions against discrimination.

Part of the growth of governmental policies can be attributed to an increase in the demands that we "the people" have placed on our government. Yet new policies and areas of governmental activity must overcome a natural inertia on the part of government officials: Why change? Why change now? Why, for example, should a private area (like health insurance) suddenly require public attention? Often, crises provide the answers.

Crises tend to push both public opinion and governmental response past their natural inertia. In response to a crisis it is easier to overcome fundamental objections to action and undertake new initiatives. For this reason, domestic policy growth in the United States has been propelled by crisis periods, characterized by intense activity, bold new laws, and precedent-shattering decisions. This pattern is not unique to the United States. In Great Britain, public policy has also been propelled by crisis periods that have corresponded neatly with those of the United States. In the twentieth century in particular, three periods stand out: the Great Depression of the 1930s, the social upheavals of the 1960s, and the conservative, anti-government sentiments of the 1980s, all of which echoed loudly on both sides of the Atlantic.

We need to look at America's response to the 1930s and 1960s in particular, because these decades produced the most explosive changes in our domestic policy agenda.

The New Deal

For millions of Americans, life in the early 1930s was terrible. Unemployment soared to 25 percent of all workers. Thousands went without food. Many thousands more were homeless. In the previous chapter, we saw how President Franklin D. Roosevelt's administration tried to respond to the economic causes of the Depression by regulating banking. In the midst of trying to guard against a repeat of the 1929 stock market crash, however, Washington produced a dizzying array of social legislation as well, forever changing how we think about the national government's duties and responsibilities to its citizens. In 1935 FDR signed into law the Social Security Act, creating for the first time a system of national retirement insurance. In 1938 the Fair Labor Standards Act created the first minimum wage and abolished child labor. As we will see later in this chapter, welfare policy has since grown from these New Deal origins to become a major function of the federal government. Without the important precedents set by FDR's New Deal, American social welfare policy would surely be far different from its present state.

At first, Roosevelt and Congress faced resistance to their expanded agenda from the Supreme Court. In 1935 the Court struck down the National Recovery Administration and limited the federal government's realm of influence by declaring both mining and farming to be state and local issues (*Schechter Poultry Corp.* v. *United States*). In response, Roosevelt attacked the Court and tried to "pack" it with up to fifteen members (at least six of whom would be new and pro–New Deal) with a 1937 judiciary reorganization bill. In the wake of both his proposal and his landslide reelection in 1936 (an electoral victory over Kansas Governor Alfred M. Landon of 523 to 8), the Court made judicial reform unnecessary by abruptly switching positions and granting the federal government broad authority over interstate commerce in *NLRB* v. *Jones and Laughlin Steel.*

In retrospect, it should not be surprising that the Supreme Court reacted more conservatively to the crisis of the Depression years. Both the president and the Congress, subject to regular elections, are extremely sensitive to public opinion. The Court traditionally is less sensitive—in theory, it is supposed to ignore entirely the public's passions of the moment. But no institution can be immune to change, and in 1937 the Court knew that its obstinacy might lead either to a packed Court or perhaps to some kind of new constitutional limitations via a congressionally passed amendment. As a result, although it took a few years longer than the other branches, the Court eventually followed the will of the public and joined the New Deal policy revolution.

The Great Society

Another crisis point that led to a greatly expanded domestic policy agenda occurred during the 1960s. The civil rights movement, student anti-war protests, and calls for reform of the electoral process all placed strong pressures on Congress and the president. In the early 1960s, President John F. Kennedy tried to launch a domestic agenda he named "The New Frontier," which called for federal aid to education, a new anti-poverty policy, and subsidized medical care for the elderly. Conservative Southern Democrats, however, joined with Republicans in Congress to block most of Kennedy's initiatives. In the wake of Kennedy's assassination in 1963, Lyndon Johnson used his experience in Congress and the country's deepening social crisis to succeed where Kennedy had failed by getting Congress to pass a dizzying series of proposals loosely referred to as his "Great Society" programs.

As it had during the New Deal period, Washington in the 1960s responded to drastic changes in public opinion; like the New Deal, it took on areas of policy making that set precedents for future activity. Between 1964 and 1966, combining the end of the 88th Congress with the 89th's "Congress of accomplished hopes . . . of realized dreams,"[1] Congress passed far-reaching legislation on civil rights (the Civil Rights Act of 1964), voting rights (the Voting Rights Act, suspending literacy requirements and encouraging registration), federal aid to education, urban mass transit subsidies, food stamps, Medicare, Medicaid, housing, urban renewal, and even clean air (see the accompanying timeline). Some of these policy areas were new: civil rights, voting rights, and clean air especially. Others represented extensions of the existing network of welfare programs, or **safety net:** food stamps, Medicare, and Medicaid.

The period since Lyndon Johnson's presidency has seen little change in the basic range of governmental domestic policy. Most major modern legislation since 1968 has

[1] Speaker of the House John McCormack (D.-Mass.), quoted in Bernand Bailyn et al., *The Great Republic,* 3rd ed. (Lexington, Mass.: Heath, 1985).

Lyndon B. Johnson, president from 1963 to 1968, was a powerful advocate of his Great Society Programs. As a former Senate majority leader, Johnson knew how to lobby individual members of Congress. He was famous for cornering people and cajoling, pleading, and threatening them in order to win their support. The blizzard of domestic policy that accompanied his presidency greatly expanded the agenda of Washington.

Lyndon Johnson's "Great Society" Speech

We have the opportunity to move not only toward the rich society and the powerful society, but upward to the Great Society. The Great Society rests on abundance and liberty for all. It demands an end to poverty and racial injustice, to which we are totally committed in our time. But that is just the beginning. It is a place where the city of man serves not only the needs of the body and the demands of commerce but the desire for beauty and the hunger for community. It is a place where man can renew contact with nature. It is a place which honors creation for its own sake and for what it adds to the understanding of the race. It is a place where men are more concerned with the quality of their goals than the quantity of their goods. But most of all, the Great Society is not a safe harbor, a resting place, a final objective, a finished work. It is a challenge constantly renewed, beckoning us toward a destiny where the meaning of our lives matches the marvelous products of our labor.

The eloquence of Lyndon Johnson's "Great Society" speech reflects the idealism and energy that spread from the social upheavals of the 1960s inward to Washington.

Major "Great Society" Programs

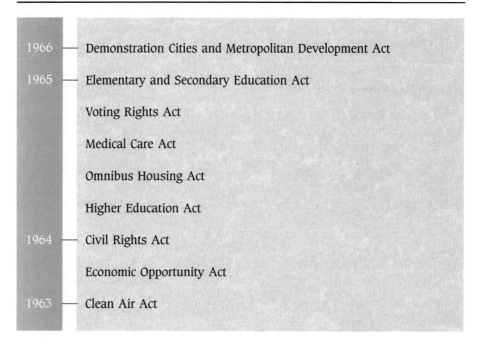

1966	Demonstration Cities and Metropolitan Development Act
1965	Elementary and Secondary Education Act
	Voting Rights Act
	Medical Care Act
	Omnibus Housing Act
	Higher Education Act
1964	Civil Rights Act
	Economic Opportunity Act
1963	Clean Air Act

re-legislated various governmental policies on civil rights, education, transportation, environmentalism, and so on. There has been one major significant twist, however: In Ronald Reagan's first term, Congress carried out a significant reduction of the federal government's expenditures in many areas. Riding the crest of an anti-government wave, Reagan and Congress scaled back income taxes and cut spending, shifting the responsibility for many programs to the states. Despite strong anti-government rhetoric, however, the 1980s saw no major areas of activity eliminated entirely. The lesson for domestic policy: Once a new policy area is born, it is unlikely ever to die.

The Policy-Making Process

As history suggests, there is a pattern to governmental domestic policy growth. First, the stage is put onto the policy agenda by changes in public opinion. (The policy "agenda" refers to those areas in which the government has chosen to make decisions.) Second, the government responds with new policy initiatives; third, these new areas set precedents for future activity. Over the years, the policy arsenal tends to grow, especially as bureaucratic institutions develop to help maintain each sphere of activity. In order to understand the process more fully, we will examine its details by using as an example the Clean Air Act Amendments of 1990.

Agenda Setting

Issues reach the government's policy agenda from the basic source of public opinion. Not all issues on the public's mind reach the depths of the Washington establishment, however. To understand why some areas stimulate policy and others do not, it is essential to examine **agenda setting,** the process by which issues become questions of policy.

Rachel Carson, whose 1962 book entitled *Silent Spring* helped focus the public's agenda on environmental hazards.

The Media. One of the first places to look for changes in public opinion is the media. In the case of clean air legislation, for example, there had been very little call for governmental intervention in the environment prior to the 1960s. The media had been largely silent on the issue because few people were making a fuss about it. In 1962, however, Rachel Carson's book, *Silent Spring,* arguing in eloquent terms against the dangers of pesticides, caught the public's eye. The public became obsessed with smokestacks and automobile exhaust.[2] Newspapers and magazines covered protests, scientific studies, and stories of polluted water and air.

Interest Groups. If an issue on the public agenda has strong enough supporters or opponents among the public, they will organize to put pressure on Washington. Issue-oriented interest groups routinely rise in response to public questions; in addition, established groups often move quickly to stake out positions on new issues. When environmentalism swept the country in the 1960s, both new and old groups responded. New groups did not mushroom as quickly as they now do, but over the course of the 1960s and 1970s, groups as specialized as the Natural Resources Defense Council, a law firm organized to intervene in environmental cases, flourished. Established groups jumped to take positions either for or against environmentalism: The United Auto Workers, for example, quickly opposed any clean air legislation because restrictions on auto pollution threatened to squeeze auto makers and cause unemployment among their employees.

Policy Entrepreneurs

Once public opinion is aroused and interest groups focus pressure on Washington to act, **policy entrepreneurs** step into the picture. Policy entrepreneurs are individuals in government who assume leadership roles in new policy areas. They can be members of Congress, the executive branch, or, occasionally, of the judiciary. They work with their

[2] Richard E. Cohen, *Washington at Work: Back Rooms and Clean Air* (New York: Macmillan, 1992), p. 11.

colleagues to build momentum on particular issues, wielding whatever power they can find. If they are members of Congress, they introduce bills and hold committee or sub-committee hearings; members of the executive branch lobby Congress or push other members to give an issue high priority within a president's administration. Members of the Supreme Court can choose to hear cases that force rulings on particular issues; they can also send signals from off the bench, as when in 1990 Chief Justice William H. Rehnquist publicly requested that Congress limit the number of *habeas corpus* appeals allowed to convicted criminals. (Writs of *habeas corpus* are court orders mandating that an officer of a state inform an individual why he or she is being held.)

In the case of clean air, the policy entrepreneurs have been both predictable and surprising. From the ranks of Congress, it was predictable that members from rural, scenic, nonmanufacturing, vacation states would take particular interest in environmentalism. One of the early champions of environmental policy, Senator Edmund S. Muskie (D.-Me.), fit this description to a tee. More recently, Senate Majority Leader George Mitchell, also a Maine Democrat, has inherited Muskie's mantle as one of the prime congressional supporters of environmental legislation.

"A Thousand Points of Light"

Since George Bush's acceptance speech at the Republican National Convention in 1988, when he floated the idea of "a thousand points of light," Bush frequently has used his office to encourage "the vast galaxy" of private individuals and corporations to help others less fortunate who normally look to the government for aid. Unlike President Ronald Reagan's administration, which skeptics believed encouraged volunteerism to justify spending cuts for the needy, the Bush administration has launched efforts to undergird volunteerism with national support.

For example, the Bush administration is pressing for legislation to help defray the expense of adopting children with handicaps. The bill would authorize a $3,000 federal tax deduction for individuals who adopt a child with special needs.

The White House has also played a leading role in trying to launch a new public-private foundation to promote volunteerism and community service. In 1990, Bush was instrumental in the creation of "A Thousand Points of Light Foundation," which works to spread successful local community service initiatives by operating a computer database of local initiatives and a telephone hotline. It oversees "Youth Entering Service to America," Bush's idea for engaging young people in community service. The foundation will try to raise $25 million from the private sector and see a $25 million appropriation from Congress.

In the meantime, Bush has issued several "point of light" awards. Award recipients have included an Appleton, Wisconsin–based initiative to educate parents about the dangers of drug and alcohol abuse; G. D. Searle & Co. of Chicago, a pharmaceutical firm that provides free drugs to needy people who have heart conditions and high blood pressure; a husband and wife team, William and Sandu Hale, both of whom have multiple sclerosis, who founded an all-volunteer medical clinic in Oklahoma City; and Aja Dyani Henderson, a Baton Rouge (Louisiana) teenager who started a library in her home.

Source: Carol F. Steinbach, "Shining a Little Light on Volunteers," *National Journal* (February 24, 1990), Vol. 22. No. 8, p. 464.

People of the Past

Mary Dewson

Mary Dewson (or "Molly," as she was widely known) entered Wellesley College in 1893 where she studied economics, history, and sociology. She was senior class president and her class predicted that she eventually would become president of the United States. She never was, but Dewson did have a profound effect on the domestic policy of the day.

After work at the Domestic Reform Committee of the Women's Educational and Industrial Union, Dewson became a superintendent of the parole department of the Massachusetts State Industrial School for Girls, a position that allowed her to take a leading role in the study of female delinquency and its prevention. She later became involved in the minimum wage movement, and in 1912 her work became the basis for the first minimum wage act passed in the United States.

Dewson became involved in Democratic Party politics and organized Democratic women to help in Franklin Roosevelt's campaign, first for New York State governor and two years later for the presidency. Taking advantage of her friendship with Franklin and Eleanor Roosevelt, Dewson urged the president to appoint many women to important positions in the New Deal. Dewson's political connections also made her a key player in gaining passage of a New York State unemployment insurance act and minimum wage laws in several states. Roosevelt appointed Dewson as a member of the Social Security Board because of her concern with unemployment and old-age insurance programs. Ill health ultimately forced her to retire, but many of the early successes of the Social Security program can be attributed to her commitment, intelligence, and skill.

Senate majority leader George Mitchell (D.-Me.) was a tireless policy entrepreneur for clean air in 1990. Policy entrepreneurs generally have strategic reasons for choosing their areas of interest. For Mitchell, clean air is a goal widely supported by the constituents of his home state of Maine, "the vacation state."

Smog over Los Angeles: Before clean air could become an important goal in Washington, enough constituencies had to come together on the issue. Environmental hazards affect many areas, causing entrepreneurs like Maine's Senator George Mitchell to be joined by allies such as Los Angeles Representative Henry Waxman (among others) to form a broad coalition.

More surprising has been the key role of two Republican presidents. Although environmentalism often runs counter to both traditional Republican pro-business interests and traditional Republican limited-government ideology, half of the four recent Republican presidents have championed clean air legislation. The first, only slightly behind Senator Muskie's lead, was Richard Nixon, who said in his 1970 State of the Union address, "The great question of the seventies is, shall we surrender to our surroundings, or shall we make our peace with nature and begin to make reparations for the damage we have done to our air, to our land and to our water?"[3] The second was George Bush, who campaigned in 1988 as an environmentalist and introduced into Congress what would eventually become the 1990 Clean Air Act Amendments.

The presidential initiatives illustrate an important lesson about the policy-making process: Presidents matter. No other individual has nearly the impact on public policy that the chief executive has. Through party leadership or adversarial tactics (such as veto threats), presidents carry tremendous influence through every stage of the policy-making process.

In the absence of Washington momentum, policy entrepreneurs often succeed at the state level. With fifty state governments to choose from, entrepreneurs often succeed in using one or more as a **policy laboratory**—a testing ground for potential national legislation. California, perhaps because of its tremendous population, often acts on the forefront of public policy, as it did in the tax revolt of the late 1970s and early 1980s. With so many governments to choose from, entrepreneurs for any particular issue tend to be scattered in many places. Figure 17-1 shows the possible entrepreneurial targets for welfare issues.

Coalition Building

No entrepreneur, not even the president, can single-handedly enact public policies. Presidents and entrepreneurs may lead the process, but they will fail unless they prove adept at building **coalitions,** alliances of individuals and groups who join forces over particular issues. Interest groups often form coalitions on the theory that they will carry more weight if they represent a larger group of constituents.

With the speed of modern communications, coalitions are easier to form than ever before. Interest groups can join forces over particular legislative battles and witness their success or failure as soon as Congress acts. They can keep coalition members "wired in" by sending reports from lobbyists' offices on a regular basis. It is not surprising, therefore, that modern large bills often generate large umbrella coalitions on each side. In the case of the 1990 Clean Air Amendments, the National Clean Air Coalition comprised most

[3] Ibid., p. 13.

Figure 17-1   Administrative Network for Selected Basic Needs Welfare Programs

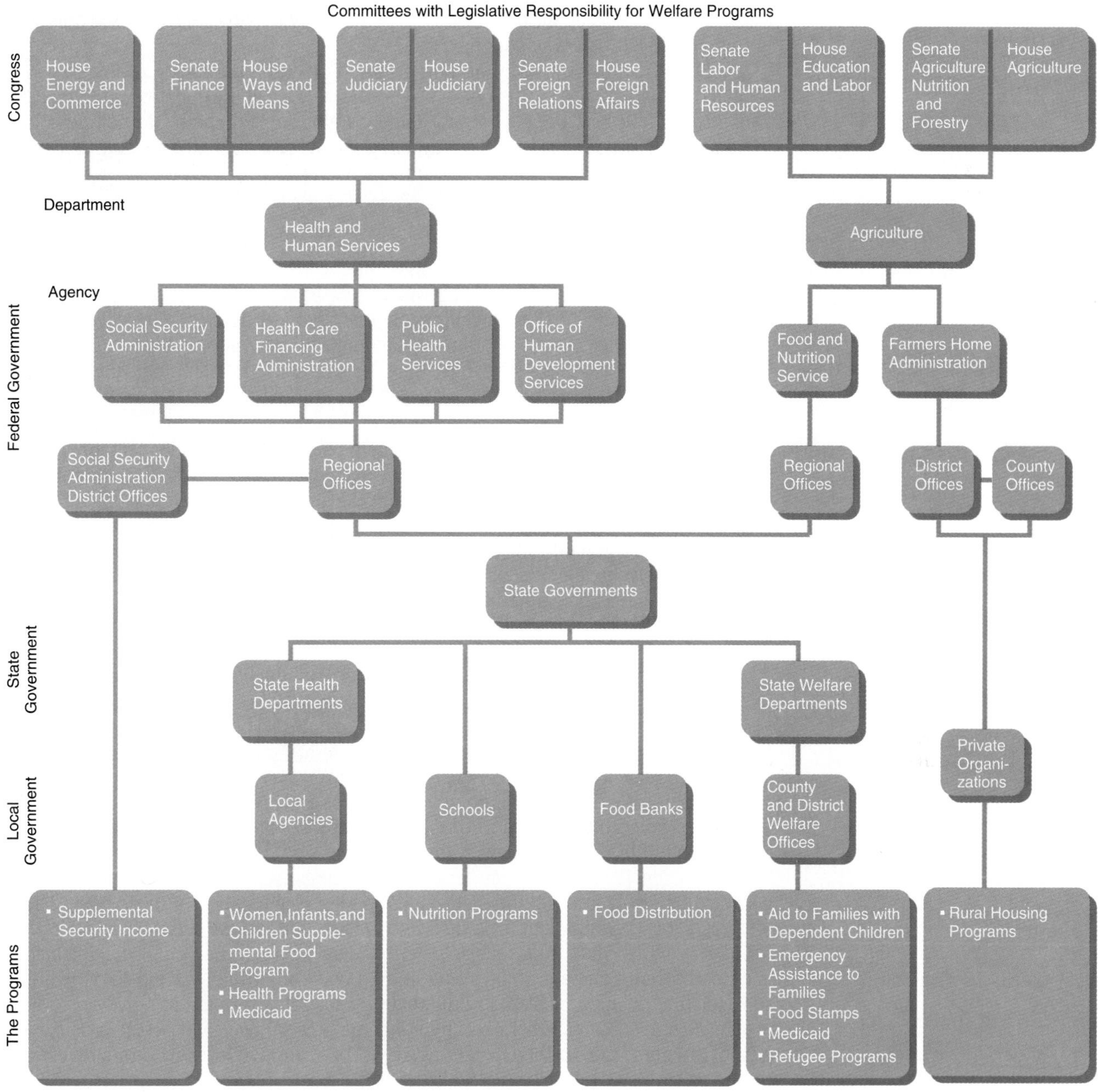

Committees with Legislative Responsibility for Welfare Programs

Source: U.S. General Accounting Office, *Welfare: Issues to Consider in Assessing Proposals for Reform* (Washington: Government Printing Office), February 1987, Figure 3, p. 20.

private pro-environment groups pushing to strengthen the bill, while the Clean Air Working Group represented business interests largely working to minimize the regulatory friction that environmental legislation inevitably creates.

Both of these coalitions exemplified modern trends by representing huge numbers of constituent interests. Earlier clean air legislation, by contrast, had not faced coalitions of anywhere near their size. In this case, at least, size proved to be a problem instead of an asset. With too many voices competing within their ranks, both the Clean Air Coalition and the Working Group had difficulty pinning down particular issues on the large legislative territory covered by the bill. In effect, they had grown to the point at which they were no more focused than was Congress itself.

Coalitions can be temporary or long-lasting. For years, a coalition of Congressional Republicans joined forces with Southern Democrats to defeat the initiatives of Democratic Party leaders. Despite the Democrats' largely uninterrupted control of Congress from 1945 onward, it took President Kennedy's assassination in 1963 to overcome Congress's conservatives and achieve major legislative victories.

Implementation

Once entrepreneurs have succeeded in mobilizing broad-based support, including congressional and presidential approval (or congressional overriding of a presidential veto), public policy becomes a matter of implementation. Without effective enforcement, laws are hardly worth the paper on which they are printed. Successful implementation involves all levels of the bureaucracy, as well as state and local governments.

The Bureaucracy. Bureaucratic enforcement can be either presidentially or congressionally managed, depending on to whom the agency in question reports. **Departmental agencies** report to the president's Cabinet and can be created by executive order. Like the departments themselves, they must obey the laws passed by Congress, but their loyalty clearly is to the president. In areas of dispute, departments and departmental agencies will always rely on the executive branch's interpretation. In 1991, for example, the Department of Education announced that it would end all federal subsidies to colleges and universities that offered minority scholarships—until President Bush personally countermanded the unpopular decision.

Nondepartmental, or independent, **agencies** include the Interstate Commerce Commission (ICC), the Securities and Exchange Commission (SEC), and the Federal Communications Commission (FCC). These and other commissions that are part of what many term the "alphabetocracy" exist because Congress has opted to delegate broad powers to them. To create a regulatory commission, Congress must delegate some of its powers to govern a particular area of the economy or business and give a bureau broad authority to make rules governing the conduct of affected businesses and individuals. Their loyalty is therefore more to Congress than to the president.

These agencies have the power not only to make rules but also to settle disputes between parties concerning the enforcement and implementation of those rules. Therefore, regulatory commissions are considered to have both **quasi-legislative** and **quasi-judicial powers.** These functions are referred to as "quasi" because law making by any body other than Congress or adjudication by a body other than the judiciary would be considered a violation of the constitutional principle of separation of powers.

The effectiveness of either executive or congressional oversight depends on the degree of attention paid to the relevant agency. There are two basic models of oversight: **police patrol** and **fire alarm.**[4] With the police patrol model, Congress (or a Cabinet member's office) regularly "patrols"—that is, gathers information on the success or failure of the regulation. With the fire alarm model, no oversight activity begins until an alarm is rung. For example, the bankruptcies of several major savings and loan associations in the late 1980s began to send alarms to Washington that the industry was in desperate need of attention.

Oversight of domestic policy implementation can be either police patrol or fire alarm style regardless of the policy area in question. With clean air, for example, Congress could

[4] Matthew D. McCubbins and Thomas Schwartz, "Congressional Oversight Overlooked: Police Patrols versus Fire Alarms," *American Journal of Political Science* 28 (February 1984).

require that the Environmental Protection Agency (EPA) gather annual data on automobile tailpipe emissions (police patrol), or it could simply wait to see if air-quality measurements suggest an abundance of exhaust (fire alarm). In practice, much oversight is the latter, simply because fire alarms cost a lot less than police patrols.

The States. In many cases, implementation of federal law can be left to the states. With the Clean Air Act Amendments, Congress specifically recognized two standards for air quality, one for the country as a whole and a stricter one desired by the state of California. Other states were allowed the option of adopting the stricter California standard if they wished. Within a year of the amendments, most of the New England states had announced they would do so, and other states seemed likely to follow. In the case of much of federal welfare policy, as we will see, the states play a key role in defining support levels and qualification standards.

The states' bureaucratic structures generally mirror those of the federal government. There are departmental and nondepartmental agencies that are variously accountable to state legislatures or governors' offices. And, as with police patrol versus fire alarm differences at the federal level, the states vary widely on the amount of attention paid to implementation.

Three Policy Areas: Welfare, Education, and Health

The remainder of this chapter examines three particular areas of domestic policy concern: welfare, education, and health. These areas will bring together many of the concerns we have raised so far: historical shifts in policy agendas, changing political processes, and complex federal-state relations. In general, it will become apparent that the United States acts more cautiously than do most other democracies in domestic arenas—see for example Figure 17-2, showing just three welfare areas in historical and comparative perspective.

Figure 17-2   Enactment of National Social Programs in Ten Nations

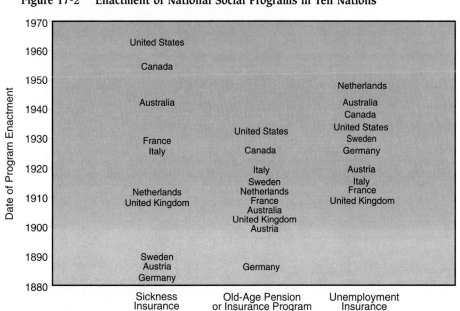

Source: D.B. Robertson and D.R. Judd, *The Development of American Public Policy* (Glenview, Ill.: Scott Foresman, 1989), p. 59.

Welfare

Welfare is a generic name that means many things to many people. It encompasses income inequality and social dependency, and it usually applies to individuals who have impaired lives and are unable to care for themselves. Welfare involves dozens of government programs administered by thousands of agencies and third-party contractors.

There are two tiers of welfare programs in the United States. The first, **Social Security,** is a federal social insurance program, administered by a centralized federal bureaucracy, providing minimum levels of income maintenance to all elderly citizens irrespective of income. It is widely supported by public opinion, and tampering with it poses significant political risks for national political figures.

The second tier includes programs targeted for the poor. These **public-assistance programs** are national only in name, for the states set both minimum requirements for eligibility and, often, benefit levels. Although the authorization of the programs might exist in federal law or through interpretations in federal court rulings, for all intents and purposes these programs rise or fall on the ability of state and local governments to fund and administer them or to delegate program delivery to third-party contractors.

To give an example of a public-assistance program, the states set the maximum income levels that determine whether a poor family will qualify for Medicaid. That means that if you live in Texas in a family of three persons, you must have an income of under $3,000 per year to qualify. In Alabama, that figure for a family of three is $1,416; in California, $8,328. These decisions rest on complex considerations of costs of living, political ideology, and competition with neighboring states. No state wants to offer so much more than its neighbors that welfare recipients will be encouraged to migrate across borders.

Politics. Welfare, like education and health, is driven by budget-balancing concerns in the federal government: It's a big money consumer. Many welfare programs are **entitlements,** with built-in growth that usually accelerates faster than the growth of the gross national product (GNP). Figure 17-3 shows entitlement growth since 1970. Entitlements

Welfare and race: With a disproportionate number of blacks in the underclass, welfare has become a code word for racial issues among some conservative white voters and politicians.

Figure 17-3   Federal Government Spending

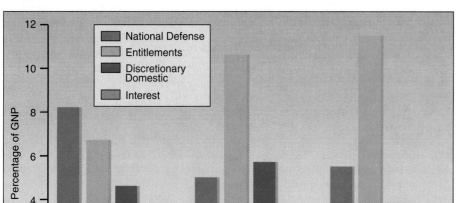

Source: Congressional Budget Office, *The Economic and Budget Outlook: Fiscal Years 1992–1996* (Washington: Government Printing Office, 1991), p. 151.

can be defined as benefits that automatically flow to certain groups, like the poor or the elderly.

Entitlement programs do not have to go through the year-to-year congressional appropriations process; instead, they are granted as a course of law. Social Security, Medicare, unemployment compensation, and other **means-tested welfare programs** (that is, availability is based on income standards) are all entitlement programs. Together, they constitute more than 75 percent of total entitlement payments.

Spending by Congress has been squeezed every year since the late 1970s by rising deficits that constrain budgets and rising entitlement costs that increase pressure to find revenue. Domestic discretionary spending has been severely cut, but the costs of mandated welfare programs are increasing.

Medicare is reputed to be the fastest-growing welfare program in the budget. It covers two parts of health care for the elderly: Part A for hospital visits is paid for out of a combination of Social Security taxes and a payroll tax taken from both employees and employers; Part B, for a part of doctor and outpatient care, is only partially funded from premiums that Social Security gets from the monthly checks of beneficiaries. Most of the cost (75 percent) is financed from the general fund from taxes paid by current workers.

Medicare does not cover long-term care, which the elderly are likely to need, and its maximum limits for benefits are not aligned with the potential catastrophic costs that can come with complex procedures and long-term illness. Congress tried to address catastrophic costs in 1988 by requiring beneficiaries to contribute to a part of the costs, but interest groups representing the elderly demanded that the law be rescinded, which it was. To paraphrase Representative Bill Gradison (R.-Ohio), ranking Republican on the Ways and Means Subcommittee on Health, "Social Security and Medicare are the third rails[5] of American politics. Touch them and you die."

[5]"Third rails" is a reference to the tracks of subway systems and other electric trains; two harmless rails serve as tracks, and an electrified third rail transmits all power.

Results. Growth in income transfers from 1960s legislation associated with the Great Society's War on Poverty has reduced the poverty rate. Income transfers refer to taxes that take income from the wealthy and divert it to the poor. This is especially true for the elderly. But changes in poverty for the non-elderly has been disappointing, especially for the working poor. There are 32 million poor people in the United States. Recent research has focused on one portion of that population: approximately 2.5 million people in 1980 called the **underclass.** They are defined as "people who live in neighborhoods where welfare dependency, female-headed families, male joblessness, and dropping out of high school are common occurrences."[6]

To break the cycle of poverty, the Urban Institute, a Washington-based think tank, has recommended several alternative economic and social policies. Suggestions range from programs to address teenage pregnancy to collecting child support and establishing and enforcing paternity and child-support laws. The report concludes that lack of education and basic skills is so glaring a deficiency as to be a root cause of poverty. Weak family structures and substantial joblessness need to be addressed. But they will require more funding and more programs constructed and applied more creatively.

Education

The Constitution makes no mention of education. Its authors felt that education was a state matter, and, indeed, most state constitutions provided for the establishment of a system of public education. In 1988, by contrast, George Bush campaigned on a pledge to be "the education president," promising to do more for education and training than any president before him. What issues led to this switch in priorities?

Politics. Debates about education cannot fail to include the question of financing. Schools are presently financed in large part by local property taxes, some 43.9 percent in 1987. The national contribution, on the other hand, has fallen from 9.8 percent of total educational outlays spent during the Carter administration (1977–81) to 6.4 percent in 1987. The Office of Management and Budget puts education and training eighth in an array of expenses of the national government, ranked behind national defense, Social Security, net interest, income security (welfare), Medicare, commerce and housing credit, and health (see Table 17-2).

States have edged up as contributors, raising their share of educational spending from 16.5 percent in the 1920s to 49.8 percent in 1987. With their increased contribution has come an increased desire to exert control over the quality and efficiency of the enterprise. But increasing control has meant that the states have become targets for a rising tide of anger over education inequality between school districts. In the 1960s this anger was channeled through the federal courts, but increasingly in the 1980s and 1990s these issues are being resolved in state courts.

The legal issue revolves around whether public financing of schools based largely on property taxes is not inherently discriminatory against poor people residing in localities that are unable to raise money for schools because of low property values. Although the Supreme Court ruled in 1973 that equal access to education is not a fundamental right guaranteed by the U.S. Constitution, the issue of spending gaps has stayed alive in the courts. During the 1970s the federal courts ordered at least twenty-five states to examine the equity of their financing systems, and in the 1980s the state courts ordered several states to overhaul the manner in which they finance education.

---

[6] Isabel V. Sawhill, "Poverty and the Underclass," in *Challenge to Leadership: Economic and Social Issues for the Next Decade,* Isabel V. Sawhill, ed. (Washington: Urban Institute, 1988), p. 229.

Table 17-2   Budget Priorities in Fiscal 1990

TEN LARGEST PROGRAM CATEGORIES	EXPENDITURES (BILLIONS OF DOLLARS)
National defense	$299.3
Social Security	248.6
Net interest	183.8
Income security	148.3
Medicare	97.7
Commerce and housing credit	67.5
Health	58.1
Education and training	37.5
Transportation	29.5
Veterans	29.1

Source: Office of Management and Budget.

Congress has traditionally been a focal point for concern for the disadvantaged in educational funding. Congress has put a lot of effort into programs directed toward remediation, job training, and early-childhood intervention and schooling, such as Head Start. The demand for a more skilled workforce in the twenty-first century, however, looms

Urban public schools have witnessed an explosion of student-owned firearms. These students stand in front of a sign warning them that they will be subject to metal detector scanning upon entering the school.

large. The average age in the workforce is rising, and the mix of workers will change dramatically. It will become older, more female, and more infused with members of disadvantaged groups like blacks and Hispanics, who will displace whites. The rivalry between Republicans and Democrats continues to stimulate both to try to gain an edge on the huge middle-class constituency that is increasingly demanding educational reform. Polls indicate that people are willing to increase funding for a reformed educational system, but are unwilling to spend one cent more for business as usual.

Results. Many states have generated higher salaries for teachers and demanded accountability of districts in how they operate. President Bush has seized on "choice" (that is, allowing parents to send their children to any district, or even to private schools at the government's expense) as a topic that will not cost the federal government any money and will encourage competitiveness among school districts. Congress is trying to counter his ability to highlight his own programs with those of their own. But so far, most of the policy results have occurred at the local and state levels, where experimentation has included more parent involvement (Chicago), some choice programs (Milwaukee), and even private management (Boston).

Health

Is there a need for a national health policy in the United States?

What does the term "health care system" really mean? What is systematic about the delivery of health services in the United States? Hospitals say they have few mechanisms to control the expensive services doctors order and patients demand. Doctors say they have no controls over hospitals. Who is in charge of the health care system, if it exists?

In 1950 Americans spent $80 per person, or $1 billion a month (4.4 percent of the GNP) on health care. In 1991 Richard Dardick, director of the U.S. Office of Management and Budget (OMB), stated that health care expenditures were 12 percent of the GNP, or $620.5 billion a year. This calculates out to be nearly $2 billion a day. By 2030 it is projected to consume 37 percent of GNP. The history of health care thus amounts to a tale of accelerating costs.

Politics. How much Americans pay for health care obscures how unfairly the health care system operates. For instance, 31 percent of its costs are paid for by private insurance companies, government at all levels picks up another 41 percent, and individuals pay approximately 26 to 28 percent of their health care bills (see Figure 17-4 on page 616). The coverage is uneven, though, as 37 million persons are uninsured, and many more are underinsured. No one is covered against catastrophic illness, and, increasingly, people who have serious diseases are finding themselves uninsurable, or insurable only at steep rates. Additionally, insurance is tied to employment for many, producing a condition of "job lock" for those who have dependents who suffer from any severe disease or suffer themselves.

The Health Care Financing Administration (HCFA) of the Department of Health and Human Services has an annual budget of $150 billion. It offers services to 59 million people—about one in five Americans. It oversees Medicare and Medicaid. Medicare, a federal program to pay for health care for the elderly, does not pay for all health costs, and it covers less than half of all persons over the age of sixty-five.

Results. Medicaid provides medical-care coverage for people living in poverty. It currently covers only 38 percent of this population. Although 25 percent of white children and 40 percent of minority children under age six in America live in families that earn less than the poverty level of income, states deny many of them Medicaid coverage because of arbitrarily set income limits. See Table 17-3 for a comparison of threshold levels for Medicaid eligibility by state, which breaks out the income ceiling needed to receive Med-

Table 17-3   Qualifying for Aid to Families with Dependent Children (AFDC)

This table shows each state's maximum allowable annual income for families with dependent children to qualify for aid. The right-hand column compares this threshold to the federal poverty level.

	AFDC FOR FAMILY OF 3	PERCENT OF POVERTY LEVEL ($10,560)		AFDC FOR FAMILY OF 3	PERCENT OF POVERTY LEVEL ($10,560)
Alabama	$ 1,416	13.4%	Nebraska	4,368	41.4
Alaska	10,152	96.1	Nevada	3,960	37.5
Arizona	3,516	33.3	New Hampshire	6,192	58.6
Arkansas	2,448	23.2	New Jersey	5,088	48.2
California	8,328	78.9	New Mexico	3,720	35.2
Colorado	5,052	47.8	New York	7,476	70.8
Connecticut	6,972	66.0	North Carolina	3,324	31.5
Delaware	3,996	37.8	North Dakota	4,812	45.6
D.C.	4,908	46.5	Ohio	4,008	38.0
Florida	3,528	33.4	Oklahoma	5,652	53.5
Georgia	4,968	47.0	Oregon	5,328	50.5
Hawaii	7,584	62.4	Pennsylvania	5,052	47.8
Idaho	3,780	35.8	Rhode Island	6,648	63.0
Illinois	4,404	41.7	South Carolina	5,280	50.0
Indiana	3,456	32.7	South Dakota	4,620	43.8
Iowa	5,112	48.4	Tennessee	4,944	46.8
Kansas	4,596	43.5	Texas	2,205	20.9
Kentucky	6,312	59.8	Utah	6,192	58.6
Louisiana	2,280	21.6	Vermont	8,148	77.2
Maine	7,824	74.1	Virginia	3,492	33.1
Maryland	4,872	46.1	Washington	6,012	56.9
Massachusetts	6,948	65.8	West Virginia	2,988	28.3
Michigan	6,900	65.3	Wisconsin	6,204	58.8
Minnesota	6,384	60.5	Wyoming	4,320	40.9
Mississippi	4,416	41.8			
Missouri	3,504	33.2			
Montana	4,440	42.0	AVG. STATE	$ 5,061	47.4%

Source: National Governor's Association (NGA), 1990.

icaid for families of three, for families of three with unusual medical needs, and for families of three that include pregnant women. In every state, families that include pregnant women are given aid more readily than the general poverty line would indicate, but otherwise families must be significantly *below* the poverty line to qualify.

Government financing for health care is very complicated. Congress finds it potentially explosive because it affects the interests of five of the most powerful organized interest groups in contemporary America: the elderly, public-sector state and local

Figure 17-4   The Nation's Health Care Dollars

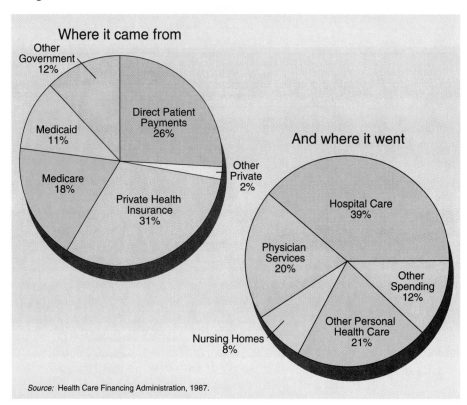

Source: Health Care Financing Administration, 1987.

officials' lobbies (that is, subnational governments who lobby the national government), hospitals, physicians, and insurers. Over and over again, policies make their way through Congress only to slip into turf battles between House and Senate, or between powerful committees such as Ways and Means, Education, or Labor in the House and Finance or Labor and Human Resources in the Senate.

Government policy makers at all levels find themselves responding more often to "hot button" health-related policy issues that have the momentum of mass movements, and not paying as much attention to the silent killers. Examples of such hot-button topics that have vocal lobbies and a flair for publicity include drunk driving, child abuse, AIDS, and abortion. Silent issues that are more difficult to address include such things as poverty, illiteracy, remedial education, and funding for preventive health and nutrition.

Toward Reform

The major issue Congress will face in the near term is that of balancing accessibility with concerns about cost. In 1990, Medicaid accounted for only 3 percent of the States' budget; now it exceeds 12 percent. How to achieve universal access is the problem. The current system is fee-for-service for physician care, and private insurance for those who can afford it. Congress has used its regulatory leverage in dispensing funds to ensure that

Mary's Place

I went to a place in Washington called Mary's Place. It is a center for Hispanic women who are pregnant and don't know much about the ways and means of caring for themselves in this country and who, because of their poverty, are indeed eligible for Medicaid. So I went through Mary's Place as though I was from San Salvador and pregnant. And the first thing I did was fill out the form. It was 33 pages long. That's not Mary's form. That is the United States Government's Medicaid application for the first time. By the time I got to page four, I was so furious that I quit. But I had written down 15 things that I would have to go home and find out from some kind of records that I kept in order to do it. This is only the first form. If you get past that and you don't get rejected, which you always do once or twice because you misspelled a word, then the next form is only three pages. But the distance between the acceptance of those two forms is two months. So now we've got four months gone by and let's say that she was three months pregnant when she came. She is now seven months pregnant. And the purpose of this is to get her into prenatal care. By the time you fill out the next form, she has delivered. And something could be done about something like that.

Former U.S. Surgeon General
C. Everett Koop

hospitals do not turn away the needy and to broaden the number of mothers and children covered by stopgap medical coverage. But assuring access to medical care for everyone is another matter.

A number of industrial countries do have national health insurance that assures access to all its citizens. In fact, the United States and South Africa are the only modern industrialized countries that do not have such universal care. Canada pays for universal access for all with a much smaller percentage of their gross national product than the United States uses of its own through private means. Public opinion polls show that the majority of Americans of all classes and races are not happy with the current system and would like one like Canada's. According to one study, 61 percent of Americans would prefer a Canadian-type of health care system.[7]

The American Medical Association has begun a concerted campaign to undermine any popular support for a movement toward a Canadian-type system. They charge that the Canadian system would be very costly and would lead to rationing of health services and abandonment of American medicine by physicians in search of higher fees and freedom from government constraints.

Theodore Marmor, a professor of public policy at Yale University's School of Organization and Management, disagrees. He compares health expenditures in the United

[7] Robert Blendon, et al., "Satisfaction with Health Systems in Ten Nations," *Health Affairs* (Summer 1990), p. 153.

Figure 17-5 **Health Expenditures in the United States and Canada as Percent of Gross National Product**

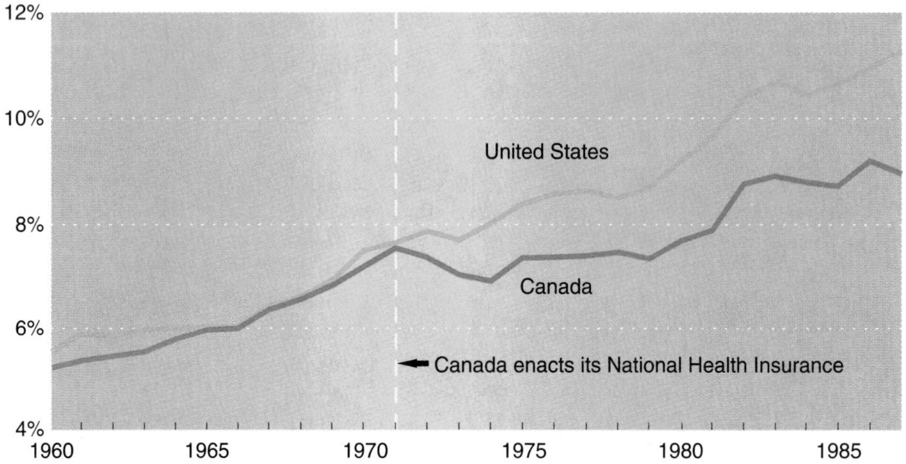

Source: Theodore R. Marmor and Jerry L. Mashaw, "Canada's Health Insurance and Ours: Real Lessons, Big Choices," *The National Voter*, April/May 1991, p. 11.

States with those in Canada (see Figure 17-5) and concludes that the Canadian system has brought within the reach of every Canadian citizen cost-effective medicine without inflationary spirals. However, not all public health care systems have produced the level of satisfaction experienced in Canada: Table 17-4 shows that nearly as many British as Americans want fundamental changes made in their health care systems.

In the near future, this debate is almost certain to loom large. In 1991, Harris Wofford used health care to beat the favored former U.S. Attorney General Dick Thornburgh in a special election for the U.S. Senate in Pennsylvania. In the 1992 presidential campaign, every Democratic candidate trumpeted support for some form of health care reform, and articles in the popular press continued to paint the high costs of health care in stark colors. Senate Majority Leader George Mitchell (D.-Me.) has publicly conjectured that a health bill may be the most important topic on Congress's agenda for 1992–93. The rest of the decade will undoubtedly see more campaigns run on the health issue.

Access to Health Care

There are many good things about the Canadian system that we could adopt—access is one and the other is their paperwork. All you have to do in Canada to get medical care is to give them a card about the size of the American Express card, which happens to be green. They stamp it and you are in and it's all over. In this country, the forms that you have to fill out are absolutely unbelievable.

Former U.S. Surgeon General C. Everett Koop

Table 17-4   The Public's Overall View of the Health Care System

	U.S.	CANADA	U.K.
On the whole the health care system works pretty well, and only minor changes are necessary to make it better.	10%	56%	27%
There are some good things in our health care system, but fundamental changes are needed to make it work better.	60	38	52
Our health care system has so much wrong with it that we need to completely rebuild it.	29	5	17
Not sure.	1	1	4

Source: Robert Blendon, Robert Leitman, Ian Morrison, and Karen Donelan, "Satisfaction with Health Systems in Ten Nations," *Health Affairs* (Summer 1990), p. 151.

Then and Now

Bernadine Healy and Benjamin Rush

Two individuals at the cutting edge of both science and health demonstrate the range of social consciousness and policy initiation on the federal level then and now. They are the new director of the National Institutes of Health (NIH), Dr. Bernadine P. Healy, and Dr. Benjamin Rush, a medical doctor renowned in Revolutionary America and signer of the Declaration of Independence.

Science magazine wrote of Healy that her name kept appearing on various short lists to head the agency. "To people who know her, that wasn't surprising. Her supporters believe she has the drive, the vision, and the political savvy to revitalize the agency and reassure the scientific community that there is an effective advocate for biomedical research inside the Bush Administration." They characterized her as "political savvy with connections," a "tough administrator who is used to getting her way."

Healy is a medical doctor, a cardiologist, who brings a mixture of high administrative and political experience. She formerly was deputy director of the White House Office of Science and Technology Policy, executive secretary of the White House Science Council's Panel on Health and Universities, and vice chair of the President's Council of Advisers on Science and Technology.

One of her first initiatives was a women's health-grant program. The new program, costing $500 million over 10 years, will emphasize a "Healthy Woman" series of research concentrating on problems of cancer, cardiovascular disease, and osteoporosis, known to shorten the life and vitality of women. This is a major breakthrough for elevating women's health concerns to national stature from its place on the back burner of normal science.

Benjamin Rush

A memoir of the American Philosophical Society on Benjamin Rush captures his qualities as a leader of science and medicine while attending to the problems of the nation in Revolutionary America. He was a friend of Thomas Jefferson's and John Adam's and a signer of the Declaration of Independence. The introduction to the memoir begins in part:

Benjamin Rush devoted his life to the quest for freedom and health—ultimately, for the growth of man's self-understanding. The search for freedom led him to oppose monarchy and to demand a republican form of government; he was also an early supporter of the anti-slavery movement. Rush actively opposed the tyranny and misery of crime, alcoholism, poverty, and ignorance. Much of his practice was among the poor; he participated in the establishment of the first public dispensary in the United States. He battled against capital punishment and sought prison reform. . . . Believing strongly in the need for education, he helped found Dickinson College, favored education for women, and propagandized for a projected series of colleges pyramiding to a national university. With a vigorous optimism characteristic of his time, Benjamin Rush worked, hoped, and prayed throughout his life for the improvement of mankind.

Bernadine Healy

Summary

Although the Framers did not expect government to take on a large number of issues aside from foreign policy, in practice the domestic policy agenda has steadily expanded to include many issues, including health, education, and welfare, among others. This expansion has occurred steadily, but two eras stand out for particularly large jumps in domestic policy making: the 1930s and the 1960s. In the former period, the economic crisis of the Depression provoked a vast expansion of social and economic policies. In the 1960s, the turbulence of the civil rights movement led to another leap in social policy.

Public policy starts with ideas that must reach the public agenda and be considered suitable for policy intervention. Once that recognition has been achieved, policy entrepreneurs try to build coalitions of support that will succeed in enacting the new laws. Once passed as legislation, policy decisions must be implemented successfully in order to have their full effect. Full implementation of the Clean Air Act, for example, has remained a distant dream, partly due to the stringency of its provisions and partly due to intentional slowdowns by the executive branch.

Three issues on the current American agenda—welfare, education, and health—have grown in importance in recent years, either through demographic causes (an aging population), worsening conditions (education), or spiraling costs. All three are certain to see changing governmental responses in the foreseeable future.

Key Terms

economic watchdog model

safety net

agenda setting

policy entrepreneurs

policy laboratory

coalitions

departmental agencies

nondepartmental agencies

quasi-legislative powers

quasi-judicial powers

police patrol oversight

fire alarm oversight

welfare

Social Security

public-assistance programs

entitlements

means-tested welfare programs

Medicare

underclass

Medicaid

Suggested Readings

Davis, Karen, Gerard Anderson, Diane Rowland, and Earl Steinberg. *Health Cost Care Containment.* Baltimore: Johns Hopkins University Press, 1990.

Derthick, Martha. *Policymaking for Social Security.* Washington: The Brookings Institution, 1979.

Finkel, Madelon Lubin, and Hirsch S. Ruchlin. *The Health Care Benefits of Retirees.* Baltimore: Johns Hopkins University Press, 1991.

Ford Foundation, *The Common Good: Social Welfare and the American Future.* New York: The Ford Foundation, May, 1984.

Kingdon, John. *Agendas, Alternatives, and Public Policies.* Glenview, Ill.: Scott, Foresman, 1984.

Lubove, Roy. *The Struggle for Social Security, 1900–1935.* Cambridge, Mass.: Harvard University Press, 1968.

Patterson, James T. *America's Struggle Against Poverty, 1900–1980.* Cambridge, Mass.: Harvard University Press, 1981.

Peterson, Paul E. *Politics of School Reform 1870–1940.* Chicago: University of Chicago Press, 1985.

Radin, Beryl A., and Willis D. Hawley. *The Politics of Federal Reorganization: Creating the U.S. Department of Education.* New York: Pergamon, 1988.

Robertson, David B., and Dennis R. Judd. *The Development of American Public Policy: The Structure of Policy Restraint.* Glenview, Ill.: Scott, Foresman, 1989.

Sawhill, Isabel V., ed. *Challenge to Leadership: Economic and Social Issues for the Next Decade.* Washington: Urban Institute, 1988.

Starr, Paul. *The Social Transformation of American Medicine.* New York: Basic Books, 1982.

Stevens, Rosemary. *In Sickness and in Wealth: American Hospitals in the Twentieth Century.* New York: Basic Books, 1989.

ccurate and

comprehensive knowledge of foreign

politics; a steady and systematic

adherence to the same views; a nice

and uniform sensibility to national

character; decision, *secrecy*, and

despatch, are incompatible with the

genius of a body so variable and

numerous.

Alexander Hamilton

FEDERALIST NO. 75

Hamilton argued that the ratification of treaties should be confined to the Senate and not to the "variable and numerous" House. But his argument recently has been taken up by the executive branch to justify excluding all of Congress from the formulation and conduct of foreign policy.

CHAPTER 18

Foreign and Military Policy

623

Although foreign policy and military policy are major concerns of the American republic today, the Framers of the Constitution did not expect to have much of either. The notion that a president would devote most of his energy to the internal affairs of Panama, Israel, Iraq, and Yugoslavia, or regularly travel abroad, or even more frequently converse with foreign heads of states, would have been almost incomprehensible in 1787.

The Origins of U.S. Foreign and Military Policy

The Framers generally agreed that the republic's foreign policy was important but limited—to keep America out of foreign countries' affairs and to keep foreign countries out of our affairs. As if to symbolize its difference from European power politics, what Europeans called a "Foreign Minister," Americans called a **Secretary of State.** For over one hundred years Americans avoided sending ambassadors abroad. **Ambassadors** are the personal representative of one head of a state to another, and because almost all heads of states were monarchs, the democratic Americans wished to avoid too close a connection with royalty. Even though Benjamin Franklin and Thomas Jefferson were among our earlier representatives abroad, they were never more than **ministers.** Not until 1893 did a president send the first ambassador abroad (to Britain). To understand the origins of American foreign policy, we must examine both the pre-constitutional era and the Constitution itself.

The Pre-Constitutional Era

In its early days, the United States had only a rudimentary military establishment. At the close of the Revolutionary War, the Continental Congress ordered the discharge of all but eighty men. This desire for a limited army was to continue; when the first Congress of the new United States eventually met, it continued the standing army authorized by the Confederation, but only at a maximum strength of 840.

At the Constitutional Convention, Elbridge Gerry wanted to write into the Constitution a provision limiting the size of an army to 2,000 or 3,000 regular soldiers. Gerry's proposal prompted George Washington to suggest, in a stage whisper, an amendment to the Constitution limiting foreign armies that might attack the United States to the same size. Nevertheless, Gerry's proposal was in keeping with American sentiment.

The Constitution

The institutional framework for foreign and defense policy is laid out in the Constitution. But in contrast to some provisions, little is spelled out in detail. The provisions governing the important question of going to war are so brief that they can be quoted here:

> *Congress shall have power . . .*
> *to declare war . . .*
> *to raise and support armies . . .*
> *to provide and maintain a navy . . . .*
>
> *The President shall be commander-in-chief of the army and navy . . . .*

Scholars agree that the Constitution intended a division of responsibility between Congress and the president. Congress alone was to *provide funds for* the army and navy—the first step toward preparation for war. Congress alone was to have the power to *initiate* war, by declaring it. Then, once the nation was at war, responsibility would shift to the president to *direct* war in his capacity as **commander-in-chief.** The president would

The Original Meaning of Commander-in-Chief

In 1792 farmers in western Pennsylvania refused to pay the new federal excise tax on whiskey. Radical elements among them terrorized the population, challenging the authority of the federal government. Militias from four states were called in to suppress the rebellion. Although strictly speaking an internal matter and not foreign policy, it was a chance for the president to act as commander-in-chief. George Washington put on his old uniform but, given his age (sixty), traveled to western Pennsylvania by coach instead of on horseback.

Washington's presence served two purposes. It emphasized that the militias were not merely forces from one region of the country acting against another but were acting as a federal army. And Washington's trustworthy reputation reassured the population that the militias would respect the lives and property of civilians. Washington himself tried to avoid much of the pomp that went with his position, often driving by back roads to steer clear of the perpetually saluting troops.

In 1977, former Governor Ronald Reagan of California commented on the charges that former President Nixon had abused his authority in the Watergate scandal. He said, "When the Commander-in-Chief of a nation finds it necessary to order employees of the government or agencies of the government to do things that would technically break the law, he has to be able to declare it legal for them to do that." Reagan's words betray an interpretation of the term "commander-in-chief" far beyond what the Framers of the Constitution had in mind or what Washington put into practice in 1792.

Source: Ronnie Dugger, *On Reagan: The Man and His Presidency* (New York: McGraw-Hill, 1983), p. 245.

also *negotiate* treaties, to end wars, but the treaties would be valid only if two-thirds of the Senate were to *grant approval.* Thus Congress was seen as having a crucial role at the beginning and end, if not in the middle, of any war.

The Early History of Foreign and Military Policy

George Washington, in his Farewell Address at the end of his presidency in 1796, warned against foreign entanglements, suggesting that it be "our true policy to steer clear of permanent alliances with any portion of the foreign world." The pre-constitutional desire for a limited foreign and defense policy therefore continued. In keeping with this policy, the standing army remained small, with most of America's military strength decentralized in the form of state **militias.** Theoretically, the Militia Act of 1792 created a universal obligation of able-bodied males to participate in the militia, but the young republic found it difficult to raise even the modest force necessary to put down rebels refusing to pay the taxes in western Pennsylvania during the Whiskey Rebellion.

This democratic distrust of armies conflicted with another tendency, the country's desire to push out its frontiers into territory technically owned by the British, French, or Spanish and inhabited mostly by a native population. Often the native population of the frontiers found both diplomatic and material support from European powers for resistance to American expansion, and frontier raids and armed conflict were common. Nevertheless, Congress was reluctant to authorize a large military establishment, and most Americans were reluctant to participate in one. They had had enough of taxes under the British. They had fought for independence from army control. Now they wanted to get on with the business of making a living. Able-bodied men had plenty of opportunity in America and, except for those living on the frontier, did not want to be troubled with military obligation.

Early Precedent: The Jay Treaty

One of the first important treaties for the early United States was the one regularizing relations with its former imperialist master and recent enemy in war, Great Britain. The treaty was generally referred to as the **Jay Treaty** after its chief negotiator, John Jay. Bitterness in the aftermath of the Revolutionary War led some members of Congress to oppose the treaty. But these diehards were in the House, not the Senate, and according to the Constitution only the Senate had the power to approve treaties.

Members of the House tried another tack to undermine the treaty. Because the House would have to appropriate funds to carry it out, members asked President Washington to submit all papers relating to the treaty. Washington refused on the constitutional grounds that the Senate alone had the power to approve treaties and on the practical grounds that successful diplomacy depended on secrecy, as Hamilton had argued (see the quotation that opens this chapter). By approving the funds despite Washington's refusal to submit papers, the House gave in, helping to establish the precedent of executive privilege—the right of the president to withhold from Congress information about the inner workings of the executive branch. The doctrine would have a long history, later to be invoked by Richard Nixon to avoid inquiry on Watergate and Ronald Reagan to avoid inquiry on secret aid to Iran.

The Monroe Doctrine

Washington had remarked in his Farewell Address that "time and habit are at least as necessary to fix the true character of governments as of other human institutions," yet in many important ways the character of the American government in regard to foreign and military policy was fixed by the time Washington left office. This was especially true by the time of the **Monroe Doctrine.** Throughout the nineteenth century, the United States played only a small role in world affairs.

Europeans were held at arm's length by the Monroe Doctrine, the name given to a statement made by President James Monroe in 1823. Monroe declared that it would be dangerous to American peace and safety for European states to attempt to extend "their system" to the Western hemisphere. In return, the United States would avoid taking part in European quarrels.

Americans have often spoken of the Monroe Doctrine as if it were a form of divine revelation. Politicians "accuse" other countries of "violating" the Monroe Doctrine. President Ronald Reagan's first Secretary of Defense, Caspar Weinberger, stated that the United States would give aid to support guerrillas seeking to overthrow the government

People of the Past

George Washington

George Washington's heritage is a part of our daily lives. His name is that of the nation's capital and its forty-second state, and his portrait appears on the nation's basic unit of currency, the dollar bill. But in many ways his most significant legacy was his Farewell Address.

It was originally printed in a newspaper, not delivered, and it reflected the ideas of Alexander Hamilton, who gave Washington editorial assistance. The key passage stated that it should be "our true policy to steer clear of permanent alliances with any portion of the foreign world." In the popular mind this sentiment was often expressed in words actually spoken by Thomas Jefferson: no "entangling alliances."

Advances in technology, particularly steam-powered ships and transoceanic cables, have seriously reduced "the foreign world," but generations of Americans schooled in Washington's remarks continue to find isolation "our true policy." Failure to participate in world affairs in the early twentieth century deprived the world of a possible moderating influence and may have made World War I more likely. Failure to join the League of Nations condemned to failure that organization's attempt to prevent future wars.

Even in the late 1930s, when the radio and the airplane had all but erased the distinction between "the foreign world" and the United States, enough members of Congress continued to cling to Washington's doctrine and prevented President Franklin D. Roosevelt from taking precautionary steps that could have averted the tragedy of World War II. It is hard to imagine that George Washington would have been so narrow-minded as to cling to advice from so distant an age.

---

of Afghanistan but would not tolerate Soviet arms supplies to guerrillas seeking to overthrow the government of El Salvador because "such aid would violate the Monroe Doctrine."[1] In fact, the Monroe Doctrine was no more than a policy preference, respected only because most European countries had no interest in expanding into the Western hemisphere and because the British navy acted as a deterrent to the few who might.

The Nineteenth Century

Despite its view of itself as uninvolved in world affairs, the nineteenth-century American republic was very active. But its foreign policy was concerned mainly with events in the Western hemisphere or with trade policy, and military activity was mainly within or on the borders of the United States—hostile relations with Canada during and following the War of 1812, war with Mexico in 1846, war with the seceding Confederate States between 1861 and 1865, and wars in the West with Native American nations (Sioux, Comanche, Apache) that resisted expansion into their territory.

The result of these wars was a country that stretched from one ocean to another. In particular, the defeat of Mexico brought California under American control. American expansion was not seen as foreign policy or military conquest but as **manifest destiny,** a divinely mandated obligation to "overspread the continent allotted by Providence for the free development of our yearly multiplying millions."[2]

---

[1] Caspar Weinberger, quoted in *The New York Times,* March 10, 1981, p. A-3.
[2] John L. O'Sullivan, writing in 1845, cited by Julius W. Pratt, "The Ideology of American Expansion," in *Essays in Honor of William E. Dodd,* ed. Avery Craven (Chicago: University of Chicago Press, 1935).

Even as the nineteenth century came to an end, however, direct participation in world events was seen as exceptional. One important exception was an international war that the United States fought with Spain in 1898, largely to win Cuba its freedom from Spanish rule. In the Pacific, for three years the United States continued fighting the inhabitants of Spain's colony in the Philippines, who had understandably although mistakenly thought that the defeat of Spain would mean their total independence and not mere transferral to the rule of the United States. This American involvement in the domestic affairs of the Philippines would later be seen by some as the beginning of a troubling theme in American foreign policy. Still, in 1898, foreign adventures remained exceptional.

World War I

When World War I broke out in Europe in 1914, many Americans were happy to stay neutral. In the words of one newspaper, "We never appreciated so keenly as now the foresight of our fathers in emigrating from Europe."[3] For a nation of immigrants, it was also politically expedient to stay out of the war, as choosing sides would inevitably anger one group or another. Many Americans of British descent favored the British, many of German descent favored the Germans, and many Irish favored any side that did not include the British.

President Woodrow Wilson ran for a second term in 1916 on the slogan "He kept us out of war," yet world events soon forced him to enter the conflict. Particularly disturbing was the German policy of "unrestricted submarine warfare," which meant that American ships carrying cargo to Britain would be sunk even though America had declared itself neutral.

Wilson tried to put the best face on his policies, talking of a "war to end all wars." He put great faith in an international organization that would be formed after the war to keep the peace. He was instrumental in writing the document that set up the **League of Nations**—the first global organization of states dedicated to preserving peace—and incorporating it into the **Versailles Peace Treaty** ending World War I. Wilson's central role was symbolized by the provision which stated that the initial meeting of the League would be convened by the president of the United States.

But Wilson had been so absorbed in foreign policy that he had neglected to build support at home. He was a Democratic president facing a Senate controlled by Republicans, and he had not courted them by such devices as including a senator among the American delegates to the Versailles Peace Conference. Many senators found membership in the new world body incompatible with the principles of George Washington's Farewell Address that they had been taught in school. Even those not totally opposed added amendments or "reservations" to the treaty, reserving to Congress the power to ratify certain League actions in regard to territory and trade, as well as declaring that the subject of the Monroe Doctrine was entirely outside the jurisdiction of the League.

When Wilson realized that the treaty was in trouble, he tried to win public opinion at home by a nationwide tour of speech making, but his efforts came too late. The Senate refused to give the necessary two-thirds vote to approve the ratification of the covenant. The United States did not participate in the new world body but retreated instead into **isolationism.**

The experience with the Versailles Treaty was an impressive display of the Senate's constitutional authority to approve or disapprove of treaties. In fact, such outright rejections are rare, as Figure 18-1 shows. But because this power has been used effectively, the threat to disapprove is a real one and is taken into account by presidents negotiating treaties.

[3]Wabash (Indiana) *Plain Dealer,* August 1914.

President Wilson (right) with Lloyd George and Clemenceau at Versailles.

Although Congress in this instance prevented presidential participation in foreign affairs, it itself was responsible for an action with major international consequences. In 1930, in order to protect American producers from falling prices, Congress passed a tariff, called the Smoot–Hawley Tariff after its sponsors. A tariff is a tax on imported goods, and Smoot–Hawley raised the average tariff to prohibitively high levels. Other countries responded by raising their tariffs as well. As might be expected, world trade began to contract until by 1932 it was only at about one-third its former level.

Because this contraction coincided with the Great Depression, the Smoot–Hawley Tariff has been linked in the public mind ever since with economic hardship. Congress

Figure 18-1   Fate of Treaties Submitted to the Senate, 1788–1988

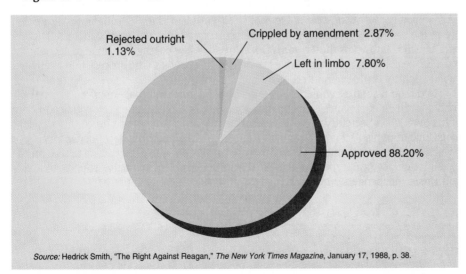

Rejected outright 1.13%

Crippled by amendment 2.87%

Left in limbo 7.80%

Approved 88.20%

Source: Hedrick Smith, "The Right Against Reagan," *The New York Times Magazine*, January 17, 1988, p. 38.

itself seemed to accept this judgment when, in 1962, it granted the president extensive authority under the Trade Expansion Act to negotiate tariff reductions, without need for congressional approval.

The Great Shift

In part because of American failure to play a responsible role in world affairs, the world found itself at war again in 1939. American isolationists, mostly Republicans, hampered the efforts of Democratic President Franklin D. Roosevelt to provide even limited assistance to those countries fighting Adolf Hitler and Benito Mussolini. The resistance of the isolationists finally crumbled when the Japanese attacked American territory in Hawaii in 1941.

But even World War II was seen as a temporary distraction from the main business of America, which, as political leaders like to repeat, was business. Even before World War II had ended, politicians competed in promising to "bring the boys home" as quickly as possible. The U.S. Army's size dropped from more than 8 million at the close of World War II in 1945 to under 1 million by 1947. Army Chief of Staff George Marshall said he did not have enough reserves to protect an airfield in Alaska.

The Origins of the Cold War

It was only when the British approached the United States in 1947 that we stepped permanently onto the world stage. The British had maintained a **sphere of influence** (an area dominated although not directly controlled) in the eastern Mediterranean, particularly Greece and Turkey, but because they had been weakened financially by the war, they did not think they could continue. At this point the British still hoped for a global role and, although they wanted American involvement, still saw the Americans as junior partners. They asked the United States to assume support for countries in the Mediterranean. The alternative was seen by both British and American leaders as having these countries slip into a Russian sphere of influence. In a flurry of activity, the State Department in a period of fifteen weeks devised a set of policies that turned the United States from isolationism to **globalism.**

The Republican chair of the Senate Foreign Relations Committee, Arthur Vandenberg of Michigan, was sympathetic to this policy shift but remembered how Republicans— Vandenberg himself among them—had resisted President Roosevelt's attempts to end isolationism before World War II. He counseled President Harry S Truman to "scare hell out of the country." Truman did, in a 1947 speech to both houses of Congress that laid out the policy known as the **Truman Doctrine.** In a key passage, Truman stated that "it must be the policy of the United States to support free peoples who are resisting attempted subjugation by armed minorities or by outside pressures."[4]

More than a century earlier John Quincy Adams had said that America "is the well-wisher to the freedom and independence of all. She is the champion and vindicator only of her own."[5] As Secretary of State under James Monroe, Adams had urged the president to exclude from his "Monroe Doctrine" address any reference to independence for Greece (which had been proclaimed a year earlier) because even verbal support might be considered interference in European affairs. Truman's speech pledging active support to maintain Greek independence marked a radical departure from such precedent.

---

[4] Henry Steel Commager, *Documents of American History,* 7th ed. (New York: Appleton-Century-Crofts, 1963), p. 525.

[5] Address given on July 4, 1821, cited in Walter LaFeber, ed., *John Quincy Adams and American Continental Empire* (Chicago: University of Chicago Press, 1965), pp. 42–46.

Isolationism: Senator Nye and Pearl Harbor

Many Americans continued to cling to the principles of Washington's Farewell Address, even though modern military technology had made the world of the twentieth century very different from Washington's days. They formed the America First Committee and tried to rally public opposition to President Franklin D. Roosevelt's policy of at least preparing to meet threats from Germany and Japan.

On December 7, 1941, a leading isolationist, Senator Gerald P. Nye (R.-N.D.), was about to address an America First rally in Pittsburgh. A few minutes before the rally began, a reporter told Nye that the White House had announced a Japanese attack on Hawaii and the Philippines. (At that moment, in fact, Japanese planes were still attacking Pearl Harbor.)

Nye suspected a hoax or at least an exaggeration; he told the reporters he would need more reliable information and rose to address the meeting. When he had finished, a reporter handed him a note telling him that while he was speaking the Japanese government had declared war on the United States.

Source: Wayne S. Cole, *Senator Gerald P. Nye and American Foreign Relations* (Minneapolis: University of Minnesota Press, 1962), pp. 198–99.

The speech was important in other ways as well. First, it created an ideological consensus, one that cut across all parties, justifying participation in world events—the consensus of **anti-communism.** Second, it created the notion of **national security** as something that Americans needed to worry about even when the world was at peace and even when no apparent military threats were directed against the United States. Third, it created the belief that public support for foreign and military policy required "scaring hell" out of the American people. President Truman's successors have tried to make

President Truman's 1947 Truman Doctrine speech, outlining the United States' new commitment to an international leadership role opposing hegemonic states, set the stage for a forty-year U.S. policy of containing communism.

external dangers as frightening as possible—the Soviets can attack us with long-range rockets (John F. Kennedy on "the missile gap"), a communist victory in Vietnam would endanger the Hawaiian islands (Lyndon B. Johnson on Vietnam), the Russian military buildup has created a "window of vulnerability" (Ronald Reagan on military spending), and, even as late as 1990, nothing that has happened in the Soviet Union should "lull us into a sense of complacency" (George Bush).

Truman's innovative words were followed by innovative actions. United States military forces were stationed permanently overseas for the first time. American naval forces' being stationed during World War II in the Mediterranean, which the United States had planned to terminate, now became a permanent presence called the Sixth Fleet. In 1948, for the first time since World War II, long-range American bombers were sent to Britain. Conscription of young men into the military service, something Americans had previously been subject to only in wartime, was now continued into peacetime—indeed, up until the creation of the all-volunteer army in 1971. And the United States for the first time entered into military alliances in peacetime.

The National Security Act

In 1947, Congress supported this new consensus with legislation appropriately named the **National Security Act.** By it Congress consolidated the army, the navy, and the new air force into one department, with the reassuring name "Department of Defense." (Previously the Cabinet office that prepared to fight wars had been named the "War Department." Henceforward, military expenditure, no matter how extravagant or foolish, would always be known as "defense.") The legislation also set up the **Central Intelligence Agency** (CIA) to collect and analyze the information deemed necessary to meet national security threats. And the legislation set up the **National Security Council,** a high-level body where State and Defense, diplomacy and military, could meet. These instruments of policy were now available to a president who already enjoyed a position of great authority in dealing with foreign and military affairs.

The Marshall Plan and NATO

President Truman through much of his time in office was an unpopular president. Initially he had not been elected to the office but had inherited it upon the death of Roosevelt. His support in the polls, high at first, dwindled. Yet he accomplished remarkable things in foreign policy. He proposed and got Congress to approve the European Recovery Program, often called the **Marshall Plan** after his Secretary of State George C. Marshall. The success of the Marshall Plan is often celebrated, particularly in calls for imitation, as in "a new Marshall Plan for the Caribbean" or "a new Marshall Plan for cities." But those who would imitate it often overlook its magnitude—it was a very expensive program. In its first year, 1948–49, the European Recovery Program gave the Europeans more than $6 billion. At that time, that amounted to 10 percent of the entire federal budget (and 2.8 percent of the gross national product). A program of equal magnitude forty years later would have cost the United States about $100 billion. Yet in 1948 Truman won support for his proposal.

Another indication of Truman's authority in foreign affairs is that the United States for the first time disregarded George Washington's advice and joined a military alliance in peacetime. The North Atlantic Treaty was signed in 1949, and the **North Atlantic Treaty Organization** (NATO) was set up the following year. Even though we were not at war and not directly threatened by any hostile state, we moved hundreds of thousands of troops to Europe (more, in fact, than we moved to Asia during the same years to fight the Korean War).

Two crises—one in Europe, the other in Asia—quickly set the stage for American policy in the postwar era. In 1948 the Soviet Union blockaded access by highway, rail,

In 1948, American and British planes were again over Berlin, this time airlifting supplies to thwart the Soviet blockade of that city.

and waterway to the Western sectors of the divided city of Berlin. Even though the Germans had recently been our enemies, Truman decided to supply the population by air. The Chief of Staff of the Air Force was reluctant to support the airlift, because so much of the United States' air transport capacity would be tied up in one vulnerable spot. The Secretary of the Army feared a policy that would provoke the Soviets into a military reaction for which the United States was not prepared. Yet despite these doubts from his advisers, even in the middle of an election year, Truman acted decisively and persisted until the Soviets lifted the blockade a year later.

Two years after winning the 1948 election, Truman was confronted with a crisis in Asia. After World War II, Korea had been partitioned into two zones, the one in the North occupied by Soviet troops, the one in the South by Americans. Disagreements between the United States and the Soviet Union prevented reunification and led to the creation of separate states instead. Then in 1950 North Korea invaded South Korea. The United States was taken by surprise, but after brief consideration Truman decided to commit U.S. forces to help South Korea resist. Even American troops did not stop the North Koreans in the first weeks, but the tide of the war was reversed by a dramatic amphibious landing staged by the American commander General Douglas MacArthur at the port city of Inchon. The tide of war reversed again when Chinese troops intervened in force in November 1950. MacArthur was responsible for the success at Inchon but was also responsible for the failure to anticipate the Chinese intervention and to counter it. MacArthur instead grumbled about restrictions on his ability to make war, hinting broadly in public that war against China, perhaps with nuclear weapons, was necessary. Despite the general's popularity as a World War II celebrity and Truman's own low standing in the polls, the president did not hesitate to release MacArthur from command.

The Cold War Era

In a short period of time, America had moved from isolationism to globalism. The actual conflict of World War II and the Cold War's possibility of conflict created a policy-making process that persisted for decades. This policy-making process, as well as the policy it produced, differed sharply from what America had known in the past. Although created in response to the sense of military threat connected with the rise of Hitler, the Japanese attack on Pearl Harbor, and the postwar policies of the Soviet leader Joseph Stalin, the institutions referred to in the foregoing section persisted because they could be used to deal with a wide variety of other issues as well. The post–World War II National Security Council, although set up to institutionalize the system by which the U.S. government conducted the war, was employed in later years to coordinate such issues as dealing with the fall from power of the Shah of Iran or negotiating a new Canal Treaty with Panama. The next section will analyze how the making of foreign policy has developed since the presidency of Harry Truman.

The Machinery of Modern Foreign Policy Making: The President

Truman was not unique in his ability to win support for his foreign and military policies. His successors have shown similar results so often that we must conclude that success flows not from the person in office but the office itself. We must conclude that the American political system bestows great power on the president in the area of relations with foreign countries and the policy areas of foreign relations and defense.

The Information Gap

One reason is that the president has almost complete control of a vital resource: information. This situation is quite unlike that of domestic politics, where many people, including those in the Congress, the media, and interest groups often have important information that bears on policy decisions. Such information is a source of power. Consider the case of speed limits. A president might decide, in the interest of reducing the need for imported oil, to press Congress to pass a reduction of the speed limit from sixty-five miles per hour to fifty-five. What the president may not know, but what groups representing truckers will know, is that there will be intense opposition to such a move, affecting as it does the livelihood of truckers. Someone well informed on the issue might anticipate truck convoys, linked by citizens' band radios, violating the lower speed limit en masse. This is in fact what happened in the 1970s.

But when dealing with foreign affairs, the president has exclusive sources of information—diplomats working for the State Department, military attachés working for the Defense Department, agents controlled by the CIA, and technical devices such as satellites controlled by the National Security Agency (that part of the Department of Defense in charge of electronic intelligence gathering). Private citizens and interest groups cannot balance the president's information with private sources of their own on issues such as the number of Soviet missiles in Cuba or the extent of Iraq's nuclear weapons program. Even the one source of information available to the president's critics, the news media, is dominated by him.

In large part what the media choose to call news (headline stories in newspapers or lead items on network news programs) is determined by the president. What the president says, or does not say, is news. News reports of major events on the other side of the globe—the dismantling of the Berlin Wall, the release of Nelson Mandela from prison—are often accompanied by the president's reaction. A measure of the importance that the news media give to the president is the more than 1,000 reporters accredited to the White House. The president, alone among persons in the United States, is able to ask major networks to relinquish prime time for major speeches or announcements and, usually, to get it.

Then and Now

Communication Technology and Foreign Policy

Traditionally the slowness of communications and the vast oceans separating the United States from the rest of the world permitted a slow and orderly reaction to world events. The war between the British and the United States that began in 1812 illustrates how slowly news traveled.

A traditional American banjo tune known as "The 8th of January" celebrates the date of the Battle of New Orleans, when General Andrew Jackson held off the British, suffering 350 casualties to the British's 2,450. But officially the War of 1812 had already been ended by a treaty signed in Belgium on December 24, 1814. The British ratified the treaty and then Americans and Britons boarded a ship in London on January 2, 1815, to bring the treaty and the British ratification to America. Because of bad weather, the ship did not arrive in New York until February 11. News did not reach the nation's capital until February 15.

By contrast, when American aircraft and cruise missiles began their opening strike against Iraq on January 17, 1991, the event was covered live on American television. Several cable network reporters in a hotel room were able to broadcast "the battle of Baghdad" as it happened. Later, television recorded Iraqi Scud mis-

CNN coverage of the 1991 Gulf War.

siles' landing in Israel, a practice criticized as providing important targeting information to the Iraqis.

A moment's reflection suggests that institutions and practices suitable for 1815 are less suitable for the 1990s.

The president's authority is enhanced by the aura of secret information available to him: diplomatic cables, CIA reports, NSA intercepts. Sometimes, to win points in debates against rivals, the president will declassify secret information. Virtually any other citizen could be prosecuted for revealing classified material, but the president may do so freely. In 1962 the presence of Soviet missiles in Cuba was a tightly held secret until President Kennedy chose to reveal it in a nationwide broadcast. In the 1980 election campaign, President Jimmy Carter, under attack from Republican opponents for neglecting America's defenses, authorized his Secretary of Defense to reveal that the United States had been developing a plane that would be invisible to radar, the Stealth bomber.

Presidential Use of the Media

Because of the deference afforded the president by the media, he has the ability to set the tone of national debate. When the Soviets launched the world's first artificial Earth satellite in 1957, President Dwight D. Eisenhower chose not to react with alarm. His first public reaction to *Sputnik* was at a press conference a full five days later, when he said, "As far as the satellite itself is concerned, that does not raise my apprehensions, not one

The 1957 Soviet *Sputnik* satellite was the first artificial object placed into orbit. In the midst of the Cold War, the *Sputnik* launch created a furor in America over the possibility of "losing the war in space."

iota. I see nothing at this moment, at this stage of development, that is significant in that development as far as security is concerned."[6] His intention was to calm public fears, and to a large measure he succeeded.

Yet Eisenhower could as easily have created a mood of national hysteria. One can easily imagine the public reaction if, instead of serene silence, Eisenhower had requested radio and television time just a few hours after *Sputnik* was launched and, in solemn tones, had begun, "My fellow Americans, I am speaking to you from the bomb shelter of the White House . . ." Had he then gone on to ask for a billion-dollar program of bomb shelters he most likely would have been granted it from a willing Congress.

In 1952, even before television stations began broadcasting a regular nightly news program, Supreme Court Justice Robert Jackson had written of the president, "In drama, magnitude and finality his decisions so far overshadow any others that almost alone he fills the public eye and ear."[7] Since that time, the already powerful image of the president has been amplified by the medium of television. Television deals in images, and the image of the president personifies the government more simply than the image of Congress. Congress, after all, consists of two houses, each with two parties and therefore four sets of leaders, and, ultimately, 535 separate individuals. The camera finds it easier to focus on the single individual occupying the White House. For the television reporter, it is against the backdrop of the White House where the president works—not the Capitol, where the Congress works—that major foreign and defense policy announcements are made. The White House has even thoughtfully placed concrete pads to support TV cameras at the best sites, so reporters can deliver their news items with the White House behind them. Congress has less ability to function as a television icon, and its authority over foreign affairs has faded in the public mind.

[6] Stephen Ambrose, *Eisenhower the President* (New York: Simon and Schuster, 1984), pp. 429–30.
[7] *Youngstown Sheet and Tube* v. *Sawyer* 343 US 579 S. Ct. 879.

Presidential Popularity

Every month, the Gallup organization asks a representative sample of Americans the same question: "Do you approve or disapprove of how [the incumbent] is handling his job as president?" Because this same question has been asked so regularly, it provides a yardstick to measure the popularity of presidents over time.

Consider these typical cases:

- At the beginning of July 1958, President Eisenhower's approval rating was 52 percent. In the middle of July, Eisenhower ordered 14,000 American troops into Lebanon to help end a civil war. In August 1958, Eisenhower's popularity was up 6 points, to 58 percent.
- At the beginning of October 1962, President Kennedy's approval rating was 61 percent. There followed, for a period of weeks, a tense confrontation with the Soviet Union over the issue of nuclear-armed missiles in Cuba. In December 1962, President Kennedy's popularity was up 11 points, to 72 percent.

On the basis of these and similar cases, we can conclude that a president's popularity goes up during foreign policy crises.

But consider also the following.

At the beginning of March 1961, President Kennedy's approval rating was 73 percent. (You will note that this is higher than his rating even after the resolution of the Cuban Missile Crisis, but it is also earlier in his term of office, when presidents traditionally fare better in the polls.) In the middle of April, Cuban opponents of the regime of Fidel Castro, trained and armed by the United States, attempted a landing in Cuba at the Bay of Pigs. They were ignominiously defeated. Yet in April 1961, Kennedy's approval rating was up 10 points, to 83 percent.

On the basis of this and similar cases, we expand our generalization to conclude that a president's popularity goes up during foreign policy crises, *even if the policy is a failure.*

If you are of a skeptical turn of mind, you might think that more than foreign policy is involved. Perhaps, you could hypothesize, it is merely the president's acting decisively that increased his popularity. So consider these cases:

- In July 1957, President Eisenhower's approval rating was 63 percent. When an attempt to integrate Central High School in Little Rock, Arkansas, met with resistance, Eisenhower put units of the National Guard under federal control to protect the pupils attempting to attend the school. In October 1957, Eisenhower's approval rating had fallen 6 points, to 57 percent.
- In June 1967, President Johnson's approval rating was 52 percent. Then riots broke out in depressed central areas in major American cities, most notably Detroit. Johnson ordered troops into several of them to restore order. By August, the president's approval rating had fallen 13 points, to 39 percent.

On the basis of these and similar cases, we can conclude that decisive domestic action does not have the same effect as foreign policy action. People feel differently about foreign policy.

Finally, consider the following case.

In October 1979, President Carter's approval rating was 31 percent. On November 4, Iranian militants in Tehran took U.S. diplomats hostage. By January 1980, President Carter's popularity had risen 25 points, to 56 percent. Once again, Americans had "rallied around the flag." But as the hostage crisis dragged on without resolution, Carter's popularity began to sink again. In March it was down to 41 percent; in April, down to 39 percent. After a failed helicopter rescue attempt in April, it rose temporarily to 43 percent, illustrating once again that the public rallies around the president even if his policies fail.

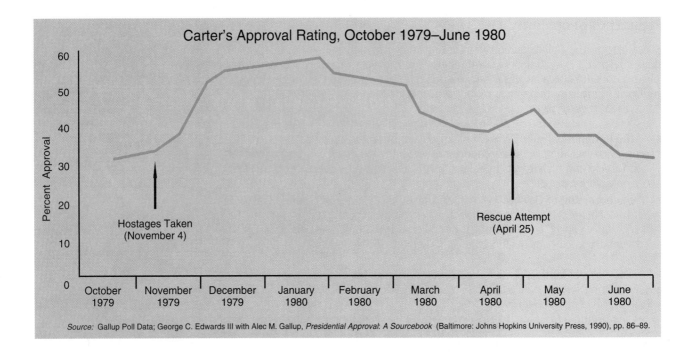

Carter's Approval Rating, October 1979–June 1980

Hostages Taken
(November 4)

Rescue Attempt
(April 25)

Source: Gallup Poll Data; George C. Edwards III with Alec M. Gallup, *Presidential Approval: A Sourcebook* (Baltimore: Johns Hopkins University Press, 1990), pp. 86–89.

British Prime Minister Margaret Thatcher as portrayed in an Argentine newspaper during the Falkland Islands war of 1982.

But by June, Carter's popularity had fallen to 32 percent—almost as low as it had been before the hostages were taken.

Therefore, we can conclude that although foreign policy crises lead to a rise in a president's popularity, the increase is temporary. People will rally around the flag, but they will not stay rallied for the long term. Similar patterns can be seen in other democracies. The Falkland Islands war in 1982 between Britain and Argentina greatly increased the popularity of Prime Minister Margaret Thatcher, whose popularity had slipped because of a slumping domestic economy. The British victory in the Falklands provided her with a theme that she used to gain a victory in the general election the following year. But British prime ministers can (within limits) call for elections when they think they will win. George Bush, by contrast, could not take advantage of his exceptionally high popularity in the wake of the Persian Gulf war but had to wait until the constitutionally ordained four-year cycle was completed.

Challenges to Presidential Power

The president is powerful in the field of foreign policy but not omnipotent. Presidents who in the minds of the public are judged to fail miserably in their foreign policy lose influence in Congress and ultimately lose office. The prospect of elections every four years is a restraint on presidential power. The cases of Harry Truman and Lyndon Johnson illustrate this restraint.

Elections

Harry Truman first completed President Roosevelt's 1945–49 term and then won election in 1948 in his own right. He was eligible to run again in 1952, but his popularity was so low that he stood no chance; seeing sure defeat, he withdrew himself from the race. The issue that made him so unpopular was one of foreign and military policy, the Korean

War. Truman had committed the United States to fight on behalf of South Korea in 1950, and by 1952 the stalemated war was still dragging on, with about 250,000 American troops committed to combat on the Korean peninsula and deaths approaching what would be their final total of 34,000. Popular dissatisfaction with the "no-win" war was very high and was a major issue in the 1952 election. The voters chose as president a military leader from World War II, General Dwight D. Eisenhower. During the campaign, Eisenhower never made it clear what he would do about Korea, beyond a vague pledge to "go there" to see for himself firsthand what was going on. The vote Eisenhower received seems to have been based mostly on the widespread belief that a general would know how to bring a war to an end.

In 1968 Lyndon Johnson decided not to run for a second term, in large part because of the unpopularity of his policy of escalating the war in Vietnam. A surprisingly strong showing for a peace candidate, Senator Eugene McCarthy (D.-Minn.), in the New Hampshire primary suggested to Johnson that although he would probably win his party's nomination, he might not win the election.

The elections in 1948 and 1968 provide evidence that the voters can check the president's power in foreign affairs. But the electorate can control the president only at set intervals—every fourth year when an election is held. Even then, this control is exercised in only the crudest of ways. The voters can approve or disapprove of an existing policy, but they can send no clear message for an alternative policy. In 1952, Eisenhower was elected to end the war in Korea, but he was as free to end it by introducing nuclear weapons (which he did not) as by negotiating an end (which he did). Richard Nixon was elected to succeed Lyndon Johnson without having made clear what he would do to end the war in Vietnam. The most that most voters knew was that some newspapers attributed to him the vague statement that "I have a plan."

Congress

As we've seen, citizens at the polling booths exercise control over the presidency only once every four years. But there is another restraint in the American system. The elected representatives returned to the House and the Senate can exercise a more consistent control over foreign policy. The Constitution appears to give a lesser role to the Congress, but a role nevertheless.

Combat in Vietnam: The unpopularity of the Vietnam War scarred American foreign policy making for years and helped create a perception that the Democratic Party could not handle foreign affairs successfully.

Platforms and Campaign Promises

Elections provide for democratic control of foreign policy only if certain conditions are met:

- The candidates have distinguishable positions on foreign policy;
- Voters know what these positions are;
- Voters cast their ballots based on that position and not some other (such as views on abortion).

These conditions are rarely met. In order to retain maximum freedom of action should they be elected, candidates try to avoid committing themselves on foreign policy issues. Even party platforms are not a reliable guide. In 1976 the Democratic platform, in a plank designed to attract supporters of Israel, called for the United States to move its embassy from Tel Aviv to Jerusalem, the city declared by Israel to be its capital but whose exact status in international law was in doubt because of Israeli annexations after the 1967 war.

Jimmy Carter said even before the election that he did not feel bound by his own party's platform. "No administration," he said, "can completely adopt the platform drawn up by its party. After all, I didn't control the Democratic platform committee. I cannot blindly accept all of it."

Two cases illustrate the power that Congress is able to exercise. Normally the president proposes a policy and Congress accepts, modifies, or rejects. But Congress has the power to develop and implement policy. When the Soviet Union launched *Sputnik,* the first artificial Earth satellite, in 1957, President Eisenhower, unlike many prominent Americans, did not treat it as a serious threat to American security. With no proposal of action from the president, Congress took the lead in developing a national program. Under the leadership of Lyndon Johnson, then a Democratic senator from Texas and the Senate Majority Leader, the Preparedness Subcommittee of the Senate Armed Services Committee held hearings on the threat posed by Soviet space potential. Having determined that there was indeed a threat, Congress reacted by setting up the National Aeronautics and Space Administration (NASA) to run a U.S. space program, and the National Defense Education Act to provide funding for science and foreign language education. Although technically civilian programs, they were seen at the time as very much part of American defense policy.

In reaction to the Soviet missile program, Congress formulated its own policy in spite of the president's disinclination to do so. A decade later, Congress moved to prevent a president from implementing his own policy on missiles. Congress's actions were unusual because they marked a departure from tradition. During World War II and in the following years, weapons became more and more complex, and Congress was willing to defer to presidential recommendations and military advice on what weapons the country needed. If the Air Force said it needed a new, higher-flying, faster-flying bomber, Congress approved the funds. But in 1969, Congress for the first time challenged a president on a major defense expenditure. President Richard Nixon proposed a nationwide system of radars and interceptor missiles to defend against incoming missiles, known at the time as the Anti-Ballistic Missiles (ABM). The Senate, relying on expert testimony by Defense Department officials who had actually tried to develop such systems and believed they would not work, came within a single vote of turning down Nixon's request.

Since 1969, we have become accustomed to congressional scrutiny of weapons, such as missiles to be transported on railroads and Stealth bombers that are invisible to radar, but such scrutiny is relatively new. It is an important check on the president's power. Indeed, in the early days of Soviet reform under First Secretary Mikhail Gorbachev, President Ronald Reagan announced that he would believe real change was occurring in the Soviet Union when a Soviet legislative body reviewed the defense budget. His yardstick was a good one, but in all fairness we should recognize that the U.S. Congress had been reviewing significant questions of nuclear strategy only since 1969.

Treaties versus Executive Agreements. The Constitution gives the Senate explicit power to approve treaties. The fate of the Versailles Treaty reminded everyone that this was a real power. Even though in U.S. history treaties have been rejected outright only seventeen times, the power is effective because presidents try to avoid direct defeats. For example, Jimmy Carter withdrew the SALT II treaty rather than let the Senate vote it down.

Presidents can avoid the treaty process altogether by using executive agreements. An executive agreement is as valid an international contract as a treaty and differs only in that Senate approval is not required. Normally executive agreements are used for routine business matters, such as purchasing and running embassies. But sometimes executive agreements have important policy implications. Several American executive agreements establishing American military bases overseas in countries such as Spain and the Philippines had the effect of allying the United States with these countries without debate or approval by the Senate.

Appropriations. Congress can also try to control foreign policy through its power to appropriate funds. The power to go to war is shared among the branches of government, but the power to appropriate funds belongs to the legislature alone. Congress has been cautious about applying this power. In the case of Vietnam, it concentrated its efforts on keeping the war from widening into the neighboring country of Cambodia. An amendment sponsored by Senators John Sherman Cooper (R.-Ky.) and Frank Church (D.-Ida.), passed in January 1971, prohibited the use of funds for "the introduction of United States ground combat troops into Cambodia." President Nixon's national security adviser, Henry Kissinger, was later to express annoyance in his memoirs at these restraints.

Another example of congressional use of its appropriation power was over activity in Nicaragua. In 1979, an insurrection, led by guerrillas named after an earlier Nicaraguan hero, Augusto Sandino, had come to power. But the policies of the Sandinistas provoked opposition from some parts of the population. Because the Sandinistas received aid from Cuba and the Soviet Union, those opposing them, known as counterrevolutionaries, or *contras,* found that the United States was willing to aid them, first secretly and then in what was called "covert operations" but in fact was openly known.

But many in the United States opposed funding the *contras,* and after much debate, Congress in December 1982 decided to cut off funding. Yet the *contras* continued to receive supplies of weapons. In 1986 it was revealed that the supplies were paid for with funds solicited from foreign states and from private individuals, as well as with proceeds from arms deals with the Khomeini regime in Iran. Exactly who was to blame for subverting the intention of Congress in cutting off funds is not clear, but the weakness of Congress is. Despite its constitutional power to appropriate—or deny—funds, Congress was not able to prevent the president from carrying out a policy he thought important.

The War Powers Act. Frustrated with their failure to influence policy on Vietnam, members of Congress tried in 1973 to prevent future foreign interventions by passing the War Powers Act. Under this act, the president was limited in his deployment of troops overseas to a sixty-day period (which could be extended for an extra thirty days to permit withdrawal) unless Congress explicitly gave its approval for a longer period. Under the act, a response to an emergency, such as a rescue of endangered Americans abroad, would be permitted, but a prolonged struggle with guerrillas would not be.

The War Powers Act became an issue in the struggle for control of foreign policy between the president and Congress for fifteen years. The act when first passed was vetoed by President Nixon and sent back to Congress. Congress overrode the president's veto in March 1973, making it the law of the land, but Nixon called it unconstitutional and said he was not bound by it. No issue arose to test the competing claims before Nixon was forced to resign in 1974, but such issues did arise under his successors. President Gerald R. Ford dispatched troops to rescue a crew of the merchant ship *Mayaguez,* captured as it sailed near Cambodia in 1975; President Carter in 1980 dispatched troops in an abortive attempt to rescue American diplomats held hostage in Iran. In neither case did the action last sixty days, and in both the presidents provided notice to Congress, as the act required, although in both instances after some delay.

The first serious test of the War Powers Act came under President Reagan. In 1982, Reagan ordered Marines into Lebanon as part of a peacekeeping mission. Because they were not in combat, Congress did not object. But after a year, they came under increasing fire from various factions in Lebanon's civil war. Marines were being killed, yet Congress was slow to force the issue. In the midst of protracted debate, a terrorist drove an explosive-filled truck into the Marine barracks in Beirut, killing 241 servicemen. Shortly thereafter, all Marines were withdrawn on the president's initiative. In 1987, Reagan dispatched ships to the Persian Gulf to protect tankers picking up oil from the hostile acts of Iran and Iraq as they warred with each other. Again, Congress did not assert itself and insist that the War Powers Act applied. By 1988, the War Powers Act was recognized as a dead letter. President Bush was able to order troops into Panama to remove General Manuel Noriega from power in 1989 without worrying about congressional attempts to restrain him.

The Press

Along with the voting public and Congress, the press provides some check on presidential power in foreign and military affairs. The press is sometimes referred to as a branch of government, under a label recalling the three estates that governed pre-revolutionary France: "the fourth estate." In the period of World War II and the early Cold War years, however, the press tended to support the president. As a rule, editors assumed that government statements were true and printed them as unquestioned fact.

The press role as a prop for foreign policy began to change in the mid-1960s. Fidel Castro had taken over Cuba in 1959 and installed a regime that he himself called Marxist–Leninist. The Democrats made much in the 1960 election of the fact that a communist regime had been set up "only 90 miles from the U.S." When an insurrection broke out in the neighboring country of the Dominican Republic in 1965, President Johnson felt under pressure to act to prevent "another Cuba." The U.S. government provided transportation to reporters to the Dominican Republic, and the U.S. embassy provided a briefing, complete with stories of atrocities committed by the rebels. But the reporters quickly discovered that the stories were not true. Relations between press and government quickly became adversarial, with reporters challenging statements at press conferences.

Critical reporting spread distrust of the president back home. In September 1965, six months after the U.S. Marines had landed, the respected chair of the Senate Foreign Relations committee, Senator William Fulbright (D.-Ark.), gave a major speech on the floor of the Senate in which he denounced the administration for what he called "the arrogance of power." Part of his critique was based on the negative press reports.

What was unusual in the Dominican Republic invasion became commonplace in the Vietnam War. The press routinely challenged government officials at briefings. The daily military briefing in Vietnam became known among the media as "the Five O'Clock Follies." Stories critical of the war ran on television. The press examined in great detail the differences between what the president was claiming and the reality. Beginning with the live coverage of parts of the Foreign Relations Committee hearings on the Vietnam War in

February 1966, dissent became a regular feature of television coverage. From 1966 on, about 20 percent of all Vietnam coverage (on CBS television, for which data are available) concerned various forms of domestic controversy.[8]

In the years since Lyndon Johnson's presidency, the news media have not been uniformly hostile to the president. During the Persian Gulf war in 1991, some press critics suggested that it was too willing to accept the government's version of events.

Yet the very fact that the media discussed their own shortcomings suggests that the country has not returned to the innocent days of the past. The relationship of trust has been replaced by an adversarial relationship. The press has come to see itself as an independent player in the game of foreign policy.

Restraint by the Public

A fourth possible check on presidential power can come from the public at large. Even when it is not an election year, or Congress is not exerting pressure, or foreign policy is not the subject of press attention, public opinion is always on the president's mind. Take the example of Ronald Reagan.

Reagan's standing in the Gallup Poll in the later years of his administration was higher than that of any of his predecessors in the past decades when polls were regularly taken. His own themes while campaigning were military strength and the restoration of American confidence. If any president had a mandate to be tough, he did. Yet Reagan and his advisers found themselves restrained by their perceptions of what the public would tolerate. Shortly after taking office in 1981, the Reagan administration emphasized the need to help the Central American government of El Salvador fight leftist insurgents trying to overthrow it. The White House saw El Salvador as an issue that would generate even more support for Reagan, playing as it did on themes of anti-communism and national security. Vandenberg's advice to Truman's to "scare hell" out of the country was echoing down the years. Yet to the White House's surprise, Reagan's standing in the polls began to go down.

The president's advisers determined that their problem was that the conflict in El Salvador was being portrayed as another Vietnam. In the words of an adviser, "We were astonished at how the news media treated it. We didn't think it was a Vietnam. But when it became apparent it was going to play that way, we had to low-key the issue."[9] Advisers quickly stopped mentioning El Salvador. The war there went on, but as the president was apparently paying no attention it ceased to be a major news item. Reagan's ratings in the polls went back up. As Eisenhower had discovered with *Sputnik* and Carter with the Iranian hostage crisis, the president could influence what went on the public's agenda but not the opinions the public would form.

Reagan's removal of a contingent of Marines from Lebanon, mentioned earlier, was motivated in part by a fear of negative public opinion. Many opponents of Ronald Reagan feared that he would be an ideological president, unable to see beyond what his own beliefs told him he was seeing. For many, those fears were confirmed when, in March 1983, he addressed a convention of evangelical clergy and referred to the Soviet Union as "the evil empire." Yet in December 1987, Reagan not only hosted the leader of that "empire" at a Washington summit conference but during the summit signed the first true disarmament agreement of the Cold War, the Intermediate Nuclear Forces (INF) Treaty. For the first time the United States and the Soviet Union agreed to physically destroy (as opposed to merely freezing the numbers of) a strategic weapon system, in this case missiles with ranges between 500 and 3,000 kilometers. Reagan's ratings in the polls continued to be high as his policies shifted from the no longer popular view of an "evil

[8] Daniel Hallin, *The "Uncensored War"* (Berkeley: University of California Press, 1989), p. 192.
[9] Sidney Blumenthal, "Marketing the President," *The New York Times Magazine,* September 13, 1981, p. 112.

empire" to the more widely accepted view that Mikhail Gorbachev had brought real change to the Soviet Union.

The authority of the president in foreign and military policy is challenged by the formal institution of Congress, by the informal institution of the press, and by citizens' expressing their will in elections and to public opinion pollsters. Yet each of these restraints on presidential authority is imperfect.

In part this comes from certain hidden advantages bestowed on the president by the Constitution. One is that the president is not only the head of government but also the head of state. Unlike in Britain, where the queen serves as head of state and the prime minister serves as head of government, in America government combines these functions. But this union has the effect of making the president not just a political actor but also the symbol of the nation.

Another hidden advantage is that the president (along with a hand-picked vice president) is the only official elected by the nation as a whole. Each senator has 99 competitors; each representative has 434. Therefore, it is not surprising that Congress, the press, and the American people look to the president as a leader. The prevailing view was summarized by one senator after a foreign policy vote: "In foreign policy initiatives, there should be a presumption in favor of supporting the President of the United States."[10]

The Search for a New Consensus

The anti-communist consensus that dominated U.S. foreign and military policy for three or four decades had some desirable results even for those who did not always share in the consensus. Without that consensus, for example, it is unlikely the Congress would ever have appropriated money for foreign aid in the quantities that it did. The large burden of the Marshall Plan was justified primarily in the name of strengthening Europe against communism. With the fading of the threat that provoked the consenus, old programs need new justification. Some people still advocate foreign aid for humanitarian reasons. But they must prevail against many others who would use the money for other purposes— sheltering America's homeless, rescuing America's savings institutions, or just reducing the deficit.

In the absence of consensus, foreign policy issues become partisan issues, provoking protracted debate between Republicans and Democrats, liberals and conservatives. Democrats in Congress are tempted to hand a Republican president a defeat on a foreign policy issue just because he is a Republican. Some partisanship in foreign policy was always present, of course, but there was a perceptible increase as the Cold War waned. In June 1989, China used tanks to crush pro-democracy demonstrators in Tiananmen Square. Americans, able to watch both demonstrations and repression on television, reacted on a range from dismay to outrage. Members of Congress who felt outrage wanted to demonstrate their feelings by permitting Chinese students currently in the United States on student visas to stay. President Bush, himself the U.S. envoy to China during the Ford administration, thought that doing so would anger the Chinese government. The resulting debate in Congress, vote in both houses, veto by the president, and finally failed attempt to override the veto was seen by political analysts as more a partisan than a foreign policy debate. In the absence of a consensus on substance, many foreign policy issues will become partisan issues.

The anti-communist consensus was one of *substance.* Over the past decades, the consensus on substance was often strong enough to provide a consensus on the *procedure* of policy making as well. But as the threat of communist expansion faded in many

---

[10] Senator Slade Gorton (R.-Wash.), after the AWACS vote, October 1981, *The New York Times,* October 29, 1981, p. Y-4, national edition.

people's minds, fundamental disagreements on procedure became more important. The Constitution states clearly that Congress declares war, yet the United States has not participated in a declared war since 1945. The major conflicts in Korea and Vietnam were never treated as wars requiring Congress's approval. In addition, presidents have dispatched U.S. forces on more than 200 occasions when combat was very likely or did occur. When these deployments became unpopular, Congress tried to stop them, using legislative devices such as the War Powers Act or amendments to bills curtailing specific foreign policy activities. Presidents at the time called these efforts an unconstitutional meddling in their authority.

The Gulf War

The invasion of Kuwait by Iraq on August 2, 1990, created a more serious situation. Even though the War Powers Act had become a dead letter, the constitutional provision that Congress declares war remained in effect. Congressional attempts to withhold funds could be circumvented, but a lengthy war would require substantial funds. Iraq was potentially a more formidable opponent than Panama or Nicaragua, and the United States would require several months of preparation before any serious military campaign could be undertaken. During the preparatory period, Congress tried to force the issue, with the Senate holding hearings on the war.

President Bush initially denied that congressional authorization was necessary, arguing that he was acting to carry out mandates of the United Nations Security Council, but he also recognized political realities. A long and costly war conducted without congressional approval would quickly become "Bush's war," just as Korea had become "Truman's war" and Vietnam had become "Johnson's war."

Bush was reluctant to ask for a resolution of support until he was certain it would pass and Congress was reluctant to act until asked. But as the January 15, 1991, deadline for Iraq to leave Kuwait—agreed to by the United Nations—approached, members of Congress took the initiative in pressing for a debate.

Congress avoided a direct declaration of war by debating instead a resolution authorizing the use of U.S. armed forces to carry out a U.N. resolution (which had itself only

House leaders prior to debate on the Gulf War resolution in January 1991.

suggested that armed force could be used but had not called for it). Congress sidestepped the issue of war powers by stating that the resolution was "consistent with" (as opposed to "pursuant to") the War Powers Act.

After several days of serious debate that raised Congress's reputation, legislators voted for the resolution by a substantial margin (250 to 183) in the House and a narrow margin (52 to 47) in the Senate. Members of Congress hastened to close ranks once the vote was taken, the Democrats who opposed the resolution declaring that they too supported the president, although some Middle Eastern experts suggested that Saddam Hussein, the ruler of Iraq, had misread the U.S. constitutional process and assumed he faced a divided and therefore irresolute opponent.[11]

Challenges to Strategic Coherence

Despite the apparent success of the Gulf war, America faces many challenges that require a coherent foreign policy. Poverty, food shortages, and economic collapse in many parts of the world are so severe that some suggest they may threaten American security. Presidents would like foreign aid to be available as a foreign policy tool but find their hands tied by what is called Congress's "earmarking" of funds, requiring that certain countries receive a large share, or that certain products be included. (For years, some of the American armed forces personnel stationed overseas were heated in winter by coal shipped from the United States, despite the availability of cheaper local supplies.)

All recent presidents have declared their support for free trade. Under authority granted to President Kennedy in the Trade Expansion Act, average tariffs have been negotiated down from around 40 percent in 1945 to about 5 percent by 1990. But as foreign imports put pressure on American business, Congress has been slowly recapturing trade policy from the president. A major milestone was the 1988 Omnibus Trade and

---

[11] This was the view of Hosni Mubarak, president of Egypt. See Elaine Sciolino, "Hussein's Errors: Complex Impulses," *The New York Times,* February 28, 1991, p. A-10.

Civil war in Yugoslavia: With the retreat of communism, local ethnic and nationalist tensions have emerged to create instability. Part of the challenge of U.S. foreign policy toward the year 2000 will be to navigate in a much more uncertain world.

Competitiveness Act, which limited presidential discretion in some areas and imposed mandatory requirements for retaliation in others. Because Congress responds readily to sectional interests such as automobile producers, the president finds it hard to develop a coherent national policy on trade.

Similarly, presidents would like to see military spending fit into a coherent strategy. With the decline of the feeling of threat, the problem facing the nation is not how to spend money but how to cut it. The president and Secretary of Defense try to justify a military spending program according to national security needs. When faced with an impending cut in the military budget, members of Congress ask first about its effect on their districts. Even members of Congress conspicuous for their vocal opposition to the vague concept of "military spending" fight to retain military bases that provide jobs for their constituents. The resulting defense budget reflects not a coherent strategy but a patchwork quilt of local interests.

A Return to Basic Principles

If we step back from the tumble of daily politics, we can see that debate on a procedural consensus has been taking place between two philosophic positions. On the one hand are those who are distrustful of too much power in the executive hands—we might call them critics of the "imperial presidency." On the other hand are their rivals bemoaning the inadequacy of Congress—we might call them critics of the "bumbling Congress." Notice that their positions are defined more by what they dislike than by what they advocate.

The debate between these two positions is very current, but many of the issues in the debate were spelled out in the eighteenth century, particularly by Alexander Hamilton in Federalist No. 75. Hamilton recognized that foreign policy was in crucial ways different from domestic policy, because it required:

1. Accurate and comprehensive knowledge of foreign politics
2. A steady and systematic adherence to the same views
3. A nice and uniform sensibility to national character
4. Decision, secrecy, and despatch [*sic*].

Let us look at each point in turn. Hamilton claims that to conduct foreign affairs one needs knowledge that is accurate and comprehensive. This is surely a commonsense assumption. Yet most American citizens will readily admit that foreign affairs are far removed from their daily concerns. Most automobile drivers would readily give you their opinion on raising gasoline taxes ten cents a gallon; few could even explain the sugar quota or the Hickenlooper Amendment, much less offer an opinion in favor of or against either. The same citizens who would never dream of entrusting tax decisions to the wisdom of the president alone happily entrust decisions on the sugar quota and the Hickenlooper Amendment, justifying that trust with the argument that the president has the facts.

Next, Hamilton writes of "adherence to the same views," or coherence in policy, or, what the Senate Foreign Relations Committee called in 1816 "unity of design." Domestic politics is the result of patchwork and compromise; policies made one year may be reversed the next. Such incoherence causes problems internally. Hamilton and his followers would argue that it causes disasters externally.

Next Hamilton suggests that foreign policy should not try what is unattainable, or what goes contrary to national wishes. But by including the word *uniform* he implies that foreign policy should rise above what is temporarily popular and look at what is best for the nation in the long run. Members of Congress think first in terms of their districts. It is standard wisdom in the halls of the Capitol that "all politics is local politics." Only the president, the followers of Hamilton argue, can speak for the nation as a whole.

Hamilton's point about "decision, secrecy, and despatch [*sic*]" may be even more persuasive in the twentieth century than it was in the eighteenth. In late summer of 1962, the Soviet Union began secretly placing nuclear missiles in Cuba. President Kennedy knew, through aerial photographs, what the Soviets were doing—although they did not know that he knew. Kennedy wanted to keep his knowledge secret while he considered what to do. By confining his decision making to a group of only fifteen trusted advisers, he succeeded. It is unlikely that within a bigger body the secret could have been kept. Kennedy also was able to decide with dispatch. After three days of deliberation, he and his advisers decided on a blockade to force the missiles out.

We can contrast the experience of President Kennedy in 1962 with that of his successor fifteen years later. In 1977 President Carter boldly announced a policy to reduce dependence on foreign energy sources, a policy that he called "the moral equivalent of war." But it took one year, six months, and nineteen days until Carter's energy bill was signed into law, and by that time it was a watered-down, much-compromised version of his original proposals. Part of the reason for the delay was that the bill had to pass through twenty-two different subcommittees and committees.

Toward Reform

Hamilton's arguments have not lost their force. Yet on the other side is a fundamental point. It is the essence of democracy that power not go unchecked. The basic principle underlying the American Revolution was the belief that the concentration of power in a single pair of hands is tyranny. Legislation must be approved by the House and the Senate. Even then the president can veto bills. But the Congress can then override the veto. Laws can be declared unconstitutional by the Supreme Court. Yet Court decisions can be nullified by constitutional amendments.

The president is checked by the need to face the electorate every four years. But in a four-year span misconceived and unpopular foreign and military policy can create disaster. Only Congress has the position within the American system to exercise ongoing checks on the president.

Several proposals for reform have been advanced. Some hope that a revised War Powers Act will provide the congressional oversight needed to restrain presidential adventurism. Others have suggested an executive committee of members of Congress to deal with foreign policy.

Whatever proposals are adopted will increase congressional participation only at the price of slowing down the decision-making process. Many Americans who find Hamilton's arguments persuasive on individual points will in the end opt for a system in which inefficiency is the price for keeping power divided and restrained.

Summary

Foreign and military policy differ in significant ways from other components of American government. Their history has not been one of continuous development. America went from a nation not "conceived in liberty" (as Abraham Lincoln put it) so much as in war and international politics. But after winning a war of national liberation, with crucial support from France, Americans withdrew behind their two-ocean moat. For more than a century, foreign and military policy played—with occasional exceptions—only a minor part in American life.

Then, during World War II and the following years of the Cold War, foreign and military policy surged to the forefront. Defense spending went from a small fraction of the federal budget to one of the biggest components—not for a few years (as in World War I), but for decades. Global affairs went from a peripheral issue of concern only to specialists to the focus of presidential attention and public debate.

It is not only in the history of their development that these issues differ. The complex balances found in many other parts of the American system are absent in foreign and military policy. One branch of government, the executive (and one individual in that branch, the president), predominates. The countervailing forces in the Congress, the media, and the public are weak. Other components of American government, such as the judicial branch and the state and local levels, play almost no role at all.

The predominance of the president has given rise to criticism of an imperial presidency, but debate about both the content and the process of foreign and military policy has been inhibited by fears of endangering the "national security." With the ending of the Cold War and the disintegration of the Soviet Union, the sense of military threat has diminished. One can expect now a more robust debate on both the content and decision-making process in foreign and military policy. As foreign affairs increasingly concern economic issues, one can expect the president's authority to diminish, both because the Constitution allocates appropriation powers to the Congress and because economic issues affect the pocketbooks of citizens in immediate and tangible ways.

Yet presidential authority does not derive from Cold War fears alone. Many of the factors that contribute to presidential predominance persist. The content of policy may change rapidly. The institutions that produce it will not.

Key Terms

Secretary of State	manifest destiny	anti-communism
ambassadors	League of Nations	national security
ministers	Versailles Peace Treaty	National Security Act
commander-in-chief	isolationism	Central Intelligence Agency
militias	sphere of influence	National Security Council
Jay Treaty	globalism	Marshall Plan
Monroe Doctrine	Truman Doctrine	North Atlantic Treaty Organization

Suggested Readings

Ambrose, Stephen. *Rise to Globalism,* 6th ed. New York: Penguin, 1991.

Barnet, Richard. *The Rockets' Red Glare.* New York: Simon and Schuster, 1990.

Bundy, McGeorge. *Danger and Survival.* New York: Random House, 1988.

Halberstam, David. *The Best and the Brightest.* New York: Random House, 1972.

Hallin, Daniel. *The "Uncensored War."* Berkeley: University of California Press, 1989.

Kennan, George. *American Diplomacy 1900–1950.* Chicago: University of Chicago Press, 1951.

Kissinger, Henry. *White House Years.* Boston: Little, Brown, 1979.

Kissinger, Henry. *Years of Upheaval.* Boston: Little, Brown, 1982.

Mueller, John E. *War, Presidents and Public Policy.* New York: Wiley, 1973.

Perret, Geoffrey. *A Country Made by War.* New York: Random House, 1989.

Schlesinger, Arthur. *The Imperial Presidency.* Boston: Houghton Mifflin, 1973, 1989.

APPENDIX I

The Declaration of Independence

In Congress, July 4, 1776

The Unanimous Declaration of the Thirteen United States of America

When in the Course of human events it becomes necessary for one people to dissolve the political bands which have connected them with another, and to assume, among the powers of the earth, the separate and equal station to which the Laws of Nature and of Nature's God entitle them, a decent respect to the opinions of mankind requires that they should declare the causes which impel them to the separation.

We hold these truths to be self-evident, that all men are created equal, that they are endowed by their Creator with certain unalienable Rights, that among these are Life, Liberty and the pursuit of Happiness. That to secure these rights, Governments are instituted among Men, deriving their just powers from the consent of the governed. That whenever any Form of Government becomes destructive of these ends, it is the Right of the People to alter or to abolish it, and to institute new Government, laying its foundation on such principles and organizing its powers in such form, as to them shall seem most likely to effect their Safety and Happiness. Prudence, indeed, will dictate that Governments long established should not be changed for light and transient causes; and accordingly all experience hath shewn that mankind are more disposed to suffer, while evils are sufferable, than to right themselves by abolishing the forms to which they are accustomed. But when a long train of abuses and usurpations, pursuing invariably the same Object evinces a design to reduce them under absolute Despotism, it is their right, it is their duty, to throw off such Government, and to provide new Guards for their future security.— Such has been the patient sufferance of these Colonies; and such is now the necessity which constrains them to alter their former Systems of Government. The history of the present King of Great Britain is a history of repeated injuries and usurpations, all having in direct object the establishment of an absolute Tyranny over these States. To prove this, let Facts be submitted to a candid world.

He has refused his Assent to Laws, the most wholesome and necessary for the public good.

He has forbidden his Governors to pass Laws of immediate and pressing importance, unless suspended in their operation till his Assent should be obtained; and when so suspended, he has utterly neglected to attend to them.

He has refused to pass other Laws for the accommodation of large districts of people, unless those people would relinquish the right of Representation in the Legislature, a right inestimable to them and formidable to tyrants only.

He has called together legislative bodies at places unusual, uncomfortable, and distant from the depository of their Public Records, for the sole purpose of fatiguing them into compliance with his measures.

He has dissolved Representative Houses repeatedly, for opposing with manly firmness his invasions on the rights of the people.

He has refused for a long time, after such dissolutions, to cause others to be elected; whereby the Legislative Powers, incapable of Annihilation, have returned to the People at large for their exercise, the State remaining in the mean time exposed to all the dangers of invasion from without, and convulsions within.

He has endeavored to prevent the population of these States; for that purpose obstructing the Laws of Naturalization of Foreigners; refusing to pass others to encourage their migration hither, and raising the conditions of new Appropriations of Lands.

He has obstructed the Administration of Justice, by refusing his Assent to Laws for establishing Judiciary powers.

He has made Judges dependent on his Will alone, for the tenure of their offices, and the amount and payment of their salaries.

He has erected a multitude of New Offices, and sent hither swarms of Officers to harass our people, and eat out their substance.

He has kept among us, in times of peace, Standing Armies without the Consent of our legislatures.

He has affected to render the Military independent of and superior to the Civil power.

He has combined with others to subject us to a jurisdiction foreign to our constitution, and unacknowledged by our laws, giving his Assent to their Acts of pretended Legislation:

For quartering large bodies of armed troops among us:

For protecting them, by a mock Trial, from punishment for any Murders which they should commit on the Inhabitants of these States:

For cutting off our Trade with all parts of the world:

For imposing Taxes on us without our Consent:

For depriving us in many cases, of the benefits of Trial by Jury:

For transporting us beyond Seas to be tried for pretended offences:

For abolishing the free System of English Laws in a neighboring Province, establishing therein an Arbitrary government, and enlarging its Boundaries so as to render it at once an example and fit instrument for introducing the same absolute rule into these Colonies:

For taking away our Charters, abolishing our most valuable Laws, and altering fundamentally the Forms of our Governments:

For suspending our own Legislatures, and declaring themselves invested with power to legislate for us in all cases whatsoever.

He has abdicated Government here, by declaring us out of his Protection and waging War against us.

He has plundered our seas, ravaged our Coasts, burnt out towns, and destroyed the lives of our people.

He is at this time transporting large Armies of foreign Mercenaries to compleat the works of death, desolation and tyranny, already begun with circumstances of Cruelty and perfidy scarcely paralleled in the most barbarous ages, and totally unworthy the Head of a civilized nation.

He has constrained our fellow Citizens taken Captive on the high Seas to bear Arms against their Country, to become the executioners of their friends and Brethren, or to fall themselves by their Hands.

He has excited domestic insurrections amongst us, and has endeavored to bring on the inhabitants of our frontiers, the merciless Indian Savages, whose known rule of warfare, is an undistinguished destruction of all ages, sexes and conditions.

In every stage of these Oppressions We have Petitioned for Redress in the most humble terms: Our repeated Petitions have been answered only by repeated injury: A Prince, whose character is thus marked by every act which may define a Tyrant, is unfit to be the ruler of a free people.

Nor have We been wanting in attention to our British brethren. We have warned them from time to time of attempts by their legislature to extend an unwarrantable jurisdiction over us. We have reminded them of the circumstances of our emigration and settlement here. We have appealed to their native justice and magnanimity; and we have conjured them by the ties of our common kindred to disavow these usurpations, which would inevitably interrupt our connections and correspondence. They too have been deaf to the voice of justice and consanguinity. We must, therefore, acquiesce in the necessity, which denounces our Separation, and hold them, as we hold the rest of mankind, Enemies in War, in Peace Friends.

We, therefore, the Representatives of the United States of America, in General Congress, Assembled, appealing to the Supreme Judge of the world for the rectitude of our intentions, do, in the Name, and by Authority of the good People of these Colonies, solemnly publish and declare, That these United Colonies are, and of Right ought to be Free and Independent States; that they are Absolved from all Allegiance to the British Crown, and that all political connection between them and the State of Great Britain, is and ought to be totally dissolved: and that as Free and Independent States, they have full power to levy War, conclude Peace, contract Alliances, establish Commerce, and to do all other Acts and Things which Independent States may of right do. And for the support of this Declaration, with a firm reliance on the protection of divine Providence, we mutually pledge to each other our Lives, our Fortunes and our sacred Honor.

JOHN HANCOCK

NEW HAMPSHIRE
Josiah Bartlett,
Wm. Whipple,
Matthew Thornton.

MASSACHUSETTS BAY
Saml. Adams,
John Adams,
Robt. Treat Paine,
Elbridge Gerry.

RHODE ISLAND
Step. Hopkins,
William Ellery.

CONNECTICUT
Roger Sherman,
Samuel Huntington,
Wm. Williams,
Oliver Wolcott.

NEW YORK
Wm. Floyd,
Phil. Livingston,
Frans. Lewis,
Lewis Morris

NEW JERSEY
Richd. Stockton,
In. Witherspoon,
Fras. Hopkinson,
John Hart,
Abra. Clark.

PENNSYLVANIA
Robt. Morris,
Benjamin Rush,
Benjamin Franklin,
John Morton,
Geo. Clymer,
Jas. Smith,
Geo. Taylor,
James Wilson,
Geo. Ross.

DELAWARE
Caesar Rodney,
Geo. Read,
Tho. M'kean.

MARYLAND
Samuel Chase,
Wm. Paca,
Thos. Stone,
Charles Caroll
    of Carrollton.

VIRGINIA
George Wythe,
Richard Henry Lee,
Th. Jefferson,
Benjamin Harrison,
Thos. Nelson, jr.,
Francis Lightfoot Lee,
Carter Braxton.

NORTH CAROLINA
Wm. Hooper,
Joseph Hewes,
John Penn.

SOUTH CAROLINA
Edward Rutledge,
Thos. Heyward, Junr.,
Thomas Lynch, jnr.,
Arthur Middleton.

GEORGIA
Button Guinnett,
Lyman Hall,
Geo. Walton.

APPENDIX II

The Constitution of the United States of America

We the People of the United States, in Order to form a more perfect Union, establish Justice, insure domestic Tranquility, provide for the common defence, promote the general Welfare, and secure the Blessings of Liberty to ourselves and our Posterity, do ordain and establish this Constitution for the United States of America.

ARTICLE I

SECTION 1. All legislative Powers herein granted shall be vested in a Congress of the United States, which shall consist of a Senate and House of Representatives.

SECTION 2. The House of Representatives shall be composed of Members chosen every second Year by the People of the several States, and the Electors in each State shall have the Qualifications requisite for Electors of the most numerous Branch of the State Legislature.

No person shall be a Representative who shall not have attained to the Age of twenty five Years, and been seven Years a Citizen of the United States, and who shall not, when elected, be an Inhabitant of that State in which he shall be chosen.

Representatives and direct Taxes shall be apportioned among the several States which may be included within this Union, according to their respective Numbers which shall be determined by adding to the whole Number of free Persons, including those bound to Service for a Term of Years, and excluding Indians not taxed, three fifths of all other Persons. The actual Enumeration shall be made within three Years after the first Meeting of the Congress of the United States, and within every subsequent Term ten Years, in such Manner as they shall by Law direct. The Number of Representatives shall not exceed one for every thirty Thousand, but each State shall have at Least one Representative; and until such enumeration shall be made, the State of New Hampshire shall be entitled to chuse three, Massachusetts eight, Rhode-Island and Providence Plantations one, Connecticut five, New-York six, New Jersey four, Pennsylvania eight, Delaware one, Maryland six, Virginia ten, North Carolina five, South Carolina five, and Georgia three.

When vacancies happen in the Representation from any State, the Executive Authority thereof shall issue Writs of Election to fill such Vacancies.

The House of Representatives shall chuse their speaker and other Officers; and shall have the sole Power of Impeachment.

SECTION 3. The Senate of the United States shall be composed of two Senators from each State chosen by the Legislature thereof, for six Years; and each Senator shall have one Vote.

Immediately after they shall be assembled in Consequence of the first Election, they shall be divided as equally as may be into three Classes. The Seats of the Senators of the first Class shall be vacated at the Expiration of the second year, of the second Class at the

Expiration of the fourth Year, and of the third Class at the Expiration of the sixth Year, so that one third may be chosen every second Year and if Vacancies happen by Resignation, or otherwise, during the Recess of the Legislature of any State, the Executive thereof may make temporary Appointments until the next Meeting of the Legislature, which shall then fill such Vacancies.

No Person shall be a Senator who shall not have attained to the Age of thirty Years, and been nine Years a Citizen of the United States, and who shall not, when elected, be an Inhabitant of that State for which he shall be chosen.

The Vice President of the United States shall be President of the Senate, but shall have no Vote, unless they be equally divided.

The Senate shall chuse their other Officers, and also a President pro tempore, in the Absence of the Vice President, or when he shall exercise the Office of President of the United States.

The Senate shall have the sole Power to try all Impeachments. When sitting for that Purpose, they shall be on Oath or Affirmation. When the President of the United States is tried, the Chief Justice shall preside: And no Person shall be convicted without the Concurrence of two thirds of the Members present.

Judgment in Cases of Impeachment shall not extend further than to removal from Office, and disqualification to hold and enjoy any Office of honor, Trust or Profit under the United States; but the Party convicted shall nevertheless be liable and subject to Indictment, Trial, Judgment and Punishment, according to Law.

SECTION 4. The Times, Places and Manner of holding Elections for Senators and Representatives, shall be prescribed in each State by the Legislature thereof; but the Congress may at any time by law make or alter such Regulations, except as to the Places of chusing Senators.

The Congress shall assemble at least once in every Year, and such Meeting shall be on the first Monday in December, unless they shall by Law appoint a different Day.

SECTION 5. Each House shall be the Judge of the Elections, Returns and Qualifications of its own Members, and a Majority of each shall constitute a Quorum to do Business; but a smaller Number may adjourn from day to day, and may be authorized to compel the Attendance of absent Members, in such Manner, and under such Penalties as each House may provide.

Each House may determine the Rules of its Proceedings, punish its Members for disorderly Behaviour, and with the Concurrence of two thirds, expel a Member.

Each House shall keep a journal of its Proceedings, and from time to time publish the same, excepting such Parts as may in their judgment require Secrecy; and the Yeas and Nays of the Members of either House on any question shall, at the Desire of one fifth of those present, be entered on the Journal.

Neither House, during the Session of Congress, shall, without the Consent of the other, adjourn for more than three days, nor to any other Place than that in which the two Houses shall be sitting.

SECTION 6. The Senators and Representatives shall receive a Compensation for their Services, to be ascertained by Law, and paid out of the Treasury of the United States. They shall in all Cases, except Treason, Felony and Breach of the Peace, be privileged from Arrest during their Attendance at the Session of their respective Houses, and in going to and returning from the same; and for any Speech or Debate in either House, they shall not be questioned in any other Place.

No Senator or Representative shall, during the Time for which he was elected, be appointed to any civil Office under the Authority of the United States, which shall have been created, or the Emoluments whereof shall have been encreased during such time; and no Person holding any Office under the United States, shall be a Member of either House during his Continuance in Office.

Section 7. All Bills for raising Revenue shall originate in the House of Representatives; but the Senate may propose or concur with Amendments as on other Bills.

Every Bill which shall have passed the House of Representatives and the Senate, shall, before it become a Law, be presented to the President of the United States; If he approves he shall sign it, but if not he shall return it, with his Objections to that House in which it shall have originated, who shall enter the Objections at large on their journal, and proceed to reconsider it. If after such Reconsideration two thirds of that House shall agree to pass the Bill, it shall be sent, together with the Objections, to the other House, by which it shall likewise be reconsidered, and if approved by two thirds of that House, it shall become a Law. But in all such Cases the Votes of both Houses shall be determined by yeas and Nays, and the Names of the Persons voting for and against the Bill shall be entered on the Journal of each House respectively. If any Bill shall not be returned by the President within ten Days (Sundays excepted) after it shall have been presented to him, the Same shall be a Law, in like Manner as if he had signed it, unless the Congress by their Adjournment prevent its Return, in which Case it shall not be a Law.

Every Order, Resolution, or Vote to which the Concurrence of the Senate and House of Representatives may be necessary (except on a question of Adjournment) shall be presented to the President of the United States; and before the Same shall take Effect, shall be approved by him, or being disapproved by him, shall be repassed by two thirds of the Senate and House of Representatives, according to the Rules and Limitations prescribed in the Case of a Bill.

Section 8. The Congress shall have Power To lay and collect Taxes, Duties, Imposts and Excises, to pay the Debts and provide for the common Defence and general Welfare of the United States; but all Duties, Imposts and Excises shall be uniform throughout the United States;

To borrow Money on the credit of the United States;

To regulate Commerce with foreign Nations, and among the several States, and with the Indian Tribes;

To establish a uniform Rule of Naturalization, and uniform Laws on the subject of Bankruptcies throughout the United States;

To coin Money, regulate the Value thereof, and of foreign Coin, and fix the Standard of Weights and Measures;

To provide for the Punishment of counterfeiting the Securities and current Coin of the United States;

To establish Post Offices and post Roads;

To promote the Progress of Science and useful Arts, by securing for limited Times to Authors and Inventors the exclusive Right to their respective Writings and Discoveries;

To constitute Tribunals inferior to the supreme Court;

To define and punish Piracies and Felonies committed on the high Seas, and Offences against the Law of Nations;

To declare War, grant Letters of Marque and Reprisal, and make Rules concerning Captures on Land and Water;

To raise and support Armies, but no Appropriation of Money to that Use shall be for a longer Term than two Years;

To provide and maintain a Navy;

To make Rules for the Government and Regulation of the land and naval Forces;

To provide for calling forth the Militia to execute the Laws of the Union, suppress Insurrections and repel Invasions;

To provide for organizing, arming, and disciplining, the Militia, and for governing such Part of them as may be employed in the Service of the United States, reserving to the States respectively, the Appointment of the Officers, and the Authority of training the Militia according to the discipline prescribed by Congress;

To exercise exclusive Legislation in all Cases whatsoever, over such District (not exceeding ten Miles square) as may, by Cession of particular States, and the Acceptance of

Congress, become the Seat of the Government of the United States, and to exercise like Authority over all Places purchased by the Consent of the Legislature of the State in which the Same shall be for the Erection of Forts, Magazines, Arsenals, dock-Yards, and other needful Buildings;—And

To make all Laws which shall be necessary and proper for carrying into Execution the foregoing Powers, and all other Powers vested by this Constitution in the Government of the United States, or in any Department or Officer thereof.

SECTION 9. The Migration or Importation of such Persons as any of the States now existing shall think proper to admit, shall not be prohibited by the Congress prior to the Year one thousand eight hundred and eight, but a Tax or duty may be imposed on such Importation, not exceeding ten dollars for each Person.

The Privilege of the Writ of Habeas Corpus shall not be suspended, unless when in Cases of Rebellion or Invasion the public Safety may require it.

No Bill of Attainder or ex post facto Law shall be passed.

No Capitation, or other direct, Tax shall be laid, unless in Proportion to the Census or Enumeration herein before directed to be taken.

No Tax or Duty shall be laid on Articles exported from any State.

No Preference shall be given by any Regulation of Commerce or Revenue to the Ports of one State over those of another; nor shall Vessels bound to, or from, one State, be obliged to enter, clear, or pay Duties in another.

No Money shall be drawn from the Treasury, but in Consequence of Appropriations made by Law; and a regular Statement and Account of the Receipts and Expenditures of all public Money shall be published from time to time.

No Title of Nobility shall be granted by the United States: And no Person holding any Office of Profit or Trust under them, shall, without the Consent of the Congress, accept of any present, Emolument, Office, or Title, of any kind whatever, from any King, Prince, or foreign State.

SECTION 10. No state shall enter into any Treaty, Alliance, or Confederation; grant Letters of Marque and Reprisal; coin Money; emit Bills of Credit; make any Thing but gold and silver Coin a Tender in Payment of Debts; pass any Bill of Attainder, ex post facto Law, or Law impairing the Obligation of Contracts, or grant any Title of Nobility.

No State shall, without the Consent of the Congress, lay any Imposts or Duties on Imports or Exports, except what may be absolutely necessary for executing its inspection Laws: and the net Produce of all Duties and Imposts, laid by any State on Imports or Exports, shall be for the Use of the Treasury of the United States, and all such Laws shall be subject to the Revision and Controul of the Congress.

No State shall, without the Consent of Congress, lay any Duty of Tonnage, keep Troops, or Ships of War in time of Peace, enter into any Agreement or Compact with another State, or with a foreign Power, or engage in War, unless actually invaded, or in such imminent Danger as will not admit of delay.

ARTICLE II

SECTION 1. The executive Power shall be vested in a President of the United States of America. He shall hold his Office during the Term of four Years, and, together with the Vice President, chosen for the same Term, be elected as follows.

Each State shall appoint, in such Manner as the Legislature thereof may direct, a Number of Electors, equal to the whole Number of Senators and Representatives to which the State may be entitled in the Congress; but no Senator or Representative, or Person holding an Office of Trust of Profit under the United States, shall be appointed an Elector.

The Electors shall meet in their respective States, and vote by Ballot for two Persons, of whom one at least shall not be an Inhabitant of the same State with themselves. And they shall make a List of all the Persons voted for, and, of the Number of Votes for each; which List they shall sign and certify, and transmit sealed to the Seat of the Government of the United States, directed to the President of the Senate. The President of the Senate shall, in the Presence of the Senate and House of Representatives, open all the Certificates, and the Votes shall then be counted. The Person having the greatest Number of Votes shall be the President, if such Number be a Majority of the whole Number of Electors appointed; and if there be more than one who have such Majority, and have an equal Number of Votes, then the House of Representatives shall immediately chuse by Ballot one of them for President; and if no Person have a Majority, then from the five highest on the List the said House shall in like Manner chuse the President. But in chusing the President, the Votes shall be taken by States, the Representation from each State having one Vote; A quorum for this Purpose shall consist of a Member or Members from two thirds of the States, and a Majority of all the States shall be necessary to a Choice. In every Case, after the Choice of the President, the Person having the greatest Number of Votes of the Electors shall be the Vice President. But if there should remain two or more who have equal Votes, the Senate shall chuse from them by Ballot the Vice President.

The Congress may determine the Time of chusing the Electors, and the Day on which they shall give their Votes; which Day shall be the same throughout the United States.

No Person except a natural born Citizen, or a Citizen of the United States, at the time of the Adoption of this Constitution, shall be eligible to the Office of President; neither shall any Person be eligible to that Office who shall not have attained to the Age of thirty five Years, and been fourteen Years a Resident within the United States.

In Case of the Removal of the President from Office, or of his Death, Resignation, or Inability to discharge the Powers and Duties of the said Office, the Same shall devolve on the Vice President, and the Congress may by Law provide for the Case of Removal, Death, Resignation or Inability, both of the President and Vice President, declaring what Officer shall then act as President, and such Officer shall act accordingly, until the Disability be removed, or a President shall be elected.

The President shall, at stated Times, receive for his Services, a Compensation, which shall neither be encreased nor diminished during the Period for which he shall have been elected, and he shall not receive within that Period any other Emolument from the United States, or any of them.

Before he enter on the Execution of his Office, he shall take the following Oath or Affirmation—"I do solemnly swear (or affirm) that I will faithfully execute the Office of President of the United States, and will to the best of my Ability, preserve, protect and defend the Constitution of the United States."

Section 2. The President shall be Commander in Chief of the Army, and Navy of the United States, and of the Militia of the several States, when called into the actual Service of the United States; he may require the Opinion, in writing, of the principal Officer in each of the executive Departments, upon any Subject relating to the Duties of their respective Offices, and he shall have Power to grant Reprieves and Pardons for Offences against the United States, except in Cases of Impeachment.

He shall have Power, by and with the Advice and Consent of the Senate, to make Treaties, provided two thirds of the Senators present concur; and he shall nominate, and by and with the Advice and Consent of the Senate, shall appoint Ambassadors, other public Ministers and Consuls, Judges of the supreme Court, and all other Officers of the United States, whose Appointments are not herein otherwise provided for, and which shall be established by Law: but the Congress may by Law vest the Appointment of such inferior Officers, as they think proper, in the President alone, in the Courts of Law, or in the Heads of Departments.

The President shall have Power to fill up all Vacancies that may happen during the Recess of the Senate, by granting Commissions which shall expire at the end of their next Session.

SECTION 3. He shall from time to time give to the Congress Information of the State of the Union, and recommend to their Consideration such Measures as he shall judge necessary and expedient; he may, on extraordinary Occasions, convene both Houses, or either of them, and in Case of Disagreement between them, with Respect to the Time of Adjournment, he may adjourn them to such Time as he shall think proper; he shall receive Ambassadors and other public Ministers; he shall take Care that the Laws be faithfully executed, and shall Commission all the Officers of the United States.

SECTION 4. The President, Vice President and all civil Officers of the United States, shall be removed from Office on Impeachment for, and Conviction of, Treason, Bribery, or other high Crimes and Misdemeanors.

ARTICLE III

SECTION 1. The judicial Power of the United States, shall be vested in one supreme Court, and in such inferior Courts as the Congress may from time to time ordain and establish. The Judges, both of the supreme and inferior Courts, shall hold their Offices during good Behaviour, and shall, at stated Times, receive for their Services, a Compensation, which shall not be diminished during their Continuance in Office.

SECTION 2. The judicial Power shall extend to all Cases, in Law and Equity, arising under this Constitution, the Laws of the United States, and Treaties made, or which shall be made, under their Authority;—to all Cases affecting Ambassadors, other public Ministers and Consuls;—to all Cases of admiralty and maritime Jurisdiction;—to Controversies to which the United States shall be a Party;—to Controversies between two or more States;—between a State and Citizens of another State;—between Citizens of different States,—between Citizens of the same State claiming Lands under Grants of different States,—and between a State, or the Citizens thereof, and foreign States, Citizens of Subjects.

In all Cases affecting Ambassadors, other public Ministers and Consuls, and those in which a State shall be Party, the supreme Court shall have original Jurisdiction. In all the other Cases before mentioned, the supreme Court shall have appellate Jurisdiction, both as to Law and Fact, with such Exceptions, and under such Regulations as the Congress shall make.

The Trial of all Crimes, except in Cases of Impeachment, shall be by Jury; and such Trial shall be held in the State where the said Crimes shall have been committed; but when not committed within any State, the Trial shall be at such Place or Places as the Congress may by Law have directed.

SECTION 3. Treason against the United States, shall consist only in levying War against them, or in adhering to their Enemies, giving them Aid and Comfort. No Person shall be convicted of Treason unless on the Testimony of two Witnesses to the same overt Act, or on Confession in open Court.

The Congress shall have Power to declare the Punishment of Treason, but no Attainder of Treason shall work Corruption of Blood, or Forfeiture except during the Life of the Person attainted.

ARTICLE IV

SECTION 1. Full Faith and Credit shall be given in each State to the public Acts, Records, and judicial Proceedings of every other State. And the Congress may by general Laws prescribe the Manner in which such Acts, Records and Proceedings shall be proved, and the Effect thereof.

SECTION 2. The Citizens of each State shall be entitled to all Privileges and Immunities of Citizens in the several States.

A Person charged in any State with Treason, Felony, or other Crime, who shall flee from Justice, and be found in another State, shall on Demand of the executive Authority of the State from which he fled, be delivered up, to be removed to the State having Jurisdiction of the Crime.

No Person held to Service or Labour in one State under the Laws thereof, escaping into another, shall, in Consequence of any Law or Regulation therein, be discharged from such Service or Labour, but shall be delivered up on Claim of the Party to whom such Service or Labour may be due.

SECTION 3. New States may be admitted by the Congress into this Union; but no new State shall be formed or erected within the Jurisdiction of any other State; nor any State be formed by the Junction of two or more States, or Parts of States, without the Consent of the Legislatures of the States concerned as well as of the Congress.

The Congress shall have Power to dispose of and make all needful Rules and Regulations respecting the Territory or other Property belonging to the United States; and nothing in this Constitution shall be so construed as to Prejudice any Claims of the United States, or of any particular State.

SECTION 4. The United States shall guarantee to every State in this Union a Republican Form of Government, and shall protect each of them against Invasion, and on Application of the Legislature, or of the Executive (when the Legislature cannot be convened) against domestic Violence.

ARTICLE V

The Congress, whenever two thirds of both Houses shall deem it necessary, shall propose Amendments to this Constitution, or, on the Application of the Legislatures of two thirds of the several States, shall call a Convention for proposing Amendments, which, in either Case, shall be valid to all Intents and Purposes, as Part of this Constitution, when ratified by the Legislatures of three fourths of the several States, or by Conventions in three fourths thereof, as the one or the other Mode of Ratification may be proposed by the Congress; Provided that no Amendment which may be made prior to the Year One thousand eight hundred and eight shall in any Manner affect the first and fourth Clauses in the Ninth Section of the first Article; and that no State, without its Consent, shall be deprived of its equal Suffrage in the Senate.

ARTICLE VI

All Debts contracted and Engagements entered into, before the Adoption of this Constitution, shall be as valid against the United States under this Constitution, as under the Confederation.

This Constitution, and the laws of the United States which shall be made in Pursuance thereof; and all Treaties made, or which shall be made, under the Authority of the United States, shall be the supreme Law of the Land; and the Judges in every State shall be bound thereby, any Thing in the Constitution or Laws of any State to the Contrary notwithstanding.

The Senators and Representatives before mentioned, and the Members of the several State Legislatures, and all executive and judicial Officers, both of the United States and of the several States, shall be bound by Oath or Affirmation, to support this Constitution; but no religious Test shall ever be required as a Qualification to any Office or public Trust under the United States.

ARTICLE VII

The Ratification of the Conventions of nine States, shall be sufficient for the Establishment of this Constitution between the States so ratifying the Same.

Done in Convention by the Unanimous Consent of the States present the Seventeenth Day of September in the Year of our Lord one thousand seven hundred and Eighty seven and of the Independence of the United States of America the Twelfth. In witness whereof we have hereunto subscribed our Names,

Go. WASHINGTON
Presid't. and deputy from Virginia

Attest
WILLIAM JACKSON
Secretary

DELAWARE
Geo. Read
Gunning Bedford jun
John Dickinson
Richard Basset
Jaco. Broom

MASSACHUSETTS
Nathaniel Gorham
Rufus King

CONNECTICUT
Wm. Saml. Johnson
Roger Sherman

NEW YORK
Alexander Hamilton

NEW JERSEY
Wh. Livingston
David Brearley
Wm. Paterson
Jona. Dayton

PENNSYLVANIA
B. Franklin
Thomas Mifflin
Robt. Morris
Geo. Clymer
Thos. FitzSimons
Jared Ingersoll
James Wilson
Gouv. Morris

NEW HAMPSHIRE
John Langdon
Nicholas Gilman

MARYLAND
James McHenry
Dan of St. Thos. Jenifer
Danl. Carroll

VIRGINIA
John Blair
James Madison, Jr.

NORTH CAROLINA
Wm. Blount
Richd. Dobbs Spaight
Hu. Williamson

SOUTH CAROLINA
J. Rutledge
Charles Cotesworth
  Pinckney
Charles Pinckney
Pierce Butler

GEORGIA
William Few
Abr. Baldwin

Articles in addition to, and amendment of the Constitution of the United States of America, proposed by Congress and ratified by the Legislatures of the several states, pursuant to the Fifth Article of the original Constitution.

(The first ten amendments were passed by Congress on September 25, 1789, and were ratified on December 15, 1791.)

Amendment I

Congress shall make no law respecting an establishment of religion, or prohibiting the free exercise thereof; or abridging the freedom of speech, or of the press; or the right of the people peaceably to assemble, and to petition the Government for a redress of grievances.

Amendment II

A well regulated Militia, being necessary to the security of a free State, the right of the people to keep and bear Arms, shall not be infringed.

Amendment III

No Soldier shall, in time of peace be quartered in any house, without the consent of the Owner, nor in time of war, but in a manner to be prescribed by law.

Amendment IV

The right of the people to be secure in their persons, houses, papers, and effects, against unreasonable searches and seizures, shall not be violated, and no warrants shall issue, but upon probable cause, supported by Oath or affirmation, and particularly describing the place to be searched, and the persons or things to be seized.

Amendment V

No person shall be held to answer for a capital, or otherwise infamous crime, unless on a presentment or indictment of a Grand Jury, except in cases arising in the land or naval forces, or in the Militia, when in actual service in time of War or public danger; nor shall any person be subject for the same offence to be twice put in jeopardy of life or limb; nor shall be compelled in any criminal case to be a witness against himself, nor be deprived of life, liberty, or property, without due process of law; nor shall private property be taken for public use, without just compensation.

Amendment VI

In all criminal prosecutions, the accused shall enjoy the right to a speedy and public trial, by an impartial jury of the State and district wherein the crime shall have been committed, which district shall have been previously ascertained by law, and to be informed of the nature and cause of the accusation; to be confronted with the witnesses against him; to have compulsory process for obtaining witnesses in his favor, and to have the assistance of counsel for his defence.

Amendment VII

In Suits at common law, where the value in controversy shall exceed twenty dollars, the right of trial by jury shall be preserved, and no fact tried by a jury, shall be otherwise re-examined in any Court of the United States, than according to the rules of the common law.

Amendment VIII

Excessive bail shall not be required, nor excessive fines imposed, nor cruel and unusual punishments inflicted.

Amendment IX

The enumeration in the Constitution, of certain rights, shall not be construed to deny or disparage others retained by the people.

Amendment x

The powers not delegated to the United States by the Constitution, nor prohibited by it to the States, are reserved to the States respectively, or to the people.

Amendment xi   *(Ratified on February 7, 1795)*

The Judicial power of the United States shall not be construed to extend to any suit in law or equity, commenced or prosecuted against one of the United States by Citizens of another State, or by Citizens or Subjects of any Foreign State.

Amendment xii   *(Ratified on June 15, 1804)*

The Electors shall meet in their respective states, and vote by ballot for President and Vice-President, one of whom, at least, shall not be an inhabitant of the same state with themselves; they shall name in their ballots the person voted for as President, and in distinct ballots the person voted for as Vice-President, and they shall make distinct lists of all persons voted for as President, and of all persons voted for as Vice-President, and of the number of votes for each, which lists they shall sign and certify, and transmit sealed to the seat of the government of the United States, directed to the President of the Senate;—The President of the Senate shall, in the presence of the Senate and House of Representatives, open all the certificates and the votes shall then be counted;—The person having the greatest number of votes for President, shall be the President, if such number be a majority of the whole number of Electors appointed; and if no person have such majority; then from the persons having the highest numbers not exceeding three on the list of those voted for as President, the House of Representatives shall choose immediately, by ballot, the President. But in choosing the President, the votes shall be taken by states, the representation from each state having one vote; a quorum for this purpose shall consist of a member or members from two-thirds of the states, and a majority of all the states shall be necessary to a choice. And if the House of Representatives shall not choose a President whenever the right of choice shall devolve upon them, before the fourth day of March next following, then the Vice-President shall act as President, as in the case of the death or other constitutional disability of the President.—The person having the greatest number of votes as Vice-President, shall be the Vice-President, if such number be a majority of the whole number of Electors appointed, and if no person have a majority, then from the two highest numbers on the list, the Senate shall choose the Vice-President; a quorum for the purpose shall consist of two-thirds of the whole number of Senators, and a majority of the whole number shall be necessary to a choice. But no person constitutionally ineligible to the office of President shall be eligible to that of Vice-President of the United States.

Amendment xiii   *(Ratified on December 6, 1865)*

SECTION 1. Neither slavery nor involuntary servitude, except as a punishment for crime whereof the party shall have been duly convicted, shall exist within the United States, or any place subject to their jurisdiction.

SECTION 2. Congress shall have power to enforce this article by appropriate legislation.

Amendment xiv   *(Ratified on July 9, 1868)*

SECTION 1. All persons born or naturalized in the United States, and subject to the jurisdiction thereof, are citizens of the United States and of the State wherein they reside.

No State shall make or enforce any law which shall abridge the privileges or immunities of citizens of the United States; nor shall any State deprive any person of life, liberty, or property, without due process of law; nor deny to any person within its jurisdiction the equal protection of the laws.

SECTION 2. Representatives shall be apportioned among the several States according to their respective numbers, counting the whole number of persons in each State, excluding Indians not taxed. But when the right to vote at any election for the choice of electors for President and Vice President of the United States, Representatives in Congress, the Executive and Judicial officers of a State, or the members of the Legislature thereof, is denied to any of the male inhabitants of such State, being twenty-one years of age, and citizens of the United States, or in any way abridged, except for participation in rebellion, or other crime, the basis of representation therein shall be reduced in the proportion which the number of such male citizens shall bear to the whole number of male citizens twenty-one years of age in such State.

SECTION 3. No person shall be a Senator or Representative in Congress, or elector of President and Vice President, or hold any office, civil or military, under the United States, or under any State, who, having previously taken an oath, as a member of Congress, or as an officer of the United States, or as a member of any State legislature, or as an executive or judicial officer of any State, to support the Constitution of the United States, shall have engaged in insurrection or rebellion against the same, or given aid or comfort to the enemies thereof. But Congress may by a vote of two-thirds of each House, remove such disability.

SECTION 4. The validity of the public debt of the United States, authorized by law, including debts incurred for payment of pensions and bounties for services in suppressing insurrection or rebellion, shall not be questioned. But neither the United States nor any State shall assume or pay any debt or obligation incurred in aid of insurrection or rebellion against the United States, or any claim for the loss or emancipation of any slave, but all such debts, obligations and claims shall be held illegal and void.

SECTION 5. The Congress shall have power to enforce, by appropriate legislation, the provisions of this article.

Amendment xv   *(Ratified on February 3, 1870)*

SECTION 1. The right of citizens of the United States to vote shall not be denied or abridged by the United States or by any State on account of race, color, or previous condition of servitude.

SECTION 2. The Congress shall have power to enforce this article by appropriate legislation.

Amendment xvi   *(Ratified on February 3, 1913)*

The Congress shall have power to lay and collect taxes on incomes, from whatever source derived, without apportionment among the several States, and without regard to any census or enumeration.

Amendment xvii   *(Ratified on April 8, 1913)*

The Senate of the United States shall be composed of two Senators from each State, elected by the people thereof, for six years; and each Senator shall have one vote. The electors in each State shall have the qualifications requisite for electors of the most numerous branch of the State legislatures.

When vacancies happen in the representation of any State in the Senate, the executive authority of such State shall issue writs of election to fill such vacancies: *Provided,* That the legislature of any State may empower the executive thereof to make temporary appointments until the people fill the vacancies by election as the legislature may direct.

This amendment shall not be so construed as to affect the election or term of any Senator chosen before it becomes valid as part of the Constitution.

Amendment xviii   *(Ratified on January 16, 1919)*

SECTION 1. After one year from the ratification of this article the manufacture, sale, or transportation of intoxicating liquors within, the importation thereof into, or the exportation thereof from the United States and all territory subject to the jurisdiction thereof for beverage purposes is hereby prohibited.

SECTION 2. The Congress and the several States shall have concurrent power to enforce this article by appropriate legislation.

SECTION 3. This article shall be inoperative unless it shall have been ratified as an amendment to the Constitution by the legislatures of the several States, as provided in the Constitution, within seven years from the date of the submission hereof to the States by the Congress.

Amendment xix   *(Ratified on August 18, 1920)*

The right of citizens of the United States to vote shall not be denied or abridged by the United States or by any State on account of sex.

Congress shall have power to enforce this article by appropriate legislation.

Amendment xx   *(Ratified on February 6, 1933)*

SECTION 1. The terms of the President and Vice President shall end at noon on the 20th day of January, and the terms of Senators and Representatives at noon on the 3d day of January, of the years in which such terms would have ended if this article had not been ratified; and the terms of their successors shall then begin.

SECTION 2. The Congress shall assemble at least once in every year, and such meeting shall begin at noon on the 3d day of January, unless they shall by law appoint a different day.

SECTION 3. If, at the time fixed for the beginning of the term of the President, the President elect shall have died, the Vice President elect shall become President. If a President shall not have been chosen before the time fixed for the beginning of his term, or if the President elect shall have failed to qualify, then the Vice President elect shall act as President until a President shall have qualified; and the Congress may by law provide for the case wherein neither a President elect nor a Vice President elect shall have qualified, declaring who shall then act as President, or the manner in which one who is to act shall be selected, and such person shall act accordingly until a President or Vice President shall have qualified.

SECTION 4. The Congress may by law provide for the case of the death of any of the persons from whom the House of Representatives may choose a President whenever the rights of choice shall have devolved upon them, and for the case of the death of any of the persons from whom the Senate may choose a Vice President whenever the right of choice shall have devolved upon them.

SECTION 5. Sections 1 and 2 shall take effect on the 15th day of October following the ratification of this article.

SECTION 6. This article shall be inoperative unless it shall have been ratified as an amendment to the Constitution by the legislatures of three-fourths of the several States within seven years from the date of its submission.

Amendment xxi   *(Ratified on December 5, 1933)*

SECTION 1. The eighteenth article of amendment to the Constitution of the United States is hereby repealed.

SECTION 2. The transportation or importation into any State, Territory, or possession of the United States for delivery or use therein of intoxicating liquors, in violation of the laws thereof, is hereby prohibited.

SECTION 3. This article shall be inoperative unless it shall have been ratified as an amendment to the Constitution by conventions in the several States, as provided in the Constitution, within seven years from the date of the submission hereof to the States by the Congress.

Amendment xxii   *(Ratified on February 27, 1951)*

No person shall be elected to the office of the President more than twice, and no person who has held the office of President, or acted as President, for more than two years of a term to which some other person was elected President shall be elected to the office of the President more than once. But this Article shall not apply to any person holding the office of President when this Article was proposed by the Congress, and shall not prevent any person who may be holding the office of President, or acting as President, during the term within which this Article becomes operative from holding the office of President or acting as President during the remainder of such term.

Amendment xxiii   *(Ratified on March 29, 1961)*

SECTION 1. The District constituting the seat of Government of the United States shall appoint in such manner as the Congress may direct:
A number of electors of President and Vice President equal to the whole number of Senators and Representatives in Congress to which the District would be entitled if it were a State, but in no event more than the least populous State; they shall be in addition to those appointed by the States, but they shall be considered, for the purposes of the election of President and Vice President, to be electors appointed by a State; and they shall meet in the District and perform such duties as provided by the twelfth article of amendment.

Section 2. The Congress shall have power to enforce this article by appropriate legislation.

Amendment xxiv   *(Ratified on January 23, 1964)*

Section 1. The right of citizens of the United States to vote in any primary or other election for President or Vice President, for electors for President or Vice President, or for Senator or Representative in Congress, shall not be denied or abridged by the United States or any State by reason of failure to pay any poll tax or other tax.

Section 2. The Congress shall have power to enforce this article by appropriate legislation.

Amendment xxv   *(Ratified on February 10, 1967)*

Section 1. In case of the removal of the President from office or of his death or resignation, the Vice President shall become President.

Section 2. Whenever there is a vacancy in the office of the Vice President, the President shall nominate a Vice President who shall take office upon confirmation by a majority vote of both Houses of Congress.

Section 3. Whenever the President transmits to the President pro tempore of the Senate and the Speaker of the House of Representatives his written declaration that he is unable to discharge the powers and duties of his office, and until he transmits to them a written declaration to the contrary, such powers and duties shall be discharged by the Vice President as Acting President.

Section 4. Whenever the Vice President and a majority of either the principal officers of the executive departments or of such other body as Congress may by law provide, transmit to the President pro tempore of the Senate and the Speaker of the House of Representatives their written declaration that the President is unable to discharge the powers and duties of his office, the Vice President shall immediately assume the powers and duties of the office as Acting President.

Thereafter, when the President transmits to the President pro tempore of the Senate and the Speaker of the House of Representatives his written declaration that no inability exists, he shall resume the powers and duties of his office unless the Vice President and a majority of either the principal officers of the executive department or of such other body as Congress may by law provide, transmit within four days to the President pro tempore of the Senate and the Speaker of the House of Representatives their written declaration that the President is unable to discharge the powers and duties of his office. Thereupon Congress shall decide the issue, assembling within forty-eight hours for that purpose if not in session. If the Congress, within twenty-one days after receipt of the latter written declaration, or, if Congress is not in session, within twenty-one days after Congress is required to assemble, determines by two-thirds vote of both Houses that the President is unable to discharge the powers and duties of his office, the Vice President shall continue to discharge the same as Acting President; otherwise, the President shall resume the powers and duties of his office.

Amendment xxvi   *(Ratified on July 1, 1971)*

Section 1. The right of citizens of the United States, who are eighteen years of age or older, to vote shall not be denied or abridged by the United States or by any State on account of age.

Section 2. The Congress shall have power to enforce this article by appropriate legislation.

Amendment xxvii   *(Ratified on May 7, 1992)*

No law varying the compensation for the services of Senators and Representatives shall take effect until an election of Representatives shall have intervened.

APPENDIX III

The Federalist No. 10

James Madison

November 22, 1787

TO THE PEOPLE OF THE STATE OF NEW YORK

Among the numerous advantages promised by a well constructed Union, none deserves to be more accurately developed than its tendency to break and control the violence of faction. The friend of popular governments, never finds himself so much alarmed for their character and fate, as when he contemplates their propensity to this dangerous vice. He will not fail therefore to set a due value on any plan which, without violating the principles to which he is attached, provides a proper cure for it. The instability, injustice and confusion introduced into the public councils, have in truth been the mortal diseases under which popular governments have every where perished; as they continue to be the favorite and fruitful topics from which the adversaries to liberty derive their most specious declamations. The valuable improvements made by the American Constitutions on the popular models, both ancient and modern, cannot certainly be too much admired; but it would be an unwarrantable partiality, to contend that they have as effectually obviated the danger on this side as was wished and expected. Complaints are every where heard from our most considerate and virtuous citizens, equally the friends of public and private faith, and of public and personal liberty; that our governments are too unstable; that the public good is disregarded in the conflicts of rival parties; and that measures are too often decided, not according to the rules of justice, and the rights of the minor party; but by the superior force of an interested and over-bearing majority. However anxiously we may wish that these complaints had no foundation, the evidence of known facts will not permit us to deny that they are in some degree true. It will be found indeed, on a candid review of our situation, that some of the distresses under which we labor, have been erroneously charged on the operation of our governments; but it will be found, at the same time, that other causes will not alone account for many of our heaviest misfortunes; and particularly, for that prevailing and increasing distrust of public engagements, and alarm for private rights, which are echoed from one end of the continent to the other. These must be chiefly, if not wholly, effects of the unsteadiness and injustice, with which a factious spirit has tainted our public administrations.

By a faction I understand a number of citizens, whether amounting to a majority or minority of the whole, who are united and actuated by some common impulse of passion or of interest, adverse to the rights of other citizens, or to the permanent and aggregate interests of the community.

There are two methods of curing the mischiefs of faction: the one, by removing its causes; the other, by controlling its effects.

There are again two methods of removing the causes of faction: the one by destroying the liberty which is essential to its existence; the other, by giving to every citizen the same opinions, the same passions, and the same interests.

It could never be more truly said than of the first remedy, that it is worse than the disease. Liberty is to faction, what air is to fire, an aliment without which it instantly expires. But it could not be a less folly to abolish liberty, which is essential to political life, because it nourishes faction, than it would be to wish the annihilation of air, which is essential to animal life, because it imparts to fire its destructive agency.

The second expedient is as impracticable, as the first would be unwise. As long as the reason of man continues fallible, and he is at liberty to exercise it, different opinions will be formed. As long as the connection subsists between his reason and his self-love, his opinions and his passions will have a reciprocal influence on each other; and the former will be objects to which the latter will attach themselves. The diversity in the faculties of men from which the rights of property originate, is not less an insuperable obstacle to a uniformity of interests. The protection of these faculties is the first object of Government. From the protection of different and unequal faculties of acquiring property, the possession of different degrees and kinds of property immediately results: and from the influence of these on the sentiments and views of the respective proprietors, ensues a division of the society into different interests and parties.

The latent causes of faction are thus sown in the nature of man; and we see them every where brought into different degrees of activity, according to the different circumstances of civil society. A zeal for different opinions concerning religion, concerning Government and many other points, as well of speculation as of practice; an attachment to different leaders ambitiously contending for pre-eminence and power; or to persons of other descriptions whose fortunes have been interesting to the human passions, have in turn divided mankind into parties, inflamed them with mutual animosity, and rendered them much more disposed to vex and oppress each other, than to co-operate for their common good. So strong is this propensity of mankind to fall into mutual animosities, that where no substantial occasion presents itself, the most frivolous and fanciful distinctions have been sufficient to kindle their unfriendly passions, and excite their most violent conflicts. But the most common and durable source of factions, has been the various and unequal distribution of property. Those who hold, and those who are without property, have ever formed distinct interests in society. Those who are creditors, and those who are debtors, fall under a like discrimination. A landed interest, a manufacturing interest, a mercantile interest, a monied interest, with many lesser interests, grow up of necessity in civilized nations, and divide them into different classes, actuated by different sentiments and views. The regulation of these various and interfering interests forms the principal task of modern Legislation, and involves the spirit of party and faction in the necessary and ordinary operations of Government.

No man is allowed to be a judge in his own cause; because his interest would certainly bias his judgment, and, not improbably, corrupt his integrity. With equal, nay with greater reason, a body of men, are unfit to be both judges and parties, at the same time; yet, what are many of the most important acts of legislation, but so many judicial determinations, not indeed concerning the rights of single persons, but concerning the rights of large bodies of citizens, and what are the different classes of legislators, but advocates and parties to the causes which they determine? Is a law proposed concerning private debts? It is a question to which the creditors are parties on one side, and the debtors on the other. Justice ought to hold the balance between them. Yet the parties are and must be themselves the judges; and the most numerous party, or, in other words, the most powerful faction must be expected to prevail. Shall domestic manufactures be encouraged, and in what degree, by restrictions on foreign manufactures? are questions which would be differently decided by the landed and the manufacturing classes; and probably by neither, with a sole regard to justice and the public good. The apportionment of taxes on the various descriptions of property, is an act which seems to require the most exact impartiality; yet, there is perhaps no legislative act in which greater opportunity and temptation are given to a predominant party, to trample on the rules of justice. Every shilling with which they over-burden the inferior number, is a shilling saved to their own pockets.

It is in vain to say, that enlightened statesmen will be able to adjust these clashing interests, and render them all subservient to the public good. Enlightened statesmen will not always be at the helm: Nor, in many cases, can such an adjustment be made at all, without taking into view indirect and remote considerations, which will rarely prevail over the immediate interest which one party may find in disregarding the rights of another, or the good of the whole.

The inference to which we are brought, is, that the *causes* of faction cannot be removed; and that relief is only to be sought in the means of controlling its *effects.*

If a faction consists of less than a majority, relief is supplied by the republican principle, which enables the majority to defeat its sinister views by regular vote: It may clog the administration, it may convulse the society; but it will be unable to execute and mask its violence under the forms of the Constitution. When a majority is included in a faction, the form of popular government on the other hand enables it to sacrifice to its ruling passion or interest, both the public good and the rights of other citizens. To secure the public good, and private rights, against the danger of such a faction, and at the same time to preserve the spirit and the form of popular government, is then the great object to which our enquiries are directed: Let me add that it is the great desideratum, by which alone this form of government can be rescued from the opprobrium under which it has so long labored, and be recommended to the esteem and adoption of mankind.

By what means is this object attainable? Evidently by one of two only. Either the existence of the same passion or interest in a majority at the same time, must be prevented; or the majority, having such co-existent passion or interest, must be rendered, by their number and local situation, unable to concert and carry into effect schemes of oppression. If the impulse and the opportunity be suffered to coincide, we well know that neither moral nor religious motives can be relied on as an adequate control. They are not found to be such on the injustice and violence of individuals, and lose their efficacy in proportion to the number combined together; that is, in proportion as their efficacy becomes needful.

From this view of the subject, it may be concluded, that a pure Democracy, by which I mean, a Society, consisting of a small number of citizens, who assemble and administer the Government in person, can admit of no cure for the mischiefs of faction. A common passion or interest will, in almost every case, be felt by a majority of the whole; a communication and concert results from the form of Government itself; and there is nothing to check the inducements to sacrifice the weaker party, or an obnoxious individual. Hence it is, that such Democracies have ever been spectacles of turbulence and contention; have ever been found incompatible with personal security, or the rights of property; and have in general been as short in their lives, as they have been violent in their deaths. Theoretic politicians, who have patronized this species of Government, have erroneously supposed, that by reducing mankind to a perfect equality in their political rights, they would, at the same time, be perfectly equalized and assimilated in their possessions, their opinions, and their passions.

A republic, by which I mean a government in which the scheme of representation takes place, opens a different prospect, and promises the cure for which we are seeking. Let us examine the points in which it varies from pure democracy, and we shall comprehend both the nature of the cure and the efficacy which it must derive from the union.

The two great points of difference, between a democracy and a republic, are, first, the delegation of the government, in the latter, to a small number of citizens, elected by the rest; secondly, the greater number of citizens, and greater sphere of country, over which the latter may be extended.

The effect of the first difference is, on the one hand, to refine and enlarge the public views, by passing them through the medium of a chosen body of citizens, whose wisdom may best discern the true interest of their country, and whose patriotism and love of justice, will be least likely to sacrifice it to temporary or partial considerations. Under such a regulation, it may well happen, that the public voice, pronounced by the representatives of the people, will be more consonant to the public good, than if pronounced by the people themselves, convened for the purpose. On the other hand the effect may be inverted. Men of factious tempers, of local prejudices, or of sinister designs, may by intrigue, by corruption, or by other means, first obtain the suffrages, and then betray the interest of the people. The question resulting is, whether small or extensive republics are most favorable to the election of proper guardians of the public weal, and it is clearly decided in favor of the latter by two obvious considerations.

In the first place, it is to be remarked that, however small the republic may be, the representatives must be raised to a certain number, in order to guard against the cabals of a few; and that however large it may be, they must be limited to a certain number, in order to guard against the confusion of a multitude. Hence, the number of representatives in the two cases not being in proportion to that of the constituents, and being proportionally greatest in the small republic, it follows, that if the proportion of fit characters be not less in the large than in the small republic, the former will present a greater option, and consequently a greater probability of a fit choice.

In the next place, as each Representative will be chosen by a greater number of citizens in the large than in the small Republic, it will be more difficult for unworthy candidates to practise with success the vicious arts, by which elections are too often carried; and the suffrages of the people being more free, will be more likely to center on men who possess the most attractive merit, and the most diffusive and established characters.

It must be confessed, that in this, as in most other cases, there is a mean, on both sides of which inconveniences will be found to lie. By enlarging too much the number of electors, you render the representative too little acquainted with all their local circumstances and lesser interests; as by reducing it too much, you render him unduly attached to these, and too little fit to comprehend and pursue great and national objects. The Federal Constitution forms a happy combination in this respect; the great and aggregate interests being referred to the national, the local and particular, to the state legislatures.

The other point of difference is, the greater number of citizens and extent of territory which may be brought within the compass of Republican, than of Democratic Government; and it is this circumstance principally which renders factious combinations less to be dreaded in the former, than in the latter. The smaller the society, the fewer probably will be the distinct parties and interests composing it; the fewer the distinct parties and interests, the more frequently will a majority be found of the same party; and the smaller the number of individuals composing a majority, and the smaller the compass within which they are placed, the more easily will they concert and execute their plans of oppression. Extend the sphere, and you take in a greater variety of parties and interests; you make it less probable that a majority of the whole will have a common motive to invade the rights of other citizens; or if such a common motive exists, it will be more difficult for all who feel it to discover their own strength, and to act in unison with each other. Besides other impediments, it may be remarked, that where there is a consciousness of unjust or dishonorable purposes, communication is always checked by distrust, in proportion to the number whose concurrence is necessary.

Hence it clearly appears, that the same advantage, which a Republic has over a Democracy, in controlling the effects of faction, is enjoyed by a large over a small Republic—is enjoyed by the Union over the States composing it. Does this advantage consist in the substitution of Representatives, whose enlightened views and virtuous sentiments render them superior to local prejudices, and to schemes of injustice? It will not be denied, that the Representation of the Union will be most likely to possess these requisite endowments. Does it consist in the greater security afforded by a greater variety of parties, against the event of any one party being able to outnumber and oppress the rest? In an equal degree does the increased variety of parties, comprised within the Union, increase this security? Does it, in fine, consist in the greater obstacles opposed to the concert and accomplishment of the secret wishes of an unjust and interested majority? Here, again, the extent of the Union gives it the most palpable advantage.

The influence of factious leaders may kindle a flame within their particular States, but will be unable to spread a general conflagration through the other States: a religious sect, may degenerate into a political faction in a part of the Confederacy but the variety of sects dispersed over the entire face of it, must secure the national Councils against any danger from that source: a rage for paper money, for an abolition of debts, for an equal division of property, or for any other improper or wicked project, will be less apt to pervade the whole body of the Union, than a particular member of it; in the same proportion as such a malady is more likely to taint a particular county or district, than an entire State.

In the extent and proper structure of the Union, therefore, we behold a Republican remedy for the diseases most incident to Republican Government. And according to the degree of pleasure and pride, we feel in being Republicans, ought to be our zeal in cherishing the spirit, and supporting the character of Federalists.

Publius

The Federalist No. 51

James Madison

February 6, 1788

TO THE PEOPLE OF THE STATE OF NEW YORK

To what expedient then shall we finally resort for maintaining in practice the necessary partition of power among the several departments, as laid down in the constitution? The only answer that can be given is, that as all these exterior provisions are found to be inadequate, the defect must be supplied, by so contriving the interior structure of the government, as that its several constituent parts may, by their mutual relations, be the means of keeping each other in their proper places. Without presuming to undertake a full development of this important idea, I will hazard a few general observations, which may perhaps place it in a clearer light, and enable us to form a more correct judgment of the principles and structure of the government planned by the convention.

In order to lay a due foundation for that separate and distinct exercise of the different powers of government, which to a certain extent, is admitted on all hands to be essential to the preservation of liberty, it is evident that each department should have a will of its own; and consequently should be so constituted, that the members of each should have as little agency as possible in the appointment of the members of the others. Were this principle rigorously adhered to, it would require that all the appointments for the supreme executive, legislative, and judiciary magistracies, should be drawn from the same fountain of authority, the people, through channels, having no communication whatever with one another. Perhaps such a plan of constructing the several departments would be less difficult in practice than it may in contemplation appear. Some difficulties however, and some additional expense, would attend the execution of it. Some deviations therefore from the principle must be admitted. In the constitution of the judiciary department in particular, it might be inexpedient to insist rigorously on the principle; first, because peculiar qualifications being essential in the members, the primary consideration ought to be to select that mode of choice, which best secures these qualifications; secondly, because the permanent tenure by which the appointments are held in that department, must soon destroy all sense of dependence on the authority conferring them.

It is equally evident that the members of each department should be as little dependent as possible on those of the others, for the emoluments annexed to their offices. Were the executive magistrate, or the judges, not independent of the legislature in this particular, their independence in every other would be merely nominal.

But the great security against a gradual concentration of the several powers in the same department, consists in giving to those who administer each department, the necessary constitutional means, and personal motives, to resist encroachments of the others. The provision for defense must in this, as in all other cases, be made commensurate to the danger of attack. Ambition must be made to counteract ambition. The interest of the man must be connected with the constitutional right of the place. It may be a reflection on human nature, that such devices should be necessary to control the abuses of government. But what is government itself but the greatest of all reflections on human nature? If men were angels, no government would be necessary. If angels were to govern men, neither external nor internal controls on government would be necessary. In framing a government which is to be administered by men over men, the great difficulty lies in this: You must first enable the government to control the governed; and in the next place, oblige it to control itself. A dependence on the people is no doubt the primary control on the government; but experience has taught mankind the necessity of auxiliary precautions.

This policy of supplying by opposite and rival interests, the defect of better motives, might be traced through the whole system of human affairs, private as well as public. We see it particularly displayed in all the subordinate distributions of power; where the constant aim is to divide and arrange the several offices in such a manner as that each may be a check on the other; that the private interest of every individual, may be a sentinel over the public rights. These inventions of prudence cannot be less requisite in the distribution of the supreme powers of the state.

But it is not possible to give to each department an equal power of self defense. In republican government the legislative authority, necessarily, predominates. The remedy for this inconveniency is, to divide the legislature into different branches; and to render them by different modes of election, and different principles of action, as little connected with each other, as the nature of their common functions, and their common dependence on the society, will admit. It may even be necessary to guard against dangerous encroachments by still further precautions. As the weight of the legislative authority requires that it should be thus divided, the weakness of the executive may require, on the other hand, that it should be fortified. An absolute negative, on the legislature, appears at first view to be the natural defense with which the executive magistrate should be armed. But perhaps it would be neither altogether safe, nor alone sufficient. On ordinary occasion, it might not be exerted with the requisite firmness; and on extraordinary occasions, it might be prefidiously abused. May not this defect of an absolute negative be supplied, by some qualified connection between this weaker department, and the weaker branch of the stronger department, by which the latter may be led to support the constitutional rights of the former, without being too much detached from the rights of its own department?

If the principles on which these observations are founded be just, as I persuade myself they are, and they be applied as a criterion, to the several state constitutions, and to the federal constitution, it will be found, that if the latter does not perfectly correspond with them, the former are infinitely less able to bear such a test.

There are moreover two considerations particularly applicable to the federal system of America, which place that system in a very interesting point of view.

First. In a single republic, all the power surrendered by the people, is submitted to the administration of a single government; and usurpations are guarded against by a division of the government into distinct and separate departments. In the compound republic of America, the power surrendered by the people, is first divided between two distinct governments, and then the portion allotted to each, subdivided among distinct and separate departments. Hence a double security arises to the rights of the people. The different governments will control each other; at the same time that each will be controlled by itself.

Second. It is of great importance in a republic, not only to guard the society against the oppression of its rulers; but to guard one part of the society against the injustice of the other part. Different interests necessarily exist in different classes of citizens. If a majority be united by a common interest, the rights of the minority will be insecure. There are but two methods of providing against this evil: The one by creating a will in the community independent of the majority, that is, of the society itself, the other by comprehending in the society so many separate descriptions of citizens, as will render an unjust combination of a majority of the whole, very improbable, if not impracticable. The first method prevails in all governments possessing an hereditary or self appointed authority. This at best is but a precarious security; because a power independent of the society may as well espouse the unjust views of the major, as the rightful interests, of the minor party, and may possibly be turned against both parties. The second method will be exemplified in the federal republic of the United States. While all authority in it will be derived from and dependent on the society, the society itself will be broken into so many parts, interests and classes of citizens, that the rights of individuals or of the minority, will be in little danger from interested combinations of the majority. In a free government, the security for civil rights must be the same as for religious rights. It consists in the one case in the multiplicity of interests, and in the other, in the multiplicity of sects. The degree of security in both cases will depend on the number of interests and sects; and this may be presumed to depend on the extent of country and number of people comprehended under the same government. This view of the subject must particularly recommend a proper federal system to all the sincere and considerate friends of republican government: Since it shows that in exact proportion as the territory of the union may be formed into more circumscribed confederacies or states, oppressive combinations of a majority will be facilitated, the best security under the republican form, for the rights of every class of citizens, will be diminished; and consequently, the stability and independence of some member of the government, the only other security, must be proportionally increased. Justice is the end of government. It is the end of civil society. It ever has been, and ever will be pursued, until it be obtained, or until liberty be lost in the pursuit. In a society under the forms of which the stronger faction can readily unite and oppress the weaker, anarchy may as truly be said to reign, as in a state of nature where the weaker individual is not secured against the violence of the stronger: And as in the latter state even the stronger individuals are prompted by the uncertainty of their condition, to submit to a government which may protect the weak as well as themselves: So in the former state, will the more powerful factions or parties be gradually induced by a like motive, to wish for a government which will protect all parties, the weaker as well as the more powerful. It can be little doubted, that if the state of Rhode Island was separated from the confederacy, and left to itself, the insecurity of rights under the popular form of government within such narrow limits, would be displayed by such reiterated oppressions of factious majorities, that some power altogether independent of the people would soon be called for by the voice of the very factions whose misrule had proved the necessity of it. In the extended republic of the United States, and among the great variety of interests, parties and sects which it embraces, a coalition of a majority of the whole society could seldom take place on any other principles than those of justice and the general good; and there being thus less danger to a minor from the will of the major party, there must be less pretext also, to provide for the security of the former, by introducing into the government a will not dependent on the latter; or in other words, a will independent of the society itself. It is no less certain than it is important, notwithstanding the contrary opinions which have been entertained, that the larger the society, provided it lie within a practicable sphere, the more duly capable it will be of self government. And happily for the *republican cause,* the practicable sphere may be carried to a very great extent, by a judicious modification and mixture of the *federal principle.*

PUBLIUS

APPENDIX IV

Presidents, Congresses and Chief Justices 1789–1992

TERM	PRESIDENT AND VICE PRESIDENT	PARTY OF PRESIDENT	CONGRESS	Majority Party		CHIEF JUSTICE OF THE UNITED STATES
				HOUSE	SENATE	
1789–1797	**George Washington** John Adams	None	1st 2d 3d 4th	(N/A) (N/A) (N/A) (N/A)	(N/A) (N/A) (N/A) (N/A)	John Jay (1789–1795) John Rutledge (1795) Oliver Ellsworth (1796–1800)
1797–1801	**John Adams** Thomas Jefferson	Federalist	5th 6th	(N/A) Fed	(N/A) Fed	Oliver Ellsworth (1796–1800) John Marshall (1801–1835)
1801–1809	**Thomas Jefferson** Aaron Burr (1801–1805) George Clinton (1805–1809)	Democratic-Republican	7th 8th 9th 10th	Dem–Rep Dem–Rep Dem–Rep Dem–Rep	Dem–Rep Dem–Rep Dem–Rep Dem–Rep	John Marshall (1801–1835)
1809–1817	**James Madison** George Clinton (1809–1812)[a] Elbridge Gerry (1813–1814)[a]	Democratic-Republican	11th 12th 13th 14th	Dem–Rep Dem–Rep Dem–Rep Dem–Rep	Dem–Rep Dem–Rep Dem–Rep Dem–Rep	John Marshall (1801–1835)
1817–1825	**James Monroe** Daniel D. Tompkins	Democratic-Republican	15th 16th 17th 18th	Dem–Rep Dem–Rep Dem–Rep Dem–Rep	Dem–Rep Dem–Rep Dem–Rep Dem–Rep	John Marshall (1801–1835)
1825–1829	**John Quincy Adams** John C. Calhoun	National-Republican	19th 20th	Admin Jack	Admin Jack	John Marshall (1801–1835)
1829–1837	**Andrew Jackson** John C. Calhoun (1829–1832)[b] Martin Van Buren (1833–1837)	Democrat	21st 22d 23d 24th	Dem Dem Dem Dem	Dem Dem Dem Dem	John Marshall (1801–1835) Roger B. Taney (1836–1864)
1837–1841	**Martin Van Buren** Richard M. Johnson	Democrat	25th 26th	Dem Dem	Dem Dem	Roger B. Taney (1836–1864)
1841	**William H. Harrison**[a] John Tyler (1841)	Whig				Roger B. Taney (1836–1864)
1841–1845	**John Tyler** (VP vacant)	Whig	27th 28th	Whig Dem	Whig Whig	Roger B. Taney (1836–1864)
1845–1849	**James K. Polk** George M. Dallas	Democrat	29th 30th	Dem Whig	Dem Dem	Roger B. Taney (1836–1864)
1849–1850	**Zachary Taylor**[a] Millard Fillmore	Whig	31st	Dem	Dem	Roger B. Taney (1836–1864)
1850–1853	**Millard Fillmore** (VP vacant)	Whig	32d	Dem	Dem	Roger B. Taney (1836–1864)
1853–1857	**Franklin Pierce** William R.D. King (1853)[a]	Democrat	33d 34th	Dem Rep	Dem Dem	Roger B. Taney (1836–1864)
1857–1861	**James Buchanan** John C. Breckinridge	Democrat	35th 36th	Dem Rep	Dem Dem	Roger B. Taney (1836–1864)
1861–1865	**Abraham Lincoln**[a] Hannibal Hamlin (1861–1865) Andrew Johnson (1865)	Republican	37th 38th	Rep Rep	Rep Rep	Roger B. Taney (1836–1864) Salmon P. Chase (1864–1873)
1865–1869	**Andrew Johnson** (VP vacant)	Republican	39th 40th	Union Rep	Union Rep	Salmon P. Chase (1864–1873)
1869–1877	**Ulysses S. Grant** Schuyler Colfax (1869–1873) Henry Wilson (1873–1875)[a]	Republican	41st 42d 43d 44th	Rep Rep Rep Dem	Rep Rep Rep Rep	Salmon P. Chase (1864–1873) Morrison R. Waite (1874–1888)
1877–1881	**Rutherford B. Hayes** William A. Wheeler	Republican	45th 46th	Dem Dem	Rep Dem	Morrison R. Waite (1874–1888)
1881	**James A. Garfield**[a] Chester A. Arthur	Republican	47th	Rep	Rep	Morrison R. Waite (1874–1888)
1881–1885	**Chester A. Arthur** (VP vacant)	Republican	48th	Dem	Rep	Morrison R. Waite (1874–1888)
1885–1889	**Grover Cleveland** Thomas A. Hendricks (1885)[a]	Democrat	49th 50th	Dem Dem	Rep Rep	Morrison R. Waite (1874–1888) Melville W. Fuller (1888–1910)

[a]Died in office.

[b]Resigned from the vice presidency.

TERM	PRESIDENT AND VICE PRESIDENT	PARTY OF PRESIDENT	CONGRESS	Majority Party		CHIEF JUSTICE OF THE UNITED STATES
				HOUSE	SENATE	
1889–1893	**Benjamin Harrison** Levi P. Morton	Republican	51st 52d	Rep Dem	Rep Rep	Melville W. Fuller (1888–1910)
1893–1897	**Grover Cleveland** Adlai E. Stevenson	Democrat	53d 54th	Dem Rep	Dem Rep	Melville W. Fuller (1888–1910)
1897–1901	**William McKinley**[a] Garret A. Hobart (1897–1899)[a] Theodore Roosevelt (1901)	Republican	55th 56th	Rep Rep	Rep Rep	Melville W. Fuller (1888–1910)
1901–1909	**Theodore Roosevelt** (VP vacant, 1901–1905) Charles W. Fairbanks (1905–1909)	Republican	57th 58th 59th 60th	Rep Rep Rep Rep	Rep Rep Rep Rep	Melville W. Fuller (1888–1910)
1909–1913	**William Howard Taft** James S. Sherman (1909–1912)[a]	Republican	61st 62d	Rep Dem	Rep Rep	Melville W. Fuller (1888–1910) Edward D. White (1910–1921)
1913–1921	**Woodrow Wilson** Thomas R. Marshall	Democrat	63d 64th 65th 66th	Dem Dem Dem Rep	Dem Dem Dem Rep	Edward D. White (1910–1921)
1921–1923	**Warren G. Harding**[a] Calvin Coolidge	Republican	67th	Rep	Rep	William Howard Taft (1921–1930)
1923–1929	**Calvin Coolidge** (VP vacant, 1923–1925) Charles G. Dawes (1925–1929)	Republican	68th 69th 70th	Rep Rep Rep	Rep Rep Rep	William Howard Taft (1921–1930)
1929–1933	**Herbert Hoover** Charles Curtis	Republican	71st 72d	Rep Dem	Rep Rep	William Howard Taft (1921–1930) Charles Evans Hughes (1930–1941)
1933–1945	**Franklin D. Roosevelt**[a] John N. Garner (1933–1941) Henry A. Wallace (1941–1945) Harry S Truman (1945)	Democrat	73d 74th 75th 76th 77th 78th	Dem Dem Dem Dem Dem Dem	Dem Dem Dem Dem Dem Dem	Charles Evans Hughes (1930–1941) Harlan F. Stone (1941–1946)
1945–1953	**Harry S Truman** (VP vacant, 1945–1949) Alben W. Barkley (1949–1953)	Democrat	79th 80th 81st 82d	Dem Rep Dem Dem	Dem Rep Dem Dem	Harlan F. Stone (1941–1946) Frederick M. Vinson (1946–1953)
1953–1961	**Dwight D. Eisenhower** Richard M. Nixon	Republican	83d 84th 85th 86th	Rep Dem Dem Dem	Rep Dem Dem Dem	Frederick M. Vinson (1945–1953) Earl Warren (1953–1969)
1961–1963	**John F. Kennedy**[a] Lyndon B. Johnson (1961–1963)	Democrat	87th	Dem	Dem	Earl Warren (1953–1969)
1963–1969	**Lyndon B. Johnson** (VP vacant, 1963–1965) Hubert H. Humphrey (1965–1969)	Democrat	88th 89th 90th	Dem Dem Dem	Dem Dem Dem	Earl Warren (1953–1969)
1969–1974	**Richard M. Nixon**[c] Spiro T. Agnew (1969–1973)[b] Gerald R. Ford (1973–1974)[d]	Republican	91st 92d	Dem Dem	Dem Dem	Earl Warren (1953–1969) Warren E. Burger (1969–1986)
1974–1977	**Gerald R. Ford** Nelson A. Rockefeller[d]	Republican	93d 94th	Dem Dem	Dem Dem	Warren E. Burger (1969–1986)
1977–1981	**Jimmy Carter** Walter Mondale	Democrat	95th 96th	Dem Dem	Dem Dem	Warren E. Burger (1969–1986)
1981–1989	**Ronald Reagan** George Bush	Republican	97th 98th 99th 100th	Dem Dem Dem Dem	Rep Rep Rep Dem	Warren E. Burger (1969–1986) William H. Rehnquist (1986–)
1989–1993	**George Bush** J. Danforth Quayle	Republican	101st 102nd	Dem Dem	Dem Dem	William H. Rehnquist (1986–)
1993–	**William J. Clinton** Albert Gore, Jr.	Democrat	103d	Dem	Dem	William H. Rehnquist (1986–)

[a] Died in office.
[b] Resigned from the vice presidency.
[c] Resigned from the presidency.
[d] Appointed vice president.

Glossary

actual representation A system in which elected members of a legislative body are considered to represent only those who elected them. (Chapter 6)

adjudication The formal process of settling a case through litigation. (Chapter 9)

administrative discretion The ability to make choices concerning the best way to implement congressional intentions. (Chapter 8)

affiliates Local television stations that are associated with national networks and supplied by them with some programming and advertising. (Chapter 14)

affirmative action A policy or program designed to redress prior discrimination. (Chapter 5)

Agenda setting The process by which issues become questions of policy. (Chapter 17)

Aid to Families with Dependent Children (AFDC) A federal assistance program that provides funds to low-income mothers. (Chapter 3)

ambassador The official representative of one head of state to another. (Chapter 18)

amicus curiae brief "Friend of the court"; a third party to a lawsuit who presents additional legal briefs for the purpose of raising additional points of view in an attempt to influence the court's decision. (Chapters, 3, 9)

anti-communism The cause of containing the spread of communism throughout the globe. (Chapter 18)

Anti-Federalists Those who opposed the ratification of the U.S. Constitution. (Chapter 2)

appellate courts Those with the legal authority to hear and review decisions of lower courts. (Chapter 9)

appellate jurisdiction The authority of a court to hear a case that already has been adjudicated in a lower court. (Chapter 9)

appropriation The earmarking of funds by Congress in particular pieces of legislation for particular programs, agencies, and so forth. (Chapter 6)

aristocracy A system of government in which control is exercised by a small ruling class, based on social, economic, or military position. (Chapter 1)

Articles of Confederation The basic framework of the new U.S. government approved by the Second Continental Congress in 1777; the Articles provided for a Congress with limited authority, and they were used to govern the United States during the Revolutionary War. (Chapter 2)

articles of impeachment When these are approved by the House of Representatives, the action initiates the process to remove the president, the vice president, or civil officers of the United States from office for "treason, bribery, or other high crimes and misdemeanors" as authorized by Article I of the U.S. Constitution. Impeachment is the political equivalent of a criminal indictment. A simple majority vote is needed. (Chapter 7)

backdoor spending Authorization by legislative committees to agencies to borrow money from the U.S. Treasury or to contract for the purchase of goods and services in the future. (Chapter 16)

bad tendency test Engaging in speech that has a tendency to induce illegal behavior; speech that is not protected by the First Amendment. (Chapter 4)

beat cop oversight A type of congressional oversight in which regular reporting creates periodic waves of information. (Chapter 17)

bicameral legislature A legislature divided into two houses; the U.S. Congress and every American state legislature are bicameral (except Nebraska's, which is unicameral). (Chapters 2, 6)

bill A proposed law. (Chapter 6)

bill of attainder Legislation that declares an act illegal and inflicts punishment without a judicial trial. (Chapter 3)

Bill of Rights The first ten amendments to the U.S. Constitution guaranteeing specific rights and liberties; ratified in 1791. (Chapters 2, 4)

Black Codes Laws denying most legal rights to newly freed slaves; passed by Southern states following the Civil War. (Chapter 5)

blanket primaries Primary elections in which voters are permitted to cast ballots in either party's primary (but not both) on an office-by-office basis. (Chapter 12)

Boston Tea Party Name given to event that occurred on December 16, 1773, when Boston citizens disguised as Native Americans boarded ships in the Boston harbor and threw the tea on those ships into the waters below to show their outrage at a tea tax that had been imposed by Britain's Parliament. (Chapter 2)

brief The collected legal written arguments in a case filed with a court prior to a hearing or trial. (Chapter 9)

Brown v. ***Board of Education of Topeka*** **(1954)** U.S. Supreme Court decision holding that school segregation is inherently unconstitutional because it violates the Fourteenth Amendment's guarantee of equal protection; marked the end of legal segregation in the United States. (Chapter 5)

bureaucracy Term used to refer to any large, complex organization; usually used here to refer to the federal bureaucracy. (Chapter 8)

bureaucratic theory The belief that all governmental and nongovernmental institutions are, in effect, controlled by an all-powerful bureaucracy. (Chapter 1)

bureaucrats Employees of the federal, state, or local governments. (Chapter 8)

business cycle Alternating periods of growth and recession in an economy, associated with higher unemployment during the recession phases. (Chapter 16)

Cabinet The secretaries or other top officials (such as the U.S. Attorney General) who head the major departments of the federal government. Appointed by the president and confirmed by the Senate, they make up a body of presidential advisers. (Chapters 7, 8)

calendar Schedule of order of business in each house of Congress. (Chapter 6)

candidate debates Direct, face-to-face, formal meetings of opposing candidates, usually carefully moderated, in order to elicit direct comparisons of their positions and records. (Chapter 13)

capitalism The economic system in which most of the means of production and distribution are operated for profit; system of government that favors free enterprise. (Chapter 1)

capture theory The idea that regulators become beholden to the industries they are designed to regulate. (Chapter 16)

Central Intelligence Agency Agency established by the 1947 National Security Act that is concerned with collecting and analyzing information deemed necessary to meet national security threats. (Chapter 18)

challenger A candidate who campaigns against an incumbent opponent. (Chapter 13)

checks and balances A governmental structure that gives each branch of government some degree of oversight and control over the actions of the others. (Chapter 2)

circuit court of appeals (court of appeals) Appellate courts empowered to review all final decisions of district courts, except in rare occasions; they also hear appeals of the orders of many federal regulatory agencies. (Chapter 9)

civil law A system of law, including private law and governmental actions, created to settle disputes that do not involve charges of criminality. (Chapter 9)

civil liberties Citizens' personal rights and freedoms, guaranteed to be immune from government restriction by constitution, law, or judicial interpretation. (Chapter 4)

civil rights Those rights guaranteeing citizens' freedom from government bias based on categories such as race, sex, national origin, age, or sexual orientation. (Chapter 4)

Civil Rights Cases Name attached to five cases brought under the Civil Rights Act of 1875. In 1883 the Supreme Court decided that discrimination in a variety of public accommodations, including theaters, hotels, and railroads, could not be prohibited by the Act because it was private and not state discrimination. (Chapter 5)

civil service laws Laws pertaining to appointed public employees. (Chapter 12)

Civil Service Reform Act of 1883 See *Pendleton Act.*

civil service system The system whereby most federal government workers are employed based on their skills or test scores (merit) and not on the basis of political favors. (Chapter 8)

Civil War Amendments Name given to the Thirteenth, Fourteenth, and Fifteenth Amendments to the Constitution, which were concerned with the rights to newly freed slaves. (Chapter 5)

class-action lawsuit A legal action brought on behalf of several similarly situated plaintiffs with a common set of claims. (Chapter 9)

clear and present danger test Used by the Supreme Court as a means of limiting freedom of expression guaranteed by the First Amendment. As the test is applied, the Court must look to see if there is an imminent danger that illegal action would occur because of the speech. (Chapter 4)

clientele agencies Executive departments directed by law to foster and promote the interests of a specific segment or group in the United States. (Chapter 8)

closed primaries Primary elections in which only a party's registered members may vote. (Chapter 12)

cloture Senate rule adopted in 1917 that allows the vote of three-fifths of all senators to cut off a filibuster. (Chapter 6)

coalition A collection of disparate groups who bond together for a specific political purpose. (Chapter 11)

Coercive Acts A series of five acts passed by Parliament in 1774 to punish the American colonists for the Boston Tea Party. (Chapter 2)

collective good A resource, benefit, or value provided for all. (Chapter 15)

commander-in-chief The leader of all combined U.S. armed forces, defined by the Constitution to be the president. (Chapter 18)

commerce clause Part of Article I, section 8, of the Constitution that gives Congress the power to regulate commerce among the states. (Chapter 3)

Committees of Correspondence Organizations created throughout each of the American colonies to keep the others abreast of developments; served as powerful molders of public opinion against the British. (Chapter 2)

common law Judge-made law based on adherence to precedents; law common to the realm in the British empire. (Chapter 2)

Common Sense Pamphlet written by Thomas Paine calling for independence from Great Britain. (Chapter 2)

communism A political system in which, at least in theory, ownership of all land and means of production is in the hands of the people, and production and distribution are controlled by the government. (Chapter 1)

Compromise of 1850 The third compromise offered by Henry Clay over slavery; among other things, California was admitted to the Union as a free state, the territories of

New Mexico and Utah were created, the issue of slavery was to be decided there on the basis of popular sovereignty, and a stricter Fugitive Slave Act was adopted. (Chapter 5)

concurrent powers Powers shared by the state and national government. Taxing is a concurrent power. (Chapter 3)

concurrent resolution Special resolution expressing the sentiment of Congress; does not need the president's signature. (Chapter 7)

concurring opinions Opinions written by justices who agree with the outcome of a case but not with the legal rationale provided for it in the majority opinion. (Chapter 9)

confederacy Type of government in which the national government derives its powers from the states; a league of independent states. (Chapters 2, 7)

confederate See *confederacy*.

conference committee Special kind of joint committee created to reconcile differences between House and Senate versions of particular pieces of legislation. (Chapter 6)

Congressional Budget Office Office created in 1974 to assist congressional budget committees. (Chapter 16)

Connecticut Compromise Proposal for a bicameral legislature made by Connecticut during the Philadelphia Convention at which the United States' Constitution was drafted. (Chapter 2)

conservatives Those who advocate streamlined government, a business sector free from government regulation, a return to traditional social values, and a priority on military needs over social needs. (Chapter 10)

constituency The individuals who reside in an area from which a representative is elected. (Chapter 6)

constituency service Array of services offered by members of Congress to those who live in their state or congressional district (constituents). (Chapter 6)

constitution Set of written laws and principles that set out a framework for governing. (Chapter 2)

constitutional courts Courts established by the Constitution in Article III or by congressional action authorized by the Constitution. (Chapter 9)

content regulation The process of governmental intervention into the content of media coverage. (Chapter 14)

contrast ads Advertising on behalf of a candidate that compares the records and proposals of the candidate with those of the opponent. (Chapter 13)

cooperative federalism The belief that because the Constitution is an agreement among people there is little distinction between the powers of the national and state governments. (Chapter 3)

Council of Economic Advisors An agency created in 1946 as part of the Executive Office of the President. (Chapter 16)

creative federalism A program that increased federal aid to state and local governments for social programs; supported by President Lyndon B. Johnson. (Chapter 3)

criminal law The branch of law dealing with crimes and their punishments. (Chapter 9)

critical elections National elections that indicate party realignments. (Chapter 12)

Declaration of Independence Document drafted by Thomas Jefferson that proclaimed the right of the American colonies to separate from Great Britain. (Chapter 2)

Declaration of Rights and Resolves Call issued by the First Continental Congress for colonial rights of petition and assembly, trial by peers, freedom from a standing army, and the selection of representative assemblies to levy taxes. (Chapter 2)

Declaration of Sentiments Statement drawn up at the Seneca Falls convention expressing the beliefs of women in attendance that they had suffered under the laws made by men. (Chapter 5)

deep background Information gathered for news stories that must be completely unsourced. (Chapter 14)

***de facto* discrimination** Racial discrimination that results from practice (such as housing patterns or other social factors) rather than law. (Chapter 5)

***de jure* discrimination** Racial segregation that is a direct result of law or official policy. (Chapter 5)

democracy A system of government in which the people, whether directly or through their elected representatives, govern. (Chapter 1)

departmental agencies Executive agencies reporting to the president's Cabinet that can be created by executive order. (Chapter 17)

deregulation A government policy to reduce or eliminate regulatory constraints on private businesses. (Chapter 8)

despot A ruler who has usurped legitimate political authority and arbitrarily uses the power seized to advance his or her own interests. (Chapter 1)

direct democracy A system of government in which members of the group meet to discuss all policy decisions and then abide by majority role. (Chapter 1)

direct mailer A professional individual hired by a candidate's campaign to supervise all mass mailing, usually for fund-raising purposes. (Chapter 13)

direct primary An election in which nominees of a political party are determined by the ballots of qualified voters, rather than at party conventions. (Chapter 11)

discharge petition A procedure by which a bill can be removed from a committee and brought to the full floor for its consideration; seldom used. (Chapter 6)

dissenting opinions Opinions written by judges who disagree with the opinion of the majority. (Chapter 9)

district courts The federal courts of original jurisdiction. (Chapter 9)

divine right of kings The belief that monarchs were given the right to govern directly from God. (Chapters 1, 2)

double jeopardy Trying an individual in court more than once for the same crime; prohibited by the U.S. Constitution. (Chapter 4)

***Dred Scott* v. *Sanford* (1857)** Supreme Court decision which ruled that a slave who had escaped to a free state enjoyed no citizenship rights and that Congress had no authority to ban slavery in the territories. (Chapter 5)

dual federalism A system of government in which states and the national government each remain supreme within their own spheres. (Chapter 3)

dualist theory The theory claiming that there has always been an underlying binary party nature to U.S. politics. (Chapter 11)

due process clause Clause contained in the Fifth and Fourteenth Amendments that over the years has been construed to guarantee to individuals a variety of rights ranging from economic liberty to criminal procedural rights to protection from arbitrary governmental action. (Chapters 3, 4)

due process rights Protections afforded to those accused of crimes by the Fourth, Fifth, Sixth, and Eighth Amendments. (Chapter 4)

economic growth The condition of an expanding economy, measured by the size of the gross national product. (Chapter 16)

economic-interest group Organization whose members have banded together to enhance their wealth or business interests. (Chapter 15)

economic watchdog model A theory of government that allows the economy to run on its own with the government standing by to solve problems and crises. (Chapter 17)

elastic clause Also "necessary and proper clause"; the final paragraph of Article 1, Section 8, of the U.S. Constitution, which gives Congress the authority to pass all laws "necessary and proper" to carry out the enumerated powers specified in the Constitution. (Chapters 2, 3)

electoral college The body of presidential electors from each state who cast their ballots in their respective state capitals for the president and vice president of the United States. (Chapters 2, 7)

electorate Those citizens eligible to vote. (Chapter 12)

electors Members of the electoral college. (Chapter 12)

electronic media The newest form of broadcast media, including television and radio. (Chapter 14)

electors The individuals who make up the electoral college. (Chapter 2)

elite theory The view that a small group of people actually makes most of the important decisions. C. Wright Mills argued that important policies were set by three loose coalitions of groups—the military, corporate leaders, and a small set of government officials—what he termed the "power elite." (Chapter 1)

Emancipation Proclamation Proclamation issued by President Abraham Lincoln in 1862; provided that all slaves in states still in active rebellion against the United States would automatically be freed on January 1, 1863. (Chapter 5)

employment The condition of having a job. (Chapter 16)

Enlightenment, the A movement that occurred in Western Europe in the 1700s that espoused rationalism, intellectual freedom, and the freedom from superstition in social and political activity. (Chapter 1)

entitlements Benefits that automatically flow to certain groups. (Chapter 17)

enumerated powers Seventeen specific powers granted to Congress under Article I, Section 8, of the U.S. Constitution; these powers include taxation, coinage of money, regulation of commerce, and the authority to provide for a national defense. (Chapters 2, 3)

Equal Employment Opportunity Commission (EEOC) Federal agency created to enforce the Civil Rights Act of 1964, which forbids discrimination on the basis of sex or race in hiring, promotion, or firing. (Chapter 5)

equal protection clause Section of the Fourteenth Amendment which guarantees that all citizens receive "equal protection of the laws"; has been used to bar discrimination against blacks and women. (Chapter 5)

equal time rule The rule that requires broadcast stations to sell campaign air time equally to all candidates if they choose to sell it to any. (Chapter 14)

establishment clause The first clause in the First Amendment; prohibits the U.S. government from establishing a national religion. (Chapter 4)

exclusionary rule Judicially created rule that prohibits police from using illegally seized evidence at trial. (Chapter 4)

executive agreement An agreement made by the president with a foreign country that has the force of a treaty but does not need the Senate's "advice and consent." (Chapter 7)

Executive Office of the President Establishment created in 1939 to help the president better oversee the bureaucracy. (Chapter 8)

executive orders Presidential directives to an agency that provide the basis for the carrying out of laws or the establishing of new policies. (Chapter 8)

executive power The authority to execute or carry out the laws of the nation; a power vested in the chief executive by Article II. (Chapters 2, 3, 7)

executive privilege The belief that, at the president's discretion, communications between him and his aides can be kept confidential from Congress and the courts. (Chapter 7)

exit polls Polls conducted by news organizations as voters leave their polling places; used to predict winners before polls close. (Chapter 10)

***ex post facto* law** Law passed after the fact, thereby making a previously legal activity illegal and subject to current penalty; prohibited by the U.S. Constitution. (Chapter 4)

express powers See *enumerated powers.*

extradite The surrender by one state of a person accused or convicted of a crime to the state in which the offense was committed. (Chapter 3)

faction Group of individuals with shared traits or common interests. (Chapters 2, 15)

fairness doctrine Rule in effect from 1949 to 1985 that required broadcasters to cover events adequately and present contrasting views on important public issues. (Chapter 14)

Federal Register A U.S. government publication that prints all presidential directives, proposals for new regulations, and executive orders. (Chapter 8)

federal system Plan of government created in the U.S. Constitution in which power is divided between the national government and the state governments. (Chapters 2, 3)

federalism See *federal system.*

The Federalist Papers A series of eighty-five political papers written by John Jay, Alexander Hamilton, and James Madison in support of ratification of the U.S. Constitution. (Chapter 2)

Federalists Supporters of the proposed U.S. Constitution; later became the first U.S. political party. (Chapter 2)

Fifteenth Amendment One of the three Civil War Amendments; specifically enfranchised blacks. (Chapter 5)

fighting words Words intended to incite or cause injury to those to whom they are addressed; not protected by the First Amendment. (Chapter 4)

filibuster Senate practice that allows for unlimited debate on any bill. (Chapter 6)

firebox oversight A type of congressional oversight in which reporting is irregular and likely to be requested only once a problem is perceived. (Chapter 17)

fiscal policy Government decisions concerning total levels of spending and taxation. (Chapter 16)

Fourteenth Amendment One of the three Civil War Amendments; guaranteed equal protection and due process of laws to all U.S. citizens. (Chapter 5)

franchise The right to vote. (Chapters 1, 5)

free exercise clause The second clause of the First Amendment; prohibits the U.S. government from interfering with a citizen's right to practice his or her religion. (Chapter 4)

free media Coverage of a candidate's campaign by news media. (Chapter 13)

free riders Those who decline to join a group while knowing that the benefits gained by the group will be offered to members and nonmembers alike; the "free rider problem" is one that most groups confront. (Chapter 15)

freedmen Name given to slaves who obtained freedom either individually (before the Emancipation Proclamation) or collectively (upon the Emancipation Proclamation and the end of the Civil War).

"freedom of choice" plan Plans enacted by Southern states in the aftermath of *Brown* v. *Board of Education* to allow parents to send their children to the school of their choice and not to the school closest to their home (especially if it had black children enrolled). (Chapter 5)

Fugitive Slave Act Originally enacted in 1793 and strengthened in 1850 as part of Compromise of 1850; purpose was to facilitate the return of fugitive slaves. (Chapter 5)

full employment Literally, when everyone willing and able to have a job is employed. In politics, the term has come to mean a policy promise to achieve that state. (Chapter 16)

full faith and credit clause Article IV, Section I of the Constitution, which holds that states cannot overrule judicial decisions and laws of other states. (Chapter 3)

gender gap The difference between the partisan choices of women and men in the aggregate. (Chapter 11)

general election campaign That part of a political campaign following a primary election, aimed at winning a general election. (Chapter 13)

general elections Elections in which voters decide which candidates will fill the nation's elective public offices. (Chapter 12)

gerrymandering Legislative process of redrawing legislative district boundaries to favor the political party that controls the state legislature. (Chapter 6)

get-out-the-vote effort An activity undertaken by a campaign close to election time, aimed at mobilizing as many favorable voters as possible. (Chapter 13)

globalism A form of foreign policy in which a country actively pursues goals throughout the world. (Chapter 18)

government The institutions and procedures by which a given nation or other territory and its people are ruled. (Chapter 1)

government corporations Businesses set up by Congress to conduct operations that could be performed by private companies. Government corporations, such as the U.S. Postal Service, charge for their services. (Chapter 8)

governmental party The office holders and candidates who run under a party's banner. (Chapter 11)

Gramm–Rudman–Hollings Act The Balanced Budget and Emergency Deficit Control Act of 1985. (Chapter 16)

grand jury The body of persons selected to serve as an investigatory body of court; they decide whether or not to indict individuals whose cases are brought before them. (Chapter 9)

grants-in-aid Programs funded by Congress that provide money to state and local governments to accomplish goals desired by the national government. (Chapter 3)

Great Compromise See *Connecticut Compromise;* a decision made during the Philadelphia Convention that gave each state the same number of representatives in the Senate regardless of size; representation in the House was to be determined by population. (Chapter 2)

Great Depression The severe recessionary period following the stock market crash of 1929. (Chapter 16)

"Great Society" President Lyndon B. Johnson's plan to end poverty in the United States through a variety of innovative programs and an end to discrimination. (Chapter 5)

gross domestic product The value of the total output of goods and services in an economy. (Chapter 16)

habeas corpus A court order demanding that individuals in official custody (usually jail or prison) be brought to court and shown the reasons for their detention. According to the U.S. Constitution, *habeas corpus* can be suspended only in times of rebellion or invasion. (Chapter 4)

Hatch Act Legislation enacted in 1939 to ban the use of federal authority to affect elections and to prohibit federal workers from making political contributions to or working for political candidates. (Chapter 8)

holds Tactic by which senators ask to be informed before a particular bill is brought to the floor; usually a way of expressing reservations in advance. (Chapter 6)

ideology The combined doctrines, assertions, and intentions of a social or political group that justify its behavior; a consistent pattern of opinion on political issues that stems from basic underlying beliefs or a set of beliefs. (Chapters 3, 11)

impeach See *impeachment.*

impeachment The power delegated to the House of Representatives in the Constitution to charge the president, vice president, or other "civil officers," including federal judges, with "Treason, Bribery, or other high Crimes and Misdemeanors." This is the first step in the constitutional process of removing such government officials from office. (Chapters 6, 9)

implementation The process of putting a law or policy into operation. (Chapter 8)

implied powers Powers of the federal government that go beyond those enumerated in the Constitution. The necessary and proper clause, combined with enumerated powers, has been construed by the Supreme Court to give Congress wide-ranging implied powers. (Chapter 3)

impoundment Refusal of the president to spend funds for programs that have been appropriated (authorized) by Congress. (Chapter 6)

income tax A tax on all money earned or accrued to individuals. (Chapter 16)

incorporation doctrine Judicially created doctrine that makes specific guarantees in the Bill of Rights applicable to the states by applying them through the due process clause of the Fourteenth Amendment. (Chapter 4)

incumbency The condition of already holding an elected office. (Chapter 12)

independent agencies Governmental units that closely resemble executive agencies but that usually have narrower areas of responsibility. (Chapter 8)

indictment A formal accusation or set of charges made after a grand jury's finding that there is probable cause to believe that a crime has been committed. (Chapter 9)

inflation The rate of increase of prices for goods and services. (Chapter 16)

in forma pauperis Literally, "in the form of a pauper"; way for an indigent or poor person to appeal a case to the U.S. Supreme Court. (Chapter 9)

inherent powers Authority claimed by the president that is not specifically granted by the Constitution. (Chapter 7)

initiative A method by which state and local voters can propose laws or constitutional amendments. Generally, special-interest groups draft initiatives and then circulate petitions that usually must attract the signatures of at least 5 to 10 percent of the registered voters in the state or community. (Chapter 10)

interest group An organized association of individuals, generally who share some values, who seek to influence governmental policy. (Chapter 15)

interest group theory The belief posited by David Truman that interest groups, not elites or bureaucrats, control the governmental process. (Chapters 1, 15)

interest group theory of democracy A descriptive and normative theory of social and political practice which argues that all politics is driven by group behavior. (Chapter 1)

Intolerable Acts See *Coercive Acts.*

iron triangles The relatively stable relationships and patterns of interaction that occur among an agency, interest groups, and congressional committees or subcommittees. (Chapter 8)

isolationism A form of foreign policy in which a country ignores activity beyond its borders. (Chapter 18)

issue network An informal network of political officials and lobbyists brought together by a proposed policy in an area of common interest. (Chapters 8, 15)

issue-oriented politics Politics that focus on specific issues, such as civil rights, tax cutting, environmentalism, and abortion, rather than on party labels. (Chapter 11)

Jay Treaty An early American pact regularizing relations with Britain. (Chapter 18)

Jim Crow laws Laws enacted by Southern states that discriminated against blacks by creating "whites only" schools, theaters, hotels, and other public accommodations. (Chapter 5)

joint committees Congressional committees formed with members from both houses to coordinate investigations or other special studies. (Chapter 6)

judicial review The authority of a court to review the acts of the legislature, the executive, or states to determine their constitutionality; enunciated by Chief Justice John Marshall in *Marbury* v. *Madison* (1803). (Chapters 2, 9)

Judiciary Act of 1789 Act establishing the basic structure of the U.S. federal courts. (Chapter 9)

laissez-faire A "hands off" governmental policy that is based on the belief that governmental regulation of the economy is wrong; first advocated by Adam Smith. (Chapter 1)

League of Nations The first global organization of states dedicated to preserving peace. (Chapter 18)

legislative courts Courts established by Congress for specialized purposes, such as the Court of Military Appeals. (Chapter 9)

legislative intent The supposed real meaning of a law as intended by its authors, which can be (sometimes) discerned from the legislative history of any statute. (Chapter 9)

legislative powers The authority of Congress to make laws as enumerated in the Constitution. (Chapter 6)

legislative veto Procedure by which one or both houses of Congress can disallow an act of an executive agency by a simple majority vote. Legislative vetoes were ruled unconstitutional by the U.S. Supreme Court in *Immigration and Naturalization Service* v. *Chadha* in 1983. (Chapter 6)

libel False statements or those tending to call someone's reputation into disrepute. (Chapter 4)

liberals Those who advocate an active government, support social welfare programs and expanded individual rights and liberties, tolerate social change and diversity, and oppose "excessive" military spending and involvement. (Chapter 10)

line-item veto The power to veto specific provisions of a bill without vetoing the bill in its entirety. (Chapter 7)

lobbying The activities of groups and associations geared toward convincing government officials of the correctness of a group's positions. (Chapter 15)

lobbyist A representative of an interest group or association. (Chapter 15)

logrolling Nickname given to the practice of vote trading on public works projects. (Chapter 6)

Magna Carta A charter of government signed by King John in 1215, guaranteeing the British people certain liberties, including landowner and tenant rights, the right to a trial by jury, and some measure of religious freedom. (Chapter 2)

majority leader The elected leader of the party controlling the most seats in the U.S. House of Representatives or the Senate; is second in authority to the Speaker of the House and in the Senate is regarded as its most powerful member. (Chapter 6)

majority party Party with most members in either house of Congress. (Chapter 6)

majority rule The right of the majority to govern themselves; a central premise of a direct democracy which requires that all policies be ratified by at least one-half of those voting. (Chapter 1)

mandate A command, indicated by an electorate's votes, for the elected officials to carry out their platforms. (Chapter 12)

manifest destiny The theory that American expansion throughout the continent was ordained by God. (Chapter 18)

margin of error The error, usually plus or minus 4 percent or less, that a survey may contain. (Chapter 10)

Margold Report Statement of the future plans of the National Association for the Advancement of Colored People (NAACP); became the basis of its test-case litigation strategy to end segregated schools. (Chapter 5)

Marshall Plan The European Recovery Program named for Secretary of State George Marshall, created in 1948 to help post–World War II reconstruction. (Chapter 18)

matching funds Donations to political campaigns from general tax revenues that are determined by the amount of private funds generated. (Chapter 13)

Mayflower Compact A covenant signed by the Pilgrims aboard the *Mayflower* on November 21, 1620, to ensure an orderly form of government upon their landing in the New World. (Chapter 1)

means-tested welfare programs Programs in which eligibility is dependent upon income standards. (Chapter 17)

media campaign That part of a political campaign (both nomination and general election) waged in the broadcast and print media. (Chapter 13)

media consultant A professional individual hired by a campaign to manage all aspects of the media campaign. (Chapter 13)

media effects The influence of the media on public opinion. (Chapter 14)

Medicaid A program of medical care—financed by the federal government and run by the states—providing coverage for low-income people. (Chapter 17)

Medicare A federal health insurance program for the elderly. (Chapter 17)

mercantilism An economic theory popular from the sixteenth through eighteenth centuries which posited that the wealth of nations was based on their possession of gold. (Chapter 2)

merit system Basing appointments to government jobs on ability or on the results of competitive exams. (Chapter 8)

midterm convention A national party gathering during midterm election years (used by the Democrats between 1974 and 1982) in order to express activists' opinions on presidential and policy matters. (Chapter 11)

militias State-sponsored standing armies. (Chapter 18)

Miller* test The Burger Court's attempt to define obscenity (as a nonprotected form of speech). It concluded that a court must ask "whether the work, taken as a whole, lacks serious literary, artistic, political or scientific value." (Chapter 4)

ministers The title given to America's earliest representatives abroad. (Chapter 18)

minority leader The elected leader of the party with the second most number of elected representatives in either the House or the Senate. (Chapter 6)

minority party Party with the second most members in either house of Congress. (Chapter 6)

Miranda* rights Statements that must be made by the police informing a suspect of his or her constitutionally protected rights, including the right to an attorney if the suspect cannot afford one. (Chapter 4)

miscegenation laws Laws passed by most Southern states in the pre–Civil War period prohibiting blacks and whites from marrying each other. (Chapter 5)

Missouri Compromise of 1820 A compromise offered by Henry Clay that attempted to maintain in the Senate a balance between slave and free states; Missouri was admitted as a slave state, and Maine as a free state. (Chapter 5)

monarchy A form of government in which power is vested in hereditary royalty. (Chapter 1)

monetarism A school of economic thought which argues that growth in the money supply should be limited to the rate of growth of the economy as a whole. (Chapter 16)

monetary policy Government decisions concerning the level of credit in the economy, implemented through changing interest rates and the money supply. (Chapter 16)

monopoly The presence of a single corporation or company in a particular field of enterprise; the absence of competition in a particular market. (Chapter 3)

Monroe Doctrine A statement by President James Monroe in 1823 that the United States' sphere of influence extends throughout the Western hemisphere but that the United States would refrain from meddling in European quarrels. (Chapter 18)

Montgomery bus boycott The first wide-scale protest against discrimination in the South; blacks refused to take buses during 1956 in response to their segregation in that city's public accommodations. (Chapter 5)

muckraking A form of newspaper publishing, in vogue in the early twentieth century, concerned with reforming government and business misconduct. (Chapter 14)

multi-issue groups Organizations that devote their resources to lobbying in several different issue areas. (Chapter 15)

multistage sampling See *stratified sampling.*

National Association for the Advancement of Colored People (NAACP) Organization created in the early 1900s to lobby for increased rights for black citizens. (Chapter 5)

national convention The quadrennial gathering of a political party during presidential election years, at which the party nominates its candidates for president and vice president. (Chapter 11)

national debt The unpaid portion of accumulated deficits over time. (Chapter 16)

National Industrial Recovery Act A New Deal act that attempted to control the economy through a combination of stronger unions and more relaxed anti-trust laws. (Chapter 16)

national party platforms Formal descriptions of political parties' positions on key issues. (Chapter 11)

national security The policy goal of maintaining safe and secure borders. (Chapter 18)

National Security Act The 1947 law that created the Department of Defense. (Chapter 18)

National Security Council A high-level body created by the National Security Act of 1947 to coordinate national security policy. (Chapter 18)

natural law The school of thought which posits that basic and God-given rules do not have to be written down so much as discovered. (Chapter 1)

necessary and proper clause The final paragraph of Article 1, Section 8, of the Constitution, authorizing Congress to pass all laws "necessary and proper" to carry out the vast number of enumerated powers set out in Article 1, Section 8, of the Constitution. (Chapter 3)

negative ads Advertising on behalf of a candidate that attacks the opponent's platform and character. (Chapter 13)

networks National broadcast sources that produce programming and sell it to local affiliated stations for airing. (Chapter 14)

New Deal The name given to the program of "Relief, Recovery, Reform" begun by President Franklin D. Roosevelt in 1933 and designed to extricate the United States from the Great Depression. (Chapter 3)

New Federalism Program that emphasizes the return of power to the states; generally heralded by Republican presidents. (Chapter 3)

newsworthiness The degree of interest in inclusion in a newscast or in the print media of a particular occurrence. (Chapter 14)

nomination campaign That part of a political campaign aimed at winning a primary election. (Chapter 13)

nondepartmental agencies Independent agencies created by legislative initiatives. (Chapter 17)

nonprobability sampling Unrepresentative samples for surveys such as straw polls; they generally are unreliable. (Chapter 10)

North Atlantic Treaty Organization The military alliance between the United States and Western Europe, created in 1950. (Chapter 18)

nullification The belief that a state can veto particular actions of the national government; the purported right of a state to nullify a federal statute; popular belief in the South prior to the Civil War. (Chapter 3)

off the record Information gathered for a news story that cannot be used at all. (Chapter 14)

off-year elections Elections in the middle of presidential terms. (Chapter 12)

Office of Management and Budget An executive branch office created in 1921 to guide all executive agencies in their budget formulations. (Chapter 16)

oligarchy A form of government in which power is concentrated in the hands of a few individuals, and the right to participate in the governing process is based on the possession of wealth or property. (Chapter 1)

one-partyism A political system in which one party dominates and wins virtually all contests. (Chapter 11)

on the record Information gathered for a news story that can be used and cited. (Chapter 14)

open primaries Primary elections in which party members, independents, and sometimes members of the other party may vote. (Chapter 12)

organizational campaign That part of a political campaign (both nomination and general election) involved in fund raising, literature distribution, and all other activities not directly involving the candidate. (Chapter 13)

organizational party The workers and activists who staff a party's formal organization. (Chapter 11)

original jurisdiction The jurisdiction of courts that hear a case first, usually in trial. Courts determine the facts of a case under their original jurisdiction. (Chapters 3, 9)

oversight The efforts of Congress to exercise some control of executive agencies through hearings, investigations, and other means. (Chapter 6)

paid media Political advertisements purchased for a candidate's campaign. (Chapter 13)

pardon power The president's constitutionally derived power to grant reprieves or forgive individuals in cases of wrongdoing, or to offer general amnesties to political insurgents and restore to them all rights and privileges. (Chapter 7)

party caucus A formal gathering of all party members used, among other things, to select party leaders. (Chapter 6)

party conference Name given to the Republican and Democratic congressional party meetings at which party leaders and committee assignments are named; held at beginning of each session in each chamber. (Chapter 6)

party identification The group label with which members of a political party identify. (Chapter 11)

party realignments A shifting of party coalition groupings in the electorate that remains in place for several elections. (Chapter 12)

party-in-the-electorate The voters who consider themselves to be allied or associated with a party. (Chapter 11)

patronage Power of elected officials to increase their political strength by appointing people of their choice to governmental or public jobs; one of the key inducements political machines use to guarantee party loyalty by rewarding supporters. (Chapters 3, 7)

patrons Those whose financial backing allows an interest group to prosper and grow. (Chapter 15)

Pendleton Act Created the bipartisan civil service system. (Chapter 8)

plaintiff The individual or organization that originally brings a lawsuit to court. (Chapter 9)

***Plessy* v. *Ferguson* (1896)** An eight-to-one Supreme Court decision upholding a Louisiana statute that made it possible to segregate blacks and whites on passenger trains; became the basis for the "separate but equal" doctrine and was used to justify passage of Jim Crow laws. (Chapter 5)

pluralist model Theory of government arguing that resources are scattered so widely in our political system that what results is a government that is mainly a competition among groups, each one pressing for its preferred policies. (Chapter 1)

pocket veto A method of killing a bill passed by both houses of Congress; the president simply refrains from signing the bill within ten days of congressional adjournment. (Chapter 6)

policy entrepreneurs Individuals in government who assume leadership roles in new policy areas. (Chapter 17)

policy laboratory A term applied to the states when they serve as testing grounds for potential national legislation. (Chapter 17)

political action committees Federally mandated, officially registered fund-raising committees that represent interest groups in the political process. (Chapter 13)

political consultants Individuals who are hired to manage campaigns and design television commercials. (Chapter 11)

political equality Government practice in which the votes of all individuals count equally. (Chapter 1)

political ideology An individual's set of beliefs about politics, public policy, and political issues. (Chapter 10)

political party A group of office holders, candidates, activists, and voters who identify with a group label and seek to elect to public office individuals who run under that label. (Chapter 11)

political socialization The process through which an individual acquires his [or her] particular orientations—his [or her] knowledge, feelings, and evaluations regarding his [or her] political world; the learning process by which people acquire their political beliefs and values. (Chapter 10)

"politically correct speech" movement Movement that developed in the late 1980s to limit free speech by banning language thought to be inappropriate or harmful. (Chapter 4)

politics The process by which policy decisions are made. (Chapter 1)

polls Surveys used to gauge public opinion. (Chapter 10)

pollster A professional individual hired by a campaign to manage all public opinion surveys undertaken by the campaign. (Chapter 13)

poll tax Method used by Southern states after the Civil War to exclude blacks from voting by imposing taxes or the payment of fees before a citizen could vote; outlawed on national elections by the Twenty-fourth Amendment in 1964 and in state elections by the Supreme Court in 1966. (Chapter 5)

popular consent The legitimation of government by the will of the people. (Chapter 1)

popular opinion Widely fluctuating changes in public support for particular programs or issues based on public reactions to particular events. (Chapter 10)

popular sovereignty The right of the majority to govern themselves. (Chapter 1)

pork barrel legislation Bills passed by Congress or other legislative bodies with expenditures targeted to local districts, so that local representatives' chances of reelection will be enhanced. (Chapter 6)

positive ads Advertising on behalf of a candidate that stresses his or her qualifications, family, and issue positions with no direct reference to the opponent. (Chapter 13)

precedent A judicial decision that serves as a rule for settling subsequent cases of a similar nature. (Chapter 9)

presidential character According to political scientist James David Barber, the patterns of behavior exhibited by presidents based on their approach to the office and energy level. (Chapter 7)

presidential style President's ability, often based on a variety of factors, to get things done. (Chapter 7)

Presidential Succession Act of 1947 Clarifies who replaces the president in case of a vacancy in the vice presidency (or in case of his inability to serve): by law first the Speaker of the House of Representatives, then the President *Pro Tempore* of the Senate, and then the Secretaries of State, Treasury, Defense, and the other Cabinet heads in order of their departments' creation. (Chapter 7)

primary elections Elections in which voters decide which of the candidates within a party will represent the party's ticket in the general election. (Chapter 12)

print press The traditional form of mass media, comprising newspapers, magazines, and journals. (Chapter 14)

prior restraint Judicial doctrine stating that the government cannot prohibit speech or publication before the fact. (Chapter 4)

pro bono Work done by a lawyer for no charge. (Chapter 9)

Progressive Movement Social movement begun around 1890 and concerned with the reform of political, economic, and social systems in the United States. (Chapter 5)

proportional representation The system of awarding legislative seats in proportion to the number of votes received. (Chapter 11)

protectionism The erection of barriers, such as tariffs, against foreign competitors. (Chapter 16)

public funds Donations to political campaigns from general tax revenues. (Chapter 13)

public-assistance programs State-administered programs for needy individuals. (Chapter 17)

public-interest group An organization whose main stated goal is to serve the interests of society as a whole; however, defining the public interest is often the subject of intense debate. (Chapter 15)

public opinion Those opinions or beliefs about politics and policy issues held by ordinary citizens. (Chapter 10)

quasi-judicial powers Effective power of agencies to settle disputes without resort to the judicial system. (Chapter 17)

quasi-legislative powers Effective law making power wielded by agencies rather than by Congress. (Chapter 17)

quorum The minimum number of members of any deliberative body that must be present before official business can be conducted. (Chapter 6)

quota sample   Sample that draws respondents based on known statistics. A particular ethnic group that constitutes 10 percent of the population will be 10 percent of those surveyed. (Chapter 10)

Radical Republicans   Members of a wing of the Republican Party which believed that the Civil War was necessary to abolish slavery; was critical of President Abraham Lincoln for his handling of the war; tried to impeach President Andrew Johnson for his conciliatory approach to the South after the war; and used Reconstruction to punish Southern states. (Chapter 5)

random sampling   A technique used in conducting a survey in which respondents are chosen by a mathematical formula to enhance the likelihood that those surveyed are representative of a much larger population. (Chapter 10)

reapportionment   The redrawing of election districts to reflect population shifts. (Chapter 6)

recall   A procedure for demanding the ouster by popular vote of an elected public official prior to the end of his or her term. (Chapter 10)

redistricting   Process of redrawing (by state legislatures) congressional districts every ten years after the national census to reflect changes in population. See *reapportionment*. (Chapter 6)

referendum   The practice of putting proposed legislation before the voters for their approval or disapproval. (Chapter 10)

regional primaries   A proposed system in which the nation would be divided into five or six geographic areas (such as the South or the Midwest), and all the states in each region would hold their presidential primary elections on the same day. (Chapter 12)

regulations   Rules that govern the operation of all government agencies. (Chapter 8)

regulatory commission   An agency of the executive branch that generally is concerned with one aspect of the economy. (Chapter 8)

representative democracy   A system of government that gives citizens the opportunity to vote for legislators who will work on their behalf. (Chapter 1)

republic   A government rooted in the consent of the governed; power is exercised by elected representatives who are ultimately responsible to the people. (Chapter 1)

republicanism   See *republic*.

retrospective judgment   A voter's evaluation of the performance of the party in power. (Chapter 12)

revenue sharing   Method of redistributing federal monies back to the states with "no strings attached"; favored by President Richard Nixon. (Chapter 3)

right-of-rebuttal rule   The rule requiring that a person attacked on a radio or television broadcast be offered the opportunity to respond on the air. (Chapter 14)

rule   Given by the House Rules Committee to legislation being reported to the floor for consideration; it contains the date the bill will come up for consideration, the time to be allotted for discussion, and often even specifications as to whether amendments to the bill may be offered. (Chapter 6)

rule making   The administrative process that results in the making of rules and regulations that have the force of law. (Chapter 8)

Rule of Four   Rule holding that at least four justices of the Supreme Court must vote to consider a case before it can be heard. (Chapter 9)

runoff primary   A secondary primary election between the two candidates who received the greatest number of votes in the first primary. (Chapter 12)

safety net   The combined set of social policies designed to cushion harsh effects of the economy. (Chapter 17)

sample   A relatively small number of individuals chosen in a survey who are interviewed for the purpose of estimating the opinions of an entire population. (Chapter 10)

sampling error A measure of the accuracy of a public opinion poll; the sample error is basically a function of sample size and is usually expressed in percentage terms. (Chapter 10)

secede To withdraw from an organization, as a state from the Union. (Chapter 3)

Secretary of State The federal cabinet position concerned with foreign policy. (Chapter 18)

secular realignment A gradual rearrangement of party coalitions, dependent less upon convulsive shocks to the political system than upon slow demographic shifts. (Chapter 12)

seditious (speech) Speech that advocates the violent overthrow of the government. (Chapter 4)

select committees Temporary congressional committees appointed for fairly specific purposes with fairly limited mandates. (Chapter 6)

selective incorporation A judicial doctrine whereby most but not all of the protections found in the Bill of Rights are made applicable to the states via the Fourteenth Amendment. (Chapter 4)

senatorial courtesy Unwritten rule in the Senate that essentially gives individual senators near–veto power over laws or appointments that affect their home states. (Chapters 6, 9)

seniority Ranking given to an elected official based on the number of years served in a particular legislative body; often the basis of special privileges, including committee assignments and election to committee chair. (Chapter 6)

separation of powers A way of dividing power among the three branches of government; developed by French political philosopher Montesquieu. (Chapters 2, 7)

single-issue groups Organizations of individuals that are committed to lobbying and gearing their efforts toward a single goal involving a single issue, such as the right to bear arms or abortion rights. (Chapter 15)

slander Spoken statements that defame an individual's character. (Chapter 4)

social contract theory The belief that people are free and equal by God-given right and that this in turn requires that all men give their consent to be governed; espoused by Thomas Hobbes and John Locke. (Chapter 1)

socialism A political philosophy that advocates public ownership and control of the means of economic production. (Chapter 1)

social regulation Regulations imposed on firms to protect the environment, to make the workplace safe and healthful, to protect consumers from unsafe products and fraud, and to end discrimination in hiring. (Chapter 16)

Social Security A federal social insurance program that provides minimum levels of income maintenance. (Chapter 17)

Solicitor General Third-ranking individual in the U.S. Justice Department (after the Attorney General and the Deputy Attorney General), responsible for appearing on behalf of the U.S. government before the Supreme Court. (Chapter 9)

Sons of Liberty A radical organization of colonists created in 1765 to express opposition to the Stamp Act. (Chapter 2)

sovereign Self-governing. (Chapter 3)

Speaker of the House The presiding officer of the House of Representatives; elected by the majority party; second in line of presidential succession, after the vice president. (Chapter 6)

special-interest caucuses Informal organizations in Congress based on party, regional, class, or special interests. (Chapter 6)

sphere of influence A geographic area dominated though not directly controlled by a country. (Chapter 18)

spoils system Nickname for practice of filling government jobs with political supporters; "to the victor goes the spoils." (Chapter 11)

spot ads Television advertising on behalf of a candidate that is broadcast in sixty-, thirty-, or ten-second durations. (Chapter 13)

stagflation The economic condition of simultaneous high inflation and high unemployment. (Chapter 16)

Stamp Act Congress Meeting of representatives of nine of the thirteen colonies held in New York City in 1765 during which representatives drafted a document to send to the king listing how their rights had been violated. (Chapter 2)

Stamp Act of 1765 A direct tax requiring the purchase of stamps as a tax to be affixed to all documents, including newspapers, magazines, and commercial papers. (Chapter 2)

standing The right of an individual to initiate a judicial proceeding. (Chapter 9)

standing committees Congressional committees that continue in each house from one session to the next. (Chapter 6)

stare decisis In court rulings, reliance on past decisions or precedents to formulate decisions in new cases. (Chapter 9)

statute Law enacted by a legislative body. (Chapter 6)

stewardship theory A theory arguing for a strong, assertive presidential role in the belief that a president has (and should have) implied powers delegated by the people unless specifically limited in the Constitution. (Chapter 7)

stratified sampling A multi-stage sampling technique that makes use of census data to determine residences to be polled in certain areas. (Chapter 10)

straw polls Unscientific surveys used to gauge public opinion on a variety of issues and policies. (Chapter 10)

strict constructionist One who believes that the U.S. Constitution should be interpreted as it was written and understood by the Framers. (Chapter 9)

suffrage The right to vote. (Chapter 2)

suffrage movement Term used to refer to drive for votes for women that took place in the United States from 1880 to 1920. (Chapters 1, 5)

Sugar Act of 1764 Act passed by Britain's Parliament to help raise revenues to pay for the French and Indian War. (Chapter 2)

sunset laws Laws that specify end dates for new programs to die unless they are further extended by Congress. (Chapter 6)

sunshine laws Laws which require that legislation be considered in public and not behind closed doors. (Chapter 6)

superdelegates Delegate slots to the Democratic Party's national convention that are reserved for elected party officials. (Chapter 12)

supply-side An adjective applied to individuals and corporations. "Supply-side policies" include tax cuts to stimulate the micro-level supplies of the economy. (Chapter 16)

supremacy clause Portion of Article IV of the U.S. Constitution which mandates that national law is supreme to (i.e., supersedes) all others passed by the states or by any other subdivision of government. (Chapter 2)

symbolic speech Symbols, signs, and other methods of expression generally also considered to be protected by First Amendment. (Chapter 4)

tariffs Taxes on goods imported to or exported from a country. (Chapter 2)

Tea Act of 1773 British law that granted to the East India Company a monopoly on the importation of tea. (Chapter 2)

test cases Cases brought by interest groups as part of a planned strategy eventually to win their point before the U.S. Supreme Court. (Chapter 15)

third-partyism A deviation from the American norm of two chief parties, in which a third party attracts enough support to have an impact on the basic two-party competition. (Chapter 11)

Thirteenth Amendment One of the three Civil War Amendments; specifically banned slavery in the United States. (Chapter 5)

Three-Fifths Compromise Agreement reached at the Constitutional Convention stipulating that slavers were to be counted as three-fifths of a white man for purposes of determining population for representation in the U.S. House of Representatives. (Chapter 2)

ticket-split The act of voting for candidates of different parties for various offices in the same election. (Chapter 11)

Title VII Section of the Civil Rights Act of 1964 that prohibits discrimination in employment based on race, creed, color, national origin, or sex. (Chapter 5)

Title XI Federal statute prohibiting sex discrimination in educational institutions receiving federal funds. (Chapter 5)

totalitarianism System of government in which the state retains total control of industry and all forms of production. (Chapter 1)

Townshend Acts Acts passed by Britain's Parliament in 1767 imposing duties on a wide variety of goods imported by the colonists, at least in part to demonstrate to the colonists Britain's continued right to tax them. (Chapter 2)

tracking polls Continuous surveys that enable a campaign to chart its daily rise or fall. (Chapter 11)

trade associations Organizations that represent firms and individuals involved in a particular industry, generally before legislative bodies or executive agencies. (Chapter 15)

trade deficits Condition created when the value of imports exceeds the value of exports. (Chapter 16)

treaty A formal agreement between nations setting forth rights and responsibilities of each. All U.S. treaties must be approved by a two-thirds vote of the Senate. (Chapter 7)

Truman Doctrine A policy established by President Harry S Truman in 1947 that the United States would support any people resisting attempted subjugation by outside pressures. (Chapter 18)

two presidencies A theory postulated by Aaron Wildavsky that there are two presidencies; in one, a president is a strong leader in foreign affairs, and in the other he is a weak one in the realm of domestic affairs. (Chapter 7)

tyranny An authoritarian government that uses cruel and oppressive means to maintain its power and authority. (Chapter 1)

Uncle Tom's Cabin Series of articles (later published as a book) written by Harriet Beecher Stowe revealing the horrors of slavery and inflaming Northern passions against it. (Chapter 5)

uncommitted delegates Delegates to a party convention whose support prior to the convention is not pledged to a particular candidate.

underclass People who live in neighborhoods where welfare dependency, female-headed families, male joblessness, and dropping out of high school are commonplace. (Chapter 17)

unicameral One-house legislature, as in the state of Nebraska. (Chapter 6)

unit rule A traditional party practice under which the majority of a state delegation can force the minority to vote for its candidate. (Chapter 12)

unitary Term applied to systems in which all power resides in the central or national government as opposed to regional (subnational) governments. (Chapter 3)

Versailles Peace Treaty   Treaty ending World War I and establishing the League of Nations. (Chapter 18)

veto   A constitutional power of the president to send a bill back to Congress with reasons for rejecting it. A two-thirds vote in each house can override a presidential veto. (Chapter 2)

virtual representation   System of government in which elected representatives are considered to most properly represent their entire nation as opposed to the more specific interests of their home district. (Chapter 6)

voter canvass   The process by which a campaign gets in touch with individual voters, either by door-to-door solicitation or by telephone. (Chapter 13)

War Powers Act   Law requiring that presidents obtain congressional approval before introducing U.S. forces into a combat situation; passed in 1973 over President Richard Nixon's veto. (Chapter 6)

Watergate   Term used to describe the events and scandal resulting from a break-in at the Democratic National Committee headquarters in 1972 (at the Watergate complex) and the subsequent cover-up of White House involvement, leading to the eventual resignation of President Richard Nixon under the threat of impeachment. (Chapter 7)

wave theory   Belief that interest groups have a tendency to form in a cyclical pattern in response to others. (Chapter 15)

welfare   The set of governmental policies designed to ameliorate individuals with impaired lives. (Chapter 17)

Whig theory   A theory prevailing in the nineteenth century that the presidency was a limited or restrained office and that the president was confined to the authority expressly granted in the Constitution. (Chapter 7)

white primary   Primary elections in which all nonwhite voters are systematically excluded from voting (no longer practiced). (Chapter 12)

wire services   National sources of news for the print media.

write of *certiorari*   A formal document issued from the Supreme Court to a lower federal or state court that calls up a case. Four of the Courts' nine justices must agree to accept the case before it is granted *certiorari.* (Chapter 9)

yellow journalism   A form of newspaper publishing in vogue in the late nineteenth century that featured pictures, comics, color, and sensationalized, oversimplified news coverage. (Chapter 14)

Index

Photo Credits

Page	Photographer/Source

Ch. 13 The Campaign Process

464	Agence France Presse
467 (top)	UPI/The Bettmann Archive
467 (bottom)	AP/Wide World Photos
468	UPI/The Bettmann Archive
470	Sandra Lee-Phipps/The Village Voice
473	James Pearson/The New York Times Modern Galleries, Philadelphia, PA
474	TO COME
P13.10	AP/Wide World Photos

Ch. 14 The News Media

496	Ewing Galloway/Courtesy of the New York Public Library
497	Historical Pictures Service
501	Gene Baker/Picture Group
503	Reuters/The Bettmann Archive
504	Charles W. Kennedy/Sygma
509	Reuters/The Bettmann Archive
510	Steve Liss/CBS News/SABA
514	R. Maiman/Sygma
517	UPI/The Bettmann Archive
519	UPI/The Bettmann Archive
521	UPI/The Bettmann Archive

Ch. 15 Interest Groups

527	Reuters/The Bettmann Archive
528	UPI/The Bettmann Archive
530	Courtesy of Handgun Control Inc.
536	Library of Congress
537	UPI/The Bettmann Archive
540	Courtesy of Common Cause
543	Reuters/The Bettmann Archive
545	National Archives

Page	Photographer/Source

| 548 | Paul Hosefros/The New York Times Pictures |
| 549 | UPI/The Bettmann Archive |

Part Opener 4: Public Policy

| 557–558 | J. L. Atlan |

Ch. 16 Economic Policy

561	The Bettmann Archive
565	The Bettmann Archive
569	UPI/The Bettmann Archive
571	Les Stone/Sygma
581	UPI/The Bettmann Archive
585	UPI/The Bettmann Archive
588	Douglas Mason/Woodfin Camp & Associates
589	AP/Wide World Photos

Ch. 17 Domestic Policy

598	Historical Pictures Service
601	UPI/Bettmann Newsphotos
603	Courtesy of Houghton
605	UPI/The Bettmann Archive
606	Curt W. Kaldor/Uniphoto
610	T. L. Litt/Impact Visuals
613	Tom McKitterick/Impact Visuals
619 (top)	Courtesy of Pennsylvania Hospital, Philadelphia, PA
619 (bottom)	UPI/The Bettmann Archive

Ch. 18 Foreign and Military Policy

625	Henry Francis du Pont Winterthur Museum
629	The Bettmann Archive
631	UPI/The Bettmann Archive
633	UPI/The Bettmann Archive
635	Courtesy of CNN America, Inc.
636	Sovfoto
638	A. Nogues/Sygma
639	C. Simonpietri/Sygma
645	AP/Wide World Photos
646	J. Langevin/Sygma